The Peptides *Volume 5*

THE PEPTIDES

Analysis, Synthesis, Biology

Treatise Editors

E. GROSS AND J. MEIENHOFER

Volume 1
Major Methods of Peptide Bond Formation

Volume 2
Special Methods in Peptide Synthesis, Part A

Volume 3
Protection of Functional Groups in Peptide Synthesis

Volume 4
Modern Techniques of Conformational, Structural, and Configurational Analysis

Volume 5
Special Methods in Peptide Synthesis, Part B

The Peptides

Analysis, Synthesis, Biology

VOLUME 5 Special Methods in Peptide Synthesis, Part B

Edited by

ERHARD GROSS

National Institutes of Health
Bethesda, Maryland

JOHANNES MEIENHOFER

Chemical Research Department
Hoffmann-La Roche Inc.
Nutley, New Jersey

1983

ACADEMIC PRESS
A Subsidiary of Harcourt Brace Jovanovich, Publishers
New York London Paris San Diego
San Francisco São Paulo Sydney Tokyo Toronto

ACADEMIC PRESS, INC.
111 Fifth Avenue, New York, New York 10003

United Kingdom Edition published by
ACADEMIC PRESS, INC. (LONDON) LTD.
24/28 Oval Road, London NW1 7DX

Library of Congress Cataloging in Publication Data

(Revised for volume 5)
Main entry under title:

The Peptides.

Includes bibliographies and indexes.
Contents: v. 1. Major methods of peptide bond formation. -- v. 2. Special methods in peptide synthesis -- [etc.] -- v. 5. Special methods in peptide synthesis, part B.
1. Peptides. I. Gross, Erhard. II. Meienhofer, Johannes. [DNLM: 1. Peptides. QU 68 P424 1979]
QP552.P4P47 574.19'245 78-31958
ISBN 0-12-304205-4 (v.5) (San Diego).

PRINTED IN THE UNITED STATES OF AMERICA

83 84 85 86 9 8 7 6 5 4 3 2 1

ERHARD GROSS, 1928–1981

Erhard Gross, the conceptual originator of this treatise, died in a traffic accident in Germany on September 12, 1981. In an instant, Gross passed away in the most productive period of his scientific work.

He had great visions about the importance of collecting any and all information on peptides and presenting it in a concise and comprehensive form to the scientific community. Many different approaches were considered, including a translation of the monumental Houben-Weyl by Erich Wünsch (Thieme, Stuttgart, 1974). Eventually, the present open-ended treatise, *The Peptides: Analysis, Synthesis, Biology,* appeared to provide the best way to generate the desired timely information transfer. Once this was decided, Gross spent countless hours on correspondence and telephone conversations in efforts to enlist authors of international reputation. We shall forever miss his inspiration and tireless pursuit of excellence in this venture.

Erhard Gross was not a novice in producing books on peptides. In the 1960s, when modern methods of peptide synthesis had undergone a dramatic expansion, Gross undertook the difficult task of translating the two volumes, *The Peptides* (E. Schröder and K. Lübke) from German into English (Academic Press, 1965/1966). Undoubtedly, the impact of these books on the explosive development of all areas of peptide research will be remembered by many colleagues. Without the English translation, progress would almost certainly have been much slower.

Erhard Gross was born in Wenings, near Frankurt am Main. He studied chemistry at the Universities of Mainz and Frankfurt and received his doctoral degree in 1958. His thesis on the synthesis of a bicyclic model peptide of the mushroom toxin phalloidin was carried out in the laboratory of Professor Theodor Wieland. Gross came to the United States in 1958. He worked for many years with Professor Bernhard Witkop at the

National Institutes of Arthritis and Metabolic Diseases, NIH, in Bethesda, Maryland. He also collaborated with Professor Lyman C. Craig, Rockefeller University, New York. These outstanding mentors, Wieland, Witkop, and Craig, profoundly influenced both Gross's direction of research and his commitment to precision and excellence in his work. In 1968 Gross was appointed Chief of the Section on Molecular Structure, Laboratory of Biomedical Sciences, and in 1973, Chief of the Section on Molecular Structure, Endocrinology and Reproduction Research Branch, National Institute of Child Health and Human Development at NIH, in Bethesda, Maryland.

The scientific work of Erhard Gross covered a wide range of subjects including development of the cyanogen bromide cleavage of methionyl peptide bonds in 1960, a method that continues to gain in importance (e.g., in genetic engineering). Gross's achievements—the difficult structure elucidation of nisin and subtilin, analytic and synthetic work on α,β-dehydroamino acids, on gramicidins A, B, and C, and their channel-forming properties as well as studies on enkephalins and chemotactic factors—may be more fully appreciated by a look at the complete bibliography of Gross, listed below.

Gross was very active in the American Peptide Symposium Committee and made major contributions to the program committees of several of the symposia. One of the most outstanding symposia was that organized by him and held at Georgetown University, Washington, D.C., in 1979. Its proceedings are recorded in the large volume entitled *Peptides: Structure and Biological Function*. The winter Gordon Conferences were regularly attended by Gross who always stimulated the discussions. He also promoted international exchange and collaboration and had students from many countries working in his laboratory.

In 1979 Gross was awarded the Alexander von Humboldt prize to carry out studies at a German University. He worked in collaboration with Professor P. Läuger at the University of Konstanz on ion transport in gramicidin-channel structures.

Gross had many extracurricular interests including literature, theater, and music. He was very sociable and fond of enjoying good food and wine in the company of his friends. Privately, he preferred to maintain a German life-style with his wife, Gertrud, and his sons, Johannes and Christoph. Every summer was spent at their German hometown, where he also found his final place of rest. Along with his family, a large number of friends and colleagues throughout the world mourn his passing and will always remember him.

BIBLIOGRAPHY

1. Wieland, Th., Freter, K., and Gross, E. (1959). Über die Giftstoffe des grünen Knollenblätterpilzes, XVII. Versuche zur Synthese Phalloin-ähnlicher Cyclopeptide. *Justus Liebigs Ann. Chem.* **626,** 154–173.
2. Patchornik, A., Lawson, W. B., Gross, E., and Witkop, B. (1960). The use of *N*-bromosuccinimide and *N*-bromoacetamide for the selective cleavage of *C*-tryptophyl peptide bonds in model peptides and glucagon. *J. Am. Chem. Soc.* **82,** 5923–5927.
3. Lawson, W. B., Gross, E., Foltz, C. M., and Witkop, B. (1961). Specific cleavage of methionyl peptides. *J. Am. Chem. Soc.* **83,** 1590.
4. Gross, E., and Witkop, B. (1961). Selective cleavage of methionyl peptide bonds in ribonuclease with cyanogen bromide. *J. Am. Chem. Soc.* **83,** 1510–1511.
5. Lawson, W. B., Gross, E., Foltz, C. M., and Witkop, B. (1962). Alkylation and cleavage of methionine peptides. *J. Am. Chem. Soc.* **84,** 1717–1718.
6. Gross, E., and Witkop, B. (1962). Nonenzymatic cleavage of peptide bonds: The methionyl residues in ribonuclease. *J. Biol. Chem.* **237,** 1856–1860.
7. Gross, E., and Witkop, B. (1965). Gramicidin IX. Preparation of gramicidin A, B, and C. *Biochemistry* **4,** 2495–2501.
8. Axen, R., Gross, E., Witkop, B., Pierce, J. V., and Webster, M. E. (1966). Release of kinin activity from human kininogens and fresh plasma by cyanogen bromide. *Biochem. Biophys. Res. Commun.* **23,** 92–95.
9. Gross, E., and Witkop, B. (1966). A convenient method for the preparation of S-peptide from bovine pancreatic ribonuclease. *Biochem. Biophys. Res. Commun.* **23,** 720–723.
10. Schöberl, A., Gross, E., Morell, J. L., and Witkop, B. (1966). The separation of optical isomers of β-methyllanthionine. *Biochim. Biophys. Acta* **121,** 4–6.
11. Gross, E., and Morell, J. L. (1966). Evidence for an active carboxyl group in pepsin. *J. Biol. Chem.* **241,** 3638–3639.
12. Kopoldova, J., Liebster, J., and Gross, E. (1967). Radiation and chemical reactions in aqueous solution of methionine and its peptides. *Radiat. Res.* **30,** 261–274.
13. Gross, E., and Witkop, B. (1967). The heterogeneity of the S-peptide of bovine pancreatic ribonuclease A. *Biochemistry* **6,** 745–748.
14. Gross, E., and Morell, J. L. (1967). The presence of dehydroalanine in nisin and its relationship to activity. *J. Am. Chem. Soc.* **89,** 2791–2792.
15. Gross, E. (1966). The cyanogen bromide reaction. *Methods Enzymol.* **11,** 238–255.
16. Gross, E. (1968). The action of cyanogen bromide on protein-bound sulfur-containing amino acids. "Proceedings, Princeton Conference, The Chemistry of Sulfides," June 29–July 1, 1966, pp. 235–256. Princeton University Press, Princeton, N.J.
17. Gross, E., Morell, J. L., and Lee, P. Q. (1968). Nonenzymatic cleavage of peptide bonds and multimolecular forms of enzymes. *Ann. N.Y. Acad. Sci.* **151,** 556–567.
18. Gross, E., Morell, J. L. (1968). The number and nature of α,β-unsaturated amino acids in nisin. *FEBS Lett.* **2,** 61–64.
19. Gross, E., and Morell, J. L. (1970). Structural studies on nisin. *In* "Peptides: Chemistry and Biochemistry" (B. Weinstein and S. Lande, eds.), pp. 389–410. Dekker, New York.
20. Gross, E., Morell, J. L., and Craig, L. C. (1969). Dehydroalanyllysine: Identical COOH-terminal structures in the peptide antibiotics nisin and subtilin. *Proc. Natl. Acad. Sci. U.S.A.* **62,** 952–956.
21. Gross, E., and Morell, J. L. (1971). Peptides with α,β-unsaturated amino acids. *In* "Peptides 1969" (E. Scoffone, ed.), pp. 356–360. North-Holland, Amsterdam.
22. Gross, E., and Morell, J. L. (1970). Nisin: The assignment of sulfide bridges of β-methyllanthionine to a novel bicyclic structure of identical ring size. *J. Am. Chem. Soc.* **92,** 2919–2920.
23. Gross, E., and Morell, J. L. (1971). The structure of nisin, *J. Am. Chem. Soc.* **93,** 4634–4635.
24. Gross, E. (1971). Structure and function of peptides with α,β-unsaturated amino acids, *Intra-Sci. Chem. Rep.* **5,** 405–408.

25. Noda, K., and Gross, E. (1972). Solid phase synthesis of the pentadecapeptides valine-gramicidin B and C. *In* "Chemistry and Biology of Peptides" (J. Meienhofer, ed.), pp. 241–250. Ann Arbor Science Publishers, Ann Arbor, Michigan.
26. Gross, E. (1972). Structural relationships in and between peptides with α,β-unsaturated amino acids. *In* "Chemistry and Biology of Peptides" (J. Meienhofer, ed.), pp. 671–678. Ann Arbor Science Publishers, Ann Arbor, Michigan.
27. Gross, E., and Kiltz, H. H. (1973). The number and nature of α,β-unsaturated amino acids in subtilin. *Biochem. Biophys. Res. Commun.* **50,** 559–565.
28. Fontana, A., and Gross, E. (1973). Solid phase synthesis of the pentadecapeptide valine-gramicidin A. *In* "Peptides 1972" (H. Hanson and H. D. Jakubke, eds.), pp. 229–234. North Holland, Amsterdam.
29. Corash, L., and Gross, E. (1973). Subcellular constituents of human placenta. Isolation and characterization of lysosomes from term tissue. *Pediatr. Res.* **7,** 798–811.
30. Mecklenburg, R. S., Noda, K., Miyachi, Y., Gross, E., and Lipsett, M. B. (1973). LH-Releasing activity of pyro-Glu-His-Trp-NH_2 and pyro-Glu-His-Trp. *Endocrinology* **93,** 993–997.
31. Gross, E., Kiltz, H. H., and Craig, L. C. (1973). Subtilin II: The amino acid composition of subtilin. *Hoppe Seyler's Z. Physiol. Chem.* **354,** 799–801.
32. Kiltz, H. H., and Gross, E. (1973). Subtilin III. Enzymatic fragmentation with trypsin and thermolysin. *Hoppe Seyler's Z. Physiol. Chem.* **354,** 802–804.
33. Kiltz, H. H., and Gross, E. (1973). Subtilin IV. Sequence and assignment of sulfide bridges in the heterodetic bicyclic peptide of amino acid residues 20–29. *Hoppe Seyler's Z. Physiol. Chem.* **354,** 805–806.
34. Nebelin, E., and Gross, E. (1973). Subtilin V. Sequence and assignment of sulfide bridges in the heterodetic tricyclic peptide of amino acid residues 3–19. *Hoppe Seyler's Z. Physiol. Chem.* **354,** 807–809.
35. Gross, E., Kiltz, H. H., and Nebelin, E. (1973). Subtilin VI. The structure of subtilin. *Hoppe Seyler's Z. Physiol. Chem.* **354,** 810–812.
36. Gross, E., Noda, K., and Nisula, B. (1973). Solid phase synthesis via α,β-unsaturated amino acids. I. Peptides with carboxyl-terminal amides-Thyrotropin-Releasing Factor (TRF). *Angew Chem.* **85,** 672–673; *Angew. Chem. Internat. Ed. Engl.* **12,** 664–665.
37. Morell, J. L., and Gross, E. (1973). The configuration of the β-carbon atoms of the β-methyllanthionine residues in nisin. *J. Am. Chem. Soc.* **95,** 6480–6481.
38. Kleinman, L. M., Tangrea, J. A., Gallelli, J. F., Brown, J. H., and Gross, E. (1973). Assay and stability of a solution of essential amino acids. *Am. J. Hosp. Pharm.* **30,** 1054–1057.
39. Boime, I., Corash, L., and Gross, E. (1974). Protein synthesis in cell-free extracts derived from first and third trimester human placenta. *Pediatr. Res.* **8,** 770–774.
40. Corash, L. M., Piomelli, S., Chen, H. C., Seaman, C., and Gross, E. (1974). Separation of erythrocytes according to age on a simplified density gradient. *J. Lab. Clin. Med.* **84,** 147–151.
41. Corash, L., and Gross, E. (1974). Subcellular constituents of human placenta, II. Isolation and density distribution of lysosomes from first trimester tissue. *Pediatr. Res.* **8,** 774–782.
42. Gross, E., and Morell, J. L. (1974). The reaction of cyanogen bromide with S-methylcysteine: fragmentation of the peptide 14-29 of bovine pancreatic ribonuclease A. *Biochem. Biophys. Res. Commun.* **49,** 1145–1150.
43. Gross, E., Noda, K., and Matsuura, S. (1975). The utility of α,β-unsaturated amino acids in peptide synthesis. *In* "Peptides 1974" (Y. Wolman, ed.), pp. 403–413. Wiley, New York.
44. Gross, E., and Matsuura, S. (1975). α,β-Unsaturated and thioether amino acids in peptide synthesis. *In* "Chemistry, Structure and Biology of Peptides" (R. Walter and J. Meienhofer, eds.), pp. 351–358., Ann Arbor Science Publishers, Ann Arbor, Michigan.
45. Gross, E. (1975). Subtilin and nisin: The chemistry and biology of peptides with α,β-unsaturated amino acids. *In* "Chemistry, Structure and Biology of Peptides" (R. Walter and J. Meienhofer, eds.), pp. 31–42. Ann Arbor Science Publishers, Ann Arbor, Michigan.
46. Bamberg, E., Gross, E., Noda, K., Läuger, P. (1976). Single channel parameters of gramicidins A, B, and C. *Biochim. Biophys. Acta* **419,** 223–228.
47. Winslow, R. M., Swenberg, M. L., Gross, E., Chervenick, P. A., Buchman, R. R., and Anderson, W. F. (1976). Hemoglobin McKees Rocks ($\alpha_2\beta_2{}^{145\text{Try}\rightarrow\text{Term}}$). *J. Clin. Invest.* **57,** 772–781.
48. Chen, H. C., Hodgen, G. D., Matsuura, S., Lin, L. J., Gross, E., Reichert, L. E., Birken, S., Canfield, R. E., and Ross, G. T. (1976). Evidence for a gonadotropin from nonpregnant subjects that has physical, immunological, and biological similarities to human chorionic gonadotropin. *Proc. Natl. Acad. Sci. U.S.A.* **73,** 2885–2889.

49. Gross, E. (1976). Nonenzymatic fragmentation of proteins and its application to molecules with rarely seen amino acids: biosynthesis and phylogentic aspects. *In* "Protein Structure and Evolution" (J. L. Fox, Z. Deyl, and A. Beazej, eds.), pp. 69–90. Dekker, New York.
50. Gross, E., and Brown, J. H. (1976). Peptides with α,β-unsaturated and thioether amino acids: DURAMCIN. *In* "Peptides 1976" (A. Loffet, ed.), pp. 183–190. Editions de l'Universite de Bruxelles, Belgium.
51. Morell, J. L., Fleckenstein, P., and Gross, E. (1977). The stereospecific synthesis of 2R, 3S-2-amino-3-mercaptobutyric acid—an intermediate for incorporation into β-methyllanthionine containing peptides. *J. Org. Chem.* **42,** 355–356.
52. Bamberg, E., Alpes, H., Apell, H. J., Benz, R., Janko, K., Kolb, H. A., Läuger, P., and Gross, E. (1977). Studies on the gramicidin channel. *In* "Biochemistry of Membrane Transport" (G. Semenza and E. Carfoli, eds.), pp. 179–201. Springer-Verlag, Berlin.
53. Gross, E. (1977). Chemistry and biology of amino acids in food proteins: lysino-alanine. *In* "Food Proteins: Improvement through Chemical and Enzymatic Modification" (R. E. Feeney and J. R. Whitaker, eds.), pp. 37–51. *A.C.S., Washington, D.C.*
54. Pert, C. B., Bowie, D. L., Pert, A., Morell, J. L., and Gross, E. (1977). Agonist-antagonist properties of N-allyl-[D-Ala]^2-Met-enkephalin. *Nature (London)* **269,** 73–75.
55. Gross, E. (1977). α,β-Unsaturated and related amino acids in peptides and proteins. *In* "Protein Crosslinking-B" (M. Friedman, ed.), pp. 131–153. Plenum, New York.
56. Grant, J. P., Cox, C. E., Klienman, L. M., Maher, M. M., Pittman, M. A., Tangrea, J. A., Brown, J. H., Gross, E., Beazley, R. M., Jones, R. S. (1977). Serum hepatic enzyme and bilirubin elevations during parenteral nutrition. *Surg. Gynecol. Obstet.* **145,** 573–580.
57. Mahley, R. W., Innerarity, T. L., Pitas, R. E., Weisgraber, K. H., Brown, J. H., and Gross, E. (1977). Inhibition of lipoprotein binding to the cell surface receptors of fibroblasts following the selective modification of arginyl residues in the arginine-rich and B apoproteins. *J. Biol. Chem.* **252,** 7279–7287.
58. Aswanikumar, S., Corcoran, B. A., Schiffmann, E., Pert, C. B., Morell, J. L., and Gross, E. (1977). Peptides with agonist and antagonist chemotactic activity. *In* "Peptides: Proceedings of the Fifth American Peptide Symposium" (M. Goodman and J. Meienhofer, eds.), pp. 141–145. Wiley, New York.
59. Pallai, P., Wakamiya, T., and Gross, E. (1977). Studies on the synthesis and biology of nisin: Ring A. *In* "Peptides, Proceedings of the Fifth American Peptide Symposium" (M. Goodman and J. Meienhofer, eds.), pp. 205–208. Wiley, New York.
60. Gross, E. (1977). Sequence determination of peptides with α,β-unsaturated and related amino acids. *In* "Solid Phase Methods in Sequence Analysis" (A. Previero and M.-A. Coletti-Previero, eds.), pp. 195–208. North Holland, Amsterdam.
61. Aswanikumar, S., Schiffmann, E., Corcoran, B. A., Pert, C. B., Morell, J. L., and Gross, E. (1978). Antibiotics and peptides with agonist and antagonist chemotactic activity. *Biochem. Biophys. Res. Commun.* **80,** 464–471.
62. Gross, E. (1978). Polypeptide antibiotics. *In* "Antibiotics. Isolation, Separation and Purification" (M. J. Weinstein and G. H. Wagman, eds.), pp. 415–462. Elsevier, New York.
63. Bamberg, E., Apell, H.-J., Alpes, H., Gross, E., Morell, J. L. Harbaugh, J. F., Janko, K., and Läuger, P. (1978). Ion channels formed by chemical analogs of gramicidin A. *Fed. Proc., Fed. Am. Soc. Exp. Biol.* **37,** 2633–2638.
64. Gross, E., and Meienhofer, J. (1979). The Peptide Bond. *In* "The Peptides" (E. Gross and J. Meienhofer, eds.), Volume 1, pp. 1–64. Academic Press, New York.
65. Gross, E., and Meienhofer, J., Eds. (1979). "The Peptides: Analysis, Synthesis, Biology." Volume 1, Major Methods of Peptide Bond Formation. Academic Press, New York.
66. Pallai, P., and Gross, E. (1979). Peptides with rare structural components: Precursors for the synthesis of nisin, lanthionine in Ring A. *In* "Peptides 1978" (I. Z. Siemion and G. Kupryszewski, eds.), pp. 357–363. Wroclaw University Press, Wroclaw, Poland.
67. Bamberg, E., Alpes, H., Apell, H. J., Läuger, P., Morell, J. L., and Gross, E. (1979). Formation of ion-transporting channels by analogs of Gramicidin A. *In* "Peptides: Structure and Biological Function" (E. Gross and J. Meienhofer, eds.), pp. 629–634. Pierce Chemical Company, Rockford, Illinois.
68. Schiffmann, E., Venkatasubramanian, K., Corcoran, B., Aswanikumar, S., Day, A., Freer, R. J., Gallin, J. I., Clark, R. A., Hirata, F., Brown, J. H., and Gross, E. (1979). Chemotactic peptides as probes of molecular events in leukocyte chemotaxis. *In* "Peptides: Structure and Biological Function" (E. Gross and J. Meienhofer, eds.), pp. 731–741. Pierce Chemical Company, Rockford, Illinois.

69. Freer, R. J., Day, A. R., Becker, E. L., Showell, H. J., Schiffmann, E., and Gross, E. (1979). Structural requirements for synthetic peptide chemoattractants and antagonists. *In* "Peptides: Structure and Biological Function" (E. Gross and J. Meienhofer, eds.), pp. 749–751. Pierce Chemical Company, Rockford, Illinois.
70. Izumiya, N., Kato, T., Aoyagi, H., Shimohigashi, Y., Yasutake, A., Lee, S., Noda, K., and Gross, E. (1979). Synthesis of cyclo-tetra-peptides, AM-toxins and analogs of CYL-2. *In* "Peptides: Structure and Biological Function" (E. Gross and J. Meienhofer, eds.), pp. 439–444. Pierce Chemical Company, Rockford, Illinois.
71. Gross, E., and Meienhofer, J., eds. (1979). "Peptides: Structure and Biological Function, Proc. Sixth American Peptide Symposium," June 17–22, 1979, Georgetown University, Washington, D.C. Pierce Chemical Company, Rockford, Illinois.
72. Noda, K., Shimohigashi, Y., Izumiya, N., and Gross, E. (1980). Synthesis of AM-toxin analogs by intramolecular condensation of pyruvyltripeptide amides. *In* "Peptide Chemistry 1979" (H. Yonehara, ed.), pp. 65–68. Protein Research Foundation, Osaka, Japan.
73. Noda, K., Shibata, Y., Shimohigashi, Y., Izumiya, N., and Gross, E. (1980). Synthesis of cyclotetrapeptides, AM-toxin analogs, containing α-hydroxyalanine. *Tetrahedron Lett.* **21,** 763–766.
74. Gross, E., and Meienhofer, J., eds. (1980). "The Peptides: Analysis, Synthesis, Biology," Volume 2, Special Methods in Peptide Synthesis, Part A. Academic Press, New York.
75. Schiffmann, E., Aswanikumar, S., Venkatasubramanian, K., Corcoran, B. A., Pert, C. B., Brown, J. H., Gross, E., Day, A. R., Freer, R. J., Showell, A. H., and Becker, E. L. (1980). Some characteristics of the neutrophil receptor for chemotactic peptides. *FEBS Lett.* **117,** 1–7.
76. Gross, E. (1980). Amino acid assemblies with rare structural components: chemical biological, and biosynthetic aspects in nucleic acids and proteins. *In* "Proceedings of Symposium on Nucleic Acids and Proteins, Shanghai, China, October 1979" (Shen Zhao-wen, ed.), pp. 70–86. Science Press, Beijing, China.
77. Gross, E., and Meienhofer, J., eds. (1981). "The Peptides: Analysis, Synthesis, Biology," Volume 3, Protection of Functional Groups in Peptide Synthesis. Academic Press, New York.
78. Noda, K., and Gross, E. (1981). Solid phase synthesis of peptides via α,β-unsaturated amino acids. Incorporation of the amide group in endo-positions. *Z. Naturforsch. B:* **36,** 1345–1347.
79. Noda, K., Shibata, Y., Gross, E., Shimohigashi, Y., and Izumiya, N. (1981). Cyclic peptides XI. Synthesis of AM-toxin analogs by intramolecular condensation of pyruvyl tripeptide amides. *Int. J. Pep. Protein Res.* **18,** 423–429.
80 Gross, E., and Meienhofer, J., eds. (1981). "The Peptides: Analysis, Synthesis, Biology," Volume 4, Modern Techniques of Conformational, Structural, and Configurational Analysis. Academic Press, New York.
81. Rich, D. H., and Gross, E., Eds. (1981). "Peptides: Synthesis, Structure, Function, Proc. Seventh American Peptide Symposium," June 14–19, 1981, University of Wisconsin, Madison, Wisconsin. Pierce Chemical Co., Rockford, Illinois.
82. Gaudreau, P., Morell, J. L., Gross, E., and St.-Pierre, S. (1981). Solid phase synthesis of COOH-terminal fragments of cholecystokinin octapeptide. *In* "Peptides: Synthesis, Structure and Function" (D. Rich and E. Gross, eds.), pp. 193–195. Pierce Chemical Company, Rockford, Illinois.
83. Gross, E., Morell, J. L., Bamberg, E., and Läuger, P. (1981). The synthesis and ion transport properties of analogs of the linear gramicidins: Valine-gramicidin A. *In* "Peptides: Synthesis, Structure and Function" (D. Rich and E. Gross, eds.), pp. 233–236. Pierce Chemical Company, Rockford, Illinois.
84. Noda, L., Gazis, D., and Gross, E. (1982). Solid phase synthesis of peptides via α,β-unsaturated amino acids. Oxytocin, simultaneous incorporation of amide functions in COOH-terminal and endo-positions. *Int. J. Pep. Protein Res.* **19,** 413–419.
85. Gaudreau, P., Morell, J. L., and Gross, E. (1982). Formation of amino-succinyl derivatives from β-phenacyl aspartyl peptides catalyzed by sodium thiophenoxide. *Int. J. Pep. Protein Res.* **19,** 280–283.
86. Morell, J. L., Gaudreau, P., and Gross, E. (1982). Cleavage of aspartyl β-phenacyl esters by selenophenol under neutral conditions. *Int. J. Pep. Protein Res.* **19,** 487–489.
87 Kolasa, T., and Gross, E. (1982). Dehydroaspartic acid derivatives. *Int. J. Pep. Protein Res.* **20,** 259–266.
88. Gross, E., and Meienhofer, J., eds. (1983). "The Peptides: Analysis, Synthesis, Biology," Volume 5, Special Methods in Peptide Synthesis, Part B. Academic Press, New York.
89. Hruby, V., ed. (1984). "The Peptides: Analysis, Synthesis, Biology" (E. Gross and J. Meienhofer, eds.), Volume 6, Physical Methods in Peptide Conformational Studies. Academic Press, New York.

Contents

List of Contributors xv
Preface xvii
Nomenclature and Abbreviations xix
Contents of Previous Volumes xxv

Chapter 1 *Synthesis of Polypeptides by Recombinant DNA Methods*

Ronald Wetzel and David V. Goeddel

I Introduction 2
II Cloning of Foreign Genes into *E. coli* 4
III Efficient Expression 22
IV Purification and Characterization of Product 41
V Synthesis of Analogs 48
VI Survey of Reports of Heterologous Gene Expression 52
VII Conclusion 57
References 58

Chapter 2 *Acidolytic Deprotecting Procedures in Peptide Synthesis*

Haruaki Yajima and Nobutaka Fujii

I Introduction 66
II Deprotecting Reagents in Peptide Synthesis 67
III Acidolytic Deprotecting Procedures 68
IV Applications in Synthesis 74

V Deprotection of Synthetic Bovine Ribonuclease A 95
VI Opportunities and Constraints 104
References 106

Chapter 3 *Side Reactions in Peptide Synthesis*

Miklos Bodanszky and Jean Martinez

I Introduction 112
II Side Reactions Characteristic of Individual Amino Acids 114
III Side Reactions in the Introduction and Removal of Protecting Groups 161
IV Side Reactions Encountered in Formation of the Peptide Bond 177
V Side Reactions in Solid-Phase Peptide Synthesis 192
VI Side Reactions in Cyclization 193
VII Instability of Peptides in Solution 194
VIII Conclusions 196
References 197

Chapter 4 *Quantitation and Sequence Dependence of Racemization in Peptide Synthesis*

N. Leo Benoiton

I Introduction 218
II Methods for Assessing Stereochemical Composition 221
III Oxazolin-5-ones from N-Substituted α-Amino Acids 235
IV Racemization of *N*-Alkoxycarbonylamino Acids 257
V Racemization during the Saponification of Esters 263
VI Racemization and Asymmetric Induction during the Aminolysis of 2,4-Dialkyl-5(4*H*)-oxazolones 263
VIII Variables Affecting α-Inversion during Coupling 268
VIIII Conclusion 278
References 279

Chapter 5 *α,β-Dehydroamino Acids and Peptides*

Kosaku Noda, Yasuyuki Shimohigashi, and Nobuo Izumiya

I	Introduction	286
II	Occurrence of Peptides Containing α,β-Dehydroamino Acids	287
III	Synthesis of α,β-Dehydroamino Acids and Introduction into Peptides	296
IV	Synthesis of Biologically Active Peptides with α,β-Dehydroamino Acids	312
V	Utility of α,β-Dehydroamino Acids in Peptide Chemistry	325
VI	Concluding Remarks	332
	References	333

Chapter 6 *Unusual Amino Acids in Peptide Synthesis*

David C. Roberts and Frank Vellaccio

I	Introduction	342
II	Isofunctional and Homofunctional Replacement	346
III	Isosteric and Homosteric Replacement	349
IV	Amino Acids Exerting Strong Conformational Influences	351
V	Reporter Groups	354
VI	Reactive Side-Chain Functionality	356
VII	Peptide Isosteres	363
	Appendix: Unusual Amino Acids	365
	References	429

Author Index 451
Subject Index 491

List of Contributors

Numbers in parentheses indicate the pages on which the authors' contributions begin.

N. Leo Benoiton (217), Department of Biochemistry, University of Ottawa, Ottawa, Ontario K1H 8M5, Canada

Miklos Bodanszky (111), Department of Chemistry, Case Western Reserve University, Cleveland, Ohio 44106

Nobutaka Fujii (65), Faculty of Pharmaceutical Sciences, Kyoto University, Kyoto, Japan

David V. Goeddel (1), Department of Molecular Biology, Genentech, Inc., South San Francisco, California 94080

Nobuo Izumiya (285), Laboratory of Biochemistry, Faculty of Science, Kyushu University, Fukuoka 812, Japan

*Jean Martinez** (111), Centre National de La Recherche Scientifique, Ecole Nationale Supérieure de Chimie, 34075 Montpellier, France

Kosaku Noda (285), Laboratory of Biochemistry, Fukuoka Women's University, Fukuoka 812, Japan

David C. Roberts (341), Department of Chemistry, Rutgers University, New Brunswick, New Jersey 08903

Yasuyuki Shimohigashi (285), National Institute of Child Health and Human Development, National Institutes of Health, Bethesda, Maryland 20205

Frank Vellaccio (341), Department of Chemistry, College of Holy Cross, Worcester, Massachusetts 01610

Ronald Wetzel† (1), Department of Protein Biochemistry, Genentech, Inc., South San Francisco, California, 94080

Haruaki Yajima (65), Faculty of Pharmaceutical Sciences, Kyoto University, Kyoto, Japan

**Present address:* Centre CNRS–INSERM de Pharmacologie–Endocrinologie, 34033 Montpellier, France

†*Present address:* Department of Chemical Sciences, Genentech, Inc., South San Francisco, California 94080

Preface

"The Peptides" is an open-ended treatise providing comprehensive and critical reviews of important developments in all areas of peptide research, including analysis, synthesis, and biology. These reviews are intended as a reference for the specialist, a guide for the novice, and a forum for all investigators concerned with peptides and proteins.

In the volumes on peptide synthesis an attempt is made to present the current state of methodology. Peptide synthesis has been variously described either as very difficult or as routine "cookbook" chemistry. The routine aspects arise from formation of the same bond whereas the difficulties are seen in the polymeric nature of peptides and proteins and their wide range of properties. Fortunately, the complete information for the three-dimensional folding of peptides and proteins is contained in the linear sequence of amino acids. The interactions between neighboring amino acid side chains determine the property of a peptide. Peptides with properties ranging from very hydrophobic to very hydrophilic, from basic to acidic, etc., arise from the extraordinary multitude of potential structures. It is the wide range of often unpredictable behavior of peptides that presents problems in synthesis and frequently requires the use of special methods.

This volume continues the survey of special approaches to peptide synthesis that was begun in Volume 2. Many of these special methods have opened up or stimulated entire new areas of investigation.

In the first chapter Ronald Wetzel and David Goeddel present exciting new ways of synthesizing peptides and proteins by recombinant DNA methods. The progress made in genetic engineering has been so rapid that more than one volume is needed for comprehensive coverage; hence only two selected examples, desacetylthymosin α_1 and human leukocyte interferon, are described. Acidolytic deprotection procedures in peptide synthesis are discussed in Chapter 2 by Haruaki Yajima and Nobutaka Fujii. These important studies have paved the way for the synthesis of fully active ribonuclease. They provide guidelines for one of the most critical steps in peptide synthesis. In Chapter 3 Miklos Bodanszky and Jean Martinez present a comprehensive discussion of side reactions that have been observed in peptide synthesis. This compilation should prove to be invaluable to the synthetic chemist. The continuing exploration of racemization during peptide synthesis has yielded very interesting new insights that are discussed in detail by N. Leo Benoiton in Chapter 4. The chemical and biological properties of α,β-dehydroamino acids and peptides are described in Chapter 5 by Kosaku Noda, Yasuyuki Shimohigashi, and Nobuo Izumiya. This interesting class of compounds will become increasingly important in peptide analog synthesis. The final chapter is also devoted to analog synthesis and contains an unprecedented collection of unusual amino acids, compiled by David C. Roberts and Frank Vellaccio.

Other special methods will be discussed in a later volume. Physical methods in peptide conformational studies will be presented in Volume 6.

Johannes Meienhofer

Nomenclature and Abbreviations

The preferred peptide size nomenclature is that using arabic numerals (M. Bodanszky, 1977), for example, "15-peptide," "31-peptide," or corticotropin-(1–24), gastrin-(5–17). Greek prefixes are retained for di- to decapeptides.

Peptides obtained by chemical or enzymatic degradation are generally termed *fragments;* however, synthetic intermediates should be referred to as *segments* and their coupling as *segment condensation.* Amino acids are of the L configuration unless otherwise indicated. In peptide structures, hyphens between D and the amino acid symbol are omitted, for example, H-Gly-DPhe-Ala-OH.

The current *Chemical Abstracts* term 5(4*H*)-oxazolone is used for azlactone [viz. *Chem. Abstr.* **83,** 3633 CS(1975)], as it is unambiguous in contrast to other (earlier) terms in the literature.

Abbreviations are kept as short as possible, preferably three letters (four or more letters only if unavoidable). Many abbreviations are those recommended by the IUPAC–IUB Commission on Biochemical Nomenclature, for example, in *J. Biol. Chem.* **242,** 6489–6497 (1970); **250,** 3215–3216 (1975).

The one-letter symbols for amino acids are as follows:

A	alanine	G	glycine	M	methionine	S	serine
C	cysteine	H	histidine	N	asparagine	T	threonine
D	aspartic acid	I	isoleucine	P	proline	V	valine
E	glutamic acid	K	lysine	Q	glutamine	W	tryptophan
F	phenylalanine	L	leucine	R	arginine	Y	tyrosine

Symbols used in this volume (except for the three-letter code of the common amino acids) are listed below.

Abbreviations

A	adenosine
AA	amino acid
ΔAA	dehydroamino acid, see D (delta)
Ac	acetyl
Acm	acetamidomethyl

Ac_2O	acetic anhydride
AcOH, HOAc	acetic acid
Ahp	2-amino-5-(4-hydroxyphenyl)pentanoic acid
Aib	α-aminoisobutyric acid
*a*Ile	*allo*-isoleucine
Ala(Cl)	2-chloroalanine
cAMP	cyclic adenosine-3′,5′-monophosphate
Amp	2-amino-5-(4-methyloxyphenyl)pentanoic acid
AP-M	aminopeptidase M
Ap^R	ampicillin-resistant gene in plasmid
App	2-amino-5-phenylpentanoic acid
ATG	start codon
ATP	adenosine triphosphate
AUG	start codon, translation initiator (coding for fmet)
*Bam*HI	*Bacillus amyloliquefacience* H restriction site
Bgl	*Bacillus globigii* restriction site (sticky end)
:B	base
bp	base pair
BK	bradykinin
Boc	*tert*-butyloxycarbonyl
Bpoc	2-(4-biphenylyl)propyl(2)oxycarbonyl
pBR322	an *Escherichia coli* expression plasmid
*t*Bu	*tert*-butyl
*t*BuOCl	*tert*-butylhypochloride
*t*BuOK	potassium *tert*-butylate
Bz	benzoyl
Bzl	benzyl
dC	deoxycitidine
CM	carboxymethyl
CNBr	cyanogen bromide
DABCO	diazabicyclooctanone, triethylenediamine
Dpr	α,β-diaminopropionic acid
DBU	1,7-diazabicyclo[5.4.0.]undec-5-ene
Dcb	2,6-dichlorobenzyl
DCC	dicyclohexylcarbodiimide (method)
DDQ	2,3-dichloro-5,6-dicyano-1,4-benzoquinone
d.e.	diastereoisomeric excess
DEAE	diethylaminoethyl
ΔAbu	α,β-dehydro-α-aminobutyric acid

ΔAla	α,β-dehydroalanine, (aminoacrylic acid)
ΔAun	α,β-dehydroundecanoic acid
ΔHis	α,β-dehydrohistidine
ΔIle	α,β-dehydroisoleucine
ΔLeu	α,β-dehydroleucine
ΔMePhe	α,β-dehydro-*N*-methylphenylalanine
ΔNle	α,β-dehydronorleucine
ΔNva	α,β-dehydronorvaline
ΔPhe	α,β-dehydrophenylalanine
ΔPro	α,β-dehydroproline
ΔThr	α,β-dehydrothreonine
ΔTrp	α,β-dehydrotryptophane
ΔTyr	α,β-dehydrotyrosine
ΔVal	α,β-dehydrovaline
DMAP	4-dimethylaminopyridine
Dmt	dimethyloxytrityl
cDNA	complementary deoxyribonucleic acid
DOPA	β-(3,4-dihydroxyphenyl)alanine
Dpm	diphenylmethyl (benzhydryl)
Dpp	diphenylphosphinoyl
DSC	disuccinimido carbonate
DTT	dithiothreitol
*Eco*Rl	GAATTC restriction site
EDA, EDAC	*N*-ethyl-*N'*-(3-dimethylaminopropyl)carbodiimide (hydrochloride)
EDT	ethanedithiol
e.e.	enantiomeric excess
EEDQ	*N*-ethyloxycarbonyl-2-ethyloxy-1,2-dihydroquinoline
Et	ethyl
Et_3N	triethylamine
Et_2NH	diethylamine
fmet	formylmethionine
Fmoc	9-fluorenylmethyloxycarbonyl
For	formyl
dG	deoxyguanosine
β-gal	β-galactosidase
GAT	codon for aspartic acid
GLC	gas–liquid chromatography
hGH	human somatotropin (growth hormone)

Hmb	2-hydroxy-3-methylbutanoic acid
HOBt	1-hydroxybenzotriazole
HOSu	*N*-hydroxysuccinimide
HPLC	high-performance liquid chromatography
hIFN-αA	human leukocyte interferon A
*i*Pr	isopropyl
ir	infrared (spectroscopy)
lac	lactose-based promoter system (operator, repressor)
*lac*Z gene	coding for β-galactosidase
LHRH	luliberin
Mbs	4-methyloxybenzenesulfonyl
MDBK	bovine kidney cell line
Me	methyl
MeAla	*N*-methylalanine
MeIle	*N*-methylisoleucine
MeLeu	*N*-methylleucine
$MeNH_2$	methylamine
MeThr	*N*-methylthreonine
Met(O)	methionine sulfoxide
MeTyr	*N*-methyltyrosine
MIF	melanostatin
Mob	4-methyloxybenzyl
Moc	methyloxycarbonyl
Moz	4-methyloxybenzyloxycarbonyl
MSA	methanesulfonic acid
α-MSH	α-melanotropin
β-MSH	β-melanotropin
Mts	mesitylene-2-sulfonyl
N^g	guanidine nitrogen
N^i	indole nitrogen
N^{im}	imidazole nitrogen
NCA	*N*-carboxyanhydride
nmr	nuclear magnetic resonance (spectroscopy)
4Np	4-nitrophenyl
Nps	2-nitrophenylsulfenyl
NSu	*N*-succinimidyl

O*t*Bu	*tert*-butyl ester
OBzl	benzyl ester
OEt	ethyl ester
OMe	methyl ester
ONp	4-nitrophenyl ester
ORD	optical rotatory dispersion (spectroscopy)
OSu(ONSu)	*N*-hydroxysuccinimide ester (*N*-succinimidoyl ester)
Orn	ornithine
OTcp	2,4,5-trichlorophenyl ester*
PAGE	polyacrylamide-gel electrophoresis
PGK	phosphorogalactosyl kinase
pGlu	pyroglutamic acid
Ph	phenyl
Pht	phthaloyl
Prot	protecting group (general)
Pst	*Providencia stuartii* (restriction site)
Py	pyridine
Pyn	*Proteus vulgaris* restriction site
RIA	radioimmunoassay
RNA	ribonucleic acid
mRNA	messenger ribonucleic acid
tRNA	transfer ribonucleic acid
$tRNA^{Trp}$	tryptophan transfer ribonucleic acid
RNase	ribonuclease (bovine)
*Sau*3a	*Staphylococcus aureus* 3a (restriction site)
SBzl	*S*-benzylthiol
S–D	Shine–Dalgarno mRNA sequence
SDS	sodium dodecyl sulfate
SMob	*S*-4-methyloxybenzyl
dT	deoxythimidine
TAA, TAG	stop codons
Tc	tetracyclin sensitive gene in plasmid
TFA	trifluoroacetic acid
Tfa	trifluoroacetyl
TFMSA	trifluoromethanesulfonic acid

*Unless a different-position isomer is indicated, for example, 2,4,6-OTcp.

TGT	codon for cysteine
pThα	an *Escherichia coli* expression plasmid
THF	tetrahydrofuran
*a*Thr	*allo*-threonine
tlc	thin-layer chromatography
Tos	4-toluenesulfonyl (tosyl)
tris-HCl	tris[hydroxymethyl]aminomethane hydrochloride
trp	tryptophan-based promoter system (operator, repressor)
trp-lac	promotor hybrid *(tac)*
Trt	triphenylmethyl (trityl)
uv	ultraviolet (spectroscopy)
VIP	vasoactive intestinal polypeptide
Wish	human amnion cell line
X-gal	5-chloro-4-bromo-3-indolyl-β-D-galactosidase
Z	benzyloxycarbonyl
Z-NH_2	benzylcarbamate

Contents of Previous Volumes

Volume 1

MAJOR METHODS OF PEPTIDE BOND FORMATION

The Peptide Bond
Erhard Gross and Johannes Meienhofer

The Formation of Peptide Bonds: A General Survey
John H. Jones

Active Esters in Peptide Synthesis
Miklos Bodanszky

The Azide Method in Peptide Synthesis
Johannes Meienhofer

The Carbodiimide Method
Daniel H. Rich and Jasbir Singh

The Mixed Carbonic Anhydride Method of Peptide Synthesis
Johannes Meienhofer

Racemization in Peptide Synthesis
D. S. Kemp

Author Index

Subject Index

Volume 2

SPECIAL METHODS IN PEPTIDE SYNTHESIS, PART A

Solid-Phase Peptide Synthesis
George Barany and R. B. Merrifield

The Liquid-Phase Method for Peptide Synthesis
Manfred Mutter and Ernst Bayer

Polymeric Reagents in Peptide Synthesis
Mati Fridkin

The Four Component Synthesis
Ivar Ugi

The Oxidation–Reduction Condensation
Teruaki Mukaiyami, Rei Matsueda, and Masaaki Ueki

Repetitive Methods in Solution
Lajos Kisfaludy

Partial Synthesis of Peptides and Proteins
Robert C. Sheppard

Racemization and Coupling Rates of N^{α}-Protected Amino Acid and Peptide Active Esters: Predictive Potential
Józef Kovács

Author Index

Subject Index

Volume 3

PROTECTION OF FUNCTIONAL GROUPS IN PEPTIDE SYNTHESIS

Amine Protecting Groups
Rolf Geiger and Wolfgang König

Carboxyl Protecting Groups
Roger W. Roeske

Sulfhydryl Group Protection in Peptide Synthesis
Richard G. Hiskey

Protection of the Hydroxyl Group in Peptide Synthesis
John M. Stewart

Differential Protection and Selective Deprotection in Peptide Synthesis
Jean-Luc Fauchère and Robert Schwyzer

Peptide Synthesis with Minimal Protection of Side-Chain Functions
John K. Inman

Dual Functional Groups
Brian J. Johnson

Author Index

Subject Index

Volume 4

MODERN TECHNIQUES OF CONFORMATIONAL, STRUCTURAL, AND CONFIGURATIONAL ANALYSIS

X-Ray Analysis: Conformation of Peptides in the Crystalline State
Isabella L. Karle

Crystal Structure Analysis of the Larger Peptide Hormones
Jennifer Gunning and Tom Blundell

Determination of the Absolute Configuration of α-Amino Acids and Small Peptides by Chiroptical Means
Voldemar Toome and Manfred Weigele

Ultramicroanalysis of Peptides and Proteins by High-Performance Liquid Chromatography and Fluorescense Detection
Stanley Stein

Amino Acid Analysis of Peptides
James R. Benson, Paul C. Louie, and Ralph A. Bradshaw

Solid-Phase Sequencing of Peptides and Proteins
Richard A. Laursen

Author Index

Subject Index

Chapter 1

Synthesis of Polypeptides by Recombinant DNA Methods

RONALD WETZEL*
Department of Protein Biochemistry
Genentech, Inc.
South San Francisco, California

DAVID V. GOEDDEL
Department of Molecular Biology
Genentech, Inc.
South San Francisco, California

I. Introduction 2
II. Cloning of Foreign Genes into *E. coli* 4
A. Source of DNA 5
1. Chemical–Enzymatic Synthesis 5
2. cDNA Approaches 14
3. Semisynthetic Genes 18
B. Gene Purification by Cloning 18
1. Selection 19
2. Screening 20
III. Efficient Expression 22
A. Replication 23
B. Transcription 23
1. Fusion Protein Synthesis 25
2. Direct Expression 27
C. Translation 28
1. Ribosome Binding Sites 28
2. Signal Sequences 29
3. mRNA Structure 30
4. Protein Product Structure 31

* Present address: Department of Chemical Sciences, Genentech, Inc., South San Francisco, California 94080.

THE PEPTIDES, VOLUME 5

ISBN 0-12-304205-4

D. *In Vivo* Stability 31
1. Stability of Fusion Proteins 32
2. Product Secretion 33
3. Analytical Detection of Low-Yield Products 37
E. Other Posttranslational Processing 37
1. Disulfide Bonds 38
2. NH_2-Terminal Methionine 39
3. NH_2-Terminal Acetylation 40
4. Glycosylation 40
5. Proteolytic Processing 40
IV. Purification and Characterization of Product 41
A. Desacetylthymosin α_1 41
B. Leukocyte Interferon A 44
C. General Considerations 45
1. Purification 45
2. Characterization 47
V. Synthesis of Analogs 48
A. Mutant DNA–Natural Amino Acids 50
1. Chemical Synthesis 50
2. Semisynthesis 50
3. Random Mutagenesis 50
4. Specific Mutagenesis 51
5. Alterations Using Restriction Sites 51
B. Chemical Semisynthesis 51
C. Biochemical Synthesis 52
1. *In Vivo* Synthesis 52
2. *In Vitro* Synthesis 52
VI. Survey of Reports of Heterologous Gene Expression 52
VII. Conclusion 57
References 58

I. INTRODUCTION

The age of recombinant DNA research can be said to have begun with the demonstration of the *in vitro* construction (Jackson *et al.*, 1972; Cohen *et al.*, 1973) and efficacy (Cohen *et al.*, 1973) of hybrid DNA molecules capable of transferring alien genetic material into an organism. Such a functional gene transfer was first accomplished between strains of bacteria. Cohen, Boyer, and co-workers (1973) transferred a structural gene, with its natural controlling elements, from the microorganism *Salmonella typhimurium* into another microorganism, *Escherichia coli*, where it was actively replicated and expressed. The success of this experiment was based upon the marriage of two relatively young areas of research: the biology of bacterial plasmids and the biochemistry of DNA-processing enzymes (Cohen, 1975).

Plasmids are naturally occurring rings of double-stranded DNA that can be taken up through bacterial cell membranes and, once internalized, be copied by the bacteria's DNA replication system and thus transferred to daughter cells after division. Since it is possible to insert new DNA fragments into plasmids, these molecules can be used as carriers, or vectors, for the stable, functional insertion of new genetic elements into bacteria. Sections of DNA can be removed from the chromosome of a cell and inserted into a plasmid by the use of a series of enzymes capable of synthesizing or hydrolyzing DNA phosphodiester bonds. Since 1973 these methods have been applied with great success to the study of the structure and organization of genes, the proteins whose syntheses they encode, and the mechanisms whereby these syntheses are regulated, both in bacteria and in higher organisms (Wetzel, 1980).

These same techniques can also be used to engineer strains of microorganisms to synthesize with high efficiency proteins not naturally produced in a given cell type (for reviews, see Gilbert and Villa-Komaroff, 1980; Wetzel, 1980). The first experiments demonstrating translational expression of foreign DNA in bacteria were not designed for efficient transcription or translation of the added DNA, nor was there any attempt to characterize rigorously the new gene product (Struhl *et al.*, 1976; Ratzkin and Carbon, 1977). These experiments were by and large extensions of the techniques of bacterial genetics. Nonetheless they clearly indicated that a coding gene sequence from another source could be expressed in *E. coli*. The gene for human somatostatin was the first cloned foreign gene to be expressed in which the structure and orientation of the added gene were engineered for efficient synthesis, under the genetic control of the host cell, of a native polypeptide (Itakura *et al.*, 1977). This was also the first protein synthesis directed by a chemically synthesized gene. Since then there have been over 80 reports of the synthesis of foreign polypeptides in microorganisms. In many of these studies, the goal was to produce in high yield a particular polypeptide resembling as closely as possible the molecule normally synthesized in another species.

This chapter concentrates on methods that have been used to synthesize polypeptides efficiently and with high fidelity in *E. coli*. The reference list at the end of this chapter is more general, however, including reports of lower-yield expression, expression of nonprocessable fusion proteins and expression of foreign polypeptides in other microorganisms, whether or not the mechanism of expression is controlled or understood. While an attempt has been made to allow easy access to the concepts and jargon of the recombinant DNA world, the uninitiated reader may find useful some of the general reviews mentioned above. For previous reviews of the recombinant DNA approach to polypeptide synthesis, see Riggs *et al.* (1980), Ross (1981),

Miozzari (1981), and Timmis (1981). Additionally, a review by Harris (1983) is now in press which covers the same material as this chapter with a somewhat different perspective.

We have attempted to cover all the aspects of this unique approach to polypeptide synthesis in this chapter. As much as possible, the points in each section are illustrated with two running examples—the synthesis of desacetylthymosin α_1, a 28-amino acid polypeptide (Goldstein *et al.*, 1977) synthesized by the fusion protein approach using chemically synthesized DNA, and of human leukocyte interferon A (IFN-αA),* a protein of about 20,000 molecular weight synthesized by direct expression from a gene comprised mostly of complementary DNA (cDNA). In both cases, a source of DNA has to be identified and then obtained through some kind of DNA synthesis. By inserting the new DNA into a plasmid and then inserting the plasmid into bacteria, the desired DNA can be purified and amplified in quantity. If the bacteria do not synthesize the desired gene product in sufficient amounts, the plasmid DNA can be further changed to try to increase efficiency. Finally, the desired protein can be isolated, purified, and characterized from cultures of the improved strain. The following sections follow this idealized project chronology.

II. CLONING OF FOREIGN GENES INTO *E. COLI*

Plasmids are rings of DNA which seem to have evolved as a mechanism by which bacteria can transfer certain genetic material, such as genes coding for resistance to certain antibiotics, from one cell to another. Simple mixing of plasmid DNA with a bacterial culture is sufficient to promote the uptake of certain plasmids by a small percentage of cells; methods have been developed for increasing the efficiency of uptake. Cells that have taken up new bits of genetic information are said to have been *transformed*. Once inside the cell, plasmid DNA is replicated by *E. coli* DNA polymerase; but, although the *E. coli* chromosome is replicated only once (just before cell division), plasmid DNA can be synthesized in 50–100 copies per cell. A culture of transformed cells can be grown up and broken open, and the plasmid DNA extracted and purified. This *amplified* DNA can be characterized, used as a substrate for enzyme-mediated alterations in its DNA sequence, and introduced into new bacterial cells.

Work at the DNA level leading up to efficient production of new polypeptides in *E. coli* proceeds in two stages. The first stage involves acquiring in a pure form a gene coding for the polypeptide of interest. DNA can be

* Also referred to as IFLrA or LeIF A.

totally synthetic (obtained by chemical synthesis using a design based on the genetic code) or natural (derived from mRNA). An important variation is one in which the gene being designed is derived from elements of both chemically synthesized and natural nucleic acid sequences. DNA obtained in any fashion is bound to be a mixture of molecules of differing sequence. This mixture of DNA is inserted into plasmids and used to transform *E. coli*; when plated out on an agar dish, individual progenitor bacterial cells grow on the plate to form colonies. Some of the colonies contain plasmids that can be shown to contain the desired inserted DNA. This *cloning* process allows identification of a cell line containing the right DNA, as well as amplification of this DNA through growth of the cells and extraction of the plasmid. Once the desired DNA is obtained, it can be further altered *in vitro* and the product repurified and amplified by a repeat of the cloning process.

A. Source of DNA

1. Chemical–Enzymatic Synthesis

The overall strategy of *de novo* gene synthesis has changed little since the pioneering work of the Khorana group on the synthesis of the tRNA Ala gene (Agarwal *et al.*, 1970). The method consists of the synthesis of relatively short oligonucleotide fragments by chemical condensation of protected nucleotides. These oligonucleotides form both the coding and noncoding strands of the synthetic gene. The purified deprotected fragments are assembled into the gene; by mixing fragments from opposite complementary strands of the DNA, their mutual affinities through base pairing can be used to help align the proper chain termini for covalent closure mediated by T4 DNA ligase (Sgaramella *et al.*, 1970).

Khorana's original method of DNA fragment synthesis, the phosphodiester method, has been largely supplanted by the variation known as the modified phosphotriester approach (Itakura *et al.*, 1975) and more recently by a number of solid-phase synthesis methods. The general features of chemical gene synthesis are illustrated in the following sections by a description of the modified triester synthesis of the gene for desacetylthymosin α_1. Following this (Section II,A,1,d) is a brief discussion of more recent developments in DNA synthesis.

a. Design of a Gene Coding for Desacetylthymosin α_1. The principal requirement for the chemical approach to obtaining a gene is a knowledge of the complete amino acid sequence of the desired polypeptide. A lesser consideration is size; although the longest polypeptide from a completely synthetic gene to be described, human leukocyte interferon (Edge *et al.*, 1981),

```
      1   2   3   4   5   6   7   8   9   10  11  12  13  14  15  16  17  18  19  20  21  22  23  24  25  26  27  28
 Met Ser Asp Ala Ala Val Asp Thr Ser Ser Glu Ile Thr Thr Lys Asp Leu Lys Glu Lys Lys Glu Val Val Glu Glu Ala Glu Asn

Eco RI                                                                                                      stop stop
<---T1---><---T2---><---T3---><---T4---><---T9---><---T10---><---T11---><---T12--->
AATTCATGTCTGATGCTGCTGTTGATACTTCTTCTGAGATTACTACTAAAGATCTTAAGGAGAAGAAGGAAGTTGTCGAAGAGGCTGAGAACTAATAG
    GTACAGACTACGACGACAACTATGAAGAAGACTCTAATGATGATTTCTAGAATTCCTCTTCTTCCTTCAACAGCTTCTCCGACTCTTGATTATCCTAG
    <---T5---><---T6---><---T7---><---T8---><---T13---><---T14---><---T15---><---T16--->
                                              Bgl II                                                  BamHI
```

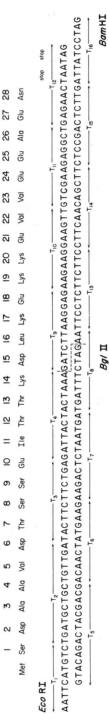

Figure 1. Design of a gene coding for Met-desacetylthymosin α_1 (Wetzel *et al*., 1980). The previously determined amino acid sequence (Low and Goldstein, 1979) is shown at the top, numbered from the number one amino acid of desacetylthymosin α_1. The gene is divided into 16 oligonucleotide fragments indicated by double-headed arrows. The 5′ ends of each strand have single-stranded cohesive termini to facilitate joining to plasmids cleaved with *Eco*RI and *Bam*HI. A *Bgl*II site in the middle of the gene assists in the analysis of recombinant plasmids. The ATG codon is added to the 5′ end of the coding strand to place a methionine at the NH_2-terminus of the peptide, allowing later cyanogen bromide cleavage of N^{α}-desacetylthymosin α_1 from the fusion protein. The stop codons TAA and TAG are added to the 3′ end of the coding strand to signal translation termination at the ribosome. Reprinted with permission from Wetzel *et al.* (1980). Copyright (1980) American Chemical Society.

is 166 amino acids long, there is in principle no limit to the lengths obtainable by chemical methods.

Figure 1 depicts a gene designed to code for the immunostimulatory thymic factor desacetylthymosin α_1 (Wetzel *et al.*, 1980, 1981a). Since most amino acids can be encoded by multiple codons, one has a good deal of flexibility in the design of a gene. Codon choice for the desacetylthymosin α_1 gene was made under a number of constraints. First, it was assumed that the best codon to use for each amino acid was the triplet favored in known *E. coli* genes. At the time the desacetylthymosin α_1 gene was designed, the only known *E. coli*-related sequences were from the genome of the bacteriophage MS2 (Fiers *et al.*, 1976), and these codon preferences were used as much as possible. Since then, several genes from the *E. coli* chromosome and from *E. coli* plasmids (Sutcliffe, 1978; Grantham *et al.*, 1980; Ikemura, 1981) have been sequenced, and the codon usage in these more typical genes has been found to differ in a number of respects from that found in MS2 phage. Despite the implication that the synthetic desacetylthymosin α_1 gene contains some codons that may be less efficiently recognized in *E. coli*, there is no evidence that this or any other synthetic gene based on MS2 codon usage is encumbered by this bias.

Once the coding strand has been designed, the noncoding strand is defined. At this point both strands are broken down into overlapping fragments which can be chemically synthesized. The sequences of these fragments are inspected for potential synthetic or other problems. For example, major concentrations of dG:dC pairs followed by dA:dT pairs are avoided, since these may lead to premature termination of transcription (Bertrand *et al.*, 1975).

The sequence of each fragment is inspected to ensure that it is not significantly self-complementary, since this association could well compete with its ability to interact properly with fragments of the opposite strand during gene assembly (Section II,A,1,c). Problem areas of the gene are treated either by using new codons or by resectioning the same sequence into new oligonucleotide fragments.

Some of the most powerful tools of recombinant DNA methods are enzymes known as restriction endonucleases. These enzymes recognize specific double-stranded DNA sequences and cleave both strands at these sites. The scissions often produce jagged termini, in which one DNA strand is cleaved about four nucleotides away from the other strand. Since the two strands in the substrate DNA were complementary, the short single strands produced by the endonuclease cleavage are as well; because of their continued complementary affinity, such endonuclease termini are called *sticky ends*. They can be exploited to mediate the covalent reassembling of restriction enzyme products (*restriction fragments*) by the same principle used to

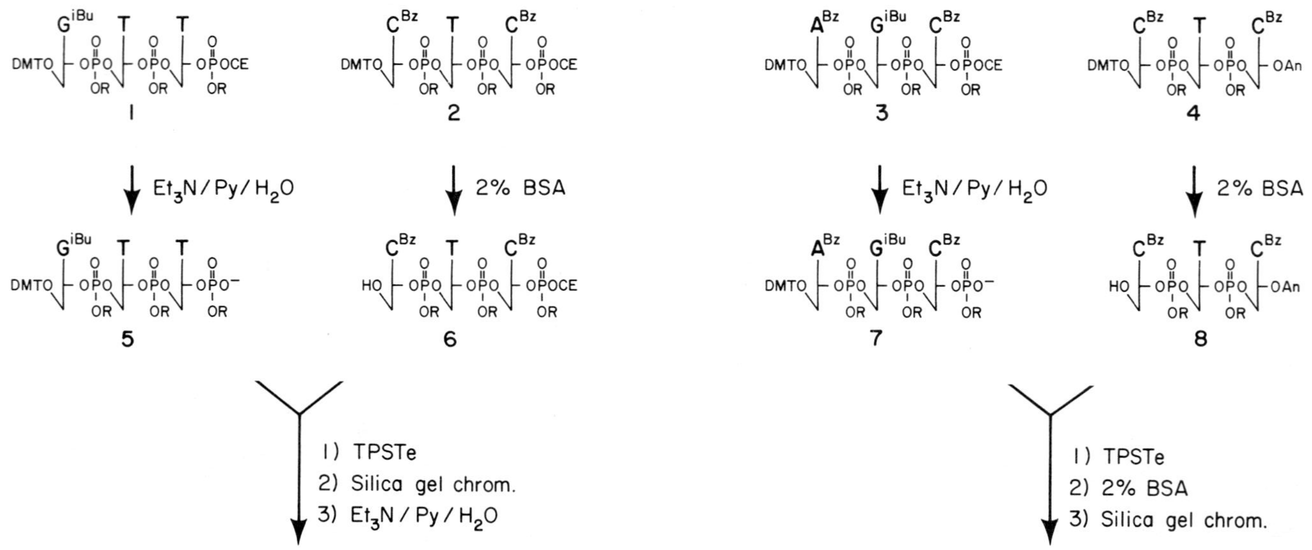

DMTO
OPOCE
OR
OPO⁻
HO
OAn
1
2
3
4
5
6
7
8
Et3N / Py / H2O
2% BSA
1) TPSTe
2) Silica gel chrom.
3) Et3N / Py / H2O
1) TPSTe
2) 2% BSA
3) Silica gel chrom.

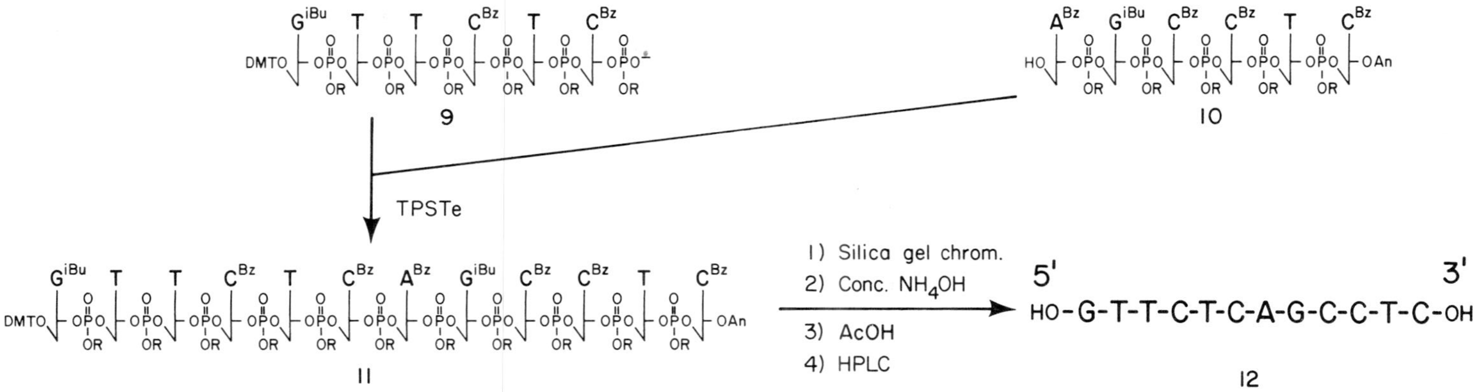

Figure 2. Synthetic route to fragment T_{15} of the N^{α}-desacetylthymosin α_1 gene (Wetzel *et al.*, 1980). Compounds **1**–**4** are typical fuliy protected trinucleotide building blocks used in the improved phosphotriester method. After deblocking the 3′-phosphate of **1** and the 5′-hydroxyl of **2**, the products (**5** and **6**) are condensed using TPSTe. A slight excess of **5** drives the reaction to completion, ensuring that the only uncharged species in the reaction mixture will be the product hexanucleotide; this allows removal of excess **5** by filtration through silica gel. The crude product is deblocked at the 3′-phosphate to give **9**. By a similar strategy, trimers **3** and **4** are deblocked and condensed, and the product is deblocked at the 5′-hydroxyl and partially purified to give **10**. The hexamers **9** and **10** are condensed, with **9** in excess, to give a reaction mixture containing mostly **11** and excess **9**. After silica gel chromatography, to remove **9**, all the protecting groups are removed to give the dodecamer **12**, which is then further purified. DMT, 4,4′-Dimethoxytrityl; BSA, benzenesulfonic acid; CE, 2-cyanoethyl; R, 4-chlorophenyl; Bz, benzoyl; An, anisoyl; i-Bu, isobutyl; TPSTe, 2,4,6-triisopropylsulfonyltetrazole; Py, pyridine; AcOH, acetic acid; Et_3N, triethylamine. Reprinted with permission from Wetzel *et al.* (1980). Copyright (1983) American Chemical Society.

align and close synthetic fragments (described above). Enzymatically derived sticky ends interact equally well with sticky ends included at the termini of chemically synthesized genes. Such genes can thus be inserted into plasmids cleaved by the appropriate enzyme(s).

The desacetylthymosin α_1 synthetic gene contains several such restriction endonuclease sites. The use of these sites, designated *Eco*RI, *Bgl*II, and *Bam*HI (see Fig. 1) in gene and plasmid construction will be described in Section II,A,c.

The codon ATG for methionine has been added to the 5′ end of the coding strand to insert methionine in position for later chemical cleavage of the protein product (Section IV,A). Tandem stop codons TAA and TAG at the 3′ end of the coding strand are signals for termination of translation by the ribosome. The designed gene was sectioned into 16 synthetic fragments, T1 through T16.

b. Fragment Synthesis and Purification. A typical scheme for the synthesis of an oligonucleotide by the modified triester approach is shown in Fig. 2, which describes the construction of fragment T15 of the desacetylthymosin in α_1 gene. The synthesis is based on a library of fully protected trinucleotide building blocks, four of which are shown at the top of the figure. These four trinucleotides are used to construct two hexanucleotides by selective deprotection of the 3′ and 5′ ends of each set of trimers, followed by condensation with the chemical coupling agent triisopropylbenzenesulfonyl tetrazole. After partial purification, the hexanucleotides are deblocked at the appropriate ends and likewise condensed to form the fully protected dodecanucleotide shown in the lower left. After partial purification this product is chemically deblocked as shown.

Following deprotection the reaction mixture is subjected to more rigorous purification. Since *E. coli* transformation can be accomplished with nanogram quantities of DNA, and because a synthetic gene, once cloned, can be easily amplified, it is only necessary to produce a small amount of the gene; this in turn requires relatively small amounts of each synthetic fragment. One consequence of these requirements is that techniques generally considered to be of only analytical utility can be employed for preparative separation. Figure 3a shows the purification of fragment T15 from the reaction mixture described above by an analytical high-performance liquid chromatography (HPLC) column. The peak at 22 min was labeled with a [^{32}P]phosphate group, purified from the phosphorylation reaction by polyacrylamide gel electrophoresis, and analyzed for purity and sequence by wandering spot sequence analysis (Jay *et al.*, 1974) as shown in Fig. 3b. Each of the synthetic fragments required was similarly synthesized, purified, and characterized.

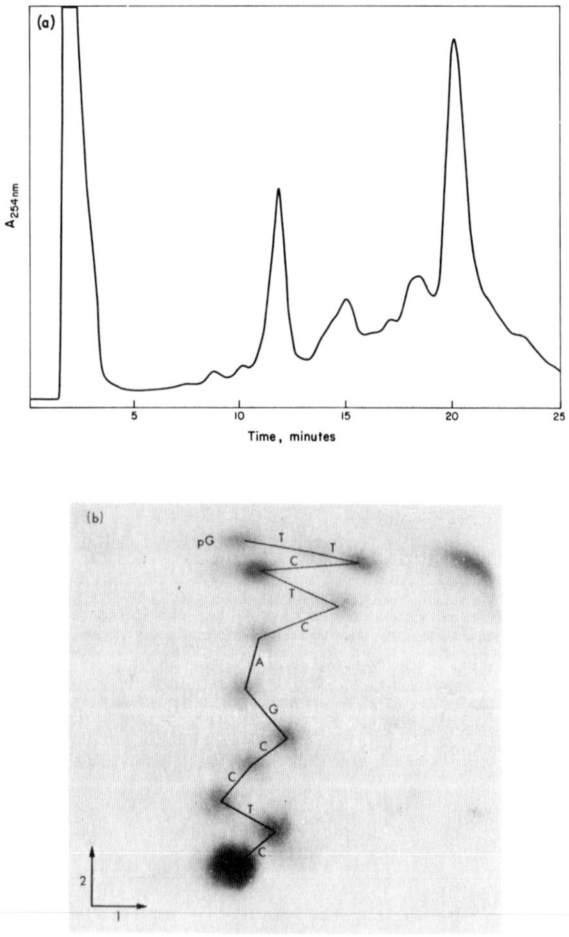

Figure 3. (a) HPLC analysis and purification of deblocked fragment T_{15} from the reaction mixture described in Fig. 2. The product was eluted from a Permaphase AAX (DuPont) column with a linear gradient of potassium chloride in phosphate buffer, pH 4.5, at 60°C. Fragment T_{15} elutes at 20.2 min. (b) Two-dimensional sequence analysis (Jay *et al.*, 1974) of T_{15} purified by HPLC and PAGE. The 5′ ^{32}P-labeled fragment was partially digested with snake venom phosphodiesterase and the resulting mixture of labeled products submitted to two-dimensional separation and autoradiography. First dimension: electrophoresis on a cellulose acetate strip at pH 3.5. Second dimension: DEAE-cellulose thin-layer chromatography developed in a solution of homologous RNA fragments. Reprinted with permission from Wetzel *et al.* (1980). Copyright (1980) American Chemical Society.

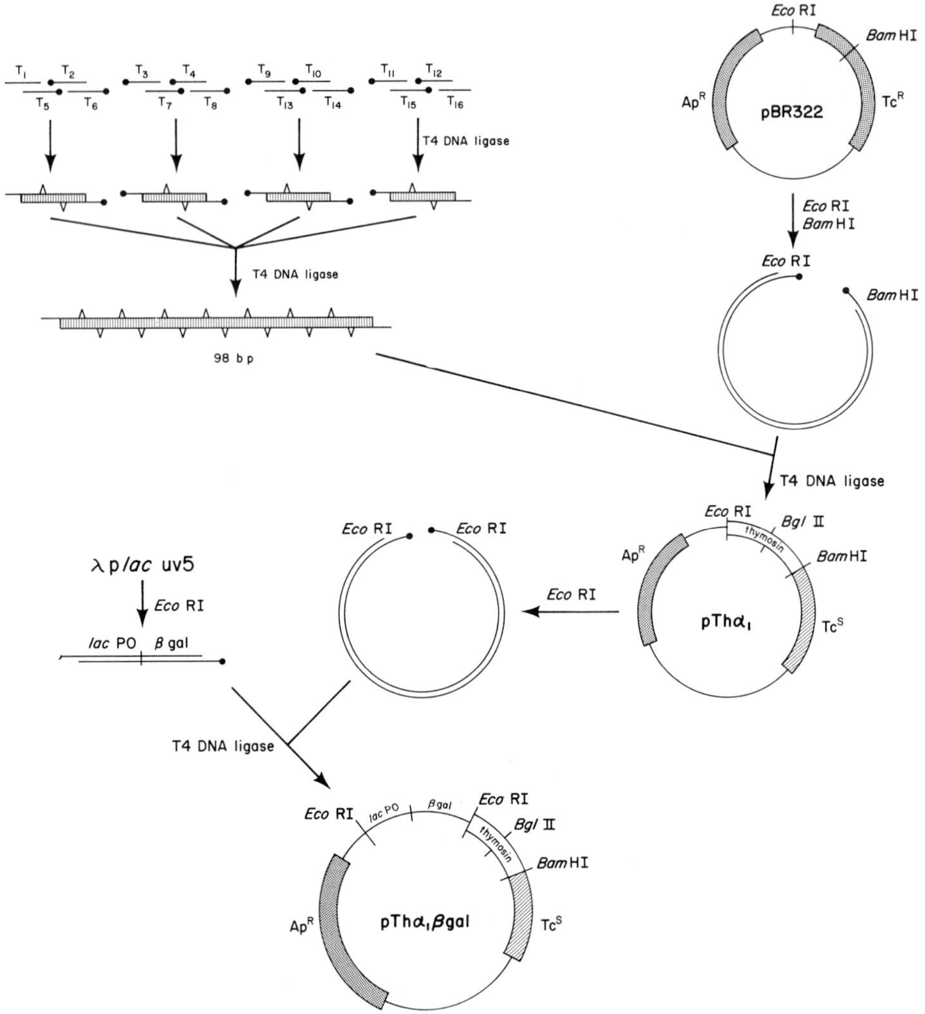

Figure 4. Ligation scheme for construction of a desacetylthymosin α_1 gene and expression vehicle. Synthetic fragments, shown at the top left with heavy dots indicating the location of 5′-phosphate groups, are mixed in groups of four with T4 DNA ligase to generate four double-stranded fragments which are purified by PAGE. These intermediates are reacted in a similar fashion to produce the double-stranded DNA shown in detail in Fig. 1. Plasmid pBR322 cleaved with restriction endonucleases *Eco*RI and *Bam*HI gives a large fragment that can combine via base-pairing complementary interactions with the synthetic gene. A covalently closed plasmid is reformed by T4 DNA ligase. This plasmid, pThα_1, is cleaved with *Eco*RI to yield an open-chain version without loss of nucleotides. The *Eco*RI fragment from λp*lac*UV5, which contains the *lac* promoter, operator, and bulk of the β-galactosidase (Z) gene, is introduced into the *Eco*RI-opened pThα_1. Closure with DNA ligase gives pTh$\alpha_1\beta$gal, which contains a replication origin (not shown), a viable ampicillin resistance (Ap^R, penicillinase) gene, a destroyed tetracycline resistance (Tc^S) gene, and a *lac* promoter–operator followed by the structural gene for a β-galactosidase–Met-desacetylthymosin α_1 fusion protein. Reprinted with permission from Wetzel *et al.* (1980). Copyright (1980) American Chemical Society.

c. Gene and Plasmid Construction. Figure 4 shows the construction of the desacetylthymosin α_1 gene and its insertion into an expression plasmid. The gene was built in two steps. In the first, sets of four oligonucleotides were mixed together in aqueous solution and joined using T4 DNA ligase. The opposite strand overlap designed into these fragments provides, via the energy of hydrogen bond formation between complementary nucleotides, a driving force for noncovalent association of the fragments. After the appropriate chain termini are brought into proximity by this association, T4 DNA ligase can catalyze efficient phosphodiester bond formation to yield contiguous DNA chains. Each double-stranded fragment obtained is purified by gel electrophoresis, and the four intermediates thus purified are mixed together and similarly ligated.

The synthetic gene can now be inserted into a plasmid that has been cleaved by one or two restriction endonucleases to generate characteristic sticky ends which should pair with the complementary termini designed into the synthetic gene. In this way, the desacetylthymosin α_1 gene was inserted into the plasmid pBR322 as shown in Fig. 4. This figure also shows further manipulations, discussed in later sections, that culminate in the synthesis of a plasmid that can direct synthesis of desacetylthymosin α_1 in *E. coli*.

d. Recent Improvements in Chemical Synthesis. The solution phosphotriester approach to oligonucleotide synthesis (Letsinger and Ogilvie, 1967) using fully protected trinucleotides (Itakura *et al*., 1975), which was used to synthesize genes that led to the expression of human somatostatin (Itakura *et al*., 1977), insulin chains (Crea *et al*., 1978), and desacetylthymosin α_1 (Wetzel *et al*., 1980), has several major advantages over other methods. Once a library of protected trinucleotides is established, oligonucleotide fragments can be synthesized in a single day. One consequence of the block condensation strategy is that most side products differ considerably in size from the desired product, allowing facile purification (Fig. 3). Both ion-exchange HPLC and gel electrophoresis separate oligonucleotides on the basis of net charge, which correlates directly with chain length. In addition to reducing the amount of side reactions normally associated with the phosphodiester approach, the phosphotriester products in the above method also lend themselves to rapid purification steps incorporated into the condensation strategy (Crea *et al*., 1978). This triester approach has been successfully modified for solid phase synthesis which should be amenable to automation (Miyoshi *et al*., 1980; Crea and Horn, 1980). Using additions of protected trimers, dimers, or monomers, it is possible to make oligomers up to 50 nucleotides in length (C. Hoyng, personal communication).

The phosphite condensation method introduced by Letsinger and Lunsford (1976) has recently become competitive with the phosphotriester method. Matteucci and Caruthers (1981) have developed a solid-phase synthesis that overcomes the previous requirement for −80°C temperatures in the condensation reaction. This method should also be amenable to automation. Presently it is possible to make oligonucleotides up to 20 bases in length using this method. Because the phosphite approach requires successive addition of monomers, side products tend to be similar in size to the desired product and thus more difficult to eliminate by purification; this problem becomes more serious with longer oligonucleotides.

Any solid-phase method generates a single-stranded oligonucleotide. With the availability of longer fragments, it has become possible to avoid total chemical synthesis of the opposite strand. For example, two strands of 30 nucleotides each might be chemically synthesized so that their 3′ ends overlap by about seven nucleotides. The remaining nucleotides can then be added using the Klenow fragment of DNA polymerase I to generate a long, double-stranded fragment (Crea *et al.*, 1982).

2. *cDNA Approaches*

If the full amino acid sequence of a desired polypeptide is unknown, it is of course not possible to design a synthetic gene coding for it. In such an instance, some natural representation of the nucleic acid coding for the polypeptide must be obtained. Once obtained, one can reengineer that DNA for expression. The most frequently used type of naturally derived nucleic acid is cDNA. Even if the protein amino acid sequence is known, the cDNA approach often can more rapidly lead to a cloned gene.

Complementary DNA is derived from reverse transcriptase-catalyzed polymerization of deoxyribonucleotide triphosphates using an RNA template and an oligodeoxynucleotide primer, followed by synthesis of the opposite strand of DNA using DNA polymerase I (Fig. 5). If the RNA is mRNA, the full-length, double-stranded cDNA transcript represents all the *coding* information necessary for synthesis of a polypeptide product.

Most cells synthesize many proteins simultaneously, which means that cDNA prepared from unfractionated mRNA is quite heterogeneous. The more enriched a DNA preparation is in the gene of interest, the more easily the gene can be located by cloning methods. One can enrich a cDNA preparation if it is possible to purify partially the template mRNA used. In some cases it may be possible to enrich the *in vivo* levels of a derived mRNA in a cell just before extraction of mRNA.

cDNA prepared from unfractionated mRNA from a cell actively synthesizing many proteins is still much less heterogeneous than total genomic

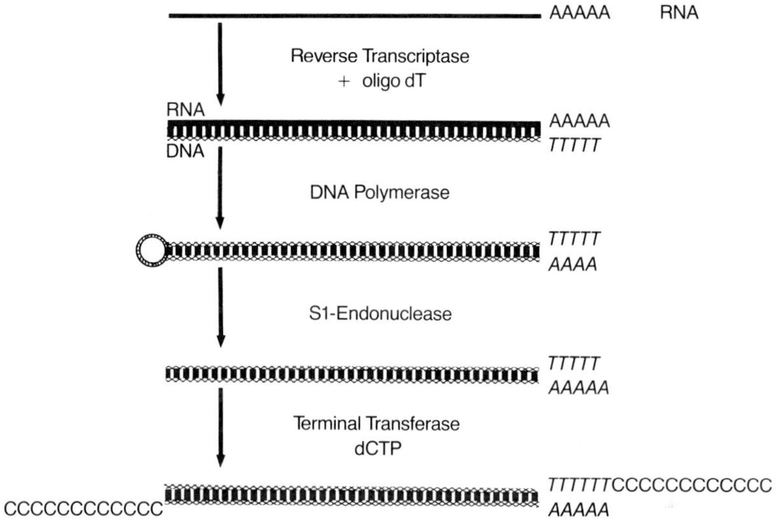

Figure 5. Synthesis of cDNA. A mixture of mRNA molecules, typically containing 3′-poly(A) sequences, is reverse-transcribed from an oligo(dT) primer to give heteroduplex DNA–RNA molecules. DNA polymerase uses these single strands of DNA as both template and primer to make the double-stranded, looped-back DNA molecules shown. The non-base-paired loops are excised by S1 nuclease. The cDNA molecules can then be extended with 5′-poly(dC) sequences using the enzyme terminal deoxynucleotidyl transferase, permitting the cDNA molecules to be introduced via base-pairing complementarity into plasmids prepared by ring opening followed by poly(dG) tailing. Reprinted with permission from Gueriguian (1981). Copyright (1981) Raven Press.

DNA. This is one reason why cDNA approaches are generally preferable to methods starting with chromosomal DNA. Another property of genomic DNA with potential disadvantages is that most eukaryotic genes contain intervening sequences of noncoding DNA interspersed within the coding regions. Such sequences inserted intact into *E. coli* cannot be expressed correctly, generating nonsense proteins. Since these intervening sequences are, however, rapidly processed out of the coding regions at the mRNA level in the eukaryotic cell, cDNA prepared from mRNA lacks intervening sequences and thus can faithfully direct the synthesis of proteins in prokaryotes.

Figure 5 summarizes the procedure involved in preparing cDNA from a pool of mRNA known to include mRNA coding for a particular protein. In this case the cDNA is inserted into a plasmid using synthetic sticky ends obtained by extending the cDNA fragments with oligo(dC) residues while "tailing" the incised plasmid with oligo(dG) residues (Jackson *et al.*, 1972; Cohen, 1975).

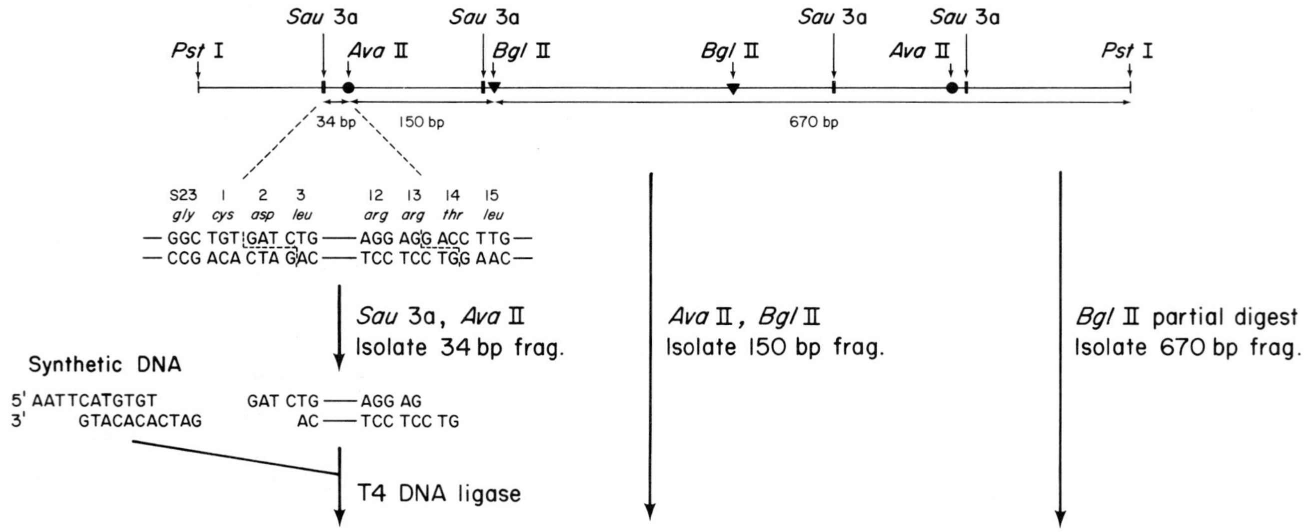

Sau 3a
Sau 3a
Sau 3a
Sau 3a
Pst I
Ava II
Bgl II
Bgl II
Ava II
Pst I
34 bp
150 bp
670 bp
S23 1 2 3 12 13 14 15
gly cys asp leu arg arg thr leu
— GGC TGT GAT CTG —— AGG AGG ACC TTG —
— CCG ACA CTA GAC —— TCC TCC TGG AAC —
Sau 3a, Ava II
Isolate 34 bp frag.
Ava II, Bgl II
Isolate 150 bp frag.
Bgl II partial digest
Isolate 670 bp frag.
Synthetic DNA
5' AATTCATGTGT
3' GTACACACTAG
GAT CTG —— AGG AG
AC —— TCC TCC TG
T4 DNA ligase

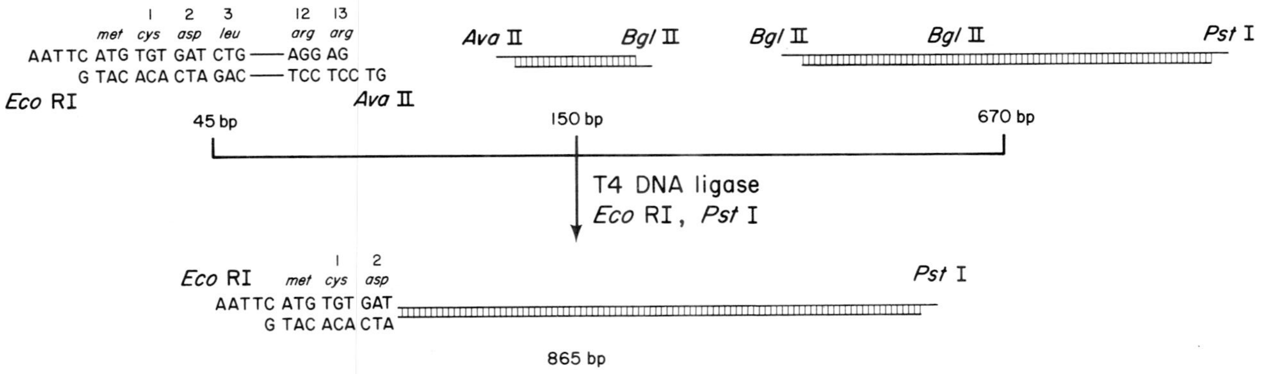

Figure 6. Construction of a gene coding for direct expression of IFN-αA (Goeddel *et al.*, 1980a). Double-stranded DNA containing the entire pre-IFN-αA gene is shown at the top with relevant restriction sites indicated. Portions of this restriction fragment were further digested as shown to give, after gel electrophoresis, gene fragments of 34, 150, and 670 base pairs (bp). As shown in the blow-up immediately under the starting material, the 34-bp fragment begins with the codon GAT for amino acid number two of the *mature* IFN-αA sequence; the IFN-αA signal sequence plus the codon for amino acid number one have been eliminated with *Sau*3a cleavage. This fragment was ligated to the synthetic fragments shown which contain the TGT codon for cysteine number one and an ATG start codon, generating a 45-bp fragment. This 45-bp fragment, which has an *Eco*RI terminus, was ligated to unaltered 150- and 670-bp fragments to generate a gene for direct expression of IFN-αA. The 865-bp product could be inserted into an expression plasmid containing the *trp* promoter and *trp* leader peptide ribosome binding site just before an *Eco*RI site. Reprinted from Goeddel *et al.*, *Nature*, Vol. 287, No. 5781, pp. 411–416. Copyright (c) 1980 Macmillan Journals Limited.

The enzyme reverse transcriptase requires a primer as well as a template. One way to enrich further for a desired gene sequence in a cDNA mixture is to prime the reverse transcription of a mRNA pool with an oligonucleotide having a sequence known (Chan *et al.*, 1979) or suspected (Houghton *et al.*, 1980) to be complementary to a region of the sought-after mRNA. If partial amino acid sequence information is known, all possible nucleotide sequences that might code for it can be predicted and synthesized. When such a mixture of oligonucleotides is used as a primer, the cDNA pool obtained should be enriched in the desired genetic information. This in turn might be used to generate a cDNA clone library (Section II,B) or to make a specific hybridization probe for screening (Section II,B,2) a preexisting cDNA clone library (Goeddel *et al.*, 1980a,b).

3. *Semisynthetic Genes*

A cDNA clone containing all of the coding region for a desired polypeptide will quite likely contain sequences detrimental to the efficient synthesis in *E. coli* of the native polypeptide (see Section III,C). For this reason, DNA sequences coding for most foreign proteins must be tailored before insertion into an expression plasmid if high yields of native product are to be obtained. One tailoring method is the semisynthetic approach, which utilizes both chemically synthesized and reverse-transcribed DNA. This method, first used in the synthesis of human growth hormone (hGH) (Goeddel *et al.*, 1979b), allows both removal of undesired eukaryotic cDNA sequences and insertion of the retained cDNA sequence at a specific point in the bacterial plasmid.

Figure 6 shows how this method was used in the processing of IFN-αA cDNA for direct expression in *E. coli*. These manipulations allowed removal of the nucleotides coding for the signal peptide of preinterferon, their replacement by the ATG start codon for protein biosynthesis, and inclusion of an *Eco*RI sticky end for later insertion into a plasmid.

B. Gene Purification by Cloning

Whatever the method for obtaining a gene, at the end of the synthetic trial there is inevitably a purification problem. The impurities in chemical synthesis tend to be mostly genes containing synthetic errors such as single-base changes. The impurities in the cDNA approach are all the other genes that were actively being transcribed in the donor cell and later were reverse-transcribed in the synthesis of the cDNA. Both methods accumulate further impurities during the enzymatic steps involved in the construction of a plasmid containing the gene.

Regardless of the impurities, the first step in gene purification is the same: Bacteria are transformed by the mixture of plasmids (differing only as their foreign DNA inserts differ), some of which contain the desired gene. A dilute suspension of the resulting genetically heterogeneous bacteria is spread on a plate of nutrient-containing agar and allowed to grow, so that each distinct bacterium gives rise to a colony of identical clones via cell division. These colonies are then screened for the presence of the correct gene.

1. Selection

Most of the plasmids used as cloning vehicles contain a functional gene for antibiotic resistance (Fig. 7). In fact, the natural history of the plasmids used in recombinant DNA research is centered on their ability to confer antibiotic resistance on an otherwise susceptible microorganism (Cohen, 1975). By including this antibiotic (e.g., ampicillin or tetracycline) in the medium of the agar plate, only bacteria that have taken up a plasmid containing such a functional antibiotic resistance *marker* will grow. Antibiotic resistance is only one possible way of making an initial selection for plasmid

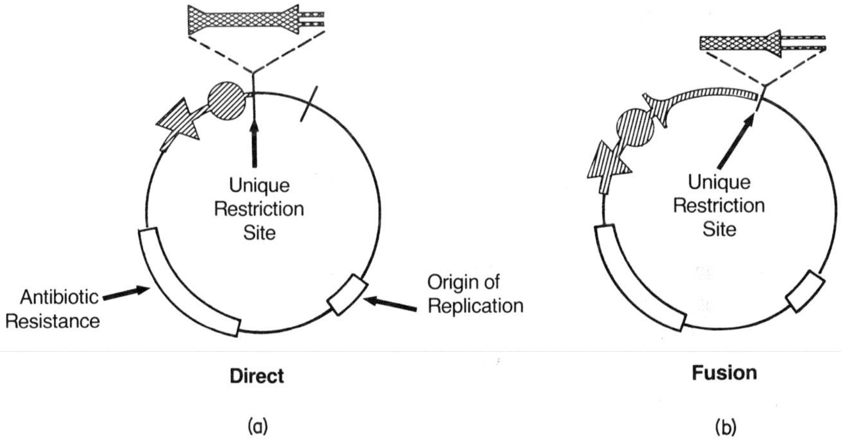

Figure 7. Vectors for the expression of foreign DNA in bacteria. Both plasmids pictured contain an origin of replication and a gene for antibiotic resistance. (a) Direct expression is accomplished by introducing a foreign gene into the plasmid at a restriction site so that the new DNA closely follows a bacterial promoter of transcription (triangle) and the ribosome binding site (circle). The figure shows that the new gene brings with it the codons for the initiation and termination of protein biosynthesis (flanged ends). (b) Fusion expression can be accomplished by introducing foreign DNA at a restriction site within the coding sequence of a bacterial gene. The new DNA brings with it only a stop codon, since the translation start codon, as well as the promoter and ribosome binding site, are provided by the bacterial gene. Expression yields a fusion protein composed of bacterial polypeptide followed by an amino acid sequence determined by the added DNA and the reading frame into which it was introduced. Reprinted with permission from Gueriguian (1981). Copyright (1981) Raven Press.

uptake. Any combination of a bacterium containing a growth-limiting mutation on its chromosome and a transforming vector containing a functional (and therefore growth-promoting) copy of the gene will, in a restrictive medium, produce the same selection effect. Selection is not only an important part of the process whereby a desired clone is initially identified, it is also a force that can be applied to ensure strain stability during fermentation.

2. *Screening*

If rigorous selective pressure has been applied, every viable colony isolated will be derived from a bacterium transformed by a plasmid. Only a few of these colonies may contain the correct plasmid, however. There exists a battery of techniques, some of general utility and some appropriate only in specific cases, for screening large numbers of colonies. Examples of different classes of screening techniques are discussed below in connection with the cloning of desacetylthymosin α_1 and leukocyte interferon genes.

a. Indicator Plates. The plasmid constructed for the expression of desacetylthymosin α_1 as part of a β-galactosidase fusion protein (Section III,D) was sought in transformed *E. coli* first by screening colonies for the multiple copies of the *lac* operator DNA expected in these cells as a result of the presence of *lac PO* sequence on the plasmid (see Fig. 4). This was accomplished with the aid of an indicator substrate, 5-chloro-4-bromo-3-indolyl-β-D-galactoside, or X-gal (Miller, 1972), which can be used directly on agar plates. The excess of *lac* operator DNA in cells containing *lac PO* plasmids binds to the limited number of *lac* repressor molecules in the cytoplasm, in direct competition with the chromosomal *lac* operator. This effectively derepresses the chromosomal *lac* operon, allowing synthesis of large (*constitutive*) amounts of β-galactosidase. When *E. coli* is making such large amounts of β-galactosidase, the enzyme hydrolyzes levels of the pseudosubstrate X-gal sufficient to turn the colony itself blue, so that it can be detected visually.

b. Restriction Mapping. In the cloning of a chemically synthesized gene, one advantage that can be exploited in screening transformants is a knowledge of the DNA sequence being sought. Restriction sites can be purposefully synthesized into the gene so that they may later be detected in cloned DNA by restriction mapping. In the case of the desacetylthymosin α_1 gene, one can predict that digestion of a plasmid containing a correctly synthesized thymosin α_1 gene (see Fig. 4) with a mixture of the restriction endonucleases *Eco*RI, *Bgl*II, and *Bam*HI will give, among other plasmid fragments, the two halves of the synthetic desacetylthymosin α_1 gene that can be detected by their length-related mobility in polyacrylamide gel electrophoresis (PAGE).

c. Hybridization Methods. The highly specific, stable interaction between two complementary oligonucleotide sequences can be exploited in a number of ways in screening for cDNA clones, even in cases where no protein or nucleic acid sequence information is available.

Short (10–15 nucleotides) oligomers of sequences known or predicted to exist in the desired DNA can be used as screening probes (Montgomery *et al.*, 1978; Noyes *et al.*, 1979; Wallace *et al.*, 1979, 1981a; Suggs *et al.*, 1981), or they can be used as primers to prepare enriched cDNA pools (Section II,A,2) as probes (Goeddel *et al.*, 1980a,b). As probes, these oligonucleotides are labeled with [^{32}P]phosphate using [γ-^{32}P]ATP and the enzyme T4 polynucleotide kinase. An agar dish containing colonies is grown and transferred to a nitrocellulose membrane filter to give a replicate array of colonies. The colonies on the filter are then lysed in such a way as to immobilize the intracellular nucleic acid on the membrane. Any complementary sequence in a lysed colony will hybridize with the radiolabeled probe. After the filter is washed, autoradiography will indicate location of the parent colony (Grunstein and Hogness, 1975).

Hybridization can be used in the absence of sequence information if one can established an *in vitro* translation system and an assay for the desired protein product. In hybrid-arrested translation (Paterson *et al.*, 1977), plasmid preparations from candidate colonies can be screened for their ability, through hybridization with natural mRNA, to interfere with product biosynthesis.

In another method, positive hybridization–translation (Harpold *et al.*, 1978), plasmid preparations from candidate colonies are immobilized on paper in an array. The paper is incubated with active mRNA under conditions promoting hybridization. Bound mRNA is then eluted from each locus, and the eluate is tested in an *in vitro* translation system coupled to an assay for the translation product.

Another variation on the hybridization approach led to the successful screening of a cDNA colony library for clones containing sequences coding for human immune interferon (γ interferon) (Gray *et al.*, 1982). In this procedure, two sets of radiolabeled cDNA probes were prepared from lymphocyte mRNA. One set was prepared from mRNA extracted from cells that had been stimulated to synthesize γ-interferon and thus should have been enriched in γ-interferon mRNA. The other cDNA probe was prepared identically, but from unstimulated (uninduced) lymphocytes. The cDNA colony library was then screened in duplicate by the Grunstein–Hogness *in situ* hybridization method described above, once with each of the two sets of probes. A few colonies were consistently positive with induced probe and negative with uninduced probe; these later turned out to contain γ-interferon sequences.

d. DNA Sequencing. Another important method of screening for the correct plasmid is to sequence the cloned DNA on the plasmid. This can be done by a chemical method such as that described by Gilbert and Maxam (1980) or by some version of DNA polymerase-based (enzymatic) sequencing as developed by Sanger and co-workers (Smith, 1980).

e. Detection of Protein; Complementation. Since the end result of the experiments covered in this chapter is the synthesis of new polypeptides in microorganisms, the ultimate screening procedure is to look for evidence of product formation in transformed cells. Chemical synthesis of genes allows one to build immediately toward an expression system (see Section III). As a consequence, the first positive clone by all other criteria will quite likely be capable of product synthesis. Immunological screening methods have been developed that permit the detection of colonies containing a specific gene product for which an antibody is available (Broome and Gilbert, 1978; Erlich *et al.*, 1978; Hitzeman *et al.*, 1980). In other cases positive clones can be detected by radioimmunoassay (RIA), perhaps after certain *in vitro* chemical steps such as those in the synthesis of insulin A and B chains (Goeddel *et al.*, 1979a). Desacetylthymosin α_1 can be detected by RIA of cyanogen bromide-treated cell debris (Wetzel *et al.*, 1980).

On the other hand, initial positive clones obtained by screening cDNA transformants may show little if any product synthesis in *E. coli.* There are many reasons for expecting activities to be low or zero, including a less than full-length cDNA clone, instability of the product, poor response from *E. coli* systems in transcription and translation of the eukaryotic DNA, and incomplete posttranslational processing of the protein in the alien microbial intracellular environment. This severely limits the value of initial colony screening based on protein activity in the cDNA approach. Nonetheless, initial screening for protein activity can sometimes be successful, especially if based on the ability of the desired protein to complement a genetic deficiency in the host cell. Most of the examples of cloned enzyme genes listed in Table III at the end of the chapter were detected by such genetic complementation screening.

III. EFFICIENT EXPRESSION

Expression levels can be influenced at any point along the biosynthetic path from gene to isolated protein. Efficient replication of the cloned gene is important, since multiple copies would be expected to boost levels of mRNA. The molecular control of transcription of these copies of DNA is very important; there is a need to understand the requirements for the strength of the promoter of transcription and any mechanisms the cell has for modulating transcription. Noncoding and, in some cases, coding sequences of the mRNA may have a lot to do with the efficiency of translation at the ribosome. Once synthesized, the gene product may fare poorly in the cell, especially since it is often of no value to the cell; steps may be needed to stabilize the desired protein. Finally, posttranslational processing mechanisms may differ in the host microbial cell and the DNA donor cell. This could lead to over- or undermodification of the gene product and thus to a possibly less useful derivative. These concerns, addressed below, have been discussed in depth in a recent review (deBoer and Shepard, 1983).

A. Replication

Once a vector such as a plasmid carries new DNA into a cell, it is replicated by the host cell; the number of copies made per cell, the *copy number*, can vary from 1 to more than 100. The copy number of a particular plasmid depends mostly on the strength of its origin of replication, a section of DNA whose sequence controls the efficiency of DNA polymerase I action on the plasmid. A high copy number is preferred, since it is expected that larger amounts of mRNA coding for a product will result from transcription of the abundant product gene.

The genome of the transducing phage λ has been used by molecular geneticists for decades to transfer genes from one bacterium to another. Much is known about the λ promoter system, which can be exploited to allow fine control over timing of gene expression in bacterial culture. The disadvantage of using λ phage as a vector is that it has an effective copy number of one. Transformed *E. coli* can proliferate and make useful amounts of product only if the phage DNA is present in a dormant (lysogenic) state; in this condition one copy of the phage DNA is integrated into the *E. coli* chromosome.

Most of the reported cases of *E. coli* expression of cloned eukaryotic genes have involved derivatives of the plasmid pBR322 (Bolivar *et al.*, 1977).

B. Transcription

Control of transcription of DNA into mRNA in bacteria can occur at several levels; gene expression in eukaryotes is far more complex and is only now being unveiled via recombinant DNA techniques. In only rare cases (see Section VI; Vapnek *et al.*, 1977; Gatenby *et al.*, 1981) is there any evidence of the efficient functioning of eukaryotic transcriptional control sequences in *E. coli.* Thus in general a eukaryotic gene must be inserted next to borrowed bacterial control sequences for expression of the foreign DNA.

Standard features of a bacterial transcriptional control region in front of a structural gene or series of related structural genes (operon) are a DNA sequence (promoter) to which the enzyme DNA-dependent RNA polymerase can bind and another sequence upstream toward the first structural gene (the operator) to which a repressor protein can bind in order to control the action of the polymerase. Only when the repressor is absent can transcription proceed; in turn, binding of a substrate or product of the enzyme system encoded on the operon controls whether or not the repressor binds to the operator. Nature has built further levels of control into some operons. In the *lac* system, a cyclic adenosine 3′,5′-monophosphate (cAMP)-binding protein must bind to the *lac* promoter next to RNA polymerase before transcription can begin. Since this protein can bind to DNA only when cAMP is bound to it, *lac* transcription is also controlled by intracellular cAMP levels (Lewin, 1974). The *trp* operon has evolved an elegant secondary control mechansim called *attenuation,* in which a significant number of the intracellular $tRNA^{Trp}$ molecules must be in the unaminoacylated form before the operon can efficiently transcribe the genes coding for tryptophan biosynthetic enzymes (Yanofsky, 1981).

Promoter strength depends ultimately not only on the strength of the binding of RNA polymerase to its binding site but also on the condition of the various control elements. One approach to maximizing promoter strength is to remove all these controls entirely. For example, in the *trp* system repressor control can be removed by using an *E. coli* mutant strain lacking the *trp* repressor, by growing the cells in a low-tryptophan medium (Doel *et al.*, 1980; Goeddel *et al.*, 1980a,b), or by the addition of a tryptophan analog such as indolacrylic acid, which derepresses the *trp* operon (Doel *et al.*, 1980; Hallewell and Emtage, 1980). Attenuation control can be removed by deleting the DNA responsible for this control from the *trp* operon sequence (Kleid *et al.*, 1981). In the *lac* system, cAMP control can be eliminated by using a mutant promoter sequence that has lost this control (Arditti *et al.*, 1968). Tandem promoters have also been employed to increase transcription (Goeddel *et al.*, 1980a,b). Repressor control of a cloned *lac* operon is under normal circumstances minimal, because the repressor protein at normal levels is titrated out by the large amounts of plasmid-encoded *lac* operators. For this reason attempts at fine induction control by timed addition of galactose analogs have been unrewarding. Such control is possible, however, in a repressor overproducing strain (Goeddel *et al.*, 1979b, 1980a).

In the compilation of examples of exogenous protein biosynthesis in Table III (p. 53), the promoter system exploited in each case, if characterized, is listed. Just as *E. coli* was the organism of choice for the first cloning experiments, the *lac* operon was the first operon utilized in finely controlled biosynthesis of proteins encoded by foreign DNA; the reason in both cases was that valuable information was already available from basic research on these systems. The first examples of *E. coli* synthesis of human hormones (Itakura *et al.*, 1977; Goeddel *et al.*, 1979a), including desacetylthymosin α_1, utilized the *lac* promoter–operator system. Another promoter used in early experiments was that for the enzyme β-lactamase. The β-lactamase promoter, which is naturally found on a plasmid, has been a popular system for the expression of foreign genes since its use requires few DNA manipulations. It generally gives low expression yields (which may have less to do with promoter strength than with translation efficiency; Section III,C) and generates fusion proteins of unpredictable activity. The P_L promoter of bacteriophage λ has been used to direct transcription leading to the synthesis of molecules related to human β-interferon (Derynck *et al.*, 1980), to maize chloroplast ribulosebisphosphate carboxylase (Gatenby *et al.*, 1981), and to a foot-and-mouth disease antigen (Kupper *et al.*, 1981). This is an attractive system because of the existence of a temperature-sensitive repressor which can be used to induce the synthesis of mRNA (and therefore protein) under the P_L control by raising the temperature of the growth medium.

Inducible promoters can be used to control the onset of product synthesis. If expression of the foreign gene in *E. coli* is deleterious to the growth of the bacterium, the culture can be grown to high density in the repressed state and then induced so that each cell makes product.

The most widely used promoter system in recent years has been the *E. coli* *trp* promoter. However, the *trp-lac* (TAC) hybrid promoters constructed by de Boer *et al.* (1982a,b) are likely to be the prototypes of future promoter systems. These TAC promoters are composed of *trp* nucleotide sequences upstream of position −20 and *lac* sequences downstream from this position. The TAC promoters combine the highly desirable features of both the *trp* (high promoter strength) and *lac* (easily controlled repression–induction) systems.

Increasing mRNA stability in the cell can be as effective as boosting transcription rates. In some cases, nuclease mutant strains can produce increased expression levels (Hautala *et al.*, 1979).

1. Fusion Protein Synthesis

Figure 7 shows plasmids that illustrate the two strategies that have evolved for the exploitation of bacterial transcription–translation systems in heterologous gene expression. In the fusion protein approach, foreign DNA is inserted into a bacterial structural gene at a restriction endonuclease site; transcription from the bacterial promoter generates a hybrid mRNA that includes the added nucleic acid sequences (Polisky *et al.*, 1976; Kourilsky *et al.*, 1977). Translation is initiated by the binding of the ribosome to the mRNA at the bacterial ribosome binding site (Section III,C,1) and the start codon, but protein synthesis proceeds through the hybrid mRNA and translates the added foreign nucleic acid sequence as well. Since any nucleotide sequence has three potential reading frames, the reading frame at the restriction site must be known if the amino acid sequence derived from the added nucleic acid sequence is to be controlled. Knowledge of the reading frame at a restriction site late in the β-galactosidase (*lac Z*) gene (Polisky *et al.*, 1976) allowed Itakura *et al.* (1977) to design and synthesize a nucleic acid sequence that upon insertion yielded somatostatin fused near the COOH-terminus of β-galactosidase. The added synthetic DNA began with the codon ATG, which led to the insertion of a methionine between the β-galactosidase and somatostatin polypeptide chains. Since somatostatin itself contains no methionine residues, cleavage with the methionine-specific reagent cyanogen bromide led to the generation of a series of fragments including somatostatin.

a. Desacetylthymosin α_1. The β-galactosidase fusion approach was used to synthesize desacetylthymosin α_1. The synthetic gene (see Fig. 1) contains, at the coding 5′ end, the codon for methionine. After the gene was constructed from synthetic fragments and inserted into a plasmid, the plasmid was cleaved with *Eco*RI at the beginning of the synthetic gene (see Fig. 4). An *Eco*RI fragment containing the *E. coli lac* promoter–operator and the bulk of the β-galactosidase (*lac Z*) gene was added by ligation to give a plasmid (pTh$\alpha_1\beta$gal) in which the synthetic gene followed the *lac* sequences in a reading frame that would translate into a Met-desacetylthymosin α_1 sequence. The correct plasmid was purified from the reaction mixture by the cloning–selection methods described in Section II,B.

b. Fusion Systems. Other promoters have been borrowed from *E. coli* for the expression of heterologous genes (see Table III). The plasmid-encoded β-lactamase gene contains a *Pst* restriction site which has been exploited to construct bacterial-eukaryotic fusion genes. Derivatives of the *trp* operon have been engineered for maximizing the levels of fusion protein expression (Kleid *et al.*, 1981). Such a system gives considerably higher yields of desacetylthymosin α_1 (Wetzel *et al.*, 1981a), because of the relative strength of the *trp* promoter and/or the relative efficiency with which the fusion protein is stably synthesized. As shown in Table III (p. 53), numerous examples of the bacterial expression of eukaryotic genes have been accomplished by a fusion protein approach, but in many cases no arrangement was made for recovery of product from the prokaryotic polypeptide leader sequence.

c. Alternate Cleavage Systems. The fusion protein approach is a good general method for stable expression of relatively short polypeptides, but it has some shortcomings. One obvious constraint on its use is the need for a site for chemical cleavage at the junction of the *E. coli* and the foreign sequence; the cyanogen bromide cleavage of methionine cannot be used efficiently for the release of methionine-containing polypeptides. In favorable cases this limitation may be overcome by the design of analogs in which the internal methionines are replaced by other amino acids.

A more attractive general solution to this problem would be the discovery of other reagents with the same degree of specificity for other amino acids. Such reagents must be highly specific, and the target sites should be relatively rare occurrences in proteins. In order for the method to be general the cleavage should occur in such a way as to leave the entire specificity site on one side of the cleavage site.

One intriguing possibility is the use of specific proteases as *in vitro* reagents for the release of peptides from fusion proteins. Two examples of such a system have already been described. After reversibly blocking all lysines, β-endorphin was cleaved from the COOH-terminus of a β-galactosidase–corticotropin–β-lipotropin fusion by trypsin cleavage at the last arginine residue (Shine *et al.*, 1980). A fusion protein composed of β-galactosidase and a proinsulin analog can also be cleaved with trypsin to generate insulin A chain (Wetzel *et al.*, 1981c). Since most polypeptides contain trypsin sites, this method may not be of general utility. On the other hand, "hot" trypsin sites composed of multibasic residues are used extensively in mammalian endocrine systems to direct the proteolytic processing of multihormone precursors and prohormones. Many hormones made in this way have other trypsin sites that are relatively resistant. It may thus not be unrealistic to hope that specially designed hot protease site may some day provide good specific cleavage points.

Although some highly specific proteases have been described, many of them are so specific as to have only one substrate. In most of these cases the substrate's target site is probably defined by tertiary structure as well as by primary sequence, precluding the use of the complementary protease as a general reagent for fusion protein cleavages.

2. *Direct Expression*

As shown in Fig. 7, an alternative to the fusion approach is direct expression, in which foreign coding DNA is inserted to take advantage of the host control elements while at the same time directing the synthesis of a polypeptide derived solely from the foreign DNA. The first example (Goeddel *et al.*, 1979a) of an efficient direct expression system was that for the synthesis of human growth hormone (Section II,3) controlled by tandem *lac* promoters (Section III,B) and the *lac* ribosome binding site (Section III,C,1). In a similar fashion the gene for human leukocyte interferon A was arranged for direct expression (see Fig. 6) behind a *trp* promoter and ribosome binding site (Goeddel *et al.*, 1980a). Other examples are listed in Table III (p. 53).

In many cases an initiator ATG must be added to the eukaryotic sequence for translation initiation (Section III,C,2). This adds an unnatural NH_2-terminal methionine to the otherwise native *E. coli* product (Section III,E,2).

C. Translation

The syntheses listed in Table III vary considerably in the finesse with which the *E. coli* translational controls were exploited. In many cases one can only guess how the protein is being translated. Foreign genes placed within the structural gene of β-lactamase might be expressed as fusion proteins, made by a translation start at the AUG for β-lactamase and read-through into the foreign gene, or by reinitiation of protein synthesis, despite the lack of an endogenous ribosome binding site (see below), at an AUG of the inserted gene. Examples of both have been reported (Villa-Komaroff *et al.*, 1978; Chang *et al.*, 1978); in many other reports of β-lactamase-linked expression, there is little or no evidence as to the actual structure of the product. At the other end of the spectrum, there are reports of highly efficient expression of polypeptide products of predictable structure. These experiments involve removing unwanted cDNA as well as precisely placing the retained cDNA or chemically synthesized DNA into the bacterial operon. The following sections describe some of the constraints on translation of eukaryotic sequences in bacteria and how they can be dealt with.

1. *Ribosome Binding Sites*

The mRNA transcribed in *E. coli* from an *E. coli* gene contains at its start a nucleic acid sequence not coding for protein (Fig. 7). One major purpose of this extra RNA is to provide a site for the binding of the mRNA to the ribosome via its complementary interaction with the 3′ end of the 16S ribosomal structural RNA. The sequence on the mRNA that is complementary to the 16S rRNA is known as the Shine–Dalgarno (1975) sequence (S-D sequence). With the mRNA properly locked in position, the mRNA AUG start codon is held so that its binding to fmet-$tRNA^{met}$ places amino-acylated tRNA in the correct orientation for the start of translation. For this reason there is not only a sequence specificity for ribosome binding but also optimal spacing of the start codon from the S-D sequence.

The problem of spacing has been attacked in a number of ways. In the fusion protein approach (Section III,B,1), the sequence from the S-D sequence to the AUG start codon is left undisturbed as part of the bacterial DNA component (see Fig. 7). In direct expression experiments (Section III,B,2), one approach has been to strive to retain the same number of nucleotides between the S-D sequence and the AUG start codon. But when this distance was adjusted to the naturally occurring seven nucleotides in the *lac* expression of human growth hormone (Goeddel *et al.*, 1979a), it was found to give lower yields of hGH than another construction containing 11 nucleotides.

Since it became clear that the natural spacing may not always be optimal, at least for expression of a foreign gene, several groups have studied the effect of spacing on expression levels. Guarente *et al.* (1980) showed the utility of an empirical approach to optimization that allows variation of nucleotide spacing and monitoring of its effect *in vivo* and *in vitro* by a simple enzyme assay. When applied to the synthesis of β-interferon (Taniguchi *et al.*, 1980), the highest producer found contained the same spacing (seven nucleotides) as the natural *E. coli lac* system. In experiments with α- and β-interferon, Shepard *et al.* (1982) systematically varied the spacing between the ribosome binding site and the AUG start and found optimal expression levels for both molecules with a nine-nucleotide spacing, compared to the seven-nucleotide spacing in the naturally occurring *trp* system.

2. *Signal Sequences*

Many eukaryotic proteins of interest, such as interferons, are synthesized at the eukaryotic ribosome as preproteins, containing very hydrophobic NH_2-terminal extensions of 20–25 amino acids. These signal sequences are involved in marking these proteins for extracellular secretion and are removed during the secretion process to yield the mature isolated protein (Blobel and Dobberstein, 1975). Although some eukaryotic signal peptides may be recognized and even processed by signal peptidases in *E. coli* (Talmadge *et al.*, 1980), no great productive advantage is conferred by the signal sequence since *E. coli*, like all gram-negative bacteria, transports even its own *secretory* proteins only as far as the periplasmic space between its inner and outer membrane. Eukaryotic signal peptide sequences are not only unnecessary for expression in *E. coli* but are generally disadvantageous. Since they may not always be efficiently processed, there is no easy way to remove the signal peptide after purification of the protein. Moreover, transport into the periplasm, the prokaryotic equivalent of the eukaryotic lysosome, may place the protein in an environment more unfavorable than the cytoplasm. This signal peptide problem can be solved by removing the nucleic acid coding for the signal peptide at the DNA level. For example, leukocyte interferon A cDNA was engineered for direct expression (Goeddel *et al.*, 1980a) of native protein by removing the signal DNA sequence plus a bit of the sequence for mature IFN-αA at any early restriction endonuclease site. A chemically synthesized DNA linker was then used to replace the lost DNA sequence information for native interferon and at the same time provide a sticky end for cloning into an efficient *trp* promoter system (see Fig. 6, Section II,A,3).

A minor problem in the above approach is that one must discard the translation initiator AUG along with the other signal peptide nucleotides. Sequences of isolated native leukocyte interferons begin with cysteine, an amino acid encoded on mRNA by the codons UGU and UGC. Since, except in rare cases (see, for example, Files *et al.*, 1974), protein biosynthesis initiates at AUG, this codon must be inserted at the front of all cloned genes except those that already begin with it. The fate and implications of the initiator formylmethionine thus added to proteins are taken up in Section III,E,2. The signal peptide-mediated secretion of a protein product might be exploited in other microorganisms that possess systems for full secretion; this is discussed in Section III,D,2.

3. *mRNA Structure*

Because degeneracies in the genetic code allow the design of many different nucleotide sequences that can code for the same amino acid sequence, it is natural to consider whether there may be better or worse nucleotide sequences from the point of view of the ribosome. Can eukaryotic mRNA be efficiently translated in prokaryotes? Is it possible to choose a poorly translatable codon in the design of a gene? Can a mRNA have too much or too little stable secondary structure?

Degenerate sequences coding for the same protein have been found to be expressed in *E. coli* with significantly different efficiencies (M. Matteucci and H. Heyneker, unpublished results). The cDNA coding for growth hormone derived from bovine pituitary mRNA, when engineered for direct expression from a prokaryotic promoter and ribosome binding site, produces relatively low levels of this hormone. If the first 66 nucleotides of the structural gene are replaced, however, with a different, chemically synthesized, sequence coding for the same amino acids, bovine growth hormone is produced in significantly larger amounts. Analysis of the less efficient eukaryotic sequence shows a good deal of stable structure at the 5′ end of the mRNA; the more efficient DNA that replaced it was designed to disfavor this structure. In the same vein, there may be mRNA sequences with greater or lesser susceptibility to nucleases by virtue of a particular stabilized structure. These considerations notwithstanding, few examples have been described in which the coding sequence of mRNA has been shown to affect levels of expression.

4. Protein Product Structure

The effects of translation product structure on expression levels are largely dealt with in Section (III,D). However, the length and character of the protein product may influence the efficiency with which it is translated, and as such these considerations are covered here. Early termination of translation can occur in the synthesis of native proteins; the enzyme peptidyl-tRNA hydrolase has the function of removing the aborted polypeptide chain from its tRNA carrier molecule. Early termination seems to be an especially serious problem with larger proteins, possibly because of steric effects arising from the juxtaposition of the growing polypeptide chain with critical parts of the ribosome (Manley, 1978). Whether by this or by other mechanisms, β-galactosidase fusion protein expression levels of small peptide hormones such as somatostatin and the insulin chains are considerably lower on a molar basis than yields of the total fusion protein estimated by PAGE (Itakura *et al.*, 1977).

Besides the possible detrimental effect of polypeptide folding there is another way yields can be lost at the translation step in hormones expressed as fusion proteins (Section III,D): Much of the energy expended for polypeptide synthesis of the cell is being wasted if, for example, every molecule of somatostatin (14 amino acids) produced requires the synthesis of a *leader sequence* of 1005 β-galactosidase amino acids. Fusion expression systems composed of shorter leader sequences should improve yields as long as the polypeptide product is stable in the cell.

D. *In Vivo* Stability

One final obstacle awaits the polypeptide product before it can be harvested—the stability of the new polypeptide in the living cell. Bacteria contain protease systems (Goldberg and St. John, 1976) that can efficiently degrade non-*E. coli* proteins (Swamy and Goldberg, 1981). Some of these proteases may be induced by the appearance of exogenous protein, denatured endogenous protein, or the onset of a nutrient-limited growth phase.

Much remains to be done in the area of yield improvement through product stabilization. Growth conditions can be altered to optimize the yield of a particular protein. Protease-deficient strains may be helpful. Some form of product (operon) induction late in the growth phase might be useful in some cases. The following discussion is confined to approaches to product stabilization and detection at the molecular biology level.

1. Stability of Fusion Proteins

In their 1977 paper, Itakura *et al.* described two β-galactosidase gene fusions with synthetic somatostatin DNA. The long fusion, with 1005 amino acids of β-galactosidase preceding somatostatin, gave significant levels of the hormone after cyanogen bromide cleavage. No activity could be detected in processed cells transformed with the other plasmid, a small fusion coding for a β-galactosidase leader of only seven amino acids. If there were no differences in the levels of stable transcripts or in the efficiencies of translation of the two hybrid mRNAs, the lack of somatostatin from the small fusion must be due to *in vivo* instability of the fusion polypeptide.

a. Length and Stability. The fusion protein approach not only allows convenient borrowing of prokaryotic DNA control elements but also is extremely useful in stabilizing polypeptide products that might otherwise be degraded *in vivo*. All attempts to stably express in *E. coli* the human peptides somatostatin (14 amino acids), insulin A chain (21 amino acids), insulin B chain (30 amino acids), desacetylthymosin α_1 (28 amino acids), and proinsulin (86 amino acids) directly or as short fusions have so far been unsuccessful (H. Heyneker, D. Kleid, and D. Goeddel, unpublished results). The smallest protein that has been stably expressed directly in *E. coli* is human immune interferon (146 amino acids). It would not be surprising to find that some foreign proteins smaller than interferon or even proinsulin may be expressed in stable form, or that some larger proteins are unstable. Undoubtedly protein conformation and sequence also play a role in susceptibility to *in vivo* degradation.

b. Mechanisms of Fusion Protein Stabilization. How is a human hormone stabilized against proteolytic degradation *in vivo* as a result of increasing its molecular weight by adding to it elements of an *E. coli* protein? One possible explanation is that the degradative pathway for proteins in *E. coli* becomes generalized below a certain molecular weight of protein. Thus larger, conformationally stable structures may be labile or stabile to proteolysis, depending on the specificity of the cell's proteolytic enzymes. But smaller polypeptides, which equilibrate among a number of solution structures, are eventually digested. A number of proteinases in *E. coli* have been characterized with respect to their molecular size, sensitivity to protease inhibitors, substrate specificity, and cofactor requirements (Swamy and Goldberg, 1981). *In vitro*, some of these *E. coli* enzymes can digest insulin and other mammalian proteins.

One possible explanation for the protective effect of fusion proteins might be that peptides such as somatostatin are stabilized by their attachment to a protein that appears essentially normal to the *E. coli* proteolytic machinery. Unfortunately the situation is not so simple: Although addition of desacetylthymosin α_1, for example, to the first 1005 amino acids of β-galactosidase generates a molecule that is still 97% β-galactosidase, the physical and enzymatic properties of the fusion protein are dramatically different from those of the native enzyme. The molecule is essentially completely insoluble under native conditions and can be solubilized only in a guanidine hydrochloride or urea solution. Even when solubilized at urea concentrations in which the native enzyme is stable, the fusion protein has no β-galactosidase activity (R. Wetzel, unpublished results). Thus it is not by maintaining a native appearance that these molecules survive in *E. coli*; in fact, at least in the case of some fusion proteins, the opposite seems to be true.

Cells producing stable β-galactosidase fusion proteins such as those described above produce intracellular organelle-like structures that appear as refractile bodies under a light microscope (Fig. 8). In the electron microscope these structures are seen as smooth, well-defined bodies with no particular subcellular localization. Similar structures have been observed when *E. coli* producing constitutive levels of β-galactosidase are grown on amino acid analogs that can be incorporated into protein (Goldberg and St. John, 1976). Claims have been made that such refractile bodies accelerate (Goldberg and St. John, 1976) or decelerate (Chang *et al.*, 1981) proteolytic degradation of the denatured protein. It may be that overproduced proteins of very poor solubility are sequestered in these bodies by an active *E. coli* process or merely by self-association–precipitation; in the authors' experience, this sequestration is associated with product stability. The situation is complicated by the fact that *E. coli* strains that produce large amounts of foreign proteins such as hGH by *direct* expression also exhibit these refractile bodies (Fig. 9). It is at present impossible to say whether refractile bodies are the agents through which some foreign proteins are stabilized, or whether stable foreign proteins produced in large amounts in *E. coli* generate refractile bodies.

2. Product Secretion

One alternative to the fusion protein approach in the *in vivo* stabilization of biosynthetic polypeptides is to arrange for the product to be secreted from the cells as it is made. Although such an approach is not possible in *E. coli* (Section III,C,2), there are other microorganisms, such as *Bacillus subtilis* and yeasts, that fully secrete some of their proteins. These proteins are either outer membrane components or proteins intended to play a role in the growth medium, physically removed from the growing cells.

The mechanisms by which the cell recognizes certain of its proteins as candidates for secretion are complex and still controversial. Secretory

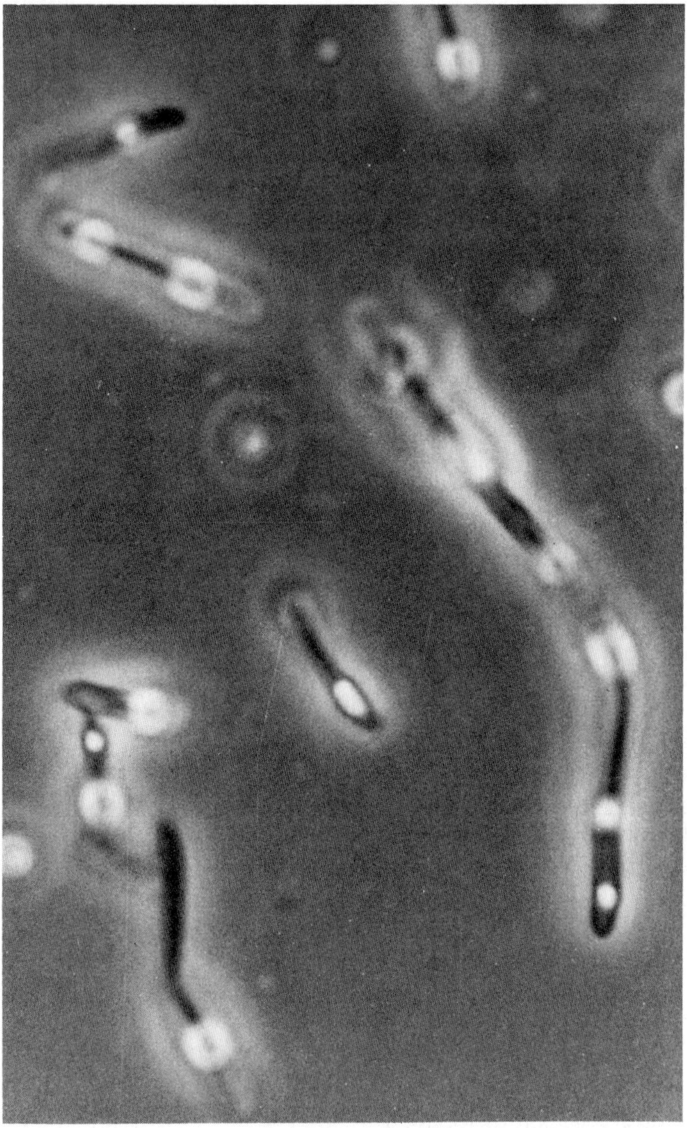

Figure 8. Phase-contrast microscopy of *E. coli* transformed with a plasmid directing the synthesis of a TrpLE–N^{α}-desacetylthymosin α_1 (Wetzel *et al.*, 1981a) fusion protein. *Escherichia coli* RV308/pthy7Δ1Δ4 (D. Kleid, unpublished) was grown from a Luria broth innoculum in mineral salts supplemented with glucose, yeast extracts, and casein hydrolysate at 37°C in an MF14 (New Brunswick) bench fermenter. Live cells taken during the fermentation at depleted tryptophan concentrations were mounted wet and photomicrographed at 500×. Refractile bodies appear after reduced tryptophan levels derepress the *trp* operon (results of N. Lin and D. Spodick).

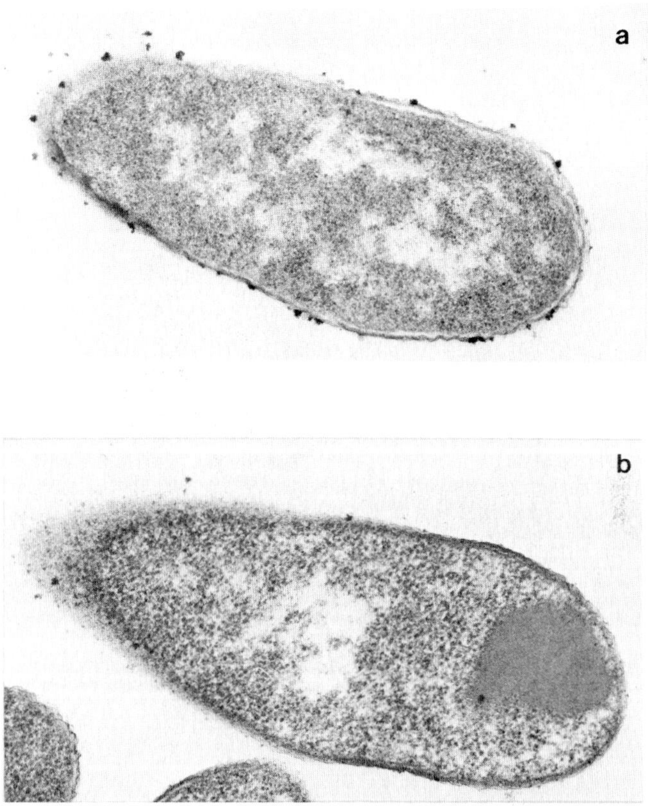

Figure 9. Electron micrographs of *E. coli* cells transformed with the plasmid pBR322 (a) or a plasmid directing the synthesis of human growth hormone (b). Cells grown under conditions identical to those described in Fig. 8 were removed from the fermenter at $A_{550} = 4$ and fixed in glutaraldehyde followed by postfixation in osmium tetroxide. The cells were embedded in Epon medium. Sections were made and stained with orange acetate and lead acetate. 39,000 ×. (Results of P. O'Connor.)

proteins often have signal peptides, hydrophobic sequences synthesized at the ribosome as a leader sequences for native proteins. These sequences somehow guide certain secretory proteins through the cell walls and membranes and in the process are proteolytically removed to generate the native molecules. However, at least in some cases, there may be further structural determinants of protein secretion involving parts of the native molecule.

If the gene to be expressed already contains a signal peptide, the protein product may be transported and processed even in the heterologous system. Thus rat preproinsulin was transported to the *E. coli* periplasm and the

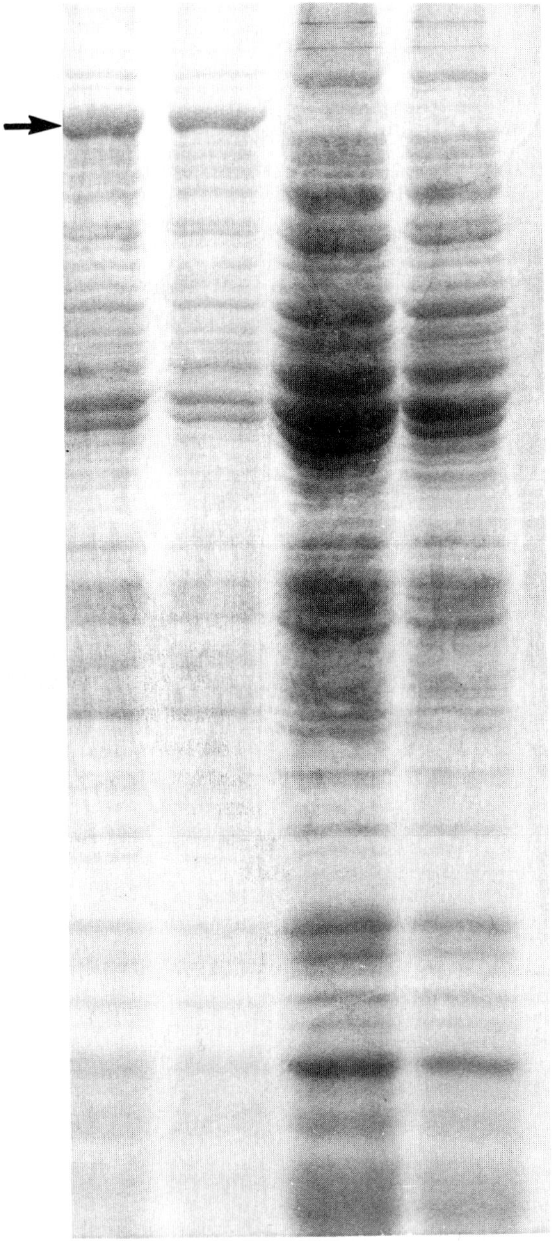

Figure 10. SDS-PAGE of protein components of *E. coli* producing β-galactosidase–desacetylthymosin α_1. The left lane shows Coomassie blue-stained material found in the pellet after centrifugation of lysed cells. The right lane shows the soluble fraction. The dark band at the top (high molecular weight end) of the left lane (arrow) is β-galactosidase–desacetylthymosin α_1. Little material was detected at the corresponding position in the right lane.

eukaryotic signal correctly removed (Talmadge *et al*., 1980), even when rat preproinsulin was expressed as an N-terminally extended fusion protein (Talmadge *et al*., 1981). The yeast *Saccharomyces cerevisiae* recognizes and correctly processes the human signal sequence of leukocyte preinterferon, secreting about 5% of the product into the growth medium (Hitzeman *et al*., 1983a). In cases in which the eukaryotic signal is incorrectly processed, it should be possible to construct a preprotein gene coding for a host system signal peptide fused to the foreign native protein. Too little is known to be able to predict how successful this approach will be in bacterial expression of foreign genes. Enough complexity has already been encountered in the study of the secretory pathway in *E. coli* (Kreil, 1981) to suggest there may be more, as yet undiscovered, constraints on protein secretion.

3. *Analytical Detection of Low-Yield Products*

Some foreign proteins are produced in *E. coli* in high enough yields that they can be clearly observed against the background of host cell protein in a sodium dodecyl sulfate (SDS) polyacrylamide gel (Fig. 10). When this is not possible, and a sufficiently sensitive functional assay for the desired protein is not available, there are methods for reducing the protein background from the host cell in order to establish if any of the desired protein is being made in stable form. Autoradiography of SDS gels loaded with immunoprecipitated radiolabeled *E. coli* protein can detect not only the desired product but also some degradation products (Goeddel *et al*., 1979a). If antibodies are unavailable, background can be decreased in other ways. The use of "mini-cells" (Meagher *et al*., 1977) and "maxi-cells" (Sancar *et al*., 1979) allows observation of only the proteins synthesized according to plasmid genes. Transformed *E. coli* can also be treated with the antibiotic chloramphenicol, which allows observation of only plasmid-directed protein synthesis (Neidhardt *et al*., 1980). This method can also be applied to the synthesis of highly radiolabeled proteins (Section V,C).

The possibility that effects other than product stability are to blame for low *in vivo* yields of a plasmid-encoded product can be explored by subjecting purified plasmid to a protease-free *in vitro* transcription–translation system (Weissbach *et al*., 1981; Brawner and Jaskunas, 1982, Shepard *et al*., 1981).

E. Other Posttranslational Processing

Although a protein's overall structure is defined largely by its amino acid sequence, and the amino acid sequence is defined by polypeptide synthesis directed by the gene sequence, posttranslational modifications can substantially modify the structure and properties of a gene product (Freedman and

Hawkins, 1980; Wold, 1981). Because of this, host metabolic pathways besides transcription and translation must be considered. Although many potential problems can be imagined, the discussion below is restricted to situations already encountered.

1. Disulfide Bonds

Disulfide bond formation *in vivo* in a nascent polypeptide chain is a process that should be controlled only by the conformation of the folding chain and the reduction potential of the cellular milieu. Although many fully reduced and denatured proteins can often properly refold *in vitro* with the correct formation of disulfide bonds, it is possible that some disulfides may be thermodynamically or kinetically favored only in the context of the nascent polypeptide chain. This folding in turn might be influenced by the structure of the ribosome on which it is made and the local steric, chemical, and enzymatic environment the growing protein is thrust into. Cell type-specific protein modifications may occur on the nascent polypeptide and may affect folding and therefore disulfide formation. In some instances, disulfide bond formation may be guided by a "disulfide interchange enzyme" (Roth and Koshland, 1981, and references therein) which could well vary with the cell type. The addition of a leader sequence, either a nonsecreted signal peptide or a longer, more complex leader of a fusion protein, may also influence folding and therefore disulfide formation. The importance of the removal of signal peptides for correct disulfide bond formation has been established for some pancreatic exocrine proteins synthesized *in vitro* (Scheele and Jacoby, 1982).

The only disulfide arrangements so far shown to be identical in a protein expressed in both a foreign cell type (*E. coli*) and in the normal cell (pituitary) are those for human growth hormone (Kohr *et al.*, 1982). Although the disulfide arrangements for one subtype of human leukocyte interferon synthesized in *E. coli* have been reported (Wetzel, 1981), the assignment in the naturally synthesized material has not as yet been made.

Mini-C proinsulin (see Section V,A) expressed at the C-terminus of a fusion protein has no appreciable RIA activity, either as fusion protein or after cyanogen bromide release (R. Wetzel, unpublished results). It is not clear whether this latter result is due to mixed disulfide formation with the *E. coli* leader sequence or to faulty folding of proinsulin induced by the leader. The protein can be properly folded *in vitro* after cyanogen bromide release (Wetzel *et al.*, 1981c). The disulfide arrangements in the protein product in the low-yield expression of rat (Talmadge *et al.*, 1980) and human (Chan *et al.*, 1981) proinsulin have not been reported.

To achieve optimal recovery of cysteine-containing proteins produced by the fusion approach, some effort is normally made to break possible disulfides between *E. coli* and foreign peptide sequences (Goeddel *et al.*, 1979a; Wetzel *et al.*, 1981c). Since *S*-sulfonates can be good intermediates for *in vitro* disulfide formation (Katsoyannis *et al.*, 1967; Frank *et al.*, 1981; Chance *et al.*, 1981a), oxidative sulfitolysis is a useful, mild, specific method for breaking possible deleterious disulfides and later forming the correct ones.

Some heterologous proteins, both directly expressed and fusions, isolated from *E. coli* in an inactive, nonnative state, have been at least partially reactivated by *in vitro* disulfide chemistry (Wetzel *et al.*, 1981c; R. Wetzel, unpublished results). Although this implies that native disulfides are not formed *in vivo*, there is at present no information on the *in vivo* structures of those products that can be regenerated by thiol–disulfide interchange.

2. NH_2-Terminal Methionine

Protein biosynthesis usually begins with an initiator methionyl-tRNA, whether or not an NH_2-terminal methionine or formylmethionine is desired in the finished bacterial product. Since many *E. coli* proteins are isolated that lack these amino-terminal groups, there must be an enzyme system that removes the formylmethionine group according to some as yet undelineated constraints of primary sequence or higher structure. The examples below of highly characterized foreign proteins directly expressed in *E. coli* are indicative of the strict constraints guiding this enzyme system. Human growth hormone does not normally contain an NH_2-terminal methionine; the *E. coli* product was found to have entirely retained the initiator methionine but to have entirely lost the formyl group (Stebbing *et al.*, 1981; Kohr *et al.*, 1982). IFN-αA was found to consist of an approximately 50/50 mixture of molecules that had lost only the formyl group and molecules that had lost the formylmethionine group (Wetzel *et al.*, 1981b; Staehelin *et al.*, 1981). A different *E. coli* strain produced a higher yield of interferon in which more than 90% of the protein had lost the entire formylmethionine group (W. Kohr and R. Wetzel, unpublished results). Since the sequence of natural mature fibroblast interferon, β interferon, after having lost its signal peptide, begins with methionine, an expression plasmid was designed with a structural gene beginning with a single ATG. The purified bacterial product was found to have lost about 80% of this (desirable) methionine (Harkins *et al.*, 1982). Thus of the three cases studied only one product, leukocyte interferon, was produced with the NH_2-terminus in the desired state. It is not known whether tandem ATGs in the fibroblast interferon gene might allow retention of a single methionine in this molecule; there is no obvious simple solution to the problem of the extra methionine in hGH produced in *E. coli*. Neither hGH nor β-interferon expressed in *E. coli* showed any change in biological activity due to the new condition of the NH_2-terminus.

3. NH_2-Terminal Acetylation

Some proteins are synthesized *in vivo* in the N^{α}-acetylated form. In some cases the addition of an acetyl group can have a distinct effect on hormonal activity (Schwyzer and Eberle, 1977; Smyth *et al*., 1979); in most cases, however, the function of the N^{α}-acetyl group is unclear (Wold, 1981). Enzymes responsible for *in vivo* acetylation have been described (Woodford and Dixon, 1979; Kido *et al*., 1981) and could possibly be utilized *in vitro* to acetylate biosynthetic products on a preparative scale. Unless the acetylation enzyme system is native to, or could be introduced by, recombinant DNA methods into the host microorganism, *in vivo* acetylation would not be possible. In any case, *in vivo* acetylation of peptides produced via the fusion protein method would be impossible, since the α-amino group is freed *in vitro* by the cyanogen bromide reaction. On the other hand, if rapid *in vivo* acetylation were to stabilize a peptide against exoproteolysis, the fusion protein approach might be rendered unnecessary.

In principle the terminal α-amino group of a polypeptide can be specifically acylated by conducting the reaction at a pH discriminatory toward the reaction of more basic lysine ε-amino groups (Means and Feeney, 1971). This approach was successful in selectively acetylating the NH_2-terminus of desacetylthymosin α_1 produced in *E. coli* (Wetzel *et al*., 1981a).

4. Glycosylation

Bacteria are not known to possess glycosylation systems similar to those found in higher organisms. Yeasts have glycosylation systems, but it is unclear how similar these systems are to those of higher eukaryotes in substrate specificity; the structures of the added carbohydrate moieties differ considerably between yeast and mammalian cells.

Fibroblast interferon is normally glycosylated, possibly at the recognition sequence for N-linked glycosylation, Asn-Glu-Thr, found at amino acid positions 80–82 predicted by the cDNA sequence. When produced in *E. coli*, no glycosylation is observed, but the antiviral activity and pharmacokinetics of the molecule are indistinguishable from those of the normal human product (Harkins *et al*., 1982).

5. Proteolytic Processing

Some degree of proteolytic processing of an initial translation product is sometimes desirable. Many prohormones are converted to active hormones by cleavage at multiple basic residues by trypsin-like activity. Human proinsulin produced in *E. coli* can be accurately processed to insulin *in vitro* (Frank *et al*., 1981) by a mixture of trypsin and carboxypeptidase B. In cases in which the prohormone differs from the hormone by an NH_2- or a COOH-terminal extension, the hormone can be made directly in *E. coli*, assuming it is stable, by merely adjusting the plasmid DNA sequence. In a case in which an interior section of the polypeptide chain must be removed post-translationally, as with proinsulin, DNA manipulations are not enough.

IV. PURIFICATION AND CHARACTERIZATION OF PRODUCT

After the early reports of successful synthesis of foreign polypeptides in *E. coli*, many protein chemists remained unconvinced that the methods would ever prove to be a practical way of making polypeptides. There are many causes for legitimate doubt: Would cyanogen bromide leave the sulfhydryls of insulin A and B chains intact so that they could later effectively be combined to form active insulin? Would it be possible to purify proteins and peptides from a new protein background? Would it be possible to reduce amounts of highly potent endotoxins to acceptable levels? How accurate, in reality, was protein biosynthesis, especially when the gene was from another organism or even chemically synthesized?

By now many of the important questions of 5 years ago have been answered. In this section some of these points will be illustrated by descriptions of the purification from *E. coli* extracts and characterization of desacetylthymosin α_1 and leukocyte IFN-αA.

A. Desacetylthymosin α_1

When *E. coli* cells containing β-galactosidase–desacetylthymosin α_1 are lysed and centrifuged, the major protein in the centrifugation pellet is the fusion protein, which is not detectable in the soluble fraction (see Fig. 10). The insolubility and/or lipophilicity of the fusion protein thus lends itself to a powerful first purification step. The fusion protein can be recovered from membranes and other cell debris in the lysis pellet by extraction into 6 *M* guanidine hydrochloride, centrifugation, and reprecipitation via dilution or dialysis to generate a low guanidine hydrochloride concentration. Although the protein is still impure at this point, it may not serve to purify this fusion protein further, since it is destined to be cut into cyanogen bromide fragments.

The cyanogen bromide reaction is carried out in aqueous formic acid; even this medium does not initially solubilize the fusion protein preparation, but cyanogen bromide eventually brings all the material into solution. Other commonly used solvents, such as aqueous hydrogen chloride, have not been

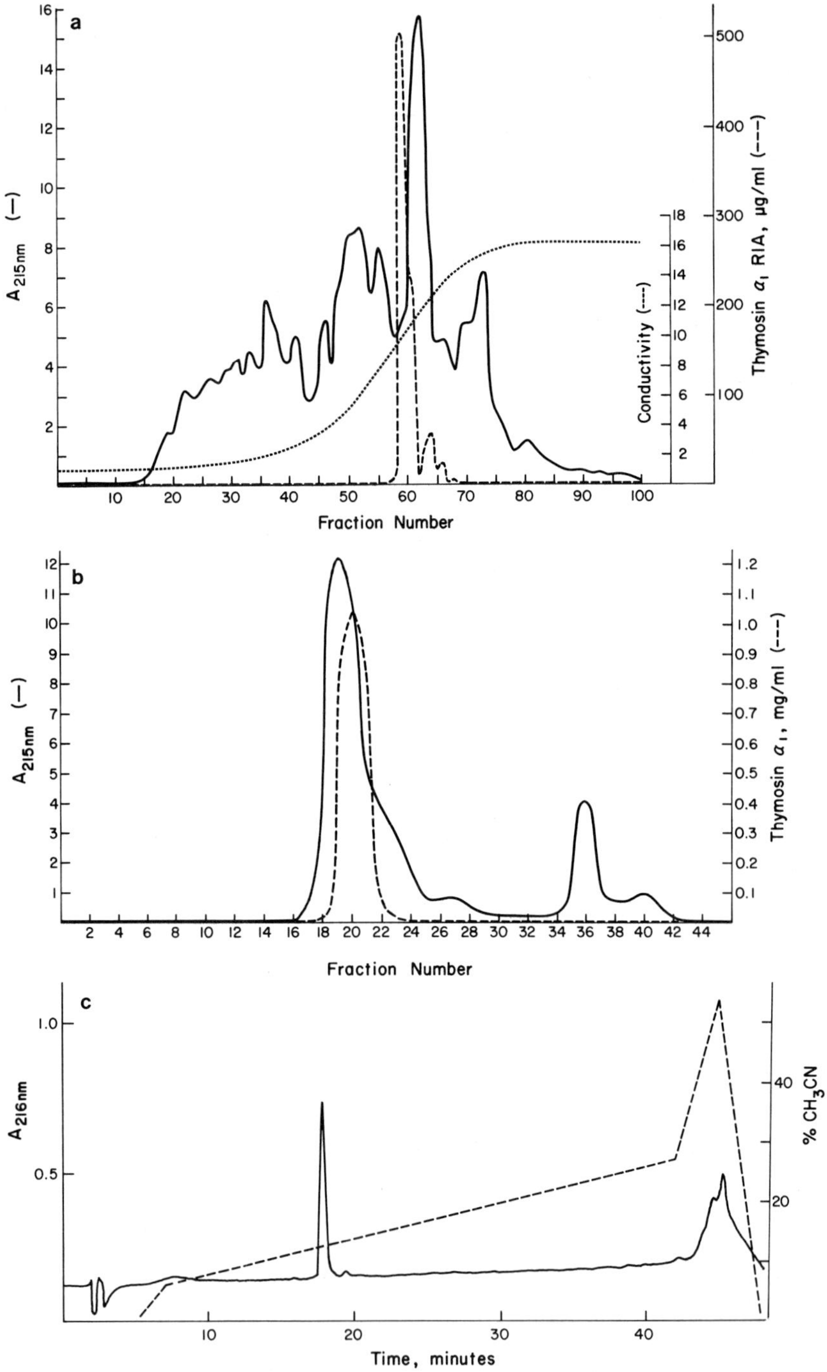

Figure 11. Purification of N^{α}-desacetylthymosin α_1 from *E. coli* extracts. (a) DEAE-cellulose chromatography of the water-soluble cyanogen bromide fragments of the lysis pellet from transformed *E. coli* (see text). The column was eluted with a linear gradient of sodium chloride in pH 7.9 buffer. The desacetylthymosin α_1 fractions, indicated by RIA (dashed line),

Table I Amino Acid Analysis of N^{α}-Desacetylthymosin α_1[a]

Residue	Theoretical	Experimental	Residue	Theoretical	Experimental[b]
Ala	3	3.18	Lys	4	4.01
Arg	0	0	Met	0	0
Asp	4	4.01	Phe	0	0
Cys	0	0	Pro	0	0
Glu	6	5.96	Ser	3	3.01
Gly	0	0	Thr	3	2.96
His	0	0	Trp	0	n.d.
Ile	1	1.05	Tyr	0	0
Leu	1	1.21	Val	3	2.61

[a] Reprinted with permission from Wetzel *et al.* (1981a).
[b] n.d., Not determined.

successful owing to the extreme insolubility of the starting material. In the case of desacetylthymosin α_1 a liberal excess of cyangen bromide (40 mol per mole of methionine) was used, since there was little danger of product decomposition. In peptides with other sulfur-containing side chains, there is evidence to suggest that too much cyanogen bromide can lead to destruction of the desired product (J. Stramondo and H. Levine, personal communication).

Many of the cyanogen bromide peptides of β-galactosidase are hydrophobic and rather poorly behaved (Fowler, 1978), which can introduce difficulties in purification. In the case of desacetylthymosin α_1 the purification was straightforward owing to the marked hydrophilic properties of the desired molecule. Suspension of the cyanogen bromide digest in a minimum of 7 *M* urea followed by dilution in a large volume of water allowed precipitation of the vast majority of β-galactosidase material while the desired product remained in solution. More hydrophobic peptide products, such as mini-C proinsulin (Wetzel *et al.*, 1981c), require stronger measures to break protein–protein interactions with β-galactosidase fragments. In the latter case even urea in the running buffer did not totally normalize the behavior of the insulin derivative in sizing chromatography.

Desacetylthymosin α_1 was purified by two chromatography steps as shown in Fig. 11. A salt gradient on DEAE-Sephadex (Fig. 11a) gave material that was already reasonably pure, as learned from size exclusion chromatography of the DEAE pool on Ultragel AcA-202 (Fig. 11b). The Ultragel pool was analyzed for purity by reverse-phase HPLC (Fig. 11c).

The peptide produced in this way had an amino acid analysis (Table I) and amino acid sequence (Wetzel *et al.*, 1980) consistent with the designed

were pooled. (b) Ultragel AcA202 gel filtration of the DEAE pool, with desacetylthymosin α_1 (dashed line) estimated by HPLC of column fractions. (c) HPLC of the Ultragel pool. The LiChrosorb (Merck) C-18, 10-μm column was eluted with a linear gradient of acetonitrile in pH 7.1 ammonium acetate. Reprinted with permission from Wetzel *et al.*, (1980). Copyright (1980) American Chemical Society.

structure. It has also been shown to free of contaminating polypeptides by HPLC, SDS-PAGE, and isoelectric focusing. Despite the absence of the N^{α}-acetyl group, the material possessed the same *in vitro* biological activity as the natural product or chemical synthesized material (Wetzel *et al.*, 1980).

B. Leukocyte Interferon-A

IFN-αA produced by *E. coli* (Goeddel *et al.*, 1980a) has been purified from *E. coli* extracts both by standard gel chromatography (Wetzel *et al.*, 1981b) and by immobilized monoclonal antibody chromatography (Stewart *et al.*, 1980; Staehelin *et al.*, 1981). In the latter approach (Staehelin *et al.*, 1981) the interferon-containing lysis supernatant was partially purified by batchwise absorption–desorption on DEAE-cellulose and then adsorbed to the antibody column directly from the DEAE elution buffer. The antibody column was then eluted with aqueous acetic acid, and the eluate further purified and concentrated by adsorption–desorption on CM-cellulose.

Immobilized antibody chromatography has special advantages when linked to recombinant DNA methods of protein synthesis. First, it can be a high-recovery process even when the desired product is present in a relatively low yield. Second, it is in principle possible to begin antibody preparation long before purified protein itself is available as an immunogen; specific antibodies can be generated by using as immunogens polypeptides predicted to contain antigenic determinants based only on a knowledge of the DNA sequence coding for the protein (Walter *et al.*, 1980; Lerner *et al.*, 1981). A monoclonal antibody useful in the purification of *E. coli*-produced human leukocyte interferon was prepared in this way (Arnheiter *et al.*, 1981).

Interferon preparations purified by the two methods had much the same chemical and biological properties. The experimental molecular weight, isoelectric point, and amino acid analysis were consistent with values predicted from the cloned DNA sequence (Goeddel *et al.*, 1980a). The sequence of the first NH_2-terminal 35 amino acids was identical to that expected from the cloned gene sequence; about 50% of the molecules retained the initiator methionine (Wetzel *et al.*, 1981a). The disulfide bonds of IFN-αA were assigned using HPLC analysis of tryptic peptide digests (Wetzel, 1981). The specific activity of the product was about 1.5×10^8 units/mg in the standard interferon antiviral assay, also consistent with values for naturally derived material. Bacterially produced IFN-αA has been found to be active *in vivo* and *in vitro* (Goeddel *et al.*, 1980a) in many animal systems as an antiviral agent and is currently being investigated as both an antiviral and an antitumor agent in clinical trials.

The sequence of the interferon molecule produced by bacteria has been determined in order to demonstrate the fidelity of replication, transcription, and translation. Peptides collected from HPLC separation of a trypsin

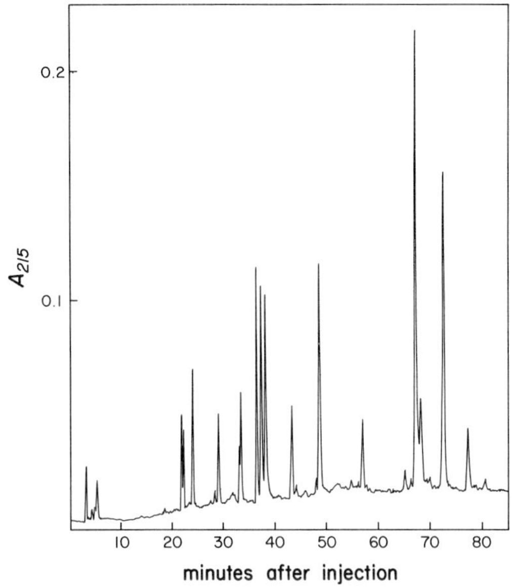

Figure 12. HPLC of a trypsin digest of IFN-αA purified from *E. coli* extracts. Five hundred micrograms of IFN-αA in 1 ml of 50mM Tris–HCl, pH 8, was digested for 17 hr at room temperature with 5 μg of L-1-tosylamide-2-phenylethyl chloromethyl ketone-treated trypsin (Worthington). The digestion was stopped by adjusting the pH to 2–3 with HCl. Fifty microliters (25 μg protein) of digest was applied to an Ultrasphere (Beckman-Altex) C-8 column and developed with a gradient of acetonitrile in aqueous sodium perchlorate, pH 2.5. The eluate was monitored at 215 nm (H. Morehead and R. Wetzel, unpublished).

digest of interferon (Fig. 12) were characterized by amino acid analysis and sequencing. All the peptides expected from the DNA sequence were accounted for (W. Kohr and R. Wetzel, unpublished).

C. General Considerations

1. Purification

As a practical matter, purity is not an absolute; for both chemists and clinicians, sensibilities toward product quality can be influenced by a number of factors, such as (1) the minimum required purity, with respect to the possible contaminants, necessary to achieve the desired results, (2) the sensitivity of available analytical systems to the contaminants, and (3) the degree to which the removal of a given contaminant is technologically possible. For a number of reasons, the criteria applied to recombinant products proposed as drugs have been much harsher than those already in effect for the equivalent natural product; this had led to the ironic situation that some recently purified recombinant preparations are a good deal more pure, for example, with respect to contaminating proteins, than the corresponding natural material used clinically in the recent past.

The two examples discussed in Section IV, A and B demonstrate that foreign polypeptides can be expressed in a stable, mature form in bacteria and purified to a high level from constituents of the bacterial cell. The above purifications could be followed by specific and sensitive assays for the desired polypeptide—for desacetylthymosin α_1, a radioimmunoassay, and for interferon, an *in vitro* antiviral biological assay. Most proteins of known function and activity have a previously established assay for their detection and purification after cloning.

In some cases, however, it may be necessary to purify for the first time a protein of unknown function and at least partly unpredictable chromatographic behavior. For example, one might discover a cDNA sequence whose unique history or homology promises an interesting gene product. Or one may synthesize a number of enzyme or hormone analogs that are of interest even though biologically inactive. One solution to this problem is to synthesize chemically a peptide predicted to be a proteolysis product of the

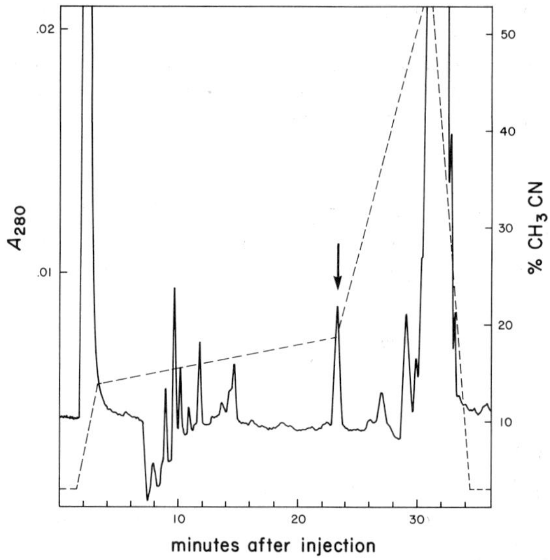

Figure 13. Trypsin–HPLC assay for monitoring the purification of mini-C proinsulin. Column chromatographic fractions were treated with trypsin (at least 1 μg/mg protein) for 1 hr at 24°C and then injected onto a Spectra-Physics C-8 10-μm analytical column and eluted with an acetonitrile gradient in 50 mM, pH 7.1, ammonium acetate. The presence of mini-C proinsulin in the fraction analyzed is indicated by the presence of insulin A chain *S*-sulfonate (arrow) among the tryptic fragments.

protein coded on the expressed gene; one can then screen chromatographic fractions for their ability to generate, upon proteolysis, a fragment that comigrates in HPLC with the synthetic peptide. Wang and Carpenter (1965) used a similar approach in an unsuccessful attempt to detect and purify proinsulin from bovine pancreas. Figure 13 shows an HPLC chromatogram of a trypsin-treated gel chromatographic fraction in the purification of a proinsulin analog that releases insulin A chain upon trypsin cleavage (Wetzel *et al.*, 1981c).

2. *Characterization*

Many purified cloned gene products have been characterized by the standard methods available to protein biochemists, and by these criteria these molecules made have not differed in any unexpected way from the naturally occurring substances. Amino acid analysis and even tryptic mapping, however, might not detect the presence of a significant amount of some analog generated by a single-base mutation during fermentation. Several polypeptides produced by recombinant DNA methods have been characterized by sequence analysis of their NH_2-termini and of HPLC-purified proteolytic fragments. The A and B chains of insulin (J. Shively, unpublished), desacetylthymosin α_1 (Wetzel *et al.*, 1980), hGH (Kohr *et al.*, 1982), and IFN-αA (W. Kohr and R. Wetzel, unpublished) have thus far been characterized. In all cases, when sequence heterogeneity (i.e., deamidation, initiator methionine) was discovered, it was not related to errors in the reading of the genetic code. Based on current evidence, the significant problems ahead do not involve questions of replicative, transcriptional, or translational fidelity, but the posttranslational events observed with many eukaryotic proteins.

What is the cross-species specificity of signal peptidases and thus what is the nature of cloned gene products secreted by *Bacillus subtilis* or yeast? How differently is a glycoprotein of a higher eukaryote glycosylated in yeast? What are the proteinaceous and nonproteinaceous components in hepatitis 22-nm particles? How do they vary in particles produced by yeast? And what are the biological consequences of the variations? Other problems of posttranslational modification, such as introduction of the N^{α}-acetyl group of thymosin α_1 and the $CONH_2$-terminal amide of calcitonin, must be dealt with *in vitro* after purification. These may be viewed as the simplest types of a series of second-generation products produced by chemical or enzymatic alteration of purified cloned gene products.

Unprotected sulfhydryls have been found to survive intact during cyanogen bromide cleavage (J. Shively, unpublished) although cysteine-containing peptides in fusion proteins can be destroyed if cyanogen bromide cleavage conditions are too harsh. If oxidized sulfhydryls are formed, they will fail to recombine [as required in A plus B insulin recombination (Chance *et al.*, 1981b) or proinsulin refolding (Frank *et al.*, 1981)] and thus at most form protein variants that can be removed during product purification.

Polypeptides produced in *E. coli* for human drug use must meet criteria other than those involving chemical identity (Gueriguian, 1981; Bristow and Bangham, 1981). The product must possess the same biological activity as the native molecule, with no additional undesirable activities such as increased immunogenicity (Stebbing *et al.*, 1981; Chance *et al.*, 1981b). An absence of bacterial endotoxins must be demonstrated (Chance *et al.*, 1981b). The early positive clinical results with bacterially produced hormones (Ahmed *et al.*, 1982) suggest that there are no systematic barriers to the manufacture of human drugs using the recombinant DNA approach.

V. SYNTHESIS OF ANALOGS

The immediate contribution of recombinant DNA methods in areas of protein research has been to allow the synthesis of protein natural products in amounts unobtainable by any other means. The same technology can make available proteins previously unobtainable in even small amounts, for example, polypeptide derivatides or analogs that are too large to be synthesized chemically. In principle, some fusion proteins such as those discussed above (Section III,B,1) might fall into this class. The great promise of this area, however, lies in the ability to create subtle and specific variants designed to test postulated mechanisms, probe suspected active sites, or provide new drugs.

Several examples of this application have already been described. One approach is to utilize restriction sites common to two homologous genes to generate by *in vitro* recombination hybrid genes coding for hybrid proteins. Two research groups have reported the synthesis and biological activities of hybrid leukocyte interferons made in this way (Streuli *et al.*, 1981; Weck *et al.*, 1981). Figure 14 shows schematically how a series of four hybrid interferon genes were constructed from two natural genes. Table II shows that these hybrid interferons can have biological properties substantially different from those of either parent molecule. The data in Table II were obtained by measuring antiviral activity of interferons synthesized using an *in vitro E. coli* transcription–translation system (Brawner and Jaskunas, 1982). Since the amount of interferon protein could be estimated in each case, specific activities did not rely on assuming 100% stability of the hybrid protein molecules *in vivo*.

In another experiment, a site-specific mutation in fibroblast interferon was introduced by synthesizing a hybrid of the wild-type gene and a mutant

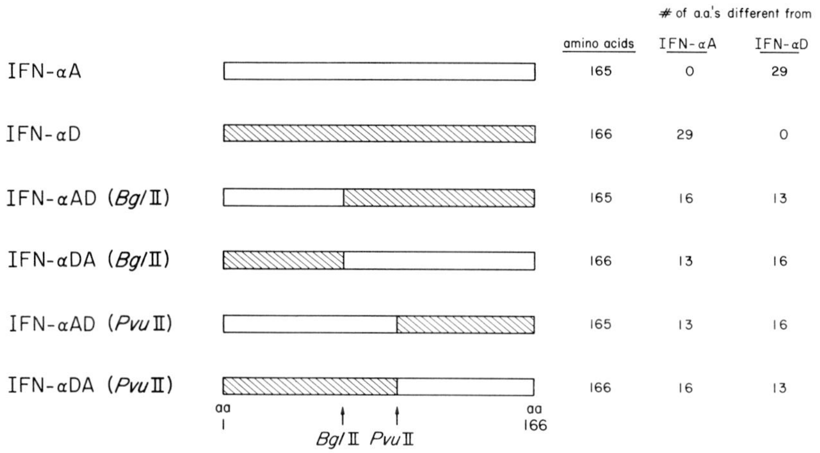

Figure 14. Construction of genes for hybrid leukocyte interferons. Plasmid-derived IFN-αA and IFN-αD DNA were cleaved with restriction endonuclease *Bgl*II or *Pvu*II and reassembled to form the indicated hybrid DNA molecules. These molecules coded for interferons that differed in amino acid composition from the parent molecules as shown. (Reproduced from Weck *et al.* (1981) by permission of IRL Press, Ltd.)

Table II. Relative Specific Activities of Interferons Produced by *in Vitro* Synthesis from Plasmid DNA[a]

IFN-α	Relative specific activity		MDBK/WISH activity ratio
	WISH	MDBK	
A	100	100	1.6
D	15	74	8.0
AD (Bgl)	190	97	0.8
AD (Pvu)	280	47	0.3
DA (Bgl)	<1	110	>160
DA (Pvu)	<2	110	>90

[a] Direct expression plasmids for each of the interferons indicated were used as substrates in a cell-free transcription–translation system. Aliquots of reaction mixtures were assayed for interferon antiviral activity *in vitro* and for interferon protein levels by scintillation counting of SDS-PAGE bands of ^{35}S-labeled protein. Adapted from Weck *et al.* (1981) by permission of IRL Press, Ltd.

gene obtained from the colony bank as a partial structural gene (Shepard *et al.*, 1981). The mutation engineered was the substitution of tyrosine for one of the cysteines presumed to be involved in a disulfide bond. When the protein product synthesized in an *in vitro* transcription–translation reaction (Brawner and Jaskunas, 1982) was assayed, no antiviral activity was detected. This supports chemical modification experiments suggesting that there is at least one essential disulfide bond in fibroblast interferon.

In another structure–function study, a proinsulin analog was synthesized in *E. coli* as directed by a chemically synthesized gene (Wetzel *et al.*, 1981c). The analog produced contained a connecting peptide of 6 amino acids instead of the 35 amino acids found in human proinsulin. Preliminary results indicated that the polypeptide chain could fold into a proinsulin-like structure despite the decreased length of the peptide connection between the A and B insulin chains.

Besides constructing analogs derived from substitutions or deletions among the 20 amino acids normally used in protein biosynthesis, it may also be possible to construct analogs containing unusual substituents by adding biochemical or chemical nuances to the basic recombinant DNA approach.

A. Mutant DNA–Natural Amino Acids

1. Chemical Synthesis

One analog has already been described using this approach, the 57-amino acid mini-C proinsulin mentioned above. Since the total synthesis of a gene for leukocyte interferon (166 amino acids) has recently been described (Edge *et al.*, 1981), there should be no size limit to genes obtainable by this method. It will be simple to design syntheses to allow permutation of particular loci within the gene.

2. Semisynthesis

If one is interested in a particular region of the gene–protein, it should be possible to design a synthesis, such as that for the hGH gene, that allows flexibility in the chemically synthesized portion but avoids the necessity of synthesizing the total gene.

3. Random Mutagenesis

Mutagenic agents have been described that allow the generation of different classes of DNA mutation in a relatively uncontrolled way. Some control may be possible by mutagenizing the gene of interest before returning it enzymatically to the vector. Any random method will require a reasonably strong selection principle, since the desired mutations will be relatively infrequent events.

4. *Specific Mutagenesis*

Site-specific mutations can be introduced into phage-enclosed (Razin *et al.*, 1978; Taniguchi and Weissmann, 1978; Hutchison *et al.*, 1978; Gillam and Smith, 1979; Gillam *et al.*, 1979; Wasylyk *et al.*, 1980) or plasmid-encoded (Wallace *et al.*, 1980, 1981b) genes using a DNA polymerase extension of "mutant" synthetic oligonucleotide primers on single-stranded DNA templates. The same synthetic oligonucleotides can then be used to screen for bacterial colonies carrying the desired mutation. Hybridization strengths differ sufficiently, that if there is a single mismatch in two complementary strands, single-site mutants can be detected (Wallace *et al.*, 1979, 1981a). A base change coding for a glutamic acid to valine mutation has been introduced by this method into a cloned β-globin gene to generate a sickle cell globin gene (Wallace *et al.*, 1981b).

The recent paper by Winter *et al.* (1982) on tyrosyl tRNA synthetase illustrates the power of these methods for addressing questions of enzyme mechanism. These authors used site specific mutagenesis to prepare a modified enzyme in which a cysteine, known by X-ray crystallographic analysis to be located at the ATP binding site, was replaced by serine. This mutant enzyme had modified catalytic properties consistent with the crystal structure: reduced ATP binding, only slightly modified V_{max}, and unchanged binding of the other small molecular weight substrate, tyrosine.

5. *Alterations Using Restriction Sites*

Besides the hybrid DNA syntheses described above, restriction sites can be used to effect deletions or insertions of relatively small numbers of nucleotides and to truncate genes through the introduction of stop codons (Yelverton *et al.*, 1983).

B. Chemical Semisynthesis

Modified amino acids might be chemically introduced into biosynthetic polypeptides in one of two ways. A chemically synthesized peptide containing the unnatural amino acid(s) might be added to a biosynthetic portion using chemical or enzymatic peptide bond formation (Offord, 1980). Alternatively, a biosynthetic polypeptide might be specifically modified posttranslationally *in vitro* at a chemical "handle," such as a cysteine, introduced into the protein by an alteration in the cloned gene.

C. Biochemical Synthesis

1. *In Vivo Synthesis*

Polypeptide analogs containing isotopically enriched amino acids can often be prepared by *in vivo* incorporation of these amino acids from an enriched growth medium. The introduction of nmr-sensitive isotopes into proteins to generate essentially native molecules has been used to study the solution properties of prokaryotic polypeptides such as alkaline phosphatase (Browne *et al.*, 1976). The same methods can now be applied to any protein being synthesized in *E. coli.* In the same way, proteins can be radiolabeled *in vivo* to generate native probes. For example, high-specific-activity leukocyte interferon was prepared for receptor binding studies by *in vivo* synthesis using [^{35}S]methionine in the growth medium in a special procedure for repressible, plasmid-encoded proteins (Estell and Powers, 1983).

It is sometimes possible to obtain polypeptide analogs *in vivo* by growing cells in the presence of an amino acid analog incorporated into a growing polypeptide chain after tRNA misaminoacylation (for review, see Sykes and Weiner, 1980). This approach is limited to analogs that resemble the natural amino acid very closely sterically and chemically. Total exclusion of the natural version of the amino acid from the product can be quite difficult, however, even after special strains, vectors, and growth conditions are developed.

2. *In Vitro Synthesis*

Thanks to the development of well-defined *in vitro* transcription–translation systems it is possible to synthesize small amounts of plasmid-encoded polypeptides in a test tube. A translation system has been described that allows the incorporation of an incorrect amino acid into a growing polypeptide chain by substitution of a mischarged tRNA in the aminoacyl-tRNA mix (Pezzuto and Hecht, 1980). It should thus be possible to incorporate any amino acid the ribosome can tolerate into a biosynthetic polypeptide in response to a specified class of codons. In turn, the placement of the target codons(s) could be controlled at the DNA synthesis level.

VI. SURVEY OF REPORTS OF HETEROLOGOUS GENE EXPRESSION

Table III is an uncritical survey, through December 1981, of all published reports of the recombinant DNA–cloning synthesis of a protein, or expression of a protein-associated activity, in microorganisms that normally do

Table III Expression of Foreign Genes in Microorganisms

Protein or peptide	Expressed in	Mode of expression	Cleavable	Molecules per cell	Reference
Aminoglycoside phosphotransferase and adenyltransferase, *S. aureus*	*E. coli*	Direct (endogenous)			Courvalin and Fiandt (1980)
Angiotensin I	*E. coli*	β-Galactosidase fusion	Yes		Kumarev *et al.* (1980)
Argininosuccinate lyase, yeast	*E. coli*	?			Clarke and Carbon (1978)
β-Endorphin, mouse	*E. coli*	β-Galactosidase fusion	Yes	80,000	Shine *et al.* (1980)
β-Galactosidase, *E. coli*	Yeast	?			Panthier *et al.* (1980)
β-Galactosidase, *Kurthia lactis*	Yeast	?			Dickson (1980)
β-Globin, rabbit	*E. coli*	Direct (*lac*)		10,000	Guarente *et al.* (1980)
β-Isopropylmalate dehydrogenase, yeast	*E. coli*	?			Ratzkin and Carbon (1977)
β-Lactamase,	*E. coli*	Direct (endogenous)			Gray and Chang (1981)
Bacillus licheniformis	*B. subtilis*	Direct (endogenous)		1,000,000	
β-Lactamase, *E. coli*	Yeast				Chevallier and Aigle (1979)
Calcitonin, human desamido-	*E. coli*	*trp LE* fusion	Yes		(W. Holmes, H. Heyneker and H. Levine, personal communication)
Catabolic dehydroquinase, *Neurospora crassa*	*E. coli*	Direct (endogenous)			Vapnek *et al.* (1977)
Chloramphenicol acetyltransferase, *E. coli*	Yeast	?			Cohen *et al.* (1980)
Desacetylthymosin α_1, human	*E. coli*	β-Galactosidase fusion	Yes	100,000	Wetzel *et al.* (1980)
Desacetylthymosin α_1, human	*E. coli*	*trp LE* fusion	Yes	2,000,000	Wetzel *et al.* (1981a); P. McKay (personal communication)
Dihydrofolate reductase, mouse	*E. coli*	Direct (*bla*)		1,000[a]	Chang *et al.* (1978)
Dihydroorotic acid dehydrogenase, yeast	*E. coli*	?			Loison and Jund (1981)
Foot-and-mouth disease virus VP_3 protein	*B. subtilis*	Fusion with erythromycin resistance gene product	No	100,000[a]	Hardy *et al.* (1981)
Foot-and-mouth disease virus VP_3 protein	*E. coli*	*trp LE* fusion	Yes[b]	2,000,000	Kleid *et al.* (1981)

(*Continued*)

Table III (*Continued*)

Protein or peptide	Expressed in	Mode of expression	Cleavable	Molecules per cell	Reference
Foot-and-mouth disease virus VP_3 protein	*E. coli*	MS2 replicase fusion (λ)	Yes[b]	1,000	Kupper *et al.* (1981)
Galactokinase, yeast	*E. coli*	?			Schell and Wilson (1979)
Glycoprotein, vesicular stomatitis virus	*E. coli*	*trp E* fusion	No		Rose and Shafferman (1981)
Growth hormone, human	*E. coli*	Direct (*lac*)		186,000	Goeddel *et al.* (1979b)
Growth hormone, human	*E. coli*	*trp D* fusion	No	300,000[a]	Martial *et al.* (1979)
Growth hormone, bovine	*E. coli*	Direct (*trp*)		1,000,000	P. Seeburg (personal communication)
Growth hormone, bovine	*E. coli*	β-Lactamase fusion	No	5,000	Keshet *et al.* (1981)
Growth hormone, rat	*E. coli*	β-Lactamase fusion	No	24,000	Seeburg *et al.* (1978)
Hemagglutinin, fowl plaque virus	*E. coli*	*trp E* fusion	No		Emtage *et al.* (1980)
Hemagglutinin, human influenza	*E. coli*	β-Galactosidase fusion	No	10,000–70,000	Davis *et al.* (1981)
Hepatitis B core and surface antigens	*E. coli*	β-Lactamase, direct or fusion			Burrell *et al.* (1979)
Hepatitis B core antigen	*B. subtilis*	Direct (erythromycin resistance gene promoter)		<10,000[a]	Hardy *et al.* (1981)
Hepatitis B core antigen	*E. coli*	Direct (*trp*)		150,000	Edman *et al.* (1981)
Hepatitis B surface antigen	*E. coli*	β-Lactamase fusion	No	170,000	Edman *et al.* (1981)
Hepatitis B surface antigen	*E. coli*	β-Galactosidase fusion	No	5,000[a]	Charnay *et al.* (1980)
Imidazole glycerol phosphate dehydratase yeast	*E. coli*	?			Ratzkin and Carbon (1977)
Imidazole glycerol phosphate dehydratase yeast	*E. coli*	?			Struhl and Davis (1977)
Immunoglobulin light chain, mouse	*E. coli*	β-Lactamase fusion	No	500	Amster *et al.* (1980)
Insulin chains, human	*E. coli*	β-Galactosidase fusion	Yes	100,000	Goeddel *et al.* (1979a)
Interferon, bovine leukocyte (α1)	*E. coli*	Direct (*trp*)		20,000	D. J. Capon and D. V. Goeddel (unpublished)
Interferon, bovine fibroblast (β2)	*E. coli*	Direct (*trp*)		60,000	D. W. Leung, D. J. Capon and D. V. Goeddel (unpublished)
Interferon, human fibroblast	*E. coli*	Direct (*trp*, *lac*)		20,000	Goeddel *et al.* (1980b)
Hepatitis B surface antigen	Yeast	Direct (ADH)		20,000[a]	Valenzuela *et al.* (1982)

Hepatitis B surface antigen	Yeast	Direct (PGK)		1,000,000[a]	Hitzeman *et al.* (1983b)
Interferon, human fibroblast	*E. coli*	β-Lactamase fusion (λ), MS2 polymerase fusion (λ)	No	25[a]	Derynck *et al.* (1980)
Interferon, human fibroblast	*E. coli*	Direct (*lac*)		50	Taniguchi *et al.* (1980)
Interferon, human immune (γ)	*E. coli*	Direct (*trp*)		10,000	Gray *et al.* (1982); D. V. Goeddel and N. Lin (unpublished results)
Interferon, human immune (γ)	Yeast	Direct (PGK)		50,000	D. V. Goeddel and R. Derynck (unpublished results)
Interferon A, human leukocyte	*E. coli*	Direct (*trp*)		12,000	Goeddel *et al.* (1980a)
Interferon A, human leukocyte (α_2)	*E. coli*	Direct (*bla*)			Streuli *et al.* (1980)
Interferon B, human leukocyte	*E. coli*	Direct (*trp*)		12,000[a]	Yelverton *et al.* (1981)
Interferon D, human leukocyte	Yeast	Direct (ADH)		1,000,000	Hitzeman *et al.* (1981)
Interferon D, human leukocyte	*E. coli*	Direct (*trp*)		20,000	Hitzeman *et al.* (1981)
Interferon analog, human fibroblast	*E. coli*	Direct (*trp*)		20,000	Shepard *et al.* (1981)
Interferon analogs, human leukocyte	*E. coli*	Direct (*trp*)		12,000[a]	Weck *et al.* (1981)
Interferon analogs, human leukocyte	*E. coli*	β-Galactosidase fusion	No		Streuli *et al.* (1981)
Leu-enkephalin	*E. coli*	β-Galactosidase fusion	Yes	50,000	Shemyakin *et al.* (1980)
Ornithine carbamoyltransferase, yeast	*E. coli*	?			Crabeel *et al.* (1980)
Orotidine-5′-phosphate decarboxylase, yeast	*E. coli*	?			Bach *et al.* (1979)
Ovalbumin, chicken	*E. coli*	β-Galactosidase fusion	No	100,000[a]	Fraser and Bruce (1978)
Ovalbumin, chicken	Yeast	β-Galactosidase fusion (*lac*)	No	1,000	Mercereau-Puijalon *et al.* (1980)
Ovalbumin, chicken	*E. coli*	β-Galactosidase fusion	No	30,000	Mercereau-Puijalon *et al.* (1978)
Plasminogen activator, human	*E. coli*	Direct (*trp*)		2,000	Pennica *et al.* (1983)
Poly(L-aspartyl-L-phenylalanine)	*E. coli*	*trp*		10,000–100,000	Doel *et al.* (1980)
Polyoma t antigen	*E. coli*	β-Galactosidase fusion	No	15,000[a]	Horwich *et al.* (1980)
Pre-interferon A, human leukocyte	*E. coli*	Direct (*trp*)		120	Goeddel *et al.* (1980a)
Pre-interferon B, human leukocyte	*E. coli*	Direct (*trp*)		15[a]	Yelverton *et al.* (1981)
Pre-interferon D, human leukocyte (α_1)	*E. coli*	Direct (*bla*)		2	Nagata *et al.* (1980)
Preinterferon D, human leukocyte (α_1)	Yeast	Direct (PGK)		300,000[d]	Hitzeman *et al.* (1983a)

(*Continued*)

Table III (*Continued*)

Protein or peptide	Expressed in	Mode of expression	Cleavable	Molecules per cell	Reference
Preinterferon, human immune (γ)	Yeast	Direct (PGK)			Hitzeman *et al.* (1983a)
Preproinsulin, human	*E. coli*	β-Lactamase fusion	Yes		Chan *et al.* (1981)
Preproinsulin, rat	*E. coli*	β-Lactamase fusion	No		Talmadge *et al.* (1980)
Proinsulin, human	*E. coli*	*trp* LE fusion	Yes	1,000,000	Ross (1981); D. Kleid and R. Wetzel (personal communication)
Proinsulin, mini-C analog	*E. coli*	β-Galactisodase fusion	Yes	>10,000[a]	Wetzel *et al.* (1981c)
Proinsulin, rat	*E. coli*	β-Lactamase fusion	No	100	Villa-Komaroff *et al.* (1978)
Proinsulin, rat	*E. coli*	β-Lactamase fusion	Yes[c]		Talmadge *et al.* (1980)
Prolactin fragments, rat	*E. coli*	β-Lactamase fusion	No		Erwin *et al.* (1980)
Rabies virus glycoprotein	*E. coli*	Direct (*trp*)		100,000	Yelverton *et al.* (1983)
Ribulosebisphosphate carboxylase, maize chloroplast	*E. coli*	Direct (λP_L)			Gatenby *et al.* (1981)
Ribulosebisphosphate carboxylase, maize chloroplast	*E. coli*	Direct (endogenous)			Gatenby *et al.* (1981)
Rous sarcoma virus $p60^{src}$	*E. coli*	β-Galactosidase fusion	No		Gilmer and Erikson (1981)
Rous sarcoma virus $p60^{src}$	*E. coli*	hGH fusion (*trp*)	No	170,000	McGrath and Levinson (1982)
SV40 t antigen	*E. coli*	Direct (*lac*)		10,000	Roberts *et al.* (1979)
SV40 t antigen	*E. coli*	Direct (*lac*)		60,000	Thummel *et al.* (1981)
Serum albumin, human	*E. coli*	Direct (*trp*)			Lawn *et al.* (1981)
Somatostatin, human	*E. coli*	β-Galactosidase fusion	Yes	10,000	Itakura *et al.* (1977)
Thymidine kinase, herpes simplex	*E. coli*	Direct (*lac*)	No	20,000[a]	Garapin *et al.* (1981)
Thymidylate synthetase, *E. coli*	*B. subtilis*	?			Rubin *et al.* (1980)
Urokinase, human	*E. coli*	β-Lactamase, fusion or direct	No		Ratzkin *et al.* (1981)

[a] Molecules per cell calculated from data presented in the reference, assuming that 100,000 molecules of a 20,000 MW protein constitutes 1% of the protein of a bacterial cell.

[b] Cyanogen bromide cleavage generates a series of VP3 fragments among which should be a fragment containing the antigenic site.

[c] *Escherichia coli* signal peptidase removes the eukaryotic presequence as well as the β-lactamase leader sequence.

[d] 5–20% of the interferon activity was secreted into the medium.

not synthesize such proteins. In most reports cited the protein product was characterized little if at all; in many cases the means by which it was expressed are poorly understood. In all cases there is some evidence for the presence of the protein, or a derivative of the protein, in the cell: chemical or immunochemical characterization, *in vivo* or *in vitro* enzymatic activity, or biological activity.

Fusion protein expression systems are characterized as "cleavable" if the system was designed for the specific generation of native product. Although there are some reports of serendipitous intracellular processing of fusion proteins to give native products, as characterized by molecular weight on SDS-PAGE, generally the evidence presented can be equally well interpreted as translation initiation at the eukaryotic start ATG (Chang *et al.*, 1980) or at other internal ATGs.

The mode of expression is characterized as being by the direct or fusion protein approach (Section III,B). Unless otherwise specified, the bacterial leader sequence of the fusion protein defines the promoter and ribosome binding site used. Promoters are tabulated in parentheses in the same column. Question marks indicate that the sequences controlling transcription and translation are obscure. The number of molecules per cell are either author's estimates or values calculated from some other indication of yield (e.g., percentage of cellular protein). The word "endogenous" refers to evidence that *E. coli* transcription and translation is being directed by eukaryotic nucleic acid sequences.

VII. CONCLUSION

It is clear that recombinant DNA methods have added a new dimension to our ability to synthesize polypeptides. Although a wide variety of structures have already been expressed in and purified from *E. coli*, intracellular expression in bacteria will not work for every protein. On the other hand, there now exist effective systems for the synthesis of novel polypeptides in other microorganisms and cultured cells of higher eukaryotes, by extensions of the techniques described here. These expression systems may succeed where *E. coli* expression fails.

Although genetic engineering methods are obviously useful at the laboratory scale, this does not guarantee success as an industrial process. By now at least five human polypeptide sequences produced in *E. coli* have been approved for clinical trials by the FDA (insulin, interferons αA, αD, and β, and growth hormone), signifying that acceptable material can be produced on the pilot plant scale. More significant is the approval for human use (in the United States and Great Britain) of human insulin produced from *E. coli* extracts, making insulin the first recombinant DNA-derived polypeptide to be marketed for human use.

To biochemists interested in protein structure–function relationships, the most exciting use of these methods is the production of polypeptide analogs. The first scattered reports, in 1982, of mechanistic studies utilizing proteins derived from specific mutagenesis of cloned genes are the seeds of a new era of research in protein chemistry and enzymology.

ACKNOWLEDGMENTS

We thank Drs. Herbert W. Boyer, Dennis G. Kleid, Charles Hoyng, and Michael J. Ross for their critical reading of parts of the manuscript, and Jeanne Arch for assistance with its preparation. We also thank Drs. Robert Hershberg, Patricia O'Connor, and Norman Lin for their preparation of *E. coli* micrographs. We are especially grateful to colleagues who communicated their results to us before publication.

REFERENCES

Agarwal, K. L., Buchi, H., Caruthers, M. H., Gupta, N., Khorana, H. G., Kleppe, K., Kumar, A., Ohtsuka, E., RajBhandary, U. L., Van de Sande, J. H., Sgaramella, V., Weber, H., and Yamada, T. (1970). *Nature* (*London*) **227**, 27–34.

Ahmed, F., Schultz, J., Smith, E. E., and Whelan, W. J., eds. (1982). "From Gene to Protein: Translation into Biotechnology." Academic Press, New York.

Amster, O., Salomon, D., Zemel, O., Zamir, A., Zeelon, E. P., Kantor, F., and Schechter, I. (1980). *Nucleic Acids Res.* **8**, 2055–2065.

Arditti, R. R., Scaife, J., and Beckwith, J. (1968). *J. Mol. Biol.* **38**, 421–426.

Arnheiter, H., Thomas, R. M., Leist, T., Fountoulakis, M., and Gutte, B. (1981). *Nature* (*London*) **294**, 278–280.

Bach, M. L., Lacroute, F., and Botstein, D. (1979). *Proc. Natl. Acad. Sci. U.S.A.* **76**, 386–390.

Bertrand, K., Korn, L., Lee, F., Platt, T., Squires, C. L., Squires, C., and Yanofsky, C. (1975). *Science* **189**, 22–26.

Blobel, G., and Dobberstein, B. (1975). *J. Cell Biol.* **67**, 835–851.

Bolivar, F., Rodriquez, R. L., Greene, P. J., Betlach, M. C., Heyneker, H. L., Boyer, H. W., Crosa, J. H., and Falkow, S. (1977). *Gene* **2**, 95–119.

Brawner, M., and Jaskunas, S. R. J. (1982). *J. Mol. Biol.* (in press).

Bristow, A. F., and Bangham, D. R. (1981). *Trends Biochem. Sci.* **6**, VI–VIII.

Broome, S., and Gilbert, W. (1978). *Proc. Natl. Acad. Sci. U.S.A.* **75**, 2746–2749.

Browne, D. T., Earl, E. M., and Otvos, J. D. (1976). *Biochem. Biophys. Res. Commun.* **72**, 398–404.

Burrell, C. J., MacKay, P., Greenaway, P. J., Hofschneider, P. H., and Murray, K. (1979). *Nature* (*London*) **279**, 43–47.

Chan, S. J., Noyes, B. E., Agarwal, K. L., and Steiner, D. F. (1979). *Proc. Natl. Acad. Sci. U.S.A.* **76**, 5036–5040.

Chan, S. J., Weiss, J., Konrad, M., Bahl, C., Yu, S. D., Marks, D., and Steiner, D. F. (1981). *Proc. Natl. Acad. Sci. U.S.A.* **78**, 5401–5405.

Chance, R. E., Hoffman, J. A., Kroeff, E. P., Johnson, M. G., Schirmer, E. W., Bromer, W. W., Ross, M. J., and Wetzel, R. (1981a). *In* "Peptides: Synthesis, Structure, Function" (D. H. Rich and E. Gross, eds.), pp. 721–728. Pierce Chemical Co., Rockford, Illinois.

Chance, R. E., Kroeff, E. P., and Hoffman, J. A. (1981b). *In* "Insulins, Growth Hormones, and Recombinant DNA Technology" (J. L. Gueriguian, ed.), pp. 71–86. Raven Press, New York.

Chang, A. C. Y., Nunberg, J. H., Kaufman, R. J., Erlich, H. A., Schimke, R. T., and Cohen, S. N. (1978). *Nature (London)* **275**, 617–624.

Chang, A. C. Y., Erlich, H. A., Gunsalvo, R. P., Nunberg, J. H., Kaufman, R. J., Schimke, R. T., and Cohen, S. N. (1980). *Proc. Natl. Acad. Sci. U.S.A.* **77**, 1442–1446.

Chang, Y. E., Kwoh, D. Y., Kwoh, T. J., Soltvedt, B. C., and Zipser, D. (1981). *Gene* **14**, 121–130.

Charnay, P., Gervais, M., Louise, A., Galibert, F., and Tiollais, P. (1980). *Nature (London)* **286**, 893–895.

Chevallier, M. R., and Aigle, M. (1979). *FEBS Lett.* **108**, 179–180.

Clarke, L., and Carbon, J. (1978). *J. Mol. Biol.* **120**, 517–532.

Cohen, J. D., Eccleshall, T. R., Needleman, R. B., Federoff, H., Buchferer, B. A., and Marmur, J. (1980). *Proc. Natl. Acad. Sci. U.S.A.* **77**, 1078–1082.

Cohen, S. N. (1975). *Sci. Am.* **233**, 24–33.

Cohen, S. N., Chang, A. C. Y., Boyer, H. W., and Helling, R. B. (1973). *Proc. Natl. Acad. Sci. U.S.A.* **70**, 3240–3244.

Courvalin, P., and Fiandt, M. (1980). *Gene* **9**, 247–269.

Crabeel, M., Messenguy, F., Lacroute, F., and Glansdorff, N. (1980). *Arch. Int. Physiol. Biochim.* **88**, B21–B22.

Crea, R., and Horn, T. (1980). *Nucleic Acids Res.* **8**, 2331–2348.

Crea, R., Kraszewski, A., Hirose, T., and Itakura, K. (1978). *Proc. Natl. Acad. Sci. U.S.A.* **75**, 5765–5769.

Crea, R., Vasser, M. P., and Struble, M. E. (1982). Submitted for publication.

Davis, A. R., Nayak, D. P., Veda, M., Hiti, A. L., Dowbenko, D., and Kleid, D. G. (1981). *Proc. Natl. Acad. Sci. U.S.A.* **78**, 5376–5380.

de Boer, H. A., Comstock, L. J., Yansura, D., and Heyneker, H. (1982a). *In* "Promoters, Structure and Function" (R. Rodriguez and M. J. Chamberlain eds.), pp. 462–481. Praeger, New York.

de Boer, H. A., Heyneker, H., Comstock, L., Wieland, A., Vasser, M., and Horn, T. (1982b). *In* "From Gene to Protein: Translation into Biotechnology" (F. Ahmed, J. Schultz, E. E. Smith, and W. J. Whelan, eds.), pp. 309–327. Academic Press, New York.

de Boer, H. A. and Shepard, H. M. (1983). Horizons in Biochemistry and Biophysics (E. Quagliarello, ed.). Wiley, New York (in press).

Derynck, R., Remaut, E., Saman, E., Stanssens, P., DeClercq, E., Content, J., and Fiers, W. (1980). *Nature (London)* **287**, 193–197.

Dickson, R. C. (1980). *Gene* **10**, 347–356.

Doel, M. T., Eaton, M., Cook, E. A., Lewis, H., Patel, T., and Carey, N. H. (1980). *Nucleic Acids Res.* **8**, 4575–4592.

Edge, M. D., Greene, A. R., Heathcliffe, G. R., Meacock, P. A., Schuch, W., Scanlon, D. B., Atkinson, T. C., Newton, C. R., and Markum, A. F. (1981). *Nature (London)* **292**, 756–762.

Edman, J. C., Hallewell, R. A., Valenzuela, P., Goodman, H. M., and Rutter, W. J. (1981). *Nature (London)* **291**, 503–506.

Emtage, J. S., Tacon, W. C. A., Catlin, G. H., Jenkins, B., Porter, A. G., and Carey, N. H. (1980). *Nature (London)* **283**, 171–174.

Erlich, H. A., Cohen, S. N., and McDevitt, H. O. (1978). *Cell* **13**, 681–689.
Erwin, C. R., Maurer, R. A., and Donelson, J. E. (1980). *Nucleic Acids Res.* **8**, 2537–2545.
Estell, D., and Powers, D. (1983). Submitted for publication.
Fiers, W., Contreras, R., Duerinck, F., Haegeman, G., Iserentant, D., Merregaert, J., Min Jou, W., Molemans, F., Raeymaekers, A., Van den Berghe, A., Volckaert, G., and Ysebaert, M. (1976). *Nature* (*London*) **260**, 500–507.
Files, J. G., Weber, K., and Miller, J. H. (1974). *Proc. Natl. Acad. Sci. U.S.A.* **71**, 667–670.
Fowler, A. V. (1978). *J. Biol. Chem.* **253**, 5499–5504.
Frank, B. H., Pettee, R. M., Zimmerman, R. E., and Burck, P. J. (1981). *In* "Peptides: Synthesis, Structure, Function" (D. H. Rich and E. Gross, eds.), pp. 729–738. Pierce Chemical Co., Rockford, Illinois.
Fraser, T. H., and Bruce, B. J. (1978). *Proc. Natl. Acad. Sci. U.S.A.* **75**, 5936–5940.
Freedman, R. B., and Hawkins, H. C., eds. (1980). "The Enzymology of Post-translational Modification of Proteins." Academic Press, New York.
Garapin, A. C., Colbere-Garapin, F., Cohen-Solal, M., Horodniceanu, F., and Kourilsky, P. (1981). *Proc. Natl. Acad. Sci. U.S.A.* **78**, 815–819.
Gatenby, A. A., Castleton, J. A., and Saul, M. W. (1981). *Nature* (*London*) **291**, 117–121.
Gilbert, W., and Maxam, A. M. (1980). *In* "Methods in Enzymology" (L. Grossmon and K. Moldave, eds.), Vol. 65, Part 1, pp. 499–560. Academic Press, New York.
Gilbert, W., and Villa-Komaroff, L. (1980). *Sci. Am.* **242**, 74–94.
Gillam, S., and Smith, M. (1979). *Gene* **8**, 81–97.
Gillam, S., Jahnke, C., Astell, C., Phillips, S., Hutchison, C. A., and Smith, M. (1979). *Nucleic Acids Res.* **6**, 2973–2985.
Gilmer, T. M., and Erikson, R. L. (1981). *Nature* (*London*) **294**, 771–773.
Goeddel, D. V., Kleid, D. G., Bolivar, F., Heyneker, H. L., Yansura, D. G., Crea, R., Hirose, T., Kraszewski, A., Itakura, K., and Riggs, A. D. (1979a). *Proc. Natl. Acad. Sci. U.S.A.* **76**, 106–110.
Goeddel, D. V., Heyneker, H. L., Hozumi, T., Arentzen, R., Itakura, K., Yansura, D. G., Ross, M. J., Miozzari, G., Crea, R., and Seeburg, P. H. (1979b). *Nature* (*London*) **281**, 544–548.
Goeddel, D. V., Yelverton, E., Ullrich, A., Heyneker, H. L., Miozzari, G., Holmes, W., Seeburg, P. H., Dull, T., May, L., Stebbing, N., Crea, R., Maeda, S., McCandliss, R., Sloma, A., Tabor, J. M., Gross, M., Familletti, P. C., and Pestka, S. (1980a). *Nature* (*London*) **287**, 411–416.
Goeddel, D. V., Shepard, H. M., Yelverton, E., Leung, D., and Crea, R. (1980b). *Nucleic Acids Res.* **8**, 4057–4074.
Goldberg, A. L., and St. John, A. C. (1976). *Annu. Rev. Biochem.* **45**, 747–803.
Goldstein, A. L., Low, T. L. K., McAdoo, M., McClure, J., Thurman, G. B., Rossio, J., Lai, C.-Y., Chang, D., Wang, S.-S., Harvey, C., Ramel, A. H., and Meienhofer, J. (1977). *Proc. Natl. Acad. Sci. U.S.A.* **74**, 725–729.
Grantham, R., Gautier, C., and Govy, M. (1980). *Nucleic Acids Res.* **8**, 1893–1912.
Gray, O., and Chang, S. (1981). *J. Bacteriol.* **145**, 422–428.
Gray, P. W., Leung, D. W., Pennica, D., Yelverton, E., Najarian, R., Simonsen, C. C., Derynck, R., Sherwood, P. J., Wallace, D. M., Berger, S. L., Levinson, A. D., and Goeddel, D. V. (1982). *Nature* (*London*) **295**, 503–508.
Grunstein, M., and Hogness, D. S. (1975). *Proc. Natl. Acad. Sci. U.S.A.* **72**, 3961–3965.
Guarente, L., Lauer, G., Roberts, T. M., and Ptashne, M. (1980). Cell **20**, 543–553.
Gueriguian, J. L., ed. (1981). "Insulins, Growth Hormone, and Recombinant DNA Technology." Raven Press, New York.
Hallewell, R. A., and Emtage, S. (1980). *Gene* **9**, 27–47.
Hardy, K., Stahl, S., and Kupper, H. (1981). *Nature* (*London*) **293**, 481–483.

Harkins, R. N., Weck, P. K., Apperson, S., Haas, P., and Agarwal, B. (1982). Submitted for publication.

Harpold, M. M., Dobner, P. R., Evans, R. M., and Bancroft, F. C. (1978). *Nucleic Acids Res.* **5**, 2039–2053.

Hautala, J. A., Bassett, C. L., Gills, N. H., and Kushner, S. R. (1979). *Proc. Natl. Acad. Sci. U.S.A.* **76**, 5774–5778.

Harris, T. J. R. (1983). *In* "Genetic Engineering" (R. Williamson, ed.), Vol. 4. Academic Press, New York (in press).

Hitzeman, R. A., Clarke, L., and Carbon, J. (1980). *J. Biol. Chem.* **255**, 12073–12080.

Hitzeman, R. A., Hagie, F. E., Levine, H. L., Goeddel, D. V., Ammerer, G., and Hall, B. D. (1981). *Nature (London)* **293**, 717–722.

Hitzeman, R. A., Leung, D. W., Perry, L. J., Kohr, W. J., Levine, H. L. and Goeddel, D. V. (1983a) *Science* **219**, 620–625.

Hitzeman, R. A., Chen, C. Y., Hagie, F. E., Patzer, E. J., Lin, C.-C., Estell, D. A., Miller, J. B., Yaffe, A., Kleid, D. G., Levinson, A. D. and Oppermann, H. (1983b). Submitted for publication.

Horwich, A., Koop, A. H., and Eckhart, W. (1980). *J. Virol.* **36**, 125–132.

Houghton, M., Stewart, A. G., Doel, S. M., Emtage, J. S., Eaton, M. A. W., Smith, J. C., Patel, T. P., Lewis, H. M., Porter, A. G., Birch, J. R., Cartwright, T., and Carey, N. H. (1980). *Nucleic Acids Res.* **8**, 1913–1931.

Hutchison, C. A., Phillips, S., Edgell, M. H., Gillam, S., Jahnke, P., and Smith, M. (1978). *J. Biol. Chem.* **253**, 6551–6560.

Ikemura, T. (1981). *J. Mol. Biol.* **146**, 1–22.

Itakura, K., Katagiri, N., Bahl, C. P., Wightman, R. H., and Narang, S. A. (1975). *J. Am. Chem. Soc.* **97**, 7327–7332.

Itakura, K., Hirose, T., Crea, R. Riggs, A. D., Heyneker, H. L., Bolivar, F., and Boyer, H. W. (1977). *Science* **198**, 1056–1063.

Jackson, D. A., Symons, R. H., and Berg, P. (1972). *Proc. Natl. Acad. Sci. U.S.A.* **69**, 2904–2909.

Jay, E., Bambara, R., Padmanabhan, P., and Wu, R. (1974). *Nucleic Acids Res.* **1**, 331–353.

Katsoyannis, P. G., Tometsko, A., Zalut, C., Johnson, S., and Trakatellis, A. C. (1967). *Biochemistry* **6**, 2635–2642.

Keshet, E., Rosner, A., Bernstein, Y., Gorecki, M., and Aviv, H. (1981). *Nucleic Acids Res.* **9**, 19–30.

Kido, H., Vita, A., Hannappel, E., and Horecker, B. L. (1981). *Arch. Biochem. Biophys.* **208**, 95–100.

Kleid, D. G., Yansura, D., Small, B., Dowbenko, D., Moore, D. M., Grubman, M. J., McKercher, P. D., Morgan, D. O., Robertson, B. H., and Bachrach, H. L. (1981). *Science* **214**, 1125–1129.

Kohr, W. J., Keck, R. G., and Harkins, R. N. (1982). Submitted for publication.

Kourilsky, P., Gros, D., Rougeon, F., and Mach, B. (1977). *Nature (London)* **267**, 637–639.

Kreil, G. (1981). *Annu. Rev. Biochem.* **50**, 317–348.

Kumarev, V. P., Rivkin, M. I., Bogachev, V. S., Baranova, L. V., Merkulov, V. M., Rybakov, V. N., Solenov, E. I., and Fedorov, V. I. (1980). *Dokl. Biochem. (Engl. Transl.)* **252**, 1–6.

Kupper, H., Keller, W., Kurz, C., Forss, S., Schaller, H., Franze, R., Strohmaier, K., Marquardt, O., Zaslavsky, V. G., and Hofschneider, P. H. (1981). *Nature (London)* **289**, 555–559.

Lawn, R. M., Adelman, J., Bock, S. C., Franke, A. E., Houck, C. M., Najarian, R. C., Seeburg, P. H., and Wion, K. L. (1981). *Nucleic Acids Res.* **9**, 6103–6128.

Lerner, R. A., Green, N., Alexander, H., Liu, F. T., Sutcliffe, J. G., and Shinnick, T. M. (1981). *Proc. Natl. Acad. Sci. U.S.A.* **78**, 3403–3407.

Letsinger, R. L., and Lunsford, W. B. (1976). *J. Am. Chem. Soc.* **98**, 3655–3661.
Letsinger, R. L., and Ogilvie, K. K. (1967). *J. Am. Chem. Soc.* **89**, 4801–4803.
Lewin, B. (1974). "Gene Expression," Vol. 1. Wiley, New York.
Loison, G., and Jund, R. (1981). *Gene* **15**, 127–137.
Low, T. L. K., and Goldstein, A. L. (1979). *J. Biol. Chem.* **254**, 987–995.
McGrath, J. P., and Levinson, A. D. (1982). *Nature (London)* **295**, 423–425.
Manley, J. L. (1978). *J. Mol. Biol.* **125**, 407–432.
Martial, J. A., Hallewell, R. A., Baxter, J. D., and Goodman, H. M. (1979). *Science* **205**, 602–607.
Matteucci, M. D. and Caruthers, M. H. (1981). *J. Amer. Chem. Soc.* **103**, 3185–3191.
Meagher, R. B., Tait, R. C., Betlach, M., and Boyer, H. W. (1977). *Cell* **10**, 521–536.
Means, G. E., and Feeney, R. E. (1971). "Chemical Modification of Proteins." Holden-Day, San Francisco.
Mercereau-Puijalon, O., Royal, A., Cami, B., Garapin, A., Krust, A., Gannon, F., and Kourilsky, P. (1978). *Nature (London)* **275**, 505–510.
Mercereau-Puijalon, O., Lacroute, F., and Kourilsky, P. (1980). *Gene* **11**, 163–167.
Miller, J. H. (1972). "Experiments in Molecular Genetics." Cold Spring Harbor Lab., Cold Spring Harbor, New York.
Miozzari, G. F. (1981). *In* "Insulins, Growth Hormone, and Recombinant DNA Technology" (J. L. Gueriguian, ed.), pp. 13–31. Raven Press, New York.
Miyoshi, K., Arentzen, R., Huang, T., and Itakura, K. (1980). *Nucleic Acids Res.* **8**, 5507–5517.
Montgomery, D. L., Hall, B. D., Gillam, S., and Smith, M. (1978). *Cell* **14**, 673–680.
Nagata, S., Taira, H., Hall, A., Johnsrud, L., Streuli, M., Ecsodi, J., Boll, W., Cantell, K., and Weissmann, C. (1980). *Nature (London)* **284**, 316–320.
Neidhardt, F. C., Wirth, R., Smith, M. W., and von Bogelen, R. J. (1980). *J. Bacteriol.* **143**, 535–537.
Noyes, B. E., Mevarech, M., Stein, R., and Agarwal, K. L. (1979). *Proc. Natl. Acad. Sci. U.S.A.* **76**, 1770–1774.
Offord, R. E. (1980). "Semisynthetic Proteins." Wiley, New York.
Panthier, J. J., Fournier, P., Heslot, H., and Rambach, A. (1980). *Curr. Genet.* **2**, 109–113.
Paterson, B. M., Roberts, B. E., and Kuff, E. L. (1977). *Proc. Natl. Acad. Sci. U.S.A.* **74**, 4370–4374.
Pennica, D., Holmes, W. E., Kohr, W. J., Harkins, R. N., Vehar, G. A., Ward, C. A., Bennett, W. E., Yelverton, E., Seeburg, P. H., Heyneker, H. L., Goeddel, D. V. and Collen, D. (1983). *Nature (London)* **301**, 214–221.
Pezzuto, J. M., and Hecht, S. M. (1980). *J. Biol. Chem.* **255**, 865–869.
Polisky, B., Bishop, R. J., and Gelfand, D. H. (1976). *Proc. Natl. Acad. Sci. U.S.A.* **73**, 3900–3904.
Ratzkin, B., and Carbon, J. (1977). *Proc. Natl. Acad. Sci. U.S.A.* **74**, 487–491.
Ratzkin, B., Lee, S. G., Schrenk, W. J., Roychoudhury, R., Chen, M., Hamilton, T. A., and Hung, P. P. (1981). *Proc. Natl. Acad. Sci. U.S.A.* **78**, 3313–3317.
Razin, A., Hirose, T., Itakura, K., and Riggs, A. D. (1978). *Proc. Natl. Acad. Sci. U.S.A.* **75**, 4268–4270.
Riggs, A. D., Itakura, K., Crea, R., Hirose, T., Kraszewski, A., Goeddel, D., Kleid, D., Yansura, D., Bolivar, F., and Heyneker, H. (1980). *Recent Prog. Horm. Res.* **36**, 261–276.
Roberts, T. M., Bikel, I., Yocum, R. R., Livingston, D. M., and Ptashne, M. (1979). *Proc. Natl. Acad. Sci. U.S.A.* **76**, 5596–5600.
Rose, J. K., and Shafferman (1981). *Proc. Natl. Acad. Sci. U.S.A.* **78**, 6670–6674.
Ross, M. J. (1981). *In* "Insulins, Growth Hormone, and Recombinant DNA Technology" (J. L. Gueriguian, ed.), pp. 33–48. Raven Press, New York.
Roth, R. A., and Koshland, M. E. (1981). *Biochemistry* **20**, 6594–6599.

Rubin, E. M., Wilson, G. A., and Young, F. E. (1980). *Gene* **10**, 227–235.
Sancar, A., Hack, A. M., and Rupp, W. D. (1979). *J. Bacteriol.* **137**, 692–693.
Scheele, G. and Jacoby, R. (1982). *J. Biol. Chem.* **257**, 12277–12282.
Schell, M. A., and Wilson, D. B. (1979). *Gene* **5**, 291–303.
Schwyzer, R., and Eberle, A. (1977). *In* "Frontiers of Hormone Research" (Tj. B. Van Wimersma Greidanus, ed.), pp. 18–25. Karger, Basel.
Seeburg, P. H., Shire, J., Martial, J. A., Ivarie, R. D., Morris, J. A., Ullrich, A., Baxter, J. D., and Goodman, H. M. (1978). *Nature (London)* **276**, 795–798.
Sgaramella, V., van de Sande, J. H., and Khorana, H. G. (1970). *Proc. Natl. Acad. Sci. U.S.A.* **67**, 1468–1475.
Shemyakin, M. F., Chestukhin, A. V., Dolganov, G. M., Khodkova, E. M., Monastyrskaya, G. S., and Sverdlov, E. D. (1980). *Nucleic Acids Res.* **8**, 6163–6174.
Shepard, H. M., Leung, D., Stebbing, N., and Goeddel, D. V. (1981). *Nature (London)* **294**, 563–565.
Shepard, H. M., Yelverton, E., and Goeddel, D. V. (1982). *DNA* **1**, 125–131.
Shine, J., and Dalgarno, L. (1975). *Nature (London)* **254**, 34–38.
Shine, J., Fettes, I., Lan, N. C. Y., Roberts, J. L., and Baxter, J. D. (1980). *Nature (London)* **285**, 456–461.
Smith, A. J. H. (1980). *In* "Methods in Enzymology" (L. Grossman and K. Moldave, eds.), Vol. 65, Part 1, pp. 560–580. Academic Press, New York.
Smyth, D. G., Massey, D. E., Zakarian, S., and Finnie, M. D. A. (1979). *Nature (London)* **279**, 252–254.
Staehelin, T., Hobbs, D. S., Kung, H., Lai, C. Y., and Pestka, S. (1981). *J. Biol. Chem.* **256**, 9750–9754.
Stebbing, N., Olson, K., Lin, N., Harkins, R. N., Snider, C., Ross, M. J., Fields, F., May, L., Fenno, J., Fodge, D., and Prender, G. (1981). *In* "Insulins, Growth Hormone, and Recombinant DNA Technology" (J. L. Gueriguian, ed.), pp. 71–86. Raven Press, New York.
Stewart, W. E., Sarkar, F. H., Taira, H., Hall, A., Nagata, S., and Weissman, C. (1980). *Gene* **11**, 181–186.
Streuli, M., Nagata, S., and Weissmann, C. (1980). *Science* **209**, 1343–1347.
Streuli, M., Hall, A., Boll, W., Stewart, W. E., Nagata, S., and Weissmann, C. (1981). *Proc. Natl. Acad. Sci. U.S.A.* **78**, 2848–2852.
Struhl, K., Cameron, J. R., and Davis, R. W. (1976). *Proc. Natl. Acad. Sci. U.S.A.* **73**, 1471–1475.
Suggs, S. V., Wallace, R. B., Hirose, T., Kawashima, E. H., and Itakura, K. (1981). *Proc. Natl. Acad. Sci. U.S.A.* **78**, 6613–6617.
Sutcliffe, J. G. (1978). *Proc. Natl. Acad. Sci. U.S.A.* **75**, 3737–3741.
Swamy, K. H. S., and Goldberg, A. L. (1981). *Nature (London)* **292**, 652–654.
Sykes, B. D., and Weiner, J. H. (1980). *In* "Magnetic Resonance in Biology" (J. S. Cohen, ed.), pp. 171–195. Wiley, New York.
Talmadge, K., Kaufman, J., and Gilbert, W. (1980). *Proc. Natl. Acad. Sci. U.S.A.* **77**, 3988–3992.
Talmadge, K., Brosius, J., and Gilbert, W. (1981). *Nature (London)* **294**, 176–178.
Taniguchi, T., and Weissmann, C. (1978). *J. Mol. Biol.* **118**, 533–565.
Taniguchi, T., Guarente, L., Roberts, T. M., Kimelman, D., Douhan, J., and Ptashne, M. (1980). *Proc. Natl. Acad. Sci. U.S.A.* **77**, 5230–5233.
Thummel, C. S., Burgess, T. L., and Tjian, R. (1981). *J. Virol.* **37**, 683–697.
Timmis, K. N. (1981). *In* "Genetics as a Tool in Microbiology" (S. W. Glover and D. A. Hopwood, eds.), pp. 49–109. Cambridge Univ. Press, London and New York.
Valenzuela, P., Medina, A., Rutter, W. J., Ammerer, G. and Hall, B. D. (1982) *Nature (London)* **298**, 347–350.

Vapnek, D., Hautala, J. A., Jacobson, J. W., Giles, N. H., and Kushner, S. R. (1977). *Proc. Natl. Acad. Sci. U.S.A.* **74**, 3508–3512.

Villa-Komaroff, L., Efstratiadis, A., Broome, S., Lomedico, P., Tizard, R., Naber, S. P., Chick, W. L., and Gilbert, W. (1978). *Proc. Natl. Acad. Sci. U.S.A.* **75**, 3727–3731.

Wallace, R. B., Shaffer, J., Murphy, R. F., Bonner, J., Hirose, T., and Itakura, K. (1979). *Nucleic Acids Res.* **6**, 3543–3557.

Wallace, R. B., Johnson, P. F., Tanaka, S., Schold, M., Itakura, K. and Abelson, J. (1980). *Science* **209**, 1396–1400.

Wallace, R. B., Johnson, M. J., Hirose, T., Miyake, T., Kawashima, E. H. and Itakura, K. (1981a). *Nucleic Acids Res.* **9**, 879–894.

Wallace, R. B., Schold, M., Johnson, M. J., Dembek, P., and Itakura, K. (1981b). *Nucleic Acids Res.* **9**, 3647–3656.

Walter, G., Scheidtmann, K. H., Carbone, A., Landano, A. P., and Doolittle, R. F. (1980). *Proc. Natl. Acad. Sci. U.S.A.* **77**, 5197–5200.

Wang, S.-S., and Carpenter, F. H. (1965). *J. Biol. Chem.* **240**, 1619–1625.

Wasylyk, B., Derbyshire, R., Guy, A., Molko, D., Roget, A., Teoule, R., and Chambon, P. (1980). *Proc. Natl. Acad. Sci. U.S.A.* **77**, 7024–7028.

Weck, P. K., Apperson, S., Stebbing, N., Gray, P. W., Leung, D., Shepard, H. M., and Goeddel, D. V. (1981). *Nucleic Acids Res.* **9**, 6153–6166.

Weissbach, H., Zarucki-Schulz, T., Kung, H., Spears, C., Redfield, B., Caldwell, P., and Brot, N. (1981). *In* "Molecular Approaches to Gene Expression and Protein Structure" M. A. Q. Siddiqui, H. Weissbach, and M. Krauskopf, eds.), pp. 215–243. Academic Press, New York.

Wetzel, R. (1980). *Am. Sci.* **68**, 664–675.

Wetzel, R. (1981). *Nature (London)* **289**, 606–607.

Wetzel, R., Heyneker, H. L., Goeddel, D. V., Jhurani, P., Shapiro, J., Crea, R., Low, T. L. K., McClure, J. E., Thurman, G. B., and Goldstein, A. L. (1980). *Biochemistry* **19**, 6096–6104.

Wetzel, R., Heyneker, H. L., Goeddel, D. V., Jhurani, P., Shapiro, J., Crea, R., Low, T. L. K., McClure, J. E., Thurman, G. B., and Goldstein, A. L. (1981a). *In* "Cellular Responses to Molecular Modulators" (L. W. Mozes, J. Schultz, W. A. Scott, and R. Werner, eds.), pp. 251–266. Academic Press, New York.

Wetzel, R., Perry, L. J., Estell, D. E., Lin, N., Levine, H. L., Slinker, B., Fields, F., Ross, M. J., and Shively, J. (1981b). *J. Interferon Res.* **1**, 381–390.

Wetzel, R., Kleid, D. G., Crea, R., Heyneker, H. L., Yansura, D. G., Hirose, T., Kraszewski, A., Riggs, A. D., Itakura, K., and Goeddel, D. V. (1981c). *Gene* **16**, 63–71.

Winter, G., Fersht, A. R., Wilkinson, A. J., Zoller, M. and Smith, M. (1982) *Nature (London)* **299**, 756–758.

Wold, F. (1981). *Annu. Rev. Biochem.* **50**, 783–814.

Woodford, T. A., and Dixon, J. E. (1979). *J. Biol. Chem.* **254**, 4993–4999.

Yanofsky, C. (1981). *Nature (London)* **289**, 751–758.

Yelverton, E., Leung, D., Weck, P., Gray, P. W., and Goeddel, D. V. (1981). *Nucleic Acids Res.* **9**, 731–741.

Yelverton, E., Norton, S., Obijeski, J. F., and Goeddel, D. V. (1983). *Science* **219**, 614–620.

Chapter **2**

Acidolytic Deprotecting Procedures in Peptide Synthesis

HARUAKI YAJIMA AND NOBUTAKA FUJII
Faculty of Pharmaceutical Sciences
Kyoto University
Kyoto, Japan

I. Introduction 66
II. Deprotecting Reagents in Peptide Synthesis. 67
III. Acidolytic Deprotecting Procedures 68
A. Dilute Hydrogen Chloride Procedure in Combination with N^{ε}-Formyllysine [Lys(For)] 68
B. Trifluoroacetic Acid Procedure in Combination with N^{ε}-*tert*-Butyloxycarbonyllysine 69
C. Liquid Hydrogen Fluoride Procedure in Combination with N^{ε}-Benzyloxycarbonyllysine 71
D. Methanesulfonic or Trifluoromethanesulfonic Acid Procedure in Combination with N^{ε}-Benzyloxy-carbonyllysine. 72
IV. Applications in Synthesis 74
A. Synthesis of Lysine-Containing Peptides 74
B. Synthesis of Methionine-Containing Peptides. 75
1. Cleavage of Ether Based on the "Hard–Soft" Concept. . 76
2. Cleavage of the Benzyloxycarbonyl Group Based on the "Push–Pull" Mechanism 77
3. Cleavage of the Methyloxycarbonyl Group. 78
4. Synthesis of Methionine-Containing Peptides without S-Protection 78
5. Synthesis of Methionine-Containing Peptides with S-Protection 79
C. Synthesis of Arginine-Containing Peptides. 80
D. Synthesis of Tyrosine-Containing Peptides. 85
E. Synthesis of Serine- or Threonine-Containing Peptides . . 86
F. Synthesis of Tryptophan-Containing Peptides. 86

THE PEPTIDES, VOLUME 5

ISBN 0-12-304205-4

G. Synthesis of Aspartic Acid-Containing Peptides 88
H. Synthesis of Cysteine-Containing Peptides 92
V. Deprotection of Synthetic Bovine Ribonuclease A 95
A. Deprotection with Methanesulfonic Acid 97
B. Deprotection by Liquid Hydrogen Fluoride 100
C. Deprotection with Trifluoromethanesulfonic Acid–Thioanisole in Trifluoroacetic Acid 101
VI. Opportunities and Constraints 104
A. Comparative Evaluation 104
B. Prognosis 105
References 106

I. INTRODUCTION

The benzyloxycarbonyl (Z) group removable by catalytic hydrogenolysis was first reported by Bergmann and Zervas (1932) in an article entitled, "Über ein allgemeines Verfahren der Peptid-Synthese." This ingenious discovery paved the way for the synthesis of optically homogeneous peptides. However, the first synthesis of a pituitary hormone, oxytocin, was achieved by du Vigneaud *et al.* (1953a) using sodium in liquid ammonia (Sifferd and du Vigneaud, 1935) as a deprotecting procedure instead of the Bergmann–Zervas technique. The presence of sulfur in the cysteine residues of oxytocin prevented the use of catalytic hydrogenolysis. It should also be remembered that the concept of a urethane-type protecting group was introduced by Emil Fischer, the father of peptide chemistry, as early as 1902. However, he had to abandon the ethyloxycarbonyl group for lack of a suitable deprotecting agent that would not simultaneously cleave the peptide bonds.

The history of peptide synthesis provides many examples of the great importance of a suitable deprotecting procedure at the final stage of synthesis in order to obtain a desired peptide in satisfactory yield and in a high degree of purity. This pertains to any peptide whether prepared by solid-phase or conventional methods, but the issue assumes critical importance for syntheses of larger peptides that contain large numbers of protecting groups. Indeed, the choice of the reagent used in the final deprotection step determines the main strategy of the synthesis. For example, the type of protection used for the N^{ε}-amino group of lysine depends directly on this choice. After reviewing several deprotecting procedures, which are examined in detail, the scope and limitations of the methanesulfonic acid (MSA) and trifluoromethanesulfonic acid (TFMSA) deprotecting procedures will be discussed.

II. DEPROTECTING REAGENTS IN PEPTIDE SYNTHESIS

After du Vigneaud's syntheses of oxytocin (1953a) and vasopressin (1953b), the sodium–liquid ammonia procedure played a major role in the final step of the synthesis of biologically active peptides during the 1950s. Syntheses of insulin in three independent laboratories [Kung *et al.*, 1965; Katsoyannis *et al.*, 1964; Zahn and collaborators (Meienhofer *et al.*, 1963)] were typical examples of this application. Information about side reactions occurring under such basic conditions was not available until Hofmann and Yajima (1961) pointed out that preferential cleavage of the proline bond took place during the sodium–liquid ammonia treatment of protected α-melanotropin (α-MSH). Later it was pointed out by Marglin and Merrified (1966) that time-dependent cleavage of the threonyl–proline bond (positions 27–28) in the insulin B chain did indeed occur with this treatment. Schwyzer *et al.* (1959) reported that β-melanotropin (β-MSH) could not be synthesized unequivocally with the use of the sodium–liquid ammonia procedure, that is, under basic conditions, mainly because of the formation of aminosuccinimide from the aspartic acid residue. The accumulated evidence warned peptide chemists against further application of the sodium–liquid ammonia procedure in the synthesis of complex peptides and indicated a need to explore new deprotecting procedures, preferably under acidic conditions.

Alternative methods were soon described for three examples: the synthesis of α-MSH by Guttmann and Boissonnas (1959), the synthesis of corticotropin (ACTH) (1–23) by Hofmann *et al.* (1961), and the synthesis of α-MSH and β-MSH by Schwyzer *et al.* (1963a,b). The benzyloxycarbonyl group was cleaved from the N^{ε}-amino group of lysine by hydrogen bromide (HBr) in

Table I. Deprotecting Reagents in Peptide Synthesis

Reagent	Reference
Catalytic hydrogenation	Bergmann and Zervas (1932)
Sodium in liquid ammonia	Sifferd and du Vigneaud (1935)
Hydrogen bromide	Ben-Ishai and Berger (1952)
Hydrochloric acid	Hofmann *et al.* (1961)
Trifluoroacetic acid	McKay and Albertson (1957)
Hydrogen fluoride	Sakakibara *et al.* (1967)
Boron tris(trifluoroacetate)	Pless and Bauer (1973)
Boron tribromide	Felix (1974)
Pyridinium poly HF	Matsuura *et al.* (1976)
Methanesulfonic acid	Yajima *et al.* (1975b)
Trifluoromethanesulfonic acid	Yajima *et al.* (1974)

glacial acetic acid (AcOH) in the first example, the formyl group by dilute hydrogen chloride (HCl) in the second example, and the *tert*-butyloxycarbonyl group by trifluoroacetic acid (TFA) in the third example. A few years later, Sakakibara *et al.* (1967) demonstrated that the benzyloxycarbonyl group could be removed by liquid hydrogen fluoride (HF). As with the sodium–liquid ammonia procedure, various side reactions were observed under these acidic conditions—mostly alkylation reactions which were not fully understood at the time. Since then, more detailed information about these side reactions has accumulated, and several other deprotecting reagents have been introduced as summarized in Table I. Of these, the TFA deprotecting procedure and the liquid HF deprotecting procedure have gained wide applicability in present-day synthesis of complex peptides (see Volume 3, Chapter 5 and Volume 2, Chapter 1, respectively).

III. ACIDOLYTIC DEPROTECTING PROCEDURES

A. Dilute Hydrogen Chloride Procedure in Combination with N^{ε}-Formyllysine [Lys(For)]

Before reviewing the TFA and liquid HF procedures, the dilute HCl deprotecting procedure employed for the synthesis of ACTH(1–23) (Hofmann *et al.*, 1961) will be briefly described. Because ACTH is known to be relatively stable toward dilute HCl (0.5 *N*), this acid was employed to remove the N^{ε}-formyl group. However, this treatment resulted in the partial cleavage of peptide bonds, preferentially at the glycyl bond. Later (Yajima *et al.*, 1968a) a mild procedure was explored for removing the N^{ε}-formyl group with hydrazine acetate [Eq. (1)] or hydroxylamine hydrochloride in pyridine (50°C for 40 hr) and was applied in the synthesis of monkey (Yajima *et al.*, 1968b) and human (Yajima *et al.*, 1969) β-MSH without observation of the fission of peptide bonds. The same idea was proposed independently by Geiger and Siedel (1968).

Similar to N^{ε}-trifluoroacetyllysine (Schallenberg and Calvin, 1955), N^{ε}-formyllysine provides an advantage in the synthesis of sulfur-containing peptides. When *tert*-butyloxycarbonyl amino acids are employed, this protecting group can be removed by TFA without affecting the N^{ε}-formyl or the N^{ε}-trifluoroacetyl groups of lysine residues. However, further application of this principle in the synthesis of complex peptides containing a large number of lysine residues seems difficult, because the cleavage reaction proceeds generally to ~95% completion in each residue but not to 100% because of an equilibrium between substrate and reagent [Eq. (1)].

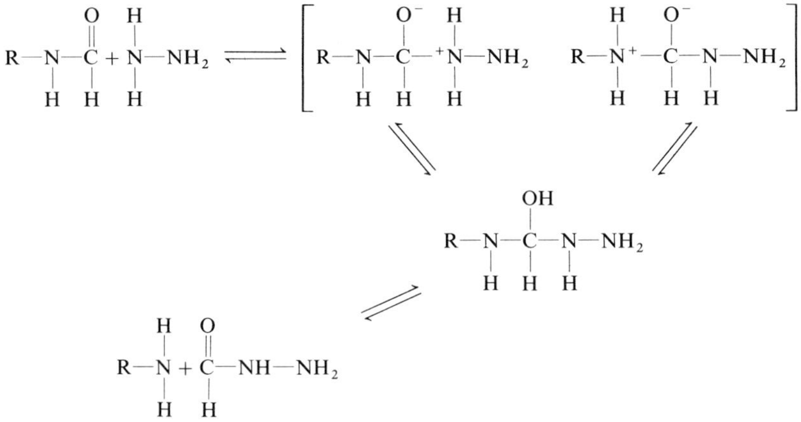

$$R-\underset{\underset{H}{|}}{N}-\underset{\underset{H}{|}}{\overset{\overset{O}{\|}}{C}} + \underset{\underset{H}{|}}{N}-NH_2 \;\rightleftharpoons\; \left[R-\underset{\underset{H}{|}}{N}-\underset{\underset{H}{|}}{\overset{\overset{O^-}{|}}{C}}-\underset{\underset{H}{|}}{\overset{+}{N}}-NH_2 \qquad R-\underset{\underset{H}{|}}{\overset{\overset{H}{|}}{N^+}}-\underset{\underset{H}{|}}{\overset{\overset{O^-}{|}}{C}}-\underset{\underset{H}{|}}{N}-NH_2 \right]$$

(1)

$$R-\underset{\underset{H}{|}}{N}-\underset{\underset{H}{|}}{\overset{\overset{OH}{|}}{C}}-\underset{\underset{H}{|}}{N}-NH_2$$

$$R-\underset{\underset{H}{|}}{\overset{\overset{H}{|}}{N}} + \overset{\overset{O}{\|}}{C}-NH-NH_2$$

B. Trifluoroacetic Acid Procedure in Combination with N^ε-*tert*-Butyloxycarbonyllysine

The *tert*-butyloxycarbonyl group removable by TFA was first reported by McKay and Albertson (1957), and this unique property opened up a new way of synthesizing complex peptides with the use of N^ε-*tert*-butyloxycarbonyllysine. A well-known example is the synthesis of α-MSH by Schwyzer *et al.* (1963a), mentioned earlier. The general principle of peptide synthesis with the use of N^ε-*tert*-butyloxycarbonyllysine can be written as shown in Fig. 1.

The use of this strategy in the synthesis of peptides whose sequences include sulfur-containing amino acids (cysteine, methionine, or both) requires an additional N^α-protecting group, removable by mild acid treatment, such as the triphenylmethyl (Trt) group (Hillmann-Elis *et al.*, 1953) or the 2-(4-biphenylyl)propyl(2)oxycarbonyl (Bpoc) group (Sieber and Iselin, 1968, 1969). For chain elongation, such a group must be cleaved without affecting the N^ε-*tert*-butyloxycarbonyl group of lysine residues. Therefore, three selectively cleavable amine protecting groups, for example, Z, Boc, and Bpoc, must be utilized to synthesize complex peptides. At present, no suitable side-chain protecting group for arginine removable by TFA is readily available. Thus, N^G-protecting groups of arginine, such as the NO_2 group, must be removed before the introduction of sulfur-containing amino acids. This situation makes it difficult to synthesize peptides with both arginine and sulfur-containing amino acid residues in their chains, especially if arginine is located on the NH_2-terminal side of methionine and cysteine residues, as in -Arg-Met-Arg-Cys-.

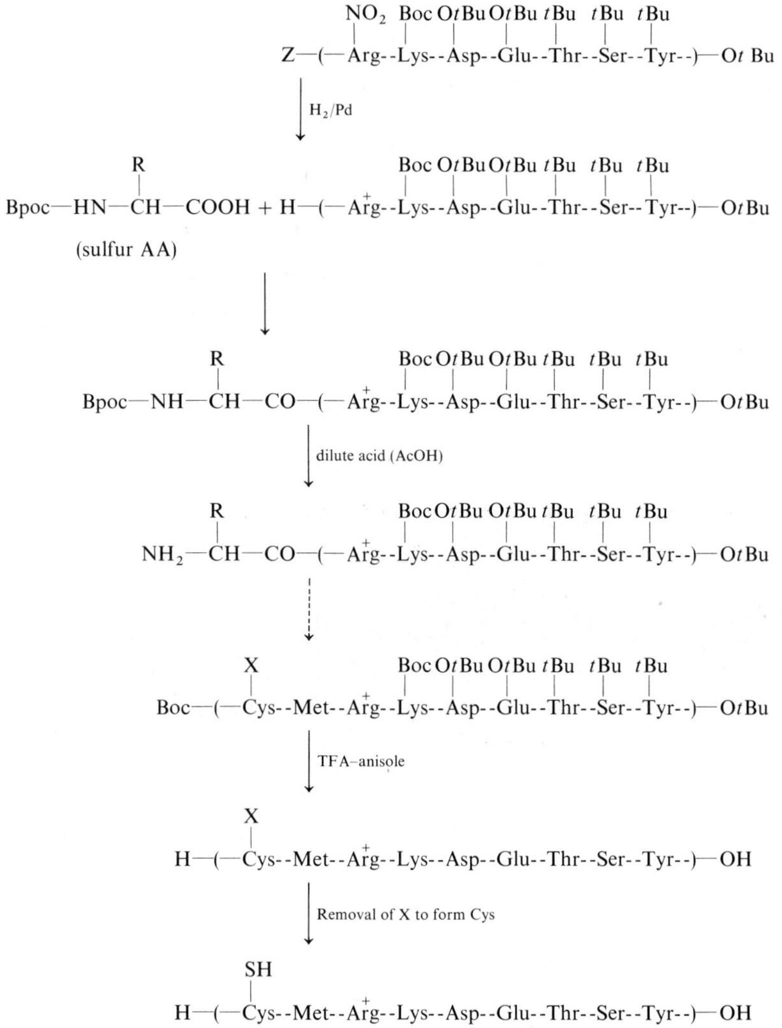

Figure 1. Principle of the trifluoroacetic acid (TFA) deprotecting procedure (Bpoc = 2-(4-biphenylyl)propyl(2)oxycarbonyl.

In spite of this difficulty, TFA is still superior to the other acid reagents listed in Table I with respect to being the least prone to undergoing side reactions during the final deprotection. The synthesis of human ACTH (Bell formula) by Schwyzer and Sieber (1963), of calcitonin by Rittel *et al.* (1968), and of glucagon by Wünch *et al.* (1968) are typical examples of its successful application.

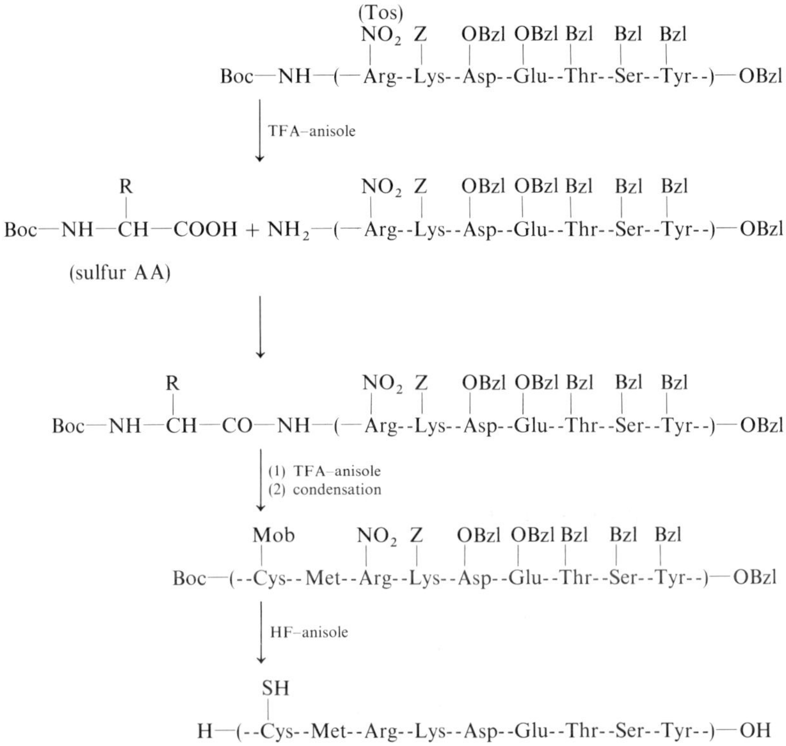

Figure 2. Principle of the liquid hydrogen fluoride (HF) deprotecting procedure (Mob = 4-methyloxybenzyl).

C. Liquid Hydrogen Fluoride Procedure in Combination with N^{ε}-Benzyloxycarbonyllysine

The general scheme of the liquid HF deprotecting procedure and the use of N^{ε}-benzyloxycarbonyllysine is illustrated in Fig. 2. Sulfur-containing amino acids are introduced as N^{α}-*tert*-butyloxycarbonyl-protected derivatives, as are other amino acids, without a need for an additional N^{α}-protecting group. Thus, the synthesis of protected peptides containing methionine and cysteine can be performed more easily than in the TFA deprotection procedure, regardless of the location of the arginine residues. N^{G}-Nitroarginine was cleaved by liquid HF (Sakakibara *et al*., 1967) as well as N^{G}-tosylarginine (Schwyzer and Li, 1958; Mazur and Plume, 1968). Because of the easy removal of N^{G}-protecting groups from arginine, liquid HF was soon adopted for the solid-phase peptide synthesis (Merrifield, 1963), replacing the initially used HBr in TFA as a deprotecting reagent for the benzyl-type protecting groups.

Several side reactions occurring during the liquid HF treatment were observed by different authors. A typical example is the γ-anisylation of the glutamic acid γ-benzyl ester residue (Sano and Kawanishi, 1975; Feinberg and Merrifield, 1975), which is due to the strong nucleophilicity of the fluoride anion, analogous to the Friedel–Crafts reaction. It has been pointed out that the NO_2 cation (deep red color) liberated from N^G-nitroarginine attacked the phenylalanine residue to form a 4-nitrophenylalanine derivative (S. Sakakibara, personal communication, 1981). These side reactions can be suppressed to an acceptable extent by lowering the reaction temperature or by selecting more effective scavengers than anisole. These problems will be discussed together with those of the MSA and TFMSA procedures in the succeeding section.

D. Methanesulfonic or Trifluoromethanesulfonic Acid Procedure in Combination with N^ε-Benzyloxycarbonyllysine

Comparison of the characteristic features of the TFA procedure and the liquid HF procedure seems to indicate that the latter is advantageous in the synthesis of protected peptides. If the benzyl-type protecting groups together with the arginine-protecting group can be removed by alternative means, instead of liquid HF, without using special equipment and possibly with fewer side reactions, the synthesis of large peptides and hopefully small proteins will become easier. Moreover, this principle can be applied, of course, to the solid-phase synthesis.

We looked for liquid organic acids and became interested in MSA and TFMSA. It is known that the tryptophan residue in proteins can be determined quantitatively by hydrolysis with 4 *N* MSA (Simpson *et al.*, 1976) or 3 *N* 4-toluenesulfonic acid (Liu and Chang, 1971). Indeed, tryptophan is rather more stable toward the action of organic sulfonic acids than toward HCl or TFA. TFMSA and MSA are 47 and 2 times stronger acids than HCl, respectively, but both lack oxidating and dehydrating properties.

As shown in Table II, both acids, MSA and TFMSA in TFA (1:3), have enough acidity to generate the parent amino acids from the corresponding derivatives currently employed in peptide synthesis within 60 min at room temperature, except for some amino acid derivatives (Yajima *et al.*, 1974, 1975b). The recovery of arginine from N^G-nitroarginine was unsatisfactory. A somewhat elevated temperature (40°C for 60–80 min) was required for quantitative recovery of arginine from N^G-tosylarginine. The recoveries of methionine and tyrosine were low–in the latter case as a result of 3-benzyl-

Table II. Removal of Various Protecting Groups by Methanesulfonic Acid (MSA) or Trifluoromethanesulfonic Acid (TFMSA)

Amino acid derivative	Parent amino acid regenerated (%)[a]	
	CH_3SO_3H	CF_3SO_3H–TFA, 1:3
NPS-Val-OH	100.5	99.9
Boc-Ser-OH	96.5	99.2
Moz-Gly-OH	99.9	99.8
Z-Trp-OH	100.0	100.9
Z-Tyr-OH	100.1	92.4
Z-Met-OH	31.5	88.3[b]
Z-Glu-OH	101.2	100.1
Z-Glu(O*t*Bu)-OH	99.5	98.8
H-Glu(OBzl)-OH	99.6	100.7
H-Asp(OBzl)-OH	100.8	100.4
H-Ser(Bzl)-OH	97.7	100.4
H-Thr(Bzl)-OH	101.6	99.0
H-Tyr(Bzl)-OH	30.2	10.5 + Tyr(3-Bzl)
H-Arg(NO_2)-OH	58.5	33.5 (incomp.)
H-Arg(Tos)-OH	49.2	93.3
Z-Arg(Z_2)-OH	100.0	
H-His(Tos)-OH	27.8	84.3
H-His(Bzl)-OH	0	
H-Cys(Bzl)-OH	32.9	98.7
H-Cys(Mob)-OH	94.6	100.0
H-Lys(For)-OH	0	

[a] Reaction at 20°C for 60 min.
[b] With dithiothreitol.

tyrosine formation, as in liquid HF treatment (Erickson and Merrifield, 1973). These results suggested that resolution of some of the aforementioned problems might open up a convenient means of peptide synthesis through the use of one of these acids as a deprotecting reagent (Fig. 3). We hoped to explore suitable conditions for readily removing many protecting groups from relatively large peptides by a brief treatment, even if the necessary acid has to be rather strong. MSA (in the presence of *m*-cresol as a scavenger) or 1 *M* TFMSA–thioanisole (1:1) in TFA (with *m*-cresol) are systems we judged to be useful for practical peptide synthesis. Several problems that needed to be overcome to reach this conclusion will be discussed in subsequent sections.

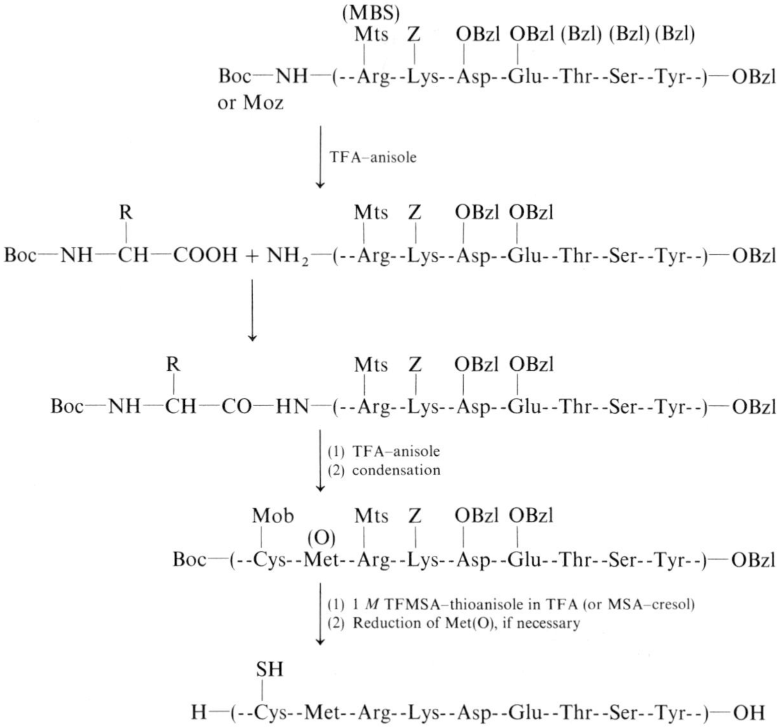

Figure 3. Principle of the methanesulfonic acid (MSA) or trifluoromethanesulfonic acid (TFMSA) deprotecting procedure (Mts = mesitylene-2-sulfonyl, Mbs = methyloxybenzenesulfonyl).

IV. APPLICATIONS IN SYNTHESIS

A. Synthesis of Lysine-Containing Peptides

TFMSA–anisole deprotection was first examined in the synthesis of neurotensin (Yajima *et al.*, 1975c), a hypothalamic peptide isolated by Carraway and Leeman (1975). Protected neurotensin, Z-pGlu-Leu-Tyr-Glu(OBzl)-Asn-Lys(Z)-Pro-Arg(Tos)-Arg(Tos)-Pro-Tyr-Ile-Leu-OH, was treated with TFMSA in the presence of anisole at 40°C for 60 min. These rather drastic conditions had to be employed in this case to ensure complete deprotection of both 4-toluenesulfonyl groups from the two arginine residues. When the deprotected peptide was subjected to gel filtration on on Sephadex G-10, we detected a small shoulder in front of the main peak

Table III. Effect of Various Cation Scavengers During the Treatment of N^{ε}-Benzyloxycarbonyllysine with Methanesulfonic Acid (MSA) or Trifluoromethanesulfonic Acid (TFMSA)

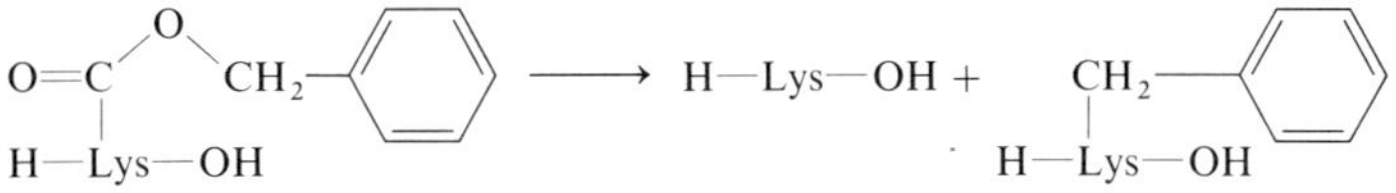

Scavenger[a]	TFMSA–TFA, 1:1 (%)		MSA (%)	
	Lys	Lys(Bzl)	Lys	Lys(Bzl)
Anisole	97.1	2.9	100	0
o-Cresol	99.6	0.4	100	0
Resorcinol	98.3	1.7	100	0
Anisole plus phenol (1: 1)	97.2	2.8	100	0
Thioanisole	100.0	0	100	0
Anisole–2% EDT	97.2	2.8	100	0
Anisole–DTT	97.6	2.4	100	0

[a] EDT, Ethanedithiol; DTT, Dithiothreitol.

and found a somewhat low recovery of lysine in its acid hydrolysate. Formation of N^{ε}-benzyllysine (~3%) during the TFMSA–TFA (1:3) treatment of N^{ε}-benzyloxycarbonyllysine had been reported by Mitchell and Merrifield (1976). This alkylation seems to be an intramolecular reaction, similar to the formation of 3-benzyltyrosine from *O*-benzyltyrosine. After surveying various scavengers (Table III), we found that this side reaction of the TFMSA system could be completely suppressed when anisole was replaced by thioanisole (Fujii *et al.*, 1977). Such an effective role of thioanisole as a cation scavenger will be discussed in Section IV,B,2. We confirmed that a weaker acid, MSA, as well as HF, did not give such an alkylation reaction, even in the presence of anisole. At this stage, the conclusion was reached that TFMSA in TFA (1:3) in the presence of thioanisole or MSA–anisole (or MSA-thioanisole) can be used for the synthesis of lysine-containing peptides without danger of N^{ε}-alkylation.

B. Synthesis of Methionine-Containing Peptides

As seen in Table II, a low recovery of methionine was noted when Z-Met-OH was treated with TFMSA in TFA (1:3) or MSA in the presence of anisole, because of the formation of a by-product, presumably the same compound detectable on the short column of an amino acid analyzer with an identical retention time for histidine and ammonia. The recovery of methionine was improved to a certain degree by the addition of sulfur compounds but still was not satisfactory.

The by-product was isolated and identified as the *S*-methylmethionine sulfonium derivative based on spectral data (Irie *et al.*, 1976, 1977). The sulfur atom of methionine trapped the methyl group of anisole. In the absence of anisole, methionine remains unchanged during treatment with TFMSA or MSA. Likewise, anisole is stable in TFMSA or MSA if methionine is absent. Cleavage of the methyl ether linkage of anisole is not due to simple acidolytic cleavage by a strong acid, such as TFMSA or MSA. This reaction seems to proceed by a sort of S_N2-type substitution reaction explainable by the "hard–soft concept" (Pearson, 1966; Pearson and Sogstad, 1967) that is, an interaction between H^+ (a hard acid)—OCH_3 (a hard base) and S (a soft base)—CH_3 (a soft acid) as shown in Eq. (2).

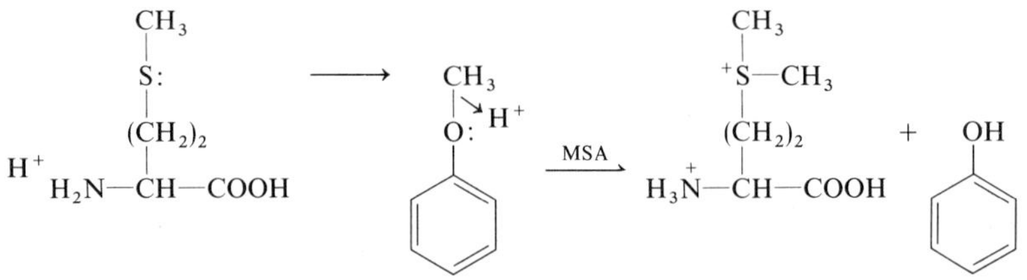

(2)

The above observation resulted in a new approach to the acidolytic deprotecting procedure and offered several ideas for the synthesis of methionine-containing peptides, as described below.

1. *Cleavage of Ether Based on the "Hard–Soft" Concept*

The facilitated cleavage of aromatic ethers can be achieved by MSA and TFMSA in the presence of a sulfur compound, such as methionine or possibly thioanisole. This idea was soon applied in the synthesis of isoquinoline alkaloids such as corypalline, thalifoline, and cherylline on the one hand (Irie *et al.*, 1980b) and the synthesis of *N*-methylenkephalinol on the other

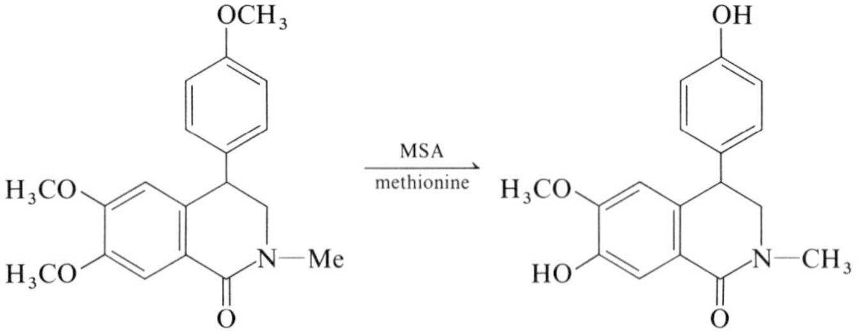

(3)

cherylline lactam

(Kiso *et al.*, 1979). In the former synthesis, methionine was used as a sulfur source (nucleophile) for the regioselective cleavage of aromatic ethers by MSA [Eq. (3)]. The oxygen atom of methyl ether located at the para position of the carbonyl moiety failed to play a role as a hard base. In the latter instance, *O*-methyltyrosine was employed, and this methyl group was removed from Boc-MeTyr(Me)-Gly-Gly-Phe-Met-OH by TFMSA in the presence of thioanisole as a sulfur source without forming the 3-alkyltyrosine derivative [Eq. (4)].

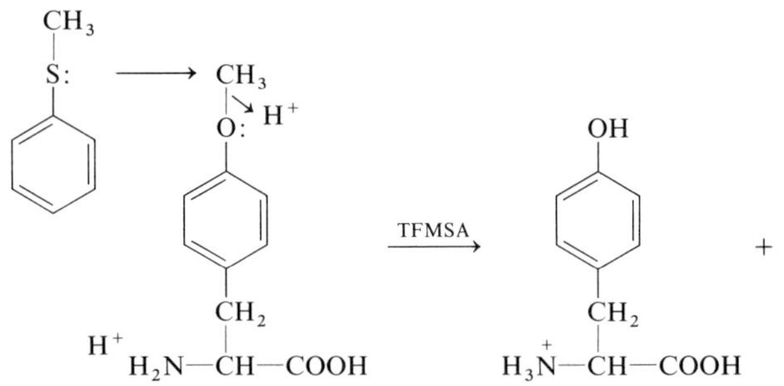

(4)

Independently, Node *et al.* (1976) and Fuji *et al.* (1980) in the same laboratory reported the easy cleavage of various ethers, as well as benzyl protecting groups, by aluminum halides or BF_3–etherate in the presence of sulfur compounds such as dimethyl sulfide, according to the hard–soft concept.

2. *Cleavage of the Benzyloxycarbonyl Group Based on the "Push–Pull" Mechanism*

Enhancement of the rate of TFA cleavage of the benzyloxycarbonyl group by dimethyl sulfide was previously observed by Brady *et al.* (1977), but quantitative data were not obtained. Kiso *et al.* (1980a) found that thioanisole was a more effective accelerator than dimethyl sulfide in TFA cleavage of the benzyloxycarbonyl group and proposed the push–pull mechanism, based on the hard–soft concept, to explain these phenomena [Eq. (5)]. The promoting effect on this cleavage reaction of the nucleophile

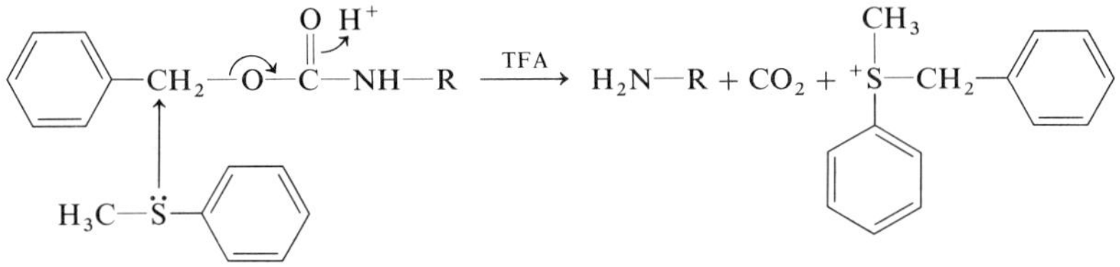

(5)

(sulfur source) followed the order: thioanisole > dimethyl sulfide > ethanedithiol (EDT). No such effects were found with phenol or anisole.

Complete cleavage of the benzyloxycarbonyl group from N^{ε}-benzyloxycarbonyllysine (0.1 mmol) was achieved by TFA (27 mmol) in the presence of thioanisole (5 mmol) at 25°C for 3 hr, whereas TFA–anisole cleavage of the benzyloxycarbonyl group was incomplete even after 27 hr at 25°C.

In the thioanisole-mediated deprotection, it was decided to use *m*-cresol as an additional scavenger to counteract the possible alkylating property of *S*-alkylthioanisole sulfonium compounds such as the *S*-benzylthioanisole sulfonium compound (Lundt *et al.*, 1978). Application of this new deprotecting procedure in practical peptide synthesis will be described in Section IV,G.

3. *Cleavage of the Methyloxycarbonyl Group*

Based on the hard–soft concept, the methyloxycarbonyl (Moc) group could be cleaved by MSA with the aid of a sulfur compound within 5 hr at 5°C [Eq. (6)]. In this instance, dimethyl sulfide was more effective than

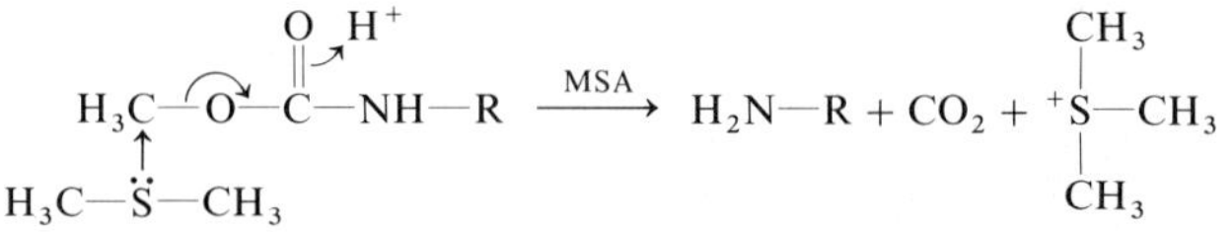

(6)

thioanisole (Irie *et al.*, 1980a). Unlike the benzyloxycarbonyl group, methyloxycarbonyl amino acids could be converted to corresponding acid chlorides and thus, using this protecting group, amide bond formation by the acid chloride method was possible as demonstrated in the synthesis of melanotropinrelease-inhibiting factor (MIF), a hypothalamic principle (Nair *et al.*, 1971; Celis *et al.*, 1971).

Despite this finding, attempts to cleave the ethyloxycarbonyl group based on the same hard–soft principle have been unsuccessful, presumably because of the subtle steric effects of an additional methyl group on the methylene carbon atom in the S_N2-type reaction (McMurry, 1976). The degree of cleavage of ethyloxycarbonylglycine by MSA–dimethyl sulfide was 12% after 6 hr at 20°C. Thus, the problem pending since Emil Fischer's work still remains to be solved.

N^{α}-*tert*-Butyloxycarbonyl-N^{ε}-methyloxycarbonyl-L-lysine was prepared. Similar to N^{ε}-formyllysine, this compound will be useful in the synthesis of relatively small peptides.

4. *Synthesis of Methionine-Containing Peptides without S-Protection*

Methionine-containing peptides can be synthesized without protection of the sulfur atom by the MSA or TFMSA procedure if anisole is replaced by *m*-cresol, thioanisole, or another scavenger devoid of alkyl donor properties, as predicted from the above reaction mechanism [Eq. (2)]. When the sulfur atom is unprotected, it follows from the above discussion that in peptides it plays a role as a promoter of acid deprotection, both in the N^{α}-deprotection step and in the final deprotection step as well. It is true that the methionine residue in peptides has a great tendency to trap alkyl cations derived from protecting groups by acid treatment. When the benzyloxycarbonyl group was removed by HBr–TFA, the formation of *S*-benzylsulfonium salt was observed (Guttmann and Boissonnas, 1959). Formation of the *S-tert*-butylsulfonium derivative during HF–anisole treatment of N^{α}-*tert*-butyloxycarbonyl-protected peptides on a polymer support was also reported (Noble *et al.*, 1976). Unlike the *S*-methyl moiety, the *S*-benzyl and the *S-tert*-butyl moieties of methionine sulfonium salts have a tendency to alkylate other functional groups such as the N^{α}-amino group. However, in most instances these substituents can be removed easily during manipulation with an organic solvent such as methanol, or by incubation with other thiols (Rothgeb *et al.*, 1977).

5. *Synthesis of Methionine-Containing Peptides with S-Protection*

Methionine sulfoxide (Iselin, 1961) is stable toward MSA and TFMSA in TFA (1:3). Thus, methionine-containing peptides can be synthesized by a combination of Met(O) and MSA or TFMSA deprotection followed by reduction of the sulfoxide with thiols. In the deprotecting step, anisole can be applied without worrying about *S*-sulfonium formation. A convenient procedure for the preparation of Met(O) derivatives was developed in our laboratory. Oxidation of benzyloxycarbonylmethionine with hydrogen peroxide (Iselin, 1961) produced its (*R*,*S*)-sulfoxide and, in most cases, the corresponding sulfone also. Among various oxidants so far examined, sodium perborate and sodium metaperiodate have been judged to be better oxidants than hydrogen peroxide, because the formation of sulfone is nearly negligible in both cases. Any sulfoxide obtained by such a method is a mixture of diastereoisomers. For confirmation, 4-methyloxybenzyloxycarbonyl-L-methionine sulfoxide prepared by sodium perborate oxidation was deprotected by TFA–anisole, and the resulting sulfoxide was submitted to an amino acid analyzer. On a long column, nearly equal amounts of the (*S*,*S*) and (*S*,*R*) diastereoisomers were detected (Fujii *et al.*, 1978).

As an example of peptide synthesis performed by a combination of methionine sulfoxide and MSA deprotection, kassinin, a frog skin peptide isolated by Anastasi *et al.* (1977), was synthesized. Construction of the entire amino acid sequence of kassinin was carried out according to the scheme in Fig. 4 (Yajima *et al.*, 1978a). In the final step, all the protecting groups, benzyloxycarbonyl, benzyl, and methyloxybenzyloxycarbonyl (Moz)

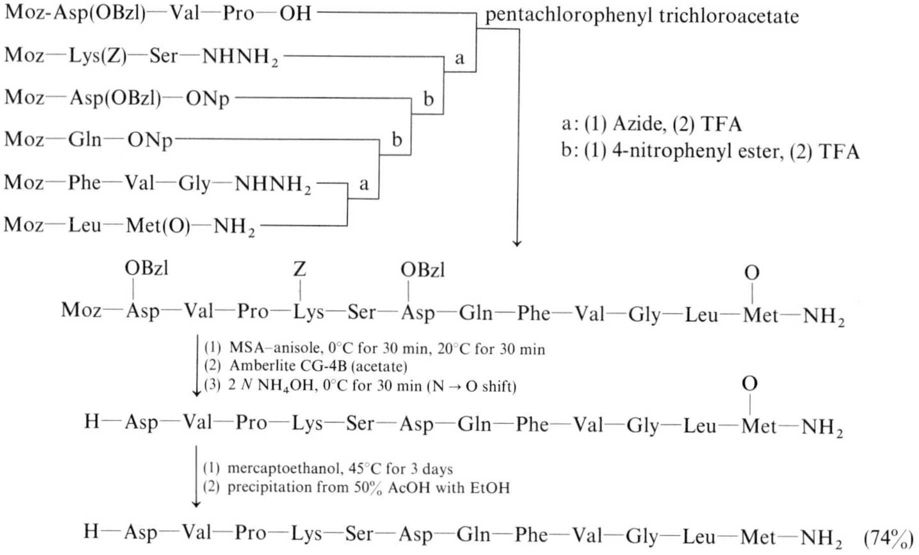

Figure 4. Scheme for the synthesis of kassinin (from *Kassina senegalensis*) as an example of the synthesis of a methionine-containing peptide by the methanesulfonic acid (MSA) procedure.

were removed by MSA–anisole (in an ice bath for 30 min and at room temperature for 30 min), and the methionine sulfoxide residue was reduced by incubation with mercaptoethanol. After purification, the desired product was obtained in 74% yield.

C. Synthesis of Arginine-Containing Peptides

The N^G-nitro group of arginine can be cleaved by HF (Sakakibara *et al.*, 1967), but not in a satisfactory manner by MSA or even TFMSA, as indicated in Table II. Cleavage of the N^G-tosyl group by these acids requires a somewhat elevated temperature, such as 40°C for 60–80 min, as reported. Such rather drastic conditions can be tolerated only in the synthesis of relatively small peptides. In an initial study, a small arginine-containing tetrapeptide, tuftsin (Nishioka *et al.*, 1972), was prepared in 88% yield by treatment of Z-Thr-Lys(Z)-Pro-Arg(Tos)-OH with TFMSA–anisole at 40°C for 45 min (Yajima *et al.*, 1975a). The synthesis of neurotensin (Yajima *et al.*, 1975c; Kitagawa *et al.*, 1976), mentioned in Section IV,A, was the second example combining N^G-tosylarginine and TFMSA deprotection. In the latter synthesis a side reaction at the lysine residue (namely, N^ε-benzyllysine formation) was noted. Thus more highly labile protecting groups for arginine were desirable. For this purpose, the 4-methyloxybenzenesulfonyl (Mbs) group

Table IV. Removal of the Mesitylene-2-sulfonyl (Mts) and 4-Methyloxybenzenesulfonyl (Mbs) Groups by Methanesulfonic Acid (MSA) or Trifluoromethanesulfonic Acid (TFMSA).

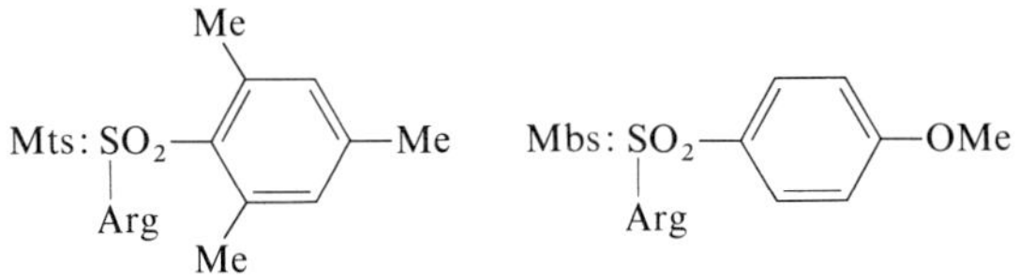

Arginine derivative	Reagent	30 min	60 min
H-Arg(Mts)-OH	MSA	93.4	98.2
	MSA–TFA (9:1)	92.6	93.7
	TFMSA–TFA (1:1)	100.0	100.0
$H\text{-}Arg(NO_2)\text{-}OH$	MSA	19.3	25.3
H-Arg(Tos)-OH	MSA	40.7	43.1
H-Arg(Mbs)-OH	MSA	71.4	88.3[a]
	MSA–TFA (9:1)	60.1	84.7
	TFMSA–TFA (1:1)	100.0	100.0
H-Arg(Mts)-OH	25% HBr–AcOH		71.5
H-Arg(Mbs)-OH	25% HBr–AcOH		0

[a] 99.1% (Nishimura and Fujino, 1976).

was used by Nishimura and Fujino (1976) and the mesitylene-2-sulfonyl (Mts) group by Yajima *et al.* (1978b,c). These two derivatives can be prepared as easily as N^G-tosylarginine by reaction of the corresponding sulfonyl chlorides with arginine. As shown in Table IV, these two groups can be cleaved smoothly by MSA, as well as by TFMSA. The N^G-mesitylene-2-sulfonyl group was judged to be more labile than the N^G-4-methyloxybenzenesulfonyl group, because the former was partially cleaved by 25% HBr in glacial AcOH but not the latter. It is interesting to note that the acid-labile N^G-mesitylene-2-sulfonyl group was found to be resistant to the action of sodium in liquid ammonia, whereas the N^G-4-methyloxybenzenesulfonyl group was not.

In our laboratory, the N^G-4-methyloxybenzenesulfonyl group was first used in the synthesis of granuliberin R, a frog skin peptide (Nakajima and Yasuhara, 1977; Nakajima *et al.*, 1978), in combination with MSA–anisole deprotection. Thus, we could perform this deprotection at room temperature within 60 min. The product was obtained in 54% yield, and we found an unexpected side reaction due to this new arginine-protecting group.

Protected granuliberin R, Moz-Phe-Gly-Phe-Leu-Pro-Ile-Tyr-Arg(Mbs)-Arg(Mbs)-Pro-Ala-Ser(Bzl)-NH_2, was treated with MSA–anisole under the conditions described above, and when the deprotected peptide was purified by column chromatography on CM-cellulose, a single peak with a small shoulder was observed. This shoulder was investigated enzymatically (Fig. 5). An aminopeptidase (AP-M) digest (this AP-M preparation digested the proline bond) contained all the amino acids in the ratios predicted by theory, except for tyrosine. Tyrosine was completely missing in the AP-M

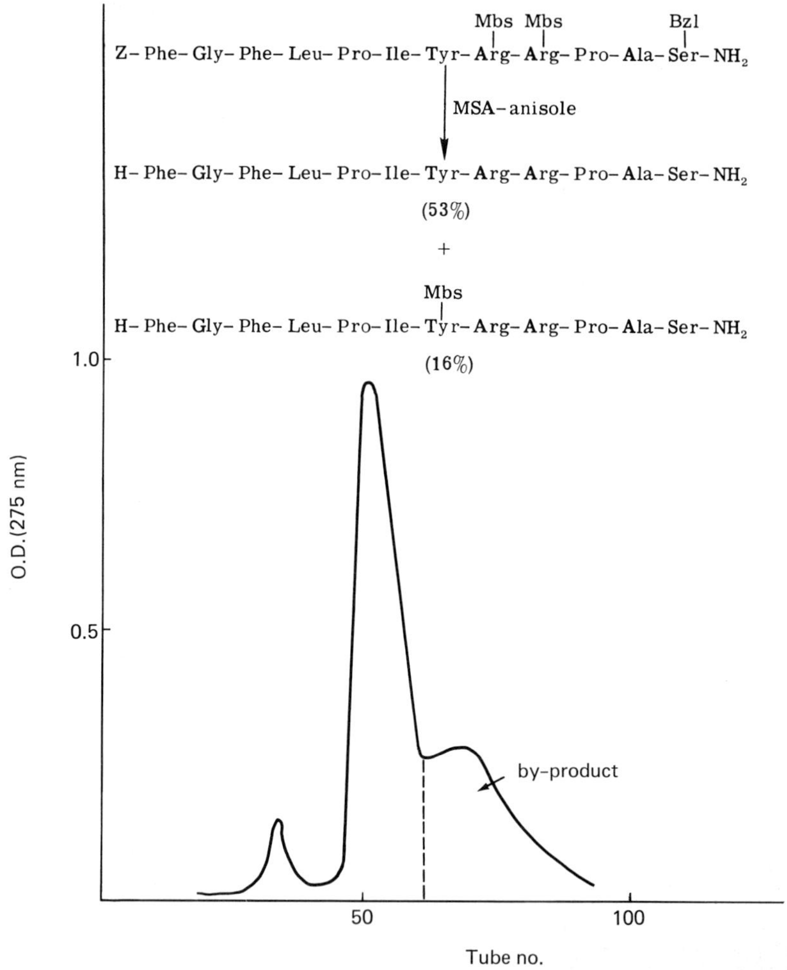

Figure 5. Isolation of a by-product derived from Arg(Mbs) during the purification of synthetic granuliberin R on CM-cellulose. Gradient: 0.2 *M* NH_4OAc, pH 6.9. The mixing flask contained 500 ml 0.01 *M* NH_4OAc.

digest, but it was fully recovered in a 6 N HCl hydrolysate. Its elemental analysis revealed the presence of atomic sulfur in 1.7%. MSA itself has no ability to sulfonate tyrosine. Then we examined this observation using two model compounds: Moz-Ile-Tyr-Arg(Mbs)-OH and Moz-Ile-Tyr-Arg(Mts)-OH. Exposure of the former peptide to MSA–anisole produced two products, one main product and a side product (ca. 30%) detectable on thin-layer chromatography (tlc). Partition chromatography on Sephadex G-25 separated the above mixture into three components. In addition to a major product, H-Ile-Tyr-Arg-OH, two side products were characterized as H-Ile-Tyr(3-*p*-methoxybenzyl)-Arg-OH (a minor component, 3%) and H-Ile-Tyr(*O*-4-methoxybenzenesulfonyl)-Arg-OH (a major by-product, 27%). The former was a predictable compound because of the intermolecular alkylation, but the latter was an unexpected compound. Treatment of the mesitylene-2-sulfonyl derivative gave nearly the same amount of the corresponding by-products. We found that HF deprotection of the 4-methyloxybenzenesulfonyl and the mesitylene-2-sulfonyl groups and, to a lesser extent, even the 4-toluenesulfonyl group produced the same type of side reaction. Later it was found that the hydroxyl groups of serine and threonine also suffered this type of O-sulfonylation, but to a lesser degree than tyrosine.

It appears that acid-labile protecting groups are apt to produce stable cations capable of attacking other functional groups. In this instance, a stable sulfonyl cation attacked the phenolic function of tyrosine as well as the hydroxyl groups of serine and threonine. Scavengers more effective than anisole were next examined. In view of the nature of this side reaction, it occurred to us that phenolic compounds, such as cresol (*o* or *m*), rather than thiol compounds should be effective in suppressing this side reaction. In the model peptides mentioned above, we could, indeed, suppress the *O*-sulfonylation to a level of less than 4% by using a mixture of scavengers, anisole–thioanisole–*m*-cresol (Table V). *m*-Cresol alone suppressed the side reaction at serine and threonine to a negligible extent during the MSA treatment. On the basis of this information, improved syntheses of substance P (yield 74%) and neurotensin (Fig. 6, yield 54%) were carried out by a combination of Arg(Mts) and MSA deprotection, in which the above scavenger system was employed (Yajima *et al.*, 1979c).

Thioanisole was not a good scavenger in the suppression of O-sulfonylation, but it did accelerate cleavage of the N^G-4-toluenesulfonyl group as well as the N^G-mesitylene-2-sulfonyl group. Kiso *et al.* (1980b) reported that the N^G-4-toluenesulfonyl group could be cleaved by TFMSA–TFA (1:4) in the presence of thioanisole (at 0°C for 30 min and then at 25°C for 3 hr) without elevating the temperature. Complete deprotection of the N^G-mesitylene-2-sulfonyl group was achieved by TFA–thioanisole at 25°C for 72 hr.

Table V. Suppression of the *O*-4-Mesitylene-2-sulfonyltyrosine Formation by Various Scavengers[a]

Moz-Ile-Tyr-Arg(Mts)-OH ⟶ [H-Ile-Tyr-Arg-OH; [H-Ile-Tyr(Mts)-Arg-OH; H-Ile-Tyr(3-Mob)-Arg-OH]]

Scavenger	Ile-Tyr-Arg (%)	By-products (%)
Anisole	70.7	29.3
Thioanisole	73.0	27.0
Dimethyl sulfide	41.8	58.2
Phenol	75.2	24.8
o-Cresol	83.3	16.7
Anisole–thioanisole (1:1)	74.0	26.0
Anisole–phenol (1:1)	88.8	11.2
Anisole–cresol (1:1)	91.0	9.0
Thioanisole–cresol (1:1)	91.3	8.7
Anisole–thioanisole–cresol (1:1:1)	96.1	3.9

[a] Tyr(3-Mob), *O*-3-methyloxybenzyltyrosine residue.

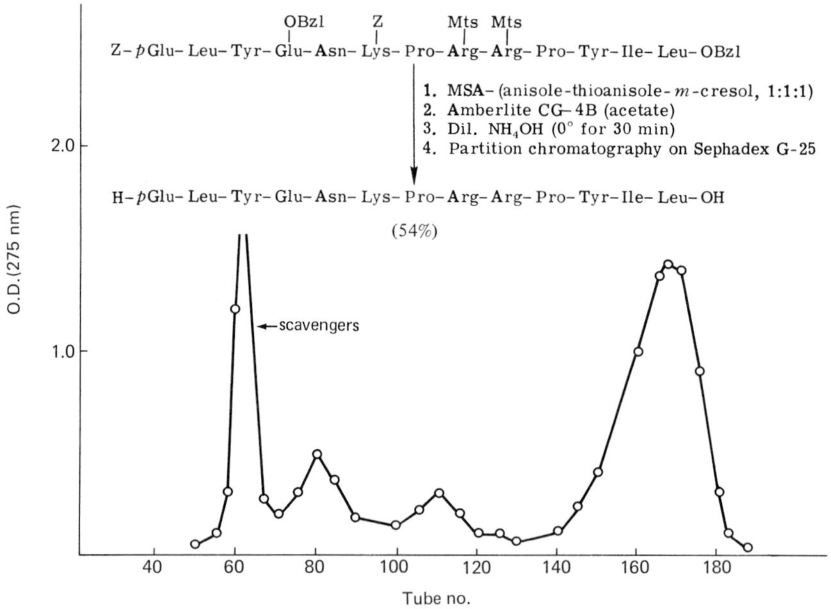

Figure 6. Application of Arg(Mts) in the synthesis of neurotensin. Partition chromatographic purification of synthetic neurotensin on Sephadex G-25.

D. Synthesis of Tyrosine-Containing Peptides

The intramolecular formation of 3-benzyltyrosine from *O*-benzyltyrosine by HF–anisole is well documented (Erickson and Merrifield, 1973; Sakakibara *et al.*, 1967). MSA and TFMSA are therefore not exceptional giving rise to this side reaction.

After surveying various tyrosine derivatives, Engelhard and Merrifield (1978) recommended the use of 2,6-dichlorobenzyltyrosine for minimization of the O–C rearrangement under HF treatment. Alternatively, Bodanszky *et al.* (1978) reported that migration of the benzyl group could be reduced by using HBr in a mixture of phenol and *p*-cresol, instead of HBr in TFA, for acidolytic deprotection. Kiso *et al.* (1980c) cleaved the *O*-benzyl group of tyrosine by TFA–thioanisole at 25°C within 3 hr and the *O*-methyl group by TFMSA–thioanisole (1979) without concomitant O–C rearrangement, based on the hard–soft concept [Eq. (7)].

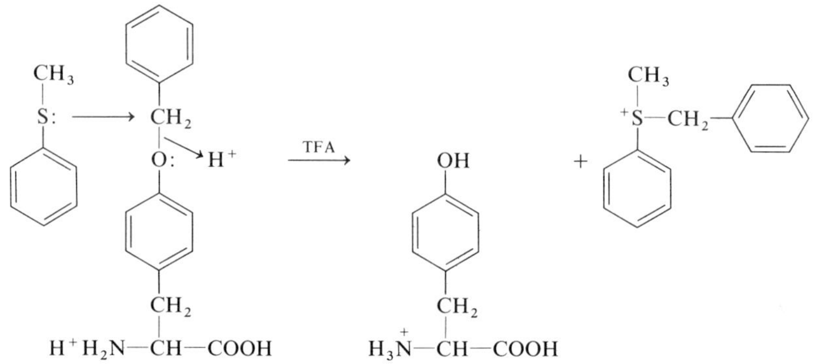

(7)

Although thioanisole again acted as an effective scavenger for alkyl cations, it was not sufficient to suppress the O-sulfonylation when N^G-mesitylene-2-sulfonyl- or 4-methyloxybenzenesulfonylarginine was present in the peptide chain as described earlier. In view of the intramolecular side reaction, the situation is the same under acidolytic conditions. Whether tyrosine-containing peptides are synthesized with or without masking the phenolic function, alkyl cations and, in addition, sulfonyl cations are capable of alkylating the 3-position and sulfonating the phenolic function, respectively. As demonstrated in the improved synthesis of neurotensin (Yajima *et al.*, 1979c), a mixed scavenger system consisting of anisole–thioanisole–*m*-cresol seems to be useful in the acidolytic deprotection of any tyrosine-containing peptide.

E. Synthesis of Serine- or Threonine-Containing Peptides

The N → O shift is the main side reaction in the HF treatment of peptides containing serine or threonine. The shift was reported to be reversed by brief treatment with dilute ammonia or urea (Sakakibara, 1971). Fujino *et al.* (1978) mentioned such a side reaction during the synthesis of mammalian glucagon, in which MSA–anisole was employed as a deprotecting reagent. They examined the possible N → O shift using a model peptide, Boc-Asn-Thr-OBzl. Treatment of this model peptide with MSA–anisole at 25°C for 60 min produced two products detectable on tlc, which upon treatment with dilute ammonium hydroxide became a single spot corresponding to an authentic sample of H-Asn-Thr-OH. We presume that the N → O shift is due to the formation of oxazoline, an intermediate in the final N → O migration, although this mechanism [Eq. (8)] has not been firmly established.

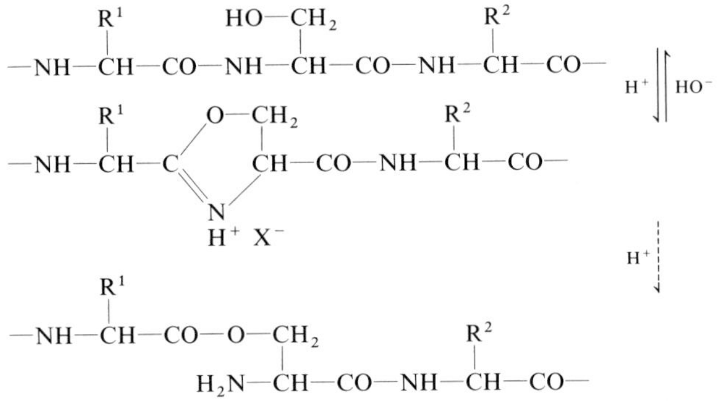

(8)

We decided to treat all peptides derived from MSA or TFMSA deprotection with dilute ammonium hydroxide for a short period (30 min at 0°C) to reverse any possible N → O shift at the serine or threonine residues, as with HF-treated peptides.

F. Synthesis of Tryptophan-Containing Peptides

Tryptophan is rather stable toward the action of MSA or TFMSA. The formation of carboline derivatives (Uphaus *et al.*, 1959) and 2-oxyindolylalanine derivatives (Theodoropoulos and Fruton, 1962) by mineral acids, and dimer formation by TFA (Omori *et al.*, 1976), have been reported. From the synthetic viewpoint, the major well-known problem with tryptophan is indole alkylation, especially during TFA cleavage of the N^{α}-*tert*-butyloxycarbonyl or 4-methyloxybenzyloxycarbonyl groups of tryptophan.

In our experience, this side reaction seems diminished when the tryptophan residue is not located at the NH_2-terminus.

Indole alkylation during TFA treatment was noted by mass spectral examination of the gastrin tetrapeptide (Alakhov *et al.*, 1970). Later Wünsch *et al.* (1977) isolated various side products formed after treatment of *tert*-butyloxycarbonyltryptophan with TFA, such as Trp(1′-*t*Bu) and Trp-(2′, 5′, 7′-tri-*t*Bu), and recommended 2-ethylindole as an effective scavenger for suppressing such side reactions. Alternatively, dimethyl sulfide was recommended by Masui *et al.* (1980) for this purpose. We also examined the side products formed from 4-methoxybenzyloxycarbonyltryptophan by TFA treatment (Ogawa *et al.*, 1978b).

In any case, complete prevention of the alkylation at tryptophan seems difficult unless a scavenger more effective than indole can be found. Cresol and thioanisole, which proved to be effective scavengers in the other cases mentioned above, were not very effective in suppressing indole alkylation (Table VI). However, considerable improvement was achieved by the use of thiol compounds such as ethanedithiol (EDT) (Sharp *et al.*, 1973). Anisole, in the presence of 2% EDT, was employed in TFA deprotection of the *tert*-butyloxycarbonyl group from intermediates in duck glucagon synthesis (Yajima *et al.*, 1977; Ogawa *et al.*, 1978a). EDT itself does not significantly accelerate cleavage of the N^{ε}-benzyloxycarbonyllysine residue present in the sequence. Alternatively, as demonstrated in the synthesis of mastoparan X, a wasp venom (Hirai *et al.*, 1979; Yajima *et al.*, 1980a), Fig. 7 represents one way of synthesizing homogeneous tryptophan-containing peptides. In this case, a COOH-terminal tryptophan peptide was selected as one of the building blocks. TFA deprotection was avoided in the synthesis of this

Table VI. Effect of Scavengers for Suppression of Indole Alkylation during Trifluoroacetic Acid Treatment.[a]

	Adduct		Boc-Trp-OH		Moz-Trp-OH		
Scavenger, 10 equiv	2% EDT	Skatole	Trp	B(1)	Trp	M(1)	M(2)
Anisole	−	−	59.4	21.9	32.5	30.0	33.8
	+	2 eq.	80.0	13.5	61.5	17.6	20.9
o-Cresol	−	−	51.2	30.7	38.8	23.5	31.7
	+	−	61.6	22.5	42.2	26.5	26.5
Thioanisole	−	−	67.6	22.5	71.0	7.0	22.0
	+	2 eq.	80.7	18.2	76.6	7.8	15.6
Dimethylsulfide	−	−	80.4	19.6	80.8	2.1	17.1
	+	2 eq.	81.7	18.3	83.0	1.5	15.5

[a] B(1),H-Trp(1′-*t*Bu)-OH. Other side products were omitted. M(1),H-Trp(1′,5′-di-Moz)-OH; M(2),H-Trp(2′-Moz)-OH.

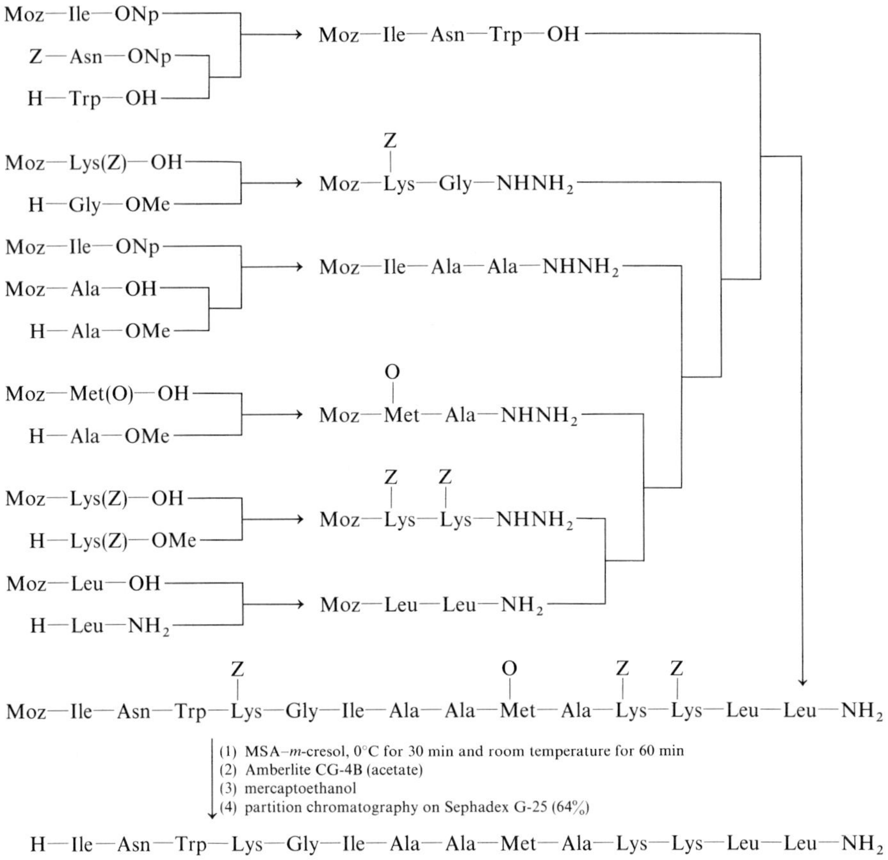

Figure 7. Scheme for the synthesis of mastoparan X.

segment, and peptide bond formation was carried out by dicyclohexylcarbodiimide–*N*-hydroxybenzotriazole (DCC–HOBt) condensation (König and Geiger, 1970). MSA in the presence of *m*-cresol was employed as a deprotecting reagent and, after partition chromatography on Sephadex G-25 (Yamashiro, 1964), the product was obtained in 64% yield.

G. Synthesis of Aspartic Acid-Containing Peptides

Formation of the γ-anisylglutamic acid derivative from γ-benzylglutamate has been noted in HF deprotection but not in MSA or TFMSA treatment. Thus, as far as the synthesis of glutamic acid-containing peptides is concerned, side reactions have not yet been observed.

However, syntheses of aspartic acid-containing peptides give rise to most disturbing problems. The β-benzyl aspartate residue in peptides has more or less of a tendency to undergo cyclization to form an aminosuccinyl derivative catalyzed by both acids and bases, as pointed out by Bodanszky and Natarajan (1975). Some additives, such as phenols, were reported to be effective in suppressing the base-catalyzed cyclization (Bodanszky *et al.*, 1978; Martinez and Bodanszky, 1978). The degree of this side reaction depends entirely on the amino acid residues (X) linked to the carboxyl site of the β-benzyl aspartate residues (Bodanszky and Kwei, 1978). This side reaction is known to be unacceptably severe when X is one of the following amino acid residues: glycine, serine, threonine, alanine, or even asparagine (Bodanszky *et al.*, 1977). If a target peptide has such a particular sequence, a homogeneous peptide can be obtained only by removing the β-benzyl group right after introduction of the β-benzyl aspartate residue into the required segment.

In the deprotecting step, acid-catalyzed cyclization of the β-benzyl aspartate residue presents an additional problem in peptide synthesis. To avoid cyclization occurring during HF deprotection, the β-phenacyl ester (Stelakatos *et al.*, 1966) was recommended (Yang and Merrifield, 1976). Alternatively the 4-nitrobenzyl group (Schwarz and Arakawa, 1959) was suggested (Suzuki and Endo, 1978). The idea was to remove this group before the HF deprotection by suitable means. However, not only is this side reaction sequence-dependent but the β-phenacyl group can also undergo base-catalyzed cyclization (Bodanszky *et al.*, 1978). Pre-removal of the β-benzyl ester group from the β-benzyl aspartate residue linked to the cyclization-prone amino acids mentioned above is again the safest way if final deprotection is to be carried out with HF, MSA, or TFMSA.

From the synthetic viewpoint, porcine (Mutt and Said, 1974) and chicken (Nilsson, 1975) vasoactive intestinal polypeptide (VIP) represent typical examples of peptides that illustrate the problem of this side reaction, since both VIP molecules possess an Asp-Ala sequence in addition to an Asp-Asn sequence. After Bodanszky's synthesis of porcine VIP (Bodanszky *et al.*, 1973b), we synthesized chicken VIP (Yajima *et al.*, 1979b, 1980c) and porcine VIP by an alternative route (Takeyama *et al.*, 1980a) (Fig. 8.).

Protected porcine VIP was obtained by coupling the fragments with unprotected aspartic acid residues, namely, Asp-Asn in segment 5 and Asp-Ala in segment 6 (Fig. 8). However, an additional problem was encountered. The aspartic acid residue with the free carboxyl group still had a tendency to undergo cyclization during the final deprotection depending on the acid employed. Before the final deprotection, two model peptides were examined corresponding to segments 6 and 5 as indicated in Tables VII and VIII. Deprotection of the fragment Moz-His-Ser(Bzl)-Asp-Ala-Val-Phe-$NHNH_2$

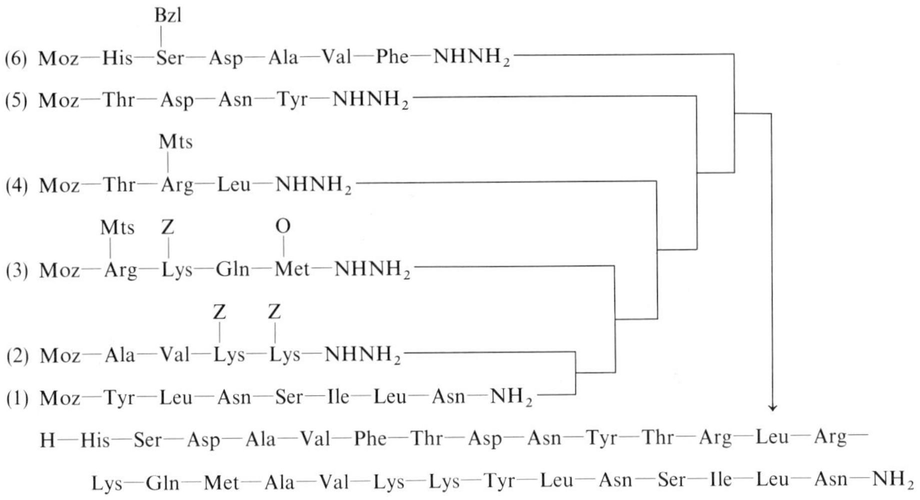

Deprotection and purification steps:
(1) Reduction of Met(O)
(2) TFA–thioanisole *m*-cresol: (1) 28°C, 10 hr; (2) 28°C, 14 hr
(3) Amberlite CG-4B (acetate)
(4) Gel filtration on Sephadex G-25
(5) CM-cellulose chromatography
(6) Isoelectrofocusing with ampholine, pH 9–11

Figure 8. Scheme for the synthesis of porcine vasoactive intestinal polypeptide (VIP).

with MSA–anisole afforded a product with low recovery of aspartic acid as determined by aminopeptidase digestion. Deprotection by HBr in glacial AcOH gave similar results, but the use of HBr in TFA improved the recovery of aspartic acid immensely. In the HF-treated sample, more than 94% of the aspartic acid was recovered after enzymatic digestion and recovery was

Table VII. Enzymatic Examination of the Products Formed by Deprotection of Moz-His-Ser(Bzl)-Asp-Ala-Val-Phe-$NHNH_2$

Reagent	R_f main, (minor)	Temp. (°C)	Scavenger	Recovery of amino acids in AP-M digest: His	Ser	Asp	Ala	Val	Phe + Ser(Bzl)
TFA	0.50	0	Anisole	1.00		0.98	1.01	0.97	2.12 (as Phe)
HBr–AcOH	0.32 (0.42)	20	Anisole	1.00	0.23	0.72	0.80	0.90	1.00 + Ser(OAc)
HBr–TFA	0.30	0	Anisole	1.00	0.97	0.95	0.97	0.93	0.96
MSA	0.30 (0.40)	20	Anisole	1.00	1.00	0.74	0.78	0.85	0.97
HF	0.30	0	Anisole	1.00	1.00	1.00	1.01	1.01	0.99
TFA (24 hr)	0.30	20	Thioanisole	1.00	0.98	0.99	0.97	0.98	1.00

Table VIII. Enzymatic Examination of the Products Formed by Deprotection of Moz-Thr-Asp-Asn-Tyr-OMe

Reagent	R_f[a]	Temp (°C)	Scavenger	Recovery of amino acids			
				Thr	Asp	Asn	Tyr
TFA	0.37	0	Anisole	1.00	0.97	0.90	0.97
HBr–AcOH	(0.37) 0.50	20	Anisole	0.78	0.30	0.37	1.00
HBr–TFA	0.37 (0.50)	0	Anisole	1.00	0.96	0.94	0.99
MSA	(0.37) 0.50	20	Anisole	1.00	0.25	0.26	0.95
HF	0.37 (0.50)	0	Anisole	1.00	0.94	0.93	1.91
TFA (24 hr)	0.37 (0.50)	20	Thioanisole	1.00	0.95	0.97	0.98

[a] Minor value is shown in parentheses.

nearly quantitative in the sample deprotected by TFA. A slight decline in the recovery was noted after prolonged treatment of the sample with TFA for 24 hr. A similar tendency was observed in the segment Moz-Thr-Asp-Asn-Tyr-OMe. The possibility of cyclization of aspartic acid residues with a free carboxyl group by acids was previously mentioned by Bodanszky *et al.* (1973a). Schön and Kisfaludy (1979) confirmed that such a reaction did indeed occur during treatment of the gastrin tetrapeptide with 4 *N* HCl.

Considering these circumstances, we employed HF deprotection in the synthesis of chicken VIP and thioanisole-mediated TFA deprotection in the alternative synthesis of porcine VIP. For the latter synthesis, Bodanszky *et al.* (1973b) used TFA deprotection of the benzyloxycarbonyl group (2.5 days at room temperature), whereas we removed the benzyloxycarbonyl group, together with the mesitylene-2-sulfonyl group from the arginine residue by repeated treatment with TFA–thioanisole (i.e., precipitation after 10 hr and treatment with fresh acid for an additional 14 hr at room temperature). Subsequently, preparative isoelectric focusing (Finlayson and Chrambach, 1971) was employed to remove a small amount of aspartimide-containing side product in both cases. The superior property of TFA as a deprotecting reagent is apparent with respect to producing fewer side reactions, but the time required for removal of the benzyloxycarbonyl group by this acid is still long, even when the cleavage is mediated by thioanisole.

Thus, it was of interest to explore the conditions of MSA and TFMSA deprotection for satisfactory removal of the aspartic acid β-benzyl ester group and minimal subsequent cyclization of the free carboxyl groups. Moz-Asp(OBzl)-Ala-OBzl and H-Asp-Ser-OH were used as model peptides. We found that 1 *M* TFMSA–thioanisole (1:1) in TFA in the presence of *m*-cresol had enough acidity to cleave various protecting groups such as benzyloxycarbonyl and its 4-methyloxy derivative, benzyl, mesitylene-2-sulfonyl, 4-methyloxybenzenesulfonyl, and *S*-methyloxybenzyl within 60 min

Table IX. Formation of Aminosuccinimide (Aspartimide) Derivatives from Two Aspartic Acid-Containing Peptides[a]

	Reagent			
Sample	MSA[b]	MSA–thioanisole, 60 equiv[b]	1 *M* TFMSA–thioanisole in TFA[c]	2 *M* TFMSA–thioanisole in TFA[c]
Moz-Asp(OBzl)-Ala-OBzl	14.6	14.2	0	6.8
H-Asp-Ser-OH	20.2	21.6	0	11.5

[a] Each reaction was performed in the presence of *m*-cresol (30 equiv). Values shown are percentages.
[b] 24°C for 60 min.
[c] 0°C for 60 min.

at 0°C. Importantly, the most satisfactory results, namely, zero aspartimide formation, were observed with the above two peptides as shown in Table IX. Increasing the concentration of TFMSA in TFA to the 2 *M* level led to the formation of increased amounts of side products. Cyclization of the free carboxyl groups seems to proceed by further protonation of the carbonyl oxygen proton if the acid employed as deprotecting agent has enough acidity. This suggests that this side reaction cannot be suppressed by a scavenger. When MSA was diluted with TFA to 50%, the acidity was also diluted, and consequently removal of the benzyl, mesitylene-2-sulfonyl, and *S*-4-methyloxybenzyl groups was incomplete within 60 min even in the presence of thioanisole.

The usefulness of 1 *M* TFMSA–thioanisole in TFA was demonstrated by the synthesis of [Glu^{8}]-porcine VIP (Takeyama *et al.*, 1980b), in which *m*-cresol was used as an additional scavenger during deprotection. We also employed these conditions in the synthesis of bovine ribonuclease A (RNase A), as described in Section V,C.

H. Synthesis of Cysteine-Containing Peptides

S-Benzylcysteine cannot be cleaved completely by HF and even by MSA within 60 min at 20°C, whereas *S*-4-methyloxybenzylcysteine is cleaved by both MSA and HF. Some decomposition of *S*-4-methyloxybenzylcysteine was noted during treatment with TFMSA-TFA (1:3) at room temperature, but 1 *M* TFMSA–thioanisole in TFA, a rather dilute reagent, afforded cysteine quantitatively at 0°C within 60 min. Synthesis of urotensin II, a

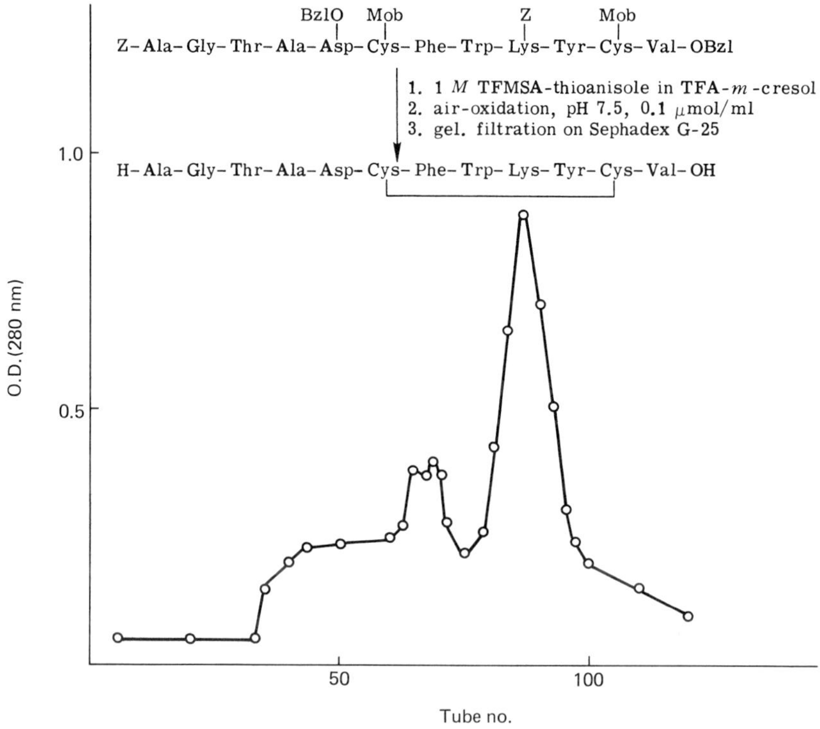

Figure 9. Scheme for the synthesis and purification of urotensin II by gel filtration on Sephadex G-25.

somatostatin-like peptide present in the caudal neurosecretory system of certain fish (Pearson *et al.*, 1980), was successfully synthesized using the latter deprotecting reagent (Akaji *et al.*, 1982) (Fig. 9).

We now describe the sulfoxide of *S*-4-methyloxybenzylcysteine, which has not as yet been reported in the literature. The problem of its formation is not serious in the synthesis of small cysteine-containing peptides but must be taken into consideration in the synthesis of relatively large peptides.

During the course of the synthesis of RNase A (Yajima and Fujii, 1980), we hydrolyzed protected intermediates containing *S*-4-methyloxybenzylcysteine and tyrosine residues with 6 *N* HCl in the presence of phenol, expecting a better recovery of tyrosine (Iselin, 1962). An unidentified peak was observed on the short column of an amino acid analyzer with a retention time of 26 min. Its appearance was accompanied by a corresponding decrease in the recovery of cysteine. This compound, *S*-4-hydroxyphenylcysteine, was derived from the sulfoxide of the *S*-4-methyloxybenzylcysteine

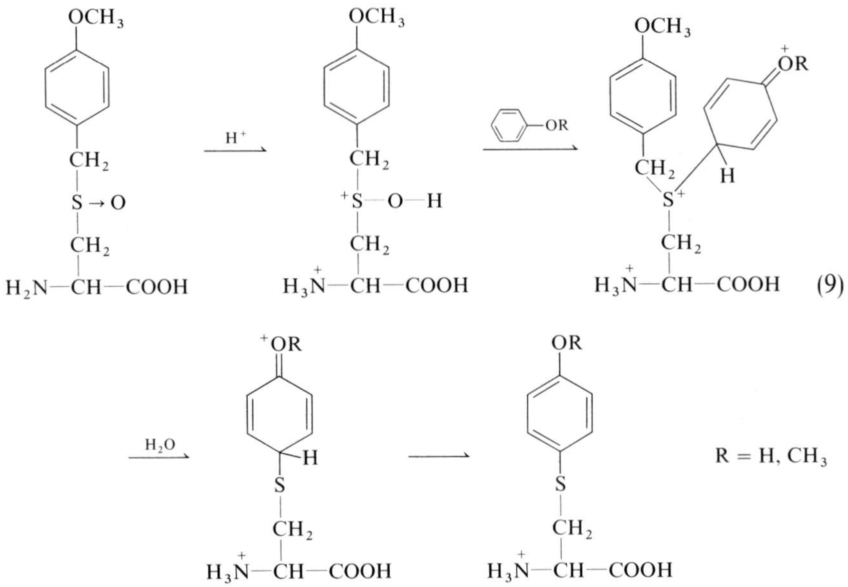

residue, which had been formed partially during the synthesis [Eq. (9)]. Whereas, *S*-benzylcysteine sulfoxide was stable toward HF and MSA, the sulfoxide of 4-methyloxybenzylcysteine was converted quantitatively to *S*-4-methyloxyphenylcysteine by MSA–anisole or by HF–anisole. Acetamidomethylcysteine sulfoxide gave an identical product, but not quantitatively, when treated with MSA or HF in the presence of anisole (Yajima *et al.*, 1979a, 1980b; Funakoshi *et al.*, 1979).

These results indicated that the sulfoxide, once formed, must be reduced before deprotection, otherwise satisfactory recovery of cysteine from *S*-4-methyloxybenzylcysteine cannot be expected. Thiophenol in organic solvents was found to be effective in reducing sulfoxides of protected peptides, except for the sulfoxide of acetamidomethylcysteine. The sulfoxide of *tert*-butyloxycarbonyl-S-acetamidomethylcysteine was converted by thiophenol to *S*-acetamidomethylphenyl sulfide and N^{α}-*tert*-butyloxycarbonyl-*S*-phenylthiocysteine [Eq. (10)]. At present, there is no suitable procedure available for reducing the sulfoxide of acetamidomethylcysteine residues if they are formed during the synthesis. *S*-Tritylcysteine (Cys(Trt)] resists oxidation by hydrogen peroxide or sodium metaperiodate, presumably because of steric hindrance created by the three phenyl residues. The occurrence of sulfoxide in synthetic peptides can be estimated by hydrolysis with 6 *N* HCl in the presence of phenol followed by identification of *S*-4-hydroxyphenylcysteine with an amino acid analyzer.

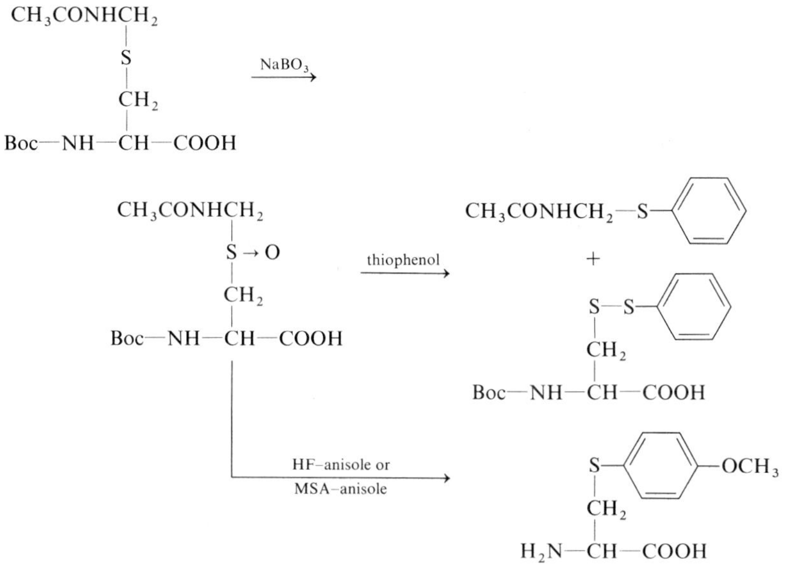

(10)

(Chemical behavior of Boc—Cys(Acm)(O)—OH)

Some uncertainty remained with respect to the stability of protected peptides under the required reducing conditions (85°C for 6 hr). However, these conditions were successfully used in the reduction of contaminating oxidized material in protected synthetic RNase before its final deprotection with MSA–*m*-cresol or with 1 *M* TFMSA–thioanisole in TFA in the presence of *m*-cresol. These experiments are described in detail in Section V.

V. DEPROTECTION OF SYNTHETIC BOVINE RIBONUCLEASE A

In this section the results of the deprotection performed in the final step of the synthesis of RNase A (Yajima and Fujii, 1980; Fujii and Yajima, 1981a–f) are summarized. At the present time, this seems to be the only example of a chemically and biologically fully characterized peptide composed of over 100 amino acids that has been synthesized in a conventional manner. Deprotection was performed not only with MSA or TFMSA but also with liquid HF. The results may offer useful information about the present status of acidolytic deprotection in the synthesis of complex disulfide-containing peptides. The target enzyme, bovine pancreatic RNase A, is the first enzyme for which the entire structure consisting of 124 amino acids was reported in the literature (Smyth *et al.*, 1963).

Previously, two groups of investigators had reported the synthesis of material with partial RNase A enzymatic activity. Gutte and Merrifield (1969, 1971) performed an automated solid-phase synthesis of RNase A and reported that they obtained a supernatant solution with a specific activity of 78% after a final ammonium sulfate fractionation of trypsin-resistant material. It was not possible to purify this product any further. The Merck group (Denkewalter *et al.*, 1969) undertook the synthesis of S-protein (21–124) in a conventional manner and obtained a solution containing 2μg of RNase S′ activity upon combination with the S-peptide(1–20) (Richards, 1958) derived from the natural source. However, the amount of material obtained was too small for chemical characterization. In both syntheses, the liquid HF deprotection procedure was used in combination with N^{ε}-benzyloxycarbonyllysine.

Our synthesis of RNase A was initially based on the strategy of using MSA as a deprotecting reagent in the final step. Thus, amino acid derivatives bearing protecting groups removable by MSA were employed, as indicated by the partial shading in Fig. 10, namely, γ-benzylglutamic acid, β-benzylaspartic acid, *S*-4-methyloxybenzylcysteine, N^{ε}-benzyloxycarbonyllysine, and N^{G}-4-methyloxybenzenesulfonylarginine. Especially, the 4-methyloxybenzenesulfonyl protecting group of arginine is cleaved more easily by MSA than by liquid HF, as described in Section IV,C. In addition, careful consideration was given to the side-chain protection of glutamic acid in position 2 and aspartic acid in position 14. *tert*-Butyl ester was employed for the former, because the use of this ester made it easier to prepare the necessary NH_2-terminal fragment than the use of the benzyl ester. The β-benzyl ester in the latter was removed during the synthesis in order to avoid aminosuccinimide formation. The entire peptide backbone of protected RNase A was constructed by assembling 30 relatively small peptide fragments of established purity. The Honzl–Rudinger azide procedure (1961) was adopted as the main tool for condensing these fragments in a stepwise manner from the COOH-terminal end. The positions of fragment condensation are indicated by the numerals in Fig. 10.

As described in Section IV,H, during synthesis the *S*-4-methyloxybenzylcysteine residues underwent partial air oxidation to sulfoxides. Therefore, these sulfoxides were reduced by thiophenol before deprotection. The artifactual sulfoxides of methionine residues were also reduced by the above treatment. Consideration of the various side reactions discussed in the preceding sections, especially at methionine, tyrosine, and aspartic acid

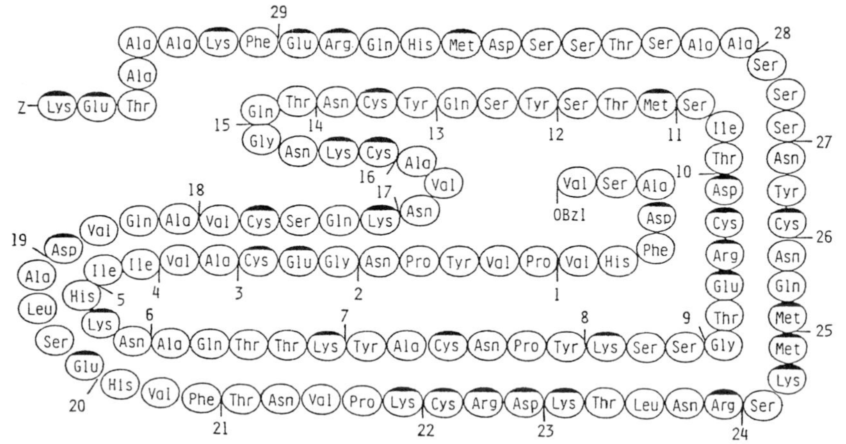

1. Reduction of Cys (Mob) (O) and Met (O) with thiophenol
2. Deprotection with MSA or HF or TFMSA-thioanisole/TFA
3. Air-oxidation
4. Sephadex G-75
5. Affinity chromatography
6. CM-cellulose chromatography

Purified RNase A.

Figure 10. Final deprotecting step in the synthesis of bovine RNase A. , Protected amino acid: Asp(OBzl), Glu(OBzl), Cys(Mob), Arg(Mts), Met(O), Glu(O*t*Bu) (position 2). The positions of fragment condensation are indicated by numerals.

residues, led to a decision to compare the effects of three different reagents in the final deprotection of protected RNase A. We first describe MSA deprotection.

A. Deprotection with Methanesulfonic Acid

Subsequent to the reductive treatment described above, the protected RNase A was exposed to MSA in the presence of *m*-cresol at 25°C for 60 min. The role of the scavenger, *m*-cresol, was discussed in Section IV,C and D, and its amount was estimated as 20 equiv per protecting group for a total of 33 protecting groups (benzyloxycarbonyl of 10 lysines and the NH_2-terminus, benzyl ester of four glutamic acids, four aspartic acids, and the COOH-terminus, *tert*-butyl ester of the glutamic acid in position 2, 4-methyloxybenzenesulfonyl of four arginines, and methyloxybenzyl of eight cysteines). Thus a total of 660 equiv of *m*-cresol were employed. In order to remove the large number of protecting groups, this treatment was repeated. We felt that drastic conditions were necessary to achieve complete removal of so many protecting groups and to avoid formation of a complicated mixture of partially deprotected peptides.

As illustrated in Fig. 10, the deprotected peptide was then reduced with 2-mercaptoethanol and dithiothreitol in 0.2 *M* Tris–HCl buffer containing 4 *M* guanidine–HCl at pH 8.6. This pH was the same as that selected by Anfinsen and Haber (1961) for reductive cleavage of the disulfides of natural RNase A. These basic conditions seemed suitable for the reversal of any possible N → O shift at the serine and threonine residues (Section IV,E). This treatment was also judged effective in the reduction of any remaining traces of methionine sulfoxide residues if present, and for removal of the S-alkyl group from the methionine residues if such products were formed during the deprotection. This treatment seemed effective also in the reduction of any aggregated disulfide complexes formed.

The reduced product was isolated as a single component by gel filtration on Sephadex G-25 with 0.1 *M* AcOH as an eluant. In order to establish the four intramolecular disulfide bridges by air oxidation, the eluants of the desired fractions were diluted in 0.05 *M* Tris–HCl buffer at pH 8.2 to a concentration of 0.02 mg/ml. The dilute solution was kept at 25°C for 2 days while the progress of the oxidation was monitored with Ellman's reagent (Ellman, 1959). The entire solution was concentrated by lyophilization, and the oxidized product was desalted by dialysis against water. Some water-insoluble material, presumably highly aggregated products or material still bearing protecting groups, was removed at this stage. The oxidized product, isolated by gel filtration on Sephadex G-75 with 0.05 *M* ammonium bicarbonate as an eluant (Fig. 11a), had 9–12% of the activity of natural RNase (Sigma) on yeast RNA (Kunitz, 1946). Starting from the protected RNase A, the yield of crude but active product was 54%.

The crude active product was next purified by affinity chromatography on Sepharose 4B–5′-(4-aminophenylphosphoryl)uridine 2′(3′)-phosphate (Wilchek and Gorecki, 1969). The material isolated from the fraction that passed through the column without retention was inactive. The product eluted with 0.2 *N* AcOH (Fig. 11b) exhibited an activity of 74–82% against yeast RNA. The yield of this purification step was 14%. Thus, in reaching this point, approximately 92% of the material was lost during conversion of the inactive protected peptide to the enzymatically active product. Various side reactions involved in the deprotection and incorrect disulfide formation might be the main reasons for the low yield. When the amino acid compositions of acid hydrolysates of active and inactive compounds were compared, no significant differences were observed, except for the number of tyrosine and cystine residues. Recoveries of these two amino acids in the active component were much closer to those for natural RNase A than those for the inactive component.

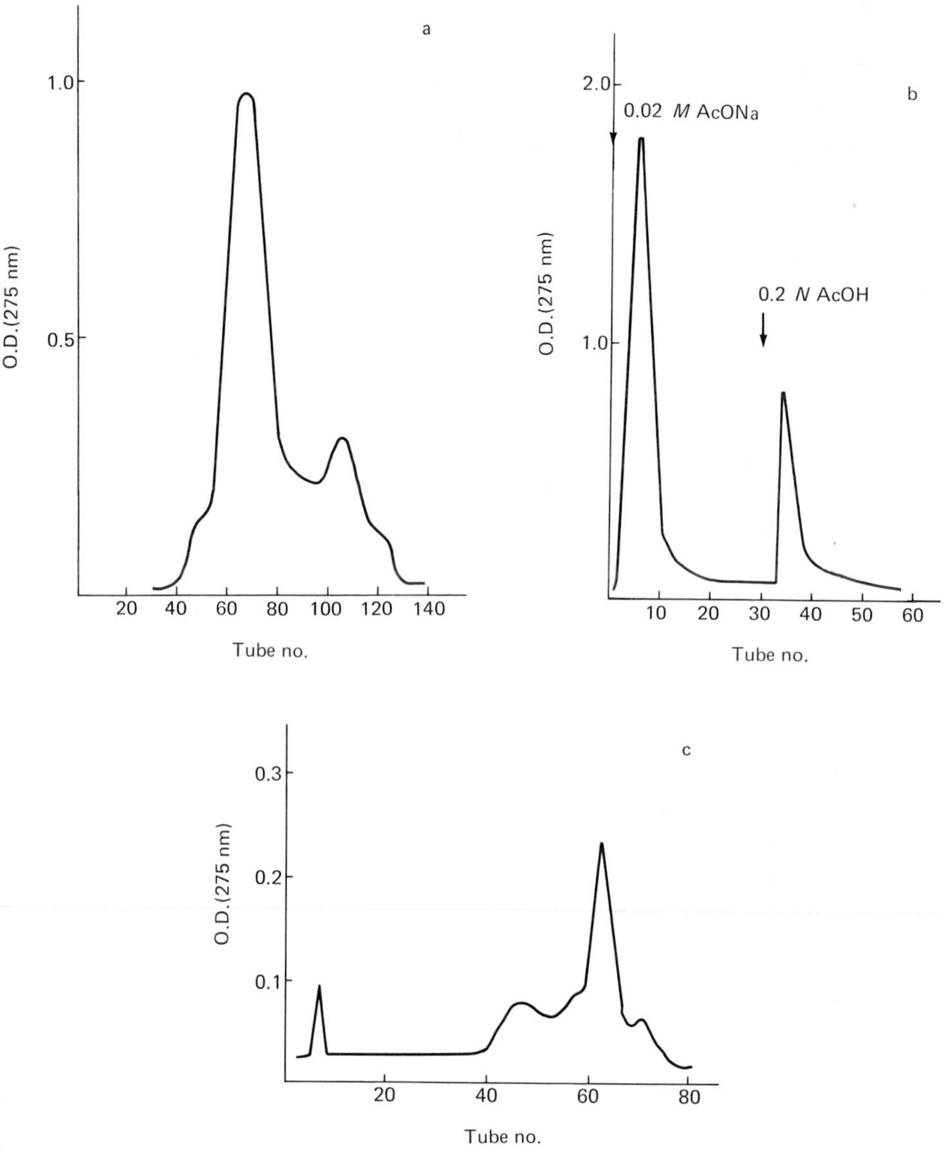

Figure 11. (a) Purification of the air-oxidized product by gel filtration on Sephadex G-75: Product eluted in tubes 57–80. (b) Purification of the Sephadex G-75-purified product by affinity chromatography: tubes 33–40. (c) Purification of the affinity-purified product by column chromatography on CM-cellulose. Gradient elution with 0.1 *M* phosphate buffer, pH 7.5: Product in tubes 59–65.

In order to remove a trace contaminant revealed by disc electrophoresis, the above product obtained from the affinity purification was next purified by ion-exchange chromatography on CM-cellulose according to the procedure of White (1961), and the main fractions were desalted by gel filtration on Sephadex G-25 (Fig. 11c). The yield of this CM-cellulose purification step was 61%, and the overall yield after deprotection followed by purification was 4.6%. The product thus purified behaved as a single component on disc electrophoresis at pH 4.3, and its mobility was identical to that of natural RNase A. The amino acid composition of the synthetic protein was in excellent agreement with that of RNase A, including the number of tyrosine and cystine residues.

The synthetic protein, with a high degree of homogeneity, exhibited essentially the same activity as natural RNase A when yeast RNA or 2′,3′-cyclic cytidine phosphate (Fruchter and Crestfield, 1965) was used as a substrate. The values obtained were in the range 104–107% in both assay systems. Examination of the physicochemical properties of the synthetic protein showed that the elution pattern of the synthetic protein after CM-cellulose chromatography was comparable to that of natural RNase A. The mobility on disc electrophoresis, specific rotation, uv absorption, and Michaelis constant (Edelhoch and Coleman, 1956) of the synthetic protein were coincident with those of natural RNase A.

From the experimental data obtained above, it can be ascertained that, with the use of the MSA deprotection procedure, the synthetic protein was obtained with a high degree of homogeneity. The target product had a series of independent physicochemical properties and specific enzymatic activity indistinguishable from those of natural RNase A.

B. Deprotection by Liquid Hydrogen Fluoride

In order to compare the results obtained from MSA deprotection, HF deprotection was performed. The protected RNase A, after reduction with thiophenol, was treated with liquid HF in the presence of *m*-cresol (660 equiv) in an ice bath for 120 min, and the product was treated in the manner mentioned above. The crude air-oxidized product isolated by gel filtration on Sephadex G-75 (yield 60%) possessed a slightly higher activity (17%) than that of the MSA-deprotected product, although the amount of water-insoluble material was somewhat greater than that in the former case. The affinity-purified product (yield 11%) was as active as that of the MSA-deprotected product (82% of natural RNase A). After purification on CM-cellulose (yield 76%), the fully active component was obtained in nearly the same yield (total yield 5.0%).

C. Deprotection with Trifluoromethanesulfonic Acid–Thioanisole in Trifluoroacetic Acid

As described in previous sections, the yield of the fully active product obtained by MSA deprotection was less than 5%. The liquid HF deprotection gave comparable results. As pointed out previously, incorrect disulfide formation and various unsuppressed side reactions during the deprotection were most likely responsible for this low yield. Among possible side reactions that may take place under acidolytic deprotecting conditions, the acid-catalyzed aminosuccinimide formation from the aspartic acid residue (Section IV,G) seems to be the major unsolved problem in the above two experiments. Thus, some improvement was obtained by using 1 *M* TFMSA–thioanisole in TFA as a deprotecting reagent in combination with a glutathione-mediated air-oxidation procedure for disulfide formation. The synthetic enzyme was finally crystallized according to Kunitz (1940).

The protected RNase A, after treatment with thiophenol, was exposed to 1 *M* TFMSA–thioanisole in TFA in an ice bath for 60 min. Again, *m*-cresol (660 equiv) was used as an additional scavenger. This treatment was repeated three times to ensure the complete removal of all protecting groups. The deprotected peptide was then incubated with mercaptoethanol and dithiothreitol at pH 8.6 as described above. After removal of the reducing agents by gel filtration on Sephadex G-25, glutathione-mediated air oxidation was performed according to Chavez and Scheraga (1980). To a dilute solution of protein (0.08 mg/ml) in 0.2 *M* Tris–HCl buffer, pH 8.0, 13.6 equiv each of reduced and oxidized glutathione were added. After adjusting the pH to 8.0, the solution was kept at 23°C for 5 days to permit disulfide bond formation. Using yeast RNA as a substrate, the solution generated RNase activity that reached a constant value of 13% after 3 days. After lyophilization and desalting by gel filtration on Sephadex G-75, the crude product with an activity of 18.9% was obtained in 65% yield. The total Kunitz units of enzyme activity obtained in this manner, 733 U, was 1.8 times higher than that obtained with the MSA procedure (389 U) and also higher than that in an experiment performed without glutathione (595 U). It can be seen that a distinct improvement has been achieved in this alternative deprotecting step and the air-oxidation step as well.

Purification procedures performed essentially as described above produced an affinity-purified product with an activity of 81% of that of natural RNase A (yield 16%). The subsequent ion-exchange chromatography on CM-cellulose provided a product that exhibited an activity of 113% of that of the natural RNase A (yield 63%).

The purity of the product thus obtained was ascertained by disc isoelectric focusing and amino acid analysis. It was also confirmed that its

Table X. Deprotection for RNase A Synthesis[a]

	Deprotection								
	MSA			HF			TFMSA–thioanisole		
Sample	Amount (mg)	Yield (%)	Activity (%)	Amount (mg)	Yield (%)	Activity (%)	Amount (mg)	Yield (%)	Activity (%)
Protected RNase	100			100			100		
G-75-purified	42.5	54	12	47.0	60	60	51.0	65	19
Affinity-purified	5.5/40.1	14	82	4.8/44.1	11	11	8.2/50.1	16	81
CMC-purified	2.8/4.6	61	105	3.0/4.0	75	106	4.6/7.4	63	113

[a] Slashes indicate purified products from starting material.

Figure 12. Crystals of synthetic RNase A.

physicochemical properties (specific rotation, extinction, uv absorption coefficient, Michaelis constant) agreed well with literature values and measured values for native RNase A. The overall yield after deprotection followed by purification was 6.6%. As summarized in Table X, a higher yield was obtained than previously by the MSA or liquid HF procedure.

Synthetic RNase A thus obtained was crystallized according to Kunitz (1940) using a salt-free procedure. A turbid solution, formed by the addition of 95% ethanol to an aqueous solution of synthetic RNase A, was kept in a refrigerator for 3 months. During this period, small crystals developed into multioriented crystals with rosette or stalagmite shapes as shown in Fig. 12 (Yajima and Fujii, 1981b).

Starting from amino acids, a protein with full RNase A activity was thus synthesized by applying the deprotecting procedures described above, and the synthetic enzyme was finally obtained in crystalline form for the first time. In view of the yield after the final deprotection followed by various purifications, it is clear that a certain amount of material was lost through formation of incorrect disulfide bonds. However, it must be realized that, if the cleavage at each protecting group were estimated to proceed at 92–93%, the final calculated yield would be no more than approximately 6%, which is equivalent to that obtained in the above experiments. These results show how difficult it is to obtain satisfactory yields in the final step of the synthesis of complex peptides.

VI. OPPORTUNITIES AND CONSTRAINTS

A. Comparitive Evaluation

Low yields are obtained in the final step of the synthesis of complex peptides clearly as a result of the difficulty of achieving complete deprotection of large numbers of protecting groups. To overcome this difficulty, synthesis of peptides with minimal protection appears to be attractive. Principally, a peptide chain can be elongated after removing the ω-carboxyl protecting groups, for example, the *tert*-butyl ester, of glutamic acid or aspartic acid residues once they are introduced into the chain. The absolutely necessary protecting groups are those for lysine and cysteine residues. However, if peptides are synthesized with such a marginal level of protection, purification of intermediates could become considerably more difficult than in the case of RNase synthesis.

In addition, the condensation of peptide segments during synthesis may have a variety of limitations that could result in less than quantitative coupling. For example, the DCC–HOBt (Geiger and Siedel, 1968) and DCC–HOSu (Wünsch and Drees, 1966) condensation procedures, useful racemization-suppressing condensation reactions, may not be applicable in certain cases. It should be borne in mind that the azide reaction, an alternative useful fragment condensation reaction (see Meienhofer, 1979) does not always proceed satisfactorily. For example, azide coupling between the NH_2-terminal portion of VIP and the amino component containing an aspartic acid residue with a free carboxyl group failed for some unknown reason (Takeyama *et al.*, 1980a).

B. Prognosis

As mentioned earlier, mild deprotecting conditions are, of course, preferable for the synthesis of biologically active peptides, but we must realize that conditions applicable in the synthesis of small peptides or used with amino acid derivatives cannot be applied directly to the synthesis of large peptides. Indeed, more rigorous conditions are needed than those employed in model experiments, otherwise unseparable mixtures of partially deprotected peptides would be produced. Thioanisole-mediated TFA deprotection, as summarized in Fig. 13, has certainly resulted in a new method of deprotection.

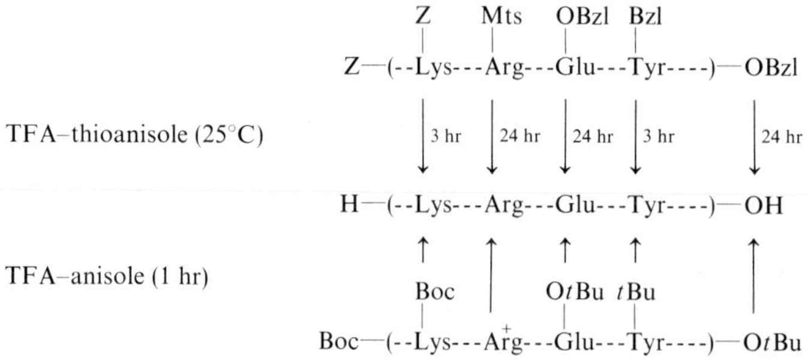

Figure 13. TFA–thioanisole deprotection.

However, even more effective procedures will be required for the synthesis of more complex peptides. The conclusion we want to draw is that there are no ideal reagents free of any side reaction available at this time. Therefore, we should not overlook the characteristic features of each reagent that are advantageous by overemphasizing small side reactions caused by these reagents.

REFERENCES

Akaji, K., Fujii, N., Yajima, H., Pearson, D. (1982). *Chem. Pharm. Bull.* **30**, 349–353.

Alakhov, Yu. B., Kiryushkin, A. A., and Lipkin, V. M. (1970). *J. Chem. Soc. Chem. Commun.* pp. 406–407.

Anastasi, A., Montecucci, P., Erspamer, V., and Visser, J. (1977). *Experientia* **33**, 857–858.

Anfinsen, C. B., and Haber, E. (1961). *J. Biol. Chem.* **236**, 1361–1363.

Ben-Ishai, D., and Berger, A. (1952). *J. Org. Chem.* **17**, 1564–1570.

Bergmann, M., and Zervas, L. (1932). *Chem. Ber.* **65**, 1192–1201.

Bodanszky, M., and Kwei, J. Z. (1978). *Int. J. Pept. Protein Res.* **12**, 69–74.

Bodanszky, M., and Natarajan, S. (1975). *J. Org. Chem.* **40**, 2495–2499.

Bodanszky, M., Sigler, G. F., and Bodanszky, A. (1973a). *J. Am. Chem. Soc.* **95**, 2352–2357.

Bodanszky, M., Klausner, Y. S., and Said, S. I. (1973b). *Proc. Natl. Acad. Sci. U.S.A.* **70**, 382–384.

Bodanszky, M., Henes, J. B., Yiotakis, A. E., and Said, S. I. (1977). *J. Med. Chem.* **20**, 1461–1464.

Bodanszky, M., Tolle, J. C., Deshmane, S. S., and Bodanszky, A. (1978). *Int. J. Pept. Protein Res.* **12**, 57–68.

Brady, S. F., Hirschmann, R., and Veber, D. F. (1977). *J. Org. Chem.* **42**, 143–146.

Carraway, R., and Leeman, S. E. (1975). *J. Biol. Chem.* **250**, 1907–1911.

Celis, M. E., Taleisnik, S., and Walter, R. (1971). *Proc. Natl. Acad. Sci. U.S.A.* **68**, 1428–1433.

Chavez, L. G., Jr., and Scheraga, H. A. (1980). *Biochemistry* **19**, 996–1004.

Denkewalter, R. F., Veber, D. F., Holly, F. W., and Hirschmann, R. (1969). *J. Am. Chem. Soc.* **91**, 502–503, and succeeding 4 papers.

du Vigneaud, V., Ressler, C., Swan, J. M., Roberts, C. W., Katsoyannis, P. G., and Gordon, S. (1953a). *J. Am. Chem. Soc.* **75**, 4879–4880.

du Vigneaud, V., Lawler, H. C., and Popenoe, E. A. (1953b). *J. Am. Chem. Soc.* **75**, 4880–4881.

Edelhoch, H., and Coleman, J. (1956). *J. Biol. Chem.* **219**, 351–363.

Ellman, G. L. (1959). *Arch. Biochem. Biophys.* **82**, 70–77.

Engelhard, M., and Merrifield, R. B. (1978). *J. Am. Chem. Soc.* **100**, 3559–3563.

Erickson, B. W., and Merrifield, R. B. (1973). *J. Am. Chem. Soc.* **95**, 3750–3756.

Feinberg, R. S., and Merrifield, R. B. (1975). *J. Am. Chem. Soc.* **97**, 3485–3496.

Felix, A. M. (1974). *J. Org. Chem.* **39**, 1427–1429.

Finlayson, G. R., and Chrambach, A. (1971). *Anal. Biochem.* **40**, 292–311.

Fischer, E. (1902). *Chem. Ber.* **35**, 1095–1106.

Fruchter, R. G., and Crestfield, A. M. (1965). *J. Biol. Chem.* **240**, 3868–3874.

Fuji, K., Kawabata, T., and Fujita, E. (1980). *Chem. Pharm. Bull.* **28**, 3662–3664.

Fujii, N., Funakoshi, S., Sasaki, T., and Yajima, H. (1977). *Chem. Pharm. Bull.* **25**, 3096–3098.

Fujii, N., and Yajima, H. (1981a). *J. Chem. Soc., Perkin Trans. I* pp. 789–796.

Fujii, N., and Yajima, H. (1981b). *J. Chem. Soc., Perkin Trans. I* pp 797–803.

Fujii, N., and Yajima, H. (1981c). *J. Chem. Soc., Perkin Trans. I* pp. 804–810.

Fujii, N., and Yajima, H. (1981d). *J. Chem. Soc., Perkin Trans. I* pp. 811–818.

Fujii, N., and Yajima, H. (1981e). *J. Chem. Soc., Perkin Trans. I* pp. 819–830.

Fujii, N., and Yajima, H. (1981f). *J. Chem. Soc., Perkin Trans. I* pp. 831–841.

Fujii, N., Sasaki, T., Funakoshi, S., Irie, H., and Yajima, H. (1978). *Chem. Pharm. Bull.* **26**, 650–653.

Fujino, M., Wakimasu, M., Shinagawa, S., Kitada, C., and Yajima, H. (1978). *Chem. Pharm. Bull.* **26**, 539–548.

Funakoshi, S., Fujii, N., Akaji, K., Irie, H., and Yajima, H. (1979). *Chem. Pharm. Bull.* **27**, 2151–2156.

Geiger, R., and Siedel, W. (1968). *Chem. Ber.* **101**, 3386–3391.

Gutte, B., and Merrifield, R. B. (1969). *J. Am. Chem. Soc.* **91**, 501–502.

Gutte, B., and Merrifield, R. B. (1971). *J. Biol. Chem.* **246**, 1922–1941.

Guttmann, S., and Boissonnas, R. A. (1959). *Helv. Chim. Acta* **42**, 1257–1264.

Hillmann-Elies, A., Gillmann, G., and Jatzkewitz, H. (1953). *Z. Naturforsch.*, **8B**, 445–446.

Hirai, Y., Kuwada, M., Yasuhara, T., Yoshida, H., and Nakajima, T. (1979). *Chem. Pharm. Bull.* **27**, 1945–1946.

Hofmann, K., and Yajima, H. (1961). *J. Am. Chem. Soc.* **83**, 2289–2293.

Hofmann, K., Yajima, H., Yanaihara, Y., Liu, T. Y., and Lande, S. (1961). *J. Am. Chem. Soc.* **83**, 487–489.

Honzl, J., and Rudinger, J. (1961). *Collect. Czech. Chem. Commun.* **26**, 2333–2344.

Irie, H., Fujii, N., Ogawa, H., and Yajima, H. (1976). *J. Chem. Soc., Chem. Commun.* pp. 922–923.

Irie, H., Fujii, N., Ogawa, H., Yajima, H., Fujino, M., and Shinagawa, S. (1977). *Chem. Pharm. Bull.* **25**, 2929–2934.

Irie, H., Nakanishi, H., Fujii, N., Mizuno, Y., Fushimi, T., Funakoshi, S., and Yajima, H. (1980a). *Chem. Lett.* pp. 705–708.

Irie, H., Shiina, A., Fushimi, T., Katakawa, J., Fujii, N., and Yajima, H. (1980b). *Chem. Lett.* pp. 875–878.

Iselin, B. (1961). *Helv. Chim. Acta* **44**, 61–78.

Iselin, B. (1962). *Helv. Chim. Acta* **45**, 1510–1515.

Katsoyannis, P. G., Fukuda, K., Tometsko, A., Suzuki, K., and Tilak, M. (1964). *J. Am. Chem. Soc.* **86**, 930–932.

Kiso, Y., Nakamura, S., Ito, K., Ukawa, K., Kitagawa, K., Akita, T., and Moritoki, H. (1979). *J. Chem. Soc., Chem. Commun.* pp. 971–972.

Kiso, Y., Ukawa, K., and Akita, T. (1980a). *J. Chem. Soc., Chem. Commun.* pp. 101–102.

Kiso, Y., Satomi, M., Ukawa, K., and Akita, T. (1980b). *J. Chem. Soc., Chem. Commun.* pp. 1063–1064.

Kiso, Y., Ukawa, K., Nakamura, S., Ito, K., and Akita, T. (1980c). *Chem. Pharm. Bull.* **28**, 673–676.

Kitagawa, K., Akita, T., Segawa, T., Nakano, M., Fujii, N., and Yajima, H. (1976). *Chem. Pharm. Bull.* **24**, 2692–2698.

König, W., and Geiger, R. (1970). *Chem. Ber.* **103**, 788–798.

Kung, Y. T. *et al.* (1965). *Sci. Sin.* **14**, 1710–1716.

Kunitz, M. (1940). *J. Gen. Physiol.* **24**, 15–32.

Kunitz, M. (1946). *J. Biol. Chem.* **164**, 563–568.

Liu, T. Y., and Chang, Y. H. (1971). *J. Biol. Chem.* **246**, 2842–2848.

Lundt, B. F., Johansen, N. L., Vølund, A., and Markussen, J. (1978). *Int. J. Pept. Protein Res.* **12**, 258–268.

McKay, F. C., and Albertson, N. F. (1957). *J. Am. Chem. Soc.* **79**, 4686–4690.

McMurry, J. (1976). *Org. React.* **24**, 187–224.

Marglin, A., and Merrifield, R. B. (1966). *J. Am. Chem. Soc.* **88**, 5051–5052.

Martinez, J., and Bodanszky, M. (1978). *Int. J. Pept. Protein Res.* **12**, 277–283.

Masui, Y., Chino, N., and Sakakibara, S. (1980). *Bull. Chem. Soc. Jpn.* **53**, 464–468.

Matsuura, S., Niu, C. H., and Cohen, J. S. (1976). *J. Chem. Soc., Chem. Commun.* pp. 451–452.

Mazur, R. H., and Plume, G. (1968). *Experientia* **24**, 661.

Meienhofer, J. (1979). *In* "The Peptides" (E. Gross and J. Meienhofer, eds.), Vol. 1, pp. 198–233. Academic Press, New York.

Meienhofer, J., Schnabel, E., Bremer, H., Brinkhoff, O., Zabel, R., Sroka, W., Klostermyer, H., Brandenburg, D., Okuda, T., and Zahn, H. (1963). *Z. Naturforsch.*, **18B**, 1120–1121.
Merrifield, R. B. (1963). *J. Am. Chem. Soc.* **85**, 2149–2154.
Mitchell, R. A., and Merrifield, R. B. (1976). *J. Org. Chem.* **41**, 2015–2019.
Mutt, V., and Said, S. I. (1974). *Eur. J. Biochem.* **42**, 581–589.
Nair, R. M. G., Kastin, A. J., and Schally, A. V. (1971). *Biochem. Biophys. Res. Commun.* **43**, 1376–1381.
Nakajima, T., and Yasuhara, T. (1977). *Chem. Pharm. Bull.* **26**, 1222–1230.
Nakajima, T., Yasuhara, T., Hirai, Y., Kitada, C., Fujino, M., Takeyama, M., Koyama, K., and Yajima, H. (1978). *Chem. Pharm. Bull.* **26**, 1222–1230.
Nilsson, A. (1975). *FEBS Lett.* **60**, 322–326.
Nishimura, O., and Fujino, M. (1976). *Chem. Pharm. Bull* **24**, 1568–1575.
Nishioka, K., Constantopoulos, A., Satoh, P. S., and Najjar, V. A. (1972). *Biochem. Biophys. Res. Commun.* **47**, 172–179.
Noble, R. L., Yamashiro, D., and Li, C. H. (1976). *J. Am. Chem. Soc.* **98**, 2324–2328.
Node, M., Hori, H., and Fujita, E. (1976). *J. Chem. Soc., Perkin Trans. I* pp. 2237–2240.
Ogawa, H., Sugiura, M., Yajima, H., Sakurai, H., and Tsuda, K. (1978a). *Chem. Pharm. Bull.* **26**, 1549–1557.
Ogawa, H., Sasaki, T., Irie, H., and Yajima, H. (1978b). *Chem. Pharm. Bull.* **26**, 3144–3149.
Omori, Y., Matsuda, S., Aimoto, S., Shimonishi, Y., and Yamamoto, M. (1976). *Chem. Lett.* pp. 805–808.
Pearson, D., Shively, J. E., Clark, B. R., Geschwind, I. I., Barkley, M., Nishioka, R. S., and Bern, H. A. (1980). *Proc. Natl. Acad. Sci. U.S.A.* **77**, 5021–5024.
Pearson, R. G. (1966). *Science* **151**, 172–177.
Pearson, R. G., and Songstad, J. (1967). *J. Am. Chem. Soc.* **89**, 1827–1836.
Pless, J., and Bauer, W. (1973). *Angew. Chem., Int. Ed. Engl.* **12**, 147–148.
Richards, F. M. (1958). *Proc. Natl. Acad. Sci. U.S.A.* **44**, 162–166.
Rittel, W., Brugger, M., Kamber, B., Riniker, B., and Sieber, P. (1968). *Helv. Chim. Acta* **51**, 924–928.
Rothgeb, T., Jones, B. N., Hayes, D. F., and Gurd, R. S. (1977). *Biochemistry* **16**, 5813–5818.
Sakakibara, S. (1971). *In* "Chemistry and Biochemistry of Amino Acids, Peptides and Proteins" (B. Weinstein, ed.), Vol. 1, pp. 51–85. Dekker, New York.
Sakakibara, S., Shimonishi, S., Kishida, Y., Okada, M., and Sugihara, H. (1967). *Bull. Chem. Soc. Jpn.* **40**, 2164–2167.
Sano, S., and Kawanishi, S. (1975). *J. Am. Chem. Soc.* **97**, 3480–3484.
Schallenberg, E. E., and Calvin, M. (1955). *J. Am. Chem. Soc.* **77**, 2779–2783.
Schön, I., and Kisfaludy, L. (1979). *Int. J. Pept. Protein Res.* **14**, 485–494.
Schwarz, H., and Arakawa, K. (1959). *J. Am. Chem. Soc.* **81**, 5691–5695.
Schwyzer, R., and Li, C. H. (1958). *Nature (London)* **182**, 1669–1670.
Schwyzer, R., Kappeler, H., Iselin, B., Rittel, W., and Zuber, H. (1959). *Helv. Chim. Acta* **42**, 1702–1708.
Schwyzer, R., and Sieber, P. (1963). *Nature (London)* **199**, 172–174.
Schwyzer, R., Costopanagiotis, A., and Sieber, P. (1963a). *Helv. Chim. Acta* **46**, 870–889.
Schwyzer, R., Iselin, B., Kappeler, H., Riniker, B., Rittel, W., and Zuber, H. (1963b). *Helv. Chim. Acta* **46**, 1975–1996.
Sharp, J. J., Robinson, A. B., and Kamen, M. D. (1973). *J. Am. Chem. Soc.* **95**, 6097–6108.
Sieber, P., and Iselin, B. (1968). *Helv. Chim. Acta* **51**, 622–632.
Sieber, P., and Iselin, B. (1969). *Helv. Chim. Acta* **52**, 1525–1531.
Sifferd, R. H., and du Vigneaud, V. (1935). *J. Biol. Chem.* **108**, 753–761.
Simpson, R. J., Neuberger, M. R., and Liu, T. Y. (1976). *J. Biol. Chem.* **251**, 1936–1940.
Smyth, D. G., Stein, W. H., and Moore, S. (1963). *J. Biol. Chem.* **238**, 227–234.

Stelakatos, G. C., Paganov, A., and Zervas, L. (1966). *J. Chem. Soc.* pp. 1191–1198.
Suzuki, K., and Endo, N. (1978). *Chem. Pharm. Bull.* **26**, 2269–2274.
Takeyama, M., Koyama, K., Inoue, K., Kawano, T., Adachi, H., Tobe, T., and Yajima, H. (1980a). *Chem. Pharm. Bull.* **28**, 1873–1883.
Takeyama, M., Koyama, K., Yajima, H., Moriga, M., Aono, M., and Murakami, N. (1980b). *Chem. Pharm. Bull.* **28**, 2265–2269.
Theodoropoulos, D. M., and Fruton, J. S. (1962). *Biochemistry* **1**, 933–937.
Uphaus, R. A., Grossweiner, L. I., Katz, J. J., and Kopple, K. D. (1959). *Science* **129**, 641–643.
White, F. H., Jr. (1961). *J. Biol. Chem.* **236**, 1353–1360.
Wilchek, M., and Gorecki, M. (1969). *Eur. J. Biochem.* **11**, 491–494.
Wünsch, E., and Drees, F. (1966). *Chem. Ber.* **99**, 110–120.
Wünsch, E., Jaeger, E., and Scharf, R. (1968). *Chem. Ber.* **101**, 3664–3670.
Wünsch, E., Jaeger, E., Kisfaludy, L., and Löw, M. (1977). *Angew. Chem.* **89**, 330–331, and other references.
Yajima, H., and Fujii, N. (1980). *J. Chem. Soc., Chem. Commun.* pp. 115–116.
Yajima, H., and Fujii, N. (1981a). *Chem. Pharm. Bull.* **29**, 600–602.
Yajima, H., and Fujii, N. (1981b). *J. Am. Chem. Soc.* **103**, 5867–5871.
Yajima, H., Kawasaki, K., Okada, Y., Minami, H., Kubo, K., and Yamashita, I. (1968a). *Chem. Pharm. Bull.* **16**, 919–928.
Yajima, H., Okada, Y., Kinomura, Y., and Minami, H. (1968b). *J. Am. Chem. Soc.* **90**, 527–528.
Yajima, H., Kawasaki, K., Minami, H., Kawatani, H., Mizokami, N., and Okada, Y. (1969). *Biochim. Biophys. Acta* **175**, 228–230.
Yajima, H., Fujii, N., Ogawa, H., and Kawatani, H. (1974). *J. Chem. Soc., Chem. Commun.* pp. 107–108.
Yajima, H., Ogawa, H., Watanabe, H., Fujii, N., Kurobe, M., and Miyamoto, S. (1975a). *Chem. Pharm. Bull.* **23**, 371–374.
Yajima, H., Kiso, Y., Ogawa, H., Fujii, N., and Irie, H. (1975b). *Chem. Pharm. Bull.* **23**, 1164–1166.
Yajima, H., Kitagawa, K., Segawa, T., Nakano, M., and Kataoka, K. (1975c). *Chem. Pharm. Bull.* **23**, 3299–3300.
Yajima, H., Ogawa, H., and Sakurai, H. (1977). *J. Chem. Soc., Chem. Commun.* pp. 909–910.
Yajima, H., Sasaki, T., Ogawa, H., Fujii, N., Segawa, T., and Nakata, Y. (1978a). *Chem. Pharm. Bull.* **26**, 1231–1235.
Yajima, H., Takeyama, H., Kanaki, J., Nishimura, O., and Fujino, M. (1978b). *Chem. Pharm. Bull.* **26**, 3752–3757.
Yajima, H., Takeyama, M., Kanaki, J., and Mitani, K. (1978c). *J. Chem. Soc., Chem. Commun.* pp. 482–483.
Yajima, H., Funakoshi, S., Fujii, N., Akaji, K., and Irie, H. (1979a). *Chem. Pharm. Bull.* **27**, 1060–1061.
Yajima, H., Takeyama, M., Koyama, K., Tobe, T., Inoue, K., Kawano, T., and Adachi, H. (1979b). *Chem. Pharm. Bull.* **27**, 3199–3201.
Yajima, H. Akaji, K., Mitani, K., Fujii, N., Funakoshi, S., Adachi, H., Oishi, M., and Akazawa, Y. (1979c). *Int. J. Pept. Protein Res.* **14**, 169–176.
Yajima, H., Kanaki, J., Funakoshi, S., Hirai, Y., and Nakajima, T. (1980a). *Chem. Pharm. Bull.* **28**, 882–886.
Yajima, H., Akaji, K., Funakoshi, S., Fujii, N., and Irie, H. (1980b). *Chem. Pharm. Bull.* **28**, 1942–1945.
Yajima, H., Takeyama, M., Koyama, K., Tobe, T., Inoue, K., Kawano, T., and Adachi, H. (1980c). *Int. J. Pept. Protein Res.* **16**, 33–47.
Yamashiro, D. (1964). *Nature (London)* **201**, 76–77.
Yang, C. C., and Merrifield, R. B. (1976). *J. Org. Chem.* **41**, 1032–1041.

Chapter **3**

Side Reactions in Peptide Synthesis

MIKLOS BODANSZKY

Department of Chemistry
Case Western Reserve University
Cleveland, Ohio

JEAN MARTINEZ*

Centre National de la Recherche Scientifique
Ecole Nationale Supérieure de Chimie
34075 Montpellier, France

I. Introduction 112
II. Side Reactions Characteristic of Individual Amino Acids . . 114
A. Glycine 114
B. Valine and Isoleucine 118
C. Proline 120
D. Phenylalanine 123
E. Tyrosine 124
F. Tryptophan 127
G. Histidine 132
H. Lysine 135
I. Arginine 137
J. Serine and Threonine 139
K. Aspartic Acid 143
L. Glutamic Acid 148
M. Asparagine and Glutamine 152
N. Cysteine and Cystine 156
O. Methionine 158

* Present address: Centre CNRS-INSERM de Pharmacologie–Endocrinologie, 34033 Montpellier, France.

THE PEPTIDES, VOLUME 5

ISBN 0-12-304205-4

III. Side Reactions in the Introduction and Removal of Protecting Groups 161
A. The Benzyloxycarbonyl (Carbobenzoxy, Z) Group . . . 161
B. The *tert*-Butyloxycarbonyl (Boc) Group 164
C. The 2-Nitrophenylsulfenyl (Nps) Group 167
D. The 4-Toluenesulfonyl (Tosyl, Tos) Group 167
E. The Phthalyl (Phthaloyl, Pht) Group 169
F. The Triphenylmethyl (Trityl, Trt) Group 170
G. The 9-Fluorenylmethyloxycarbonyl (Fmoc) Group . . . 170
H. Protection of the Carboxyl Group 173
I. Protection of Side-Chain Functions and the Final Deprotection 175
IV. Side Reactions Encountered in Formation of the Peptide Bond 177
A. The Azide Method 177
1. Preparation of Azides 178
2. Curtius Rearrangement 180
B. Anhydrides 182
1. Symmetrical Anhydrides 183
2. Mixed Anhydrides (Asymmetrical Anhydrides) 184
3. *N*-Carboxy (Leuchs') Anhydrides 187
C. Carbodiimides 189
D. Active Esters 192
V. Side Reactions in Solid-Phase Peptide Synthesis 192
VI. Side Reactions in Cyclization 193
VII. Instability of Peptides in Solution 194
VIII. Conclusions 196
References 197

I. INTRODUCTION

In the synthesis of organic compounds, with few exceptions, a single product is expected. Ideally synthetic reactions are unequivocal; they proceed through a distinct mechanism and result in the desired material, essentially in pure form. There are some procedures that approach or even attain this ideal, for example, catalytic hydrogenation or esterification of a carboxylic acid with diazomethane. However, in the majority of synthetic steps at least some unreacted starting materials have to be separated from the product of the reaction, and quite frequently a process yields not one but two or more products and the desired substance has to be isolated from the complex mixture of accompanying materials, often by time-consuming procedures. Such difficulties render organic synthesis an interesting or even exciting endeavor. In peptide synthesis, however, because of the size of the molecules to be prepared and the sometimes exceedingly large number of steps to be performed, the cumulative effect of such problems can become overwhelming or prohibitive. Moreover, the complexity of the intermediates and the limitations of the analytical procedures hinder the detection of by-products resulting from side reactions. The similarity of the by-products to the desired material, together with the poor solubility of many intermediates, makes their separation sometimes almost impossible. Thus, it becomes imperative to seek unequivocal reactions in all phases of peptide synthesis.

The literature abounds with reports on novel side reactions and undetected by-products. A closer scrutiny often reveals that the newly discovered side reaction is not so novel, and that the by-products have been noted before but were unknown to the investigator reporting them. He or she should not be blamed too much for overlooking earlier accounts: There is no obvious approach by which an already encountered side reaction or by-product can be located in the literature. The field is already extensive and growing at an exponential rate. The authors of this chapter, therefore, are faced with the same difficulties as the investigator just mentioned: We found many but certainly not all reports on side reactions that should be mentioned in a complete review. Yet, we hope that even an incomplete summary of side reactions will help peptide chemists in their efforts to obtain pure products, or in less fortunate cases assist them in finding out what went wrong.

This is certainly not the first attempt to provide such information. Several papers (e.g., Kisfaludy, 1979, 1981) have dealt with special aspects of side reactions in peptide synthesis. A review by the present authors (Bodanszky and Martinez, 1981) concentrated on side reactions characteristic of individual amino acids. Simultaneously and independently the same point of view prevailed in a major article, "Solid-Phase Peptide Synthesis," by Bárány and Merrifield, in Vol. 2 of this treatise. The editors of *The Peptides* feel, however, that a comprehensive treatment of side reactions not restricted to a special technique or a special aspect is still warranted. Therefore, we will try to present a review encompassing side reactions related to activation, coupling, and the introduction and removal of protecting groups including final deprotection, and also an overview of the cases characteristic of individual amino acids. We must apologize beforehand, since our presentation cannot be as comprehensive as we would like it to be.* However, we hope that it will serve a useful purpose, that it will help peptide chemists to recognize or, better, to anticipate and avoid side reactions. A search for unequivocal pathways in the ever increasing array of methods of activation,

* An important side reaction, racemization, is not included in this chapter because excellent treatments of this subject appear in Chap. 4 (this volume) and in Vol. 1 (Kemp, 1979) and Vol. 2 (Kovács, 1980) of this treatise.

coupling, protection, and deprotection should bring us closer to the unquestionable aim of peptide synthesis, the production of pure peptides.

A word of encouragement must be added here. Full awareness of side reactions might prompt some investigators to abandon their intentions and to seek, instead of synthesis, alternative routes to the peptides they need. Synthesis in the organic laboratory remains, however, a viable approach, and many important peptides have been secured this way in pure form. The well-informed researcher, by avoiding or at least suppressing side reactions, will achieve his or her goals without excessive purification of intermediates or final products.

II. SIDE REACTIONS CHARACTERISTIC OF INDIVIDUAL AMINO ACIDS

A. Glycine

Glycine is certainly the simplest amino acid. The absence of a side chain has suggested to many investigators the absence of complicating factors such as steric or electronic effects of side chains. Hence, they chose glycine for model experiments in peptide chemistry. This view is not fully warranted. In simple model compounds, functional groups other than those involved in the problem under study should indeed be absent. In this respect, however, any monoaminomonocarboxylic acid is suitable. Among these, as we shall see in the subsequent section, valine and isoleucine represent a special class with rather exceptional steric hindrance caused by branching of the aliphatic side chain at the β-carbon atom. Of the 20 common constituents of proteins this leaves only alanine and leucine as typical amino acids for model experiments. However, glycine is quite atypical. It is the only amino acid among the building components of proteins that lacks a chiral center. Even more significant is the absence of steric limitation due to the presence of a side chain in all other amino acids. For instance, the hydrogen atoms on the α-carbon do not prevent diacylation of the amino group. In contrast, no diacylamides form, at least not under mild conditions, in the interaction of acylating agents with all other amino acids, including alanine. A characteristic case of diacylation was noted by Wieland and Heinke (1956) in the reaction of benzyloxycarbonylglycine with phosphorus oxychloride. The unexpected diacylamide, *N*-benzyloxycarbonyl-*N*-(benzyloxycarbonylglycyl)glycine (**1**) was obtained in 30% yield. The same material (**1**) was formed, on exposure to a tertiary base, from the symmetrical anhydride of benzyloxycarbonylglycine (Kotake and Saito, 1966). Activation and coupling of glycine via mixed anhydrides can also result in similar diacylamides such

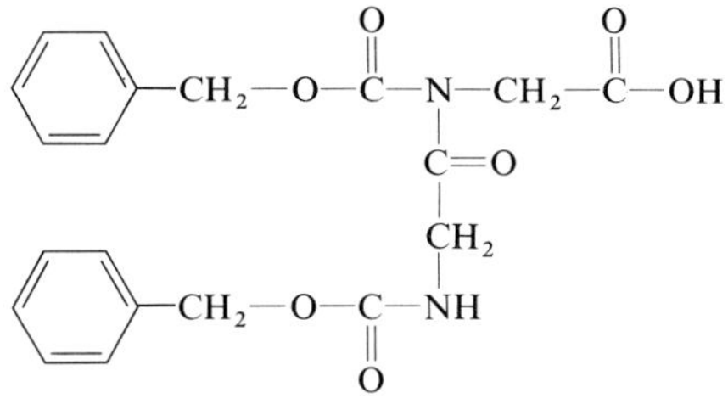

(1)

as **2** (Kopple and Renick, 1958; Schellenberg and Ullrich, 1959; cf. also Wieland and Mohr, 1956).

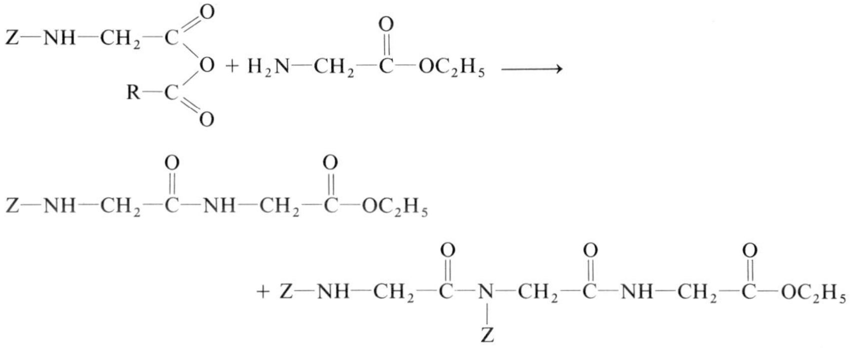

(2)

In an analogous manner the mixed anhydride of 4-toluenesulfonylglycine, prepared with the help of *sec*-butyl chlorocarbonate in pyridine, gave rise on reaction with aniline to a series of products, among them *N*-tosylglycyltosylglycine anilide (**3**) in a significant amount (Zaoral and Rudinger, 1961):

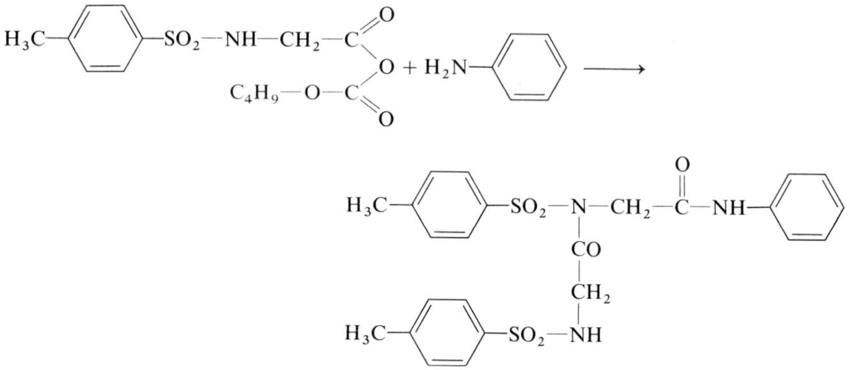

(3)

Several cyclization reactions characteristic of glycine derivatives are also based on the ready formation of diacylamides. The production of hydantoin derivative **4** in the attempted saponification of ethoxycarbonylglycyl-glycine ethyl ester (Fischer, 1902; cf also Wessely and Kemm, 1928; Wessely *et al.*, 1929) was the earliest observation of this phenomenon. (**4** was cleaved by excess alkali to yield **5**.) Subsequently hydantoins were noted in the reaction

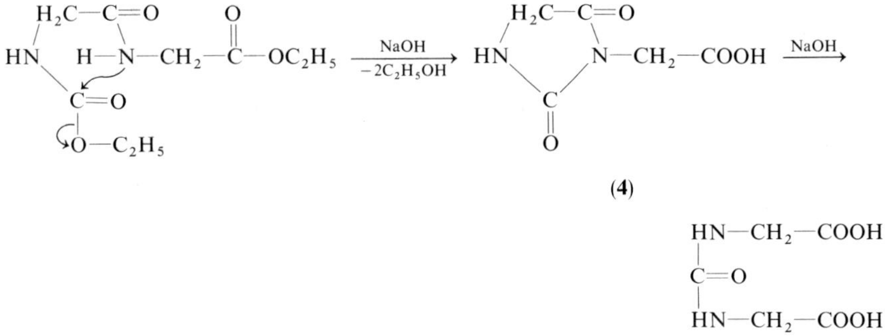

(**4**)

(**5**)

of benzyloxycarbonyl-L-phenylalanylglycine ethyl ester with methanolic ammonia (Fruton and Bergmann, 1942). Thus abstraction of a proton from the amide nitrogen of acylglycines does not even require sodium hydroxide, and it can take place under the influence of less strong bases as well:

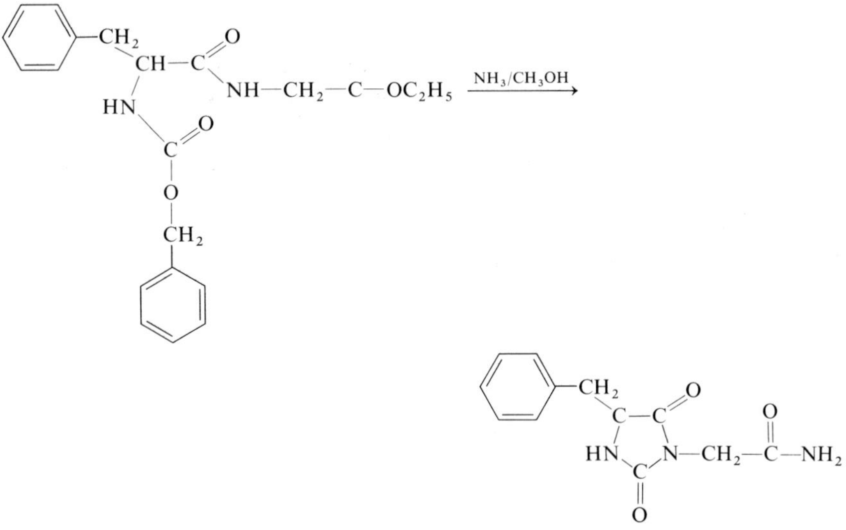

(**6**)

The production of hydantoin derivatives such as **6** is not limited to one specific sequence. Analogous reactions, starting with benzyloxycarbonyl-alanyl-glycylhydroxyproline ethyl ester (Heyns and Legler, 1960) and with benzyloxycarbonyl-L-tryptophylglycine ethyl ester (Davis, 1956) demonstrate that the possible formation of hydantoin derivatives must be considered when *peptides with glycine as the second residue in their sequence* are exposed to the action of bases (Goldschmidt and Wick, 1952; Wessely *et al.*, 1952; Schlögl and Fabitschowitz, 1953; MacLaren, 1958; Bodanszky *et al.*, 1963a).

Ring formation through intramolecular attack by the amide grouping in acylglycine derivatives is not limited to the formation of five-membered cycles. This is demonstrated in the production of an *N*-acylpiperazine-2,5-dione in the decomposition of benzyloxycarbonylglycyl-L-proline 4-nitrophenyl ester (**7**). Elimination of 4-nitrophenol yields a benzyloxycarbonyl derivative of glycylproline diketopiperazine (**8**) (Goodman and Steuben, 1962a):

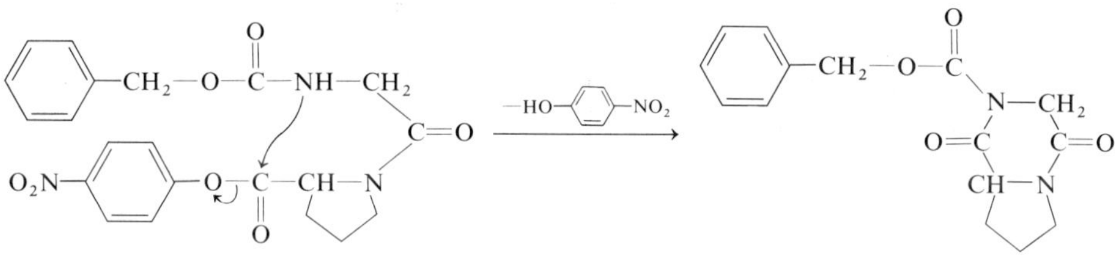

(**7**) (**8**)

The facile formation of the diketopiperazine cyclo(glycylglycyl) (Rothe and Mazdanek, 1972) is also noteworthy.

The addition of ethyl glycinate to one of the two double bonds of dicyclohexylcarbodiimide leads to a substituted guanidine (**9**) which then undergoes cyclization to 1-cyclohexyl-2-cyclohexylamino-4,5-dihydroimidazolin-5-one (**10**) (Muramatsu *et al.*, 1963):

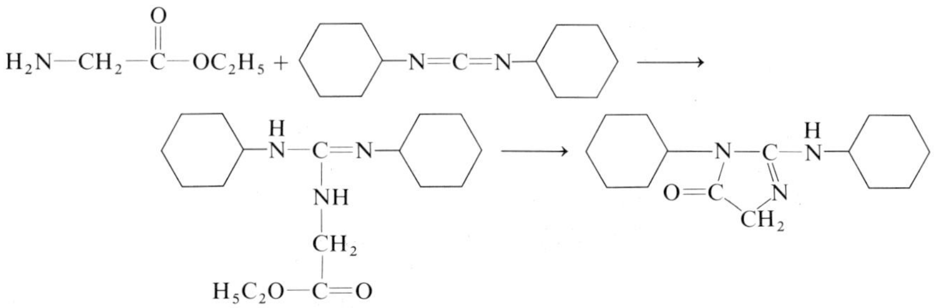

(**9**) (**10**)

An unusual tendency for rearrangement is exhibited by Leuchs' anhydride of glycine (**11**). Isocyanate (**12**) thus formed reacts with amines and generates hydantoic acids (**13**) instead of the expected glycyl derivatives (Dewey *et al.*,

1968):

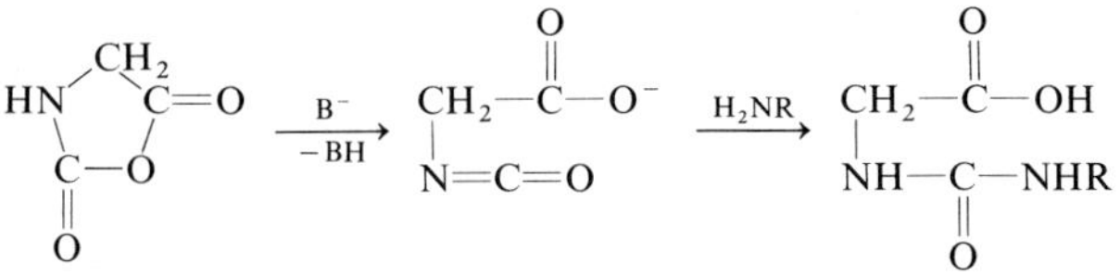

(11) (12) (13)

B. Valine and Isoleucine

With respect to steric hindrance valine and isoleucine (**14** and **15**) are in a separate class among the 20 amino acids that are constituents of proteins. Only in these two is there branching of the side chain at the β-carbon atom; in all other cases, shown here using leucine (**16**) as an example, branching, if any, occurs at the γ-carbon of the amino acid skeleton. In terms of bulkiness the hydroxyl group of threonine (**17a**) competes with a methyl group, hence

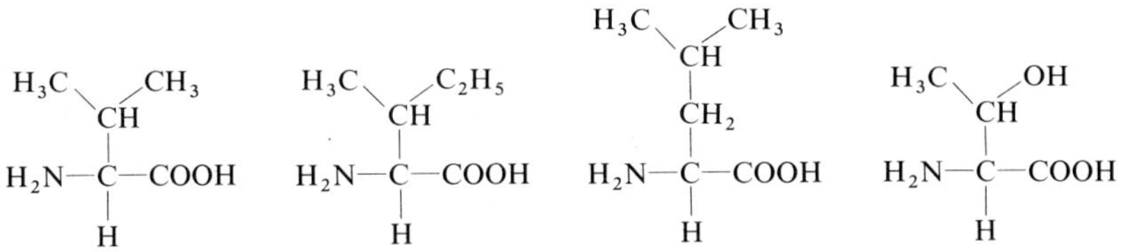

(14) (15) (16) (17a)

threonine in this regard is analogous to valine. The bulky side chains obviously affect the availability of the carbonyl group for nucleophilic attack in activated derivatives of these amino acids. Acylation reactions proceed unusually slowly, and competing reactions cause more difficulties than in the case of less hindered amino acids (Harris and Work, 1950; Weygand and Obermeier, 1968; Esko *et al.*, 1968). To mention a characteristic example, the Curtius rearrangement of azides, a unimolecular reaction, is more pronounced when valine or isoleucine is activated in this form (Hinman *et al.*, 1950). Also, the formation of dicyclohexylureides by O → N migration in *O*-acylisoureas, the reactive intermediates in dicyclohexylcarbodiimide-mediated couplings (Sheehan and Hess, 1955), is more serious when the activated carboxyl groups belong to valine or isoleucine than in the case of less hindered amino acids (e.g., Shankman and Schvo, 1958). This situation is further aggravated if the activated intermediates are brought into reaction with only moderately reactive nucleophiles. For instance, in the esterification of protected amino acids with 4-nitrophenol, *N*-acylurea derivatives are mostly negligible by-products. When, however, 4-nitrophenol is replaced by 2-nitrophenol, in which the hydroxyl group is less available because of an intramolecular hydrogen bond, the formation of ureides (**17b**) is more significant and with derivatives of valine and isoleucine they can become the main product of the attempted esterification:

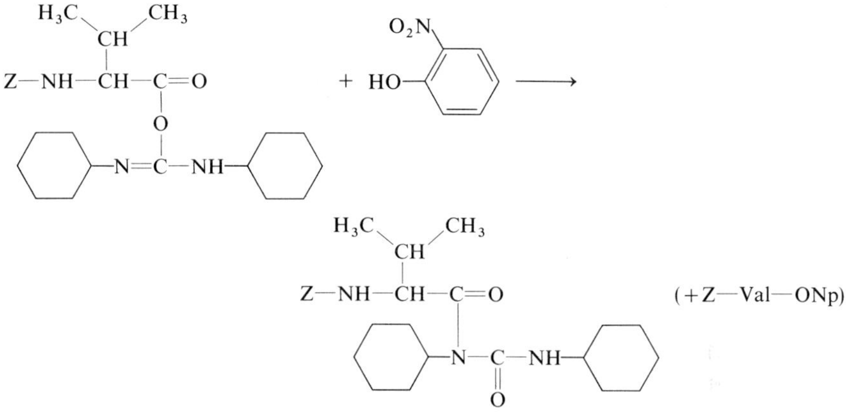

(**17b**)

The extent of the side reaction must be diminished by increasing the rate of the desired reaction, for example, by carrying out the esterification in pyridine, a solvent that can enhance the nucleophilicity of 2-nitrophenol (Bodanszky *et al*., 1973a).

The hydrolysis (Shankman and Higa, 1962), aminolysis (Losse and Müller, 1961), and hydrazinolysis (M. Bodanszky, unpublished) of alkyl esters of valine and isoleucine are unusually slow. Also, in the formation of the valyl–tryosine bond O-acylation competes with the expected aminolysis (Paul and Anderson, 1962). A more general competing reaction was noted in a reexamination of the mixed anhydride method (Bodanszky and Tolle, 1977). With isobutyl chlorocarbonate as activating reagent, in most cases less than 1% of the total products consisted of the undesired urethanes. However, the mixed anhydrides of protected valine or isoleucine produced 6–8% "second-acylation products" such as **18**:

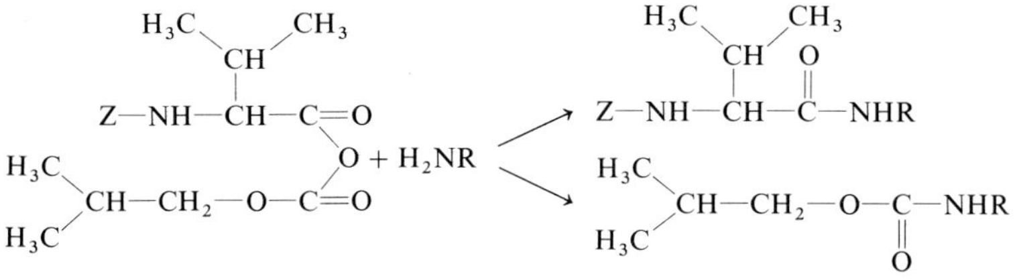

(**18**)

When valine is the NH_2-terminal residue of a peptide that serves as the amino component in a coupling reaction, its bulky side chain still might interfere with the outcome of the synthesis. For instance, polycondensation of the *N*-hydroxysuccinimide ester of valylvalylglycine proceeds less well than the analogous reaction with peptides with less hindered NH_2-termini (Katakai, 1977). Also, the steric effects noted in derivatives of valine and isoleucine are quite pronounced in *tert*-leucine (Pospisek and Blaha, 1977). If branching takes place at the α-carbon atom, for example, in the derivatives of α-methylalanine (Leplawy *et al.*, 1960), the hindrance becomes extreme.

C. Proline

Proline is unique among the 20 amino acid constituents of proteins because it is the only secondary amine. Thus, it is an imino rather than an amino acid. Furthermore, the side chain of proline is also the alkyl substituent on its amino group, and the ensuing ring structure is the cause of severe steric restrictions. A conspicuous example of the side reactions resulting from steric hindrance in proline was reported by Savrda (1977). In the reaction of the *N*-hydroxysuccinimide ester of *tert*-butyloxycarbonyl-L-proline with proline, the nucleophile could not readily approach the active ester carbonyl and therefore it reacted with one of the carbonyl groups of the succinimide ring. Thus, in addition to the expected product, *tert*-butyloxycarbonyl-L prolyl-L-proline, a by-product (**19**), was also isolated. The same steric hindrance leads to the formation of more than the usual small amount of

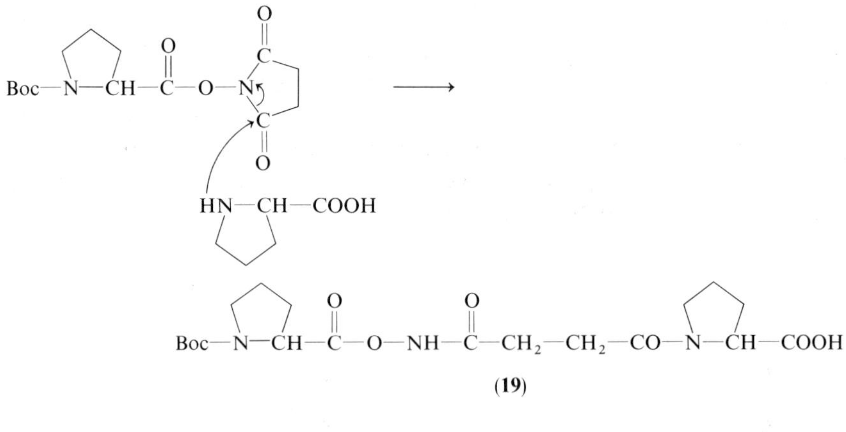

(**19**)

N-acyldicyclohexylurea (**20**) in acylations with protected proline and dicyclohexylcarbodiimide (Merrifield, 1964a).

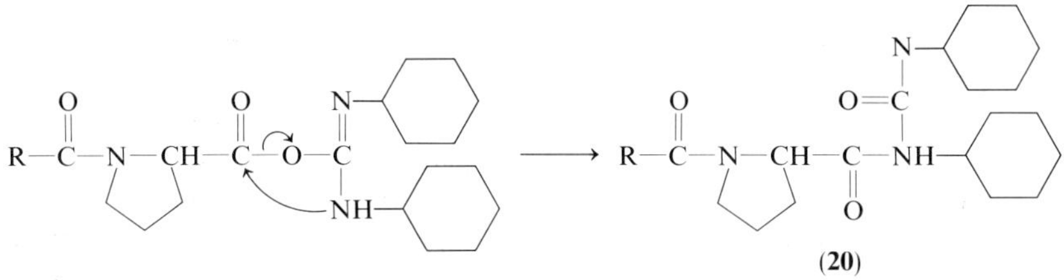

(20)

The geometry of proline residues is also conducive to the generation of rings, particularly to the production of diketopiperazines (Abderhalden and Nienburg, 1933; Smith and Bergmann, 1944; Neumann and Smith, 1951; Wieland and Heinke, 1958; Sakakibara and Nagai, 1960; Ondetti *et al.*, 1971), sometimes even at the expense of fragmentation of the peptide chain (Meienhofer, 1970; Lucente *et al.*, 1971; Gerig and McLeod, 1976). This tendency can also be recognized in the formation of *N*-acyldiketopiperazines on storage of protected and activated derivatives of glycyl-proline such as benzyloxycarbonylglycyl-L-proline 4-nitrophenyl ester (Goodman and Steuben, 1962b; cf. also Conti *et al.*, 1973). The same sort of ring closure was encountered (Gisin and Merrifield, 1972; Khosla *et al.*, 1972) in solid-phase peptide synthesis (Merrifield, 1963), where COOH-terminal aminoacyl-proline sequences (**21**) attached through an ester bond to the insoluble polymeric support can be lost from the resin as a result of cyclization (**22**).

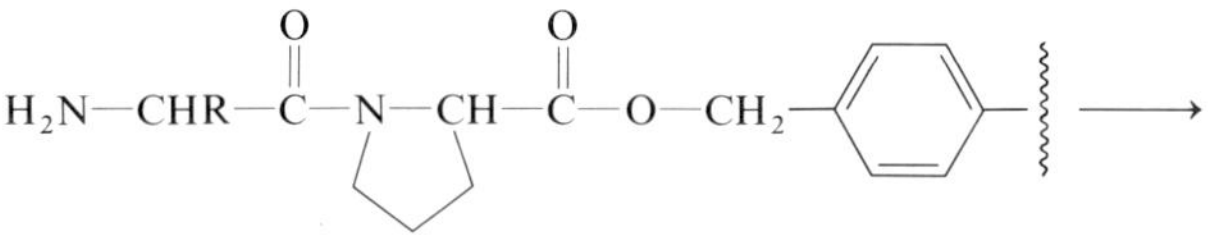

(**21**)

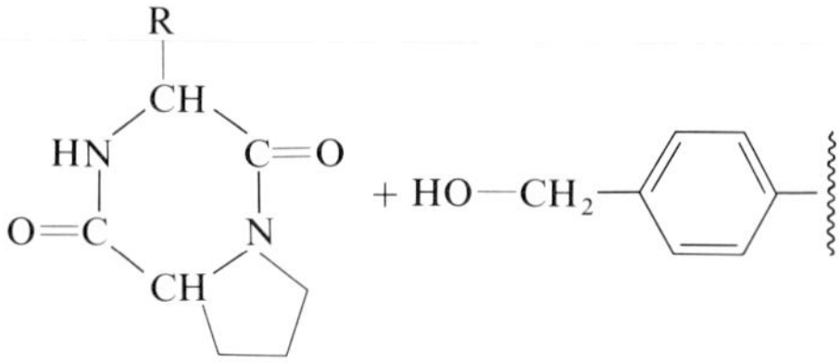

(**22**)

The loss of a COOH-terminal dipeptide is quite serious if it consists of two proline residues (Rothe and Mazanek, 1972, 1974). Diketopiperazine formation is also facile in dipeptides in which one residue has the L and the other the D configuration. The well-known reason for this is the interference of the two side chains which in LL- and DD-diketopiperazines are on the same side of the general plane of the ring. Bulky substituents seem to provide additional enhancement of cyclization; the diketopiperazine from DVal-L-Pro was reported as a by-product in two independent syntheses (Meienhofer, 1970; Gisin and Merrifield, 1972).

The peptide bond between proline and the preceding amino acid is a secondary amide, and therefore it can be cleaved by a strong reducing agent such as $LiAlH_4$. Such a reductive cleavage has been utilized in the sequence determination of peptides but not in peptide synthesis. On the other hand, reduction with sodium in liquid ammonia in the presence of hydrogen donors can also split the peptide bond (Hofmann and Yajima, 1961) [Eq. (1)].

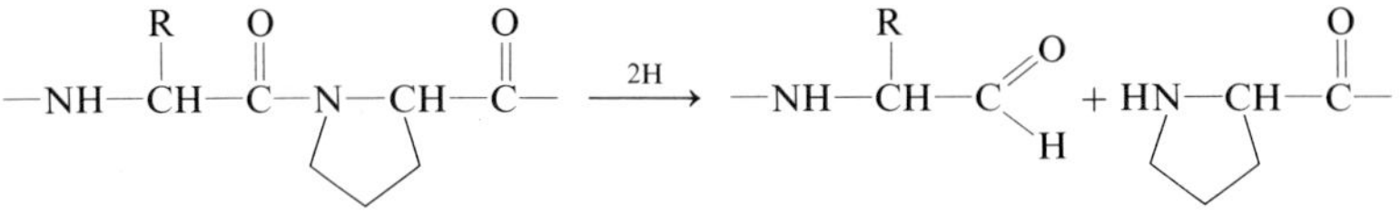
(1)

Because treatment with sodium in liquid ammonia is commonly used in the removal of protecting groups, the question whether or not this method of deblocking can cause fission of the assembled peptide chain must be raised. In a continued effort to answer this question fragmentation during deprotection with sodium in liquid ammonia has been studied in several laboratories (e.g., Patchornik, 1963; Wilchek *et al*., 1965; Benisek and Cole, 1965; Ramachandran *et al*., 1965; Ressler and Kashelikar, 1966; Marglin and Merrifield, 1966; Jošt and Rudinger, 1967a; Katsoyannis *et al*., 1971; Marglin, 1972; Bossert and Jaquenoud, 1975). Some investigators (Guttmann, 1963; Bajusz and Medzihradszky, 1963) were able to avoid this side reaction under carefully maintained conditions. It is at least likely that the presence or absence of hydrogen donors [cf. Eq. (1)] is responsible for discrepancies in the literature. Traces of water or alcohols in the mixture or the presence of tosylamides can cause significant fission of the aminoacyl–proline bond. Of course the source of hydrogen can be the peptide itself: Alcoholic hydroxyl groups of serine and threonine or the phenolic hydroxyl of tyrosine can participate in the reductive cleavage (cf. Marglin, 1972). The nature of the amino acid preceding the proline residue also has an influence on the rate or extent of chain fragmentation (Benisek *et al*., 1967), and NH_2-terminal residues are split off more readily than midchain peptide bonds. A particularly sensitive link between threonine and proline in the B-chain of insulin was noted by Merrifield and Marglin (1967). The addition of *excess* sodium amide, which probably reacts with hydrogen donors, prevents fission of the aminoacyl–proline bond (Katsoyannis *et al*., 1971).

Proline, as a secondary amine, is more readily N-alkylated than other amino acids, which are primary amines. In solid-phase peptide synthesis, chain termination occurred as a result of the reaction of unreacted chloromethyl groups with NH_2-terminal proline residues (Schou *et al*., 1976) as shown in Scheme 1.

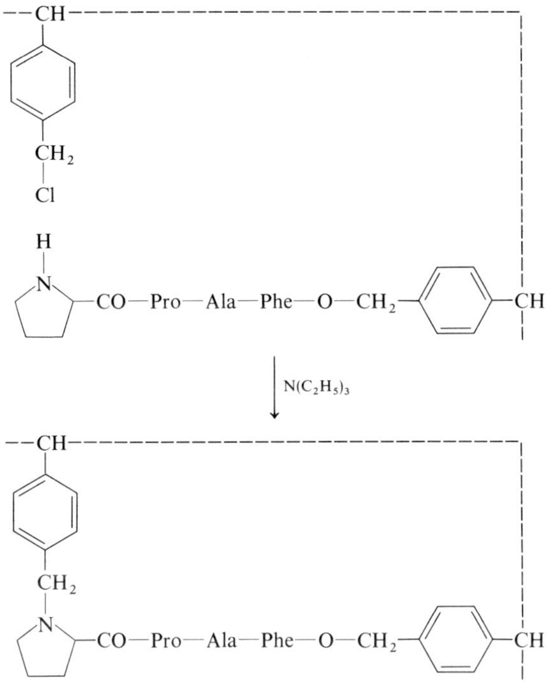

Scheme 1

D. Phenylalanine

The aromatic ring in phenylalanine has no substituents that increase its reactivity. Because of the relative inertness of the phenylalanine side chain, the side reactions characteristic of this amino acid are rarely mentioned in the literature. The benzenoid ring is resistant to oxidation and also to catalytic hydrogenation at least under the conditions usually applied in the removal of benzyl or benzyloxycarbonyl groups. Thus, treatment with hydrogen in the presence of a palladium catalyst at room temperature for a few hours leaves phenylalanine residues more or less intact (Keil *et al.*, 1962). If for the removal of a somewhat resistant protecting group, such as the benzyl group on the imidazole nucleus of histidine, the time of hydrogenation is extended (Ondetti *et al.*, 1968), saturation of the ring can occur. In such a case (Windridge and Jorgensen, 1971) the prolonged hydrogenation was carried out at elevated pressure and in the presence of an unusually high amount of catalyst, and most of the phenylalanine in the peptide was converted to hexahydrophenylalanine (or β-cyclohexylalanine) before the histidine side chain was completely deblocked. Saturation of phenylalanine side chains by hydrogenation, extended for 10 days, was achieved (Schafer *et al.*, 1971), yielding cyclohexylalanine analogs of bradykinin.

During the introduction of the most classic protecting group, in the reaction of phenylalanine (sodium salt) with benzyl chlorocarbonate, the formation of a complex between the expected benzyloxycarbonyl-L-phenylalanine and its sodium salt was noted (Grassmann and Wünsch, 1958; Grommers and Arens, 1959; Goodman and Steuben, 1959a). The complex has a higher melting point than the desired benzyloxycarbonyl-amino acid, and it is soluble in organic solvents such as ethyl acetate. It cannot be readily changed into the desired acid, therefore its formation should be prevented (cf. Brown and Wade, 1962). Similar complexes were observed with benzyloxycarbonylglycine, benzyloxycarbonylalanine, benzyloxycarbonyl-L-lysine, and their potassium or sodium salts (Grommers and Arens, 1959) and also between the sodium salts of benzyloxycarbonyl-L-valine (Grassmann and Wünsch, 1958), benzyloxycarbonyl-DL-phenyllanine, formyl-DL-phenylalanine (Goodman and Steuben, 1959a), benzyloxycarbonyl-L-serine (Brown and Wade, 1962), and benzyloxycarbonyl-L-tryptophan (M. Bodanszky, unpublished observations, 1959) and the corresponding acids.

E. Tyrosine

The presence of a hydroxyl group in the aromatic ring of the tyrosine side chain renders the nucleus sensitive to electrophilic aromatic substitution. Alkylation of the ring occurred on heating tyrosine-containing peptides with trifluoroacetic acid in order to remove benzyl and benzyloxycarbonyl groups (Weygand and Steglich, 1959). Benzyl trifluoroacetate was assumed to be the reactive intermediate in the substitution reaction, which could be suppressed by the addition of phenol, anisole, or resorcinol. Subsequently, the presence of 3-benzyltyrosine (**23**) was noted on paper chromatograms when tyrosine-containing peptides protected with benzyl or benzyloxycarbonyl groups were hydrolyzed with hot hydrochloric acid (HCl) (Iselin, 1962).

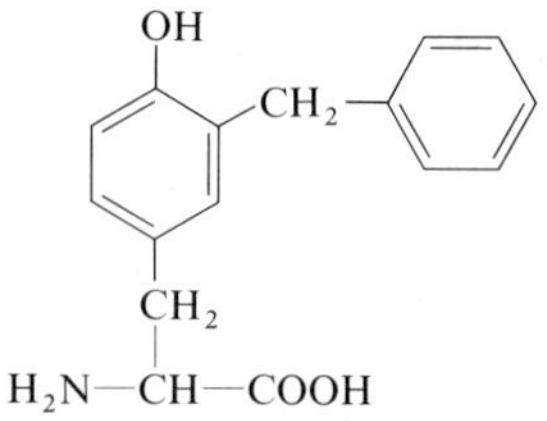

(23)

This side reaction, however, is not limited to treatment with hot acids. Under the usual, relatively mild conditions of acidolysis used for the removal of acid-labile protecting groups similar alkylation of tyrosine was observed time and again. Although, interestingly, deblocking with hydrobromic acid (HBr) in glacial *acetic acid* (Ben Ishai and Berger, 1952) leads to no noticeable C-benzylation of tyrosine, HBr in *trifluoroacetic acid* (Guttmann and Boissonnas, 1959) can produce considerable amounts of 3-benzyltyrosine (**23**). In neat trifluoroacetic acid *O*-benzyltyrosine suffers fairly rapid loss of the benzyl group with its concomitant migration to the carbon atom ortho to the hydroxyl group. Loss of protection and aromatic substitution are suppressed in a 7:3 mixture of trifluoroacetic acid and acetic acid. In liquid hydrogen fluoride (HF) this side reaction must be prevented by the addition of scavengers (Sakakibara *et al.*, 1967). The scavenger most frequently used, anisole, however, is not really suitable for capturing the benzyl group in HF because it can lose the methyl group in strong acids and cause methylation for example, on the sulfur atom of methionine (Irie *et al.*, 1977), without completely preventing substitution of tyrosine (Trudelle and Spach, 1972). A more useful scavenger is methyl ethyl sulfide or dithiothreitol (Yajima *et al.*, 1974) or the recently recommended thioanisole (Bauer and Pless, 1975; Kiso *et al.*, 1978; Yajima *et al.*, 1979a; Kiso *et al.*, 1980).

Benzylation is not the only substitution that can affect the aromatic nucleus of tyrosine. The ring can also be attacked by nitrous acid (Schnabel and Zahn, 1957; Bonnet and Nicolaidou, 1979) during the conversion of hydrazides to azides. The O-acylation of tyrosine by the 4-methoxybenzenesulfonyl group used for protection of the guanidino function in arginine side chains (Nishimura and Fujino, 1976; Takeyama *et al.*, 1979) could be the cause of subsequent C-acylation as well. Even the hindered *tert*-butyl group can alkylate the tyrosine side chain (Lundt *et al.*, 1979). Hydroxyl protecting groups that can be removed by methods other than acidolysis hold more promise in this respect. For instance, the 4-dimethylcarbamoylbenzyl group (Chauhan *et al.*, 1980) proposed for protection of the side-chain functions in serine, threonine, and tyrosine residues is removable by hydrogenolysis, but it is more resistant to acids than the unsubstituted benzyl group.

In solid-phase peptide synthesis (Merrifield, 1963) where long chains often have to be assembled, mostly by stepwise strategy (Bodanszky, 1960), the cumulative effect of C-alkylation of several tyrosine residues is a cause for serious concern (cf. Sørup *et al.*, 1979). Therefore, new protecting groups have been designed for masking of the phenolic hydroxyl group in tyrosine by investigators active in this area. Benzyl groups with halogen substituents were proposed simultaneously by Yamashiro and Li (1973a) and by Erickson and Merrifield (1973). A series of cycloalkyl ethers were also examined

(Engelhard and Merrifield, 1978) from the point of view of their readiness or inertness in the substitution reaction, and the cyclohexyl ether of tyrosine was selected as the least likely to cause this, much feared, side reaction.

Although C-benzylation of tyrosine during acidolytic deprotection of *O*-benzyltyrosine residues is often called "benzyl migration," the reaction, at least under the conditions of peptide synthesis, is probably more inter- than intramolecular. The observation that this side reaction can be suppressed by scavengers or practically eliminated in appropriately selected solvents suggests a mainly intermolecular pathway (cf. also Spanninger and von Rosenberg, 1972). Therefore, not only the protecting group used for the hydroxyl in tyrosine but all other protecting groups as well must be chosen judiciously in tyrosine-containing peptides: They should not give rise to alkylating agents during their removal. Alternatively, deprotection must be carried out in the presence of efficient scavengers or in a solvent such as acetic acid (Ben Ishai and Berger, 1952) or a mixture of phenol and 4-cresol (Bodanszky *et al.*, 1978), which can capture the alkyl cations generated during acidolysis.

The nucleophilic character of the phenolic hydroxyl group, particularly in the presence of base, is sufficient to permit it to compete with the amino group for acylating agents. Thus, the reaction of 4-toluenesulfonyl chloride with tyrosine under alkaline conditions yields *N*,*O*-ditosyltyrosine (Fischer, 1915), and benzyl chlorocarbonate affords *N*,*O*-dibenzyloxycarbonyltyrosine (Abderhalden and Bahn, 1933; Katchalski and Sela, 1953). However, *O*-acylation of tyrosine also occurs with less powerful acylating agents, for example, in dicyclohexylcarbodiimide-mediated couplings (Okawa, 1956) and in acylations with carbonyldiimidazole (Paul, 1963). When used in excess and in the presence of base, even such moderately reactive reagents as active esters can acylate the phenolic hydroxyl of tyrosine (Ramachandran and Li, 1963; Agarwal *et al.*, 1969b). The conditions conducive to this latter version of the side reaction, the effect of solvents, the nature of the active ester used, and so on, were the subject of a sustained study by Girin and Shvachkin (1977a,b, 1978a,b, 1979a,b). Since O-acylation of tyrosine seems to require abstraction of the proton from the hydroxyl group, compounds with a higher affinity for the tertiary amines present in the reaction mixture can prevent or at least considerably suppress this undesired side reaction. Pentachlorophenol and 2,4-dinitrophenol are quite effective in this respect (Martinez *et al.*, 1979a). Also, one should not forget that, although O-acylation of tyrosine is indeed undesirable, the acyl groups can still be readily removed from the peptide by alkaline hydrolysis, ammonolysis, hydrazinolysis, and so on, under rather mild conditions.*

* Of course removal of such an acyl group by aminolysis, that is, acylation of α-amino groups, is also possible. For the same reason, acyl groups are not really suitable for the protection of tyrosine side chains.

F. Tryptophan

The well-known sensitivity of indole to oxidation under acidic conditions often leads to more-or-less severe decomposition of tryptophan. For instance, the usual acid hydrolysis of peptides or proteins necessary for amino acid analysis results in a mixture lacking tryptophan, and if the tryptophan content of the sample has to be determined in a hydrolysate, special precautions must be taken, such as hydrolysis in the complete absence of air. Alternatively, chemically pure hydrochloric acid must be used or sulfonic acids, rather than the hydrochloric acid usually employed in hydrolysis. Acidolytic cleavage of protecting groups can cause similar decomposition. This side reaction is less serious if acidolysis is carried out at a low temperature and in an inert atmosphere (e.g., Yajima *et al.*, 1970). The addition of scavengers can further suppress oxidative decomposition (Marshall, 1968; Li and Yamashiro, 1970; Blake *et al.*, 1972; Noda and Gross, 1972; Stewart and Matsueda, 1972; Sharp *et al.*, 1973; Bauer and Pless, 1975). A whole series of reducing agents, various mercaptans, phenols, thiophenol, thioanisole, dialkyl sulfides, and so on, have been recommended, and of course the harm can be "diluted" by the addition of indole or skatole. Selection of the acid used for acidolytic deblocking should be guided by the presence or absence of tryptophan residue(s) in the protected peptide. Thus, although considerable damage to tryptophan can occur in solutions of HBr in acetic or in trifluoroacetic acid (Theodoropoulos and Fruton, 1962; Wünsch, 1959), deprotection with neat trifluoroacetic acid or with HCl in formic acid (Ohno *et al.*, 1972a,b) or with organic sulfonic acids (Loffet and Dremier, 1971; Suzuki *et al.*, 1978) is relatively harmless. The noxious effect of HBr in acetic or trifluoroacetic acid may be due to the free bromine that forms in these reagents. The addition of phenol or triethyl phosphite eliminates this harmful impurity (Boissonnas *et al.*, 1958; Wünsch, 1959; Neumann *et al.*, 1959).

Substitution of the indole ring with acyl groups on the nitrogen atom can reduce its sensitivity to oxidative degradation. So far only the formyl group has been used as an easily removable protecting group (Previero *et al.*, 1967), and its effectiveness is not beyond question (Rees and Offord, 1976). Nevertheless, experience in several laboratories (Yamashiro and Li, 1973b; Ohno *et al.*, 1973; Lemaire *et al.*, 1976; Löw and Kisfaludy, 1979) indicates that protected tryptophan residues have at least some advantages over unprotected ones. Introduction of the formyl group with HCl in formic acid yields the formyl derivative (**24**) in a straightforward manner, but removal of the formyl protection with nucleophiles such as liquid ammonia, hydrazine, tertiary amines, or aqueous piperidine can cause some transfer of the formyl group from the indole to an α-amino group (Yamashiro and Li, 1973b):

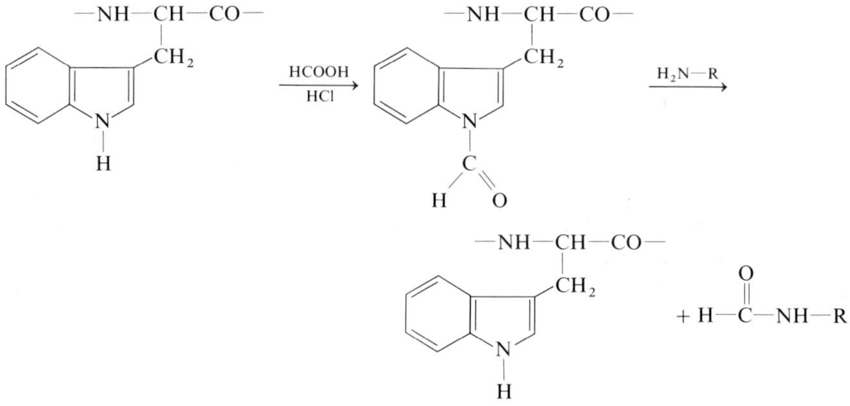

(24)

When catalytic hydrogenation is used for deprotection, reduction of the ring to 2,3-dihydroindole derivatives can occur (Löw and Kisfaludy, 1979).* Catalytic reduction of the nucleus in the presence of platinum oxide had been known earlier (Keil *et al.*, 1962). Because of these shortcomings of formyl protection, attempts to develop other blocking groups for the tryptophan side chain are certainly justified. Protection of the indole nitrogen by the benzyloxycarbonyl group (Chorev and Klausner, 1976) can be carried out in the presence of crown ethers, but the value of this new application of the benzyloxycarbonyl group still has to be established in actual syntheses.

Protection of the indole through acylation of its nitrogen atom, in addition to inhibiting oxidative degradation, might also prevent electrophilic substitution in the aromatic system. Thus, *tert*-butylation of the ring did not occur during acidolytic removal of protecting groups based on formation of the *tert*-butyl cation (Löw and Kisfaludy, 1979) if N^i-formyltryptophan rather than tryptophan was used in the synthesis. The occurrence of *tert*-butylation has been noted before (Kessler and Iselin, 1966; Sieber, 1968; Alakhov *et al.*, 1970; Wünsch *et al.*, 1972). It is quite pronounced in trifluoroacetic acid, and less so in solutions of HCl in ethyl acetate or in acetic acid. The nature of the alkylating agent was studied by Lundt *et al.* (1978) who showed that *tert*-butylation was due not to isobutene or to the direct action of *tert*-butyl cations but rather to the action of *tert*-butyl trifluoroacetate. This is in agreement with the assumptions of Weygand and Steglich (1959) who postulated the formation of benzyl trifluoroacetate in the removal of benzyl or benzyloxycarbonyl groups with hot trifluoroacetic acid and

* Hydrogenation over extended periods can lead to complete saturation of the indole side chain (Bajusz *et al.*, 1973).

attributed the observed benzylation of tyrosine to the alkylating effect of the ester. An extensive study carried out by two laboratories in collaboration (Wünsch *et al.*, 1977; Löw *et al.*, 1978a,b; Jaeger *et al.*, 1978a,b,c) was reviewed by Kisfaludy (1979). Alkylation of tryptophyl residues by *tert*-butyl groups was followed by nmr spectroscopy and concluded with isolation of the alkylated derivatives. Surprisingly, it was found that over and above the already known substitution of the nitrogen atom of the indole nucleus (**25**) alkylation proceeded even to the production of 2,5,7-trisubstituted indoles. The trisubstituted tryptophan (**26**) was isolated in crystalline form. The same

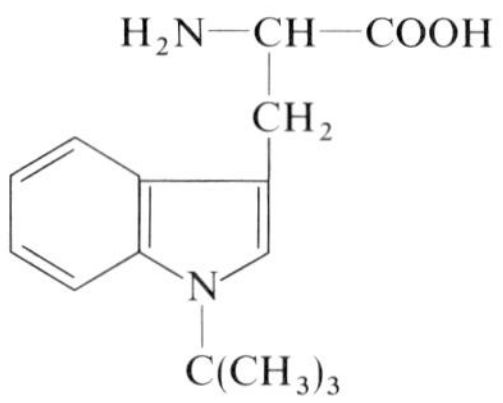

(**25**)

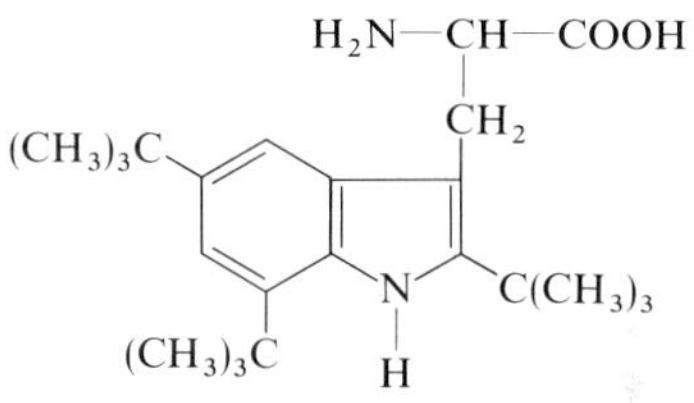

(**26**)

investigations revealed that alkylation was particularly severe when HF or boron tris(trifluoroacetate) (Pless and Bauer, 1973) was used as an acidic reagent in the removal of protecting groups, and that much less substitution took place in trifluoroacetic acid but the side reaction was still serious. Solutions of mercaptosulfonic acids, for example, mercaptoethanesulfonic acid (Loffet and Dremier, 1971), cause less harm and alkylation is negligible if HCl in acetic acid is used for cleavage. The situation is quite different, however, in the presence of scavengers (Masui *et al.*, 1980): The addition of 1,2-ethanedithiol in excess completely suppresses alkylation in HF but not in trifluoroacetic acid. In the latter however, *tert*-butylation can be avoided with a combination of two scavengers, 1,2-ethanedithiol and dimethyl sulfide. The experience gained with the use of scavengers suggested that the N^i-*tert*-butyl derivative is the alkylating intermediate in C-substitution of the ring. Of course other electrophiles can also cause substitution of the indole in the tryptophan side chain. For example, removal of 4-methoxybenzyloxycarbonyl groups with trifluoroacetic acid produced tryptophyl residues substituted by 4-methoxybenzyl groups in position 2′ and others with substituents in positions 2′ and 5′ or in 2′, 5′, and 7′, but not in position 1′ (Ogawa *et al.*, 1978). A scavenger system consisting of thioanisole, 1,2-ethanedithiol, and skatole reduced the extent of the side reaction in trifluoroacetic acid, and was even more effective when ethanesulfonic acid was used for acidolysis.

Because of the well-known sensitivity of 3-substituted indoles to sulfenyl halides (Wieland *et al.*, 1954) it is not too surprising that the highly reactive

2-nitrophenylsulfenyl chloride that forms during removal of the 2-nitrophenylsulfenyl (Nps) group with HCl in organic solvents attacks the side chain of tryptophan residues. A quantitative reaction of this sulfenyl chloride with the indole nucleus resulting in 2-(2-nitrophenylsulfenyl)indole derivatives (**27**) was reported by Anderson *et al.* (1965). The same side reaction

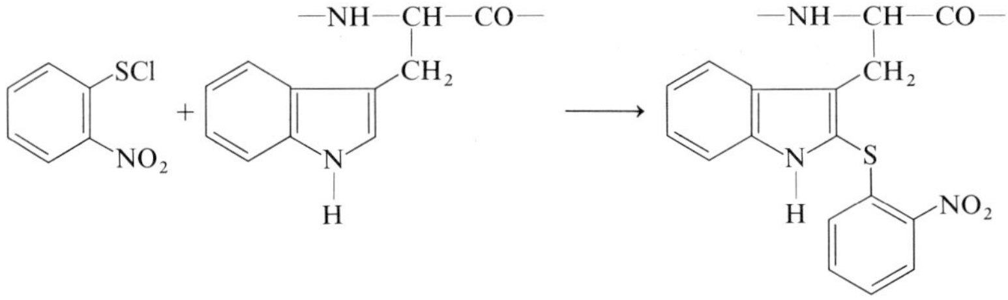

(**27**)

received more attention in subsequent studies (Wünsch *et al.*, 1967; Scoffone *et al.*, 1968). The formation of 2-(2-nitrophenylsulfenyl)tryptophan (**28**) in the attempted preparation of Nps-Trp from the sulfenyl chloride and the amino acid was also observed (Fontana *et al.*, 1966b):

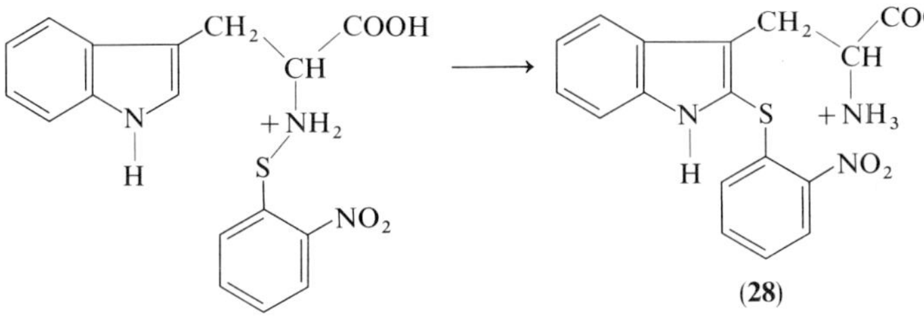

(**28**)

Nevertheless, the presence of tryptophan residues in a peptide should not exclude use of the 2-nitrophenylsulfenyl group in the protection of the α-amino function of other amino acid constituents of the target molecule. If, instead of HCl in an organic solvent, a nucleophilic reagent such as thioacetamide (Kessler and Iselin, 1966), thiophenol, or thioglycolic acid (Fontana *et al.*, 1966a,c; Wünsch *et. al.*, 1967) is used for deprotection, no sulfenyl halide will form, hence the side reaction described here does not occur. More recently, improved nucleophilic reagents were used for the same purpose, namely, 3-nitro-4-mercaptobenzoic acid (Juillerat and Bargetzi, 1976) and 2-mercaptopyridine (pyridine-2-thione) (Tun-Kyi, 1978) which eliminate the 2-nitrophenyl-sulfenyl group in the form of innocuous disulfides. A more general consideration of the sensitivity of tryptophan toward substitution is also possible. Protecting groups that on acidolytic removal do not generate alkylating or acylating agents (Kenner *et al.*, 1976) could become important tools in the synthesis of tryptophan-containing peptides. An even greater advantage can be expected from the use of a base-sensitive protecting group such as the 9-fluorenylmethyloxycarbonyl group (Carpino and Han, 1972), which does not involve exposure of the peptide to acids and hence circumvents the oxidative degradation problem as well.

The effect of acidic media prevailing during deprotection by acidolysis extends beyond oxidative degradation or substitution in the indole ring. For instance, N^{α}-acetyltryptophan can cyclize in trifluoroacetic acid to give 1-methyl-3,4-dihydro-β-carboline-3-carboxylic acid (**29**) which on exposure to light and oxygen is dehydrogenated to 1-methylcarboline-3-carboxylic acid (**30**) (Uphaus *et al.*, 1959):

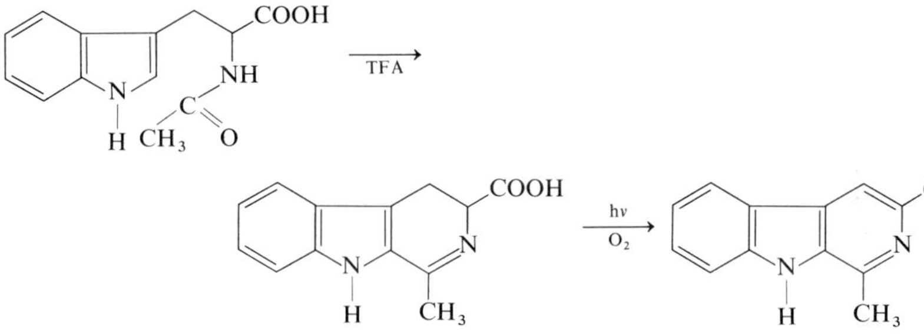

(**29**) (**30**)

In an analogous manner N^{α}-formyltryptophan (**31**) in the presence of HCl in anhydrous formic acid yields N^{α},N^{i}-diformyltryptophan (**32**) together with 3,4-dihydrocarboline-3-carboxylic acid (**33**) (Previero *et al.*, 1968). In aqueous HCl–HCOOH **32** is partially deformylated to **31** which in turn is cyclized to **33**. Peptides with tryptophan at their NH_2-terminus are also prone to such conversions.

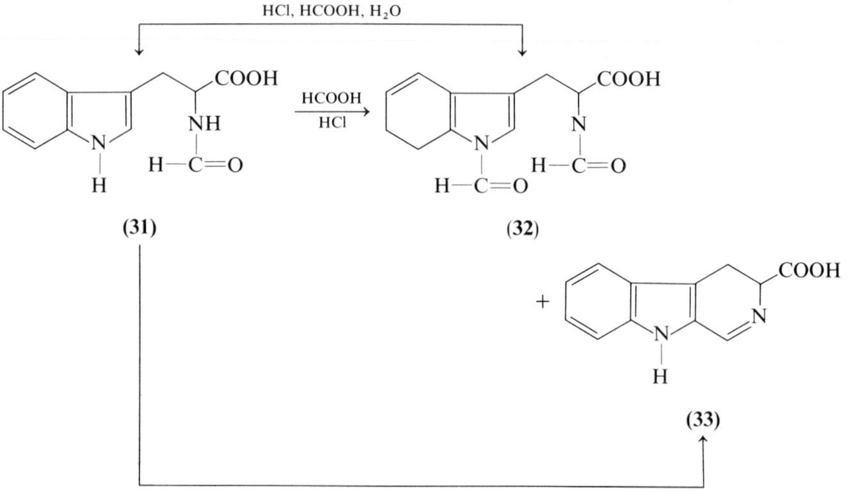

Reactions that may affect the integrity of tryptophan residues are reported time and again in the literature: conversion of the 2-acyl derivatives into β-carbolines (Previero *et al.*, 1972), photocyclization to pyrroloindoles (**34**)

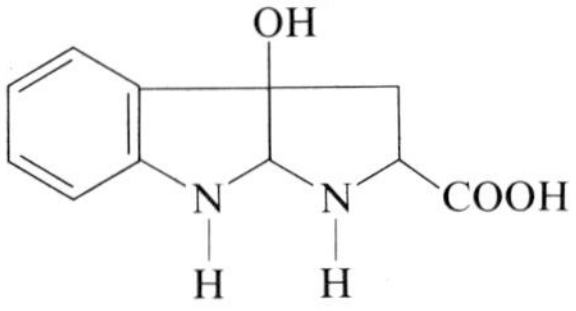

(**34**)

during acid hydrolysis or exposure to near-uv light (Sun and Zigman, 1979), and conversion of the methyl ester of N^{α}-acetyltryptophan in trifluoroacetic acid (Omori *et al.*, 1976) to **35** and its geometric isomer (Hashizume and Shimonishi, 1980) **36**. These reports call for concern and care when otherwise

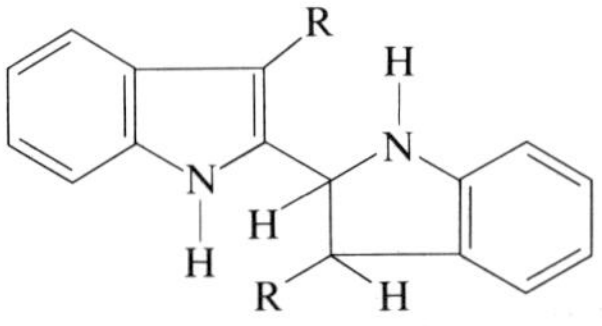

(**35**)

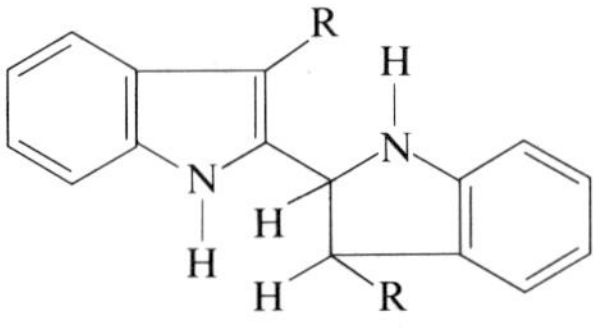

(**36**)

$$R = CH_3{-}CO{-}NH{-}\overset{|}{C}H{-}COOCH_3$$

perhaps innocuous operations are carried out on tryptophan-containing peptides. Similarly, the effect of nitrous acid on tryptophan residues (Zahn and Brandenburg, 1966; Agarwal *et al.*, 1969a) must be kept in mind when the azide method is applied.

The chemistry of tryptophan in peptides and proteins has been reviewed (Fontana and Toniolo, 1976).

G. Histidine

The imidazole ring in the side chain of histidine is often left without protection. Yet, neither the basic character nor the nucleophilicity of the two nitrogen atoms in an aromatic system can be completely ignored. On the other hand, the various groups used to protect the histidine side chain usually suffer from some disadvantages. For instance, the most well-known group, the *im*-benzyl group, is relatively resistant to hydrogenolysis. Although no problems were encountered in several laboratories where the *im*-benzyl group was smoothly removed by catalytic hydrogenation (e.g., Theodoropoulos, 1956), other investigators (e.g., Bricas and Nicot-Cutton, 1960; Kappeler, 1961; Kopple *et al.*, 1963) found this cleavage sluggish or incomplete even after extended reaction times. The discrepancy among the experiences of different researchers might be due to subtle experimental details, but it could also be caused by the presence of the two possible *im*-benzyl derivatives of histidine (**37** and **38**) in varying amounts (Fletcher *et al.*, 1979;

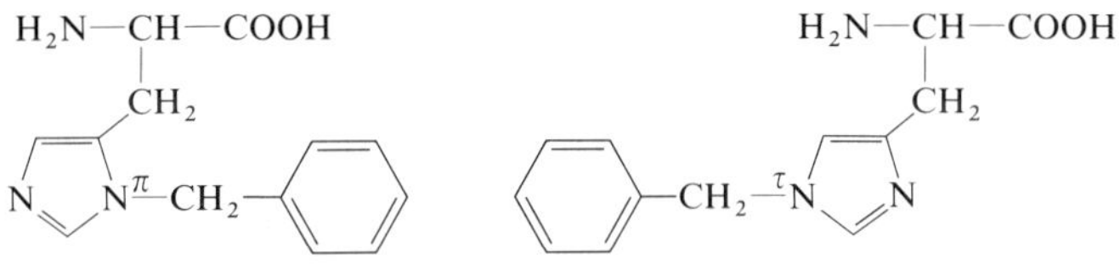

(**37**) (**38**)

π = N^{im}-pros protection
τ = N^{im}-tele protection

Grønvald *et al.*, 1981). The two derivatives might differ with respect to the formation of palladium complexes devoid of catalytic activity, as are unprotected imidazoles, depending on their position. For example, removal of the benzyl group from NH_2-terminal histidine residues is quite slow (Li *et al.*, 1960). The influence of steric factors on the hydrogenolysis of *im*-benzyl groups has already been postulated (Kopple *et al.*, 1963).

Several more imidazole-protecting groups have been mentioned in the literature (Geiger and König, 1981; Brown and Jones, 1981; Brown *et al.*, 1982) but not enough experience has accumulated so far to allow a fair evaluation of most of them. Thus, methods of protection such as the *im*-toluenesulfonyl group (Fujii *et al.*, 1976) and blocking by the 4-methoxybenzenesulfonyl group (Kitagawa *et al.*, 1979) require further scrutiny before they can be fully accepted for peptide synthesis in general. One should keep in mind that acylimidazoles are powerful acylating agents and therefore, with any *im*-acyl group used for protection, the possibility of premature loss with concomitant transfer to α-amino groups has to be considered. In this connection the lability of *im*-*tert*-butyloxycarbonyl groups toward amines (Penke *et al.*, 1973) and the limited shelf-life of N^{α},N^{im}-dibenzyloxycarbonylhistidine (Sakiyama, 1962) should serve as warning. The reactivity of acylimidazoles is also demonstrated in the lactam (**39**) produced in the reaction of N^{α}-protected histidine with dicyclohexylcarbodiimide (Sheehan *et al.*,

1959):

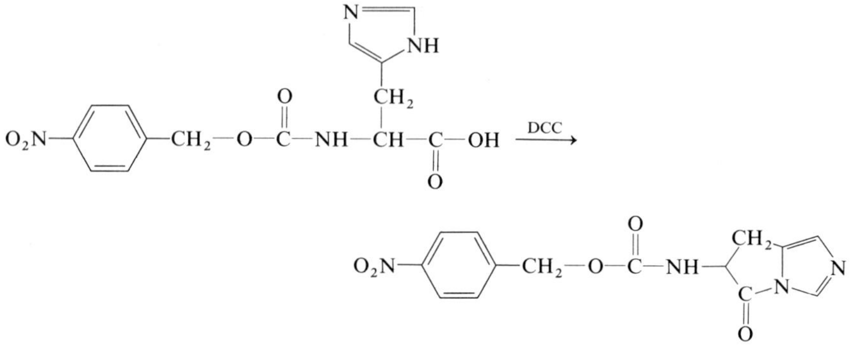

(**39**)

The lactam ring of **39** is opened up by nucleophiles, and it can be used as an acylating agent in the preparation of peptides.*

Because protection of the imidazole moiety in histidine is still in the developmental stage, one might prefer to work with histidine derivatives unprotected in their side chains. Unfortunately, such derivatives also can cause several side reactions. The catalytic effect of imidazole in transesterification reactions (cf., e.g., Stewart, 1968b) leads to significant O-acylation of serine residues in histidine-containing peptides if these are lengthened with the help of active esters (Bodanszky *et al.*, 1977). Also, the addition of imidazole to dicyclohexylcarbodiimide (Rink and Riniker, 1974) resulting in the substituted guanidine (**40**) occurs with derivatives of histidine, for example,

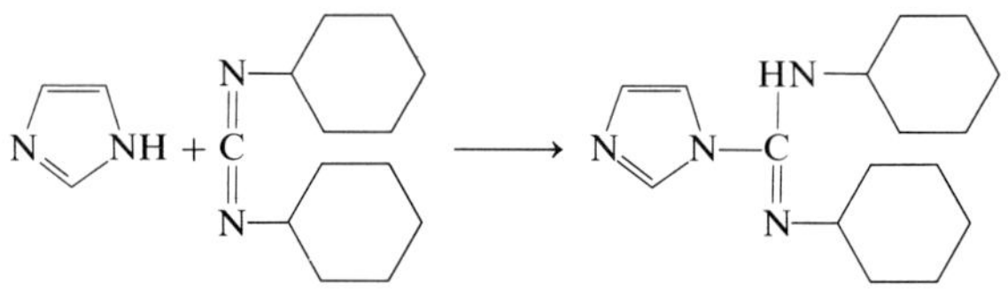

(**40**)

tert-butyloxycarbonylhistidine methyl ester as well. Although the addition product can be cleaved with trifluoroacetic acid, with liquid HF (Ivanov *et al.*, 1976), and also with hot methanol (Rink and Riniker, 1974), it should still cause some concern because of the extreme basicity of derivatives of guanidine. Last but not least, unprotected imidazoles are good catalysts of hydrolytic processes (Bruice and Bruno, 1962), hence they can effect autolytic

* An analogous lactam formation involving an acid azide and the NH group of an unprotected histidine side chain was observed (Merrifield and Woolley, 1956) in Z-Ser-His-N_3.

cleavage of the chain in histidine-containing peptides. This not too rarely observed phenomenon is exemplified here in the splitting of and concomitant diketopiperazine formation from histidylprolylphenylalanine methyl ester (Mazur and Schlatter, 1963) in aqueous acetic acid:

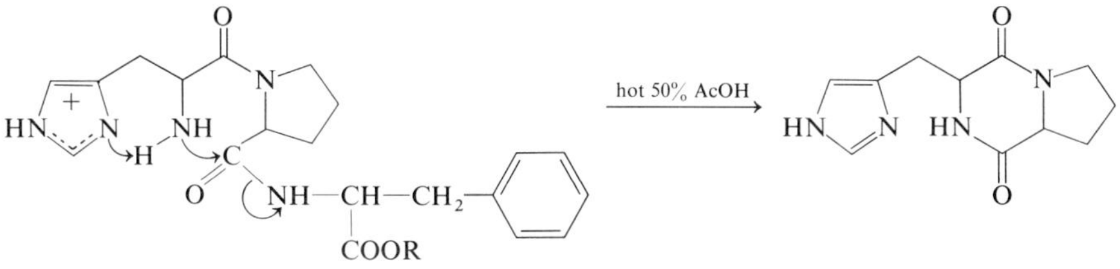

H. Lysine

The need to protect the ε-amino group in the lysine side chain is obvious. With respect to basicity or nucleophilic character this group is too similar to α-amino groups to permit selective acylation of one of them. For instance, during the addition of protecting groups to the ε-amino function of lysine its α-amino group must be complexed with copper. A notable exception is trifluoroacetylation of the ε-amino of lysine with ethyl thiotrifluoroacetate (Schallenberg and Calvin, 1955). The ε-amino group, being at the end of a four-carbon side chain, is readily accessible to acylating and alkylating agents. Therefore its protection must be given careful consideration. As classic solution to the problem of semipermanent blocking of the lysine side chain function, the 4-toluenesulfonyl group seems to be excellent, because it remains unaffected during the removal of α-amino protecting groups by acidolysis or hydrogenolysis. However, sulfonamides are not inert: The remaining hydrogen atom of the amino group is rather acidic and, if abstracted by base, allows the introduction of a second substituent. At least in one instance such a side reaction was noted (Cipera, 1961). Complete protection of the lysine side chain can be achieved by diacylation, for example, by the phthalyl group, except for a serious disadvantage of phthalyl protection, shared by several other blocking groups, that is, a decrease in the solubility of the protected intermediates in organic solvents, including dimethylformamide. A reasonable compromise is the use of a urethane-type protecting groups, such as the benzyloxycarbonyl (Z) group which, unlike the tosyl group, does not increase the reactivity of the amide. Branching of peptide chains at lysine residues protected by the benzyloxycarbonyl group indeed does not occur, although some substitution of the amino groups by benzyl groups in the process of deprotection by acidolysis has been observed

(Mitchell and Merrifield, 1976). Alkylation can be suppressed by the use of methanesulfonic acid in the presence of thioanisole (Fujii *et al.*, 1977).

The most frequently encountered side reaction in connection with lysine is the branching of the peptide chain caused by partial loss of ε-amino protection followed by ε-acylation during incorporation of the next amino acid or peptide (e.g., Yaron and Schlossman, 1968). The combination of *tert*-butyloxycarbonyl (Boc) protection for α-amino groups and benzyloxycarbonyl blocking of the lysine side chain function was found to be imperfect by several investigators who tried and recommended various remedies. The use of 98% formic acid for the removal of *tert*-butyloxycarbonyl groups was proposed by Halpern and Nitecki (1967), and a solution of 2-mercaptoethanesulfonic acid by Loffet and Dremier (1971). Solutions of HCl in acetic acid were found to be more selective than trifluoroacetic acid in one laboratory (Grahl-Nielsen and Tritsch, 1969), but not in another (Yaron and Schlossman, 1968). Deblocking of α-amino groups with trifluoroacetic acid (a reagent with excellent solvent properties) could be obtained with only slight damage to N^{ε}-benzyloxycarbonyl groups when the reagent was diluted with water (Schnabel *et al.*, 1971) or acetic acid (Klausner and Bodanszky, 1973). Complete prevention of the loss of protection of the N^{ε}-benzyloxycarbonyl group could not be achieved with such dilution techniques. Some premature removal of the blocking occurs also in mixtures of trifluoroacetic acid and dichloromethane (Gutte and Merrifield, 1971). More satisfactory resistance to acidolysis by trifluoroacetic acid was achieved by the introduction of benzyloxycarbonyl groups provided with electron-withdrawing substituents. The *p*-chlorobenzyloxycarbonyl (Boissonnas and Preitner, 1953) and 4-nitrobenzyloxycarbonyl groups (Carpenter and Gish, 1952) were known to be quite stable toward acids, and a reexamination of benzyloxycarbonyl groups carrying various halogen substituents led to selection of the 2-bromobenzyloxycarbonyl group (Yamashiro and Li, 1973c) and the 2-chlorobenzyloxycarbonyl (and also the 2,4- and 3,4-dichlorobenzyloxycarbonyl) groups (Erickson and Merrifield, 1973). Additional acid-resistant blocking groups can be found, such as the diisopropylmethyloxycarbonyl group (Sakakibara *et al.*, 1970), that are removable by HF. A general problem related to these acid-resistant blocking groups is that they require extremely strong acids for their removal and, even with HF, a longer treatment or higher temperature might be necessary than is desirable for the integrity of the product. Therefore it seems to be more promising to turn to protecting groups that can semipermanently block the lysine side-chain function because they are completely inert to acids and yet are readily removed by the action of bases or nucleophiles under mild conditions. The trifluoroacetyl group (Weygand and Csendes, 1952), the methylsulfonylethyloxycarbonyl group (Tesser and Balvert-Geers, 1975), and the 9-fluorenylmethyloxycarbonyl group (Carpino and Han, 1972) are particularly promising in this respect.

I. Arginine

The guanidino group is rather exceptional among organic bases: Only under extreme conditions does it exist in an unprotonated form. Therefore, although acylation of the guanidine nitrogens can be achieved (Photaki and Yiotakis, 1976), it does not occur as a side reaction in the mildly basic milieu that prevails in most coupling reactions. On the other hand, intramolecular acylation of the guanidino group, yielding δ-lactams, is very common in activated derivatives of arginine. Protonation of the guanidino group is not sufficient to prevent this cyclization. Moreover, lactam formation takes place even in arginine derivatives with protected side chains. Thus, the classic method of protection, nitration of the guanidino group, does not exclude its intramolecular acylation. This might be the reason for the limited use of nitroarginine for a long period after its introduction in peptide synthesis. It served as an amino component but could not be used in acylation until the advent of mild methods of activation (cf. Gish and Carpenter, 1953; Hofmann *et al.*, 1953; Van Orden and Smith, 1954). Yet, even with moderate activation cyclization can occur, as shown by the formation of piperidone **41** (Bodanszky and Sheehan, 1960; Paul *et al.*, 1961) during the attempted

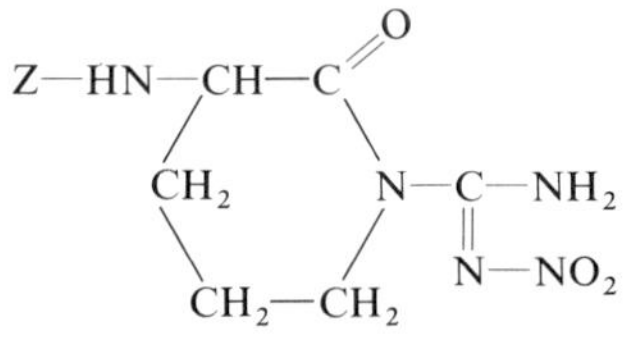

(41)

preparation of active esters of benzyloxycarbonylnitroarginine. An analogous piperidone is generated in the activation of the hindered N^{α}-tritylnitroarginine (Rittel, 1962) as well. Still, cyclization of activated derivatives of nitroarginine and the production of lactams do not exclude their use in peptide synthesis. It merely necessitates their application in sufficient excess to allow complete acylation of the amino component. Removal of the lactam side products is usually a simple operation. The nitro group, unlike several other protecting groups proposed for blocking the guanidino function, improves the solubility of arginine peptides in organic solvents. Therefore, it is rather unfortunate that masking the side-chain function in arginine by the nitro group suffers from additional shortcomings as well. The resonance stabilization of guanidine is only slightly affected by alkyl substituents, and thus it is fairly intact in arginine which is sensitive only to supernucleophiles such as hydrazine. In nitroarginine, however, this stabilization is greatly reduced and the nitroguanidino group is readily attacked by acids and bases. Acid hydrolysis of nitroarginine-containing peptides results in a hydrolysate in which, in addition to nitroarginine, its degradation products, arginine and ornithine, are also present. Even more concern must be felt about the effect of nucleophiles. Hydrazinolysis of esters of nitroarginine-containing peptides fails to yield the expected hydrazides (McKay, 1952) but leads to the formation of ornithine residues (Boissonnas *et al.*, 1960). Decomposition of the nitroguanidino group also takes place during ammonolysis (Künzi *et al.*, 1974) and during reduction with sodium in liquid ammonia (Tritsch and Wooley, 1960). However, not only activation and coupling of nitroarginine-containing peptides is fraught with difficulties: The removal of this protecting group is often less than straightforward. Deblocking by catalytic hydrogenation follows a complex course (Iselin, 1966); it is slow (Bergmann *et al.*, 1934; Berse *et al.*, 1960) and can produce, in addition to arginine derivatives, some aminoguanidine-containing residues (Gros *et al.*, 1961; Scopes *et al.*, 1965; Turan *et al.*, 1975). Similar side products also appear in the electrolytic reduction of nitroarginine peptides (Gros *et al.*, 1961; Scopes *et al.*, 1965) and even in the process of deblocking with zinc in acetic acid (Turan *et al.*, 1975). Better results were reported for reduction with stannous chloride in formic acid (Hayakawa *et al.*, 1967) and titanium trichloride in methanol (Freidinger *et al.*, 1978).

The shortcomings of protection of the guanidino group in the form of nitroarginine prompted numerous attempts to develop more efficient methods of protection. Thus, N^g-toluenesulfonyl- or tosylarginine is less conducive to the formation of ornithine derivatives than nitroarginine in the final deblocking of peptides with liquid HF (Yamashiro *et al.*, 1972). Electrolytic reduction of the tosyl group, however, failed to prevent the loss of tosylguanyl groups and the appearance of ornithine residues (Pless and Guttmann, 1967). The 4-methoxybenzenesulfonyl group (Nishimura and Fujino, 1976), although more readily removable by acidolysis than the related but very acid-resistant tosyl group, was found to have been transferred during acidolysis to the phenolic hydroxyl of tyrosine residues. A further modified version of tosyl protection, the N^g-mesitylene-2-sulfonyl group (Yajima *et al.*, 1978, 1979b), causes less O-acylation.

A priori it seems that acyl groups derived from carbonic acid half-esters should produce more inert guanidines than substitution with aromatic sulfonic acids, yet N^α,N^g-dibenzyloxycarbonylarginine is not exempt from lactam formation (Zervas *et al.*, 1959b), and the tribenzyloxycarbonyl derivative can lose one of the protecting groups to yield the same unsafe dibenzyloxycarbonylarginine (Nicolaides and De Wald, 1961). Blocking with bulky protecting groups brings about some improvements. Thus, triadamantyloxycarbonylarginine is better protected against side reactions characteristic of arginine than the corresponding benzyloxycarbonyl compound (Geiger *et al.*, 1969). Protection of the guanidine with the isobornyloxycarbonyl group interfered, however, with hydrogenolytic removal of the benzyloxycarbonyl group on the α-amino group of the same arginine residue (Jäger and Geiger, 1973).

J. Serine and Threonine

The alcoholic hydroxyl groups in the side chains of serine and threonine residues are not strong enough nucleophiles to compete efficiently with the amino group for the acylating agent. Therefore, at least in principle, these hydroxyl groups might be left unprotected. Indeed, for a considerable time it was generally believed that acylation of a peptide with moderately activated derivatives of amino acids, such as active esters, did not require protection of hydroxyl groups. Also, coupling reactions with dicyclohexylcarbodiimide as a condensing agent were successfully carried out on peptides containing unprotected serine or threonine residues (Sheehan *et al.*, 1956). However, with highly reactive derivatives of carboxyl components, such as the ones generated by carbodiimides, O-acylation can be avoided only if the acylating agent is used in an amount equimolar to the amino component. An *excess* of the acylating intermediate, used to ensure complete acylation of the amine (Bodanszky, 1971), will obviously cause O-acylation of serine and threonine side chains. The primary hydroxyl group of serine is more sensitive in this respect, whereas the secondary hydroxyl in threonine, shielded by the bulky methyl group, undergoes substitution less readily. In the presence of bases, for instance, tertiary amines often present in coupling mixtures, even moderately reactive intermediates such as active esters, can produce O-acylation because the alcohols are converted, in part, to alcoholates which are better nucleophiles [Eq. (2)]. This kind of O-acylation can be prevented by the

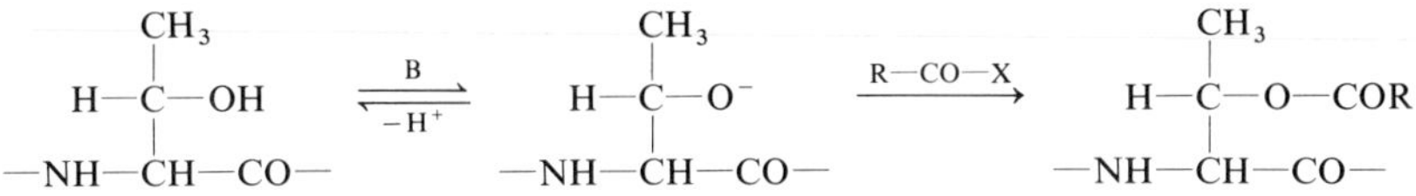

(2)

addition of compounds that have a specific affinity for tertiary bases and thus are able to interfere with proton abstraction from alcoholic hydroxyls. Pentachlorophenol and 2,4-dinitrophenol were found (Martinez *et al.*, 1979a) to be quite efficient in this respect. On the other hand O-acylation by active esters (Zahn *et al.*, 1965b; Garner *et al.*, 1971) is promoted by imidazole (Stewart, 1968b) or 1-hydroxybenzotriazole and can be rather extensive in histidine-containing peptides (Bodanszky *et al.*, 1977; Girin and Shvachkin, 1978a,b; 1979a,b). Such examples of undesired participation of the side chains of hydroxyamino acids suggest that the principle of minimal protection is not always applicable and that in many syntheses global protection is necessary (Sakakibara, 1977). This view prevails among practitioners of solid-phase peptide synthesis, who recommend protection of the less sensitive threonine residue (Hogue-Angeletti *et al.*, 1974; Hagenmaier and Frank, 1972b). Acylation of the hydroxyl group can be intramolecular as well. Thus lactone formation was noted on several occasions (Bodanszky and Ondetti, 1966; Young *et al.*, 1967).

For protection of the hydroxyl function its blocking in the form of benzyl ether is the most obvious solution. This method is indeed satisfactory as long as catalytic hydrogenation is used for the removal of protecting groups. In acidolysis, however, the classic reagent HBr in acetic acid (Ben Ishai and Berger, 1952) in addition to removing the benzyl group also causes some acetylation of the liberated hydroxyl, particularly in serine residues. This undesired acetylation is avoidable: It does not occur in solutions of HBr in trifluoroacetic acid (Guttmann and Boissonnas, 1959). Unfortunately this change in the medium enhances alkylation of the aromatic nucleus of tyrosine side chains, a side reaction that is neglible in HBr–acetic acid solutions. Of course O-acetylation (Okawa, 1957; Nicolaides and De Wald, 1963; Nicolaides *et al.*, 1963) is not an irreversible event. The acetyl group can be removed by the action of hydrazine or another nucleophile. At this point it should be mentioned that *O*-acetyl derivatives of serine peptides are formed even without the intervention of acetylating agents or catalysis by a strong acid such as HBr. The mere storage of an intermediate in solution in acetic acid can produce a considerable amount of *O*-acetyl derivatives with time. Such esterification, which is due to ester equilibrium, is much less extensive in threonine-containing peptides.

Intramolecular O-acylation of hydroxyl groups takes place in activated derivatives of serine. For instance, *N*-tritylserine was converted by carbodiimides (Sheehan *et al.*, 1959; Sheehan, 1960) to the corresponding lactone (**42**); such *β*-lactones are good acylating agents [Eq. (3)]. From *N*-benzyl-

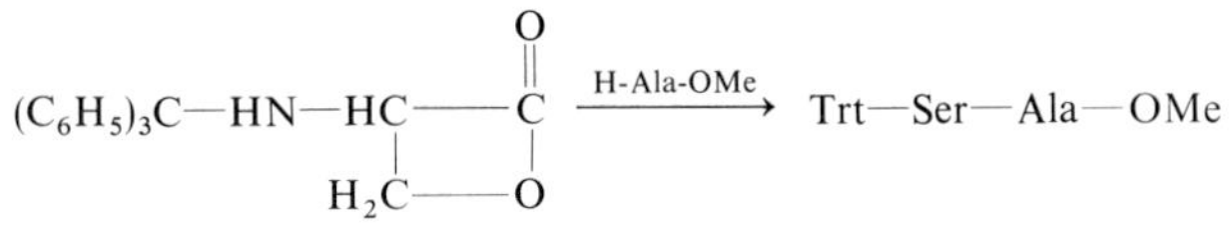

(3)

(**42**)

oxycarbonyl-L-serine an analogous lactone was obtained in good yield through the action of dicyclohexylcarbodiimide and 1-hydroxybenzotriazole (König and Geiger, 1970).

Ring closure involving the alcoholic hydroxyl group of serine might be preceded by Curtius rearrangement of an azide. This often observed side reaction (Fruton, 1942; Baer *et al.*, 1956; Schnabel, 1962; Katsoyannis *et al.*, 1967) must be prevented by carrying out the azide coupling at low temperature. Otherwise incorporation of the urea (**43**) rather than of a protected serine residue will occur [Eq. (4)].

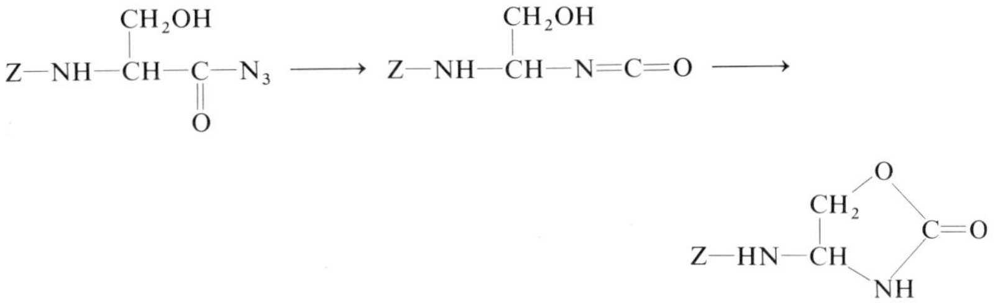

(4)

(**43**)

An unusual rearrangement was observed with the *N*-carboxyanhydride (Leuchs' anhydride) of serine (Saito, 1964). This compound (**44**) forms a 2-oxazolidone derivative (**45**).

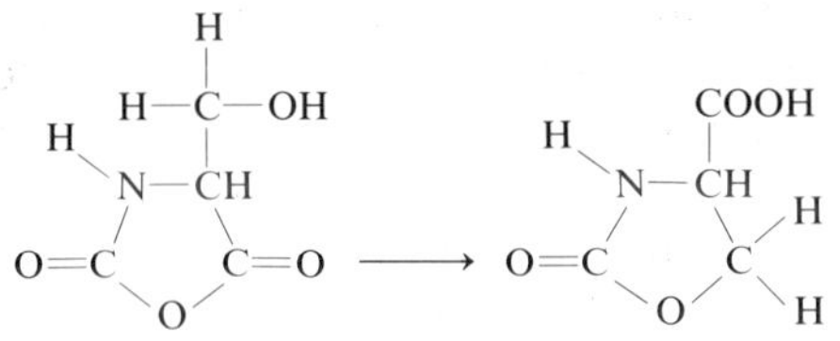

(**44**) (**45**)

Disruption of the peptide chain by an $N \rightarrow O$ acyl migration turned into a real danger in solid-phase synthesis when extremely strong acids, such as liquid HF, were used for complete deblocking and for cleavage of a completed peptide chain from the supporting polymer. The shift from N to O is reversible [Eq. (5)], and thus the damage can be repaired by dissolving the

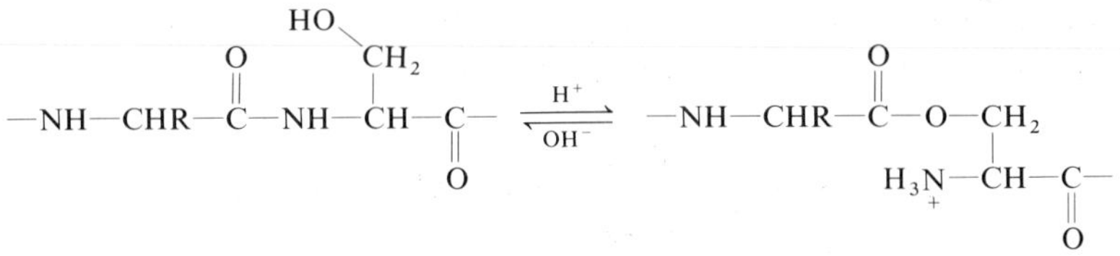

(5)

material in an aqueous solution of sodium bicarbonate. Still, some hydrolysis of a peptide bond might result from this process. This is a much studied reaction for which a mechanism involving the cyclic intermediate **46a** was usually postulated (Bergmann *et al.*, 1923; Bergmann and Miekeley, 1924; Bailey, 1955; Theodoropoulos *et al.*, 1959; Cohen and Witkop, 1961) [Eq. (6)]. The same shift also occurs in concentrated sulfuric acid (Elliott, 1952), methanesulfonic acid (Fujino *et al.*, 1978), and formic acid (Narita, 1959) and is not limited to serine, but occurs in threonine-containing peptides

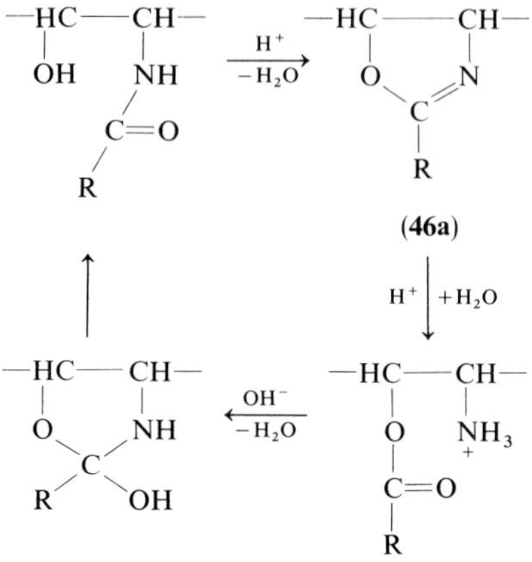

(6)

as well (Fujiwara *et al.*, 1962). The N → O shift in liquid HF was used for selective cleavage of peptide chains (Shin *et al.*, 1962; Sakakibara *et al.*, 1962; Iwai and Ando, 1967). It is a reaction that can occur under a variety of conditions for example, cyclic derivatives similar to **46a** will result from treatment of serine- or threonine-containing peptides with thionyl chloride, phosphorus pentachloride, or trifluoroacetic anhydride (Weygand and Rinno, 1959). The possibility of reversing the shift with a base such as piperidine (Lenard and Hess, 1964) is reassuring, but the inversion of configuration observed in some cases (Wakamiya *et al.*, 1973, 1974) should raise further concern.

Hydrolysis of ester groups by alkali must be carried out with care on serine- or threonine-containing peptides. Excess base might cause the elimination of water and consequently the formation of dehydroamino acid residues (Harris and Fruton, 1951; Zahn and Schnabel, 1957; Inouye and Otsuka, 1961). If the hydroxyl groups are acylated with the tosyl group or another good leaving group (Riley *et al.*, 1957; Photaki, 1963; Benoiton *et al.*, 1964), β-elimination will become even more facile [Eq. (7)].

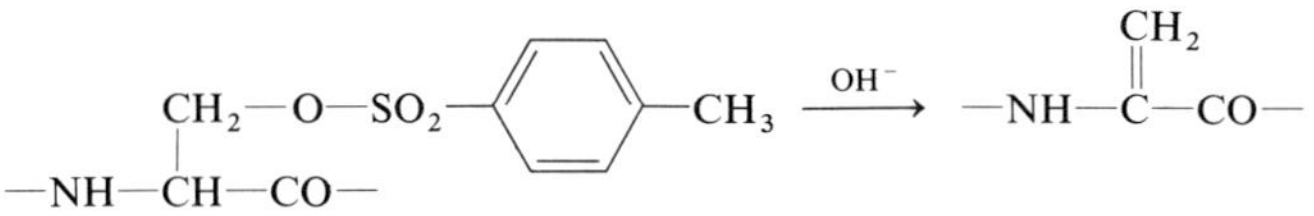

(7)

In view of the role of serine residues at the active sites of, for examples, proteolytic enzymes (cf. Bruice and Fife, 1962; Bender *et al.*, 1963), the various inter- and intramolecular reactions of the hydroxyl groups of hydroxyamino acids should not be too surprising. Because of their reactivity and the ensuing side reactions, a continued effort (Girin and Shvachkin, 1979a,b, and references therein) to clarify the effects of the hydroxyl groups on different reactants is certainly warranted.

As an interesting observation, formation of a complex during the preparation of benzyloxycarbonyl-DL-serine should be mentioned (Brown and Wade, 1962). The complex consists of the sodium salt of the protected amino acid and the benzyloxycarbonylamino acid itself and resists acidification of the mixture, hence precautions are necessary to prevent formation of the complex (Brown and Wade, 1962).

K. Aspartic Acid

Protection of the β-carboxyl group before activation of the α-carboxyl is absolutely necessary in aspartic acid-containing peptides. Otherwise, either or both carboxyl groups could be activated and a mixture of α- and β-aspartyl peptides would ensue [Eq. (8)]. The same result would be achieved in cases where activation affords a cyclic anhydride such as compound **46b**

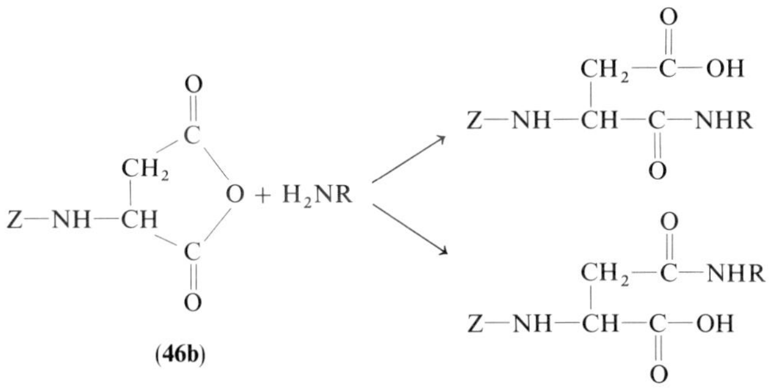

(8)

(King and Kidd, 1951; Tanenbaum, 1953; Buchanan *et al.*, 1966). For a long time it was generally believed that, because the amino component need not be activated, the side-chain carboxyls of its aspartyl residues could be left unprotected. Moreover, it was expected that the pronounced tendency of the aspartyl moiety to form derivatives of aspartimide was absent in residues with a free β-carboxyl group. Unfortunately, gradually accumulating evidence shows that this is not so. Ring closure occurs in unprotected midchain aspartyl residues on treatment with hydrazine (Mitsuyasu *et al.*, 1970), on exposure to acidic reagents like HCl in acetic acid (Schön and Kisfaludy, 1979), and even on storage in aqueous solution (Bodanszky *et al.*, 1973b). On the other hand, protection, such as esterification with various alcohols, instead of reducing the rate of cyclization might further increase the formation of aspartimides [Eq. (9)]. Although ring closure can be spontaneous, obviously because of the thermodynamic stability of the five-membered aspartimide ring, the latter is nonetheless reactive and opens up readily (Titherley and Stubbs, 1914) under attack by nucleophiles. In part the desired α-aspartyl peptides are produced in this reaction, and in part the

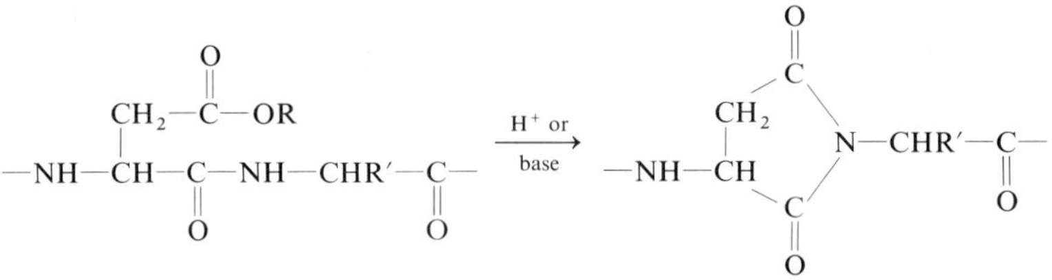 (9)

mostly undesired β-aspartyl peptides. Under most conditions the peptide with β-aspartyl linkage dominates in the mixture (Battersby and Robinson, 1955), [Eq. (10)]. The rate of ring closure depends, to a considerable degree,

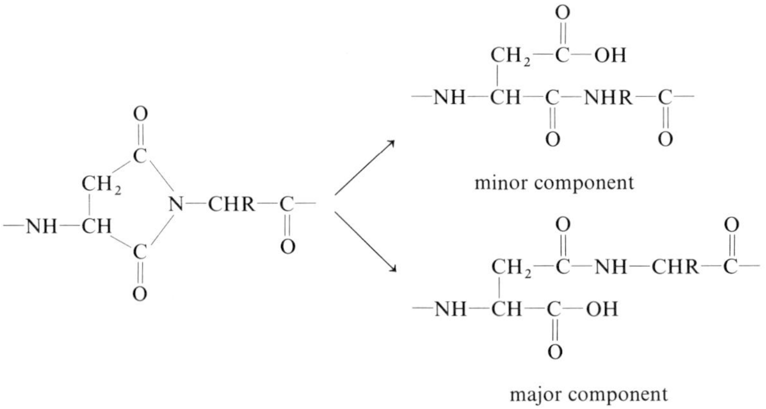

(10)

on the amino acid that follows the aspartyl residue in the sequence (Bodanszky *et al.*, 1967; Bodanszky and Kwei, 1978). It is particularly fast with -Asp-Ser- and with -Asp-Gly- sequences (Iselin and Schwyzer, 1962). Accordingly, it is not too surprising that the dipeptide (**47**), β-aspartylglycine,

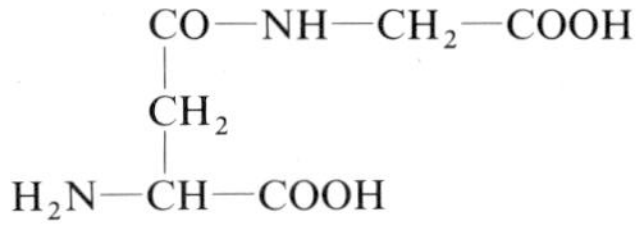

(**47**)

occurs in human urine (Haley *et al.*, 1966) as a product of rearrangement followed by proteolysis, because the human organism has no enzyme that can cleave this "unnatural" peptide bond. The Asp-Pro sequence is particularly sensitive to acid hydrolysis (Fraser *et al.*, 1972).

Beyond the effect of the sequence, the nature of the substituent on the carboxyl group of aspartyl side chains also has a major influence on the rate of succinimide formation. One of the most commonly used methods for blocking the carboxyl function involves benzyl esters. Because of its relative resistance to acids the benzyl group provides semipermanent protection which persists throughout the chain-lengthening process if the latter relies on blocking of α-amino functions with more acid-sensitive groups such as the *tert*-butyloxycarbonyl group. A combination of protecting groups with different sensitivities to acids entails, however, the use of strong acids for final deprotection. Under the strongly acidic conditions needed for the acidolytic cleavage of benzyl esters the loss of benzyl alcohol is accompanied by the formation of succinimide derivatives and thus not all the formerly blocked carboxyl groups are set free [Eq. (11)]. Among the acids that

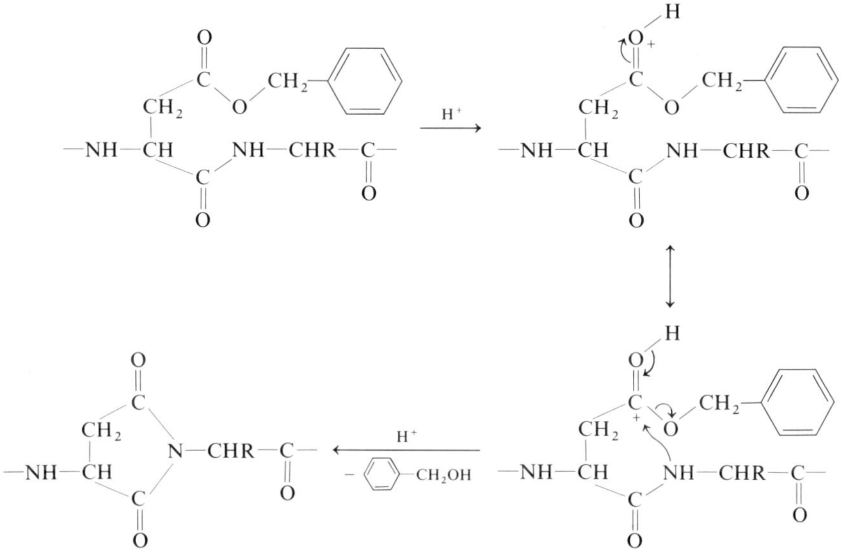

(11)

catalyze this ring closure reaction, HBr in acetic acid, and liquid HF, were found (Merrifield, 1967; Baba *et al.*, 1973; Wang *et al.*, 1974; Suzuki *et al.*, 1976) to be particularly harmful, whereas HBr in trifluoroacetic acid caused only moderate damage ((Ondetti *et al.*, 1968; Bodanszky *et al.*, 1978). The replacement of benzyl esters by 4-nitrobenzyl esters (Suzuki *et al.*, 1976) or by phenacyl esters (**48**) provides only a partial remedy. Selective removal of

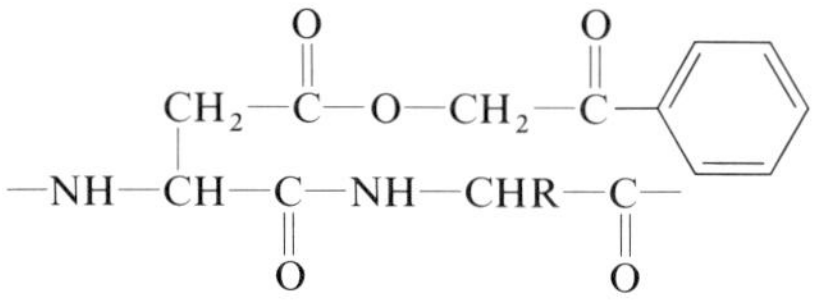

(**48**)

the phenacyl group before final deblocking indeed suppressed (Yang and Merrified, 1976) the acid-catalyzed reaction [Eq. (11)]. However, possible ring closure in acidic media cannot be excluded even with free carboxyl groups (Schön and Kisfaludy, 1979).

The sensitivity of phenacyl esters (and probably also of 4-nitrobenzyl esters) to intramolecular nucleophilic attack is more pronounced than that of benzyl esters (Bodanszky and Martinez, 1978). Cyclopentyl esters (Blake, 1979) and cyclohexyl esters (Tam *et al.*, 1979) might provide satisfactory protection for aspartyl side chains.

A more general solution to the problem of acid-catalyzed ring closure of aspartyl derivatives is to avoid strongly acidic conditions during the entire process. This is possible if instead of the *tert*-butyloxycarbonyl group a more acid-sensitive blocking, such as the one provided by the 2-(4-biphenylyl)propyl(2)oxycarbonyl group (Sieber and Iselin, 1968) is employed. Because the latter can be removed under extremely mild acidic cleavage, the side-chain functions are best masked by protecting groups based on the stability of the *tert*-butyl cation. An alternative solution is the use of α-amino protecting groups requiring nucleophiles for their removal, for example, the 9-fluorenylmethyloxycarbonyl group (Carpino and Han, 1972). Once again, the side-chain carboxyl groups can be protected in the form of their *tert*-butyl esters, and acidolytic removal of the latter by trifluoroacetic acid is practically harmless (Kenner and Seely, 1972) with respect to the side reaction involving the β-carboxyl group of aspartyl residues.

Ring closure in β-benzylaspartyl residues is also catalyzed by bases. The addition of a tertiary amine in order to liberate the amino component from its salt generates conditions that are conducive to aspartimide formation [Eq. (12)]. The amino acid residue that follows aspartic acid in the sequence has a major effect on the outcome of this reaction:

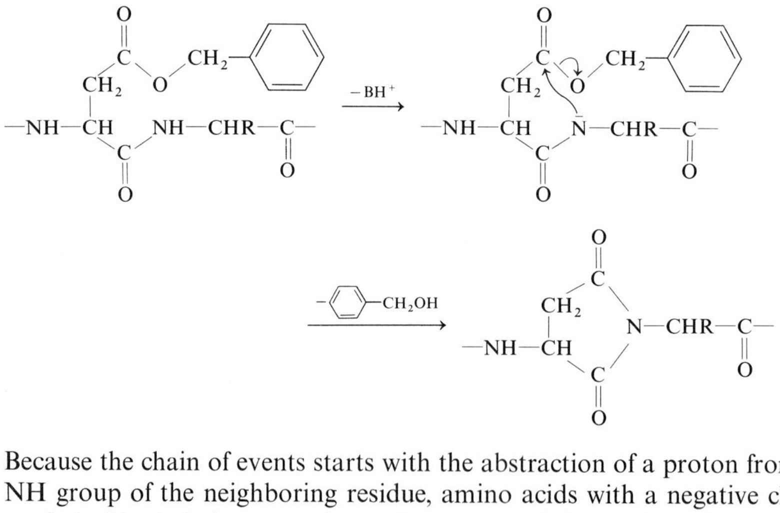

(12)

Because the chain of events starts with the abstraction of a proton from the NH group of the neighboring residue, amino acids with a negative charge on their side chain (e.g., tyrosine and unprotected glutamyl residues) impede ring closure because they interfere with the formation of a second anionic center. Similarly, closing of the succinimide ring is hindered by amino acids with a bulky side chain. Accordingly, aspartimide derivatives form from β-benzylaspartyl residues very slowly in Asp-Val or Asp-Ile sequences, whereas ring closure is fast in Asp-Gly- and particularly rapid in Asp-Ser-containing peptides (Bodanszky and Kwei, 1978; cf. also Bernhard *et al.*, 1962; Schneider, 1963; Shalitin and Bernhard, 1964, 1966; Theodoropoulos and Souchleris, 1964). This side reaction, ring closure of β-benzylaspartyl residues in basic media, can be suppressed by the addition of compounds with a higher affinity for the tertiary bases present in the mixture than the NH group of the next residue. Thus, the abstraction of a proton from this group is prevented, and thereby the undesired ring closure as well. From a number of weak acids tested (Martinez and Bodanszky, 1978) 2,4-dinitrophenol and pentachlorophenol were found to have the best effect.

Unlike β-benzyl esters, the β-*tert*-butyl esters of aspartyl residues are fairly resistant to nucleophile attack. The bulkiness of the protecting group combined with its inherent electron release diminish the reactivity of the ester carbonyl to such an extent that it remains inert under the usually mild conditions of peptide synthesis (Bodanszky *et al.*, 1978). However, strong bases can hydrolyze *tert*-butyl esters (Schwyzer *et al.*, 1963; Bajusz *et al.*, 1964; Wünsch and Drees. 1966), and they are also eliminated by the action of supernucleophiles such as hydrazine (Wünsch and Zwick, 1963; Chillemi, 1966). In both cases the formation of α- *and* β-aspartyl derivatives points to cyclic intermediates. Thus, the loss of protection is due to anchimeric assistance provided by the NH group. Similar observations were also made in the ammonolysis of benzyloxycarbonyl-β-benzyl-L-aspartyl-L-serine methyl ester (Hanson and Rydon, 1964; Fölsch, 1966) [Eq. (13)].

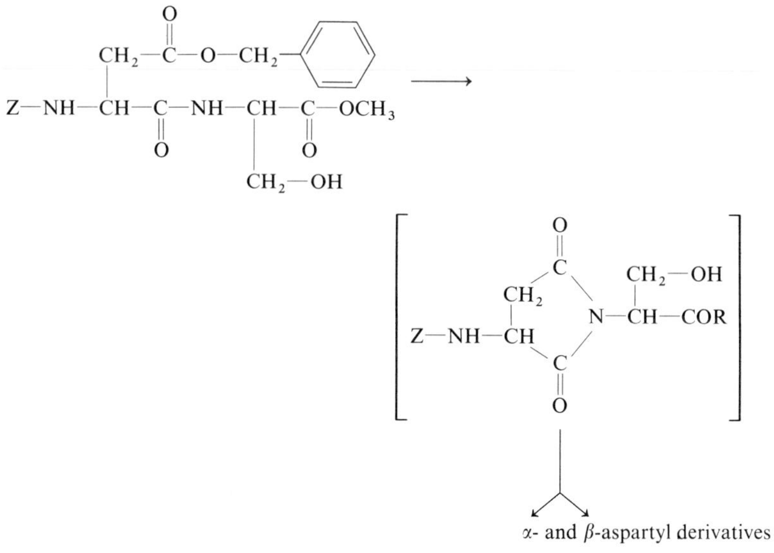

(13)

As a note of consolation one might add here that the separation of α- and β-aspartyl peptides is generally feasible, for example, by chromatography (Riniker and Schwyzer, 1964a).

Earlier in this section we saw that an unprotected carboxyl group in the amine component is no safeguard against aspartimide formation during acidolytic deprotection. Such ring closure can also take place during coupling, for instance, in the process of chain lengthening with active esters (Bodanszky and Natarajan, 1975). Presumably, mixed anhydrides or active esters (**49** and **50**) play the role of reactive intermediates in the process which is enhanced by the presence of tertiary bases (Scheme 2). Intermediate **49**

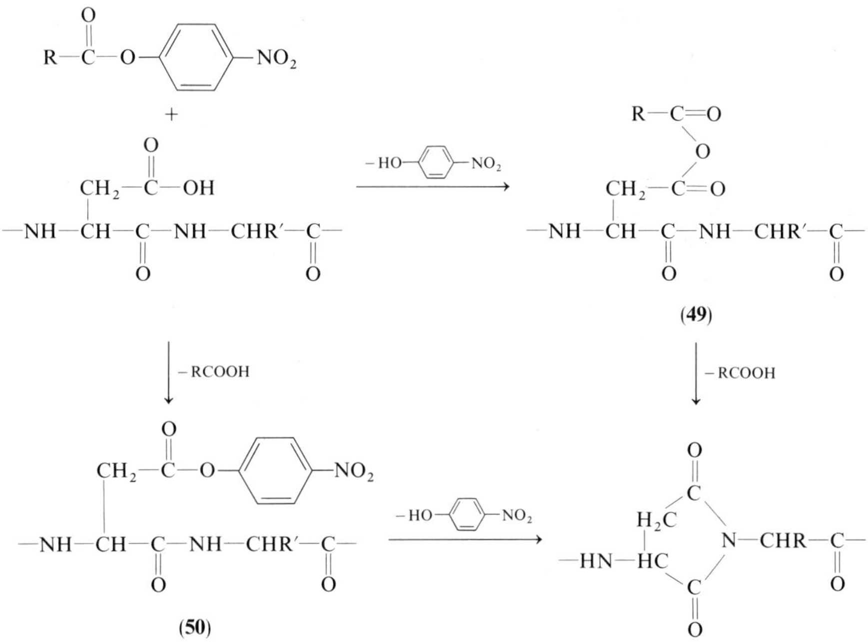

Scheme 2

or **50** can react with a second molecule of the amino component to yield a branched peptide (Natarajan and Bodanszky, 1976).

L. Glutamic Acid

The need to protect side-chain carboxyl functions in carboxyl components before their activation is fairly obvious: Unprotected side-chain carboxyl groups will also be activated, and a branched peptide will result from the coupling reaction. It was more surprising to realize that the γ-carboxyl group of glutamyl residues is turned into an acyl cation during deprotection with HF (Sakakibara and Shimonishi, 1965) and that this reactive intermediate readily participates in electrophilic aromatic substitution reactions. With anisole added as a cation scavenger ketones such as **51** are formed. This side

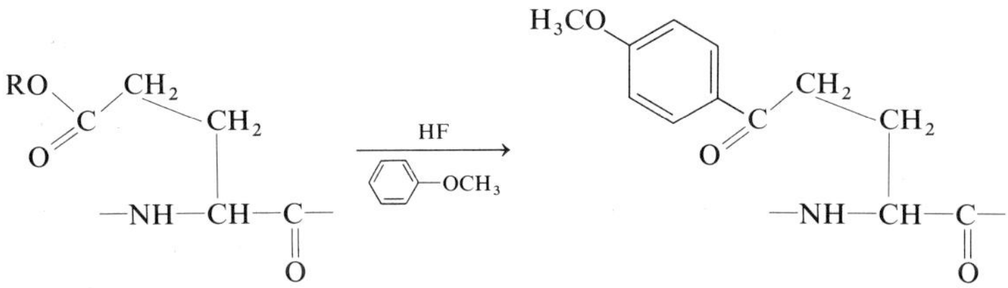

(51)

reaction was recognized (Polzhofer and Ney, 1970; Sano and Kawanishi, 1973) by the low glutamic acid content of hydrolysates of peptides cleaved from insoluble supports (Merrifield, 1963) and explained by the Friedel–Crafts reaction shown here (Sano and Kawanishi, 1975; Feinberg and Merrifield, 1975). If the conditions of cleavage with HF are carefully controlled, this serious side reaction can be avoided. For example, it does not occur to major extent when treatment with HF is carried out at 0°C or below and exposure of the peptide lasts less than 0.5 hr. However, the removal of several protecting groups requires longer cleavage times and temperatures as high as 25°C. An alternative solution to this problem can be found (Suzuki *et al.*, 1977) in the use of protecting groups such as phenacyl esters and 4-nitrobenzyl esters which remain on the side-chain function of glutamyl residues during cleavage with HF and are removed subsequently in a separate operation.

Although intermolecular acylation via the γ-carboxyl group of glutamic acid takes place only exceptionally and requires activation of the carboxyl group or a catalyst such as HF, intramolecular reactions of the side-chain carboxyl group are more facile and, therefore, also more general. Thus, the stable five-membered ring of a pyrrolidone forms on mere heating of glutamic acid.* Hence the name "pyroglutamic acid" for 2-pyrrolidone-5-carboxylic acid (**52**):

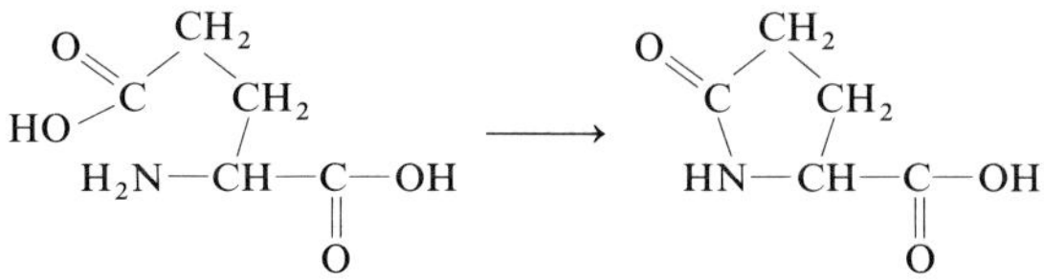

(52)

* Exposure to a strongly acidic ion exchanger (in the hydrogen cycle) can cause the same conversion (Das and Roy, 1962).

Ring closure to derivatives of pyroglutamic acid also occurs in *N*-acyl derivatives of glutamic acid if their γ-carboxyl group is activated (Rudinger, 1954; Stedman, 1957; Gibian and Klieger, 1960; Taschner *et al.*, 1960) and under the influence of acidic or basic catalysts in peptides where the glutamyl residue is at the NH_2-terminus (Hubert *et al.*, 1963; Bonora *et al.*, 1974). Opening of the pyrrolidone ring by ammonolysis is a well-established route to the incorporation of glutamine residues.

An alternative cyclization can also take place in the activation of glutamyl residues if their γ-carboxyl group is left without protection. This reaction involves the amino group of the residue that follows glutamic acid in the sequence and produces derivatives of glutarimide such as **53** (Battersby and

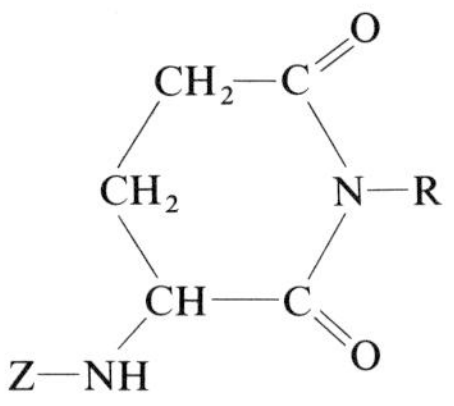

(53)

Robinson, 1956; Clayton *et al.*, 1956). The six-membered ring of these piperidine-2,6-diones opens up more readily under the attack of alkali or amines than the five-membered ring of pyrrolidones (such as **52**). Therefore ring closure followed by ring opening is an often noted side reaction (Clayton and Kenner, 1953; Kovacs *et al.*, 1954; Bruckner *et al.*, 1955, 1958; Bruckner and Kovacs, 1957; Bruckner and Kajtar, 1959 leading to the formation of γ-glutamyl peptides from α-glutamyl peptides, and vice versa [Eq. (14)].

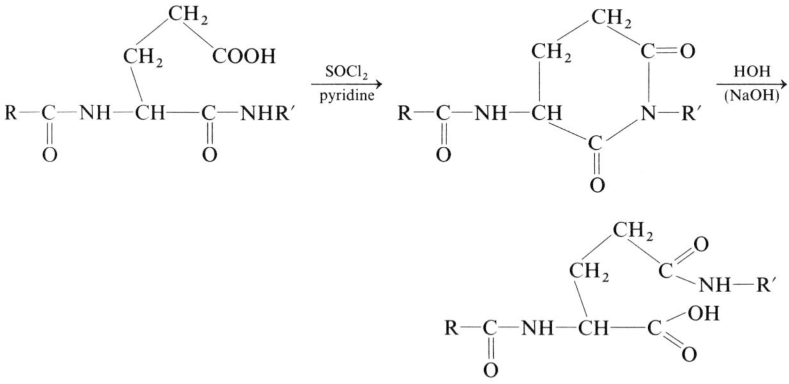

(14)

The extent of rearrangement or transpeptidation is influenced by steric factors and depends, therefore, on the nature of the residue that follows glutamic acid in the sequence (Battersby and Reynolds, 1961): It is more pronounced in Glu-Gly than in Glu-Phe. A mixture of α- and γ-glutamyl peptides was obtained also in coupling via N-protected glutamic acid monohydrazides and monoazides (Sachs and Brand, 1954; Rowlands and Young, 1957; Kisfaludy, 1960) [Eq. (15)]. Analogous problems arise in the opening

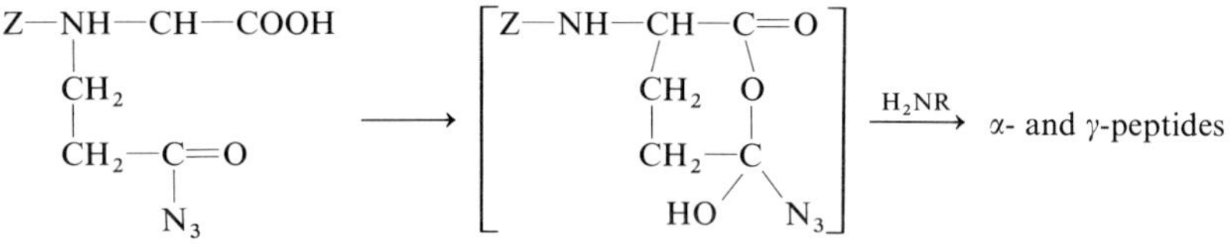

(15)

of cyclic anhydrides (e.g., **54**) of glutamic acid. In the resulting mixture of α- and γ-derivatives the latter are present in higher amounts (Melville, 1935; Bergmann *et al.*, 1936; LeQuesne and Young, 1950). An unusually unequivocal ring opening occurs in the case of the anhydride of phthalylglutamic acid (**55**): Both aminolysis and alcoholysis produce only the γ-derivative

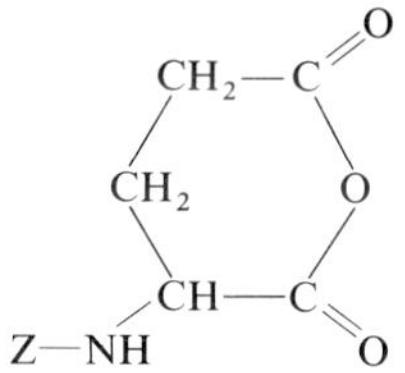

(54)

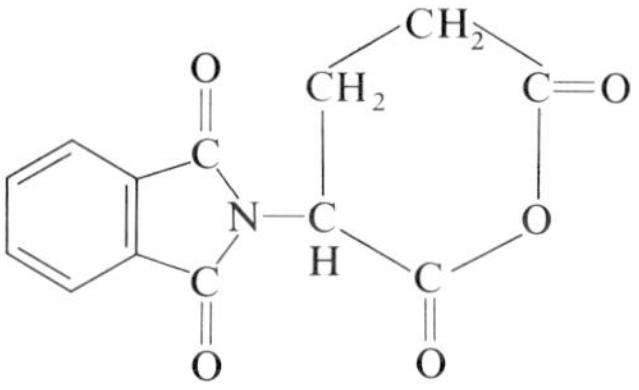

(55)

(King and Kidd, 1949; King *et al.*, 1951, 1954b, 1957). Perhaps less surprising is the straightforward ring opening of the *N*-carboxyanhydride of glutamic acid (**56**) which, when attacked by aminocomponents, yields exclusively α-peptides (Denkewalter *et al.*, 1966).

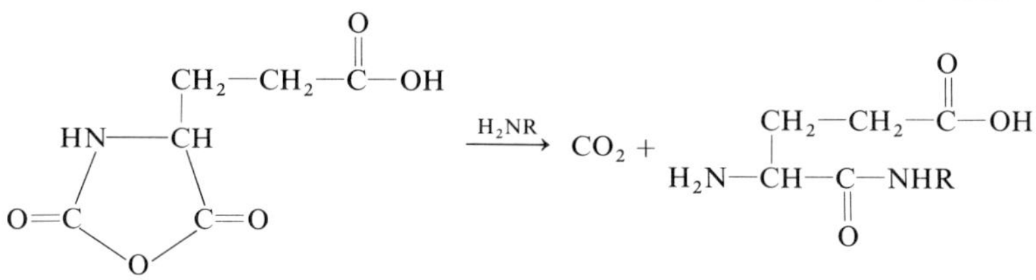

(56)

Transpeptidation also occurs during alkaline hydrolysis of glutamic acid esters (Liefländer, 1960; Shiba and Kaneko, 1960), but it can be efficiently suppressed by the addition of copper(II) hydroxide (Bruckner *et al.*, 1959). Cyclic intermediates are also implicated in the sensitivity of γ-*tert*-butyl esters to hydrazine (Zahn *et al.*, 1965a; Shiba and Kanebo, 1960). The relatively rapid deprotection of γ-benzyl esters of glutamic acid by HBr in acetic acid (Bayer *et al.*, 1961) or by aqueous trifluoroacetic acid (Schnabel *et al.*, 1971) probably involves cyclic transition states. Rapid acidolysis of γ-esters was also noted in connection with polyamino acids (Balasubramanian and Subramanian, 1973) and in solid-phase peptide synthesis (Krumdieck and Baugh, 1969).

M. Asparagine and Glutamine

A simultaneous discussion of these two amino acid residues seems to be justified, because in several of their side reactions, for example, dehydration of the carboxamide group and formation of cyclic imides, complete parallelism exists. There are, however, notable exceptions among such similarities; for instance, ring closure involving the α-amino group of the same residue occurs in derivatives of glutamine where a stable pyrrolidone can form, but not with compounds containing asparagine residues where a strained four-membered ring would result from analogous cyclization [Eq. (16)]. The

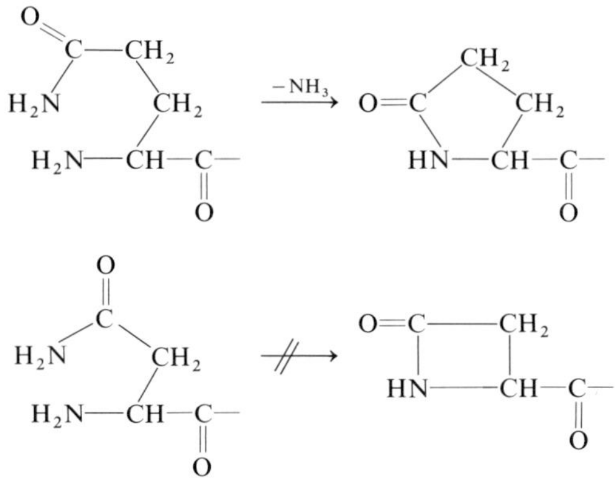

(16)

formation of pyroglutamyl residues was mentioned in Section II,L, but it is more pronounced in glutaminyl peptides. In such compounds, mere boiling with water can cause a loss of ammonia and concomitant ring closure (Chibnall and Westall, 1932; Vickery *et al.*, 1935; Rudinger and Pravda, 1958; Blömback, 1967). This conversion would present no problem in peptide synthesis if it also did not take place under conditions that commonly occur in conventional processes. Thus, the removal of acid-labile protecting groups from NH_2-terminal glutamine residues with HCl in acetic acid can lead to pyroglutamic acid formation and thereby to chain termination (Takashima *et al.*, 1968; Manning, 1968). The same reaction occurs, although to a lesser extent, in mixtures of trifluoroacetic acid and dichloromethane (Bárány and Merrifield, 1973). Interestingly, in HCl–acetic acid not the HCl component, but acetic acid, acts as the catalyst in deamidation–cyclization

(Beyerman *et al.*, 1973). Hence, the side reaction can be suppressed by the use of HCl in dioxane (Potts *et al.*, 1971; Dorman *et al.*, 1972). Catalysis of ring closure by the imidazole ring of a neighboring histidine residue was also observed (Kappeler, 1961; Geiger *et al.*, 1963; Schnabel *et al.*, 1967). Complete prevention of pyroglutamic acid formation can be achieved (Pietta *et al.*, 1971) by protecting the carboxamide nitrogen with the 2,4-dimethoxybenzyl group, the 4,4′-dimethoxydiphenylmethyl, or the xanthenyl group, but only at the expense of forming additional alkylating agents during acidolytic deprotection.

Cyclizations involving the (activated) α-carboxyl group and the side-chain carboxamide produce succinimides (such as **57**) from asparagine and similarly stable glutarimides or piperidine-2,6-diones (**58**) from glutamine residues.

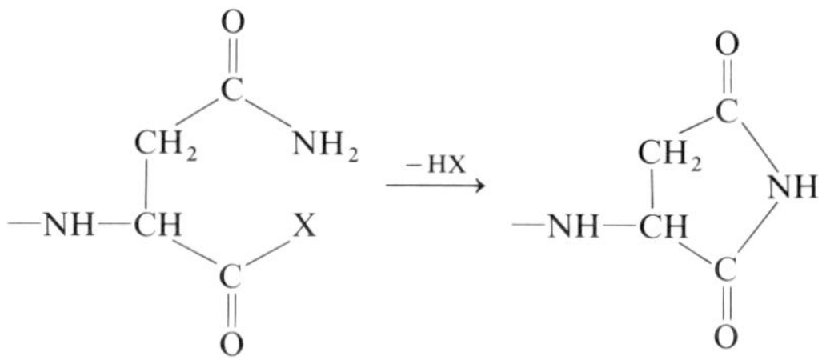

(57)

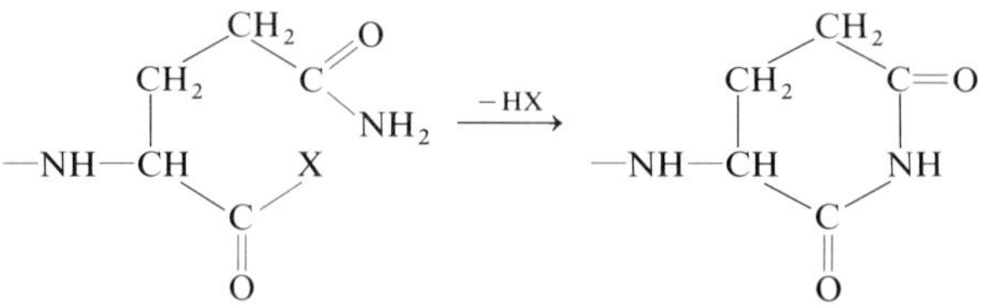

(58)

Several side reactions characteristic of asparagine and glutamine proceed through such cyclic intermediates. Thus, ammonolysis of β-methylaspartate yields both asparagine and isoasparagine (Inukai *et al.*, 1968). Similarly, alkaline hydrolysis of esters of N^{α}-acylasparagine leads to both α- and β-amides [Eq. (17)] or to α- and γ-amides in the case of N^{α}-acylglutamine esters (Sondheimer and Holley, 1954a, 1957; cf. also König and Volk, 1977).

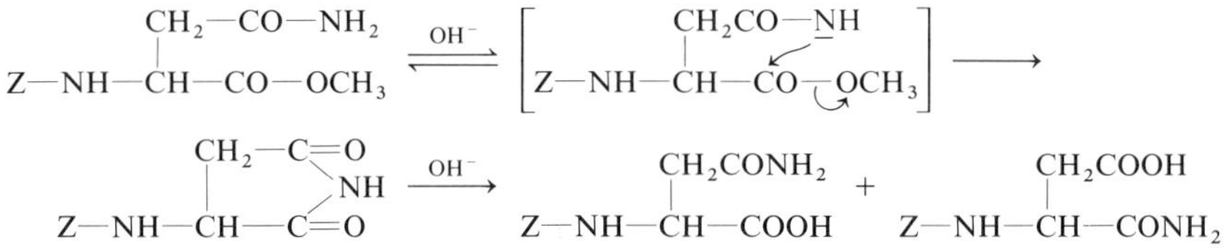

(17)

A succinimide intermediate was proposed (Roeske, 1963) to explain the surprising hydrolysis of the *tert*-butyl ester of asparagine by alkali under mild conditions. This observation foreshadowed the loss of *tert*-butyl groups from the β-carboxyl group of midchain aspartyl residues, a reaction assisted by the nearby amide group. The sensitivity of ω-amides to both acid- and base-catalyzed hydrolysis (Schwyzer *et al.*, 1958; Riniker and Schwyzer, 1961; Robinson *et al.*, 1970; McKerrow and Robinson, 1971, 1974; Robinson and Tedro, 1973; Robinson, 1974) is obviously due to anchimeric assistance. The acid-catalyzed alcoholysis of side-chain carboxamides, for example, during the removal of formyl groups with methanolic HCl (Sondheimer and Semeraro, 1961), probably belongs to the same category of side reactions.

Transpeptidation took place in asparagine-containing peptides even in the absence of nucleophilic reagents when their aqueous solutions were heated (Riniker *et al.*, 1962). On the other hand, it was possible to prepare benzyloxycarbonylglutamine hydrazide without side reactions (Sondheimer and Holley, 1954b), but only under mild conditions. An attempt to remove the phthalyl group from asparagine peptides with the use of hydrazine led to complications (Leach and Lindley, 1954).

Activation of the carboxyl group of COOH-terminal asparagine and glutamine residues is even more likely to cause cyclization to the corresponding imide. Poor results in the coupling of such asparagine peptides via mixed anhydrides were attributed to succinimide formation (Boissonnas *et al.*, 1955). The synthesis of 2-nitrophenylsulfenylglutamine *N*-hydroxysuccinimide ester (Dewey *et al.*, 1969; Meyers *et al.*, 1969) with the aid of dicyclohexylcarbodiimide can be carried out at low temperature, but the active ester is gradually converted to the glutarimide on storage in solution with dimethylformamide, particularly in the presence of a tertiary base. The same kind of transformation to glutarimide (**60**) also takes place in the case of *tert*-butyloxycarbonylglutamine *N*-hydroxysuccinimide ester (**59**) (Dewey *et al.*, 1969):

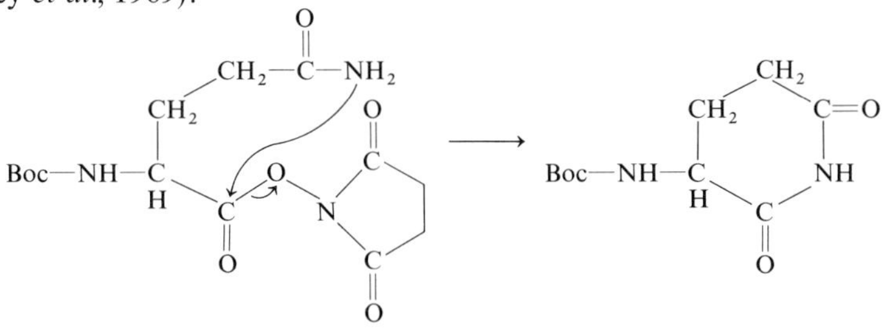

(**59**) (**60**)

In a similar fashion, the pentafluorophenyl ester of benzyloxycarbonylasparagine cyclized, in dimethylformamide, to benzyloxycarbonylaminosuccinimide at room temperature in a fairly short time (Kisfaludy *et al.*, 1972).

A serious side reaction affecting the side chain of asparagine and, to a lesser extent, that of glutamine is the loss of water during activation and coupling [Eq. (18)]. The incorporation of β-cyanoalanine was observed

$$
\begin{array}{c}
\underset{\substack{| \\ -NH-CH-C-X \\ \| \\ O}}{\overset{\substack{O \\ \| \\ CH_2-C-NH_2}}{}} + H_2NR \xrightarrow[-H_2O]{-HX} \underset{\substack{| \\ -NH-CH-C-NHR \\ \| \\ O}}{\overset{CH_2-CN}{}}
\end{array}
$$

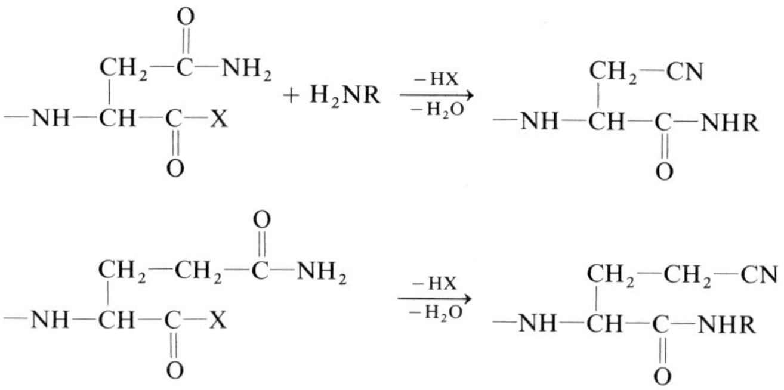

(18)

$$
\begin{array}{c}
\underset{\substack{| \\ -NH-CH-C-X \\ \| \\ O}}{\overset{\substack{O \\ \| \\ CH_2-CH_2-C-NH_2}}{}} \xrightarrow[-H_2O]{-HX} \underset{\substack{| \\ -NH-CH-C-NHR \\ \| \\ O}}{\overset{CH_2-CH_2-CN}{}}
\end{array}
$$

(Gish *et al.*, 1956; Ressler, 1956) in the synthesis of analogs of oxytocin and vasopressin (cf. also Katsoyannis *et al.*, 1957). The formation of γ-cyano-α-aminobutyric acid residues was also noted (Katsoyannis *et al.*, 1958). The same kind of dehydration takes place in the preparation of active esters as well (Bodanszky and du Vigneaud, 1959), but it is relatively easy to separate the active esters of (N^{α}-protected) asparagine or glutamine from the accompanying nitriles by fractional crystallization (Bodanszky *et al.*, 1963b). Thus, it is possible to use the pure active esters for the actual synthesis and thereby avoid the incorporation of nitriles. Once the residues with carboxamide side chains become part of a peptide chain, the usual operations of peptide synthesis cause no more dehydration (Kashelikar and Ressler, 1964). A strong dehydrating agent such as *p*-toluenesulfonyl chloride in pyridine can produce nitriles from carboxamides (Zaoral and Rudinger, 1959). The conversion of carboxamides to nitriles also occurs under the influence of phosphorus oxychloride (Liberek, 1961) or dicyclohexylcarbodiimide (Ressler and Ratzkin, 1961). The reaction of phosgene with asparagine yielded the *N*-carboxyanhydride of β-cyanoalanine (**61**), and the homologous Leuchs' anhydride was obtained from glutamine (**62**) (Wilchek *et al.*, 1968). Because the dehydration reaction occurs in the carboxyl-activated intermediates, a cyclic transition state has to be assumed (Stammer, 1961; Liberek, 1962; Kashelikar and Ressler, 1964; Paul and Kende, 1964; Kisfaludy *et al.*, 1975).

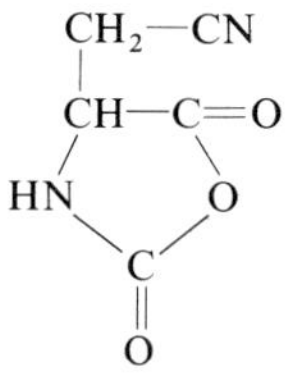

$$
\begin{array}{cc}
\underset{\substack{HN \quad\;\; O \\ \diagdown\;\; \diagup \\ C \\ \| \\ O}}{\overset{\substack{CH_2-CN \\ | \\ CH-C=O \\ \diagup \quad\;\; \diagdown}}{}} & \underset{\substack{HN \quad\;\; O \\ \diagdown\;\; \diagup \\ C \\ \| \\ O}}{\overset{\substack{CH_2-CH_2-CN \\ | \\ CH-C=O \\ \diagup \quad\;\; \diagdown}}{}} \\
(\mathbf{61}) & (\mathbf{62})
\end{array}
$$

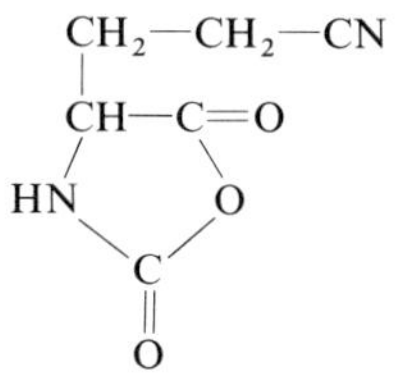

Finally a note of hope should be added to allay our worries with respect to dehydration. The loss of water can be reversed by hydration with strong acids (Mojsov *et al.*, 1980) or by treatment of cyanoamino acid-containing peptides with alkaline hydrogen peroxide (Liberek, 1961).

N. Cysteine and Cystine

It is probably impractical to attempt the synthesis of cysteine-containing peptides without first protecting the SH group in the cysteine side chains. The nucleophilic character of mercaptans renders them strong competitors of amino groups for acylating agents. Also, free mercaptans are readily alkylated during deprotection processes in which carbo-cations are generated. The SH groups are oxidized, even by air, to disulfides, and thiols are smoothly added to the indole nucleus of tryptophan. These dangers do not appear if, instead of cysteine, the disulfide cystine is incorporated in peptides chains (Lunkenheimer and Zahn, 1970), but the procedure is safe only in the preparation of symmetrical disulfides. Nonsymmetrical disulfides (**63**) disproportionate to afford two symmetrical compounds (**64** and **65**).

$$2\,R{-}S{-}S{-}R' \rightleftharpoons R{-}S{-}S{-}R + R'{-}S{-}S{-}R'$$

(63) **(64)** **(65)**

Under close to neutral conditions this dismutation is catalyzed by mercaptans (Sanger, 1953; Ryle and Sanger, 1955; Zervas *et al.*, 1959a), but it also occurs in strong acids (Benesch and Benesch, 1958). Free SH groups can cause the transfer of 2-nitrophenylsulfenyl groups from N to S (Phocas *et al.*, 1967; Scoffone *et al.*, 1968), and this migration is not prevented by some S-protecting groups, for example, the *S*-acetamidomethyl group (Kessler and Iselin, 1966; Zervas *et al.*, 1967; Shchukina *et al.*, 1970; Guarneri *et al.*, 1971). The obvious transacylation from S to N makes a careful selection of S-protecting groups really mandatory. Thus, the *S*-acetyl and *S*-benzoyl groups are efficient acylating agents (cf. coenzyme A) and can cause, via S → N migration, premature termination of peptide chains (Hiskey *et al.*, 1966).

The classic protection of the SH function, the *S*-benzyl group, is remarkably stable. For its removal by acids, only extremely acidic conditions such as those found in liquid HF are sufficient. Its resistance to catalytic hydrogenation is similarly extreme and, because sulfides are known poisons in the catalytic effect of platinum metals, the *S*-benzyl group interferes with hydrogenolytic removal of benzyloxycarbonyl and *O*-benzyl groups as well. A careful selection of catalyst might overcome the poisoning effect (Kuhn and Haas, 1955), but a more general remedy was found in a new technique—

hydrogenation with liquid ammonia as the solvent (Meienhofer and Kuromizu, 1974). The synthesis of peptide hormones (Kuromizu and Meienhofer, 1974; Felix *et al.*, 1977) proved the practicality of this new approach. An amino-protecting group, the 1,1-dimethyl-2-propynyloxycarbonyl group, was designed to be removed by catalytic hydrogenation from sulfur-containing peptides (Southard *et al.*, 1971).

An interesting counterpart of the *S*-benzyl group is the *S*-4-nitrobenzyl group (Berse *et al.*, 1957), which seemed to be removable by hydrogenolysis. Further investigations have revealed that, during hydrogenation, instead of removal only reduction to the 4-aminobenzyl group takes place (Ondetti and Bodanszky, 1962) but the latter is cleaved in a second step by treatment with mercury(II) salts (Bachi and Ross-Petersen, 1972).

The best established method for removal of the *S*-benzyl group, reduction with sodium in liquid ammonia (du Vigneaud *et al.*, 1930), gave excellent results in the synthesis of oxytocin, vasopressin, and their numerous analogs. However, in similar deblocking of insulin chains (Katsoyannis, 1966), the conversion of cysteine to alanine was noted. The concomitant racemization suggests that reduction was preceded by the elimination of benzylmercaptan [Eq. (19)]. Such β-elimination is also caused by alkali, alkoxides, and even hydrazine (Clarke and Inouye, 1931; Berger *et al.*, 1956; du Vigneaud *et al.*, 1957; Swan, 1957; MacLaren *et al.*, 1958; Sokolovsky *et al.*, 1964; Hiskey *et al.*, 1970; Zervas and Ferderigos, 1973):

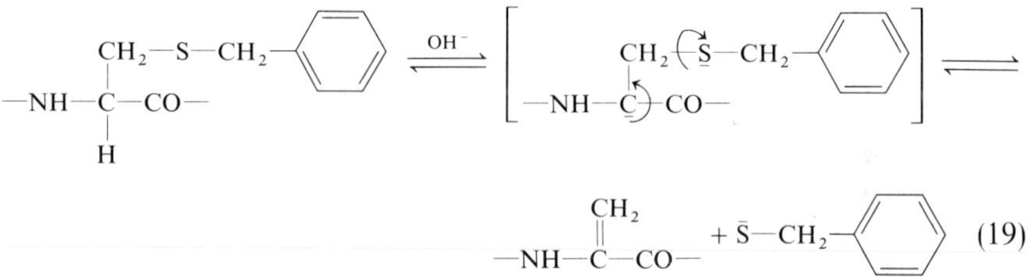

(19)

Elimination of mercaptans from protected cysteine side chains is not limited to the *S*-benzyl group. The loss of the *S*-triphenylmethyl (trityl) group (Hiskey *et al.*, 1970) suggests that it is a rather general phenomenon. The formation of alanine in the sodium–liquid ammonia reduction of the insulin A chain (Katsoyannis, 1966; Manning *et al.*, 1972) should caution against generalizations in connection with S-protecting groups. An additional complication, the oxidation of S-protected cysteine residues to the corresponding sulfoxides (Honzl and Rudinger, 1961) has also received recent attention (Yajima *et al.*, 1979c, 1980). Fortunately, this oxidation is reversible by reduction with thiophenol.

An unexpected enhancement of amide formation, usually a minor side reaction in the case of other residues, occurs in the activation of peptides with COOH-terminal cysteine through their hydrazides and azides (Hegedüs, 1948; Holland and Cohen, 1958; Roeske *et al.*, 1956). The production of amides can be kept at a minimum if the azides are prepared at low temperature, at low pH, under anhydrous conditions, and with alkyl nitrites as nitrosating agents (Honzl and Rudinger, 1961).

O. Methionine

Methionine residues usually suffer no damage during activation, but they interfere with the removal of protecting groups in more than one way. They prevent deblocking by catalytic hydrogenation, because sulfides are well-known poisons of platinum metal catalysts. Furthermore, the methionine side chain itself can undergo changes such as desulfurization and alkylation. Over and above these complications the mere handling of methionine-containing peptides in air can cause oxidation to the sulfoxide.

The catalyst-poisoning effect of methionine does not completely prevent the removal of benzyloxycarbonyl groups or benzyl esters by catalytic hydrogenation. Repeated addition of the catalyst and an extended reaction time are often sufficient to remedy the situation, (Dekker *et al.*, 1949; Li *et al.*, 1961; Medzihradszky *et al.*, 1962) although these measures can lead to desulfurization and thus to the formation of α-aminobutyric acid (butyrine) residues. The addition of freshly prepared palladium black (Merrifield, 1964b) or boron trifluoride (Yajima *et al.*, 1968) was found to be useful in the deprotection of methionine-containing peptides by hydrogenolysis. In the presence of an organic base such as triethylamine or cyclohexylamine catalytic reduction of methionine-containing peptides proceeded smoothly (Medzihradszky-Schweiger and Medzihradszky, 1966), but only benzyloxycarbonyl and benzyl ester groups were cleaved under these conditions: In a basic medium benzyl ethers are completely resistant to catalytic reduction (Medzihradszky-Schweiger, 1973).

Alkylation is probably the most serious of the side reactions affecting the methionine side chain. Acidolytic removal of many protecting groups is based on the stability of carbocations generated by protonation. An obvious consequence of such deprotection is alkylation of the sulfur in methionine either through direct action of the cations or more plausibly via alkylating agents produced in the process. Thus, in the cleavage of *tert*-butyloxycarbonyl groups, *tert*-butyl esters, and ethers, *S*-*tert*-butylation was observed (Sieber *et al.*, 1970) mediated by *tert*-butyl trifluoroacetate (Lundt *et al.*, 1978). Deblocking of *tert*-butyl-based groups with HF might produce *tert*-butyl fluoride as an alkylating agent (Veber *et al.*, 1969). Fortunately this alkylation is reversible: The thioether is regenerated by storage under fairly mild conditions (Noble *et al.*, 1976) [Eq. (20)].

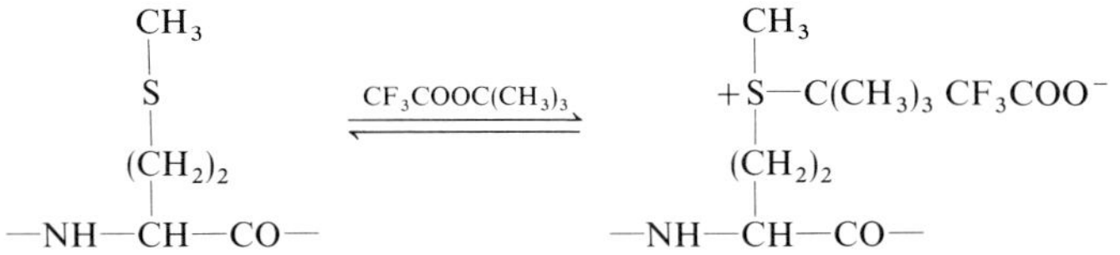
(20)

The presence of methylating agents in the reaction mixtures of acidolytic deprotection is less obvious. However, the commonly used scavenger anisole is the source of methyl cations that readily alkylate the methionine side chain (Irie *et al.*, 1976, 1977). It is possible to undo this damage, because sulfonium salts can be reduced to the parent sulfides with thiols (Naider *et al.*, 1972; Naider and Bohak, 1972) or thiosulfate (Ramirez *et al.*, 1973). However, the harm caused by the benzylation of methionine side chain is irreversible. The well-studied (Dekker and Fruton, 1948) conversion of benzylsulfonium salts of methionine to *S*-benzylhomocysteine (**66**) explains why this alkylation

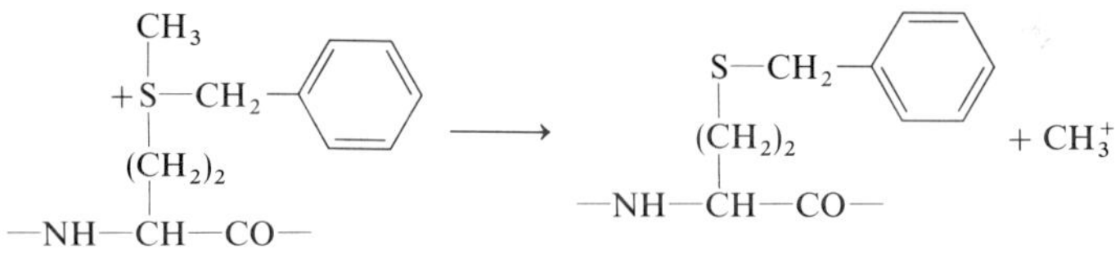
(**66**)

should be avoided (cf. also Toennies and Kolb, 1945; Albertson and McKay, 1953; Gawron and Draus, 1958, 1959). The analogous alkylation of the methionine side chain by the "chloromethyl" groups of the Merrifield resin (Zhukova *et al.*, 1970) is similarly irreversible because this resin is a polymeric form of (substituted) benzyl chloride [Eq. (21)].

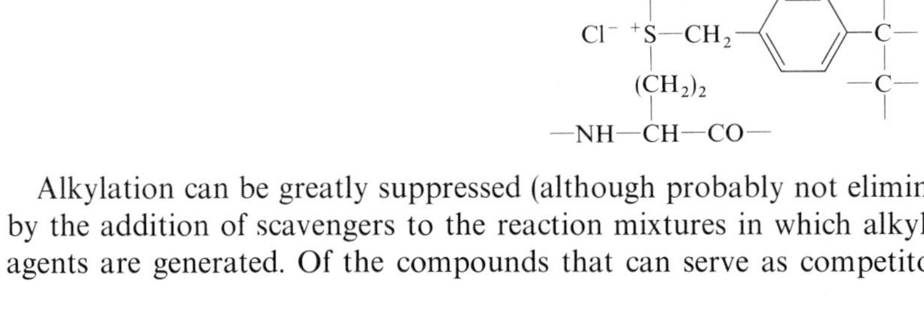
(21)

Alkylation can be greatly suppressed (although probably not eliminated) by the addition of scavengers to the reaction mixtures in which alkylating agents are generated. Of the compounds that can serve as competitors of methionine for the alkylating agent, methylethyl sulfide is well established (Guttmann and Boissonnas, 1958, 1959; Chillemi, 1963; Merrifield 1964b), but a great variety of sulfides have been proposed, among them methionine itself (Marglin and Merrifield, 1966; Bayer *et al.*, 1968; Syrier and Beyerman, 1975; Yajima *et al.*, 1976), *N*-acetylmethionine *n*-butylester (Bodanszky *et al.*, 1979a, 1980), and thioanisole (Bauer and Pless, 1975; Kiso *et al.*, 1978, 1979), although the latter might transfer the captured alkyl groups to other receptors (Lundt *et al.*, 1978). Mercaptans such as mercaptoethanol (Blake and Li, 1968) and ethane-1,2-dithiol (Sharp *et al.*, 1973; Lundt *et al.*, 1978; Chino *et al.*, 1978) are efficient scavengers and can reduce the extent of S-alkylation considerably. An alternative solution is precipitation of the deblocked products soon after completion of the deprotection reaction (Sieber, 1968). Evaporation of the volatile components of the mixture results in prolonged exposure of the nucleophilic centers to alkylating agents such as benzyl trifluoroacetate (Weygand and Steglich, 1959) and thus in enhancement of the side reaction.

Although acidolytic deprotection of methionine-containing peptides is likely to entail alkylation at the sulfur atom, the same sulfur can also be the site of dealkylation, more precisely demethylation, in the treatment of peptides with *excess* sodium in liquid ammonia (Stekol, 1941; Brenner and Pfister, 1951; Hofmann *et al.*, 1957) [Eq. (22)]. This side reaction does not occur if an excess of sodium is avoided (Hofmann *et al.*, 1957) and can also be reversed by alkylation of the homocysteine residue thus formed with methyl iodide (Brenner and Pfister, 1951).

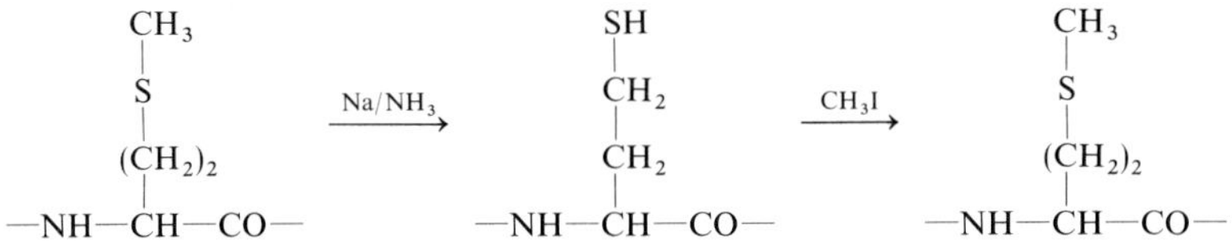

(22)

Oxidation of the sulfide in the methionine side chain is usually only a minor side reaction if it is accomplished by the manipulation of intermediates in air (Hofmann *et al.*, 1965). Of course it can be avoided by working in an inert atmosphere, for example, under nitrogen (Norris *et al.*, 1971), although argon or dithiothreitol (Polzhofer and Ney 1971) might provide better protection. More extensive oxidation takes place in peptides exposed to an oxidating agent such as *N*-bromosuccinimide (Omenn *et al.*, 1970). Luckily, oxidation to sulfoxides can be reversed, and the more final conversion to sulfones requires strong oxidants or catalysts. However, sulfones form on thin-layer plates where the spots are exposed to air over a large surface and where trace metals which are probably present might catalyze the reaction.

Oxidation to the sulfoxide also represents a method for protecting the methionine side chain (Iselin, 1961). Although the protection offered by this approach is considerable, there are certain shortcomings connected with it. Thus, in sulfoxides the sulfur atom becomes chiral and the intermediates of the synthesis are, therefore, not homogeneous but mixtures of diastereoisomers. Furthermore, the polar sulfoxide group often contributes to the insolubility of peptides in organic solvent and can aggravate a sometimes already serious difficulty. Finally, reduction of the sulfoxide to the parent thiol ether is not as smooth as would be desirable in the removal of a temporary protecting group. The originally proposed reagent for the reduction, thioglycolic (mercaptoacetic) acid (Iselin, 1961), can cause mercaptoacetylation of amino groups (Houghten and Li, 1977). Better results were reported with dithiothreitol (Polzhofer and Ney, 1971; Yamashiro and Li, 1973c), and optimal results were obtained with *N*-methylmercaptoacetamide (Houghten and Li, 1977).

III. SIDE REACTIONS IN THE INTRODUCTION AND REMOVAL OF PROTECTING GROUPS

The temporary and semipermanent protecting groups proposed for the masking of functional groups of amino acids are too numerous to be treated in an exhaustive manner. We will, therefore, limit the discussion of side reactions related to blocking groups and their removal to relatively few protection methods, essentially to those that have gained general acceptance in peptide synthesis. In fact, only in connection with frequently used protecting groups has enough experience accumulated to allow a meaningful discussion of side reactions.

A. The Benzyloxycarbonyl (Carbobenzoxy, Z) Group

Both the introduction (via Schotten–Baumann acylation with benzyl chlorocarbonate) and removal by catalytic hydrogenation of this classic protecting group (Bergmann and Zervas, 1932) are relatively free of side reactions.* The isolation of a carbamate salt (Schön and Kisfaludy, 1978) in the hydrogenolysis of benzyloxycarbonylglycinamide in methanol demonstrates the mechanism of deprotection but cannot be regarded as evidence of a side reaction, since the salts (e.g., **67**) readily decompose on

* A notable exception, formation of complexes between benzyloxycarbonylamino acids and their salts, has been discussed in connection with phenylalanine and serine.

acidification to yield the desired product:

$$2 \text{C}_6\text{H}_5\text{—CH}_2\text{—O—CO—NH—CH}_2\text{—CO—NH}_2 \xrightarrow{\text{H}_2/\text{Pd}}$$

$$\overset{+}{\text{H}_3\text{N}}\text{—CH}_2\text{—CO—NH}_2 \quad \text{OOC—NH—CH}_2\text{—CO—NH}_2 \; (+\text{CO}_2 + 2\, \text{C}_6\text{H}_5\text{—CH}_3)$$

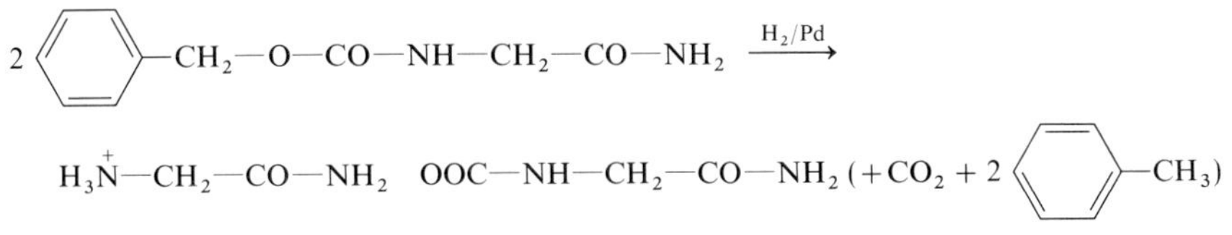

(67)

Premature loss of the benzyloxycarbonyl group during alkaline hydrolysis or in the ammonolysis of ester groups is more or less limited to peptides with glycine as the second amino acid in their sequence. These side reactions involve the formation of hydantoin derivatives such as **5** and **6** which were discussed in more detail in Section II,A.

In contrast to the smooth, elegant removal of the benzyloxycarbonyl group by hydrogenolysis, acidolytic deblocking is often accompanied by side reactions. The most frequently used reagent, HBr in acetic acid (Ben Ishai and Berger, 1952), should be free of bromine, otherwise substitutions can take place and brominated products be obtained (Schröder and Gibian, 1961; Greenbaum and Hosoda, 1963). Additives such as phenol (Neumann *et al.*, 1959) and diethyl phosphite can, of course, trap the free bromine. More serious problems are presented by the alkylating action of benzyl bromide, the by-product of fission by HBr. Amino acids with nucleophilic centers in their side chains are endangered in the deblocking reaction, S-alkylation of methionine being a particularly noteworthy example (cf. the side reactions related to methionine, Section II,O). Electrophilic aromatic substitution can also occur (see Section II,E), and alkylation of tryptophan was observed in removal of the 4-methoxybenzyloxycarbonyl group with trifluoroacetic acid (Ogawa *et al.*, 1978). Acidolysis with trifluoroacetic acid (Weygand and Steglich, 1959; Khosla and Anand, 1963) or with HBr in trifluoroacetic acid (Guttmann and Boissonnas, 1959) is more conducive to alkylation than with HBr in acetic acid.*

The selective removal of benzyloxycarbonyl groups in the presence of benzyl esters is less than perfect. Using HBr in acetic acid (Rudinger and Pravda, 1958; Kisfaludy *et al.*, 1960; Homer *et al.*, 1965) a fraction of benzyl esters is simultaneously cleaved. The benzyloxycarbonyl group itself is not as stable as would be desirable. For instance some unwanted deprotection

---

* The conversion of cyanomethyl esters to carboxamidomethyl esters ($R\text{—CO—OCH}_2\text{CN} \rightarrow R\text{—CO—OCH}_2\text{CONH}_2$) by HBr in acetic acid, observed by Goodman and Steuben (1959b) during the removal of benzyloxycarbonyl groups, suggests a beneficial effect of this acidolytic reagent. The analogous reconversion of β-cyanoalanine residues to asparagine residues can be regarded as a desirable side reaction.

of the ε-amino group of lysine residues occurred during the esterification of peptides with BF_3–alcohol mixtures (Coggins *et al.*, 1970).

In view of the problems arising with removal of the benzyloxycarbonyl group by acidolysis it is understandable that new attempts have been made to revive hydrogenolysis. Transfer hydrogenation with various donors, such as hydrazine, is a promising approach (Anwar *et al.*, 1978), although it seems to have some limitations. For instance, although the benzyloxycarbonyl group, benzyl esters, the nitro group, and even the *O*-benzyl group on the tyrosine side chain were cleaved, removal of the *O*-benzyl group from serine ran into difficulties. In deblocking with hydrazine and palladium at a elevated temperature some scission of peptide bonds occurred (Watanabe *et al.*, 1965). A search for novel protecting groups that are removable by hydrogenation even from sulfur-containing peptides is certainly justified. The 1,1-dimethyl-2-propynyloxycarbonyl group (Southard *et al.*, 1971) might receive more attention in the future.*

Removal of benzyloxycarbonyl groups by reduction with sodium in liquid ammonia (Sifferd and du Vigneaud, 1935; Loring and du Vigneaud, 1935) is not only a practical but often also an elegant method of deblocking. Nevertheless, proline-containing peptides in the presence of proton donors can suffer reductive scission of the chain (Hofmann and Yajima, 1961; Marglin and Merrifield, 1966; Bossert and Jaquenoud, 1975; Flegel *et al.*, 1976). In one case even the opening of the proline ring was observed. Reduction of acetylproline *tert*-butyl ester with sodium in liquid ammonia yielded acetyl-δ-aminovaleric acid and its *tert*-butyl ester (Ramachandran, 1965).

Activation of benzyloxycarbonylamino acids or peptides usually does not cause side reactions. Benzyloxycarbonylamino acid chlorides, however, are transformed on heating or during storage at room temperature to *N*-carboxyanhydrides (Bergmann and Zervas, 1932) [Eq. (23)]. In connection

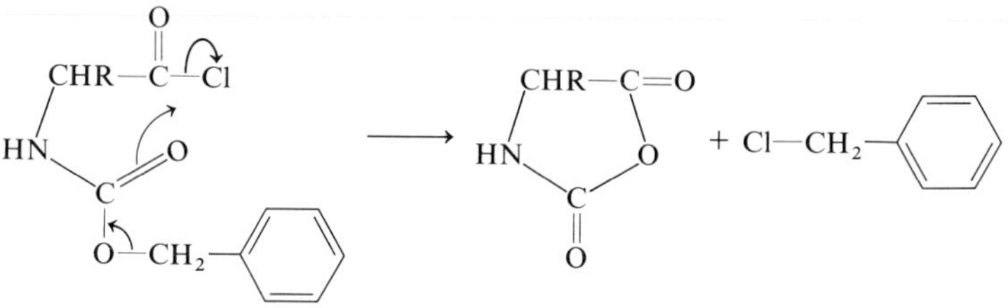

(23)

with activation it is interesting to note that a possible and even likely side reaction, the formation of mixed anhydrides from the salts of benzyloxycarbonylamino acids and benzyl chlorocarbonate used in their preparation

* Catalyst poisons, however, need not originate from the peptide itself. They can be present in the contaminated atmosphere of the laboratory or stem from the reagents used in the synthesis, for example, the activating agents derived from phosphorus (Goldschmidt, 1959).

[Eq. (24)] occurs only exceptionally (conf. ref 15 in Kopple *et al.*, 1969). Yet,

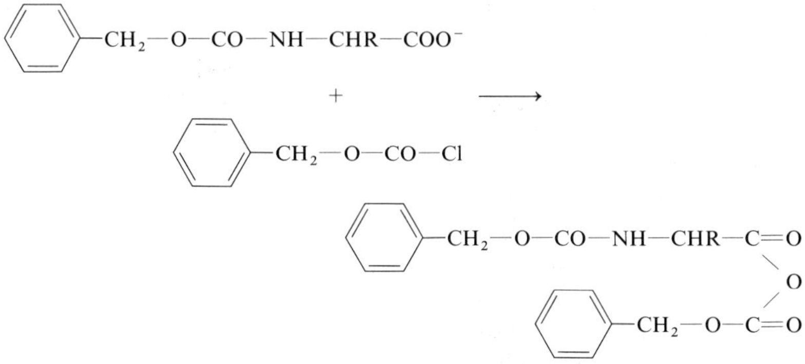
(24)

in the acylation of tripeptides such as Leu-Phe-Ala and Phe-Leu-Gly with benzyl chlorocarbonate, *N*-protected oligomers, for example, Z-(Leu-Phe-Ala)$_2$, Z-(Leu-Phe-Ala)$_3$, and Z-(Phe-Leu-Gly)$_5$, were obtained (Kopple *et al.*, 1969) in significant amounts, suggesting that the carboxylate can indeed compete with the amino group for the acylating agent.

The benzyloxycarbonyl group remains one of the mainstays of peptide chemistry. There are other groups that can be removed by a variety of procedures, for example, the formyl group which is cleaved by hydrogenolysis (Losse and Nadolski, 1964) as well as by other reductive methods and also by oxidation, with acids and with nucleophiles. Yet the benzyloxycarbonyl group, with few exceptions, prevents racemization of the activated amino acid, and this characteristic has secured an important place for it among protecting groups in peptide synthesis.

B. The *tert*-Butyloxycarbonyl (Boc) Group

The wide acceptance of this valuable method of protection (Carpino, 1957; McKay and Albertson, 1957; Anderson and McGregor, 1957) rests on the relative stability of the *tert*-butyloxycarbonyl group which is readily removable with moderately strong acids such as HCl in acetic acid and particularly with trifluoroacetic acid, an excellent solvent for most peptide derivatives. Since *tert*-butyl chlorocarbonate is not stable enough to be used for introduction of the *tert*-butyloxycarbonyl group, a continued effort to obtain better reagents resulted in many compounds of which only two di-*tert*-butyl dicarbonate (Tarbell *et al.*, 1972) (**68**) and 2-*tert*-butyloxycarbonyl-oxyimino-2-phenylacetonitrile (Itoh *et al.*, 1975) (**69**), are mentioned here as examples of commercially available acylating agents. (For a more detailed

$(CH_3)_3C{-}O{-}CO{-}O{-}CO{-}O{-}C(CH_3)_3$

(68)

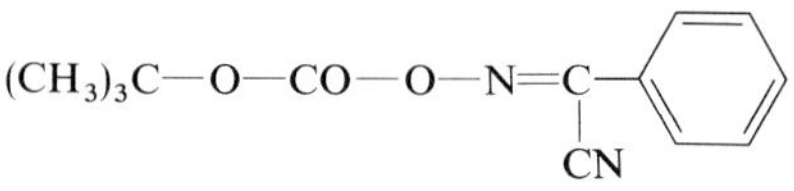

(69)

overview of reagents proposed for the *tert*-butyloxycarbonylation of amino acids we refer the reader to Bodanszky *et al.*, 1976, Table 3 on pp 32–33.) Interestingly, the closely related amyloxycarbonyl group (Sakakibara *et al.*, 1965) can be introduced via the chlorocarbonate (**70**), but in the case of

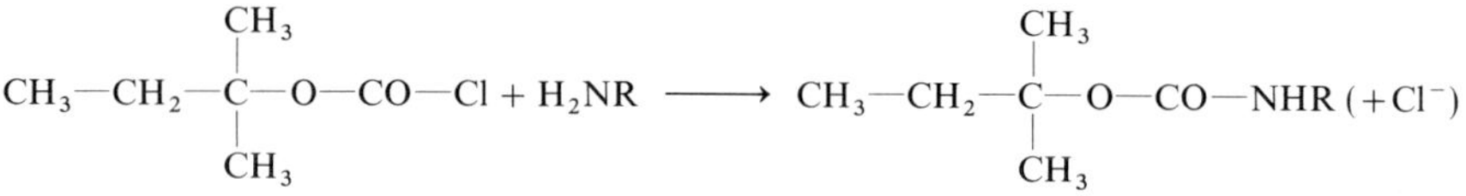

(70)

asparagine, glutamine, and nitroarginine the reaction was accompanied by side reactions and the yields and the purity of the products were less than satisfactory (Sakakibara *et al.*, 1969). No major side reactions were reported, however, in the use of an active ester of *tert*-butylcarbonic acid such as **69**.

Removal of the *tert*-butyloxycarbonyl group is less trouble-free than its introduction. Alkylation by *tert*-butyl trifluoroacetate (Lundt *et al.*, 1978) has been discussed in some detail in connection with the side reactions characteristic of methionine, tyrosine, and tryptophan. There is no reason to assume that deblocking with acids other than trifluoroacetic acid will produce no alkylating agents. Esters of *tert*-butanol are probably generally harmful in this respect, although perhaps not equally noxious. As mentioned before, *tert*-butyl fluoride and *tert*-butyl esters of various sulfonic acids all can affect the purity of deprotected peptides. The more volatile compounds are eliminated early in the work-up; the less volatile ones remain during concentration of the reaction mixture and cause more harm. The use of scavengers and precipitation of the product without prior concentration of the mixture provides at least a partial remedy.

The inherent promise in the use of the *tert*-butyloxycarbonyl group, that it can be removed without the loss of benzyloxycarbonyl and benzyl groups used for the masking of side-chain functions, has not been completely fulfilled. Neat trifluoroacetic acid (Kappeler and Schwyzer, 1960) slowly but steadily cleaves the benzyloxycarbonyl groups from the ε-amino group of lysine residues (Schnabel *et al.*, 1971), and even the more acid-stable benzyl esters and benzyl ethers do not necessarily remain intact in the process (Rzeszotarska and Kmiecik-Chmura, 1977). The desired selectivity can be approached by dilution of trifluoroacetic acid with dichloromethane (Gutte and Merrifield, 1969; Karlsson *et al.*, 1970; Gutte, 1975), water (Schnabel *et al.*, 1971), or acetic acid (Klausner and Bodanszky, 1973), or by the use of formic acid (Halpern and Nitecki, 1967) for acidolytic deblocking. Greater selectivity, however, might be counterbalanced by slow or imperfect cleavage (Dorman and Markley, 1971).

In the activation of *tert*-butyloxycarbonylamino acids, for example, with dicyclohexylcarbodiimide or other coupling reagents, the formation of impurities which on exposure to moisture give rise to ninhydrin-positive materials was observed (Bodanszky *et al.*, 1975). The free amino acid, its oligomers, and the amino acid *tert*-butyl ester were identified as products of the decomposition. The latter probably proceeds through the oxonium intermediate **71** which can collapse to form the isocyanate **72** or the *N*-carboxyanhydride **73**. Hydrolysis of **72** yields the *tert*-butyl ester of the amino acid, whereas the free amino acid and its oligomers are produced in the reaction of **73** with water or with the already liberated molecules of the amino acid (Scheme 3). Fortunately, this side reaction involves only a small fraction of the activated material. Thus, it merely interferes with examination of the reaction mixture on thin-layer chromatograms but does not seriously

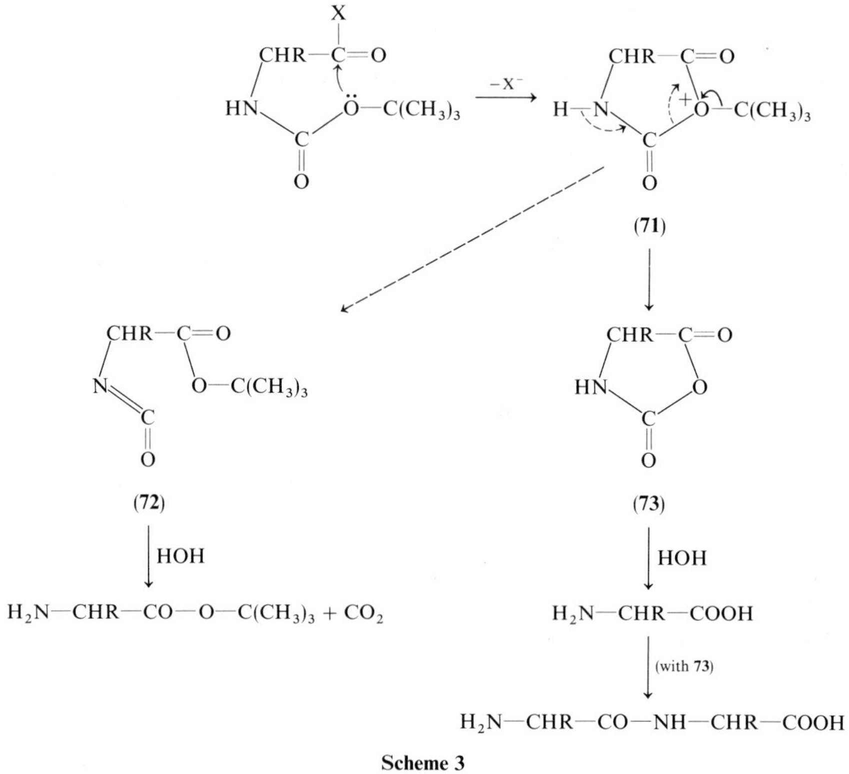

Scheme 3

affect the yield or the purity of the main product of the reaction. On the other hand, decomposition of Boc-amino acids should serve as a warning against overactivation: When a solution of a *tert*-butyloxycarbonylamino acid in ethyl acetate is treated with phosphorus pentoxide, the corresponding *N*-carboxyanhydride is generated (Bodanszky *et al.*, 1975).

Of the acid-labile protecting groups proposed for peptide synthesis the 4-methoxybenzyloxycarbonyl group (McKay and Albertson, 1957; Weygand and Hunger, 1962) and the 2-(4-biphenylyl)propyl(2)oxycarbonyl (Bpoc) group (Sieber and Iselin, 1968) have gained major importance. Since the removal of these groups by moderately strong acids under mild conditions is based on the stability of the carbo-cations formed on protonation, side reactions similar to those reported for the *tert*-butyloxycarbonyl group, particularly alkylation, must be anticipated in their use.

C. The 2-Nitrophenylsulfenyl (Nps) Group

The principal side reaction in connection with the 2-nitrophenylsulfenyl group, addition of its cleavage product, 2-nitrophenylsulfenyl chloride, to the indole nucleus of tryptophan, has been discussed in detail in Section II,F. The new trend toward using nucleophilic reagents rather than HCl (in organic solvents) for removal of the 2-nitrophenylsulfenyl group was also mentioned. Such deblocking, however, can occur unintentionally and prematurely as a result of the presence of 1-hydroxybenzotriazole (Geiger *et al.*, 1973) in dicyclohexylcarbodiimide-mediated couplings. Similarly, the 2-nitrophenylsulfenyl group is removed by and transferred to the amino group of amino acid esters used as nucleophilic components (Kulikov *et al.*, 1977; Lashkov and Vlasov, 1978) [Eq. (25)]. Several side products were

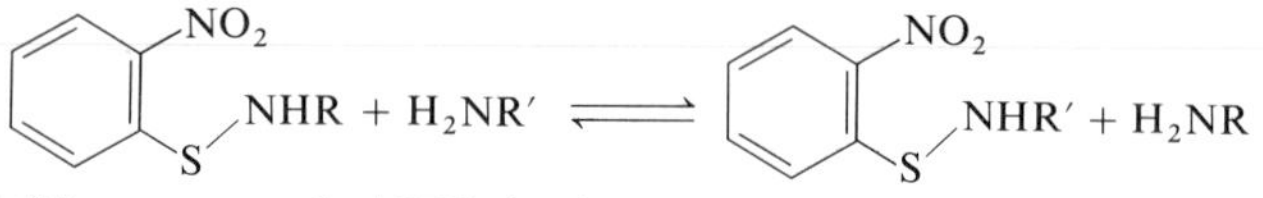

(25)

identified (Vegners *et al.*, 1979) in the preparation of 2-nitrophenylsulfenyl-amino acids, for example, di-2-nitrophenyl sulfide, the corresponding disulfide, and sulfones. These impurities may have been formed on oxidation by the solvent, aqueous dioxane (perhaps not free of peroxides), or caused by the presence of nitro groups in alkaline media.

D. The 4-Toluenesulfonyl (Tosyl, Tos) Group

The protection of the amino function provided by the tosyl group is less than perfect. Acylation of primary amines with sulfonic acids leads to amides with rather acidic NH groups. Abstraction of the proton from the latter results in potent nucleophiles. This is shown, for instance, in the cyclization of active esters of tosyl dipeptides to substituted diketopiperazines (Lucente and Frattesi, 1972) such as **74**. Similarly, attempted preparation of the 4-

$$H_3C-\langle\rangle-SO_2-NH-CHR-CO-NH-CHR'-CO-O-\langle\rangle-NO_2 \xrightarrow[\text{aqueous alkali}]{\text{pyridine or}}$$

$$\left[H_3C-\langle\rangle-SO_2-\bar{N}-CHR-CO-NH-CHR'-CO-O-\langle\rangle-NO_2\right] \longrightarrow$$

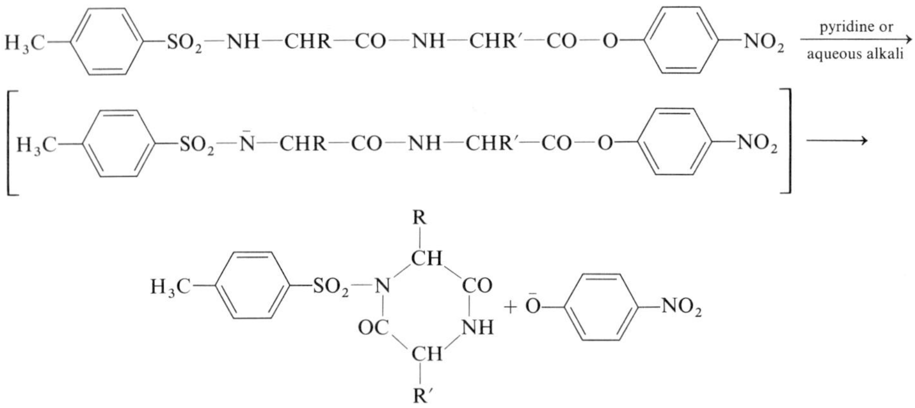

(74)

nitrophenyl ester from tosylglycine with dicyclohexylcarbodiimide yielded only 1,4-ditosylpiperazine-2,5-dione (Berse *et al.*, 1963). Active ester or peptide bond formation failed in every case in these experiments, except when tosylproline and tosylpyroglutamic acid were activated: they have no abstractable proton on the tosylamido group.

In an analogous but intramolecular attack tosylglutamic acid bischloride (**75**) is converted to tosylpyroglutamic acid chloride (**76**) (Stedman, 1957),

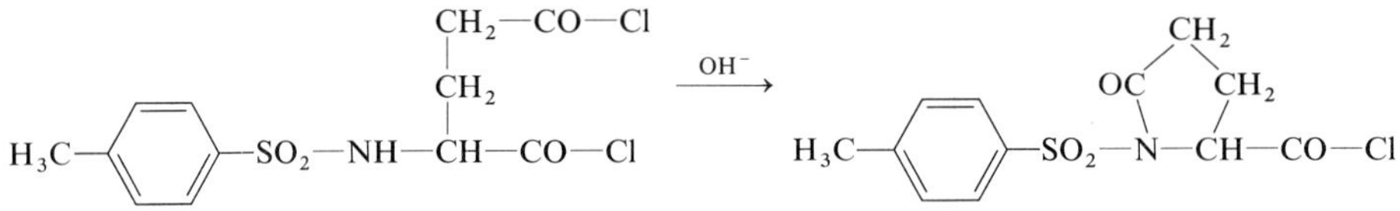

(75)   (76)

and spontaneous lactam formation occurs in carboxyl-activated derivatives of N^δ-tosylornithine (Zaoral and Rudinger, 1959). The difficulties reported (Hillmann and Hillmann, 1951) in the coupling of tosylamino acids via mixed anhydrides are probably related to the nucleophilic center in their molecules. The problem, however, was solved by the use of tosylamino acid–trimethylacetic acid mixed anhydrides (Zaoral, 1962).

The tosylamido grouping is the probable source of protons that can cause the cleavage of peptide bonds (particularly between proline and the preceding amino acid) in reduction with sodium in liquid ammonia (Guttmann, 1963; Jošt and Rudinger, 1967a). The most remarkable consequence of the ready proton abstraction from tosylamino acids is decomposition of the acid chlorides (Beecham, 1955, 1957, 1963): On treatment with alkali, tosylamino acid chlorides lose carbon monoxide and HCl and are converted to an aldehyde and 4-toluenesulfonamide [Eq. (26)]. A similar decomposition

$$H_3C-\underset{}{\bigcirc}-SO_2-NH-CHR-CO-Cl \xrightarrow{OH^-}$$

$$\left[H_3C-\underset{}{\bigcirc}-SO_2-\overset{+}{N}-CHR-CO-Cl \right] \longrightarrow \quad (26)$$

$$H_3C-\underset{}{\bigcirc}-SO_2-N=CHR \ (+CO+Cl^-) \xrightarrow{HOH}$$

$$H_3C-\underset{}{\bigcirc}-SO_2-NH_2 + OHC-R$$

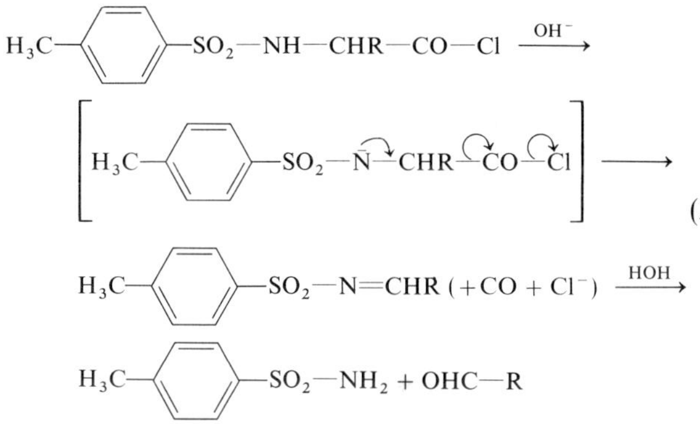

takes place with tosylamino acid azides. Notable exceptions are tosylproline and tosylpyroglutamic acid: They both lack an abstractable NH proton.

E. The Phthalyl (Phthaloyl, Pht) Group

Introduction of the phthalyl group into amino acids with bulky side chains (isoleucine, α-methylalanine) via 2-carbomethoxybenzoyl chloride is hindered (Hoogwater *et al.*, 1973). The reaction stops at the intermediate 2-carbomethoxybenzoylamino acid. In connection with phthalylation with *N*-carboethoxyphthalimide (Nefkens, 1960; Nefkens *et al.*, 1960) no such difficulties were reported.

The main problem in working with phthalyl-protected intermediates is the sensitivity of the protecting group to aqueous alkali (Sheehan *et al.*, 1952; Hanson and Illhardt, 1954; Grassmann and Wünsch, 1956; Goodman and Kenner, 1957; Rudinger *et al.*, 1960). The ring is opened, albeit slowly, even by solutions of sodium bicarbonate in water [Eq. (27)].

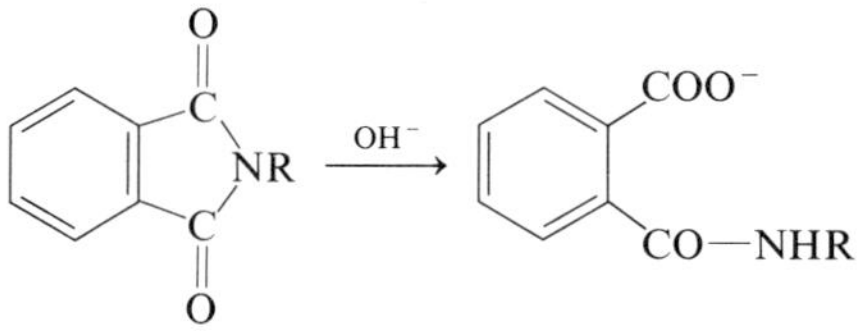

$$\underset{}{\bigcirc}\overset{O}{\underset{O}{\overset{\parallel}{C}}}NR \xrightarrow{OH^-} \underset{}{\bigcirc}\overset{COO^-}{\underset{CO-NHR}{}} \quad (27)$$

F. The Triphenylmethyl (Trityl, Trt) Group

The bulkiness of the trityl group leads to severe limitations on its application in peptide synthesis. Saponification of esters of tritylglycine proceeds readily, but esters of other amino acids protected by the trityl group can be hydrolyzed only slowly with alkali. The rates seem to depend on the size of the side chain (Zervas and Theodoropoulos, 1956). Similarly, tritylglycine esters react with hydrazine to yield tritylglycine hydrazide (**77**), but hydra-

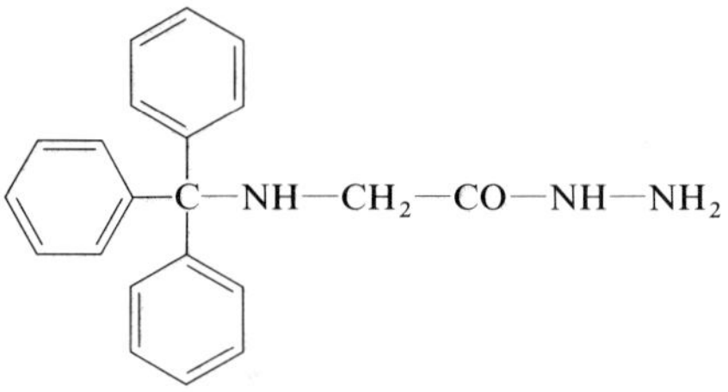

(**77**)

zinolysis generally fails with other amino acid esters (Hillmann-Elies *et al.*, 1953). Nevertheless, it is possible to use tritylamino acids in peptide synthesis because they can be coupled (Stelakatos *et al.*, 1959), for example, by the dicyclohexylcarbodiimide method, and trityl dipeptides can be activated in the form of their mixed anhydrides.

G. The 9-Fluorenylmethyloxycarbonyl (Fmoc) Group

The possibility of deblocking through an attack by nucleophilic reagents rather than by acidolysis was tempting for a long time. The trifluoroacetyl group (Weygand and Csendes, 1952), which could be removed from the amino function by mild alkaline hydrolysis or with aqueous piperidine (Goldberger and Anfinsen, 1962), could be a more generally applied tool of peptide synthesis if its introduction were not complicated by the formation of mixed anhydrides (Weygand and Geiger, 1956; Weygand *et al.*, 1956) or if, like urethane-type protecting groups it prevented the loss of chiral purity during coupling. A whole series of carboxyl protecting groups is based on the abstraction of an acidic proton from the β-carbon atom of ethyl esters bearing an electron-withdrawing substituent on this carbon atom. The resulting carbo-anion is then stabilized by the elimination of a carboxylate group and the formation of a vinyl derivative (for reviews, cf. Carpino, 1973; Bodanszky *et al.*, 1979b) [Eq. (28)]. The same principle was also applied in the protection of amino groups simply by converting the latter to a carbamoic acid (e.g., Tesser and Balvert-Geers, 1975) [Eq. (29)]. An

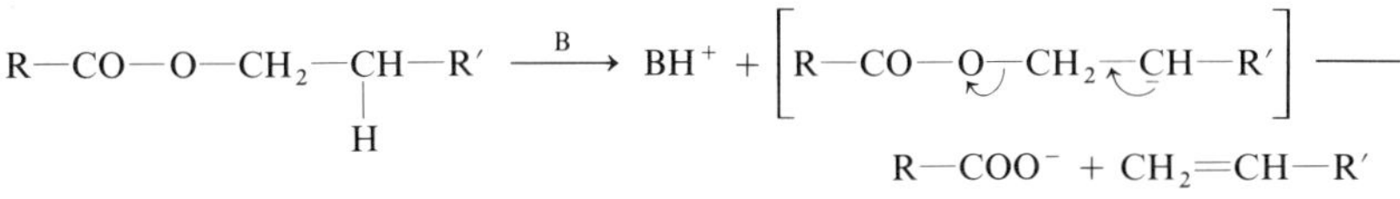

$$R-CO-O-CH_2-\underset{\underset{H}{|}}{CH}-R' \xrightarrow{B} BH^+ + \left[R-CO-O-CH_2-CH-R'\right] \longrightarrow$$

$$R-COO^- + CH_2{=}CH-R' \quad (28)$$

$$R-NH-CO-O-CH_2-\underset{\underset{H}{|}}{CH}-\underset{\underset{O}{\overset{O}{\|}}}{S}-CH_3 \xrightarrow{NaOH}$$

$$\left[R-NH-CO-O-CH_2-CH-\underset{\underset{O}{\overset{O}{\|}}}{S}-CH_3\right] \longrightarrow \quad (29)$$

$$R-NH-COO^- + CH_2{=}CH-\underset{\underset{O}{\overset{O}{\|}}}{S}-CH_3 \longrightarrow R-NH_2 + CO_2$$

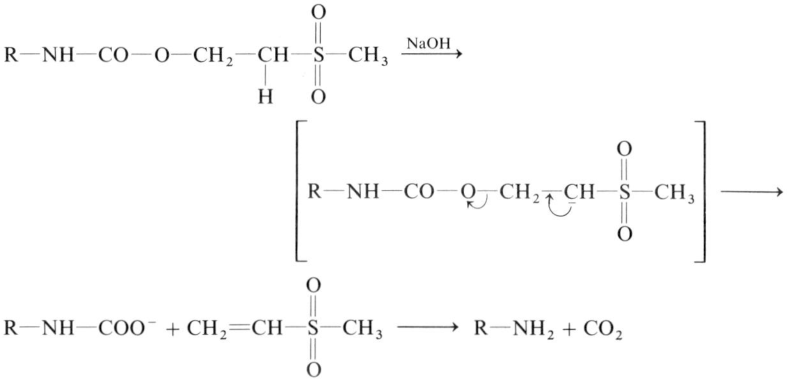

excellent illustration of this concept involves the 9-fluorenylmethyloxy-carbonyl group (Carpino and Han, 1972), because the effect of the fluorenyl system renders the proton on its C-9 so readily abstractable that even relatively weak bases such as ammonia and particularly secondary amines, for example, piperidine, are sufficient for the generation of a carbo-anion. The latter yields dibenzofulvene (**78**) and a carbamate which on acidification, and even on standing or evaporation of the solvent, decomposes to carbon dioxide and the free amine [Eq. (30)].

$$+ \; {}^-OCONHR \longrightarrow H_2NR + CO_2$$

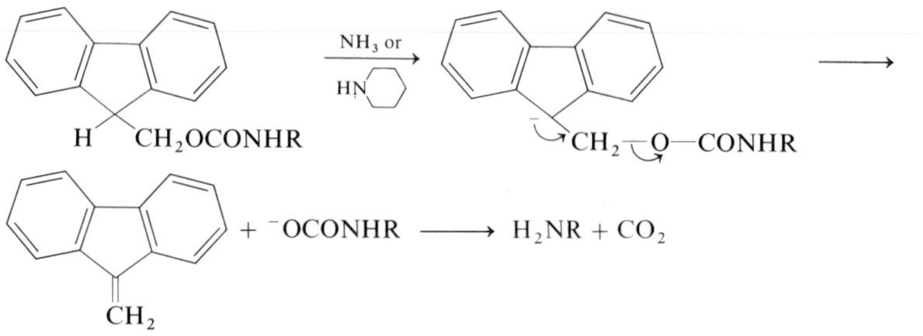

(**78**)

(30)

These attractive features prompted laboratories engaged in solid-phase peptide synthesis to use the 9-fluorenylmethyloxycarbonyl group in protecting the α-amino function, in combination with side-chain-protecting groups based on the *tert*-butyl cation, mostly with quite satisfactory results (Chang and Meienhofer, 1978; Atherton *et al*., 1978; Chang *et al*., 1980; Meienhofer *et al*., 1979). The new protecting group also worked well in syntheses carried out in solution (e.g., Bodanszky *et al*., 1980). However, some general concern must be felt about cleavage of the 9-fluorenylmethyloxycarbonyl group by amines under mild conditions. The question must be raised whether or not the primary amines set free in the process are sufficiently basic to effect removal of the 9-fluorenylmethyloxycarbonyl group. Such a premature deblocking would have undesirable consequences, such as double incorporation. A study of this problem (Bodanszky *et al*., 1979b) revealed that the 9-fluorenylmethoxycarbonyl was indeed removed by esters of amino acids, particularly by glycine ethyl ester or proline *tert*-butyl ester, but the extent of loss of protection was moderate unless prolonged reaction times were necessary in the coupling reactions. Fortunately, in condensations with potent coupling reagents such as dicyclohexylcarbodiimide, exposure of the 9-fluorenylmethoxycarbonyl derivative to the basic amino component is rather brief and the risk of premature deblocking is further reduced by the presence of the acidic carboxyl componet. During acylations with active esters, which are neutral materials, the basic character of the amino component should indeed give cause for concern. However, as the reaction progresses, the gradually diminishing concentration of the amino component attenuates the danger, and the acidity of the (protonated) leaving group, for example, 4-nitrophenol, should also have a favorable effect. Nevertheless, it is highly desirable to accelerate the aminolysis of active esters, for example, with 1-hydroxybenzotriazole (König and Geiger, 1973), and thus limit the exposure of the 9-fluorenylmethoxycarbonyl group to basic conditions.

According to the investigations of Carpino and Han (1972) the 9-fluorenylmethoxycarbonyl group is resistant to catalytic hydrogenation. This finding was supported by careful experiments and also by the nonbenzylic character of the CH_2 group at C-9 of the fluorene system. Therefore, it is surprising that complete hydrogenolysis of the 9-fluorenylmethoxycarbonyl group was observed in two laboratories (Atherton *et al*., 1979; Martinez *et al*., 1979b). The isolation of 9-methylfluorene (**79**) in quantitative yield leaves no doubt about cleavage of the 9-fluorenylmethoxycarbonyl group by catalytic hydrogenation, but the reaction still awaits an explanation.

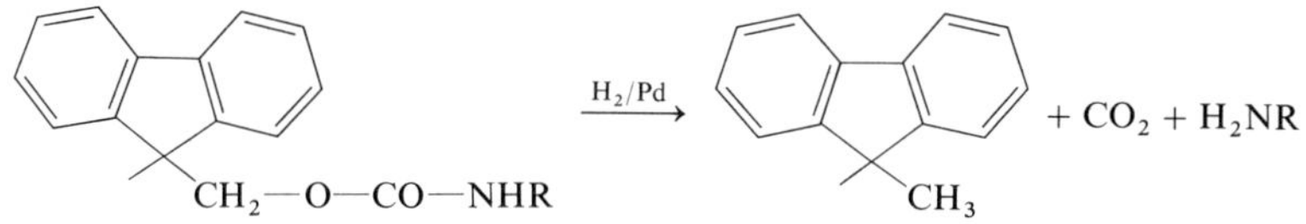

(**79**)

H. Protection of the Carboxyl Group

The obvious and general approach to the protection of carboxyl functions involves their conversion to esters that are readily cleaved. The simplest of these are methyl and ethyl esters, which are easily prepared and stable under a variety of conditions and can be hydrolyzed, with alkali, under mild conditions. The effect of bulky side chains on the rate of saponification has been discussed in connection with valine and isoleucine. It is possible to enhance the rate of nucleophilic attacks by adding electron-withdrawing substituents to the alkyl group of the ester moiety or by replacing the alkyl group by an aryl group. Of course, such a replacement results in carboxyls that are not as fully protected; in fact, they are somewhat activated. Thus the phenyl esters proposed by Kenner and Seely (1972) for the protection of carboxyl groups, although readily cleaved with alkali, must also be sensitive to aminolysis [Eq. (31)]. Catalysis of the alkaline hydrolysis with hydrogen

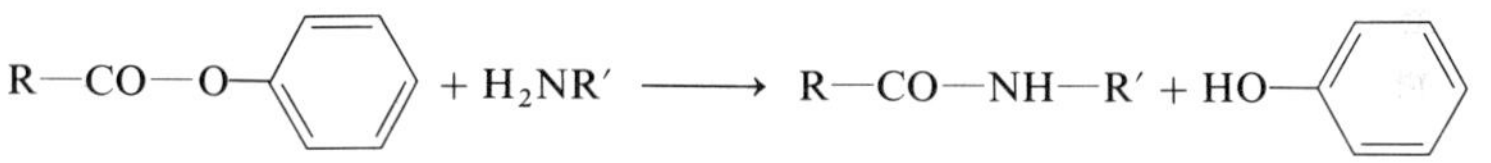

(31)

peroxide cannot be regarded as harmless: Oxidation of sensitive amino acids, such as tryptophan, must be prevented, for example, by the addition of dimethyl sulfide. The borderline between protection and activation is similarly vague in 2,2,2-trichloroethyl esters (Woodward *et al.*, 1966) and in 3-nitrophenyl esters (Ito, 1979). In such partially activated esters the risk of intermolecular aminolysis is rather obvious. One usually feels safer when unsubstituted alkyl esters are used. Yet, even methyl, ethyl, and benzyl esters are less than inert when they are attacked by an intramolecular nucleophile. The formation of diketopiperazines or piperazine-2,5-diones from dipeptide esters has been well known since the beginnings of peptide synthesis (Fischer and Fourneau, 1901; Fischer, 1901, 1906; Fischer and Suzuki, 1905) and has been encountered again and again. The tendency toward cyclization is so pronounced in dipeptide esters that protonation by acetic acid does not prevent the reaction (McGregor and Carpenter, 1961). Thus catalytic reduction of 4-nitrobenzyloxycarbonyl-L-leucyl-L-alanine ethyl ester in a mixture of methanol and acetic acid yields the substituted diketopiperazine (**80**).

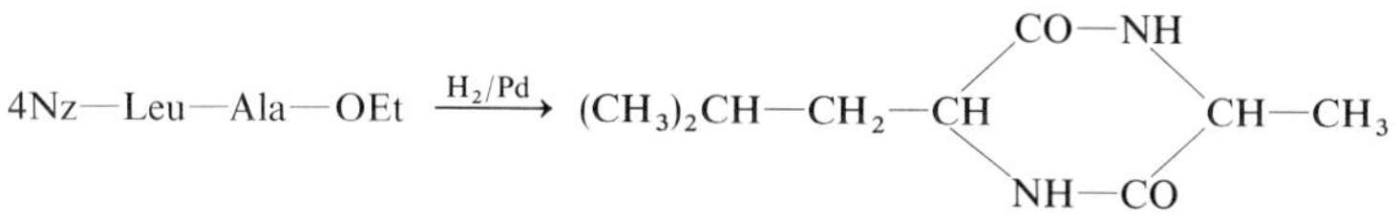

(**80**)

Diketopiperazines are also formed via cyclization of dipeptide amides (acetate salts) (Huang and Niemann, 1950). In esters the rate of ring closure depends on the nature of the amino acid constituents of the dipeptide: For instance, it is fast in glycine-containing compounds and rapid in glycyl-sarcosine methyl ester (Purdie and Benoiton, 1973). In the alkaline hydrolysis of glycyl-glycine ethyl ester, ring closure competes with saponification (Meresar and Agren, 1968), and diketopiperazines are also produced during hydrazinolysis of trifluoroacetyl dipeptide esters (Weygand and Swodenk, 1960).

Side reactions can also take place during the preparation of esters of amino acids or peptides. In acid-catalyzed transesterification with *tert*-butyl acetate, alkylation of the carboxamide nitrogen in asparagine or glutamine can occur (Schnabel and Schüssler, 1965). In esterification with triethyloxonium fluoroborate (Yonemitsu *et al.*, 1969) alkylation of the sulfur atom in methionine and of the NH group in the imidazole ring of histidine was observed. In the case of amino acids that are not easily converted to their *tert*-butyl esters by treatment with isobutene in strong acids (Roeske, 1959, 1963), the use of 2,4,6-trimethylbenzyl esters (Ledger and Stewart, 1968) remains a good alternative. It should be noted here that, in addition to esters, hydrazides can also be used as protected forms of the COOH-terminal carboxyl group (Cheung and Blout, 1965). With mild acylating agents, used in the calculated amount, no acylation of the second amino group of the hydrazide should occur. With an excess of acylating agent, however, the formation of diacylhydrazines is a distinct possibility.

Removal of carboxyl blocking groups by hydrolysis is obviously a risky operation. With nucleophilic reagents side reactions, such as the hydantoin formation discussed in Section II,A, can easily occur. In saponification with alkali the chiral purity of the formerly protected residue is also endangered. It is more surprising to note that such a gentle method as catalytic hydrogenation can take an unexpected course. However, in the removal of benzyl esters by hydrogenolysis, transesterification by the solvent, ethanol, was observed (Crofts *et al.*, 1959). The side reaction could be prevented by the use of *tert*-butanol.

The sophisticated dealkylation of esters with iodotrimethylsilane (Ho and Olah, 1976; Jung and Lyster, 1977) still awaits application in the synthesis of complex peptides.

The side reactions encountered in the protection and deprotection of carboxyl groups show that no perfect solution has been found so far for the blocking of this function. Masking of the carboxyl group in the form of 2-trimethylsilylethyl ester (Sieber *et al.*, 1977), which is cleaveable by fluoride ions, is a good example of the promising new methods in this area. Many more carboxyl protecting groups, some of them potentially useful in peptide synthesis, are described in a comprehensive review by Haslam (1980).

I. Protection of Side-Chain Functions and the Final Deprotection

The protection of reactive groups in amino acid side chains has been discussed in connection with the side reactions characteristic of individual amino acids. Here we call attention mainly to the general problems arising in the final removal of blocking groups. Since the masking of the COOH-terminal carboxyl function and the functional groups in the side chains of amino acid residues requires semipermanent protecting groups, removal of these blocking groups often calls for more drastic conditions or more efficient reagents than those applied in removal of the protection from α-amino groups before chain lengthening. In some exceptional cases final deblocking by hydrogenolysis is quite practical* (cf., e.g., Bodanszky *et al.*, 1967), but the majority of peptide syntheses have to be concluded by acidolysis, usually with a strong acid such as HF (Sakakibara and Shimonishi, 1965). Under mild conditions, such as 0°C and a reaction time of less than $\frac{1}{2}$ hr, this reagent is relatively safe, but for full exploitation of its deblocking ability in the removal of acid-resistant groups such as the *S*-benzyl group or the nitro group on the guanidines of arginine residues, more extended treatment and a somewhat higher temperature are necessary. Under such conditions several side reactions can occur. Noteworthy among these is the acylmigration from N to O [Eq. (32)], because it can disrupt the peptide

$$\begin{array}{r} HO-CH_2 \\ | \quad \\ -NH-CHR-CO-NH-CH-CO- \end{array} \xrightarrow{HF} \begin{array}{r} -NH-CHR-CO-O-CH_2 \\ | \quad \\ H_2N-CH-CO- \end{array} \qquad (32)$$

chain. This well-studied reaction (cf., e.g., Sakakibara *et al.*, 1962; Shin *et al.*, 1962) need not be fatal, since the rearrangement can be reversed by exposure to mild alkaline conditions, for example, by dissolving the product in aqueous sodium bicarbonate. Nevertheless, some damage to the peptide chain should be expected because of the susceptibility of the newly formed ester group to hydrolysis, even in bicarbonate solutions. Regrettably, there are also other side reactions related to this otherwise very effective method of final deprotection. Thus, cleavage of the bond between methionine and glycine (Lenard *et al.*, 1964) has been reported. Alkylation of tyrosine side chains and the

* Some side-chain protecting groups, however, require for their removal prolonged periods of catalytic reduction, elevated temperatures, or a more than usual amount of catalyst. Under such conditions significant saturation of the aromatic nuclei of phenylalanine, tyrosine, and particularly of tryptophan can take place (Bajusz *et al.*, 1973; Schafer *et al.*, 1971; Windridge and Jorgensen, 1971).

sulfur in methionine were mentioned in connection with these amino acids, as was the ring closure to form a succinimide derivative noted in Section II,K. The harmful effect of anisole in HF was treated in Section II,L. The latter side reaction was suppressed by the addition of pyridine (Sugano *et al.*, 1978), but it remains questionable whether or not all the other shortcomings of the procedure were eliminated. The use of Lewis acids for deblocking is equally risky. For instance, boron tribromide caused partial degradation of asparagine and glutamine residues (Felix, 1974). Novel reagents proposed for general deprotection, for example, trimethylsilyl iodide (Lott *et al.*, 1979), await the judgment of those who use them in the synthesis of complex peptides.

Having seen the damage that can be caused by strong acids, one would be inclined to give thought to deprotection under alkaline conditions. Unfortunately no remedy can be found in such an approach. Not only partial hydrolysis of the carboxamide groups on the side chains of asparagine and glutamine must be expected, but even their protected forms (e.g., by the 2,4-dimethoxybenzyl group) suffer decomposition with alkali (Pietta *et al.*, 1971). The sensitivity of disulfides to alkali (cf., e.g., Gawron and Odstrchel, 1967) is a further obstacle. Thus, one has to return to the idea of acidic deblocking, except that acids milder than HF should be more advantageous. Acidolysis with trifluoroacetic acid might be an attractive solution, although it presupposes the protection of α-amino functions by blocking groups that are sensitive to very weak acids (e.g., Bpoc) or can be removed by nucleophiles under mild conditions (e.g., Fmoc).

Because of the individuality of peptides, final deprotection remains problematic even when well-established protecting groups are removed by commonly used methods. For instance, some *tert*-butyl ester groups of protected β-endorphin resisted the action of trifluoroacetic acid (Meienhofer and Chang, 1979). Difficulties caused in the deprotection of cysteine side chains are particularly notorious. The *S*-4-methoxybenzyl group, which is readily cleaved by HF, could be removed only incompletely from a peptide derivative with the sequence of the A chain of insulin (Berndt, 1976). A similar experience was reported (Rocchi *et al.*, 1979) in connection with the cleavage of *S*-acetamidomethyl groups with mercury(II) acetate from a protected pancreatic trypsin inhibitor. Extended treatment of the peptide with the mercury reagent can cause substitution of tyrosine side chains. Compound **81** was isolated after a 30-hr exposure of benzyloxycarbonyltyrosinamide to mercury(II) acetate followed by precipitation with sodium chloride (Williams and Young, 1979). Oxidative removal of *S*-trityl groups (with iodine) afforded, in addition to the desired disulfide, a substituted indole derivative of the type shown in **82** (Sieber *et al.*, 1980). In an analogous manner removal of S-protecting groups with HF can lead to the formation

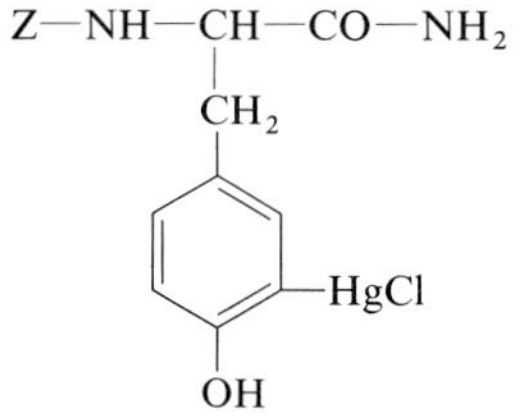

(81)

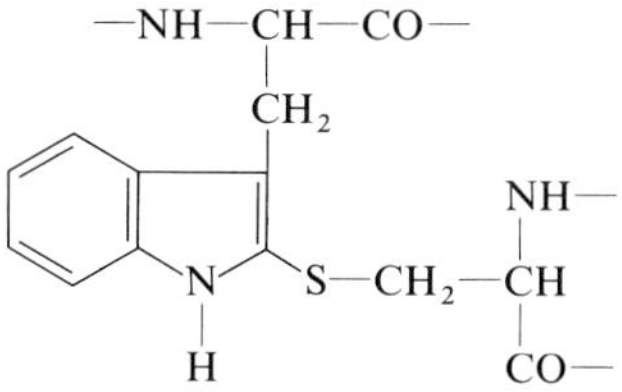

(82)

of γ-thiol esters of glutamyl residues as shown in **83** (Tregear *et al.*, 1981). A dire consequence of this side reaction is polymerization of the product*

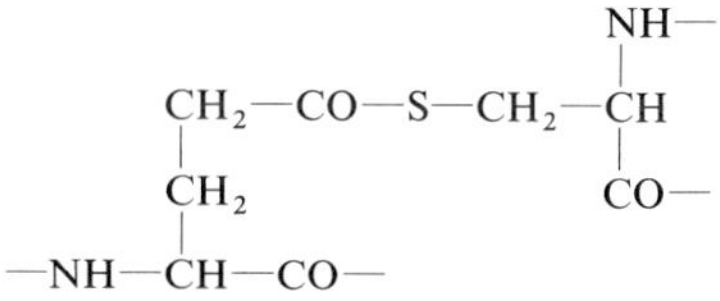

(83)

Simultaneous removal of all blocking groups from the protected form of oxytocin was achieved (du Vigneaud *et al.*, 1953) by reduction with sodium in liquid ammonia. The same elegant procedure was also used in the concluding steps of the syntheses of vasopressins and in numerous analogs of these pituitary hormones. An extension of the method for the final deprotection of the B chain of insulin resulted in extensive scission of the peptide between proline and the preceding residue unless special precautions (Marglin and Merrifield, 1966) were taken. Reductive cleavage of the peptide bond was discussed in Section II,C. Here we point out the discrepancy in experiences reported with the same method in the deblocking of different peptides. The conspicuous sensitivity of the Thr-Pro and Ser-Pro bonds to reduction with sodium in liquid ammonia also serves as a warning against generalizations in peptide chemistry.

IV. SIDE REACTIONS ENCOUNTERED IN FORMATION OF THE PEPTIDE BOND

A. The Azide Method

Since its introduction at the turn of the century (Curtius, 1902) the azide method has been an important approach to peptide bond formation. Various aspects of the procedure including the side reactions associated with azide

* The reactivity of newly liberated SH groups can lead to still further side reactions. For example, alkylation of the cysteine SH group by benzyl bromide was observed (Jŏst and Rudinger, 1967b) during synthetic operations.

coupling were treated in reviews (Klausner and Bodanszky, 1974; Meienhofer, 1979a), and Schnabel (1962, 1963) dedicated two articles solely to such side reactions. Nevertheless, because of the significance of the method and of a few recent observations a brief discussion of the azide procedure seems to be justified in this chapter.

1. Preparation of Azides

The classic route to azides of protected amino acids or peptides proceeds through esters and hydrazides (Scheme 4), and is applicable in many cases. Some amino acid side chains, however, are sensitive to hydrazine, which is a powerful reducing agent. Thus, nitroguanidine in protected arginine

$$\mathrm{R{-}CO{-}OCH_3 + H_2NNH_2 \longrightarrow R{-}CO{-}NHNH_2\ (+\ CH_3OH)}$$

$$\downarrow \text{HONO or RONO}$$

$$\mathrm{R{-}CO{-}N{=}\overset{}{\underset{+}{N}}{=}\underset{-}{N}}$$

Scheme 4

might be reduced to aminoguanidine (McKay, 1952). Because hydrazine is also an excellent nucleophile, it is not surprising that substituted guanidines from which the resonance stabilization of guanidine itself is absent are readily decomposed during the hydrazinolysis of esters. Nitroarginine moieties, for instance, are converted to ornithine residues. An interesting transfer of the tosyl group can take place in tosylarginine derivatives (**84**) (Danho and Li, 1971).

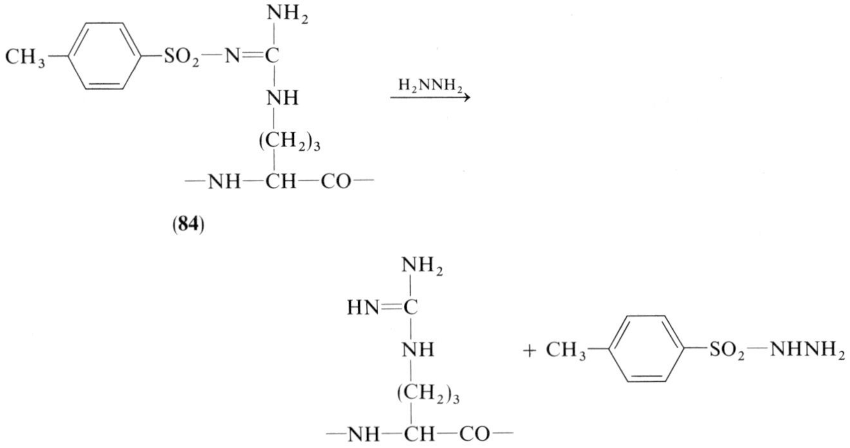

(**84**)

Side-chain carboxamides remain intact if hydrazinolysis is carried out under mild conditions (Sondheimer and Holley, 1954b), but hydrolysis

(Bajusz *et al.*, 1964) and hydrazinolysis (Chillemi, 1966; Schwyzer *et al.*, 1963) of β-*tert*-butyl esters of aspartyl residues are distrubing side reactions. Aspartyl and glutamyl peptides can rearrange to β- or γ-peptides under the influence of hydrazine (Naithani, 1973) even if the side-chain carboxyls are free (Mitsuyasu *et al.*, 1970).

The risk of hydrazinolysis of the peptide bond (Akabori *et al.*, 1952) eliminates the use of neat hydrazine, but the reagent still must be used in considerable excess to avoid the formation of diacylhydrazines* (**85**) (Woolley, 1948; Schneider, 1960) [Eq. (33)]. Potentially the same type of compound can also form in the conversion of hydrazides to azides if the already activated compound reacts with unchanged hydrazide [Eq. (34)]. An alternative to ester hydrazinolysis is the use of protected hydrazides as starting points of chain building (Hofmann *et al.*, 1950) [Eq. (35)]. This is

$$2\ \mathrm{R{-}CO{-}OCH_3 + H_2NNH_2 \longrightarrow R{-}CO{-}HNNH{-}CO{-}R\ (+2CH_3OH)} \quad (33)$$

(**85a**)

$$\mathrm{R{-}CO{-}N_3 + H_2NNH{-}CO{-}R \longrightarrow R{-}CO{-}HNNH{-}COR\ (+HN_3)} \quad (34)$$

(**85b**)

$$\begin{aligned} &\mathrm{Z{-}NH{-}CHR{-}CO{-}HNNH{-}Boc \longrightarrow H_2N{-}CHR{-}CO{-}HNNH{-}Boc} \\ &\mathrm{Boc{-}NH{-}CHR{-}CO{-}HNNH{-}Z \longrightarrow H_2N{-}CHR{-}CO{-}HNNH{-}Z} \end{aligned} \quad (35)$$

an elegant procedure that has often been applied in the synthesis of peptides having polyfunctional amino acid residues. A certain concern must be felt however, about the possibility of rearrangements of *N*-acyl-*N'*-aminoacyl hydrazines that are intermediates in these syntheses. The insertion reaction discovered by Brenner and Hofer (1961) involves analogous starting materials [Eq. (36)]. Various other ways of preparing acid hydrazides have been explored, such as the reaction of free carboxylic acids with hydrazine and

$$\mathrm{R{-}CO{-}HNNH{-}CO{-}CHR'{-}NH_2 \longrightarrow R{-}CO{-}NH{-}CHR'{-}CO{-}HNNH_2} \quad (36)$$

dicylohexylcarbodiimide, preferably in the presence of 1-hydroxybenzotriazole (Wang *et al.*, 1978) and enzyme-catalyzed coupling of the carboxyl component with hydrazine (Chou *et al.*, 1979). The hydrazide stage can be circumvented by interaction of the carboxylic acid with diphenylphosphoryl azide (Shioiri and Yamada, 1974), yielding the acid azide directly. These alternatives help to avoid side reactions associated with the hydrazinolysis of esters, yet at a price: The esters represent protected forms of the carboxyl

* The possibility, however, that peptide amides were mistakenly identified as diacylhydrazines cannot be excluded.

group, and it is no small advantage to be able to convert a protecting group to an activating group at a preselected stage of the synthesis.

The harmful effect of nitrous acid used in the conversion of hydrazides to azides was mentioned in Section II,E and F in connection with tyrosine and tryptophan, which undergo substitution, and in the discussion of cysteine (Section II,N) which in its *S*-alkyl derivatives is oxidized to the corresponding sulfoxides. Here we call attention to the potential danger to acid-labile protecting groups that might be cleaved, at least in part, by the acid (usually HCl) present in the reaction mixture. However, many peptides carrying *tert*-butyloxycarbonyl groups were exposed to such conditions without serious damage. The low temperatures maintained during azide formation seem to provide a sufficient safeguard against premature deprotection. At -20 to $-25°C$ even hydrazides of trityl peptides could be transformed to the desired azides (Iselin, 1958).

An important side reaction that takes place during the preparation of azides from hydrazides, the formation of acid amides, has been observed time and again (Prelog and Wieland, 1946; Olsen and Enkemeyer, 1948; Fruton *et al.*, 1951; Brenner and Burckhardt, 1951; Erlanger *et al.*, 1959; Rudinger and Honzl, 1960; Wieland and Determann, 1963). The somewhat puzzling amide production is best explained by decomposition of the (hypothetical) nitrosohydrazide intermediate **86**. Elimination of water from **86** yields the desired azide, but loss of N_2O results in formation of the amide

$$R{-}\overset{\overset{\displaystyle O}{\|}}{C}{-}NHNH_2 \xrightarrow[-H_2O]{HONO} \underset{(\mathbf{86})}{R{-}\overset{\overset{\displaystyle O}{\|}}{C}{-}NH{-}NH{-}NO} \xrightarrow{-N_2O} R{-}\overset{\overset{\displaystyle O}{\|}}{C}{-}NH_2 \quad (37)$$

[Eq. (37)]. An alternative possibility involving α-nitrosation of the hydrazide was proposed by Klausner (cf. Klausner and Bodanszky, 1974). Amide formation can be greatly diminished by the use of alkyl nitrites or nitrosyl chloride rather than nitrous acid in the generation of azides from hydrazides and by carrying out the reaction in organic solvents (Honzl and Rudinger, 1961). Even under such conditions some amides might be formed (Waki *et al.*, 1968). A note of caution should be added to this discussion of amides as by-products of the azide method. The elemental compositions of amides and diacylhydrazines are so similar that analysis can sometimes lead to erroneous identification (Simmonds *et al.*, 1951).

2. *Curtius Rearrangement*

The decomposition of carboxylic acid azides discovered by Curtius (1890; cf. also Curtius, 1904; Curtius and Curtius, 1904) is cause for serious concern in applications of the azide method. Elimination of nitrogen from azides of carboxylic acids (**87**) is a spontaneous process yielding highly

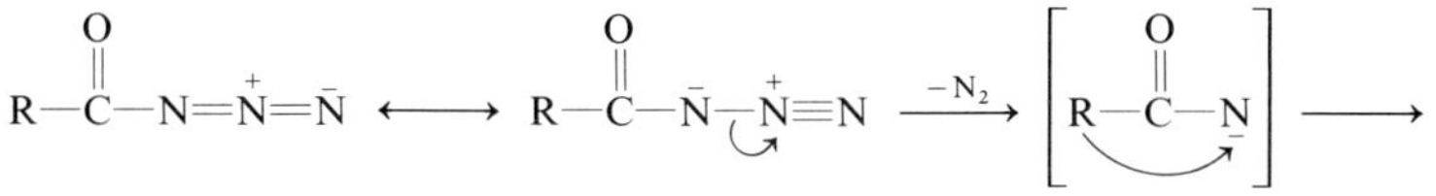

(**87**) (**87**)

$$R{-}N{=}C{=}O$$

(**88**)

reactive isocyanates (**88**). Isocyanates (**88**) are hydrolyzed by water to amines (**89**); they add to alcohols to produce urethanes (**90**) and react with amines to yield urea derivatives (**91**). Azides of protected serine (**92**) are slowly converted, via isocyanates (**93**), to cyclic urethanes (**94**), as discussed in Section II,J. An analogous formation of cyclic urea derivatives has been

$$R{-}N{=}C{=}O + HOH \longrightarrow R{-}NH_2 + CO_2$$

(**88**) (**89**)

(**88**) (**90**)

(**88**) (**91**)

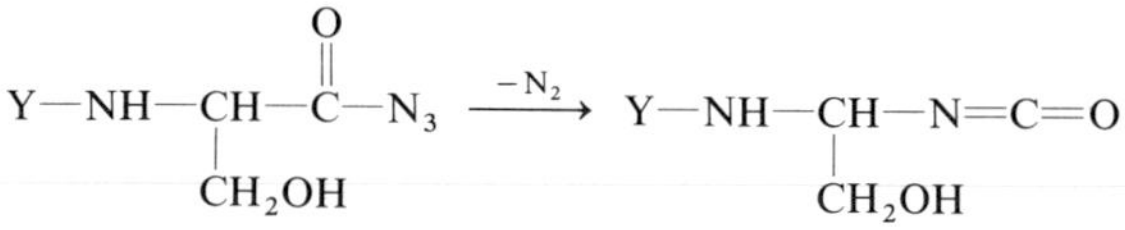

(**92**) (**93**)

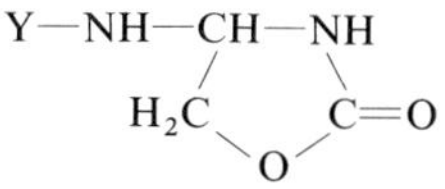

(**94**)

mentioned in connection with histidine (Schneider, 1960; Shin and Inouye, 1978).* The best way to avoid the Curtius rearrangement is coupling at a

* The reversible intramolecular attack of the imidazole NH group on the azide itself has been treated by Meienhofer in Vol. 1 of this treatise (p. 219) and also by Kemp, in the same volume (p. 356).

low temperature (for a recent study, cf. Okada *et al.*, 1980). Room temperature is conducive to the elimination of nitrogen from azides of carboxylic acids, although considerable differences exist in this respect between the azides of various amino acids and also among different peptides. The formation of isocyanates can be detected by a characteristic change in their spectrum. Azides exhibit a strong band at 4.75, whereas the band characteristic for isocyanates appears at 4.5 μm (Schwyzer and Kappeler, 1961). It is also possible to recognize the presence of a urea derivative in a peptide prepared by the azide procedure: The residue, which was activated in the form of an azide, is absent from the hydrolysate, and this is indicated by quantitative amino acid analysis. Separation, however, of the desired material from the side product might be quite difficult. In some instances, particularly in the case of longer peptides, the similarity of the target compound (**95**) to the urea-containing side product (**96**) can be a major obstacle (Hofmann *et al.*, 1960; Riniker and Schwyzer, 1964b; Inouye *et al.*, 1977). Because of

$$\text{—NH—CHR—CO—NH—CHR'—CO—N}_3 + \text{H}_2\text{N—CHR''—CO—NH—CHR'''—CO—} \longrightarrow$$

$$\text{—NH—CHR—CO—NH—CHR'—CO—NH—CHR''—CO—NH—CHR'''—CO—} \; +$$

(95)

$$\text{—NH—CHR—CO—NH—CHR'—NH—CO—NH—CHR''—CO—NH—CHR'''—CO—}$$

(96)

such difficulties, it is fortunate that acidic reagents such as HF, formic acid, trifluoroacetic acid, and HBr in acetic acid decompose the rearranged product (**96**) (Inouye and Watanabe, 1977) and that the conditions needed for cleavage of the urea derivatives are similar to those used in the removal of protecting groups by the same reagents.

The Curtius rearrangement is the most important but not the only side reaction affecting peptide azides. For instance, their hydrolysis during coupling has also been reported (Blanot *et al.*, 1979).

B. Anhydrides

The side reactions recognized in connection with activation and coupling through symmetrical, mixed, and *N*-carboxyanhydrides have been discussed in review articles by Albertson (1962) and by Tarbell (1969) and also in various monographs on peptide synthesis. A quite substantial treatment of this topic can be found in Chapter 6 of Vol. 1 of this treatise (Meienhofer, 1979). Therefore, we will limit ourselves to a brief account of the major side reactions encountered in the use of anhydrides of amino acids or peptides.

1. Symmetrical Anhydrides

It seems a priori that symmetrical anhydrides are the least likely to cause side reactions, because acylation with these compounds should lead to a single product [Eq. (38)]. Also, symmetrical anhydrides were obtained,

$$R{-}\underset{\underset{O}{\|}}{C}{-}O{-}\underset{\underset{O}{\|}}{C}{-}R + H_2N{-}R' \longrightarrow R{-}CO{-}NH{-}R' + R{-}COOH \qquad (38)$$

although often unintentionally, in various activation processes. Thus, disproportionation of mixed anhydrides (Sheehan and Frank, 1950; Wieland *et al.*, 1950) resulted in the formation of symmetrical anhydrides, and the latter were obtained in crystalline form by Schüssler and Zahn as early as 1962. However, it took several more years until symmetrical anhydrides were considered for general use in chain building (Weygand *et al.*, 1967). The reason for this delay probably lies in the economy of the procedure. As long as protected amino acids were regarded as too expensive to be wasted in a method involving the loss (or regeneration) of half of the original material, symmetrical anhydrides were not used as general tools of peptide synthesis. Protected amino acids, however, gradually became less costly and the simplicity of the procedure more convincing. Thus, the addition of 1 mol of dicyclohexylcarbodiimide to a solution of 2 mol (or more) of protected amino acid is generally regarded as preparation of symmetrical anhydrides. Since the solution contains other reactive intermediates, such as *O*-acylisoureas (Khorana, 1955) as well, this expression is an oversimplification of a complex phenomenon. Yet, for all practical purposes, acylations carried out with such solutions are equivalent to the application of isolated symmetrical anhydrides. It is interesting to note that, in spite of the availability of several symmetrical anhydrides in pure form (Schüssler and Zahn, 1962; Chen *et al.*, 1978), in the actual practice of peptide synthesis with symmetrical anhydrides the latter are used without isolation (Wieland *et al.*, 1971; Flor *et al.*, 1973; Hagenmaier and Frank, 1972a; etc). The reason for this might be found in the high reactivity of acid anhydrides in general. Crystalline symmetrical anhydrides are known in the case of protected amino acids and peptides (Bodanszky and Birkhimer, 1962), but generally with inert side chains. In the presence of nucleophilic centers in the amino acid side chains intra- or intermolecular attacks limit the shelf-life of a reactive intermediate even if it can be isolated in pure form. An additional limiting factor could be the lability of the *tert*-butyloxycarbonyl group in activated derivatives of amino acids (Bodanszky *et al.*, 1975). Thus, it might be not only simpler but also safer to use symmetrical anhydrides without isolation. Apart from the acylation of protected glycine residues (cf. Section II,A) no major side reaction should be expected in the use of symmetrical anhydrides. A general improvement in the results achieved in solid-phase peptide synthesis must be attributed to their widely accepted use. The ready accessibility of symmetrical anhydrides from protected amino acids, in smooth reactions with alkoxyacetylenes (Panneman *et al.*, 1959), ynamines (Viehe *et al.*, 1964; Weygand *et al.*, 1967), and water-soluble carbodiimides (Benoiton and Chen, 1979), suggests a further increase in their use, including syntheses carried out in solution.

2. *Mixed Anhydrides (Asymmetrical Anhydrides)*

Although the first peptide bond formation between two amino acid residues involved a mixed anhydride as the reactive intermediate (Curtius, 1881, 1902), the planned, intentional application of mixed anhydrides followed much later, about the middle of this century (Chantrenne, 1947, 1948, 1949, 1950; Sheehan and Frank, 1950; Wieland *et al.*, 1950; Wieland and Sehring, 1950; Wieland and Bernhard, 1951; Vaughan and Osato, 1951; Boissonnas, 1951). An unusually large number of various mixed anhydrides were proposed for peptide synthesis (cf., e.g., Bodanszky *et al.*, 1976; Jones, 1979), but only a few of these gained practical significance; outstanding among these are mixed carbonic anhydrides, for example, **97**, in which protected amino acids or peptides are activated by half-esters of carbonic acid.

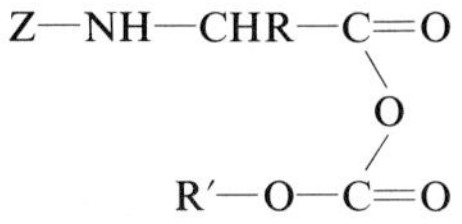

Particularly successful were anhydrides in which R′ is isobutyl: $(CH_3)_2CH—CH_2—$ (Vaughan, 1951; Vaughan and Osato, 1952).* In an excellent review in this treatise (Meienhofer, 1979b) the mixed carbonic anhydride method is discussed in considerable detail, including side reactions associated with this procedure. Therefore, to reduce duplication to a minimum, we will limit ourselves to some important points.

There are several side reactions related to mixed anhydrides that generally do not occur under the mild conditions of peptide synthesis. For instance, disproportionation of symmetrical anhydrides (Einhorn, 1909; Leister and Tarbell, 1958) [Eq. (39)] has not been observed at -10 to $-15°C$, the temperature range mostly used for the generation of and during coupling with mixed anhydrides (Wieland *et al.*, 1962; Beyerman, 1972). The same seems to be true in the disproportionation of carbonic acid mixed anhydrides: The reaction [Eq. (40)] proceeds only at elevated temperatures, as does the

* Slightly better results were obtained with mixed anhydrides prepared with the aid of *sec*-butyl chlorocarbonate.

alternative decomposition of these anhydrides (Leister and Tarbell, 1958) [Eq. (41)].

$$2\,R{-}\overset{\displaystyle O}{\overset{\|}{C}}{-}O{-}\overset{\displaystyle O}{\overset{\|}{C}}{-}R' \longrightarrow R{-}\overset{\displaystyle O}{\overset{\|}{C}}{-}O{-}\overset{\displaystyle O}{\overset{\|}{C}}{-}R + R'{-}\overset{\displaystyle O}{\overset{\|}{C}}{-}O{-}\overset{\displaystyle O}{\overset{\|}{C}}{-}R' \qquad (39)$$

$$2\,R{-}CO{-}O{-}CO{-}OR' \longrightarrow CO_2 + R{-}CO{-}O{-}CO{-}R + R'{-}O{-}CO{-}O{-}R' \qquad (40)$$

$$R{-}CO{-}O{-}CO{-}O{-}R' \longrightarrow R{-}CO{-}O{-}R' + CO_2 \qquad (41)$$

Whereas the decomposition of mixed anhydrides is usually not encountered in the praxis of peptide synthesis, a "wrong-side attack" of the nucleophile on the molecule of a mixed anhydride is an often reported side reaction. In fact, one should a priori expect *two products* in acylations with mixed anhydrides (Emery and Gold, 1950), their ratio being determined by the relative electrophilic character of the two carbonyl groups in the anhydride (Scheme 5). With judiciously chosen R′ groups the extent of the wrong-side

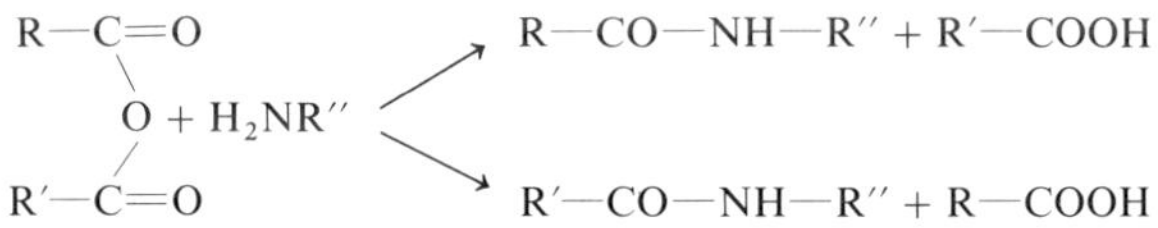

Scheme 5

attack is greatly diminished, but it is unlikely that this side reaction can be completely eliminated. Thus, pronounced electron release by R′ combined with its bulkiness in the interesting and sometimes quite valuable pivalic acid mixed anhydrides (**98**) (Zaoral, 1962) should lead to very little if any second-acylation product (**99**). However, the same material (**99**) will

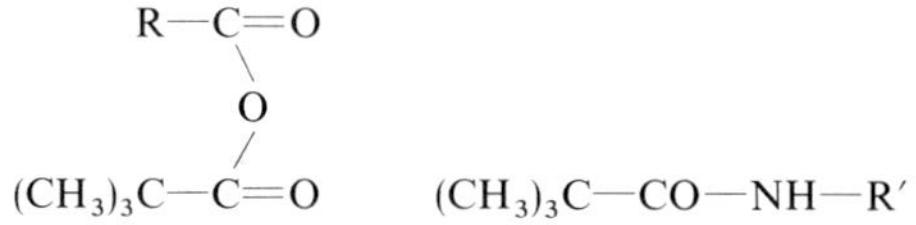

(**98**) (**99**)

result from a reaction between any unreacted anhydride-forming reagent (pivalic acid chloride) and the nucleophile $H_2N{-}R'$. The same factors that render the $(CH_3)_3C{-}C{=}O$ group unreactive in **98** will also interfere with the ready formation of **98**. Hence, production of **99** via direct acylation by the reagent is not unlikely and should be taken into consideration in application of the pivalic anhydride method.

In the most popular and best studied (Wieland, 1959; Gillessen *et al.*, 1963) carbonic acid mixed anhydrides the second-acylation product is a urethane

(**100**) and often is designated as such (e.g., Albertson, 1962). The relative amount of **100** may be affected by several factors. Some investigators attributed an increase in the wrong-side attacks to the basicity of the amino

$$
\begin{array}{ccc}
Z—NH—CHR—C{=}O & & Z—NH—CHR—CO—NH—R' \\
\diagdown & & \\
O + H_2N—R' \longrightarrow & & + \\
\diagup & & \\
(CH_3)_2CH—CH_2—O—C{=}O & & (CH_3)_2CH—CH_2—O—CO—NH—R'
\end{array}
$$

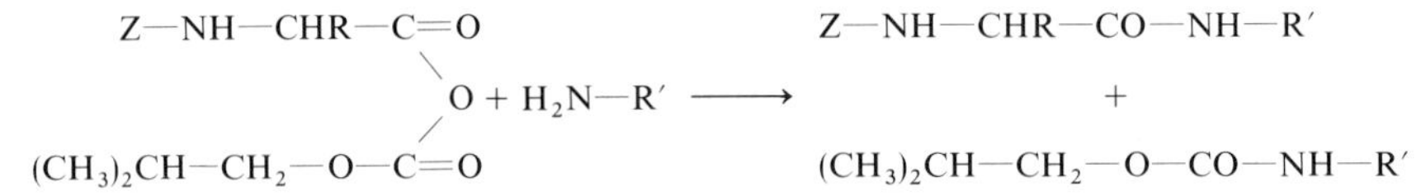

(**100**)

component (Vaughan and Osato, 1951; Kenner, 1955), whereas steric effects in the amine were suspected by others (Leister and Tarbell, 1958; Losse and Demuth, 1961). Urethane formation is particularly pronounced when the imino group of a proline residue has to be acylated (Beyerman, 1972; Yajima *et al.*, 1969). In a more recent study (Bodanszky and Tolle, 1977) the influence of the amino component appeared to be less important, whereas steric hindrance, combined with electron release in the mixed carbonic acid anhydrides, played a major role. Thus, Boc-Gly and Boc-Leu activated with isobutyl chlorocarbonate produced less than 1% urethane, independent of whether glycine or valine residues were acylated, but the same activation in the case of Boc-Val and Boc-Ile resulted in the formation of 5–8% urethane. A wrong-side attack leads to chain termination in stepwise chain lengthening (Jakubke and Baumert, 1974). Therefore, the prediction that, in the construction of long peptide chains by stepwise strategy (Bodanszky and du Vigneaud, 1959), mixed anhydrides are less than ideal acylating agents seems to be vindicated and their use (Tilak, 1970; van Zon and Beyerman, 1973, 1976; cf. also Sarges and Witkop, 1965) in a systematic fashion not fully justified. If chain building by the stepwise strategy (Bodanszky, 1960) must be executed with acylating agents that are more reactive than the originally proposed nitrophenyl esters, then very active esters, such as pentafluorophenyl esters (Kisfaludy *et al.*, 1970) or symmetrical anhydrides, should be better choices than mixed anhydrides with their inherent ambiguity.

It is not surprising that reactive intermediates such as mixed anhydrides are attacked not only by the amino group of the amino component but also by nucleophiles in amino acid side chains and even by the protected amino group of the activated residue itself.* Protecting groups that facilitate the abstraction of a proton from the amide can interfere with the intended process. Thus, difficulties were encountered with mixed anhydrides of 4-

---

* Highly active acylating agents, such as mixed or symmetrical anhydrides, used in excess react even with very weak nucleophiles including the NH group in amides. Hence the formation of diacylimides, particularly in the case of acylglycines as mentioned in Section II,A (cf. also Kopple and Renick, 1958; Zaoral and Rudinger, 1961; Determan and Kahle, 1969; Merrifield *et al.*, 1974).

toluenesulfonyl- (tosyl)amino acids (Wieland *et al*., 1950; Barass and Elmore, 1957; Theodoropoulos and Craig, 1955; Zaoral, 1959), probably on account of the deprotonated species **101** which competes with the nucleophilic component for the acylating agent. Problems were also noted with formyl-amino acids (King *et al*., 1954a).

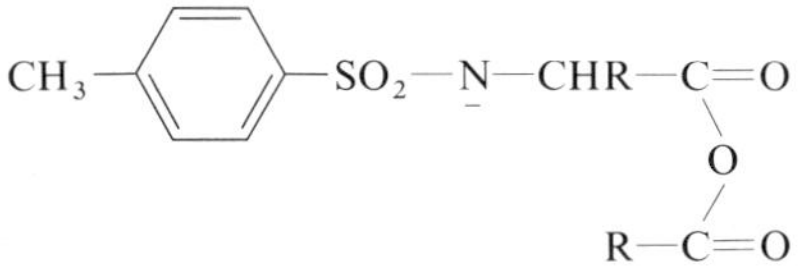

(**101**)

An ingenious method for the generation of mixed anhydrides was proposed by Belleau and Malek (1968) [Eq. (42)]. 1-Ethoxycarbonyl-2-ethoxy-1,2-dihydroquinoline (EEDQ, **102**) can activate the carboxyl component in the absence of acid binding agents needed when mixed anhydrides are

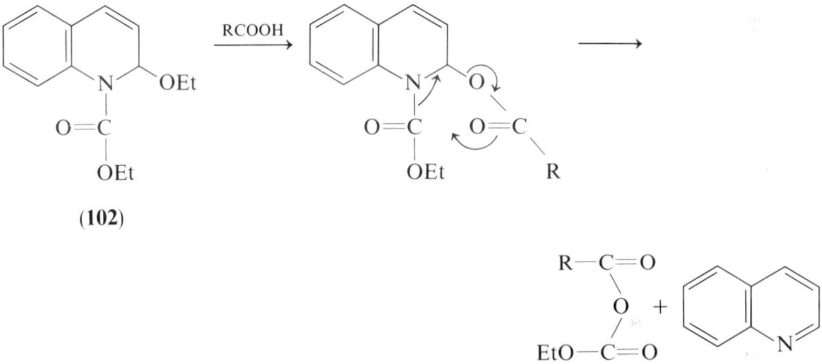

(**102**)

(42)

formed with the help of acid chlorides or alkyl chlorocarbonates. Several advantages follow from this seemingly small difference, and also a reduced tendency for racemization in the activated residue. Still, this innovation, which was further improved by Kiso and Yajima (1972), does not dispense with some problems associated with mixed anhydrides. Thus, the wrong-side attack—the formation of urethanes—remains to be reckoned with (Lombardino *et al*., 1978).

3. N-Carboxyanhydrides (Leuchs') Anhydrides

An unusually attractive feature of *N*-carboxyanhydrides (NCA), (**103**) is the simplicity of the mixture obtained in acylation with these potent intermediates. The sole by-product is carbon dioxide, and the principal product is ready for the next operation [Eq. (43)]. Because of this possibility, the inherent difficulties, for example, the sensitivity of NCAs to moisture, did

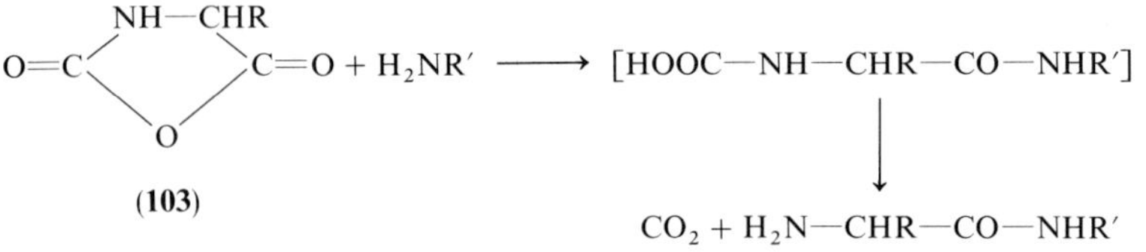

$$\underset{(103)}{O=C\overset{NH-CHR}{\underset{O}{\diagdown}}C=O} + H_2NR' \longrightarrow [HOOC-NH-CHR-CO-NHR']$$

$$\downarrow \tag{43}$$

$$CO_2 + H_2N-CHR-CO-NHR'$$

not deter generations of investigators who attempted the use of NCAs in stepwise chain building. Careful handling and storage are necessary to avoid polymerization (or, more exactly, polycondensation) of NCAs, but this is not impossible and these powerful reagents were and remain the favorite starting materials of researchers who use polyamino acids in their studies. A more insiduous side reaction results from the abstraction of a proton from NCAs by bases such as sodium alkoxides under anhydrous conditions. The resulting anions rearrange to isocyanates [Eq. (44)], which in turn

$$O=C\overset{NH-CHR}{\underset{O}{\diagdown}}C=O + R'-O^- \longrightarrow O=C\overset{NH-CHR}{\underset{O}{\diagdown}}C=O \longrightarrow$$

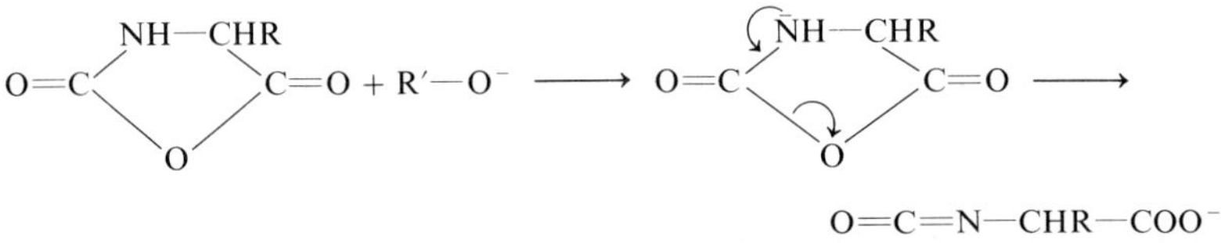

$$O=C=N-CHR-COO^- \tag{44}$$

combine with alcohols or amines to yield urethanes or urea derivatives (Berger *et al.*, 1953; Kopple, 1957; Szwarc, 1965). The fundamental problem, however, associated with the systematic use of NCAs in peptide synthesis is premature decarboxylation of the carbamoic acid intermediate, the loss of amino protection during coupling, resulting in double (or triple) incorporation of residues (Bartlett and Jones, 1957; Bartlett and Dittmer, 1957). After early attempts to prevent premature decarboxylation (Hunt and du Vigneaud, 1938; Bailey, 1949; 1950), Hirschmann and his associates (1967, 1971) initiated a new effort and determined the conditions under which this flaw could be avoided or at least kept at a minimum. Although they were able to use NCAs with considerable success, the special conditions, including a narrow pH range, an aqueous environment, extremely vigorous stirring, and a short reaction time, are perhaps too demanding for general acceptance of the procedure.

In spite of some additional difficulties, such as the dehydration of carboxamides to nitriles by phosgene in the preparation of NCAs (Speciale and Smith, 1963; Yanagida *et al.*, 1969) and the rearrangement of the NCA of serine to an oxazolidone (cf. Section II,J) Leuchs' anhydrides remain intriguing material. This is shown by recent publications on their ability to form cyclic peptides (Rothe *et al.*, 1981) and on their use in the preparation of dipeptides (Kircher *et al.*, 1980).

C. Carbodiimides

Beyond doubt carbodiimides are the most important activating reagents in peptide synthesis. In addition to being efficient tools for direct formation of the peptide bond between the carboxyl component and the amino component they can serve the same purpose through reactive intermediates, such as symmetrical anhydrides and active esters. Therefore a detailed presentation of the side reactions that accompany the use of carbodiimides seems to be justified. However, the chemistry of carbodiimides was reviewed (Khorana, 1953) even before their introduction in peptide synthesis (Sheehan and Hess, 1955) and treated in considerable mechanistic detail in Vol. 1 of this treatise (Rich and Singh, 1979). Therefore we confine our discussion of the carbodiimide-related side reactions to a few important aspects.

The most commonly encountered side reaction in the activation of carboxylic acids is the formation of acylureas. The addition product of a carboxylic acid and a carbodiimide, the *O*-acylisourea derivative **104** (Khorana, 1953) is unstable and in the absence of external nucleophiles rearranges, via intramolecular nucleophilic attack, to the *N*-acylurea derivative **105**. This rearrangement, which also occurs in the presence of external

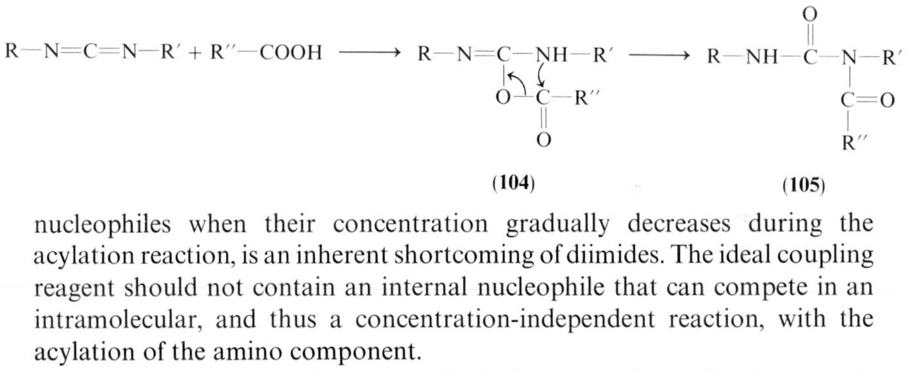

(104) **(105)**

nucleophiles when their concentration gradually decreases during the acylation reaction, is an inherent shortcoming of diimides. The ideal coupling reagent should not contain an internal nucleophile that can compete in an intramolecular, and thus a concentration-independent reaction, with the acylation of the amino component.

Early observations of acylurea (**105**) formation (e.g., Sheehan *et al.*, 1956; Zahn and Diehl, 1957; Merrifield and Woolley, 1958; Helferich and Böshagen, 1959; Habermann, 1961; Suzuki and Abiko, 1966; etc.) usually included some suggestions regarding, for example, choice of solvents, working at a low temperature, and the conditions less conducive to this very undesirable side reaction. Both these reports and a series of papers on more systematic investigations (Vajda *et al.*, 1965; Izdebski *et al.*, 1975, 1977, 1978, 1980a; Arendt *et al.*, 1976; Arendt and Kojodziejczyk, 1978) of acylurea formation are centered around the reaction of dicyclohexylcarbodiimide (Schmidt *et al.*, 1938) with carboxylic acids, because this compound was recommended as the reagent of choice in peptide synthesis (Sheehan and

Hess, 1955). In retrospect, however, it seems that the advantages of dicyclohexylcarbodiimide, such as crystallinity and stability, are outweighed by the ease with which it yields acylureas and perhaps also by the fact that it is a strong allergen. Some other carbodiimides might be equally efficient coupling reagents and not have such drawbacks. For instance, the amount of acylurea (**105**) was considerably reduced, when ethyl benzylcarbodiimide rather than dicyclohexylcarbodiimide was used (Ito *et al.*, 1977). It is at least conceivable that this side reaction would be further suppressed in a sterically hinderea carbodiimide, such as di-*tert*-butylcarbodiimide (Schmidt *et al.*, 1948). In this connection it is interesting to note that diisopropylcarbodiimide (Schmidt and Striewsky, 1941), in contrast to dicyclohexylcarbodiimide, yields relatively stable *O*-acylisoureas (**104**) that can be isolated (Bates *et al.*, 1980) in pure form.* Some *N*-acylurea formation, however, occurs also with *O*-acyl- diisopropylisoureas (Izdebski *et al.*, 1980b). From the point of view of *N*-acylurea formation water-soluble carbodiimides (Sheehan and Hlavka, 1956) have the advantage that the ureides are also water-soluble and thus readily separated from the coupling product.

Carbodiimides are clearly highly reactive reagents, and it is not surprising that they participate in a variety of side reactions. The *O*-acylisourea derivatives (**104**) are not only efficient acylating agents of amines, but also react with carboxylic acids to generate symmetrical anhydrides (Khorana, 1955). Their intramolecular reactions produce, in addition to *N*-acylureas (**105**), azlactones (**106**) (Siemion and Nowak, 1960, 1961), surprisingly in the case of amino acids with urethane protecting groups (Benoiton and Chen, 1981; Bates *et al.*, 1981). The dimerization of dicyclohexylcarbodiimide, in the presence of 1-hydroxybenzotriazole, to the diazetidine **107** was noted (Jakubke and Klessen, 1977), although dimerization and polymerization of carbodiimides in general had been known earlier (Khorana, 1953). Undesired trifluoroacetylation was observed in coupling reactions in which the amino component was used in the form of its trifluoroacetate salt (Fletcher *et al.*,

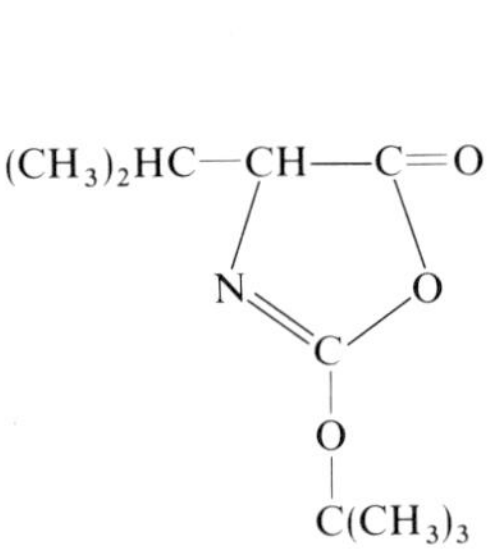

(**106**)

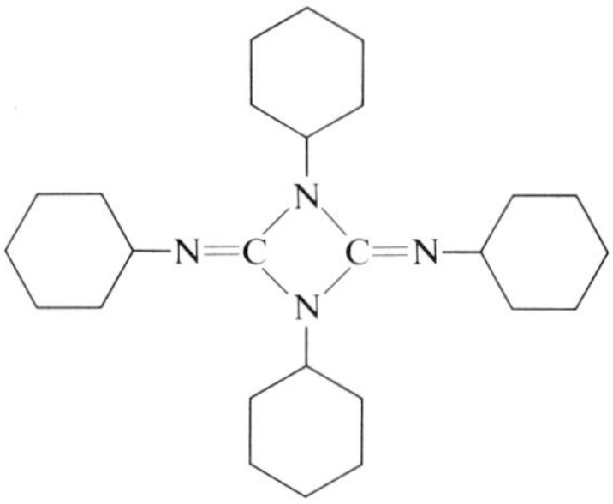

(**107**)

* Subsequent studies by Benoiton indicate that not an *O*-acylisourea but compound **106** was obtained.

1973), yet this possibility was clearly pointed out by Weygand and Steglich (1959). Similarly, several side reactions should have been anticipated from the known chemistry of carbodiimides. For instance, in spite of favorable experience (Sheehan *et al.*, 1956) with dicyclohexylcarbodiimide-mediated coupling of amino acids with an unprotected alcoholic hydroxyl group in their side chains, acylation of hydroxyls occurs when the acylating agent is present in excess or when the reaction is catalyzed by bases or 1-hydroxybenzotriazole, imidazole, 4-dimethylaminopyridine, and so on. The formation of isourea ethers from phenols and carbodiimides (Kovacs *et al.*, 1967; Stewart, 1968a) is analogous to the reaction of diphenylcarbodiimide with picric acid (Bush *et al.*, 1909). Novel, however, is the recognition, that these phenyl ethers are useful esterifying reagents.

The overreactive *O*-acylisourea derivatives can undergo undesired reactions, also with excess carbodiimide. For instance, dehydration of asparagine residues to *β*-cyanoalanine derivatives can occur (as discussed in more detail in Section II,M). Of course, the same process can be considered useful when preparation of *β*-cyanoalanine is the objective (Liberek *et al.*, 1966). Most of these side reactions can be effectively suppressed by the addition of compounds for which the expression "auxiliary nucleophiles" is proposed. Such materials, *N*-hydroxysuccinimide (Wünsch and Drees, 1966) and 1-hydroxybenzotriazole (König and Geiger, 1970), counteract the effect of the decreasing concentration of the amino component and, because they are regenerated during the acylation reaction, provide a safeguard against intramolecular (and hence unimolecular) competing side reactions. The significance of auxiliary nucleophiles in peptide synthesis cannot be overemphasized. Nevertheless, one must call attention also to some potential pitfalls related to the use of these additives. Thus, dicyclohexylcarbodiimide reacts with *N*-hydroxysuccinimide (Löw and Kisfaludy, 1965; Gross and Bilk, 1968) to produce a reactive derive of *β*-alanine (**108**). In the presence of polyethylene glycol dicyclohexycarbodiimide reacted with 1-hydroxybenzotriazole to yield the ether **109** (Hemassi and Bayer, 1977). Such a list

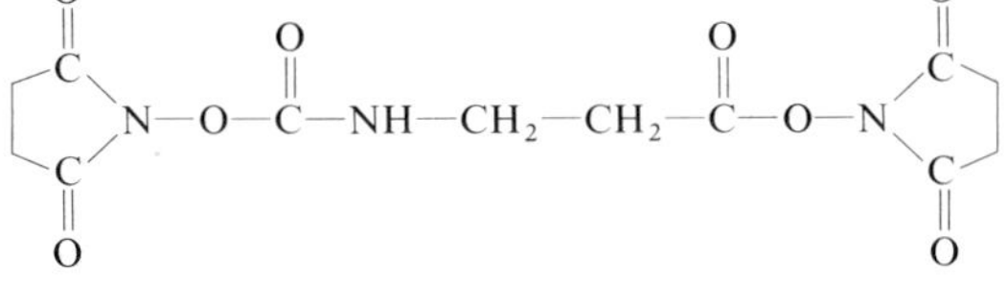

(**108**)

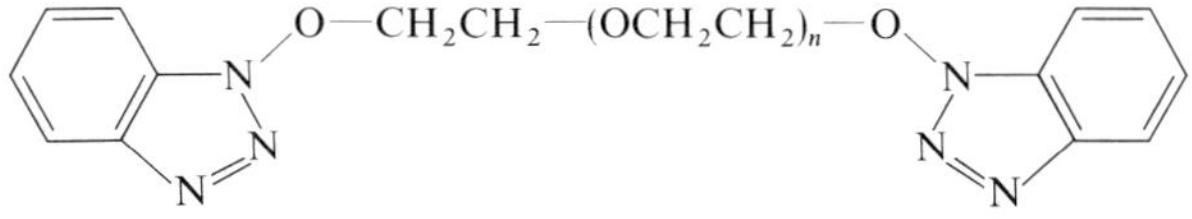

(**109**)

of side reactions, all due to overactivation by carbodiimides, might give the uninitiated reader a false impression. An experienced peptide chemist knows the value of the dicyclohexylcarbodiimide method and the convenience of the execution of couplings with carbodiimides. A true coupling reagent should react only with the amino or with the carboxyl component, but not with both. This selectivity allows addition of the reagent to a mixture of the segments to be coupled. In contrast to the fast addition of carboxylates to carbodiimides, the latter are almost inert toward amines and only exceptional cases have been reported (Muramatsu *et al.*, 1963; Rink and Riniker, 1974) where guanidines (**110**) formed. This is not true for all coupling reagents. Thus, the potent carbonyldiimidazole (Staab, 1957; Anderson and Paul, 1958), if applied in excess, reacts with amines in the reaction mixture to produce substituted ureas (**111**).

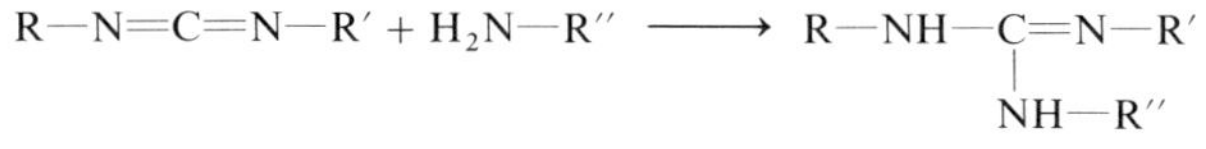

(**110**)

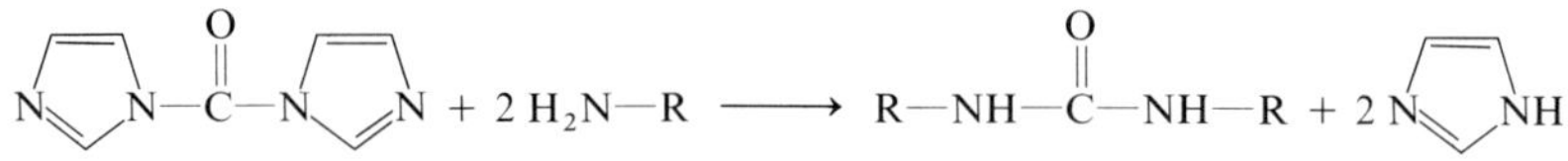

(**111**)

D. Active Esters

In Vol. 1 of this treatise a chapter on active esters (Bodanszky, 1979) included a major section on side reactions. Therefore, a discussion of this area is omitted here.

V. SIDE REACTIONS IN SOLID-PHASE PEPTIDE SYNTHESIS

A multifaceted extensive review of solid-phase peptide synthesis was presented by Barany and Merrifield (1980) in Vol. 2 of this treatise. Side reactions were considered by these authors in connection with every aspect of the solid-phase approach. Therefore we limit this section to the addition of recent developments.

The most commonly used coupling reagent, dicyclohexylcarbodiimide is the source of a relatively harmless by-product, *N,N′*- dicyclohexylurea. In spite of its inertness this urea derivative can cause minor difficulties, because it is very insoluble in most solvents and often incompletely removed by washing. A search for carbodiimides (Tartar and Gesquiere, 1979) that retain the efficiency of dicyclohexylcarbodiimide but yield substituted ureas soluble in dichloromethane included a comparison of diisopropyl-, phenyl ethyl-, benzyl ethyl-, and benzyl isopropyl carbodiimides. Some of the ureas produced were more soluble in dichloromethane than the dicyclohexyl derivative.

The application of mixed anhydrides in conjunction with a high-pressure flow reactor produced peptides uncontaminated by deletion sequences or products from incorrect opening of the mixed anhydrides (Chaturvedi *et al.*, 1981). A similarly efficient flow system was described by Lucas *et al.* (1981).

VI. SIDE REACTIONS IN CYCLIZATION

The often less than satisfactory results of attempted cyclizations are mainly due to cyclodimerization (Schwyzer and Sieber, 1958; Schwyzer and Gorup, 1958) and polymerization. With the notable exception of dipeptides, which readily form diketopiperazines, small peptides resist cyclization. The presence of proline and glycine in the sequence permits cyclic conformations in the open-chain precursors (Schwyzer *et al.*, 1970) and, therefore, favor the cyclization reactions. Similarly, cyclic pentapeptides are obtained in good yield when D and L residues alternate in the sequence (Bodanszky and Henes, 1975) because of the β-turn-stabilized cyclic conformation of the "linear" peptide (Ramachandran and Chandrasekaran, 1972). Otherwise pentapeptides show a pronounced tendency toward cyclodimerization (Kato and Izumiya, 1974). The method of activation is not without influence on the outcome of cyclization reactions: The azide method favors cyclization of monomers over cyclodimerization. The doubling reaction is caused by association of the linear peptides through hydrogen bonds for example, in a sheetlike β-structure, but steric hindrance can also inhibit the formation of cyclic monomers (Schwyzer *et al.*, 1964). The same factors play an even more decisive role in the cyclization of tetrapeptides (Titlestad, 1972). The distribution of monomers, dimers, and hydrogen bond-stabilized polymers in the cyclization of a hexapeptide 4-nitrophenyl ester was studied by Kopple *et al.* (1977).

In the preparation of heterodetic peptides special problems can arise, such as premature oxidation of the reduced form of oxytocin (oxytocein, **112**) to the disulfide. If oxidation takes place before dilution to a very low concentration of the sulfhydro compound can be achieved, in addition to the monomer (oxytocin, **113**), the two dimers (**114** and **115**) are produced in significant amounts. Exclusion of atmospheric oxygen before dilution and oxidation with $K_3Fe(CN)_6$ changed the ratio of **113** to **114** + **115** from

4:1 to 11:1 (Wälti and Hope, 1973).

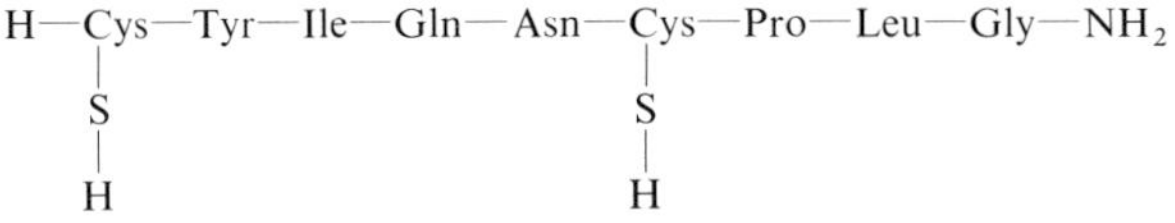

(112)

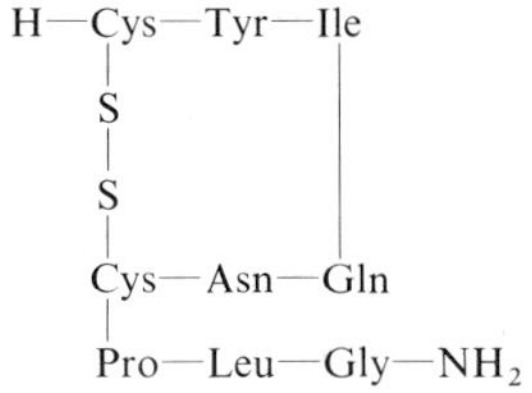

(113)

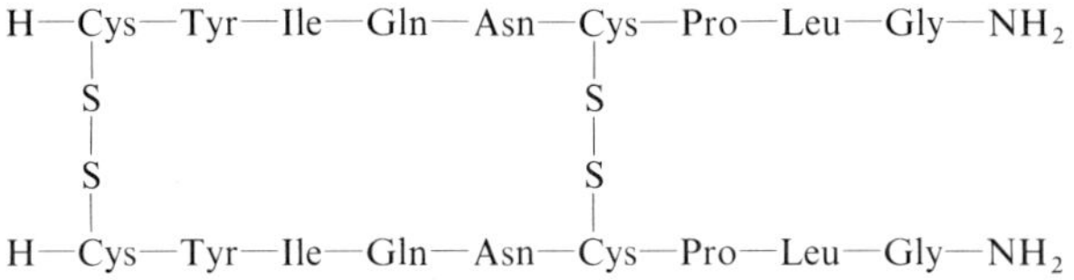

(114)

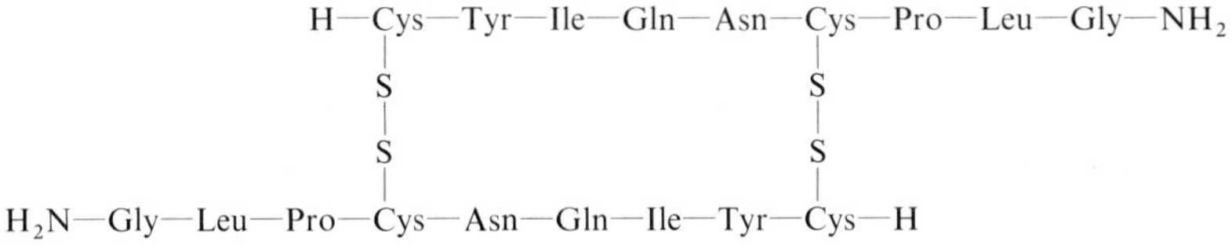

(115)

VII. INSTABILITY OF PEPTIDES IN SOLUTION

In the absence of acids or bases most peptides can be stored in aqueous solution without decomposition. Hydrolysis can occur, however, if the solution is contaminated by microorganisms that produce proteolytic enzymes. Metal ions can similarly catalyze hydrolysis of the peptide bond (Meriwether and Westheimer, 1956). In some special cases the energy required for cleavage of an amide or a peptide bond is provided by the formation of a diketopiperazine. Thus, Phe-Gly-NH_2 undergoes ring closure sure to 3-benzyl-2,5-diketopiperazine without catalysis (Meriwether and Westheimer, 1956). Diketopiperazines are produced from tripeptide esters, particularly with glycine and proline in their sequences (Rydon and Smith, 1956). The tripeptide derivative H-His-Pro-Phe-OMe was cleaved under mild acid conditions to yield His-Pro diketopiperazine and H-Phe-OMe (Mazur and Schlatter, 1963). During the synthesis of actinomycine D (Meienhofer *et al.*, 1970) the diketopiperazine of DVal-LPro formed from DVal-LPro-Sar simply on storage of its solutions at room temperature. In this case ring closure might have been facilitated by the circumstance that the two residues, valine and proline, have different configuration, but the reaction [Eq. (45)] has also been observed in other instances and cannot be ignored

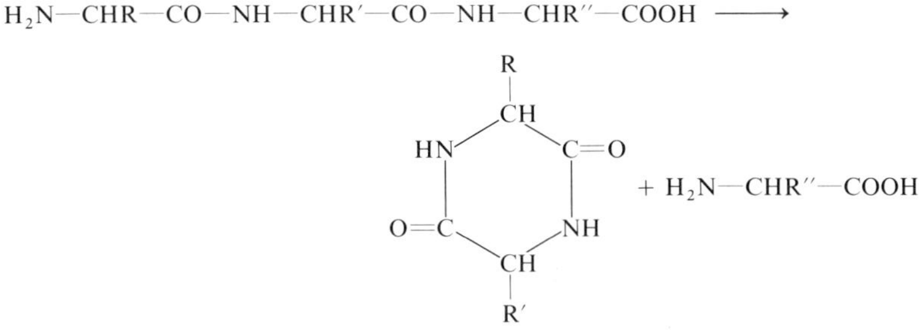

(45)

as a possibility when tripeptides or their derivatives are kept in solution or are formed, for example, during deprotection by catalytic hydrogenation (Gerig and McLeod, 1976). Over and above the presence of proline, sarcosine and/or glycine (Rothe *et al.*, 1972; Titlestad, 1972), bulky substituents such as the side chain of valine or 2-methylalanine seem to facilitate cyclization.

The general limitations in the stability of peptides containing aspartic acid, asparagine, glutamic acid, or glutamine residues follow from the side reactions discussed in connection with these amino acids. Thus peptides with glutamine as the NH_2-terminal residue are gradually converted to pyroglutamyl peptides if stored in aqueous solution. Transpeptidation via cyclic intermediates is also well studied. As an interesting example of the instability of peptides in aqueous solution we mention here the gastrointestinal hormone secretin, which is known to lose its activity on storage. This inactivation could be traced mainly to ring closure of an aspartic acid residue followed by a glycine moiety and subsequent ring opening to a β-aspartyl derivative (Jäger *et al.*, 1974; Beyerman *et al.*, 1981). However, not all loss of biological activity is due to such chemical transformations. From dilute aqueous solutions a significant portion of the peptide can be adsorbed on the surface of a glass container. Glass has a measurable ion-exchange capacity and can bind oligo-cations, such as secretin, by chemosorption. Interestingly, the same peptide is bound also to polyethylene, probably by hydrophobic interaction.

The inactivation of oxytocin by acetone (Yamashiro *et al.*, 1965) is caused by the formation of a substituted 2,2-dimethyl-4-imidazolidinone (**116**) [Eq. (46)]. This condensation reaction was studied in considerable detail (Yamashiro and du Vigneaud, 1968; Yamashiro *et al.*, 1968; Hruby *et al.*, 1968; Havran and du Vigneaud, 1969; Hruby and du Vigneaud, 1969; Takashima and du Vigneaud, 1970). Formation of 4-imidazolidinone, however, is not

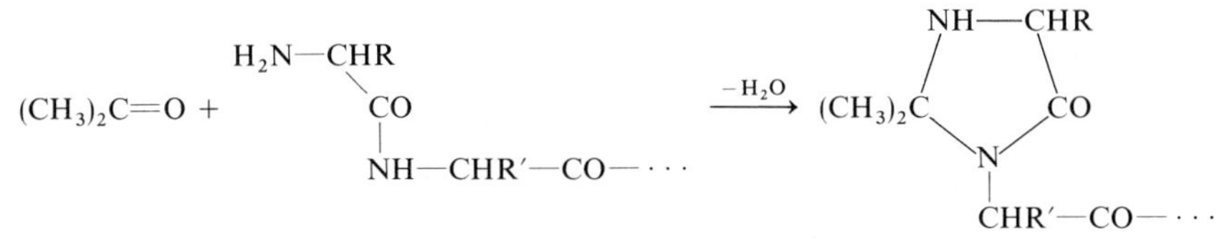

$$(CH_3)_2C{=}O \; + \quad \begin{matrix} H_2N{-}CHR \\ \diagdown \\ CO \\ | \\ NH{-}CHR'{-}CO{-}\cdots \end{matrix} \quad \xrightarrow{-H_2O} \quad (CH_3)_2C \begin{matrix} NH{-}CHR \\ \diagup \qquad \diagdown \\ \qquad CO \\ \diagdown \qquad \diagup \\ N \\ | \\ CHR'{-}CO{-}\cdots \end{matrix}$$

(116)

(46)

limited to oxytocin or to acetone. Other peptides with free amino termini and also other carbonyl compounds can participate in analogous condensations (Cardinaux and Brenner, 1973). Therefore, the presence of aldehydes in alcohols used as solvents is not without risk to the integrity of peptide preparations.

VIII. CONCLUSIONS

The numerous pitfalls created by side reactions cause peptide chemists to seek a general remedy against them. Although an entire group of side products, such as those generated by alkylation in acidolytic deprotection, can be avoided, for example, by changing from acidolysis to deprotection with weak bases, no solution to the problems involving all side reactions exists and probably no one will be found. However, because many side reactions are intra- and therefore unimolecular, it is possible to reduce the extent of the harm they cause by carrying out the operations of peptide synthesis, the coupling reaction in particular, at high concentrations of the reactants. This is practical only if one of the components, usually the acylating agent, is used in excess. This "principle of excess" (Bodanszky, 1971) is now generally accepted in solid-phase peptide synthesis where the dilution caused by the insoluble support is compensated for by an excess of the activated carboxyl component, for example, a symmetrical anhydride, sometimes a very large excess. It is almost certain that application of the same principle in syntheses carried out in solution will have similarly beneficial effects. The extent of many side reactions can be reduced by the use of auxiliary nucleophiles such as 1-hydroxybenzotriazole. However, complete avoidance of side reactions remains nearly impossible. Therefore, they must be considered challenges that should be known and then met one by one. We hope that this review provides some help in this endeavor.

ACKNOWLEDGMENTS

One of the authors (M.B.) thanks Professor Dr-ing. Helmut Zahn for helpful discussions and for encouragement during the preparation of this chapter, at the Deutsches Wollforschungsinstitut an der Rheinisch-Westfälischen Technischen Hochschule in Aachen, where M.B., as an awardee of the Alexander von Humboldt Foundation, was a guest of the Federal Government of Germany. The studies of side reactions were supported from grants from the U.S. Public Health Service (NIH-HL 14187) and from the National Science Foundation (CHE-7615652). The work of J.M. was funded by Le Centre National de la Recherche Scientifique, France.

The authors also thank Mrs. Agnes A. Bodanszky for her valuable help in preparing the manuscript.

REFERENCES

Abderhalden, E., and Bahn, A. (1933). *Hoppe-Seyler's Z. Physiol. Chem.* **219**, 72–81.
Abderhalden, E., and Nienburg, H. (1933). *Fermentforschung* **13**, 573–596.
Agarwal, K. L., Kenner, G. W., and Sheppard, R. C. (1969a). *J. Chem. Soc. C.* pp. 954–958.
Agarwal, K. L., Kenner, G. W., and Sheppard, R. C. (1969b). *J. Chem. Soc. C* pp. 2213–2217.
Akabori, S., Ohno, K., and Narita, K. (1952). *Bull. Chem. Soc. Jpn.* **25**, 214–218.
Alakhov, Yu. B., Kiryushkin, A. A., Lipkin, V. M., and Milne, G. W. A. (1970). *J. Chem. Soc., Chem. Commun.* pp. 406–407.
Albertson, N. F. (1962). *Org. React.* **12**, 151–355.
Albertson, N. F., and McKay, F. C. (1953). *J. Am. Chem. Soc.* **75**, 5323–5326.
Anderson, G. W., and McGregor, A. C. (1957). *J. Am. Chem. Soc.* **79**, 6180–6183.
Anderson, G. W., and Paul, R. (1958). *J. Am. Chem. Soc.* **80**, 4423.
Anderson, J. C., Barton, M. A., Hardy, P. M., Kenner, G. W., McLeod, J. K., Preston, J., and Sheppard, R. C. (1965). *Acta Chim. Acad. Sci. Hung.* **44**, 187–195.
Anwar, M. K., Khan, S. A., and Sivanandaiah, K. M. (1978). *Synthesis* **10**, 751–752.
Arendt, A., and Kolodziejczyk, A. M. (1978). *Tetrahedron Lett.* pp. 3867–3868.
Arendt, A., Kolodziejczyk, A., and Sokolowska, T. (1976). *Tetrahedron Lett.* pp. 447–448.
Atherton, E., Fox, H., Harkiss, D., Logan, C. J., Sheppard, R. C., and Williams, B. J. (1978). *J. Chem. Soc., Chem. Commun.* pp. 537–540.
Atherton, E., Bury, C., Sheppard, R. C., and Williams, B. J. (1979). *Tetrahedron Lett.* pp. 3041–3042.
Baba, T., Sugiyama, H., and Seto, S. (1973). *Chem. Pharm. Bull.* **21**, 207–209.
Bachi, M. D., and Ross-Petersen, K. J. (1972). *J. Org. Chem.* **37**, 3550–3551.
Baer, E., Maurukas, J., and Clarke, D. D. (1956). *Can. J. Chem.* **34**, 1182–1188.
Bailey, J. L. (1949). *Nature (London)* **164**, 889.
Bailey, J. L. (1950). *J. Chem. Soc.* pp. 3461–3466.
Bailey, J. L., (1955). *Biochem. J.* **60**, 173–176.
Bajusz, S., and Medzihradszky, K. (1963). *In* "Peptides 1962" (G. T. Young, ed.), pp. 49–52. Pergamon, Oxford.
Bajusz, S., Lázár, T., and Paulay, Z. (1964). *Acta Chim. Acad. Sci. Hung.* **41**, 329–330.
Bajusz, S., Turán, A., Fauszt, I., and Juhász, A. (1973). *In* "Peptides 1972" (H. Hanson and H.-D. Jakubke, eds.), pp. 93–96. North-Holland Publ., Amsterdam.

Balasubramanian, D., and Subramanian, V. H. (1973). *Indian J. Biochem. Biophys.* **10**, 61–62.
Barany, G., and Merrifield, R. B. (1973). *Cold Spring Harbor Symp. Quant. Biol.* **37**, 121–126.
Barany, G., and Merrifield, R. B. (1980). *In* "The Peptides" (E. Gross and J. Meienhofer, eds.), Vol. 2, Part A, pp. 1–284. Academic Press, New York.
Barass, B. C., and Elmore, D. T. (1957). *J. Chem. Soc.* pp. 3134–3139.
Bartlett, P. D., and Dittmer, D. C. (1957). *J. Am. Chem. Soc.* **79**, 2159–2160.
Bartlett, P. D., and Jones, R. H. (1957). *J. Am. Chem. Soc.* **79**, 2153–2159.
Bates, H. S., Jones, J. H., and Witty, M. J. (1980). *J. Chem. Soc., Chem. Commun.* pp. 773–774.
Bates, H. S., Jones, J. H., Ramage, W. I., and Witty, M. J. (1981). *In* "Peptides 1980" (K. Brunfeldt, ed.), pp. 185–190. Scriptor, Copenhagen.
Battersby, A. R., and Reynolds, J. J. (1961). *J. Chem. Soc.* pp. 524–530.
Battersby, A. R., and Robinson, J. C. (1955). *J. Chem. Soc.* pp. 259–269.
Battersby, A. R., and Robinson, J. C. (1956). *J. Chem. Soc.* pp. 2076–2084.
Bauer, W., and Pless, J. (1975). *In* "Peptides: Chemistry, Structure and Biology" (R. Walter and J. Meienhofer, eds.), pp. 341–345. Ann Arbor Sci. Publ., Ann Arbor, Michigan.
Bayer, E., Jung, G., and Hagenmaier, H. (1968). *Tetrahedron* **24**, 4853–4860.
Bayer, J., Dualszky, S., and Kisfaludy, L. (1961). *J. Chromatogr.* **6**, 155–158.
Beecham, A. F. (1955). *Chem. Ind. (London)* pp. 1120–1121.
Beecham, A. F. (1957). *J. Am. Chem. Soc.* **79**, 3251–3261, 3262–3263.
Beecham, A. F. (1963). *Aust. J. Chem.* **16**, 889–895.
Belleau, D., and Malek, G. (1968). *J. Am. Chem. Soc.* **90**, 1651–1652.
Bender, M. L., Kezdy, F. J., and Zerner, B. (1963). *J. Am. Chem. Soc.* **85**, 3017–3024.
Benesch, R. E., and Benesch, R. (1958). *J. Am. Chem. Soc.* **80**, 1666–1669.
Benisek, W. F., and Cole, R. D. (1965). *Biochem. Biophys. Res. Commun.* **20**, 655–660.
Benisek, W. F., Raftery, M. A., and Cole, R. D. (1967). *Biochemistry* **6**, 3780–3790.
Ben Ishai, D., and Berger, A. (1952). *J. Org. Chem.* **17**, 1564–1570.
Benoiton, L., Hanson, R. W., and Rydon, H. N. (1964). *J. Chem. Soc.* pp. 824–836.
Benoiton, N. L., and Chen, F. M. F. (1979). *In* "Peptides: Structure and Biological Function" (E. Gross and J. Meienhofer, eds.), pp. 261–264. Pierce Chemical Co., Rockford, Illinois.
Benoiton, N. L., and Chen, F. M. F. (1981). *Can. J. Chem.* **59**, 384–389.
Berger, A., Sela, M., and Katchalski, E. (1953). *Anal. Chem.* **25**, 1554–1555.
Berger, A., Noguchi, J., and Katchalski, E. (1956). *J. Am. Chem. Soc.* **78**, 4483–4488.
Bergmann, M., and Miekeley, A. (1924). *Hoppe-Seyler's Z. Physiol. Chem.* **140**, 128–145.
Bergmann, M., and Zervas, L. (1932). *Ber. Dtsch. Chem. Ges.* **65**, 1192–1201.
Bergmann, M., Brand, E., and Weinman, F. (1923). *Hoppe-Seyler's Z. Physiol. Chem.* **131**, 1–17.
Bergmann, M., Zervas, L., and Rinke, H. (1934). *Hoppe-Seyler's Z. Physiol. Chem.* **224**, 40–44.
Bergmann, M., Zervas, L., and Fruton, J. S. (1936). *J. Biol. Chem.* **115**, 593–611.
Berndt, H. (1976). *In* "Peptides 1976" (A. Loffet, ed.), p. 230. Editions de l'Université de Bruxelles, Belgium.
Bernhard, S. A., Berger, A., Carter, J. H., Katchalski, E., Sela, M., and Shalitin, Y. (1962). *J. Am. Chem. Soc.* **84**, 2421–2434.
Berse, C., Boucher, R., and Piché, L. (1957). *J. Org. Chem.* **22**, 805–808.
Berse, C., Piché, L., and Uchiyama, A. (1960). *Can. J. Chem.* **38**, 1946–1950.
Berse, C., Massiah, T., and Piché, L. (1963). *Can. J. Chem.* **41**, 2767–2773.
Beyerman, H. C. (1972). *In* "Chemistry and Biology of Peptides" (J. Meienhofer, ed.), pp. 351–357. Ann Arbor Sci. Publ., Ann Arbor, Michigan.
Beyerman, H. C., Lie, T. S., and Van Veldhuizen, C. J. (1973). *In* "Peptides 1971" (H. Nesvadba, ed.), pp. 162–164. North-Holland, Publ., Amsterdam.

Beyerman, H. C., Kranenburg, P., and Voskamp, D. (1981). *In* "Peptides 1980" (K. Brunfeldt, ed.), pp. 282–287. Scriptor Copenhagen.
Blake, J. (1979). *Int. J. Pept. Protein Res.* **13**, 418–425.
Blake, J., and Li, C. H. (1968). *J. Am. Chem. Soc.* **90**, 5882–5884.
Blake, J., Wang, K. T., and Li, C. H. (1972). *Biochemistry* **11**, 438–441.
Blanot, D., Martinez, J., Auger, G., and Bricas, E. (1979). *Int. J. Pept. Protein Res.* **14**, 41–56.
Blombäck, B. (1967). *In* "Methods of Enzymology" (C. H. W. Hirs, ed.), Vol. 11, pp. 398–411. Academic Press, New York.
Bodanszky, M. (1960). *Ann. N.Y. Acad. Sci.* **88**, 655–664.
Bodanszky, M. (1971). *In* "Prebiotic and Biochemical Evolution" (A. P. Kimball and J. Oro, eds.), pp. 217–222. North-Holland Publ. Amsterdam.
Bodanszky, M. (1979). *In* "The Peptides" (E. Gross and J. Meienhofer, eds.), Vol. 1, pp. 105–196. Academic Press, New York.
Bodanszky, M., and Birkhimer, C. A. (1962). *Chem. Ind.* (*London*) pp. 1620–1622.
Bodanszky, M., and du Vigneaud, V. (1959). *J. Am. Chem. Soc.* **81**, 5688–5691.
Bodanszky, M., and Henes, J. B. (1975). *Biorg. Chem.* **4**, 212–218.
Bodanszky, M., and Kwei, J. Z. (1978). *Int. J. Pept. Protein Res.* **12**, 69–74.
Bodanszky, M., and Martinez, J. (1978). *J. Org. Chem.* **43**, 3071–3073.
Bodanszky, M., and Martinez, J. (1981). *Synthesis* **5**, 333–356.
Bodanszky, M., and Natarajan, S. (1975). *J. Org. Chem.* **40**, 2495–2499.
Bodanszky, M., and Ondetti, M. A. (1966). *Chem. Ind.* (*London*) pp. 26–27.
Bodanszky, M., and Sheehan, J. T. (1960). *Chem. Ind.* (*London*) pp. 1268–1269.
Bodanszky, M., and Tolle, J. C. (1977). *Int. J. Pept. Protein Res.* **10**, 380–384.
Bodanszky, M., Sheehan, J. T., Ondetti, M. A., and Lande, S. (1963a). *J. Am. Chem. Soc.* **85**, 991–997.
Bodanszky, M., Denning, G. S., Jr., and du Vigneaud, V. (1963b). *Biochem. Prep.* **10**, 122–125.
Bodanszky, M., Ondetti, M. A., Levine, S. D., and Williams, N. J. (1967). *J. Am. Chem. Soc.* **89**, 6753–6757.
Bodanszky, M., Funk, K. W., and Fink, M. L. (1973a). *J. Org. Chem.* **38**, 3565–3570.
Bodanszky, M., Sigler, G. F., and Bodanszky, A. (1973b). *J. Am. Chem. Soc.* **95**, 2352–2357.
Bodanszky, M., Klausner, Y. S., and Bodanszky, A. (1975). *J. Org. Chem.* **40**, 1507–1508.
Bodanszky, M., Klausner, Y. S., and Ondetti, M. A. (1976). *In* "Peptide Synthesis," 2nd ed. Wiley, New York.
Bodanszky, M., Fink, M. L., Klausner, Y. S., Natarajan, S., Tatemoto, K., Yiotakis, A. E., and Bodanszky, A. (1977). *J. Org. Chem.* **42**, 149–152.
Bodanszky, M., Tolle, J. C., Deshmane, S. S., and Bodanszky, A. (1978). *Int. J. Pept. Protein* Res. **12**, 57–68.
Bodanszky, M., Chandramouli, N., and Martinez, J. (1979a). *J. Med. Chem.* **22**, 270–273.
Bodanszky, M., Deshmane, S. S., and Martinez, J. (1979b). *J. Org. Chem.* **44**, 1622–1625.
Bodanszky, M., Tolle, J. C., Gardner, J. D., Walker, M. D., and Mutt, V. (1980). *Int. J. Pept. Protein Res.* **16**, 402–411.
Boissonnas, R. A. (1951). *Helv. Chim. Acta* **34**, 874–879.
Boissonnas, R. A., and Preitner, G. (1953). *Helv. Chim. Acta* **36**, 875–886.
Boissonnas, R. A., Guttmann, S., Jacquenoud, P. A., and Waller, J. P. (1955). *Helv. Chim. Acta* **38**, 1491–1501.
Boissonnas, R. A., Guttmann, S., Huguenin, R. L., Jacquenoud, P. A., and Sandrin, E. (1958). *Helv. Chim. Acta* **41**, 1867–1882.
Boissonnas, R. A., Guttmann, S., and Jacquenoud, P. A. (1960). *Helv. Chim. Acta* **43**, 1349–1358.
Bonnet, R., and Nicolaidou, P. (1979). *J. Chem. Soc., Perkin Trans. 1* pp. 1969–1977.

Bonora, G. M., Toniolo, C., Fontana, A., Dibello, C., and Scoffone, E. (1974). *Biopolymers* **13**, 157–167.
Bossert, H. W., and Jacquenoud, P. A. (1975). *In* "Peptides 1974" (Y. Wolman, ed.), pp. 233–237. Wiley, New York.
Brenner, M., and Burckhardt, C. H. (1951). *Helv. Chim. Acta* **34**, 1070–1083.
Brenner, M., and Hofer, W. (1961). *Helv. Chim. Acta* **44**, 1794–1798.
Brenner, M., and Pfister, R. W. (1951). *Helv. Chim. Acta* **34**, 2085–2096.
Bricas, E., and Nicot-Cutton, C. (1960). *Bull. Soc. Chim. Fr.* **26**, 466–472.
Brown, S. S., and Wade, R. (1962). *J. Chem. Soc.* pp. 3280–3281.
Brown, T., and Jones, J. H. (1981). *J. Chem. Soc. Chem. Commun.*, pp. 648–649.
Brown, T., Jones, J. H., and Richards, J. D. (1982). *J. Chem. Soc. Perkin Trans. 1*, pp. 1553–1561.
Bruckner, V., and Kajtar, M. (1959). *Acta Chim. Acad. Sci. Hung.* **21**, 417–425.
Bruckner, V., and Kovács, J. (1957). *Acta Chim. Acad. Sci. Hung.* **12**, 363–404.
Bruckner, V., Kovács, J., and Medzihradszky, K. (1955). *Naturwissenschaften* **42**, 96–97.
Bruckner, V., Kajtar, M., Kovács, J., Nagy, H., and Wein, J. (1958). *Tetrahedron* **2**, 211–235.
Bruckner, V., Kotai, A., and Kovács, K. (1959). *Acta Chim. Acad. Sci. Hung.* **21**, 427–443.
Bruice, T. C., and Bruno, J. J. (1962). *J. Am. Chem. Soc.* **84**, 2128–2132.
Bruice, T. C., and Fife, T. H. (1962). *J. Am. Chem. Soc.* **84**, 1973–1979.
Buchanan, D. L., Haley, E. E., Dorer, F. E., and Corcoran, B. J. (1966). *Biochemistry* **5**, 3240–3245.
Bush, M., Blume, G., and Pungs, E. (1909). *J. Prakt. Chem.* **79**, 513–546.
Cardinaux, F., and Brenner, M. (1973). *Helv. Chim. Acta* **56**, 339–347.
Carpenter, F. H., and Gish, D. T. (1952). *J. Am. Chem. Soc.* **74**, 3818–3821.
Carpino, L. A. (1957). *J. Am. Chem. Soc.* **79**, 4427–4431.
Carpino, L. A. (1973). *Acc. Chem. Res.* **6**, 191–198.
Carpino, L. A., and Han, G. Y. (1972). *J. Org. Chem.* **37**, 3404–3409.
Chang, C. D., and Meienhofer, J. (1978). *Int. J. Pept. Protein Res.* **11**, 246–249.
Chang, C. D., Felix, A. M., Jimenez, M. H., and Meienhofer, J. (1980). *Int. J. Pept. Protein Res.* **15**, 485–494.
Chantrenne, H. (1947). *Nature (London)* **160**, 603–604.
Chantrenne, H. (1948). *Biochim. Biophys. Acta* **2**, 286–293.
Chantrenne, H. (1949). *Nature (London)* **164**, 576–577.
Chantrenne, H. (1950). *Biochim. Biophys. Acta* **4**, 484–492.
Chaturvedi, N., Sigler, G., Fuller, W., Verlander, M., and Goodman, M. (1981). *Dev. Biochem.*, pp. 169–177.
Chauhan, V. S., Ratcliffe, S. J., and Young, G. T. (1980). *Int. J. Pept. Protein Res.* **15**, 96–101.
Chen, F. M., Kuroda, K., and Benoiton, N. L. (1978). *Synthesis* pp. 928–929.
Cheung, H. T., and Blout, E. R. (1965). *J. Org. Chem.* **30**, 315–316.
Chibnall, A. C., and Westall, R. G. (1932). *Biochem. J.* **26**, 122–132.
Chillemi, F. (1963). *Gazz. Chim. Ital.* **93**, 1079–1092.
Chillemi, F. (1966). *Gazz. Chim. Ital.* **96**, 359–374.
Chino, N., Masui, Y., and Sakakibara, S. (1978). *In* "Peptide Chemistry 1977" (T. Shiba, ed.), pp. 27–32. Protein Res. Found., Osaka, Japan.
Chorev, M., and Klausner, Y. S. (1976). *J. Chem. Soc., Chem. Commun.* p. 596.
Chou, S. H., Wong, C. H., Chen, S. T., and Wang, K. T. (1979). *J. Chin. Chem. Soc. (Taipei)* **26**, 11–15.
Cipera, J. D. (1961). *J. Org. Chem.* **26**, 206–209.
Clarke, H. T., and Inouye, J. M. (1931). *J. Biol. Chem.* **94**, 541–550.
Clayton, D. W., and Kenner, G. W. (1953). *Chem. Ind. (London)* p. 1205.
Clayton, D. W., Kenner, G. W., and Sheppard, R. C. (1956). *J. Chem. Soc.* pp. 371–380.
Coggins, J., Demayo, R., and Benoiton, N. L. (1970). *Can. J. Chem.* **48**, 385–387.

Cohen, L. A., and Witkop, B. (1961). *Angew. Chem.* **73**, 253–271.

Conti, F., Lucente, G., Romeo, A., and Zanotti, G. (1973). *Int. J. Pept. Protein Res.* **5**, 353–357.

Crofts, P. C., Markes, J. H. H., and Rydon, H. N. (1959). *J. Chem. Soc.* pp. 3610–3616.

Curtius, T. (1881). *J. Prakt. Chem.* **24**, 239–240.

Curtius, T. (1890). *Ber. Dtsch. Chem. Ges.* **23**, 3023–3033.

Curtius, T. (1902). *Ber. Dtsch. Chem. Ges.* **35**, 3226–3228.

Curtuis, T. (1904). *J. Prakt. Chem.* **70**, 57–128.

Curtius, T., and Curtius, H. (1904). *J. Prakt. Chem.* **70**, 158–194.

Danho, W., and Li, C. H. (1971). *Int. J. Protein Res.* **3**, 81–92.

Das, H. K., and Roy, S. C. (1962). *Biochim. Biophys. Acta* **62**, 590–591.

Davis, N. C. (1956). *J. Biol. Chem.* **223**, 935–947.

Dekker, C. A., and Fruton, J. S. (1948). *J. Biol. Chem.* **173**, 471–477.

Dekker, C. A., Taylor, S. P., Jr., and Fruton, J. S. (1949). *J. Biol. Chem.* **180**, 155–173.

Denkewalter, R. G., Schwam, H., Strachan, R. G., Beesley, T. E., Veber, D. F., Schoenewaldt, E. F., Barkemeyer, H., Palaveda, W. J., Jr., Jacob, T., and Hirschmann, R. (1966). *J. Am. Chem. Soc.* **88**, 3163–3164.

Determann, H., and Kahle, I. (1969). *Justus Liebig's Ann. Chem.* **670**, 203–211.

Dewey, R. S., Schoenewaldt, E. F., Joshua, H., Palaveda, W. J., Jr., Schwam, H., Barkemeyer, H., Arison, B. H., Veber, D. F., Denkewalter, R. G., and Hirschmann, R. (1968). *J. Am. Chem. Soc.* **90**, 3254–3255.

Dewey, R. S., Barkemeyer, H., and Hirschmann, R. (1969). *Chem. Ind. (London)* p. 1632.

Dorman, L. C., and Markley, L. D. (1971). *J. Med. Chem.* **14**, 5–9.

Dorman, L. C., Nelson, D. A., and Chow, R. C. L. (1972). *In* "Progress in Peptide Research" (S. Lande, ed.), pp. 65–68. Gordon & Breach, New York.

du Vigneaud, V., Audrieth, L. F., and Loring, H. S. (1930). *J. Am. Chem. Soc.* **52**, 4500–4504.

du Vigneaud, V., Ressler, C., Swan, J. M., Roberts, C. W., Katsoyannis, P. G., and Gordon, S. (1953). *J. Am. Chem. Soc.* **75**, 4879–4880.

du Vigneaud, V., Bartlett, M. F., and Jöhl, A. (1957). *J. Am. Chem. Soc.* **79**, 5572–5575.

Einhorn, A. (1909). *Ber. Dtsch. Chem. Ges.* **42**, 2772–2773.

Elliott, D. F. (1952). *Biochem. J.* **50**, 542–550.

Emery, A. R., and Gold, V. (1950). *J. Chem. Soc.* pp. 1443–1447.

Engelhard, M., and Merrifield, R. B. (1978). *J. Am. Chem. Soc.* **100**, 3559–3563.

Erickson, B. W., and Merrifield, R. B. (1973). *J. Am. Chem. Soc.* **95**, 3750–3756, 3757–3763.

Erlanger, B. F., Curran, W. V., and Kokowsky, N. (1959). *J. Am. Chem. Soc.* **81**, 3055–3058.

Esko, K., Karlsson, S., and Poráth, J. (1968). *Acta Chem. Scand.* **22**, 3342–3343.

Feinberg, R. S., and Merrifield, R. B. (1975). *J. Am. Chem. Soc.* **97**, 3485–3496.

Felix, A. M. (1974). *J. Org. Chem.* **39**, 1427–1429.

Felix, A. M., Jimenez, M. H., and Meienhofer, J. (1977). *In* "Peptides: Proceedings of the Fifth American Peptide Symposium" (M. Goodman and J. Meienhofer, eds.), pp. 532–535. Wiley, New York.

Fischer, E. (1901). *Ber. Dtsch. Chem. Ges.* **34**, 433–454.

Fischer, E. (1902). *Ber. Dtsch. Chem. Ges.* **35**, 1095–1106.

Fischer, E. (1906). *Ber. Dtsch. Chem. Ges.* **39**, 2893–2931.

Fischer, E. (1915). *Ber. Dtsch. Chem. Ges.* **48**, 93–102.

Fischer, E., and Fourneau, E. (1901). *Ber. Dtsch. Chem. Ges.* **34**, 2868–2877.

Fischer, E., and Suzuki, V. (1905). *Ber. Dtsch. Chem. Ges.* **38**, 4173–4196.

Flegel, M., Barth, T., and Zaoral, M. (1976). *In* "Peptides 1976" (A. Loffet, ed.), pp. 511–515. Editions de l'Université de Bruxelles, Belgium.

Fletcher, G. A., Löw, M., and Young, G. T. (1973). *J. Chem. Soc., Perkin Trans. 1* pp. 1162–1164.

Fletcher, R., Jones, J. H., Ramage, W. I., and Stachulski, A. V. (1979). *In* "Peptides 1978"

(I. Z. Siemion and G. Kupryszewski, eds.) pp. 169–171. Wroclaw Univ. Press, Wroclaw, Poland.
Flor, F., Birr, C. and Wieland, T. (1973). *Justus Liebig's Ann. Chem.* pp. 1601–1605.
Fölsch, G. (1966). *Acta Chem. Scand.* **20**, 459–473.
Fontana, A., and Toniolo, C. (1976). *Prog. Chem. Org. Nat. Prod.* **33**, 309–449.
Fontana, A., Marchiori, F., Rocchi, R., and Pajetta, P. (1966a). *Gazz. Chim. Ital.* **96**, 1301–1312.
Fontana, A., Marchiori, F., Moroder, L., and Scoffone, E. (1966b). *Gazz. Chim. Ital.* **96**, 1313–1321.
Fontana, A., Marchiori, F., Moroder, L., and Scoffone, E. (1966c). *Tetrahedron Lett.* pp. 2985–2987.
Fraser, K. J., Poulsen, K., and Haber, E. (1972). *Biochemistry* **11**, 4974–4977.
Freidinger, R. M., Hirschmann, R., and Veber, D. F. (1978). *J. Org. Chem.* **43**, 4800–4803.
Fruton, J. S. (1942). *J. Biol. Chem.* **146**, 463–470.
Fruton, J. S., and Bergmann, M. (1942). *J. Biol. Chem.* **145**, 253–265.
Fruton, J. S., Johnston, R. B., and Fried, M. (1951). *J. Biol. Chem.* **190**, 39–53.
Fujii, N., Funakoshi, S., Sasaki, T., and Yajima, H. (1977). *Chem. Pharm. Bull.* **25**, 3096–3098.
Fujii, T., Kimura, T., and Sakakibara, S. (1976). *Bull. Chem. Soc. Jpn.* **49**, 1595–1601.
Fujino, M., Wakamitsu, M., Shinagawa, S., Kitada, C., and Yajima, H. (1978). *Chem. Pharm. Bull.* **26**, 539–548.
Fujiwara, S., Morinaga, S., and Narita, K. (1962). *Bull. Chem. Soc. Jpn.* **35**, 438–442.
Garner, R., Schafer, D. J., and Young, G. T. (1971). *In* "Peptides 1969" (E. Scoffone, ed.), pp. 102–108. North-Holland Publ., Amsterdam.
Gawron, O., and Draus, F. (1958). *J. Org. Chem.* **23**, 1040–1041.
Gawron, O., and Draus, F. (1959). *J. Org. Chem.* **24**, 1392–1393.
Gawron, O., and Odstrchel, G. (1967). *J. Am. Chem. Soc.* **89**, 3263–3267.
Geiger, R., and König, W. (1981). *In* "The Peptides" (E. Gross and J. Meienhofer, eds.), Vol. 3, pp. 1–99. Academic Press, New York.
Geiger, R., Sturm, K., and Siedel, W. (1963). *Chem. Ber.* **96**, 1080–1087.
Geiger, R., Jäger, G., König, W., and Volk, A. (1969). *Z. Naturforsch., B: Anorg. Chem., Org. Chem., Biochem., Biophys., Biol.* **24**, 999–1004.
Geiger, R., Treuth, G., and Burow, F. (1973). *Chem. Ber.* **106**, 2339–2346.
Gerig, J. T., and McLeod, R. S. (1976). *J. Org. Chem.* **41**, 1653–1655.
Gibian, H., and Klieger, E. (1960). *Angew. Chem.* **72**, 708.
Gillessen, D., Schnabel, E., and Meienhofer, J. (1963). *Justus Liebig's Ann. Chem.* **667**, 164–171.
Girin, S. K., and Shvachkin, Yu. P. (1977a). *J. Gen. Chem. USSR (Engl. Transl.)* **47**, 1085–1090.
Girin, S. K., and Shvachkin, Yu. P. (1977b). *J. Gen. Chem. USSR (Engl. Transl.)* **47**, 1950–1953.
Girin, S. K., and Shvachkin, Yu. P. (1978a). *J. Gen. Chem. USSR (Engl. Transl.)* **48**, 823–828.
Girin, S. K., and Shvachkin, Yu. P. (1978b). *J. Gen. Chem. USSR (Engl. Transl.)* **48**, 1720–1724.
Girin, S. K., and Shvachkin, Yu. P. (1979a). *J. Gen. Chem. USSR (Engl. Transl.)* **49**, 395–399.
Girin, S. K., and Shvachkin, Yu. P. (1979b). *J. Gen. Chem. USSR (Engl. Transl.)* **49**, 606–613.
Gish, D. T., and Carpenter, F. H. (1953). *J. Am. Chem. Soc.* **75**, 5872–5877.
Gish, D. T., Katsoyannis, P. G., Hess, G. P., and Stedman, R. J. (1956). *J. Am. Chem. Soc.* **78**, 5954–5955.
Gisin, B. F., and Merrifield, R. B. (1972). *J. Am. Chem. Soc.* **94**, 3102–3106.
Goldberger, R. F., and Anfinsen, C. B. (1962). *Biochemistry* **1**, 401–405.

Goldschmidt, S. (1959). *Collect. Czech. Chem. Commun.* **24**, 15.
Goldschmidt, S., and Wick, M. (1952). *Justus Liebig's Ann. Chem.* **575**, 217–231.
Goodman, M., and Kenner, G. W. (1957). *Adv. Protein Chem.* **12**, 465–638.
Goodman, M., and Steuben, K. C. (1959a). *J. Org. Chem.* **24**, 112–113.
Goodman, M., and Steuben, K. C. (1959b). *J. Am. Chem. Soc.* **81**, 3980–3983.
Goodman, M., and Steuben, K. C. (1962a). *J. Am. Chem. Soc.* **84**, 1279–1283.
Goodman, M., and Steuben, K. C. (1962b). *J. Org. Chem.* **27**, 3409–3415.
Grahl-Nielsen, O., and Tritsch, G. L. (1969). *Biochemistry* **8**, 187–192.
Grassmann, W., and Wünsch, E. (1956). *Fortschr. Chem. Org. Naturst.* **13**, 444–559.
Grassmann, W., and Wünsch, E. (1958). *Chem. Ber.* **91**, 462–465.
Greenbaum, L. M., and Hosoda, T. (1963). *Biochem. Pharmacol.* **12**, 325–330.
Grommers, E. P., and Arens, J. F. (1959). *Recl. Trav. Chim. Pays-Bas* **78**, 558–565.
Grønvald, F. C., Lundt, B. F., and Johansen, N. L. (1981). *In* "Peptides 1980" (K. Brunfeldt, ed.), pp. 706–710. Scriptor, Copenhagen.
Gros, C., de Garilhe, M. P., Costopanagiotis, A., and Schwyzer, R. (1961). *Helv. Chim. Acta* **44**, 2042–2048.
Gross, H., and Bilk, L. (1968). *Tetrahedron* **24**, 6935–6939.
Guarneri, M., Benassi, C. A., Ferroni, R., Guggi, A., Tomatis, R., and Rocchi, R. (1971). *Gazz. Chim. Ital.* **101**, 375–386.
Gutte, B. (1975). *J. Biol. Chem.* **250**, 889–904.
Gutte, B., and Merrifield, R. B. (1969). *J. Am. Chem. Soc.* **91**, 501–502.
Gutte, B., and Merrifield, R. B. (1971). *J. Biol. Chem.* **246**, 1922–1941.
Guttmann, S. (1963). *In* "Peptides 1962" (G. T. Young, ed.), p. 41. Pergamon, Oxford.
Guttmann, S., and Boissonnas, R. A. (1958). *Helv. Chim. Acta* **41**, 1852–1867.
Guttmann, S., and Boissonnas, R. A. (1959). *Helv. Chim. Acta* **42**, 1257–1264.
Habermann, E. (1961). *Naunyn-Schmiedebergs Arch. Exp. Pathol. Pharmakol.* **241**, 543–544.
Hagenmaier, H., and Frank, H. (1972a). *Hoppe-Seyler's Z. Physiol. Chem.* **353**, 1973–1976.
Hagenmaier, H., and Frank, H. (1972b). *J. Chromatogr. Sci.* **10**, 663–667.
Haley, E. E., Corcoran, B. J., Dorer, F. E., and Buchanan, D. L. (1966). *Biochemistry* **5**, 3229–3235.
Halpern, B., and Nitecki, D. E. (1967). *Tetrahedron Lett.* pp. 3031–3033.
Hanson, H., and Illhardt, R. (1954). *Hoppe-Seyler's Z. Physiol. Chem.* **298**, 210–218.
Hanson, R. W., and Rydon, H. N. (1964). *J. Chem. Soc.* pp. 836–842.
Harris, J. I., and Fruton, J. S. (1951). *J. Biol. Chem.* **191**, 143–151.
Harris, J. I., and Work, T. S. (1950). *Biochem. J.* **46**, 582–589.
Hashizume, K., and Shimonishi, Y. (1980). *In* "Peptide Chemistry 1979" (H. Yonehara, ed.), pp. 77–82. Protein Res. Found., Osaka, Japan.
Haslam, E. (1980). *Tetrahedron* **36**, 2409–2433.
Havran, R. T., and du Vigneaud, V. (1969). *J. Am. Chem. Soc.* **91**, 2696–2698.
Hayakawa, T., Fujiwara, Y., and Noguchi, J. (1967). *Bull. Chem. Soc. Jpn.* **40**, 1205–1208.
Hegedüs, B. (1948). *Helv. Chim. Acta* **31**, 737–748.
Helferich, B., and Böshagen, H. (1959). *Chem. Ber.* **92**, 2813–2827.
Hemassi, B., and Bayer, E. (1977). *Tetrahedron Lett.* pp. 1599–1602.
Heyns, K., and Legler, G. (1960). *Hoppe-Seyler's Z. Physiol. Chem.* **321**, 161–183.
Hillmann, A., and Hillmann, G. (1951). *Z. Naturforsch., B: Anorg. Chem., Org. Chem., Biochem., Biophys., Bio.* **6B**, 340–341.
Hillmann-Elies, A., Hillmann, G., and Jatzkewitz, H. (1953). *Z. Naturforsch., B: Anorg. Chem., Org. Chem., Biochem., Biophys., Biol.* **8B**, 445–446.
Hinman, J. W., Caron, E. L., and Christensen, H. N. (1950). *J. Am. Chem. Soc.* **72**, 1620–1626.

Hirschmann, R., Strachan, R. G., Schwam, H., Schoenewaldt, E. F., Joshua, H., Barkemeyer, B., Veber, D. F., Palaveda, W. J., Jr., Jacob, T. A., Beesley, T. E., and Denkewalter, R. G. (1967). *J. Org. Chem.* **32**, 3415–3425.

Hirschmann, R., Schwam, H., Strachan, R. G., Schoenewaldt, E. F., Barkemeyer, H., Miller, S. M., Conn, J. B., Garsky, V., Veber, D. F., and Denkewalter, R. G. (1971). *J. Am. Chem. Soc.* **93**, 2746–2754.

Hiskey, R. G., Mizogucchi, T., and Inui, T. (1966). *J. Org. Chem.* **31**, 1192–1195.

Hiskey, R. G., Upham, R. A., Beverly, G. M., and Jones, W. C., Jr. (1970). *J. Org. Chem.* **35**, 513–515.

Ho, T. L., and Olah, G. A. (1976). *Angew. Chem., Int. Ed. Engl.* **15**, 774.

Hofmann, K., and Yajima, H. (1961). *J. Am. Chem. Soc.* **83**, 2289–2293.

Hofmann, K., Magee, M. Z., and Lindenmann, A. (1950). *J. Am. Chem. Soc.* **72**, 2814–2815.

Hofmann, K., Rheiner, A., and Peckham, W. D. (1953). *J. Am. Chem. Soc.* **75**, 6083–6084.

Hofmann, K., Johl, A., Furlenmeier, A. E., and Kappeler, H. (1957). *J. Am. Chem. Soc.* **79**, 1636–1641.

Hofmann, K., Thompson, T. A., Yajima, H., Schwartz, E. I., and Inouye, H. (1960). *J. Am. Chem. Soc.* **82**, 3715–3721.

Hofmann, K., Haas, W., Smithers, M. J., and Zanetti, G. (1965). *J. Am. Chem. Soc.* **87**, 631–639.

Hogue-Angeletti, R., Bradshaw, R. A., and Marshall, G. R. (1974). *Int. J. Pept. Protein Res.* **6**, 321–328.

Holland, G. F., and Cohen, L. A. (1958). *J. Am. Chem. Soc.* **80**, 3765–3769.

Homer, R. B., Moodie, R. B., and Rydon, H. N. (1965). *J. Chem. Soc.* pp. 4403–4409.

Honzl, J., and Rudinger, J. (1961). *Collect. Czech. Chem. Commun.* **26**, 2333–2344.

Hoogwater, D. A., Reinhoudt, D. N., Lie, T. S., Gunneweg, J. J. and Beyerman, H. C. (1973). *Recl. Trav. Chim. Pays-Bas* **92**, 819–825.

Houghten, R. A., and Li, C. H. (1977). *In* "Peptides: Proceedings of the Fifth American Peptide Symposium" (M. Goodman and J. Meienhofer, eds.), pp. 458–460. Wiley, New York.

Hruby, V. J., and du Vigneaud, V. (1969). *J. Am. Chem. Soc.* **91**, 3624–3628.

Hruby, V. J., Yamashiro, D., and du Vigneaud, V. (1968). *J. Am. Chem. Soc.* **90**, 7106–7110.

Huang, H. T., and Niemann, C. (1950). *J. Am. Chem. Soc.* **72**, 921–922.

Hubert, A. J., Buyle, R., and Hargitay, B. (1963). *Helv. Chim. Acta* **46**, 1429–1445.

Hunt, M. and du Vigneaud, V. (1938). *J. Biol. Chem.* **124**, 699–707.

Inouye, K., and Otsuka, H. (1961). *Bull. Chem. Soc. Jpn.* **34**, 1–3.

Inouye, K., and Watanabe, K. (1977). *J. Chem. Soc., Perkin Trans. 1* pp. 1911–1915.

Inouye, K., Watanabe, K., and Shin, M. (1977). *J. Chem. Soc., Perkin Trans. 1* pp. 1905–1911.

Inukai, N., Nakano, K., and Murakami, M. (1968). *Bull. Chem. Soc. Jpn.* **41**, 182–186.

Irie, H., Fujii, N., Ogawa, H., Yajima, H., Fujino, M., and Shinagawa, S. (1976). *J. Chem. Soc., Chem. Commun.* pp. 922–923.

Irie, H., Fujii, N., Ogawa, H., Yajima, H., Fujino, M., and Shinagawa, S. (1977). *Chem. Pharm. Bull.* **25**, 2929–2934.

Iselin, B. M. (1958). *Arch. Biochem. Biophys.* **78**, 532–538.

Iselin, B. M. (1961). *Helv. Chim. Acta* **44**, 61–68.

Iselin, B. M. (1962). *Helv. Chim. Acta* **45**, 1510–1515.

Iselin, B. M. (1966). *In* "Peptides 1963" (L. Zervas, ed.), pp. 27–33. Pergamon, Oxford.

Iselin, B. M., and Schwyzer, R. (1962). *Helv. Chim. Acta* **45**, 1499–1509.

Ito, H. (1979). *Synthesis* pp. 465–467.

Ito, H., Takamatsu, N., and Ichikizaki, I. (1977). *Chem. Lett.* **5**, 539–542.

Itoh, M., Hagiwara, D., and Kamiya, T. (1975). *Tetrahedron Lett.* pp. 4393–4394.

Ivanov, V. T., Mikhaleva, I. I., Volpina, O. M., Myagkova, M. A., and Deigin, V. I. (1976).

In "Peptides 1976" (A. Loffet, ed.), pp. 219–231. Editions de l'Université de Bruxelles, Belgium.
Iwai, K., and Ando, T. (1967). *In* "Methods in Enzymology" (C. H. W. Hirs, ed.), Vol. 11, pp. 263–282. Academic Press, New York.
Izdebski, J., Drabarek, S., and Lebek, M. (1975). *Rocz. Chem.* **49**, 1535–1540; *Chem. Abstr.* **84**, 905604.
Izdebski, J., Lebek, M., and Drabarek, S. (1977). *Rocz. Chem.* **51**, 81–88.
Izdebski, J., Kubiak, T., Kunce, D., and Drabarek, S. (1978). *Pol. J. Chem.* **52**, 539–545.
Izdebski, J., Kunce, D., Pelka, J., and Drabarek, S. (1980a). *Pol. J. Chem.* **54**, 117–120.
Izdebski, J., Kunce, D., and Drabarek, S. (1980b). *Pol. J. Chem.* **54**, 413–418.
Jaeger, E., Thamm, P., Schmidt, I., Knof, S., Moroder, L., and Wünsch, E. (1978a). *Hoppe-Seyler's Z. Physiol. Chem.* **359**, 155–164.
Jaeger, E., Thamm, P., Knof, S., Wünsch, E., Löw, M., and Kisfaludy, L. (1978b). *Hoppe-Seyler's Z. Physiol. Chem.* **359**, 1617–1628.
Jaeger, E., Thamm, P., Knof, S., and Wünsch, E. (1978c). *Hoppe-Seyler's Z. Physiol. Chem.* **359**, 1629–1636.
Jäger, G., and Geiger, R. (1973). *Justus Liebig's Ann. Chem.* pp. 1928–1933.
Jäger, G., König, W., Wissmann, H., and Geiger, R. (1974). *Chem. Ber.* **107**, 215–231.
Jakubke, H. D., and Baumert, A. (1974). *J. Prakt. Chem.* **316**, 67–74.
Jakubke, H. D., and Klessen, C. (1977). *J. Prakt. Chem.* **319**, 159–162.
Jones, J. H. (1979). *In* "The Peptides" (E. Gross and J. Meienhofer, eds.), Vol. 1, pp. 65–104. Academic Press, New York.
Jošt, K., and Rudinger, J. (1967a). *Collect. Czech. Chem. Commun.* **32**, 1229–1241.
Jošt, K., and Rudinger, J. (1967b). *Collect. Czech. Chem. Commun.* **32**, 2485–2490.
Juillerat, M., and Bargetzi, J. R. (1976). *Helv. Chim. Acta* **59**, 855–866.
Jung, M. E., and Lyster, M. A. (1977). *J. Am. Chem. Soc.* **99**, 968–969.
Kappeler, H. (1961). *Helv. Chim. Acta* **44**, 476–491.
Kappeler, H., and Schwyzer, R. (1960). *Helv. Chim. Acta* **43**, 1453–1459.
Karlsson, A., Lindeberg, G., Poráth, J., and Ragnarsson, U. (1970). *Acta Chem. Scand.* **24**, 1010–1014.
Kashelikar, D. V., and Ressler, C. (1964). *J. Am. Chem. Soc.* **86**, 2467–2473.
Katakai, R. (1977). *Bull. Chem. Soc. Jpn.* **50**, 1173–1178.
Katchalski, E., and Sela, M. (1953). *J. Am. Chem. Soc.* **75**, 5284–5289.
Kato, T., and Izumiya, N. (1974). *Chem. Biochem. Amino Acids, Pept. Proteins* **2**, 1–38.
Katsoyannis, P. G. (1966). *Am. J. Med.* **40**, 652–661.
Katsoyannis, P. G., Gish, D. T., Hess, G. P., and du Vigneaud, V. (1957). *J. Am. Chem. Soc.* **79**, 4516–4520.
Katsoyannis, P. G., Gish, D. T., Hess, G. P., and du Vigneaud, V. (1958). *J. Am. Chem. Soc.* **80**, 2558–2562.
Katsoyannis, P. G., Tometsko, A. M., and Zalut, C. (1967). *J. Am. Chem. Soc.* **89**, 4505–4513.
Katsoyannis, P. G., Zalut, C., Tometsko, A., Tilak, M., Johnson, S., and Trakatellis, A. C. (1971). *J. Am. Chem. Soc.* **93**, 5871–5877.
Keil, B., Zikan, J., Rexona, L., and Šorm, F. (1962). *Collect. Czech. Chem. Commun.* **27**, 1678–1686.
Kemp, D. S. (1979). *In* "The Peptides" (E. Gross and J. Meienhofer, eds.), Vol. 1, pp. 315–383. Academic Press, New York.
Kenner, G. W. (1955). *Spec. Publ.—Chem. Soc.* **2**, 103–113.
Kenner, G. W., and Seely, J. H. (1972). *J. Am. Chem. Soc.* **94**, 3259–3260.
Kenner, G. W., Moore, G. A., and Ramage, R. (1976). *Tetrahedron Lett.* pp. 3623–3626.
Kessler, W., and Iselin, B. M. (1966). *Helv. Chim. Acta* **49**, 1330–1344.

Khorana, H. G. (1953). *Chem. Rev.* **53**, 145–166.
Khorana, H. G. (1955). *Chem. Ind.* (*London*) pp. 1087–1088.
Khosla, M. C., and Anand, N. (1963). *Indian J. Chem.* **1**, 49–50.
Khosla, M. C., Smeby, R. R., and Bumpus, F. M. (1972). *J. Am. Chem. Soc.* **94**, 4721–4724.
King, F. E., and Kidd, D. A. A. (1949). *J. Chem. Soc.* pp. 3315–3319.
King, F. E., and Kidd, D. A. A. (1951). *J. Chem. Soc.* pp. 2976–2978.
King, F. E., Jackson, B. S., and Kidd, D. A. A. (1951). *J. Chem. Soc.* pp. 243–246.
King, F. E., Clark-Lewis, J. W., Kidd, D. A. A., and Smith, G. R. (1954a). *J. Chem. Soc.* pp. 1039–1043.
King, F. E., Clark-Lewis, J. W., and Smith, G. R. (1954b). *J. Chem. Soc.* pp. 1044–1046.
King, F. E., Clark-Lewis, J. W., and Wade, R. (1957). *J. Chem. Soc.* pp. 880–885, 886–894.
Kircher, K., Berndt, H., and Zahn, H. (1980). *Justus Liebig's Ann. Chem.* pp. 275–284.
Kisfaludy, L. (1960). *Acta Chim. Acad. Sci. Hung.* **24**, 309–319.
Kisfaludy, L. (1979). *In* "Peptides 1978" (I. Z. Siemion and G. Kupryszewski, eds.), pp. 25–40. Wroclaw Univ. Press, Wroclaw, Poland.
Kisfaludy, L. (1981). *In* "Perspectives in Peptide Chemistry" (A. Eberle, R. Geiger and T. Wieland, eds.), pp. 58–66. Karger, Basel.
Kisfaludy, L., Dualszky, S., and Bayer, J. (1960). *Chimia* **14**, 368.
Kisfaludy, L., Roberts, J. E., Johnson, R. H., Mayers, G. L., and Kovacs, J. (1970). *J. Org. Chem.* **35**, 3563–3565.
Kisfaludy, L., Low, M., Szirtes, T., Schön, I., Sárközi, M., Bajusz, S., Turán, A., Juhász, A., and Beke, R. (1972). *In* "Chemistry and Biology of Peptides" (J. Meienhofer, ed.), pp. 299–303. Ann Arbor Sci. Publ., Ann Arbor, Michigan.
Kisfaludy, L., Schön, I., Renyei, M., and Görög, S. (1975). *J. Am. Chem. Soc.* **97**, 5588–5589.
Kiso, Y., and Yajima, H. (1972). *J. Chem. Soc., Chem. Commun.* pp. 942–943.
Kiso, Y., Isawa, H., Kitagawa, K., and Akita, T. (1978). *Chem. Pharm. Bull.* **26**, 2562–2564.
Kiso, Y., Ito, K., Nakamura, S., Kitagawa, K., Akita, T., and Moritoki, H. (1979). *Chem. Pharm. Bull.* **27**, 1472–1475.
Kiso, Y., Ukawa, K., Nakamura, S., Ito, K., and Akita, I. (1980). *Chem. Pharm. Bull.* **28**, 673–676.
Kitagawa, K., Kitade, K., Kiso, Y., Akita, T., Funakoshi, S., Fujii, N., and Yajima, H. (1979). *J. Chem. Soc., Chem. Commun.* pp. 955–956.
Klausner, Y. S., and Bodanszky, M. (1973). *Bioorg. Chem.* **2**, 354–362.
Klausner, Y. S., and Bodanszky, M. (1974). *Synthesis* pp. 549–559.
König, W., and Geiger, R. (1970). *Chem. Ber.* **103**, 788–798.
König, W., and Geiger, R. (1973). *Chem. Ber.* **106**, 3626–3635.
König, W., and Volk, A. (1977). *Chem. Ber.* **110**, 1–11.
Kopple, K. D. (1957). *J. Am. Chem. Soc.* **79**, 6442–6446.
Kopple, K. D., and Renick, R. J. (1958). *J. Org. Chem.* **23**, 1565–1567.
Kopple, K. D., Jarabak, R. R., and Bhatia, P. L. (1963). *Biochemistry* **2**, 958–964.
Kopple, K. D., Saito, T., and Ohnishi, M. (1969). *J. Org. Chem.* **34**, 1631–1635.
Kopple, K. D., Feng, M. C., and Go, A. (1977). *In* "Peptides: Proceedings of the Fifth American Peptide Symposium (M. Goodman and J. Meienhofer, eds.), pp. 333–336. Wiley, New York.
Kotake, H., (1980) and Saito, T. (1966). *Bull. Chem. Soc. Jpn.* **39**, 853.
Kovács, J., (1980). *In* "The Peptides" (E. Gross and J. Meienhofer, eds.) Vol. 2., pp. 486–539. Academic Press, New York.
Kovács, J., Medzihradszky, K., and Bruckner, V. (1954). *Naturwissenschaften* **41**, 450.
Kovács, J., Kisfaludy, L., and Ceprini, M. Q. (1967). *J. Am. Chem. Soc.* **89**, 183–184.
Krumdieck, C. L., and Baugh, C. M. (1969). *Biochemistry* **8**, 1568–1572.
Kuhn, R., and Haas, H. J. (1955). *Angew. Chem.* **67**, 785.

Kulikov, S. V., Vlasov, G. P., Ginzburg, O. F., and Tsukerman, B. V. (1977). *J. Org. Chem. USSR* (*Engl. Transl.*) **13**, 2023–2025.

Künzi, H., Manneberg, M., and Studer, R. O. (1974). *Helv. Chim. Acta* **57**, 566–572.

Kuromizu, K., and Meienhofer, J. (1974). *J. Am. Chem. Soc.* **95**, 4978–4981.

Lashkov, V. N., and Vlasov, G. P. (1978). *J. Gen. Chem. USSR* (*Engl. Transl.*) **48**, 1710–1717.

Leach, S. J., and Lindley, H. (1954). *Aust. J. Chem.* **7**, 173–180.

Ledger, R., and Stewart, F. H. C. (1968). *Aust. J. Chem.* **21**, 1101–1105.

Leister, N. A., and Tarbell, D. S. (1958). *J. Org. Chem.* **23**, 1152–1155.

Lemaire, S., Yamashiro, D., and Li, C. H. (1976). *J. Med. Chem.* **19**, 373–376.

Lenard, J., and Hess, G. P. (1964). *J. Biol. Chem.* **239**, 3275–3281.

Lenard, J., Schally, A. V., and Hess, G. P. (1964). *Biochem. Biophys. Res. Commun.* **14**, 498–502.

Leplawy, M. T., Jones, D. S., Kenner, G. W., and Sheppard, R. C. (1960). *Tetrahedron* **11**, 39–51.

Lequesne, W. J., and Young, G. T. (1950). *J. Chem. Soc.* pp. 1954–1959.

Li, C. H., and Yamashiro, D. (1970). *J. Am. Chem. Soc.* **92**, 7608–7609.

Li, C. H., Schnabel, E., and Chung, D. (1960). *J. Am. Chem. Soc.* **82**, 2062–2067.

Li, C. H., Meienhofer, J., Schnabel, E., Chung, D., Lo, T. B., and Ramachandran, J. (1961). *J. Am. Chem. Soc.* **83**, 4449–4457.

Liberek, B., Jr. (1961). *Chem Ind.* (*London*) pp. 987–989.

Liberek, B., Jr. (1962). *Bull. Acad. Pol. Sci., Ser. Sci. Chim.* **10**, 227–231. *Chem. Abstr.* **59**, 4031 g.

Liberek, B., Jr., Buczel, Cz., and Grzonka, Z. (1966). *Tetrahedron* **22**, 2302–2306.

Liefländer, M. (1960). *Hoppe-Seyler's Z. Physiol. Chem.* **320**, 35–57.

Loffet, A., and Dremier, C. (1971). *Experientia* **27**, 1003–1004.

Lombardino, J. G., Anderson, S. L., and Norris, C. P. (1978). *J. Heterocycl. Chem.* **15**, 655–656.

Loring, H. S., and du Vigneaud, V. (1935). *J. Biol. Chem.* **111**, 385–392.

Losse, G., and Demuth, E. (1961). *Chem. Ber.* **94**, 1762–1766.

Losse, G., and Müller, G. (1961). *Chem. Ber.* **94**, 2768–2778.

Losse, G., and Nadolski, D. (1964). *J. Prakt. Chem.* **24**, 118–124.

Lott, R. S., Chauhan, V. S., and Stammer, C. H. (1979). *J. Chem. Soc., Chem. Commun.* pp. 495–496.

Löw, M., and Kisfaludy, L. (1965). *Acta Chim. Acad. Sci. Hung.* **44**, 61–66.

Löw, M., and Kisfaludy, L. (1979). *Hoppe-Seyler's Z. Physiol. Chem.* **360**, 13–18.

Löw, M., Kisfaludy, L., Jaeger, E., Thamm, P., Knof, S., and Wünsch, E. (1978a). *Hoppe-Seyler's Z. Physiol. Chem.* **359**, 1637–1642.

Löw, M., Kisfaludy, L., and Sohár, P. (1978b). *Hoppe-Seyler's Z. Physiol. Chem.* **359**, 1643–1651.

Lucas, T. J., Prystowsky, M. B., and Erickson, B. W. (1981). *Proc. Natl. Acad. Sci. U.S.A.* **78**, 2790–2795.

Lucente, G., and Frattesi, P. (1972). *Tetrahedron Lett.* pp. 4283–4286.

Lucente, G., Fiorentini, G., and Rossi, D. (1971). *Gazz. Chim. Ital.* **101**, 109–116.

Lundt, B. F., Johansen, N. L., Volund, A., and Markussen, J. (1978). *Int. J. Pept. Protein Res.* **12**, 258–268.

Lundt, B. F., Johansen, N. L., and Markussen, J. (1979). *Int. J. Pept. Protein Res.* **14**, 344–346.

Lunkenheimer, W., and Zahn, H. (1970). *Justus Liebig's Ann. Chem.* **740**, 1–17.

McGregor, W. H., and Carpenter, F. H. (1961). *J. Org. Chem.* **26**, 1849–1854.

McKay, F. C. (1952). *Chem. Rev.* **51**, 301–346.

McKay, F. C., and Albertson, N. F. (1957). *J. Am. Chem. Soc.* **79**, 4686–4690.

McKerrow, J. H., and Robinson, A. B. (1971). *Anal. Biochem.* **42**, 565–568.
McKerrow, J. H., and Robinson, A. B. (1974). *Science* **183**, 85.
MacLaren, J. A. (1958). *Aust. J. Chem.* **11**, 360–365.
MacLaren, J. A., Savige, W. E., and Swan, M. J. (1958). *Aust. J. Chem.* **11**, 345–359.
Manning, M. (1968). *J. Am. Chem. Soc.* **90**, 1348–1349.
Manning, M., Marglin, A., and Moore, S. (1972). *In* "Progress in Peptide Research" (S. Lande, ed.), pp. 173–183. Gordon & Breach, New York.
Marglin, A. (1972). *Int. J. Pept. Protein Res.* **4**, 47–55.
Marglin, A., and Merrifield, R. B. (1966). *J. Am. Chem. Soc.* **88**, 5051–5052.
Marshall, G. R. (1968). *In* "Pharmacology of Hormonal Polypeptides and Proteins" (N. Back, L. Martini, and R. Paoletti, eds.), pp. 48–52. Plenum, New York.
Martinez, J., and Bodanszky, M. (1978). *Int. J. Pept. Protein Res.* **12**, 277–283.
Martinez, J., Tolle, J. C., and Bodanszky, M. (1979a). *Int. J. Pept. Protein Res.* **13**, 22–27.
Martinez, J., Tolle, J. C., and Bodanszky, M. (1979b). *J. Org. Chem.* **44**, 3596–3598.
Masui, Y., Chino, N., and Sakakibara, S. (1980). *Bull. Chem. Soc. Jpn.* **53**, 464–468.
Mazur, R. H., and Schlatter, J. M. (1963). *J. Org. Chem.* **28**, 1025–1029.
Medzihradszky, K., Bruckner, V., Kajtár, M., Löw, M., Bajusz, S., and Kisfaludy, L. (1962). *Acta Chim. Acad. Sci. Hung.* **30**, 105–108.
Medzihradszky-Schweiger, H. (1973). *Acta Chim. Acad. Sci. Hung.* **76**, 437–440.
Medzihradszky-Schweiger, H., and Medzihradszky, K. (1966). *Acta Chim. Acad. Sci. Hung.* **50**, 339–350.
Meienhofer, J. (1970). *J. Am. Chem. Soc.* **92**, 3771–3777.
Meienhofer, J. (1979a). *In* "The Peptides" (E. Gross and J. Meienhofer, eds.), Vol. 1, pp. 197–239. Academic Press, New York.
Meienhofer, J. (1979b). *In* "The Peptides" (E. Gross and J. Meienhofer, eds.), Vol. 1, pp. 263–314. Academic Press, New York.
Meienhofer, J., and Chang, C. D. (1979). *In* "Peptides 1978" (I. Z. Siemion and G. Kupryszewski, eds.), pp. 573–575. Wroclaw Univ. Press, Wroclaw, Poland.
Meienhofer, J., and Kuromizu, K. (1974). *Tetrahedron Lett.* pp. 3259–3262.
Meienhofer, J., Sano, Y., and Patel, R. P. (1970). *In* "Peptides: Chemistry and Biochemistry" (B. Weinstein and S. Lande, eds.), pp. 419–434. Dekker, New York.
Meienhofer, J., Waki, M., Heimer, E. P., Lambros, T. J., Makofske, R. C., and Chang, C. D. (1979). *Int. J. Pept. Protein Res.* **13**, 35–42.
Melville, J. (1935). *Biochem. J.* **29**, 179–186.
Meresar, U., and Agren, A. (1968). *Acta Pharm. Suec.* **5**, 85–94.
Meriwether, L., and Westheimer, F. H. (1956). *J. Am. Chem. Soc.* **78**, 5119–5123.
Merrifield, R. B. (1963). *J. Am. Chem. Soc.* **85**, 2149–2154.
Merrifield, R. B. (1964a). *Biochemistry* **3**, 1385–1390.
Merrifield, R. B. (1964b). *J. Org. Chem.* **29**, 3100–3102.
Merrifield, R. B. (1967). *Recent Prog. Horm. Res.* **23**, 451–482.
Merrifield, R. B., and Marglin, A. (1967). *In* "Peptides 1966" (H. C. Beyerman, A. van de Linde, and W. Maassen van den Brink, eds.), pp. 85–90. North-Holland Publ., Amsterdam.
Merrifield, R. B., and Woolley, D. W. (1956). *J. Am. Chem. Soc.* **78**, 4646–4649.
Merrifield, R. B., and Woolley, D. W. (1958). *J. Am. Chem. Soc.* **80**, 6635–6639.
Merrifield, R. B., Mitchell, A. R., and Clarke, J. E. (1974). *J. Org. Chem.* **39**, 660–668.
Meyers, C., Havran, R. T., Schwartz, I. L., and Walter, R. (1969). *Chem. Ind.* (*London*) pp. 136–137.
Mitchell, A. R., and Merrifield, R. B. (1976). *J. Org. Chem.* **41**, 2015–2019.
Mitsuyasu, N., Waki, M., Kato, T., and Izumiya, N. (1970). *Mem. Fac. Sci., Kyushu Univ., Ser. C* **7**, 97–101; *Chem. Abstr.* **73**, 88154.
Mojsov, S., Mitchell, A. R., and Merrifield, R. B. (1980). *J. Org. Chem.* **45**, 555–560.

Muramatsu, I., Hirabayashi, T., and Hagitani, A. (1963). *Nippon Kagaku Zasshi* **84**, 855–860; *Chem. Abstr.* **60**, 12100c.
Naider, F., and Bohak, Z. (1972). *Biochemistry* **11**, 3208–3211.
Naider, F., Bohak, Z., and Yariv, J. (1972). *Biochemistry* **11**, 3202–3207.
Naithani, V. K. (1973). *Hoppe-Seyler's Z. Physiol. Chem.* **354**, 659–672.
Narita, K. (1959). *J. Am. Chem. Soc.* **81**, 1751–1756.
Natarajan, S., and Bodanszky, M. (1976). *J. Org. Chem.* **41**, 1269–1272.
Nefkens, G. H. L. (1960). *Nature (London)* **185**, 309.
Nefkens, G. H. L., Tesser, G. I., and Nivard, R. J. F. (1960). *Recl. Trav. Chim. Pays-Bas* **79**, 688–698.
Neumann, H., Levin, Y., Berger, A., and Katchalski, E. (1959). *Biochem. J.* **73**, 33–41.
Neumann, R. E., and Smith, E. L. (1951). *J. Biol. Chem.* **193**, 97–111.
Nicolaides, E. D., and De Wald, H. A. (1961). *J. Org. Chem.* **26**, 3872–3876.
Nicolaides, E. D., and De Wald, H. A. (1963). *J. Org. Chem.* **28**, 1926–1927.
Nicolaides, E. D., Craft, M. K., and De Wald, H. A. (1963). *J. Med. Chem.* **6**, 524–528.
Nishimura, O., and Fujino, M. (1976). *Chem. Pharm. Bull.* **24**, 1568–1575.
Noble, R. L., Yamashiro, D., and Li, C. H. (1976). *J. Am. Chem. Soc.* **98**, 2324–2328.
Noda, K., and Gross, E. (1972). *In* "Chemistry and Biology of Peptides" (J. Meienhofer, ed.), pp. 241–250. Ann Arbor Sci. Publ., Ann Arbor, Michigan.
Norris, K., Halström, J., and Brunfeldt, K. (1971). *Acta Chem. Scand.* **25**, 945–954.
Ogawa, H., Sasaki, T., Irie, H., and Yajima, H. (1978). *Chem. Pharm. Bull.* **26**, 3144–3149.
Ohno, M., Tsukamoto, S., Makisumi, S., and Izumiya, N. (1972a). *Bull. Chem. Soc. Jpn.* **45**, 2852–2855.
Ohno, M., Tsukamoto, S., and Izumiya, N. (1972b). *J. Chem. Soc., Chem. Commun.* pp. 663–664.
Ohno, M., Tsukamoto, S., Sato, S., and Izumiya, N. (1973). *Bull. Chem. Soc. Jpn.* **46**, 3280–3285.
Okada, Y., Tsuda, Y., and Yagyu, M. (1980). *Chem. Pharm. Bull.* **28**, 2254–2258.
Okawa, K. (1956). *Bull. Chem. Soc. Jpn.* **29**, 488–489.
Okawa, K. (1957). *Bull. Chem. Soc. Jpn.* **30**, 976–978.
Olsen, S., and Enkemeyer, E. M. (1948). *Chem. Ber.* **81**, 359–361.
Omenn, G. S., Fontana, A., and Anfinsen, C. B. (1970). *J. Biol. Chem.* **245**, 1895–1902.
Omori, Y., Matsuda, Y., Aimoto, S., Shimonishi, Y., and Yamamoto, M. (1976). *Chem. Lett.* pp. 805–808.
Ondetti, M. A., and Bodanszky, M. (1962). *Chem. Ind. (London)* pp. 697–698.
Ondetti, M. A., Deer, A., Sheehan, J. J., Pluscec, J., and Kocy, O. (1968). *Biochemistry* **7**, 4069–4075.
Ondetti, M. A., Williams, N. J., Sabo, E. F., Pluscec, J., Weaver, E. R., and Kocy, O. (1971). *Biochemistry* **10**, 4033–4039.
Panneman, H. J., Marx, A. F., and Arens, J. F. (1959). *Recl. Trav. Chim. Pays-Bas.* **78**, 487–511.
Patchornik, A. (1963). *In* "Peptides 1962" (G. T. Young, ed.), p. 54. Pergamon, Oxford.
Paul, R. (1963). *J. Org. Chem.* **28**, 236–237.
Paul, R., and Anderson, G. W. (1962). *J. Org. Chem.* **27**, 2094–2099.
Paul, R., and Kende, A. S. (1964). *J. Am. Chem. Soc.* **86**, 741–742, 4162–4166.
Paul, R., Anderson, G. W., and Callahan, F. M. (1961). *J. Org. Chem.* **26**, 3347–3350.
Penke, B., Dombi, G., and Kovács, K. (1973). *Acta Phys. Chem.* **19**, 165–169.
Phocas, I., Yovanidis, P. C., Photaki, I., and Zervas, L. (1967). *J. Chem. Soc. C.* pp. 1506–1509.
Photaki, I. (1963). *J. Am. Chem. Soc.* **85**, 1123–1126.
Photaki, I., and Yiotakis, A. E. (1976). *J. Chem. Soc., Perkin Trans 1* pp. 259–264.

Pietta, P. G., Cavallo, P., and Marshall, G. R. (1971). *J. Org. Chem.* **36**, 3966–3970.
Pless, J., and Bauer, W. (1973). Angew. Chem., Int. Ed. Engl. **12**, 147–148.
Pless, J., and Guttmann, S. (1967). *In* "Peptides 1966" (H. C. Beyerman, A. van de Linde, and W. Maasen van den Brink, eds.), pp. 50–54. North-Holland Publ., Amsterdam.
Polzhofer, K. P., and Ney, K. H. (1970). *Tetrahedron* **26**, 3221–3226.
Polzhofer, K. P., and Ney, K. H. (1971). *Tetrahedron* **27**, 1997–2001.
Pospisek, J., and Blaha, K. (1977). *Collect. Czech. Chem. Commun.* **42**, 1069–1076.
Potts, J. T., Tregear, G. W., Keutman, H. T., Niall, H. D., Saver, R., Deftos, L. J., Dawson, B. F., Hogan, M. L., and Auerbach, G. D. (1971). *Proc. Natl. Acad. Sci. U.S.A.* **68**, 63–67.
Prelog, V., and Wieland, P. (1946). *Helv. Chim. Acta* **29**, 1128–1132.
Previero, A., Coletti-Previero, M. A., and Cavadore, J. C. (1967). *Biochim. Biophys. Acta* **147**, 453–461.
Previero, A., Coletti-Previero, M. A., and Barry, L. G. (1968). *Can. J. Chem.* **46**, 3404–3407.
Previero, A., Prota, G., and Coletti-Previero, M. A. (1972). *Biochim. Biophys. Acta* **285**, 269–278.
Purdie, J. E., and Benoiton, N. L. (1973). *J. Chem. Soc., Perkin Trans. 2* pp. 1845–1852.
Ramachandran, G. N., and Chandrasekaran, R. (1972). *In* "Progress in Peptide Research" (S. Lande, ed.), Vol. 2, pp. 195–215. Gordon & Breach, New York.
Ramachandran, J. (1965). *Nature (London)* **206**, 927–928.
Ramachandran, J., and Li, C. H. (1963). *J. Org. Chem.* **28**, 173–177.
Ramachandran, J., Chung, D., and Li, C. H. (1965). *J. Am. Chem. Soc.* **87**, 2696–2708.
Ramirez, F., Finnan, J. L., and Carlson, M. (1973). *J. Org. Chem.* **38**, 2597–2600.
Rees, A. R., and Offord, R. E. (1976). *Biochem. J.* **159**, 467–479.
Ressler, C. (1956). *J. Am. Chem. Soc.* **78**, 5956–5957.
Ressler, C., and Kashelikar, D. V. (1966). *J. Am. Chem. Soc.* **88**, 2025–2035.
Ressler, C., and Ratzkin, H. (1961). *J. Org. Chem.* **26**, 3356–3360.
Rich, D. H., and Singh, J. (1979). *In* "The Peptides" (E. Gross and J. Meienhofer, eds.), Vol. 1, pp. 241–261. Academic Press, New York.
Riley, G., Turnbull, J. H., and Wilson, W. (1957). *J. Chem. Soc.* pp. 1373–1379.
Riniker, B., and Schwyzer, R. (1961). *Helv. Chim. Acta* **44**, 685–692.
Riniker, B., and Schwyzer, R. (1964a). *Helv. Chim. Acta* **47**, 2357–2374.
Riniker, B., and Schwyzer, R. (1964b). *Helv. Chim. Acta* **47**, 2375–2384.
Riniker, B., Brunner, H., and Schwyzer, R. (1962). *Angew. Chem.* **74**, 469.
Rink, H., and Riniker, B. (1974). *Helv. Chim. Acta* **57**, 831–835.
Rittel, W. R. (1962). *Helv. Chim. Acta* **45**, 2465–2473.
Robinson, A. B. (1974). *Proc. Natl. Acad. Sci. U.S.A.* **71**, 885–888.
Robinson, A. B., and Tedro, S. (1973). *Int. J. Pept. Protein Res.* **5**, 275–278.
Robinson, A. B., McKerrow, J. H., and Cary, P. (1970). *Proc. Natl. Acad. Sci. U.S.A.* **66**, 753–757.
Rocchi, R., Guggi, A., Menegatti, E., Salvatori, S., Scatturin, A., and Tomatis, R. (1979). *In* "Peptides 1978" (I. Z. Siemion and G. Kupryszewski, eds.), pp. 649–653. Wroclaw Univ. Press, Wroclaw, Poland.
Roeske, R. (1959). *Chem. Ind. (London)* pp. 1121–1122.
Roeske, R. (1963). *J. Org. Chem.* **28**, 1251–1253.
Roeske, R., Stewart, F. H. C., Stedman, R. J., and du Vigneaud, V. (1956). *J. Am. Chem. Soc.* **78**, 5883–5887.
Rothe, M., and Mazanek, J. (1972). *Angew. Chem., Int. Ed. Engl.* **11**, 293–294.
Rothe, M., and Mazanek, J. (1974). *Justus Liebig's Ann. Chem.* pp. 439–459.
Rothe, M., Theysohn, R., Mühlhausen, D., Eisenkeiss, F., and Schindler, W. (1972). *In* "Chemistry and Biology of Peptides" (J. Meienhofer, ed.), pp. 51–57. Ann Arbor Sci. Publ., Ann Arbor, Michigan.

Rothe, M., Frank, E., and Schmidtberg, G. (1981). *In* "Peptides 1980" (K. Brunfeldt, ed.), pp. 258–263. Scriptor, Copenhagen.

Rowlands, D. A., and Young, G. T. (1957). *Biochem. J.* **65**, 516–519.

Rudinger, J. (1954). *Collect. Czech. Chem. Commun.* **19**, 365–374.

Rudinger, J., and Honzl, J. (1960). *Chimia* **14**, 367.

Rudinger, J., and Pravda, Z. (1958). *Collect. Czech. Chem. Commun.* **23**, 1947–1957.

Rudinger, J., Krupicka, J., Zaoral, M., and Cernik, V. (1960). *Collect. Czech. Chem. Commun.* **25**, 3338–3343.

Rydon, H. N., and Smith, P. W. G. (1956). *J. Chem. Soc.* pp. 3642–3650.

Ryle, A. P., and Sanger, F. (1955). *Biochem. J.* **60**, 535–540.

Rzeszotarska, B., and Kmiecik-Chmura, H. (1977). *Rocz. Chem.* **51**, 1523–1526.

Sachs, H., and Brand, E. (1954). *J. Am. Chem. Soc.* **76**, 1815–1817.

Saito, T. (1964). *Bull. Chem. Soc. Jpn.* **37**, 624–628.

Sakakibara, S. (1977). *In* "Peptides: Proceedings of the Fifth American Peptide Symposium" (M. Goodmann and J. Meienhofer, eds.), pp. 436–447. Wiley, New York.

Sakakibara, S., and Nagai, Y. (1960). *Bull. Chem. Soc. Jpn.* **33**, 1537–1542.

Sakakibara, S., and Shimonishi, Y. (1965). *Bull. Chem. Soc. Jpn.* **38**, 1412–1413.

Sakakibara, S., Shin, K. H., and Hess, G. P. (1962). *J. Am. Chem. Soc.* **84**, 4921–4928.

Sakakibara, S., Shin, M., Fujino, M., Shimonishi, Y., Inouye, S., and Inukai, N. (1965). *Bull. Chem. Soc. Jpn.* **38**, 1522–1525.

Sakakibara, S., Shimonishi, Y., Kishida, Y., Okada, M., and Sugihara, H. (1967). *Bull. Chem. Soc. Jpn.* **40**, 2164–2167.

Sakakibara, S., Honda, I., Takada, K., Miyoshi, M., Ohnishi, T., and Okumura, K. (1969). *Bull. Chem. Soc. Jpn.* **42**, 808–811.

Sakakibara, S., Fukuda, T., Kishida, Y., and Honda, I. (1970). *Bull. Chem. Soc. Jpn.* **43**, 3322.

Sakiyama, F. (1962). *Bull. Chem. Soc. Jpn.* **35**, 1943–1950.

Sanger, F. (1953). *Nature (London)* **171**, 1025–1026.

Sano, S., and Kawanishi, S. (1973). *Biochem. Biophys. Res. Commun.* **51**, 46–51.

Sano, S., and Kawanishi, S. (1975). *J. Am. Chem. Soc.* **97**, 3480–3484.

Sarges, R., and Witkop, B. (1965). *J. Am. Chem. Soc.* **87**, 2020–2027.

Savrda, J. (1977). *J. Org. Chem.* **42**, 3199–3201.

Schafer, D. J., Young, G. T., Elliott, D. F., and Wade, R. (1971). *J. Chem. Soc. C* pp. 46–49.

Schallenberg, E. E., and Calvin, M. (1955). *J. Am. Chem. Soc.* **77**, 2779–2783.

Schellenberg, P., and Ullrich, J. (1959). *Chem. Ber.* **92**, 1276–1287.

Schlögl, K., and Fabitschowitz, H. (1953). *Monatsh. Chem.* **84**, 937–955.

Schmidt, E., and Striewszky, W. (1941). *Ber. Dtsch. Chem. Ges.* **74**, 1285–1296.

Schmidt, E., Hitzler, F., and Lahde, E. (1938). *Ber. Dtsch. Chem. Ges.* **71**, 1933–1938.

Schmidt, E., Striewszky, W., and Hitzler, F. (1948). *Justus Liebig's Ann. Chem.* **560**, 222–231.

Schnabel, E. (1962). *Justus Liebig's Ann. Chem.* **659**, 168–184.

Schnabel, E. (1963). *In* "Peptides 1962" (G. T. Young ed.), pp. 77–82. Pergamon, Oxford.

Schnabel, E., and Schüssler, H. (1965). *Justus Liebig's Ann. Chem.* **686**, 229–238.

Schnabel, E., and Zahn, H. (1957). *Monatsh. Chem.* **88**, 646–651.

Schnabel, E., Klostermeyer, H., Dahlmans, J., and Zahn, H. (1967). *Justus Liebig's Ann. Chem.* **707**, 227–241.

Schnabel, E., Klostermeyer, H., and Berndt, H. (1971). *Justus Liebig's Ann. Chem.* **749**, 90–108.

Schneider, F. (1960). *Hoppe-Seyler's Z. Physiol. Chem.* **321**, 38–48; 82–91.

Schneider, F. (1963). *Hoppe-Seyler's Z. Physiol. Chem.* **332**, 38–53.

Schön, I., and Kisfaludy, L. (1978). *Z. Naturforsch., B: Anorg. Chem., Org. Chem.* **33B**, 1196–1197.

Schön, I., and Kisfaludy, L. (1979). *Int. J. Pept. Protein Res.* **14**, 485–494.

Schou, O., Bucher, D., and Nebelin, E. (1976). *Hoppe-Seyler's Z. Physiol. Chem.* **357**, 103–106.
Schröder, E., and Gibian, H. (1961). *Justus Liebig's Ann. Chem.* **649**, 168–182.
Schüssler, H., and Zahn, H. (1962). *Chem. Ber.* **95**, 1076–1080.
Schwyzer, R., and Gorup, B. (1958). *Helv. Chim. Acta* **41**, 2199–2205.
Schwyzer, R., and Kappeler, H. (1961). *Helv. Chim. Acta* **44**, 1991–2002.
Schwyzer, R., and Sieber, P. (1958). *Helv. Chim. Acta* **41**, 2186–2189; 2190–2199.
Schwyzer, R., Iselin, B., Kappeler, H., Riniker, B., Rittel, W., and Zuber, H. (1958). *Helv. Chim. Acta* **41**, 1273–1286.
Schwyzer, R., Iselin, B., Kappeler, H., Riniker, B., Rittel, W., and Zuber, H. (1963). *Helv. Chim. Acta* **46**, 1975–1996.
Schwyzer, R., Carrion, J. P., Gorup, B., Nolting, H., and Tun-Kyi, A. (1964). *Helv. Chim. Acta* **47**, 441–464.
Schwyzer, R., Tun-Kyi, A., Caviezel, M., and Moser, P. (1970). *Helv. Chim. Acta* **53**, 15–27.
Scoffone, E., Fontana, A., and Rocchi, R. (1968). *Biochemistry* **7**, 971–979.
Scopes, P. M., Walshaw, K. B., Welford, M., and Young, G. T. (1965). *J. Chem. Soc.* pp. 782–786.
Shalitin, Y., and Bernhard, S. A. (1964). *J. Am. Chem. Soc.* **86**, 2291–2292.
Shalitin, Y., and Bernhard, S. A. (1966). *J. Am. Chem. Soc.* **88**, 4711–4721.
Shankman, S., and Higa, S. (1962). *J. Pharm. Sci.* **51**, 137–140.
Shankman, S., and Schvo, Y. (1958). *J. Am. Chem. Soc.* **80**, 1164–1168.
Sharp, J. J., Robinson, A. B., and Kamen, M. D. (1973). *J. Am. Chem. Soc.* **95**, 6097–6108.
Shchukina, L. A., Davankova, L. A., Suvorov, N. N., and Neklyudov, A. D. (1970). *J. Gen. Chem. USSR* (*Engl. Transl.*) **40**, 1657.
Sheehan, J. C. (1960). *Ann. N.Y. Acad. Sci.* **88**, 665–668.
Sheehan, J. C., and Frank, V. S. (1950). *J. Am. Chem. Soc.* **72**, 1312–1316.
Sheehan, J. C., and Hess, G. P. (1955). *J. Am. Chem. Soc.* **77**, 1067–1068.
Sheehan, J. C., and Hlavka, J. J. (1956). *J. Org. Chem.* **21**, 439–441.
Sheehan, J. C., Chapman, D. W., and Roth, R. W. (1952). *J. Am. Chem. Soc.* **74**, 3822–3825.
Sheehan, J. C., Goodman, M., and Hess, G. P. (1956). *J. Am. Chem. Soc.* **78**, 1367–1369.
Sheehan, J. C., Hasspacher, K., and Yeh, Y. L. (1959). *J. Am. Chem. Soc.* **81**, 6086.
Shiba, T., and Kaneko, T. (1960). *Bull. Chem. Soc. Jpn.* **33**, 1721–1731.
Shin, K. H., Sakakibara, S., Schneider, W., and Hess, G. P. (1962). *Biochem. Biophys. Res. Commun.* **8**, 288–293.
Shin, M., and Inouye, K. (1978). *In* "Peptide Chemistry 1977" (T. Shiba, ed.), pp. 67–72. Protein Res. Found., Osaka, Japan.
Shioiri, T., and Yamada, S. (1974). *Chem. Pharm. Bull.* **22**, 849–854.
Sieber, P. (1968). *In* "Peptides 1968" (C. E. Bricas, ed.), p. 236. North-Holland Publ., Amsterdam.
Sieber, P., and Iselin, B. (1968). *Helv. Chim. Acta* **51**, 614–622; 622–632.
Sieber, P., Riniker, B., Brugger, M., Kamber, B., and Rittel, W. (1970). *Helv. Chim. Acta* **53**, 2135–2150.
Sieber, P., Andreatta, R. H., Eisler, K., Kamber, B., Riniker, B., and Rink, H. (1977). *In* "Peptides: Proceedings of the Fifth American Peptide Symposium" (M. Goodman and J. Meienhofer, eds.), pp. 543–548. Wiley, New York.
Sieber, P., Kamber, B., Riniker, B., and Rittel, W. (1980). *Helv. Chim. Acta* **63**, 2358–2363.
Siemion, I. Z., and Nowak, K. (1960). *Rocz. Chem.* **34**, 1479–1482; *Chem. Abstr.* **55**, 21096.
Siemion, I. Z., and Nowak, K. (1961). *Rocz. Chem.* **35**, 979–984; *Chem. Abstr.* **56**, 6084d.
Sifferd, R. H., and du Vigneaud, V. (1935). *J. Biol. Chem.* **108**, 753–761.
Simmonds, S., Harris, J. I., and Fruton, J. S. (1951). *J. Biol. Chem.* **188**, 251–262.
Smith, E. L., and Bergmann, M. (1944). *J. Biol. Chem.* **153**, 627–651.

Sokolovsky, M., Wilchek, M., and Patchornik, A. (1964). *J. Am. Chem. Soc.* **86**, 1202–1206.
Sondheimer, E., and Holley, R. W. (1954a). *J. Am. Chem. Soc.* **76**, 2467–2470.
Sondheimer, E., and Holley, R. W. (1954b). *J. Am. Chem. Soc.* **76**, 2816–2818.
Sondheimer, E., and Holley, R. W. (1957). *J. Am. Chem. Soc.* **79**, 3767–3770.
Sondheimer, E., and Semeraro, R. J. (1961). *J. Org. Chem.* **26**, 1847–1849.
Sørup, P., Braae, H., Villemoes, P., and Christensen, T. (1979). *Acta Chem. Scand.* **333**, 653–663.
Southard, G. L., Zaborowsky, B. R., and Pettee, J. M. (1971). *J. Am. Chem. Soc.* **93**, 3302–3303.
Spanninger, P. A., and von Rosenberg, J. L. (1972). *J. Am. Chem. Soc.* **94**, 1973–1978.
Speciale, A. J., and Smith, L. R. (1963). *J. Org. Chem.* **28**, 1805–1811.
Staab, H. A. (1957). *Justus Liebig's Ann. Chem.* **609**, 75–83.
Stammer, J. (1961). *J. Org. Chem.* **26**, 2556–2560.
Stedman, R. J. (1957). *J. Am. Chem. Soc.* **79**, 4691–4694.
Stekol, J. A. (1941). *J. Biol. Chem.* **140**, 827–831.
Stelakatos, G. C., Theodoropoulos, D. M., and Zervas, L. (1959). *J. Am. Chem. Soc.* **81**, 2884–2887.
Stewart, F. H. C. (1968a). *Aust. J. Chem.* **21**, 477–482.
Stewart, F. H. C. (1968b). *Aust. J. Chem.* **21**, 1639–1649.
Stewart, J. M., and Matsueda, G. R. (1972). *In* "Chemistry and Biology of Peptides" (J. Meienhofer, ed.), pp. 221–224. Ann Arbor Sci. Publ., Ann Arbor, Michigan.
Sugano, H., Taguchi, Y., Kwai, H., and Miyoshi, M. (1978). *In* "Peptide Chemistry 1977" (T. Shiba, ed.), pp. 23–26. Protein Res. Found., Osaka, Japan.
Sun, M., and Zigman, S. (1979). *Photochem. Photobiol.* **29**, 893–897.
Suzuki, K., and Abiko, T. (1966). *Chem. Pharm. Bull.* **14**, 1017–1023.
Suzuki, K., Nitta, K., and Sasaki, Y. (1976). *Chem. Pharm. Bull.* **24**, 3025–3033.
Suzuki, K., Endo, N., and Sasaki, Y. (1977). *Chem. Pharm. Bull.* **25**, 2613–2616.
Suzuki, K., Endo, N., Kazuo, N., and Sasaki, Y. (1978). *Chem. Pharm. Bull.* **26**, 2198–2204.
Syrier, J. L. M., and Beyerman, H. C. (1975). *In* "Peptides 1974" (Y. Wolman, ed.), pp. 105–111. Wiley, New York.
Swan, J. M. (1957). *Nature (London)* **180**, 643–645.
Szwarc, M. (1965). *Fortschr. Hochpolym.-Forsch.* **4**, 1–65.
Takashima, H., and du Vigneaud, V. (1970). *J. Am. Chem. Soc.* **92**, 2501–2504.
Takashima, H., du Vigneaud, V., and Merrifield, R. B. (1968). *J. Am. Chem. Soc.* **90**, 1323–1325.
Takeyama, M., Koyama, K., and Yajima, H. (1979). *In* "Peptide Chemistry 1978" (N. Izumiya, ed.), pp. 1–4. Protein Res. Found., Osaka, Japan.
Tam, J. P., Wong, T. W., Riemen, M. W., Tjoeng, F. S., and Merrifield, R. B. (1979). *Tetrahedron Lett.* pp. 4033–4036.
Tanenbaum, S. W. (1953). *J. Am. Chem. Soc.* **75**, 1754–1756.
Tarbell, D. S. (1969). *Acc. Chem. Res.* **2**, 296–300.
Tarbell, D. S., Yamamoto, Y., and Pope, B. M. (1972). *Proc. Natl. Acad. Sci. U.S.A.* **69**, 730–732.
Tartar, A., and Gesquiere, J. C. (1979). *J. Org. Chem.* **44**, 5000–5002.
Taschner, E., Wasielewski, C., Biernat, J. F., and Sokolovska, T. (1960). *Chimia* **14**, 371.
Tesser, G. I., and Balvert-Geers, I. C. (1975). *Int. J. Pept. Protein Res.* **7**, 295–305.
Theodoropoulos, D. (1956). *J. Org. Chem.* **21**, 1550–1551.
Theodoropoulos, D., and Craig, L. C. (1955). *J. Org. Chem.* **20**, 1169–1172.
Theodoropoulos, D., and Souchleris, I. (1964). *Biochemistry* **3**, 145–151.
Theodoropoulos, D., Bennich, H., and Mellander, O. (1959). *Nature (London)* **184**, 270–271.
Theodoropoulos, D. and Fruton, J. S. (1962). *Biochemistry* **1**, 933–937.

Tilak, M. A. (1970). *Tetrahedron Lett.* pp. 849–854.
Titherley, A. W., and Stubbs, L. (1914). *J. Chem. Soc.* **105**, 299–309.
Titlestad, K. (1972). *In* "Chemistry and Biology of Peptides" (J. Meienhofer, ed.), pp. 59–65. Ann Arbor Sci. Publ., Ann Arbor, Michigan.
Toennis, G., and Kolb, J. J. (1945). *J. Am. Chem. Soc.* **67**, 849–851, 1141–1144.
Tregear, G. W., Fagan, C., Reynolds, H., Scanlon, D., Jones, P., Kemp, B., Niall, H. D. and Du, Y. C. (1981). *In* "Peptides: Synthesis, Structure. Function" (D. H. Rich and E. Gross, eds.), pp. 249–252. Pierce Chemical Co., Rockford, Illinois.
Tritsch, G. L., and Wooley, D. W. (1960). *J. Am. Chem. Soc.* **82**, 2787–2793.
Trudelle, Y., and Spach, G. (1972). *Tetrahedron Lett.* pp. 3475–3478.
Tun-Kyi, A. (1978). *Helv. Chim. Acta* **61**, 1086–1090.
Turán, A., Patthy, A., and Bajusz, S. (1975). *Acta Chim. Acad. Sci. Hung.* **85**, 327–332.
Uphaus, R. A., Grossweiner, L. I., Katz, J. J., and Kopple, K. D. (1959). *Science* **129**, 641–642.
Vajda, T., Kuziel, A., Ruff, F., Rzeszotarska, B., and Taschner, E. (1965). *Acta Chim. Acad. Sci. Hung.* **44**, 45–50.
Van Orden, H. O., and Smith, E. L. (1954). *J. Biol. Chem.* **208**, 751–764.
van Zon, A., and Beyerman, H. C. (1973). *Helv. Chim. Acta* **56**, 1729–1740.
van Zon, A., and Beyerman, H. C. (1976). *Helv. Chim. Acta* **59**, 1112–1126.
Vaughan, J. R., Jr. (1951). *J. Am. Chem. Soc.* **73**, 3547.
Vaughan, J. R., Jr., and Osato, R. L. (1951). *J. Am. Chem. Soc.* **73**, 5553–5555.
Vaughan, J. R., Jr., and Osato, R. L. (1952). *J. Am. Chem. Soc.* **74**, 676–678.
Veber, D. F., Varga, S. L., Milkowski, J. D., Joshua, H., Conn, J. B., Hirschmann, R., and Denkewalter, R. G. (1969). *J. Am. Chem. Soc.* **91**, 506–507.
Vegners, R., Cipens, G., and Perkone, I. (1979). *Bioorg. Chim.* **5**, 645–650.
Vickery, H. B., Pucher, G. W., Clark, H. E., Chibnall, A. C., and Westall, R. G. (1935). *Biochem. J.* **29**, 2710–2720.
Viehe, H. G., Fuks, R., and Reinstein, M. (1964). *Angew. Chem.* **76**, 571.
Wakamiya, T., Tarumi, Y., and Shiba, T. (1973). *Chem. Lett.* **3**, 233–236.
Wakamiya, T., Tarumi, Y., and Shiba, T. (1974). *Bull. Chem. Soc. Jpn.* **47**, 2686–2689.
Waki, M., Mitsuyasu, N., Kato, T., Makisumi, S., and Izumiya, N. (1968). *Bull. Chem. Soc. Jpn.* **41**, 669–672.
Wälti, M., and Hope, D. B. (1973). *Experientia* **29**, 389.
Wang, S. S., Yang, C. C., Kulesha, I. D., Sonenberg, M., and Merrifield, R. B. (1974). *Int. J. Pept. Protein Res.* **6**, 103–109.
Wang, S. S., Kulesha, I. D., Winter, D. P., Makofske, R., Kutny, R., and Meienhofer, J. (1978). *Int. J. Pept. Protein Res.* **11**, 297–300.
Watanabe, H., Kutawa, S., and Tada, M. (1965). *Nippon Kagaku Zasshi* **86**, 631–632; *Chem. Abstr.* **65**, 797c (1966).
Wessely, F., and Kemm, E. (1928). *Hoppe-Seyler's Z. Physiol. Chem.* **174**, 306–318.
Wessely, F., Kemm, E., and Mayer, J. (1929). *Hoppe-Seyler's Z. Physiol. Chem.* **180**, 64–74.
Wessely, F., Schlögl, K., and Korger, G. (1952). *Nature (London)* **169**, 708–709.
Weygand, F., and Csendes, E. (1952). *Angew. Chem.* **64**, 136.
Weygand, F., and Geiger, R. (1956). *Chem. Ber.* **89**, 647–652.
Weygand, F., and Hunger, K. (1962). *Chem. Ber.* **95**, 1–6.
Weygand, F., and Obermeier, R., (1968). *Z. Naturforsch., B*: **23B**, 1390.
Weygand, F., and Rinno, H. (1959). *Chem. Ber.* **92**, 517–527.
Weygand, F., and Steglich, W. (1959). *Z. Naturforsch., B: Anorg. Chem., Org. Chem., Biochem., Biophys., Biol.* **14B**, 472–473.
Weygand, F., and Swodenk, W. (1960). *Chem. Ber.* **93**, 1693–1696.
Weygand, F., Geiger, R., and Glockler, U. (1956). *Chem. Ber.* **89**, 1543–1549.

Weygand, F., Huber, P., and Weiss, K. (1967). *Z. Naturforsch., B: Anorg. Chem., Org. Chem., Biochem., Biophys., Biol.* **22B**, 1084–1085.
Wieland, T. (1959). *Collect. Czech. Chem. Commun.* **24**, Suppl., 6–14.
Wieland, T., and Bernhard, H. (1951). *Justus Liebig's Ann. Chem.* **572**, 190–194.
Wieland, T., and Determann, H. (1963). *Angew. Chem., Int. Ed. Engl.* **7**, 358–370.
Wieland, T., and Heinke, B. (1956). *Justus Liebig's Ann. Chem.* **599**, 70–80.
Wieland, T., and Heinke, B. (1958). *Justus Liebig's Ann. Chem.* **615**, 184–202.
Wieland, T., and Mohr, H. (1956). *Justus Liebig's Ann. Chem.* **599**, 222–232.
Wieland, T., Kern, W., and Sehring, R. (1950). *Justus Liebig's Ann. Chem.* **569**, 117–121.
Wieland, T., Weiber, O., Fischer, E., and Horlein, G. (1954). *Justus Liebig's Ann. Chem.* **587**, 146–161.
Wieland, T., Heinke, B., Vogler, K., and Morimoto, H. (1962). *Justus Liebig's Ann. Chem.* **655**, 189–194.
Wieland, T., Birr, C., and Flor, F. (1971). *Angew. Chem.* **83**, 333–334.
Wilchek, M., Sarid, S., and Patchornik, A. (1965). *Biochim. Biophys. Acta* **104**, 616–618.
Wilchek, R., Ariely, S., and Patchornik, A. (1968). *J. Org. Chem.* **33**, 1258–1259.
Williams, B. J., and Young, G. T. (1979). *In* "Peptides: Structure, Biology and Function" (E. Gross and J. Meienhofer, eds.), pp. 321–324. Pierce Chemical Co., Rockford, Illinois.
Windridge, G. C., and Jorgensen, E. C. (1971). *J. Am. Chem. Soc.* **93**, 6318–6319.
Woodward, R. B., Heusler, K., Gosteli, J., Naegeli, P., Oppolzer, W., Ramage, R., Ranganathan, S., and Vorbrueggen, H. (1966). *J. Am. Chem. Soc.* **88**, 852–853.
Woolley, D. W. (1948). *J. Biol. Chem.* **172**, 71–81.
Wünsch, E. (1959). *Collect. Czech. Chem. Commun.* **24**, 60–74.
Wünsch, E., and Drees, F. (1966). *Chem. Ber.* **99**, 110–120.
Wünsch, E., and Zwick, A. (1963). *Hoppe-Seyler's Z. Physiol. Chem.* **333**, 108–113.
Wünsch, E., Fontana, A., and Drees, F. (1967). *Z. Naturforsch., B*: **22B**, 607–609.
Wünsch, E., Jaeger, E., Deffner, M., and Scharf, R. (1972). *Hoppe-Seyler's Z. Physiol. Chem.* **353**, 1716–1720.
Wünsch, E., Jaeger, E., Kisfaludy, L., and Löw, M. (1977). *Angew. Chem., Int. Ed. Engl.* **16**, 317–318.
Yajima, H., Kawasaki, K., Kinomura, Y., Oshima, T., Kimoto, S., and Okamoto, M. (1968). *Chem. Pharm. Bull.* **16**, 1342–1350.
Yajima, H., Mikozami, N., Okada, Y., and Kawasaki, K. (1969). *J. Pharm. Bull.* **17**, 1958–1962.
Yajima, H., Kawatani, H., and Watanabe, H. (1970). *Chem. Pharm. Bull.* **18**, 1279–1283.
Yajima, H., Fujii, N., Ogawa, H., and Kawatani, H. (1974). *Chem. Commun.* pp. 107–108.
Yajima, H., Koyama, K., Kiso, Y., Tanaka, A., and Nakamura, M. (1976). *Chem. Pharm. Bull.* **24**, 492–499.
Yajima, H., Takeyama, M., Kanaki, J., Nishimura, O., and Fujino, M. (1978). *Chem. Pharm. Bull.* **26**, 3752–3757.
Yajima, H., Akaji, K., Saito, H., Adachi, H., Oishi, M., and Akazawa, Y. (1979a). *Chem. Pharm. Bull.* **27**, 2238–2242.
Yajima, H., Akaji, K., Mitani, K., Fujii, N., Funakoshi, S., Adachi, H., Oishi, M., and Akazawa, Y. (1979b). *Int. J. Pept. Protein Res.* **14**, 169–176.
Yajima, H., Akaji, K., Funakoshi, S., Fujii, N., and Irie, H. (1980). *Chem. Pharm. Bull.* **28**, 1942–1945.
Yamashiro, D., and du Vigneaud, V. (1968). *J. Am. Chem. Soc.* **90**, 487–490.
Yamashiro, D., and Li, C. H. (1973a). *J. Org. Chem.* **38**, 591–592.
Yamashiro, D., and Li, C. H. (1973b). *J. Org. Chem.* **38**, 2594–2597.
Yamashiro, D., and Li, C. H. (1973c). *J. Am. Chem. Soc.* **95**, 1310–1315.
Yamashiro, D., Aanning, H. L., and du Vigneaud, V. (1965). *Proc. Natl. Acad. Sci. U.S.A.* **54**, 166–171.

Yamashiro, D., Aanning, H. L., Branda, L. A., Cash, W. D., Murti, V. V. S., and du Vigneaud, V. (1968). *J. Am. Chem. Soc.* **90**, 4141–4144.
Yamashiro, D., Blake, J., and Li, C. H. (1972). *J. Am. Chem. Soc.* **94**, 2855–2859.
Yanagida, S., Hayama, H., and Komori, S. (1969). *J. Org. Chem.* **34**, 4180–4181.
Yang, C. C., and Merrifield, R. B. (1976). *J. Org. Chem.* **41**, 1032–1041.
Yaron, A., and Schlossman, S. F. (1968). *Biochemistry* **7**, 2673–2681.
Yonemitsu, O., Hamada, T., and Kanaoka, Y. (1969). *Tetrahedron Lett.* pp. 1819–1820.
Young, J. D., Benjamini, E., Stewart, J. M., and Leung, C. Y. (1967). *Biochemistry* **6**, 1455–1460.
Zahn, H., and Brandenburg, D. (1966). *Justus Liebig's Ann. Chem.* **622**, 220–230.
Zahn, H., and Diehl, J. F. (1957). *Z. Naturforsch., B*: **12B**, 85–92.
Zahn, H., and Schnabel, E. (1957). *Justus Liebig's Ann. Chem.* **605**, 212–232.
Zahn, H., Bremer, H., Sroka, W., and Meienhofer, J. (1965a). *Z. Naturforsch., B*: **20B**, 646–649.
Zahn, H., Bremer, H., and Zabel, R. (1965b). *Z. Naturforsch., B*: **20B**, 653–660.
Zaoral, M. (1959). *Angew. Chem.* **71**, 743.
Zaoral, M. (1962). *Collect. Czech. Chem. Commun.* **27**, 1273–1277.
Zaoral, M., and Rudinger, J. (1959). *Collect. Czech. Chem. Commun.* **24**, 1993–2012.
Zaoral, M., and Rudinger, J. (1961). *Collect. Czech. Chem. Commun.* **26**, 2316–2332.
Zervas, L., and Ferderigos, N. (1973). *Experientia* **29**, 262.
Zervas, L., and Theodoropoulos, D. M. (1956). *J. Am. Chem. Soc.* **78**, 1359–1363.
Zervas, L., Benoiton, L., Weiss, E., Winitz, M. and Greenstein, J. P. (1959a). *J. Am. Chem. Soc.* **81**, 1729–1734.
Zervas, L., Otani, T. T., Winitz, M., and Greenstein, J. P. (1959b). *J. Am. Chem. Soc.* **81**, 2878–2884.
Zervas, L., Photaki, I., Yovanidis, C., Taylor, J., Phocas, I. and Bardakos, V. (1967). *In* "Peptides 1966" (H. C. Beyermann, A. van de Linde and W. Maassen van den Brink, eds.), pp. 28–37. North-Holland Publ., Amsterdam.
Zhukova, G. F., Ravdel, G. A., and Shchukina, L. A. (1970). *J. Gen. Chem. USSR* (*Engl. Transl.*) **40**, 2750–2753.

Chapter **4**

Quantitation and Sequence Dependence of Racemization in Peptide Synthesis*

N. LEO BENOITON
Department of Biochemistry,
University of Ottawa,
Ottawa, Ontario,
Canada

I. Introduction 218
II. Methods for Assessing Stereochemical Composition . . . 221
A. Optical Purity of Amino Acids 222
1. L-Amino Acid Oxidase 222
2. Conversion to Diastereomeric Dipeptides 222
3. Gas–Liquid Chromatography on a Chiral Stationary Phase 225
B. Model Systems for Studying Racemization 227
1. Isoleucine as a Test Residue 227
2. Acylamino Acids 228
3. Protected Dipeptides 230
4. Comparison of Model Systems 234
III. Oxazolin-5-ones from N-Substituted α-Amino Acids . . . 235
A. Introduction 235
B. 2,4-Dialkyl-5(4*H*)-oxazolones 236
C. 4-Alkyl-5(2*H*)-oxazolones 238
D. 2-Alkoxy-4-alkyl-5(4*H*)-oxazolones 239
1. Introduction 239
2. Preparation of 2-Alkoxy-5(4*H*)-oxazolones Using Chloride-Forming Reagents 241
3. Preparation of 2-Alkoxy-5(4*H*)-oxazolones Using Soluble Carbodiimide 242
4. Reactions and Chiral Properties of 2-Alkoxy-5(4*H*)-oxazolones 244

* The work cited from my laboratory was supported by grants from the Medical Research Council of Canada, of which I am a Career Investigator.

THE PEPTIDES, VOLUME 5

ISBN 0-12-304205-4

5. Formation of 2-*tert*-Butoxy-5(4*H*)-oxazolones from Symmetrical Anhydrides and Tertiary Amines . . . 247
6. Formation of 2-Alkoxy-5(4*H*)-oxazolones from Symmetrical Anhydrides and Carbodiimides 248
7. Implication of 2-Alkoxy-5(4*H*)-oxazolones in Carbodiimide-Mediated Reactions in the Absence of Nitrogen Nucleophiles 249
8. Implication of 2-Alkoxy-5(4*H*)-oxazolones in Carbodiimide-Mediated Coupling Reactions 251
9. Conclusions 251
E. Do Symmetrical Anhydrides of Acylamino Acids and N-Protected Peptides Exist? 252
IV. Racemization of *N*-Alkoxycarbonylamino Acids 257
A. Introduction 257
B. Racemization of *N*-Alkoxycarbonylamino Acids during Coupling in the Presence of Bases 257
1. Racemization during Esterification to Resin Supports 257
2. Racemization during Peptide Bond Formation . . . 259
3. Conclusion 259
C. Racemization of N^{α}-Protected Histidine 260
V. Racemization during the Saponification of Esters 263
VI. Racemization and Asymmetric Induction during the Aminolysis of 2,4-Dialkyl-5(4*H*)-oxazolones 263
A. Introduction 263
B. Variables Affecting Asymmetric Induction 265
VII. Variables Affecting α-Inversion during Coupling 268
A. Internal Factors 268
1. Side Chain of the Activated Residue 268
2. N-Substituent on the Activated Residue 271
3. Side Chain of the Penultimate Residue 272
4. The Attacking Nucleophile 273
5. Configuration of the Residues 273
B. External Factors 275
1. Temperature 275
2. Solvent Polarity 276
3. Coupling Method 277
VIII. Conclusion 278
References 279

I. INTRODUCTION

Readers of this treatise are aware that the general subject of racemization was comprehensively and elegantly reviewed by Kemp (1979) in Vol. 1. A second chapter on racemization dealt with the predictive potential of data on the racemization and coupling rates of activated esters of N^{α}-protected amino acids and peptides (Kovacs, 1980). The appearance of an additional chapter on racemization so soon after these reviews will seem surprising to many. However, we believe it is warranted by several developments including the discovery of 5(4*H*)-oxazolones derived from *N*-alkoxycarbonylamino acids, the recognition that asymmetric induction is a major factor contributing to the α-inversion accompanying any coupling reaction, and the use of series of model peptides instead of individual racemization tests for collecting data on racemization. Much of this progress is an outgrowth of exploitation of the very simple observation, made during studies on the mechanism of action of the coupling reagent *N*-ethoxycarbonyl-2-ethoxy-1,2-dihydroquinoline (EEDQ), that symmetrical anhydrides of N^{α}-*tert*-butoxycarbonylamino acids survive the usual reaction workup involving washing with aqueous solutions (Chen and Benoiton, 1978). This finding led to the development of a simple method of obtaining chemically and optically pure symmetrical anhydrides of N^{α}-alkoxycarbonylamino acids (Chen *et al.*, 1978) and 2-alkyl-5(4*H*)-oxazolones from acylamino acids and protected dipeptides (Chen *et al.*, 1979) using the soluble carbodiimide *N*-ethyl-*N'*-(γ-dimethylaminopropyl)carbodiimide hydrochloride (EDC). This in turn led to the discovery that 2-alkoxy-5(4*H*)-oxazolones (Jones and Witty, 1977, 1979) are intermediates in some carbodiimide-mediated reactions (Benoiton and Chen, 1979, 1981a), the demonstration that racemization can occur when *N*-alkoxycarbonylamino acids are coupled in the presence of basic catalysts (Benoiton *et al.*, 1981a), the discovery of 5(2*H*)-oxazolones obtained from N^{α}-formylamino acids (Benoiton and Chen, 1982) and the importance of asymmetric induction in the stereochemical course of coupling reactions (Benoiton *et al.*, 1981c).

Progress in the acquisition of useful data on racemization has emerged from the design of several series of model peptides each incorporating one variable residue only (Benoiton *et al.*, 1979a,b,c; Castro *et al.*, 1978, 1979). Using these systems, it has been possible to carry out, for the first time, studies on the relative sensitivity to racemization of different residues under practical coupling conditions. The work has so far been limited to amino acids with unfunctionalized side chains (Benoiton *et al.*, 1979b; Benoiton and Kuroda, 1981; Le Nguyen *et al.*, 1981), but the approach can be extended to other residues and to the collection of data on other aspects of the sequence dependence of racemization. An interesting side light of the studies by Benoiton *et al.* is the revelation that conclusions based on data acquired using couplings of N^{α}-acylamino acids can sometimes be misleading because they do not always apply to the couplings of small peptides.

This chapter reviews new information on the chemistry of 5(4*H*)-oxazolones particularly as it relates to the stereochemical course of coupling reactions, new racemization tests and approaches available for collecting data, and data that have been acquired since the previous review (Kemp, 1979). The central theme is the sequence dependence of racemization. A comprehensive survey of the racemization associated with new coupling methods and racemization suppressants has not been attempted. Duplication of the previous discussion (Kemp, 1979) has been avoided as much as possible.

Natural amino acids are chiral molecules by virtue of their asymmetric α-carbon atom. Occasionally when they or their derivatives are manipulated, some of the molecules temporarily lose this chirality. As a result, after the manipulation the same compound contains molecules of opposite chirality. This change in stereochemistry is commonly referred to as racemization. Racemization is usually defined as the conversion of one enantiomer into an equimolar mixture of the two enantiomers but can also be defined as the transformation of one configuration (*R* or *S*, D or L) into the two possible configurations in equal amounts. It is understood that the process occurs through an achiral intermediate. The product mixture is a racemate, provided the compound contains only one asymmetric carbon atom. The racemization may be partial or complete, depending on whether part or all of the starting material is converted into racemate.

In practice, the molecule undergoing racemization usually contains more than one chiral center or combines with a second chiral molecule. The products generated by the racemization are then diastereoisomeric, and because only one configuration in the two products is different, they are epimers. If the epimers are generated before the coupling, and the coupling is with an achiral molecule, the epimeric content of the product will correspond to the extent of racemization. However if the coupling is to another chiral molecule, the epimeric content of the product will not correspond to the extent of racemization because the second substance will couple at different rates with the optical antipodes of the racemizing intermediate which are in equilibrium, thus generating one isomer in excess of the other. This phenomenon is referred to as asymmetric induction, and it plays an important role in determining the isomeric content of the reaction product.

The reader might note that the term *epimerization* does not appear in the above discussion. In a general sense epimerization denotes a stereochemical change from one configuration into the other in a molecule containing more than one chiral center. In a strict sense, it implies a process of inversion through an S_N2 mechanism. The other mechanism through which a configurational change occurs is racemization. I contend that, if it is understood that it refers to the process occurring at one particular chiral center, whether the products form a racemate or not, *racemization* is still the more precise term for expressing the chiral change that initially occurs in peptide synthesis, and it is used in this sense in this review. The term *stereomutation* is used to express the total change in configuration. It is generally applicable and is an all-encompassing term.

An additional but rare source of stereomutation in amino acid chemistry is isoracemization where the configurational change occurs without ionization of the α-proton (Kovacs *et al.*, 1971; Cram and Gosser, 1964; see Kemp, 1979).

II. METHODS FOR ASSESSING STEREOCHEMICAL COMPOSITION

The objective of peptide synthesis is to produce a product that is both chemically and chirally homogeneous. The latter can be achieved only if the starting amino acids or derivatives are of established chiral integrity which is preserved throughout the synthesis. It is a straightforward operation for assessing the optical purity of amino acids and their derivatives, and the methods in common use are discussed here. However, peptide synthesis without racemization is not always straightforward. A great deal of effort has been expended trying to define the circumstances under which racemization can be eliminated or minimized. The methods used to study racemization are addressed here in detail. Once the peptide has been constructed, there still remains the challenge of proving that the objective has been achieved. In addition to establishing the homogeneity of products by an analytical technique such as high-performance liquid chromatography (HPLC), two general approaches are used to confirm the absence of D-residues in an all-L-peptide. One is to look for evidence of incomplete digestion by proteolytic enzymes. This approach has been reviewed by Finn and Hofmann (1976) and is not considered here. The other approach is to analyze for the enantiomers after hydrolysis of the peptide. Unfortunately the hydrolysis operation itself causes slight racemization of the component amino acids, at separate stages, before rupture of the peptide bonds and after. An approximation of the racemization produced after liberation of the amino acids can be obtained by subjecting a similar amino acid mixture to identical hydrolytic conditions. However, it is not presently possible to estimate the amount of racemization produced prior to the hydrolysis, because it depends on the nature of the adjacent residues in the peptide chain. For example, during the hydrolysis of a simple dipeptide, a COOH-terminal phenylalanyl residue racemized nearly twice as much when it was adjacent to valine as when it was adjacent to glycine (Smith and Silva de Sol, 1980). In order to correct for racemization that occurs during the hydrolysis of peptides (see Kemp, 1979), Manning (1970) introduced the use of tritiated hydrochloric acid as the hydrolyzing medium. Because racemization occurs concomitant with removal of the α-proton, the amount of enantiomer created during the hydrolysis corresponds to the amount of isotope incorporated. The radioactivity of each amino acid is measured with a flow-cell scintillation counter attached to an amino acid analyzer. The enantiomeric content of each amino acid is determined chromatographically after the sample is coupled with an L-amino acid *N*-carboxyanhydride (see Section II,A,2). Any additional enantiomer detected was present before the hydrolysis. The method is restricted to amino acids whose side-chain hydrogens are not exchangeable during acid hydrolysis. Aspartic and glutamic acids, histidine, phenylalanine, and tyrosine are excluded. For whatever reason, few laboratories seem to have adopted this method. A promising variation involves tagging the created enantiomers with the stable heavier isotope, deuterium, followed by analysis exclusively for the untagged enantiomers by mass spectrometry (Kusumoto *et al.*, 1981; Liardon *et al.*, 1981).

A. Optical Purity of Amino Acids

1. L-Amino Acid Oxidase

Snake venom L-amino acid oxidase and hog kidney D-amino acid oxidase were used routinely for determining the optical purity of amino acids (Greenstein and Winitz, 1961) before the method of Manning and Moore (1968) was introduced. These enzymes with the help of oxygen and water convert amino acids into α-oxoacids, ammonia, and hydrogen peroxide. The change in gas volume was measured in a Warburg apparatus. The main shortcoming of this method was that it required milligram quantities of substrate. The indirect approach for determining optical purity is to destroy the L-residue(s) with the L-directed enzyme from *Crotalus adamanteus* and to measure the amount of residual D-residue with an amino acid analyzer (Sieber *et al.*, 1970). Serine, threonine, aspartic acid, and glutamic acid are poor substrates for this enzyme (Greenstein and Winitz, 1961; Lichtenberg and Wellner, 1968), but contrary to generally held notions based on these same studies, lysine is not a poor substrate. Diamino acids are oxidized over a narrow pH range which does not include the neutral pH normally used, but at pH 8.6 lysine and ornithine are excellent substrates for the enzyme (Paik and Kim, 1965). Precise details for the determination of histidine have been elaborated (Jones and Ramage, 1979).

2. Conversion to Diastereomeric Dipeptides

Reaction to give diastereomeric dipeptides followed by analysis with an amino acid analyzer is the most common method of determining amino acid enantiomers. First introduced by Manning and Moore (1968), this method rendered a valuable service to the research community. According to Manning and Moore, L-leucine *N*-carboxyanhydride is added to the amino acid (Yyy) in solution in cold borate buffer at pH 10.4, and then the mixture is agitated vigorously for 2 min and acidified quickly with hydrochloric acid. The epimeric peptides H-Leu-Yyy-OH and H-Leu-DYyy-OH are then analyzed with a Beckmann analyzer using the same buffers as for amino acid analysis (Spackman *et al.*, 1958). The separation of leucyl dipeptides by ion-exchange chromatography had been examined in detail before this by Noda *et al.* (1968). Some H-Leu_2-OH or H-Leu_2-Yyy-OH is sometimes formed as a side product of the reaction, but it does not usually interfere with the analysis. To avoid excessively long retention times, phenylalanine, tryptophan, histidine, and arginine are determined as their glutamyl peptides after reaction with L-glutamic acid *N*-carboxyanhydride. Other than its simplicity, the main attractive feature of the method is that the amino acid does not have to be isolated or purified in order to be assessed. The method can even be applied to a mixture of amino acids provided that the product peaks do not overlap. The modified amino acids *S*-carboxymethylcysteine (Manning and Moore, 1968), *O*-methylserine (Hodges and Merrifield, 1974), and several ring-substituted phenylalanines (2-OH, 3-OH, 3,4-diOH, 4-Cl as their alanine dipeptides, Tong *et al.*, 1971) have been examined by this method. There have also been studies on the chiral integrity of histidine in synthetic peptides after isolation from hydrolysates by fractionation on a Dowex-50 column. Detection of the amino acid was facilitated by the addition of [^{3}H]histidine as a tracer, and the glutamyl peptides were separated with a Durrum 500 analyzer (Galardy *et al.*, 1976).

HPLC has also been used as the technique for analyzing the peptides. Dipeptide pairs obtained with racemic leucine or phenylalanine *N*-carboxyanhydride have been separated using a 0.4 × 15 cm Nucleosil $5C_{18}$ (Macherey, Nagel & Co.) column eluted with mixtures of acetonitrile (0–20%) and aqueous potassium hydrogen phosphate at various pH values below neutrality (Takaya and Sakakibara, 1980; Takaya *et al.*, 1981). Despite the different selectivities that obtain during preparation of the reference compounds, this method of analysis still permits determination of enantiomers to an accuracy of $\pm 0.01\%$ because it was found that the selectivity quotient for any particular amino acid was constant for mixtures at all levels of enantiomeric excess. Of the many commercially obtained amino acids that were examined, only D-glutamic acid (1.0%), D-leucine (1.0%), and L-serine (1.9, 1.2%) contained $>0.10\%$ of the other isomer. And, surprisingly, the contamination was greatly reduced when they were converted to the *N-tert*-butoxycarbonyl derivatives.

The main drawback of the Manning and Moore method concerns the accessibility of the reagents. The commercial availability of *N*-carboxyanhydrides has been erratic, they deteriorate on storage, and the preparation of L-glutamic acid *N*-carboxyanhydride is not straightforward. In order to eliminate these obstacles, Mitchell *et al.* (1978) introduced the use of Boc-Leu-ONSu instead of *N*-carboxyanhydrides as the reagent. Conditions for the separation of H-Leu-Yyy-OH diastereomers for Yyy = Phe, Tyr, His, Arg were also defined. These authors report that commercially obtained L- and D-amino acids generally contain $<0.1\%$ of the other isomer, except for D-threonine and D-isoleucine which often are partially (up to 10%) epimerized. Users of the method of Mitchell *et al.* (1978) should bear in mind the claim of Takaya *et al.* (1981) that the amino acid being tested undergoes slight racemization during acylation by the succinimidyl ester.

The stereochemical purity of amino acid derivatives can be established using the Manning and Moore method after deprotection. Of the commercially available *N-tert*-butoxycarbonylamino acids, only Boc-Ser(Bzl)-OH seems occasionally not to be optically pure (Mitchell *et al.*, 1978). An alternative approach (Benoiton *et al.*, 1979c) involves direct coupling of the derivative, with H-Lys(Z)-OBzl for N-protected amino acids and Z-Lys(Z)-OH for amino acid esters, followed by deprotection by hydrogenolysis (and acidolysis if necessary) to give the epimeric lysyl dipeptide pairs H-Xxx-Lys-OH/H-DXxx-Lys-OH and H-Lys-Yyy-OH/H-Lys-DYyy, respectively. These diastereomeric pairs for Xxx or Yyy = Ala, Leu, Val, Phe, Ile are well separated by elution of a 0.9 × 15 cm Aminex A-5 resin column with pH 6.50 buffer (pH 7.50 for Phe). The coupling can be done by any procedure that is racemization-free. This method has been used to examine derivatives of hydroxyamino acids and their *O*-methyl ethers (Benoiton *et al.*, 1979c) and some activated forms of Boc-Val-OH and Z-Val-OH, namely, 2-alkoxy-4-isopropyl-5(4*H*)-oxazolones (Benoiton and Chen, 1979, 1981a).

Extension to the lysyl dipeptide Lys-Yyy proved to be a simple method of assessing the racemization accompanying the 4-dimethylaminopyridine-catalyzed esterification of the first residue to a hydroxymethylphenyl-polymer (Benoiton *et al.*, 1981a). Fmoc-Yyy-oxymethylphenoxy-resin was deprotected by a base cycle, Boc-Lys(Boc)-OH was coupled via the symmetrical anhydride, and the dipeptide was deprotected and liberated at the same time using 95% aqueous trifluoroacetic acid. Reference peptides were similarly obtained using the racemic lysine derivative. The H-Lys-Yyy-OH/H-DLys-Yyy-OH peptides for Yyy = Ala, Leu, Val, Phe, Ile were well separated by the standard chromatographic system of a Beckmann model 119CL analyzer (N. L. Benoiton, E. Brown, and V. Woolley, unpublished). The Aminex A-5 resin is therefore not crucial to the method of analysis of lysyl peptides (Benoiton *et al.*, 1979c).

The method of Manning and Moore (1968) is not generally applicable for determining the enantiomeric purity of N^{α}-methylamino acids (see Cheung and Benoiton, 1977b). The reaction is sluggish at best, and the dipeptide products generate a ninhydrin color yield even lower (McDermott and Benoiton, 1973c) than the low color yield of the *N*-methylamino acid. The latter can be dramatically increased by increasing the reaction time in the coil of an analyzer (Coggins and Benoiton, 1970). It was to overcome this impasse that the idea of coupling to lysine emerged. The ε-amino group of lysine would provide the ninhydrin color for the peptides. As the best route to *N*-methylamino acids is by methylation of the *N*-alkoxycarbonylamino acid (McDermott and Benoiton, 1973a; Cheung and Benoiton, 1977a), derivatization is not necessary because it is from the derivative that the *N*-methylamino acid is generated. Thus N-protected *N*-methylamino acids and *N*-methylamino acid esters can be examined for optical purity by coupling with the appropriate esters of lysine as for the corresponding unmethylated residues (Cheung and Benoiton, 1977b; Benoiton *et al.*, 1979c). Free *N*-methylamino acids can be assessed after conversion to their *N*-benzyloxycarbonyl derivatives (Cheung and Benoiton, 1977b,c).

Other amino acid derivatives whose optical purity might require scrutiny are N^{α}-benzoylamino acids. These can be coupled in dichloromethane with H-Lys(Z)-OMe using dicyclohexylcarbodiimide (DCC) in the presence of 1-hydroxybenzotriazole as reagent. The epimeric peptide products can be distinguished by nmr spectroscopy by inspection of their ester methyl singlets which do not coincide (Benoiton *et al.*, 1979b). No racemization occurs during the coupling if dichloromethane is used as solvent.

A test for confirming and studying the unusual chiral instability of the histidyl residue (see Section IV,C) was developed (Windridge and Jorgensen, 1971b) following the lead of Izumiya and Muraoka (1969) and available information on the separation of epimeric peptides by ion-exchange chromatography (Manning and Moore, 1968). Boc-His(Bzl)-OH was coupled with H-Glu(OBzl)-OBzl, and the partially deprotected H-His(Bzl)-Glu-OH epimers were determined with an amino acid analyzer.

3. Gas–Liquid Chromatography on a Chiral Stationary Phase

Amino acids can be determined by gas–liquid chromatography (glc) after derivatization (Roach and Gerke, 1969). Because of the individuality of amino acids, strict reproduction of derivatization conditions is required, and any change in chromatographic conditions requires a redetermination of response factors. For the same reason, any internal standard is unsatisfactory for more than one or at best a few amino acids. Frank *et al.* (1978) exploited the idea that the ideal internal standard would be the optical antipode of each amino acid. The necessary requirement for implementing this idea was a chromatographic system that separated all enantiomeric pairs. This was met by introduction of the chiral stationary phase Chirasil-Val, a polysiloxane containing valine (Frank *et al.*, 1977). The method devised involves the addition of a known amount of optical antipode as an internal standard before any manipulations are executed. Both sample and standard undergo identical treatment. Variations due to the individuality of amino acids are completely eliminated. The method is based on the premise that optical antipodes exhibit identical chemical and physical properties in a nonchiral environment and is referred to as enantiomeric labeling. The amino acids are determined as their *N*-pentafluoropropionyl isopropyl ester derivatives which are separated on glass capillaries (20 m × 0.3 mm) coated with Chirasil-Val (0.1 μm film thickness) using hydrogen as the carrier gas. The column is maintained at 87°C for 5 min, and then the temperature is raised to 200°C at a rate of 4°C/min. By using separately both the L- and D-isomers of any amino acid as the standards, the two enantiomers can be determined and thus the racemization sustained by any residue. Satisfactory procedures for derivatizing histidine and arginine were lacking.

Another method allowing determination of histidine involves conversion of the isomers to aspartic acid by reaction with ozone followed by analysis after esterification with (+)-3-methyl-2-butanol, and trifluoroacetylation (Rahn *et al.*, 1976). The method of Frank *et al.* (1978) has been adopted by the Hoffmann–La Roche research group (Meienhofer, 1981) as a routine procedure for the determination of racemization during synthetic work. Results are available within a day, and this includes hydrolysis of the peptides, derivatization, and analysis. Cognizant of racemization produced during hydrolysis, they examined several systems and obtained the least racemization in a mixture of amino acids subjected to the hydrolytic conditions of Scotchler *et al.* (1970) involving 6 *N* hydrochloric acid–propionic acid (1:1) at 150°C for 15 min. These conditions caused the following racemization expressed as percent D-amino acids: Ile, 1.0%; Leu, 1.6%; Ser, 0.8%;Asp, 4.2%; Cys, 8.9%; Phe, 2.1%; Glu, 2.9%; Met, 2.4%; Tyr, 1.8%; Lys, 2.2%; Arg, 2.8%; His, 3.9%. Substantially more racemization occurred for glutamic (3.3%), lysine (2.8%), and aspartic (7.3%) acids in 6 *N* hydrochloric acid at 110°C for 24 h. Recently, satisfactory analyses of arginine and histidine were achieved by a third derivatization step using diethyl pyrocarbonate in benzene and a modified temperature program starting at 180°C for 5 min followed by a 4°C/min gradient to 220°C.

A similar approach to separating enantiomers by glc has been described by Liardon *et al.* (1981) and Kusumoto *et al.* (1981) who used 2,4-bis(Val-Val-O*i*Pr)-6-ethoxy-*s*-triazine as the chiral stationary phase. The novelty of this procedure resides in the method of eliminating the uncertainty created in a racemization determination by the hydrolysis operation. By effecting the hydrolysis in deuterium chloride, all newly generated enantiomers are tagged at the α-carbon atom by a heavy isotope. After separation, the D/L ratio of untagged molecules is determined by mass spectrometry. Chiral purity has been determined with an accuracy of 0.2%. The method is applicable to all amino acids except proline, arginine, and histidine and is therefore superior to that of Manning (1970), which is restricted to amino acids that undergo tritium exchange only at the α-carbon atom.

B. Model Systems for Studying Racemization

Information on racemization accompanying peptide couplings is obtained by preparing selected peptides whose stereochemical purities are established by analytical methods peculiar to each model system. Different systems are commonly referred to as racemization tests. They can be classified into two broad categories: those involving activation of an acylamino acid and those involving activation of a protected peptide.

1. *Isoleucine as a Test Residue*

The unique nature of L-isoleucine whereby its α-inversion product D-*allo*-isoleucine is a diastereomer provides a simple option for assessing the racemization accompanying selected reaction conditions. The two epimers are readily separated by ion-exchange chromatography using an amino acid analyzer (Spackman *et al.*, 1958). The initial application of this method was the introduction of the model Ac-Ile-OH + H-Gly-OEt followed by acid hydrolysis as a test for racemization during coupling (Bodanszky and Conklin, 1967). A recent modification uses Z-Phe-Ile-OH instead of the acylamino acid (Fujino *et al.*, 1972). Variation of the amino acid ester provides information on the effect of the nature of the incoming nucleophile on the extent of racemization (Itoh *et al.*, 1978). The compounds Z-Me-Ile-OMe and Z-Ile-OMe and the free acids were used to establish that *N*-methylamino acids and derivatives racemize much more than the corresponding unmethylated derivatives under conditions of saponification and acidolytic cleavage by hydrogen bromide in acetic acid (McDermott and Benoiton, 1973b). An interesting side light of this study was that benzyloxycarbonylmethylisoleucine epimerized seven times more than benzyloxycarbonylmethyl-*allo*-isoleucine under the acidic conditions, demonstrating that the two epimers are different compounds even with respect to sensitivity to α-inversion. In solid-phase synthesis, one method of attaching the first residue to the support is by reaction of the alkoxycarbonylamino acid with the hydroxymethylphenyl-polymer. This esterification is more difficult to achieve than the subsequent peptide bond-forming reactions, so it became common practice to add 4-dimethylaminopyridine (DMAP) as a catalyst (Wang *et al.*, 1974; Atherton *et al.*, 1979). Assessment using isoleucine as the test residue revealed that racemization occurred under some of these conditions (Benoiton *et al.*, 1981a).

Racemization during the coupling of isoleucine in peptides (Z-Phe-Ile-OH, Fujino *et al.*, 1972; Boc-Leu-Ile-OH, Kitada and Fujino, 1978) has been assessed by determination of the *allo*-isoleucine after hydrolysis of the products. This is an extension of the test involving Ac-Ile-OH (Bodanszky and Conklin, 1967).

Racemization at threonine was similarly determined after coupling Boc-Asp(O*t*Bu)-Thr-OH with several dipeptide esters (Kitada and Fujino, 1978). An interesting point emerged. The system is not suitable as a racemization test because very little α-inversion occurs (0.6–3.4% for DCC-mediated couplings), but the demonstration that threonine has a low tendency to racemize is valuable information in itself.

2. *Acylamino Acids*

The most widely used test implicating an acylamino acid is the Young test (Williams and Young, 1963) which involves coupling Bz-Leu-OH with H-Gly-OEt followed by determination of the specific rotation of the product. The extent of racemization is confirmed by saponifying the ester and crystallizing out the racemic benzoyl dipeptide acid. Two percent or more of the racemate can be detected. The test is subject to error when the coupling product is not chemically homogeneous. Pure product can be obtained by preparative thin-layer chromatography (tlc) (Izdebski, 1975). Application of a multiple-isotope dilution procedure increases the sensitivity of the Young test by several orders of magnitude (Kemp *et al.*, 1970). The Bz-Leu-OH + H-Gly-OEt system is superior to its analogous forerunner, Ac-Leu-OH + H-Gly-OEt (Smart *et al.*, 1960), whose product was not always easy to crystallize. Use of the analogous For-Leu-OH + H-Gly-OEt system also led to the conclusion that the racemization-promoting effect of *N*-acyl sustituents is in the order benzoyl > acetyl > formyl (Heard and Young, 1963). The synthesis of For-Phe-Gly-OEt that proved to be optically pure served as a test for appraising the mixed-anhydride method of coupling (Anderson *et al.*, 1966). The coupling of Tfa-Val-OH with H-Val-OMe followed by analysis of the products by glc is one of the original racemization tests (Weygand *et al.*, 1963). The use of Ac-Ile-OH + H-Gly-OEt as a test (Bodanszky and Conklin, 1967) has been alluded to earlier.

A racemization test based on the coupling of For-Phe-OH with H-Phe-OMe (Arendt *et al.*, 1976a, 1978a, 1979) emerged from an in-depth study on the chromatography of protected dipeptide diastereomers on thin-layer plates of silica gel (Arendt *et al.*, 1976b). The study revealed that the best separations of epimers were achieved when the protecting groups were small. For the test, the formylamino acid is labeled with tritium, the diastereomeric products are separated by tlc, the areas surrounding the spots that have been visualized with a uv lamp are scraped off, and the radioactivity contained therein is measured with a counter. A variation where the acetylamino acid replaces the formylamino acid (Ac-Leu-OH + H-Leu-OMe) has been used to study the influence of the configuration of the residues on racemization during coupling (Arendt *et al.*, 1978b). Additional studies using a dozen different dipeptide pairs led to the conclusion that couplings between residues with identical configurations are accompanied by more racemization (Arendt *et al.*, 1979). Separation by paper chromatography of the epimeric peptides formed by coupling For-Phe-OH with H-Val-O*t*Bu, and quantitation by planimetry after straining the chromatograms, had previously been described as a method for studying racemization (Rzeszotarska *et al.*, 1966).

The idea of using proton nmr as a tool for determining racemization was introduced by Weinstein (1970). Variation of the chemical shifts of the side-chain methyl group protons in alanine dimers and trimers is small. However, in protected peptides, particularly if an aromatic residue is adjacent to a COOH-terminal alanyl residue, the variation is sufficient (5–9 Hz) to allow quantitation of the two stereomers. The methyl doublet of the L-L-peptide is at lower field than that of the D-L-peptide. From this emerged the choice of the system Ac-Phe-OH + H-Ala-OMe as a test for racemization (Weinstein and Pritchard, 1972) and also data showing that the racemizing tendency of N-substituents is in the order benzoyl > acetyl > Z-Gly-Gly > Z-Gly > formyl (Weinstein, 1970). The routine method using a 60-MHz instrument can detect down to 3% of the other isomer.

Subsequent work by Davies *et al.* (1975) has shown that an NH_2-terminal benzoyl, but not a benzyloxycarbonyl, group in dipeptide methyl esters promotes sufficient differential in the chemical shift of the ester methyl proton singlets to allow detection and quantitation of epimers by nmr. The effect is solvent dependent, because the phenomenon occurs in deuterochloroform but not in hexadeuterated dimethyl sulfoxide. Separations of 7 cps, with the L-L-isomer downfield from the D-L-isomer, were observed for the four peptides containing alanine and valine. Couplings of Bz-Ala-OH and Bz-Val-OH with the methyl esters can serve as tests for racemization (Davies *et al.*, 1975; Davies and Thomas, 1978). Racemization of the corresponding *N*-methylamino acids was examined by the same approach (Davies and Thomas, 1979, 1981).

The separation of the ester methyl signals in the nmr spectrum of Bz-DLAla-Lys(Z)-OMe, the chemical precursor of a carboxypeptidase B substrate, had been noticed in our laboratory. Further investigation revealed that the 60-MHz spectra of all diastereomeric pairs, except for Yyy = Ala, of the derivatives Bz-DLXxx-Lys(Z)-OMe and Bz-DLLys(Z)-Yyy-OMe for Xxx and Yyy = Ala, Leu, Val, Phe, Ile showed ester methyl singlets separated by 5–7 cps (Benoiton *et al.*, 1979a,b). These dipeptide series were characterized with the intended objective of acquiring data on the relative sensitivity to racemization of residues Xxx and the influence of the nature of Yyy on the racemization at Xxx during couplings. This was the first serious attempt to carry out such studies. The results obtained from couplings of Bz-Xxx-OH with H-Lys(Z)-OMe demonstrated for the first time that valine and isoleucine racemize more readily that the other aliphatic amino acids when coupled in a polar solvent and that *N*-benzoylamino acids can be coupled without racemization if the reagent is DCC in the presence of 1-hydroxybenzotriazole and the solvent is dichloromethane (Benoiton *et al.*, 1979b). This method of studying racemization has also been written in the form of a laboratory experiment suitable for senior undergraduates (Benoiton *et al.*, 1980). It requires the use of a simple 60-MHz spectrometer and can detect down to about 1.5% of the other isomer. The dramatic effects of temperature and polarity of the solvent on the asymmetric induction occurring during amination of a 5(4*H*)-oxazolone have been demonstrated using this method of analysis (Benoiton *et al.*, 1981c).

The nmr method for assessing racemization based on quantitation of ester methyl signals can give misleading data in cases where other methyl esters are formed as side products of the coupling reaction (Benoiton *et al.*, 1979b). One example is the urethane product, EtOCO-Lys(Z)-OMe in this case, formed during amination of the mixed anhydrides of protected amino acids. Its ester methyl peak coincides with that of Bz-DXxx-Lys(Z)-OMe. Another possible source of misleading data is the ester formed as a side product from *N*-hydroxysuccinimide-assisted carbodiimide reactions (see Benoiton *et al.*, 1979b).

Separation of the isomeric product arising from the coupling of an acylamino acid using HPLC has been limited. The coupling of Bz-Phe-OH with either the methyl or benzyl ester of alanine has been suggested as a test for racemization (Goodman *et al.*, 1977). The diastereomeric products have been separated by a 60-cm Microporasil column eluted with chloroform containing 0.7 and 0.6% of 95% aqueous ethanol, respectively. The solvent composition is crucial to the separation. This method can detect as little as 0.1% of the other isomer.

3. Protected Dipeptides

The first racemization test involving activation of a peptide emerged from the assessment of phosphites (chloro- and tetraethylpyrophosphite) as coupling reagents (Anderson and Young, 1952; Anderson *et al.*, 1952). It was found that any D-isomer in the coupling product Z-Gly-Phe-Gly-OEt crystallized out as the racemate from a 2% solution in ethanol. As little as 1% racemization in the coupling of Z-Gly-Phe-OH + H-Gly-OEt can be detected. The sensitivity of this Anderson test can be increased substantially by use of the multiple-isotope dilution procedure (Kemp *et al.*, 1970). A second widely used test implicating phenylalanine as the activated residue involves coupling Z-Leu-Phe-OH with H-Val-OtBu (Weygand *et al.*, 1966c). Racemization is assessed by determination of the derivatized epimeric COOH-terminal dipeptide units Tfa-Phe-Val-OMe by glc. These are obtained by deprotection of the coupling product using hot trifluoroacetic acid, partial peptide bond cleavage, and esterification using 8.5 *N* HCl in methanol followed by acylation using methyl trifluoroacetate. In recent studies on new approaches to peptide bond formation, the racemization of Z-Ala-Phe-OH during coupling to give Z-Ala-Phe-Val-OMe (Berndt, 1980) and Z-Ala-Phe-Gly-Phe-Gly-OMe (Matoni and Berndt, 1980) was determined by HPLC (silica gel column) of the products using chloroform containing 1–1.5% methanol as eluting agent.

The well-known Izumiya test involving the separation of tripeptide isomers by ion-exchange chromatography with an amino acid analyzer became available after a fruitless attempt to find a suitable candidate among the NH_2-terminal glycyl tripeptides containing both a basic and an acidic residue (Muraoka *et al.*, 1968). Isomers of the simpler peptides H-Gly-Ala-Leu-OH and H-Gly-Ala-Val-OH could be completely separated. The Z-Gly-Ala-OH + H-Leu-OBzl system, followed by deprotection by catalytic hydrogenation, was chosen as the preferred test because the deprotected dipeptide and amino acid do not overlap with the tripeptide (Izumiya and Muraoka, 1969; Izumiya *et al.*, 1971). Down to 0.2% racemization can be detected by this method. Use of partition chromatography prior to ion-exchange chromatography increases the limit of detection by two orders of magnitude (Yamashiro and Blake, 1981). A modified test determines the protected isomers Moz-Gly-Ala-Phe-OBzl* (from Moz-Gly-Ala-OH + H-Phe-OBzl) by HPLC on a μBondapak column eluted with methanol–water (55:45) (Kiso *et al.*, 1981). Racemization at alanine could also be established by coupling Prot-Leu-Ala-OH with H-Gly-Val-OR followed by deprotection, as Kent *et al.* (1978) have described the separation of H-Leu-DLAla-Gly-Val-OH isomers by ion-exchange chromatography (pH 3.49 buffer) as a means of assessing racemization occurring during solid-phase synthesis. Not more that 0.04% racemization occurred at either the alanine or leucine residues during the synthesis of this peptide on a solid support according to the Merrifield procedure (Kent *et al.*, 1978).

* Moz, 4-methoxybenzyloxycarbonyl.

Tripeptide systems analogous to those used in the Izumiya test include Boc-Gly-Ala-OH coupled with H-Leu-OR (Yamashiro and Blake, 1981) and Z-Ala-Leu-OH and Z-Ala-MeLeu-OH coupled with H-Gly-OBzl (McDermott and Benoiton, 1973c), the deprotected tripeptide isomers being determined with an amino acid analyzer. Use of these allowed the demonstration that an *N*-methylamino acid residue racemizes more readily than the corresponding unmethylated residue during coupling (McDermott and Benoiton, 1973c). A novel approach for assessing racemization at leucine involved coupling Boc-Ala-Met-Leu-OH with H-Yyy-OtBu for Yyy = Leu, Ile, Asp(OtBu), followed by deprotection with trifluoracetic acid, cleavage of the tetrapeptides with cyanogen bromide, and analysis of the H-Leu-Yyy-OH isomers with an analyzer (Kitada and Fujino, 1978). H-Asp(O*t*Bu)-OtBu gave rise to two to three times more epimerization than the other esters.

The single test implicating the valyl residue to assess racemization (Tfa-Pro-Val-OH + H-Pro-O*t*Bu, Weygand *et al.*, 1968) involves determination of the epimeric products by glc. The remarkable racemization-suppressing effect of the Lewis acid zinc chloride was discovered using this test (Jakubke *et al.*, 1978). Modifications of the method have included the use of Boc-Pro-Val-OH as the activated component coupled with H-Pro-OMe (Tomida *et al.*, 1973) or H-Pro-Val-OMe (Tomida and Nishimura, 1980) followed by N-deprotection and subsequent trifluoracetylation before analysis. Six other epimeric trifluoracetyltetrapeptide methyl esters containing two prolyl residues are readily separated by the same glc system (Tomida and Nishimura, 1980).

The racemization tests available at the time of the previous review (Kemp, 1979) had provided a wealth of data on the relative merits of different reagents, methods, and conditions as they affect the stereochemical course of coupling reactions. Several different amino acids were implicated as the activated residues in the numerous tests. However, it was still not possible to draw conclusions about the relative tendency of different residues to racemize because of the variety in the nature of the N-substituents (acyl and protected aminoacyl) on the activated residues as well as in the nature of the amino components used in the tests. What was lacking was a series of racemization tests involving A-Www-Xxx-OH + H-Yyy-B, where Xxx was variable but all other components were constant. Our own and Castro's laboratory had already embarked on programs with this in mind.

The series Bz-Xxx-OH + H-Lys(Z)-OMe, with the epimeric products determined by nmr spectroscopy (Benoiton *et al.*, 1979b), has been described above. Extension of the lysyl dipeptide series H-DLXxx-Lys-OH (Benoiton *et al.*, 1979c) by a glycyl residue has provided the test series Z-Gly-Xxx-OH + H-Lys(Z)-OBzl → → H-Gly-DLXxx-Lys-OH where deprotection is carried out by hydrogenolysis and the isomeric products are determined with an amino acid analyzer using a similar chromatographic system (a 15-cm Aminex A-5 resin column eluted with sodium citrate buffer, pH 5.50; pH 7.50 for phenylalanine) (Benoiton *et al.*, 1979c). Peptides with Xxx = Ala, Leu, Phe, Val, Ile, Pro are well separated (> 10-min interval). The various applications of these series of tests are described later. The analogous series Z-Gly-Lys(Z)-OH + H-Yyy-OBzl → → H-Gly-DLLys-Yyy-OH (Benoiton *et al.*, 1979c) is also available for comparing the effect of Yyy on racemization at the activated residue or on the asymmetric induction occurring during coupling. Castro *et al.* (1978, 1979) and Le Nguyen *et al.* (1981) devised the analogous series Boc-Www-Ala-OH + H-Ala-OMe, Boc-Ala-Xxx-OH + H-Ala-OMe, and Boc-Ala-Ala-OH + H-Yyy-OMe, where Www, Xxx, Yyy = Ala, Leu, Phe, Val, Ile. Using 250-MHz nmr spectroscopy and couplings under a single set of conditions, they compared the sensitivity to racemization of Xxx residues and the contributions to racemization of Www and Yyy residues. On the basis of these data and extradynamic assumptions, they have proposed an equation whose use allows prediction of the sequence dependence of racemization.

When glc, HPLC, and nmr spectroscopy are employed for determining isomeric peptides, the methods give directly the relative amounts of the compounds in solution because the two isomers produce the same response in the detector. However, the situation is different for analyses carried out with an amino acid analyzer. The reaction of ninhydrin with diastereomeric peptides produces different color yields (Noda *et al.*, 1968; Manning and Moore, 1968), so a correction to compensate for this must be applied. The correction factor must be obtained from a mixture of known composition which, unfortunately, is not easy to come by. Because some selectivity occurs in many cases, coupling an L-residue with a racemic amino acid does not always give a 1:1 mixture of products, even if an excess of the enantiomer is used to try to force the reaction to go to completion. The only way to determine accurately the absolute or relative color yields of two isomers is to synthesize them separately. When one racemization test is in question, this is feasible, but if a series of tests are involved, this synthetic work adds a substantial burden to the project. But if the objective is to establish trends and not to place importance on absolute amounts of racemization, then the use of color yield ratios determined from mixtures prepared by coupling with the racemic form of one of the components can still allow the execution of valid studies. The work by Benoiton *et al.*, (1979c, 1981a,b,c) is an example of this, and it must be remembered when examining the data that all values are subject to correction. To eliminate this inherent shortcoming of the analyzer method of determining peptide isomers, several series of model peptides have been adapted to analysis by reversed-phase HPLC. Good separations of the H-Gly-DLXxx-Lys-OH isomeric pairs have been achieved on a μBondapak C_{18} column using purely aqueous 0.01 *M* ammonium acetate (pH 6.6) as solvent (Steinauer *et al.*, 1982). Addition of 3% acetonitrile to a pH 4.0 buffer gave a similar separation of the epimers of H-Gly-Ala-Leu-OH and H-Gly-Leu-Ala-OH.

4. Comparison of Model Systems

The nature of the model system used to study racemization has a bearing on the degree of racemization observed. For any selected coupling method or condition, a test based on the coupling of an acylamino acid will indicate more racemization than a test based on the coupling of a protected dipeptide. Based on nine cases, Kemp *et al.*, (1970) found an average ratio between the Young test (Bz-Leu-OH + H-Gly-OEt, Williams and Young, 1963) and the Anderson test (Z-Gly-Phe-OH + H-Gly-OEt, Anderson and Young, 1952) of about 10, and this figure has often been quoted in discussing these tests. This ratio is a manifestation of the higher tendency of benzoylamino than N-substituted aminoacylamino acids to form the racemizing intermediate 5(4*H*)-oxazolone, but it also incorporates the differences in the tendencies of the leucyl and phenylalanyl residues to racemize. Recent work by Benoiton's group has provided data that eliminate these differences between residues and thus permit a more valid comparison of the racemizing tendency of benzoylamino acids versus N-protected glycylamino acids (Benoiton and Kuroda, 1981). On the basis of 17 experiments involving 4 coupling methods and 5 different residues, they obtained an average ratio of 6, with only a few widely deviating values of 1.2 and 27. The ratios depended on the coupling methods and the residues implicated. Lower ratios were obtained for DCC-mediated couplings in dichloromethane than for the same couplings in the presence of 1-hydroxybenzotriazole in dimethylformamide. Unfortunately, these data also cannot be taken as the final word on the relative sensitivity of the two types of models. The data of Benoiton *et al.*, (1979b) and Benoiton and Kuroda (1981) are observed racemization and do not take into account the contribution of asymmetric induction which is much more pronounced in the coupling of benzoylamino acids (Section IV,B). After appropriate correction the ratios would be reduced for experiments done in dichloromethane in which the induction is negative (excess D-L-isomer produced) and increased for those done in dimethylformamide in which the induction is positive (more L-L-isomer produced) (Benoiton *et al.*, 1981c). The complexity of the issue can be illustrated further by considering a comparison of the relative sensitivities to racemization of benzoyl- versus trifluoroacetylamino acid. The Weygand (Tfa-Val-OH + H-Val-OMe, Weygand *et al.*, 1963) and the Davies (Bz-Val-OH + H-Val-OMe, Davies *et al.*, 1975) tests seem appropriate for the purpose. However, racemization in the former case is accompanied by a positive induction in tetrahydrofuran; in the latter case it is accompanied by a negative induction (Steglich *et al.*, 1967). Therefore a true comparison would have to take the asymmetric induction into account.

The high tendency of benzoylamino acids to racemize when coupled, combined with the simplicity with which the stereomutation can be assessed, such as by nmr spectroscopy, makes them attractive models for studying racemization. The Young test in particular has provided valuable information to the peptide community. However, recent reports by Benoiton and co-workers indicate that caution is in order when interpreting results acquired with the use of model systems that are based on the coupling of acylamino acids. Several examples have come to light where the conclusions did not apply to the coupling of protected dipeptides. Using two series of models involving coupling of benzoylamino acids and benzyloxycarbonylglycylamino acids (Section II,B,2 and 3), Benoiton and Kuroda (1981) found the former to indicate that 1-hydroxybenzotriazole was not an effective racemization suppressant for ethyl γ-dimethylaminopropylcarbodiimide-mediated couplings in dichloromethane, whereas the latter indicated that it was. Similarly, the benzoylamino acid series showed *N*-hydroxysuccinimide to be superior to 1-hydroxybenzotriazole as a racemization suppressant in dimethylformamide, whereas the peptide series showed the opposite. But the most significant irregularity concerned the relative susceptibility to racemization of L- and D-residues. In line with another report (Arendt *et al.*, 1978b) based on the use of acetylamino acids, Benoiton *et al.* (1981b) found that benzoyl-L-amino acids racemized more than benzoyl-D-amino acids when coupled with an L-amino acid ester. However, when the issue was examined using benzyloxycarbonylglycylamino acids, the results were opposite, that is, the activated D-residues underwent more stereomutation than the activated L-residues. Because it is logical that information on racemization acquired with the use of small peptides is more likely to apply to the real case in peptide synthesis than that acquired with the use of acylamino acids, the model systems based on coupling peptides are generally preferable.

III. OXAZOLINE-5-ONES FROM N-SUBSTITUTED α-AMINO ACIDS

A. Introduction

Racemization in peptide synthesis may occur via two mechanisms, simple enolization [Eq. (1)], which may be acid- or base-catalyzed, and 5(4*H*)-oxazolone formation [Eq. (2)], which is base-catalyzed when it is implicated

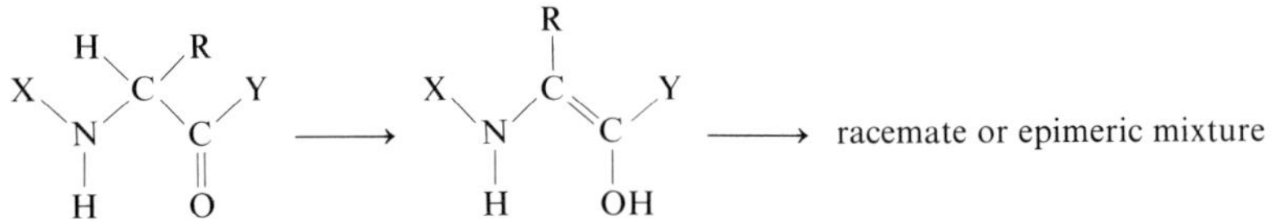

(1)

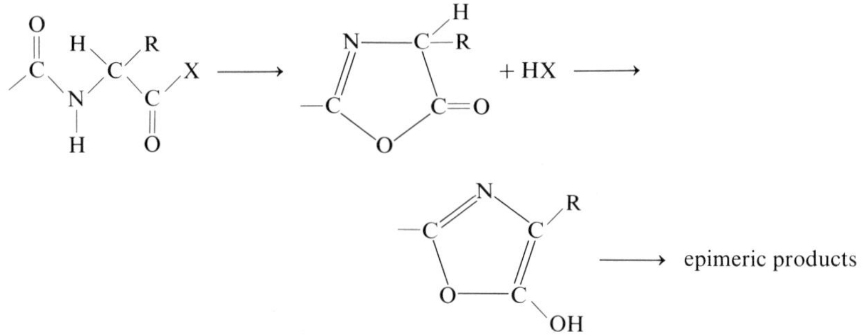

(2)

in coupling reactions (see Kemp, 1979). An example of racemization via acid-catalyzed enolization is the racemization of N-substituted *N*-methylamino acids by anhydrous hydrogen bromide in acetic acid (McDermott and Benoiton, 1973b). Examples of racemization via base-catalyzed enolization are racemization accompanying the saponification of esters (Section V), and couplings by the acyl azide method (Kemp and Rebek, 1970). 5(4*H*)-Oxazolone formation can also be acid-catalyzed, as in the cyclization of acylamino acids in the presence of acetic anhydride (Mohr and Geis, 1908). Acid-catalyzed formation of 5(4*H*)-oxazolones has been proposed to account for the racemization occurring during the methanolysis of small peptides (Weygand *et al.*, 1966a) and the acidolytic cleavage of benzoylamino acid anilides by hydrogen bromide (Chen and Benoiton, 1978). Both the enolization mechanism and the 5(4*H*)-oxazolone mechanism may be implicated in the racemization process associated with a single coupling reaction.

B. 2,4-Dialkyl-5(4*H*)-oxazolones

2,4-Dialkyl-5(4*H*)-oxazolones* (**1**) have been known since the turn of the century, but it is through contributions from the laboratories of Young in Oxford, Goodman in San Diego, and Siemion in Wroclaw that their role in peptide synthesis was revealed (Kemp, 1979). They can be prepared from acylamino acids using acetic anhydride (Mohr and Geis, 1908) or DCC

* The 5(4*H*)-oxazolones from peptides, referred to as peptide 5(4*H*)-oxazolones, which are really 2-(*N*-substituted-α-aminoalkyl)-4-alkyl-5(4*H*)-oxazolones, are included in the term 2,4-dialkyl-5(4*H*)-oxazolone.

(Siemion and Nowak, 1960), but the products have not always been easy to purify. Distillation or recrystallization has usually led to major losses and partial or complete racemization. DCC also gives 5(4*H*)-oxazolones from protected dipeptides, but the compounds obtained from Z-Gly-Phe-OH (Schnabel, 1965; DeTar *et al.*, 1966) and Z-Gly-Cys(Bzl)-OH (Kovacs *et al.*, 1979) were either partially racemized or of uncertain optical purity. The method of Goodman and Levine (1964) using an acetic anhydride–dioxane mixture gave crystalline 5(4*H*)-oxazolones of high optical purity from Z-Aib-Phe-OH* and Z-Pro-Val-OH (Jakubke *et al.*, 1978) but not from Z-Aib-Ala-OH (Goodman and Levine, 1964). 5(4*H*)-Oxazolones react with hydrazine to give hydrazides without loss of chirality (Siemion and Morawiec, 1964; Goodman and Glaser, 1970), so their stereochemical purity can be assessed by comparison of the specific rotations of these products with those of hydrazides obtained from the corresponding esters.

Difficult access to 5(4*H*)-oxazolones that are both chemically and optically pure has been a severe obstacle to progress in attempts to understand the stereochemical course of events in coupling reactions. The work of Chen *et al.* (1979) may have eliminated this obstacle. Taking advantage of the simple but significant observation that 5(4*H*)-oxazolones can be washed with cold neutral or weakly alkaline aqueous solutions without deleterious effects, they have devised a general procedure by which chemically pure 5(4*H*)-oxazolones can be obtained from the parent acid with a minimum of manipulation [Eq. (3)]. At 0°C, 1 equiv of the water-soluble carbodiimide

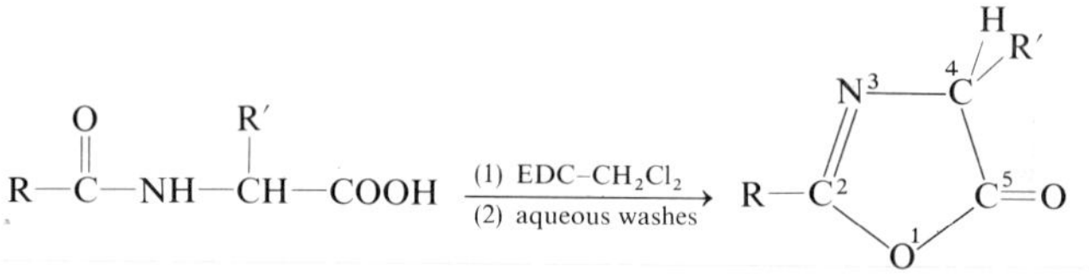

(3)

(1)

EDC (Sheehan *et al.*, 1961) is added to the acid in dichloromethane, and after 15 min the solution is washed successively with ice-cold water, aqueous sodium bicarbonate, and water. Removal of the dried solvent by evaporation gives the pure products. All side products are removed by the aqueous washes. About 20 5(4*H*)-oxazolones (**1**) from acetyl-, benzoyl-, formyl-, and benzyloxycarbonylglycylamino acids have been obtained by this procedure (Chen *et al.*, 1979; Benoiton *et al.*, 1982; Benoiton and Chen, 1982). Based on a comparison of the specific rotations of their hydrazides with those of reference compounds, the products from N-substituted L-leucine were

* Aib, α-Aminoisobutyric acid.

optically pure. The optical purity of the five urethane-substituted 5(4*H*)-oxazolones was examined further (Benoiton *et al*., 1982). Each was converted to the hydrazide which was coupled by the acyl azide procedure with a lysine derivative, thus allowing determination of the diastereomers by a routine procedure (Benoiton *et al*., 1979c; see Section II,B,3). All were optically pure except that from Z-Gly-DAla-OH, which could not be obtained optically pure despite repeated attempts to do so. Whether the racemization occurred before or during the hydrazinolysis could not be established. The D-isomer of alanine had been used to overcome an analytical obstacle. Except for the uncertainty with alanine, the results provided confirmatory evidence for the thesis that hydrazinolysis of 5(4*H*)-oxazolones proceeds without loss of chiral integrity and put it on a firmer experimental basis.

The difficulties encountered with alanine by our group and by Goodman and Levine (1964) suggest the possibility that its 5(4*H*)-oxazolones might be more prone to autoracemization than those of other residues. A very slow autoracemization was observed for the 5(4*H*)-oxazolone from acetylleucine (Chen *et al*., 1979). Siemion and Dzugaj (1966) have proposed that autoracemization results from abstraction of the α-proton of one molecule of the 5(4*H*)-oxazolone by the basic nitrogen atom of a second molecule [Eq. (4)].

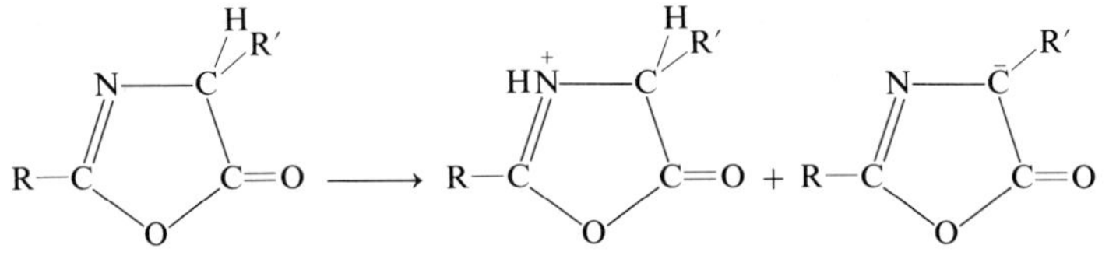

(4)

C. 4-Alkyl-5(2*H*)-oxazolones

4-Alkyl-5(4*H*)-oxazolones (**2**) are also formed by the reaction of DCC (Siemon and Nowak, 1961; Schnabel, 1965) or EDC (Benoiton and Chen, 1982) with formylamino acids. Their behavior resembles that of the corresponding 2,4-disubstituted 5(4*H*)-oxazolones in most respects, but in the presence of a base such as triethylamine they are converted into the achiral 4-alkyl-5(2*H*)-oxazolones (**3**) (Benoiton and Chen, 1982) [Eq. (5)]. Whether

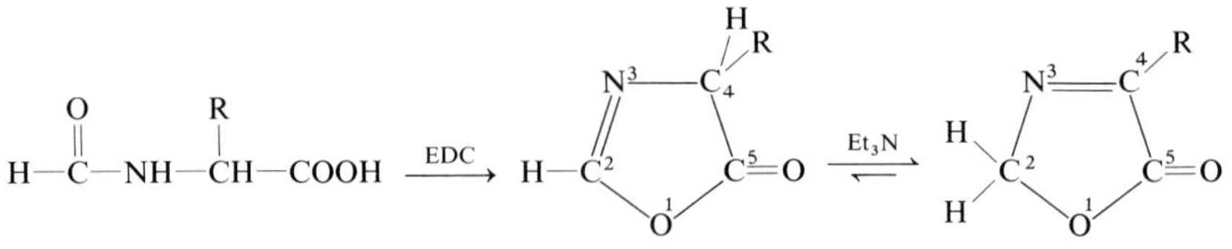

(**2**) (**3**)

(5)

or not racemization precedes the proton transfer is open to speculation. The conversion was complete for 4-isobutyl-5(4*H*)-oxazolone* but incomplete for 4-isopropyl-5(4*H*)-oxazolone. The reaction is not reversed by acetic acid or hydrogen chloride. Methylamine reacted with 4-isopropyl-5(2*H*)-oxazolone to give formylvaline *N*-methylamide, probably through the 5(4*H*)-oxazolone. However, a 10% yield of a second neutral product was also formed, so the reaction course is uncertain. 4-Alkyl-5(2*H*)-oxazolones are characterized by a single nmr signal at $\delta = 5.7$ ppm for two ring protons which show the same long-range five-bond coupling with the exocyclic protons at C-6 as exhibited by the protons in 4-methyloxazoline (**4**) (Meese *et al.*, 1974). The new oxazolone is the same as the so-called pseudooxazolones (**5**) formed by cyclization of trifluoracetylamino acids (Weygand *et al.*, 1963). 2,4-Disubstituted 5(4*H*)-oxazolones do not undergo the conversion described in Eq. (5).

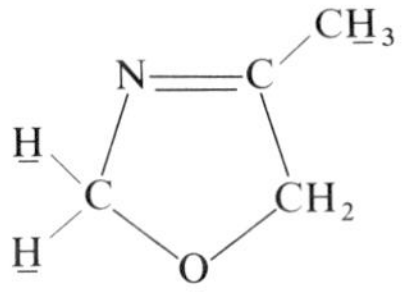

(**4**)

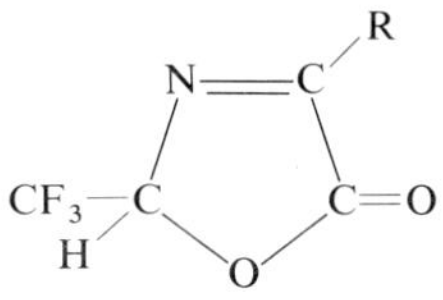

(**5**)

D. 2-Alkoxy-4-alkyl-5(4*H*)-oxazolones

1. Introduction

Activated acylamino acids and N-blocked peptides form 5(4*H*)-oxazolones far more rapidly than they enolize, consequently racemization during coupling occurs primarily through the 5(4*H*)-oxazolone mechanism. As described by Kemp (1979) this mechanism involves a base-catalyzed rate-determining cyclization to give the 5(4*H*)-oxazolone which then racemizes via a resonance-stabilized tautomer and rapidly reacts with nucleophiles at its acyl carbon to form a mixture of enantiomers or epimers [Eq. (6)]. It is known from experience, however, that if the activated component is an *N*-alkoxycarbonylamino acid (**7**), except for unusual cases where the side chain intervenes, the coupling proceeds without any change in stereochemistry. It is for this reason that peptide chains are built up by incremental addition starting from the COOH-terminal end of the chain, and it is based on this premise that the successful synthesis of stereochemically pure peptides has been achieved. The reason put forth and generally accepted in explaining the preservation of chirality has been that the corresponding 2-alkoxy-5(4*H*)-oxazolones (**6**) do not or cannot form. Cyclization has been considered

* Designation as 4-*sec*-butyl-5(4*H*)-oxazolone in Benoiton and Chen (1982) was an error.

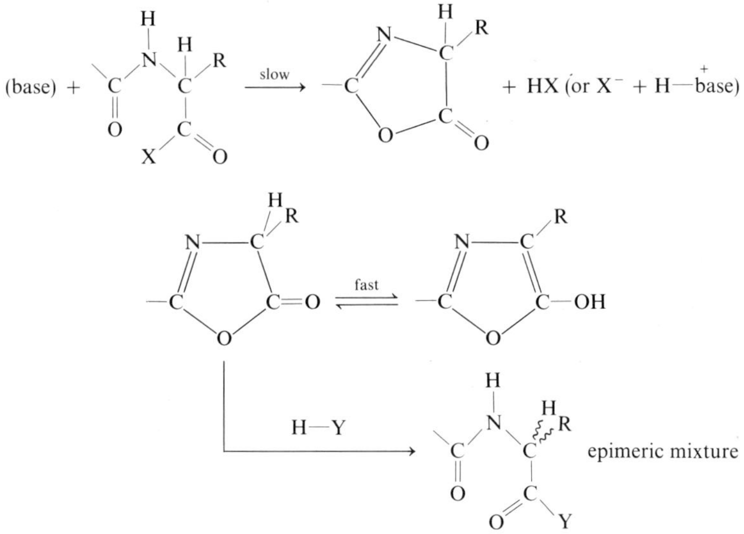

(6)

possible only if X is an extremely good leaving group, and then only with formation of the *N*-carboxyanhydride (**8**) and not the 5(4*H*)-oxazolone (Kemp, 1979; Bodanszky *et al*., 1976) [Eq. (7)]. "The 5(4*H*)-oxazolone mechanism is relevant to the epimerizations of acylamino acids, but not to urethane-protected amino acids [Kemp, 1979, p. 339]."

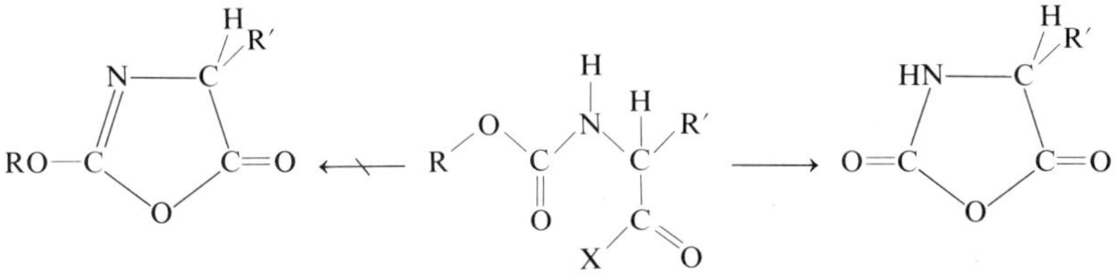

(7)

(**6**) (**7**) (**8**)

It now transpires that 2-alkoxy-5(4*H*)-oxazolones from *N*-alkoxycarbonylamino acids indeed do exist (Jones and Witty, 1977, 1979), that they had been prepared earlier from the acid using thionyl chloride and triethylamine but their structures had been misassigned (Miyoshi, 1970, 1973a), that they can be obtained from some *tert*-butyloxycarbonylamino acids using EDC (Benoiton and Chen, 1979) and can even be isolated from incomplete carbodiimide-mediated coupling reactions (Benoiton and Chen, 1981a). They are chirally more stable than 2-alkyl-5(4*H*)-oxazolones (Jones and Witty, 1979; Benoiton and Chen, 1979, 1981a), and this explains why *N*-alkoxycarbonylamino acids normally couple without undergoing racemization. However, 2-alkoxy-5(4*H*)-oxazolones do racemize when coupled in the presence of a tertiary amine base (Benoiton and Chen, 1979, 1981a), so *N*-alkoxycarbonylamino acids cannot be coupled indiscriminately without regard to the possibility of racemization.

2. *Preparation of 2-Alkoxy-5(4H)-oxazolones Using Chloride-Forming Reagents*

No reaction occurs within 30 min between equivalent amounts of benzyloxycarbonylphenylalanine (**9**) and thionyl chloride in tetrahydrofuran at −25°C, but a change in absorbance is observed after the addition of 1 equiv of triethylamine (Miyoshi, 1973a), probably due to formation of the acid chloride (**10**) [Eq. (8)]. Addition of a second equivalent of triethylamine

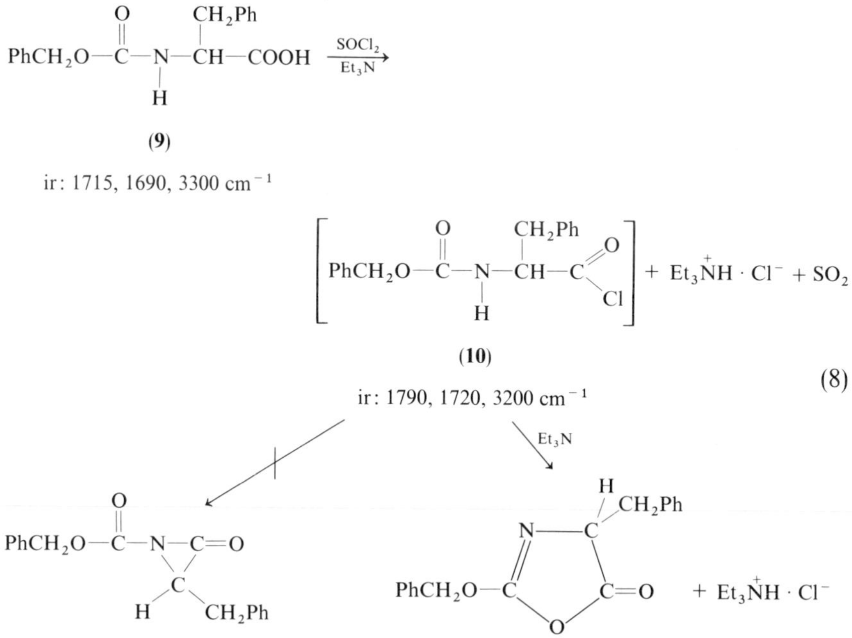

(**9**)

ir: 1715, 1690, 3300 cm^{-1}

(**10**)

ir: 1790, 1720, 3200 cm^{-1}

(8)

(**11**)

(**12**)

ir: 1840, 1690

mp: 73°C, $[\alpha]_D = -36$°C (THF)

followed by removal of the triethylamine hydrochloride and solvent gave an optically active crystalline cyclodehydration product to which was assigned the aziridinone structure (**11**) on the basis of its ir absorbance, nmr spectrum, and other considerations (Miyoshi, 1973a). The product reacted with oxygen and nitrogen nucleophiles to give optically active esters and amides and optically pure protected dipeptide esters (Miyoshi, 1973b). Coupling with retention of all the optical activity induced Miyoshi to reject the 5(4*H*)-oxazolone structure (**12**) on the grounds that the reaction of such compounds with amines would be accompanied by racemization. Five years later, Jones and Witty (1977) argued that the latter was a nonsequitur and indeed proved that the compound prepared by Miyoshi was the 2-benzyloxy-4-benzyl-5(4*H*)-oxazolone (**12**). The proof was provided by the fact that in the proton-decoupled ^{13}C-nmr spectrum of the ^{15}N-labeled compound, ^{13}C–^{15}N coupling was observed for only one of the two low-field (>C=) carbons. The aziridinone (**11**) has two carbonyl carbons which would display ^{13}C–^{15}N coupling. The same product is obtained using phosgene or phosphorus oxychloride (Miyoshi, 1973a) or phosphorus pentachloride (Jones and Witty, 1977). The other characterized 2-benzyloxy-4-alkyl-5-(4*H*)-oxazolones prepared by this method are those from 4-bromobenzyloxycarbonyl-L-phenylalanine (mp 87°C), 4-chlorobenzyloxycarbonyl-L-phenylalanine (mp 82°C) (Miyoshi, 1973a), benzyloxycarbonyl-DL-phenylalanine (mp 53°C), and benzyloxycarbonyl-DL-valine, (oil) (Jones and Witty, 1979).

3. *Preparation of 2-Alkoxy-5(4H)-oxazolones Using Soluble Carbodiimide*

In contrast to the reaction of acylamino acids and protected peptide acids with carbodiimides, which gives 2,4-disubstituted 5(4*H*)-oxazolones (Section III,B), *N*-alkoxycarbonylamino acids give symmetrical anhydrides (**13**) under the same conditions (Schüssler and Zahn, 1962; see Rich and Singh, 1979). These symmetrical anhydrides are good acylating agents, and their use without isolation (Hagenmeier and Frank, 1972) in solid-phase peptide synthesis has become common practice (see Barany and Merrifield, 1980). Prompted by the claim that in solid-phase peptide synthesis the active form of the coupling residue is in fact the symmetrical anhydride, and the recommendation that purified anhydrides might eliminate side reactions (Rebek and Feitler, 1974), Chen *et al.*, (1978) devised a routine procedure by which chemically pure symmetrical anhydrides of *N*-alkoxycarbonylamino acids can be obtained [Eq. (9)]. The method consists of adding 0.5 equiv of the

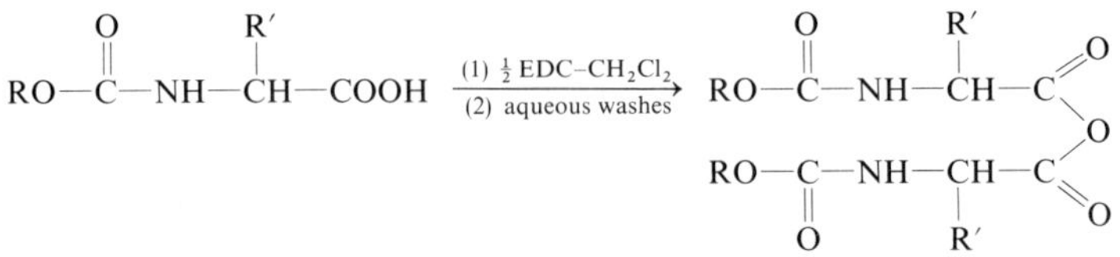

(9)

(**13**)

soluble carbodiimide EDC to the acid in dichloromethane (10 ml/mmol) at 0°C for *tert*-butyloxycarbonylamino acids and 23°C for benzyloxycarbonylamino acids. After stirring for 1 hr, the solution is washed with cold aqueous solutions of citric acid, water, and sodium bicarbonate. Evaporation of the solvent gives the pure anhydrides, all the side products having been removed by the aqueous washes. The original description (Chen *et al.*, 1978) indicated replacement of the solvent by ethyl acetate before the extraction, but this is unnecessary (F. M. F. Chen and N. L. Benoiton, unpublished). *N*-9-Fluorenylmethyloxycarbonylamino acid anhydrides have also been prepared by this procedure (Heimer *et al.*, 1981). Pure symmetrical anhydrides have been used for the synthesis of a tetrapeptide in 80% aqueous dimethylformamide (Benoiton and Chen, 1981e).

Chen *et al.* (1978) observed that the yields of anhydrides from Boc-Val-OH and Boc-Ile-OH were considerably lower than those from other derivatives. Attempts to increase the yield of $(Boc\text{-}Val)_2O$ (**14**) by using more EDC (1 equiv) produced a second stable neutral compound that could be obtained pure after removal of the solvent by precipitating out the anhydride with light petroleum. The product (oil, 20% yield) was identified as 2-*tert*-butoxy-4-isopropyl-5(4*H*)-oxazolone (**15**) on the basis of its ir absorbance (1845 and 1700 cm^{-1}), nmr spectrum (sharp α-proton doublet), elemental analysis, and reaction with methylamine to give Boc-Val-$NHCH_3$ (Benoiton and Chen, 1979, 1981a). The analogous 2-benzyloxy-4-isopropyl-5(4*H*)-oxazolone (**16**)

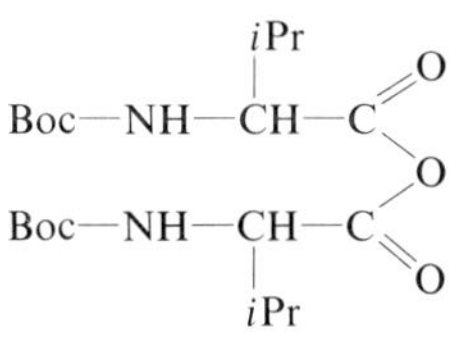

(**14**)

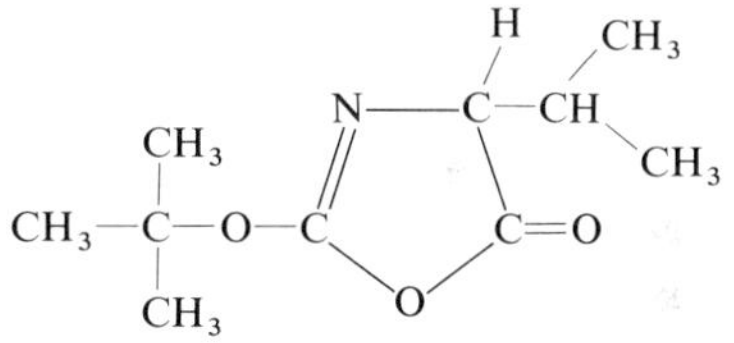

(**15**)

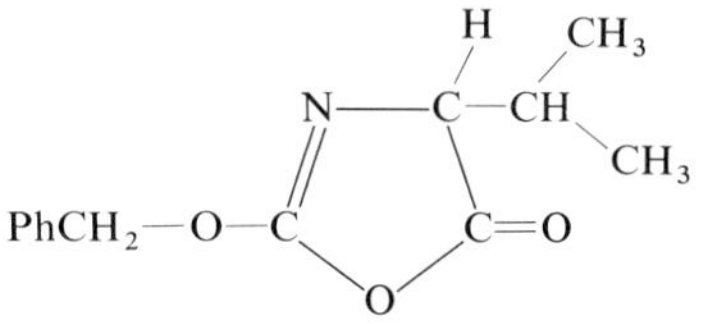

(**16**)

was obtained from Z-Val-OH. Both were shown to be optically pure (<0.1% D-isomer) by analysis of the products of the reaction with a lysine derivative (Benoiton *et al.*, 1979c). The aziridinone structures were rejected on the basis of the mass spectra and the absence of absorption for a urethane carbonyl group (1750–1770 cm^{-1}) in the ir spectra.

2-Alkoxy-5(4*H*)-oxazolones can be readily detected and quantitated in mixtures by nmr spectroscopy by virtue of the unique chemical shifts of their *tert*-butoxy and methylenoxy protons which are downfield by 0.13 and 0.20 ppm, respectively, from those of urethanes and esters. A 60-MHz instrument suffices in most cases. And in particular for 5(4*H*)-oxazolones obtained from valine derivatives, the α-proton doublet also serves as a diagnostic peak.

The two 2-alkoxy-5(4*H*)-oxazolones (**15** and **16**) were obtained in yields of 55% by adding a solution of the acid dropwise to a dilute solution containing excess EDC. Other 2-*tert*-butoxy-5(4*H*)-oxazolones could not be isolated pure because the symmetrical anhydrides could not be precipitated out completely, but evidence for their formation, using 1 equiv of EDC, was obtained for the following amino acids (percentage yield): alanine (15), leucine (5), isoleucine (45), and phenylalanine (15) (Benoiton and Chen, 1981a). 2-Ethoxy- and 2-(9-fluorenylmethyloxy)-4-isopropyl-5(4*H*)-oxazolones have also been prepared (A. Paquet, F. M. F. Chen, and N. L. Benoiton, unpublished). The latter decomposes on standing, liberating dibenzofulvene.

4. Reactions and Chiral Properties of 2-Alkoxy-5(4H)-Oxazolones

2-*tert*-Butoxy-4-isopropyl-5(4*H*)-oxazolone is stable in deuterochloroform at −5°C for 5 days or in dimethylformamide at 23°C for several hours. It slowly decomposes in solutions containing water, giving rise to *tert*-butanol, and is converted to valine *N*-carboxyanhydride (**17**) on standing in *tert*-butanol, anhydrous acid, or *in vacuo* (Benoiton and Chen, 1981a). 2-Benzyloxy-4-isopropyl-5(4*H*)-oxazolone is more stable, not decomposing on standing in *tert*-butanol and giving the ethyl ester after 36 hr in ethanol. Catalytic hydrogenation transforms it into the *N*-carboxyanhydride (Benoiton and Chen, 1979, 1981a; Miyoshi, 1973a) [Eq. (10)]. Both 2-

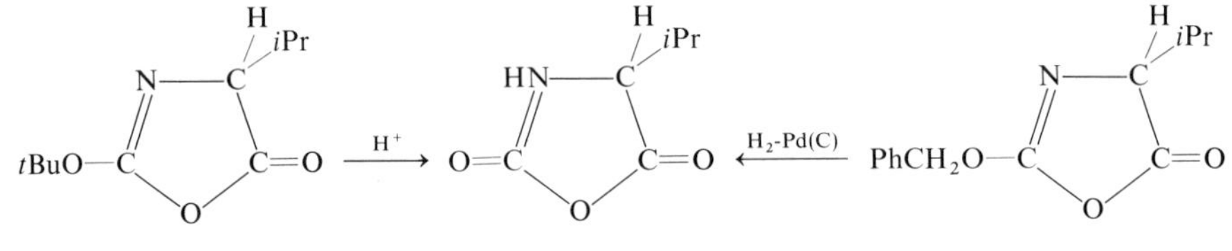

(**17**)

(10)

alkoxy-5(4*H*)-oxazolones react with the parent acid to give the symmetrical anhydride (**18**) (Benoiton and Chen, 1979, 1981a) [Eq. (11)], the benzyloxy compound also giving the anhydride by reaction with water (Miyoshi, 1973b), no doubt via formation of the parent acid which reacts with a second mole-

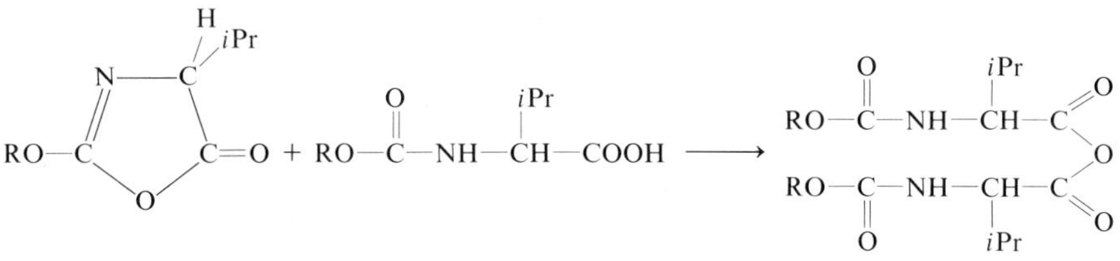

(18)

(11)

cule. 2-Alkoxy-5(4*H*)-oxazolones react with *N*-acylamino acids and N-blocked dipeptide acids through the unsymmetrical* anhydride (**19**), which is postulated as a transient intermediate, to give the *N*-alkoxycarboxylamino acid and the 2-alkyl-5(4*H*)-oxazolone of the starting acid (Benoiton and Chen, 1982) [Eq. (12)]. All the starting material is consumed by the reaction.

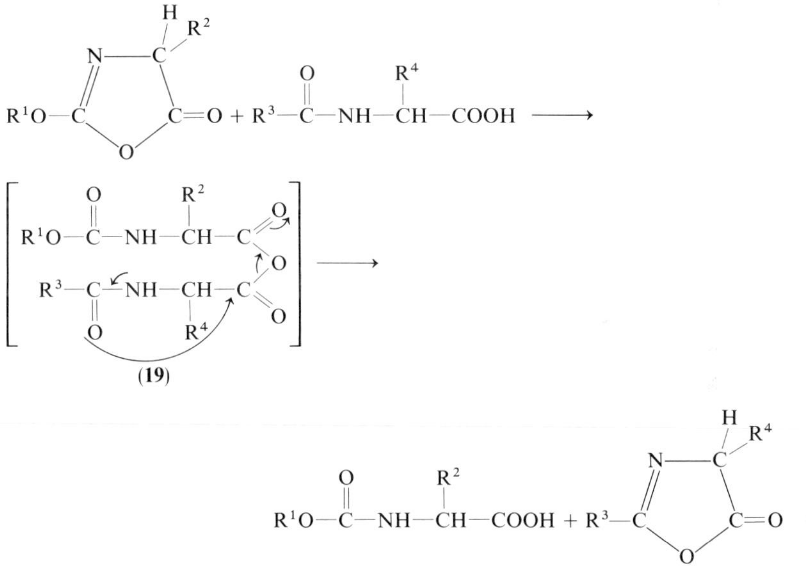

(19)

(12)

2-Benzyloxy-5(4*H*)-oxazolones prepared *in situ* reacted with several amino acid esters to give *N*-benzyloxycarbonyl dipeptide esters with no apparent loss in chiral integrity (Miyoshi, 1973b). The 2-alkoxy-5(4*H*)-oxazolones from Boc-Val-OH and Z-Val-OH also gave optically pure (>99.9%) products when reacted with H-Lys(Z)-OBzl, even in the presence

* The term "mixed anhydride" is reserved for anhydrides containing only one N-substituted amino acid moiety.

of salts (Benoiton and Chen, 1979, 1981a). The chiral stability of 2-alkoxy-5(4*H*)-oxazolones therefore contrasts with that of 2-alkyl-5(4*H*)-oxazolones which cannot be coupled, except with hydrazine, without extensive racemization (see Kemp, 1979). However, 2-alkoxy-5(4*H*)-oxazolones do undergo racemization when coupled in the presence of a tertiary amine base. Racemization of 6 and 15%, respectively, was observed for couplings of 2-*tert*-butoxy- and 2-benzyloxy-4-isopropyl-5(4*H*)-oxazolones in the presence of 0.2 equiv of triethylamine. Fifty percent racemization occurred for a coupling of the latter in the presence of 1 equiv of triethylamine (Benoiton and Chen, 1979, 1981a). The difference in the chiral stabilities of the two types of 5(4*H*)-oxazolones is therefore one of degree.

The extent of racemization associated with the amination of 5(4*H*)-oxazolones depends on the relative rates of ring opening versus racemization caused by the basicity of the attacking nucleophile (see Kemp, 1979). 2-Alkyl-5(4*H*)-oxazolones racemize severely when coupled because the rate of racemization far exceeds the rate of ring opening (Goodman and Levine, 1964). Rate constant data indicate that 2-alkoxy-5(4*H*)-oxazolones racemize much more slowly in the presence of base and ring-open much more quickly than the corresponding 2-alkyl-5(4*H*)-oxazolones (Jones and Witty, 1979) (Table I). The combination of these two differences accounts for the absence of racemization during the amination of 2-alkoxy-5(4*H*)-oxazolones in the absence of excess base. In addition, it follows that, if 2-alkoxy-5(4*H*)-oxazolones retain their configuration during aminolysis, the phenomenon of asymmetric induction should not be pertinent to the aminolysis of this type of 5(4*H*)-oxazolone. Asymmetric induction is the consequence of the equilibration of two chirally unstable 5(4*H*)-oxazolone antipodes, one of which is being consumed at a faster rate (see Section VI).

That 2-alkoxy-5(4*H*)-oxazolones are chirally stable means that the proton at position 4 resists ionization. This is also manifested by the failure of 2-alkoxy-5(4*H*)-oxazolones to react with electrophiles at position 4, as do

Table I. Relative Rates of Racemization and Ring Opening of 2-Substituted 4-Phenyl-5(4*H*)-oxazolones[a]

2-Substituent	Racemization	Ring opening
Phenyl	850	1
Methyl	21	25
Benzyloxy	1	250

[a] Racemization by diisopropylamine and ring opening by 4-bromoaniline. Calculated from the data of Jones and Witty (1979).

2-alkyl-5(4*H*)-oxazolones (Witty, 1979). This behavior is in accord with that of 2-alkoxy-5(4*H*)-thiazolones which are less reactive than 2-alkyl-5(4*H*)-thiazolones (Davies *et al.*, 1972).

5. Formation of 2-tert-Butoxy-5(4H)-oxazolones from Symmetrical Anhydrides and Tertiary Amines

2-*tert*-Butoxy-5(4*H*)-oxazolones react with the parent acid to give the symmetrical anhydride [see Eq. (11)]. In the presence of tertiary amines such as triethylamine, pyridine, or 4-dimethylaminopyridine, these symmetrical anhydrides undergo the reverse reaction, producing the 2-*tert*-butoxy-5(4*H*)-oxazolone and the amine salt of the parent acid (**20**) (Benoiton and Chen, 1981c,d) [Eq. (13)]. The reaction proceeds in chloroform or

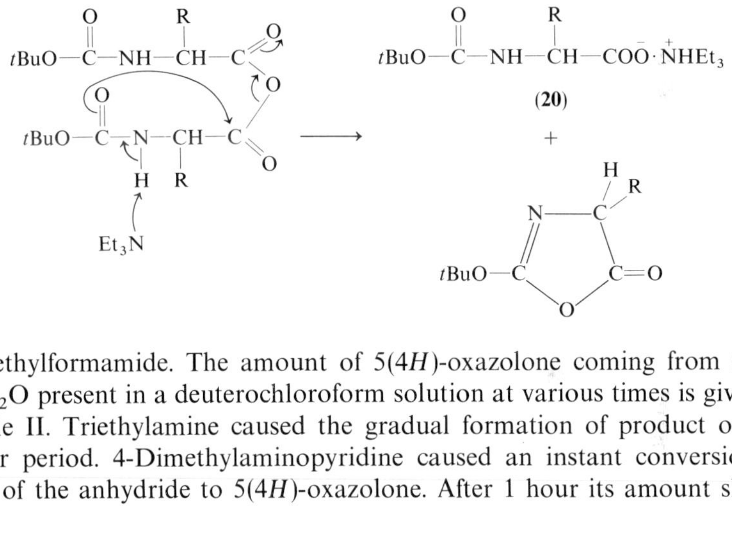

(13)

dimethylformamide. The amount of 5(4*H*)-oxazolone coming from (Boc-Val)$_2$O present in a deuterochloroform solution at various times is given in Table II. Triethylamine caused the gradual formation of product over a 24-hr period. 4-Dimethylaminopyridine caused an instant conversion of half of the anhydride to 5(4*H*)-oxazolone. After 1 hour its amount slowly

Table II. Amount of 2-*tert*-Butoxy-4-isopropyl-5(4*H*)-oxazolone Present in a Solution of *tert*-Butyloxycarbonylvaline Anhydride and an Amine Base in Deuterochloroform at Ambient Temperature at Various Times[a]

Base, 1.2 equiv	0 hr	1 hr	5 hr	25 hr
No base	0	2	7	1.5
Triethylamine	2	17	37	72
Pyridine	11	26	27	29
4-Dimethylaminopyridine	47	53	44	27

[a] From Benoiton and Chen (1981c).

decreased. The reaction seems to be general for Boc-amino acids, (Boc-Phe)$_2$O giving 100% of 5(4*H*)-oxazolone within 30 min in the presence of triethylamine. No 5(4*H*)-oxazolone could be detected after the addition of triethylamine to (Z-Val)$_2$O, but a reaction did occur.

6. *Formation of 2-Alkoxy-5(4H)-oxazolones from Symmetrical Anhydrides and Carbodiimides*

2-Alkoxy-5(4*H*)-oxazolones are also formed from symmetrical anhydrides in the presence of carbodiimides, the second product of the reaction being the *N*-acyl-*N*,*N*′-dialkylurea (Benoiton and Chen, 1981d) [Eq. (14)]. Even

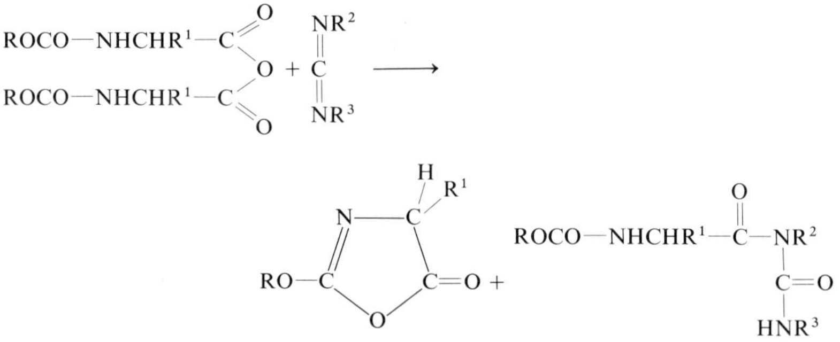

(14)

(21) (22)

though closely related studies had been effected (DeTar *et al.*, 1966) the reaction of carbodiimides with symmetrical anhydrides had not previously been described (see Rich and Singh, 1979). The basic nature of carbodiimides is known (DeTar *et al.*, 1966), so their reaction with anhydrides is consistent with the reaction of amines with anhydrides [see Eq. (13)]. Isolated yields of 65–70% have been obtained for reactions between Boc-Val-OH or Z-Val-OH and dicyclohexylcarbodiimide or diisopropylcarbodiimide (Benoiton and Chen, 1981d). The soluble carbodiimide EDC also reacts with symmetrical anhydrides to give 2-alkoxy-5(4*H*)-oxazolones, indicating that its basic property is still manifested in the presence of the trialkylammonium chloride group. To account for the reaction, F. M. F. Chen and N. L. Benoiton (unpublished) propose a mechanism involving a six-atom transition state intermediate (**23**) giving rise to the *N*,*O*-dialkylurea (**24**) followed by an intra- or extramolecular base-catalyzed cyclization accompanied by expulsion of the *N*-acylurea [Eq. (15)]. Note that this proposal explains *N*-acylurea formation without implicating the commonly held *O*-acyl → *N*-acyl transfer mechanism (see Rich and Singh, 1979).

Discovery of the reaction of symmetrical anhydrides with carbodiimides arose from a closer examination of the reaction of Boc-Val-OH with 1 equiv of DCC, which gives, after 15 min at ambient temperature, 80% anhydride,

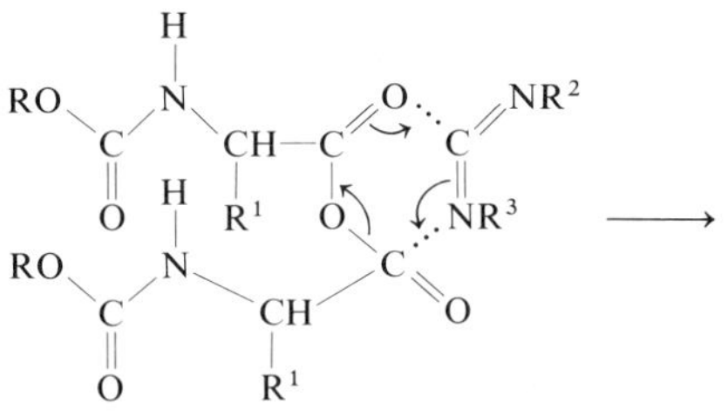

(**23**)

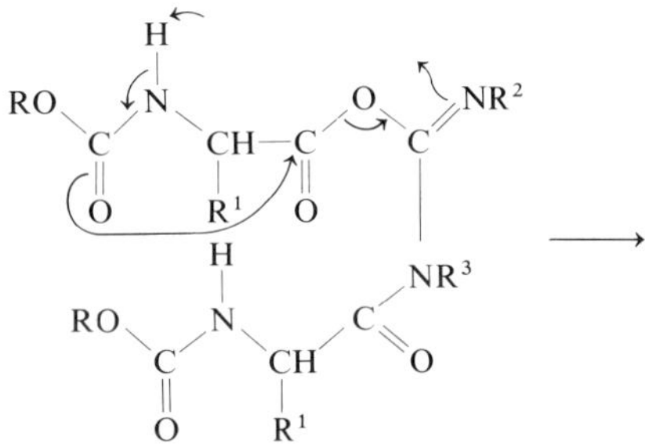

21 + **22** (15)

(**24**)

3% 5(4*H*)-oxazolone, 53% *N*,*N*′-dialkylurea, 6% *N*-acylurea, and 40% unconsumed carbodiimide (Benoiton and Chen, 1981d). This superseded the report that this reaction produced an equimolar mixture of anhydride, urea, and unconsumed carbodiimide (Benoiton and Chen, 1981b). In fact, the reaction continues over several hours, generating 38% 5(4*H*)-oxazolone and 40% *N*-acylurea at the expense of the anhydride and carbodiimide. The claim that the reaction of Z-Val-OH with diisopropylcarbodiimide gives the stable *O*-acylisourea (**25**) (Bates *et al.*, 1980) has been withdrawn (see Benoiton and Chen, 1981b).

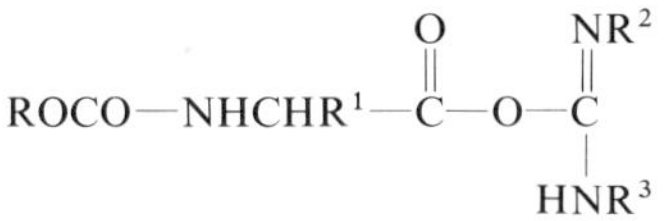

(**25**)

7. *Implication of 2-Alkoxy-5(4H)-oxazolones in Carbodiimide-Mediated Reactions in the Absence of Nitrogen Nucleophiles*

When an *N*-alkoxycarbonylamino acid is reacted with 0.5 equiv of EDC and the neutral product is isolated after 30 min, the sole product is the symmetrical anhydride [see Eq. (9)]. However, when such a reaction with Boc-Val-OH was terminated after 3 min, in addition to the anhydride (yield,

24% of theory), a 12% yield of 2-*tert*-butoxy-5(4*H*)-oxazolone was present (Benoiton and Chen, 1981a). Since the 5(4*H*)-oxazolone reacts with the parent acid [see Eq. (11)], and since it is stable for at least 30 min in the solvent used to effect the reaction, Benoiton and Chen (1981a) concluded that the 5(4*H*)-oxazolone is an intermediate in the synthesis of the anhydride, its immediate precursor being the *O*-acylisourea (**25**). The *O*-acylisourea, which remains elusive (see Section III,D,5), is recognized as the initial product of carbodiimide reactions (see Rich and Singh, 1979). Part of the *O*-acylisourea formed reacts with acid to form the anhydride, and part of it cyclizes to the 5(4*H*)-oxazolone which also reacts with acid to give the anhydride. If there is enough acid to consume the 5(4*H*)-oxazolone, it disappears. If not (i.e., if there is >0.5 equiv of carbodiimide), it accumulates, and the excess slowly reacts with the anhydride to generate 5(4*H*)-oxazolone and *N*-acylurea [see Eq. (14)]. These reactions, which occur when a carbodiimide is added to an *N*-alkoxycarbonylamino acid in chloroform or dichloromethane in the absence of a nitrogen nucleophile, are described in Schemes 1 and 2. The nature of the amino acid has some bearing on the

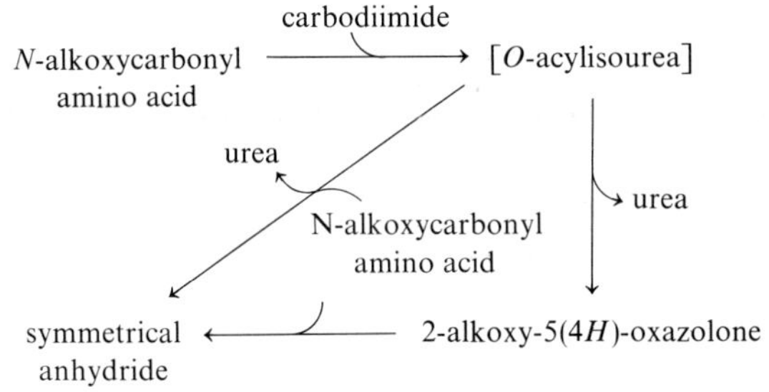

$\leq \frac{1}{2}$ equiv of carbodiimide

Scheme 1

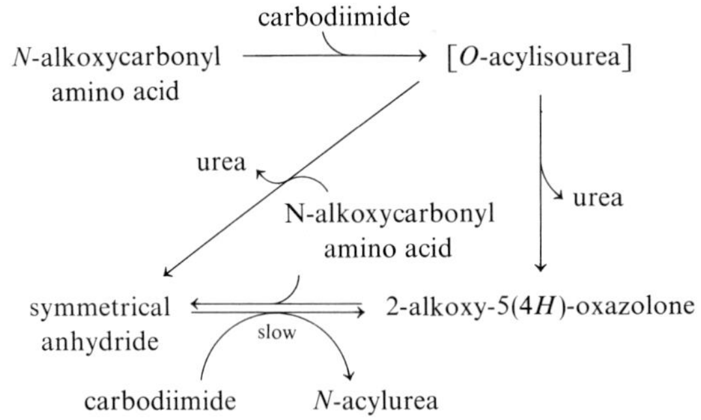

$> \frac{1}{2}$ equiv of carbodiimide

Scheme 2

course of events. More 5(4*H*)-oxazolone can be isolated from reactions beginning with valine and isoleucine derivatives (Benoiton and Chen, 1981a).

8. Implication of 2-Alkoxy-5(4H)-oxazolones in Carbodiimide-Mediated Coupling Reactions

Having succeeded in isolating 2-*tert*-butoxy-4-isopropyl- 5(4*H*)-oxazolone from a reaction mixture containing an oxygen nucleophile, Benoiton and Chen (1981a) examined normal coupling reaction mixtures for their 2-alkoxy-5(4*H*)-oxazolone content. Couplings with amino acid esters in dichloromethane were terminated after 3 mins by the addition of aqueous citric acid. 5(4*H*)-Oxazolone was obtained in 6–11% yield from reactions involving Boc-Val-OH or Boc-Ile-OH and DCC or EDC at 23°C. As the 5(4*H*)-oxazolone is known to react with amino acid esters to give the peptide, and because no 5(4*H*)-oxazolone is present in the reaction mixtures after 30 min, Benoiton and Chen (1981a) concluded that the 5(4*H*)-oxazolone must be an intermediate in the coupling reactions. Yields of $\simeq 1\%$ were obtained for the same reactions at 0°C, from the benzyloxycarbonyl derivatives, and from Boc-Leu-OH at 23°C. No 5(4*H*)-oxazolone was obtained from reactions of the latter at 0°C, but this could be due to the fact that these 5(4*H*)-oxazolones undergo aminolysis faster than they are formed. The nature of the carbodiimide had no influence on the amount of 5(4*H*)-oxazolone isolated, except that those isolated from DCC-mediated reactions were contaminated with substituted ureas.

9. Conclusions

According to a generally held tenet of peptide chemistry, *N*-alkoxycarbonylamino acids can be coupled without racemization because they do not form 5(4*H*)-oxazolones (see Kemp, 1979; Bodanszky *et al.*, 1976). It is obvious from the above discussion that 2-alkoxy-5(4*H*)-oxazolones exist, and moreover, that they are formed under some common reaction conditions of peptide synthesis. This tenet must therefore be rejected. The reason that *N*-alkoxycarbonylamino acids can be coupled without racemization is that, even if the 5(4*H*)-oxazolone is formed, it does not racemize under normal coupling conditions. However, it is important to recognize that the 5(4*H*)-oxazolone *can* racemize in the presence of a tertiary amine base. Therefore prudence dictates that extreme caution be exercised when coupling *N*-alkoxycarbonylamino acids in the presence of bases. The danger of racemization is real, and racemization has already been observed in some cases (Section IV).

The reasons put forth for the apparent reluctance of *N*-alkoxycarbonylamino acids to cyclize to the 5(4*H*)-oxazolone are the lower acidity of the

N—H group (Jones and Witty, 1979; Young, 1967) and the lower nucleophilicity of the carbonyl (Determann *et al.*, 1966) of the urethane group. Cyclization of the protected acid was considered to require an exceptionally good leaving group such as chloride at the carboxyl group (Bodanszky *et al.*, 1976; Jones and Witty, 1979) and, until the report by Jones and Witty, was considered to be accompanied by expulsion of the alkyl group, giving rise to the *N*-carboxyanhydride (Bodanszky *et al.*, 1976). Cyclization without loss of the alkyl group obviously does occur, and it occurs under conditions less forcing than previously thought. In fact, the conditions used to make 2-alkoxy-5(4*H*)-oxazolones using EDC are the same as those used to make 2-alkyl-5(4*H*)-oxazolones [see Eq. (3)] except that 0°C is used in the latter case to avoid racemization. The differences in nature between the amide and urethane groups of the two substrates are therefore of little consequence in the cyclization. A more significant difference resides in the fate of the products once formed. The 2-alkyl-5(4*H*)-oxazolone undergoes no apparent reaction with the substrate (see Section III, E), whereas the 2-alkoxy-5(4*H*)-oxazolone reacts to give the symmetrical anhydride [see Eq. (11)].

It is interesting to consider reasons why 2-alkoxy-5(4*H*)-oxazolones were not discovered until recently. The belief that they do not form, and that 5(4*H*)-oxazolones racemize readily certainly dissuaded researchers from searching for them. This was epitomized by the case of their initial discoverer (Miyoshi, 1970; see Section III,D,2) who failed to recognize that he had the 2-alkoxy-5(4*H*)-oxazolones in hand. Failure to recognize that activated forms of N-substituted amino acids such as 5(4*H*)-oxazolones and symmetrical anhydrides survive washing by aqueous solutions (see Section III,D,3) contributed to the delay, because use of this information facilitates purification of the compounds. The fact that 2-alkoxy-5(4*H*)-oxazolones are more reactive to nucleophiles than 2-alkyl-5(4*H*)-oxazolones made them less likely to be detected. Finally, the fact that the latter are the endproducts of the reaction of the parent acid with carbodiimide, whereas the 2-alkoxy-5(4*H*)-oxazolones are not, made the latter more elusive.

The fact that 2-*tert*-butoxy-5(4*H*)-oxazolones are generated by the action of tertiary amines on symmetrical anhydrides (Section D,5), combined with the fact that they racemize partially during aminolysis in the presence of these bases (Section D,4), has implications in peptide synthesis. First, it means there is a danger of racemization when symmetrical anhydrides are coupled in the presence of tertiary amines. Second, it means there is a danger of racemization when reactants that generate the symmetrical anhydride as an intermediate are coupled in the presence of tertiary amines. The danger is greater when the coupling rate is lower. Unfortunately, it is usually when a coupling rate is low that an organic base is introduced into the system to act as a catalyst. Typical examples of this are the use of the very basic 4-

dimethylaminopyridine to enhance esterification of the first residue to resin supports in peptide synthesis (Wang *et al.*, 1974; Atherton *et al.*, 1979) and to hydroxy acids in depsipeptide synthesis (Gilon *et al.*, 1979). This compound causes immediate formation of the 5(4*H*)-oxazolone from the anhydride, and racemization has indeed been observed in the former case (Benoiton *et al.*, 1981a; see Section IV). Even enhancement of coupling to a nitrogen nucleophile [Boc-Phe-OH + H-Glu(OBzl)-OCH_2-resin] caused some racemization (Wang *et al.*, 1981).

E. Do Symmetrical Anhydrides of Acylamino Acids and N-Protected Peptides Exist?

It is known that *N*-alkoxycarbonylamino acids react with 0.5 equiv of carbodiimide to give the symmetrical anhydrides (Section III,D,3) and that acylamino acids or protected dipeptides react with 1 equiv of carbodiimide to give the 2-substituted 5(4*H*)-oxazolones (Section III,B). The question arises whether two molecules of acylamino acid or protected peptide can react together to form symmetrical anhydrides. Do such compounds exist? The weight of experience suggests that they do not, but indications to the contrary appear in the literature. Both Jones (1979) and Meienhofer (1979) allude to symmetrical anhydrides of peptides in recent reviews. Albeit without giving supporting details, Arendt and Kolodziejczyk (1978) reported using the anhydride of formylphenylalanine, which was distinct from the 5(4*H*)-oxazolone, as a reference compound, and Schnabel (1965) suggested that the reaction of Z-Phe-Gly-OH with DCC gave the symmetrical anhydride. The situation has been somewhat unclear, and only now has some light been shed on the matter.

Benoiton and Chen (1982) have addressed the question directly, using the following protocol and reasoning. Model compound acids were reacted with 0.5 equiv of EDC in dichloromethane, and the yields of neutral products obtained after washing the mixtures with water and aqueous sodium bicarbonate and the amounts of methylamide and methylamine salt of the acid generated by reaction of the products with excess methylamine were determined (Scheme 3). Products produced in 50% yield that generate 1 mol of methylamide and no acid salt are 5(4*H*)-oxazolones (**26**) (path A). Products produced in 100% yield that generate $\frac{1}{2}$ mol of methylamide and $\frac{1}{2}$ mol of acid salt are symmetrical anhydrides (**27**) (path B). In practice, the yields of products were 45 or 85–90%. The amount of acid salt generated by the second reaction is a measure of the amount of symmetrical anhydride present in the products. $(Z\text{-}Val)_2O$ was used as a control. Down to 1% of symmetrical anhydride can be detected, as not more than 1% of acid salt is

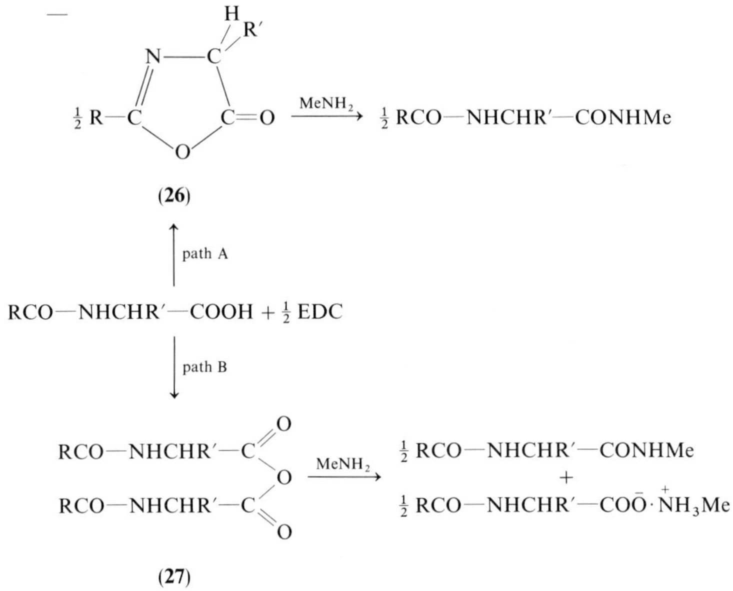

Scheme 3

generated by the hydrolysis of 5(4*H*)-oxazolones during the workup. Both pure and crude products can be examined by this method.

Based on the preparation and analysis of crude and chemically pure products, Benoiton and Chen (1982) concluded that the reaction of EDC with Z-Gly-Leu-OH, Z-Leu-Gly-OH, formylvaline, and formylphenylalanine gives exclusively the 5(4*H*)-oxazolones and that Z-Gly-Pro-OH gives the symmetrical anhydride. The 5(4*H*)-oxazolone structure for the product obtained from Z-Leu-Gly-OH is also indicated by the clear glycine α-proton singlet in the nmr spectrum, which otherwise would be replaced by a doublet. Reactions of the peptides with DCC are believed to give the same products, but the proof for the absence of anhydride in the 5(4*H*)-oxazolone products is less convincing because of the difficulties introduced by the slightly soluble ureas. But the two formylamino acids definitely do not give symmetrical anhydrides (i.e., $<1\%$) after reaction with DCC.

Independent evidence that symmetrical anhydrides of acylamino and protected peptide acids, except for N-substituted prolines, are not isolatable compounds was also provided by the results of studies on the reactions of 5(4*H*)-oxazolones with the parent acids (Benoiton and Chen, 1982). 2-Benzyloxy-4-isopropyl-5(4*H*)-oxazolone reacts with the parent acid to give the symmetrical anhydride [Eq. (16)]. However, when added to acylamino acids or protected dipeptide acids, it converts them into the 2-alkyl-5(4*H*)-oxazolones, itself picking up the water molecule to give Z-Val-OH [Eq. (17)].

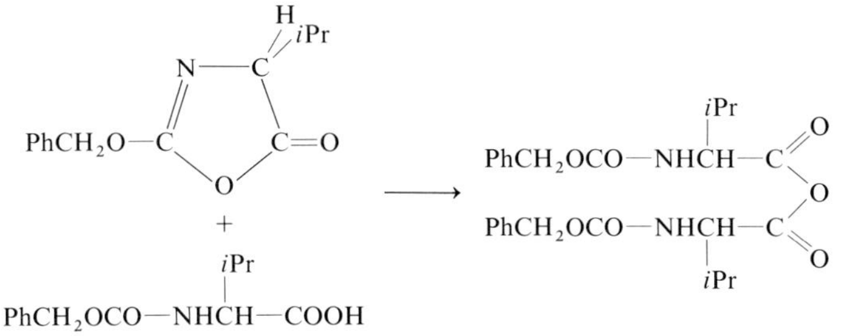

(16)

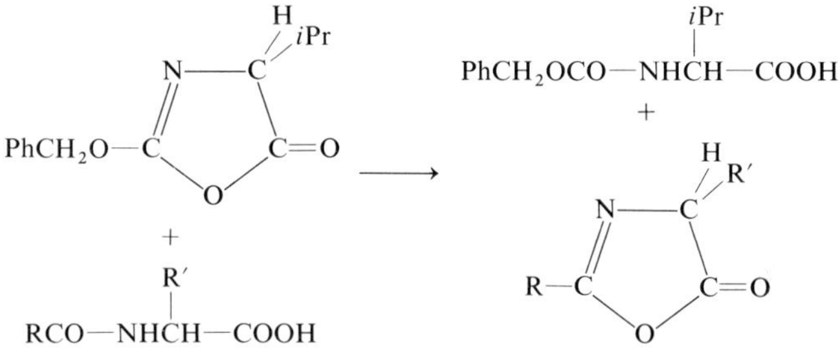

(17)

2-Phenyl-4-isopropyl-5(4*H*)-oxazolone undergoes no apparent reaction with benzoylvaline, however, when it is added to another acylamino acid or a protected dipeptide acid, an equilibrium mixture of the two 5(4*H*)-oxazolones and the two acids is obtained [Eq. (18)]. The unsymmetrical*

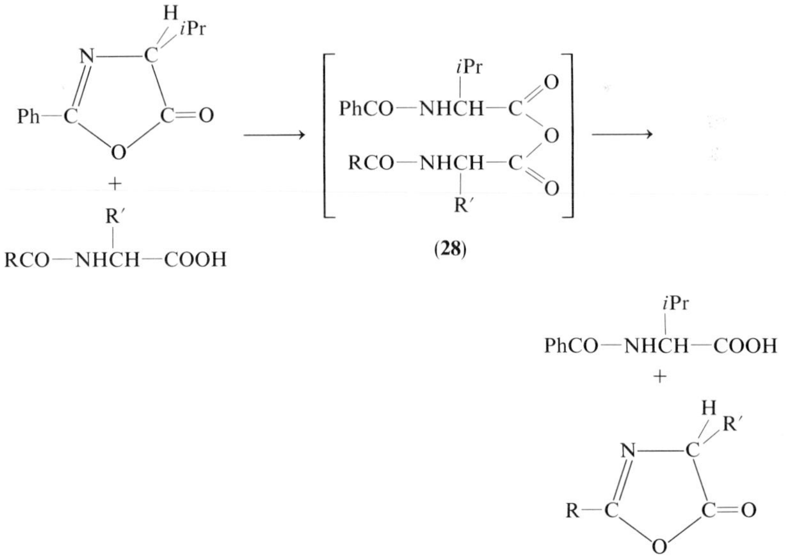

(28)

(18)

* The term "mixed anhydride" is reserved for anhydrides containing only one N-substituted amino acid moiety.

anhydride (**28**) has been postulated as the intermediate to account for the event (Benoiton and Chen, 1982). The thesis that emerges is that, if one of the components of a bis-carboxylic acid anhydride (**29**) is an acylamino acid moiety (**30**), as distinguished from an alkoxycarbonylamino acid moiety (**31**), the anhydride will immediately cyclize to the 5(4*H*)-oxazolone. Cyclization is assisted by the carbonyl of the other moiety that abstracts the N—H proton. The fate of a mixed acylamino acid–carbonic acid anhydride (**32**) is not known.* The oxygen atom adjacent to the carbonyl of the carbonic acid moiety might repress its basicity enough to stabilize the compound. When the oxygen atom is adjacent to the other carbonyl that participates in the reaction, that is, in the urethane group (**31**), it stabilizes the compound, an example being the mixed anhydride with pivalic acid (**33**) (Leplawy *et al.*, 1960). On the other hand, if the activation is through the *O*-acylisourea (**34**), the molecule still cyclizes to the 5(4*H*)-oxazolone (Section III,D,7).

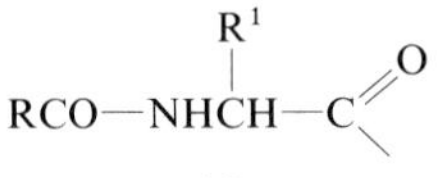

(**30**)

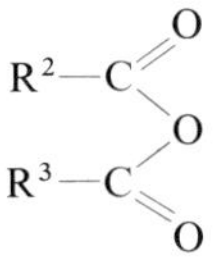

(**29**)

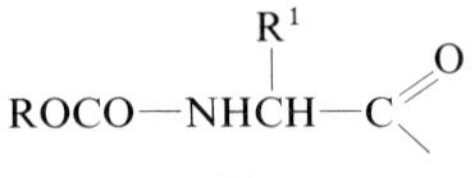

(**31**)

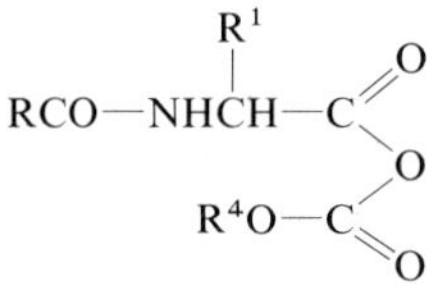

(**32**)

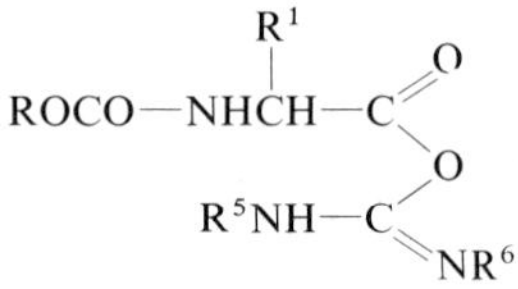

(**34**)

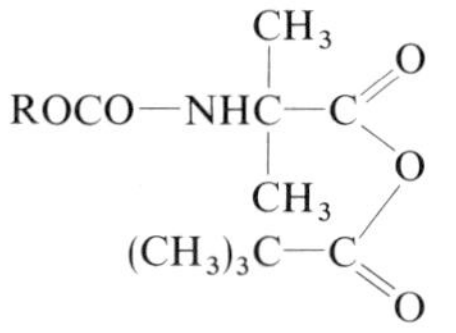

(**33**)

The 5(4*H*)-oxazolones from formylvaline and formylphenylalanine showed no apparent reaction with the parent acids, so the conclusion is that formylamino acids are not exceptions to the thesis described above.

Equation (17) provides a new method of preparing 2,4-disubstituted 5(4*H*)-oxazolones using a 2-alkoxy-5(4*H*)-oxazolone as reagent. Our group is currently exploring the possibility of using a 2-alkoxy-5(4*H*)-oxazolone as a coupling reagent.

* See note added in proof (p. 284).

IV. RACEMIZATION OF *N*-ALKOXYCARBONYLAMINO ACIDS

A. Introduction

N-Alkoxycarbonylamino acids have traditionally been the derivatives of choice for peptide synthesis because they were assumed to undergo no stereomutation during coupling. On the basis of this premise, the strategy of chain elongation by incremental addition starting from the COOH-terminus has been devised, and successful syntheses have been achieved. Until now, the absence of racemization has been explained by the inability of *N*-alkoxycarbonylamino acids to form 5(4*H*)-oxazolones (Bodanszky *et al.*, 1976; Kemp, 1979). The discovery that 2-alkoxy-5(4*H*)-oxazolones (Jones and Witty, 1977) indeed can be formed under commonly used reaction conditions (Benoiton and Chen, 1979) does not alter the basic premise, but it calls for a new interpretation of the observed results.* It is of considerable practical significance because it drew attention to the possibility that *N*-alkoxycarbonylamino acids might not resist racemization when coupled in the presence of bases, a situation that was not a rarity at the time since it was becoming popular to accelerate slow reactions of *N*-alkoxycarbonylamino acids by the addition of the very basic 4-dimethylaminopyridine. Typical examples were enhancement of the esterification of these acids to resin supports in solid-phase peptide synthesis (Wang *et al.*, 1974; Wang, 1975; Atherton *et al.*, 1979) and to hydroxy acids in depsipeptide synthesis (Gilon *et al.*, 1979).

B. Racemization of *N*-Alkoxycarbonylamino Acids during Coupling in the Presence of Bases

1. Racemization during Esterification to Resin Supports

Indeed, suspicion that racemization might have occurred during attachment of the first residue to a polymer support was evoked by the finding that the amino acid composition of an HPLC-separable minor product, which was incompletely degraded by enzymes, was apparently identical with that of the major product in syntheses of three gastrin peptides (Brown

* At first glance, the discovery appeared to be of questionable significance. At the September 1979, meeting of the Peptide and Protein Group, in Gregynog, Wales, a recognized researcher commented "this is the most exciting development reported at the meeting, but it is of no practical significance." How wrong this researcher was became apparent within a short time.

et al., 1980). The COOH-terminal phenylalanine residue had been introduced as the *tert*-butoxycarbonylamino acid symmetric anhydride in the presence of 4-dimethylaminopyridine. A systematic examination of the racemization attending the attachment of isoleucine to the 4-hydroxymethylphenoxy-acetyl–polydimethylacrylamide-resin was undertaken (Benoiton *et al.*, 1981a). According to the standard procedure (Atherton *et al.*, 1979) a solution containing an excess of the symmetrical anhydride, obtained by reaction of the acid with DCC in dichloromethane followed by filtration and evaporation of the solvent, was added to a reaction flask containing functionalized resin and 1 equiv of 4-dimethylaminopyridine in the same solvent. After a time on a rotating agitator, the resin was washed, the amino acid was liberated using 95% trifluoroacetic acid, and the *allo*-isoleucine content of the product was determined with an amino acid analyzer. About 4.5–6.5% *allo*-isoleucine was found for couplings of the *tert*-butoxycarbonyl derivative in dimethyl-acetamide, dimethylformamide, and dichloromethane, and for couplings of the benzyloxycarbonyl and 9-fluorenylmethyloxycarbonyl derivatives in dimethylacetamide. A critical factor contributing to the racemization was the time of contact between the anhydride and the base, a 5-min incubation of the two before mixing with the resin, raising the *allo*-isoleucine level to 20%. Racemization could be halved by adding the 4-dimethylaminopyridine to the resin *after* the anhydride and reduced further to 3.0–3.5% by using a catalytic amount (0.1 equiv) of the base supplemented with 1 equiv of *N*-methylmorpholine, a tactic suggested in the original paper on 4-dimethyl-aminopyridine (Steglich and Höfle, 1969). Under the original conditions (Atherton *et al.*, 1979), alanine, phenylalanine, and valine also showed 7.5–10.5% racemization when attached to the polymer as their 9-fluorenyl-methyloxycarbonyl derivatives, whereas leucine showed 3.5% racemization (N. L. Benoiton, E. Atherton, and R. C. Sheppard, unpublished). The enantiomers were determined as their NH_2-terminal lysyl dipeptides (Benoiton *et al.*, 1979c; see Section II,A,2). Benoiton *et al.* (1981a) concluded that slight racemization at the COOH-terminal amino acid residue is of no consequence when the single resulting diastereomer may be separated from the desired optically pure product, but clearly the absence of any diastereo-meric peptide is the preferred objective. No stereochemical change occurred during esterification of hydroxymethylphenyl-polymers using *tert*-butyloxy-carbonylisoleucine 4-nitrophenyl ester in the presence of imidazole (Bodan-szky and Fagan, 1977; Benoiton *et al.*, 1981a) or 4-dimethylaminopyridine (Benoiton *et al.*, 1981a). However, the latter did cause some racemization (3.0–5.0%, Benoiton *et al.*, 1981a; 1.2–1.7%, Wang *et al.*, 1981) when used to catalyze the reaction of Boc-Ile-OH and DCC (Wang *et al.*, 1974) with hydroxymethylphenyl-polymer. On the other hand, *tert*-butyloxycarbonyl-*O*-benzylthreonine retained its stereochemistry when coupled under the same conditions (Wang *et al.*, 1981). The latter is probably exceptionally resistant to racemization. The evidence suggests that some racemization is likely to accompany the esterification of *N*-alkoxycarbonylamino acids to hydroxymethyl-resin supports if the reaction is enhanced by 4-dimethylaminopyridine unless activation is through a conventional activated ester.

2. Racemization during Peptide Bond Formation

It has become popular to enhance difficult couplings of *N*-alkoxycarbonylamino acids by adding 4-dimethylaminopyridine (Steglich and Höfle, 1969) as a catalyst (Section IV,A). The second component in the reaction has been a hydroxy group. However, couplings with amino groups are also sometimes slow if hindered residues are involved. Wang *et al.* (1981) have examined the use of 4-dimethylaminopyridine to enhance difficult peptide bond-forming reactions in solid-phase synthesis. On the basis of synthesis of a model heptapeptide-resin, they concluded that of four coupling methods examined, which included DCC, DCC plus 1-hydroxybenzotriazole, and symmetrical anhydrides, only DCC plus 4-dimethylaminopyridine (3 equiv each) gave the desired near quantitative couplings in cycles involving sterically hindered amino acids. No racemization was detectable for a coupling of Boc-Ile-OH with valyloxymethyl-resin or for a synthesis of leucyl-alanyl-glycyl-valine from the valyloxymethyl-resin using this procedure. However, significant racemization, 7% in dichloromethane and 11.5% in dimethylformamide, was observed for couplings of Boc-Phe-OH with γ-benzylglutamyloxymethyl resin. In another coupling variation, which was successful in achieving high coupling efficiency, reaction of the symmetrical anhydride in the presence of 0.6 equiv of 4-dimethylaminopyridine showed 8% racemization. Premixing the anhydride and the base for 2 min led to a startling 36% racemization. It is clear that base-catalyzed racemization of activated *tert*-butyloxycarbonylamino acids by 4-dimethylaminopyridine can occur under certain coupling conditions. Phenylalanine seems to be an unusually susceptible residue, but more data will be required before firm conclusions can be drawn.

3. Conclusion

In some cases, when symmetrical anhydrides of *N*-alkoxycarbonylamino acids are coupled in the presence of 4-dimethylaminopyridine, racemization of the activated residue occurs (Benoiton *et al.*, 1981a; Wang *et al.*, 1981). The extent of racemization, which is independent of the nature of the N-protecting group, depends on the amount of base and time of contact with the base before the coupling reaction. It is known that bases such as triethylamine and 4-dimethylaminopyridine generate 2-alkoxy-5(4*H*)-oxazolones from *tert*-butyloxycarbonylamino acid anhydrides, the amount increasing with time (Benoiton and Chen, 1981d). It is also known that 2-alkoxy-5(4*H*)-oxazolones racemize when aminolyzed in the presence of triethylamine (Benoiton and Chen, 1981a). It is therefore logical to conclude that the racemization that accompanies the coupling of *N*-alkoxycarbonylamino acids in the presence of 4-dimethylaminopyridine occurs through the formation and racemization of the 2-alkoxy-5(4*H*)-oxazolone. The 5(4*H*)-oxazolone provides an explanation for the racemization, and the racemization provides evidence that the 5(4*H*)-oxazolone is implicated as an intermediate in the reaction. It must be pointed out, however, that the possibility that some of the racemization arises from enolization is not rigorously excluded by the argument.

Racemization has also been observed for the carbodiimide-mediated reaction of Boc-Ile-OH with hydroxymethyl resin in the presence of 4-dimethylaminopyridine (Benoiton *et al.*, 1981a; Wang *et al.*, 1981). The *O*-acylisourea is the activated species in carbodiimide-mediated reactions, but the symmetrical anhydride is a second and probably the predominating active form in solid-phase synthesis (see Rich and Singh, 1979). It follows that the racemization observed in this case can be accounted for by the same mechanism, formation of the 2-*tert*-butoxy-5(4*H*)-oxazolone from the anhydride (Benoiton and Chen, 1981d) or directly from the *O*-acylisourea (Benoiton and Chen, 1981a). Again, the racemization observed provides supportive evidence for the intermediary of the 2-alkoxy-5(4*H*)-oxazolones in carbodiimide-mediated reactions (Benoiton and Chen, 1981a).

4-Dimethylaminopyridine is so far the only base shown to cause racemization of *N*-alkoxycarbonylamino acids. It can be expected that weaker bases might also have deleterious effects in some cases. Prudence dictates that careful monitoring is in order if any base is used to enhance reactions of *N*-alkoxycarbonylamino acids. The situation remains unchanged for couplings of *N*-alkoxycarbonylamino acids in the absence of a tertiary amine or another base.

C. Racemization of N^{α}-Protected Histidine

There is one exception to the tenet that *N*-alkoxycarbonylamino acids do not racemize when coupled in the absence of bases. Even when bearing a stable side-chain protecting group, and in particular during solid-phase synthesis, histidine undergoes considerable racemization under circumstances when other residues are unaffected (see Kemp, 1979). When coupled using various reagents, Boc-His(Bzl)-OH underwent 20–50% racemization during reaction with resin-bound γ-benzyl glutamate (Windridge and Jorgensen, 1971b). Racemization could be reduced to $<0.2\%$ using DCC in the presence of *N*-hydroxysuccinimide (Windridge and Jorgensen, 1971b) or

1-hydroxybenzotriazole (Windridge and Jorgensen, 1971a). The racemizing effects of benzylimidazole and imidazole are documented and can be attributed to their basicity (see Kemp, 1979). Veber (1975) considered possible mechanisms to account for the racemization of COOH-terminal histidine and suggested that an N(π)-substituted derivative would be the least susceptible to racemization. It has been recognized that the location of the side-chain substituent in histidine derivatives has not been defined and that most substituents are probably in the N(τ)-position (see Veber, 1975). The validity of the thesis that π-substituted derivatives racemize the least has now been confirmed by the group of Jones (Jones and Ramage, 1978; Fletcher *et al.*, 1979) who examined the tendency of N(π)- and N(τ)-derivatives to racemize. When **35** and **36** were preincubated with DCC in dimethylformamide at 0°C for 1 hr and then added to proline amide, the N(π)-derivative underwent no racemization (<2% D), whereas the N(τ)-derivative gave 35% D-isomer.

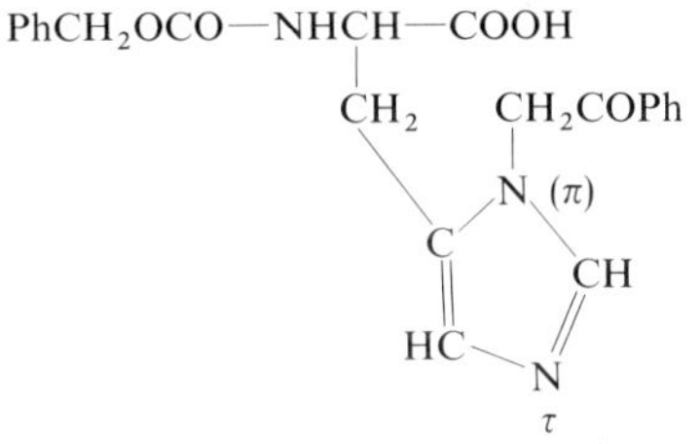

(35)

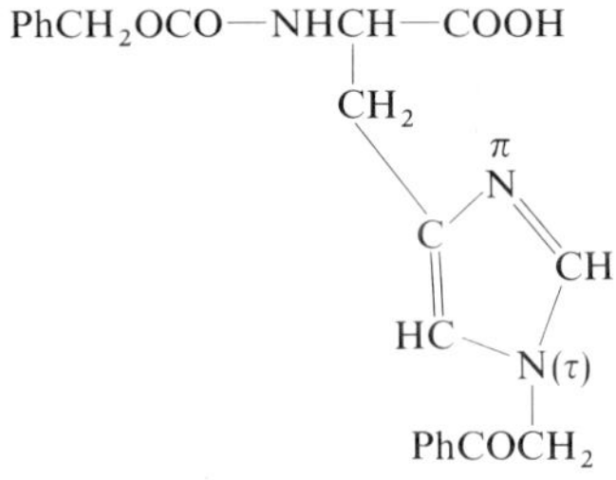

(36)

And on the basis of the relationship between the degree of racemization and the preactivation time, Jones *et al.* (1980) concluded that the racemization of *N*(τ)-substituted derivatives is the result of an intramolecular process whereby the α-proton of the *O*-acylisourea intermediate (**25**), which is in equilibrium with the substrate and the carbodiimide, is abstracted by the π-nitrogen [Eq. (19)]. Thus racemization of *N*-alkoxycarbonylhistidine

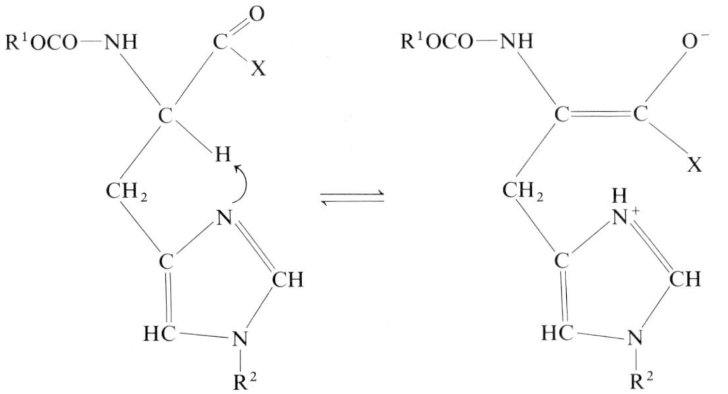

(19)

Table III. Racemization during Saponification of Esters

Substrate	Racemization	Alkali	Reference
Z-Gly-Cys(Bzl)-OEt	74	1 equiv *N* NaOH–EtOH	Maclaren (1958)
Z-Cys(Bzl)-Gly-OEt	Nil	1 equiv *N* NaOH–EtOH	Maclaren (1958)
Z-Cys(Trt)-Gly-OMe	Some	Unspecified	Schlingloff (1976)
Z-Ala-Pro-OMe	<0.2	1.1 equiv NaOH–MeOH	McDermott and Benoiton (1973b)
Z-Ala-Leu-OMe	<0.2	1.1 equiv NaOH–MeOH	McDermott and Benoiton (1973b)
Z-Ala-MeLeu-OMe	22.2	2 equiv 4 *N* NaOH–MeOH	McDermott and Benoiton (1973b)
Z-Leu-Ala-OMe	0.8	1 equiv 0.25 *N* NaOH–acetone	Kenner and Seely (1972)
Z-Ala-Phe-OMe	2.8	1 equiv 0.25 *N* NaOH–acetone	Kenner and Seely (1972)
Boc-Gly-Phe-OMe	16	Unspecified	Rapacka *et al.* (1976)
Z-Pro-Gly-Phe-OMe	Nil	Unspecified	Rapacka *et al.* (1976)
Boc-Leu-Val-OMe	0.4	2 equiv *N* NaOH–*t*BuOH	Rapacka *et al.* (1976)

can be effectively eliminated by protection of the imidazole ring at the N(π)-position. For practical reasons, N^{α}-*tert*-butoxycarbonyl-$N^{im(\pi)}$-benzyloxymethyl-L-histidine is proposed as the compound of choice for synthetic work (Brown and Jones, 1981). The side-chain protecting group can be cleaved by catalytic hydrogenation or acidolysis using hydrogen bromide in trifluoroacetic acid.

V. RACEMIZATION DURING THE SAPONIFICATION OF ESTERS

It has been known since the work of Maclaren (1958) on dipeptides containing *S*-benzylcysteine and glycine that racemization may accompany the saponification of peptide esters. A peptide ester with *S*-benzylcysteine (Maclaren, 1958) or an *N*-methylamino acid (McDermott and Benoiton, 1973b) at the COOH-terminus is likely to be substantially epimerized during saponification. However, this is the extent to which generalizations can be made with confidence. The limited data on the subject are compiled in Table III. Note the confusion introduced by the apparently conflicting results of Rapaka *et al.* (1976) who found a marked difference in the chiral stabilities of a dipeptide and a tripeptide with identical COOH-terminal residues. A systematic study defining the conditions and circumstances under which a stereomutation does or does not occur during saponification would be very valuable.

VI. RACEMIZATION AND ASYMMETRIC INDUCTION DURING THE AMINOLYSIS OF 2,4-DIALKYL-5(4*H*)-OXAZOLONES

A. Introduction

As illustrated in Scheme 4, during reaction of an activated acylamino acid with an amino acid ester to give a peptide (k_1), 5(4*H*)-oxazolone may be formed (k_2) as a side product. The optically active 5(4*H*)-oxazolone, which is an activated form of the residue, can also combine with the amine component to give the peptide (k'_3). However, in the presence of the basic amino group with which it reacts, the 5(4*H*)-oxazolone tautomerizes to the achiral form (k_4), which is in equilibrium (k_{-4}) with the two optically active forms. Subsequent aminolysis (k_3, k_5) gives the peptide containing the two configurations of the activated residue. For discussion purposes, it is convenient to separate the two aminolysis reactions, before and after tautomerization, of the (*S*)-5(4*H*)-oxazolone, bearing in mind that $k_3 = k'_3$.

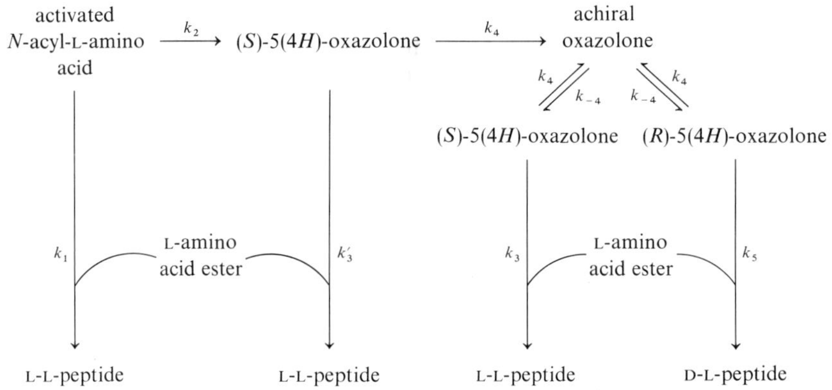

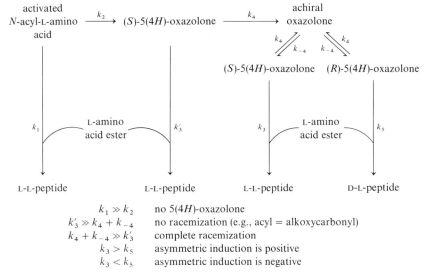

$k_1 \gg k_2$	no 5(4*H*)-oxazolone
$k'_3 \gg k_4 + k_{-4}$	no racemization (e.g., acyl = alkoxycarbonyl)
$k_4 + k_{-4} \gg k'_3$	complete racemization
$k_3 > k_5$	asymmetric induction is positive
$k_3 < k_5$	asymmetric induction is negative

Scheme 4

The ratio k_4/k'_3 determines the extent of racemization. Since the work of Goodman and Levine (1964), it is generally considered that $k_4 + k_{-4} \gg k'_3$, and thus that a 2-alkyl-5(4*H*)-oxazolone racemizes severely if not completely before it is aminolyzed. This raises the question whether or not any peptide is actually formed from the 5(4*H*)-oxazolone before it is racemized. The answer is yes in some cases. For example, (*S*)-2-phenyl-4-isobutyl-5(4*H*)-oxazolone reacts with aniline to give a product that is only 50% racemized (N. L. Benoiton and F. M. F. Chen, unpublished). Here half of the peptide is formed directly from the starting 5(4*H*)-oxazolone. The remaining 5(4*H*)-oxazolone generates equal amounts of enantiomeric products.

The relative amounts of products derived from the tautomerized 5(4*H*)-oxazolone are determined by the ratio k_3/k_5. In the above case $k_3 = k_5$, because the attacking amine is not a chiral molecule. In Scheme 4, because the amino acid ester is chiral, $k_3 \neq k_5$, and because the 5(4*H*)-oxazolone antipodes are in equilibrium through their achiral form, the epimeric peptides are formed in unequal amounts. This process is known as asymmetric induction and was first recognized in peptide chemistry by Weygand *et al.* (1966d). A prerequisite for asymmetric induction is a chirally unstable (or a prochiral) reactant. 2-Alkoxy-5(4*H*)-oxazolones are chirally stable (Section III,D,4), therefore the phenomenon of asymmetric induction is not pertinent to the aminolysis of these compounds.

When $k_3 > k_5$ (Scheme 4), more LL-isomer is formed than in the absence of induction. The diastereomer with residues of identical chirality is the "positive" isomer (Ugi, 1965), so the induction is positive. When $k_3 < k_5$, more D-L- or "negative" isomer is formed, and the induction is negative. The amount of asymmetric induction can be expressed in terms of the excess of predominating isomer, referred to as the diastereomeric excess (d.e.) (Benoiton *et al.*, 1981c). The term "epimeric excess" is not used to avoid confusion with "enantiomeric excess" (e.e.). For a mixture of 60% D-L- and 40% L-L-isomers, $\text{d.e.}_{(\text{D-L})} = 60 - 40 = 20\%$. Asymmetric induction can be examined experimentally by determining the products of the reaction of an amino acid ester with a racemic 2-alkyl-5(4*H*)-oxazolone (Weygand *et al.*, 1966d; Benoiton *et al.*, 1981c). The use of available ligand constants (Ugi, 1965) plus the quotient %L-L/%D-L (k_3/k_5) determined for one amino acid ester allows one to calculate the quotient for a different residue (see Weygand *et al.*, 1966d).

Asymmetric induction is implicated whenever racemization accompanies the coupling of two chiral residues, and it has a bearing on the change in configuration actually observed. If the induction is negative, it corresponds to additional racemization if two residues of identical chirality are involved. If it is positive, it corresponds to a diminution of racemization, or deracemization. So the racemization observed is really the sum of the true racemization and the stereomutation due to induction, which equals the d.e.:

$$\text{rac}_{\text{obs}}\ (\%) = \text{rac}_{\text{true}}\ (\%) + \text{d.e.}\ (\%)$$

When the induction is negative, d.e. has a positive value; when the induction is positive, d.e. has a negative value. Alternatively, this can be expressed by saying that the percentage of epimer obtained in any reaction is equal to the sum of the percentage of epimer produced by the racemization and the d.e. Most if not all of the data on racemization reported in the literature for reactions involving two chiral residues are for observed racemization. Only when d.e. = 0 is the racemization observed equal to the true extent of racemization that occurred in any particular case.

B. Variables Affecting Asymmetric Induction

Experimental data on asymmetric induction are far from plentiful, so our discussion must be based on limited data. There are two aspects of induction to consider, namely, its extent and its direction. Both can be affected by solvent polarity and temperature (Benoiton *et al.*, 1981c), so these are addressed first. For the two cases examined (Table IV), at room temperature the direction of induction was opposite depending on whether the solvent was polar or apolar. In polar solvents it was positive (excess L-L-isomer);

Table IV. Effect of Solvent, Temperature, and 2-Substituent on Asymmetric Induction in the Aminolysis of (*R*, *S*)-2,4-Dialkyl-5(4*H*)-oxazolones (**37**)[a]

		Diastereomeric excess (%)			
		5(4*H*)-Oxazolone from			
		Bz-DLLeu-OH[b]		Z-Gly-DLLeu-OH[c]	
Solvent	Temperature (°C)	L-L	D-L	L-L	D-L
Tetrahydrofuran	23		30		12
Dichloromethane	35		28		
Dichloromethane	23		24		2
Dichloromethane	5		18	6	
Dichloromethane	−10	12			
Dimethylformamide	35	22		10	
Dimethylformamide	23	36		16	
Dimethylformamide	5	54		28	
Dimethyl sulfoxide	23	32		20	

[a] From Benoiton *et al.* (1981c).
[b] Reacting with H-Lys(Z)-OMe.
[c] Reacting with H-Lys(Z)-OBzl.

in apolar solvents, it was negative (excess D-L-isomer). However, in dichloromethane the direction was reversed to positive by lowering the temperature. This effect of a lower temperature favoring formation of the L-L-isomer was observed also in dimethylformamide, so it is probably a general phenomenon. It is well known that the degree of racemization in a coupling is diminished by lowering the temperature (see Kemp, 1979). It follows that one of the reasons for this is that the lower temperature reduces the amount of D-L-isomer generated by reaction of the amine with the racemized 5(4*H*)-oxazolone (Benoiton *et al.*, 1981c). It would be interesting to see if less racemization might be observed at 23 than at 0°C for a coupling between residues of opposite chirality. If the pronounced solvent effect is a general phenomenon, it means that for coupling reactions carried out in dichloromethane the observed racemization is less than the true racemization. Similarly, the racemization observed for couplings in dimethylformamide is greater than the true racemization.

There are four internal variables, R^1 and R^2 of the 5(4*H*)-oxazolone (**37**) and R^3 and R^4 of the amino acid nucleophile (**38**), that can have an influence on the extent of asymmetric induction. The contribution, if any, of R^4 is not known. The influence of R^2 seems to be minimal, typical data (Table V) showing a difference in d.e. of only 8% among four residues examined. The nature of R^1 has a drastic effect on the induction (Tables IV and V), being

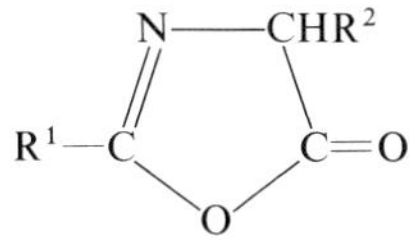

(37)

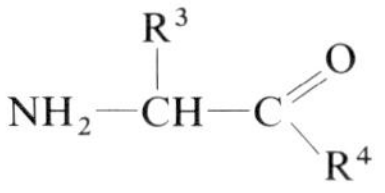

(38)

Table V. Effect of Internal Variables on the Aminolysis of (*R*, *S*)-2,4-Dialkyl-5(4*H*)-oxazolones (**37**)[a]

5(4*H*)-Oxazolone from R^1CO-Val-OH reacting with H-Val-OMe[b]		5(4*H*)-Oxazolone from Bz-NHCHR^2-COOH reacting with H-Lys(Z)-OMe[c]		5(4*H*)-Oxazolone from Bz-Val-OH reacting with NH_2-CHR^3-COOMe[b]	
R^1	d.e.[d]	R^2	d.e.	R^3	d.e.
Ph	67	CH_2Ph	30	*i*Pr	67
CH_2NHZ	35	*i*Bu	30	*i*Bu	57
Me	22	*i*Pr	28	CH_2Ph	49
CF_3[e]	40	Me	22	Me	22
				CH_2COOMe	0

[a] % d.e.$_{(\text{D-L})}$ = % D-L − % L-L, in tetrahydrofuran at room temperature.
[b] Steglich *et al.* (1967).
[c] N. L. Benoiton, K. Kuroda, and F. M. Chen, unpublished.
[d] d.e., Diastereomeric excess.
[e] 5(2*H*)-Oxazolone.

greater when it originates from a benzoylamino acid, less from benzyloxycarbonylglycine, and least from an acetylamino acid. 5(2*H*)-Oxazolones from trifluoroacetylamino acids under the same conditions generate the opposite or positive isomer (L-L) in excess. The effect of branching at the α-carbon atom of R^1 (influence of the nature of the residue adjacent to the activated residue in a coupling) is not known. The greatest effect on induction in the synthesis of peptides is probably contributed by the side-chain R^3 of the amine (Table V), the d.e. ranging from 67 to 0% for the reaction of 2-phenyl-4-isopropyl-5(4*H*)-oxazolone with various amino acid methyl esters in the order valine > leucine > phenylalanine > alanine > β-methyl aspartate. The peculiar result with the dicarboxylic acid makes it impossible to generalize at present. Furthermore, it must be remembered that the data are for one solvent only. Related to the effects of R^3 are the results of Tomida *et al.* (1976) showing that, in the aminolysis of 2-trifluoromethyl-5(2*H*)-oxazolones, in contrast to the other amino acid esters that generated the positive isomer in excess, proline methyl ester produced more negative isomer.

VII. VARIABLES AFFECTING α-INVERSION DURING COUPLING

When racemization accompanies peptide bond formation, the stereomutation produced as a result of 5(4*H*)-oxazolone formation is dictated by the values of the rate constants k_1, the rate of coupling of the activated residue; k_2, the rate of its conversion to 5(4*H*)-oxazolone; k'_3, the rate of aminolysis of the unracemized 5(4*H*)-oxazolone; $k_4 + k_{-4}$, the rates of tautomerism of the 5(4*H*)-oxazolone to and from its achiral form; and the ratio k_3/k_5, the ratio of the rates of aminolysis of the two 5(4*H*)-oxazolone antipodes (Scheme 4, $k'_3 = k_3$). Constants k_1 and k_2 depend on the type of activation; k_1, k_3, and k_5 depend on the configurations of the residues involved in the coupling; and all five constants depend to a greater or lesser extent on the temperature, the solvent polarity, and the nature of the side chains of the activated residue Xxx, the penultimate residue Www, and the aminolyzing residue Yyy for a coupling of Www-Xxx-OH with H-Yyy. How the kinetic constants are affected by a change in any one of these variables is a complex issue. Peptide chemistry has yet to develop to the stage where this question can be discussed intelligently. Data on the influence of the nature of Xxx on the coupling rate k_1 and the racemization rate, which incorporates k_2 and $k_4 + k_{-4}$, have been collected, and the potential of using these data for predicting relative extents of racemization has been discussed (Kovacs, 1980). But in the main we have only been able to observe the influence of the variables on the final outcome of a coupling reaction. And even here, information on the influence of the structural variables or the sequence dependence of racemization is not plentiful. This section addresses this question based on the available data which are mostly observed racemization data.

A. Internal Factors

1. Side Chain of the Activated Residue

The most notable development to emerge since the previous review (Kemp, 1979) is that the order of sensitivity to racemization of activated residues can vary depending on whether the solvent is polar or less polar and that the difference between any two residues can depend on the method of coupling (Benoiton *et al.*, 1979b; Benoiton and Kuroda, 1981). Conclusions are based on numerous reactions of benzoylamino acids and benzyloxycarbonylglycyl dipeptides that were coupled using carbodiimides with and without additives, and *N*-ethyl-5-phenylisoxazolium-3′-sulfonate. The main generalization to be made is that, in polar solvents such as dimethylformamide, the hindered residues valine and isoleucine racemize more (3 to 10 times) than the unhindered residues alanine, leucine, and phenylalanine. In dichloromethane, the situation is the opposite, with valine and isoleucine being the least susceptible to racemization. Phenylalanine racemizes more than alanine and leucine in most cases. The difference between isoleucine and valine is marginal, or the former racemizes more. The difference between alanine and leucine was unclear, but subsequent work (R. Steinauer, F. M. F. Chen, and N. L. Benoiton, unpublished) favored leucine as the more resistant of the two to racemization. In summary, Benoiton *et al.* found the order Ile $\geq$ Val $>$ Phe $>$ Ala $\geq$ Leu in polar solvents, and Phe $>$ Ala $>$ Leu $>$ Ile $>$ Val in apolar solvents. Their conclusion for apolar solvents is based on fewer data because, in these solvents, racemization is completely suppressed by the additives. Their conclusion for polar solvents is corroborated by the work of Le Nguyen *et al.* (1981) who found the order Ile $>$ Val $\gg$ Phe $>$ Ala $>$ Leu for couplings of protected dipeptides using benzotriazolyloxytris(dimethylamino)phosphonium hexafluorophosphate in dimethylformamide. The higher sensitivity of the hindered residues has not been confirmed by any work with longer segments, the only data pertinent to this discussion being the results from work on human insulin where, albeit for couplings with different nucleophiles, activated *O-tert*-butyltyrosine underwent three times as much racemization as leucine (Riniker *et al.*, 1979); Sieber *et al.*, 1977).

The order in apolar solvents generally held also for couplings by the acyl azide method, phenylalanine showing the most and valine and isoleucine the least racemization (Benoiton *et al.*, 1982). Previous work had shown four times as much racemization for phenylalanine as for leucine for similar couplings of hexapeptides (Sieber and Riniker, 1973). But there is one apparent discrepancy in the results for racemization in apolar solvents. Tomida *et al.* (1973) reported the order Ile $>$ Val $\gg$ Ala for DCC-mediated couplings of Z-Pro-Xxx-OH with a proline ester in tetrahydrofuran.

The racemization for couplings of 9-fluorenylmethyloxycarbonylamino acid anhydrides with the hydroxymethyl group of a polymer in dimethylformamide in the presence of 1 equiv of 4-dimethylaminopyridine according to Atherton *et al.* (1979) (see Section IV,B) was 10% for alanine and valine, 7.5% for phenylalanine, and 3.5% for leucine (N. L. Benoiton, E. Atherton, and R. C. Sheppard, unpublished). This follows the order for normal couplings except for alanine. A similar anomaly was found for alanine during the preparation of hydrazides from 5(4*H*)-oxazolones. For the usual five residues, only the hydrazide from Z-Gly-Ala-OH could not be obtained stereochemically pure (Benoiton *et al.*, 1982). On the other hand, alanine behaved normally during acyl azide couplings (Benoiton *et al.*, 1982), a result that contradicts the previous claim by Mitin and Maksimov (1973) that alanine racemizes during hydrazinolysis.

With respect to our attempts to identify the residues that are least sensitive to racemization, an observation in the work of Kitada and Fujino (1978) may be significant. They found *O*-unprotected threonine to be unusually chirally stable, DCC-mediated reactions of Z-Asp(O*t*Bu)-Thr-OH with several dipeptide esters yielding not more than 3.5% racemization which is considerably less than is usually encountered. Even an *O*-protected threonine derivative was stable in other work, Bpoc-Thr(Bzl)-OH undergoing no racemization during esterification in the presence of 4-dimethylamino-pyridine (Wang *et al.*, 1981). Devoting further attention to the chiral lability of activated threonine is certainly in order.

On the basis of experience and theoretical consideration, namely, that acylproline cannot form 5(4*H*)-oxazolone by the base-catalyzed mechanism (see Kemp, 1979), proline is the residue least likely to racemize during peptide synthesis. Two cases of partial racemization of acylproline derivatives under unusual circumstances have been recorded (See Kemp, 1979). Racemization of proline under normal reaction conditions has now been reported for the coupling of Z-Aib-Pro-OH with H-Aib-Ala-OMe (Nagaraj and Balaram, 1981). The conclusion was based on the presence of two sets of quartets corresponding to the benzyl methylene protons in the 100-MHz nmr spectrum of the protected tetrapeptide acids, combined with the fact that the addition of *N*-hydroxysuccinimide to a carbodiimide-mediated reaction eliminated the signal for the D-isomer. It is proposed that the methyl groups of the adjacent aminoisobutyryl residue stabilize and favor formation of the positively charged 5(4*H*)-oxazolone, thus rendering the C-4 proton labile [Eq. (20)]. Evidence for the intermediacy of such a charged

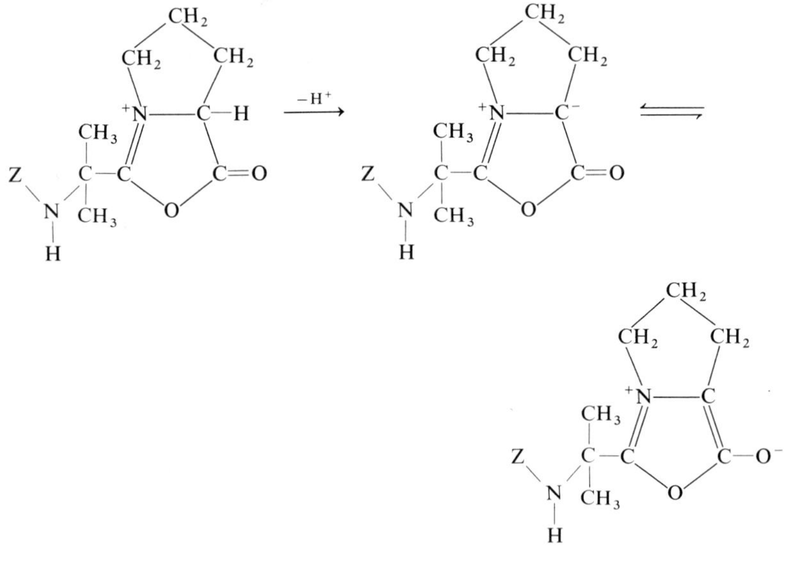

(20)

5(4*H*)-oxazolone in the activation of *N*-methylamino acids exists (McDermott and Benoiton, 1973c). Confirmation by an independent method of the phenomenon reported by Nagaraj and Balaram (1981) is awaited with interest.

In a discussion of the tendency of activated residues to racemize, glycine is excluded because it is not chiral. However, there is one pertinent implication of using glycine as the activated residue in a coupling. Racemization can also occur at the residue adjacent to the activated residue (see Kemp, 1979, and Section VII,A,3), and it transpires that more occurs when the activated residue has no side chain (Dzieduszycka *et al.*, 1979). So couplings at glycine may not be as safe with respect to the preservation of stereochemistry as is generally believed.

The finding that activated valine and isoleucine racemize more readily than other difunctional amino acids in polar solvents and less readily in apolar solvents, and that phenylalanine racemizes more readily than leucine and alanine in both types of solvents, invites attempts to rationalize. Available evidence indicates that the answer cannot be found in the side chain and solvent effects related to asymmetric induction (Section VI,B). It must therefore lie in the mechanisms of racemization, enolization, and 5(4*H*)-oxazolone formation, either one or both of which are operative in any given situation (Section III,A). Experience reveals that bulky or hindered side chains favor cyclization such as 5(4*H*)-oxazolone formation more than less bulky side chains. On the other hand, direct α-proton abstraction or enolization is promoted by electron-withdrawing side chains. The phenyl group of phenylalanine is both bulky and electron-withdrawing. Phenylalanine racemizes more readily than other residues when coupled in apolar solvents, and also when coupled by the acyl azide method, a method for which it is known that part of the racemization originates from enolization (see Kemp, 1979). It is therefore proposed that, in polar solvents that facilitate charge separation, the side-chain effect of promoting cyclization manifests itself more, that is, the 5(4*H*)-oxazolone mechanism predominates, whereas in apolar solvents, the electronic effect, and consequently enolization, plays a more significant role.

2. *N*-Substituent on the Activated Residue

The racemization-promoting effect of *N*-acyl or *N*-peptidyl (protected aminoacyl) substituents on an activated residue is in the order benzoyl > acetyl > Z-Gly-Gly-OH > Z-Gly-OH > formyl (Weinstein, 1970). This conclusion is corroborated by the results of Heard and Young (1963) (benzoyl > acetyl > formyl), Determann (1966) (benzoyl > Z-Gly-OH > acetyl), Arendt *et al.* (1979) (acetyl > formyl), and Benoiton and Kuroda (1981) (benzoyl > Z-Gly-OH). The difference between the effects of two substituents can vary depending on the type of activation and the residue activated, the most frequent ratio between benzoyl and Z-Gly-OH being about 6 (Benoiton and Kuroda, 1981). Activated residues bearing an *N*-alkoxycarbonyl substituent do not racemize under normal operating conditions, but they can in the presence of tertiary amines, the benzyloxycarbonyl group allowing 2.5–4 times more racemization than the *tert*-butoxycarbonyl group (Kovacs *et al.*, 1975; Benoiton and Chen, 1981a). Other types of protecting groups such as 2-nitrophenylsulfenyl, 4-toluenesulfonyl, triphenylmethyl, and phthaloyl do not permit the 5(4*H*)-oxazolone to form, so derivatives containing these substituents cannot racemize by the same mechanism as the *N*-acyl and *N*-alkoxycarbonyl derivatives. On the other hand an *N,N*-diacyl derivative such as a phthaloylamino acid becomes more susceptible to racemization by the enolization mechanism than a monoacylamino acid. And finally, if two N-substituents include an acyl and a methyl group, the chirally labile 5(4*H*)-oxazolium cation corresponding to the 5(4*H*)-oxazolone can form and the protected *N*-methylamino acid racemizes more readily than the *N*-acylamino acid during coupling (McDermott and Benoiton, 1973c).

3. *Side Chain of the Penultimate Residue*

When 5(4*H*)-oxazolone is formed and racemization occurs during the coupling of a peptide, the carbonyl group of the penultimate residue participates in the cyclization, so that it can be expected that the nature of the side chain of the latter will affect both reactions. Little information is available on this aspect of racemization.

For DCC-mediated couplings under comparable conditions, valine as the penultimate residue led to twice as much racemization at the activated residue as alanine (Kuwata *et al.*, 1981), and proline, $1\frac{1}{2}$ times as much as alanine (Tomida *et al.*, 1973). According to Le Nguyen *et al.* (1981), the racemization to be expected at an activated residue decreases depending on the adjacent residue in the order valine > isoleucine > alanine > leucine > phenylalanine. For couplings by the acyl azide method in the presence of tertiary amines Z-Asp(O*t*Bu)-Phe-OH underwent twice as much racemization as Z-Gly-Phe-OH (Sieber and Riniker, 1973). But here, racemization occurs via both the 5(4*H*)-oxazolone and enolization mechanisms (Kemp, 1979). Obviously, more data will be required before a valid generalization can be made.

The penultimate residue itself also can undergo α-inversion during coupling (Weygand *et al.*, 1966b) via tautomerism of the imide bond of the adjacent 5(4*H*)-oxazolone [Eq. (21)], phenylalanine undergoing twice as much racemization as valine during mixed-anhydride activation in the presence of triethylamine (Dzieduszycka *et al.*, 1979).

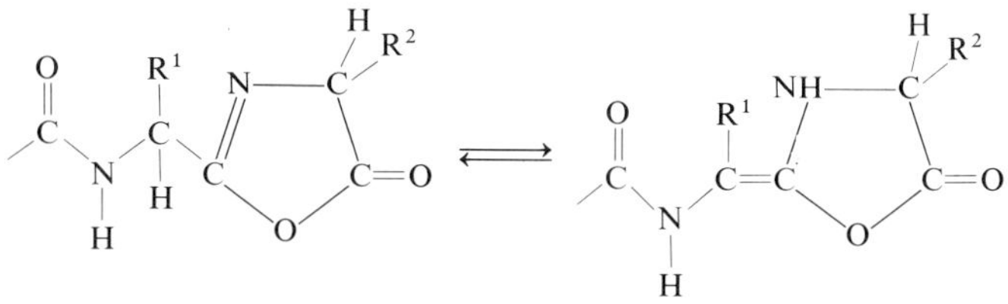

(21)

4. The Attacking Nucleophile

For couplings of formylamino acids to form dipeptide esters, racemization varied according to the amino acid ester in the order leucine ≥ alanine ≥ phenylalanine (Arendt *et al.*, 1979). For couplings of a protected dipeptide and tripeptide, the order was valine > alanine > asparagine > leucine, and *β-tert*-butyl aspartate > isoleucine > leucine, respectively (Kitada and Fujino, 1978). This is in general agreement with the results of Le Nguyen *et al.* (1981) showing valine ≫ phenylalanine > alanine > isoleucine ≫ leucine. Proline esters give rise to more racemization than other amino acid esters (Fujino *et al.*, 1972; Itoh *et al.*, 1978). *tert*-Butyl esters generate more than methyl esters (Tomida *et al.*, 1973). For couplings by the acyl azide procedure in the presence of triethylamine, glycinate led to 30% more racemization than valinate (Sieber and Riniker, 1973). The order may be affected by the nature of the solvent (Benoiton *et al.*, 1979a). It reflects in part the varying effect of the amine nucleophile on the stereomutation resulting from asymmetric induction (Section VI,B).

5. Configuration of the Residues

Peptide bond formation usually involves coupling between two residues of the same configuration but sometimes between residues of opposite configuration. When the same residues are implicated in both cases, the products are diastereoisomers that are not likely to form at the same rates, and consequently the α-inversion expected in the two cases will not be the same. Surprisingly, at the time of writing of the previous review (Kemp, 1979), it was not yet possible to state which coupling, that between residues of equal or opposite configuration, would give rise to more α-inversion. An indication was, however, apparent from the work of Rapaka *et al.* (1976) on the synthesis of sequential polypeptides.

Analysis of the D-isomer content of products obtained from the polymerization of H-Pro-Gly-Phe-ONp in dimethyl sulfoxide had revealed that the higher molecular weight polymers contained less DPhe than the lower molecular weight polymers, one containing 8% DPhe. As pointed out by Rapaka *et al.* (1976), this implied a slower reaction between epimeric

Table VI. Racemization during Coupling of Configurational Isomers

Subtrates	Solvent	Xxx[a]					
		LLeu	DLeu	LPhe	DPhe	LVal	DVal
For-Xxx-OH + H-LLeu-OMe (Arendt *et al.*, 1979)	Dioxane	9.6	7.5	9.3	8.6		
For-LVal-OH + H-Xxx-OMe (Arendt *et al.*, 1979)	Dioxane	38	21	22	14.5		
Ac-LLeu-OH + H-Xxx-OMe (Arendt *et al.*, 1979)	Dioxane	81	26	71	42		
Bz-Xxx-OH + H-LLys(Z)-OBzl (Benoiton *et al.*, 1980)	Dichloromethane	104	65	115	71	72	31
Z-Gly-Xxx-OH + H-LLys(Z)-OBzl (Benoiton *et al.*, 1981b)	Dichloromethane	24	56	28	58	16	34
Z-Gly-Xxx-OH + H-LLys(Z)-OBzl (Benoiton *et al.*, 1981b)	Dimethylformamide	35	70	42	62	64	106

[a] Values are percent racemization for dicyclohexylcarbidiimide-mediated reactions.

peptides than between peptides of identical configuration. But the opposite was found when a test system involving the coupling of Ac-Leu-OH was examined. Arendt *et al.* (1978b) found, by assessing the course of a DCC-mediated reaction at different times, that Ac-Leu-OH coupled more slowly with H-Leu-OMe than with H-DLeu-OMe, that more racemization accompanied the slower reaction, and that the relative amount of epimer formed increased as the coupling progressed. This means in effect that an activated L-residue is more susceptible to racemization than a D-residue when they are coupled to an L-residue. This was confirmed by Benoiton *et al.* (1980) who used several benzoylamino acids as test substances. On the other hand, when the same question was examined using protected glycyl dipeptides as the activated components, the exact opposite was found for DCC-mediated couplings in dichloromethane or dimethylformamide (Benoiton *et al.*, 1981b). Data from the two laboratories appear in Table VI. For the activated dipeptides, the α-inversion obtaining for the L-isomers was about half that obtaining for the D-isomers. The available evidence therefore allows the general conclusion that couplings between residues of identical configuration are accompanied by more racemization when the activated component is an acylamino acid, and less racemization when the activated component is a protected glycylamino acid, than when the couplings are between residues of opposite configuration.

Assuming that a chiral residue instead of glycine at the penultimate position of an activated peptide does not alter the course of events, it follows that more α-inversion will occur for a coupling at a D-residue, whether it be the COOH-terminus or the NH_2-terminus, than in normal peptide synthesis. It must be added that the data in Table VI are a true reflection of the relative susceptibility to racemization of L- and D-residues only if the solvent and temperature were such that no selectivity occurred during aminolysis of the racemized 5(4*H*)-oxazolone by the amino acid ester (see Section VI).

B. External Factors

1. Temperature

Racemization during coupling is promoted by an increase in temperature (Kemp, 1979), but the variation can depend on the residue in question. The increase was twice as much for Z-Gly-Ile-OH as for Z-Gly-Leu-OH for couplings in dimethylformamide using DCC in the presence of 1-hydroxybenzotriazole (Benoiton and Kuroda, 1981). The increase for couplings of Boc-His(Bzl)-OH using DCC in dichloromethane (Windridge and Jorgensen, 1971b) was less than that for the leucyl dipeptide above. The possibility that asymmetric induction contributes to the temperature effect has been suggested (Section VI,B). Further discussion on this is premature.

2. Solvent Polarity

The prevalent notion is that an increase in solvent polarity increases the extent of racemization during coupling (Kemp, 1979). It is now apparent that the issue is complex and that this generalization is not always valid. Two important points have emerged. First, depending on the method of coupling, the nature of the residue may or may not have a crucial influence on the solvent effect (Benoiton and Kuroda, 1981). For couplings of Z-Gly-Xxx-OH mediated by DCC in the presence of additives, racemization increased as expected in going from dimethylformamide to 67% aqueous dimethylformamide for Xxx = Leu, Phe, Val, and Ile. However, for couplings mediated by DCC alone, valine and isoleucine showed a five- to sixfold increase in going from dichloromethane to dimethylformamide, but leucine and phenylalanine showed a 15% decrease. This phenomenon issues from the fact that in dimethylformamide, valine and isoleucine have a greater tendency to racemize then leucine and phenylalanine, but the opposite is true in dichloromethane (Benoiton and Kuroda, 1981; Section VII,A,1). A similar high (10-fold) solvent effect was reported for couplings of Z-Pro-Val-OH (Tomida *et al.*, 1973), whereas less racemization in dimethylformamide than in dichloromethane was observed for couplings of benzoylphenylalanine (Goodman *et al.*, 1977). Another aspect of the solvent effect was found in DCC-mediated couplings of Boc-His(Bzl)-OH (Windridge and Jorgensen, 1971b). Racemization was twice as much in dichloromethane as in dimethylformamide for reactions in solution, and half as much for reactions with the nucleophile on a solid support.

The second point to emerge is that in some cases, for practical purposes, the difference in racemization in going from a polar solvent to a less polar solvent is not one of degree but of kind. In particular, DCC-mediated couplings of protected dipeptides in the presence of *N*-hydroxysuccinimide, 1-hydroxybenzotriazole or 3-hydroxy-4-oxo-3,4-dihydro-1,2,3-benzotriazine proceeded with no racemization in dichloromethane, but some racemization in dimethylformamide (Benoiton and Kuroda, 1981). Similarly, 1-hydroxybenzotriazole suppressed racemization during couplings of benzoylamino acids in dichloromethane, but not in dimethylformamide (Benoiton *et al.*, 1979b). Whether this phenomenon applies to other methods of coupling is not certain, but the possibility that it does must be recognized. It follows that it is imperative when examining the racemization associated with any new coupling reagent or technique that the performance be assessed in a polar solvent.

The following observations are also related to solvent effects. Polar solvents produce a positive (excess L-L isomer) asymmetric induction, less polar solvents, a negative induction, during aminolysis of 5(4*H*)-oxazolones (Benoiton *et al.*, 1981c; Section VI,B). Less racemization was caused in dimethylformamide than in dichloromethane-ethyl acetate by excess organic base during couplings by the acyl azide method (Benoiton *et al.*, 1982). Concentration of a solution of protected tripeptide in dimethylformamide by evaporation of solvent under reduced pressure below 40°C after a coupling using diphenylphosphoro azide produced about 1.5% of epimeric peptide (Kuwata *et al.*, 1981).

3. Coupling Method

In the previous review (Kemp, 1979), the results of chiral purity determinations obtained by numerous researchers using various methods were tabulated. In this section, instead of giving more data, I present selected conclusions drawn on the basis of new data obtained by two or more laboratories which are complementary, or data acquired using more than one model peptide under several reaction conditions. For minimizing racemization during DCC-mediated reactions of small peptides, 1-hydroxybenzotriazole is superior to *N*-hydroxysuccinimide as an additive (Kitada and Fujino, 1978; Benoiton and Kuroda, 1981; Kuwata *et al.*, 1981). 1-Hydroxybenzotriazole allows racemization-free couplings of benzoylamino acids in dichloromethane (Benoiton *et al.*, 1979b), but *N*-hydroxysuccinimide is superior as an additive for coupling benzoylamino acids in dimethylformamide (Izdebski, 1975; Benoiton *et al.*, 1979b). Both additives are superior to *N*-hydroxy-5-norborene-2,3-dicarboximide (Kitada and Fujino, 1978; Kuwata *et al.*, 1981), but the most effective of all is 3-hydroxy-4-oxo-3,4-dihydro-1,2,3-benzotriazine (Izdebski, 1975; Benoiton and Kuroda, 1981). *N*-Ethyl-*N'*-(γ-dimethylaminopropyl)carbodiimide produces more racemization than DCC whether used alone or in the presence of 1-hydroxybenzotriazole (Benoiton *et al.*, 1979b; Benoiton and Kuroda, 1981). Diethylphosphoro cyanide produces less racemization than diphenylphosphoro azide (Tomida and Nishimura, 1980). With regard to all of the above however, it must be borne in mind that different situations can alter the course of events. For example, instead of having a favorable effect, 1-hydroxybenzotriazole promoted racemization during DCC-mediated coupling of *N*-benzoyl-*N*-methylalanine (Davies and Thomas, 1979) and of a protected pentapeptide acid (80% racemization) which reacted very sluggishly (Wendlberger *et al.*, 1979).

The common hydroxylamine-derived additives suppress racemization by trapping the *O*-acylisourea before it cyclizes, or the 5(4*H*)-oxazolone before it racemizes (see Kemp, 1979; Rich and Singh, 1979). An interesting new proposal suggests that in polar solvents in particular, 5(4*H*)-oxazolones exist as bis-hydrogen-bonded bimolecular complexes, and that additives, besides inhibiting cyclization, decrease racemization by interfering with complexation by substituting for one of the components of the complex (Przybylski *et al.*, 1977). Lewis acids are a new type of additive claimed to be superior to 1-hydroxybenzotriazole and *N*-hydroxysuccinimide (Jakubke *et al.*, 1978). When added to a DCC-mediated coupling in dimethylformamide, zinc chloride reduced racemization during the synthesis of Tfa-Pro-Ala-Pro-OMe to 14%, and led to an 80% yield of optically pure Z-Gly-Phe-Gly-OEt. It also reduced racemization during aminolysis of the 5(4*H*)-oxazolone of Z-Pro-Ala-OH from 82 to 15%. Other Lewis acids were even more efficient racemization suppressants, but they are not of practical use for synthesis.

The most promising development related to coupling methods is the demonstration that thiol acids undergo very little racemization when coupled using DCC alone (Yamashiro and Blake, 1981). When reacted with leucyl-oxymethyl-resin in dimethylformamide at 24°C, Boc-Gly-Ala-SH gave only 0.04% of epimer compared to 16.5% for Boc-Gly-Ala-OH. The latter was reduced to 0.13% by the addition of 1-hydroxybenzotriazole, but racemization of the thiol acid increased ninefold in the presence of the additive. It follows that the activated thiol acid forms little or no 5(4*H*)-oxazolone during coupling, so it must racemize more than the activated carboxylic acid by the other mechanism which is enolization, promoted by the basic property of the additive. If this and previous reasoning (Section VII,A,1) is correct, the hindered residues valine and isoleucine will not racemize more than alanine when used as thiol acids for coupling.

A note of caution to those who acylate free amino acids or peptides in aqueous solution using an activated ester. Takaya *et al.* (1981) claim that the COOH-terminal unactivated residue undergoes appreciable racemization during the reaction.

VIII. CONCLUSION

The following points emerge from the review:

1. There are now numerous racemization tests at the disposal of researchers. With the possible exception of some peptides containing proline or an *N*-methylamino acid, it is likely that most stereoisomeric peptides can be separated by reversed-phase HPLC using aqueous buffers at neutral or acidic pH containing small amounts of organic modifier for neutral peptides. Therefore, unless it is designed for a unique purpose, a new racemization test is hardly a novelty.

2. There are many methods that effect racemization-free couplings in apolar solvents such as dichloromethane. However, achieving racemization-free couplings in the more useful polar solvents remains a challenge. Consequently, any new coupling reagent, additive, or method should be assessed for its performance in both types of solvents.

3. A seeming multitude of factors contribute to the stereomutation obtaining in any particular case. It is therefore preferable that conclusions on racemization be based on data acquired using several tests and reaction conditions. When pertinent, conclusions based on reactions of acylamino acids should be challenged using a test involving an activated peptide acid in order to establish their generality.

4. The tenet that an *N*-alkoxycarbonylamino acid does not racemize when coupled remains valid only for reactions carried out in the absence of tertiary amine and probably other bases. There is a danger of racemization when a base is added to catalyze the reaction.

5. The demonstrated potential of HPLC for determining epimeric peptides and the ready accessibility of chemically pure 2,4-disubstituted-5(4*H*)-oxazolones of established stereochemistry are two important practical developments which, alone or combined, render feasible a host of systematic studies on the sequence dependence of racemization.

REFERENCES

Anderson, G. W., and Young, R. W. (1952). *J. Am. Chem. Soc.* **74**, 5307–5309.

Anderson, G. W., Blodinger, J., and Welcher, A. D. (1952). *J. Am. Chem. Soc.* **74**, 5309–5312.

Anderson, G. W., Zimmerman, J. E., and Callahan, F. M. (1966). *J. Am. Chem. Soc.* **88**, 1338–1339.

Arendt, A., and Kolodziejczyk, A. M. (1978). *Tetrahedron Lett.* pp. 3867–3868.

Arendt, A., Kolodziejczyk, A., and Sokolowska, T. (1976a). *Chromatographia* **9**, 123–126.

Arendt, A., Kolodziejczyk, A., and Sokolowska, T. (1976b). *Tetrahedron Lett.* pp. 447–448.

Arendt, A., Kolodziejczyk, A. M., and Sokolowska, T. (1978a). *Pol. J. Chem.* **52**, 1959–1966.

Arendt, A., Kolodziejczyk, A. M., and Sokolowska, T. (1978b). *Tetrahedron Lett.* pp. 2711–2712.

Arendt, A., Kolodziejczyk, A. M., and Sokolowska, T. (1979). *Pol. J. Chem.* **53**, 2209–2212.

Atherton, E., Gait, M. J., Sheppard, R. C., and Williams, B. J. (1979). *Bioorg. Chem.* **8**, 351–370.

Barany, G., and Merrifield, R. B. (1980). *In* "The Peptides" (E. Gross and J. Meienhofer, eds.), Vol. 2, pp. 1–284. Academic Press, New York.

Bates, H. S., Jones, J. H., and Witty, M. J. (1980). *J. Chem. Soc., Chem. Commun.* pp. 773–774.

Benoiton, N. L., and Chen, F. M. F. (1979). *In* "Peptides, Structure and Biological Function" (E. Gross and J. Meienhofer, eds.), pp. 261–264. Pierce Chemical Co., Rockford, Illinois.

Benoiton, N. L., and Chen, F. M. F. (1981a). *Can. J. Chem.* **59**, 384–389.

Benoiton, N. L., and Chen, F. M. F. (1981b). *J. Chem. Soc., Chem. Commun.* pp. 543–545.

Benoiton, N. L., and Chen, F. M. F. (1981c). *In* "Peptides: Synthesis, Structure, Function" (D. H. Rich and E. Gross, eds.), pp. 105–108. Pierce Chemical Co., Rockford, Illinois.

Benoiton, N. L., and Chen, F. M. F. (1981d). *J. Chem. Soc., Chem. Commun.* pp. 1225–1227.
Benoiton, N. L., and Chen, F. M. F. (1981e). *FEBS Lett.* **125**, 104–106.
Benoiton, N. L., and Chen, F. M. F. (1982). *In* "Peptides 1982" (K. Blaha and P. Malon, eds.). de Gruyter, Berlin.
Benoiton, N. L., and Kuroda, K. (1981). *Int. J. Pept. Protein Res.* **17**, 197–204.
Benoiton, N. L., Kuroda, K., and Chen, F. M. F. (1979a). *In* "Peptides 1978" (I. Z. Siemion and G. Kupryszewski, eds.), pp. 165–168. Wroclaw Univ. Press, Wroclaw, Poland.
Benoiton, N. L., Kuroda, K., and Chen, F. M. F. (1979b). *Int. J. Pept. Protein Res.* **13**, 403–408.
Benoiton, N. L., Kuroda, K., Cheung, S. T., Chen, F. M. F. (1979c). *Can. J. Biochem.* **57**, 776–781.
Benoiton, N. L., Kuroda, K., and Chen, F. M. F. (1980). *Int. J. Pept. Protein Res.* **15**, 475–479.
Benoiton, N. L., Atherton, E., Brown, E., Sheppard, R. C., and Williams, B. J. (1981a). *J. Chem. Soc., Chem. Commun.* pp. 336–337.
Benoiton, N. L., Kuroda, K., and Chen, F. M. F. (1981b). *Tetrahedron Lett.* **22**, 3359–3360.
Benoiton, N. L., Kuroda, K., and Chen, F. M. F. (1981c). *Tetrahedron Lett.* **22**, 3361–3364.
Benoiton, N. L., Kuroda, K., and Chen, F. M. F. (1982). *Int. J. Pept. Protein Res.* **20**, 81–86.
Berndt, H. (1980). *Tetrahedron Lett.* **21**, 3265–3268.
Bodanszky, M., and Conklin, L. F. (1967). *Chem. Commun.* pp. 773–774.
Bodanszky, M., and Fagan, D. T. (1977). *Int J. Pept. Protein Res.* **10**, 375–379.
Bodanszky, M., Klausner, Y. S., and Ondetti, M. A. (1976). "Peptide Synthesis," 2nd ed., pp. 137–157. Wiley, New York.
Brown, E., Williams, B. J., and Sheppard, R. C. (1980). *J. Chem. Soc., Chem. Commun.* pp. 1093–1094.
Brown, T., and Jones, J. H. (1981). *J. Chem. Soc., Chem. Commun.* pp. 648–649.
Castro, B., Dormoy, J. R., and Le Nguyen, D. (1978). *Tetrahedron Lett.* pp. 4419–4420
Castro, B., Dormoy, J. R., and Le Nguyen, D. (1979). *In* "Peptides 1978" (I. Z. Siemion and G. Kupryszewski, eds.), pp. 155–158. Wroclaw Univ. Press, Wroclaw, Poland.
Chen, F. M. F., and Benoiton, N. L. (1978). *Can. J. Biochem.* **56**, 38–42.
Chen, F. M. F., Kuroda, K., and Benoiton, N. L. (1978). *Synthesis* 928–929; (1979) *Synthesis* 232.
Chen, F. M. F., Kuroda, K., and Benoiton, N. L. (1979). *Synthesis* pp. 230–232.
Cheung, S. T., and Benoiton, N. L. (1977a). *Can. J. Chem.* **55**, 906–910.
Cheung, S. T., and Benoiton, N. L. (1977b). *Can. J. Chem.* **55**, 911–915.
Cheung, S. T., and Benoiton, N. L. (1977c). *Can. J. Chem.* **55**, 916–921.
Coggins, J. R., and Benoiton, N. L. (1970). *J. Chromatogr.* **52**, 251–256.
Cram, D. J., and Gosser, L. (1964). *J. Am. Chem. Soc.* **86**, 5457–5465.
Davies, J. H., Davis, R. H., and Carrington, R. A. G. (1972). *J. Chem. Soc., Perkin Trans. 1* pp. 1983–1985.
Davies, J. S., and Thomas, W. A. (1978). *J. Chem. Soc., Perkin Trans. 2* pp. 1157–1163.
Davies, J. S., and Thomas, R. J. (1979). *In* "Peptides 1978" Siemion and G. Kupryszewski, eds.), pp. 173–177. Wroclaw Univ. Press, Wroclaw, Poland.
Davies, J. S., and Thomas, R. J. (1981). *J. Chem. Soc., Perkin Trans. 1* pp. 1639–1646.
Davies, J. S., Thomas, R. J., and Williams, M. K. (1975). *J. Chem. Soc., Chem. Commun.* pp. 76–77.
DeTar, D. F., Silverstein, R., and Rogers, F. F. (1966). *J. Am. Chem. Soc.* **88**, 1024–1030.
Determann, H. (1966). *In* "Peptides 1963" (L. Zervas, ed), pp. 160–161, Pergamon, Oxford.
Determann, H., Heuer, J., Pfaender, P., and Reinartz, M. L. (1966). *Justus Liebigs Ann. Chem.* **694**, 190–199.
Dzieduszycka, M., Smulkowski, M. and Taschner, E. (1979). *Pol. J. Chem.* **53**, 1095–1102.
Finn, F. M. and Hofmann, K. (1976). *In* "The Proteins" (H. Neurath and R. L. Hill, eds.), 3rd ed., Vol. 2, pp. 183–189. Academic Press, New York.

Fletcher, A. P., Jones, J. H., Ramage, W. I., and Stachulski, A. V. (1979). *J. Chem. Soc., Perkin Trans. 1* pp. 2261–2267.
Frank, H., Nicholson, G. J., and Bayer, E. (1977). *J. Chromatogr. Sci.* **15**, 174–176.
Frank, H., Nicholson, G. J., and Bayer, E. (1978). *J. Chromatogr.* **167**, 187–196.
Fujino, M., Kobayashi, S., Fukuda, T., Obayashi, M., and Shinagawa, S. (1972). *In* "Peptide Chemistry 1971" (J. Noguchi, ed.), pp. 7–10. Protein Res. Found., Osaka, Japan.
Galardy, R. E., Bleich, H. E., Ziegler, P., and Craig, L. C. (1976). *Biochemistry* **15**, 2303–2309.
Gilon, C., Klausner, Y., and Hassner, A. (1979). *Tetrahedron Lett.* pp. 3811–3814.
Goodman, M., and Glaser, C. B. (1970). *J. Org. Chem.* **35**, 1954–1962.
Goodman, M., and Levine, L. (1964). *J. Am. Chem. Soc.* **86**, 2918–2922.
Goodman, M., Keogh, P., and Anderson, H. (1977). *Bioorg. Chem.* **6**, 239–247.
Greenstein, J. P., and Winitz, M. (1961). "Chemistry of the Amino Acids," pp. 715–760, 2118–2122. Wiley, New York.
Hagenmaier, H., and Frank, H. (1972). *Hoppe-Seyler's Z. Physiol. Chem.* **353**, 1973–1976.
Heard, A. L., and Young, G. T. (1963). *J. Chem. Soc.* pp. 5807–5810.
Heimer, E. P., Chang, C. D., Lambros, T., and Meienhofer, J. (1981). *Int. J. Pept. Protein Res.* **18**, 237–241.
Hodges, R. S., and Merrifield, R. B. (1974). *J. Org. Chem.* **39**, 1870–1874.
Itoh, M., Nojima, H., Notani, J., Hagiwara, D., and Takai, K. (1978). *Bull. Chem. Soc. Jpn.* **51**, 3320–3329.
Izdebski, J. (1975). *Rocz. Chem.* **49**, 1097–1103.
Izumiya, N., and Muraoka, N. (1969). *J. Am. Chem. Soc.* **91**, 2391–2392.
Izumiya, N., Muraoka, N., and Aoyagi, H. (1971). *Bull. Chem. Soc. Jpn.* **44**, 3391–3395.
Jakubke, H. D., Klessen, C., Berger, E., and Neubert, K. (1978). *Tetrahedron Lett.* pp. 1497–1500.
Jones, J. H. (1979). *In* "The Peptides" (E. Gross and J. Meienhofer, eds.), Vol. 1, p. 71. Academic Press, New York.
Jones, J. H., and Ramage, W. I. (1978). *J. Chem. Soc., Chem. Commun.* pp. 472–473.
Jones, J. H., and Ramage, W. I. (1979). *Int. J. Pept. Protein Res.* **14**, 65–67.
Jones, J. H., and Witty, M. J. (1977). *J. Chem. Soc., Chem. Commun.* pp. 281–282.
Jones, J. H., and Witty, M. J. (1979). *J. Chem. Soc., Perkin Trans. 1* pp. 3203–3206.
Jones, J. H., Ramage, W. I., and Witty, M. J. (1980). *Int. J. Pept. Protein Res.* **15**, 301–303.
Kemp, D. S. (1979). *In* "The Peptides" (E. Gross and J. Meienhofer, eds.), Vol. 1, pp. 315–383. Academic Press, New York.
Kemp, D. S., and Rebek, J. (1970). *J. Am. Chem. Soc.* **92**, 5792–5793
Kemp, D. S., Wang, S. W., Busby, G., and Hugel, G. (1970). *J. Am. Chem. Soc.* **92**, 1043–1055.
Kenner, G. W., and Seely, J. H. (1972). *J. Am. Chem. Soc.* **94**, 3259.
Kent, S. B. H., Mitchell, A. R., Barany, G., and Merrifield, R. B. (1978). *Anal. Chem.* **50**, 155–159.
Kiso, Y., Satomi, M., Miyazaki, T., Hiraiwa, H., and Akita, T. (1981). *In* "Peptide Chemistry 1980" (K. Okawa, ed.), pp. 71–74. Protein Res. Found., Osaka, Japan.
Kitada, C., and Fujino, M. (1978). *Chem. Pharm. Bull.* **26**, 585–590.
Kovacs, J. (1980). *In* "The Peptides" (E. Gross and J. Meienhofer, eds.), Vol. 2, pp. 485–539. Academic Press, New York.
Kovacs, J., Cortegiano, H., Cover, R. E., and Meyers, G. L. (1971). *J. Am. Chem. Soc.* **93**, 1541–1543.
Kovacs, J., Cover, R., Jham, G., Hsieh, Y., and Kalas, T. (1975). *In* "Peptides: Chemistry, Structure and Biology" (R. Walter and J. Meienhofer, eds.), pp. 317–324. Ann Arbor Sci. Publ., Ann Arbor, Michigan.
Kovacs, J., Hsieh, Y., Holleran, E. M., and Ting, Y. F. (1979). *In* "Peptides 1978" (I. Z. Siemion and G. Kupryszewski, eds.), pp. 159–164. Wroclaw Univ. Press, Wroclaw, Poland.

Kusumoto, S., Matsukura, M., and Shiba, T. (1981). *Biopolymers* **20**, 1869–1875.
Kuwata, S., Yamada, T., Miyazawa, T., Dejima, K. and Watanabe, K. (1981). *In* "Peptide Chemistry 1080" (K. Okawa, ed), pp. 65–70. Protein Res. Found., Osaka, Japan.
Le Nguyen, D., Dormoy, J. R., Castro, B., and Prevot, D. (1981). *Tetrahedron* **37**, 4229–4238.
Leplawy, M. T., Jones, D. S., Kenner, G. W., and Sheppard, R. C. (1960) *Tetrahedron* **11**, 39–51.
Liardon, R., Ledermann, S., and Ott, U. (1981). *J. Chromatogr.* **76**, 2839–2841.
Lichtenberg, L. A., and Wellner, D. (1968). *Anal. Biochem.* **26**, 313–319.
McDermott, J. R., and Benoiton, N. L. (1973a). *Can. J. Chem.* **51**, 1915–1919.
McDermott, J. R., and Benoiton, N. L. (1973b). *Can. J. Chem.* **51**, 2555–2561.
McDermott, J. R., and Benoiton, N. L. (1973c). *Can. J. Chem.* **51**, 2562–2570
Maclaren, J. A. (1958). *Aust. J. Chem.* **11**, 360–365.
Manning, J. M. (1970). *J. Am. Chem. Soc.* **92**, 7449–7454.
Manning, J. M., and Moore, S. (1968). *J. Biol. Chem.* **243**, 5591–5597.
Matoni, Y. and Berndt, H. (1980). *Tetrahedron Lett.* **22**, 37–40.
Meese, C. O., Walter, W., and Berger, M. (1974). *J. Am. Chem. Soc.* **96**, 2259–2260.
Meienhofer, J. (1979). *In* "The Peptides" (E. Gross and J. Meienhofer, eds.), Vol. 1, p. 306. Academic Press, New York.
Meienhofer, J. (1981). *Biopolymers* **20**, 1761–1784.
Mitchell, A. R., Kent, S. B. H., Chu, Y. I., and Merrifield, R. B. (1978). *Anal. Chem.* **50**, 637–640.
Mitin, Y. V., and Maksimov, E. E. (1973). *Zh. Obshch. Khim.* **43**, 203–207.
Miyoshi, M. (1970). *Bull. Chem. Soc. Jpn.* **43**, 3321.
Miyoshi, M. (1973a). *Bull. Chem. Soc. Jpn.* **46**, 212–218.
Miyoshi, M. (1973b). *Bull. Chem. Soc. Jpn.* **46**, 1489–1496.
Mohr, E., and Geis, T. (1908). *Ber. Dtsch. Chem. Ges.* **41**, 798–799.
Muraoka, M., Yoshida, N., Noda, K., and Izumiya, N. (1968). *Bull. Chem. Soc. Jpn.* **41**, 2134–2140.
Nagaraj, R., and Balaram, P. (1981). *Tetrahedron* **37**, 2001–2005.
Noda, K., Okai, H., Kato, T., and Izumiya, N. (1968). *Bull. Chem. Soc. Jpn.* **41**, 401–407.
Paik, W. K., and Kim, S. (1965). *Biochim. Biophys. Acta* **96**, 66–74.
Przybylski, J., Jeschkeit, H. and Kupryszewski, G. (1977). *Rocz. Chem.* **51**, 939–949.
Rahn, W., Eckstein, H. and König, W. A. (1976). *Hoppe-Seyler's Z. Physiol. Chem.* **357**, 1223–1227.
Rapaka, R. S., Bhatnagar, R. S., and Nitecki, D. E. (1976). *Biopolymers* **15**, 317–324.
Rebek, J., and Feitler, D. (1974). *J. Am. Chem. Soc.* **96**, 1606–1607.
Rich, D. H., and Singh, J. (1979). *In* "The Peptides" (E. Gross and J. Meienhofer, eds.), Vol. 1, pp. 241–261. Academic Press, New York.
Riniker, B., Eisler, K., Kamber, B., Müller, H., Rittel, W., and Sieber, P. (1979). *In* "Peptides 1978" (I. Z. Siemion and G. Kypryszewski, eds.), pp. 631–634. Wroclaw Univ. Press, Wroclaw, Poland.
Roach, D., and Gerke, C. W. (1969) *J. Chromatogr.* **44**, 269–278.
Rzeszotarska, B., Taschner, E., and Kuziel, A. (1966). *In* "Peptides 1963" (L. Zervas, ed.), pp. 131–133. Pergamon, Oxford.
Schlingoff, G. (1976). *In* "Peptides 1976" (A. Loffet, ed.), p. 116. Editions de l'Université de Bruxelles, Brussels.
Schnabel, E. (1965). *Justus Liebig's Ann. Chem.* **688**, 238–249.
Schüssler, H. and Zahn, H. (1962). *Chem. Ber.* **95**, 1076–1080.
Scotchler, J., Lozier, R., and Robinson, A. B. (1970). *J. Org. Chem.* **35**, 3151–3152.
Sheehan, J. C., Cruikshank, P. A., and Boshart, G. L. (1961). *J. Org. Chem.* **26**, 2525–2528.

Sieber, P., and Riniker, B. (1973). *In* "Peptides 1971" (H. Nesvadba, ed.), pp. 49–53. North-Holland Publ., Amsterdam.
Sieber, P., Riniker, B., Brugger, M., Kamber, B., and Rittel, W. (1970). *Helv. Chim. Acta* **53**, 2135–2150.
Sieber, P., Kamber, B., Hartmann, A., Johl, A., Riniker, B., and Rittel, W. (1977). *Helv. Chim. Acta* **60**, 27–37.
Siemion, I. Z., and Dzugaj, A. (1966). *Rocz. Chem.* **40**, 1699–1705.
Siemion, I. Z., and Morawiec, J. (1964). *Bull. Acad. Pol. Sci., Ser. Sci. Chim.* **12**, 295–298.
Siemion, I. Z., and Nowak, K. (1960). *Rocz. Chem.* **34**, 1479–1482.
Siemion, I. Z., and Nowak, K. (1961). *Rocz. Chem.* **35**, 979–984.
Smart, N. A., Young, G. T., and Williams, M. W. (1960). *J. Chem. Soc.* pp. 3902–3912.
Smith, G. C., and Silva de Sol, B. (1980). *Science* **207**, 765–767.
Spackman, D. H., Stein, W. H., and Moore, S. (1958). *Anal. Chem.* **30**, 1190–1205.
Steglich, W., and Höfle, G. (1969). *Angew. Chem., Int. Ed. Engl.* **8**, 981.
Steglich, W., Mayer, D., Barocio de la Lama, X., Tanner, H., and Weygand, F. (1967). *In* "Peptides 1966" (H. C. Beyerman, A. van de Linde and W. Maassen van den Brink, eds.) pp. 67–72. North-Holland Publ., Amsterdam.
Steinauer, R., Chen, F. M. F., and Benoiton, N. L. (1982). Second Int. Symposium on HPLC of Proteins, Peptides and Polynucleotides Dec., Baltimore, Maryland
Takaya, T., and Sakakibara, S. (1980). *In* "Peptide Chemistry 1979" (Y. Yonehara, ed.), pp. 139–144. Protein Res. Found., Osaka, Japan.
Takaya, T., Kishida, Y., and Sakakibara, S. (1981). *J. Chromatogr.* **215**, 279–287.
Tomida, I., and Nishimura, N. (1980). *Agric. Biol. Chem.* **44**, 1241–1244.
Tomida, I., Kayahara, H., and Iriye, R. (1973). *Agric. Biol. Chem.* **37**, 2557–2563.
Tomida, T., Senda, S., Kuwabara, T., and Katayama, T. (1976). *Agric. Biol. Chem.* **40**, 2033–2036.
Tong, J. H., Petitclerc, C., D'Iorio, A., and Benoiton, N. L. (1971). *Can. J. Biochem.* **49**, 877–881.
Ugi, I. (1965). *Z. Naturforsch.*, **20B**, 405–409.
Veber, D. F. (1975). *In* "Peptides: Chemistry Structure and Biology" (R. Walter and J. Meienhofer, eds.), pp. 307–316. Ann Arbor Sci. Publ., Ann Arbor, Michigan.
Wang, S. S. (1975). *J. Org. Chem.* **40**, 1235–1239.
Wang, S. S., Yang, C. C., Kulesha, I. D., Sonenburg, M., and Merrifield, R. B. (1974). *Int. J. Pept. Protein Res.* **6**, 103–109.
Wang, S. S., Tam, J. P., Wang, B. S. H., and Merrifield, R. B. (1981). *Int. J. Pept. Protein Res.* **18**, 459–467.
Weinstein, B. (1970). *In* "Peptides: Chemistry and Biochemistry" (B. Weinstein and S. Lande, eds.), pp. 371–387. Dekker, New York.
Weinstein, B., and Pritchard, A. E. (1972). *J. Chem. Soc., Perkin Trans. 1* pp. 1015–1020.
Wendlberger, G., Moroder, L., Hallet, A., and Wünsch, E. (1979). *Monatsh. Chem.* **110**, 1407–1428.
Weygand, F., Prox, A., Schmidhammer, L. and König, W. (1963). *Angew. Chem., Int. Ed. Engl.* **2**, 183–188.
Weygand, F., König, W., Prox, A., and Burger, K. (1966a). *Chem. Ber.* **99**, 1443–1445.
Weygand, F., Prox, A., and König, W. (1966b). *Chem. Ber.* **99**, 1446–1450.
Weygand, F., Prox, A., and König, W. (1966c). *Chem. Ber.* **99**, 1451–1459.
Weygand, F., Steglich, W., and Barocio de la Lama, X. (1966d). *Tetrahedron, Suppl.* **8**, Part 1, 9–13.
Weygand, F., Hoffmann, D., and Prox, A. (1968). *Z. Naturforsch.*, **23B**, 279–281.
Williams, M. W., and Young, G. T. (1963). *J. Chem. Soc.* pp. 881–889.

Windridge, G. C., and Jorgensen, E. C. (1971a). *J. Am. Chem. Soc.* **93**, 6318–6319.
Windridge, G. C., and Jorgensen, E. C. (1971b). *Intra-Sci. Chem. Rep.* **5**, 375–380.
Witty, M. J. (1979). Ph. D. Thesis, University of Oxford.
Yamashiro, D., and Blake, J. (1981). *Int. J. Pept. Protein Res.* **18**, 383–392.
Young, G. T. (1967). *In* "Peptides 1966" (H. C. Beyerman, A. van de Linde and W. Maassen van den Brink, eds.) pp. 55–66. North-Holland, Amsterdam.

NOTE ADDED IN PROOF

We have found that mixed anhydrides (**32**) (R = R′O), p. 256, are as stable as symmetrical anhydrides (**13**) (R = *t*Bu), p. 242, and can be isolated pure in the same manner by washing a reaction mixture in dichloromethane with aqueous acid and sodium hydrogen carbonate followed by evaporation of the solvent. In addition, *N*-methylpiperidine is preferable to *N*-methylmorpholine as the base in mixed anhydride couplings because it diminishes the side reactions of racemization and urethane formation (F. M. F. Chen, R. Steinauer and N. L. Benoiton, unpublished; reported at the Eighth American Peptide Symposium, Tucson, Arizona, May 22–27, 1983).

Chapter 5

α,β-Dehydroamino Acids and Peptides

KOSAKU NODA
Laboratory of Biochemistry,
Fukuoka Women's University,
Fukuoka 813, Japan

YASUYUKI SHIMOHIGASHI
National Institutes of Health,
National Institute of Child Health and Human Development
Bethesda, Maryland

NOBUO IZUMIYA
Laboratory of Biochemistry,
Faculty of Science,
Kyushu University,
Fukuoka 812, Japan

I. Introduction 286
II. Occurrence of Peptides Containing α,β-Dehydroamino Acids . 287
A. Natural Peptides with α,β-Dehydroamino Acids 287
B. Structure and Activity of α,β-Dehydropeptides 291
1. Neoechinulins 292
2. Stendomycin 293
3. Heptamycins 294
4. Subtilin 295
III. Synthesis of α,β-Dehydroamino Acids and Introduction into Peptides 296
A. Procedures for Synthesis of α,β-Dehydroamino Acids . . . 297
1. Dehydroalanine 297
2. Dehydroaminobutyric Acid 300
3. Dehydrovaline. 302
4. Dehydroleucine 303
5. Dehydrophenylalanine 305
6. α,β-Dehydroamino Acids with Other β-Substituents . . 308
B. Coupling Reactions of α,β-Dehydroamino Acid Derivatives 309

THE PEPTIDES, VOLUME 5

ISBN 0-12-304205-4

C. Analytical Methods for Confirmation of the α,β-Dehydroamino Acid Moiety 310
1. Identification of the α,β-Dehydroamino Acid Moiety . . 310
2. Determination of *Z*- and *E*-Configurations 311
IV. Synthesis of Biologically Active Peptides with α,β-Dehydroamino Acids 312
A. Biologically Active Dehydropeptides 313
1. Tentoxin. 313
2. AM-Toxins. 316
3. Nisin 320
B. Peptide Hormone Analogs Substituted by α,β-Dehydroamino Acids. 323
V. Utility of α,β-Dehydroamino Acids in Peptide Chemistry . . . 325
A. Synthesis of Peptide Amides via Dehydroalanine. 326
1. Peptides with a COOH-Terminal Amide 326
2. Peptides with an Amide in the Endo Position 327
B. Asymmetric Hydrogenation of α,β-Dehydroamino Acids in Cyclic Peptides 330
1. Asymmetric Hydrogenation of Cyclic Dehydropeptides. 330
2. Preparation of Optically Pure α-Amino Acids. 332
VI. Concluding Remarks 332
References 333

I. INTRODUCTION*

The chemistry of α,β-dehydroamino acids was studied extensively during the 1930s, notably by M. Bergmann and his co-workers (Bergmann and Grafe, 1930) and by J. P. Greenstein and associates (Greenstein and Winitz, 1961). For a long time after that, α,β-dehydroamino acids received rather little attention, although some investigators dealt with them in studies on nonenzymatic fragmentation of peptides and of proteins at serine or cysteine residues by β-elimination and subsequent hydrolysis (Photaki, 1963; Patchornik and Sokolovsky, 1963, 1964).

During the past decade, numerous α,β-dehydropeptides, many of them possessing biological activity, have been isolated from natural sources and characterized. This rapid progress was a result of improved isolation techniques and the development of new methods of analysis. Chemical synthesis of dehydropeptides has also become possible through the recent development of new methods. These peptides have aroused interest among investigators involved in peptide chemistry.

* Dedicated to the memory of our mentor and dear friend, Dr. Erhard Gross.

α,β-Dehydropeptides have unique chemical and stereochemical properties that must be considered in any discussion of dynamic structure–activity relationships. It is clear that the α,β-dehydroamino acid moiety affects both the chemical reactivity and the conformation. A better understanding of the roles of dehydropeptides generally requires the synthesis of new analogs and elucidation of the structures of these peptides by careful analysis before biological examination.

The aim of this chapter is to survey naturally occurring α,β-dehydropeptides, as well as α,β-dehydroamino acids, and standard methods of chemical synthesis. The synthesis of some bioactive dehydropeptides will also be described. Previous reviews covering this field include those by Gross (1976, 1977), Shimohigashi and Izumiya (1978b), Shin (1979), Schmidt *et al.* (1979), and Stammer (1982).

II. OCCURRENCE OF PEPTIDES CONTAINING α,β-DEHYDROAMINO ACIDS

A. Natural Peptides with α,β-Dehydroamino Acids

The majority of α,β-dehydroamino acids have been found in relatively low-molecular-weight peptides from microbial sources, most of which have a cyclic structure and possess a variety of biological activities. Table I summarizes naturally occurring α,β-dehydroamino acids and α,β-dehydropeptides together with some of their characteristics. The structures and biological activities of some of these dehydropeptides will be described in detail in Section II,B.

The presence of α,β-dehydroamino acids is, however, not necessarily restricted to peptides of low molecular weight nor to those of microbial origin. Dehydroalanine (ΔAla), for instance, has been identified in histidine ammonia lyase of both bacterial (Givot *et al.*, 1969; Wickner, 1969) and mammalian origin (Givot and Abeles, 1970) and also in phenylalanine ammonia lyase from a plant source (Hanson and Havir, 1970).

In addition, α,β-dehydroamino acids may well be of greater physiological significance than is presently appreciated. They may be precursors of a number of biologically active substances and may play significant roles in metabolic pathways. The formation and natural existence of α-mercapto-α-amino acids and α-hydroxy-α-amino acids, the primary addition products to the α,β-double bond, are discussed in a review by Schmidt *et al.* (1979). α,β-Dehydroamino acids are also important precursors in the formation

Table I. Natural Peptides Containing α,β-Dehydroamino Acids[a]

Peptide	Number of amino acid residues	ΔAmino acid involved	Biological activity	Reference	
				Structure	Synthesis
Amino acids					
Asparenomycin A, B and C	1	ΔPro derivative	Antibacterial	Shoji *et al.* (1982)	
Hydroxyminaline	1	ΔPro derivative		Minagawa (1945)	
Minaline	1	ΔPro derivative		Minagawa (1946)	
Oxaline	1	ΔHis derivative		Nagel *et al.* (1976)	
Pencolide	1	ΔAbu		Birkinshaw *et al.* (1963)	
Primocarcin	1	ΔAla derivative	Antitumor	Isono (1962)	Bowman *et al.* (1965)
Thienamycin	1	ΔPro derivative	Antibacterial	Albers-Schönberg *et al.* (1978)	
Versimide	1	ΔAla		Brown (1970)	Atkins and Kay (1971)
Piperazinediones					
Albonoursin	2	ΔLeu, ΔPhe	Antitumor	Khoklov and Lokshin (1963)	Shin *et al.* (1969)
Austamide	2	ΔPro	Toxic	Steyn (1971)	
cyclo(MeTrp-ΔAbu)	2	ΔAbu	Transcriptase inhibitory	Kakinuma and Rinehart (1974)	Izumiya *et al.* (1977)
cyclo(ΔPhe-ΔPhe)	2	2 ΔPhe		Brown *et al.* (1965)	
cyclo(ΔPhe-Phe)	2	ΔPhe		Brown *et al.* (1965)	
Isoechinulin A	2	ΔTrp derivative	Growth inhibit.	Nagasawa *et al.* (1976)	
Isoechinulin B and C	2	ΔAla, ΔTrp derivative		Nagasawa *et al.* (1976)	
Mycerianamide	2	ΔTyr derivative	Antibacterial	Birch *et al.* (1956)	
Neoechinulin	2	ΔTrp derivative		Barbetta *et al.* (1969)	
Neoechinulin A	2	ΔTrp derivative		Itokawa *et al.* (1973)	Nakatsuka *et al.* (1980)
Neoechinulin B and C	2	ΔAla, ΔTrp derivative		Dossena *et al.* (1974) Cardillo *et al.* (1974)	

Neoechinulin D	2	ΔTrp derivative		Dossena *et al.* (1975)	
Neoechinulin E	2	ΔTrp derivative		Marchelli *et al.* (1977)	
Roquefortine	2	ΔHis		Scott *et al.* (1976)	
Oligopeptides					
Kikumycin A and B	2	ΔPro derivative	Antibacterial	Takahashi *et al.* (1972)	
Netropsin	2	ΔPro derivative	Antibacterial	Nakamura *et al.* (1964)	Julia and Preau (1963)
Anthelvencin A and B	3	2 ΔPro derivatives	Antibacterial	Probst *et al.* (1965)	
C-2801X	3	ΔVal derivative	Antibacterial	Hasegawa *et al.* (1976)	
Celenamide A and B	3	ΔPhe derivative	Alkaloid	Stonard and Anderson (1980)	
Cephalosporin C	3	ΔVal derivative	Antibacterial	Abraham and Newton (1961)	Woodward *et al.* (1966)
Cephamycin A and B	3	ΔVal derivative	Antibacterial	Albers-Schönberg *et al.* (1972)	
Deacetoxycephalosporin C	3	ΔVal derivative	Antibacterial	Higgins *et al.* (1974)	
Deacetylcephalospolin C	3	ΔVal derivative	Antibacterial	Fujisawa *et al.* (1973)	
Distamycin A	3	3 ΔPro derivatives	Antibacterial	Arcamone *et al.* (1964)	Arcamone *et al.* (1964)
7-Methoxycephalosporin C	3	ΔPro derivative	Antibacterial	Fujisawa *et al.* (1975)	
Oganomycins	3	ΔVal derivative	Antibacterial	Gushima *et al.* (1981)	
WS-3442B	3	ΔVal derivative	Antibacterial	Fujisawa *et al.* (1975)	
AM-toxin I	4	ΔAla	Toxic	Okuno *et al.* (1974)	Shimohigashi *et al.* (1977b)
AM-toxin II	4	ΔAla	Toxic	Ueno *et al.* (1975a)	Shimohigashi *et al.* (1977c)
AM-toxin III	4	ΔAla	Toxic	Ueno *et al.* (1975b)	Kanmera *et al.* (1981)
Griseoviridin	4	ΔAla derivative	Antibacterial	Fallona *et al.* (1962)	
Lasiodine A	4	ΔVal	Alkaloid	Marchand *et al.* (1969)	
Nocobactin NA	4	ΔThr derivative		Ratledge and Snow (1974)	
Ostreogrycin A	4	ΔPro, ΔSer derivative	Antibacterial	Delpierre *et al.* (1966) Crooy and DeNeys (1972)	
Tentoxin	4	ΔMePhe	Toxic	Meyer *et al.* (1974a)	Rich and Mathiaparanam (1974)
Capreomycin IIA and IIB	5	ΔAla derivative	Antibacterial	Nomoto *et al.* (1977)	
Coumermycin A_1	5	3 ΔPro derivatives	Antibacterial	Kawaguchi *et al.* (1965a)	
Coumermycin A_2	5	3 ΔPro derivatives	Antibacterial	Kawaguchi *et al.* (1965b)	
Capreomycin IA and IB	6	ΔAla derivative	Antibacterial	Nomoto *et al.* (1977)	Nomoto *et al.* (1978)

(continued)

Table 1 *(continued)*

Peptide	Number of amino acid residues	ΔAmino acid involved	Biological activity	Reference	
				Structure	Synthesis
Tuberactinomycin A	6	ΔAla derivative	Antibacterial	Yoshioka *et al.* (1971)	
Tuberactinomycin B	6	ΔAla derivative	Antibacterial	Noda *et al.* (1972)	
Tuberactinomycin N	6	ΔAla derivative	Antibacterial	Yoshioka *et al.* (1971)	Shiba *et al.* (1980)
Tuberactinomycin O	6	ΔAla derivative	Antibacterial	Yoshioka *et al.* (1971)	Teshima *et al.* (1976)
Antrimycin	7	ΔIle	Antibacterial	Morimoto *et al.* (1981)	
Heptamycin A	7	ΔAbu	Antibacterial	Ogawa *et al.* (1977)	
Heptamycin B	7	ΔAbu	Antibacterial	Nakagawa *et al.* (1975)	
Nosiheptide	9	ΔAla, ΔAbu derivative	Antibacterial	Prange *et al.* (1977)	
Polypeptides					
Micrococcin P_1 and P_2	10	2 ΔAbu	Antibacterial	Bycroft and Gowland (1978)	
Berninamycin A	10	5 ΔAla	Antibacterial	Liesch and Rinehart (1977)	
Thiocillin I, II and III	10	2 ΔAbu	Antibacterial	Shoji *et al.* (1981)	
A-128-OP and A-128-P	11	ΔTrp	Antibacterial	Silaev *et al.* (1971)	
Siomycin B	11	2 ΔAla, ΔAbu derivative	Antibacterial	Tori *et al.* (1981)	
Telomycin	11	ΔTrp	Antibacterial	Sheehan *et al.* (1968)	
Thiostrepton B	11	ΔAla, ΔAbu derivative	Antibacterial	Hensens and Albers-Schönberg (1978)	
Siomycin A	13	4 ΔAla, ΔAbu derivative	Antibacterial	Tori *et al.* (1976)	
Siomycin C	13	4 ΔAla, ΔAbu derivative	Antibacterial	Tori *et al.* (1981)	
Siomycin D_1	13	4 ΔAla, ΔAbu derivative	Antibacterial	Tokura *et al.* (1980)	
Thiopeptin A_1 and B	13	3 ΔAla, ΔAbu derivative	Antibacterial	Hensens and Albers-Schönberg (1978)	
Thiostrepton	13	3 ΔAla, ΔAbu derivative	Antibacterial	Anderson *et al.* (1970)	
Stendomycin	14	ΔAbu	Antibacterial	Bodanszky *et al.* (1969a)	
Subtilin	32	2 ΔAla, ΔAbu	Antibacterial	Gross *et al.* (1973b)	
Nisin	34	2 ΔAla, ΔAbu	Antibacterial	Gross and Morell (1971a)	
L-Histidine ammonia lyase	>100	ΔAla derivative	Enzyme	Givot *et al.* (1969)	
L-Phenylalanine ammonia lyase	>100	ΔAla derivative	Enzyme	Hanson and Havir (1970)	

[a] ΔAbu, α,β-dehydro-α-aminobutyric acid; ΔAla, α,β-dehydroalanine (aminoacrylic acid); ΔHis, α,β-dehydrohistidine; ΔIle, α,β-dehydroisoleucine; ΔLeu, α,β-dehydroleucine; ΔMePhe, α,β-dehydro-*N*-methylphenylalanine; ΔPhe, α,β-dehydrophenylalanine; ΔPro, α,β-dehydroproline; ΔVal, α,β-

of cross-links in peptides and proteins (Friedman, 1977). Lanthionine (1) and β-methyllanthionine (2), the constituents of nisin (Gross and Morell, 1970,

$$\underset{NH_2}{\overset{\textstyle}{HOOC-CH}}-CH_2-S-\underset{NH_2}{\overset{\textstyle R}{CH}}-CH-COOH$$

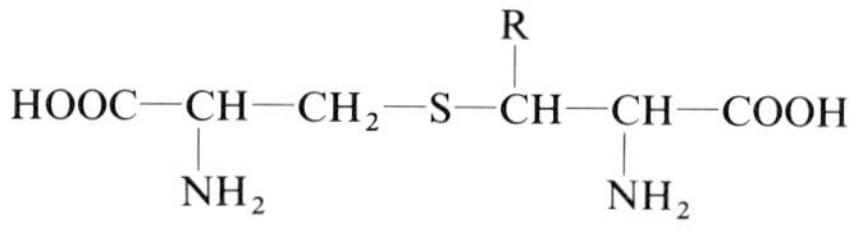

(1) R = H
(2) R = CH$_3$

1971a) and subtilin (Gross *et al.*, 1973a), are presumed to be formed by addition of the sulfhydryl group of cysteine residues across the double bond of ΔAla and dehydro-α-aminobutyric acid (ΔAbu), respectively (Gross, 1977; Asquith and Carthew, 1972). The addition appears to be stereospecific, as it was observed that all α-carbon atoms of one of the alanine moieties in the lanthionine residues and the α-aminobutyric acid moieties in the β-methyllanthionines had the D configuration.

The antibiotics cinnamycin and duramycin contain lysinoalanine (3) in addition to 1 and 2 (Gross, 1977). The formation of the imino bridge is attributed to addition of the ε-amino group of a lysine residue across the

$$\underset{NH_2}{\overset{\textstyle}{HOOC-CH}}-CH_2-NH-CH_2-CH_2-CH_2-CH_2-\underset{NH_2}{\overset{\textstyle}{CH}}-COOH$$

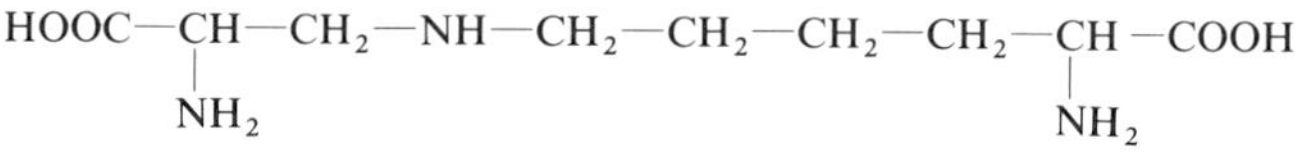

(3)

α,β-unsaturated bond of ΔAla. Bycroft (1969) indicated that a possible pathway for the biosynthesis of D-amino acids in microorganisms may proceed through the dehydration–rehydration of L-amino acids.

B. Structure and Activity of α,β-Dehydropeptides

The discovery of a variety of biological activities has facilitated the isolation and characterization of α,β-dehydropeptides from various sources. Some of these that are of particular interest because of their potential pharmacological and physiological usefulness are described here. The natural occurrence of several α,β-dehydroamino acid derivatives has also been reported. An example is primocarcin, whose structure (4) (Isono, 1962) was confirmed by chemical synthesis (Bowman *et al.*, 1965).

$$CH_3CO-NH-\overset{\textstyle \overset{CH_2}{\|}}{C}-CO-CH_2-CH_2-CONH_2$$

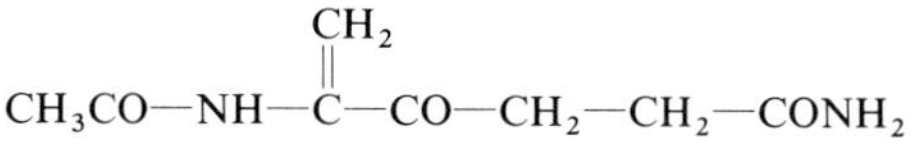

(4)

1. Neoechinulins

Neoechinulin was isolated as a metabolic product of *Aspergillus amstelodami* and identified as a cyclic compound (**5a**) containing a dehydrotryptophan (ΔTrp) unit with isoprenyl groups on the indole ring (Barbetta *et al.*, 1969). A number of analogous piperazinediones, such as neoechinulin A (**5b**) (Itokawa *et al.*, 1973; Stipanovic and Schroeder, 1976), B (**5c**), C (**5d**) (Dossena *et al.*, 1974; Cardillo *et al.*, 1974), D (**5e**) (Dossena *et al.*, 1975), and E (**5f**) (Marchelli *et al.*, 1977), have been isolated and characterized in recent years. Nagasawa *et al.* (1976) also reported the isolation of similar derivatives, isoechinulin A (**5g**), B (**5h**), and C (**5i**), in which the isoprenyl group is linked to the indole ring at position 5 (R^1).

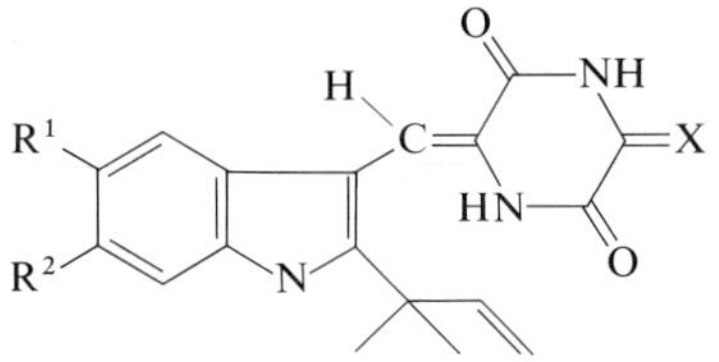

(5a–i)

	R^1	R^2	X
Neoechinulin (**5a**)	H	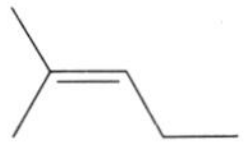	O
Neoechinulin A (**5b**)	H	H	H, CH_3
Neoechinulin B (**5c**)	H	H	CH_2
Neoechinulin C (**5d**)	H	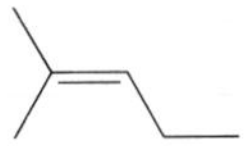	CH_2
Neoechinulin D (**5e**)	H	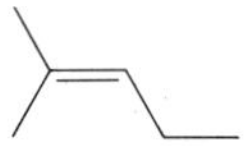	H, CH_3
Neoechinulin E (**5f**)	H	H	O
Isoechinulin A (**5g**)	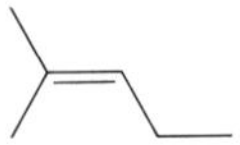	H	H, CH_3
Isoechinulin B (**5h**)	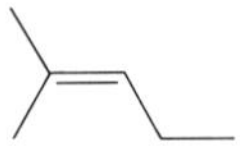	H	CH_2
Isoechinulin C (**5i**)	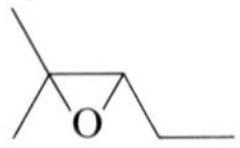	H	CH_2

The geometrical configuration arising from the α,β-double bond of ΔTrp was determined to be of the *Z* type (**6**) by ^{1}H-nmr study (Marchelli *et al.*, 1977) and ^{13}C-nmr study (Cardillo *et al.*, 1975) (see Section III,C,2). It was

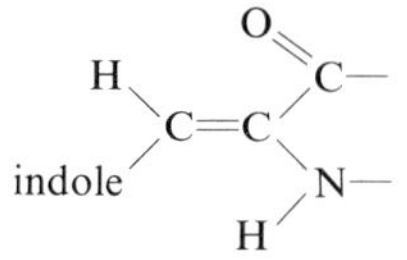

(6)

shown that the α,β-double bond of neoechinulins could not be hydrogenolyzed by platinum-catalyzed reduction, in contrast to other double bonds in the molecule. This was probably caused by steric hindrance from the indol isoprenyl group. The biosynthetic pathways of these peptides were investigated by Cardillo *et al.* (1975) and Marchelli *et al.* (1975). It was suggested that *cyclo*(Trp-Ala) is the precursor of **5a** and that peptides **5b**–**5f** are the intermediates in the following mechanisms: successive dehydrogenation, substitution on the indole nucleus, and oxidation of the ΔAla residue.

Nagasawa *et al.* (1975) reported that isoechinulin A inhibited the growth of silkworms, however, the full biological activity spectrum of neoechinulins has not been determined.

Before neoechinulins were discovered, isolation of the closely related compound echinulin was reported. Its structure is *cyclo*(LTrp-LAla) with three isoprenyl groups in the 2, 5, and 7 positions of the indole ring (Cardani *et al.*. 1959; Nakashima and Slater, 1971).

2. Stendomycin

Stendomycin, produced by *Streptomyces endus*, is an antimycotic peptide that prevents the growth of *Aspergillus*, *Penicillium*, *Trichlophyton*, *Candida*, and *Saccharomyces* (Thompson and Hughes, 1963). The primary structure of stendomycin was determined to be a tetradecapeptide (**7**) with a hetero-

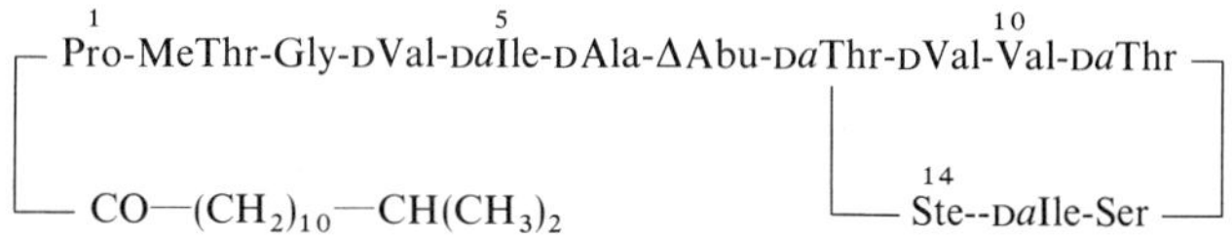

(7)

detic cyclic structure (Bodanszky *et al.*, 1968a, 1969a). The presence of ΔAbu in the peptide was established by obtaining α-ketobutyric acid from the acid hydrolysate and α-aminobutyric acid from the acid hydrolysate of dihydrostendomycin (Bodanszky *et al.*, 1968b). A new basic amino acid, L-stendomycidine (**8**), was also found to be a constituent (Bodanszky *et al.*, 1969b; Marconi and Bodanszky, 1970). The amino acid abbreviations used hereafter refer to the L-configuration unless otherwise noted. There are additional

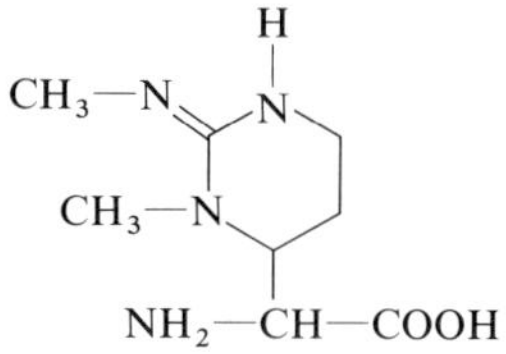

Ste = L-stendomycidine Ste (**8**)

derivatives with lower *N*-acyl groups, and analogs in which D-*allo*-isoleucine (DaIle) has been replaced by D-valine or D-leucine also exist. Dihydrostendomycin obtained by hydrogenation of ΔAbu[7] also prevents the growth of *Blastomycetes* (Bodanszky *et al.*, 1969a).

Optical rotary dispersion (ORD) measurements showed that stendomycin and its dihydro derivative gave the same Cotton effect, whereas such a Cotton effect could not be observed for the inactive stendomycinic acid obtained by saponification of **7**. This indicates that a specific conformation may be fixed by the lactone ring that is essential to the biological activity (Bodanszky *et al.*, 1969a; Bodanszky and Bodanszky, 1968). Conformational nmr studies on **7** have also been reported (Pitner and Urry, 1972; Urry, 1972). The addition of thioglycolic acid to the ΔAbu[7] residue and subsequent acid hydrolysis gave a carboxymethylthio derivative (**9**) that contained only two optical isomers, rather than the four possible isomers, indicating that the thiol addition might take place from the less sterically hindered side in the plane formed by ΔAbu (Bodanszky *et al.*, 1969b).

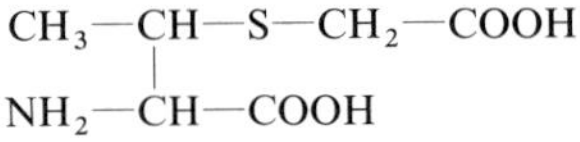

(**9**)

3. Heptamycins

Heptamycins are antibiotic peptides produced by *Bacillus subtilis*, which inhibit the growth of gram-positive bacteria. The primary structure of heptamycins was investigated independently by two groups. Shoji and coworkers isolated an antibiotic peptide termed TL-119 from the culture broth of *B. subtilis* and proposed a structure for the peptide except for its stereochemistry (Shoji *et al.*, 1975; Nakagawa *et al.*, 1975). Ogawa *et al.*, (1977) isolated two antibiotics, A-3302-A and A-3302-B, from the same strain and

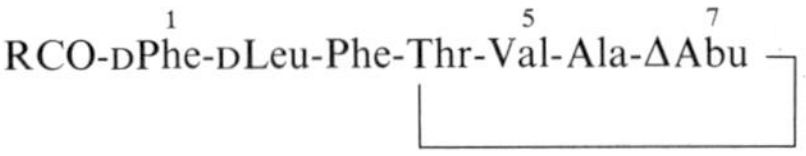

(**10a**) R = CH_3
(**10b**) R = CH_3CH_2

determined their chemical and stereochemical structures. Eventually, A-3302-B was suggested to be identical to TL-119. The names heptamycin A and B have been proposed for these peptides by one of the present authors (N.I.). Work toward synthesis of these peptides is in progress.

Heptamycin A (**10a**) and B (**10b**) are heterodetic heptapeptides with acetyl and propionyl groups at the NH_2-terminus, respectively. The D-configurations of the two NH_2-terminal amino acid residues were confirmed by the biological method using *Lactobacillus plantarum* and *Streptococcus faecalis*, and by the gas chromatographic method. The geometrical arrangement of ΔAbu^7 in **10a** and **10b** was determined to be of the (*Z*) type by nmr studies, since the chemical shifts of methyl and vinyl protons of ΔAbu in these peptides showed a better correspondence with those in authentic Z-LAla-(*Z*)-ΔAbu-OMe rather than with those in Z-LAla-(*E*)-ΔAbu-OMe (Ogawa *et al.*, 1977).

4. Subtilin

This basic polypeptide antibiotic was isolated from *B. subtilis* and inhibits the growth of *Sarcina lutea*, *Staphylococcus aureus*, *Mycobacterium phlei*, and other microorganisms (Jansen and Hirschman, 1944; Stracher and Craig, 1959). The occurrence of the sulfur-containing amino acids lanthionine and β-methyllanthionine in nature was first established in this peptide (Alderton, 1953). Treatment of subtilin with HCl–AcOH liberated pyruvyllysine, which was also released from the antibiotic nisin by the same reaction (Gross and Morell, 1967). This immediately established the COOH–terminal sequence ΔAla-Lys to be identical to the two terminating residues of nisin (Gross *et al.*, 1969). An additional residue of ΔAla and one of ΔAbu were recognized subsequent to mercaptan addition to subtilin or subtilin fragments (Gross and Kiltz, 1973) after tryptic and thermolytic fragmentation (Kiltz and Gross, 1973). With the use of the methods developed for nisin (Gross and Morell, 1970, 1971a), the primary structure of subtilin was determined to be a heterodetic pentacyclic peptide (**11**) (Gross *et al.*, 1973b).

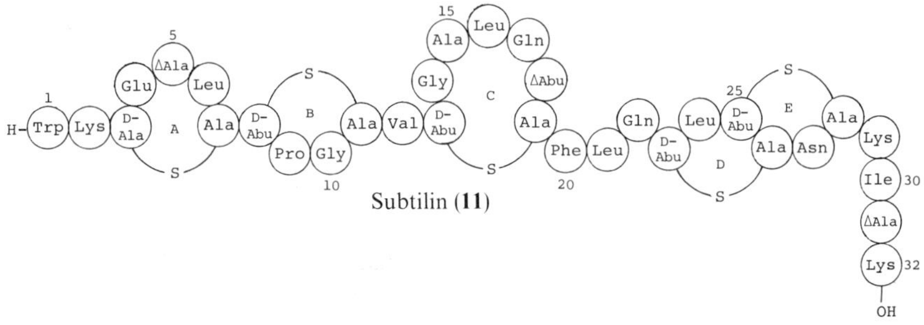

Subtilin (**11**)

The close relationship between the structures of nisin (**61**, see Section IV,A,3) and subtilin (**11**) is evident from the figures. Both peptides contain equal numbers of residues of ΔAla (two each), ΔAbu (one each), lanthionine (one each), and β-methyllanthionine (four each), besides identical COOH-terminal sequences of ΔAla-Lys. All amino acids participating in sulfide bridges in subtilin are found in positions identical to those in nisin, and consequently all rings are of the same size as those in nisin. Amino acid exchanges obviously occurred in a number of places. The phylogenetic questions to be asked are numerous. One of these concerns the reasons for the preservation of structure in two microorganisms—a spore-forming *Bacillus* and a *Streptococcus*—that are no longer so closely related (Gross, 1977).

Gross proposed a working hypothesis for the biological action of peptides with α,β-dehydroamino acids that calls for the addition of essential sulfhydryl groups across the double bond in α,β-dehydroamino acids. Indeed, it was found that nisin and nisin fragments exhibited a variety of biological activities: (1) They displayed antimalarial activity (Gross and Morell, 1967), presumably by depriving the parasite of the necessary supply of coenzyme A through the host organism; (2) they caused the *in vitro* release of lysosomal enzymes, presumably by interacting with sulfhydryl group-dependent proteins and/or enzymes located in the organellar membrane; (3) they induced fetal resorption and/or inhibited implantation of the ovum via mechanisms as yet not adequately studied (Gross and Morell, 1971b; Gross, 1975).

III. SYNTHESIS OF α,β-DEHYDROAMINO ACIDS AND INTRODUCTION INTO PEPTIDES

The first synthesis of an α,β-dehydroamino acid was carried out 100 years ago by Plöchl (1883) who prepared the azlactone of dehydrophenylalanine (ΔPhe). This approach, via an Erlenmeyer synthesis, was further developed by Bergmann (Bergmann *et al.*, 1926) and used to synthesize a series of ΔPhe-containing peptides. However, by the early 1960s, few dehydropeptides containing other dehydroamino acids had been prepared because of the instability of azlactones with alkyl substituents.

Recently, more facile and effective methods have been developed for the preparation of dehydroamino acids. The reason for this revival of interest has been the discovery of many dehydroamino acids in nature. Moreover, incorporation of dehydroamino acid residues into peptide antibiotics, peptide hormones, and enzymes has provided analogs exhibiting modified bioactivity that have been useful for establishing structure–activity relationships.

Methods for the synthesis of several dehydroamino acids are described in this section. General procedures that can be applied to the preparation of most dehydroamino acids, such as N-chlorination–dehydrochlorination or pseudoazlactone procedures are also discussed.

A. Procedures for Synthesis of α,β-Dehydroamino Acids

1. Dehydroalanine

ΔAla has no substituents on the β-carbon and should be the most electrophilic dehydroamino acid. Consequently, ΔAla is the most reactive dehydroamino acid toward nucleophiles, and it forms additives and polymerizes. Saturated amino acids such as serine, cysteine, alanine, and α,β-diaminopropionic acid are usually utilized as precursors of ΔAla.

a. ΔAla from Serine. α-Protected serine is most frequently used as a starting material in generating ΔAla. Photaki (1963) introduced the efficient β-elimination method using *O*-tosylserine as shown in Scheme 1. Alternative

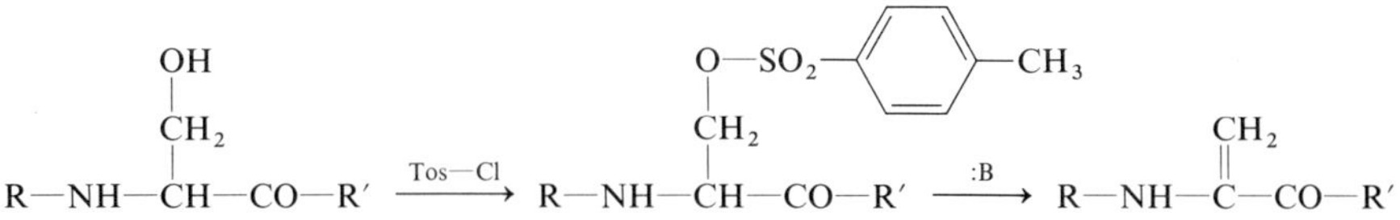

Scheme 1

β-leaving groups for serine *O*-sulfonate have been reported such as the phenylmethanesulfonyl ($SO_2CH_2C_6H_5$) (Ako *et al.*, 1972a,b) and methanesulfonyl (SO_2CH_3) groups (Shimohigashi and Izumiya, 1968a; Shin *et al.*, 1978). These have been used successfully in introducing the ΔAla residue into several peptide toxins (see Section IV,A,2), hormones (see Section IV,B), and enzymes such as trypsin (Ako *et al.*, 1972b) and chymotrypsin (Weiner *et al.*, 1966; Ako *et al.*, 1972a). Srinivasan *et al.*, (1977a) reported the replacement of β-hydroxy by the chloro group followed by α,β-dehydrochlorination to yield the ΔAla residue (Scheme 2).

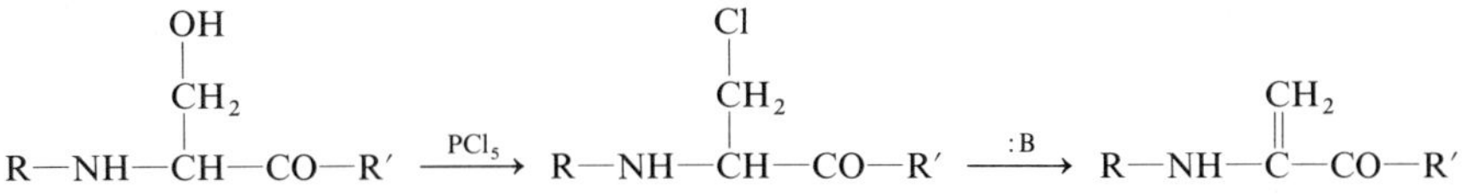

Scheme 2

Other reported β-leaving groups for the serine residue are diphenylphosphoryl [$(C_6H_5O)_2P{=}O$] (Photaki, 1963) and *tert*-butoxycarbonyl (Schnabel *et al.*, 1971). However, in these β-elimination methods, the side reactions sometimes encountered may result in poor yields and formation of inseparable mixtures. The possible side reactions have been reviewed (Schmidt *et al.*, 1979) and include oxazoline formation, aziridine formation, hydantoin formation, and nucleophilic substitutions. A disadvantage of these methods is also the generation of unstable intermediates.

These problems have been resolved by Miller (1980) who developed the direct isourea-mediated β-elimination process for serine and cysteine to yield the ΔAla residue (Scheme 3). In the presence of copper(I) chloride

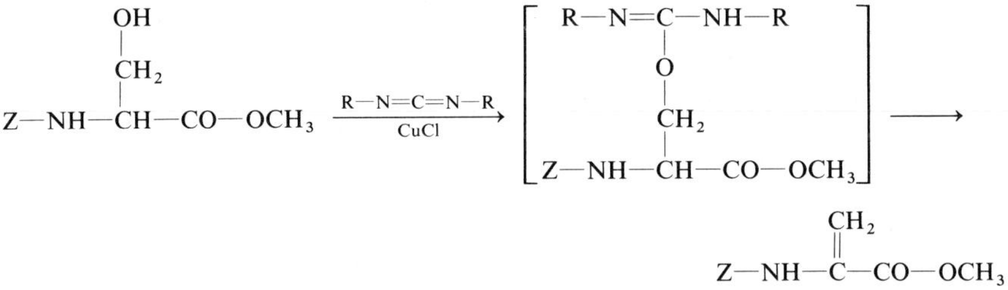

Scheme 3

catalyst (30 mol%) the treatment of serine peptides with a carbodiimide (1.1 equiv) afforded the corresponding ΔAla peptides in yields of 80–95%.

Direct β-elimination also takes place in 90% yield by treatment of a serine peptide with an equimolar amount of disuccinimido carbonate (DSC) (**12**) and triethylamine (Scheme 4) under rather mild conditions (Ogura *et al.*, 1981).

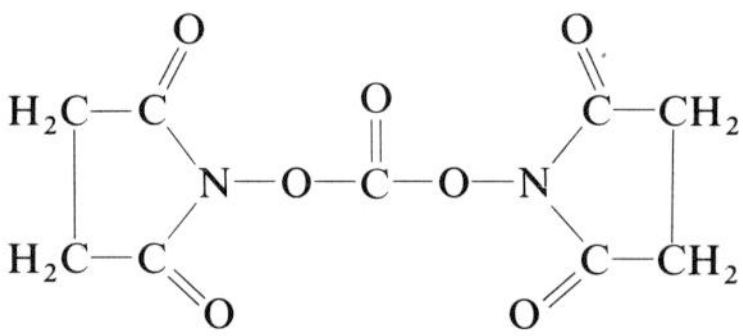

(**12**)

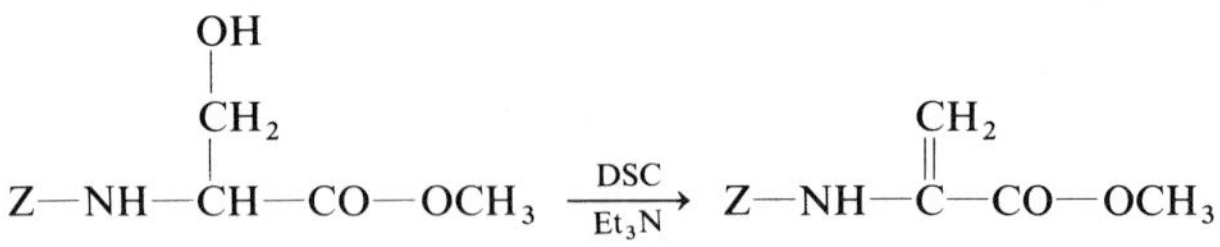

Scheme 4

The use of two equimolar amounts of DSC (**12**) for Z-Ser-OH affords Z-ΔAla-OSu (in 80% yield) which can serve directly in the coupling with amino acid esters (Scheme 5).

Z-Ser-OH $\xrightarrow{\text{2 DSC}}$ Z-ΔAla-OSu $\xrightarrow{\text{H-Gly-OEt}}$ Z-ΔAla-Gly-OEt

Scheme 5

b. ΔAla from Cysteine and Other Amino Acids. Thiol-substituted cysteine residues are susceptible to β-elimination reactions that give rise to ΔAla residues (Scheme 6). Several leaving groups (X) including sulfur have

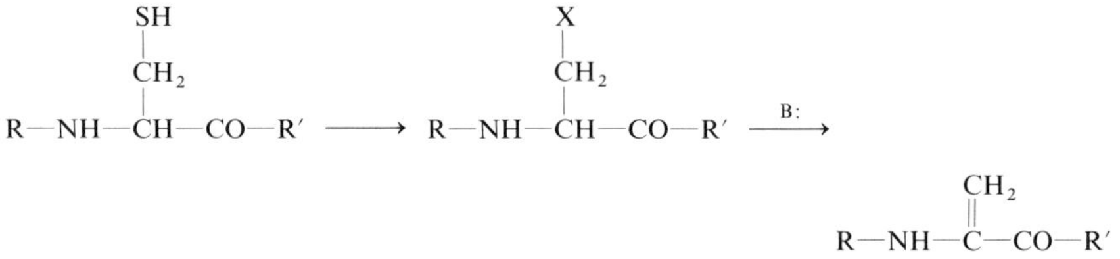

Scheme 6

been reported: sulfoxide (Rich and Tam, 1977), sulfone (Gross *et al.*, 1975), *S,S*-dimethylsulfonium $[-\overset{+}{S}(CH_3)_2]$ (Sokolovsky *et al.*, 1964; Öhler and Schmidt, 1977), *S*-2,4-dinitrophenyl (Sokolovsky *et al.*, 1964), and *S*-dimethylphosphinothioyl (Ueki *et al.*, 1981).

Oxidation of the selenocysteine derivative produces the ΔAla derivative, presumably through its selenoxide-like sulfoxide, as shown in Scheme 7 (Walter and Roy, 1971).

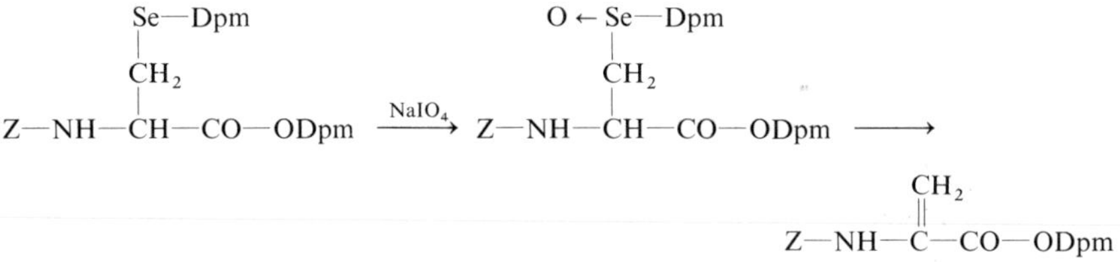

Dpm = $CH(C_6H_5)_2$

Scheme 7

Nomoto *et al.* (1979) reported the direct formation of a ΔAla residue from an α,β-diaminopropionic acid residue, mediated by Hofmann degradation utilizing methyl iodide and potassium bicarbonate (Scheme 8). The isolation of the resulting ΔAla peptides in 60–95% yield is rather easy because of the basic properties of the starting material and intermediates.

One of the possible pathways for production of the dehydroamino acid unit *in vivo* is the formation of an imino acid unit which is readily rearranged to an enamino acid, that is, the dehydroamino acid unit, by N-hydroxylation and subsequent dehydration. Herscheid *et al.* (1981) has reported that this hypothesis works well in chemical synthesis. The *N*-hydroxyamic derivative

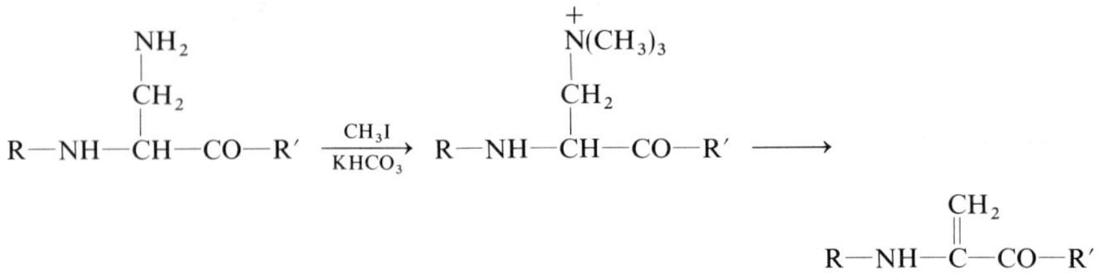

Scheme 8

of alanine was acetylated and then deacetylated by treatment with 1,7-diazabicyclo[5.4.0]undec-5-ene (DBU) to yield a rearranged enamine, that is, the ΔAla moiety in 70–95% yield (Scheme 9).

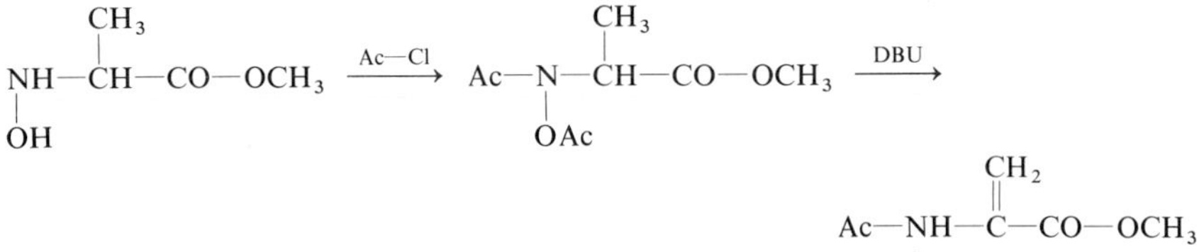

Scheme 9

Many synthetic methods for preparing ΔAla peptides have been reported in recent years: condensation between amides and pyruvates (see Section III,A,4), dehydrobromination of bromopseudoazlactones (see Section III,A,5), and others.

2. Dehydroaminobutyric Acid

a. ΔAbu from Threonine. ΔAbu, which has a methyl group at the *β*-carbon, can be derived from threonine by essentially the same methods used for the synthesis of ΔAla from serine. However, because of this methyl group on the *β*-carbon, two geometrical isomers with *Z*- (methyl and C=O, trans) (**13a**) and *E*- (methyl and C=O, cis) (**13b**) configurations are formed. Therefore, either stereoselective synthesis or separation of the isomers must be taken into consideration.

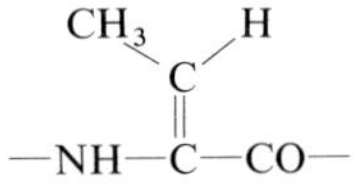

(*Z*) (**13a**)

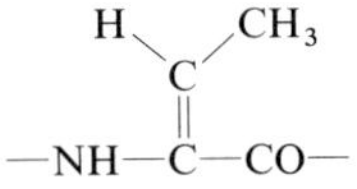

(*E*) (**13b**)

Srinivasan *et al.* (1977b) reported detailed stereochemical studies on *β*-elimination of threonine derivatives. *N*-Acyl-DL-threonine methyl ester (threo type) (**14**) gives only the stable *Z*-isomer of *N*-acylaminobutenate (**15**) upon O-tosylation and subsequent elimination by triethylenediamine (DABCO) as base (Scheme 10). The underlying mechanism may be trans

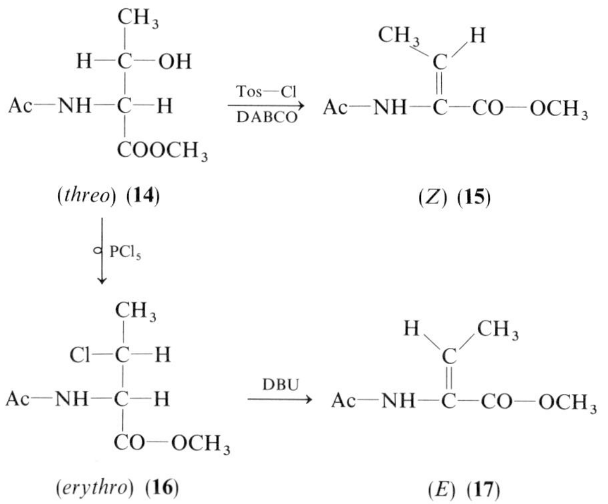

Scheme 10

E_2-elimination. α-Acylamino-β-chloro-DL-butyric acid methyl ester (erythro) (**16**), which is derived from **14** by chlorination with inversion of configuration of the β-carbon, yields predominantly the *E*-isomer (**17**) by brief treatment with DBU as base. A prolonged reaction time and use of the base DABCO cause a significant amount of isomerization to the *Z*-isomer. Lee *et al.* (1979) have confirmed the stereospecific formation of the ΔAbu from *O*-tosylthreonine derivatives: that is, *Z*-isomer from the threo type and *E*-isomer from the erythro type. It should be noted, however, that extensive side reactions such as aziridine formation may occur with certain *O*-tosylthreonine peptides by treatment with base (Nakagawa *et al.*, 1972).

Using DSC for direct β-elimination, Ogura *et al.* (1981) found only the *Z*-isomer (**19**) of the ΔAbu unit from Z-Thr-OMe (**18**) in 70% yield. In contrast, the isourea-mediated β-elimination method for threonine peptides (Miller, 1980), which involved carbodiimide and CuCl catalysis (see Section III,A,1), formed a mixture of *Z*- and *E*-isomers in a 2:3 ratio.

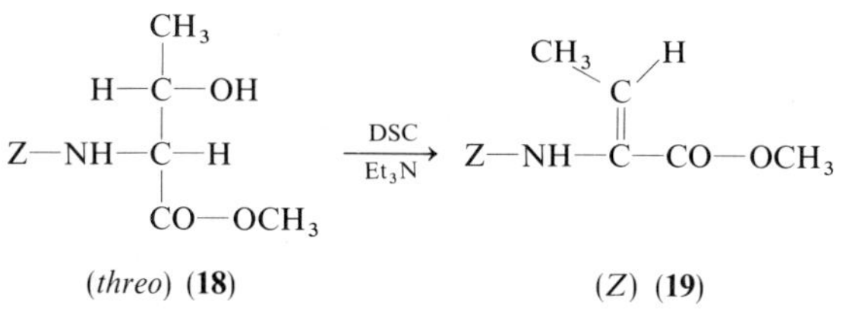

b. ΔAbu from Other Derivatives. Rich and Tam (1977) reported the stereospecific thermolytic elimination of β-alkylsulfinyl derivatives of 2-aminobutyrate in about 80% yield. The threo isomer of Boc-Abu(3-S(O)Bzl)OMe (**20**) gave exclusively the (*E*)-ΔAbu derivative (**21**), whereas the erythro isomer yielded exclusively the (*Z*)-ΔAbu derivative, suggesting that elimination proceeded by the cis mechanism.

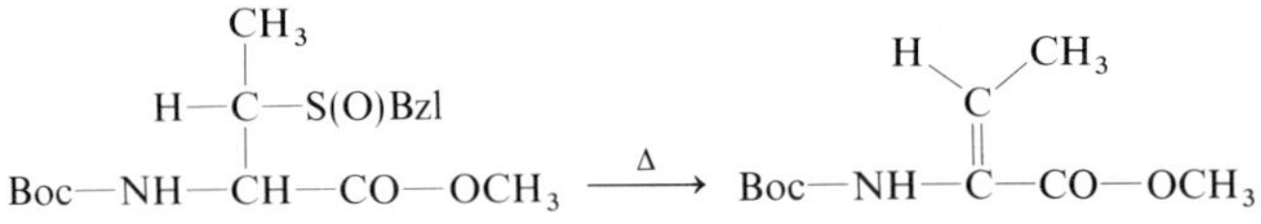

(*threo*) (**20**) (*E*) (**21**)

The ΔAbu unit can be formed by the N-hydroxylation–dehydration method (see Section III,A,1) or the N-chlorination–dehydrochlorination (see Section III,A,3) method. A condensation method (amide and pyruvate derivative, Section III,A,4) also forms the ΔAbu unit.

3. Dehydrovaline

Dehydrovaline (ΔVal) has no geometrical isomers because of the two methyl groups on the β-carbon. Consequently, it may serve as a sterically bulky dehydroamino acid. Grigg and Kemp (1977) have reported that the benzylidene derivative (**22**) of H-Val-OMe was dehydrogenated with diethyl azodicarboxylate (EtOOC—N=N—COOEt) to afford the ΔVal derivative (**23**). This procedure probably involved an ene reaction and was also successfully used for the preparation of (*Z*)-ΔPhe and of ΔIle with a mixture of *Z*- and *E*-isomers.

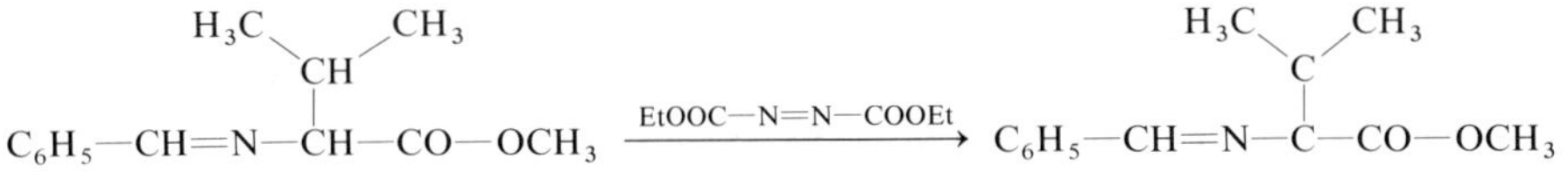

(**22**) (**23**)

A possible *in vivo* synthetic pathway for dehydroamino acids, mediated by N-hydroxylation–dehydration (see Section III,A,1) has been successfully extended by Schmidt and co-workers (Schmidt and Öhler, 1977; Poisel and Schmidt, 1976; Poisel, 1977a,b) to the N-chlorination–dehydrochlorination method. Acylvaline esters are N-chlorinated with *tert*-butylhypochloride (*t*BuOCl). The use of DBU as a base eliminates HCl to yield an acylimino ester which is spontaneously rearranged to the acyldehydroamino acid (ΔVal) ester by DBU as shown in Scheme 11. The treatment of *N*-chloro derivatives with methoxide ion in methanol resulted in the formation of α-acylamino-α-methoxy acid derivatives. These α-alkoxy intermediates can be converted into ΔVal esters by acid- or base-catalyzed elimination.

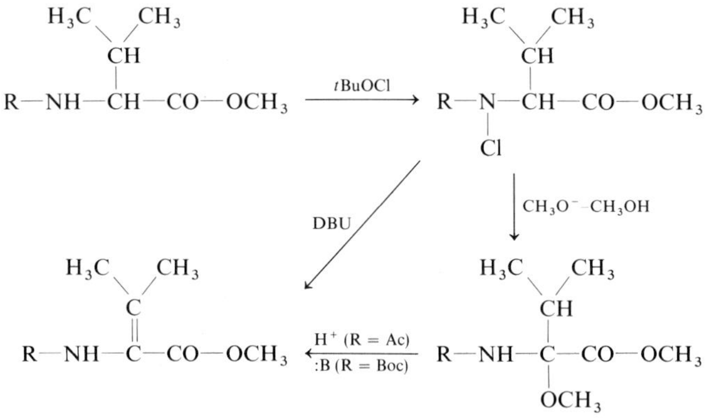

Scheme 11

Shin *et al.* (1971) reported the preparation of 2-imino-3-methylbutyric acid ethyl ester (**25**) in 40% yield by condensation of α-keto ester (**24**) with triphenylphosphine imine. The isolated imine (**25**) was converted into the enamino (ΔVal) derivative (**26**) by acylation with chloroacetyl chloride. The α-imino acid ester can be rearranged to the enamino form by treatment with HCl–ether at −70°C according to the procedure of Schmidt and Öhler (1977).

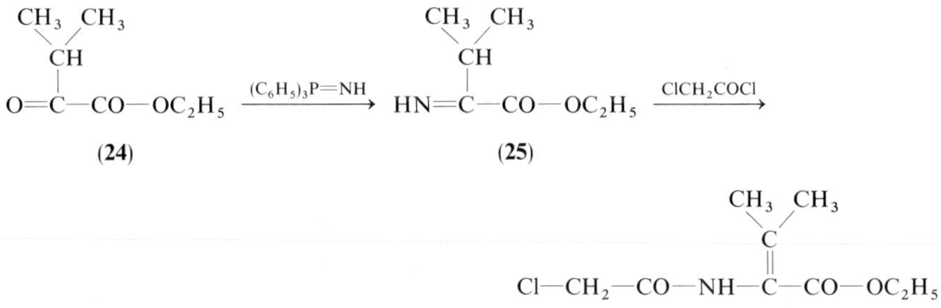

(**24**) (**25**) (**26**)

4. Dehydroleucine

Two geometric isomers with *Z*- and *E*-configurations are possible for dehydroleucine (ΔLeu): *Z*, isopropyl and C=O, trans; *E*, isopropyl and C=O, cis. It seems, however, that ordinary chemical reactions form exclusively the *Z*-isomer. This is presumably due to the orientation of its bulky isopropyl group in a trans position away from the carbonyl group, thus stabilizing the less hindered structure. The ΔLeu derivatives can be prepared by essentially the same methods as described for ΔVal. Among these, the N-chlorination–dehydrochlorination method appears to be most efficient.

Schmidt and Öhler (1977) reported the preparation of ΔLeu esters with free amino groups as shown in Scheme 12. The α-imino acid ester was rearranged into the hydrochloride of H-ΔLeu-OMe by treatment with HCl–ether at a very low temperature (−70°C).

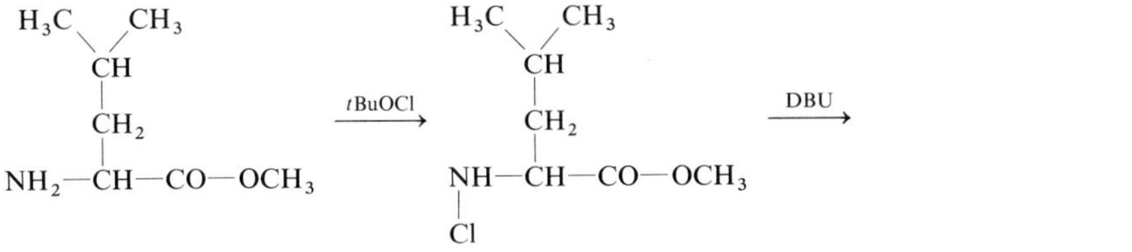

Scheme 12

The condensation reaction of α-keto acids with amides has been frequently applied in the synthesis of dehydroamino acid derivatives (Scheme 13). This process is also a possible *in vivo* pathway for producing dehydroamino

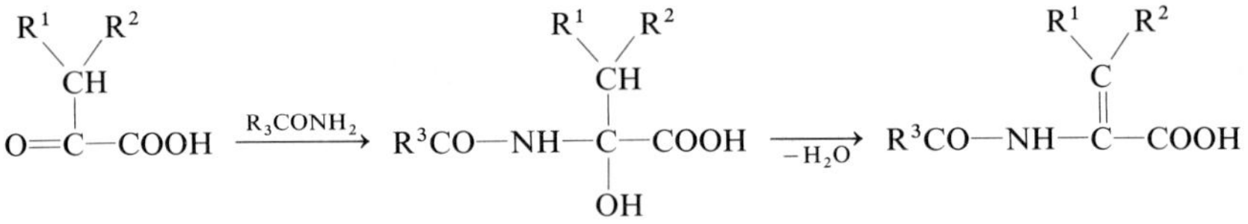

Scheme 13

acids. When benzyl carbamate ($C_6H_5CH_2OCONH_2$) was used as an amide component for the α-keto acid (**27**), N^{α}-benzyloxycarbonyldehydroamino acid (**28**) was directly prepared in 80–90% yield with the *Z*-configuration

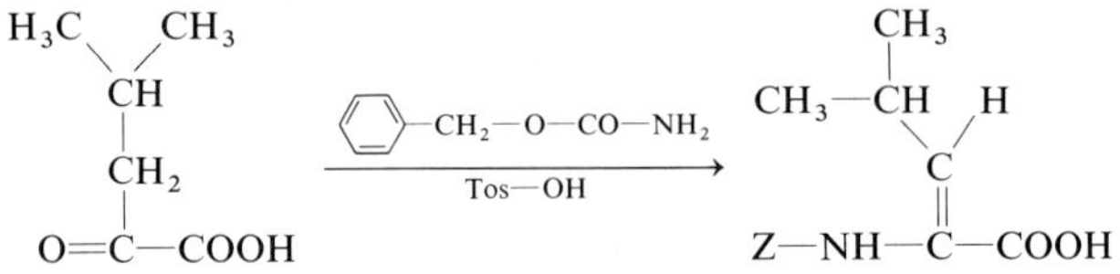

(**27**) (*Z*) (**28**)

(Shin *et al.*, 1979). 4-Toluenesulfonic acid served as a catalyst for the dehydration of the α-hydroxy intermediate. This method is also suitable for the preparation of (*Z*)-ΔAbu, (*Z*)-dehydronorvaline (ΔNva), (*Z*)-dehydronorleucine (ΔNle), and (*Z*)-ΔPhe. A wide variety of procedures for the condensation of α-keto acids with amides and nitriles have been described in the reviews by Greenstein and Winitz (1961), Shin (1979), and Schmidt *et al.* (1979).

5. *Dehydrophenylalanine*

ΔPhe is one of the most frequently used, and well-studied dehydroamino acids. ΔPhe has two geometrical isomers: *Z*, phenyl ring and C=O, trans; *E*, phenyl ring and C=O, cis.

a. ΔPhe Azlactone from Glycine. Employing unsaturated azlactone derivatives (**29**) of phenylalanine, Bergmann *et al.* (1926) applied the Erlenmeyer condensation in the syntheses of a series of ΔPhe peptides as shown in Scheme 14 (Doherty *et al.*, 1943; also reviewed by Greenstein and

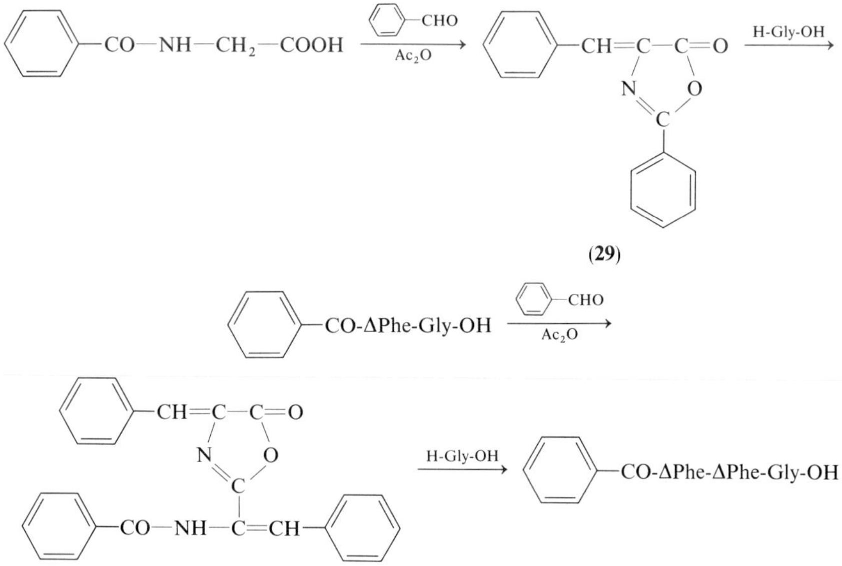

Scheme 14

Winitz, 1961). In such a continuous synthesis, the concomitant formation of stereoisomers has been suggested because of the possibility of cis–trans isomerization at the α,β-double bond. A wide range of azlactone derivatives of ΔPhe have been reviewed by Rao and Filler (1975).

b. ΔPhe Azlactone from β-Phenylserine and Other Amino Acids. β-Phenylserine peptides (**30**) can be converted into the corresponding azlactones (**31**) of ΔPhe peptides in 70% yields by treatment with an acetic

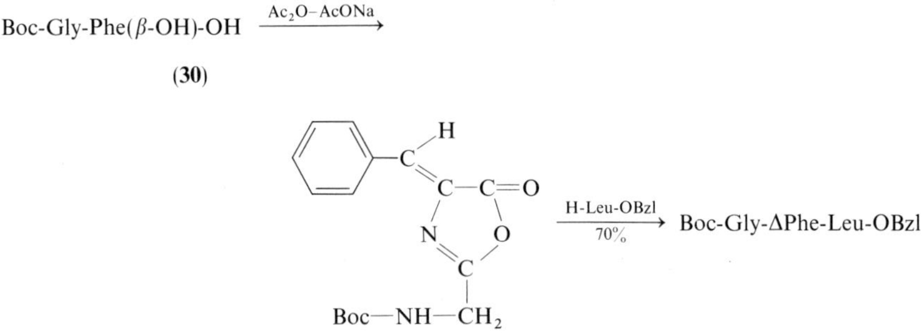

(**30**)

(*Z*) (**31**)

acid–sodium acetate solution (Konno and Stammer, 1978; Shimohigashi and Stammer, 1982). An attempt to prepare such azlactones using the Erlenmeyer condensation gave less than 5% of the desired product. The incubation of the azlactone (**31**) and the free base of leucine benzyl ester produced the tripeptide N^{α}-*tert*-butyloxycarbonyl-glycyl-dehydrophenyl-alanyl-leucine benzyl ester. The oxidation of saturated azlactones (**32**) by 2,3-dichloro-5,6-dicyano-1,4-benzoquinone (DDQ) or *O*-chloranil, in the presence of collidine as a weak base, afforded the α,β-unsaturated azlactone (**33**) in 40–50% yield (Konno and Stammer, 1978).

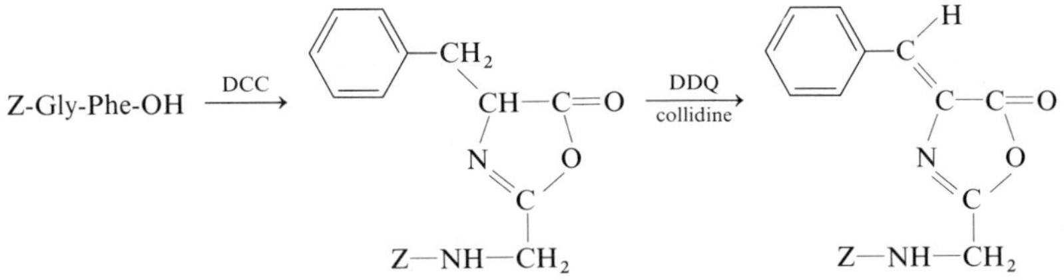

(**32**) (*Z*) (**33**)

Breitholle and Stammer (1976) reported the preparation of an unsaturated azlactone (**35**) by dehydrobromination of the bromo pseudoazlactone (**34**) as shown in Scheme 15. This procedure is applicable to the preparation of derivatives of ΔAla, ΔAbu, ΔVal, and ΔLeu, however, in these cases, the N^{α}-Tfa group was not deblocked by gaseous ammonia.

c. Other Methods and *Z-E* Isomerism. The N-chlorination–dehydrochlorination method can be used for incorporation of the ΔPhe unit. Grim

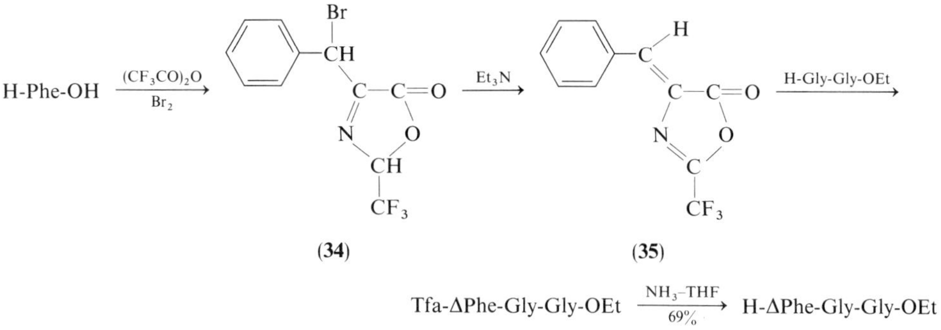

Scheme 15

et al. (1981) applied it even in the preparation of a dipeptide containing an α,β-dehydrophenylalanine residue (Scheme 16). Z-(*Z*)-ΔPhe-OH was pre-

$$\text{Z-pGlu-Phe-O}t\text{Bu} \xrightarrow[\text{DABCO}]{t\text{BuOCl}} \text{Z-pGlu-}(Z)\text{-}\Delta\text{Phe-O}t\text{Bu}$$

Scheme 16

pared by the condensation of β-phenylpyruvic acid with benzyl carbamate (see Section III,A,4, Shin *et al.*, 1979).

The azlactone of Bz-(*Z*)-ΔPhe-OH (**36**) is isomerized to its *E*-isomer (**37**) by irradiation with a 3650 Å beam, resulting in the formation of a

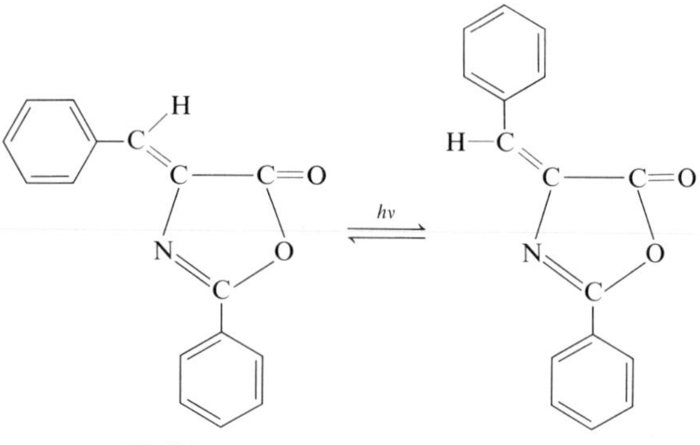

(*Z*) (**36**) (*E*) (**37**)

mixture of the *Z*- and *E*-isomers. The mixtures of geometrical isomers may be separated by silica gel column chromatography, high-performance liquid chromatography (HPLC), or fractional precipitation. Nitz *et al.* (1981) has prepared a mixture of the *Z*- and *E*-isomers of Z-ΔPhe-OEt by rearrangement of a vinyl isocyanate with benzyl alcohol. The pure Z-(*E*)-ΔPhe-OEt isolated by silica gel column was examined for its thermal and chemical stability, and it has been suggested that the *E*-isomer probably cannot survive under the conditions of usual peptide synthesis by the standard methods.

6. Dehydroamino Acids with Other β-Substituents

Application of the chemical synthetic procedures described above, in principle, allows the preparation of many other α,β-dehydroamino acids with different substituents. In particular, the *N*-chlorination–dehydrochlorination method, the condensation of α-keto acids (or esters) with benzyl carbamate (Z-NH_2), and the azlactone methods appear to be the most well-established synthetic procedures. N^{α}-*tert*-butyloxycarbonyl-*O*-dichlorobenzyldehydrotyrosine methyl ester [Boc-ΔTyr(Dcb)-OMe] was prepared by the N-chlorination method (Shimohigashi and Stammer, 1982). ΔNva and ΔNle were obtained by the condensation method (Shin *et al.*, 1979, 1981), and α,β-dehydroaminoundecanoic acid (ΔAun) was obtained by the azlactone method (Hallinan and Mazur, 1979), *N*-Acyl-ΔTrp esters were synthesized by the reaction of 3-[(1-pyrolidinyl)methylene]-3*H*-indole with *N*-acylglycine esters (Moriya *et al.*, 1982).

2,3-Dehydroproline (ΔPro) (**38**) was prepared from 1,2-ΔPro (**39**) by the addition of acetyl chloride and subsequent elimination (Poisel and Schmidt, 1975b). The latter compound was obtained by N-chlorination–dehydrochlorination of proline (Poisel and Schmidt, 1975a) and also by cyclization of 5-azido-2-oxovaleric acid (Öhler and Schmidt, 1975).

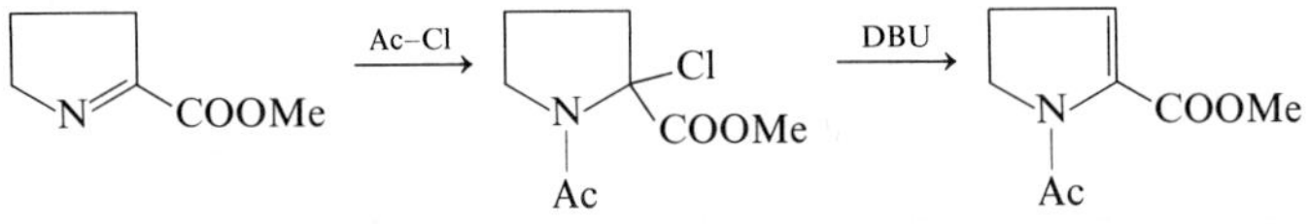

(**39**) (**38**)

Piperazinediones containing glycine residue(s) can be condensed with aldehydes on the α-methylene of the glycine residue (Sasaki, 1921; Akabori *et al.*, 1952). Gallina and Liberatori (1973) extended this approach and activated the α-methylene group in advance by N-acetylation (Scheme 17).

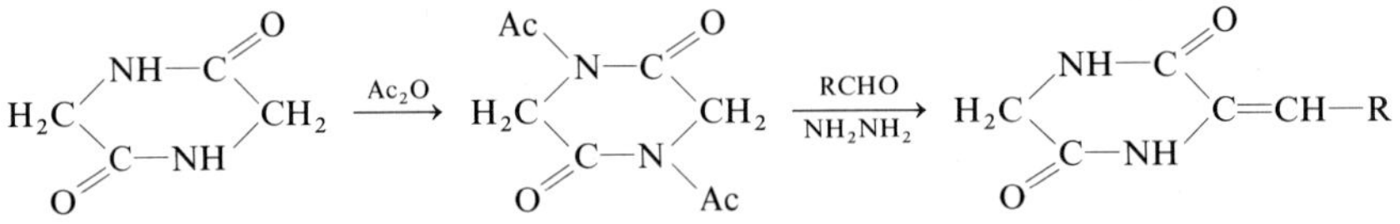

Scheme 17

Utilizing this procedure for piperazinediones containing glycine and L-amino acids, Kanmera *et al.* (1979) prepared a variety of unsaturated derivatives (ΔAbu, ΔVal, ΔPhe, ΔApp, and ΔTrp). Many dehydropiperazinediones have been found as metabolites of bacteria. Several different synthetic approaches are possible because of their six-membered cyclic structure. Schmidt *et al.* (1979) reviewed these condensation methods and the synthetic opportunities offered by α,β-dehydropiperazinediones.

B. Coupling Reactions of α,β-Dehydroamino Acid Derivatives

The coupling reactions utilizing α,β-dehydroamino acid derivatives as amine and/or acid components have not been studied frequently or in detail. When α,β-dehydroamino acid esters are used as an amine component, the coupling must be inefficient, since the amino group of enamino acid esters is less nucleophilic than that of amino acid esters: Therefore the tautomer (imino form) may be produced and interfere with the reaction. Although such coupling methods as those involving an acid chloride (Shin *et al.*, 1967, 1971) or mixed anhydrides (McCapara and Roth, 1972; Poisel, 1970a) have been used in the acylation of enamino acid esters, Shin *et al.* (1981) showed that the dicyclohexylcarbodiimide (DCC) method could also be employed for the preparation of dipeptides. Z-Ser(or Thr)-OH was coupled in 20–50% yield with several α,β-dehydroamino acid esters by the DCC method. The water-soluble carbodiimide (EDAC)–HOBt was found to be an effective method for the coupling of Boc-Phe-OH and H-ΔLeu-OBzl in 50% yield (Shimohigashi and Stammer, 1982).

When N-blocked α,β-dehydroamino acids are used as acid components, the usual coupling procedures are applicable, for example, the mixed-anhydride (Poisel and Schmidt, 1976; Konno and Stammer, 1978), *N*-carboxyanhydride (NCA) (Kurita *et al.*, 1968), or DCC (Shin *et al.*, 1981) methods. The EDAC–HOBt method was efficient in coupling Boc-ΔTyr(Dcb)-OH with tetrapeptide esters in 80–90% yield (Shimohigashi and Stammer, 1982).

The coupling of N-blocked α,β-dehydroamino acids with α,β-dehydroamino acid esters in about 50% yield was carried out by the usual acid chloride method as shown in Scheme 18 (Shin *et al.*, 1981).

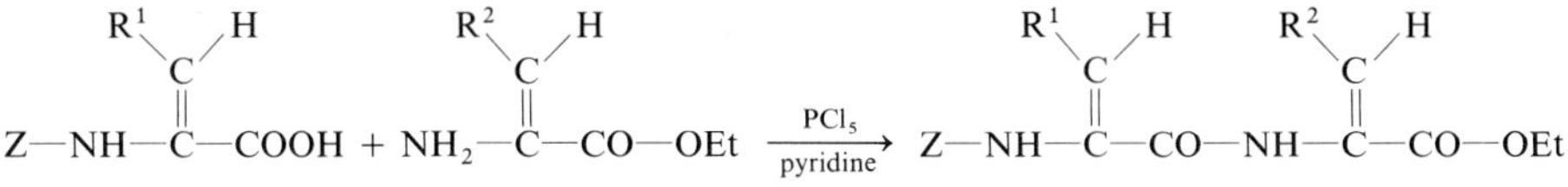

R^1, R^2 = Me, Me; Me, Et; Me, *i*Pr; Et, *i*Pr; etc.

Scheme 18

For the successful synthesis of dehydropeptides, it is important to decide when and where dehydroamino acid residues should be incorporated in a peptide sequence. The ΔAla residue should be introduced close to the final step because of its high reactivity. Peroxide-free solvents are required for both the reaction and workup to avoid polymerization of the ΔAla moiety. In order to perform chain elongation of dehydropeptides, the chemical and stereochemical stability of the α,β-unsaturated moiety must be considered in both deblocking and coupling reactions. (*Z*)-ΔLeu and (*Z*)-ΔPhe residues have been shown to be quite stable toward acids and bases (Shimohigashi and Stammer, 1982). Dehydropeptides survive the HF-anisole treatment in the final deblocking to liberate the free peptides even if ΔAla residues are present. However, as mentioned before (see Section III,A,5), it is unlikely that the *E*-configuration can be maintained during the usual peptide synthesis (Nitz *et al.*, 1981).

C. Analytical Methods for Confirmation of the α,β-Dehydroamino Acid Moiety

After the introduction of α,β-dehydroamino acids into peptides or total synthesis of dehydropeptides, it is essential to ascertain both the presence and the stereochemical properties of each unsaturated amino acid residue in the final product by careful physicochemical characterization.

1. Identification of the α,β-Dehydroamino Acid Moiety

The main characteristics used in the identification of α,β-dehydroamino acid residues are their reactivity toward nucleophiles and a variety of spectroscopic techniques that respond to the α,β-double bond. Acid hydrolysis of dehydropeptides converts the α,β-dehydroamino acid residue into the peptide or amino acid amide (finally yielding ammonia) and the ninhydrin-negative pyruvic acid derivative (α-keto acid) as shown in Scheme 19. Consequently, evidence for the presence of an α,β-dehydroamino

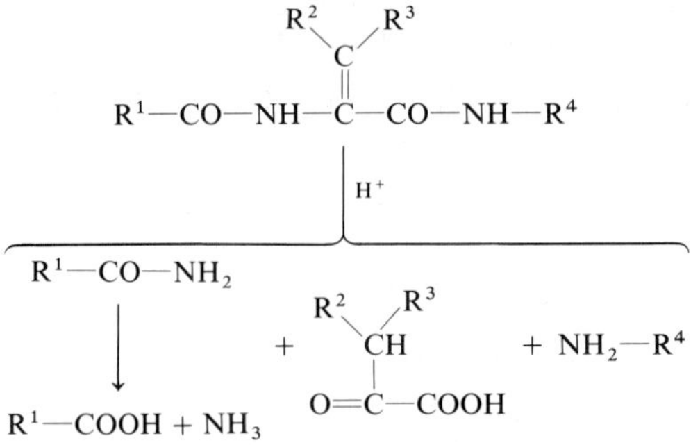

Scheme 19

acid residue in a peptide sequence can only be obtained indirectly by amino acid analysis. Hydrogenation of the dehydroamino acid moiety generates the saturated amino acid residue, which can be detected by hydrolysis and amino acid analysis (Fisher *et al.*, 1981; Shimohigashi *et al.*, 1981b). Thus, amino acid analysis, before and after hydrogenation of the α,β-unsaturated bond, provides strong proof for the presence of an α,β-dehydroamino acid residue in a peptide.

Patchornik and Sokolovsky (1964) suggested quantitative determination of the α-keto acid. Reductive tritiation with sodium borohydride yielding a saturated and labeled residue (Wickner, 1969; Hanson and Havir, 1970) and addition of thioglycolic acid (Bodanszky and Bodanszky, 1974) or nitromethane (Givot *et al.*, 1969) have been used to identify dehydroamino acid moieties in natural products.

Shimohigashi *et al.* (1981a) reported determination of the uv absorption of dehydroamino acid moieties by difference spectroscopy, in which the uv spectrum of an unsaturated peptide was scanned using the saturated analog as a reference. Three types of α,β-dehydroamino acid were characterized by their uv difference spectra: ΔAla (no β-substituents), peaks at 200 and 240 nm; (*Z*)-ΔLeu (β-alkyl substituent), peaks at 200 and 220–230 nm; and (*Z*)-ΔPhe (β-aryl substituent), peaks at 200, 220, and 280 nm. Since the saturated reference peptides can be obtained by chemical synthesis or just by hydrogenation of the samples, this method can be used to determine the presence of a dehydroamino acid moiety. In ^{1}H-nmr spectra of dehydropeptides, some profiles resulting from the α,β-unsaturated moiety can be observed: the distinct peak of the vinyl proton at 5–8 ppm and, especially, the downfield shift of the amide proton peak in DMSO-d_6 (Shimohigashi *et al.*, 1979).

2. Determination of Z- and E-Configurations

When two geometric isomers of the α,β-double bond in dehydropeptides are indicated (ΔAbu, ΔLeu, ΔPhe, etc.), it is important to determine the stereochemical structure in the *Z*-, *E*-, or *Z*, *E*-mixed configuration. Such a structural examination can be made directly by X-ray analysis of the peptide (see the review by Schmidt *et al.*, 1979). However, ^{1}H- or ^{13}C-nmr spectroscopy is usually used for this purpose. The following empirical regularities have been developed in recent years.

(1) A difference in the chemical shift of the β-vinyl and amide protons (Shin *et al.*, 1978) and the β-alkyl proton (Srinivasan *et al.*, 1976; Poisel, 1977b): The *E*-isomer appears 0.2–0.7 ppm downfield from the *Z*-isomer. (2) A change in the chemical shift (Δδ) of the vinyl proton when measured

in $CDCl_3$ and trifluoroacetic acid (TFA) (Srinivasan *et al.*, 1976): *Z*-isomer, $\Delta\delta = 0.34–0.54$ ppm downfield shift; *E*-isomer, $\Delta\delta = 0.18–0.32$ ppm upfield shift. (3) A comparison of the chemical shifts of the vinyl proton before and after N-methylation (Srinivasan *et al.*, 1976; Nitz *et al.*, 1981): *Z*-isomer, almost no change; *E*-isomer, 0.7–0.9 ppm unfield shift. (4) A difference in the vicinal coupling constant (J_{CH}) between the carbonyl carbon and the vinyl proton in the coupled nuclear Overhauser enhanced ^{13}C-nmr spectrum (Vleggaar and Wessels, 1980, and references therein): *Z*-isomer, $J = \sim 5$ Hz; *E*-isomer, $J = \sim 10$ Hz. (5) A differential nuclear overhauser effect (Noe) between the vinyl and amide protons (Shimohigashi *et al.*, 1982b): *Z*-isomer, Noe = 0%; *E*-isomer, Noe = 26–37%.

Rich and Mathiaparanam (1974) reported the uv absorption peak of the ΔPhe peptides in assigning the *Z*-configuration ($\varepsilon = 18{,}400$ at 276 nm) and the *E*-configuration ($\varepsilon = 9080$ at 282 nm). Such a difference in the intensity of the peak was not observed for the isomers of N-blocked ΔPhe-OH and its esters (Rao and Filler, 1975; Shimohigashi *et al.*, 1981a). Since spectroscopic pictures are often sensitive to environmental factors around the α,β-double bond, the use of several combined measurements is recommended for structural examinations.

IV. SYNTHESIS OF BIOLOGICALLY ACTIVE PEPTIDES WITH α,β-DEHYDROAMINO ACIDS

Because of the frequent occurrence of cyclic structures with ester bonds and uncommon amino acids besides α,β-dehydroamino acids, the chemical synthesis of naturally occurring dehydropeptides is in itself a challenging and attractive area of peptide chemistry. The synthesis of saturated analogs is obviously essential in clarifying the roles of α,β-dehydroamino acids in bioactivity. It has been shown, however, that hydrogenation of the α,β-double bond is usually associated with changes in the conformation, which is a disadvantage because the conformation is one of the important factors in the bioactivity. How the α,β-dehydroamino acid moiety takes part in the mode of action of peptides remains unclear in almost all cases.

The incorporation of α,β-dehydroamino acids into normal bioactive peptides has become another interesting objective. Indiscriminate incorporation into small peptides is now feasible. However, it is essential to substitute precisely those amino acid residues by dehydro units that are located at the active and binding sites. Interest in the synthetic aspects of natural dehydropeptides and also in unsaturated analogs of peptide hormones has increased considerably in recent years.

A. Biologically Active Dehydropeptides

1. Tentoxin

Tentoxin is a phytotoxic metabolite produced by *Alternaria tenuis*, which causes chlorosis in germinating seedlings of many flowering plants (Templeton *et al.*, 1967). The primary structure of tentoxin was determined to be a cyclotetrapeptide (**40**) by nmr and mass spectrometry (Meyer *et al.*,

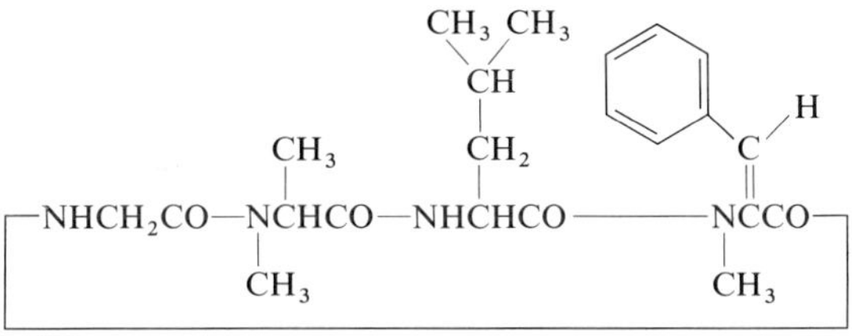

(**40**)

1974a, 1975) and confirmed by X-ray diffraction (Meyer *et al.*, 1974b). The α,β-double bond of α,β-dehydro-*N*-methylphenylalanine (ΔMePhe) was found to be in the [*Z*]-configuration.

a. Synthesis of Tentoxin. The chemical synthesis of tentoxin was achieved by Rich and his associates (Rich and Mathiaparanam, 1974; Rich *et al.*, 1975a; Rich, 1976) as shown in Scheme 20. Using 3-benzylthio-DL-phenylalanine [DLPhe(3-SBzl)] as a precursor of ΔPhe in a linear tetrapeptide (**41**), the ΔPhe residue was introduced by oxidation of the 3-benzylthio group followed by pyrolysis (Rich *et al.*, 1974). The resulting geometrical isomers with *Z*- and *E*-configurations were separated by partition chromatography. The ΔPhe residue of the isolated *Z*-isomer (**42a**) was selectively N-methylated (Rich *et al.*, 1975b) to give **43**, which was then converted to the trichlorophenyl ester (**44**). After removal of the *tert*-butyloxycarbonyl group, the peptide was cyclized to **40** which was found to be identical to natural tentoxin.

Rich *et al.* (1978) also prepared **40** from the linear tetrapeptide (**41**) in several different ways. The *Z*-isomer in the mixture of **42a** and **42b** was selectively N-methylated under mild condition to afford **43**. Attempts were made to introduce the (*Z*)-MeΔPhe moiety stereoselectively. Boc-*threo*-MePhe(3-SBzl)-OH (**45**) was S-methylated to form a sulfonium salt which was susceptible to base-catalyzed trans-elimination to give the desired (*Z*)-ΔMePhe compound.

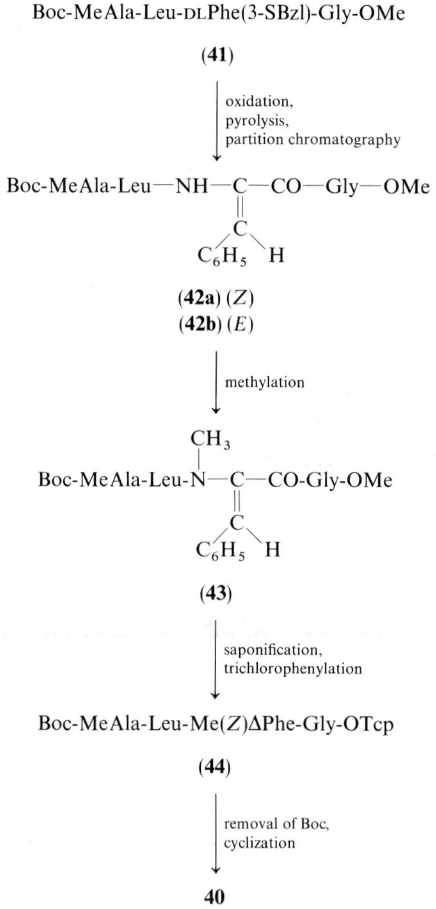

Scheme 20

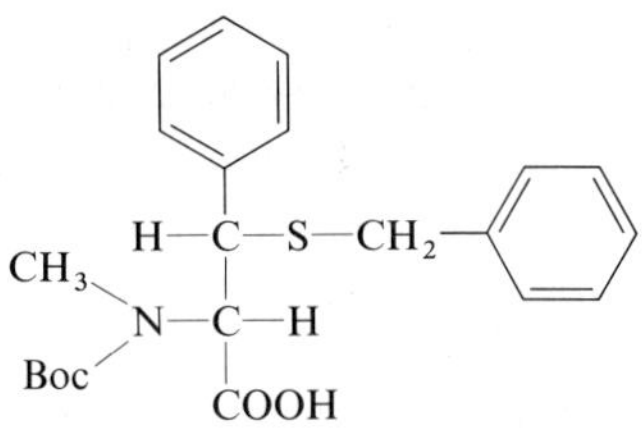

(45)

b. Structure–Activity Relationships. Several analogs of tentoxin have been prepared by chemical synthesis and by modification of tentoxin in order to study the relationships between structure, conformation, and biological activity. [DMePhe^4]Tentoxin (**46**), selectively obtained by catalytic hydrogenation of tentoxin, was shown to be inactive (Meyer *et al.*, 1974a, 1975). Nmr studies showed that the conformation of **46** differed from that of **40** (Rich *et al.*, 1975a). [LMePhe^4]Tentoxin (**47**), [DMeAla^2, LMePhe^4]tentoxin (**48**), and [DMeAla^2]tentoxin (**49**) were prepared by procedures similar to that used for **40**. It was shown that **47** and **48** were biologically inactive, whereas **49** was active (Rich and Mathiaparanam, 1974; Rich *et al.*, 1975a).

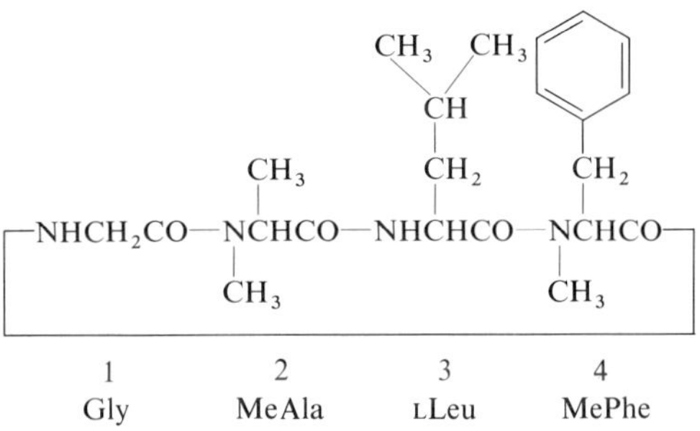

	MeAla^2	MePhe^4
(**46**)	L	D
(**47**)	L	L
(**48**)	D	L

(**49**)

Rich and Bhatnagar (1978a) studied in detail the conformation of tentoxin together with those of [LPro^2]tentoxin and ^{13}C-labeled [LMeAla^2]tentoxin using ^{1}H and ^{13}C nmr. These three compounds have essentially the same conformation and inhibitory activity. The conformations were shown to be of a "ring-flipped" nature with a cis-trans-cis-trans backbone structure. On the basis of these data, the authors corrected the centrosymmetric conformation of tentoxin previously reported.

The configurational modification at position 2 in **49** does not influence the activity. However, two conformers exist for **49** and can be separated by tlc (Rich and Bhatnagar, 1978b). It was shown that the activity of one of these conformers approached that of tentoxin, whereas the other was much less active. Based on a comparison of the conformation of **49** and that of its dihydro analogs, Rich and Bhatnagar (1978b) indicated that α,β-dehydroamino acid residues could restrict the conformational space available to a peptide.

2. *AM-Toxins*

A destructive disease of apples is caused by a pathogenic strain of *Alternaria mali*; apple cultivars such as Indo and Delicious are known to be susceptible, whereas Jonathan is resistant to the disease. Okuno *et al.* (1974) succeeded in isolating the host-specific toxin from a culture broth and named the crystalline toxin alternariolide. They characterized it as a cyclic tetradepsipeptide (**50**).

Ueno and his co-workers isolated three toxic peptides from *A. mali* designated AM-toxins I, II, and III. They reported the structures of AM-toxins I (**50**) (Ueno *et al.*, 1975a), II (**51**) (Ueno *et al.*, 1975a), and III (**52**) (Ueno *et al.*, 1975b), determined mainly by mass and nmr spectroscopy. Subsequently, it was found that AM-toxin I was identical to alternariolide, the name AM-toxin I will be used hereafter in this discussion.

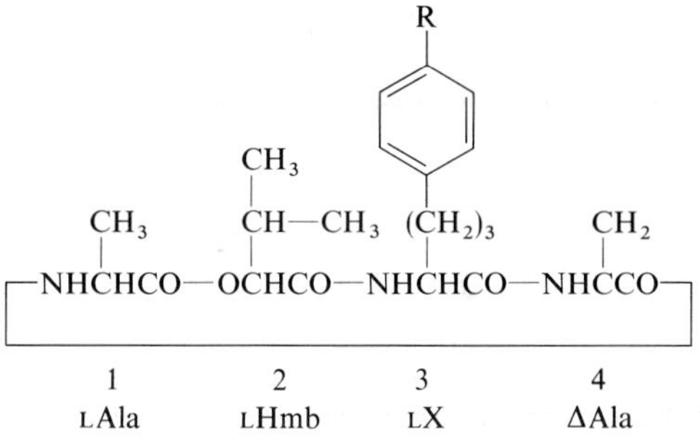

	R	X
AM-toxin I (**50**)	OMe	Amp
AM-toxin II (**51**)	H	App
AM-toxin III (**52**)	OH	Ahp

Hmb = 2-hydroxy-3-methylbutanoic acid

Amp = 2-amino-5-(4-methoxyphenyl)pentanoic acid

App = 2-amino-5-phenylpentanoic acid

Ahp = 2-amino-5-(4-hydroxyphenyl)pentanoic acid

a. Synthesis of AM-Toxins. Photaki (1963) described the preparation of Z-ΔAla-Gly-OEt from Z-LSer-Gly-OEt by tosylation and subsequent treatment with diethylamine, suggesting that a cyclic depsipeptide with a serine residue might be converted into the corresponding peptide with a ΔAla residue. Before synthetic confirmation of the structure of AM-toxin I, Izumiya and his associates selected L-*O*-methyltyrosine [LTyr(Me)^{3}]AM-toxin I as a model peptide in searching for an effective synthetic route (Shimohigashi *et al.*, 1977a), because of the greater ease of preparation of LTyr(Me) compared to that of L-2-amino-5-(4-methoxyphenyl)pentanoic acid (LAmp).

Table II. Cyclization of Linear Tetradepsipeptide Active Esters Related to AM-Toxin I[a]

Linear tetradepsipeptide active ester	Ratio of cyclic product	
	Monomer	Dimer
Me H-LTyr^{3}-LSer^{4}-LAla^{1}-LHmb^{2}-OSu (**53**)	5	95
Me H-LSer^{4}-LAla^{1}-LHmb^{2}-LTyr^{3}-OSu (**54**)	60	40
Me H-LAla^{1}-LHmb^{2}-LTyr^{3}-LSer^{4}-OSu (**55**)	7	93

[a] Hmb, 2-hydroxy-3-methylbutanoic acid; OSu, *N*-hydroxysuccinimide ester; Tyr(Me), *O*-methyltyrosine.

In order to investigate a feature of cyclization, three linear tetrapeptide active esters (**53**–**55**) were treated with pyridine (Shimohigashi *et al.*, 1977a). Since only one peptide (**54**) afforded appreciable amounts of the monomer (see Table II) a similar tetrapeptide active ester (**56**) with LAmp^{3} instead of the LTyr(Me)^{3} residue was subjected to cylization (Shimohigashi *et al.*, 1977b) (Scheme 21). The cyclic monomer (**57**) was converted to cyclic dehydropeptide (**58**) which was identical to natural AM-toxin I, whereas an interesting cyclodimeric dehydropeptide (**60**) was obtained from the corresponding cyclic peptide (**59**).

Shimohigashi *et al.* (1978) found that a linear tetrapeptide active ester with the sequence DLLL affords exclusively a cyclic monomer in good yield. This finding was applied to the synthesis of AM-toxin II as shown in Scheme 22 (Shimohigashi and Izumiya, 1978a).

Since AM-toxin III contains a phenolic group in the LAhp residue, a synthesis of AM-toxin III seemed to be difficult by Photaki's method which

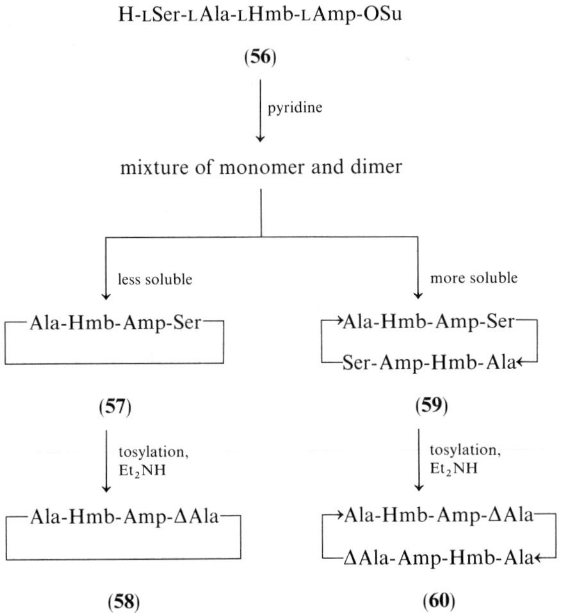

Scheme 21

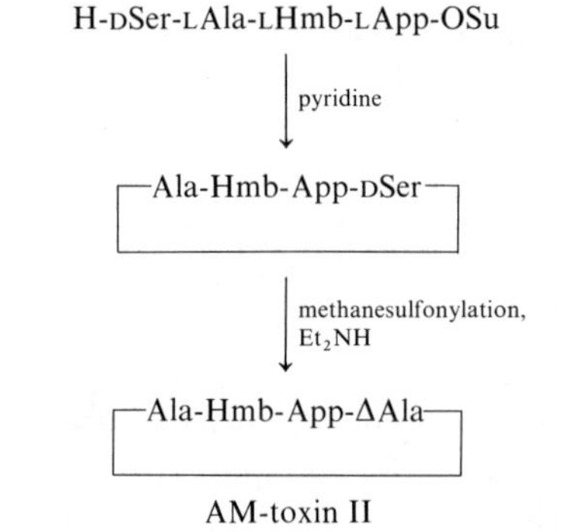

Hmb = 2-hydroxy-3-methylbutanoic acid
App = 2-amino-5-phenylbutanoic acid

Scheme 22

had been applied in the synthesis of AM-toxins I and II. However, AM-toxin III was successfully synthesized by use of the Hofmann degradation procedure (see Section III,A,1), by which an α,β-diaminopropionic acid (Dap) residue was converted into ΔAla as shown in Scheme 23 (Kanmera *et al.*, 1981).

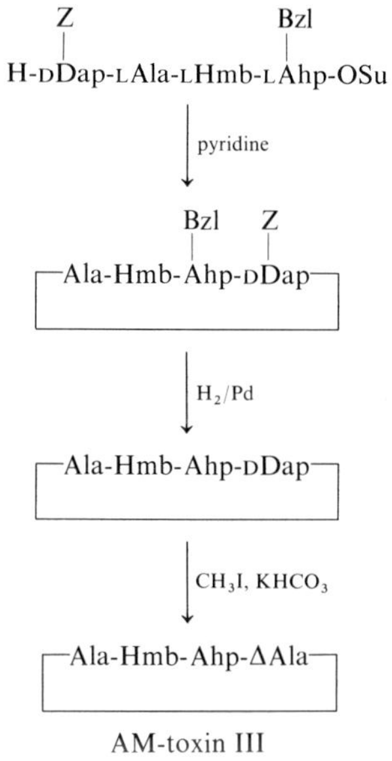

Scheme 23

b. Structure–Activity Relationships. The levels of necrotic activity of AM-toxins and their analogs on an apple leaf are summarized in Table III. It should be pointed out that structural requirements of AM-toxins for the expression of activity are very strict. As shown in Table III, not only the ring size (Shimohigashi *et al.*, 1977b) but also the presence of the bulky

Table III. Necrotic Activity on Apple Leaf of AM-Toxins and Their Analogs[a]

AM-Toxins and analogs	Minimum necrotic concentration for Indo apple leaf (μg/ml)
AM-toxin I (natural or synthetic)	0.002
Dimer (**60**) of AM-toxin I	25
[LTyr(Me)^3]AM-toxin I	25
[LAla^4]AM-toxin I	>100
[DAla^4]AM-toxin I	10
AM-toxin II (natural or synthetic)	0.02
[LPhe^3]AM-toxin II	50
AM-toxin III (natural or synthetic)	0.01
[LTyr^3]AM-toxin III	50

[a] Tyr(Me), *O*-methyltyrosine.

side chain of an L-aromatic amino acid residue such as LAmp (Shimohigashi *et al.*, 1977a) are important in the exhibition of biological activity. In other words, the interaction between an AM-toxin and a possible receptor on an apple leaf is very specific.

Catalytic hydrogenation of the double bond in an AM-toxin resulted in a lowering of the activity by about 20,000–50,000 times. Table III shows that synthetic [DAla[4]]AM-toxin I retained very low but recognizable activity, whereas [LAla[4]]AM-toxin I no longer showed any activity (Shimohigashi *et al.*, 1978). This shows that the presence of an α,β double bond is of importance, but it is not the only factor affecting the activity.

3. Nisin

Nisin is an antibiotic peptide produced by *Streptococcus lactis* (Rogers and Wittier, 1928). The primary structure of nisin was determined by Gross and Morell (1971a) to be a heterodetic pentacyclic peptide (**61**) with 34 amino acid residues. It contains three α,β-dehydroamino acids, namely, two ΔAla residues and one ΔAbu residue. The five cross-linking bonds are the sulfide bridges of one lanthionine residue (**1**) and four β-methyllanthionine residues (**2**). Five of the amino acids occupying positions 3, 8, 13, 23, and 25 that join in the cross-linkages show the D-configuration. The five rings in the molecule are termed rings A–E, respectively.

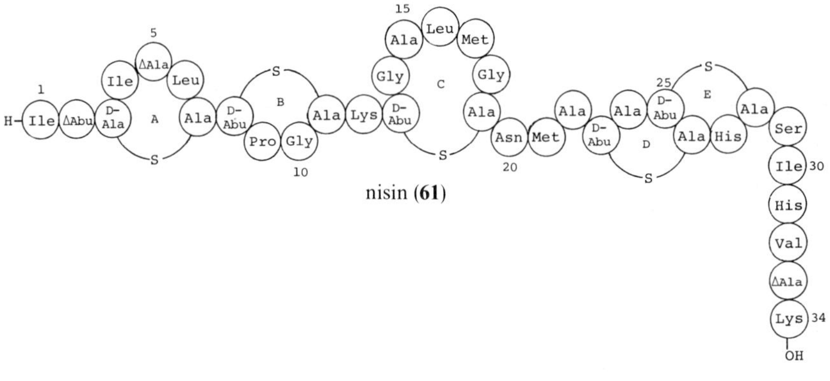

nisin (**61**)

Attempts to synthesize this particular peptide have been made independently by three groups—those of Zervas, Gross, and Shiba. The main difficulties encountered in the synthesis are related to (1) incorporation of α,β-dehydroamino acids into the peptide chain, and (2) chemical differentiation of the two amino and two carboxyl groups of the lanthionines.

a. Synthesis of Ring A by Zervas and Collaborators. Zervas and his associates (Photaki *et al.*, 1975, 1979; Zervas and Ferderigos, 1973, 1974) prepared several lanthionine derivatives by using L- or *meso*-lanthionine with different protection at the amino and carboxyl groups. For example, **62** was obtained by the condensation of Z-Ala(Cl)-OH and H-Cys-OH to give N^{α}-benzyloxycarbonyllanthionine (**63**) by subsequent conversion of **63**

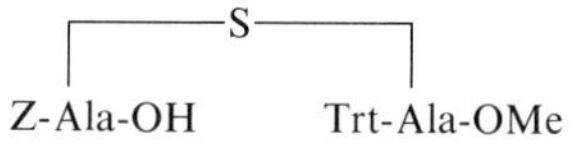

(**62a**) (α,α′: LL)
(**62b**) (α,α′: DL)
(**62c**) (α,α′: LD)

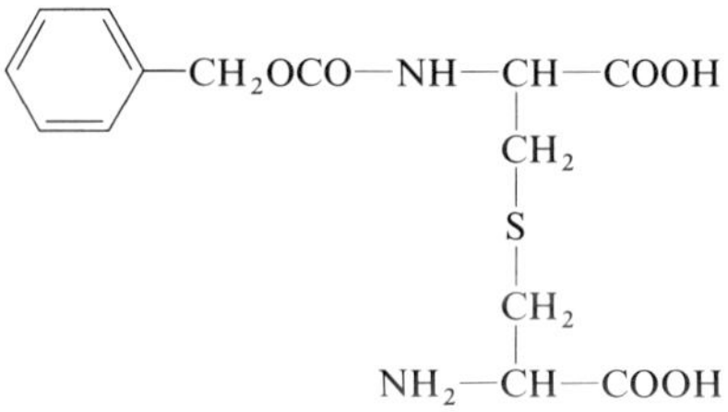

(**63**)

through a series of reactions. Photaki *et al.* (1980) reported the synthesis of a protected derivative (**64**) of ring A of nisin starting with the protected *meso*-lanthionine (**62b**) and H-Ile-Ser-Leu-OMe (**65**) as shown in Scheme 24. The ΔAla residue was incorporated by diphenylphosphorylation of the serine residue followed by a β-elimination reaction before cyclization. The authors reported that an attempted diphenylphosphorylation of the serine residue after cyclization and cyclization of the diphenylphosphinoyl peptide both failed, presumably because of steric hindrance.

b. Synthesis of Ring A by E. Gross and Collaborators. Pallai *et al.* (1977) reported synthesis of the same compound (**64**) via a different route. They prepared protected *meso*-lanthionine (**66**), with different protective groups, by condensation of Z-DAla(Cl)-OH and Boc-LCys(Bz)-OMe with *t*BuOK or with NaH. A precursor (**67**) for cyclization to **64** was obtained by removal of the *tert*-butyloxycarbonyl group of **66** followed by coupling with Boc-Ile-ΔAla-Leu-OSu (**68**). The ΔAla residue was incorporated into **68** by conversion of the *S*-methylcysteine residue to the sulfonium salt with fluorosulfonic acid methyl ester (Rich and Tam, 1975) followed by

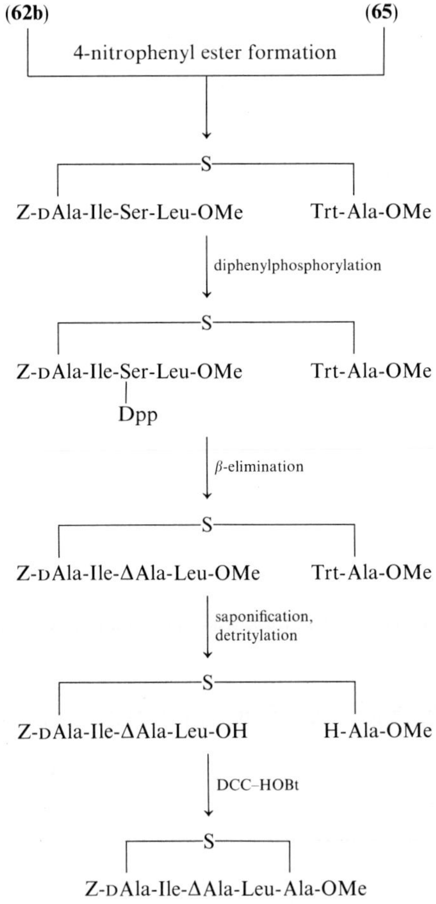

(64)

Scheme 24

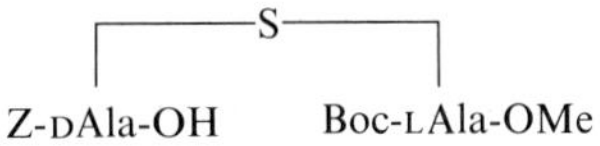

(66)

triethylamine-catalyzed β-elimination as shown in Scheme 25. After *N*-hydroxysuccinylation and subsequent removal of the *tert*-butyloxycarbonyl group, the precursor (**67**) was cyclized to **64**. The authors also prepared a precursor (**69**) for cyclization via sulfide bridge formation.

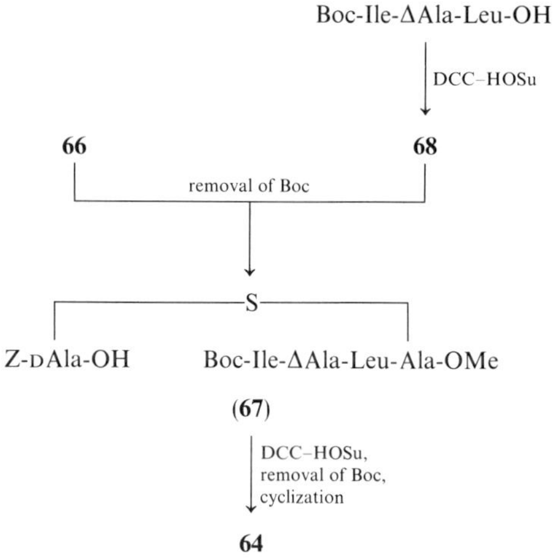

Scheme 25

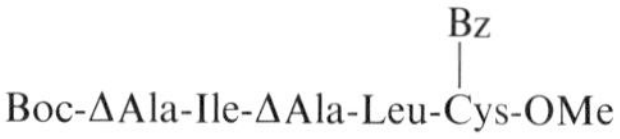

(69)

c. Synthesis of Ring A by Shiba and Collaborators. Recently, Shiba and his associates succeeded in synthesizing ring A, in which the thioether bond was generated by removal of one sulfur atom of the disulfide linkage by treatment with hexaethylphosphoramide $P(NEt_2)_3$ (Harpp *et al.*, 1968), and the ΔAla residue was incorporated by Hofmann degradation of the α,β-diaminopropionic acid residue (Sano *et al.*, 1981).

B. Peptide Hormone Analogs Substituted by α,β-Dehydroamino Acids

The incorporation of dehydroamino acids provides the peptide with a unique profile: rigidity, increased hydrophobicity, electrophilic reactivity, restricted orientation of β-substituents, and resistance to enzymatic degradation. By taking advantage of these properties, many α,β-dehydroamino acid-containing analogs of bioactive peptides have been synthesized in recent years. Replacement of an amino acid residue by an α,β-dehydroamino acid in a peptide hormone could lead to elucidation of the structural requirements of receptor interactions if the substitution was made at or close to the active or binding sites of the hormone (Walter, 1977). Many peptide hormone analogs containing α,β-dehydroamino acids have been synthesized and their biological activity reported. Several examples are described below.

a. Angiotensin. [Sar^1, Ala^8]Angiotensin II (**70**), saralasine, is an antagonist of angiotensin II (AII). The alanine residue in position 8 was replaced by ΔAla, ΔVal, ΔPhe, and ΔAun, and the agonist and antagonist behavior

$$\overset{1}{\text{H-Sar}}\text{-Arg-Val-Tyr-}\overset{5}{\text{Ile}}\text{-His-Pro-}\overset{8}{\underline{\text{Ala}}}\text{-OH}$$

(**70**)

of each dehydropeptide was evaluated for inhibition of aldosterone biosynthesis using isolated cells (Hallinan and Mazur, 1979). [Sar^1,ΔAla^8]AII was the most active AII inhibitor, being almost 35-fold more active than saralasine. [Sar^1,ΔVal^8]AII was less active than [Sar^1,ΔAla^8]AII, and [Sar^1,ΔAun^8]AII was a mixed agonist–antagonist. However, [Sar^1,ΔPhe^8]-AII was an agonist.

b. Bradykinin. Fisher *et al.* (1981) synthesized the unsaturated analogs of the vasodilator peptide hormone bradykinin (BK) (**71**). [ΔPhe^5]BK showed a high biological activity in its blood pressure-lowering effects,

$$\text{H-}\overset{1}{\text{Arg}}\text{-Pro-Pro-Gly-}\overset{5}{\underline{\text{Phe}}}\text{-Ser-Pro-}\underline{\text{Phe}}\text{-}\overset{9}{\text{Arg}}\text{-OH}$$

(**71**)

being 23-fold more potent than BK. On the other hand, [ΔPhe^8]BK was less potent than BK, and [ΔPhe^5,ΔPhe^8]BK had effects comparable to those of BK. It has been suggested that the high potency may be the result of increased resistance to enzymatic degradation and, perhaps, conformational factors.

c. Enkephalin. Enkephalin (**72**) was found in brain as an opiate-like neuropeptide. English and Stammer (1978) reported the synthesis of a highly potent [DAla^2,ΔPhe^4,Met^5]enkephalin amide that was fivefold more potent

$$\text{H-}\overset{1}{\text{Tyr}}\text{-}\underline{\text{Gly}}\text{-}\underline{\text{Gly}}\text{-}\underline{\text{Phe}}\text{-}\overset{5}{\underline{\text{Leu}}}\text{(or Met)-OH}$$

(**72**)

than the saturated analog. Shimohigashi and Stammer (1981, 1982a,b) prepared a series of unsaturated [DAla^2,Leu^5]enkephalin analogs: [ΔAla^2]-, [DAla^2,ΔAla^3]-, [DAla^2,ΔPhe^4]-, and [DAla^2, ΔLeu^5]enkephalins. These analogs exhibited almost the full receptor activity (Shimohigashi *et al.*, 1981b).

It has been shown that [ΔPhe[4]]- and [ΔLeu[5]]-enkephalins have unchanged δ-enkephalin receptor selectivity. Furthermore, it has been suggested that the phenyl ring of ΔPhe[4], oriented in the Z-configuration, is important for the interaction with the δ-receptors (Shimohigashi et al., 1982a). These unsaturated enkephalins were examined for their resistance to enzymatic hydrolysis employing carboxypeptidase Y and amino acid analysis. α,β-Dehydroamino acid residues are completely resistant to an enzyme at the amino side, whereas in spite of considerable resistance the peptide bond at the carboxyl side can be cleaved slowly (Shimohigashi et al., 1982c).

These studies have shown clearly the usefulness and significance of the incorporation of α,β-dehydroamino acids in peptide hormones. Further work should lead to the establishment of useful structure–activity relationships. Moreover, analogs suitable for the study of in vivo receptor interaction may be developed. Thus, the synthesis of biologically active peptides containing α,β-dehydroamino acids provides an opportunity for detailed examinations of their biological activities.

V. UTILITY OF α,β-DEHYDROAMINO ACIDS IN PEPTIDE CHEMISTRY

The dynamic chemical properties intrinsic to α,β-dehydroamino acids are applied with advantage to peptide chemistry. Among these, the acid-catalyzed conversion to amide and α-keto acid [Eq. (1)] and the reversible addition–elimination reaction [Eq. (2)] have been well investigated.

$$
\begin{array}{cc}
\underset{\text{C}}{\overset{R\diagdown\diagup R}{\|}} & \underset{\text{CH}}{\overset{R\diagdown\diagup R}{|}} \\
-\text{CO}-\text{NH}-\text{C}-\text{CO}- + \text{H}_2\text{O} \rightleftharpoons -\text{CO}-\text{NH}_2 + \text{O}=\text{C}-\text{CO}- & (1)
\end{array}
$$

$$
\begin{array}{cc}
\underset{\text{C}}{\overset{R\diagdown\diagup R}{\|}} & \overset{R}{\underset{R-\text{C}-\text{X}}{|}} \\
-\text{CO}-\text{NH}-\text{C}-\text{CO}- + \text{HX} \rightleftharpoons -\text{CO}-\text{NH}-\text{CH}-\text{CO}- & (2)
\end{array}
$$

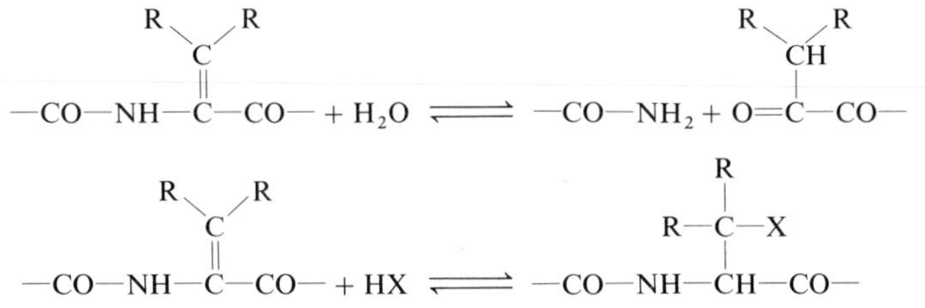

Earlier analytical endeavors, aimed at the development of methods for the conversion of β-substituted amino acids, such as serine (Photaki, 1963; Patchornik and Sokolovsky, 1963) and cysteine (Patchornik and Sokolovsky, 1964; Gross et al., 1968), to dehydroamino acids for the purpose of non-enzymatic fragmentation of peptides and proteins, now find their counterpart in the application of α,β-dehydroamino acids in peptide synthesis and its utility there.

In the following section, two examples of such applications are described: synthesis of peptide amides using ΔAla, and asymmetric reduction of dehydropiperazinediones.

A. Synthesis of Peptide Amides via Dehydroalanine

The structural elucidation of nisin (Gross and Morell, 1971a) and subtilin (Gross *et al.*, 1973b) necessitated detailed studies on the chemistry of α,β-dehydroamino acids. Each of the two peptides contains two residues of ΔAla and one residue of ΔAbu. A lead to the detection of ΔAla in nisin was obtained during purification when pyruvyllysine was found to be present in the commercially available preparation (Gross and Morell, 1967). Pyruvyllysine had been generated by cleavage of the NH—$^{\alpha}$C bond of the ΔAla residue in the penultimate position of the molecule. The acid-catalyzed conversion of acyl-ΔAla-OH to an amide and an α-keto acid [Eq. (1)] suggested the application of this reaction to peptide synthesis.

Dehydroalanine may serve (1) as a vehicle for the attachment of peptides to solid supports in the solid-phase method (Merrifield, 1963), and (2) simultaneously as pseudoprotection for the amide function by donating its amino group to the peptide during the course of cleavage.

1. Peptides with a COOH-Terminal Amide

The solid-phase synthesis of peptides with a COOH-terminal amide via ΔAla requires attachment of the growing peptide chain to the support such that the amide-carrying COOH-terminal amino acid is followed by the ΔAla residue. The carboxyl group of ΔAla may be linked to the support via an ester or amide bond. Since ΔAla itself is not stable, a suitably N-protected aminoacyl-ΔAla derivative is necessary for conducting peptide synthesis on a solid support.

The applicability of the method was demonstrated with the synthesis of H-Leu-Ala-Gly-NH_2. A ΔAla resin (**75**) with an ester-type linkage between the α,β-dehydroamino acid and the support was readily prepared from Boc-Gly-ΔAla-OH (**73**) and chloromethylated styrene–divinylbenzene copolymer (**74**). Following removal of the protecting group from **75** with TFA in dichloromethane, the peptide chain was elongated in two conventional solid-phase synthesis steps. Treatment of the resulting peptide resin (**76**) with 1 *M* HCl–AcOH in the presence of water cleaved the tripeptide (**77**) from the support with simultaneous introduction of the terminal amide and removal of the *tert*-butyloxycarbonyl group.

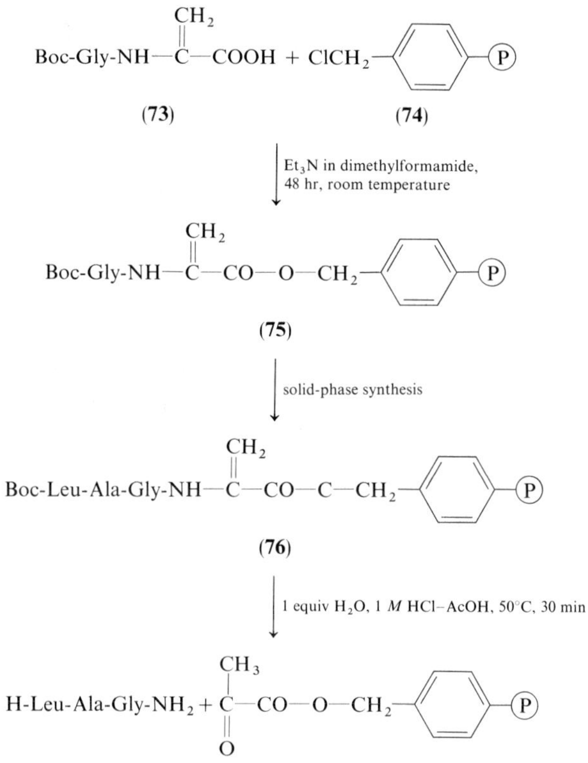

With the same procedure, thyrotropin-releasing hormone (Gross *et al.*, 1973c), pGlu-His-Trp-NH_2, the NH_2-terminal tripeptide amide of luteinizing hormone-releasing hormone (Mecklenberg *et al.*, 1973), and oxytocin analogs (Rosamond and Ferger, 1976) have been synthesized. Each peptide showed the full complement of chemical and physical properties and biological activity when compared with a standard preparation.

2. *Peptides with an Amide in the Endo Position*

The ω-amide functions of asparagine and glutamine have also been introduced via this method (Gross *et al.*, 1975; Noda and Gross, 1981). During stepwise peptide synthesis, the ω-carboxyl groups of the monoaminodicarboxylic acids are linked to ΔAla alkylamide, for example, Glu (ΔAla-NHMe). Two model peptides, H-Leu-Asn-Gly-NH_2 (**78**) and H-Leu-Gln-Gly-NH_2

(**79**), have been synthesized via the solid-phase technique using (1) ΔAla resin (**75**) to incorporate the amide function of the COOH-terminal residue,

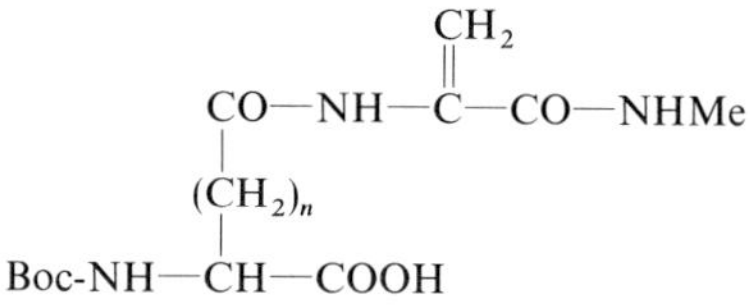

(**80**) $n = 1$
(**81**) $n = 2$

and (2) the methylamide of ΔAla attached to the ω-carboxyl groups **80** and/or **81** to introduce the amide functions of asparagine and/or glutamine as shown in Scheme 26.

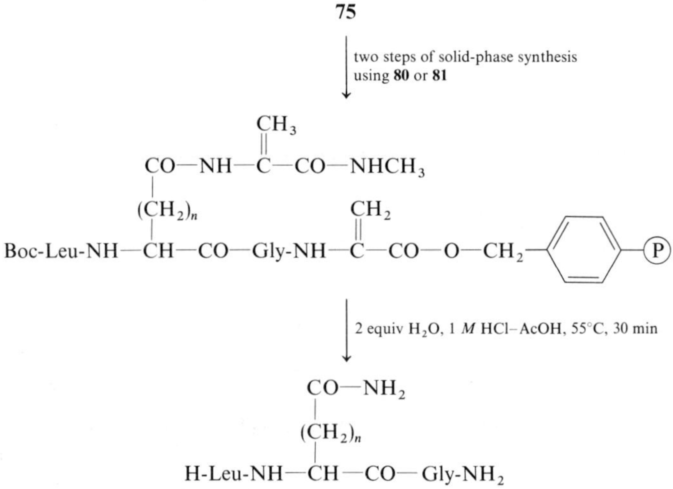

(**78**) $n = 1$
(**79**) $n = 2$

Scheme 26

The applicability of the method in the synthesis of bioactive peptide amides was demonstrated by the solid-phase synthesis of oxytocin as shown in Scheme 27 (Noda *et al.*, 1982). After attachment of **73** to aminomethylated styrene–divinylbenzene copolymer (**82**) (Mitchell *et al.*, 1976; Sparrow, 1976) via the *N*-hydroxysuccinimide ester method, the amino acid sequence of oxytocin was completed in a stepwise manner using Boc-Asp(ΔAla-NHEt)-OH and Boc-Glu(ΔAla-NHEt)-OH as precursors of Asn^5 and Gln^4,

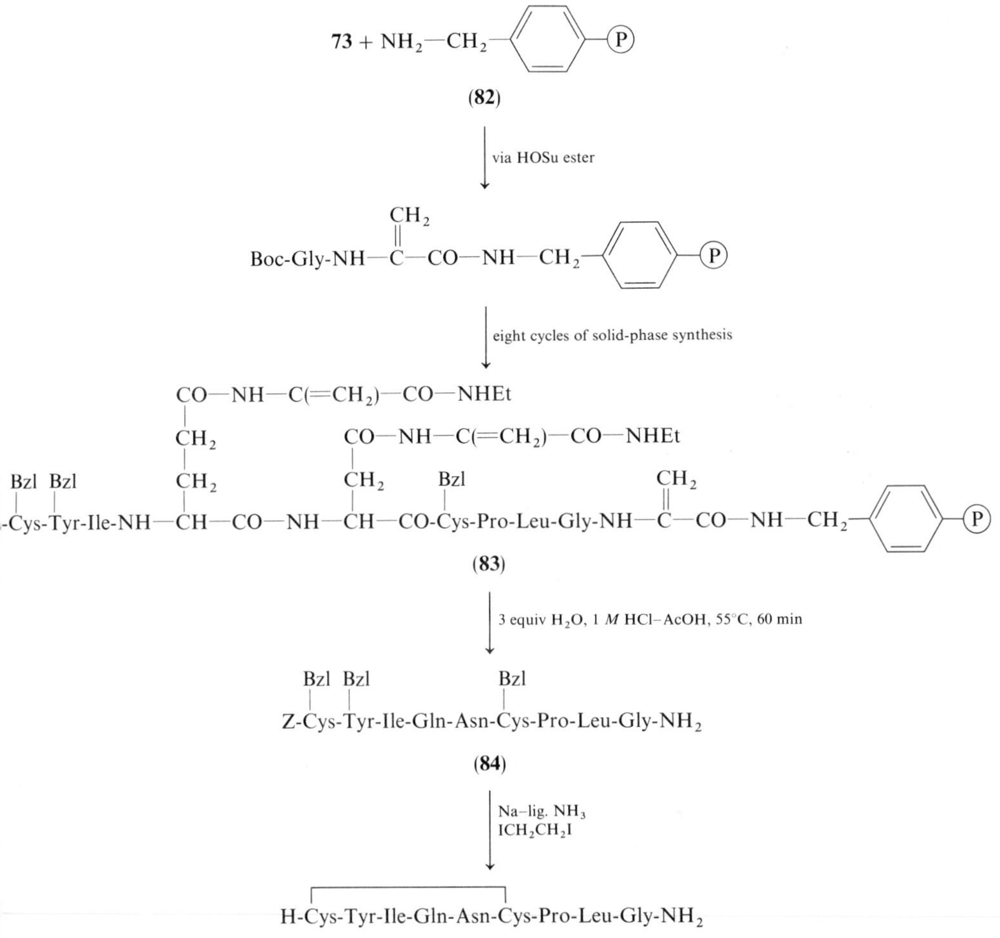

Scheme 27

respectively. Treatment of the protected [Glu(ΔAla-NHEt)^4,Asp(ΔAla-NHEt)^5] oxytocin-ΔAla-$NHCH_2$ resin (**83**) with 1 *M* HCl–AcOH in the presence of 3 equiv of water removed the peptide from the support with simultaneous formation of the amide functions at the COOH-terminal residue and the ω-carboxyl groups of Gln^4 and Asn^5 to give the protected oxytocin (**84**). After deprotection and subsequent oxidation, the purified product, obtained in 30% yield, displayed the chemical and physical properties and biological activity of a standard preparation of oxytocin.

B. Asymmetric Hydrogenation of α,β-Dehydroamino Acids in Cyclic Peptides

Izumiya and associates planned to prepare a diastereomeric mixture of [LAla^4]- and [DAla^4]AM-toxin I by hydrogenation of AM-toxin I (**50**). As a preliminary study, Izumiya *et al.* (1977) hydrogenated *cyclo*(ΔAla-LLeu) and observed unexpectedly high asymmetric induction, affording pure *cyclo*(LAla-LLeu). They proposed an interesting mechanism of asymmetric hydrogenation and have prepared many unusual L- and D-α-amino acids by this procedure (Izumiya *et al.*, 1977; Kanmera *et al.*, 1980).

1. *Asymmetric Hydrogenation of Cyclic Dehydropeptides*

A series of *cyclo*(ΔAla-LAA) were synthesized by the Photaki method (Photaki, 1963) from a corresponding *cyclo*(LSer-LAA) (where LAA represents one of various L-α-amino acids). As shown in Scheme 28, Kanmera *et al.* (1980) developed a facile route for synthesizing *cyclo*(ΔAA′-LAA) (**87**) from *cyclo*(Gly-LAA) (**85**) and the corresponding aldehyde via **86**.

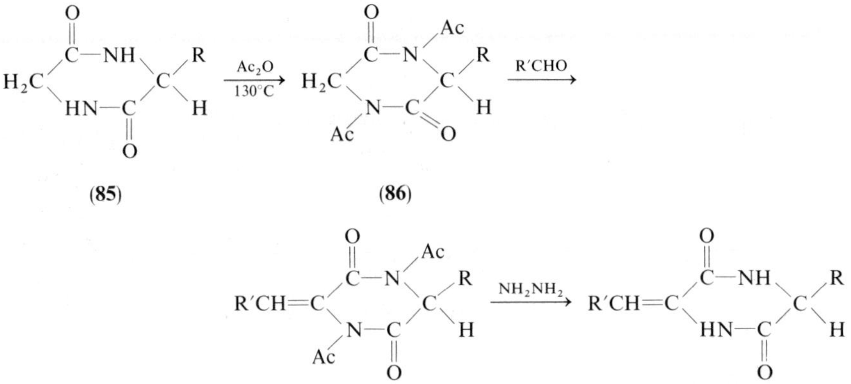

(**85**) (**86**) (**87**)

Scheme 28

These cyclic α,β-dehydrodipeptides were subjected to hydrogenation with several catalysts such as palladium black or platinum oxide and various solvents such as methanol, acetic acid, or dimethylformamide. Generally, high chiral inductions were observed. Typical results (Kanmera *et al.*, 1980; Hashimoto *et al.*, 1983) are shown in Table IV. Hydrogenation of ΔPhe or ΔTrp in *cyclo*(ΔPhe-AA) or *cyclo*(ΔTrp-LAA) resulted in a slightly lower asymmetric induction at 25 and 50°C. However, *cyclo*(ΔPhe-LAla) was hydrogenated with high chiral induction at a low temperature (0°C) (Hashimoto *et al.*, 1983).

Table IV. Chiral Induction of cyclo(ΔAA′-LAA)[a] by Catalytic Hydrogenation in Methanol at 25°C

cyclo(ΔAA′-LAA)[a]	Chiral induction (%)[b]
cyclo(ΔAla-LAla)	94.6
cyclo(ΔAla-LVal)	98.4
cyclo(ΔAla-LLeu)	95.8
cyclo(ΔAla-LPhe)	94.6
cyclo(ΔAla-LPro)	84.8
cyclo((*Z*)-ΔAbu-LAla)	99.1
cyclo((*E*)-ΔAbu-LAla)	99.0
cyclo(ΔVal-LAla)	96.2
cyclo(ΔLeu-LAla)	97.8
cyclo(ΔLeu-LLeu)	98.0
cyclo(ΔPhe-LAla)	88
cyclo(ΔPhe-LAla)	97[c]
cyclo(ΔHomophe-LAla)	95.7
cyclo(ΔTrp-LAla)	71

[a] ΔAA′, α,β-dehydroamino acid; LAA, L-α-amino acid; Δ Homophe, α,β-dehydrohomophenylalanine.
[b] Defined as %LAA′ minus %DAA′ in hydrogenated cyclodipeptides.
[c] At 0°C.

The mechanism of the chiral inductions has been discussed by Izumiya and his associates (Izumiya *et al.*, 1977; Kanmera *et al.*, 1980). In *cyclo*(ΔAla-LAA) or cyclo(ΔLeu-LAA), the rigid, planar structure of the diketopiperazine ring and the side chain containing the double bond is an important factor inducing high asymmetry. In *cyclo*(ΔPhe-LAA) or *cyclo*(ΔTrp-LAA), however, the diketopiperazine ring and the aromatic ring cannot be coplanar; and less stereoselectivity in the adsorption of the diketopiperazine ring on palladium black is assumed to lower the degree of asymmetric hydrogenation.

Shimohigashi *et al.* (1978) reported that hydrogenation of the constituent ΔAla residue in AM-toxin I (**50**) yielded a nearly racemic alanine residue. On the contrary, Ando *et al.* (1982) observed that the ΔAla residue in [LOrn-(Boc)$^{2,2'}$, ΔAla^{4}, DSer$^{4'}$]gramicidin S (**88**) was asymmetrically hydrogenated to D-alanine. This was attributed by the authors to a possible conformation

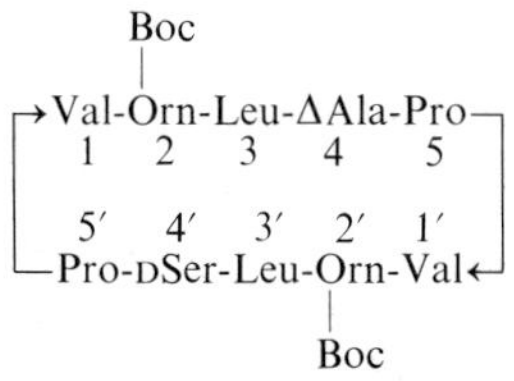

(**88**)

of **88** that might favor asymmetric hydrogenation to produce D-alanine from ΔAla.

2. *Preparation of Optically Pure α-Amino Acids*

Izumiya and his associates have developed a procedure for preparing common as well as unusual α-amino acids in optically pure form by the asymmetric hydrogenation of cyclic dehydrodipeptides. For example, LAbu is obtained on a preparative scale from the cyclic α,β-dehydrodipeptide (**89**) as shown in Scheme 29 (Kanmera *et al.*, 1980).

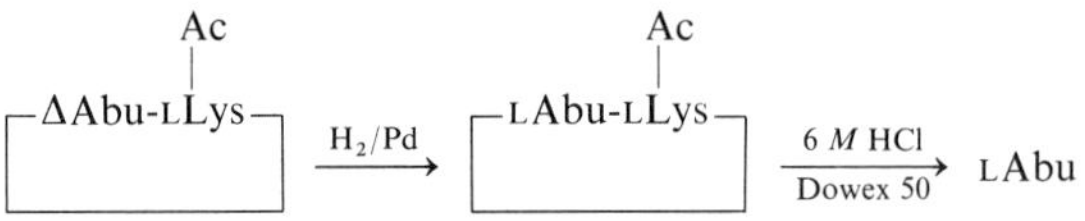

(**89**)

Scheme 29

Pure L-2-amino-5-phenylpentanoic acid (LApp) was prepared from *cyclo*(ΔApp-LAla) and used in the synthesis of AM-toxin II (**51**) (Shimohigashi and Izumiya, 1978a). [$^2H_2$] D-Phenylalanine was prepared from *cyclo*[ΔPhe-DLys(Ac)] and deuterium at 0°C (Hashimoto *et al.*, 1983), and synthetic [$^2H_2$-DPhe$^{4,4'}$] gramicidin S has been used in nmr investigations by Izumiya and co-workers.

VI. CONCLUDING REMARKS

α,β-Dehydroamino acids are now recognized as key constituents of certain peptides and proteins. As this chapter shows, their occurrence is firmly established in a number of peptides. Chemical synthesis of these compounds has also been made possible with the recent development of new methods.

Investigations of the structure–bioactivity relationships of dehydropeptides are of great interest, because they contain the highly reactive α,β-double bond. Biologically active α,β-dehydropeptides may be divided into two classes: (1) those that lose their activity completely upon saturation of the double bond, for example, by hydrogenation or by mercaptan addition, as in AM-toxin and tuberactinomycin; and (2) those that retain their activity more or less upon saturation, for example in nisin and tentoxin. This indicates a certain diversity of the role of α,β-double bonds. In the first group of dehydropeptides double bonds may play important direct roles in the expression of activity, whereas in the second group α,β-double bonds are assumed to provide overall stability to the peptides, such as rigidity, increased hydrophobicity, and restricted orientation of β-substituents, to maintain their conformation and resistance toward enzymatic degradation.

These properties of α,β-dehydroamino acids are being utilized in the chemical synthesis of dehydro analogs of peptide hormones, peptide antibiotics, and other bioactive peptides in order to elucidate the structural requirements of the interactions with their receptor and thus to develop therapeutically useful medicinal agents.

With such burgeoning interest, the chemistry of α,β-dehydropeptides will undoubtedly become an increasingly important area of research.

ACKNOWLEDGMENT

We want to thank Dr. T. Kato, Dr. H. Aoyagi, and Dr. M. Waki, Kyushu University, for their helpful discussions during the preparation of the manuscript for this chapter.

The preparation of a chapter on dehydropeptides for Vol. 5 of *The Peptides* was originally proposed by Dr. E. Gross who asked us to join him as co-authors, and the article was expected to be dedicated to Prof. N. Izumiya. Shortly after the tragic death of Dr. Gross, we received a letter from Dr. J. Meienhofer that the chapter was still expected to be written by us. We then proceeded to complete it with the participation of Professor Izumiya as a tribute to Dr. Gross. We shall miss him very much in the years to come.

K. N. and Y. S.

REFERENCES

Abraham, E. P., and Newton, G. C. F. (1961). *Biochem. J.* **79**, 377–393.

Akabori, S., Ikenaka, T., and Matsumoto, K. (1952). *Nippon Kagaku Kaishi* **73**, 112–115.

Ako, H., Ryan, C. A., and Foster, R. J. (1972a). *Biochem. Biophys. Res. Commun.* **46**, 1639–1645.

Ako, H., Ryan, C. A., and Foster, R. J. (1972b). *Biochem. Biophys. Res. Commun.* **47**, 1402–1407.

Albers-Schönberg, G., Arison, B. H., and Smith, J. L. (1972). *Tetrahedron Lett.* pp. 2911–2914.

Albers-Schönberg, G., Arison, B. H., Hensens, O. D., Hirshfield, J., Hoogsteen, K., Kaczka, E. A., Rhodes, R. E., Kahan, J. S., Kahan, F. M., Ratcliffe, R. W., Walton, E., Ruswinkle, L. J., Morin, R. B., and Christensen, B. G. (1978). *J. Am. Chem. Soc.* **100**, 6491–6499.

Alderton, G. (1953). *J. Am. Chem. Soc.* **75**, 2391–2392.

Anderson, B., Hodgkin, D. C., and Viswamitra, M. A. (1970). *Nature (London)* **225**, 233–235.

Ando, S., Aoyagi, H., Waki, M., Kato, T., Izumiya, N., Okamoto, K., and Kondo, M. (1982). *Tetrahedron Lett.* **23**, 2195–2198.

Arcamone, F., Pence, S., Orezzi, P., Nicolella, V., and Pirelli, A. (1964). *Nature (London)* **203**, 1064–1065.

Asquith, R. S., and Carthew, P. (1972). *Biochem. Biophys. Acta* **278**, 8–14.

Atkins, P. R., and Kay, I. T. (1971). *J. Chem. Soc., Chem. Commun.* p. 430.

Barbetta, M., Casnati, G., Pochini, A., and Selva, A. (1969). *Tetrahedron Lett.* pp. 4457–4460.

Bergmann, M., and Grafe, K. (1930). *Hoppe-Seyler's Z. Physiol. Chem.* **187**, 187–195.

Bergmann, M., Stern, F., and Witte, C. (1926). *Justus Liebig's Ann. Chem.* **449**, 277–302.

Birch, A. J., Massy-Westropp, R. A., and Rickards, R. W. (1956). *J. Chem. Soc.* pp. 3717–3721.
Birkinshaw, J. H., Kalyanhur, M. G., and Stickings, C. E. (1963). *Biochem. J.* **86**, 237–243.
Bodanszky, M., and Bodanszky, A. (1968). *Nature (London)* **220**, 73–74.
Bodanszky, M., and Bodanszky, A. (1974). *J. Antibiot.* **27**, 312–315.
Bodanszky, M., Muramatsu, I., Bodanszky, A., Lukin, M., and Doubler, M. R. (1968a). *J. Antibiot.* **21**, 77–78.
Bodanszky, M., Marconi, G. G., and Colman, G. C. (1968b). *J. Antibiot.* **21**, 668–670.
Bodanszky, M., Izdebski, J., and Muramatsu, I. (1969a). *J. Am. Chem. Soc.* **91**, 2351–2358.
Bodanszky, M., Marconi, G. G., and Bodanszky, A. (1969b). *J. Antibiot.* **22**, 40–41.
Bowman, R. E., Closier, M. D., and Islip, P. J. (1965). *J. Chem. Soc.* pp. 470–473.
Breitholle, E. G., and Stammer, C. H. (1976). *J. Org. Chem.* **41**, 1344–1349.
Brown, A. G. (1970). *J. Chem. Soc. C* pp. 2572–2573.
Brown, R., Kelly, C., and Wiberley, S. E. (1965). *J. Org. Chem.* **30**, 277–280.
Bycroft, B. W. (1969). *Nature (London)* **224**, 595–596.
Bycroft, B. W., and Gowland, M. S. (1978). *J. Chem. Soc., Chem. Commun.* pp. 256–258.
Cardani, C., Casnati, G., Piozzi, L., and Quilico, A. (1959). *Tetrahedron Lett.* pp. 1–8.
Cardillo, R., Fuganti, C., Gatti, G., Ghiringhelli, D., and Grasselli, P. (1974). *Tetrahedron Lett.* pp. 3163–3166.
Cardillo, R., Fuganti, C., Ghiringhelli, D., and Grasselli, P. (1975). *J. Chem. Soc., Chem. Commun.* pp. 778–779.
Crooy, P., and DeNys, R. (1972). *J. Antibiot.* **25**, 371–372.
Delpierre, G. R., Eastwood, F. W., Gream, G. E., Kingston, D. G. I., Sarin, P. S., Todd, L., and Williams, D. H. (1966). *J. Chem. Soc. C* pp. 1653–1669.
Doherty, D. G., Tietzmann, J. E., and Bergmann, M. (1943). *J. Biol. Chem.* **147**, 617–637.
Dossena, A., Marchelli, R., and Pochini, A. (1974). *J. Chem. Soc., Chem. Commun.* pp. 771–772.
Dossena, A., Marchelli, R., and Pochini, A. (1975). *Experientia* **31**, 1249.
English, M. L., and Stammer, C. H. (1978). *Biochem. Biophys. Res. Commun.* **85**, 780–782.
Fallona, M. C., McMorris, T. C., Demayo, P., Money, T., and Stoessl, A. (1962). *J. Am. Chem. Soc.* **84**, 4162–4163.
Fisher, G. H., Berryer, P., Ryan, J. W., Chauhan, V., and Stammer, C. H. (1981). *Arch. Biochem. Biophys.* **211**, 269–275.
Friedman, M. (1977). "Protein Crosslinking, Nutritional and Medical Consequences." Plenum, New York.
Fujisawa, Y., Shirafuji, H., Kida, M., Nara, K., Yoneda, M., and Kanzaki, T. (1973). *Nature New Biol.* **246**, 154–155.
Fujisawa, Y., Kitano, K., and Kanzaki, T. (1975). *Agric. Biol. Chem.* **39**, 2049–2055.
Gallina, C., and Liberatori, A. (1973). *Tetrahedron Lett.* pp. 1135–1136.
Givot, I. L., and Abeles, R. H. (1970). *J. Biol. Chem.* **245**, 3271–3273.
Givot, I. L., Smith, T. A., and Abeles, R. H. (1969). *J. Biol. Chem.* **244**, 6341–6353.
Greenstein, J. P., and Winitz, M. (1961). *In* "Chemistry of the Amino Acids," Vol. II, pp. 823–860. Wiley, New York.
Grigg, R., and Kemp, J. (1977). *J. Chem. Soc., Chem. Commun.* pp. 125–126.
Grim, M. D., Chauhan, V., Shimohigashi, Y., Kolar, A. J., and Stammer, C. H. (1981). *J. Org. Chem.* **46**, 2671–2673.
Gross, E. (1975). *In* "Peptides: Chemistry, Structure and Biology" (R. Walter and J. Meienhofer, eds.), pp. 31–42. Ann Arbor Sci. Publ., An Arbor, Michigan.
Gross, E. (1976). *In* "Handbook of Biochemistry and Molecular Biology" (G. D. Fasman, ed.), 3rd ed., Vol. 1, pp. 175–176. Chem. Rubber Publ., Co., Cleveland, Ohio.
Gross, E. (1977). *Adv. Exp. Med. Biol.* **86B**, 131–153.
Gross, E., and Kiltz, H. H. (1973). *Biochem. Biophys. Res. Commun.* **50**, 559–565.
Gross, E., and Morell, J. L. (1967). *J. Am. Chem. Soc.* **89**, 2791–2792.

Gross, E., and Morell, J. L. (1970). *J. Am. Chem. Soc.* **92**, 2919–2920.
Gross, E., and Morell, J. L. (1971a). *J. Am. Chem. Soc.* **93**, 4634–4635.
Gross, E., and Morell, J. L. (1971b). *In* "Peptides 1969" (E. Scoffone, ed.), pp. 356–360. North-Holland Publ., Amsterdam.
Gross, E., Morell, J. L., and Lee, P. Q. (1968). *Proc. Int. Congr. Biochem., 7th, 1967* pp. 535–536.
Gross, E., Morell, J. L., and Craig, L. C. (1969). *Proc. Natl. Acad. Sci. U.S.A.* **62**, 952–956.
Gross, E., Kiltz, H. H., and Craig, L. C. (1973a). *Hoppe-Seyler's Z. Physiol. Chem.* **354**, 799–801.
Gross, E. Kiltz, H. H., and Nebelin, E. (1973b). *Hoppe-Seyler's Z. Physiol. Chem.* **354**, 810–812.
Gross, E., Noda, K., and Nisula, B. (1973c). *Angew. Chem., Int. Ed. Engl.* **12**, 664–665.
Gross, E., Noda, K., and Matsuura, S. (1975). *In* "Peptides 1974" (Y. Wolman, ed.), pp. 403–413. Wiley, New York.
Gushima, H., Watanabe, S., Saito, T., Sasaki, T., Eiki, H., Oka, Y., and Osano, T. (1981). *J. Antibiot.* **34**, 1507–1512.
Hallinan, E. A., and Mazur, R. H. (1979). *In* "Peptides: Structure and Biological Function" (E. Gross and J. Meienhofer, eds.), pp. 475–477. Pierce Chemical Co., Rockford, Illinois.
Hanson, K. R., and Havir, E. A. (1970). *Arch. Biochem. Biophys.* **141**, 1–17.
Harpp, D. N., Gleason, J. C., and Snyder, J. P. (1968). *J.* Am. Chem. Soc. **90**, 4181–4182.
Hasegawa, T., Hatano, K., Iwasaki, H., and Yoneda, M. (1976). *J. Antibiot.* **29**, 113–120.
Hashimoto, Y., Aoyagi, H., Waki, M., Kato, T., and Izumiya, N. (1983). *Int. J. Pept. Protein Res.* **21**, 11–15.
Hensens, O. D., and Albers-Schönberg, G. (1978). *Tetrahedron Lett.* pp. 3649–3652.
Herscheid, J. D. M., Scholton, H. P. H., Tijhuis, M. W., and Ottenheijm, H. C. J. (1981). *Recl. Trav. Chim. Pays-Bas* **100**, 73–78.
Higgins, C. E., Hamill, R. L., Sands, T. H., Hoehn, M. M., Davis, N. E., Nagarajan, R., and Boeck, L. D. (1974). *J. Antibiot.* **27**, 298–300.
Isono, K. (1962). *J. Antibiot.* **A15**, 80–87.
Itokawa, H., Akita, Y., and Yamasaki, M. (1973). *Yakugaku Zasshi* **93**, 1251–1252.
Izumiya, N., Lee, S., Kanmera, T., and Aoyagi, H. (1977). *J. Am. Chem. Soc.* **99**, 8346–8348.
Jansen, E. F., and Hirschman, D. J. (1944). *Arch. Biochem. Biophys.* **4**, 297–309.
Julia, M., and Preau, J. N. (1963). *C. R. Hebd. Seances Acad. Sci.* **257**, 1115–1118.
Kakinuma, M., and Rinehart, K. L. (1974). *J. Antibiot.* **27**, 733–737.
Kanmera, T., Lee, S., Aoyagi, H., and Izumiya, N. (1979). *Tetrahedron Lett.* pp. 4483–4486.
Kanmera, T., Lee, S., Aoyagi, H., and Izumiya, N. (1980). *Int. J. Pept. Protein Res.* **16**, 280–290.
Kanmera, T., Aoyagi, H., Waki, M., Kato, T., Izumiya, N., Noda, K., and Ueno, T. (1981). *Tetrahedron Lett.* **22**, 3625–3628.
Kawaguchi, H., Naito, T., and Tsukiura, H. (1965a). *J. Antibiot. Ser. A* **18**, 11–25.
Kawaguchi, H., Miyake, T., and Tsukiura, H. (1965b). *J. Antibiot., Ser. A* **18**, 220–222.
Khoklov, A. S., and Lokshin, G. B. (1963). *Tetrahedron Lett.* pp. 1881–1885.
Kiltz, H. H., and Gross, E. (1973). *Hoppe-Seyler's Z. Physiol. Chem.* **354**, 802–804.
Konno, S., and Stammer, C. H. (1978). *Int. J. Pept. Protein Res.* **12**, 222–231.
Kurita, H., Chigira, Y., Masaki, M., and Ohta, M. (1968). *Bull. Chem. Soc. Jpn.* **41**, 2758–2762.
Lee, S., Kanmera, T., Aoyagi, H., and Izumiya, N. (1979). *Int. J. Pept. Protein Res.* **13**, 207–217.
Liesch, J. M., and Rinehart, K. L. (1977). *J. Am. Chem. Soc.* **99**, 1645–1646.
McCapara, F., and Roth, M. (1972). *J. Chem. Soc., Chem. Commun.* pp. 894–895.
Marchand, J., Pais, M., Monseur, X., and Jarreau, F. X. (1969). *Tetrahedron* **25**, 937–954.
Marchelli, R., Dossena, A., and Casnati, G. (1975). *J. Chem. Soc., Chem. Commun.* pp. 779–780.
Marchelli, R., Dossena, A., Pochini, A., and Dradi, E. (1977). *J. Chem. Soc., Perkin Trans. 1* pp. 713–717.
Marconi, G. G., and Bodanszky, M. (1970). *J. Antibiot.* **23**, 120–124.
Mecklenberg, R. S., Noda, K., Miyachi, Y., Gross, E., and Lipsett, M. (1973). *Endocrinology* **93**, 993–997.

Merrifield, R. B. (1963). *J. Am. Chem. Soc.* **85**, 2149–2154.
Meyer, W. L., Kuyper, L. F., Lewis, R. B., Templeton, G. E., and Woodhead, S. H. (1974a). *Biochem. Biophys. Res. Commun.* **56**, 234–240.
Meyer, W. L., Kuyper, L. F., Phelps, D. N., and Cordes, A. W. (1974b). *J. Chem. Soc., Chem. Commun.* pp. 339–340.
Meyer, W. L., Templeton, G. E., Grable, C. I., Jones, R., Kuyper, L. F., Lewis, R. B., Sigel, C. W., and Woodhead, S. H. (1975). *J. Am. Chem. Soc.* **97**, 3802–3809.
Miller, M. J. (1980). *J. Org. Chem.* **45**, 3131–3132.
Minagawa, T. (1945). *Proc. Imp. Acad.* (*Tokyo*) **21**, 37–43.
Minagawa, T. (1946). *Proc. Imp. Acad.* (*Tokyo*) **22**, 131–138.
Mitchell, A. R., Erickson, B. W., Ryabtsev, M. N., Hodges, R. S., and Merrifield, R. B. (1976). *J. Am. Chem. Soc.* **98**, 7357–7362.
Morimoto, K., Shimada, N., Naganawa, H., Kakita, T., and Umezawa, H. (1981). *J. Antibiot.* **34**, 1615–1618.
Moriya, T., Yoneda, N., Miyoshi, M., and Matsumoto, K. (1982). *J. Org. Chem.* **47**, 94–98.
Nagasawa, H., Isogai, A., Ikeda, K., Sato, S., Murakoshi, S., Suzuki, A., and Tamura, S. (1975). *Agric. Biol. Chem.* **39**, 1901–1902.
Nagasawa, H., Isogai, A., Suzuki, A., and Tamura, S. (1976). *Tetrahedron Lett.* pp. 1601–1604.
Nagel, D. W., Pachler, K. G. R., Steyn, P. S., Vleggaar, R., and Wessels, P. L. (1976). *Tetrahedron* **32**, 2625–2631.
Nakagawa, T., Tsuno, T., Nakajima, K., Iwai, M., Kawai, H., and Okawa, K. (1972). *Bull. Chem. Soc. Jpn.* **45**, 1162–1167.
Nakagawa, T., Nakazawa, T., and Shoji, J. (1975). *J. Antibiot.* **28**, 1004–1005.
Nakamura, S., Yonehara, H., and Umezawa, H. (1964). *J. Antibiot. Ser. A* **17**, 220–221.
Nakashima, R., and Slater, G. R. (1971). *Tetrahedron Lett.* pp. 2649–2650.
Nakatsuka, S., Miyazaki, H., and Goto, T. (1980). *Tetrahedron Lett.* **21**, 2817–2820.
Nitz, T. J., Holt, E. M., Rubin, B., and Stammer, C. H. (1981). *J. Org. Chem.* **46**, 2667–2671.
Noda, K., and Gross, E. (1981). *Z. Naturforsch.*, **36B**, 1345–1347.
Noda, T., Take, T., Nagata, A., Wakamiya, T., and Shiba, T. (1972). *J. Antibiot.* **25**, 427–428.
Noda, K., Gazis, D., and Gross, E. (1982). *Int. J. Pept. Protein Res.* **19**, 413–419.
Nomoto, S., Teshima, T., Wakamiya, T., and Shiba, T. (1977). *J. Antibiot.* **30**, 955–959.
Nomoto, S., Teshima, T., Wakamiya, T., and Shiba, T. (1978). *Tetrahedron* **34**, 921–927.
Nomoto, S., Sano, A., and Shiba, T. (1979). *Tetrahedron Lett.* pp. 521–522.
Ogawa, Y., Mori, H., Ishihashi, M., Ueno, T., Nakashima, T., Fukami, H., Nakajima, R., and Ida, H. (1977). *In* "Peptide Chemistry 1976" (T. Nakajima, ed.), pp. 123–126. Protein Res. Found., Osaka, Japan.
Ogura, H., Sato, O., and Takeda, K. (1981). *Tetrahedron Lett.* **22**, 4817–4818.
Öhler, E., and Schmidt, U. (1975). *Chem. Ber.* **108**, 2907–2916.
Öhler, E., and Schmidt, U. (1977). *Chem. Ber.* **110**, 921–941.
Okuno, T., Ishita, Y., Sawai, K., and Matsumoto, T. (1974). *Chem. Lett.* pp. 635–638.
Pallai, P., Wakamiya, T., and Gross, E. (1977). *In* "Peptides" (M. Goodman and J. Meienhofer, eds.), pp. 205–208. Wiley, New York.
Patchornik, A., and Sokolovsky, M. (1963). *In* "Peptides 1962" (G. T. Young, ed.), pp. 253–257. Pergamon, Oxford.
Patchornik, A., and Sokolovsky, M. (1964). *J. Am. Chem. Soc.* **86**, 1206–1212.
Photaki, I. (1963). *J. Am. Chem. Soc.* **85**, 1123–1126.
Photaki, I., Samouilidis, I., and Zervas, L. (1975). *In* "Peptides 1974" (Y. Wolman, ed.), pp. 415–418. Wiley, New York.
Photaki, I., Samouilidis, I., Caranikas, S., and Zervas, L. (1979). *J. Chem. Soc., Perkin Trans. 1* pp. 2599–2605.

Photaki, I., Caranikas, S., Samouilidis, I., and Zervas, L. (1980). *J. Chem. Soc., Perkin Trans. 1* pp. 1965–1970.

Pitner, T. P., and Urry, D. W. (1972). *Biochemistry* **11**, 4132–4137.

Plöchl, J. (1883). *Ber. Dtsch. Chem. Ges.* **16**, 2815–2825.

Poisel, H. (1977a). *Chem. Ber.* **110**, 942–947.

Poisel, H. (1977b). *Chem. Ber.* **110**, 948–953.

Poisel, H., and Schmidt, U. (1975a). *Chem. Ber.* **108**, 2547–2553.

Poisel, H., and Schmidt, U. (1975b). *Chem. Ber.* **108**, 2917–2922.

Poisel, H., and Schmidt, U. (1976). *Angew. Chem., Int. Ed. Engl.* **15**, 294–295.

Prange, T., Ducruix, A., and Pascard, C. (1977). *Nature (London)* **265**, 189–190.

Probst, G. W., Hoehn, M. M., and Woods, B. L. (1965). *Antimicrob. Agents Chemother.* pp. 789–795.

Rao, Y. S., and Filler, R. (1975). *Synthesis* pp. 749–765.

Ratledge, C., and Snow, G. A. (1974). *Biochem. J.* **139**, 407–413.

Rich, D. H. (1976). *In* "Specificity in Plant Diseases" (R. K. S. Woods and A. Granti, eds.), pp. 169–183. Plenum, New York.

Rich, D. H., and Bhatnagar, P. K. (1978a). *J. Am. Chem. Soc.* **100**, 2212–2218.

Rich, D. H., and Bhatnagar, P. K. (1978b). *J. Am. Chem. Soc.* **100**, 2218–2224.

Rich, D. H., and Mathiaparanam, P. (1974). *Tetrahedron Lett.* pp. 4037–4040.

Rich, D. H., and Tam, J. P. (1975). *Tetrahedron Lett.* pp. 211–212.

Rich, D. H., and Tam, J. P. (1977). *J. Org. Chem.* **42**, 3815–3820.

Rich, D. H., Tam, J. P., Mathiaparanam, P., Grant, J. A., and Mabuni, C. (1974). *J. Chem. Soc., Chem. Commun.* pp. 897–898.

Rich, D. H., Mathiaparanam, P., Grant, J. A., and Bhatnagar, P. (1975a). *In* "Peptides: Chemistry, Structure and Biology" (R. Walter and J. Meienhofer, eds.), pp. 943–948. Ann Arbor Sci. Publ., Ann Arbor, Michigan.

Rich, D. H., Tam, J. P., Mathiaparanam, P., and Grant, J. A. (1975b). *Synthesis* pp. 402–403.

Rich, D. H., Bhatnagar, P., Mathiaparanam, P., Grant, J. A., and Tam, J. P. (1978). *J. Org. Chem.* **43**, 296–302.

Rogers, L. A., and Wittier, E. O. (1928). *J. Bacteriol.* **16**, 211–229.

Rosamond, J. D., and Ferger, M. F. (1976). *J. Med. Chem.* **19**, 873–876.

Sano, A., Shinho, K., Wakamiya, T., and Shiba, T. (1981). *Abst. 43rd Annu. Meet. Chem. Soc. Jpn, 1981*, Vol. II.

Sasaki, T. (1921). *Ber. Dtsch. Chem. Ges.* **54**, 163–168.

Schmidt, U., and Öhler, E. (1977). *Angew. Chem., Int. Ed. Engl.* **16**, 327–328.

Schmidt, U., Häusler, J., Öhler, E., and Poisel, H. (1979). *Prog. Chem. Org. Nat. Prod.* **37**, 252–327.

Schnabel, E., Stoltefuss, J., Offe, H. A., and Klauke, E. (1971). *Justus Liebigs Ann. Chem.* **743**, 57–68.

Scott, P. M., Merrien, M.-A., and Polonsky, J. (1976). *Experientia* **32**, 140–142.

Sheehan, J. C., Mania, D., Nakamura, S., Stock, J. A., and Maeda, K. (1968). *J. Am. Chem. Soc.* **90**, 462–470.

Shiba, T., Ando, T., and Teshima, T. (1980). *In* "Peptide Chemistry 1979" (H. Yonehara, ed.), pp. 83–88. Protein Res. Found., Osaka, Japan.

Shimohigashi, Y., and Izumiya, N. (1978a). *Int. J. Pept. Protein Res.* **12**, 7–16.

Shimohigashi, Y., and Izumiya, N. (1978b). *Yuki Gosei Kagaku Kyokaishi* **36**, 1023–1038.

Shimohigashi, Y., and Stammer, C. H. (1981). *In* "Peptides: Synthesis, Structure, Function" (D. H. Rich and E. Gross, eds.), pp. 645–648. Pierce Chemical Co., Rockford, Illinois.

Shimohigashi, Y., and Stammer, C. H. (1982a). *Int. J. Pept. Protein Res.* **19**, 54–62.

Shimohigashi, Y., and Stammer, C. H. (1982b). *Int. J. Pept. Protein Res.* **20**, 199–206.

Shimohigashi, Y., Lee, S., Aoyagi, H., Kato, T., and Izumiya, N. (1977a). *Int. J. Pept. Protein Res.* **10**, 197–205.
Shimohigashi, Y., Lee, S., Aoyagi, H. Kato, T., and Izumiya, N. (1977b). *Int. J. Pept. Protein Res.* **10**, 323–327.
Shimohigashi, Y., Lee, S., Kato, T., Izumiya, N. Ueno, T., and Fukami, H. (1977c). *Chem. Lett.* pp. 1411–1414.
Shimohigashi, Y., Lee, S., Kato, T., and Izumiya, N. (1978). *Bull. Chem. Soc. Jpn.* **51**, 584–588.
Shimohigashi, Y., Kato, T., Kang, S., Minematsu, Y., Waki, M., and Izumiya, N. (1979). *Tetrahedron Lett.* pp. 1327–1328.
Shimohigashi, Y., Dunning, J. W., Jr., Grim, M. D., and Stammer, C. H. (1981a). *J. Chem. Soc., Perkin Trans. 2* pp. 1171–1175.
Shimohigashi, Y., Costa, T., and Stammer, C. H. (1981b). *FEBS Lett.* **133**, 269–271.
Shimohigashi, Y., English, M. L., Stammer, C. H., and Costa, T. (1982). *Biochem. Biophys. Res. Commun.* **104**, 583–590.
Shimohigashi, Y., Nitz, T. J., Stammer, C. H., and Inubushi, T. (1982b). *Tetrahedron Lett.* **23**, 3235–3236.
Shimohigashi, Y., Chen, H. C., and Stammer, C. H. (1982c). *Peptides* **3**, 985–987.
Shin, C. (1979). *Yuki Gosei Kagaku Kyokaishi* **37**, 830–842.
Shin, C., Masaki, M., and Ohta, M. (1967). *J. Org. Chem.* **32**, 1860–1863.
Shin, C., Chigira, Y., Masaki, M., and Ohta, M. (1969). *Bull. Chem. Soc. Jpn.* **42**, 191–193.
Shin, C., Masaki, M., and Ohta, M. (1971). *Bull. Chem. Soc. Jpn.* **44**, 1657–1660.
Shin, C., Hayakawa, M., Suzuki, T., Ohtsuka, A., and Yoshimura, J. (1978). *Bull. Chem. Soc. Jpn.* **51**, 550–554.
Shin, C., Yonezawa, Y., Unoki, K., and Yoshimura, J. (1979). *Tetrahedron Lett.* pp. 1049–1050.
Shin, C., Yonezawa, Y., Takahashi, M., and Yoshimura, J. (1981). *Bull. Chem. Soc. Jpn.* **54**, 1132–1136.
Shoji, J., Hinoo, H., Wakasaka, Y., Koizumi, K., and Mayama, M. (1975). *J. Antibiot.* **28**, 126–128.
Shoji, J., Kato, T., Yoshimura, Y., and Tori, K. (1981). *J. Antibiot.* **34**, 1126–1136.
Shoji, J., Hinoo, H., Sakazaki, R., Tsuji, N., Nagashima, K., Matsumoto, K., Takahashi, Y., Kozuki, S., Hattori, T., Kondo, E., and Tanaka, K. (1982). *J. Antibiot.* **35**, 24–31.
Silaev, A. B., Katrukha, G. S., Trifonova, Zh. P., Li, R. I., and Melenteva, T. M. (1971). *Khim. Prir. Soedin.* **7**, 130–131.
Sokolovsky, M., Sadeh, T., and Patchornik, A. (1964). *J. Am. Chem. Soc.* **86**, 1212–1217.
Sparrow, J. T. (1976). *J. Org. Chem.* **41**, 1350–1353.
Srinivasan, A., Richards, K.D., and Olsen, R. K. (1976). *Tetrahedron Lett.* pp. 891–894.
Srinivasan, A., Stephensen, R. W., and Olsen, R. K. (1977a). *J. Org. Chem.* **42**, 2253–2256.
Srinivasan, A., Stephensen, R. W., and Olsen, R. K. (1977b). *J. Org. Chem.* **42**, 2256–2260.
Stammer, C. H. (1982). *Chem. Biochem. Amino Acids, Pept. Proteins* **6**, 33–74.
Steyn, P. S. (1971). *Tetrahedron Lett.* pp. 3331–3334.
Stipanovic, R. D., and Schroeder, H. W. (1976). *Trans. Br. Mycol. Soc.* **66**, 178–179.
Stonard, R. J., and Anderson, R. J. (1980). *J. Org. Chem.* **45**, 3687–3691.
Stracher, A., and Craig, L. C. (1959). *J. Am. Chem. Soc.* **81**, 696–700.
Takahashi, T., Sugawara, Y., and Suzuki, M. (1972). *Tetrahedron Lett.* pp. 1873–1876.
Templeton, G. E., Meyer, W. L., Grable, C. I., and Sigel, C. W. (1967). *Phytopathology* **57**, 833.
Teshima, T., Nomoto, S., Wakamiya, T., and Shiba, T. (1976). *Tetrahedron Lett.* pp. 2342–2346.
Thompson, R. Q., and Hughes, M. S. (1963). *J. Antibiot. Ser. A* **16**, 187–194.
Tokura, K., Tori, K., Yoshimura, Y., Okabe, K., Otsuka, H., Matsushita, K., Inagami, F., and Miyazawa, T. (1980). *J. Antibiot.* **33**, 1563–1567.
Tori, K., Tokura, K., Okabe, K., Ebata, M., and Otsuka, H. (1976). *Tetrahedron Lett.* pp. 185–188.

Tori, K., Tokura, K., Yoshimura, Y., Terui, Y., Okabe, H., Otsuka, H., Matsushita, K., Inagami, F., and Miyazawa, T. (1981). *J. Antibiot.* **34**, 124–129.

Ueki, M., Shinozaki, K., and Inazu, T. (1981). *In* "Peptide Chemistry 1980" (K. Okawa, ed.), pp. 37–40. Protein Res. Found., Osaka, Japan.

Ueno, T., Nakashima, T., Hayashi, Y., and Fukami, H. (1975a). *Agric. Biol. Chem.* **39**, 1115–1122.

Ueno, T., Nakashima, T., Hayashi, Y., and Fukami, H. (1975b). *Agric. Biol. Chem.* **39**, 2081–2082.

Urry, D. W. (1972). *Proc. Natl. Acad. Sci. U.S.A.* **69**, 1610–1614.

Vleggaar, R., and Wessels, P. L. (1980). *J. Chem. Soc., Chem. Commun.* pp. 160–162.

Walter, R. (1977). *Fed. Proc. Fed. Am. Soc. Exp. Biol.* **36**, 1872–1878.

Walter, R., and Roy, J. (1971). *J. Org. Chem.* **36**, 2561–2563.

Weiner, H., White, W. H., Hoare, D. G., and Koshland, D. E., Jr. (1966). *J. Am. Chem. Soc.* **88**, 3851–3859

Wickner, R. B. (1969). *J. Biol. Chem.* **244**, 6550–6552.

Woodward, R. B., Heusler, K., Gosteli, J., Naegeli, P., Oppolzer, W., Ramage, R., Ranganathan, S., and Vorbruggen, H. (1966). *J. Am. Chem. Soc.* **88**, 852–853.

Yoshioka, H., Aoki, T., Goto, H., Nakatsu, K., Noda, T., Sakakibara, H., Take, T., Nagata, A., Abe, J., Wakamiya, T., Shiba, T., and Kaneko, T. (1971). *Tetrahedron Lett.* pp. 2043–2046.

Zervas, L., and Ferderigos, N. (1973). *Experientia* **29**, 262.

Zervas, L., and Ferderigos, N. (1974). *Isr. J. Chem.* **12**, 139–152.

Chapter **6**

Unusual Amino Acids in Peptide Synthesis

DAVID C. ROBERTS
Department of Chemistry,
Rutgers University,
New Brunswick,
New Jersey

FRANK VELLACCIO
Department of Chemistry,
College of the Holy Cross,
Worcester, Massachusetts

I. Introduction 342
  A. Literature Sources 342
  B. Types of Structural Variants of Peptides 343
  C. Scope of This Review 343
  D. Reasons for Using Unusual Amino Acids 344
II. Isofunctional and Homofunctional Replacement 346
  A. Fatty Amino Acids 346
  B. Aromatic Series 347
  C. Large Aryl Side Chains 348
  D. Organometallic Amino Acids 348
III. Isosteric and Homosteric Replacement 349
  A. Histidine Isosteres 349
  B. Pyridylalanines as Isologs of Phenylalanine and Histidine . 350
  C. Tetrazole-Containing Amino Acids 350
  D. Functional Variants of Sulfur-Containing Amino Acids . . 350
IV. Amino Acids Exerting Strong Conformational Influences . . . 351
  A. Proline Isologs 352
  B. 1-Aminocycloalkane-1-carboxylic Acids and Bicyclic Congeners 353
  C. Conformationally Constrained Dipeptide Units 353
V. Reporter Groups 354
  A. Fluorinated Amino Acids in nmr Studies of Peptides . . . 354
  B. Spin Labels 355
  C. Radioactive Labels 356

THE PEPTIDES, VOLUME 5

ISBN 0-12-304205-4

VI. Reactive Side-Chain Functionality 356
A. Receptor Interactions 356
1. Alkylating Agents 357
2. Photoaffinity Labeling 358
B. Synthetic Transformations on Side-Chain Groups 359
1. Aromatic Side Chains 361
2. Sulfur-Containing Side Chains 361
3. Unsaturated Side Chains 362
VII. Peptide Isosteres 363
Appendix: Unusual Amino Acids 365
References 429

I. INTRODUCTION

In a 1972 review article, Josef Rudinger concluded that the design of peptide hormone analogs would prove more fruitful if chemists were to be "less reluctant ... to abandon the facile use of ready-made bricks, the protein-constituent amino acids, and to undertake sometimes quite intricate syntheses to meet the designs which will best answer a given purpose." It is apparent that this view has since gained increasing acceptance within the peptide community; it is the authors' purpose in writing this review to assess what has actually been done to date in the development and use of non-standard building blocks in peptides and to compile a reference list of unusual amino acids that have been or might be used in peptide synthesis.

We have not attempted to be exhaustive in our coverage but rather have presented selected examples illustrating the various motivations and strategies behind the use of unusual amino acids in peptides. We apologize to the authors of many important articles which, because of space and time limitations, are mentioned very briefly or cited only as references. We also warn the reader that this review was implicitly written from the standpoint of peptide hormone-based medicinal chemistry. Specialized topics such as the synthesis of peptide antibiotics containing unusual hydroxyamino acids have not been included.

A. Literature Sources

The literature on unusual amino acids prior to 1960 has been covered by Greenstein and Winitz (1961); the authors also call the reader's attention to a number of review articles with a natural product emphasis (Meister, 1965; Fowden, 1964, 1970; Fowden *et al.*, 1979; Vickery, 1972; Lea, 1978). As our sources, we have relied heavily on the annual *Specialist Periodical Reports on Amino Acids, Peptides, and Proteins* (Chemical Society), supplemented by the *MTP International Review of Science—Organic Chemistry* Series, the compendia of Pettit (1970, 1973, 1975, 1976), and a review by Mooz (1974), along with standard literature search sources. None of these sources address the present subject in a comprehensive way. It is the authors' hope that this chapter will provide peptide chemists with an awareness of existing capabilities for structural variation in peptides and open the door to strategies of drug design previously employed only in more traditional areas of medicinal chemistry.

B. Types of Structural Variants of Peptides

Departures from the sole use of the coded amino acids in peptide structures may involve relatively straightforward procedures such as modification (acylation, alkylation, etc.) of side-chain functional groups of coded amino acids, acylation of the NH_2-terminus with simple carboxylic acids or attachment of amines to the COOH-terminus, and replacement of one or more amino acids in a chain with a noncoded counterpart. This category, being for the most part available within the confines of standard procedures for peptide synthesis (including solid-phase techniques), is perhaps the most straightforward means by which peptide chemists can expand their repertoire of available structural variation and therefore provides the main focus of this review.

A number of more radical measures are also available to chemists. These include the use of α-azaamino (Dutta and Morley, 1975; Powers and Gupton, 1977) and α-dehydroamino (Chapter 5, this volume) acids, which require special treatment owing to their chemical constitution. The synthesis of retro-inverso sequences (Goodman and Chorev, 1981), which involves the use of malonic acid derivatives and *gem*-diamines, also requires unusual procedures. Replacement of the peptide linkage at a particular position with some more or less isosteric but chemically distinct functionality (esters, ethers, etc.), may also require some involved synthetic transformations. Finally, major surgery of the sort so dramatically demonstrated by the Merck group in the case of somatostatin, in which a large fragment was replaced with a simple linkage that fulfilled the same role in maintaining the active conformation (Veber *et al.*, 1979; Veber, 1981), provides a striking recent example.

C. Scope of This Review

The table of amino acids in the Appendix includes only α-amino acids, and (with a few exceptions) only those for which syntheses have been reported in the literature. Amino acids cited by Greenstein and Winitz (1961) are referenced to that review and not to the original work or (with a few exceptions) to any more recent works. We have further excluded certain types of α-amino acids which, in our opinion, would not have substantially increased the value of the chapter but would have added a great deal of bulk; see the introduction to the Appendix for details. In the text of the present chapter, the authors have occasionally overstepped these boundaries in the interests of historical and logical continuity; in addition, we have incorporated a brief overview of dipeptide isosteres, which can often be treated as simple amino acids for the purposes of peptide synthesis and represent an especially exciting modern development. We have attempted in the text to give a comprehensive overview of the various applications that call for unusual amino acids, and have chosen examples for discussion that illuminate these applications. We have not attempted to discuss all noteworthy amino acids, and many important pieces of work are omitted or only briefly mentioned in the text. We have, however, attempted to give complete, up-to-date reviews of those applications that are covered. Aside from a few more recent works, the literature through 1981 is covered.

D. Reasons for Using Unusual Amino Acids

Traditional peptide structure–activity studies employing coded amino acids have had as their goal, and have often realized, some of the potential benefits outlined in Table I. However, many previously unavailable possibilities are opened up when such studies embrace the incorporation of groups sterically and functionally different from those present in the coded amino acids. Techniques such as affinity labeling, studies with spectroscopic probes, and novel chemical modifications are now possible through the incorporation of appropriate functional groups. Furthermore, the transport and metabolism of peptide analogs can be affected much more dramatically by departing from the sole use of coded amino acids, and the much wider range of available molecular shapes and chemical functionality enhances the likelihood of further optimization of receptor binding and of other pharmacological properties. These capabilities, and the impressive successes they have made possible, should serve to reassure chemists who fear that recombinant DNA technology and its inevitable success in the production of natural peptides will render their services obsolete.

It has been pointed out by Rudinger (1972) and others that structure–activity data are more easily interpreted if structural changes are made isosteric or "isofunctional" whenever possible. The use of unusual amino acids makes newly possible many such substitutions; indeed many of the unusual amino acids reviewed here seem to have been developed just for

Table I. Benefits To Be Gained by Using Unusual Amino Acids and Other Unnatural Structural Variations of Peptides

- Improved drug–receptor interactions
  - Study of strength and nature of binding (including selecting out certain types of activity)
    - Effects on fit
      - Steric compatibility of active conformation with receptor site
      - Enhancement of active conformation relative to others
    - Effects on strength of chemical interactions
      - Electrostatic polar interactions
      - Hydrophobic interactions
  - Irreversible binding
    - Affinity labeling of allosteric binding sites
    - Prolonged pharmacological activity due to irreversible receptor binding
- Improved pharmacokinetic properties
  - Interactions with peptide-processing enzymes
    - Resistance to enzymatic degradation
    - Pharmacological effects resulting from inhibition of peptide-processing enzymes
  - Effects on drug delivery and excretion
    - Effects on solubility, mobility, tissue specificity
    - Slow chemical release of active species
- Development of tools for study of peptide chemistry and biology
  - Spectroscopic probes of peptide conformations and interactions
  - Affinity labeling as probe for enzymes and receptors
  - Radiolabeled peptides for anatomical and pharmacological studies
- Facilitated chemical synthesis of peptides
  - Improved stability and physical properties of product
  - Structural variation that allows retention of activity in smaller, simpler molecules
  - Easy modification of side-chain functionality following incorporation into a peptide chain
- Unusual amino acid required as component of a natural product (and needed for any of the above reasons)

such purposes. Although analogs containing them might not themselves show dramatically improved activity, they can impart order to the structure–activity data and ultimately lead to the rational formulation of analogs possessing the sought characteristics.

Ideally, an article such as this would provide its readers with easily applied information as to how a given unusual amino acid may be expected to function in affecting the activity of an analog. The authors hesitate to attempt this, as available activity data often reflect structural changes in ways that are not obvious. A change in structure may function differently in different situations—in receptor binding or even at the level of gene expression from which the distribution of enzymes and receptors themselves may be affected. A statement such as, "Pyridylalanines function as six-ring analogs of histidine," although simplifying matters neatly, may not only be untrue but is likely to cause readers to ignore other possible analogies. In many cases, however, it may be clear that the investigator's *intent* was to use, for example, pyridylalanines as functional analogs of histidine; this review will attempt to limit itself to these more harmless interpretations.

II. ISOFUNCTIONAL AND HOMOFUNCTIONAL REPLACEMENT

Perhaps the most subtle way to vary the structure of a peptide hormone is to change only its steric properties and leave its functional groups intact and in the same approximate relative geometry. Although in a few cases it is possible to do this by substituting one coded amino acid for another (e.g., threonine for serine, aspartic acid for glutamic acid), most such modifications require the introduction of a noncoded amino acid. Simple homologs, that is, structures that contain greater or lesser numbers of methylene groups in the side chain than the natural amino acid or are otherwise functionally similar, are known for most amino acids. Much of the early work with noncoded amino acids involved substitutions of this type, some of which have seen extensive use in peptides. In general, changing the steric properties of a peptide hormone does not result in a significant improvement of potency and in many cases lowers potency severely. Its most useful application is in cases where the spectrum of physiological activity is altered by modification (i.e., suppression of one type of activity while preserving another).

A. Fatty Amino Acids

The use of unnatural fatty (hydrocarbon) amino acids as steric probes of the receptor site was pioneered by Rudinger and co-workers (Eisler *et al.*, 1966) in their studies on oxytocin analogs; they found, as have many other investigators, that natural fatty and aromatic residues can often be replaced by unnatural analogs without sacrificing biological activity. In some cases, stability to enzymatic cleavage can be introduced in this way without sacrificing biological activity, as in the case of [adamantylalanine^5]-enkephalin analogs (Do and Schwyzer, 1981). The reader is cautioned that certain fatty amino acids, notably *tert*-alkylglycines, may be expected to pose problems in synthesis as a result of the steric bulk of the side chain; for example, difficulty was encountered in coupling active esters of protected *tert*-leucine (β-methylvaline), whereas acylation of the amino acid proceeded satisfactorily (Pospíšek and Bláha, 1977).

Although substitutions of this type do not appear to afford significant improvement in activity over that of the natural hormone, they can result in substantially modified activity. For example, Khosla *et al.* (1972) found striking antagonistic activity in angiotensin II analogs containing a cyclohexylalanine residue in place of phenylalanine. This replacement is not strictly isofunctional because of the electronic properties of the aromatic ring in phenylalanine. In fact, such replacements have been used as probes of biological requirements for aromaticity (Fletcher and Young, 1972), and a similar use has been described for partially saturated phenylalanines (Ressler *et al.*, 1979). Differences in activity are sufficiently minor as to be attributable to the steric nonequivalence of the hydrogenated phenylalanine derivatives relative to phenylalanine. To the authors' knowledge, there are no cases where a functional requirement for aromaticity per se has been demonstrated. The steric similarity between cyclohexylalanine and phenylalanine has been used in polyamino acid CD studies where the interference of the chromophoric side chain causes problems (Peggion *et al.*, 1970).

B. Aromatic Series

Replacement of an aromatic residue with a nonnatural counterpart produces a common type of structural variant. Abrupt changes in functionality (e.g., replacing phenylalanine with tyrosine) often result in a loss of activity; however, more nearly isofunctional replacements often result in preserved or even enhanced activity. A series of substituted phenylalanines, including alkyl and alkoxy, were employed as replacements at position 2 of oxytocin, and the bulkier groups were found to impart a strong antagonist activity to the analogs (Rudinger, 1972). Typically, replacement of phenylalanine with sterically similar substituted aromatic residues does not grossly affect the activity; for example, Morley and co-workers (Morley, 1968; Gregory *et al.*, 1968) have found that para substitution of the phenylalanine residue in gastrin tetrapeptide with various types of groups (methyl, methoxy, nitro, fluoro) can be done without sacrificing activity. 4-Fluorophenylalanine (Nicolaides *et al.*, 1963) is very nearly isosteric with phenylalanine and has found considerable application in adjusting hormonal activity. 4-Nitrophenylalanine has also been used extensively; enhanced activity of enkephalin analogs containing this amino acid appears to stem from the electron-poor character of the aromatic ring (Fauchère and Schiller, 1981; Schwyzer, 1980). 3-Tyrosine is another interesting isofunctional variant that has been used (Bernardi *et al.*, 1966). An unusual phenylalanine homolog that has found considerable application is 3-(2-thienyl)alanine (du Vigneaud *et al.*, 1945; Dunn and Stewart, 1971).

C. Large Aryl Side Chains

Larger or fused-ring aromatic amino acids have been used as replacements for both phenylalanine and tryptophan residues. The naphthylalanines and various other tryptophan isologs employed by Yabe *et al.* (1976) generally provide analogs with reduced activity. Tesser and co-workers have used pentamethylphenylalanine as a replacement for tryptophan in several types of hormone analogs, including those of α-melanotropin (α-MSH), which exhibit useful potency (Van Nispen *et al.*, 1977b); they have found that more nearly isosteric but less electron-rich tryptophan isologs give less active peptides and have concluded that strong π-donor properties of tryptophan isologs are more important than steric equivalence in preserving hormonal activity. This is apparently not always the case, as seen in studies by Rajh *et al.* (1980). Extensive studies on the replacement of Trp^6 in luliberin (LHRH) analogs have been carried out in a search for antifertility agents. A series of bulky carbocyclic (Nestor *et al.*, 1981, 1982a) and heteroaromatic (Nestor *et al.*, 1982b) amino acids, some representing considerable steric and electronic deviation from tryptophan, provided analogs with potent super-agonist activity.

Other large aromatic amino acids of potential interest are styrylphenylalanine (Jones and Wright, 1971), with a photoisomerizable double bond, and anthracene derivatives of possible use in photophysical studies (Ben-Ishai *et al.*, 1978; Nestor *et al.*, 1982a; Schreiber and Lautsch, 1965).

D. Organometallic Amino Acids

Amino acids with side chains incorporating polyhedral carboranes and organometallic "sandwich" complexes have been proposed or utilized as homologs of phenylalanine or other bulky hydrophobic amino acids. Schwyzer and co-workers have, in the course of studies on unusual hydrophobic amino acids, introduced 3-*o*-carboranylalanine, which is claimed to occupy a space nearly equal to that swept by a 180° rotation of the phenylalanine aryl group. Their studies show that analogs containing this unusual group can exhibit enhanced activity in some cases (Fauchère *et al.*, 1979) and, interestingly, that this may be a result more of the electron deficiency of the carborane nucleus than its steric bulk (Schwyzer, 1980; Fauchère and Schiller, 1981).

Greater deviations in shape from that of phenylalanine are seen in amino acids with organometallic π-complexes incorporated into their side chains. Ferrocenylalanine has been incorporated into peptide structures and exhibits the interesting ability to undergo a reversible one-electron oxidation to provide a cationic side chain that imparts water solubility and a deep-green color to derivatives (Cuingnet *et al.*, 1980; Pospíšek *et al.*, 1980). Also of interest are amino acids with cyclobutadiene, cyclopentadienyl (Brunet *et al.*, 1981a), and benzene (Brunet *et al.*, 1981b) metal carbonyl complexes. These are of interest for their unusual steric properties and for their possible use in photoaffinity labeling, which results from the known ability of various groups (e.g., amines) to replace CO in such complexes under photolysis.

III. ISOSTERIC AND HOMOSTERIC REPLACEMENT

The role of functional group interactions in allosteric binding of peptide hormones is at least equal in importance to steric fit and is undoubtedly the source of most of the specificity characteristic of these interactions. Although hormone–receptor binding is optimized both sterically and functionally by evolution within the limitations of the coded amino acids, it is in principle possible, by employing functional groups other than those in the coded amino acids, to create interactions significantly stronger than those present in the natural system; for this reason it seems that functional variants of peptides are more likely than steric variants to provide analogs with enhanced or modified activity. Below are outlined some of the more extensively studied functional variants of amino acids.

A. Histidine Isosteres

An early example of isosteric substitution in investigating the effects of functional changes is the use of histidine isologs in which the imidazole ring is replaced with a pyrazole nucleus (Hofmann *et al.*, 1968). This involves a change in the arrangement of nitrogen atoms relative to those in histidine, as well as a significant lowering of their basicity; steric changes are insignificant. It was found that the catalytic activity of ribonuclease S was entirely lost when the enzyme was reconstituted using an analog of S-peptide containing a β-(3-pyrazolyl)alanine residue in place of the catalytically functional histidine (Hofmann *et al.*, 1970). In contrast to this the activity of a variety of peptide hormones was retained (although it was often significantly weakened) in analogs containing pyrazolylalanines in place of a histidine residue. It has been concluded from such studies that the basicity of the histidine residue per se is not a requisite for activity, however, it may in some cases contribute to the strength of binding. A fair variety of other histidine isosteres have been reported, but most of them have not yet been incorporated into peptides.

B. Pyridylalanines as Isologs of Phenylalanine and Histidine

Although a fair variety of derivatives of (2-, 3-, and 4-pyridyl)alanines have been reported, surprisingly little has been done to investigate their usefulness as components of peptides. Watanabe *et al.* (1968) report difficulties with coupling methods other than the dicyclohexylcarbodiimide (DCC) method in syntheses of β-(2-pyridyl)alanine-containing dipeptides. Veselova and Chaman (1973) successfully prepared a tripeptide from this amino acid. Especially attractive as isologs of tyrosine are the *N*-oxides of pyridylalanines (Sullivan *et al.*, 1968), although only their synthesis was reported.

C. Tetrazole-Containing Amino Acids

Following Morley's observation (1968) of the close steric and functional similarity between the tetrazole group and the carboxyl group, progress has been made in studying incorporation of the tetrazole nucleus at the sites of both side-chain and COOH-terminal carboxyl groups in peptides. Morley (1969) incorporated a tetrazole derivative of aspartic acid into an analog of gastrin tetrapeptide. Further studies reported by Grzonka's group involve synthesis of the γ-tetrazole derivative of glycine (Van Thach *et al.*, 1977, and references therein) and evidence from enzyme studies that the tetrazole–carboxyl similarity may not be as close as previously thought.

D. Functional Variants of Sulfur-Containing Amino Acids

Cysteine occurs in small peptides exclusively in the form of disulfide-bridged cystine, often serving to cyclize an otherwise linear peptide in order to stabilize an active conformation. Replacement of the cystine disulfide linkage with sterically similar linkages such as CH_2CH_2 and CH_2S was found not to lower hormonal activity in ground-breaking studies with oxytocin (Rudinger and Jošt, 1964; Jošt and Rudinger, 1967). This trend was subsequently confirmed for vasopressins and somatostatin. It was therefore not surprising that the selenium isolog of cysteine should function as a good substitute for this amino acid in such hormones, as a result of its tendency to form Se—Se and S—Se bonds which are chemically similar to disulfide linkages. Walter (1973) reported extensive structural and conformational studies of the selenium analog of oxytocin, in which the activity was comparable to that of the native hormone despite differing dihedral angles in the dichalcogenide linkage. Zdansky (1973) has reviewed the field of selenium-containing amino acids, including selenocysteine, selenomethionine, and various side-chain-methylated derivatives.

Functional variants of methionine are an especially interesting class of amino acids; unlike other amino acids, whose chemical functions are quite well understood, methionine remains something of a mystery with regard to the function of the sulfur atom. Although in some hormones, such as corticotropin, replacement of methionine with a sterically similar fatty amino acid such as norleucine can be made without sacrifice of activity, this is apparently not the case in gastrin tetrapeptide and others (reviewed by Rudinger, 1972); in general, *S*-ethylcysteine functions well as a substitute for methionine. The separate biological roles of Leu- and Met-enkephalins and their precursors are also striking when one considers their structural and functional similarity. It may be that the hydrocarbon-like steric and hydrophobic properties of methionine will not in themselves be sufficient to explain these differences.

IV. AMINO ACIDS EXERTING STRONG CONFORMATIONAL INFLUENCES

Any type of structural modification of a peptide might categorically be expected to influence the range of available conformations and/or the degree to which a given active conformation is preferred relative to others. This may in some cases be the primary means by which structural changes affect activity. Certain types of amino acid substitutions have been known for some time to exert powerful effects in this regard. As residues in a peptide chain, N-substituted amino acids including proline and its isologs function uniquely in that the amino nitrogen cannot serve as a hydrogen bond donor when incorporated into an amide linkage, which in turn lacks a marked preference for the trans conformation characteristic of the unsubstituted CONH linkage. Substitution of a proline residue in place of another (N-unsubstituted) amino acid of similar steric bulk (or vice versa) is therefore not as subtle a change as it might as first seem. α,α-Disubstituted amino acids also exert strong influences on conformation, directly by limiting the allowable values of the dihedral angles of bonds to the α-carbon. By the same token, glycine, being an α,α-unsubstituted amino acid, gives greater conformational freedom. From the standpoint of analog design, substitutions that preserve the gross conformational influences of the constituent amino acids in most cases prove to be the best strategy.

Because of space limitations, acyclic *N*-alkyl and acyclic α,α-disubstituted amino acids have been excluded from this review; the considerations above give the present authors some hope that this omission will not seriously detract from the usefulness of the chapter.

A. Proline Isologs

A fair variety of substituted prolines are known, as there has been considerable interest in them as antimetabolites in collagen biosynthesis. Most of these variants have yet to be employed as components of peptides, with the notable exception of naturally occurring 4-hydroxyproline (Adams, 1977). One of the most popular replacements for proline is the 3,4-dehydro derivative; this amino acid was introduced by Robertson and Witkop (1962) and was claimed to be somewhat susceptible to racemization. Replacement of proline with this amino acid in bioactive peptides can, as a rule, be done without substantial loss of activity and in some cases enhances activity markedly, as in position 7 of oxytocin (Moore *et al.*, 1977a), in angiotensin-converting enzyme inhibitors (Fisher and Ryan, 1979; Natarajan *et al.*, 1979), and in angiotensin II (Moore, 1981). It also appears that this substitution can confer resistance to enzymatic degradation on a peptide (Fisher *et al.*, 1978). These effects are apparently mediated by the enhanced planarity imparted to the proline ring by the double bond, although the decreased steric bulk and enhanced polarizability of the π-cloud may contribute to the enhanced receptor affinity observed (Moore *et al.*, 1977a). Epoxidation of this amino acid provides another very interesting proline derivative which has not yet found application in peptide synthesis (Hudson *et al.*, 1975).

Thiazolidine-4-carboxylic acid and its 2-substituted derivatives are readily available as thioaminals from cysteine, and the unsubstituted version has found application as an isolog of proline in peptides, where it can provide enhanced activity and/or selectivity (Felix *et al.*, 1973; Rosamond and Ferger, 1976; Moore, 1981). This residue probably allows somewhat greater conformational freedom than proline itself. A variety of ring homologs of proline, with ring sizes varying from 3 to 15, are available, and some of them, notably azetidine-2-carboxylic acid and pipecolic acid, have been incorporated into peptide analogs in place of proline. This as a rule results in a significant loss of activity, at least in the neurohypophyseal hormone series (Barber *et al.*, 1979; Chaturvedi *et al.*, 1970; Neubert *et al.*, 1972) and verifies the crucial relationship between conformation and activity. Peptides incorporating the 6-ring and higher homologs will enjoy significantly enhanced conformational freedom; small-ring homologs will maintain rigidity, but bond angles differ. The latter still appear, on these grounds, to be promising as replacements for proline since few data to the contrary are presently available. By the same token, bicyclic prolines (Fujimoto *et al.*, 1971; Hughes *et al.*, 1980; Pirrung, 1980) appear promising as well.

A considerable number of benzo-fused cyclic imino acids are available, many of which are structurally related to biogenic amines. One noteworthy example is 1,2,3,4-tetrahydroquinoline-2-carboxylic acid, whose *N*-acyl or *N*-peptidyl derivatives can be caused to undergo dehydration–isomerization under mild conditions to give *O*-acylaminals potentially hydrolyzable to the peptide aldehyde (Zecchini and Paradisi, 1979).

B. 1-Aminocycloalkane-1-carboxylic Acids and Bicyclic Congeners

Although they do not correspond structurally to any of the coded amino acids, the sheer variety of cyclic α,α-disubstituted amino acids available in the literature warrants a close look by peptide chemists. Comparatively little has been done in the way of peptide chemistry involving these compounds, and the results have been disappointing [e.g., see angiotensin II analogs described by Park *et al.* (1974) and Hsieh *et al.* (1979)], as would be expected owing to conformational effects. A large number of interesting amino acids in this class, including various fused aromatic derivatives, were reviewed by Ross *et al.* (1961) following an exhaustive search for anticancer agents. More recently, several bicyclic amino acids have been reported. These include 2-aminoadamantane-2-carboxylic acid, whose peptides can serve as inhibitors of leucine aminopeptidase (Nagasawa *et al.*, 1975). The corresponding norbornane amino acid and its peptides are readily prepared by a Diels–Alder reaction between cyclopentadiene and α-dehydroalanine derivatives, including peptides (Horikawa *et al.*, 1980). The latter process suggests that, given a variety of reactive dienes, a variety of peptide analogs incorporating unusual bicyclic amino acids can be obtained from a single dehydroalanine peptide.

C. Conformationally Constrained Dipeptide Units

A very recent development in the design of peptide hormone analogs is the introduction of bridging groups into an otherwise normal peptide, which provide a secondary linkage between adjacent residues and thereby restrict conformational freedom. This would be expected to enhance receptor affinity if the resulting analog were to approximate the receptor-bound conformation of the native hormone. This type of structural change may also confer resistance to enzymatic degradation on the analogs.

Analysis of the structural relationship between morphine alkaloids and enkephalins led Di Maio *et al.* (1979) to synthesize a series of enkephalin analogs possessing either a methylene bridge between the tyrosine amino nitrogen and the Gly^2 α-carbon, or an ethano bridge between the same nitrogen and the Gly^2 nitrogen. The resulting Tyr-Gly units can be treated as simple imino acids for the purpose of peptide synthesis. These investigators reported that one of the analogs exhibited potent analgesic activity *in vivo*, the others being inactive (Di Maio *et al.*, 1979; Di Maio and Schiller, 1980).

Some very encouraging results along similar lines have been obtained by the Merck peptide group with LHRH analogs. Following prior evidence of a β-turn at positions 6 and 7 in the active conformation of LHRH, Freidinger, and co-workers (1980) sought to lock the molecule into this conformation by introducing an ethano bridge between the α-carbon of Gly^6 and the nitrogen of Leu^7. The corresponding dipeptide unit was prepared conveniently from Boc-Met-Leu-OMe via a sulfonium salt; this unit was incorporated into positions 6 and 7 of gonadoliberin LHRH using traditional methods. The resulting analog exhibited significantly greater potency *in vitro* and *in vivo* than the native hormone, apparently because of greater receptor affinity. A number of related conformational constraints have been reported (Freidinger, 1981; Freidinger *et al.*, 1982) employing hydrocarbon or thioether bridges in five-, six-, and seven-ring structures, some of which are readily derived from ordinary amino acids. Enkephalin analogs with such bridges between adjacent glycine residues were reported, and some of them exhibited weak but significant activity.

V. REPORTER GROUPS

A. Fluorinated Amino Acids in Nmr Studies of Peptides

A large number of fluorinated derivatives of coded amino acids have been introduced as antimetabolites and antibacterial agents. Among the more interesting fluorinated amino acids available for study are pentafluorophenylalanine and tetrafluorotyrosine (Filler *et al.*, 1969), trifluoromethionine (Dannley and Taborsky, 1957), and aliphatic amino acids bearing CF_3 groups (Lazar and Sheppard, 1968). Although the acidity or basicity of proximal groups is often affected by fluorine substitution, steric differences are minimal. For these reasons, Fauchère and Schwyzer (1971), in describing a synthesis of pentafluorophenylalanine, proposed the use of fluoroamino acids as nmr-active probes that avoid the complexities and interferences in the interpretation of proton nmr data of peptides. Conformational changes occurring upon molecular association, kinetics of association, and nonbonded interactions are all potentially amenable to study using ^{19}F nmr, although very little has been done to date; Schwyzer and Ludescher (1968) have discussed the relevant methodology in a paper describing the use of proton nmr reporter groups in peptides, and Dwek (1972) has reviewed the use of ^{19}F-nmr probes in the study of macromolecules.

Gerig and McLeod (1976) used a monofluoroproline in proton nmr studies on a tripeptide; the fluorine substituent dispersed the chemical shifts of the proline protons and facilitated the interpretation of individual coupling constants from which the time-averaged ring conformation could be calculated. Blumenstein *et al.* (1981) reported the use of a 3-fluorotyrosine analog of oxytocin in their studies on the binding of neurohypophyseal hormones to neurophysins: The affinity was unchanged by the fluorine substituent; the data indicated that the amino acid residue was conformationally constrained upon binding but experienced a polarity environment similar to that present in the free hormone.

The potential of silicon-containing amino acids for proton nmr studies is also worth mentioning in this context; certain protons in these amino acids will appear considerably upfield from the range in which peptides generally fall and are therefore amenable to convenient study.

B. Spin Labels

Many of the advantages of ^{19}F nmr also apply to esr spectroscopy, with the added advantage of very high sensitivity, resulting in very low working concentrations of the odd-electron species necessary for observation. Stable free radicals are rather limited structurally, and it is not easy to incorporate a radical grouping into a peptide without significant secondary steric and functional perturbation. Weinkam and Jorgensen (1971a,b) have introduced an amino acid approximating histidine in structure, where the imidazole ring is replaced with a dioxyimidazoline structure (nitronyl-nitroxide radical). In simple derivatives, pH-dependent conformational changes were observed and characterized via coupling constants to the β-hydrogens. A series of analogs based on the COOH-terminal three-residue sequence (His-Pro-Phe) of angiotensin II were prepared; standard synthetic techniques were applicable with some restrictions, although the products were generally noncrystalline (possibly because of diastereoisomerism) and required chromatographic purification. pH-dependent ion–dipole interactions of the odd-electron group with the COOH-terminus were observed and interpreted in terms of conformational preferences; the interaction was shown to be dependent on the presence of a proline residue in the sequence. The temperature dependence of the line broadening allowed the determination of activation energies for rotamer interconversion. The functional differences between histidine and the spin-labeled amino acid used in these studies might lead one to question their relevance to the native hormone;

in this case, proton nmr and other studies with the native hormone reinforce these interpretations.

A method of introducing a spin label onto a cysteine residue using a nitroxide-functionalized maleimide was introduced by Möschler and Schwyzer (1974), who also applied the technique to the study of angiotensin II. Here steric differences are considerably greater.

C. Radioactive Labels

The most straightforward labeling technique, namely, the incorporation of a previously radioactively labeled amino acid into a peptide, requires multiple manipulations of radioactively labeled intermediates (a disadvantage and potential hazard), which may cause concomitant loss of label in the case of rapid decay isotopes. Unusual amino acids offer the possibility of incorporating a specific radioactive label at a final stage in the synthesis of a peptide analog, which was formerly achieved only in the case of tyrosine labeling with iodine isotopes. The introduction of tritium via catalytic hydrogenation of unsaturated groups (Felix *et al.*, 1977) or hydrogenolysis of halogenated aromatic amino acids (Eberle and Schwyzer, 1976) may potentially be extended to many of the amino acids of these structural types listed in the Appendix.

In addition to the standard types of radiolabeling, incorporation of unusual isotopes is possible using nonstandard amino acids. Firnau *et al.* (1973) prepared a very hot ^{18}F-labeled β-(3,4-dihydroxyphenyl)alanine (dopa) derivative via a diazonium salt intermediate. The process is potentially applicable to peptides, and the isotope is a γ-emitter suitable for scintigraphic organ imaging. Although exotic, further application of the technique could prove very useful in studying endocrinological processes. A series of ^{123m}Te-labeled amino acids analogous to cysteine and methionine have also been introduced (Knapp *et al.*, 1978).

VI. REACTIVE SIDE-CHAIN FUNCTIONALITY

A. Receptor Interactions

Covalent attachment of a peptide hormone analog to a receptor, enzyme, or other binding site is a highly desirable goal. On the one hand, it makes possible the labeling of such sites with radioactive or fluorescent tags, facilitating isolation and/or structural studies on the binding protein. On the other hand, long-lasting agonist or antagonist activity may result from such binding; besides being desirable from the standpoint of medicinal chemistry, this allows the study of receptor turnover and other compensatory physiological mechanisms that affect the pharmacology of the system. Two basic strategies exist for bringing about such irreversible binding. The reactive group, such as an alkylating agent, may be present initially, in which case it must be relatively inert to nonspecific side reactions which might take place while the substance is en route to the receptor. Alternatively, the reactive group can be generated at the binding site from a relatively inert precursor. This is most often done photochemically (photoaffinity labeling) but may take place via action of functional groups at the binding site (suicide inactivators), the latter process being generally restricted to enzymes.

1. *Alkylating Agents*

Amino acids incorporating an alkylating agent in the side chain are known both as natural products (antibiotics), or components thereof, and as synthetic substances originally of interest as potential antitumor compounds. Alkylating functionalities available as components of amino acids include simple alkyl halides, α-halo carbonyl compounds, nitrogen mustards, epoxides, and Michael acceptors. The simple haloaliphatic amino acids are in most cases too unreactive to be practical in this regard, although such effects have apparently never been specifically sought in their derivatives. The other groupings are considerably more reactive and show promise in this application.

Following the introduction of 4-bis(2-chloroethyl)aminophenylalanine (melphalan) as an experimental antitumor agent (Bergel and Stock, 1954; Bergel *et al.*, 1955), a series of related amino acids have appeared that contain the nitrogen mustard grouping. Little has been done in the way of incorporating this amino acid into peptides, and the results are not promising (e.g., 0.3% of the pressor activity of angiotensin II in the 8-melphalan analog), possibly because of steric differences. Still there is a possibility that an irreversible receptor attachment might be demonstrable, not to mention the intriguing possibility that the antitumor (cytotoxic) activity of the amino acid might be channeled much more specifically into hormone-sensitive tumor cells by incorporation of the residue into an appropriate hormone analog. Karpavicius *et al.* (1973) have determined the stability of several such mustards in dioxane–water at 60°C, obtaining rate constants for hydrolysis in the neighborhood of 10^{-3} min^{-1}; this bodes well for the applications referred to above. A handful of epoxy-functionalized amino acids are known, some as components of antibiotics (e.g., chlamydocin, bacilysin) or as antibiotics themselves (anticapsin). Since their antibiotic activity may result from the alkylating ability of the epoxide group, it seems possible that epoxide-containing peptides could function as irreversibly binding hormone analogs. Olefinic amino acids and their derivatives are potential sources of additional new epoxide structures.

Since Walter *et al.* (1972) reported that placing an α-bromoacetyl group on the NH_2-terminus of oxytocin converted it into an irreversible antagonist of oxytocin-dependent adenylate cyclase, several research groups have been concerned with pursuing similar strategies via modified amino acid side chains. Pliška and Marbach (1978) prepared an oxytocin analog containing a 4-bromoacetamidophenylalanine residue at position 2 (tyrosine) and observed characteristics of irreversible antagonist activity. An isosteric analog of this (CH_3 replacing bromine) gave typical reversible behavior, but the results were not unequivocal. Similar studies were performed with analogs of arginine–vasopressin (Fahrenholz and Thierauch, 1980; Fahrenholz *et al.*, 1980), which were found to have activity similar to that of the native hormone, although irreversibility was not confirmed. The retention of activity in both these cases despite increased steric bulk is encouraging. A bromoketone variant on this amino acid is also known and seems to be a likely candidate for similar experiments.

Among the alkylating agents under discussion, maleimides are unique in being relatively "soft"; in biological systems, they are essentially specific for the free thiol function, with which they undergo Michael addition. Maleimides derived from the ω-amino group of ornithine and lysine have been reported by Keller and Rudinger (1975); the ω-amino group of an ornithine or lysine residue in a peptide can be so functionalized. Applications of these compounds in affinity labeling and in the preparation of conjugates have been suggested.

2. Photoaffinity Labeling

Photoaffinity labeling requires a substrate or hormone analog that bears an inert but photochemically activated functional group, giving rise to covalent attachment to a group at the binding site when irradiated in the bound state. This offers several advantages over the "alkylating agent" strategy: The analog remains stable up until the irradiation step, allowing traditional binding studies to be carried out and eliminating ambiguities arising from partial degradation. The reactive species (usually a carbene or a nitrene) can link to almost all types of proximal groups, including unactivated C—H bonds. Limitations of the method include the necessity of working in the dark for most such compounds, possible side reactions in the protein induced by irradiation, and the general inapplicability of the method to in vivo studies. Some very impressive results have been obtained using this method, primarily with enzymes. In peptide chemistry, aryl azides have been exclusively used for this purpose. Although in some instances an extra azidoaryl group has been attached to a hormone structure to provide a photoaffinity labeling agent, the incorporation of an azido derivative of phenylalanine in place of phenylalanine or tyrosine (or perhaps tryptophan or another amino acid) has the advantage of causing minimal steric differences between the analog and the native hormone.

Schwyzer and Caviezel (1971) introduced 4-azidophenylalanine expressly for such purposes, and succeeding papers from Schwyzer's group illustrate some of its successful applications. For example, chymotrypsin (Escher and Schwyzer, 1974) was successfully labeled using azidophenylalanine-containing tripeptide substrate analogs, which, surprisingly, were in some cases bound more tightly to the enzymes than the corresponding phenylalanine peptide. Variants on this theme, the 3-azido- and 4-azido-3-nitro derivatives, were described and shown to function similarly. A method for introducing a tritium label in the course of synthesizing such photoaffinity peptides was later described and applied in the preparation of a photoactive α-MSH analog (Eberle and Schwyzer, 1976).

Higher degrees of covalent linkage, shorter irradiation times, and longer wavelengths are possible with nitroazidophenylalanine derivatives (perhaps at some sacrifice of binding strength). In one experiment, a 2′-nitro-4′-azido derivative provided 75% labeling in 3 min, as opposed to 40% in 30 min for the corresponding 4′-azido compound (Fahrenholz and Schimmack, 1975). Surprisingly, the nitro group alone was found to give rise to covalent attachment in experiments with chymotrypsin and substrate analogs (Escher and Schwyzer, 1974). This report should be of some interest considering the numerous nitrophenylalanine peptides already described in the literature. Also reported were photoaffinity derivatives of antamanide (Wieland *et al.*, 1971), a leucine aminopeptidase substrate (Escher *et al.*, 1974), a neurophysin-binding tripeptide (Klausner *et al.*, 1978), and arginine–vasopressin (Fahrenholz and Thierauch, 1980).

Several methods are available for introducing the azidophenylalanine residue into a peptide. These include incorporating the preformed azido compound with the use of traditional peptide synthesis (requiring special treatment because of the lability of the azido group toward catalytic hydrogenation and strong acids) or by carrying out transformations on a nitro- or protected aminophenylalanine residue after incorporation into the peptide structure (see Fahrenholz and Thierauch, 1980, for a brief review).

B. Synthetic Transformations on Side-Chain Groups

The development of peptide-based medicinal chemistry has followed a significantly different path from, say, the chemistry of steroids and alkaloids: Derivatization is the exception rather than the rule, and most structural variants of peptides have been prepared by incorporating a substitute amino acid at an appropriate point in the synthesis. In marked contrast to traditional organic chemistry, each structural variant is prepared via a separate synthesis. Although this may be facilitated by automated techniques or by the sharing of common intermediates in separate syntheses, it remains cumbersome relative to the straightforward reactions by which analogs and congeners are often made in the alkaloid or steroid series. Drug development is facilitated when numerous derivatives are available for testing, increasing the likelihood of a chance discovery, which is still a major route to new drugs. It therefore seems prudent to consider synthetic transformations of side-chain groups as an alternate, and perhaps less costly, strategy for the preparation of analogs of peptides.

A considerable variety of functional-group modification reactions of applicability to the more reactive side chains of the coded amino acids have been developed for use in protein chemistry (Glazer, 1976), and most of these are sufficiently mild by nature as to be directly applicable to typical peptides. Unfortunately, many of these modifications are inappropriate from the standpoint of analog design (many involve the introduction of excessively bulky groups and/or radical changes in functionality); furthermore, multiple reactive sites on a peptide pose problems in some cases. Nevertheless, this approach can provide peptide analogs with desirable biological activity. Rudinger (1972) points out that increasing the steric bulk of selected residues in a peptide hormone often imparts antagonist activity to the analog; clearly such side-chain modifications lend themselves well to this sort of application, and Rudinger cites a large number of successful examples. More recently, as a compelling example of this approach, various modifications of Lys^{12}, His^{1}, and Ser^{2} residues in glucagon were carried out, and some highly potent antagonists were obtained (Hruby *et al.*, 1981; Bregman *et al.*, 1980).

Unusual amino acids can lend themselves to functional group transformations upon preformed peptides. By proper choice of the functional group, the advantages of high selectivity, mild reaction conditions, residue specificity, and a wide choice of modification reactions can be realized, thereby avoiding some of the separation and structure determination problems that beset modifications of native residues. An amino acid with such a specially functionalized side chain may be incorporated into an appropriate position in a peptide structure using traditional methods; the resulting analog serves as a mutual precursor of a series of related analogs obtained by applying a group of specific transformations in parallel. The requirements for such a scheme are that the amino acid be compatible with typical methods of peptide syntheses and that the side-chain transformations are all compatible with the remainder of the peptide structure.

Further advantages of this approach are that sensitive functional groups, which would not survive the conditions used in standard peptide synthesis, may be introduced at a final stage, and that all the analogs in a series have nearly identical chemical histories, lending further credence to comparisons of biological activity (e.g., error sequences and epimerization during construction of the peptide would remain invariant among analogs).

1. Aromatic Side Chains

Two basic types of strategies for modifying an aryl residue on a peptide side chain are presently available, although other possibilities exist besides these. The nitro-amino-diazonium sequence provides a reactive grouping that can be (and has been) nucleophilically substituted in a variety of ways, most notably by azide (Eberle and Schwyzer, 1976) and halide (e.g., Firnau *et al.*, 1973; Houghten and Rapoport, 1974), with other possibilities such as cyano, hydroxy, alkoxy, and "onium" salts suggesting themselves from classical chemistry. Furthermore, the aryl ring at the amino stage may be substituted electrophilically in a variety of ways, only a few of which have been explored. Much of this chemistry is compatible with peptide structures, given proper precautions.

A second strategy involves metallo derivatives of the aryl ring. A series of silylated phenylalanines has been introduced (e.g., Frankel *et al.*, 1963, 1968; Gertner *et al.*, 1963) which, given the known ease of electrophilic substitutions ipso to the silyl group (Eaborn, 1975), may provide for a variety of substitutions with such groups as hydrogen (and its isotopes), heavy metals such as mercury, and iodine and other halogens (possibly in masked form). Similar possibilities exist for boronic acid-functionalized phenylalanine (Roberts *et al.*, 1980) which, after incorporation into a peptide (apparently without interference from the boronic acid group) can be converted under very mild conditions (aqueous, pH $\sim$ 9) to a phenylalanine or tyrosine residue with silver cation or H_2O_2, respectively. An additional asset of the boronic acid group is that it can serve as a "handle" for extractive purification of its derivatives (Kemp and Roberts, 1975). As in the case of silyl derivatives, further known electrophilic substitutions of the boronic group, such as heavy metal reactions, are of potential use in broadening the scope of this strategy.

2. Sulfur-Containing Side Chains

Much of the thiol derivatization chemistry developed for proteins is applicable to cysteine and related residues in peptides. Usually such residues as they occur naturally are components of disulfide bridges; useful application of the divergent modification strategy would probably be limited to the introduction of a cysteine residue in place of another, followed by the use of various transformations on this residue to provide a series of analogs. Just a few of the many relevant transformations cited by Glazer (1976) include oxidative sulfonation (providing a glutamic acid isolog), reaction with ethyleneimine (giving a "thialysine"), iodoacetic acid (giving a "homothiaglutamic" residue), and peracid oxidation (giving an aspartic acid isolog). Introduction of a spin label grouping is also possible (Möschler and Schwyzer, 1974). Many of the resulting amino acids are known in the uncombined state and have been well-characterized. In some cases, these have been incorporated, using traditional methods, into peptides whose biological activity has been determined. For example, Hermann and Zaoral (1965) found that a thialysine residue (from cysteine and ethyleneimine) in vasopressin greatly decreased pressor activity and enhanced antidiuretic activity of the resulting analog relative to the native lysine–vasopressin. It therefore appears that these variants of amino acids can provide useful analogs.

Further possibilities result from oxidation at the sulfur atom in such "thia" amino acids; this has been done for free thialysine and thiahomoglutamic acid, giving sulfoxides and sulfones (Hermann *et al.*, 1970), but this should be readily applicable to the residue in a peptide as well. Some "selena" analogs of these thia amino acids are known (e.g., DeMarco *et al.*, 1975), and some of the sulfur chemistry is applicable here.

As a further extension of this technology, Wright and Rodbell (1980) have introduced a sulfhydryl group at the 2′-position of tryptophan residues (in this case, in glucagon) and used this grouping in the preparation of conjugates or immobilization of the hormone. Some of the functionalizations of cysteine should apply here also.

3. Unsaturated Side Chains

Quite a variety of unsaturated amino acids have been reported in the literature, containing olefin, diene, allene, and acetylene groups of various types. Little has been done to exploit the reactions of these groups, however. A number of them have been proposed or used as a convenient means of introducing deuterium or tritium labels into a peptide (Jansen *et al.*, 1970; Felix *et al.*, 1977). Other processes of potential use that have for the most part been applied only to the amino acid itself and that are known from traditional olefin chemistry (e.g., cyclopropanation, epoxidation, hydroxylation, oxidative cleavage, cycloaddition reactions, metal complex formation) offer a wide range of mild transformations.

In a conscious attempt to employ the "pluripotential" strategy in the preparation of peptide analogs, Synodis and Roberts (1981) made use of the terminal acetylene grouping in propargylglycine (Schwyzer *et al.*, 1976). Model studies showed that the ethynyl hydrogen could be replaced with silver under mild conditions, and from this deuterio, iodo, and mercuric derivatives could be prepared. Mild hydration to the methyl ketone and partial or total hydrogenation could be carried out as well. No problems were encountered incorporating the residue into an enkephalin analog, and a series of five related enkephalin analogs were prepared by carrying out transformations on the acetylene grouping.

Some especially interesting individual examples of unsaturated amino acids include vinylglycine (Baldwin *et al.*, 1977), a series of allenic amino acids (e.g., Black and Landor, 1968a,b), and a group of structurally related amino acids derived from 2′,5′-dihydro-*O*-methyltyrosine (Kaminski and Sokolowska, 1973). In this last case, the dihydroamino acid (obtained by Birch reduction of the aromatic amino acid) can be selectively transformed to provide a choice of saturated or unsaturated ketones or vinyl ethers: These in turn could in principle be used to provide numerous derivatives based on transformations of ketone or olefin groups.

These are a few selected examples of what may develop into a cohesive and well-worked-out chemistry of functional group transformations in peptides. The reader is invited to explore the structures in the Appendix to this chapter, which may suggest themselves for further applications of this strategy.

VII. PEPTIDE ISOSTERES

A relatively recent approach to the design of peptide hormone analogs that departs from the use of coded amino acids is based on modifications of the peptide backbone. This is usually done with the intention of imparting hydrolytic stability or even enzyme inhibitory activity to the analog. Use of β-amino and α-hydrazino acids, often structurally derived from coded amino acids, results in the insertion of an extra atom into the peptide chain, thereby altering the steric relationships between side chains; nevertheless, in some cases, useful biological activity results, and resistance to enzymes is often imparted. This strategy is even employed in nature, as in the carboxyl proteinase inhibitor bestatin. Other minor backbone modifications include reversal of one or more amide linkages (Goodman and Chorev, 1981) and the employment of α-azaamino acids (carbazic acid derivatives).

Replacement of the amide linkage with a sterically similar grouping represents a more formidable synthetic challenge but has the advantage of completely eliminating (rather than displacing) the hydrolytically susceptible grouping while preserving the steric relationships between side chains. This strategy requires the availability of preformed units bearing the appropriate side chains and incorporating the modified linkage, which have been referred to as dipeptide isosteres or pseudodipeptides. These are formally δ-amino acids and can be incorporated into peptides using traditional methods in most cases. Information concerning sites of *in vivo* enzymatic degradation, which has recently become available for a number of peptide hormones (see, for example, Marks, 1978), greatly assists in suggesting sites for amide bond replacement.

Early efforts along these lines centered on reduced linkages in which the CONH group is replaced with or reduced to a CH_2NH functionality (Zaoral *et al.*, 1967; Atherton *et al.*, 1971; Roeske *et al.*, 1976; Szelke *et al.*, 1977). This introduces a basic or protonated amine at a formerly neutral site and requires protection for further elaboration. More recently, Yankeelov *et al.* (1978) have introduced the CH_2S linkage as an amide bond replacement. Their methods appear applicable to a variety of amino acid starting materials and can preserve chirality at the α-carbon bearing the sulfur. This approach has provided LHRH analogs with high *in vitro* potency (Spatola *et al.*, 1980). More recently, variants on this theme involving CH_2SO, $C(CH_3)S$, and $C(CH_3)SO$ linkages have been introduced (Spatola *et al.*, 1981). A further interesting variant is the thioamide linkage (which may not in fact impart hydrolytic stability), which has been introduced into various peptide structures (Ried and Schmidt, 1966; Jones *et al.*, 1973; Clausen *et al.*, 1981).

Recently, some of the more synthetically challenging amide bond replacements have appeared. Hann *et al.* (1980) prepared an active enkephalin analog employing a trans olefin linkage. Almquist *et al.* (1980) synthesized a potent angiotensin-converting enzyme inhibitor containing a $COCH_2$ linkage at a site corresponding to that which would undergo enzymatic cleavage in the natural substrates. Ondetti's group have overcome some formidable synthetic problems in introducing new methods for preparing dipeptide isosteres involving trans $CH{=}CH$ and $C({=}CH_2)CH_2$ linkages, among others (Natarajan *et al.*, 1981).

There is some question as to the degree to which various amide bond replacements affect the conformation space available to a peptide analog. Marshall *et al.* (1981) have introduced procedures by which an analog can be compared to its true peptide congener; they find, for example, the surprising result that the trans olefin linkage is a better mimic of an amide than a retro amide linkage. It is worth mentioning in this context the conformationally constrained dipeptide units introduced by Di Maio *et al.* (1979) and by Freidinger *et al.* (1980) which, like the dipeptide isosteres, may be incorporated into peptides similarly to ordinary amino acids. Farmer (1980) has provided an interesting overview of the "no-man's land" lying between the traditional areas of organic chemistry and peptide chemistry; his viewpoint focuses on the design and synthesis of "nonpeptidic peptidomimetics." It appears that, especially with molecular modeling capabilities such as those used so effectively by the Merck group (Gund *et al.*, 1980), success in the design of such molecules will become sufficiently likely as to justify attempts to solve the formidable synthetic problems they pose.

ACKNOWLEDGMENTS

The authors wish to thank those of our colleagues who kindly made manuscripts and other information available to us for inclusion in this review. Frank Vellaccio is indebted to the Chemistry Department at the University of California, San Diego, for a visiting associate professorship (1981–1982) during which much of this work was completed.

APPENDIX

The following tabulation is designed to provide chemists with information about the variety of amino acids available by chemical synthesis. The authors have attempted complete coverage of the literature within certain limitations, as follows: (1) Only α-amino carboxylic acids are included; (2) the parent amino acid is listed in cases where only simple derivatives were reported; (3) all α,α-disubstituted amino acids, with the exception of 1-amino-1-carboxycycloalkanes and related cyclic structures, are excluded; (4) all α-dehydro- and α-azaamino acids are excluded; (5) all simple heteroatom-functionalized (e.g., protected, N-alkylated, etc.) derivatives of genetically coded amino acids are excluded; (6) all noncoded stereoisomers of coded amino acids are excluded; (7) with a few exceptions, all amino acids for which no chemical synthesis exists are excluded; (8) all references to the patent literature are excluded. For some classes of amino acids, explicit listings have been omitted due to the large number of related structures; in these cases, all references are included with a general descriptive term and/or generalized structure.

All physical, chemical, and stereochemical data on the amino acids have been omitted from the table, but these may generally be obtained from the cited references. No attempt has been made to prioritize the references, to include all references to original work, or to give exhaustive bibliographies on each entry. The references were chosen so as to provide the reader with synthetic procedures for each amino acid and examples of its use in peptide synthesis when such use exists. Ultimately, the contents of the table will reflect the subjective opinions of the authors, who are solely responsible for any deficiencies or omissions that may inconvenience the reader, and we apologize for such that may exist.

The entries in the table have been arranged according to a system of 20 structural categories, which are listed below; within each category, the authors have attempted to arrange the entries in a systematic and convenient order, although this was not possible in all cases. Amino acids that fall into more than one category are cross-referenced to the additional categories.

Structural categories of amino acids:

Aliphatic

I	Saturated, p. 366
II	Unsaturated, p. 368
III	Halogenated, p. 371
IV	Chalcogen-containing, p. 374
V	Oxygenated, p. 378
VI	Aminopolycarboxylic acids and derivatives, p. 384
VII	Polyamino mono- and polycarboxylic acids and derivatives, p. 387
VIII	Guanido- and amidino-containing, p. 391
IX	1-Aminocycloalkane-1-carboxylic acids and related compounds, p. 393
X	Miscellaneous carbocyclic, p. 396

Aromatic

XI	Phenylglycine derivatives, p. 398
XII	Phenylalanine derivatives, p. 399
XIII	Miscellaneous, p. 405

Heterocyclic

XIV	Imino acids, including proline analogs, p. 408
XV	Pyridine-derived, p. 415
XVI	3-Azolylalanines and related compounds, p. 416
XVII	Indolylalanines and other fused hetarylalanines, p. 418
XVIII	Purine- and pyrimidine-containing, p. 424
XIX	Miscellaneous, p. 426
XX	Carbohydrate-containing, p. 429

Structure and name	References
Aliphatic: saturated (I)	
I-1 $CH_3(CH_2)_nCH(NH_2)CO_2H$ $n = 1–8, 11, 15$ 2-Aminoalkanoic acids	Greenstein and Winitz, 1961
I-2 $(CH_3)_3C—CH(NH_2)CO_2H$ 2-Amino-3,3-dimethylbutanoic acid (*tert*-butylglycine, *tert*-leucine)	Yamada *et al.*, 1977; Pospíšek and Bláha, 1976; Steglich *et al.*, 1971; Pracejus and Winter, 1964
I-3 $(CH_3)_3CCH_2—CH(NH_2)CO_2H$ 2-Amino-4,4-dimethylpentanoic acid	Fauchère and Petermann, 1981
I-4 $CH_3(CH_2)_nCHCH(NH_2)CO_2H$ (with CH_3 on the CH) $n = 2–5$ 2-Amino-3-methylalkanoic acids	Greenstein and Winitz 1961

Structure and name	References
I-5 $CH_3CH_2CH(CH_3)CH_2—CH(NH_2)CO_2H$ 2-Amino-4-methylhexanoic acid (homoisoleucine)	Gellert *et al.*, 1978
I-6 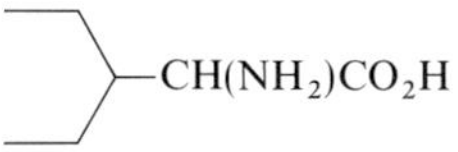 β,β-Diethylalanine	Greenstein and Winitz, 1961
I-7 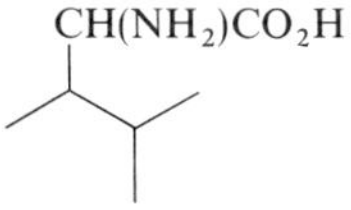 β-Methylleucine	Sheehan and Ledis, 1973; Oki *et al.*, 1970
I-8 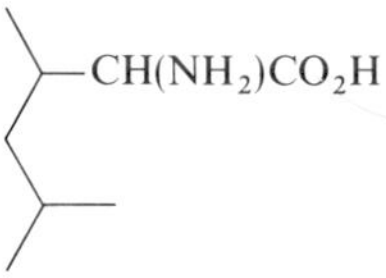 2-Amino-3,5-dimethylhexanoic acid	Greenstein and Winitz, 1961
I-9 $R^2—C(R^1)(R^3)—CH(NH_2)CO_2H$ *tert*-Alkylglycines R^1 = Me, R^2 = Me, R^3 = Et*; R^1 = Et, R^2 = Et, R^3 = Et; R^1, R^2 = $(CH_2)_5$, R^3 = Et	Schöllkopf and Meyer, 1975; 1977; *See also Jorgensen *et al.*, 1971.
I-10 $(CH_3)_2CH(CH_2)_n—CH(NH_2)CO_2H$ $n = 2, 3, 4$ α-Amino-(ω-1)-methylalkanoic acids (mono-, bis-, and trishomoleucines)	Shiba *et al.*, 1975
I-11  α-Cyclopentylglycine	Hill and Dunn, 1965, 1969; Eisler *et al.*, 1966; Ohno and Izumiya, 1965

(continued)

Structure and name	References
I-12 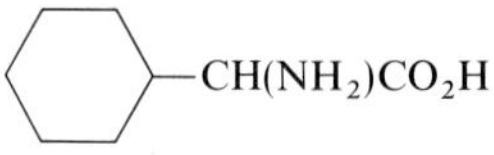 α-Cyclohexylglycine	Tamura and Harada, 1978; Eisler *et al.*, 1966
I-13 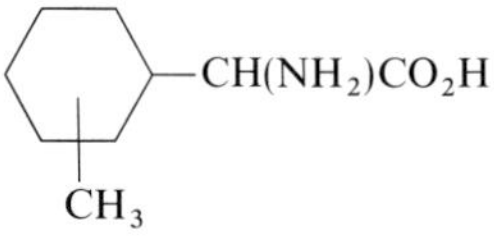 Methylcyclohexylglycines	Greenstein and Winitz, 1961
I-14 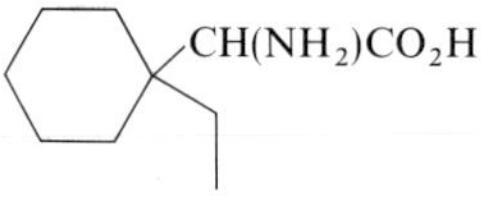 α-(1-Ethylcyclohexyl)glycine	Horner and Schwahn, 1955
I-15 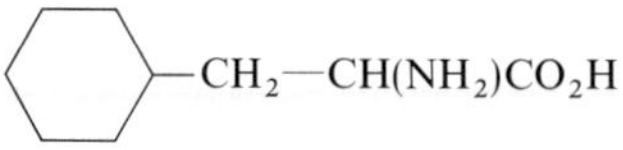 3-Cyclohexylalanine	Wieland *et al.*, 1977a; Borin *et al.*, 1977; Kunzi *et al.*, 1974; Fletcher and Young, 1972, 1974; Khosla *et al.*, 1972
I-16 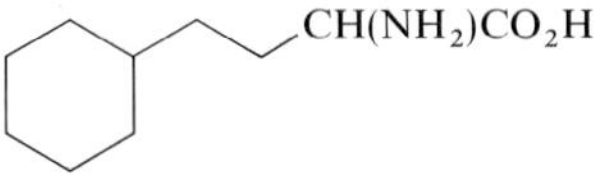 2-Amino-4-cyclohexylbutanoic acid	Greenstein and Winitz, 1961
I-17 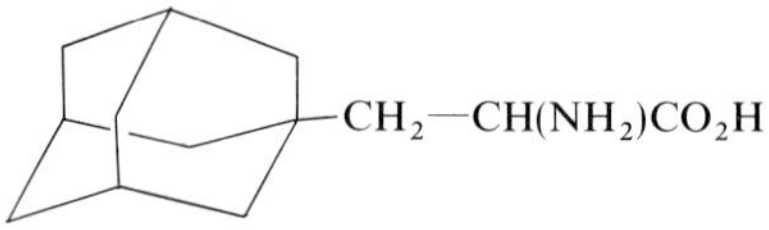 3-(1-Adamantyl)alanine	Do and Schwyzer, 1981; Do *et al.*, 1979
See also compounds IX-1–12; X-13; XIV-1–4, 26–33	
Aliphatic: unsaturated (II)	
II-1 $CH_2{=}CH{-}CH(NH_2)CO_2H$ 2-Amino-3-butenoic acid (α-vinylglycine)	Afzali-Ardakani and Rapoport, 1980; Baldwin *et al.*, 1977
II-2 $CH_2{=}C(CH_3){-}CH(NH_2)CO_2H$ 2-Amino-3-methyl-3-butenoic acid (α-isopropenylglycine)	Baldwin *et al.*, 1977; Levenberg, 1968

Structure and name	References
II-3 $CH_2{=}CHCH_2{-}CH(NH_2)CO_2H$ 2-Amino-4-pentenoic acid (Allylglycine)	Fushiya *et al.*, 1981
II-4 $CH_3CH{=}CH(CH_2)_nCH(NH_2)CO_2H$ $n = 1, 2$ 2-Amino-4-hexenoic acid (2-Amino-5-heptenoic acid)	Greenstein and Winitz, 1961
II-5 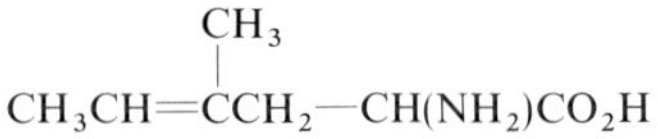 2-Amino-4-methyl-4-hexenoic acid	Edelson *et al.*, 1959
II-6 $(CH_3)_2C{=}CHCH_2{-}CH(NH_2)CO_2H$ 2-Amino-5-methyl-4-hexenoic acid	Letham and Young, 1971; Dardenne *et al.*, 1968
II-7 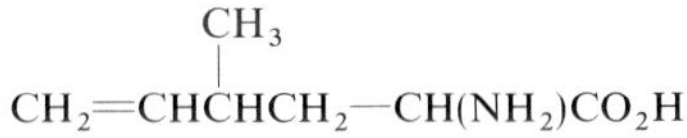 2-Amino-4-methyl-5-hexenoic acid	Snider and Duncia, 1981
II-8 $CH_2{=}CH(CH_2)_3{-}CH(NH_2)CO_2H$ 2-Amino-6-heptenoic acid	Karwoski *et al.*, 1978
II-9 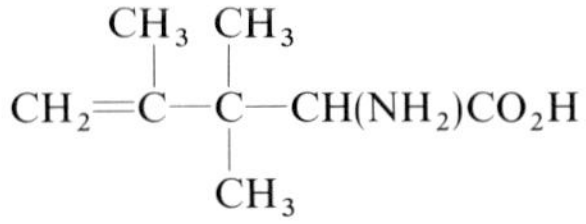 2-Amino-3,3,4-trimethyl-4-pentenoic acid	Altman *et al.*, 1975
II-10 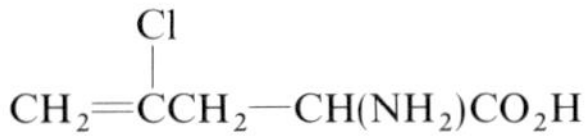 2-Amino-4-chloro-4-pentenoic acid	Hatanaka *et al.*, 1974
II-11 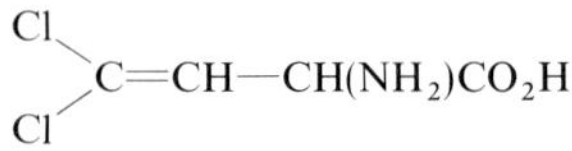 2-Amino-4,4-dichloro-3-butenoic acid	Iwasaki *et al.*, 1976; Urabe *et al.*, 1975
II-12 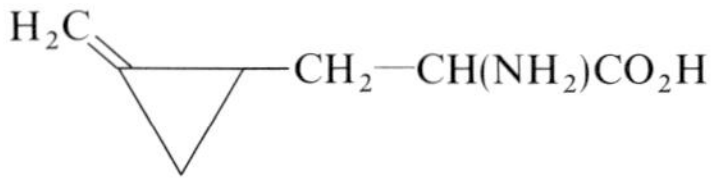 2-Amino-3-(2-methylenecyclopropyl)-propanoic acid	Black and Landor, 1968c

(continued)

	Structure and name	References
II-13	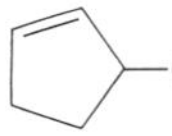 $-CH(NH_2)CO_2H$ 2-(2-Cyclopentenyl)glycine	Santoso *et al.*, 1981b
II-14	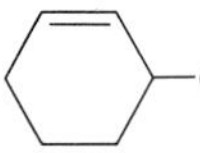 $-CH(NH_2)CO_2H$ 2-(2-Cyclohexenyl)glycine	Santoso *et al.*, 1981a; Dzieduszycka *et al.*, 1978
II-15	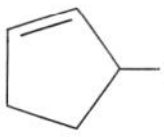 $-CH_2-CH(NH_2)CO_2H$ 3-(2-Cyclopentenyl)alanine, also the 3-enyl derivative	Porter *et al.*, 1968
II-16	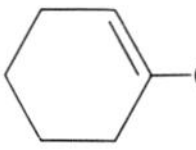 $-CH_2-CH(NH_2)CO_2H$ 3-(1-Cyclohexenyl)alanine (3′,4′,5′,6′-Tetrahydrophenylalanine), also the 2-enyl derivative*	Kaminski and Sokolowska, 1973; *Porter *et al.*, 1968; Snow *et al.*, 1968
II-17	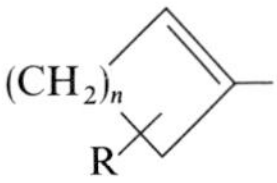 $-CH(NH_2)CO_2H$ α-(1-Cycloalkenyl)glycines $n = 2, 3, 4, 5$ and R = H; $n = 3$ and R = 4-Me	Nunami *et al.*, 1979; Suzuki *et al.*, 1978
II-18	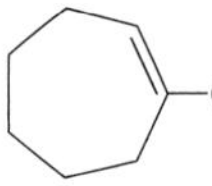 $-CH_2-CH(NH_2)CO_2H$ 3-(1-Cycloheptenyl)alanine	Porter *et al.*, 1968
II-19	 $-CH_2-CH(NH_2)CO_2H$ 3-(1,4-cyclohexadienyl)alanine (2′,5′-dihydrophenylalanine)	Banerjee *et al.*, 1979; Ressler *et al.*, 1979; Nagarajan *et al.*, 1973; Snow *et al.*, 1968
II-20	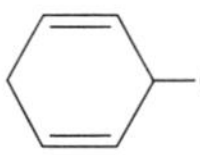 $-CH_2-CH(NH_2)CO_2H$ 3-(2,5-Cyclohexadienyl)alanine (1′,4′-dihydrophenylalanine)	Scholz and Schmidt, 1974

Structure and name	References
II-21  $-CH(NH_2)CO_2H$ 2-(7-Cycloheptatrienyl)glycine	Hanessian and Schütze, 1969
II-22 $H_2C{=}C{=}CHCH_2{-}CH(NH_2)CO_2H$ 2-Amino-4,5-hexadienoic acid (β-allenylalanine); similar amino acids with the ketene functional group can be found in these references	Black and Landor, 1968a,b
II-23 $HC{\equiv}C{-}CH(NH_2)CO_2H$ 2-Amino-3-butynoic acid (ethynylglycine)	Fauchère *et al.*, 1979
II-24 $HC{\equiv}CCH_2CH(NH_2)CO_2H$ Propargylglycine	Schwyzer *et al.*, 1976; Synodis and Roberts, 1981
II-25 $CH_3C{\equiv}CCH_2{-}CH(NH_2)CO_2H$ 2-Amino-4-hexynoic acid	Hatanaka *et al.*, 1972
II-26 $HC{\equiv}CCH{=}CHCH_2{-}CH(NH_2)CO_2H$ 2-Amino-4-hepten-6-ynoic acid	Black and Landor, 1968b
See also structures IV-14, 15; V-20, 36–41; VI-10, 11, 21, 23; VII-13, 14; X-14; XII-81; XIII-5; XIV-9–11, 30; XVIII-4	
Aliphatic: halogenated (III)	
III-1 $FCH_2{-}CH(NH_2)CO_2H$ 3-Fluoroalanine	Kollonitsch *et al.*, 1979; Dolling *et al.*, 1978; Gal *et al.*, 1977; Kollonitsch and Barash, 1976
III-2 $F_3C{-}CH(NH_2)CO_2H$ 3,3,3-Trifluoroalanine	Uskert *et al.*, 1973; Weygand *et al.*, 1966, 1967, 1970b
III-3 $CH_3CH(F){-}CH(NH_2)CO_2H$ 2-Amino-3-fluorobutanoic acid	Kollonitsch *et al.*, 1979; Loy and Hudlicky, 1976

(continued)

Structure and name	References
III-4 $CH_3(CH_2)_nCHCH(NH_2)CO_2H$ (F on C-3) $n = 1, 2$ 2-Amino-3-fluoroalkanoic acids	Gershon *et al.*, 1973
III-5 $RCF_2—CH(NH_2)CO_2H$ 2-Amino-3,3-difluorobutanoic acid, 2-amino-3,3-difluoro-3-phenylpropanoic acid (β,β-difluorophenylalanine) R = Me, Ph	Wade and Khéribet, 1980; Wade and Guedj, 1979
III-6 $CF_3CF_2—CH(NH_2)CO_2H$ 2-Amino-3,3,4,4,4-pentafluorobutanoic acid (α-perfluoroethylglycine)	Weygand *et al.*, 1970a
III-7 $F(CF_2)\ CH_2—CH(NH_2)CO_2H$ $n = 2, 3$ 3-Perfluoroalkylalanines	Steglich *et al.*, 1967
III-8 $(CH_3)_2C—CH(NH_2)CO_2H$ (F on C) β-Fluorovaline	Gershon *et al.*, 1973
III-9 $(CH_2F)_2CH—CH(NH_2)CO_2H$ 2-Amino-3-fluoromethyl-4-fluorobutanoic acid (ω,ω'-difluorovaline)	Lettré and Wölcke, 1967
III-10 $CF_3(CH_2)_2—CH(NH_2)CO_2H$ 2-Amino-5,5,5-trifluoropentanoic acid	Babb and Bollinger, 1970
III-11 $CF_3CH—CH(NH_2)CO_2H$ (CH_3 on CH) 2-Amino-3-methyl-4,4,4-trifluorobutanoic acid (ω,ω,ω-trifluorovaline)	Babb and Bollinger, 1970; Loncrini and Walborsky, 1964
III-12 $(CF_3)_2CH—CH(NH_2)CO_2H$ 2-Amino-3-trifluoromethyl-4,4,4-trifluorobutanoic acid (ω-hexafluorovaline)	Knunyants and Cheburkov, 1960; Vine *et al.*, 1981
III-13 $CF_3CF_2CF_2—CH(NH_2)CO_2H$ 2-Amino-3,3,4,4,5,5,5-heptafluoropentanoic acid	Weygand *et al.*, 1970a

	Structure and name	References
III-14	$\overset{CH_3}{\overset{\mid}{}}$ $FCH_2CH_2CH{-}CH(NH_2)CO_2H$ (with CH_3 on the third C) 2-Amino-3-methyl-5-fluoropentanoic acid (ω-fluoroisoleucine)	Hudlicky *et al.*, 1970
III-15	F and CH_3 above $CH_3CHCH{-}CH(NH_2)CO_2H$ 2-Amino-3-methyl-4-fluoropentanoic acid (γ-fluoroisoleucine)	Gershon *et al.*, 1978
III-16	$CH_3CF_2CH_2CH_2{-}CH(NH_2)CO_2H$ 2-Amino-5,5-difluorohexanoic acid	Hudlicky, 1967
III-17	$(CH_2F)_2CHCH_2{-}CH(NH_2)CO_2H$ 2-Amino-4-(fluoromethyl)-5-fluoropentanoic acid (ω,ω′-difluoroleucine)	Lettré and Wölcke, 1967
III-18	$(CF_3)_2CHCH_2{-}CH(NH_2)CO_2H$ 2-Amino-4-trifluoromethyl-5,5,5-trifluoropentanoic acid (ω-hexafluoroleucine)	Lazar and Sheppard, 1968
III-19	$RRCF{-}CH(NH_2)CO_2H$ 3-Fluoro-substituted aliphatic amino acids $R = R' = Me$; $R = Me$ and $R' = Et, Ph$; $R = R' = (CH_2)_4, (CH_2)_5$	Ayi *et al.*, 1981
III-20	$ClCH_2{-}CH(NH_2)CO_2H$ 2-Amino-3-chloropropanoic acid (3-chloroalanine)	Srinivasan *et al.*, 1977; Okumura *et al.*, 1972
III-21	Cl above $CH_3CH{-}CH(NH_2)CO_2H$ 2-Amino-3-chlorobutanoic acid	Srinivasan *et al.*, 1977
III-22	$Cl_2CHCH_2{-}CH(NH_2)CO_2H$ 2-Amino-4,4-dichlorobutanoic acid	Iwasaki *et al.*, 1976; Urabe *et al.*, 1975
III-23	$Cl_3CCH_2{-}CH(NH_2)CO_2H$ 2-Amino-4,4,4-trichlorobutanoic acid	Iwasaki *et al.* 1976; Urabe *et al.*, 1974

(continued)

Structure and name	References
III-24 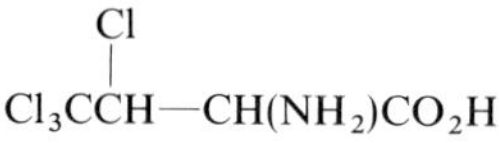 2-Amino-3,4,4,4-tetrachlorobutanoic acid	Urabe *et al.*, 1974
III-25 $ClCH_2—(CH_2)_3—CH(NH_2)CO_2H$ 2-Amino-6-chlorohexanoic acid	Effenberger and Karlheinz, 1979
III-26 $Br—CH_2CH_2—CH(NH_2)CO_2H$ 2-Amino-4-bromobutanoic acid	Nollet *et al.*, 1969
III-27 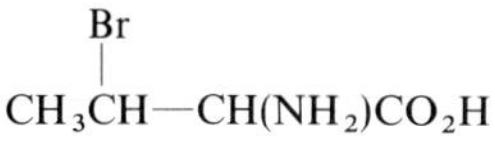 2-Amino-3-bromobutanoic acid	Wieland *et al.*, 1977b
See also structures II-10, 11; V-18, 19, 35; VI-12–15; VII-15, 16; VIII-8; IX-19; XI-1, 4; XII-5–9, 13, 14, 21, 22, 26, 35–39, 41, 42, 48, 49, 53–58; XIII-14, 16; XIV-5–8; XV-4, 5, 12; XVI-5, 7; XVII-2–7, 22, 34; XIX-7, 8	
Aliphatic: chalcogen-containing (IV)	
IV-1  2-Amino-3-mercaptobutanoic acid (β-methylcysteine)	Morell *et al.*, 1977
IV-2 $HS\text{-}CH_2CH_2CH(NH_2)CO_2H$ Homocysteine	Greenstein and Winitz, 1961
IV-3 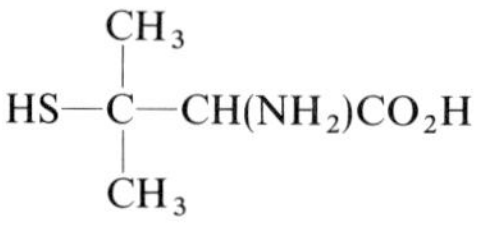 Penicillamine (3-mercaptovaline)	Sheehan and Yang, 1958 (see also Greenstein and Winitz, 1961)
IV-4 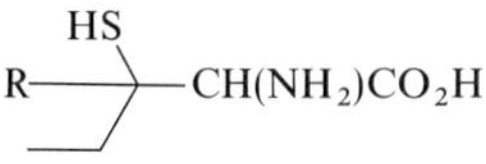 3-Mercaptonorvaline (3-mercaptoisoleucine) $R = H, CH_3$	Greenstein and Winitz, 1961

	Structure and name	References
IV-5	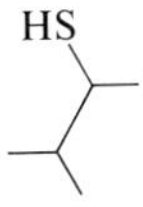 $CH(NH_2)CO_2H$ 3-Mercaptoleucine	Greenstein and Winitz, 1961
IV-6	CH_3 CH_3 $HSCH—CH—CH(NH_2)CO_2H$ 2-Amino-3-methyl-4-mercapto-pentanoic acid	Zdansky, 1968a
IV-7	CH_3 $HSCCH_2CH_2—CH(NH_2)CO_2H$ CH_3 2-Amino-5-mercapto-5-methyl-hexanoic acid	Dilbeck *et al.*, 1978
IV-8	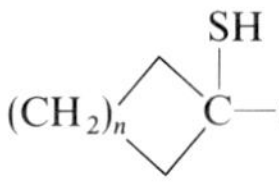 $n = 1, 2, 3$ (1-Mercaptocycloalkyl)glycines	Leclercq *et al.*, 1978
IV-9	$CH_3S(CH_2)_3CH(NH_2)CO_2H$ Homomethionine	Greenstein and Winitz, 1961
IV-10	$CH_3S(CH_2)_4—CH(NH_2)CO_2H$ 2-Amino-6-(methylthio) hexa-noic acid (bishomomethionine)	Lee and Serif, 1970
IV-11	$CH_3SCH_2CHCH(NH_2)CO_2H$ C_6H_5 β-Phenylmethionine	Greenstein and Winitz, 1961
IV-12	R^1 R $Et—S\text{-}CCH_2CH—CH(NH_2)CO_2H$ R^2 Also *S*-*n*-butyl derivatives $R' = Me, R = R^2 = H$; $R' = Me, R = R^2 = Me$; $R' = Ph, R = R^2 = H$; $R' = H, R = R^2 = H$	Rakhshinda and Khan, 1978

(continued)

Structure and name	References
IV-13 $R{-}CH(NH_2)CO_2H$ "Thia" amino acids R = amino acid side chain in which a sulfur atom replaces a CH_2 group	Hermann, 1981
IV-14 $CH_3CH{=}CHS(\rightarrow O)CH_2{-}CH(NH_2)CO_2H$ 3-(1-Propenesulfinyl)alanine, also the 2-enyl derivative (alliine)	Nishimura *et al.*, 1975; Stoll and Seebeck, 1951
IV-15 $CH_3SCH{=}CH{-}CH(NH_2)CO_2H$ 2-Amino-4-(methylthio)-3-butenoic acid (Δ^3-dehydromethionine)	Balenovic and Deljac, 1973
IV-16 $PhCH_2S{-}CH(NH_2)CO_2H$ α-(Benzylthio)glycine	Matthies, 1978; Petrzilka and Fehr, 1973
IV-17 $CH_3S(CH_2)_2CH(OH){-}CH(NH_2)CO_2H$ 2-Amino-3-hydroxy-5-(methylthio)-pentanoic acid	Otani and Briley, 1974
IV-18 $HOCH_2CH_2C(CH_3)_2SCH_2{-}CH(NH_2)CO_2H$ *S*-(2-Methyl-4-hydroxy-2-butyl)cysteine	Schöberl *et al.*, 1968; Trippett, 1957
IV-19 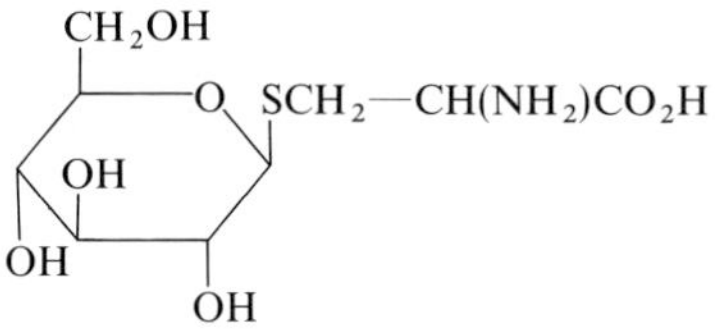 *S*-(*β*-Glucopyranosyl)cysteine	Monsigny *et al.*, 1977
IV-20 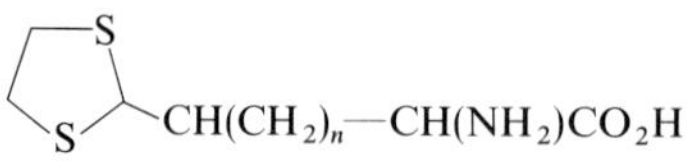 $n = 0, 1, 2$ α-Amino-1,3-dithiolane-2-alkanoic acids	Mertes and Ramsey, 1969

	Structure and name	References
IV-21	$H_2NC(=S)CH_2—CH(NH_2)CO_2H$ 2-Aminobutanedioic acid 4-thionamide (γ-thioasparagine)	Ressler and Banerjee, 1976
IV-22	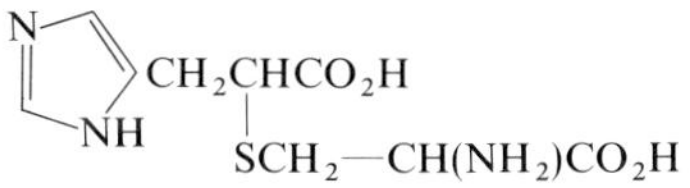 *S*-[1-Carboxy-2-(4-imidazolyl)ethyl]cysteine	Yankeelov and Jolley, 1972
IV-23	$PhSO_2—CH(NH_2)CO_2H$ α-Benzenesulfonylglycine	Matthies, 1978
IV-24	$RCH_2SO_2CH_2CH(NH_2)CO_2H$ γ-Thialysine and -homoglutamic acid *S,S*-dioxides $R = H_2NCH_2$, HO_2C	Hermann *et al.*, 1970
IV-25	$HO_3SCH_2—CH(NH_2)CO_2H$ Cysteic acid	Bodanszky *et al.*, 1977
IV-26	$XO_2S—CH_2—CH(NH_2)CO_2H$ Cysteic acid derivatives $X = NH_2$ $X = NHR$ or $NH—NHR$ $X = Cl$ $X = SH$	Aleksiev *et al.*, 1971 Brynes *et al.*, 1978 Stoev *et al.*, 1973 DeMarco and Coletta, 1961
IV-27	$CH(NH_2)CO_2H$ | CH_2SO_2H Cysteine sulfinic acid (β-sulfinylalanine)	Gordon, 1973
IV-28	$HS—SO_2—CH_2CH_2—CH(NH_2)CO_2H$ 2-Amino-4-thiosulfobutanoic acid	DeMarco and Luchi, 1972
IV-29	$HSeCH_2—CH(NH_2)CO_2H$ Selenocysteine	Shrift *et al.*, 1976; for a review, see Walter, 1973; Zdansky, 1973

(continued)

Structure and name	References
IV-30 $HSeCH(CH_3)CH(CH_3)—CH(NH_2)CO_2H$ 2-Amino-3-methyl-4-hydroselenopentanoic acid	Zdansky, 1968a
IV-31 $RSeCH_2CH_2—CH(NH_2)CO_2H$ Selenomethionine and Se-alkyl congeners R = Me, Et, Bzl	Zdansky, 1968b; Jakubke *et al.*, 1968
IV-32 $CH_3SeCH_2CH(CH_3)—CH(NH_2)CO_2H$ 2-Amino-3-methyl-4-(methylseleno)butanoic acid	Zdansky, 1967
IV-33 $RCH_2SeCH_2CH(NH_2)CO_2H$ γ-Selenalysine, R = H_2NCH_2 γ-Selenahomoglutamic acid, R = HO_2C	DeMarco *et al.*, 1975 Rinaldi *et al.*, 1976
IV-34 $H_2N(CH_2)_3SeCH_2—CH(NH_2)CO_2H$ 3-(3-Aminopropylseleno)alanine (γ-selenahomolysine)	DeMarco *et al.*, 1976
IV-35 $CH_3TeCH_2CH_2—CH(NH_2)CO_2H$ Telluromethionine	Knapp, 1979
See also structures VII-24, 25; IX-13; XI-4; XII-82; XIV-12, 13, 44–50; XVI-10; XVII-11, 19; 14; XVIII-14	
Aliphatic: oxygenated (V)	
V-1 $HOCH_2CH_2—CH(NH_2)CO_2H$ 2-Amino-4-hydroxybutanoic acid	Turan and Manning, 1977
V-2 $CH_3CH_2CH(OH)CH_2CH(NH_2)CO_2H$ γ-Hydroxynorleucine (also δ and ε)	Greenstein and Winitz, 1961
V-3 $CH_3(CH_2)_nCHOHCH(NH_2)CO_2H$ $n = 1, 2, 14$ 2-Amino-3-hydroxyalkanoic acids	Ariyoshi and Sato, 1971; Ichikawa *et al.*, 1971; Greenstein and Winitz, 1961

Structure and name	References
CH_3 | V-4 $HOCH_2CH{-}CH(NH_2)CO_2H$ 2-Amino-3-methyl-4-hydroxybutanoic acid (homothreonine)	Usher, 1980
OH | V-5 $(CH_3)_2C{-}CH(NH_2)CO_2H$ 3-Hydroxyvaline (3-methylthreonine)	Scott and Wilkinson, 1981; Berse and Bessette, 1971; Ohhashi and Harada, 1966
V-6 $HO(CH_2)_4{-}CH(NH_2)CO_2H$ 2-Amino-6-hydroxyhexanoic acid	Dreyfuss, 1974; Davis and Bailey, 1972
OH | V-7 $CH_3CH_2CHCH_2{-}CH(NH_2)CO_2H$ 2-Amino-4-hydroxyhexanoic acid (also 4-oxo derivative)	Barry and Roark, 1964
OH | V-8 $(CH_3)_2CHCH{-}CH(NH_2)CO_2H$ 3-Hydroxyleucine	Futagawa *et al.*, 1971
OH | V-9 $CH_3CH_2C{-}CH(NH_2)CO_2H$ | CH_3 3-Hydroxyisoleucine (3-ethylthreonine)	Dobson and Vining, 1968
CH_3 | V-10 $HOCH_2C{-}CH(NH_2)CO_2H$ | CH_3 3-(Hydroxymethyl)valine	Ackermann and Shive, 1948
OH | V-11 $R{-}CH{-}CH(NH_2)CO_2H$ Various β-hydroxyamino acids R = H, Me, Et, $CH(CH_3)_2$, CO_2H, Ph, *p*-Ph-NO_2, 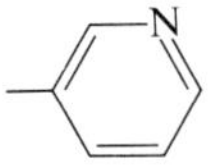	Ozaki *et al.*, 1979b

(continued)

	Structure and name	References
V-12	 α-(1-Hydroxycyclopropyl)glycine (3,4-methylenethreonine)	Kato *et al.*, 1980
V-13	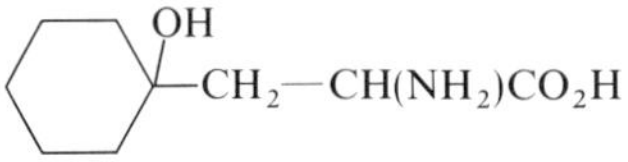 3-(1-Hydroxycyclohexyl) alanine	Snow *et al.*, 1968
V-14	$PhCH(OH)—CH(NH_2)CO_2H$ β-Hydroxyphenylalanine (β-phenylserine)	Arold and Reissmann, 1970
	carbohydrate derivative	Weiss, 1977
V-15	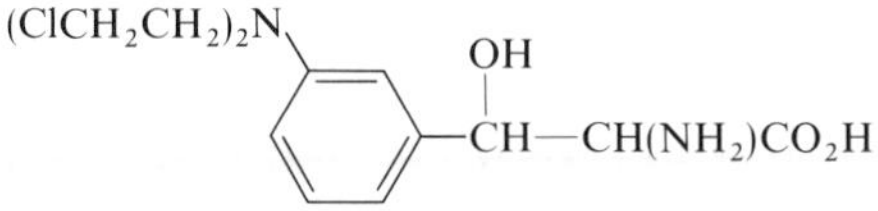 3-Hydroxy-3′-(bis(2-chloroethyl)amino)-phenylalanine, also para derivative	Straukas *et al.*, 1971
V-16	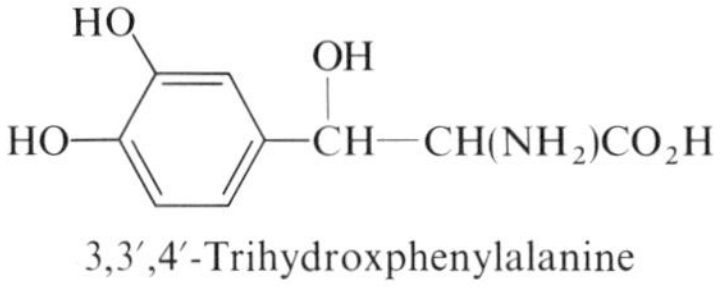 3,3′,4′-Trihydroxphenylalanine (β-hydroxydopa)	Hegedüs *et al.*, 1975
V-17	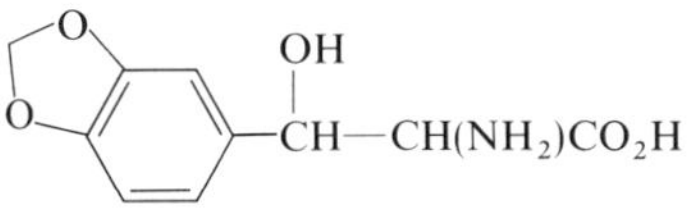 3-Hydroxy-3′,4′-methylenedioxyphenylalanine, many other derivatives	Eisele, 1975
V-18	$CH_2(F)CH(OH)—CH(NH_2)CO_2H$ 4-Fluorothreonine	Lettré and Wölcke, 1967
V-19	$Cl_3CCH(OH)—CH(NH_2)CO_2H$ 4,4,4-Trichlorothreonine	Iwasaki *et al.*, 1976

Structure and name	References
V-20 $CH_3C{\equiv}\overset{OH}{\overset{\vert}{C}}H—CH(NH_2)CO_2H$ 2-Amino-3-hydroxy-4-hexynoic acid	Nimura and Hatanaka, 1974
V-21 $HOCH_2(CHOH)_nCH(NH_2)CO_2H$ $n = 1, 3$ 2-Amino-3,4-dihydroxybutanoic acid (2-amino-3,4,5,6-tetrahydroxyhexanoic acid	Greenstein and Winitz, 1961
V-22 $HOCH_2\overset{OH}{\overset{\vert}{C}}H\underset{CH_3}{\underset{\vert}{C}}H—CH(NH_2)CO_2H$ 2-Amino-4,5-dihydroxy-3-methylpentanoic acid	Georgi and Wieland, 1966
V-23 $HOCH_2\overset{OH}{\overset{\vert}{C}}H(CH_2)_2—CH(NH_2)CO_2H$ 2-Amino-5,6-dihydroxyhexanoic acid	Davis and Bailey, 1972 Mechanic and Tanzer, 1970
V-24 $(HOCH_2)_2CHCH_2—CH(NH_2)CO_2H$ ω,ω'-Dihydroxyleucine	Bory *et al.*, 1979
V-25 $(HOCH_2)_2\overset{OH}{\overset{\vert}{C}}CH_2—CH(NH_2)CO_2H$ 2-Amino-4,5-dihydroxy-4-hydroxymethyl-pentanoic acid	Weygand and Mayer, 1968
V-26 $PhCH_2OCH_2CH_2\overset{OH}{\overset{\vert}{C}}H—CH(NH_2)CO_2H$ 2-Amino-3-hydroxy-5-benzyloxypentanoic acid	Wakamiya *et al.*, 1981
V-27 $H_2N(CH_2)_2—O—CH_2—CH(NH_2)CO_2H$ O-(2-Aminoethyl)serine (4-oxalysine)	Tesser and Nefkens, 1959
V-28 $H_2N(CH_2)_2—O—(CH_2)_2—CH(NH_2)CO_2H$ 2-Amino-4-(2-aminoethoxy)butanoic acid (5-oxahomolysine)	Liu *et al.*, 1978
V-29 $H\overset{O}{\overset{\Vert}{C}}CH_2—CH(NH_2)CO_2H$ Aspartic γ-semialdehyde (β-formylalanine)	Fushiya *et al.*, 1981; Westerik and Wolfenden, 1974

(continued)

	Structure and name	References
V-30	$\mathrm{RC(=O)—CH(NH_2)CO_2H}$ Various β-keto α-amino acids (reduction gives corresponding β-hydroxy compound) R = Me, *i*Pr, Ph, Bzl	Kirihata *et al.*, 1978; Ben-Ishai *et al.*, 1975b
V-31	$\mathrm{H_3CC(=O)—CH(CH_3)—CH(NH_2)CO_2H}$ 4-Oxoisoleucine	Perlman *et al.*, 1977
V-32	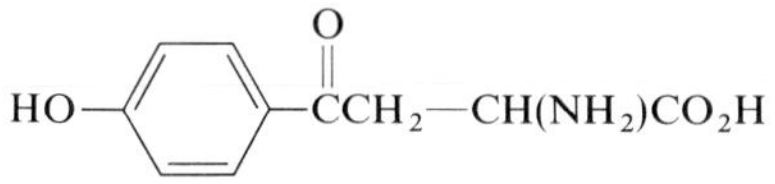 β-(*p*-Hydroxybenzoyl)alanine [2-amino-4-oxo-4-(4-hydroxyphenyl) butanoic acid	Keller-Schierlein and Joos, 1980
V-33	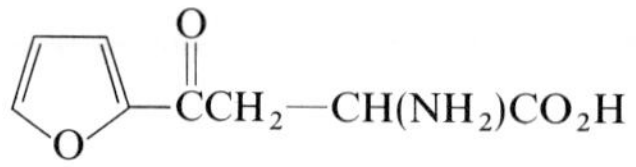 2-Amino-4-oxo-4-(2-furyl)butanoic acid	Ichihara *et al.*, 1973; Couchman *et al.*, 1973
V-34	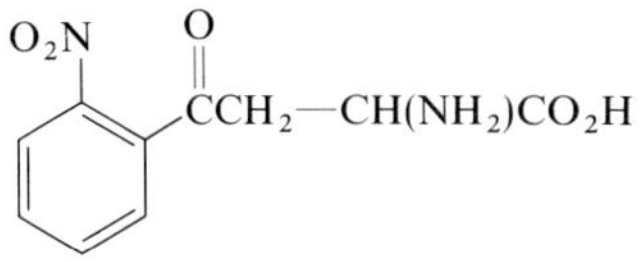 2-Amino-4-oxo-4-(2-nitrophenyl)butanoic acid	Rivett and Stewart, 1976
V-35	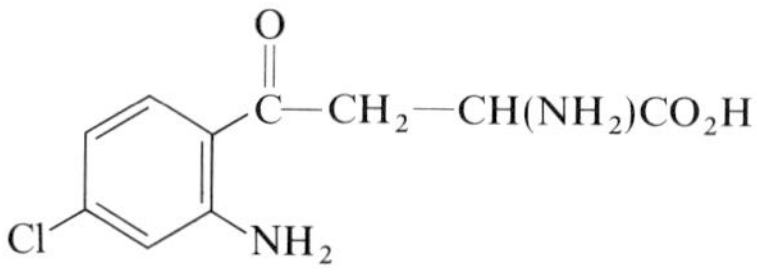 2-Amino-4-oxo-4-(2-amino-4-chlorophenyl)-butanoic acid	Kawashima *et al.*, 1980
V-36	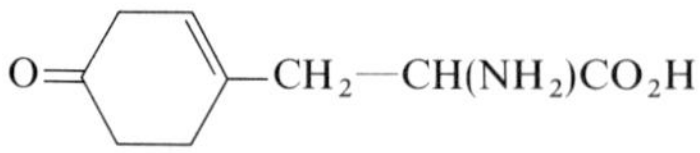 3-(4-Oxo-1-cyclohexenyl)alanine, also saturated compound	Kaminski and Sokolowska, 1973

	Structure and name	References
V-37	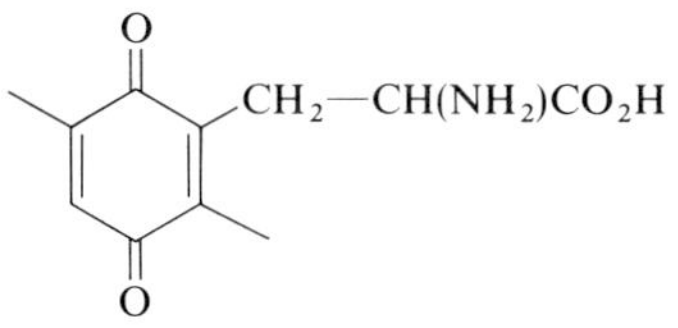 3-(2,5-Dimethyl-3,6-dioxo-1, 4-cyclohexadienyl)alanine	Martynov *et al.*, 1967
V-38	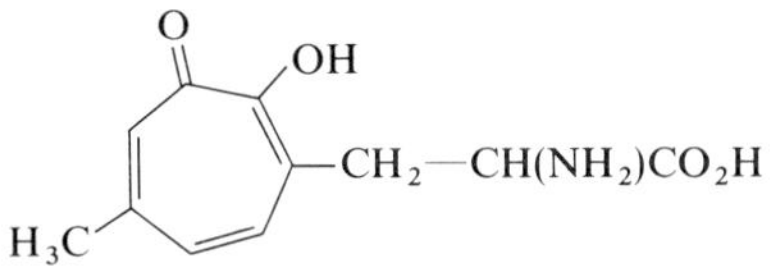 3-(1-Hydroxy-5-methyl-7-oxo- cyclohepta-1,3,5-trien-2-yl)alanine	Teitei, 1979
V-39	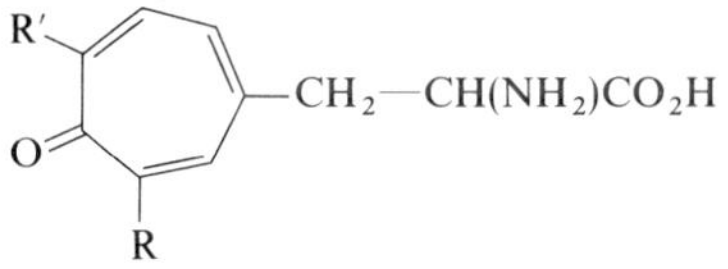 3-(1-Hydroxy-7-oxo-cyclohepta-1,3,5-trien- 3-yl)alanine (also 4-yl isomer) R = H, R′ = OH; R = OH, R′ = H	Teitei and Harris 1979
V-40	ROCH=CH—CH(NH_2)CO_2H Various 2-amino-4-alkoxy-3-butenoic acids R = Me R = $CH_2CH_2NH_2$ R = $CH_2CH(NH_2)CH_2OH$	Keith *et al.*, 1978a Keith *et al.*, 1978b Keith *et al.*, 1975
V-41	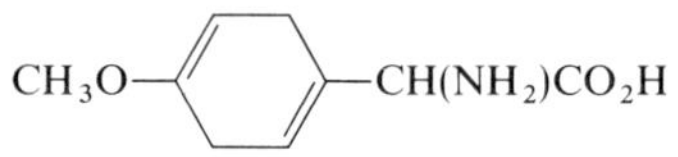 2′,5′-Dihydro-O-methyltyrosine, also 4,5-saturated analog	Kaminski and Sokolowska, 1973
V-42	(EtO_2CH—CH(NH_2)CO_2H 2-Aminomalonic acid semialdehyde diethyl acetal (3,3-diethoxyalanine)	Teshima *et al.*, 1976
V-43	$(MeO)_2CHCH_2$—CH(NH_2)CO_2H Aspartic acid γ-semialdehyde dimethyl acetal	Altman *et al.*, 1975

(continued)

Structure and name	References
V-44 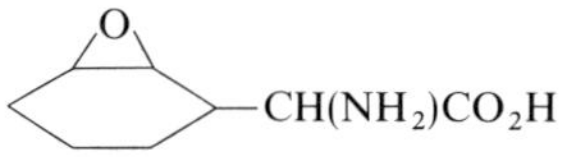 α-(2,3-Epoxycyclohexyl)glycine	Dzieduszycka *et al.*, 1978
V-45 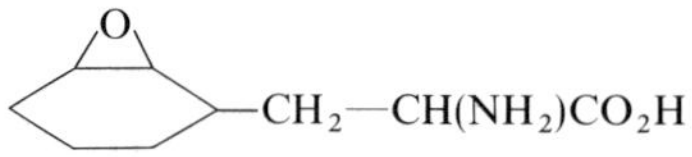 3-(2,3-Epoxycyclohexyl)alanine	Borowski *et al.*, 1979
V-46 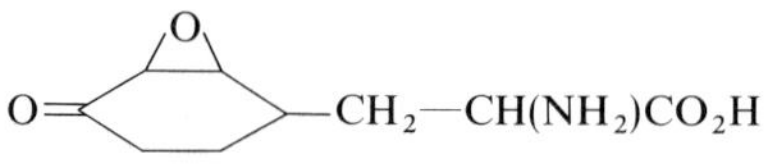 3-(2,3-Epoxy-4-oxocyclohexyl)alanine	Laguzza and Ganem, 1981; Richards *et al.*, 1977
V-47 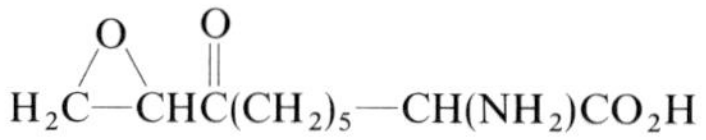 2-Amino-8-oxo-9,10-epoxydecanoic acid	Closse and Huguenin, 1974
See also structures IV-17–20; VI-16–21, 26; VII-17–19, 26, 27; VIII-9–10; IX-17; X-5–8; XII-60; XIII-6; XIV-14–20, 35, 36, 42, 43, 50; XV-11; XIX-1, 2; XX-1	
Aliphatic: aminopolycarboxylic acids and derivatives (IV)	
VI-1 $HO_2C—CH(NH_2)CO_2H$ Aminomalonic acid	Fujino *et al.*, 1976
VI-2 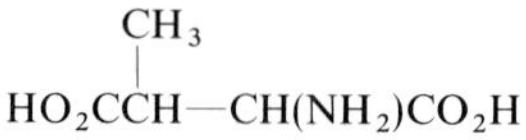 β-Methylaspartic acid	Traynham and Williams, 1962; Barber *et al.*, 1959
VI-3 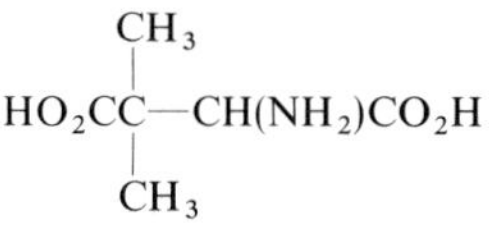 β,β-Dimethylaspartic acid	Greenstein and Winitz, 1961
VI-4 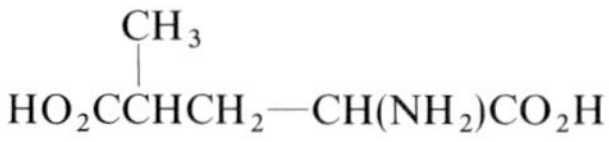 γ-Methylglutamic acid	Done and Fowden, 1952

Structure and name	References
VI-5 $HO_2CCH_2CHCH(NH_2)CO_2H$ R (on the β-CH) Various 3-substituted glutamic acid derivatives $R = CH_3, C_6H_5, OH, CO_2H$	Greenstein and Winitz, 1961
R (on the γ-C) VI-6 $HO_2CCHCH_2—CH(NH_2)CO_2H$ Various γ-alkylglutamic acids R = Et, *n*Pr, isoamyl, Ph	Shakhnazaryan *et al.*, 1968
VI-7 $HO_2C(CH_2)_nCH(NH_2)CO_2H$ $n = 3, 4, 7$ 2-Aminoalkanedioic acids	Greenstein and Winitz, 1961
VI-8 $HO_2C(CH_2)_5—CH(NH_2)CO_2H$ 2-Aminooctanedioic acid	Veber *et al.*, 1976; Hase *et al.*, 1968
VI-9 $HO_2C(CH_2)_9—CH(NH_2)CO_2H$ 2-Aminododecanedioic acid	Fabrichnyi *et al.*, 1979
CH_2 (double bond to C) VI-10 $HO_2CC—CH(NH_2)CO_2H$ β-Methyleneaspartic acid	Dowd and Kaufman, 1979
CH_2 (double bond to C) VI-11 $HO_2CCCH_2—CH(NH_2)CO_2H$ γ-Methyleneglutamic acid	Marcus *et al.*, 1963
F VI-12 $HO_2CCH—CH(NH_2)CO_2H$ β-Fluoroaspartic acid	Matsumoto *et al.*, 1979
F VI-13 $HO_2CCHCH_2—CH(NH_2)CO_2H$ γ-Fluoroglutamic acid	Tolman and Veres, 1966

(continued)

	Structure and name	References
VI-14	F | HO_2CC—$CH(NH_2)CO_2H$ | F β,β-Difluoroaspartic acid	Hageman *et al.*, 1977
VI-15	Cl | HO_2CCH_2CH—$CH(NH_2)CO_2H$ β-Chloroglutamic acid	Alekseeva *et al.*, 1968
VI-16	OH | HO_2CCH—$CH(NH_2)CO_2H$ β-Hydroxyaspartic acid	Jones *et al.*, 1969; Inui *et al.*, 1968; Liwschitz *et al.*, 1962, 1968a,b; Hedgcoth and Skinner, 1963
VI-17	OH | HO_2CCHCH_2—$CH(NH_2)CO_2H$ γ-Hydroxyglutamic acid	Kusumi *et al.*, 1978; Lee and Kaneko, 1973b; Kaneko *et al.*, 1962
VI-18	OH | $HO_2CCH_2CHCH_2$—$CH(NH_2)CO_2H$ 2-Amino-4-hydroxyhexanedioic acid (other similar amino acids in this reference)	Kristensen *et al.*, 1980
VI-19	$HO_2C(CHOH)_2CH(NH_2)CO_2H$ 3,4-Dihydroxyglutamic acid	Greenstein and Winitz, 1961
VI-20	CO_2H | $HO(CH_2)_3CH$—$CH(NH_2)CO_2H$ 3-(3-Hydroxypropyl)aspartic acid	Kuss, 1967a
VI-21	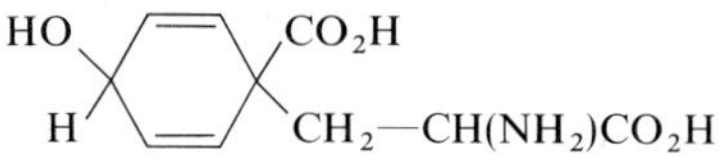 3-(1-Carboxy-4-hydroxy-2-cyclodienyl)-alanine	Danishefsky *et al.*, 1981
VI-22	R | EtO_2CCH—$CH(NH_2)CO_2H$ 3-Substituted aspartic acids R = Ac, CN	Ozaki *et al.*, 1979a

Structure and name	References
VI-23 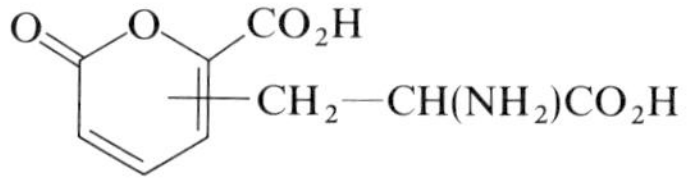 3-(2-Carboxy-6-oxo-6*H*-pyranyl)alanines	Senoh *et al.*, 1964, 1967; Imamoto *et al.*, 1966
VI-24 $(HO_2C)_2CH{-}CH(NH_2)CO_2H$ β-Carboxyaspartic acid	Henson *et al.*, 1981
VI-25 $(HO_2C)_2CHCH_2{-}CH(NH_2)CO_2H$ γ-Carboxyglutamic acid	Zee-Cheng and Olson, 1980; Danishefsky *et al.*, 1979; Hiskey and Boggs, 1977; Märki *et al.*, 1977; Oppliger and Schwyzer, 1977
VI-26 $H_2NC(=O)CH(OH){-}CH(NH_2)CO_2H$ β-Hydroxyasparagine	Singerman and Liwschitz, 1968
VI-27 $H_2NC(=O)CH(R){-}CH(NH_2)CO_2H$ Various β-substituted asparagines; R = Me; R = NH_2, Ph, 	Brain, 1963; Chang *et al.*, 1973
See also structures IV-21, 22, 24, 33; VII-20–22, VIII-12; IX-14, 19; XI-7, 12; XII-30, 44, 62; XIV-23; XV-13; XVI-20, 21	
Aliphatic: polyamino mono- and polycarboxylic acids and derivatives (VII)	
VII-1 $H_2NCH_2{-}CH(NH_2)CO_2H$ β-Aminoalanine	Waki *et al.*, 1981; Wakamiya *et al.*, 1977; Asquith and Carthew, 1972; Kitagawa *et al.*, 1969; McCord *et al.*, 1968; Asquith *et al.*, 1977
VII-2 $CH_3CH(NH_2)CH(NH_2)CO_2H$ 2,3-Diaminobutanoic acid	Atherton and Meienhofer, 1972

(continued)

Structure and name	References
VII-3 $H_2NCH_2CH_2—CH(NH_2)CO_2H$ 2,4-Diaminobutanoic acid	Ferderigos and Katsoyannis, 1977; El-Maghraby, 1976; Hase *et al.*, 1972; Poduška and Rudinger, 1966
CH_3 | VII-4 $H_2NCH_2—CH—CH(NH_2)CO_2H$ 2,4-Diamino-3-methylbutanoic acid Also (along with 3-phenyl)	Shaw *et al.*, 1981 Greenstein and Winitz, 1961
$NHCH_3$ | VII-5 $CH_3CH—CH(NH_2)CO_2H$ 2-Amino-3-methylaminobutanoic acid	McCord *et al.*, 1967
VII-6 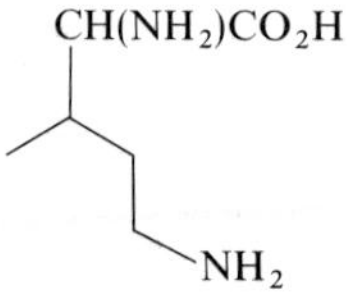 β-Methylornithine	Skinner and Johansson, 1972
VII-7 $H_2N(CH_2)_5CH(NH_2)CO_2H$ Homolysine	Bodanszky and Lindeberg, 1971
VII-8 $H_2N—CHCH_2CH(NH_2)CO_2H$ | C_3H_7 2,4-Diaminoheptanoic acid	Greenstein and Winitz, 1961
VII-9 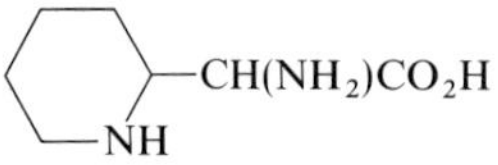 α-(2-Piperidyl)glycine	Golding and Smith, 1980
VII-10 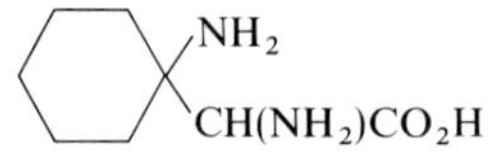 α-(1-Aminocyclohexyl)glycine	Rakhshinda and Khan, 1979
NH_2 | VII-11 Ph—CH—$CH(NH_2)CO_2H$ β-Aminophenylalanine	Ali and Khan, 1978

Structure and name	References
VII-12 R—$CHCH(NH_2)CO_2H$ | NH_2 Various α,β-diamino acids R = 4-HOC_6H_4; 4-$MeOC_6H_4$; 4-$Me_2NC_6H_4$; 3,4-$(MeO)_2C_6H_3$; 3,4-methylenedioxy-C_6H_3; 3-MeO-4-HOC_6H_3; $PhCH_2CH_2$; n-C_3H_7, 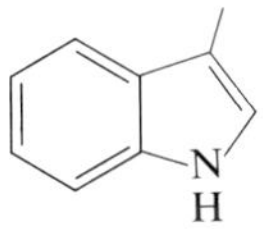	Rakhshinda and Khan, 1979
VII-13 $H_2NCH_2CH{=}CHCH_2$—$CH(NH_2)CO_2H$ 2,6-Diamino-4-hexenoic acid (4,5-dehydrolysine)	Davis *et al.*, 1973
VII-14 $NH_2CH_2C{\equiv}CCH_2$—$CH(NH_2)CO_2H$ 2,6-Diamino-4-hexynoic acid	Sasaki and Bricas, 1980; Jansen *et al.*, 1969, 1970
F | VII-15 $H_2NCH_2CH(CH_2)_n$—$CH(NH_2)CO_2H$ $n = 1, 2$ 4-Fluoroornithine (5-fluorolysine)	Tolman and Benes, 1976
VII-16 $H_2NCH_2CX_2CH_2CH_2$—$CH(NH_2)CO_2H$ 5,5-Dimethyllysine (5,5-difluorolysine) X = F or Me	Shirota *et al.*, 1977b
OH | VII-17 $H_2N(CH_2)_nCH$—$CH(NH_2)CO_2H$ $n = 2$ $n = 3$ β-Hydroxyornithine and -lysine	Wakamiya *et al.*, 1977; Tomlinson and Viswanatha, 1973 Stammer and Webb, 1969
VII-18 $H_2N(CH_2)_nCHCH_2CH(NH_2)CO_2H$ | OH $n = 1$ $n = 2$ γ-Hydroxyornithine and -lysine	Greenstein and Winitz, 1961 Fujita *et al.*, 1965

(continued)

Structure and name	References
VII-19 $H_2NCH_2CH_2C(=O)CH_2—CH(NH_2)CO_2H$ 4-Oxolysine	Hider and John, 1972
VII-20 $(—CH_2CH_2CH(NH_2)CO_2H)_2$ 2,7-Diaminooctanedioic acid	Jošt and Rudinger, 1967; Rudinger and Jošt, 1964
VII-21 $H_2N(CH_2)_3CH(CO_2H)—CH(NH_2)CO_2H$ 3-Carboxylysine	Kuss, 1967b
VII-22 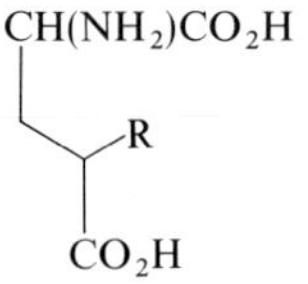 3-Substituted glutamic acid derivatives	
R = CH_2NH_2, $CH_2CH_2N(C_2H_5)_2$	Alekseeva *et al.*, 1971c
R = $N(C_2H_5)_2$, 	Alekseeva *et al.*, 1971a
R = 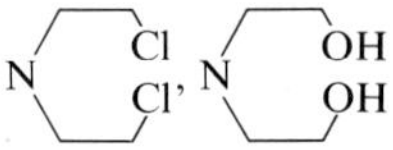	Alekseeva *et al.*, 1971b
VII-23 $H_2NCH_2CH_2CH(NH_2)—CH(NH_2)CO_2H$ *β*-Aminoornithine	Wakamiya *et al.*, 1978
VII-24 $H_2N(CH_2)_2—X—CH_2—CH(NH_2)CO_2H$ *γ*-Aza-, thia-, and selenalysines X = NH X = S X = Se	Kolc, 1969; Hermann *et al.*, 1970; Hermann and Zaoral, 1965 Sadeh *et al.*, 1976
VII-25 $CH_2CH_2CH(NH_2)CO_2H$ | $SCH_2CH(NH_2)CO_2H$ Cystathionine	Jošt and Rudinger, 1967; Rudinger and Jošt, 1964; see also Greenstein and Winitz, 1961
VII-26 $H_2NOCH_2CH_2CH(NH_2)CO_2H$ 2-Amino-4-aminooxybutanoic acid (canaline)	Greenstein and Winitz, 1961

Structure and name	References
VII-27 $HONH{-}(CH_2)_3CH(NH_2)CO_2H$ N^{δ}-hydroxyornithine	Isowa *et al.*, 1972
VII-28 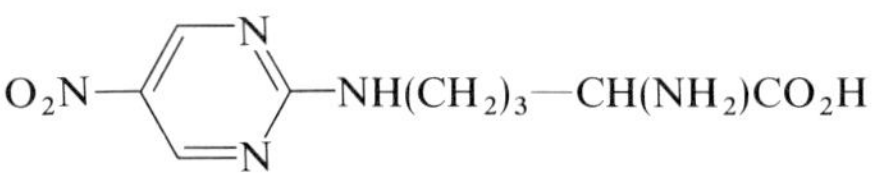 N^{δ}(5-Nitro-2-pyrimidinyl)ornithine	Signor *et al.*, 1971
VII-29 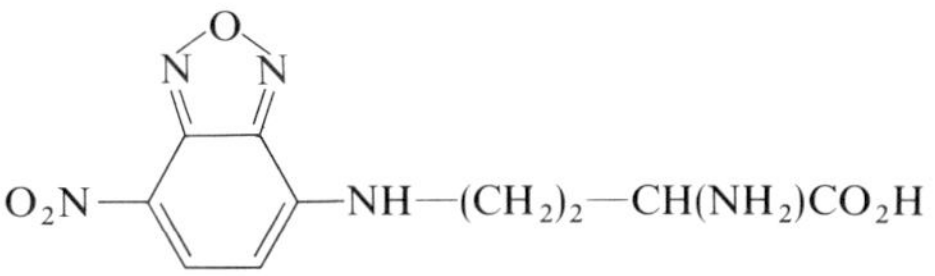 2-Amino-4-(7-nitro-2,1,3-benzoxadiazol-4-ylamino)-butanoic acid	Moore, 1978
See also structures IV-24, 33, 34; V-27, 28, 35, 40; VI-23; IX-15, 16; X-7; XI-8; XII-19, 21, 22, 44, 49; XIV-21, 22, 34; XVI-7, 19; XVII-12, 13; XIX-20	
Aliphatic: guanido- and amidino-containing (VIII)	
VIII-1 $H_2NC(=NH)NHCH_2{-}CH(NH_2)CO_2H$ β-Guanidoalanine	Zaoral *et al.*, 1979; Brtník and Zaoral, 1976
VIII-2 $H_2NC(=NH)NHCH(CH_3){-}CH(NH_2)CO_2H$ 2-Amino-3-guanidobutanoic acid	Brtník and Zaoral 1976
VIII-3 $H_2NC(=NH)NH(CH_2)_2{-}CH(NH_2)CO_2H$ 2-Amino-4-guanidobutanoic acid	Van Nispen *et al.*, 1977a; Van Nispen and Tesser, 1972
VIII-4 $H_2NC(=X)NH(CH_2)_4CH(NH_2)CO_2H$ Homoarginine, homocitrulline X = NH, O	Greenstein and Winitz, 1961

(continued)

Structure and name	References
VIII-5 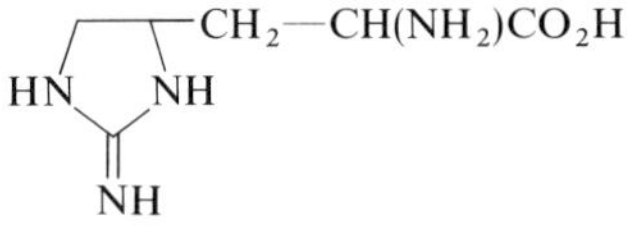 3(2-Iminoimidazolin-4-yl)-alanine (γ-cycloarginine, enduracididine)	Tsuji *et al.*, 1975
VIII-6 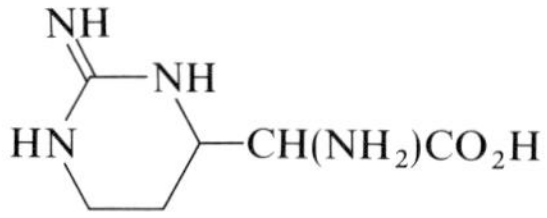 α-(2-Iminohexahydropyrimidin-4-yl)glycine (β-cycloarginine)	Wakamiya *et al.*, 1978; Shiba *et al.*, 1977; Bycroft *et al.*, 1968, 1971
VIII-7 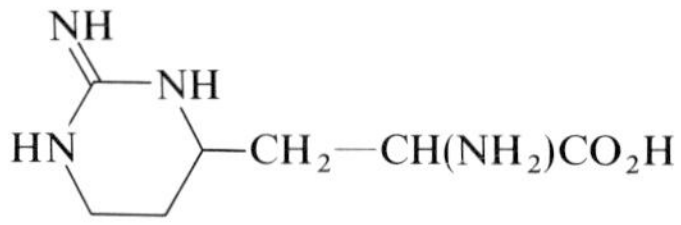 3-(2-Iminohexahydropyrimidin-4-yl)alanine	Iinuma *et al.*, 1977; Tsuji *et al.*, 1975
VIII-8 $H_2NC(=NH)NHCH_2CH(F)CH_2-CH(NH_2)CO_2H$ γ-Fluoroarginine	Tolman and Benes, 1976
VIII-9 $H_2NC(=NH)NHCH_2CH(OH)CH_2-CH(NH_2)CO_2H$ γ-Hydroxyarginine	Mizusaki and Makisumi, 1981; Bell, 1961
VIII-10 $H_2NC(=NH)NHOCH_2CH_2CH(NH_2)CO_2H$ 2-Amino-4-guanidooxybutanoic acid (canavanine)	Greenstein and Winitz, 1961; for derivative, see Rosenthal, 1975
VIII-11 $H_2NC(=NH)NHC(=O)NH(CH_2)_3-CH(NH_2)CO_2H$ N^{ω}-Amidinocitrulline	Ito and Hashimoto, 1969
VIII-12 $NH_2C(=NH)(CH_2)_4-CH(NH_2)CO_2H$ 2-Aminoheptanedioic acid 7-monoamidine	Culvenor *et al.*, 1969, 1971

Structure and name	References
VIII-13 $CH_3C(=NH)NH(CH_2)_3—CH(NH_2)CO_2H$ N^{δ}-Acetimidoylornithine	Pinker *et al.*, 1975
See also structures X-9, 10; XII-23; XIV-54	
Aliphatic: 1-aminocycloalkane-1-carboxylic acids and related compounds (IX)	
IX-1  1-Aminocyclopropanecarboxylic acid	Rich and Tam, 1978; Bregovec and Jakovčić, 1972
IX-2 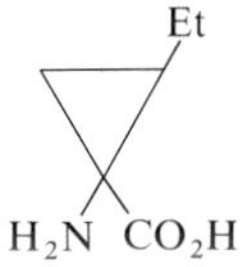 1-Amino-2-ethylcyclopropanecarboxylic acid	Ichihara *et al.*, 1977; Shiraishi *et al.*, 1977
IX-3 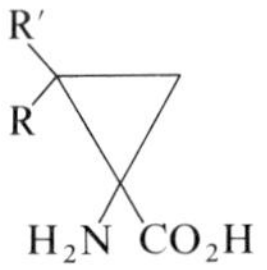 Various 2,2-disubstituted 1-amino-cyclopropanecarboxylic acids	Schöllkopf *et al.*, 1973
IX-4  1-Aminocyclopentanecarboxylic acid (cycloleucine)	Park *et al.*, 1974; Diehl and Bowen, 1965
IX-5  1-Aminocyclohexanecarboxylic acid	Kenner *et al.*, 1965
IX-6 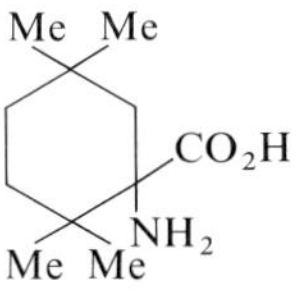 1-Amino-2,2,5,5-tetramethyl-cyclohexanecarboxylic acid	Cremlyn *et al.*, 1970

(continued)

Structure and name	References
IX-7 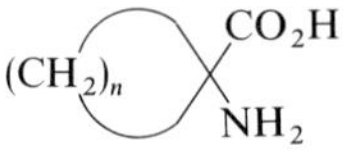 $n = 7, 9$ 1-Aminocycloheptane- and -nonanecarboxylic acids	Cremlyn *et al.*, 1970
IX-8  2-Aminoindan-2-carboxylic acid	Hsieh *et al.*, 1979
IX-9 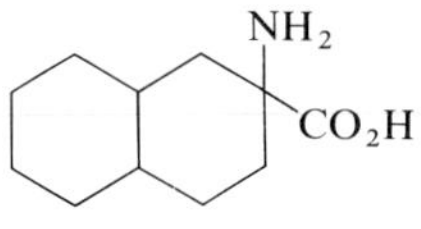 2-Aminodecalin-2-carboxylic acid	Chisholm *et al.*, 1967
IX-10 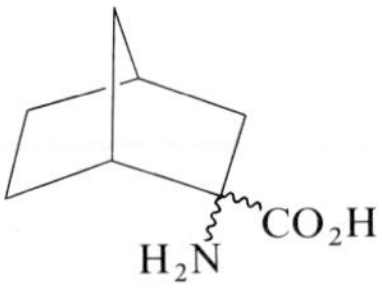 2-Aminonorbornane-2-carboxylic acid	Horikawa *et al.*, 1980
IX-11 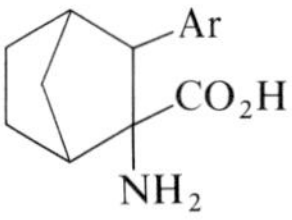 3-Aryl-2-aminonorbornane-2-carboxylic acids	Kinoshita *et al.*, 1969
IX-12 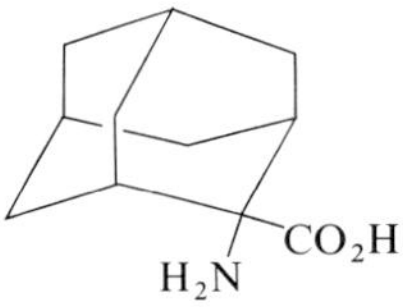 2-Aminoadamantane-2-carboxylic acid	Nagasawa *et al.*, 1975
IX-13 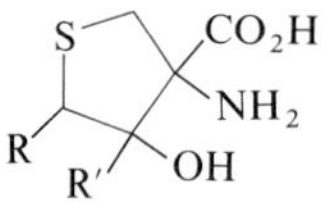 Substituted 3′-aminotetrahydrothiophene-3-carboxylic acids $R = R' = (CH_2)_4$; $R = H$, $R' = Ph$	Field, 1979

	Structure and name	References
IX-14	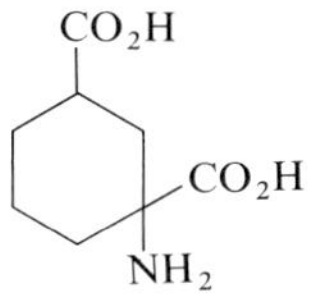 1-Amino-1,3-cyclohexanedicarboxylic acid	Gass and Meister, 1970
IX-15	 3-Aminopyrrolidine-3-carboxylic acid	Monteiro, 1973
IX-16	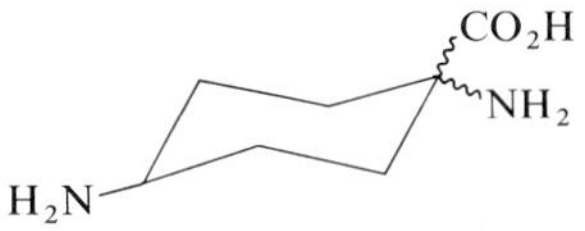 1,4-Diaminocyclohexanecarboxylic acid	Bey *et al.*, 1978
IX-17	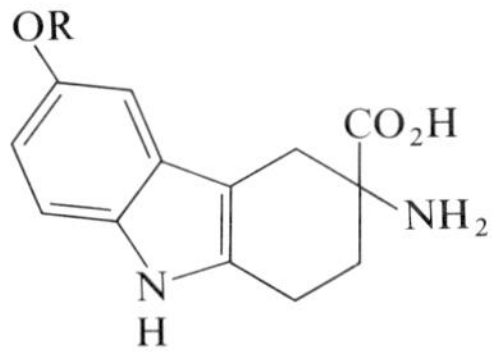 6-Alkoxy-3-amino-1,2,3,4-tetrahydrocarbazole-3-carboxylic acids	Maki *et al.*, 1973
IX-18	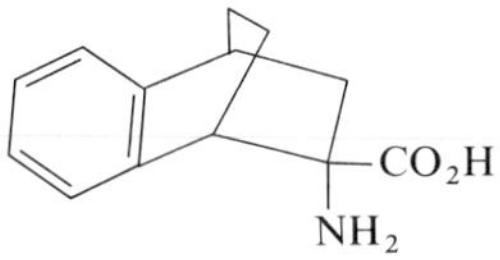 2-Aminobenzobicyclo[2.2.2]octane-2-carboxylic acid	Grunewald *et al.*, 1980
IX-19	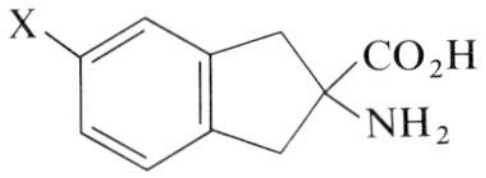 5-Substituted 2-aminoindan-2-carboxylic acids X = OH, OMe, CO_2H, Cl, Br, I	Pinder *et al.*, 1971
IX-20	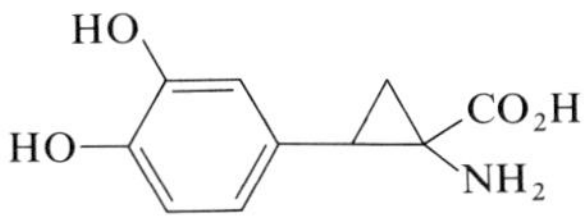 1-Amino-2-(3,4-dihydroxyphenyl)cyclopropanecarboxylic acid (2,3-methylene-dopa)	Hines *et al.*, 1976

(continued)

Structure and name	References
IX-21 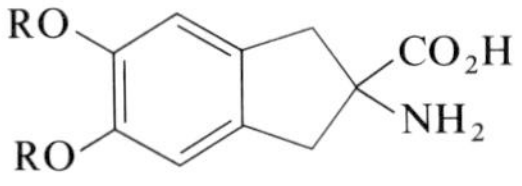 5,6-Dialkoxy-2-aminoindan-2-carboxylic acids	Taylor *et al.*, 1970
IX-22 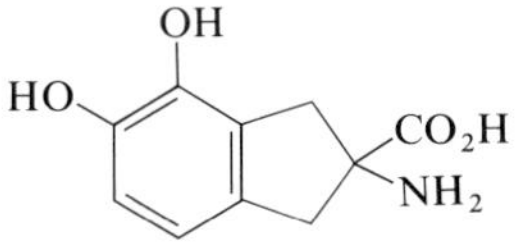 4,5-Dihydroxy-2-aminoindan-2-carboxylic acid	Cannon *et al.*, 1974
IX-23 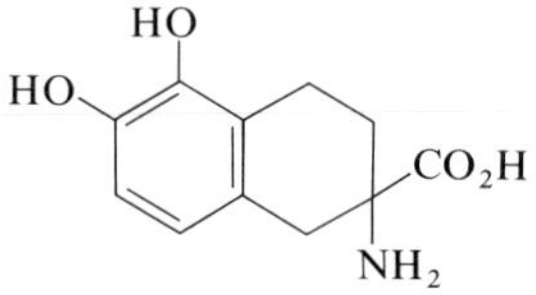 5,6-Dihydroxy-2-aminotetralin-2-carboxylic acid	Cannon *et al.*, 1974
See also structure XIV-33. Additional examples in this structural class have been cited by Ross *et al.*, 1961.	
Aliphatic: miscellaneous (X)	
X-1 $NCCH(NH_2)CO_2H$ Aminomalonic acid mononitrile (α-cyanoglycine)	Warren *et al.*, 1974
X-2 $NCCH_2CH(NH_2)CO_2H$ Aspartic acid 4-nitrile	Wilchek *et al.*, 1968; Liberek *et al.*, 1966
X-3 $NCCH_2CH_2—CH(NH_2)CO_2H$ Glutamic acid 5-nitrile	Wilchek *et al.*, 1968
X-4 $O_2N—(CH_2)_n—CH(NH_2)CO_2H$ $n = 3$ $n = 4$ 2-Amino-ω-nitroalkanoic acids	Maurer and Keller-Schierlein, 1969; Keller-Schierlein and Maurer, 1969; Bayer and Schmidt, 1973
X-5 $N_2CH_2\overset{O}{\overset{\Vert}{C}}OCH_2—CH(NH_2)CO_2H$ *O*-Diazoacetylserine (azaserine)	Curphey and Daniel, 1978; Moore *et al.*, 1954

Structure and name	References
X-6 $N_2CH_2\overset{O}{C}CH_2CH_2$—$CH(NH_2)CO_2H$ 2-Amino-5-oxo-6-diazohexanoic acid	Dion *et al.*, 1956
X-7 $H_2NOCH_2CH_2$—$CH(NH_2)CO_2H$ 2-Amino-4-aminooxybutanoic acid (δ-oxaornithine)	Korpela *et al.*, 1977; Gilon *et al.*, 1967
X-8 $ON\overset{OH}{N}CH_2$—$CH(NH_2)CO_2H$ 2-Amino-3-(*N*-nitrosohydroxylamino)propanoic acid	Eaton *et al.*, 1973; Isowa *et al.*, 1973
X-9 $H_2N\overset{O}{C}NHCH_2$—$CH(NH_2)CO_2H$ β-Ureidoalanine	Kjaer and Larsen, 1959
X-10 $H_2N\overset{O}{C}NH(CH_2)_2$—$CH(NH_2)CO_2H$ Norcitrulline	Izumiya and Kitagawa, 1958
X-11 $(HO)_2\overset{X}{P}CH_2$—$CH(NH_2)CO_2H$ β-Phosphoalanine, thiophosphoalanine X = O, S	Varlet *et al.*, 1979
X-12 $H_3C\overset{OH}{\underset{O}{P}}CH_2CH_2$—$CH(NH_2)CO_2H$ 2-Amino-4-methanephosphonylbutanoic acid	Gruszecka *et al.*, 1979; Ogawa *et al.*, 1973
X-13 R—CH_2—$\overset{CH_3}{\underset{CH_3}{Si}}CH_2$—$CH(NH_2)CO_2H$ β-Trimethylsilylalanine (R = H); also β-Dimethyl(trimethylsilylmethyl)silylalanine (R = $(CH_3)_3Si$)	Birkofer and Ritter, 1958; Porter and Shive, 1968
X-14 Me_3Si—C≡C—$CH(NH_2)CO_2H$ 2-Amino-4-trimethylsilyl-3-butynoic acid	Casara and Metcalf, 1978
See also structure XII-28, 50; XIII-21–24	

(continued)

Structure and name	References
Carbocyclic aromatic: phenylglycine derivatives (XI)	
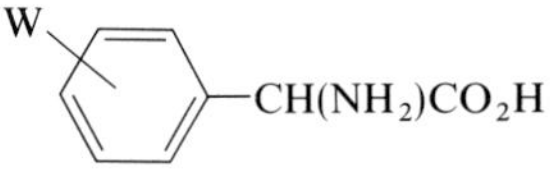	
XI-1 W = H, *m*-Cl, *p*-Cl, *o*-F, *m*-F, *p*-F, *m*-Me, *p*-Me, *p*-OMe	Compere and Weinstein, 1977
XI-2 W = H, *o*-Me	Greenstein and Winitz, 1961
XI-3 W = *p*-OMe	Weinges *et al.*, 1980
XI-4 W = *p*-CH_2Cl, *p*-CH_2OH, *p*-CH_2SMe, *p*-CH_2Br, *p*-CH_2OMe, *p*-CH_2NHBzl	Ben-Ishai *et al.*, 1977a,b
See also	Ben-Ishai *et al.*, 1975a
XI-5 W = *p*-OH	Yamada *et al.*, 1978, 1979
XI-6 W = *m*-OH	Müller and Schütte, 1968
XI-7 W = *m*-CO_2H	Larsen and Wieczorkowska, 1977; Irreverre *et al.*, 1961
XI-8 W = *p*-NH_2, *p*-N_3	Eberle *et al.*, 1981; Fahrenholz and Thierauch, 1980

XI-9 W = 3-*t*Bu-4-OH	Lundt *et al.*, 1979
XI-10 W = 3,5-di-F-4-OH	Kirk, 1980
XI-11 W = 3,5-di-OH	Müller and Schütte, 1968
XI-12 W = 3-CO_2H-4-OH	Larsen and Wieczorkowska, 1977
XI-13 W = 3,5-di-*t*Bu-4-OH	Teuber *et al.*, 1978; Hewgill and Webb, 1977

Structure and name	References
Carbocyclic aromatic: phenylalanine derivatives (XII)	
Ring-substituted phenylalanines	
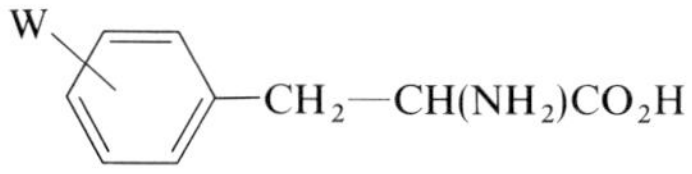	
XII-1 W = *o*-Me	Berger *et al.*, 1973
XII-2 W = *p*-Et	Zhuze *et al.*, 1964
XII-3 W = *p*-C_6H_5	Yabe *et al.*, 1976
XII-4 W = *p*-CH_2Ph	Podkoscielny *et al.*, 1978
XII-5 W = *m*-F, *p*-Me	Bosshard and Berger 1973; Maki *et al.*, 1977
XII-6 W = *p*-F	Borin *et al.*, 1977; Maki *et al.*, 1977 Bosshard and Berger, 1973; Nicolaides *et al.*, 1963
XII-7 W = *p*-Cl	Houghten and Rapoport, 1974
XII-8 W = *o*-Cl	Greenstein and Winitz, 1961
XII-9 W = *p*-Br, *o*-Br	Faulstich *et al.*, 1973
XII-10 W = *m*-OH	Bernardi *et al.*, 1966
XII-11 W = *o*-OH	Greenstein and Winitz, 1961
XII-12 W = *p*-SH	Greenstein and Winitz, 1961
XII-13 W = *m*-CF_3	Nicolaides and Lipnik, 1966; Maki *et al.*, 1977; Nestor *et al.*, 1982a
XII-14 W = *p*-CF_3	Nestor *et al.*, 1982a for additional fluorinated phenylalanines, see Maki *et al.*, 1977

(continued)

Structure and name	References
XII-15 W = p-CH_2OH	Smith and Sloane, 1967
XII-16 W = m-CH_2OH, m-CH_2NH_2	Larsen and Wieczorkowska, 1977
XII-17 W = m-CO_2H	Thompson *et al.*, 1961
XII-18 W = p-NO_2	Fauchère and Schiller, 1981; Massey and Fessler, 1976; Houghten and Rapoport, 1974; Coy *et al.*, 1974
XII-19 W = p-$NH_2(N_3)$	Klausner *et al.*, 1978; Sakarellos *et al.*, 1976; Houghten and Rapoport, 1974; Coy *et al.*, 1974; Schwyzer and Caviezel, 1971
XII-20 W = p-CN, p-$COCH_3$	Cleland, 1969
XII-21 W = p-$N(CH_2CH_2Cl)_2$	Hsieh and Marshall, 1981; Park *et al.*, 1974; Bergel *et al.*, 1955; Bergel and Stock, 1954
XII-22 W = p-$N(CH_2CH(Cl)CH_3)_2$	Karpavicius *et al.*, 1973
XII-23 W = p-guanidino	Moore *et al.*, 1977b
XII-24 W = p-N=N—Ph	Goodman and Kossoy, 1966
XII-25 W = p-$CH{=}CHC_6H_5$	Jones and Wright, 1971
XII-26 W = p-$COCH_2Br$, p-$NHCOCH_2Br$, m-$NHCOCH_2Cl$	Degraw *et al.*, 1968
XII-27 W = p-$(HO)_2B$	Snyder *et al.*, 1958; Roberts *et al.*, 1980
XII-28 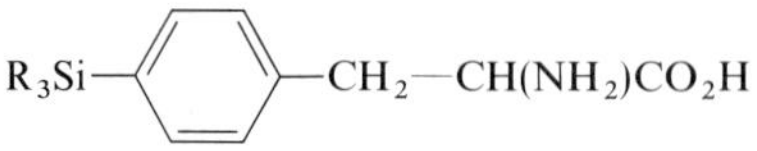 Ortho derivative	Frankel *et al.*, 1963, 1967, 1968; Gertner *et al.*, 1963; for other related derivatives, see Rotman *et al.*, 1967

Structure and name	References
XII-29 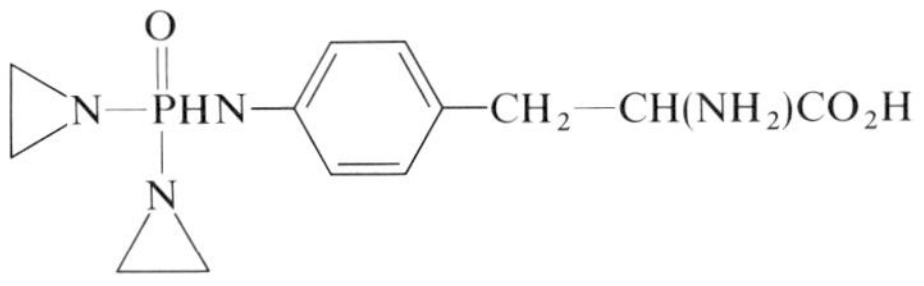	Poskiene *et al.*, 1976
XII-30 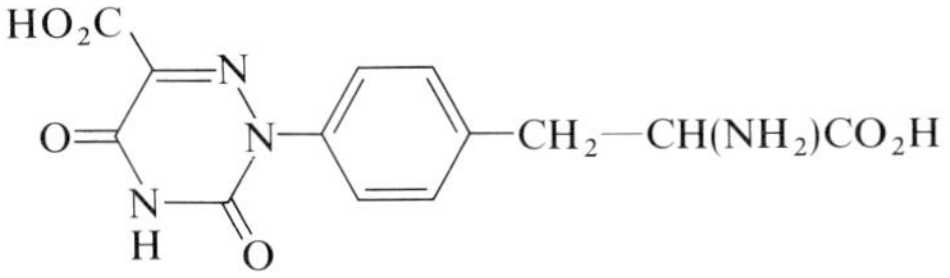	Slouka, 1978
Ring-polysubstituted phenylalanines 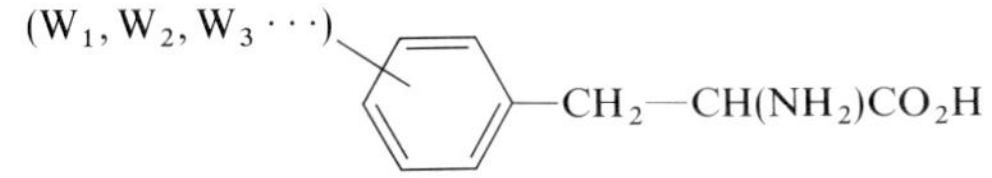	
XII-31 W = 2,4-di-Me; 2,3-di-Me; 2,5-di-Me; 2,6-di-Me; 3,5-di-Me	Greenstein and Winitz, 1961
XII-32 W = 2,4,6-tri-Me	Greenstein and Winitz, 1961
XII-33 W = 3,4,5-tri-Me	Nestor *et al.*, 1982a
XII-34 W = 2,3,4,5,6-penta-Me	Van Nispen *et al.*, 1977b; Coy *et al.*, 1974; Carrion *et al.*, 1968
XII-35 W = 2,4-di-F; 3,4-di-F; 3,5-di-F; 2,5-di-F; 2,6-di-F; 2,3,5,6-tetra-F; 3,5-di-Cl-2,4,6-tri-F	Prudchenko, 1970
XII-36 W = 2,3-di-F; 2,4-di-F; 2,3-bis-CF_3; 2,4-bis-CF_3; 2-Cl-5-CF_3; 4-Cl-5-CF_3; 2,5-di-F	Märki *et al.*, 1977
XII-37 W = 2,3,4,5,6-penta-F	Kaurov and Smirnova, 1977; Bosshard and Berger, 1973; Fauchère and Schwyzer, 1971; Filler *et al.*, 1969
XII-38 W = 2,3-Br; 2,5-Br; 3,4-Br	Faulstich *et al.*, 1973
XII-39 W = 3,4,5-tri-I	Schatz *et al.*, 1968
XII-40 W = 2,3-di-OH; 2,5-di-OH; 2,6-di-OH	Greenstein and Winitz, 1961

(continued)

Structure and name	References
XII-41 W = 3-Br-5-OMe	Crooij and Eliaers, 1969
XII-42 W = 2,5-di-OMe; 2,5-di-OMe-4-Me; 4-Br-2,5-di-OMe	Coutts and Malicky, 1974
XII-43 W = 2,5-di-OMe-4-Me	Lee *et al.*, 1971
XII-44 W = 3-CO_2H-4-OH; 3-CO_2H-4-NH_2	Larsen and Wieczorkowska, 1977
XII-45 W = 2-OH-5-NO_2; 2-OEt-5-NO_2	Greenstein and Winitz, 1961
XII-46 W = 3,4,5-tri-OMe	Nestor *et al.*, 1982a
XII-47 W = 2-NO_2-4-N_3	Fahrenholz and Schimmack, 1975
XII-48 W = 3-$NHCOCH_2Cl$-4-F	Degraw *et al.*, 1968
XII-49 W = 4-$N(CH_2CH_2Cl)_2$-2-OMe	Teng and Pang, 1978
XII-50 W = 2,4-bis-$SiMe_3$	Frankel *et al.*, 1968
Ring-substituted tyrosines	
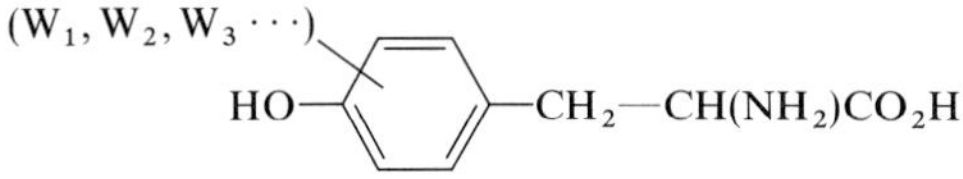	
XII-51 W = 3,5-di-*t*Bu	Teuber and Krause, 1978; Teuber *et al.*, 1978
XII-52 W = 3,5-di-Me (O-Me derivative)	Jean and Anatol, 1969
XII-53 W = 3-$CH_2C_6H_5$; 3-$CH_2C_6H_3Cl_2$	Erickson and Merrifield, 1973
XII-54 W = 3-F	Blumenstein *et al.*, 1981
XII-55 W = tetra-F	Filler and Kang, 1965
XII-56 W = 3,5-di-Cl	Brody and Spencer, 1968
XII-57 W = 3-I	Harington and Rivers, 1944
XII-58 W = 3,5-di-I	Lemaire *et al.*, 1977
XII-59 W = 2-OH	Greenstein and Winitz, 1961

Structure and name	References
XII-60 W = 3-CH_2OH	Wang and Vida, 1974
XII-61 W = 2-OH-6-Me	Schneider, 1958
XII-62 W = 3-CO_2H	Arnold and Larsen, 1977; Leonard *et al.*, 1965; Larsen and Kjaer, 1962
XII-63 W = 3,5-di-NO_2	Brundish and Wade, 1973
XII-64 W = 3-^{211}At-5-I	Visser *et al.*, 1979
XII-65 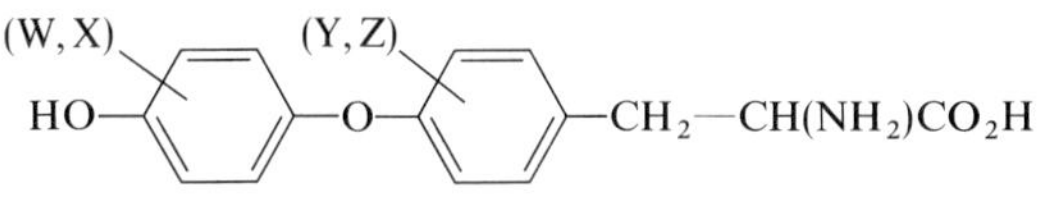 Variously substituted thyronines	Jorgensen *et al.*, 1969, 1974; Cox *et al.*, 1974; Block and Coy, 1972; Jorgensen and Berteau, 1971; Jorgensen and Wright, 1970a,b; Matsuura *et al.*, 1968, 1969
Ring-substituted dihydroxyphenylalanine (dopa) derivatives 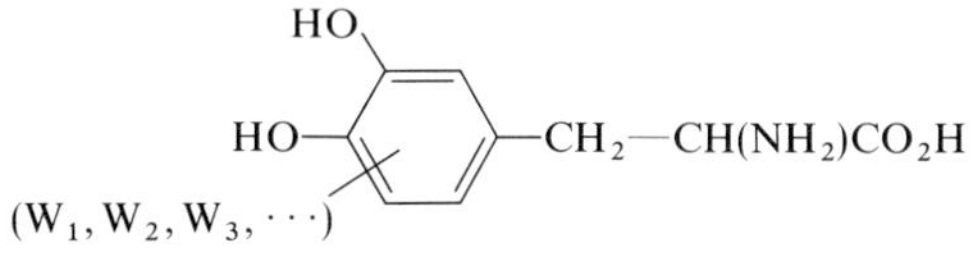	
XII-66 W = 2-Cl; 2-Br; 2-F; 2-NO_2	Greenstein and Winitz, 1961
XII-67 W = 2-Me; 2-Et; 2-iPr; 2-*t*Bu-4,5-di-OH	Morgenstern *et al.*, 1971
XII-68 W = 3-F-4,5-di-OH	Firnau *et al.*, 1973
XII-69 W = 2-F-4,5-di-OH	Firnau *et al.*, 1980
XII-70 W = 2,5,6-tri-F-3,4-di-OH	Filler and Rickert, 1981
XII-71 W = 2,6-di-Br-3,4-di-OH; 5,6-di-Br-3,4-di-OH	Anhovry *et al.*, 1974
XII-72 W = 2,4,5-tri-OH	Ong *et al.*, 1969; Langemann and Scheer, 1969
XII-73 W = 2,3,4-tri-OH	Rapp *et al.*, 1975

(continued)

Structure and name	References
XII-74 W = 5-OMe-3,4-di-OH	Sethi *et al.*, 1973
Miscellaneous phenylalanine congeners	
XII-75 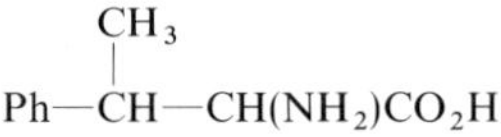 β-Methylphenylalanine	Cativiela and Melendez, 1981; Yamada *et al.*, 1977; Kataoka *et al.*, 1976; Arold *et al.*, 1969, 1974; Waisuisz *et al.*, 1957
XII-76 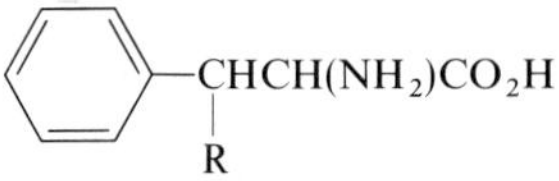 Various β-substituted phenylalanine derivatives; R = C_2H_5, i-C_3H_7, *n*-C_4H_9, $PhCH_2$, $PhCH_2CH_2$, *p*-ClC_6H_4, *p*-$MeOC_6H_4$	Horner and Schwahn, 1955
XII-77 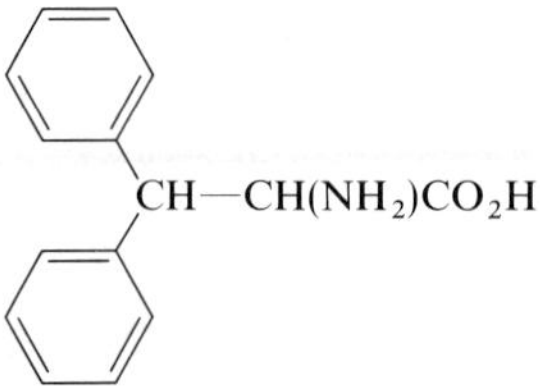 β,β-Diphenylalanine	Filler and Rao, 1961
XII-78 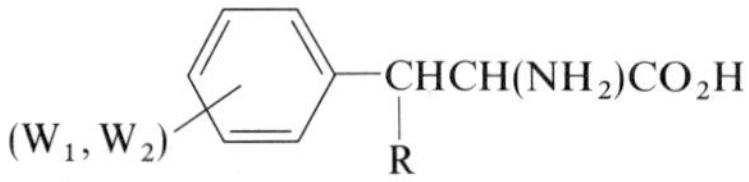 Ring-substituted β-alkylphenylalanines; R = *n*-C_4H_9, W = *p*-NEt_2; R = C_2H_5, W = *p*-NEt_2; R = C_2H_5, W = 3,4-$(MeO)_2$; R = C_2H_5, W = 3,4-$(OH)_2$	Horner and Schwahn, 1955
XII-79 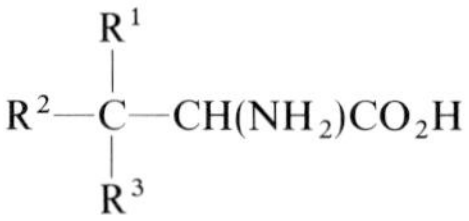 Various *tert*-aralkyl glycines; R^1 = Me, R^2 = Me, R^3 = Ph; R^1 = Et, R^2 = Et, R^3 = Ph; R^1 = Me, R^2 = Ph, R^3 = Et; R^1 = Me, R^2 = Ph, R^3 = Ph; R^1 = $(CH_2)_5$, R^2 = $(CH_2)_5$, R^3 = Ph	Schöllkopf and Meyer, 1975, 1977

Structure and name	References
XII-80 $PhCH(F)—CH(NH_2)CO_2H$ *β*-Fluorophenylalanine	Tsushima *et al.*, 1980; Kollonitsch *et al.*, 1979; Wade *et al.*, 1979
XII-81 $CH_2{=}C(Ph)—CH(NH_2)CO_2H$ *β*-Methylenephenylalanine	Chari and Wemple, 1979
XII-82 $CH_3SCH(C_6H_5)(CH_2)_nCH(NH_2)CO_2H$ $n = 0, 1$ 3-(Methylmercapto)phenylalanine, also *γ*-phenylmethionine	Greenstein and Winitz, 1961
See also structures II-19, 20; III-5; IV-11; V-11, 14–17, 30, 36, 37, 41; VI-5, 21, 27; VII-4, 11, 12; XIV-37, 39–41	
Carbocyclic aromatic: miscellaneous (XIII)	
XIII-1 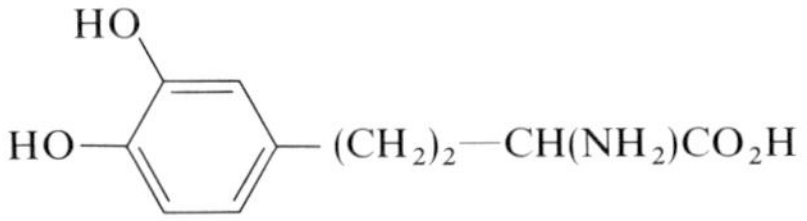 2-Amino-4-(3,4-dihydroxyphenyl)butanoic acid (homo-dopa) also the 3,4,5-trihydroxy derivative	Winn *et al.*, 1975
XIII-2 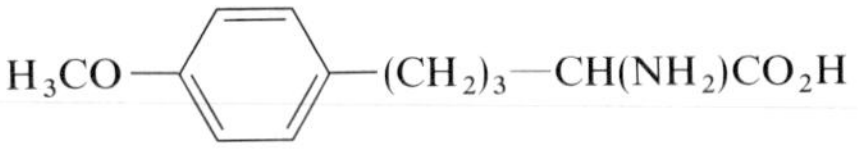 2-Amino-5-(4-methoxyphenyl)pentanoic acid	Shimohigashi *et al.*, 1976, 1977
XIII-3 $C_6H_5(CH_2)_nCH(NH_2)CO_2H$ $n = 2, 3$ 2-Amino-*ω*-phenylalkanoic acids	Greenstein and Winitz, 1961
XIII-4 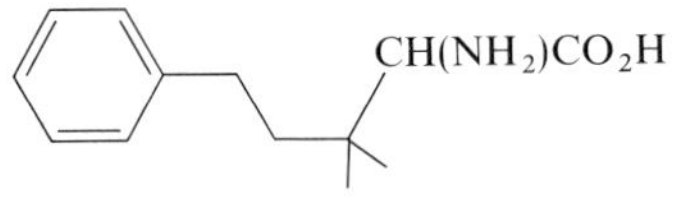 2-Amino-3,3-dimethyl-5-phenylpentanoic acid	Horner and Schwahn, 1955
XIII-5 $PhCH{=}CH—CH(NH_2)CO_2H$ 2-Amino-4-phenyl-3-butenoic acid (styrylglycine)	Hines *et al.*, 1976

(continued)

Structure and name	References
XIII-6 $C_6H_5O(CH_2)_nCH(NH_2)CO_2H$ $n = 2, 3$ 2-Amino-ω-phenoxyalkanoic acids	Greenstein and Winitz, 1961
XIII-7 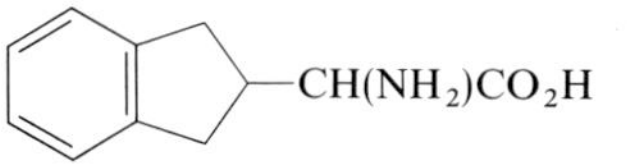 α-(2-Indanyl)glycine	Porter and Shive, 1968
XIII-8 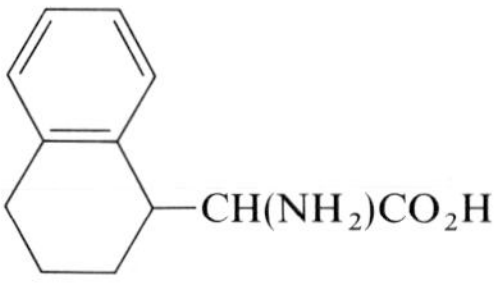 α-(1-Tetralyl)glycine	Reimann and Voss, 1977; Milkowski *et al.*, 1970
XIII-9 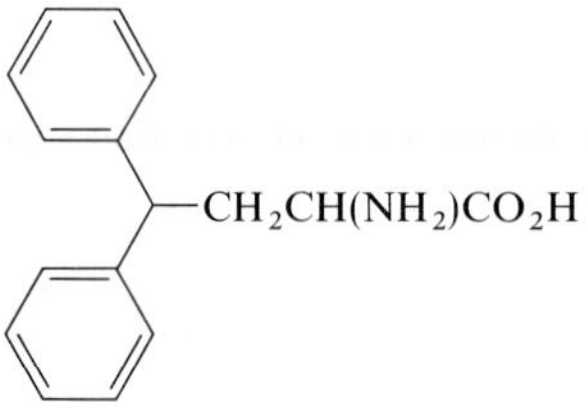 Benzhydrylalanine	Nestor *et al.*, 1982a
XIII-10 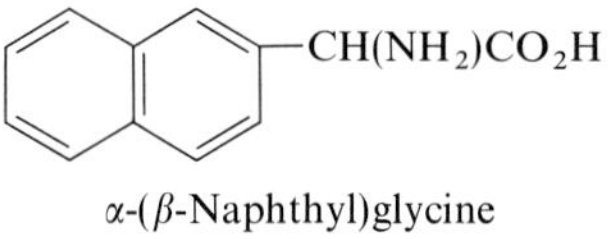 α-(β-Naphthyl)glycine	Compere and Weinstein, 1977; Ben-Ishai *et al.*, 1975a
XIII-11 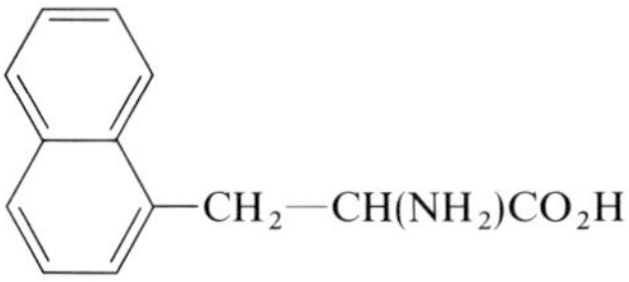 3-(1-Naphthyl)alanine	Yabe *et al.*, 1976, 1977, 1978; Nestor *et al.*, 1982a
XIII-12 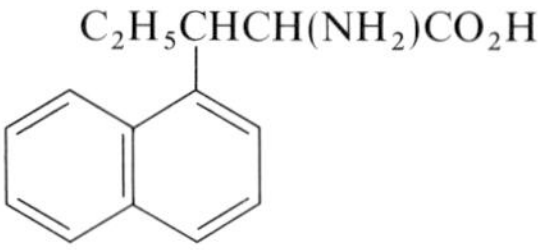 2-Amino-3-(1-naphthyl)pentanoic acid	Horner and Schwahn, 1955

	Structure and name	References
XIII-13	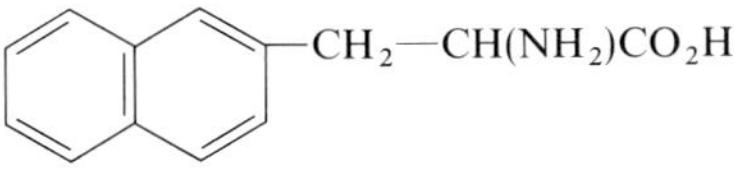 3-(2-Naphthyl)alanine	Yabe *et al.*, 1976, 1977, 1978; Berger *et al.*, 1973
XIII-14	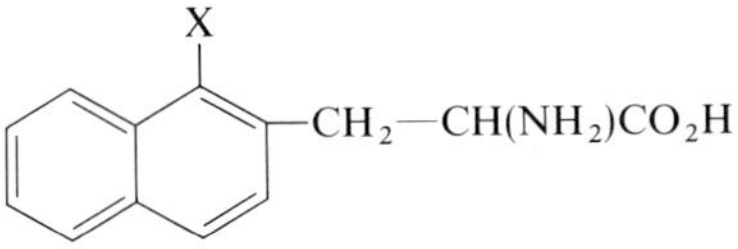 3-(1-Chloro-2-naphthyl)alanine, also the bromo derivative:	McCord *et al.*, 1976 see also Nestor *et al.*, 1982a
XIII-15	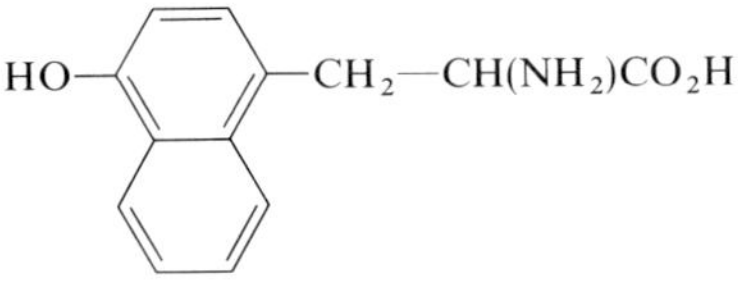 3-(4-Hydroxy-1-naphthyl)alanine	Tsou *et al.*, 1966
XIII-16	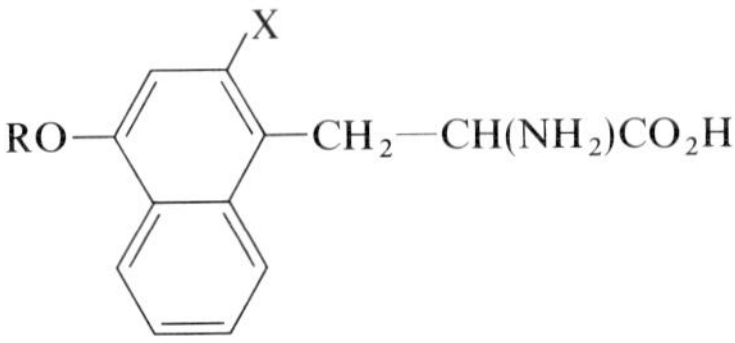 Various substituted 3-(1-naphthyl)alanines R = H, X = H; R = Me, X = H; R = H, X = Cl; R = Me, X = Cl	Ablewhite and Wooldridge, 1967
XIII-17	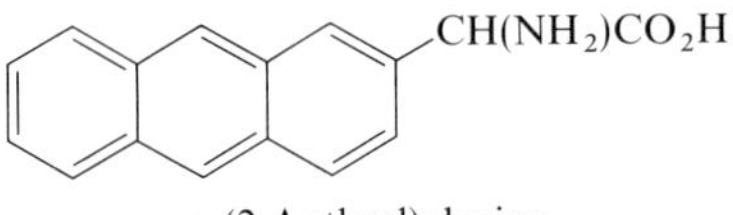 α-(2-Anthryl)glycine	Ben-Ishai *et al.*, 1975a
XIII-18	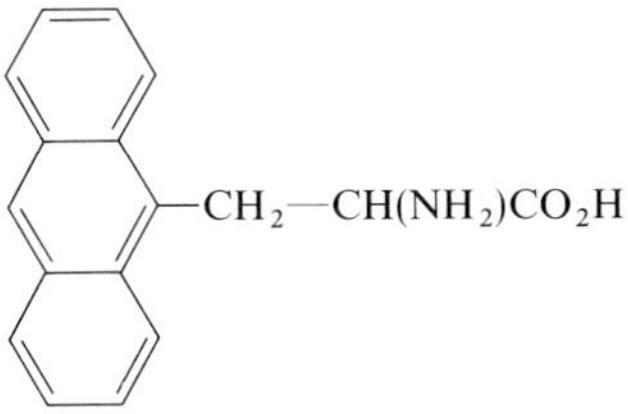 β-(9-Anthryl)alanine	Schreiber and Lautsch, 1965; Nestor *et al.*, 1982a

(continued)

	Structure and name	References

XIII-19

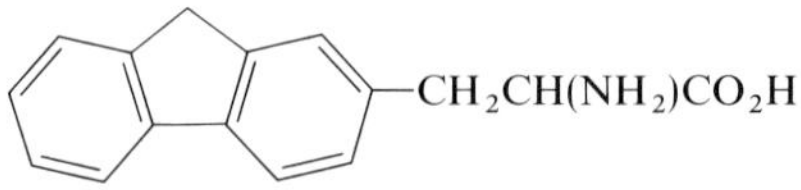

3-(2-Fluorenyl)alanine

Nestor *et al.*, 1982a

XIII-20

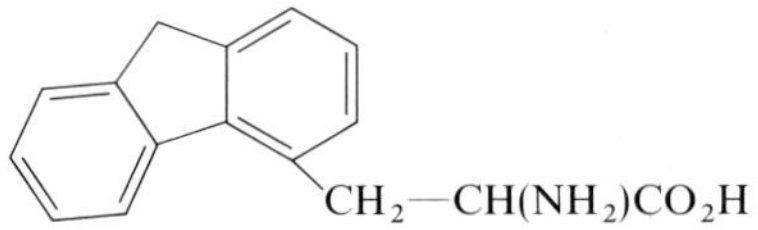

3-(4-Fluorenyl)alanine

Morrison, 1965

XIII-21

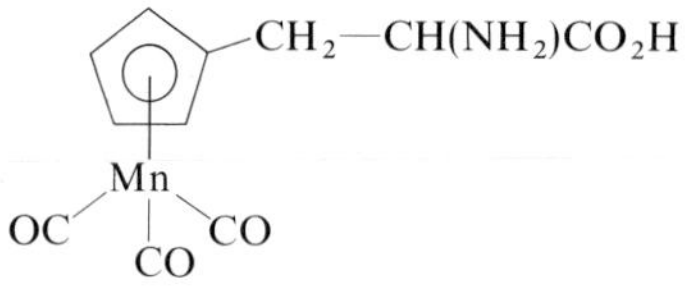

2-Amino-2-carboxyethylcyclopentadienyl manganese tricarbonyl

Brunet *et al.*, 1981a

XIII-22

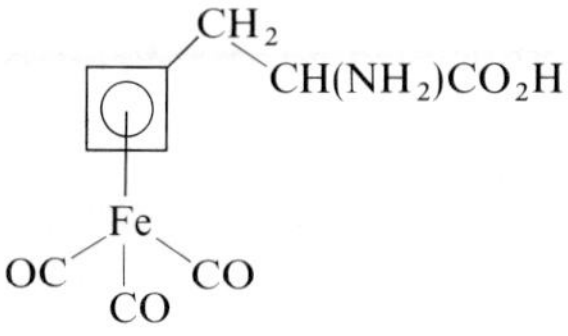

2-Amino-2-carboxyethylcyclobutadiene iron tricarbonyl

Brunet *et al.*, 1981a

XIII-23

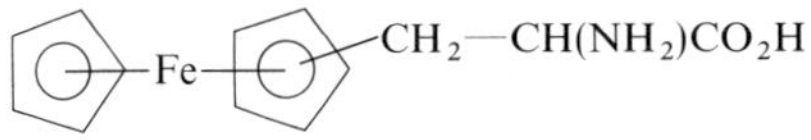

β-Ferrocenylalanine

Pospíšek *et al.*, 1980; Cuingnet *et al.*, 1980; Hanzlik *et al.*, 1979; Osgerby and Pauson, 1958.

XIII-24 $(B_{10}C_2H_{11})CH_2CH(NH_2)CO_2H$

β-*o*-Carboranylalanine

Schwyzer *et al.*, 1981; Fauchère *et al.*, 1979; Leukart *et al.*, 1976

See also structures IV-12, 16, 23; V-32, 34, 35; VI-6; VII-12; IX-11, 13, 18–23; XIV-37–41, 49; XVI-18; XIX-11, 12

Heterocyclic: imino acids, including proline analogs (XIV)

Substituted prolines

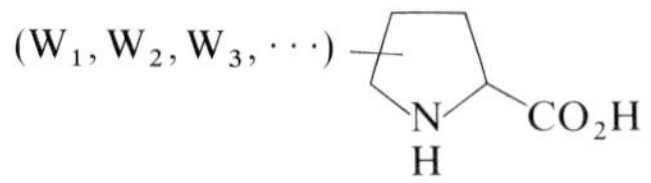

Structure and name	References
XIV-1 W = 3-Me	Mauger *et al.*, 1966
XIV-2 W = 4-Me	Dalby *et al.*, 1962
XIV-3 W = 5-Me	Overberger *et al.*, 1972
XIV-4 W = 4,4-di-Me	Shirota *et al.*, 1977a
XIV-5 W = 4-F	Gerig and McLeod, 1973
XIV-6 W = 4,4-di-F	Shirota *et al.*, 1977a
XIV-7 W = 4-Br	Wieland *et al.*, 1977b
XIV-8 W = 4-Cl; 4-Br; 4-NH_2	Andreatta *et al.*, 1967
XIV-9 W = 3,4-Dehydro	Dormoy *et al.*, 1980; Scott *et al.*, 1980, Fisher *et al.*, 1978; Moore *et al.*, 1977a; Corbella *et al.*, 1969; Robertson and Witkop, 1962
XIV-10 W = 3,4-Dehydro; 4-OH; 4-Me	Felix *et al.*, 1973; McGee *et al.*, 1973
XIV-11 W = 4-Methylene	Bethell and Kenner, 1965; Burgstahler *et al.*, 1964; Wittig *et al.*, 1958
XIV-12 W = 4-SH	Eswarakrishnan and Field, 1981
XIV-13 W = 4-S-*p*-OMe-Bzl	Verbiscar and Witkop, 1970
XIV-14 W = 4-CH_2OH	Bethell *et al.*, 1963; Burgstahler and Aiman, 1962; Bethell and Kenner, 1965
XIV-15 W = 3-OH	Philip and Robertson, 1977; Irreverre *et al.*, 1962; Ogle *et al.*, 1962; Sheehan and Whitney, 1962
XIV-16 W = 4-OH	Lee and Kaneko, 1973a; Hara *et al.*, 1981
XIV-17 W = 3-OH, 5-Me	Mauger and Stuart, 1977

(continued)

Structure and name	References
XIV-18 W = 3,4-di-OH	Kahl and Wieland, 1981; Adams, 1976; Hudson *et al.*, 1968, 1975
XIV-19 W = 3-OPh	Haeusler and Schmidt, 1979
XIV-20 W = 3,4-Epoxy	Hudson *et al.*, 1968, 1975
XIV-21 W = 2-NH_2; 5-NH_2	Gallina *et al.*, 1970
XIV-22 W = 3-$NHCO_2R$	Haeusler, 1981
XIV-23 W = 4-CN-5-Me-5-CO_2H; 4-CO_2Me-5-Me-5-CO_2H	Casella *et al.*, 1979
XIV-24 W = 4-CO_2H-5-*p*-HOC_6H_4	Belokon *et al.*, 1977
XIV-25 W = 4-Adeninyl, guaninyl, hypoxanthinyl	Kaspersen and Pandit, 1975
XIV-26 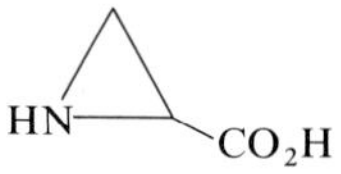 2-Aziridinecarboxylic acid	Okawa *et al.*, 1982; Okawa and Nakajima, 1981; Nakajima *et al.*, 1978; Harada and Nakamura, 1978
XIV-27 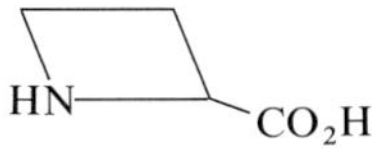 2-Azetidinecarboxylic acid	Barber *et al.*, 1979; Vičar *et al.*, 1977; Felix *et al.*, 1973; McGee *et al.*, 1973
XIV-28 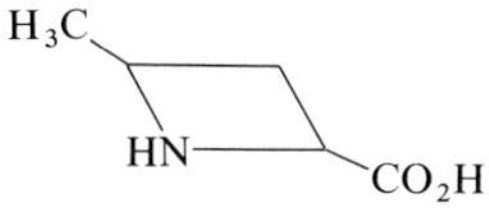 4-Methyl-2-azetidinecarboxylic acid	Soriano *et al.*, 1980
XIV-29 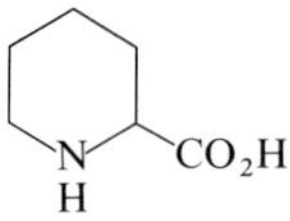 Pipecolic acid	Balaspiri *et al.*, 1972; Neubert *et al.*, 1972

Structure and name	References
XIV-30 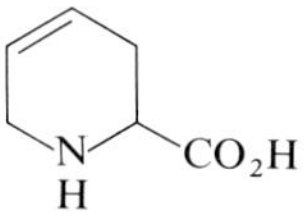 1,2,3,6-Tetrahydropicolinic acid	Greenstein and Winitz, 1961
XIV-31 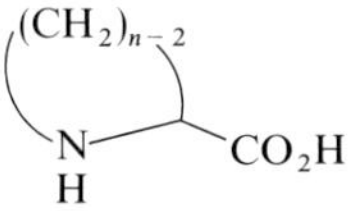 Various azacycloalkane-2-carboxylic acids $n = 7, 8, 9, 10, 11$ $n = 12, 13, 14, 15$	Nagasawa *et al.*, 1971; Nagasawa and Elberling, 1966 Elberling and Nagasawa, 1972
XIV-32 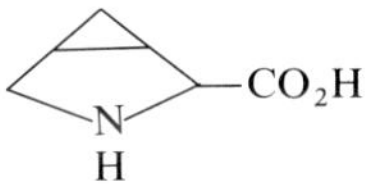 3,4-Methyleneproline (5-azabicyclo[3.1.0]hexane-4-carboxylic acid)	Fujimoto *et al.*, 1971
XIV-33 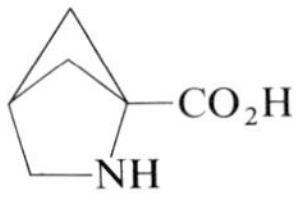 2,4-Methyleneproline (5-azabicyclo[2.1.1]hexane-1-carboxylic acid)	Hughes *et al.*, 1980; Pirrung, 1980
XIV-34 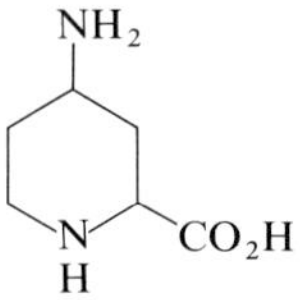 4-Aminopipecolic acid	Schenk and Schütte, 1961
XIV-35 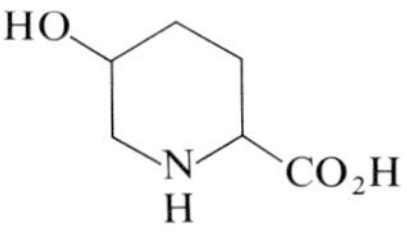 5-Hydroxypipecolic acid	Greenstein and Winitz, 1961

(continued)

	Structure and name	References
XIV-36	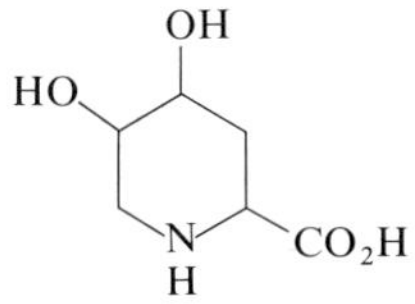 4,5-Dihydroxypipecolic acid	Marlier *et al.*, 1972
XIV-37	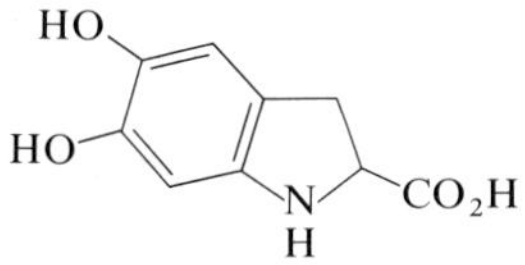 5,6-Dihydroxy-2,3-dihydroindole-2-carboxylic acid	Büchi and Kamikawa, 1977; Wyler and Chiovini, 1968
XIV-38	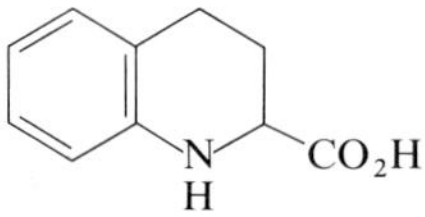 1,2,3,4-Tetrahydroquinoline-2-carboxylic acid	Zecchini and Paradisi, 1979
XIV-39	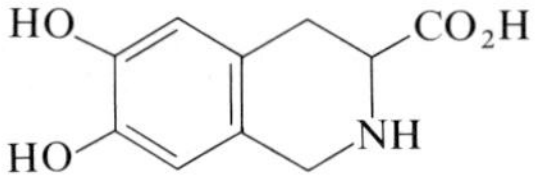 6,7-Dihydroxy-1,2,3,4-tetrahydroisoquinoline-3-carboxylic acid	Bell *et al.*, 1971
XIV-40	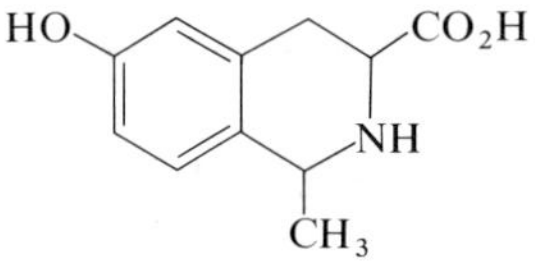 6-Hydroxy-1-methyl-1,2,3,4-tetrahydroisoquinoline-3-carboxylic acid	Müller and Schütte, 1968
XIV-41	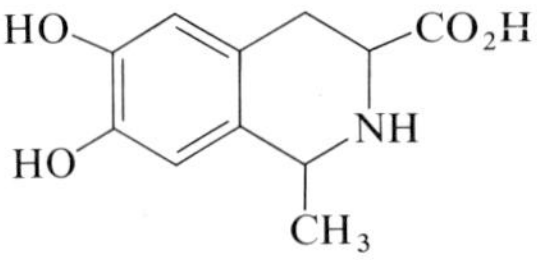 6,7-Dihydroxy-1-methyl-1,2,3,4-tetrahydroisoquinoline-3-carboxylic acid	Daxenbichler *et al.*, 1972

Structure and name	References
XIV-42 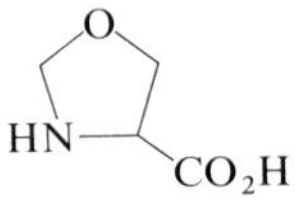 1,3-Oxazolidine-4-carboxylic acid	Wolfe *et al.*, 1979
XIV-43 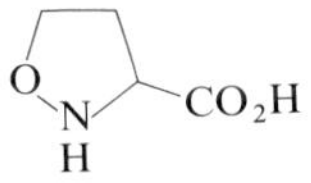 1,2-Oxazolidine-3-carboxylic acid	Vasella and Voeffray, 1981
XIV-44 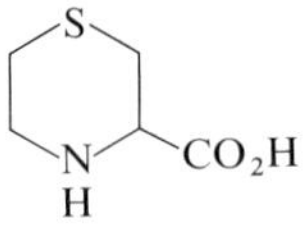 Perhydro-1,4-thiazine-3-carboxylic acid	Daebritz and Virtanen, 1965; Carson and Wong, 1964
XIV-45 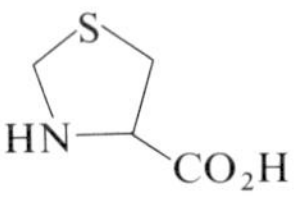 Thiazolidine-4-carboxylic acid	Barber and Jones, 1977; Felix *et al.*, 1973; McGee *et al.*, 1973; Ratner and Clark, 1937
XIV-46 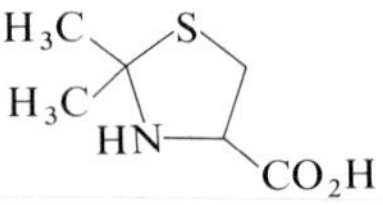 2,2-Dimethylthiazolidine-4-carboxylic acid	Sheehan and Yang, 1958
XIV-47 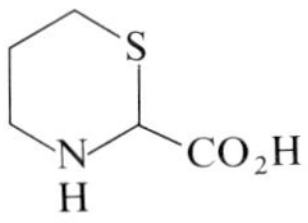 Perhydro-1,3-thiazine-2-carboxylic acid	Foppoli *et al.*, 1980
XIV-48 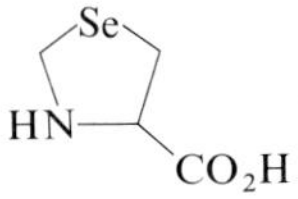 Selenazolidine-4-carboxylic acid	DeMarco *et al.*, 1977

(continued)

	Structure and name	References
XIV-49	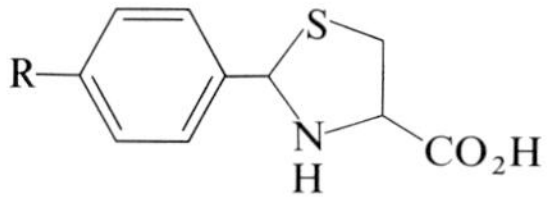 2-Phenyl- and 2-(*p*-tolyl)thiazolidine-4-carboxylic acid R = H, Me	Szilagyi and Gyorgydeak, 1979
XIV-50	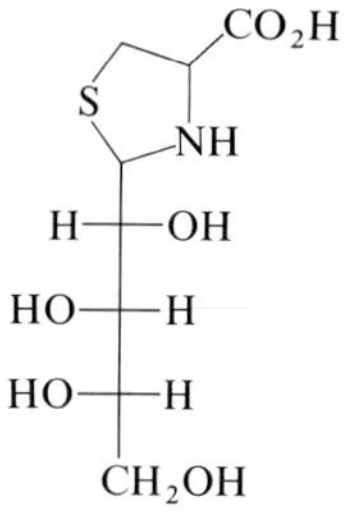 Arabinose cysteine thioaminal	Bognar *et al.*, 1976
XIV-51	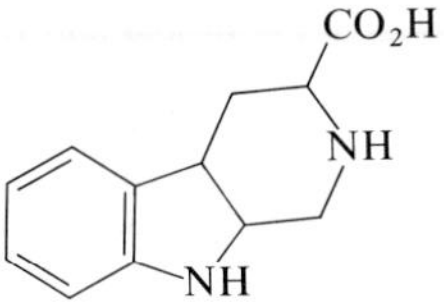 1,2,3,4,4*a*,9*a*-Hexahydro-*β*-carboline-3-carboxylic acid	Yabe *et al.*, 1978
XIV-52	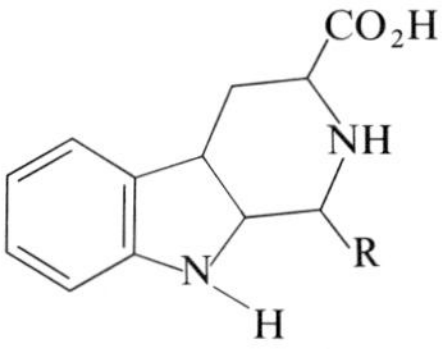 1-(4-Dimethylaminophenyl)-1,2,3,4,4*a*,9*a*-hexahydro-*β*-carboline-3-carboxylic acid R = 4-$Me_2NC_6H_4$	Pindur, 1978
XIV-53	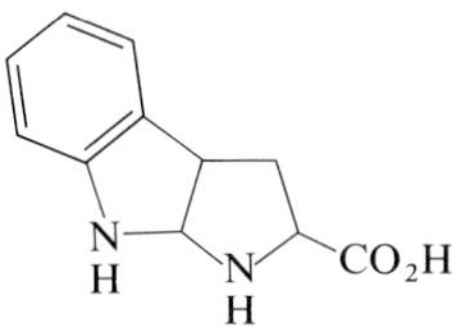 2,3,3*a*,8*a*-Tetrahydropyrrolo(2,3*b*)indole-2-carboxylic acid	Taniguchi and Hino, 1981; Nakagawa *et al.*, 1981

Structure and name	References
XIV-54 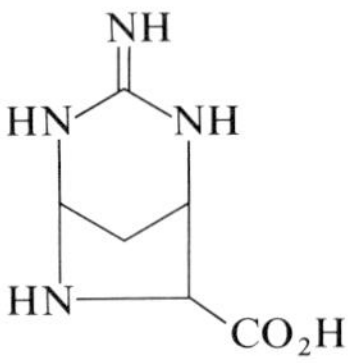 6-Imino-2,5,7-triazabicyclo[3.2.1]octane-3 carboxylic acid	Wakamiya *et al.*, 1981
Heterocyclic: pyridine-derived (XV)	
3-(Pyridyl)alanines (some references also to *N*-oxides)	
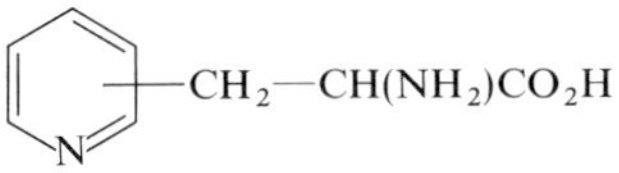	
XV-1 2-Pyridyl	Veselova and Chaman, 1973: Sullivan *et al.*, 1968; Watanabe *et al.*, 1968
XV-2 3-Pyridyl	Voskuyl-Holtkamp and Schattenkerk, 1979; Sullivan *et al.*, 1968
XV-3 4-Pyridyl	Hoes *et al.*, 1979; Sullivan *et al.*, 1968
Substituted pyridylalanines	
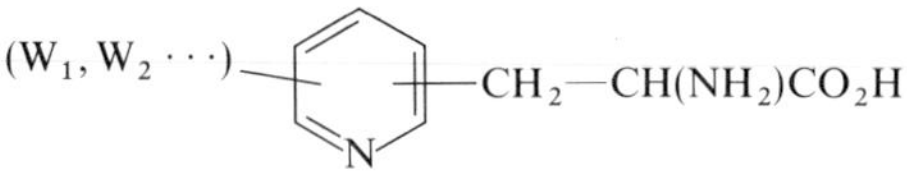	
XV-4 W = 2-Br-3, 4-, 5-, or 6-pyridyl; 2-Cl- 3-, 4-, 5-, or 6-pyridyl	Sullivan and Norton, 1971
XV-5 W = 2-F-3-, 5-, or 6-pyridyl; 1,2-di-hydro-2-oxo-3-, 4-, 5-, or 6-pyridyl	Sullivan *et al.*, 1971
XV-6 W = 5-OH-2-pyridyl	Norton *et al.*, 1961
XV-7 W = 4,5-di-OH-2-pyridyl	Norton and Sanders, 1967
XV-8 W = 5-OH-6-I-2-pyridyl	Norton and Sullivan, 1970

(continued)

Structure and name	References
XV-9 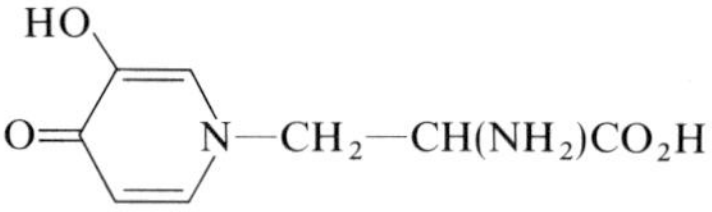 3-(3-Hydroxy-4-oxo-1,4-dihydro-1-pyridyl)alanine analogs	Harris, 1976a; Spencer and Notation, 1962 Harris and Teitei, 1977
XV-10 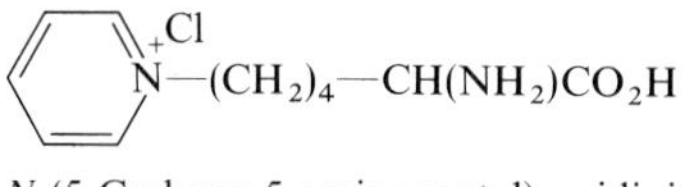 *N*-(5-Carboxy-5-aminopentyl)pyridinium chloride	Hardy *et al.*, 1976
XV-11 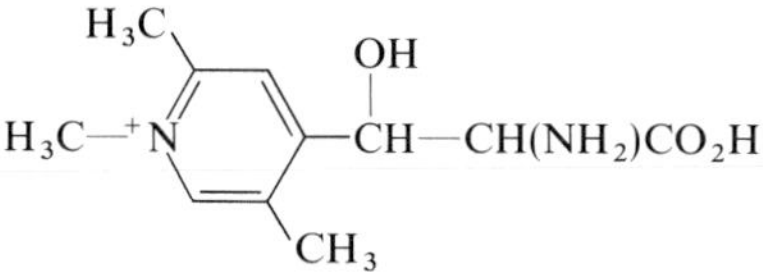 1,2,5-Trimethyl-4-(2-amino-2-carboxy-1-hydroxyethyl)pyridinium salt	Thanassi, 1970
XV-12 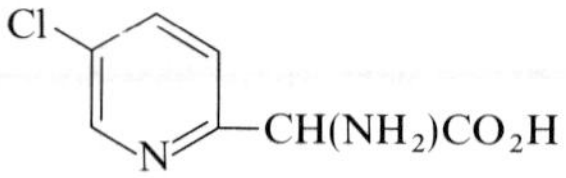 2-(5-Chloro-2-pyridyl)glycine	Edgar *et al.*, 1979
XV-13 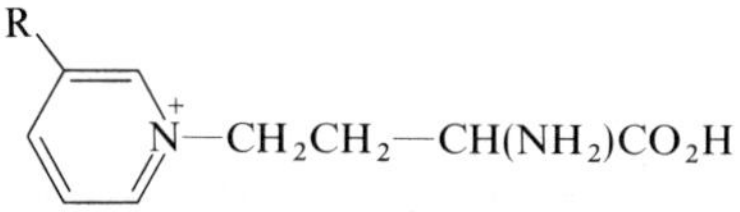 *N*-(3-Amino-3-carboxypropyl)pyridinium salts $R = H, COO^-$	Noguchi *et al.*, 1968
See also structure V-11	
Heterocyclic: 3-azolylalanines and related compounds (XVI)	
XVI-1 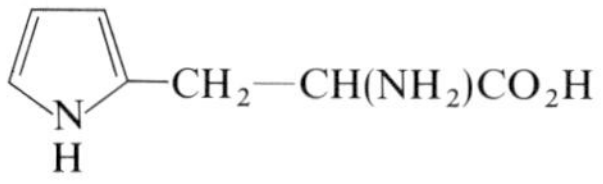 3-(2-Pyrryl)alanine	Hanck and Kutscher, 1964
XVI-2 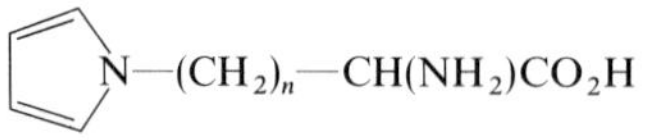 $n = 1, 2, 3$ 2-Amino-ω-(1-pyrryl)alkanoic acids	Poduška *et al.*, 1969

Structure and name	References
Substituted histidines	
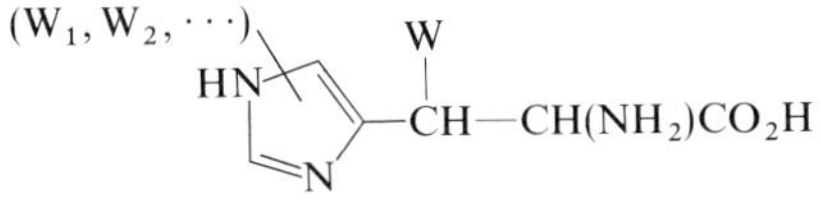	
XVI-3 W = β-Me; β-Et; β-*n*-hexyl	Kelley *et al.*, 1977
XVI-4 W = 4-NO_2; 4-Me; 2-Me	Trout, 1972
XVI-5 W = 4-F	Kirk and Cohen, 1971
XVI-6 W = β-OH	Hecht *et al.*, 1979
XVI-7 W = 2-F; 2-NH_2; 2—N═N—$C_6H_4\beta$r	Nagai *et al.*, 1973
XVI-8 W = 1-Me-2-NO_2; 1-Me-4-NO_2; 1-Me-5-NO_2	Tautz *et al.*, 1973
XVI-9 W = 2-SH	Greenstein and Winitz, 1961
XVI-10 2-$SCH_2CH(NH_2)CO_2H$	Ito *et al.*, 1981
XVI-11 2-*p*-N═$NPhCO_2H$, 4-*p*-N═$NPhCO_2H$	Montagnoli *et al.*, 1977
XVI-12 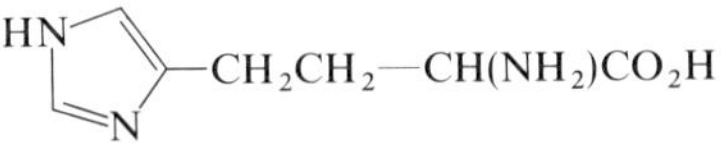 Homohistidine	Bloemhoff and Kerling, 1975
XVI-13 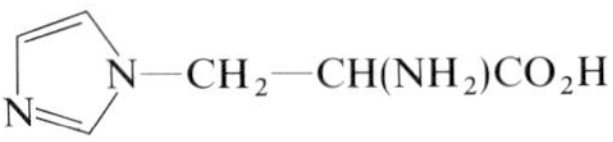 3-(1-Imidazolyl)alanine	Trout, 1972
XVI-14 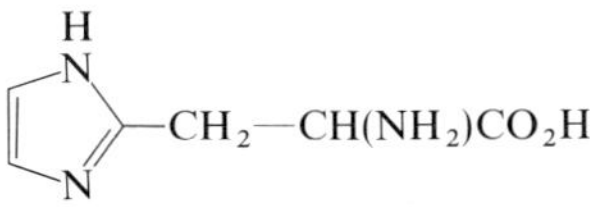 3-(2-Imidazolyl)alanine	Trout, 1972
XVI-15 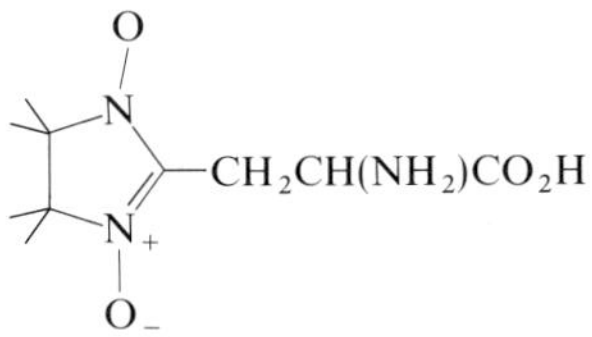 (1,3-Dioxy-4,4,5,5-tetramethylimidazolin-2-yl)alanine	Weinkam and Jorgensen, 1971a,b

(continued)

Structure and name	References
XVI-16 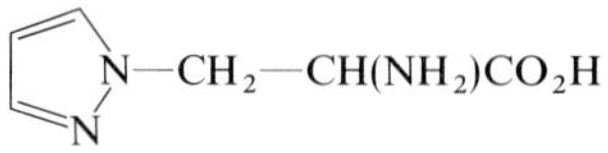 3-(1-Pyrazolyl)alanine	Coy *et al.*, 1975; Murakoshi *et al.*, 1972; Hofmann *et al.*, 1968; Dunnill and Fowden, 1963
XVI-17 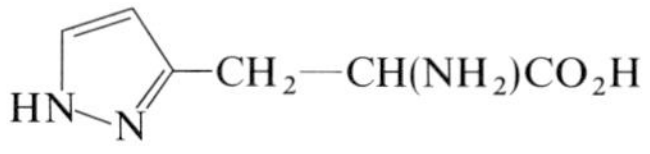 3-(3-Pyrazolyl)alanine	Seeman *et al.*, 1972; Hofmann *et al.*, 1968; Finn and Hofmann, 1967; Hofmann and Bohn, 1966
XVI-18 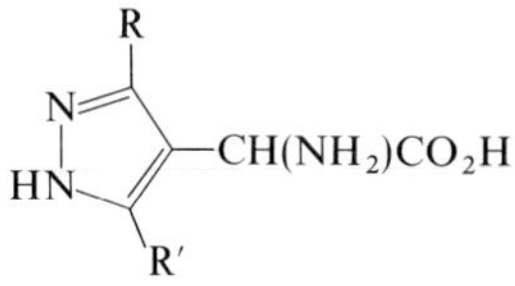 Substituted α-(4-pyrazolyl)glycines R or R′ = Me or Ph	Ben-Ishai *et al.*, 1978
XVI-19 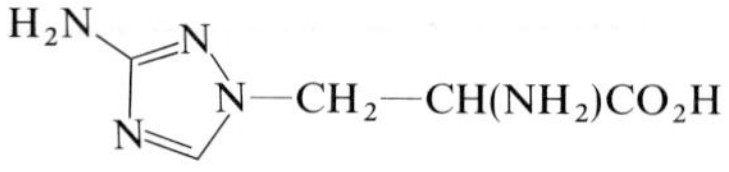 3-(3-Amino-1,2,4-triazol-1-yl)alanine	Murakoshi *et al.*, 1974
XVI-20 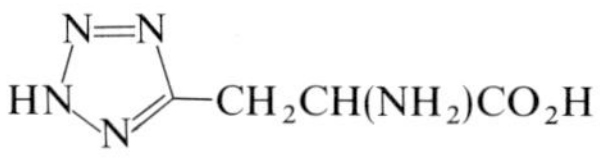 β-(Tetrazol-5-yl)alanine	Morley, 1969
XVI-21 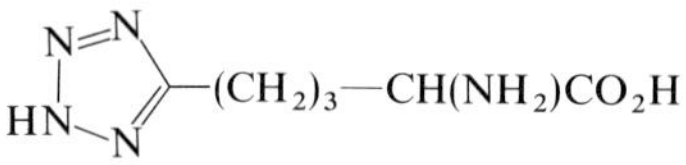 2-Amino-4-(5-tetrazolyl)butanoic acid	Grzonka *et al.*, 1977; Van Thach *et al.*, 1977
Heterocyclic: indolylalanines and other fused hetarylalanines (excluding purines) (XVII)	
Substituted tryptophans	
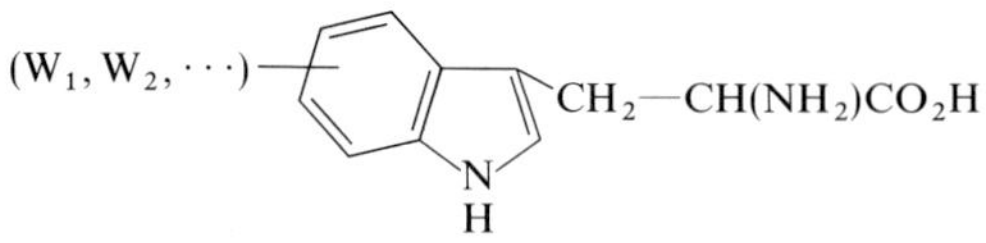	
XVII-1 W = 6-Me	Hengartner *et al.*, 1979
XVII-2 W = 4-F; 5-F; 6-F	Bentov and Roffman, 1969

Structure and name	References
XVII-3 W = 5-F; 6-F; 4,5,6,7-tetra-F	Rajh *et al.*, 1979, 1980
XVII-4 W = 5-Cl	Shiba *et al.*, 1975
XVII-5 W = 6-Cl	Moriya *et al.*, 1975
XVII-6 W = 7-Cl	Van Pee *et al.*, 1981
XVII-7 W = 5-Br; 7-Br	Allen *et al.*, 1980
XVII-8 W = 2-OH	Nakazawa *et al.*, 1972
XVII-9 W = 5-OH	Iriuchijima and Tsuchihashi, 1978
XVII-10 W = 7-OH	Greenstein and Winitz, 1961
XVII-11 W = 2-SR	DaSettimo, 1962; Wieland *et al.*, 1974, 1978
XVII-12 W = 6-NH_2	Goodman *et al.*, 1965
XVII-13 W = 6-$N(CH_2CH_2Cl)_2$; 7-$N(CH_2CH_2Cl)_2$; 5-$N(CH_2CH_2Cl)_2$	Goodman *et al.*, 1965; Barclay *et al.*, 1964
XVII-14 W = 4-NO_2; 7-NO_2	Ohno *et al.*, 1974
XVII-15 W = 4-CO_2H	Greenstein and Winitz, 1961
XVII-16 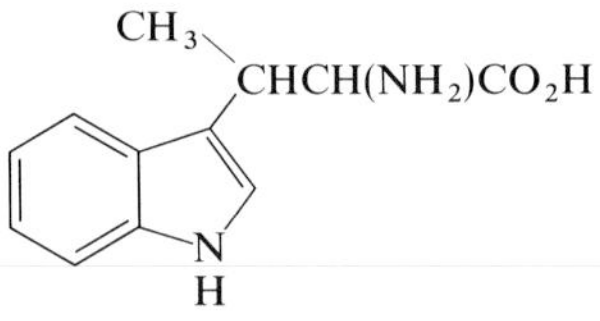 β-Methyltryptophan	Greenstein and Winitz, 1961
XVII-17 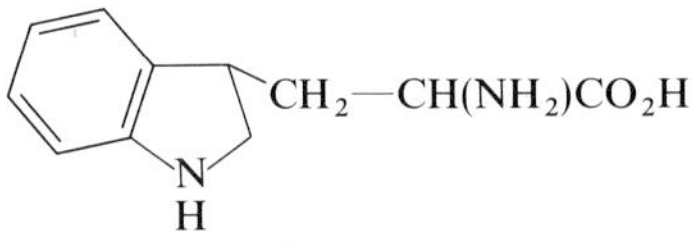 2′,3′-Dihydrotryptophan	Kikugawa *et al.*, 1979; Kikugawa, 1978; Bakhra *et al.*, 1973
XVII-18 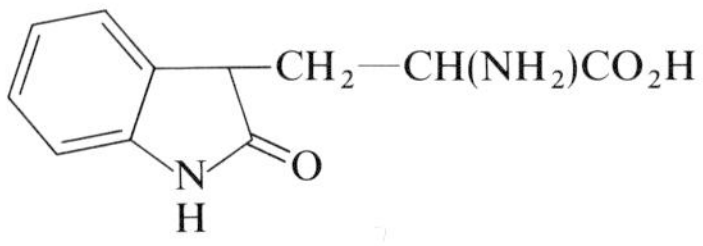 2′-Oxo-2′,3′-dihydrotryptophan	Nakai and Ohta, 1976

(continued)

	Structure and name	References
XVII-19	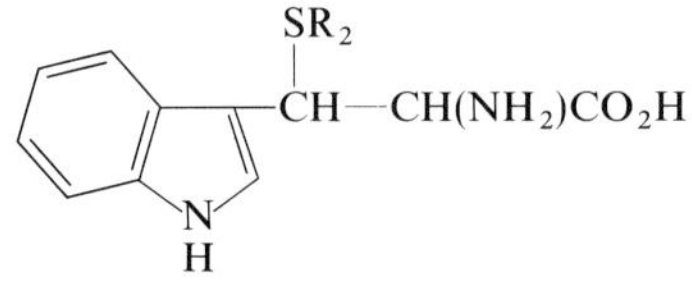 3-Alkylthiotryptophans	Vinograd *et al.*, 1974
XVII-20	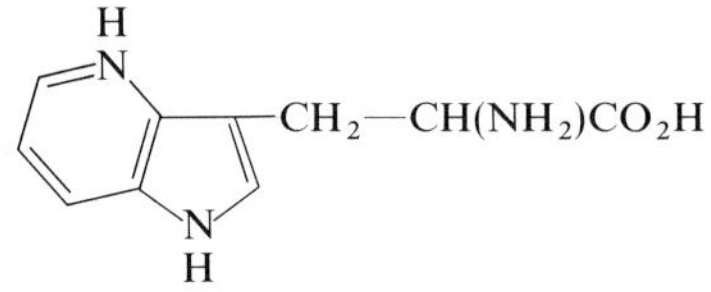 4′-Azatryptophan	Azimov *et al.*, 1968
XVII-21	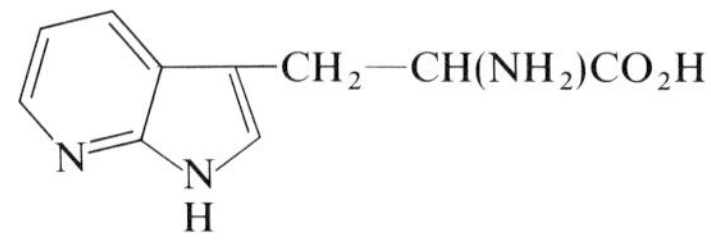 7′-Azatryptophan	Yabe *et al.*, 1976
XVII-22	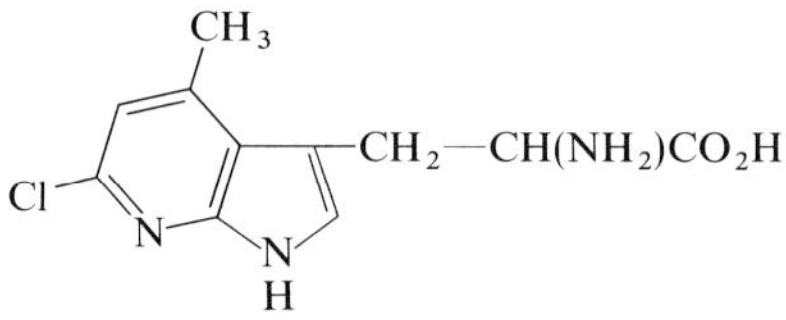 6-Chloro-4-methyl-7-azatryptophan	Azimov *et al.*, 1968
XVII-23	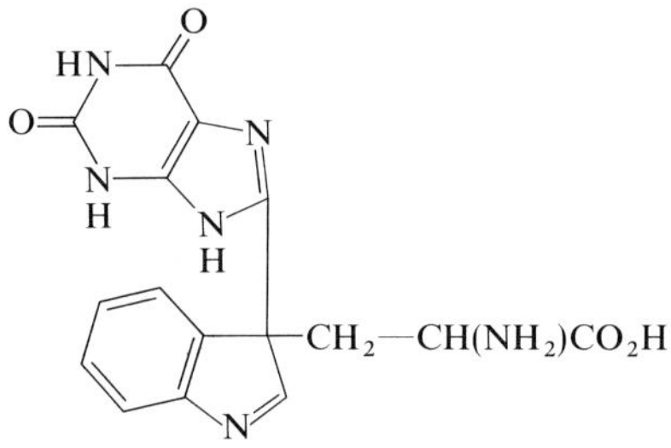 3′-(8-Xanthinyl)-3′*H*-tryptophan	Stöhrer *et al.*, 1973
XVII-24	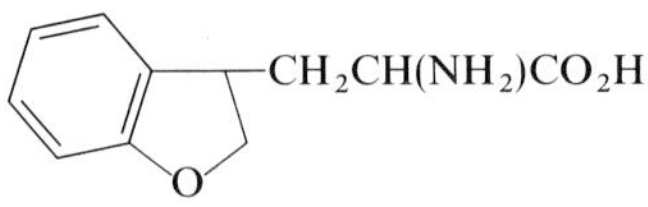 3-(2,3-Dihydrobenzofuran-3-yl)alanine	Rajh *et al.*, 1979

	Structure and name	References
XVII-25	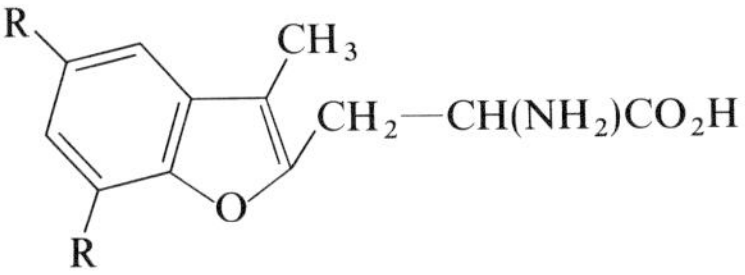 3-(3-Methyl-5,7-dialkylbenzofuran-2-yl)alanines	Sila *et al.*, 1973; Sila, 1964
XVII-26	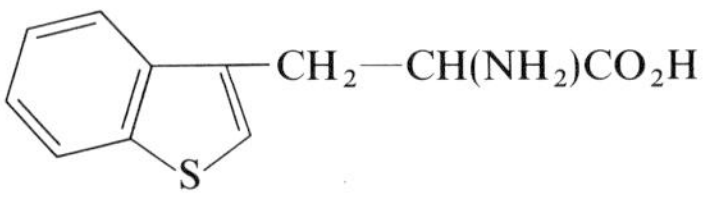 3-(Benzothiophen-3-yl)alanine	Rajh *et al.*, 1979; Yabe *et al.*, 1976
XVII-27	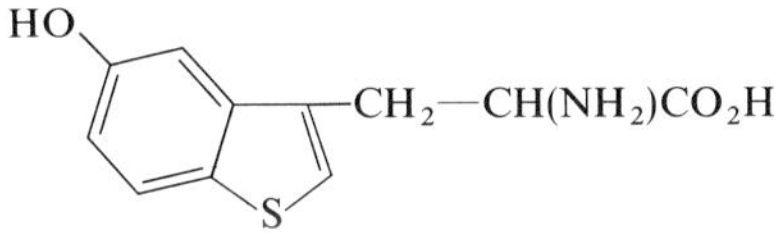 3-(5-Hydroxybenzothiophen-3-yl)alanine	Campaigne and Dinner, 1970
XVII-28	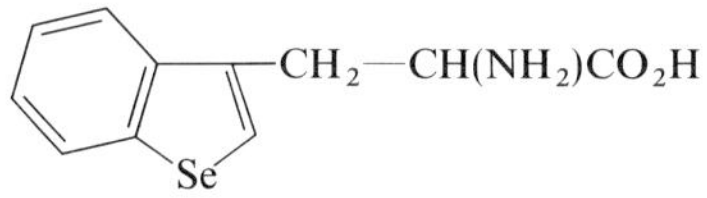 3-(Benzoselenol-3-yl)alanine	Laitem and Christiaens, 1976
XVII-29	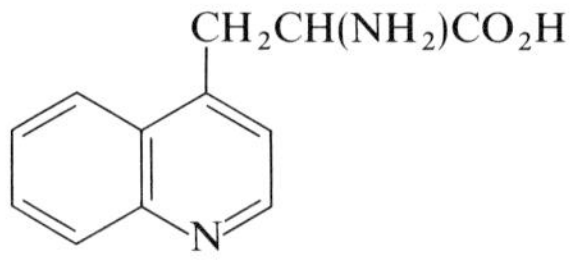 3-(4-Quinolyl)alanine	Greenstein and Winitz, 1961
XVII-30	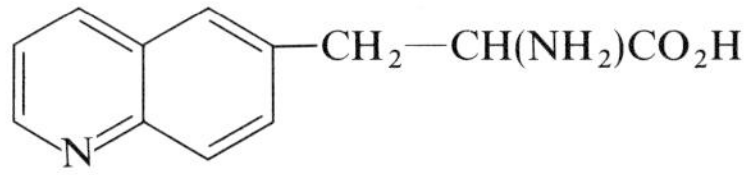 3-(6-Quinolyl)alanine	Berger *et al.*, 1973
XVII-31	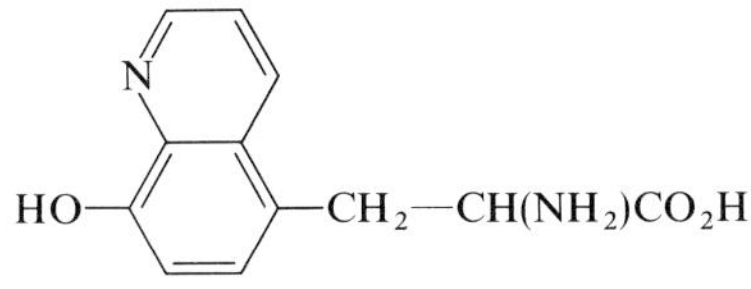 3-(8-Hydroxy-5-quinolyl)alanine	Matsumura *et al.*, 1969

(continued)

	Structure and name	References
XVII-32	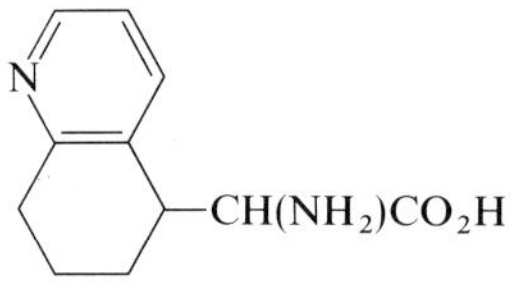 2-(5,6,7,8-Tetrahydroquinol-5-yl)glycine	Reimann and Voss, 1977
XVII-33	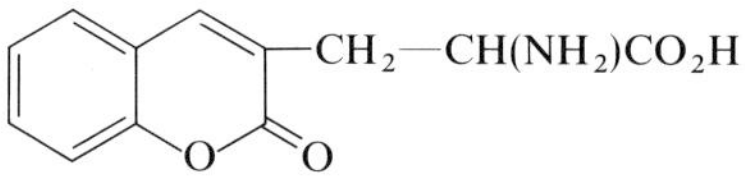 3-(3-Coumarinyl)alanine	Belokon *et al.*, 1977
XVII-34	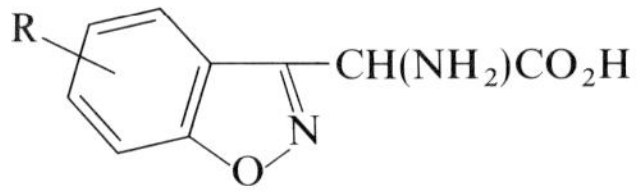 Substituted 2-(benzisoxazol-3-yl)glycines R = H, 5-Me, 6-Me, 7-Me, 5-Br	Giannella *et al.*, 1972
XVII-35	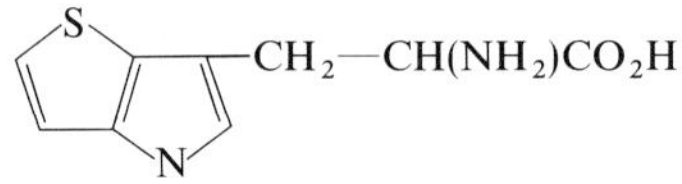 3-(Thieno-[3,2*b*]pyrrol-3-yl)alanine	Humphries *et al.*, 1972
XVII-36	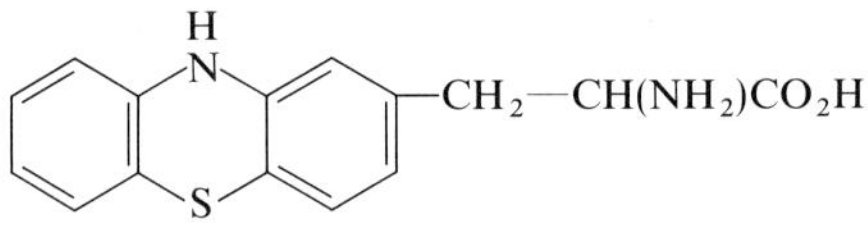 3-(2-Phenothiazinyl)alanine	Fattorusso, 1965
XVII-37	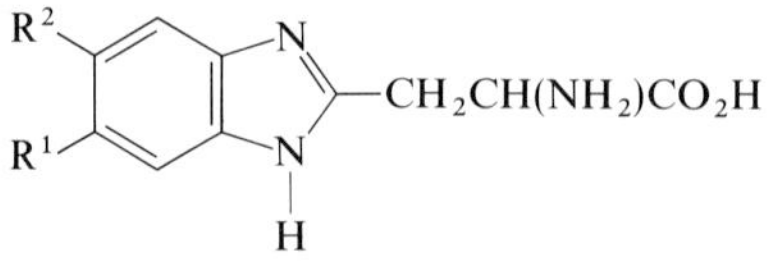 Substituted benzimidazol-2-ylalanines R^1, R^2 = H, H; Cl, Cl; Me, Me; 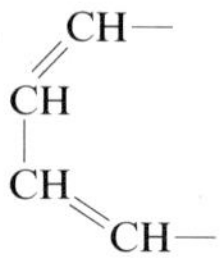	Nestor *et al.*, 1982b

	Structure and name	References
XVII-38	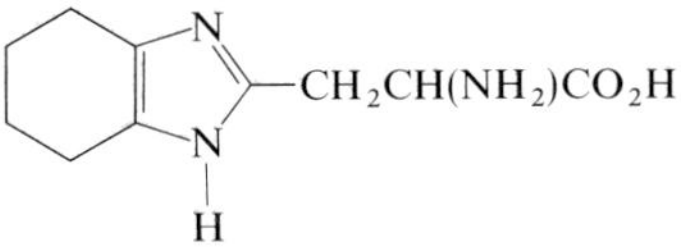 4,5,6,7-Tetrahydrobenzimidazol-2-ylalanine	Nestor *et al.*, 1982b
XVII-39	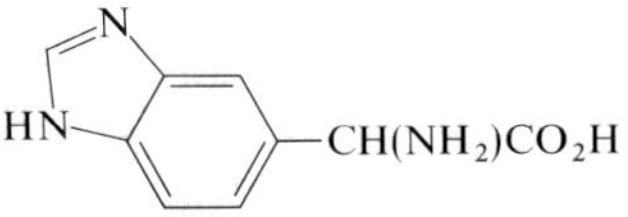 2-(Benzimidazol-5-yl)glycine	Milkowski *et al.*, 1970
XVII-40	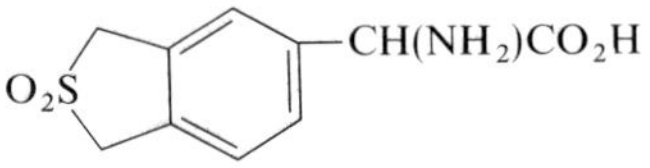 2-(1,3-Dihydro-2,2-dioxoisobenzothiophen-5-yl)glycine	Edwards, 1980
XVII-41	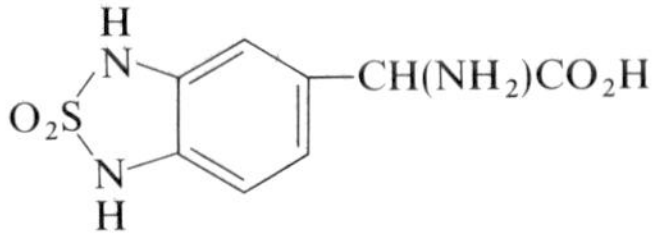 2-(1,3-Dihydro-2,2-dioxo-2,1,3-benzothiadiazol-5-yl)glycine	Edwards, 1980
XVII-42	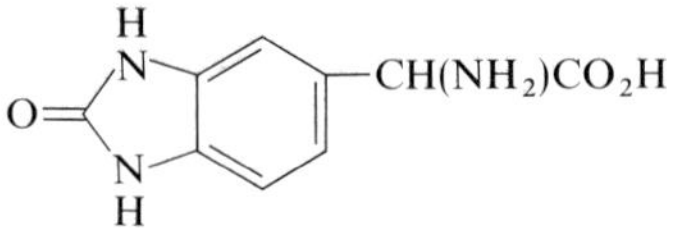 2-(2-Oxobenzimidazol-5-yl)glycine	Edwards, 1980
XVII-43	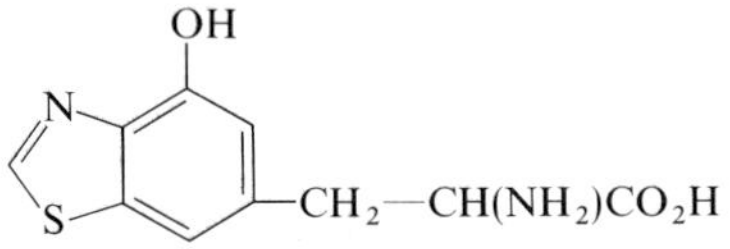 3-(4-Hydroxybenzothiazol-6-yl)alanine	Ismail *et al.*, 1980
XVII-44	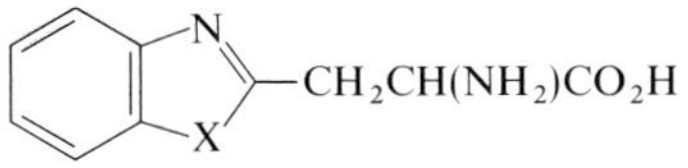 Benzoxazol-2-ylalanines, benzothiazol-2-ylalanines X = O, S	Nestor *et al.*, 1982b

See also structures VII-12; IX-17; XIV-51–53

(continued)

	Structure and name	References
Heterocyclic: purine- and pyrimidine-containing (XVIII)		
XVIII-1	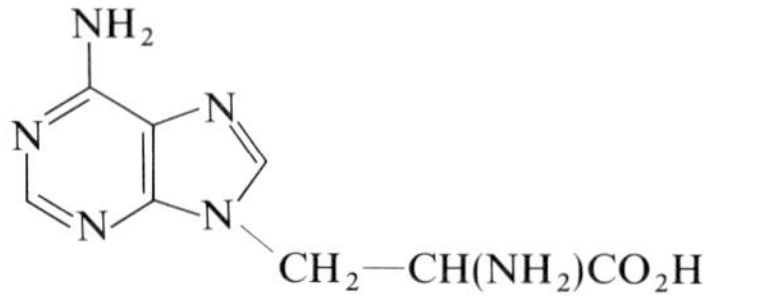 3-(9-Adeninyl)alanine, similar amino acids	Shvachkin and Olsuf'eva, 1979; Draminski and Pitha, 1978; Doel *et al.*, 1969, 1974; Nollet and Pandit, 1969a; Lidaks *et al.*, 1968, 1970, 1971a,b; Nollet *et al.*, 1969
XVIII-2	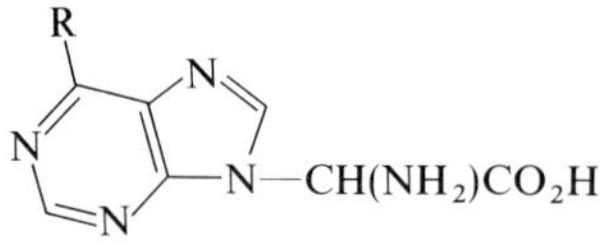 2-(6-Substituted-9-purinyl)glycines R = Cl, NH_2	Nishitani *et al.*, 1979
XVIII-3	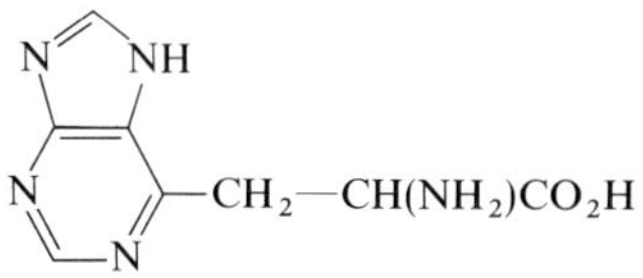 3-(6-Purinyl)alanine	Woenckhaus and Stock, 1965
XVIII-4	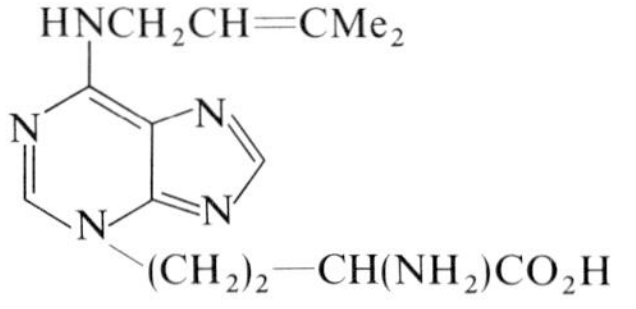 4-(6-(3-methyl-2-butenylamino)-purin-3-yl)-butyrine	Seela and Hasselmann, 1979; Uchiyama and Abe, 1977; for a related structure see also MacLeod *et al.*, 1975
XVIII-5	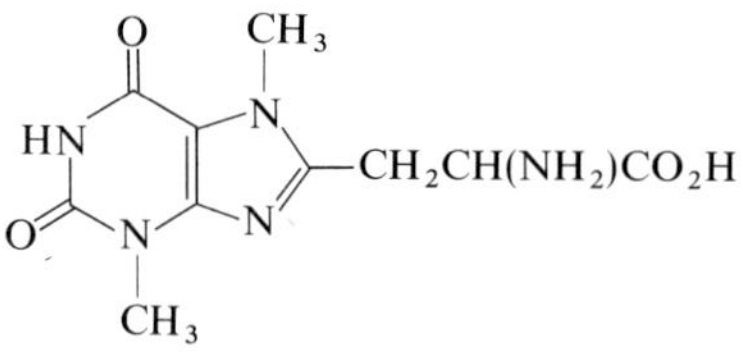 3-(8-Theobrominyl)alanine	Vdovina and Karpova, 1968

Structure and name	References
XVIII-6 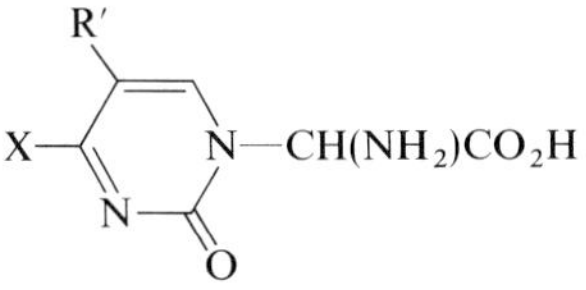 Substituted 2-(1-uracilyl)- and (1-cytosinyl)glycines; X = OH or NH_2; R = H, Me, F	Nishitani *et al.*, 1979
XVIII-7 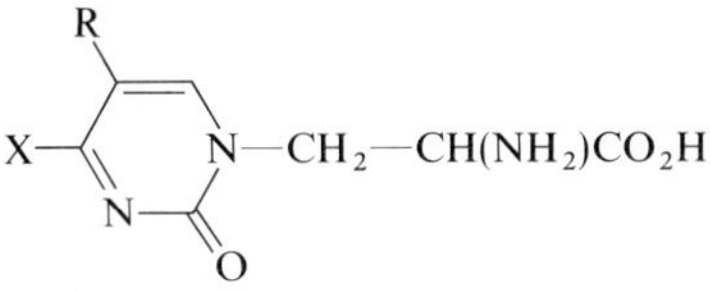 Substituted 3-(1-uracilyl)- and (1-cytosinyl)alanines; X = OH or NH_2; Uridine derivative	Shvachkin and Olsuf'eva, 1979; Draminski and Pitha, 1978; Doel *et al.*, 1969, 1974; Lidaks *et al.*, 1971b; Dewar and Shaw, 1962; Martinez *et al.*, 1968 Ohashi *et al.*, 1974
XVIII-8 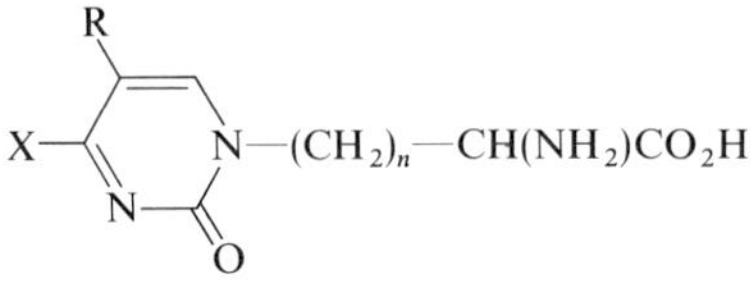 Substituted 2-amino-ω-(1-pyrimidinyl)alkanoic acids; X = OH or NH_2; $n = 2$; X = OH or NH_2; $n = 3, 4, 5$	Nollet and Pandit, 1969b; Tjoeng *et al.*, 1976
XVIII-9 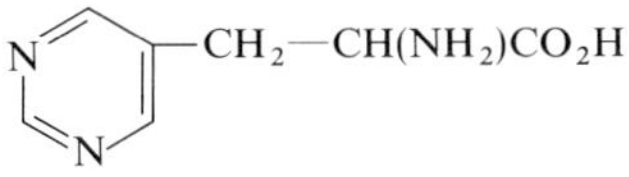 3-(5-Pyrimidinyl)alanine	Haggerty *et al.*, 1965
XVIII-10 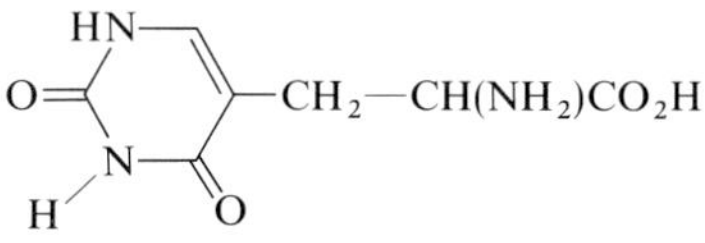 3-(6-Uracilyl)alanine (and others)	Vincze *et al.*, 1968; Springer *et al.*, 1965

(continued)

Structure and name	References
XVIII-11 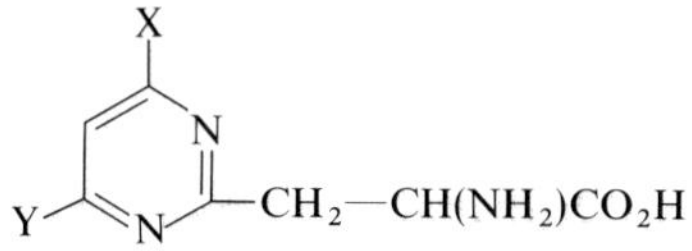 Substituted 3-(2-pyrimidinyl)alanines $X = Cl, Y = NH_2$ $X = OH, Y = H$	Shvachkin and Syrtsova, 1963 Shvachkin *et al.*, 1963a,b
XVIII-12 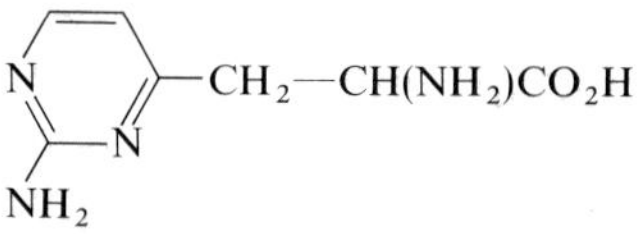 3-(2-Amino-4-pyrimidinyl)alanine	Shvachkin *et al.*, 1968; Whitlock *et al.*, 1965; Shvachkin and Berestenko, 1964
XVIII-13 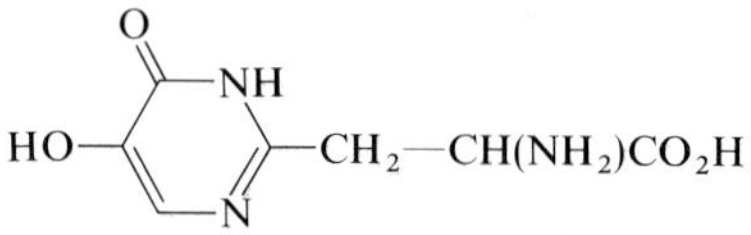 3-(4,5-Dihydroxypyrimidin-2-yl)alanine	Harris, 1976b
XVIII-14 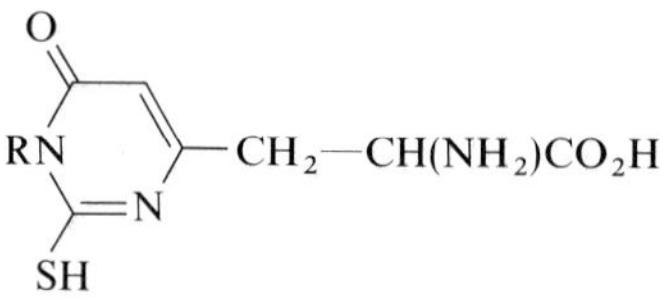 3-(2-Thiouracil-6-yl)alanines	Hong *et al.*, 1968
See also structures VII-28; XII-30; XIV-25; XVII-23	
Heterocyclic: miscellaneous (XIX)	
XIX-1 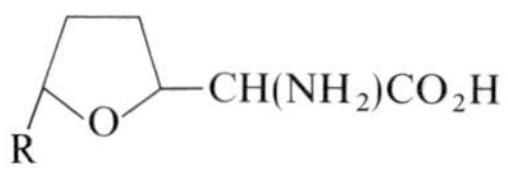 2-(5-Alkyl-2-tetrahydrofuryl)glycines	Ben-Ishai *et al.*, 1976
XIX-2 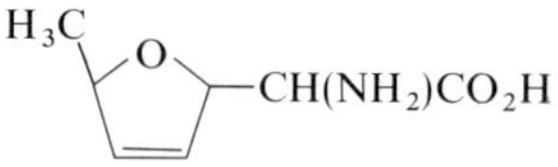 2-(5-Methyl-2,5-dihydro-2-furyl)glycine	Semple *et al.*, 1980; Masamune and Ono, 1975
XIX-3 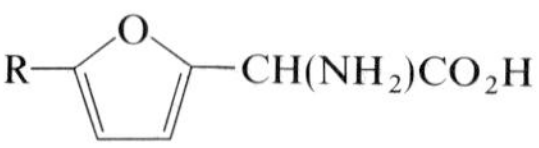 2-(5-Alkyl-2-furyl)glycines	Ben-Ishai *et al.*, 1976

	Structure and name	References
XIX-4	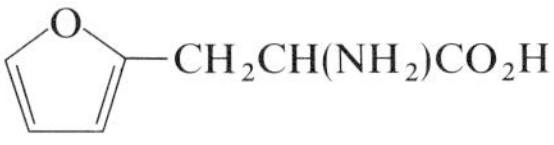 β-(2-Furyl)alanine	Greenstein and Winitz, 1961
XIX-5	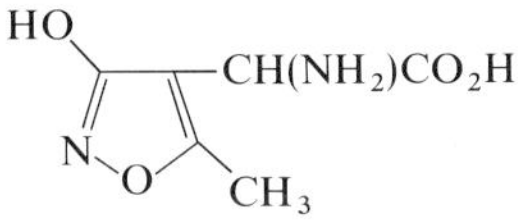 2-(3-Hydroxy-5-methyl-4-isoxazolyl)glycine	Christensen and Larsen, 1978
XIX-6	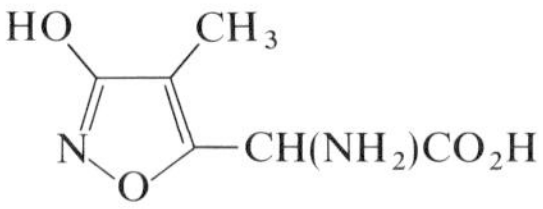 2-(3-Hydroxy-4-methyl-5-isoxazolyl)glycine	Hansen and Krogsgaard-Larsen, 1980
XIX-7	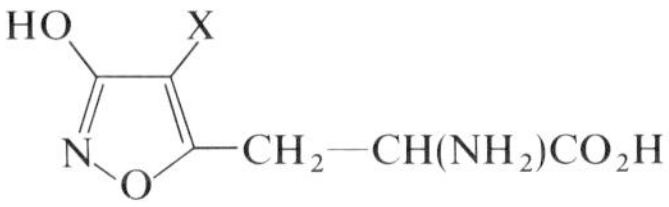 3-(4-Substituted-3-hydroxy-5-isoxazolyl)alanines X = H, Br, Me	Hansen and Krogsgaard-Larsen, 1980
XIX-8	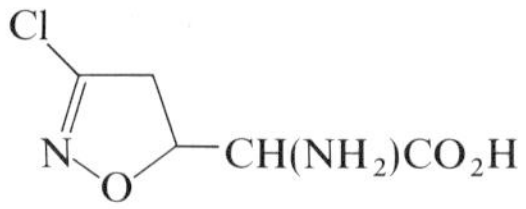 2-(3-Chloro-Δ^2-isoxazolin-5-yl)glycine	Silverman and Holladay, 1981; Kelly *et al.*, 1979; Baldwin *et al.*, 1976
XIX-9	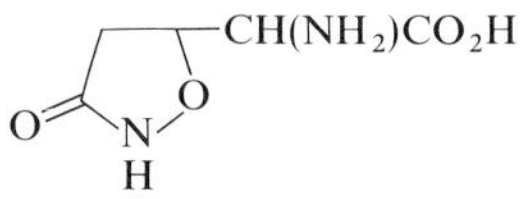 2-(3-Oxo-5-isoxazolidinyl)glycine (tricholomic acid)	Silverman and Holladay, 1981; Iwasaki *et al.*, 1969a,b; Kamiya, 1969
XIX-10	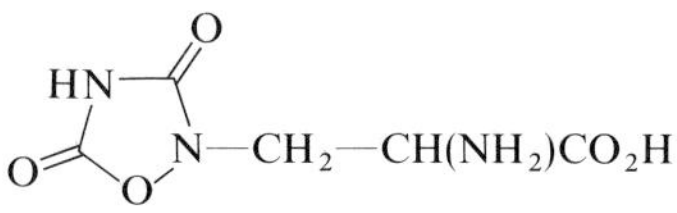 3-(3,5-Dioxo-1,2,4-oxadiazolin-2-yl)alanine	Takemoto *et al.*, 1975

(continued)

Structure and name	References

XIX-11

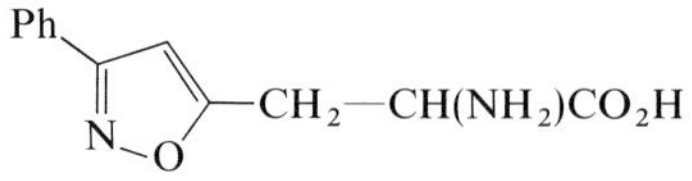

3-(3-Phenyl-5-isoxazolyl)alanine

Vecchio *et al.*, 1963

XIX-12

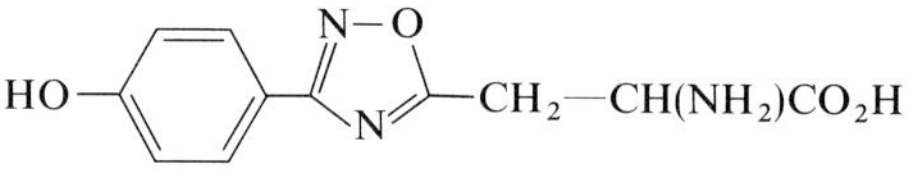

3-(3-(4-Hydroxyphenyl)-1,2,4-oxadiazol-5-yl)alanine

Moussebois *et al.*, 1977

XIX-13

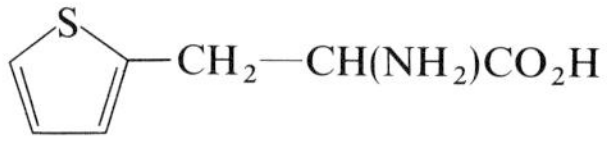

3-(2-Thienyl)alanine

Lipkowski and Flouret, 1980; Smith *et al.*, 1975, 1978; Bellocq *et al.*, 1977; Sievertsson *et al.*, 1973; Dunn and Stewart, 1971; Hill and Dunn, 1969; Dunn, 1963; du Vigneaud *et al.*, 1945

XIX-14

2-(2-Furyl)glycine, 2-(2-thienyl)glycine

X = O, S

Divanfard *et al.*, 1978

XIX-15

2-(2-Thiazolyl)glycine

Hatanaka and Ishimaru, 1973

XIX-16

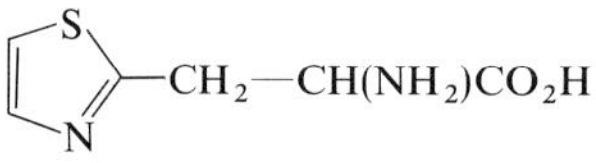

3-(2-Thiazolyl)alanine

Seto *et al.*, 1974

XIX-17

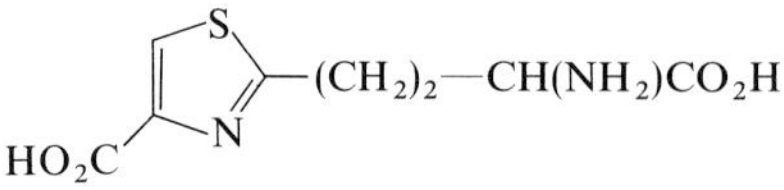

2-Amino-4-(4-carboxy-2-thiazolyl)-butanoic acid

Jadot *et al.*, 1969

Structure and name	References
XIX-18 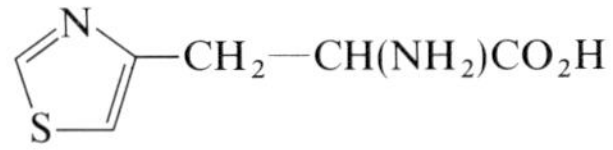 3-(4-Thiazolyl)alanine	Watanabe *et al.*, 1966
See also compounds IV-22 and VII-28	
XIX-19 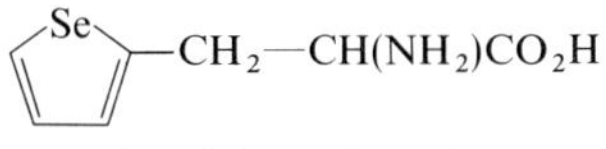 3-(2-Selenolyl)alanine	Frejd *et al.*, 1980; Jacobs and Davis, 1979
XIX-20 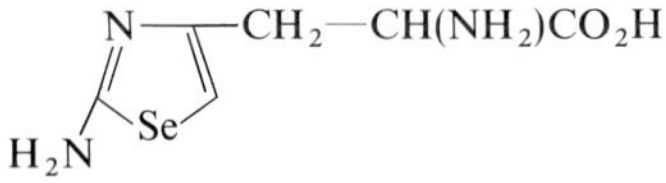 3-(2-Amino-4-selenazolyl)alanine	Hanson and Davis, 1981
See also structures V-33,44–47; VI-23; VII-9, 29; and XIV-42–50	
Heterocyclic: carbohydrate-containing (XX)	
XX-1 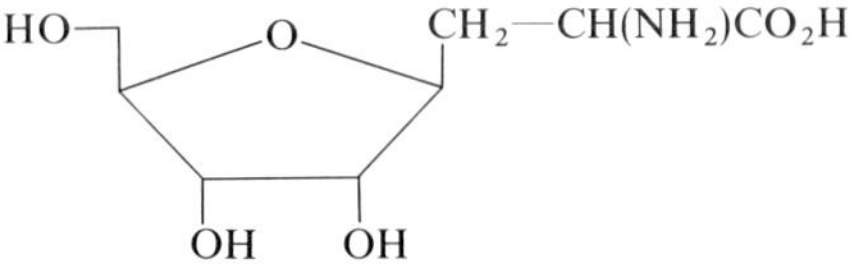 3-(*β*-Ribofuranosyl)alanine, other carbohydrate containing amino acids	Rosenthal and Brink, 1976b; Divanfard *et al.*, 1978; Rosenthal and Dooley, 1978; Rosenthal and Ratcliffe, 1977; Rosenthal and Brink, 1976a; Bischofberger *et al.*, 1975; Kum, 1969
See also structures IV-19; V-21; and XIV-50	

REFERENCES

Ablewhite, A. J., and Wooldridge, K. R. H. (1967). *J. Chem. Soc.* C pp. 2488–2491.
Abshire, C. J., and Planet, G. (1972). *J. Med. Chem.* **15**, 226–229.
Ackermann, W. W., and Shive, W. (1948). *J. Biol. Chem.* **175**, 867–870.
Adams, E. (1976). *Int. J. Pept. Protein Res.* **8**, 503–516.
Adams, E. (1977). *Int. J. Pept. Protein Res.* **9**, 293–309.
Afzali-Ardakani, A., and Rapoport, H. (1980). *J. Org. Chem.* **45**, 4817–4820.

Alekseeva, L. V., Burde, N. L., and Lundin, B. N. (1968). *Zh. Obshch. Khim.* **38**, 1687–1691.
Alekseeva, L. V., Burde, N. L., and Bilim, G. V. (1971a). *J. Org. Chem. USSR* (*Engl. Transl.*) **7**, 653–655.
Alekseeva, L. V., Burde, N. L., and Pushkareva, Z. V. (1971b). *J. Org. Chem. USSR* (*Engl. Transl.*) **7**, 656–659.
Alekseeva, L. V., Burde, N. L., and Tatarinova, G. P. (1971c). *J. Org. Chem. USSR* (*Engl. Transl.*) **7**, 1442–1444.
Aleksiev, B., Nisanjan, P., Stoev, S., and Doseva, V. (1971). *Hoppe-Seyler's Z. Physiol. Chem.* **352**, 1411–1416.
Ali, R. M., and Khan, N. H. (1978). *Synth. Commun.* **8**, 497–510.
Allen, M. C., Brundish, D. E., and Wade, R. (1980). *J. Chem. Soc., Perkin Trans. 1* pp. 1928–1932.
Almquist, R., Chao, W., Ellis, M., and Johnson, H. (1980). *J. Med. Chem.* **23**, 1392–1398.
Altman, J., Moshberg, R., and Ben-Ishai, D. (1975). *Tetrahedron Lett.* pp. 3737–3740.
Andreatta, R. H., Nair, V., Robertson, A. V., and Simpson, W. R. J. (1967). *Aust. J. Chem.* **20**, 1493–1509.
Anhovry, M. L., Crooy, P., Neys, R. D., and Eliaers, J. (1974). *Bull. Soc. Chim. Belg.* **83**, 117–132.
Ariyoshi, Y., and Sato, N. (1971). *Bull. Chem. Soc. Jpn.* **44**, 3435–3437.
Arnold, Z., and Larsen, P. O. (1977). *Acta Chem. Scand., Ser. B* **31**, 826–828.
Arold, H., and Reissmann, S. (1970). *J. Prakt. Chem.* **312**, 1130–1144, see also pp. 1145–1160.
Arold, H., Eule, M., and Reissmann, S. (1969). *Z. Chem.* **9**, 447–449; *Chem. Abstr.* **72**, 55859d (1970).
Arold, H., Reissmann, S., and Eule, M. (1974). *J. Prakt. Chem.* **316**, 93–102.
Asquith, R. S., and Carthew, P. (1972). *Tetrahedron* **28**, 4769–4773.
Asquith, R. S., Yeung, K. W., and Otterburn, M. S. (1977). *Tetrahedron* **33**, 1633–1635.
Atherton, E., and Meienhofer, J. (1972). *J. Am. Chem. Soc.* **94**, 4759–4761.
Atherton, E., Lau, H. D., Moore, S., Elliott, D. P., and Wade, R. (1971). *J. Chem. Soc. C*, pp. 3393–3396.
Ayi, A. L., Remli, M., and Guedj, R. (1981). *Tetrahedron Lett.* **22**, 1505–1508.
Azimov, V. A., Uritskaya, M. Y., and Yakhontov, L. N. (1968). *Zh. Khim. Farm.* **2**, 16–19.
Babb, R. M., and Bollinger, F. W. (1970). *J. Org. Chem.* **35**, 1438–1440.
Bakhra, M., Katrukha, G. S., and Silaev, A. B. (1973). *Khim. Prir. Soedin.* pp. 280–281; *Chem. Abstr.* **79**, 19087m (1973).
Balaspiri, L., Papp, G., and Kovacs, K. (1972). *Monatsh. Chem.* **103**, 581–585.
Baldwin, J. E., Hoskins, C., and Kruse, L. (1976). *J. Chem. Soc., Chem. Commun.* pp. 795–796.
Baldwin, J. E., Haber, S. B., Hoskins, C., and Kruse, L. (1977). *J. Org. Chem.* **42**, 1239–1241.
Balenović, K., and Deljac, A. (1973). *Recl. Trav. Chim. Pays-Bas* **92**, 117–122.
Banerjee, S. N., Diamond, L., Ressler, C., and Sawyer, W. H. (1979). *J. Med. Chem.* **22**, 1487–1492.
Barber, H. A., Smyth, R. D., Wilson, R. M., and Weissbach, H. (1959). *J. Biol. Chem.* **234**, 320–328.
Barber, M., and Jones, J. H. (1977). *Int. J. Pept. Protein Res.* **9**, 269–271.
Barber, M., Jones, J. H., Stachulski, A. V., Bisset, G. W., Chowdrey, H. S., and Hudson, A. L. (1979). *Int. J. Pept. Protein Res.* **14**, 247–261.
Barclay, R., Phillipps, M., Perri, G., and Kanematsu, S. (1964) *Cancer Res.* **24**, 1324–1330.
Barry, G. T., and Roark, E. (1964). *J. Biol. Chem.* **239**, 1541–1544.
Bayer, E., and Schmidt, K. (1973). *Tetrahedron Lett.* pp. 2051–2054.
Bell, E. A. (1961). *Nature* (*London*) **199**, 70–71.
Bell, E. A., Nulu, J. R., and Cone, C. (1971). *Phytochemistry* **10**, 2191–2194.

Bellocq, A., Castensson, S., and Sievertsson, H. (1977). *Biochem. Biophys. Res. Commun.* **74**, 577–583.
Belokon, Y. N., Faleev, N. G., Belikov, U. M., Maksakov, V. A., and Petrovskii, P. V. (1977). *Izv. Akad. Nauk SSSR, Ser. Khim.* pp. 2536–2539.
Ben-Ishai, D., Satati, I., and Berler, Z. (1975a). *J. Chem. Soc., Chem. Commun.* pp. 349–350.
Ben-Ishai, D., Berler, Z., and Altman, J. (1975b). *J. Chem. Soc., Chem. Commun.* pp. 905–906.
Ben-Ishai, D., Satati, I., and Bernstein, Z. (1976). *Tetrahedron* **32**, 1571–1573.
Ben-Ishai, D., Altman, J., and Peled, N. (1977a). *Tetrahedron* **33**, 2715–2717.
Ben-Ishai, D., Altman, J., and Peled, N. (1977b). *J. Chem. Soc., Chem. Commun.* pp. 2715–2717.
Ben-Ishai, D., Altman, J., Bernstein, Z., and Peled, N. (1978). *Tetrahedron* **34**, 467–473.
Bentov, M., and Roffman, C. (1969). *Isr. J. Chem.* **7**, 835–837.
Bergel, F., and Stock, J. A. (1954). *J. Chem. Soc.* pp. 2409–2417.
Bergel, F., Burnop, V., and Stock, J. A. (1955). *J. Chem. Soc.* pp. 1223–1230.
Berger, A., Smolarsky, M., Kurn, N., and Bosshard, H. R. (1973). *J. Org. Chem.* **38**, 457–460.
Bernardi, L., Bosisio, G., Chillemi, F., de Caro, G., de Castiglione, R., Erspamer, V., Glaesser, A., and Goffredo, O. (1966). *Experientia* **22**, 29–31.
Berse, C., and Bessette, P. (1971). *Can. J. Chem.* **49**, 2610–2611.
Bethell, M. J., and Kenner, G. W. (1965). *J. Chem. Soc.* pp. 3850–3854.
Bethell, M. J., Bigley, D. B., and Kenner, G. W. (1963). *Chem. Ind. (London)* pp. 653–654.
Bey, P., Danzin, C., van Dorsselaer, V., Mamont, P., Jung, M., and Tardif, C. (1978). *J. Med. Chem.* **21**, 50–55.
Birkofer, L., and Ritter, A. (1958). *Justus Liebigs Ann. Chem.* **612**, 22–33.
Bischofberger, K., Hall, R. H., and Jordan, A. (1975). *J. Chem. Soc., Chem. Commun.* pp. 806–807.
Black, D. K., and Landor, S. R. (1968a). *J. Chem. Soc. C* pp. 281–283.
Black, D. K., and Landor, S. R. (1968b). *J. Chem. Soc. C* pp. 283–287.
Black, D. K., and Landor, S. R. (1968c). *J. Chem. Soc. C* pp. 288–290.
Bloemhoff, W., and Kerling, E. T. (1975). *Recl. Trav. Chim. Pays-Bas* **94**, 182–185.
Blumenstein, M., Hruby, V. J., and Viswanatha, V. (1981). *In* "Peptides: Synthesis, Structure, Function" (D. H. Rich and E. Gross, eds.), pp. 363–365. Pierce Chemical Co., Rockford, Illinois
Block, P., and Coy, D. H. (1972). *J. Chem. Soc., Perkin Trans. I* pp. 633–634.
Bodanszky, M., and Lindeberg, G. (1971). *J. Med. Chem.* **14**, 1197–1199.
Bodanszky, M., Natarajan, S., Hahne, W., and Gardner, J. D. (1977). *J. Med. Chem.* **20**, 1047–1450.
Bognar, R., Gyorgydeak, Z., Szilagyi, L., Horvath, G., Czira, G., and Radics, L. (1976). *Liebigs Ann. Chem.* pp. 450–462.
Borin, G., Filippi, B., Moroder, L., Santoni, C., and Marchiori, F. (1977). *Int. J. Pept. Protein Res.* **10**, 27–38.
Borowski, E., Smulkowski, M., Dzieduszycka, M., Sawlewicz, P., Chmara, H., and Milewski, S. (1979). *In* "Peptides: Structure and Biological Function" (E. Gross and J. Meienhofer, eds.), pp. 563–566. Pierce Chemical Co., Rockford, Illinois.
Bory, S., Gaudry, M., Marquet, A., and Azerad, R. (1979). *Biochem. Biophys. Res. Commun.* **87**, 85–91.
Bosshard, H. R., and Berger, A. (1973). *Helv. Chim. Acta* **56**, 1836–1845.
Brain, F. H. (1963). *J. Chem. Soc.* pp. 632–640.
Bregman, M. D., Trivedi, D., and Hruby, V. J. (1980). *J. Biol. Chem.* **255**, 11725–11731.
Bregovec, I., and Jakovčić, T. (1972). *Monatsh. Chem.* **103**, 288–291.
Brody, K. R., and Spencer, R. P. (1968). *J. Org. Chem.* **33**, 1665–1666.

Brtník, F., and Zaoral, M. (1976). *Collect. Czech. Chem. Commun.* **41**, 2969–2977.
Brundish, D. E., and Wade, R. (1973). *J. Chem. Soc., Perkin Trans. I* pp. 2875–2879.
Brunet, J. C., Cuingnet, E., Gras, H., Marcincal, P., Mocz, A., Sergheraert, C., and Tartar, A. (1981a). *J. Organomet. Chem.* **216**, 73–77.
Brunet, J. C., Cuingnet, E., Dautrevaux, M., Marcincal, P., Sergheraert, C., and Tartar, A. (1981b). Poster session delivered at *7th* American Peptide Symposium, Madison, WIS.
Brynes, S., Burckart, G. J., and Mokotoff, M. (1978). *J. Med. Chem.* **21**, 45–49.
Büchi, G., and Kamikawa, T. (1977). *J. Org. Chem.* **42**, 4153–4154.
Burgstahler, A. W., and Aiman, C. E. (1962). *Chem. Ind.* (*London*) pp. 1430–1431.
Burgstahler, A. W., Trollope, M. L., and Aiman, C. E. (1964). *Nature* (*London*) **202**, 388–389.
Bycroft, B. W., Cameron, D., Croft, L. R., and Johnson, A. W. (1968). *J. Chem. Soc., Chem. Commun.* pp. 1301–1302.
Bycroft, B. W., Cameron, D., and Johnson, A. W. (1971). *J. Chem. Soc. C* pp. 3040–3047.
Campaigne, E., and Dinner, A. (1970). *J. Med. Chem.* **13**, 1205–1208.
Cannon, J. G., O'Donnell, J. P., Rosazza, J. P., and Hoppin, C. R. (1974). *J. Med. Chem.* **17**, 565–568.
Carrion, J. P., Deranleau, D. A., Donzel, B., Esko, K., Moser, P., and Schwyzer, R. (1968). *Helv. Chim. Acta* **51**, 459–481.
Carson, J. F., and Wong, F. F. (1964). *J. Org. Chem.* **29**, 2203–2205.
Casara, P., and Metcalf, B. W. (1978). *Tetrahedron Lett.* pp. 1581–1584.
Casella, L., Gullotti, M., Pasini, A., and Psaro, R. (1979). *Synthesis* pp. 150–151.
Cativiela, C., and Melendez, E. (1981). *Synthesis* pp. 805–807.
Chang, P. K., Sciarini, L. J., and Handschumacher, R. E. (1973). *J. Med. Chem.* **16**, 1277–1280.
Chari, R. V. J., and Wemple, J. (1979). *Tetrahedron Lett.* pp. 111–114.
Chaturvedi, N., Park, W., Smeby, R. R., and Bumpus, F. M. (1970). *J. Med. Chem.* **13**, 177–181.
Chisholm, M., Cremlyn, R. J. W., and Taylor, P. J. (1967). *Tetrahedron Lett.* pp. 1373–1378.
Christensen, S. B., and Larsen, P. K. (1978). *Acta Chem. Scand., Ser. B* **32**, 27–30.
Clausen, K., Thorsen, M., and Lawesson, S.-O. (1981). *Tetrahedron* **37**, 3635–3639.
Cleland, G. H. (1969). *J. Org. Chem.* **34**, 744–747.
Closse, A., and Huguenin, R. (1974). *Helv. Chim. Acta* **57**, 533–545.
Compere, E. L., Jr., and Weinstein, D. A. (1977). *Synthesis* pp. 852–853.
Corbella, A., Gariboldi, P., Jommi, G., and Mauri, F. (1969). *Chem. Ind.* (*London*) pp. 583–584.
Couchman, R., Eagles, J., Hegarty, M. P., Laird, W. M., Self, R., and Synge, L. M. (1973). *Phytochemistry* **12**, 707–718.
Coutts, R. T., and Malicky, J. L. (1974). *Can. J. Chem.* **52**, 390–394.
Cox, M. T., Bowness, W. G., and Holohan, J. J. (1974). *J. Med. Chem.* **17**, 1125–1127.
Coy, D. H., Coy, E. J., Hirotsu, Y., Vichez-Martinez, J. A., Schally, A., Van Nispen, J., and Tesser, G. (1974). *Biochemistry* **13**, 3550–3553.
Coy, D. H., Hirotsu, Y., Redding, T. W., Coy, E. J., and Schally, A. V. (1975). *J. Med. Chem.* **18**, 948–949.
Cremlyn, R. J. W., Ellam, R. M., and Mitra, T. K. (1970). *Indian J. Chem.* **8**, 218–220.
Crooij, P., and Eliaers, J. (1969). *J. Chem. Soc. C* pp. 559–563.
Cuingnet, E., Sergheraert, C., Tartar, A., and Dautrevaux, M. (1980). *J. Organomet. Chem.* **195**, 325–329.
Culvenor, C. C. J., Foster, M. C., and Hegarty, M. P. (1969). *J. Chem. Soc., Chem. Commun.* p. 1091.
Culvenor, C. C. J., Foster, M. C., and Hegarty, M. P. (1971). *Aust. J. Chem.* **24**, 371–375.

Curphey, T. J., and Daniel, D. S. (1978). *J. Org. Chem.* **43**, 4666–4668.
Daebritz, E., and Virtanen, A. J. (1965). *Chem. Ber.* **98**, 781–788.
Dalby, J. S., Kenner, G. W., and Sheppard, R. C. (1962). *J. Chem. Soc.* pp. 4387–4396.
Danishefsky, S., Berman, E., Clizbe, L. A., and Hirama, M. (1979). *J. Am. Chem. Soc.* **101**, 4385–4386.
Danishefsky, S., Morris, J., and Clizbe, L. (1981). *J. Am. Chem. Soc.* **103**, 1602–1604.
Dannley, R. L., and Taborsky, R. G. (1957). *J. Org. Chem.* **22**, 1275–1276.
Dardenne, G., Casimar, J., and Jadot, J. (1968). *Phytochemistry* **7**, 1401–1406.
DaSettimo, A. (1962). *Ann. Chim.* (*Rome*) **52**, 17–24.
Davis, A. L., Cavitt, M. B., McCord, T. J., Vickrey, P. E., and Shire, W. (1973). *J. Am. Chem. Soc.* **95**, 6800–6802.
Davis, N. R., and Bailey, A. J. (1972). *Biochem. J.* **129**, 91–96.
Daxenbichler, M. E., Kleiman, R., Weisleder, D., Van Etten, C. H., and Carlson, K. D. (1972). *Tetrahedron Lett.* pp. 1801–1802.
Degraw, J. L., Cory, M., Skinner, W. A., Theisen, M. C., and Mitoma, C. (1968). *J. Med. Chem.* **11**, 225–227.
DeMarco, C., and Coletta, M. (1961). *Biochim. Biophys. Acta* **47**, 257–261.
DeMarco, C., and Luchi, P. (1972). *Anal. Biochem.* **48**, 346–352.
DeMarco, C., Rinaldi, A., Dernini, S., and Cavallini, D. (1975). *Gazz. Chim. Ital.* **105**, 1113–1115.
DeMarco, C., Dernini, S., Rinaldi, A., and Cavallini, D. (1976). *Gazz. Chim. Ital.* **106**, 211–213.
DeMarco, C., Coccia, R., Rinaldi, A., and Cavallini, D. (1977). *Ital. J. Biochem.* **26**, 51–58.
Dewar, J. H., and Shaw, G. (1962). *J. Chem. Soc.* pp. 583–585.
Diehl, J. F., and Bowen, D. O. (1965). *J. Med. Chem.* **8**, 274.
Dilbeck, G. A., Field, L., Gallo, A. A., and Gargiulo, R. J. (1978). *J. Org. Chem.* **43**, 4593–4596.
Di Maio, J., and Schiller, P. W. (1980). *Proc. Natl. Acad. Sci. U.S.A.* **77**, 7162–7166.
Di Maio, J., Schiller, P. W., and Belleau, B. (1979). *In* "Peptides: Structure and Biological Function" (E. Gross and J. Meienhofer, eds.), pp. 889–892. Pierce Chemical Co., Rockford, Illinois.
Dion, H. W., Fusari, S. A., Jakubowski, Z. L., Zora, J. G., and Bartz, Q. R. (1956). *J. Am. Chem. Soc.* **78**, 3075–3077.
Divanfard, H. R., Lysenko, Z., Wang, P.-C., and Joullie, M. M. (1978). *Synth. Commun.* **8**, 269–273.
Do, K. Q., and Schwyzer, R. (1981). *Helv. Chim. Acta* **64**, 2084–2089.
Do, K. Q., Thanei, P., Caviezel, M., and Schwyzer, R. (1979). *Helv. Chim. Acta* **62**, 956–964.
Dobson, T. A., and Vining, L. C. (1968). *Can. J. Chem.* **46**, 3007–3012.
Doel, M. T., Jones, A. S., and Taylor, N. (1969). *Tetrahedron Lett.* pp. 2285–2288.
Doel, M. T., Jones, A. S., and Walker, R. T. (1974). *Tetrahedron Lett.* pp. 2755–2759.
Dolling, U. H., Douglas, A. W., Grabowski, E. J. J., Schoenewaldt, E. F., Sohar, P., and Sletzinger, M. (1978). *J. Org. Chem.* **43**, 1634–1640.
Done, T., and Fowden, L. (1952). *Biochem. J.* **51**, 451–458.
Dormoy, J. R., Castro, B., Chappuis, G., Fritschi, U. S., and Grogg, P. (1980). *Angew. Chem.* **92**, 761.
Dowd, P., and Kaufman, C. (1979). *J. Org. Chem.* **44**, 3956–3957.
Draminski, M., and Pitha, J. (1978). *Makromol. Chem.* **179**, 2195–2200.
Dreyfuss, P. (1974). *J. Med. Chem.* **17**, 252–255.
Dunn, F. W. (1963). *Biochem. Prep.* **10**, 159–165.
Dunn, F. W., and Stewart, J. M. (1971). *J. Med. Chem.* **14**, 779–781.

Dunnill, P. M., and Fowden, L. (1963). *J. Exp. Bot.* **14**, 237–248.
Dutta, A. S., and Morley, J. S. (1975). *J. Chem. Soc., Perkin Trans. I* pp. 1712–1720.
du Vigneaud, V., McKennis, H., Jr., Simmonds, S., Dittmer, K., and Brown, G. B. (1945). *J. Biol. Chem.* **159**, 385–394.
Dwek, R. A. (1972). *In* "Carbon-Fluorine Compounds. Chemistry, Biochemistry, and Biological Activities," Ciba Found. Symp., pp. 239–271. Associated Scientific Publishers, Amsterdam.
Dzieduszycka, M., Smulkowski, M., Czarnomska, T., and Borowski, E. (1978). *Pol. J. Chem.* **52**, 933–939; *Chem. Abstr.* **89**, 163944n.
Eaborn, C. (1975). *J. Organomet. Chem.* **100**, 43–57.
Eaton, C. N., Denney, G. H., Ryder, M. A., Ly, M. G., and Babson, R. D. (1973). *J. Med. Chem.* **16**, 289–290.
Eberle, A., and Schwyzer, R. (1976). *Helv. Chim. Acta* **59**, 2421–2431.
Eberle, A. N., DeGraan, P. N. E., and Huebscher, W. (1981). *Helv. Chim. Acta* **64**, 2645–2653.
Edelson, J., Skinner, C. G., Ravel, J. M., and Shive, W. (1959). *J. Am. Chem. Soc.* **81**, 5150–5153.
Edgar, M. T., Pettit, G. R., and Krupa, T. S. (1979). *J. Org. Chem.* **44**, 396–400.
Edwards, M. L. (1980). *J. Heterocycl. Chem.* **17**, 383–384.
Effenberger, F., and Karlheinz, D. (1979). *Angew. Chem.* **91**, 504–505.
Eisele, K. (1975). *Z. Naturforsch., C: Biosci.* **30C**, 538–540.
Eisler, K., Rudinger, J., and Šorm, F. (1966). *Collect. Czech. Chem. Commun.* **31**, 4563–4580.
Elberling, J. A., and Nagasawa, H. T. (1972). *J. Heterocycl Chem.* **9**, 411–414.
El-Maghraby, M. A. (1976). *J. Indian Chem. Soc.* **53**, 496–497.
Erickson, B. W., and Merrifield, R. B. (1973). *J. Am. Chem. Soc.* **95**, 3750–3756.
Escher, E., and Schwyzer, R. (1974). *FEBS Lett.* **46**, 347–350.
Escher, E., Jošt, R., Zuber, H., and Schwyzer, R. (1974). *Isr. J. Chem.* **12**, 121–138.
Eswarakrishnan, V., and Field, L. (1981). *J. Org. Chem.* **46**, 4182–4187.
Fabrichnyi, B. P., Shalavina, I. F., and Goldfarb, Y. L. (1979). *Zh. Org. Khim.* **15**, 1536–1540.
Fahrenholz, F., and Schimmack, G. (1975). *Hoppe-Seyler's Z. Physiol. Chem.* **356**, 469–471.
Fahrenholz, F., and Thierauch, K. H. (1980). *Int. J. Pept. Protein Res.* **15**, 323–330.
Fahrenholz, F., Thierauch, K. H., and Crause, P. (1980). *Hoppe-Seyler's Z. Physiol. Chem.* **361**, 153–157.
Farmer, P. S. (1980). *In* "Drug Design" (E. J. Ariens, ed.), Vol. 10, pp. 119–143. Academic Press, New York.
Fattorusso, E. (1965). *Rend. Accad. Sci. Fis. Mat. Naples* [4] **32**, 150–155.
Fauchère, J.-L., and Petermann, C. (1981). *Int. J. Pept. Protein Res.* **18**, 249–255.
Fauchère, J.-L., and Schiller, P. W. (1981). *Helv. Chim. Acta* **64**, 2090–2094.
Fauchère, J.-L., and Schwyzer, R. (1971). *Helv. Chim. Acta* **54**, 2078–2080.
Fauchère, J.-L., Leukart, O., Eberle, A., and Schwyzer, R. (1979). *Helv. Chim. Acta* **62**, 1385–1395.
Faulstich, H., Smith, H. O., and Zobeley, S. (1973). *Justus Liebigs Ann. Chem.* pp. 765–771.
Felix, A. M., Jimenez, M. H., Vergona, R., and Cohen, M. R. (1973). *Int. J. Pept. Protein Res.* **5**, 201–206.
Felix, A. M., Wang, C. T., Liebman, A. A., Delaney, C. M., Mowles, T., Burghardt, B. A., Charnecki, A. M., and Meienhofer, J. (1977). *Int. J. Pept. Protein Res.* **10**, 299–310.
Ferderigos, N., and Katsoyannis, P. G. (1977). *J. Chem. Soc., Perkin Trans. I* pp. 1299–1305.
Field, G. F. (1979). *J. Org. Chem.* **44**, 825–827.
Filler, R., and Kang, H. H. (1965). *J. Chem. Commun.* pp. 626–627.
Filler, R., and Rao, Y. S. (1961). *J. Org. Chem.* **26**, 1685.
Filler, R., and Rickert, R. C. (1981). *J. Fluorine Chem.* **18**, 483–495.
Filler, R., Ayyangar, N. R., Gustowski, W., and Kang, H. H. (1969). *J. Org. Chem.* **34**, 534–538.

Finn, F. M., and Hofmann, K. (1967). *J. Am. Chem. Soc.* **89**, 5298–5300.
Firnau, G., Nahmias, C., and Garnett, S. (1973). *J. Med. Chem.* **16**, 416–418.
Firnau, G., Chirakal, R., Sood, S., and Garnett, S. (1980). *Can. J. Chem.* **58**, 1449–1450.
Fisher, G. H. and Ryan, J. W. (1979). *FEBS Lett.* **107**, 273–276.
Fisher, G. H., Marlborough, D. J., Ryan, J. W., and Felix, A. M. (1978). *Arch. Biochem. Biophys.* **189**, 81–85.
Fletcher, G. A., and Young, G. T. (1972). *J. Chem. Soc., Perkin Trans. 1* pp. 1867–1874.
Fletcher, G. A., and Young, G. T. (1974). *J. Chem. Soc., Perkin Trans. 1* pp. 1867–1874.
Foppoli, C., Cini, C., Blarzino, C., and DeMarco, C. (1980). *Ital. J. Biochem.* **29**, 251–259.
Fowden, L. (1964). *Annu. Rev. Biochem.* **33**, 173–204.
Fowden, L. (1970). *Prog. Phytochem.* **2**, 203–266.
Fowden, L., Lea, P. J., and Bell, E. A. (1979). *Adv. Enzymol.* **50**, 117–175.
Frankel, M., Gertner, D., Shenhar, A., and Zilkha, A. (1963). *J. Chem. Soc.* pp. 5049–5051.
Frankel, M., Gertner, D., Shenhar, A., and Zilkha, A. (1967). *J. Chem. Soc.* pp. 1334–1336.
Frankel, M., Shenhar, A., Gertner, D., and Zilkha, A. (1968). *Isr. J. Chem.* **6**, 921–925.
Freidinger, R. (1981). *In* "Peptides: Synthesis, Structure, Function" (D. A. Rich and E. Gross, eds.), pp. 673–683. Pierce Chemical Co., Rockford, Illinois.
Freidinger, R., Veber, D., Perlow, D., Brooks, J., and Saperstein, R. (1980). *Science* **210**, 656–658.
Freidinger, R., Perlow, D., and Veber, D. (1982). *J. Org. Chem.* **47**, 104–109.
Frejd, T., Davis, M. A., Gronowitz, S., and Sadeh, T. (1980). *J. Heterocycl. Chem.* **17**, 759–761.
Fujimoto, Y., Irreverre, F., Karle, J. M., Karle, I. L., and Witkop, B. (1971). *J. Am. Chem. Soc.* **93**, 3471–3477.
Fujino, M., Wakimasu, M., Mano, M., Tanaka, K., Nakajima, N., and Aoki, H. (1976). *Chem. Pharm. Bull.* **24**, 2112–2117.
Fujita, Y., Kollonitsch, J., and Witkop, B. (1965) *J. Am. Chem. Soc.* **87**, 2030–2033.
Fushiya, S., Nakatsuyama, S., Sato, Y., and Nozoe, S. (1981). *Heterocycles* **15**, 819–822.
Futagawa, S., Nakahara, M., Inui, T., Katsura, H., and Kaneko, T. (1971). *Nippon Kagaku Zasshi* **92**, 374–376; *Chem. Abstr.* **76**, 25554r (1972).
Gal, G., Chemerda, J. M., Reinhold, D. F., and Purick, R. M. (1977). *J. Org. Chem.* **42**, 142–143.
Gallina, C., Petrini, F., and Romeo, A. (1970). *J. Org. Chem.* **35**, 2425–2426.
Gass, J. D., and Meister, A. (1970). *Biochemistry* **9**, 842–846.
Gellert, E., Halpern, B., and Rudzats, R. (1978). *Phytochemistry* **17**, 802.
Georgi, V., and Wieland, T. (1966). *Justus Liebigs Ann. Chem.* **700**, 149–156.
Gerig, J. T., and McLeod, R. S. (1973). *J. Am. Chem. Soc.* **95**, 5725–5729.
Gerig, J. T., and McLeod, R. S. (1976). *J. Am. Chem. Soc.* **98**, 3970–3975.
Gershon, H., McNeil, M. W., and Bergmann, E. D. (1973). *J. Med. Chem.* **16**, 1407.
Gershon, H., Shanks, L., and Clarke, D. D. (1978). *J. Pharm. Sci.* **67**, 715–717.
Gertner, D., Shenhar, A., and Zilkha, A. (1963). *Isr. J. Chem.* *1*, 142–146.
Giannella, M., Gualtieri, F., Melchiorre, C., and Orlandoni, A. (1972). *Chim. Ther.* **7**, 127–132; *Chem. Abstr.* **77**, 114838z.
Gilon, C., Knobler, Y., and Sheradsky, T. (1967). *Tetrahedron* **23**, 4441–4447.
Glazer, A. N. (1976). *In* "The Proteins" (H. Neurath and R. Hill, eds.), 3rd ed., Vol. 2, pp. 2–103. Academic Press, New York.
Golding, B. T., and Smith, A. J. (1980). *J. Chem. Soc., Chem. Commun.* pp. 702–703.
Goodman, M., and Chorev, M. (1981). *In* "Perspectives in Peptide Chemistry" (A. Eberle, R. Geiger, and T. Wieland, eds.), pp. 283–294. Karger, Basel/New York.
Goodman, M., Spencer, R., Casini, G., Crews, O., and Reist, E. (1965). *J. Med. Chem.* **8**, 251–252.
Goodman, M., and Kossoy, A. (1966). *J. Am. Chem. Soc.* **88**, 5010–5015.

Gordon, P. G. (1973). *Aust. J. Chem.* **26**, 1771–1780.
Greenstein, J., and Winitz, M. (1961). "Chemistry of the Amino Acids," Vol. I, p. 37. Wiley, New York.
Gregory, H., Jones, D. S., and Morley, J. S. (1968). *J. Chem. Soc. C* pp. 531–540.
Grunewald, G. L., Kuttab, S. H., Pleiss, M. A., Mangold, J. B., and Soine, P. (1980). *J. Med. Chem.* **23**, 754–758.
Gruszecka, E., Soroka, M., and Mastalerz, P. (1979). *Pol. J. Chem.* **53**, 937–939.
Grzonka, Z., Kojro, E., Palacz, Z, Willhardt, I., and Herman, P. (1977). *In* "Peptides: Procedings of the Fifth Amererican Peptide Symposium" (M. Goodman and J. Meienhofer, eds.), pp. 153–156. Wiley, New York.
Gund, P., Andose, J. D., Rhodes, J. B., and Smith, G. M. (1980). *Science* **208**, 1425–1431.
Haeusler, J. (1981). *Liebigs. Ann. Chem.* pp. 1073–1088.
Haeusler, J., and Schmidt, U. (1979). *Liebigs Ann. Chem.* pp. 1881–1889.
Hageman, J. J. M., Wanner, M. J., Koomen, G. J., and Pandit, U. K. (1977). *J. Med. Chem. Chem.* **20**, 1677–1679.
Haggerty, W. J., Jr., Springer, R. H., and Cheng, C. C. (1965). *J. Heterocycl. Chem.* **2**, 1–6.
Hanck, A., and Kutscher, W. (1964). *Hoppe-Seyler's Z. Physiol. Chem.* **338**, 272–275.
Hanessian, S., and Schütze, G. (1969). *J. Med. Chem.* **12**, 347.
Hann, M., Sammes, P., Kennewell, P., and Taylor, J. (1980). *J. Chem. Soc., Chem. Commun.* pp. 234–235.
Hansen, J. J., and Krogsgaard-Larsen, P. (1980). *J. Chem. Soc., Perkin Trans. 1* pp. 1826–1833.
Hanson, R. N., and Davis, M. A. (1981). *J. Heterocycl. Chem.* **18**, 205–206.
Hanzlik, R. P., Soine, P., and Soine, W. H. (1979). *J. Med. Chem.* **22**, 424–428.
Hara, J. Inouye, Y., and Kakisawa, H. (1981). *Bull. Chem. Soc. Jpn.* **54**, 3871–3872.
Harada, K., and Nakamura, I. (1978). *J. Chem. Soc., Chem. Commun.* pp. 522–523.
Hardy, P. M., Hughes, G. J., and Rydon, H. N. (1976). *J. Chem. Soc., Chem. Commun.* pp. 157–158.
Harington, C. R., and Rivers, R. V. P. (1944). *Biochem. J.* **38**, 320–321.
Harris, R. L. N. (1976a) *Aust. J. Chem.* **29**, 1329–1334.
Harris, R. L. N. (1976b). *Aust. J. Chem.* **29**, 1335–1339.
Harris, R. L. N., and Teitei, T. (1977). *Aust. J. Chem.* **30**, 649–655.
Hase, S., Kiyoi, R., and Sakakibara, S. (1968). *Bull. Chem. Soc. Jpn.* **41**, 1266–1267.
Hase, S., Schwartz, I. L., and Walter, R. (1972). *J. Med. Chem.* **15**, 126–128.
Hatanaka, M., and Ishimaru, T. (1973). *Bull. Chem. Soc. Jpn.* **46**, 3600–3601.
Hatanaka, S.-I., Nimura, Y., and Taniguchi, K. (1972). *Phytochemistry* **11**, 3327–3329.
Hatanaka, S.-I., Kuneko, S., Niimura, V., Kinoshita, F., and Soma, G.-I. (1974). *Tetrahedron Lett.* **45**, 3931–3932.
Hecht, S. M., Rupprecht, K. M., and Jacobs, P. M. (1979). *J. Am. Chem. Soc.* **101**, 3982–3983.
Hegedüs, B., Krassó, A. F., Noack, K., and Zeller, P. (1975). *Helv. Chim. Acta* **58**, 147–162.
Hedgcoth, C., and Skinner, C. G. (1963). *Biochem. Prep.* **10**, 67–72.
Hengartner, U., Valentine, D., Jr., Johnson, K. K., Larscheid, M. E., Pigott, F., Scheidl, F., Scott, J. W., Sun, R. C., and Townsend, J. M. (1979). *J. Org. Chem.* **44**, 3741–3747.
Henson, E. B., Gallop, P. M., and Hauschka, P. U. (1981). *Tetrahedron* **37**, 2561–2562.
Hermann, P. (1981). *Org. Sulfur Chem., Invit. Lect. Int. Symp., 9th, 1980* pp. 51–62; *Chem. Abstr.* **95**, 11595y.
Hermann, P., and Zaoral, M. (1965). *Collect. Czech. Chem. Commun.* **30**, 2817–2825.
Hermann, P., Stalla, K., Schwimmer, J., Willhardt, I., and Kutschera, I. (1970). *J. Prakt. Chem.* **311**, 1018–1028.
Hewgill, F. R., and Webb, R. J. (1977). *Aust. J. Chem.* **30**, 2565–2569.
Hider, R. C., and John, D. I. (1972). *J. Chem. Soc., Perkin Trans. 1* pp. 1825–1830.

Hill, J. T., and Dunn, F. W. (1965). *J. Org. Chem.* **30**, 1321–1322.

Hill, J. T., and Dunn, F. W. (1969). *J. Med. Chem.* **12**, 737–740.

Hines, J. W., Breitholle, E. G., Sato, M., and Stammer, C. H. (1976). *J. Org. Chem.* **41**, 1466–1467.

Hiskey, R. G., and Boggs, N. T., III (1977). *In* "Peptides: Proceedings of the Fifth American Peptide Symposium" (M. Goodman and J. Meienhofer, eds.) pp. 465–467. Wiley, New York.

Hoes, C., Hoogerhout, P., Bloemhoff, W., and Kerling, K. E. T. (1979). *Recl. Trav. Chim. Pays-Bas* **98**, 137–139.

Hofmann, K., and Bohn, H. (1966). *J. Am. Chem. Soc.* **88**, 5914–5919.

Hofmann, K., Andreatta, R., and Bohn, H. (1968). *J. Am. Chem. Soc.* **90**, 6207–6212.

Hofmann, K., Visser, J. P., and Finn, F. M. (1970). *J. Am. Chem. Soc.* **92**, 2900–2909.

Hofmann, K., Chang, J. K., Folkers, K., and Bowers, C. Y. (1972). *J. Med. Chem.* **15**, 219–224.

Hong, C. I., Piantadosi, C., and Irvin, J. L. (1968). *J. Med. Chem.* **11**, 588–591.

Horikawa, H., Nishitani, T., Iwasaki, T., Mushika, Y., Inoue, I., and Miyoshi, M. (1980). *Tetrahedron Lett.* pp. 4101–4104.

Horner, L., and Schwahn, H. (1955). *Liebigs Ann. Chem.* **591**, 99–107.

Houghten, R. A., and Rapoport, H. (1974). *J. Med. Chem.* **17**, 556–558.

Hruby, V. J., Bregman, M. D., Trivedi, D., Johnson, D. G., and Ulichny, C. (1981). *In* "Peptides: Synthesis, Structure, Function" (D. H. Rich and E. Gross, eds.), pp. 813–816. Pierce Chemical Co., Rockford, Illinois.

Hsieh, K.-H., and Marshall, G. (1981). *J. Med. Chem.* **24**, 1304–1310.

Hsieh, K.-H., Jorgensen, E. C., and Lee, T. C. (1979). *J. Med. Chem.* **22**, 1038–1044.

Hudlicky, M. (1967). *Collect. Czech. Chem. Commun.* **32**, 453–457.

Hudlicky, M., Jelinek, V., Eisler, K., and Rudinger, J. (1970). *Collect. Czech. Chem. Commun.* **35**, 498–503.

Hudson, C. B., Robertson, A. V., and Simpson, W. R. (1968). *Aust. J. Chem.* **21**, 769.

Hudson, C. B., Robertson, A. V., and Simpson, W. R. (1975). *Aust. J. Chem.* **28**, 2479–2498.

Hughes, P., Martin, M., and Clardy, J. (1980). *Tetrahedron Lett.* **21**, 4579–4580.

Humphries, A. J., Keener, R. L., Yano, K., Skelton, F. S., Freiter, E., and Snyder, H. R. (1972). *J. Org. Chem.* **37**, 3626–3629.

Ichihara, A., Hasegawa, H., Sato, H., Koyama, M., and Sakamura, S. (1973). *Tetrahedron Lett.* pp. 37–38.

Ichihara, A., Shiraishi, K., and Sakamura, S. (1977). *Tetrahedron Lett.* pp. 269–272.

Ichikawa, T., Maeda, S., Okamoto, T., Araki, Y., and Ishido, Y. (1971). *Bull. Chem. Soc. Jpn.* **44**, 2779–2786.

Iinuma, K., Kondo, S., Maeda, K., and Umezawa, H. (1977). *Bull. Chem. Soc. Jpn.* **50**, 1850–1857.

Imamoto, S., Maeno, Y., Senoh, S., Tokuyama, T., and Sakan, T. (1966). *Nippon Kagaku Zasshi* **87**, 1230–1235; *Chem. Abstr.* **67**, 22125e (1967).

Inui, T., Ohta, Y., Ujike, T., Katsura, H., and Kaneko, T. (1968). *Bull. Chem. Soc. Jpn.* **41**, 2148–2150.

Iriuchijima, S., and Tsuchihashi, G. (1978). *Agric. Biol. Chem.* **42**, 843–845.

Irreverre, F., Kny, H., Asen, S., Thompson, J. F., and Morris, C. J. (1961). *J. Biol. Chem.* **236**, 1093–1094.

Irreverre, F., Morita, K., Robertson, A. V., and Witkop, B. (1962). *Biochem. Biophys. Res. Commun.* **8**, 453–455.

Ismail, I. A., Sharp, D. E., and Chedekel, M. R. (1980). *J. Org. Chem.* **45**, 2243–2246.

Isowa, Y., Takashima, T., Ohmori, M., Kurita, S., Sato, M., and Mori, K. (1972). *Bull. Chem. Soc. Jpn.* **45**, 1461–1464, 1464–1466.

Isowa, Y., Kurita, M., Ohmori, M., Sato, M., and Mori, K. (1973). *Bull. Chem. Soc. Jpn.* **46**, 1847–1850.

Ito, K., and Hashimoto, Y. (1969). *Agric. Biol. Chem.* **33**, 237–241.

Ito, S., Inoue, S., Yamamoto, Y., and Fujita, K. (1981). *J. Med. Chem.* **24**, 673–677.

Iwasaki, H., Kamiya, T., Oka, O., and Ueyanagi, J. (1969a). *Chem. Pharm. Bull.* **17**, 866–872.

Iwasaki, H., Kamiya, T., Hatanaka, C., Sunada, Y., and Ueyanagi, J. (1969b). *Chem. Pharm. Bull.* **17**, 873–878.

Iwasaki, T., Urabe, Y., Ozaki, Y., Miyoshi, M., and Matsumoto, K. (1976). *J. Chem. Soc., Perkin Trans. 1* pp. 1019–1022.

Izumiya, J., and Kitagawa, K. (1958). *J. Chem. Soc. Jpn.* **79**, 65–68.

Jacobs, P. M., and Davis, M. A. (1979). *J. Org. Chem.* **44**, 178–179.

Jadot, J., Casimir, J., and Warin, R. (1969). *Bull. Soc. Chim. Belg.* **78**, 299–308.

Jakubke, H.-D., Fischer, J., Jošt, K., and Rudinger, J. (1968). *Collect. Czech. Chem. Commun.* **33**, 3910–3912.

Jansen, A. C. A., Weustink, R. J. M., Kerling, K. E. T., and Havinga, E. (1969). *Recl. Trav. Chim. Pays-Bas* **88**, 819–827.

Jansen, A. C. A., Kerling, K. E. T., and Havinga, E. (1970). *Recl. Trav. Chim. Pays-Bas* **89**, 861–864.

Jean, A., and Anatol, J. (1969). *C. R. Hebd. Seances Acad. Sci. Ser. C* **268**, 1307–1309; *Chem. Abstr.* **71**, 39361j (1969).

Jones, C. W., Leyden, D. E., and Stammer, C. H. (1969). *Can J. Chem.* **47**, 4363–4366.

Jones, G., and Wright, S. (1971). *J. Chem. Soc. C* pp. 141–142.

Jones, W. C., Nestor, J. J., and du Vigneaud, V. (1973). *J. Am. Chem. Soc.* **95**, 5677–5679.

Jorgensen, E. C., and Berteau, P. F. (1971). *J. Med. Chem.* **14**, 1199–1202.

Jorgensen, E. C., and Wright, J. (1970a). *J. Med. Chem.* **13**, 367–370.

Jorgensen, E. C., and Wright, J. (1970b). *J. Med. Chem.* **13**, 745–747.

Jorgensen, E. C., Muhlhauser, R. O., and Wiley, R. A. (1969). *J. Med. Chem.* **12**, 689–691.

Jorgensen, E. C., Rapaka, S. R., Windridge, G. C., and Lee, T. C. (1971). *J. Med. Chem.* **14**, 899–903.

Jorgensen, E. C., Murray, W., and Block, P., Jr. (1974). *J. Med. Chem,* **17**, 434–439.

Jošt, K., and Rudinger, J. (1967). *Collect, Czech. Chem. Commun.* **32**, 1229–1241.

Kahl, J. D., and Wieland, T. (1981). *Liebigs Ann. Chem.* pp. 1445–1450.

Kaminski, K., and Sokolowska, T. (1973). *Rocz. Chem.* **47**, 1091–1093: *Chem. Abstr.* **79**, 42819k.

Kamiya, T. (1969). *Chem. Pharm. Bull.* **17**, 886–889, 879–885, 895–900.

Kaneko, T., Lee, Y. K., and Hanafusa, T. (1962). *Bull. Chem. Soc. Jpn.* **35**, 875–878.

Karpavicius, K., Prasmickiene, G., Gurviciene, L., and Kil'disheva, O. V. (1973). *Izv. Akad. Nauk SSSR, Ser. Khim. pp.* 1887–1889.

Karwoski, G., Galione, M., and Starcher, B. (1978). *Biopolymers* **17**, 1119–1127.

Kaspersen, F. M., and Pandit, U. K. (1975). *J. Chem. Soc., Perkin Trans. 1* pp. 1617–1622.

Kataoka, Y., Seto, Y., Yamamoto, M., Yamada, T., Kuwata, S., and Watanabe, H. (1976). *Bull. Chem. Soc. Jpn.* **49**, 1081–1084.

Kato, K., Takita, T., and Umezawa, H. (1980). *Tetrahedron Lett.* **21**, 4925–4926.

Kaurov, O., and Smirnova, M. (1977). *Khim. Prir. Soedin.* pp. 392–398; *Chem. Abstr.* **87**, 202079q.

Kawashima, K., Itoh, H., Yoneda, N., Hagio, K., Moriya, T., and Chibata, I. (1980). *J. Agric. Food Chem.* **28**, 1340–1342.

Keith, D. D., Tortora, J. A., Ineichen, K., and Leimgruber, W. (1975). *Tetrahedron* **31**, 2633–2636.

Keith, D. D., Tortora, J. A., and Yang, R. (1978a). *J. Org. Chem.* **43**, 3711–3713.

Keith, D. D., Yang, R., Tortora, J. A., and Weigele, M. (1978b). *J. Org. Chem.* **43**, 3713–3716.
Keller, O., and Rudinger, J. (1975). *Helv. Chim Acta* **58**, 531–541.
Keller-Schierlein, W., and Joos, B. (1980). *Helv. Chim. Acta* **63**, 250–254.
Keller-Schierlein, W., and Maurer, B. (1969). *Helv. Chim. Acta* **52**, 603–610.
Kelley, J. L., Miller, C. A., and McLean, E. W. (1977). *J. Med. Chem.* **20**, 721–723.
Kelly, R. C., Schletter, I., Stein, S. J., and Wierenga, W. (1979). *J. Am. Chem. Soc.* **101**, 1054–1056.
Kemp, D. S., and Roberts, D. C. (1975). *Tetrahedron Lett.* pp. 4629–4632.
Kenner, G. W., Preston, J., and Sheppard, R. C. (1965). *J. Chem. Soc.* (*London*) pp. 1239–1244.
Khosla, M. C., Leese, R. A., Maloy, W. L., Ferreira, A. T., Smeby, R. R., and Bumpus, F. M. (1972). *J. Med. Chem.* **15**, 792–795.
Kikugawa, Y. (1978). *J. Chem. Res., Synop.* pp. 184–185.
Kikugawa, Y., Tachibana, S., and Araki, K. (1979). *In* "Peptide Chemistry 1978," pp. 17–20. Protein Res. Found., Osaka, Japan; *Chem. Abstr.* **93**, 186776f (1980).
Kinoshita, M., Yanagisawa, H., Doi, S., Kaji, E., and Umezawa, S. (1969). *Bull. Chem. Soc. Jpn.* **42**, 194–199.
Kirihata, M., Jokumor, H., Ichimoto, I., and Ueda, H. (1978). *Nippon Nogei Kagaku Kaishi* **52**, 271–276; *Chem. Abstr.* **89**, 146371f.
Kirk, K. L. (1980). *J. Org. Chem.* **45**, 2015–2016.
Kirk, K. L., and Cohen, L. A. (1971). *J. Am. Chem. Soc.* **93**, 3060–3061.
Kitagawa, T., Ozasa, T., and Taniyama, H. (1969). *Yakugaku Zasshi* **89**, 285–286; *Chem. Abstr.* **70**, 115524m (1969).
Kjaer, A., and Larsen, P. O. (1959). *Acta Chem. Scand.* **13**, 1565–1574.
Klausner, Y. S., McCormick, W. M., and Chaiken, I. M. (1978). *Int. J. Pept. Protein Res.* **11**, 82–90.
Knapp, F. F., Jr. (1979). *J. Org. Chem.* **44**, 1007–1009.
Knapp, F. F., Jr., Ambrose, K. R., and Callahan, A. P. (1978). *Energy Res. Abstr.* **3**, No. 55587; *Chem. Abstr.* **90**, 204459z.
Knunyants, I. L., and Cheburkov, Yu. (1960). *Izv. Akad. Nauk SSSR, Otd. Khim. Nauk* pp. 2162–2167.
Kolc, J. (1969). *Collect. Czech. Chem. Commun.* **34**, 630–634.
Kollonitsch, J., and Barash, L. (1976). *J. Am. Chem. Soc.* **98**, 5591–5593.
Kollonitsch, J., Marburg, S., and Perkins, L. M. (1979). *J. Org. Chem.* **44**, 771–777.
Korpela, T., Lundell, J., and Pasanen, P. (1977). *Org. Prep. Proced. Int.* **9**, 57–62.
Kristensen, E. P., Larsen, L. M., Olsen, O., and Sørensen, H. (1980). *Acta Chem. Scand., Ser. B* **34**, 497–504.
Kum, K. (1969). *Carbohydr. Res.* **11**, 269–272.
Kunzi, H., Gillessen, D., Trzeciak, A., and Studer, R. O. (1974). *Helv. Chim. Acta* **57**, 231–232.
Kuss, E. (1967a). *Hoppe-Seyler's Z. Physiol. Chem.* **348**, 1589–1595.
Kuss, E. (1967b). *Hoppe-Seyler's Z. Physiol. Chem.* **348**, 1596–1601.
Kusumi, T., Kakisawa, H., Suzuki, S., Harada, K., and Kashima, C. (1978). *Bull. Chem. Soc. Japan* **51**, 1261–1262.
Laguzza, B. C., and Ganem, B. (1981). *Tetrahedron Lett.* **22**, 1483–1486.
Laitem, L., and Christiaens, L. (1976). *Bull. Soc. Chim. Fr.* pp. 2294–2296.
Langemann, A., and Scheer, M. (1969). *Helv. Chim. Acta* **52**, 1095–1097.
Larsen, P. O., and Kjaer, A. (1962). *Acta Chem. Scand.* **16**, 142–148.
Larsen, P. O., and Wieczorkowska, E. (1977). *Acta Chem. Scand., Ser. B* **31**, 109–113.
Lazar, J., and Sheppard, W. A. (1968). *J. Med. Chem.* **11**, 138–140.
Lea, P. J. (1978). *Int. Rev. Biochem.* **18**, 1–47.

Leclercq. J., Cossement, E., Boydens, R., Rodriguez, L. A. M., Brouwers, L., DeLaveleye, F., and Libert, W. (1978). *J. Chem. Soc., Chem. Commun.* pp. 46–47.
Lee, C. J., and Serif, G. S. (1970). *Biochemistry* **9**, 2068–2071.
Lee, F. G. H., Dickson, D. E., and Manian, A. A. (1971). *J. Med. Chem.* **14**, 266–268.
Lee, Y. K., and Kaneko, T. (1973a). *Bull. Chem. Soc. Jpn.* **46**, 2924–2926.
Lee, Y. K., and Kaneko, T. (1973b). *Bull. Chem. Soc. Jpn.* **46**, 3494–3498.
Lemaire, S., Yamashiro, D., Behrens, C., and Li, C. H. (1977). *J. Am. Chem. Soc.* **99**, 1577–1580.
Leonard, F., Wajngurt, A., Tschannen, W., and Block, F. B. (1965). *J. Med. Chem.* **8**, 812–815.
Letham, D. S., and Young, H. (1971). *Phytochemistry* **10**, 23–28.
Lettré, H., and Wölcke, U. (1967). *Justus Liebigs Ann. Chem.* **708**, 75–85.
Leukart, O., Caviezel, M., Eberle, A., Escher, E., Tun-Kyi, A., and Schwyzer, R. (1976). *Helv. Chim. Acta* **59**, 2184–2187.
Levenberg, B. (1968). *J. Biol. Chem.* **243**, 6009–6013.
Liberek, B., Buczel, C. Z., and Grzonka, Z. (1966). *Tetrahedron* **22**, 2303–2306.
Lidaks, M., Sluke, J., and Shvachkin, Y. P. (1968). *Khim. Geterotsikl. Soedin.* pp. 955–956.
Lidaks, M., Sluke, J., Poritere, S., and Shvachkin, Y. P. (1970). *Khim. Geterotsikl. Soedin.* pp. 529–533.
Lidaks, M., Sluke, J., Poritere, S., and Shvachkin, Y. P. (1971a). *Khim. Geterotsikl. Soedin.* pp. 427–428.
Lidaks, M., Paegle, R., Plata, M., and Shvachkin, Y. P. (1971b). *Khim. Geterotsikl. Soedin.* pp. 530–534.
Lipkowski, A. W., and Flouret, G. (1980). *Pol. J. Chem.* **54**, 2221.
Liu, Y. Y., Thern, E., and Liebman, A. A. (1978). *Can. J. Chem.* **56**, 2853–2855.
Liwshitz, Y., Rabinsohn, Y., and Haber, A. (1962). *J. Chem. Soc.* pp. 3589–3591.
Liwshitz, Y., Singerman, A., and Wiesel, Y. (1968a). *Isr. J. Chem.* **6**, 647–650.
Liwshitz, Y., Singerman, A., and Sokoloff, S. (1968b). *J. Chem. Soc. C* pp. 1843–1845.
Loncrini, D. F., and Walborsky, H. M. (1964). *J. Med. Chem.* **7**, 369–370.
Loy, R. S., and Hudlicky, M. (1976). *J. Fluorine Chem.* **7**, 421–426.
Lundt, B. F., Johansen, N. L., and Markussen, J. (1979). *Int. J. Pept. Protein Res.* **14**, 344–346.
McCord, T. J., Foyt, D. C., Kirkpatrick, J. L., and Davis, A. L. (1967). *J. Med. Chem.* **10**, 353–355.
McCord, T. J., Booth, L. D., and Davis, A. L. (1968). *J. Med. Chem.* **11**, 1077–1078.
McCord, T. J., Watson, R. N., DuBose, C. E., Hulme, K. L., and Davis, A. L. (1976). *J. Med. Chem.* **19**, 429–430.
McGee, J. O'D., Jimenez, M. H., Felix, A. M., Cardinale, G. J., and Udenfriend, S. (1973). *Arch. Biochem. Biophys.* **154**, 483–487.
MacLeod, J. K., Summons, R. E., Parker, C. W., and Letham, D. S. (1975). *J. Chem. Soc., Chem. Commun.* pp. 809–810.
Maki, Y., Masugi, T., Hiramitsu, T., and Ogiso, T. (1973). *Chem. Pharm. Bull.* **21**, 2460–2465.
Maki, Y., Fujii, S., and Inukai, K. (1977). *Yuki Gosei Kagaku Kyokaishi* **35**, 421–424; *Chem. Abstr.* **87**, 118052t (1977).
Marcus, A., Feeley, J., and Shannon, L. M. (1963). *Arch. Biochem. Biophys.* **100**, 80–85.
Märki, W., Oppliger, M., Thanei, P., and Schwyzer, R. (1977). *Helv. Chim. Acta* **60**, 798–806.
Marks, N. (1978). *In* "Frontiers in Neuroendocrinology," Vol. 5 (W. F. Ganong and L. Martini, eds.), pp. 329–377. Raren Press, New York.
Marlier, M., Dardenne, A., and Casimir, J. (1972). *Phytochemistry* **11**, 2597–2599.
Marshall, G. R., Humblet, C., Van Opdenbosch, N., and Zabrocki, J. (1981). *In* "Peptides: Synthesis, Structure, Function" (D. H. Rich and E. Gross, eds.), pp. 669–672. Pierce Chemical Co., Rockford, Illinois.
Martinez, A. P., Lee, W. W., and Goodman, L. (1968). *J. Med. Chem.* **11**, 60–62.
Martynov, V. S., Makarova, A. N., and Berlin, A. Y. (1967). *Zh. Obshch. Khim.* **37**, 70–76.

Masamune, T., and Ono, M. (1975). *Chem. Lett.* pp. 625–626.
Massey, T. H., and Fessler, D. C. (1976). *Biochemistry* **15**, 4906–4912.
Matsumoto, K., Ozaki, Y., Iwasaki, F., Horikawa, H., and Miyoshi, M. (1979). *Experientia* **35**, 850–851.
Matsumura, K., Takomasa, K., and Tashiro, H. (1969). *Bull. Chem. Soc. Jpn.* **42**, 1741–1743.
Matsuura, T., Nagamachi, T., Matsuo, K., and Nishinaga, A. (1968). *J. Med. Chem.* **11**, 899–900.
Matsuura, T., Nagamachi, T., and Nishinaga, A. (1969). *Chem. Pharm. Bull.* **17**, 2176–2177.
Matthies, D. (1978). *Synthesis* pp. 53–54.
Mauger, A. B., and Stuart, O. (1977). *J. Org. Chem.* **42**, 1000–1005.
Mauger, A. B., Irreverre, F., and Witkop, B. (1966). *J. Am. Chem. Soc.* **88**, 2019–2024.
Maurer, B., and Keller-Schierlein, W. (1969). *Helv. Chim. Acta* **52**, 388–396.
Mechanic, G., and Tanzer, M. L. (1970). *Biochem. Biophys. Res. Commun.* **41**, 1597–1604.
Meister, A. (1965). "Biochemistry of the Amino Acids," 2nd ed., Vol. 1, pp. 60–62. Academic Press, New York.
Mertes, M. P., and Ramsey, A. A. (1969). *J. Med. Chem.* **12**, 342–343.
Milkowski, J. D., Miller, F. M., Johnson, E. M., and Zenker, N. (1970). *J. Med. Chem.* **13**, 741–742.
Mizusaki, K., and Makisumi, S. (1981). *Bull. Chem. Soc. Jpn.* **54**, 470–472.
Monsigny, M. L. P., Delay, D., and Vaculik, M. (1977). *Carbohydr. Res.* **59**, 589–593.
Montagnoli, G., Pieroni, O., Nannicinni, L., and Muttini, A. (1977). *Gazz. Chim. Ital.* **107**, 409–414.
Monteiro, H. J. (1973). *J. Chem. Soc., Chem. Commun.* p. 2.
Moore, G. J. (1981). *In* "Peptides: Synthesis, Structure, Function" (D. H. Rich and E. Gross, eds.), pp. 245–248. Pierce Chemical Co., Rockford, Illinois.
Moore, J. A., Dice, J. R., Nicolaides, E. P., Westland, R. D., and Wittle, E. C. (1954). *J. Am. Chem. Soc.* **76**, 2884–2887, 2887–2891.
Moore, R. R. (1978). *Semisynth. Pept. Proteins, Pap. Int. Meet. Protein Semisynth., 1977* pp. 361–371.
Moore, S., Felix, A., Meienhofer, J., Smith, C. W., and Walter, R. (1977a). *J. Med. Chem.* **20**, 495–500.
Moore, S., Law, H. D., Brundish, D. E., Elliot, D. F., and Wade, R. (1977b). *J. Chem. Soc., Perkin Trans. 1* pp. 2025–2030.
Mooz, E. D. (1974). *In* "Handbook of Biochemistry and Molecular Biology" (G. Fasman, ed.), 3rd ed., Vol. 1, pp. 111–174. Chem. Rubber Publ. Co., Cleveland, Ohio.
Morell, J. L., Fleckenstein, P., and Gross, E. (1977). *J. Org. Chem.* **42**, 355–356.
Morgenstern, A. P., Schvijt, C., and Nauta, W. T. (1971). *J. Chem. Soc. C* pp. 3706–3712.
Moriya, T., Hagio, K., and Yoneda, N. (1975). *Bull. Chem. Soc. Jpn.* **48**, 2217–2218.
Morley, J. S. (1968). *Proc. R. Soc. London, Ser. B* **170**, 97–111.
Morley, J. S. (1969). *J. Chem. Soc. C* pp. 809–813.
Morrison, D. C. (1965). *J. Chem. Soc.* pp. 2264–2265.
Möschler, H. J., and Schwyzer, R. (1974). *Helv. Chim. Acta* **57**, 1576–1584.
Moussebois, C., Heremans, J. F., Merenyi, R., and Rennerts, W. (1977). *Helv. Chim. Acta* **60**, 237–242.
Müller, P., and Schütte, H. R. (1968). *Z. Naturforsch.*, **23B**, 491–493, 659.
Murakoshi, I., Ohmiya, S., and Haginiwa, J. (1972). *Chem. Pharm. Bull.* **20**, 609–611.
Murakoshi, I., Kato, F., and Haginiwa, J. (1974). *Chem. Pharm. Bull.* **22**, 480–481.
Nagai, W., Kirk, K. L., and Cohen, L. A. (1973). *J. Org. Chem.* **38**, 1971–1974.
Nagarajan, G. R., Diamond, L., and Ressler, C. (1973). *J. Org. Chem.* **38**, 621–624.
Nagasawa, H. T., and Elberling, J. A. (1966). *Tetrahedron Lett.* **44**, 5393–5399.
Nagasawa, H. T., Elberling, J. A., and Fraser, P. S. (1971). *J. Med. Chem.* **14**, 501–508.

Nagasawa, H. T., Elberling, J. A., and Shirota, F. N. (1975). *J. Med. Chem.* **18**, 826–830.
Nakagawa, M., Kato, S., Nakano, K., and Hino, T. (1981). *J. Chem. Soc., Chem. Commun.* pp. 855–856.
Nakajima, K., Takai, E., Tanaka, T., and Okawa, K. (1978). *Bull. Chem. Soc. Jpn.* **51**, 1577–1578.
Nakazawa, H., Enei, H., Okumura, S., Yoshida, H., and Yamada, H. (1972). *FEBS Lett.* **25**, 43–45.
Nakai, T., and Ohta, T. (1976). *Biochim. Biophys. Acta* **420**, 258–264.
Natarajan, S., Condon, M. E., Cohen, M. S., Reid, J., Cushman, D., Rubin, B., and Ondetti, M. (1979). *In* "Peptides: Structure and Biological Function" (E. Gross and J. Meienhofer, eds.), pp. 463–466. Pierce Chemical Co., Rockford, Illinois.
Natarajan, S., Condon, M., Nakane, M., Reid, J., Gordon, E., Cushman, D., and Ondetti, M. (1981). *In* "Peptides: Synthesis, Structure, Function" (D. H. Rich and E. Gross, eds.), pp. 429–433. Pierce Chemical Co., Rockford, Illinois.
Nestor, J. J., Jr., Ho, T. L., Simpson, R., Horner, B. L., Jones, G., McRae, G., and Vickery, B. (1981). *In* "Peptides: Synthesis, Structure, Function" (D. H. Rich and E. Gross, eds.), pp. 109–112. Pierce, Chemical Co., Rockford, Illinois.
Nestor, J. J., Jr., Ho, T. L., Simpson, R., Horner, B. L., Jones, G., and McRae, G., Vickery, B. (1982a). *J. Med. Chem.* **25**, 795–801.
Nestor, J. J., Jr., Horner, B. L., Ho, T. L., Tahilraman, R., Jones, G., McRae, G., and Vickery, B. (1982b). *Winter Gordon Res. Conf. Pept. 1982* Poster presentation.
Neubert, K., Balaspiri, L., and Losse, G. (1972). *Monatsh. Chem.* **103**, 1575–1584.
Nicolaides, E. D., and Lipnik, M. (1966). *J. Med. Chem.* **9**, 958–960.
Nicolaides, E. D., Craft, M. K., and DeWald, H. A. (1963). *J. Med. Chem.* **6**, 524–528.
Nimura, Y., and Hatanaka, S. I. (1974). *Phytochemistry* **13**, 175–178.
Nishimura, H., Mizuguchi, A., and Mizutani, J. (1975). *Tetrahedron Lett.* pp. 3201–3202.
Nishitani, T., Iwasaki, T., Mushika, Y., and Miyoshi, M. (1979). *J. Org. Chem.* **44**, 2019–2023.
Noguchi, M., Sakuma, H., and Tamaki, E. (1968). *Phytochemistry* **7**, 1861–1866.
Nollet, A. J. H., and Pandit, U. K. (1969a). *Tetrahedron* **25**, 5983–5987.
Nollet, A. J. H., and Pandit, U. K. (1969b). *Tetrahedron* **25**, 5989–5994.
Nollet, A. J. H., Huting, C. M., and Pandit, U. K. (1969). *Tetrahedron* **25**, 5971–5981.
Norton, S. J., and Sanders, E. (1967). *J. Med. Chem.* **10**, 961–963.
Norton, S. J., and Sullivan, P. T. (1970). *J. Hetereocycl. Chem.* **7**, 699–702.
Norton, S. J., Skinner, C. G., and Shive, W. (1961). *J. Org. Chem.* **26**, 1495–1498.
Nunami, K., Suzuki, M., and Yoneda, N. (1979). *J. Chem. Soc., Perkin Trans. 1* pp. 2224–2229.
Ogawa, Y., Tsuruoka, T., Inoue, S., and Nida, T. (1973). *Meiji Seika Kenkyu Nempo* **13**, 42–48; *Chem. Abstr.* **81**, 37806r (1974).
Ogle, T. D., Artinghaus, R. B., and Logan, M. A. (1962). *J. Biol. Chem.* **237**, 3667–3673.
Ohashi, Z., Maeda, M., McCloskey, J. A., and Nishimura, S. (1974). *Biochemistry* **13**, 2620–2625.
Ohhashi, J., and Harada, K. (1966). *Bull. Chem. Soc. Jpn.* **39**, 2287–2289.
Ohno, M., and Izumiya, N. (1965). *Bull. Chem. Soc. Jpn.* **38**, 1831–1840.
Ohno, M., Spande, T. F., and Witkop, B. (1974). *J. Org. Chem.* **39**, 2635–2637.
Okawa, K., and Nakajima, K. (1981). *Biopolymers* **20**, 1785–1791.
Okawa, K., Nakajimi, K., Tanaka, T., and Neya, M. (1982). *Bull. Chem. Soc. Jpn.* **55**, 174–176.
Oki, K., Suzuki, K., Tuchida, S., Saito, T., and Kotake, H. (1970). *Bull. Chem. Soc. Jpn.* **43**, 2554–2558.
Okumura, K., Iwasaki, T., Okawara, T., and Matsumoto, K. (1972). *Bull. Inst. Chem. Res., Kyoto Univ.* **50**, 209–215; *Chem. Abstr.* **77**, 165045w (1972).
Ong, H. H., Creveling, C. R., and Daly, J. W. (1969). *J. Med. Chem.* **12**, 458–461.
Oppliger, M., and Schwyzer, R. (1977). *Helv. Chim. Acta* **60**, 43–47.

Osgerby, J., and Pauson, P. (1958). *J. Chem. Soc.* pp. 656–660.
Otani, T. T., and Briley, M. R. (1974). *J. Pharm. Sci.* **63**, 1253–1256.
Overberger, C. G., David, K. H., and Moore, J. A. (1972). *Macromolecules* **5**, 368–372.
Ozaki, Y., Iwasaki, T., Miyoshi, M., and Matsumoto, K. (1979a). *J. Org. Chem.* **44**, 1714–1716.
Ozaki, Y., Maeda, S., Miyoshi, M., and Matsumoto, K. (1979b). *Synthesis* pp. 316–317.
Park, W. K., Choi, C., Rioux, F., and Regoli, D. (1974). *Can. J. Biochem.* **52**, 113–119.
Peggion, E., Strasorier, L., and Cosani, A. (1970). *J. Am. Chem. Soc.* **92**, 381–386.
Perlman, D., Perlman, K. L., Bodanszky, M., Bodanszky, A., Foltz, R. L., and Matthews, H. W. (1977). *Bioorg. Chem.* **6**, 263–271.
Petrzilka, T., and Fehr, C. (1973). *Helv. Chim. Acta* **56**, 1218–1224.
Pettit, G. R. (1970). "Synthetic Peptides," Vol. 1. Van Nostrand-Reinhold, Princeton, New Jersey.
Pettit, G. R. (1973). "Synthetic Peptides," Vol. 2. Van Nostrand-Reinhold, Princeton, New Jersey.
Pettit, G. R. (1975). "Synthetic Peptides," Vol. 3. Academic Press, New York.
Pettit, G. R. (1976). "Synthetic Peptides," Vol. 4. Elsevier, Amsterdam.
Philip, R. P., and Robertson, A. V. (1977). *Aust. J. Chem.* **30**, 123–130.
Pinder, R. M., Butcher, B. H., Buxton, D. A., and Howells, D. J. (1971). *J. Med. Chem.* **14**, 892–893.
Pinder, U. (1978). *Arch. Pharm. (Weinheim, Ger.)* **311**, 615–621.
Pinker, T. G., Young, G. T., Elliot, D. F., and Wade R. (1975). *J. Chem. Soc., Perkin Trans. 1* pp. 220–228.
Pirrung, M. C. (1980). *Tetrahedron Lett.* pp. 4577–4578.
Pliška, V., and Marbach, P. (1978). *Eur. J. Pharmacol.* **49**, 213–222.
Podkoscielny, W., Podgorski, M., and Smulkowska, E. (1978). *Pol. J. Chem.* **52**, 2455–2459.
Poduška, K., and Rudinger, J. (1966). *Collect. Czech. Chem. Commun.* **31**, 2938–2954.
Poduška, K., Rudinger, J., Gloede, J., and Gross, H. (1969). *Collect. Czech. Chem. Commun.* **34**, 1002–1006.
Porter, T. H., and Shive, W. (1968). *J. Med. Chem.* **11**, 402–403.
Porter, T. H., Gipson, R. M., and Shive, W. (1968). *J. Med. Chem.* **11**, 263–266.
Poskiene, R., Karpavicius, K., Pozerauskas, A., Kildisheva, O. V., and Knunyants, I. L. (1976). *Izv. Akad. Nauk. SSSR, Ser. Khim.* pp. 407–411.
Pospišek, J., and Bláha, K. (1976). *In* "Peptides 1976" (A. Loffet, ed.), pp. 95–100. Editions de l'Université de Bruxelles, Belgium.
Pospíšek, J., and Bláha, K. (1977). *Collect. Czech. Chem. Commun.* **42**, 1069–1076.
Pospíšek, J., Toma, S., Fric, I., and Bláha, K. (1980). *Collect. Czech. Chem. Commun.* **45**, 435–441.
Powers, J. C., and Gupton, B. F. (1977). *In* "Methods in Enzymology" (W. B. Jakoby and M. Wilchek, eds.), Vol. 46, pp. 208–216. Academic Press, New York.
Pracejus, H., and Winter, S. (1964). *Chem. Ber.* **97**, 3173–3182.
Prudchenko, A. T. (1970). *Izv. Sib. Otd. Akad. Nauk SSSR, Ser. Khim. Nauk* pp. 95–100; *Chem. Abstr.* **75**, 6265k (1971).
Rajh, H. M., Uitzetter, J. H., Westerhuis, L. W., Van denDrics, C. L., and Tesser, G. I. (1979). *Int. J. Pept. Protein Res.* **14**, 68–79.
Rajh, H. M., Mariman, E. C. M., Tesser, G. I., and Nivard, R. J. F. (1980). *Int. J. Pept. Protein Res.* **15**, 200–210.
Rakhshinda, M. A., and Khan, N. H. (1978). *Indian J. Chem., Sect. B* **16B**, 634–635.
Rakhshinda, M. A., and Khan, N. H. (1979). *Synth. Commun.* **9**, 351–361.
Rapp, P., Kumagai, H., Yamada, H., Ueno, T., and Fukami, H. (1975). *Biochem. Biophys. Res. Commun.* **64**, 241–247.
Ratner, S., and Clark, H. T. (1937). *J. Am. Chem. Soc.* **59**, 200–206.

Reimann, E., and Voss, D. (1977). *Arch. Pharm.* (*Weinheim, Ger.*) **310**, 102–109.
Ressler, C., and Banerjee, S. N. (1976). *J. Org. Chem.* **41**, 1336–1340.
Ressler, C., Banerjee, S. N., Tsutsumi, M., Diamond, L., and Sawyer, W. (1979). *In* "Peptides: Structure and Biological Function" (E. Gross and J. Meienhofer, eds.), pp. 217–220. Pierce Chemical Co., Rockford, Illinois.
Rich, D. H., and Tam, J. P. (1978). *Synthesis* p. 46.
Richards, R. W., Rodwell, J. L., and Schmalzl, K. J. (1977). *J. Chem. Soc., Chem. Commun.* pp. 849–850.
Ried, W., and Schmidt, E. (1966). *Justus Liebigs Ann. Chem.* **695**, 217–225, and references therein.
Rinaldi, A., Cosso, P., and De Marco, C. (1976). *J. Chromatogr.* **120**, 221–223.
Rivett, D. E., and Stewart, F. H. C. (1976). *Aust. J. Chem.* **29**, 2095–2100.
Roberts, D., Suda, K., Samanen, J., and Kemp, D. S. (1980). *Tetrahedron Lett.* **21**, 3435–3438.
Robertson, A. V., and Witkop, B. (1962). *J. Am. Chem. Soc.* **84**, 1697–1701.
Roeske, R. W., Weitl, F. L., Prasad, K. U., and Thompson, R. M. (1976). *J. Org. Chem.* **41**, 1260–1261.
Rosamond, J. D., and Ferger, M. F. (1976). *J. Med. Chem.* **19**, 873–876.
Rosenthal, A., and Brink, A. J. (1976a). *Carbohydr. Res.* **46**, 289–292.
Rosenthal, A., and Brink, A. J. (1976b). *Carbohydr. Res.* **47**, 332–336.
Rosenthal, A., and Dooley, K. (1978). *Carbohydr. Res.* **60**, 193–199.
Rosenthal, A., and Ratcliffe, M. (1977). *J. Carbohydr., Nucleosides, Nucleotides* **4**, 199–214.
Rosenthal, G. A. (1975). *Anal. Biochem.* **65**, 60–65.
Ross, R. B., Noll, C. I., Ross, W. C. J., Nadkarni, M. V., Morrison, B. H., Jr., and Bond, H. W. (1961). *J. Med. Pharm. Chem.* **3**, 1–23.
Rotman, A., Gertner, D., and Zilkha, A. (1967). *Can. J. Chem.* **45**, 2469–2471.
Rudinger, J. (1972). *In* "Drug Design" (E. J. Ariens, ed.), Vol. 2, pp. 319–419. Academic Press, New York.
Rudinger, J., and Jošt, K. (1964). *Experientia* **20**, 570–571.
Sadeh, T., Davis, M. A., and Giese, R. W. (1976). *J. Pharm. Sci.* **65**, 623–625.
Sakarellos, C., Donzel, B., and Goodman, M. (1976). *Biopolymers* **15**, 1835–1840.
Santoso, S., Kemmer, T., and Trowitzsch, W. (1981a). *Liebigs Ann. Chem.* pp. 642–657.
Santoso, S., Kemmer, T., and Trowitzsch, W. (1981b). *Liebigs Ann. Chem.* pp. 658–667.
Sasaki, A. W., and Bricas, E. (1980). *Tetrahedron Lett.* pp. 4263–4264.
Schatz, V. B., O'Brien, B. C., and Sandusky, W. R. (1968). *J. Med. Chem.* **11**, 140–142.
Schenk, W., and Schütte, H. R. (1961). *Naturwissenschaften* **48**, 223.
Schlögl, K. (1957). *Monatsh. Chem.* **88**, 601–621.
Schneider, G. (1958). *Biochem. Z.* **330**, 428–432.
Schöberl, A., Borchers, J., and Hantzsch, D. (1968). *Chem. Ber.* **101**, 373–374.
Schöllkopf, U., and Meyer, R. (1975). *Angew. Chem.* **87**, 624–625.
Schöllkopf, U., and Meyer, R. (1977). *Liebigs Ann. Chem.* pp. 1174–1182.
Schöllkopf, U., Harms, R., and Hoppe, D. (1973). *Liebigs Ann. Chem.* pp. 611–618.
Scholz, D., and Schmidt, U. (1974). *Chem. Ber.* **107**, 2295–2298.
Schreiber, W., and Lautsch, W. (1965). *Hoppe-Seyler's Z. Physiol. Chem.* **340**, 95–96.
Schwyzer, R. (1980). *Proc. R. Soc. London, Ser. B* **210**, 5–20.
Schwyzer, R., and Caviezel, M. (1971). *Helv. Chim. Acta* **54**, 1395–1400.
Schwyzer, R., and Ludescher, U. (1968). *Biochemistry* **7**, 2514–2518.
Schwyzer, R., Tun-Kyi, A., Escher, E., Eberle, A. N., Caviezel, M., and Leukart, O. (1976). *Helv. Chim. Acta* **59**, 2181–2183.
Schwyzer, R., Do, K. Q., Eberle, A. N., and Fauchère, J.-L. (1981). *Helv. Chim. Acta* **64**, 2078–2083.

Scott, A. I., and Wilkinson, T. J. (1981). *J. Labelled Compd. Radiopharm.* **18**, 347–352.
Scott, J. W., Focella, A., Hengartner, U. O., Parrish, P. R., and Valentine, D., Jr. (1980). *Synth. Commun.* **10**, 529–540.
Seela, F., and Hasselmann, D. (1979). *Chem. Ber.* **112**, 3072–3080.
Seeman, N. C., McGandy, E. L., and Rosenstein, R. D. (1972). *J. Am. Chem. Soc.* **94**, 1717–1720.
Semple, J. E., Wang, D. C., Lysenko, Z., and Joullie, M. M. (1980). *J. Am. Chem. Soc.* **102**, 7505–7510.
Senoh, S., Imamoto, S., Maeno, Y., Tokuyama, T., Sakan, T., Komamine, A., and Hattori, S. (1964). *Tetrahedron Lett.* pp. 3431–3436.
Senoh, S., Maeno, Y., Imamoto, S., Komamine, A., Shizuo, H., Yamashita, K., and Matsui, M. (1967). *Bull. Chem. Soc. Jpn.* **40**, 379–384.
Sethi, M. L., Rao, G. S., and Kapadia, G. J. (1973). *J. Pharm. Sci.* **62**, 1802–1806.
Seto, Y., Torii, K., Bori, K., Inabata, K., Kuwata, S., and Watanabe, H. (1974). *Bull. Chem. Soc. Jpn.* **47**, 151–155.
Shakhnazaryan, G. M., Saakyan, L. A., and Dangyan, M. (1968). *Zh. Org. Khim.* **4**, 1914–1919; *Chem. Abstr.* **70**, 29258w (1969).
Shaw, G. J., Ellingham, P. J., and Nixon, L. N. (1981). *Phytochemistry* **20**, 1853–1855.
Sheehan, J. C., and Ledis, S. L. (1973). *J. Am. Chem. Soc.* **95**, 875–879.
Sheehan, J. C., and Whitney, J. G. (1962). *J. Am. Chem. Soc.* **84**, 3980.
Sheehan, J. C., and Yang, D. D. H. (1958). *J. Am. Chem. Soc.* **80**, 1158–1164.
Shiba, T., Mukunoki, Y., and Akiyama, H. (1975). *Bull. Chem. Soc. Jpn.* **48**, 1902–1906.
Shiba, T., Ukita, T., Mizuno, K., Teshima, T., and Wakamiya, T. (1977). *Tetrahedron Lett.* pp. 2681–2684.
Shimohigashi, Y., Lee, S., and Izumiya, N. (1976). *Bull. Chem. Soc. Japan* **49**, 3280–3284.
Shimohigashi, Y., Lee, S., Aoyagi, H., Kato, T., and Izumiya, N. (1977). *Int. J. Pept. Protein Res.* **10**, 323–327.
Shiraishi, K., Ichihara, A., and Sakamura, S. (1977). *Agric. Biol. Chem.* **41**, 2497–2498.
Shirota, F. N., Nagasawa, H. T., and Elberling, J. A. (1977a). *J. Med. Chem.* **20**, 1176–1181.
Shirota, F. N., Nagasawa, H. T., and Elberling, J. A. (1977b). *J. Med. Chem.* **20**, 1623–1627.
Shrift, A., Bechard, D., Harcup, C., and Fowden, L. (1976). *Plant Physiol.* **58**, 248–252.
Shvachkin, Y. P., and Berestenko, M. K. (1964). *Zh. Obshch. Khim.* **34**, 3506–3507.
Shvachkin, Y. P., and Olsuf'eva, E. N. (1979). *Zh. Obshch. Khim.* **49**, 1133–1138; see also pp. 1139–1146, 1147–1150, 1151–1156, 1157–1161.
Shvachkin, Y. P., and Syrtsova, L. A. (1963). *Zh. Obshch. Khim.* **33**, 3805–3810.
Shvachkin, Y. P., Syrtsova, L. A., and Filatova, M. P. (1963a). *Zh. Obshch. Khim.* **33**, 2487–2493.
Shvachkin, Y. P., Novikova, M. A., Reznikova, M. B., and Padyukova, N. Sh. (1963b). *Zh. Obshch. Khim.* **33**, 4022–4023.
Shvachkin, Y. P., Korshunova, G. A., Bashkirova, N. A., and Prokof'ev, M. A. (1968). *Dokl. Akad. Nauk SSSR* **179**, 1127–1128; *Chem. Abstr.* **69**, 67595r (1968).
Sievertsson, H., Cartensson, S., Bowers, C. Y., Friesen, H. G., and Folkers, K. (1973). *Acta Pharm. Suec.* **10**, 297–308.
Signor, A., Bonora, G. M., Biondi, L., Nisato, D., Marzotto, A., and Scoffone, E. (1971). *Biochemistry* **10**, 2748–2752.
Sila, B. (1964). *Rocz. Chem.* **38**, 1387–1391; *Chem. Abstr.* **64**, 19756d.
Sila, B., Wojtanis, J., and Lesiak, T. (1973). *Rocz. Chem.* **47**, 1281–1284; *Chem. Abstr.* **80**, 15164g.
Silverman, R. B., and Holladay, M. W. (1981). *J. Am. Chem. Soc.* **103**, 7357–7358.
Singerman, A., and Liwschitz, Y. (1968). *Tetrahedron Lett.* pp. 4733–4734.
Skinner, W. A., and Johansson, J. G. (1972). *J. Med. Chem.* **15**, 427–428.
Slouka, J. (1978). *Pharmazie* **33**, 426–428.

Smith, C. W., Ferger, M. F., and Chan, W. Y. (1975). *J. Med. Chem.* **18**, 822–825.
Smith, C. W., Skala, G., and Walter, R. (1978). *J. Med. Chem.* **21**, 115–117.
Smith, S. C., and Sloane, N. H. (1967). *Biochim. Biophys. Acta* **148**, 414–422.
Snider, B. B., and Duncia, J. V. (1981). *J. Org. Chem.* **46**, 3223–3226.
Snow, M. L., Lauinger, C., and Ressler, C. (1968). *J. Org. Chem.* **33**, 1774–1780.
Snyder, H., Reedy, A., and Lennarz, W. (1958). *J. Am. Chem. Soc.* **80**, 835–838.
Soriano, D. S., Podraza, K. F., and Cromwell, N. H. (1980). *J. Heterocycl. Chem.* **17**, 623–624.
Spatola, A. F., Agarwal, N. S., Bettag, A. L., Yankeelov, J. A., Bowers, C. Y., and Vale, W. W. (1980). *Biochem. Biophys. Res. Commun.* **97**, 1014–1023.
Spatola, A. F., Bettag, A., Agarwal, N., Saneii, H., Anwer, M., Edwards, J., and Owen, T. (1981). *In* "Peptides: Synthesis, Structure, Function" (D. H. Rich and E. Gross, eds.), pp. 613–616. Pierce Chemical Co., Rockford, Illinois.
Spencer, I. D., and Notation, A. D. (1962). *Can. J. Chem.* **40**, 1374–1379.
Springer, R. H., Haggerty, W. J., Jr., and Cheng, C. C. (1965). *J. Heterocycl. Chem.* **2**, 49–52.
Srinivasan, A., Stephenson, R. W., and Olsen, R. (1977). *J. Org. Chem.* **42**, 2253–2256, also 2256–2260.
Stammer, C. H., and Webb, R. G. (1969). *J. Org. Chem.* **34**, 2306–2311.
Steglich, W., Heininger, H. V., Dworschak, H., and Weygand, F. (1967). *Angew. Chem., Int. Ed. Engl.* **6**, 807–808.
Steglich, W., Frauendorfer, E., and Weygand, F. (1971). *Chem. Ber.* **104**, 687–690.
Stoev, S. B., Vulkova, A. T., and Aleksiev, B. V. (1973). *Dokl. Bolg. Akad. Nauk* **26**, 1633–1636; *Chem. Abstr.* **80**, 133802m (1974).
Stöhrer, G., Salemnick, G., and Brown, G. B. (1973). *Biochemistry* **12**, 5084–5086.
Stoll, A., and Seebeck, E. (1951). *Helv. Chim. Acta* **34**, 481–487.
Straukas, I., Dirvyanskite, N., and Degutis, Y. (1971). *Zh. Org. Khim.* **7**, 1390–1396.
Sullivan, P. T., and Norton, S. J. (1971). *J. Med. Chem.* **14**, 557–558.
Sullivan, P. T., Kester, M., and Norton, S. J. (1968). *J. Med. Chem.* **11**, 1172–1176.
Sullivan, P. T., Sullivan, C. B., and Norton, S. J. (1971). *J. Med. Chem.* **14**, 211–214.
Suzuki, M., Nunami, K., and Yoneda, N. (1978). *J. Chem. Soc., Chem. Commun.* pp. 270–271.
Synodis, J., and Roberts, D. (1981). *In* "Peptides: Synthesis, Structure, Function" (D. H. Rich and E. Gross, eds.), pp. 101–104. Pierce Chemical Co., Rockford, Illinois.
Szelke, M., Hudson, D., Sharpe, R., MacIntyre, I., Fink, G., and Pickering, A. (1977). *In* "Molecular Endocrinology" (I. MacIntyre and M. Szelke, eds.), pp. 57–70. Elsevier/North Holland, Amsterdam.
Szilagyi, L., and Gyorgydeak, Z. (1979). *J. Am. Chem. Soc.* **101**, 427–432.
Takemoto, T., Kuike, K., Nakajima, T., and Arihara, S. (1975). *Yakugaku Zasshi* **95**, 448–452; *Chem. Abstr.* **83**, 97875p (1975).
Tamura, M., and Harada, K. (1978). *Synth. Commun.* **8**, 345–351.
Taniguchi, M., and Hino, T. (1981). *Tetrahedron* **37**, 1487–1494.
Tautz, W., Teitel, S., and Brossi, A. (1973). *J. Med. Chem.* **16**, 705–707.
Taylor, J. B., Lewis, J. W., and Jacklin, M. (1970). *J. Med. Chem.* **13**, 1226–1227.
Teitei, T. (1979). *Aust. J. Chem.* **32**, 1631–1634.
Teitei, T., and Harris, R. L. N. (1979). *Aust. J. Chem.* **32**, 1329–1337.
Teng, T. A., and Pang, P. C. (1978). *Hua Hsueh Hsueh Pao* **36**, 233–237; *Chem. Abstr.* **90**, 204445s (1979).
Teshima, T., Nomoto, S., Wakamiya, T., and Shiba, T. (1976). *Tetrahedron Lett.* pp. 2343–2346.
Tesser, G. I., and Nefkens, G. H. L. (1959). *Recl. Trav. Chim. Pays-Bas* **78**, 404–407.
Tesser, G. I., Slits, H. G. A., and Van Nispen, J. W. (1973). *Int. J. Pept. Protein Res.* **5**, 119–122.
Teuber, H. J., and Krause, H. (1978). *Liebigs Ann. Chem.* pp. 1311–1326.
Teuber, H. J., Krause, H., and Berariu, V. (1978). *Liebigs Ann. Chem.* pp. 757–770.

Thanassi, J. W. (1970). *Biochemistry* **9**, 525–532.
Thompson, J. F., Morris, C. J., Asen, S., and Irreverre, F. (1961). *J. Biol. Chem.* **236**, 1183–1185.
Tjoeng, F., Ekkehard, K., Breitmaier, E., and Jung, G. (1976). *Chem. Rev.* **109**, 2615–2621.
Tolman, V., and Beneš, J. (1976). *J. Fluorine Chem.* **7**, 397–407.
Tolman, V., and Vereš K. (1966). *Tetrahedron Lett.* pp. 3909–3912.
Tomlinson, G., and Viswanatha, T. (1973). *Can. J. Biochem.* **51**, 754–763.
Traynham, J. G., and Williams, U. R. (1962). *J. Org. Chem.* **27**, 2959–2960.
Trippett, S. (1957). *J. Chem. Soc.* (*London*) pp. 1929–1930.
Trout, G. E. (1972). *J. Med. Chem.* **15**, 1259–1261.
Tsou, K. C., Su, H. C. F., Turner, R. B., and Mirachi, U. (1966). *J. Med. Chem.* **9**, 57–60.
Tsuji, S., Kusumoto, S., and Shiba, T. (1975). *Chem. Lett.* pp. 1281–1284.
Tsushima, T., Nishikawa, J., Seto, T., Tanida, H., Tori, K., Tsuji, T., Misaki, S., and Suefuji, M. (1980). *Tetrahedron Lett.* pp. 3593–3594.
Turan, A., and Manning, M. (1977). *J. Med. Chem.* **20**, 1169–1172.
Uchiyama, M., and Abe, H. (1977). *Agric. Biol. Chem.* **41**, 1549–1551.
Urabe, Y., Okawara, T., Okurkura, K., Miyoshi, M., and Matsumoto, K. (1974). *Synthesis* p. 440.
Urabe, Y., Iwaski, T., Matsumoto, K., and Miyoshi, M. (1975). *Tetrahedron Lett.* pp. 997–1000.
Usher, J. J. (1980). *J. Chem. Res., Synop.* p. 30.
Uskert, A., Neder, A., and Kasztreiner, E. (1973). *Magy. Kem. Foly.* **79**, 333–334; *Chem. Abstr.* **79**, 79147r (1973).
Van Nispen, J. W., and Tesser, G. I. (1972). *Synth. Commun.* **2**, 207–210.
Van Nispen, J. W., Tesser, G. I., and Nivard, R. J. F. (1977a). *Int. J. Pept. Protein Res.* **9**, 193–202.
Van Nispen, J. W., Smeets, P. J. H., Poll, E. H. A., and Tesser, G. I. (1977b). *Int. J. Pept. Protein Res.* **9**, 203–212.
Van Pee, K. H., Salcher, O., and Lingens, F. (1981). *Liebigs Ann. Chem.* pp. 233–239.
Van Thach, T., Kojro, E., and Grzonka, Z. (1977). *Tetrahedron* **33**, 2299–2302.
Varlet, J. M., Collignon, N., and Savignac, P. (1979). *Can. J. Chem.* **57**, 3216–3220.
Vasella, A., and Voeffray, R. (1981). *J. Chem. Soc., Chem. Commun.* pp. 97–98.
Vdovina, R. G., and Karpova, A. V. (1968). *Chem. Natur. Compounds* **4**, 35–39.
Veber, D. F. (1981). *In* "Peptides: Synthesis, Structure, Function" (D. H. Rich and E. Gross, eds.), pp. 685–694. Pierce Chemical Co., Rockford, Illinois.
Veber, D. F., Strachan, R. G., Bergstrand, S. J., Holly, F. W., Homnick, C. F., Hirschmann, R., Torchiana, M. L., and Saperstein, R. (1976). *J. Am. Chem. Soc.* **98**, 2367–2369.
Veber, D. F., Holly, F. W., Nutt, R. F., Bergstrand, S., Brady, S. F., Hirschmann, R., Glitzer, M. S., and Saperstein, R. (1979). *Nature* (*London*) **280**, 512–514.
Vecchio, G. L., Conti, M. P., and Cum, G. (1963). *Biochem. Appl.* **10**, 192–206.
Verbiscar, A. J., and Witkop, B. (1970). *J. Org. Chem.* **35**, 1924–1927.
Veselova, L. N., and Chaman, E. S. (1973). *Zh. Obshch. Khim.* **43**, 1637–1640.
Vičar, J., Maloň, P., Trka, A., Smolikova, J., Fric, I., and Blaha, K. (1977). *Collect. Czech. Chem. Commun.* **42**, 2701–2717.
Vickery, H. B. (1972). *Adv. Protein Chem.* **26**, 81–171.
Vincze, A., Lachman, C., and Cohon, S. (1968). *Isr. J. Chem.* **6**, 641–646.
Vine, W. H., Hsieh, K., and Marshall, G. R. (1981). *J. Med. Chem.* **24**, 1043–1047.
Vinograd, L. K., Shalygina, O. D., Kostyuchenko, N. P., and Suvorov, N. N. (1974). *Khim. Geterotsikl. Soedin.* pp. 1236–1239; *Chem. Abstr.* **82**, 57514t (1975).
Visser, G. W. M., Diemer, E. L., and Kaspersen, F. M. (1979). *Int. J. Appl. Radiat. Isot.* **30**, 749–752.
Voskuyl-Holtkamp, I., and Schattenkerk, C. (1979). *Int. J. Pept. Protein Res.* **13**, 185–194.

Wade, T. N., and Guedj, R. (1979). *Tetrahedron Lett.* pp. 3953–3954.
Wade, T. N., and Khéribet, R. (1980). *J. Org. Chem.* **45**, 5333–5335.
Wade, T. N., Gaymard, F., and Guedj, R. (1979). *Tetrahedron Lett.* pp. 2681–2682.
Waisuisz, J. M., van der Hoeven, M. G., and Nijenhuis, B. (1957). *J. Am. Chem. Soc.* **79**, 4524–4527.
Wakamiya, T., Teshima, T., Sakakibara, H., Fukukawa, K., and Shiba, T. (1977). *Bull. Chem. Soc. Jpn.* **50**, 1984–1989.
Wakamiya, T., Mizuno, K., Ukita, T., Teshima, T., and Shiba, T. (1978). *Bull. Chem. Soc. Jpn.* **51**, 850–854.
Wakamiya, T., Konishi, K., Chaki, H., Teshima, T., and Shiba, T. (1981). *Heterocycles* **15**, 999–1005.
Waki, M., Kitajima, Y., and Izumiya, N. (1981). *Synthesis* pp. 266–268.
Walter, R. (1973). *In* "Organic Selenium Compounds: Their Chemistry and Biology" (D. L. Klayman, ed.), pp. 601–627. Wiley, New York.
Walter, R., Schwartz, J. L., Hechter, A., Dousa, T., and Hoffmann, P. J. (1972). *Endocrinology* **91**, 213–222.
Wang, T. S. T., and Vida, J. A. (1974). *J. Med. Chem.* **17**, 1120–1122.
Warren, C. B., Minard, R. D., and Matthews, C. N. (1974). *J. Org. Chem.* **39**, 3375–3378.
Watanabe, H., Kuwata, S., Sakata, T., and Matsumura, K. (1966). *Bull. Chem. Soc. Jpn.* **39**, 3473–3476.
Watanabe, H., Kuwata, S., Naoe, K., and Nishida, Y. (1968). *Bull. Chem. Soc. Jpn.* **41**, 1634–1638.
Weinges, K., Brune, G., and Droste, H. (1980). *Liebigs Ann. Chem.* pp. 212–218.
Weinkam, R. J., and Jorgensen, E. C. (1971a). *J. Am. Chem. Soc.* **93**, 7028–7033
Weinkam, R. J., and Jorgensen, E. C. (1971b). *J. Am. Chem. Soc.* **93**, 7033–7038.
Weiss, B. (1977). *Chem. Phys. Lipids* **19**, 347–355.
Westerik, J. O., and Wolfenden, R. (1974). *J. Biol. Chem.* **249**, 6351–6353.
Weygand, F., and Mayer, F. (1968). *Chem. Ber.* **101**, 2065–2068.
Weygand, F., Steglich, W., Oettmeier, W., Maierhofer, A., and Coy, R. S. (1966). *Angew. Chem. Int. Ed. Engl.* **5**, 600–601.
Weygand, F., Steglich, W., and Fraunberger, F. (1967). *Angew. Chem., Int. Ed. Engl.* **6**, 808.
Weygand, F., Wolfgang, S., and Oettmeier, W. (1970a). *Chem. Ber.* **103**, 818–826.
Weygand, F., Steglich, W., and Oettmeier, W. (1970b). *Chem. Ber.* **103**, 1655–1663.
Whitlock, B. J., Lipton, S. H., and Strong, F. M. (1965). *J. Org. Chem.* **30**, 115–118.
Wieland, T., Dungen, A., and Birr, C. (1971). *Justus Liebigs Ann. Chem.* **752**, 109–114.
Wieland, T., Jorden de Urries, M. P., Indest, H., Faulstich, H., Gieren, A., Sturm, M., and Hoppe, W. (1974). *Liebigs Ann. Chem.* pp. 1570–1579.
Wieland, T., Rohr, G., Faulstich, H., Zobeley, S., and Trischmann, H. (1977a). *Liebigs Ann. Chem.* pp. 381–386.
Wieland, T., Schermer, D., Rohr, G., and Faulstich, H. (1977b). *Liebigs Ann. Chem.* pp. 806–810.
Wieland, T., Birr, C., and Zanotti, G. (1978). *Angew. Chem.* **90**, 67–68.
Wilchek, M., Ariely, S. and Patchornik, A. (1968). *J. Org. Chem.* **33**, 1258–1259.
Winn, M., Rasmussen, R., Minard, F., Kynel, J., and Plotnikoff, N. (1975). *J. Med. Chem.* **18**, 434–437.
Wittig, G., Eggers, H., and Duffner, P. (1958). *Justus Liebigs Ann. Chem.* **619**, 10–27.
Woenckhaus, C., and Stock, A. (1965). *Z. Naturforsch.*, **20B**, 400.
Wolfe, S., Militello, G., Ferrari, C., Hasan, S. K., and Lee, S. L. (1979). *Tetrahedron Lett.* pp. 3913–3916.
Wright, D. E., and Rodbell, M. (1980). *J. Biol. Chem.* **255**, 10884–10887.

Wyler, H., and Chiovini, J. (1968). *Helv. Chim. Acta* **51**, 1476–1494.
Yabe, Y., Miura, C., Horikoshi, H., and Baba, Y. (1976). *Chem. Pharm. Bull.* **24**, 3149–3153.
Yabe, Y., Morita, A., Miura, C., Kobayashi, S., and Baba, Y. (1977). *Chem. Pharm. Bull.* **25**, 2731–2734.
Yabe, Y., Miura, C., Baba, Y., and Sawano, S. (1978). *Chem. Pharm. Bull.* **26**, 993–997.
Yamada, S., Hongo, C., and Chibata, I. (1978). *Agric. Biol. Chem.* **42**, 1521–1526.
Yamada, S., Hongo, C., Yoshioka, R., and Chibata, I. (1979). *Agric. Biol. Chem.* **43**, 395–396.
Yamada, T., Takashima, K., Miyazawa, T., Kuwata, S., and Watanabe, H. (1977). *Bull. Chem. Soc. Jpn.* **51**, 878–883.
Yankeelov, J. A., and Jolley, G. J. (1972). *Biochemistry* **11**, 159–163.
Yankeelov, J. A., Fok, K. F., and Carothers, D. J. (1978). *J. Org. Chem.* **43**, 1623–1624.
Zaoral, M., Kolc, J., Korenicki, F., Černěckij, V., and Šorm, F. (1967). *Collect. Czech. Chem. Commun.* **32**, 843–853.
Zaoral, M., Krchnak, V., Brtník, F., Machova, A., and Shopkova, J. (1979). *Collect. Czech. Chem. Commun.* **44**, 2443–2450.
Zdansky, G. (1967). *Ark. Kemi* **27**, 447–452; *Chem. Abstr.* **68**, 13332p (1968).
Zdansky, G. (1968a). *Ark. Kemi* **29**, 47–56; *Chem. Abstr.* **69**, 67684u (1968).
Zdansky, G. (1968b). *Ark. Kemi* **29**, 437–442, 443–448; *Chem. Abstr.* **69**, 87433q, 87434r (1968).
Zdansky, G. (1973). *In* "Organic Selenium Compounds: Their Chemistry and Biology" (D. L. Klayman, ed.), pp. 579–600. Wiley, New York.
Zecchini, G. P., and Paradisi, M. P. (1979). *J. Heterocycl. Chem.* **16**, 1587–1597.
Zee-Cheng, R. K. Y., and Olson, R. E. (1980). *Biochem. Biophys. Res. Commun.* **94**, 1128–1132.
Zhuze, A. L., Jošt, K., Kasafirek, E., and Rudinger, J. (1964). *Collect. Czech. Chem. Commun.* **29**, 2648–2662.
Zilkha, A., Friedman, G., and Gertner, D. (1967). *Can. J. Chem.* **45**, 2979–2985.

Author Index

A

Aanning, H. L., 195, *215*
Abderhalden, E., 121, 126, *197*
Abe, H., 424, *447*
Abe, J., 290, *339*
Abeles, R. H., 287, 290, 311, *334*
Abelson, J., 51, *64*
Abiko, T., 189, *213*
Ablewhite, A. J., 407, *429*
Abraham, E. P., 289, *333*
Abshire, C. J., *429*
Ackermann, W. W., 379, *429*
Adachi, H., 83, 85, 89, 105, *109,* 125, 138, *215*
Adams, E., 352, 409, *429*
Adelman, J., 56, *61*
Afzali-Ardakani, A., 368, *429*
Agarwal, B., 39, 40, *61*
Agarwal, K. L., 5, 18, 21, *58, 62,* 126, 132, *197*
Agarwal, N. S., 364, *446*
Agren, A., 174, *208*
Ahmed, F., 48, *58*
Aigle, M., 53, *59*
Aiman, C. E., 409, *432*
Aimoto, S., 86, *108,* 132, *209*
Akabori, S., 179, *197,* 308, *333*
Akazawa, Y., 83, 85, *109,* 125, 138, *215*
Akaji, K., 83, 85, 93, 94, *106, 107, 109,* 125, 138, 157, *215*
Akita, I., 125, *206*
Akita, K., 77, 80, 83, *107*
Akita, T., 85, *107,* 125, 133, 160, *206,* 231, *281*
Akita, Y., 288, 292, *335*
Akiyama, H., 367, 419, *445*
Ako, H., 297, *333*
Alakhov, Yu. B., 87, *106,* 128, *197*
Albers-Schönberg, G., 288, 289, 290, *333, 335*
Albertson, N. F., 67, 69, *107,* 159, 164, 167, 182, 186, *197, 207*
Alderton, G., 295, *333*
Alexander, H., 44, *61*
Alekseeva, L. V., 386, 390, *430*
Aleksiev, B. V., 377, *446*
Ali, R. M., 388, *430*
Allen, M.C., 419, *430*
Almquist, R., 364, *430*
Altman, J., 348, 369, 382, 383, 398, 418, *430, 431*
Ambrose, K. R., 356, *439*
Ammerer, G., 54, 55, *61, 63*
Amster, O., 54, *58*
Anand, M., 162, *206*
Anastasi, A., 79, *106*
Anatol, J., 402, *438*
Anderson, B., 290, *333*
Anderson, G. W., 119, 137, 164, 192, *197, 209,* 228, 230, 234, *279*
Anderson, H., 230, 276, *281*
Anderson, J. C., 130, *197*
Anderson, R. J., 289, *338*
Anderson, S. L., 187, *207*
Ando, S., 331, *333*
Ando, T., 142, *205,* 290, *337*
Andose, J. D., 365, *436*
Andreatta, R. H., 174, *212,* 349, 409, 418, *430, 437*
Anfinsen, C. B., 98, *106,* 160, 170, *202, 209, 210*
Anhovry, M. L., 403, *430*
Anwar, M. K., 163, *197*
Anwer, M., 364, *446*
Aoki, H., 384, *435*
Aoki, T., 290, *339*
Aono, M., 92, *109*
Aoyagi, H., 231, *281,* 288, 289, 301, 308, 317, 318, 319, 320, 330, 331, 332, *333, 335, 338,* 405, *445*
Apperson, S., 39, 40, 48, 49, 55, *61, 64*
Arakawa, K., 89, *108*
Araki, K., 419, *439*
Araki, Y., 378, *437*
Arcamone, F., 289, *333*
Arditti, R. R., 24, *58*
Arendt, A., 189, *197,* 228, 229, 235, 253, 271, 273, 274, 275, *279*
Arens, J. F., 124, 184, *203, 209, 210*

Arentzen, R., 13, 18, 24, 54, *60, 62*
Ariely, S., 155, *215*, 396, *448*
Arihara, S., 427, *446*
Arison, B. H., 117, *201*, 288, 289, *333*
Ariyoshi, Y., 378, *430*
Arnheiter, H., 44, *58*
Arnold, Z., 403, *430*
Arold, H., 380, 404, *430*
Artinghaus, R. B., 409, *442*
Asen, S., 398, 400, *437, 447*
Asquith, R. S., 291, *333*, 387, *430*
Astell, C., 51, *60*
Atherton, E., 172, *197*, 219, 224, 228, 233, 253, 257, 258, 259, 260, 269, *279, 280*, 364, 387, *430*
Atkins, P. R., 288, *333*
Atkinson, T. C., 5, 50, *59*
Audrieth, L. F., 157, *201*
Auger, G., 182, *199*
Averbach, G. D., 153, *210*
Aviv, H., 54, *61*
Ayi, A. L., 373, *430*
Ayyanger, N. R., 354, 401, *434*
Azerad, R., 381, *431*
Azimov, V. A., 420, *430*

B

Baba, T., 145, *197*
Baba, Y., 348, 399, 406, 407, 414, 420, 421, *449*
Babb, R. M., 372, *430*
Babson, R. D., 397, *434*
Bach, M. L., 55, *58*
Bachi, M. D., 157, *197*
Bachrach, H. L., 24, 26, 53, *61*
Baer, E., 140, *197*
Bahl, C., 38, *59*
Bahl, C. P., 5, 13, 56, *61*
Bahn, A., 126, *197*
Bailey, A. J., 379, 381, *433*
Bailey, J. L., 141, 188, *197*
Bajusz, S., 122, 128, 138, 147, 154, 158, 175, 179, *197, 206, 207, 208, 214*
Bakhra, M., 419, *430*
Balaram, P., 270, 271, *282*
Balaspiri, L., 352, 410, *430, 442*
Balasubramanian, D., 152, *198*
Baldwin, J. E., 363, 368, *430*
Balenović, K., 376, *430*
Balvert-Geers, I. C., 136, 171, *213*
Bambara, R., 10, 11, *61*
Bancroft, F. C., 21, *61*
Banerjee, S. N., 347, 370, 377, *430, 444*
Bangham, D. R., 48, *58*
Baranova, L. V., 53, *61*
Barany, G., 113, 152, 192, *198*, 231, 242, *279, 281*
Barash, L., 371, *439*
Barass, B. C., 187, *198*
Barber, H. A., 384, *430*
Barber, M., 352, 410, 413, *430*
Barbetta, M., 288, 292, *333*
Barclay, R., 419, *430*
Bardakos, V., 156, *216*
Bargetzi, J. R., 130, *205*
Barkeley, M., 93, *108*
Barkemeyer, H., 117, 151, 154, 188, *201, 204*
Barocio de la Lama, X., 235, 264, 265, 267, *283*
Barry, G. T., 379, *430*
Barry, L. G., 131, *210*
Barth, T., 163, *201*
Bartlett, M. F., 157, *201*
Bartlett, P. D., 188, *198*
Barton, M. A., 130, *197*
Bartz, Q. R., 397, *433*
Bashkirova, N. A., 426, *445*
Bassett, C. L., 25, *61*
Bates, H. S., 190, *198*, 249, *279*
Battersby, A. R., 144, 150, 151, *198*
Bauer, W., 67, *108*, 125, 127, 129, 160, *198, 210*
Baugh, C. M., 152, *206*
Baumert, A., 186, *205*
Baxter, J. D., 27, 53, 54, *63*
Bayer, E., 160, 191, *198, 203*, 225, 226, *281*, 396, *430*
Bayer, J., 152, 162, *198, 206*
Bechard, D., 377, *445*
Beckwith, J., 24, *58*
Beecham, A. F., 169, *198*
Beesley, T. E., 151, 188, *201, 204*
Behrens, C., 402, *440*
Beke, R., 154, *206*
Belikov, U. M., 410, 422, *431*
Bell, E. A., 342, 392, 412, *430, 435*
Belleau, B., 187, *198*, 353, 354, 364, *433*
Bellocq, A., 428, *431*
Belokon, Y. N., 410, 422, *431*
Benassi, C. A., 156, *203*
Bender, M. L., 142, *198*
Beneš, J., 389, 392, *447*
Benesch, R., 156, *198*
Benesch, R. E., 156, *198*

Benisek, W. F., 122, *198*
Ben-Ishai, D., 67, *106*, 125, 126, 140, 162, *198*, 348, 369, 382, 383, 398, 406, 407, 418, 426, *430, 431*
Benjamini, E., 140, *216*
Bennett, W. E., 55, *62*
Bennich, H., 141, *213*
Benoiton, N. L., 142, 156, 163, 173, 183, 184, 190, *198, 200, 210, 216*, 219, 223, 224, 225, 227, 228, 230, 232, 233, 234, 235, 236, 237, 238, 240, 241, 242, 243, 244, 245, 246, 247, 248, 249, 250, 251, 253, 254, 256, 257, 258, 259, 260, 262, 263, 265, 266, 268, 269, 271, 272, 273, 274, 275, 276, 277, *279, 280, 282, 283*
Bentov, M., 418, *431*
Berariu, V., 398, 402, *446*
Berestenko, M. K., 426, *445*
Berg, P., 2, 15, *61*
Bergel, F., 357, 400, *431*
Berger, A., 67, *106*, 125, 126, 127, 140, 147, 157, 162, 188, *198, 209*, 399, 401, 407, 421, *431*
Berger, E., 232, 237, 278, *281*
Berger, M., 239, *282*
Berger, S. L., 21, 55, *60*
Bergmann, E. D., 372, *435*
Bergmann, M., 66, 67, *106*, 116, 121, 138, 141, 151, 161, 163, *198, 202, 212*, 286, 296, 305, *333, 334*
Bergstrand, S. J., 343, 385, *447*
Berler, Z., 382, 398, 406, 407, *431*
Berlin, A. Y., 383, *440*
Berman, E., 387, *433*
Bern, H. A., 93, *108*
Bernardi, L., 347, 399, *431*
Berndt, H., 152, 153, 165, 175, 188, *198, 206, 211*, 231, *280, 282*
Bernhard, H., 184, *215*
Bernhard, S. A., 147, *198, 212*
Bernstein, Y., 54, *61*
Bernstein, Z., 348, 426, *431*
Berryer, P., 311, 324, *334*
Berse, C., 138, 157, 168, *198*, 379, *431*
Berteau, P. F., 403, *438*
Bertrand, K., 7, *58*
Bessette, P., 379, *431*
Bethell, M. J., 409, *431*
Betlach, M. C., 23, 37, *58, 62*
Bettag, A. L., 364, *446*
Beverly, G. M., 157, *204*
Bey, P., 395, *431*
Beyerman, H. C., 153, 160, 169, 184, 186, 195, *198, 199, 204, 213, 214*
Bhatia, P. L., 132, *206*
Bhatnagar, P. K., 313, 315, 316, *337*
Bhatnagar, R. S., 262, 263, 273, *282*
Biernat, J. F., 150, *213*
Bigley, D. B., 409, *431*
Bikel, I., 56, *62*
Bilim, G. V., 390, *430*
Bilk, L., 191, *203*
Biondi, L., 390, *445*
Birch, A. J., 288, *334*
Birch, J. R., 18, *61*
Birkhimer, C. A., 183, *199*
Birkinshaw, J. H., 288, *334*
Birkofer, L., 397, *431*
Birr, C., 183, *201, 202, 215*, 359, 419, *448*
Bischofberger, K., 429, *431*
Bishop, R. J., 25, *62*
Bisset, G. W., 352, 410, *430*
Black, D. K., 363, 369, 371, *431*
Bláha, K., 120, *210*, 346, 349, 366, 408, 410, *443, 447*
Blake, J., 127, 138, 146, 160, *199, 216*, 231, 232, 278, *284*
Blanot, D., 182, *199*
Blarzino, C., 413, *435*
Bleich, H. E., 223, *281*
Blobel, G., 29, *58*
Block, F. B., 403, *440*
Block, P., Jr., 403, *431, 438*
Blodinger, J., 230, *279*
Bloemhoff, W., 415, 417, *431, 437*
Blombäck, B., 152, *199*
Blout, E. R., 174, *200*
Blume, G., 191, *200*
Blumenstein, M., 355, 402, *431*
Bock, S. C., 56, *61*
Bodanszky, A., 85, 89, 91, *106*, 126, 134, 139, 143, 145, 147, 166, 167, 183, *199*, 293, 294, 311, *334*, 382, *443*
Bodanszky, M., 85, 89, 91, *106, 107*, 113, 117, 119, 125, 126, 134, 136, 137, 139, 140, 143, 144, 145, 146, 147, 148, 155, 157, 160, 162, 166, 167, 170, 172, 175, 178, 180, 183, 184, 186, 192, 193, 196, *199, 206 208, 209*, 227, 228, 240, 251, 252, 257, 258, *280*, 290, 293, 294, 311, *334, 335*, 377, 382, 388, *431, 443*
Boeck, L. D., 289, *335*
Böshagen, H., 189, *203*
Bogachev, V. S., 53, *61*

Boggs, N. T., 387, *437*
Bognar, R., 414, *431*
Bohak, Z., 159, *209*
Bohn, H., 349, 418, *437*
Bolivar, F., 3, 13, 22, 23, 25, 26, 27, 29, 31, 32, 37, 39, 54, 56, *58, 60, 61, 62*
Boissonnas, R. A., 67, 79, *107,* 125, 127, 136, 138, 140, 154, 160, 162, 184, *199, 203*
Boll, W., 48, 55, *62, 63*
Bollinger, F. W., 372, *430*
Bond, H. W., 353, *444*
Bonner, J., 21, 51, *64*
Bonnet, R., 125, *199*
Bonora, G. H., 150, *200,* 391, *445*
Booth, L. D., 387, *440*
Borchers, J., 376, *444*
Bori, K., 428, *445*
Borin, G., 368, 399, *431*
Borowski, E., 370, 384, *431, 434*
Bory, S., 381, *431*
Boshart, G. L., 237, *282*
Bosisio, G., 347, 399, *431*
Bossert, H. W., 122, 163, *200*
Bosshard, H. R., 399, 401, 407, 421, *431*
Botstein, D., 55, *58*
Boucher, R., 157, *198*
Bowen, D. O., 393, *433*
Bowers, C. Y., 364, 428, *437, 445, 446*
Bowman, R. E., 288, 291, *334*
Bowness, W. G., 403, *432*
Boydens, R., 375, *440*
Boyer, H. W., 2, 3, 13, 23, 25, 26, 31, 32, 37, 56, *58, 59, 61, 62*
Braae, H., 125, *213*
Bradshaw, R. A., 140, *204*
Brady, S. F., 77, *106,* 343, *447*
Brain, F. H., 387, *431*
Brand, E., 140, 151, *198, 211*
Branda, L. A., 195, *216*
Brandenburg, D., 67, *108,* 132, *216*
Brawner, M., 37, 48, 50, *58*
Bregman, M. D., 360, *431, 437*
Bregovec, I., 393, *431*
Breitholle, E. G., 306, *334,* 395, 405, *437*
Breitmaier, E., 425, *447*
Bremer, H., 67, *108,* 139, 151, *216*
Brenner, M., 160, 179, 180, 196, *200*
Bricas, E., 133, 182, *199, 200,* 388, *444*
Briley, M. R., 376, *443*
Brink, A. J., 429, *444*
Brinkhoff, O., 67, *108*
Bristow, A. F., 48, *58*
Brody, K. R., 402, *431*
Bromer, W. W., 39, *59*
Brooks, J., 364, *435*
Brooks, O., 354, *435*
Broome, S., 22, 28, 56, *58, 64*
Brosius, J., 37, 56, *63*
Brossi, A., 417, *446*
Brot, N., 37, *64*
Brouwers, L., 375, *440*
Brown, A. G., 288, *334*
Brown, E., 219, 224, 228, 233, 253, 257, 258, 260, *280*
Brown, G. B., 347, 420, 428, *434, 446*
Brown, R., 288, *334*
Brown, S. S., 124, 142, 143, *200*
Brown, T., 133, *200,* 263, *280*
Browne, D. T., 52, *58*
Brtník, F., 391, *432, 449*
Bruce, B. J., 55, *60*
Bruckner, V., 150, 151, 158, *200, 206, 208*
Brugger, M., 70, *108,* 158, *212,* 222, 269, *283*
Bruice, T. C., 134, 142, *200*
Brundish, D. E., 400, 403, 419, *432, 441*
Brune, G., 398, *448*
Brunet, J. C., 349, 408, *432*
Brunfeldt, K., 160, *209*
Brunner, H., 154, *210*
Bruno, J. J., 134, *200*
Brynes, S., 377, *432*
Buchanan, D. L., 143, 144, *200, 203*
Buchferer, B. A., 53, *59*
Bucher, D., 122, *212*
Buchi, H., 5, *58*
Buczel, Cz., 191, *207,* 396, *440*
Büchi, G., 412, *432*
Bumpus, F. M., 121, *206,* 347, 352, 368, *432, 439*
Burck, P. J., 39, 40, *60*
Burckart, G. J., 377, *432*
Burckhardt, C. H., 180, *200*
Burde, N. L., 386, 390, *430*
Burger, K., 236, *283*
Burgess, T. L., 56, *63*
Burghardt, B. A., 356, 413, *434*
Burgstahler, A. W., 409, *432*
Burnop, V., 357, 400, *431*
Burow, F., 167, *202*
Burrell, C. J., 54, *58*
Bury, C., 172, *197*
Busby, G., 228, 231, 234, *281*

Bush, M., 190, *200*
Butcher, B. H., 395, *443*
Buxton, D. A., 395, *443*
Buyle, R., 150, *204*
Bycroft, B. W., 290, 291, *334*, 392, *432*

C

Caldwell, P., 37, *64*
Callahan, A. P., 356, *439*
Callahan, F. M., 137, *209, 210*, 228, *279*
Calvin, M., 68, *108*
Cameron, D., 392, *432*
Cameron, J. R., 3, *63*
Cami, B., 55, *62*
Campaigne, E., 421, *432*
Cannon, J. G., 396, *432*
Cantell, K., 55, *62*
Caranikas, S., 321, *336, 337*
Carbon, J., 3, 22, 53, 54, *59, 61, 62*
Carbone, A., 44, *64*
Cardillo, R., 288, 292, 293, *334*
Cardinale, G. J., 409, 410, 413, *440*
Cardinaux, F., 196, *200*
Cardini, C., 293, *334*
Carey, N. H., 18, 24, 54, 55, *59, 61*
Carlson, K. D., 412, *433*
Carlson, M., 159, *210*
Caron, E. L., 118, *203*
Carothers, D., 364, *449*
Carpenter, F. H., 47, *64*, 136, 137, 173, *200, 202, 207*
Carpino, L. A., 131, 136, 146, 164, 170, 171, 172, *200*
Carraway, R., 74, *106*
Carrington, R. A. G., 247, *280*
Carrion, J. P., 193, *212*, 401, *432*
Carson, J. F., 413, *432*
Cartensson, S., 428, *445*
Carter, J. H., 147, *198*
Carthew, P., 291, *333*, 387, *430*
Cartwright, T., 18, *61*
Caruthers, M. H., 5, 14, *58, 62*
Cary, P., 154, *210*
Casara, P., 397, *432*
Casella, L., 410, *432*
Cash, W. D., 195, *216*
Casimar, J., 369, *433*
Casimir, J., 412, 428, *438, 440*
Casini, G., 419, *435*
Casnati, G., 288, 292, 293, *333, 334*
Castensson, S., 428, *431*
Castleton, J. A., 23, 25, 56, *60*
Castro, B., 219, 233, 269, 272, 273, *280, 282*, 409, *433*
Cativiela, C., 404, *432*
Catlin, G. H., 54, *59*
Cavadore, J. C., 127, *210*
Cavallini, D., 362, 377, 413, *433*
Cavallo, P., 153, 176, *210*
Caviezel, M., 193, *212*, 359, 363, 368, 371, 400, 408, *433, 440, 444*
Cavitt, M. B., 389, *433*
Celis, M. E., 78, *106*
Ceprini, M. Q., 191, *206*
Černěckij, V., 364, *449*
Cernik, V., 169, *211*
Chaiken, I. M., 359, 400, *439*
Chaki, H., 381, 415, *448*
Chaman, E. S., 350, 415, *447*
Chambon, D., 51, *64*
Chan, S. J., 18, 38, 56, *58, 59*
Chan, W. Y., 428, *446*
Chance, R. E., 39, 48, *59*
Chandramouli, N., 160, *199*
Chandrasekaran, R., 193, *210*
Chang, A. C. Y., 2, 28, 53, 57, *59*
Chang, C. D., 172, 176, *200, 208*, 243, *281*
Chang, D., 4, *60*
Chang, P. K., 387, *432*
Chang, S., 53, *60*
Chang, Y. E., 33, *59*
Chang, Y. H., 72, *107*
Chantrenne, H., 184, *200*
Chao, W., 364, *430*
Chapman, D. W., 169, *212*
Chappuis, G., 409, *433*
Chari, R. V. J., 405, *432*
Charnay, P., 54, *59*
Charnecki, A. M., 356, 413, *434*
Chaturvedi, N., 193, *200*, 352, *432*
Chauhan, V. S., 125, 176, *200, 207*, 306, 311, 324, *334*
Chavez, L. G., Jr., 101, *106*
Cheburkov, Yu., 372, *439*
Chedekel, M. R., 423, *437*
Chemerda, J. M., 371, *435*
Chen, C. Y., 55, *61*
Chen, F. M. F., 183, 184, 190, *198, 200*, 219, 224, 225, 230, 232, 233, 234, 235, 236, 237, 238, 240, 241, 242, 243, 244, 245, 246, 247, 248, 249, 250, 251, 254, 256, 257, 258, 260, 265, 266, 268, 269, 272, 273, 274, 275, 276, 277, *279, 280, 283*

Chen, H. C., 325, *338*
Chen, M., 56, *62*
Chen, S. T., 179, *200*
Cheng, C. C., 425, *436, 446*
Chestukhin, A. V., 55, *63*
Cheung, H. T., 174, *200*
Cheung, S. T., 219, 224, 225, 232, 233, 238, 243, 258, *280*
Chevallier, M. R., 53, *59*
Chibata, I., 382, 398, *438, 449*
Chibnall, A. C., 152, *200, 214*
Chick, W. L., 28, 56, *64*
Chigira, Y., 288, 309, *335, 338*
Chillemi, F., 147, 160, 179, *200,* 347, 399, *431*
Chino, N., 87, *107,* 129, 160, *200, 208*
Chiovini, J., 412, *449*
Chirakal, R., 403, *435*
Chisholm, M., 394, *432*
Chmara, H., 384, *431*
Choi, C., 353, 393, 400, *443*
Chorev, M., 128, *200,* 343, 363, *435*
Chou, S. H., 179, *200*
Chow, R. C. L., 153, *201*
Chowdrey, H. S., 352, 410, *430*
Chrambach, A., 91, *106*
Christensen, B. G., 288, *333*
Christensen, H. N., 118, *203*
Christensen, S. B., 427, *432*
Christensen, T., 125, *213*
Christiaens, L., 421, *439*
Chu, Y. I., 224, *282*
Chung, D., 122, 133, 158, *207, 210*
Cini, C., 413, *435*
Cipens, G., 167, *214*
Cipera, J. D., 135, *200*
Clardy, J., 352, 411, *437*
Clark, B. R., 93, *108*
Clark, H. E., 152, *214*
Clarke, D. D., 140, *197,* 373, *436*
Clarke, H. T., 157, *200,* 413, *443*
Clarke, J. E., 186, *208*
Clarke, L., 22, 53, *59, 61*
Clark-Lewis, J. W., 151, 187, *206*
Clausen, K., 364, *432*
Clayton, D. W., 150, *200*
Cleland, G. H., 400, *432*
Clizbe, L. A., 386, 387, *433*
Closier, M. D., 288, 291, *334*
Closse, A., 384, *432*
Coccia, R., 413, *433*
Coggins, J. R., 163, *200,* 225, *280*
Cohen, J. D., 53, *59*
Cohen, J. S., 67, *107*
Cohen, L. A., 141, 158, *201, 204,* 417, *439, 441*
Cohen, M. R., 352, 362, 409, 410, *434*
Cohen, M. S., 352, 364, *442*
Cohen, S. N., 2, 15, 19, 22, 28, 53, 57, *59*
Cohen-Solal, M., 56, *60*
Cohon, S., 425, *447*
Colbere-Garapin, F., 56, *60*
Cole, R. D., 122, *198*
Coleman, J., 100, *106*
Coletta, M., 377, *433*
Coletti-Previero, M. A., 127, 131, 132, *210*
Collen, D., 55, *62*
Collignon, N., 397, *447*
Colman, G. C., 293, *334*
Compere, E. L., Jr., 398, 406, *432*
Comstock, L. J., 25, *59*
Condon, M. E., 352, *442*
Cone, C., 412, *430*
Conklin, L. F., 227, 228, *280*
Conn, J. B., 158, 188, *204, 214*
Constantopoulos, A., 80, *108*
Content, J., 25, 55, *59*
Conti, F., 121, *201*
Conti, M. P., 428, *447*
Contreras, R., 7, *60*
Cook, E. A., 24, 55, *59*
Corbella, A., 409, *432*
Corcoran, B. J., 143, 144, *200, 203*
Cordes, A. W., 313, 315, *336*
Cortegiano, H., 221, *281*
Cory, M., 400, 402, *433*
Cosani, A., 347, *443*
Cossement, E., 375, *440*
Cosso, P., 378, *444*
Costa, T., 311, 324, 325, *338*
Cory, M., 400, *433*
Costopanagiotis, A., 67, 69, *108,* 138, *203*
Couchman, R., 382, *432*
Courvalin, P., 53, *59*
Coutts, R. T., 402, *432*
Cover, R. E., 221, 272, *281*
Cox, M. T., 403, *432*
Coy, D. H., 400, 401, 403, 418, *431, 432*
Coy, E. J., 400, 401, 418, *432*
Coy, R. S., 371, *446*
Crabeel, M., 55, *59*
Craft, M. K., 140, *209,* 347, 399, *442*

Craig, L. C., 187, *213*, 223, *281*, 291, 295, *335*, *338*
Cram, D. J., 221, *280*
Crause, P., 358, *434*
Crea, R., 3, 6, 7, 8, 11, 12, 13, 14, 17, 18, 21, 22, 24, 25, 26, 27, 28, 30, 31, 32, 34, 37, 38, 39, 40, 42, 43, 44, 47, 50, 53, 54, 55, 56, *59*, *60*, *61*, *62*, *64*
Cremlyn, R. J. W., 393, 394, *432*
Crestfield, A. M., 100, *106*
Creveling, C. R., 403, *442*
Crews, O., 419, *435*
Croft, L. R., 392, *432*
Crofts, P. C., 174, *201*
Cromwell, N. H., 410, *446*
Crooij, P., 402, *432*
Crooy, P., 289, *334*, 403, *430*
Crosa, J. H., 23, *58*
Cruikshank, P. A., 237, *282*
Csendes, E., 136, 170, *214*
Cuingnet, E., 349, 408, *432*
Culvenor, C. C. J., 392, *432*
Cum, G., 428, *447*
Curphey, T. J., 396, *433*
Curran, W. V., 180, *201*
Curtius, H., 180, *201*
Curtius, T., 177, 180, 184, *201*
Cushman, D., 352, 364, *442*
Czarnomska, T., 370, 383, *434*
Czira, G., 414, *431*

D

Daebritz, E., 413, *433*
Dalby, J. S., 409, *433*
Dahlmans, J., 136, 153, *211*
Dalgarno, L., 28, *63*
Daly, J. W., 403, *442*
Dangyan, M., 385, *445*
Danho, W., 178, *201*
Daniel, D. S., 396, *433*
Danishefsky, S., 386, 387, *433*
Dannley, R. L., 354, *433*
Danzin, C., 395, *431*
Dardenne, A., 412, *440*
Dardenne, G., 369, *433*
Das, H. K., 149, *201*
DaSettimo, A., 419, *433*
Dautrevaux, M., 349, 408, *432*
Davankova, L. A., 156, *212*
David, K. H., 409, *443*
Davies, J. S., 229, 234, 247, 277, *280*
Davis, A. L., 387, 388, 389, 407, *433*, *440*
Davis, A. R., 54, *59*
Davis, M. A., 390, 429, *435*, *436*, *438*, *444*
Davis, N. C., 117, *201*
Davis, N. E., 289, *335*
Davis, N. R., 379, 381, *433*
Davis, R. H., 247, *280*
Davis, R. W., 31, *63*
Dawson, B. F., 153, *210*
Daxenbichler, M. E., 412, *433*
de Boer, H. A., 25, *59*
de Caro, G., 347, 399, *431*
de Castiglione, R., 347, 399, *431*
DeClercq, E., 25, 55, *59*
Deer, A., 123, 145, *209*, *210*
Deffner, M., 128, *215*
Deftos, L. J., 153, *210*
de Garilhe, M. P., 138, *203*
DeGraan, P. N. E., 398, *434*
Degraw, J. L., 400, 402, *433*
Degutis, Y., 380, *446*
Deigin, V., 134, *204*
Dejima, K., 272, 277, *282*
Dekker, C. A., 158, 159, *201*
Delaney, C. M., 356, 413, *434*
DeLaveleye, F., 375, *440*
Delay, D., 376, *441*
Deljac, A., 376, *430*
Delpierre, G. R., 289, *334*
DeMarco, C., 362, 377, 378, 413, *433*, *435*, *444*
Demayo, P., 289, *334*
Demayo, R., 163, *200*
Dembeck, P., 51, *64*
Demuth, E., 186, *207*
Denkewalter, R. F., 96, *106*
Denkewalter, R. G., 117, 151, 158, 188, *201*, *204*, *214*
Denney, G. H., 397, *434*
Denning, G. S., Jr., 155, *199*
DeNys, R., 289, *334*
Deranleau, D. A., 401, *432*
Derbyshire, R., 51, *64*
Dernini, S., 362, 377, *433*
Derynck, R., 21, 25, 55, *59*, *60*
Deshmane, S. S., 85, 89, *106*, 126, 145, 147, 170, 172, *199*
DeTar, D. F., 237, 248, *280*
Determann, H., 180, 186, *201*, *215*, 252, 271, *280*

De Wald, H. A., 138, 140, *209*, 347, 399, *442*
Dewar, J. H., 425, *433*
Dewey, R. S., 117, 154, *201*
Diamond, L., 347, 370, *430*, *441*, *444*
Dibello, C., 150, *200*
Dice, J. R., 396, *441*
Dickson, D. E., 402, *440*
Dickson, R. C., 53, *59*
Diehl, J. F., 189, *216*, 393, *433*
Diemer, E. L., 403, *447*
Dilbeck, G. A., 375, *433*
D'Iorio, A., 223, *283*
Di Maio, J., 353, 354, 364, *433*
Dinner, A., 421, *432*
Dion, H. W., 397, *433*
Dirvyanskite, N., 380, *446*
Dittmer, D. C., 188, *198*
Dittmer, K., 347, 428, *434*
Divanfard, H. R., 428, 429, *433*
Dixon, J. E., 40, *64*
Do, K. Q., 346, 368, 408, *433*, *444*
Dobberstein, B., 29, *58*
Dobner, P. R., 21, *61*
Dobson, T. A., 379, *433*
Doel, M. T., 24, 25, *59*, 424, 425, *433*
Doel, S. M., 18, *61*
Doherty, D. G., 305, *334*
Doi, S., 394, *439*
Dolganov, G. M., 55, *63*
Dolling, U. H., 371, *433*
Dombi, G., 133, *209*
Done, T., 384, *433*
Donelson, J. E., 56, *60*
Donzel, B., 400, 401, *444*
Dooley, K., 429, *444*
Doolittle, R. F., 44, *64*
Dorer, F. E., 143, 144, *200*, *203*
Dorman, L. C., 153, 166, *201*
Dormoy, J. R., 219, 232, 269, 272, 273, *280*, *282*, 409, *433*
Doseva, V., 377, *430*
Dossena, A., 288, 289, 292, 293, *334*, *335*
Doubler, M. R., 293, *334*
Douglas, A. W., 371, *433*
Douhan, J., 29, 55, *63*
Dousa, T., 358, *448*
Dowbenko, D., 24, 26, 53, 54, *59*, *61*
Dowd, P., 385, *433*
Drabarek, S., 189, 190, *205*
Dradi, E., 289, 292, *335*
Draminski, M., 424, 425, *433*
Draus, F., 159, *202*
Drees, F., 105, *109*, 130, 147, 191, *215*
Dremier, C., 127, 129, 136, *207*
Dreyfuss, P., 379, *433*
Droste, H., 398, *448*
Du, Y. C., 177, *214*
Dualszky, S., 152, 162, *198*, *206*
DuBose, C. E., 407, *440*
Ducruix, A., 290, *337*
Duerinck, F., 7, *60*
Duffner, P., 409, *448*
Dull, T., 17, 18, 21, 24, 28, 30, 44, 55, *60*
Duncia, J. V., 369, *446*
Dunn, F. W., 347, 367, 428, *433*, *437*
Dungen, A., 359, *448*
Dunnill, P. M., 418, *434*
Dunning, J. W., Jr., 311, 312, *338*
Dutta, A. S., 343, *434*
du Vigneaud, V., 66, 67, *106*, *108*, 152, 155, 157, 158, 163, 177, 186, 188, 195, *199*, *201*, *203*, *204*, *205*, *207*, *210*, *212*, *213*, *215*, *216*, 347, 364, 428, *434*, *438*
Dwek, R. A., 355, *434*
Dworschak, H., 372, *446*
Dzieduszycka, M., 271, 272, *280*, 370, 384, *431*, *434*
Dzugaj, A., 238, *283*

E

Eaborn, C., 361, *434*
Eagles, J., 382, *432*
Earl, E. M., 52, *58*
Eastwood, F. W., 289, *334*
Eaton, C. N., 397, *434*
Eaton, M. A. W., 18, 24, 55, *59*, *61*
Ebata, M., 290, *338*
Eberle, A. N., 40, *63*, 348, 356, 359, 361, 363, 371, 398, 408, *434*, *440*, *444*
Eccleshall, T. R., 53, *59*
Eckhart, W., 55, *61*
Eckstein, H., 228, *282*
Ecsodi, J., 55, *62*
Edelhoch, H., 100, *106*
Edelson, J., 369, *434*
Edgar, M. T., 416, *434*
Edge, M. D., 5, 50, *59*
Edgell, M. H., 51, *61*
Edman, J. C., 54, *59*
Edwards, J., 364, *446*

Edwards, M. L., 423, *434*
Effenberger, F., 374, *434*
Efstratiadis, A., 28, 56, *64*
Eggers, H., 409, *448*
Eiki, H., 289, *335*
Einhorn, A., 184, *201*
Eisele, K., 380, *434*
Eisenkiss, F., 195, *210*
Eisler, K., 174, *212*, 269, *282*, 346, 367, 368, 373, *434*, *437*
Ekkehard, K., 425, *447*
Elberling, J. A., 353, 389, 394, 409, 411, *434*, *441*, *442*, *445*
Eliaers, J., 402, 403, *430*, *432*
Ellam, R. M., 393, 394, *432*
Ellingham, P. J., 388, *445*
Elliott, D. F., 124, 141, 175, *201*, *211*, 393, 400, *441*, *443*
Elliott, D. P., 364, *430*
Ellis, M., 364, *430*
El-Magharaby, M. A., 388, *434*
Ellman, G. L., 98, *106*
Elmore, D. T., 187, *198*
Emery, A. R., 185, *201*
Emtage, J. S., 18, 54, *59*, *60*, *61*, 124
Endo, N., 89, *109*, 127, 149, *213*
Enei, H., 419, *442*
Engelhard, M., 85, *106*, 126, *201*
English, M. L., 324, 325, *334*, *338*
Enkemeyer, E. M., 180, *209*, *210*
Erickson, B. W., 73, 85, *106*, 125, 136, 193, *201*, *207*, 328, *336*, 402, *434*
Erikson, R. L., 56, *60*
Erlanger, B. F., 180, *201*
Erlich, H. A., 22, 28, 53, 57, *59*
Erspamer, V., 79, *106*, 347, 399, *431*
Erwin, C. R., 56, *60*
Escher, E., 359, 363, 371, 408, *434*, *440*, *444*
Esko, K., 118, *201*, 401, *432*
Estell, D., 52, *60*
Estell, D. A., 55, *61*
Estell, D. E., 39, 44, *64*
Eswarakrishnan, V., 409, *434*
Eule, M., 404, *430*
Evans, R. M., 21, *61*

F

Fabitschowitz, H., 117, *211*
Fabrichnyi, B. P., 385, *434*
Fagan, C., 177, *214*
Fagan, D. T., 258, *280*
Fahrenholz, F., 358, 359, 398, 402, *434*
Faleev, N. G., 410, 422, *431*
Falkow, S., 23, *58*
Fallona, M.C., 289, *334*
Familletti, P. C., 17, 18, 21, 24, 38, 30, 44, 55, *60*
Farmer, P. S., 364, *434*
Fattorusso, E., 422, *434*
Fauchère, J.-L., 347, 348, 354, 356, 371, 400, 401, 408, *434*, *444*
Faulstich, H., 368, 374, 399, 401, 409, 419, *434*, *448*
Fauszt, I., 128, 175, *197*
Federoff, H., 53, *59*
Federov, V. I., 53, *61*
Feeley, J., 385, *440*
Feeney, R. E., 40, *62*
Fehr, C., 376, *443*
Feinberg, R. S., 72, *106*, 149, *201*
Feitler, D., 242, *282*
Felix, A. M., 67, *106*, 157, 172, 176, *200*, *201*, 352, 356, 362, 409, 410, 413, *434*, *435*, *440*, *441*
Feng, M. C., 193, *206*
Fenno, J., 39, 48, *63*
Ferderigos, N., 157, *216*, 321, *339*, 388, *434*
Ferger, M. F., 327, *337*, 352, 428, *444*, *446*
Ferrari, C., 413, *448*
Ferreira, A. T., 347, 368, *439*
Ferroni, R., 156, *203*
Fersht, A. R., 51, *64*
Fessler, D . C., 400, *441*
Fettes, I., 27, 53, *63*
Fiandt, M., 53, *59*
Field, G. F., 394, *434*
Field, L., 375, 409, *433*, *434*
Fields, F., 39, 44, 48, 50, 63, *64*
Fiers, W., 7, 25, 55, *59*, *60*
Fife, T. H., 142, *200*
Filatova, M. P., 426, *445*
Files, J. G., 30, *60*
Filippi, B., 368, 399, *431*
Filler, R., 305, 312, *337*, 354, 401, 402, 403, 404, *434*
Fink, G., 364, *446*
Fink, M. L., 119, 134, 139, *199*
Finlayson, G. R., 91, *106*
Finn, F. M., 221, *280*, 349, 418, *435*, *437*
Finnan, J. L., 159, *209*, *210*
Finnie, M. D. A., 40, *63*

Fiorentini, G., 121, *207*
Firnau, G., 356, 361, 403, *435*
Fischer, E., 66, *106,* 116, 126, 129, 173, *201, 215*
Fischer, J., 378, *438*
Fisher, G. H., 311, 324, *334,* 352, 409, *435*
Fleckenstein, P., 374, *441*
Flegel, M., 163, *201*
Fletcher, A. P., 261, *281*
Fletcher, G. A., 190, *201,* 347, 368, *435*
Fletcher, R., 133, *201*
Flor, F., 183, *201, 202, 215*
Flouret, G., 428, *440*
Focella, A., 409, *445*
Fodge, D., 39, 48, *63*
Fok, K. F., 364, *449*
Folkers, K., 428, *437, 445*
Folsch, G., 147, *202*
Foltz, R. L., 382, *443*
Fontana, A., 130, 132, 150, 156, 160, *199, 200, 202, 209, 210, 212, 215*
Foppoli, C., 413, *435*
Forss, S., 25, 54, *61*
Foster, M. C., 392, *432*
Foster, R. J., 297, *333*
Fountoulakis, M., 44, *58*
Fourneau, E., 173, *201*
Fournier, P., 53, *62*
Fowden, L., 342, 377, 384, 418, *433, 434, 435, 445*
Fowler, A. V., 43, *60*
Foyt, D. C., 388, *440*
Fox, H., 172, *197*
Frank, B. H., 39, 40, 48, *60*
Frank, E., 188, *211*
Frank, H., 140, 183, *203,* 225, 226, 242, *281*
Frank, V. S., 183, 184, *212*
Franke, A. E., 56, *61*
Frankel, M., 361, 400, 402, *435*
Franze, R., 25, 54, *61*
Fraser, K. J., 144, *202*
Fraser, P. S., 411, *441*
Fraser, T. H., 55, *60*
Frattesi, P., 167, 207
Frauendorfer, E., 366, *446*
Fraunberger, F., 371, *448*
Freedman, R. B., 37, *60*
Freidinger, R., 354, 364, *435*
Freidinger, R. M., 138, *202*
Freiter, E., 422, *437*
Frejd, T., 429, *435*
Fric, I., 349, 408, 410, *443, 447*
Fried, M., 180, *202*
Friedman, M., 291, *334*
Fritschi, U. S., 409, *433*
Friesen, H. G., 428, *445*
Fruchter, R. G., 100, *106*
Fruton, J. S., 86, *109,* 116, 127, 140, 142, 151, 158, 159, 180, *198, 201, 202, 203, 212, 213*
Fuganti, C., 288, 292, 293, *334*
Fuji, K., 77, *106*
Fujii, N., 67, 72, 75, 76, 78, 79, 80, 83, 85, 93, 94, 95, 104, *106, 107,* 125, 133, 136, 157, 159, *202, 204, 206, 215*
Fujii, S., 399, *440*
Fujii, T., 133, *202*
Fujimoto, Y., 352, 411, *435*
Fujino, M., 75, 81, 86, *106, 108,* 125, 138, 141, 159, 165, *202, 204, 209, 215,* 227, 228, 232, 270, 273, 277, *281,* 384, *435*
Fujisawa, Y., 289, *334*
Fujita, E., 77, *106, 108*
Fujita, K., 417, *438*
Fujita, Y., 389, *435*
Fujiwara, Y., 138, 142, *202, 203*
Fukada, K., 67, *107*
Fukada, T., 136, *211,* 227, 228, 273, *281*
Fukukawa, K., 387, 389, *448*
Fukami, H., 289, 290, 294, 295, 316, *336, 338, 339,* 403, *443*
Fuks, R., 184, *214*
Fuller, W., 193, *200*
Funk, K. W., 119, *199*
Funakoshi, S., 75, 79, 83, 85, 87, 94, *106, 107, 109,* 133, 136, 138, 157, *202, 206, 215*
Funkoshi, S., 78, *107*
Furlenmeier, A. E., 160, *204*
Fusari, S. A., 397, *433*
Fushimi, T., 76, 78, *107*
Fushiya, S., 369, 381, *435*
Futagawa, S., 379, *435*

G

Gait, M. J., 228, 253, 257, 258, *279, 280*
Gal, G., 371, *435*
Galardy, R. E., 223, *281*
Galibert, F., 54, *59*
Galione, M., 369, *438*
Gallina, C., 308, 410, *334, 435*

Gallo, A. A., 375, *433*
Gallop, P. M., 387, *436*
Ganem, B., 384, *439*
Gannon, F., 55, *62*
Garapin, A. C., 55, 56, *60, 62*
Gardner, J. D., 160, 172, *199,* 377, *431*
Gargiulo, R. J., 375, *433*
Gariboldi, P., 409, *432*
Garner, R., 139, *202*
Garnett, S., 356, 361, 403, *435*
Garsky, V., 188, *204*
Gass, J. D., 395, *435*
Gatenby, A. A., 23, 25, 56, *60*
Gatti, G., 288, 292, *334*
Gaudry, M., 381, *431*
Gautier, C., 7, *60*
Gawron, O., 159, 176, *202*
Gaymard, F., 405, *448*
Gazis, D., 328, *336*
Geiger, R., 68, 88, 105, *107,* 133, 138, 139, 140, 153, 167, 170, 172, 191, 195, *202, 205, 206*
Geis, T., 236, *282*
Gelfand, D. H., 25, *62*
Gellert, E., 367, *435*
Georgi, V., 381, *435*
Gerig, J. T., 121, 195, *202,* 355, 409, *435*
Gerke, C. W., 225, *282*
Gerschon, H., 372, 373, *435*
Gertner, A., *444*
Gertner, D., 361, 400, 402, *435, 444*
Gervais, M., 54, *59*
Geschwind, I. I., 93, *108*
Gesquiere, J. C., 192, *213*
Ghiringhelli, D., 288, 292, 293, *334*
Giannella, M., 422, *435*
Gibian, H., 150, 162, *202, 212*
Gieren, A., 419, *448*
Giese, R. W., 390, *444*
Gilbert, W., 3, 22, 28, 29, 37, 38, 55, 56, *58, 60, 63, 64*
Giles, N. H., 23, 53, *64*
Gillam, S., 21, 51, *60, 61, 62*
Gillessen, D., 185, *202,* 368, *431*
Gillmann, G., 69, *107*
Gills, N. H., 25, *61*
Gilmer, T. M., 56, *60*
Gilon, C., 253, 257, *281,* 397, *435*
Ginzburg, O. F., 167, *207*
Gipson, R. M., 370, *443*
Girin, S. K., 126, 139, 142, *202*
Gish, D. T., 136, 137, 155, *200, 202, 205*
Gisin, B. F., 121, 122, *202*
Givot, I. L., 287, 290, 311, *334*
Glaesser, A., 347, 399, *431*
Glansdorff, N., 55, *59*
Glaser, C. B., 237, *281*
Glazer, A. N., 360, 362, *435*
Gleason, J. C., 323, *335*
Glitzer, M. S., 343, *447*
Glockler, U., 170, *214*
Gloede, J., 416, *443*
Görög, S., 155, *206*
Goffredo, O., *431*
Go, A., 193, *206*
Goeddel, D. V., 3, 6, 7, 8, 11, 12, 13, 17, 18, 21, 22, 24, 25, 26, 27, 28, 29, 30, 34, 37, 38, 39, 40, 42, 43, 44, 47, 48, 49, 50, 53, 54, 55, 56, *60, 61, 62, 63, 64*
Goffredo, O., 347, 399, *431*
Gold, V., 185, *201*
Goldberg, A. L., 31, 32, 33, *60*
Goldberger, R. F., 170, *202*
Gol'dfarb, Y. L., 385, *434*
Golding, B. T., 388, *435*
Goldschmidt, S., 117, *203*
Goldstein, A. L., 4, 6, 7, 8, 11, 12, 13, 22, 26, 34, 40, 42, 43, 44, 47, 53, *60, 62, 64*
Goodman, H. M., 54, *59, 62, 63*
Goodman, M., 117, 121, 124, 139, 169, 189, 190, *200, 203, 212,* 230, 237, 238, 246, 264, 276, *281,* 343, 363, 400, 419, *435, 444*
Gordon, E., 364, *442*
Gordon, P. G., 377, *436*
Gordon, S., 66, 67, *106,* 157, 177, *201*
Gorecki, M., 54, *61,* 98, *109*
Gorup, B., 193, *212*
Gosser, L., 221, *280*
Gosteli, J., 173, *215,* 289, *339*
Goto, H., 290, *339*
Goto, T., 288, *336*
Govy, M., 7, *60*
Gowland, M. S., 290, *334*
Grable, C. I., 313, 315, *336*
Grabowski, E. J. J., 371, *433*
Grafe, K., 286, *333*
Grahl-Nielsen, O., 136, *203*
Grant, J. A., 313, 315, *337*
Grantham, R., 7, *60*

Gras, H., 349, 408, *432*
Grasselli, P., 288, 292, 293, *334*
Grassman, W., 124, 169, *203*
Gray, O., 53, *60*
Gray, P. W., 21, 48, 49, 55, *60, 64*
Gream, G. E., 289, *334*
Green, N., 44, *61*
Greenaway, P. J., 54, *58*
Greenbaum, L. M., 162, *203*
Greene, A. R., 5, 50, *59*
Greene, P. J., 23, *58*
Greenstein, J. P., 138, 156, 216, 222, *281,* 286, 305, *334,* 342, 343, 366, 367, 368, 369, 374, 375, 378, 380, 384, 385, 386, 388, 389, 390, 391, 392, 398, 399, 401, 402, 403, 405, 406, 411, 417, 419, 421, 427, *436*
Gregory, H., 347, *436*
Grigg, R., 302, *334*
Grim, M. D., 306, 311, 312, *334, 338*
Grønvald, F. C., 133, *203*
Grogg, P., 409, *433*
Grommers, E. P., 124, *203*
Gronowitz, S., 429, *435*
Gros, C., 138, *203*
Gros, D., 26, *61*
Gross, E., 127, *209,* 287, 290, 291, 295, 296, 299, 320, 321, 325, 326, 327, 328, *334, 335, 336,* 374, *441*
Gross, H., 191, *203,* 416, *443*
Gross, M., 17, 18, 21, 24, 28, 30, 44, 55, *60,* 127, *209*
Grossweiner, L. I., 86, *109,* 131, *214*
Grubman, M. J., 24, 26, 53, *61*
Grunewald, G. L., 395, *436*
Grunstein, M., 21, *60*
Gruszecka, E., 397, *436*
Grzonka, Z., 191, *207,* 350, 396, 418, *440, 447*
Gualtieri, F., 422, *435*
Guarente, L., 29, 53, 55, *60, 63*
Guarneri, M., 156, *203*
Guedj, R., 372, 373, 405, *430, 448*
Guggi, A., 156, 176, *203, 210*
Gullotti, M., 410, *432*
Gunneweg, J. J., 165, *204*
Gunsalvo, R. P., 53, 56, *59*
Gund, P., 365, *436*
Gupta, N., 5, *58*
Gupton, B. F., 343, *443*
Gurd, R. S., 79, *108*
Gurviciene, L., 357, 400, *438*
Gushima, H., 289, *335*
Gustowski, W., 354, 401, *434*
Gutte, B., 44, *57,* 96, *107,* 136, 165, *203*
Guttman, S., 67, 79, *107,* 122, 125, 127, 138, 140, 154, 160, 162, 168, *199, 203, 210*
Guy, A., 51, *64*
Gyorgydeak, Z., 414, *431, 446*

H

Haas, H. J., 156, *206*
Haas, P., 39, 40, *61*
Haas, W., 160, *204*
Haber, A., 386, *440*
Haber, E., 98, *106,* 144, *202*
Haber, S. B., 363, 368, *430*
Habermann, E., 189, *203*
Hack, A. M., 37, *63*
Haegeman, G., 7, *60*
Häusler, J., 287, 298, 305, 309, 311, *337,* 410, *436*
Hageman, J. J. M., 386, *436*
Hagenmaier, H., 140, 160, 183, *198, 203, 242, 281*
Haggerty, W. J., Jr., 425, *436, 446*
Hagie, F. E., 55, *61*
Haginiwa, J., 418, *441*
Hagio, K., 382, 419, *438, 441*
Hagitani, A., 117, 192, *209*
Hagiwara, D., 164, *204,* 227, 273, *281*
Hahne, W., 377, *431*
Haley, E. E., 143, 144, *200, 203*
Hall, A., 44, 48, 55, *62, 63*
Hall, B. D., 21, 54, 55, *61, 62, 63*
Hall, R. H., 429, *431*
Hallet, A., 277, *283*
Hallewell, R. A., 24, 54, *59, 60, 62*
Hallinan, E. A., 308, 324, *335*
Halpern, B., 136, 166, *203,* 367, *435*
Halström, J., 160, *209*
Hamada, T., 174, *216*
Hamill, R. L., 289, *335*
Hamilton, T. A., 56, *62*
Han, G. Y., 131, 136, 146, 171, 172, *200*
Hanafusa, T., 386, *438*
Hanck, A., 416, *436*
Handschumacher, R. E., 387, *432*

Hanessian, S., 371, *436*
Hann, M., 364, *436*
Hannappel, E., 40, *61*
Hansen, J. J., 427, *436*
Hanson, H., 169, *203*
Hanson, K. R., 287, 290, 311, *335*
Hanson, R. N., 429, *436*
Hanson, R. W., 142, 147, *198, 203*
Hantzsch, D., 376, *444*
Hanzlik, R. P., 408, *436*
Hara, J., 409, *436*
Harada, K., 368, 379, 386, 410, *436, 439, 442, 446*
Harcup, C., 377, *445*
Hardy, K., 52, 54, *60*
Hardy, P. M., 130, *197,* 416, *436*
Hargitay, B., 150, *204*
Harington, C. R., 402, *436*
Harkins, R. N., 38, 39, 40, 47, 48, 55, *61, 62, 63*
Harkiss, D., 172, *197*
Harms, R., 393, *444*
Harpold, M. M., 21, *61*
Harpp, D. N., 323, *335*
Harris, J. I., 118, 142, 180, *203, 212*
Harris, R. L. N., 383, 416, 426, *436, 446*
Harris, T. J. R., 4, *61*
Hartmann, A., 269, *283*
Harvey, C., 4, *60*
Hasan, S. K., 413, *448*
Hase, S., 385, 388, *436*
Hasegawa, H., 382, *437*
Hasegawa, T., 289, *335*
Hashimoto, Y., 330, 332, *335,* 392, *438*
Hashizume, K., 132, *203*
Haslam, E., 174, *203*
Hasselmann, D., 424, *445*
Hassner, A., 253, 257, *281*
Hasspacher, K., 133, 140, *212*
Hatanaka, C., 427, *438*
Hatanaka, M., 428, *436*
Hatanaka, S.-I., 369, 371, 381, *436, 442*
Hatano, K., 289, *335*
Hattori, S., 387, *445*
Hattori, T., 288, *338*
Hauschka, P. U., 387, *436*
Hautala, J. A., 23, 25, 53, *61, 64*
Havinga, E., 362, 389, *438*
Havir, E. A., 287, 290, 311, *335*
Havran, R. T., 154, 195, *203, 208*
Hawkins, H. C., 37, *60*
Hayakawa, M., 297, 311, *333*
Hayakawa, T., 138, *203*
Hayama, H., 188, *216*
Hayashi, Y., 289, 316, *339*
Hayes, D. F., 78, *108*
Heard, A. L., 228, 271, *281*
Heathcliffe, G. R., 5, 50, *59*
Hecht, S. M., 52, *62,* 417, *436*
Hechter, A., 358, *448*
Hedgcoth, C., 386, *436*
Hegarty, M.P., 382, 392, *432*
Hegedüs, B., 158, *203,* 380, *436*
Heimer, E. P., 172, *208,* 243, *281*
Heininger, H. V., 372, *446*
Heinke, B., 114, 121, 184, *215*
Helferich, B., 189, *203*
Helling, R. B., 2, *59*
Hemassi, B., 191, *203*
Henes, J. B., 89, *106,* 193, *199*
Hengartner, U. O., 409, 418, *436, 445*
Hensens, O. D., 288, 290, *333, 335*
Henson, E. B., 387, *436*
Heremans, J. F., 428, *441*
Herman, P., 418, *436*
Hermann, P., 362, 376, 377, 390, *436*
Herscheid, J. D. M., 299, *335*
Heslot, H., 53, *62*
Hess, G. P., 118, 139, 142, 155, 175, 188, 189, 190, *202, 207, 211, 212*
Heuer, J., 252, *280*
Heusler, K., 173, *215,* 289, *339*
Hewgill, F. R., 398, *436*
Heyneker, H. L., 3, 6, 7, 8, 11, 12, 13, 17, 18, 21, 22, 23, 24, 25, 26, 27, 28, 29, 30, 31, 32, 34, 37, 38, 39, 40, 42, 43, 44, 47, 50, 53, 54, 55, 56, *58, 59, 60, 61, 62, 64*
Heyns, K., 117, *203*
Hider, R. C., 390, *436*
Higa, S., 119, *212*
Higgins, C. E., 289, *335*
Hill, J. T., 367, 428, *437*
Hillmann, A., 168, *203*
Hillmann, G., 168, 170, *203*
Hillmann-Elis, A., 69, *107,* 170, *203*
Hines, J. W., 395, 405, *437*
Hinman, J. W., 118, *203*
Hino, T., 414, *442, 446*
Hinoo, H., 288, 294, *338*

Hirabayashi, T., 117, 192, *209*
Hirai, Y., 81, 87, *107, 108, 109*
Hiraiwa, H., 231, *281*
Hirama, M., 387, *433*
Hiramatsu, T., 395, *440*
Hirose, T., 3, 13, 21, 22, 24, 25, 26, 27, 29, 31, 32, 37, 38, 39, 43, 47, 50, 51, 54, 56, *59, 60, 61, 62*
Hirotsu, Y., 400, 401, 418, *432*
Hirschmann, D. J., 295, *335*
Hirschmann, R., 77, 96, *106,* 117, 138, 151, 154, 158, 188, *201, 202, 204, 214,* 343, 385, *447*
Hirshfield, J., 288, *333*
Hiskey, R. G., 156, 157, *204,* 387, *437*
Hiti, A. L., 54, *59*
Hitzeman, R. A., 22, 37, 55, 56, *61*
Hitzler, F., 189, 190, *211*
Hlavka, J. J., 190, *212*
Ho, T. L., 174, *204,* 348, 399, 401, 402, 406, 407, 408, 422, 423, *442*
Hoare, D. G., 297, *339*
Hobbs, D. S., 39, 44, *63*
Hodges, R. S., 223, *281,* 328, *336*
Hodgkin, D. C., 290, *333*
Höfle, G., 258, 259, *283*
Hoehn, M. M., 289, *335, 337*
Hoes, C., 415, *437*
Hofer, W., 179, *200*
Hoffman, J. A., 39, 48, *59*
Hoffmann, D., 232, *283*
Hoffmann, P. J., 358, *448*
Hofmann, K., 67, 68, *107,* 122, 137, 160, 163, 179, 182, *204,* 221, *280,* 349, 418, *435, 437*
Hofschneider, P. H., 25, 54, *58, 61*
Hogan, M. L., 153, *210*
Hogness, D. S., 21, *60*
Hogue-Angeletti, R., 140, *204*
Holladay, M. W., 427, *445*
Holland, G. F., 158, *204*
Holleran, E. M., 237, *281*
Holley, R. W., 153, 154, 178, *213*
Holly, F. W., 96, *106,* 343, 385, *447*
Holmes, W. E., 17, 18, 21, 24, 28, 30, 44, 55, *60, 62*
Holohan, J. J., 403, *432*
Holt, E. M., 307, 310, 312, *336*
Homer, R. B., 162, *204*
Homnick, C. F., 385, *447*
Honda, I., 136, 165, *211*
Hong, C. I., 426, *437*
Hongo, C., 398, *449*
Honzyl, J., 96, *107,* 157, 158, 180, *204, 211*
Hoogerhout, P., 415, *437*
Hoogwater, D. A., 169, *204*
Hoogsteen, K., 288, *333*
Hope, D. B., 194, *214*
Hoppe, D., 393, *444*
Hoppe, W., 419, *448*
Hoppin, C. R., 396, *432*
Horecker, B. L., 40, *61*
Hori, H., 77, *108*
Horikawa, H., 353, 385, 394, *437, 441*
Horikoshi, H., 348, 399, 406, 407, 420, 421, *449*
Horlein, G., 129, *215*
Horn, T., 13, 25, *59*
Horner, B. L., 348, 399, 401, 402, 406, 407, 408, 422, 423, *442*
Horner, L., 368, 404, 405, 406, *437*
Horodniceanu, F., 56, *60*
Horvath, G., 414, *431*
Horwich, A., 55, *61*
Hoskins, C., 363, 368, *430*
Hosoda, T., 162, *203*
Houck, C. M., 56, *61*
Houghten, R. A., 161, *204,* 361, 399, 400, *437*
Houghton, M., 18, *61*
Howells, D. J., 395, *443*
Hozumi, T., 18, 24, 54, *60*
Hruby, V. J., 195, *204,* 355, 360, 402, *431, 437*
Hsieh, K.-H., 312, 353, 394, 400, *437, 447*
Hsieh, Y., 237, 272, *281*
Huang, H. T., 173, *204*
Huang, T., 13, *62*
Huber, P., 183, 184, *215*
Hubert, A. J., 150, *204*
Hudlicky, M., 371, 373, *437, 440*
Hudson, A. L., 352, 410, *430*
Hudson, C. B., 352, 410, *437*
Hudson, D., 364, *446*
Huebscher, W., 398, *434*
Hugel, G., 228, 231, 234, *281*
Hughes, G. J., 416, *436*
Hughes, M. S., 293, *338*
Hughes, P., 352, 411, *437*
Huguenin, R., 384, *432*
Huguenin, R. L., 127, *199*
Hulme, K. L., 407, *440*

Humblet, C., 364, *440*
Humphries, A. J., 422, *437*
Hung, P. P., 13, 56, *62*
Hunger, K., 167, *214*
Hunt, M., 188, *204*
Hutchinson, C. A., 51, *60, 61*
Huting, C. M., 374, 424, *442*

I

Ichihara, A., 382, 393, *437, 445*
Ichikawa, T., 378, *437*
Ichikizaki, I., 190, *204*
Ichimoto, I., 382, *439*
Ida, H., 290, 294, 295, *336*
Iinuma, K., 392, *437*
Ikeda, K., 293, *336*
Ikemura, T., 7, *61*
Ikenaka, T., 308, *333*
Illhardt, R., 169, *203*
Imamoto, S., 387, *437, 445*
Inabata, K., 428, *445*
Inagami, F., 290, *338, 339*
Inazu, T., 299, *339*
Indest, H., 419, *448*
Ineichen, K., 383, *438*
Inoue, I., 353, 394, *437*
Inoue, K., 89, 105, *109*
Inoue, S., 397, 417, *438, 442*
Inouye, J. M., 157, *200*
Inouye, H., 182, *204*
Inouye, K., 142, 181, 182, *204, 212*
Inouye, S., 165, *211*
Inouye, Y., 409, *436*
Inubushi, T., 312, *338*
Inui, T., 156, *204*, 379, 386, *435, 437*
Inukai, K., 399, *440*
Inukai, N., 153, 165, *204, 211*
Irie, H., 68, 72, 75, 76, 78, 79, 87, 94, *106, 107, 108*, 125, 129, 157, 159, *204, 209, 215*
Iriuchijima, S., 419, *437*
Iriye, R., 232, 269, 272, 273, 276, *283*
Irreverre, F., 352, 398, 400, 409, 411, *435, 437, 441, 447*
Irvin, J. L., 426, *437*
Isawa, H., 125, 160, *206*
Iselin, B. M., 67, 69, 79, 93, *107, 108*, 124, 128, 130, 138, 142, 146, 147, 154, 156, 161, 167, 179, 180, *204, 205, 212*
Iserentant, D., 7, *60*
Ishido, Y., 378, *437*
Ishihashi, M., 290, 294, 295, *336*
Ishimaru, T., 428, *436*
Ishita, Y., 289, 316, *336*
Islip, P. J., 288, 291, *334*
Ismail, I. A., 423, *437*
Isogai, A., 288, 292, 293, *336*
Isono, K., 288, 291, *335*
Isowa, Y., 391, 397, *437, 438*
Itakura, K., 3, 5, 13, 18, 21, 22, 24, 25, 26, 27, 29, 31, 32, 37, 38, 39, 43, 47, 50, 51, 54, 56, *59, 60, 61, 62*
Ito, H., 173, 190, *204*
Ito, K., 77, 85, *107*, 125, 160, *206*, 392, *438*
Ito, S., 417, *438*
Itoh, H., 382, *438*
Itoh, M., 164, *204*, 227, 273, *281*
Itokawa, H., 288, 292, *335*
Ivanov, V. T., 134, *204*
Ivarie, R. D., 54, *62*
Iwai, K., 142, *205*
Iwai, M., 301, *336*
Iwasaki, F., 385, *441*
Iwasaki, H., 289, *335*, 427, *438*
Iwasaki, T., 353, 369, 373, 374, 380, 386, 394, 424, 425, *438, 442, 443, 447*
Izdebski, J., 189, 190, *205*, 228, 277, *281*, 290, 293, 294, *334*
Izumiya, J., 397, *438*
Izumiya, N., 127, 143, 179, 180, 193, *205, 208, 209, 214*, 223, 225, 231, 233, *281, 282*, 287, 288, 289, 297, 301, 308, 311, 317, 318, 319, 320, 330 331, 332, *333, 335, 337, 338*, 367, 387, 405, *442, 445, 448*

J

Jacklin, M., 396, *446*
Jackson, B. S., 151, *206*
Jackson, D. A., 2, 15, *61*
Jacob, T. A., 151, 188, *201, 204*
Jacobs, P. M., 417, 429, *436, 438*
Jacobson, J. W., 23, 53, *64*
Jacoby, R., 38, *63*
Jacquenoud, P. A., 122, 127, 138, 154, 163, *199, 200*
Jadot, J., 369, 428, *433, 438*
Jaeger, E., 70, 85, *109*, 128, 129, *205, 207, 215*
Jäger, G., 138, 139, 195, *202, 205*

Jahnke, C., 51, *60*
Jahnke, P., 51, *61*
Jakovčić, T., 393, *431*
Jakubke, H. D., 186, 190, *205*, 232, 237, 278, *281*, 378, *438*
Jakubowski, Z. L., 397, *433*
Jansen, A. C. A., 362, 389, *438*
Jansen, E. F., 295, *335*
Jarabak, R. R., 133, *206*
Jarreau, F. X., 289, *335*
Jaskunas, S. R. J., 37, 48, 50, *58*
Jatzkewitz, H., 69, *107*, 170, *203*
Jay, E., 10, 11, *61*
Jean, A., 402, *438*
Jelinek, V., 373, *437*
Jenkins, B., 54, *59*
Jeschkeit, H., 278, *282*
Jham, G., 272, *281*
Jhurani, P., 6, 7, 8, 11, 12, 13, 22, 26, 37, 40, 42, 43, 44, 47, 53, *64*
Jimenez, M. H., 157, 172, *200*, *201*, 352, 362, 409, 410, 413, *434*, *440*
Johansen, N. L., 78, *107*, 125, 128, 133, 158, 160, 165, *203*, *207*, 398, *440*
Johansson, J. G., 388, *445*
Jöhl, A., 157, 160, *201*, *204*, 269, *283*
John, D. I., 390, *436*
Johnson, A. W., 392, *432*
Johnson, D. G., 360, *437*
Johnson, E. M., 406, 423, *441*
Johnson, H., 364, *430*
Johnson, K. K., 418, *436*
Johnson, M. G., 39, *59*
Johnson, M. J., 21, 51, *64*
Johnson, P. F., 51, *64*
Johnson, R. H., 186, *206*
Johnson, S., 39, *61*, 122, *205*
Johnsrud, L., 55, *62*
Johnston, R. B., 180, *202*
Jokumor, H., 382, *439*
Jolley, G., 377, *449*
Jommi, G., 409, *432*
Jones, A. S., 424, 425, *433*
Jones, B. N., 78, *108*
Jones, C. W., 386, *438*
Jones, D. S., 120, *207*, 256, *282*, 347, *436*
Jones, G., 348, 399, 400, 401, 402, 406, 407, 408, 422, 423, *438*, *442*
Jones, J. H., 133, 184, 190, *198*, *200*, *201*, *205*, 219, 222, 240, 242, 246, 249, 252, 253, 257, 261, 262, 263, *279*, *280*, *281*, 352, 410, 413, *430*
Jones, P., 177, *214*
Jones, R., 313, 315, *336*
Jones, R. H., 188, *198*
Jones, W. C., 364, *438*
Jones, W. C., Jr., 157, *204*
Joos, B., 382, *439*
Jordan, A., 429, *431*
Jorden de Urries, M. P., 419, *448*
Jorgensen, E. C., 123, 175, *215*, 225, 260, 261, 275, 276, *284*, 353, 355, 367, 394, 403, 417, *437*, *438*, *448*
Joshua, H., 117, 158, 188, *204*, *214*
Jošt, K., 122, 168, 177, *205*, 350, 378, 390, 399, *438*, *444*, *449*
Jošt, R., 359, *434*
Joullie, M. M., 426, 428, 429, *433*, *445*
Juhász, A., 128, 154, 175, *197*, *206*
Juillerat, M., 130, *205*
Julia, M., 289, *335*
Jund, R., 53, *62*
Jung, G., 160, *198*, 425, *447*
Jung, M., 395, *431*
Jung, M. E., 174, *205*

K

Kaczka, E. A., 288, *333*
Kahan, F. M., 288, *333*
Kahan, J. S., 288, *333*
Kahl, J. D., 410, *438*
Kahle, I., 186, *201*
Kaji, E., 394, *439*
Kajtár, M., 150, 158, *200*, *208*
Kakata, W., *109*
Kakinuma, M., 288, *335*
Kakisawa, H., 386, 409, *436*, *439*
Kalas, T., 272, *281*
Kalyanhur, M. G., 288, *334*
Kamber, B., 70, *108*, 158, 174, 176, *212*, 222, 269, *282*, *283*
Kamen, M. D., 87, *108*, 127, 160, *212*
Kamikawa, T., 412, *432*
Kaminski, K., 363, 370, 382, 383, *438*
Kamiya, T., 164, *204*, 427, *438*
Kanaki, J., 81, 87, *109*, 138, *215*
Kanaoka, Y., 174, *216*
Kaneko, T., 151, *212*, 290, *339*, 379, 386, 409, *435*, *437*, *438*, *440*
Kanematsu, S., 419, *430*
Kang, H. H., 354, 401, 402, *434*
Kang, S., 311, *338*
Kaniguchi, K., 371, *436*

Kanmera, T., 288, 289, 301, 308, 318, 330, 331, 332, *335*
Kantor, F., 54, *58*
Kanzaki, T., 289, *334*
Kapadia, G. J., 404, *445*
Kappeler, H., 67, *108*, 132, 147, 153, 154, 160, 165, 179, 182, *204*, *205*, *212*
Karle, I. L., 352, 411, *435*
Karle, J. M., 352, 411, *435*
Karlheinz, D., 374, *434*
Karlsson, A., 165, *205*
Karlsson, S., 118, *201*
Karpavicius, K., 357, 400, 401, *438*, *443*
Karpova, A. V., 424, *447*
Karwoski, G., 369, *438*
Kasafirek, E., 399, *449*
Kashelikar, D. V., 122, 155, *205*, *210*
Kashima, C., 386, *439*
Kaspersen, F. M., 403, 410, *438*, *447*
Kastin, A. J., 78, *108*
Kasztreiner, E., 371, *447*
Katagiri, N., 5, 13, *61*
Katakai, R., 120, *205*
Katakawa, J., 76, *107*
Kataoka, K., 74, 80, *109*
Kataoka, Y., 404, *438*
Katayama, T., *283*
Katchalski, E., 126, 127, 147, 157, 162, 188, *198*, *205*, *209*
Kato, F., 418, *441*
Kato, K., 380, *438*
Kato, S., 414, *442*
Kato, T., 143, 179, 193, *205*, *208*, *214*, 223, 233, *282*, 289, 290, 311, 317, 318, 319, 320, 330, 331, 332, *333*, *335*, *338*, 405, *445*
Katrukha, G. S., 290, *338*, 419, *430*
Katsoyannis, P. G., 39, *61*, 66, 67, *106*, *107*, 122, 140, 155, 157, 177, *201*, *202*, *205*, 388, *434*
Katsura, H., 379, 386, *435*, *437*
Katz, J. J., 86, *109*, 131, *214*
Kaufman, C., 385, *433*
Kaufman, J., 38, 57, *63*
Kaufman, R. J., 28, 53, 56, *59*
Kaurov, O., 401, *438*
Kawabata, T., 77, *106*
Kawaguchi, H., 289, *335*
Kawai, H., 301, *336*
Kawanishi, S., 72, *108*, 149, *211*
Kawano, T., 89, 105, *109*
Kawasaki, K., 68, *109*, 158, 186, *215*
Kawashima, E. H., 21, 51, *63*, *64*
Kawashima, K., 382, *438*
Kawatani, H., 67, 68, 72, *109*, 125, 127, *215*
Kay, I. T., 288, *333*
Kayahara, H., 232, 269, 272, 273, 276, *283*
Kazuo, N., 127, *213*
Keck, R. G., 38, 39, 47, *61*
Keener, R. L., 422, *437*
Keil, B., 123, 128, *205*
Keith, D. D., 383, *438*, *439*
Keller, O., 358, *439*
Keller, W., 25, 54, *61*
Keller-Schierlen, W., 382, 396, *439*, *441*
Kelley, J. L., 417, *439*
Kelly, C., 288, *334*
Kelly, R. C., 427, *439*
Kemmer, T., 370, *444*
Kemm, E., 116, *214*
Kemp, B., 177, *214*
Kemp, D. S., 113, *205*, 218, 220, 221, 228, 231, 232, 234, 235, 236, 239, 240, 246, 251, 257, 260, 261, 266, 268, 270, 271, 272, 273, 275, 276, 277, 278, *281*, 361, 400, *439*, *444*
Kemp, J., 302, *334*
Kende, A. S., 155, *209*, *210*
Kenner, G. W., 120, 126, 130, 132, 146, 150, 169, 173, 186, *197*, *200*, *203*, *205*, 252, 262, *281*, *282*, 393, 409, *431*, *433*, *439*
Kent, S. B. H., 224, 231, *281*, *282*
Kennewell, P., 364, *436*
Keogh, P., 230, 276, *281*
Kerling, K. E. T., 362, 389, 415, 417, *431*, *437*, *438*
Kern, W., 183, 184, 187, *215*
Keshet, E., 54, *61*
Kessler, W., 128, 130, 156, *205*
Kester, M., 350, 415, *446*
Keutman, H. T., 153, *210*
Kezdy, F. J., 142, *198*
Khan, N. H., 375, 388, 389, *430*, *443*
Khan, S. A., 163, *197*
Khéribet, R., 372, *448*
Khodkova, E. M., 55, *63*
Kohklov, A. S., 288, *335*
Khorana, H. G., 5, *58*, *63*, 183, 189, 190, *206*
Khosla, M. C., 121, 162, *206*, 347, 368, *439*
Kida, M., 289, *334*
Kidd, D. A. A., 143, 151, 187, *206*
Kido, H., 40, *61*

Kikugawa, Y., 419, *439*
Kildisheva, O. V., 357, 400, 401, 438, *443*
Kiltz, H. H., 290, 291, 295, 326, *334, 335*
Kim, S., 222, *282*
Kimura, T., 133, *202*
Kimelman, D., 29, 55, *63*
Kimoto, S., 158, *215*
King, F. E., 143, 151, 187, *206*
Kingston, D. G. I., 289, *334*
Kinomura, Y., 68, *109*, 158, *215*
Kinoshita, F., 369, *436*
Kinoshita, M., 394, *439*
Kircher, K., 188, *206*
Kirihata, M., 382, *439*
Kirk, K. L., 398, 417, *439, 441*
Kirkpatrick, J. L., 388, *440*
Kiryushkin, A. A., 87, *106*, 128, *197*
Kisfaludy, L., 87, 91, *108, 109*, 113, 127, 128, 129, 143, 145, 151, 152, 154, 155, 158, 161, 162, 186, 191, *198, 205, 206, 207, 208, 211, 215*
Kishida, Y., 67, 68, 70, 85, *108*, 125, 136, *211*, 223, 224, 278, *283*
Kiso, Y., 67, 72, 77, 83, 85, *107, 109*, 125, 133, 160, 187, *206, 215*, 231, *281*
Kitada, C., 81, 86, *106, 108*, 141, *202*, 228 232, 270, 273, 277, *281*
Kitade, K., 133, *206*
Kitajima, Y., 387, *448*
Kitagawa, K., 74, 77, 80, *107, 109*, 125, 133, 160, *206*, 397, *438*
Kitagawa, T., 387, *439*
Kitano, K., 289, *334*
Kiyoi, R., 385, *436*
Kjaer, A., 397, 403, *439*
Klauke, E., 298, *337*
Klausner, Y. S., 89, 91, *106*, 128, 134, 136, 139, 165, 166, 167, 178, 180, 183, 184, *199*, 206, 240, 251, 252, 253, 257, *280*, 281, 359, 400, *439*
Kleid, D. G., 3, 22, 24, 25, 26, 27, 29, 37, 38, 39, 43, 47, 50, 53, 54, 55, 56, *59, 60, 61, 62, 64*
Kleiman, R., 412, *433*
Kleppe, K., 5, *58*
Klessen, C., 190, *205*, 232, 237, 278, *281*
Klieger, E., 150, *202*
Klostermeyer, H., 67, *108*, 136, 152, 153, 165, *211*
Kmiecik-Chmura, H., 165, *211*
Knapp, F. F., Jr., 356, 378, *439*
Knobler, Y., 397, *435*
Knof, S., 129, *205, 207*
Knunyants, I. L., 372, 401, *439, 443*
Kny, H., 398, *437*
Kobayashi, S., 227, 228, 273, *281*, 406, 407, *449*
Kocy, O., 121, 123, 145, *209, 210*
Kohr, W. J., 37, 38, 39, 47, 55, 56, *61, 62*
Koizumi, K., 294, *338*
Kojro, E., 350, 418, *436, 447*
Kokowsky, N., 180, *201*
Kolar, A. J., 306, *334*
Kolb, J. J., 159, *214*
Kollonitsch, J., 371, 389, 405, *435*
Kolc, J., 364, 390, *439, 449*
Kolodziejczyk, A. M., 189, *197*, 228, 229, 235, 253, 269, 271, 273, 274, 275, *279*
Komamine, A., 387, *445*
Komori, S., 188, *216*
Kondo, E., 288, *338*
Kondo, M., 331, *333*
Kondo, S., 392, *437*
König, W. A., 88, *107*, 133, 138, 140, 153, 172, 191, 195, *202, 205, 206*, 226, 228, 231, 234, 236, 239, 272, *282, 283*
Konishi, K., 381, 415, *448*
Konno, S., 306, 309, *335*
Konrad, M., 38, 56, *59*
Koomen, G. J., 386, *436*
Koop, A. H., 55, *61*
Kopple, K. D., 86, *109*, 115, 131, 133, 164, 186, 188, 193, *206, 214*
Korenicki, F., 364, *449*
Korger, G., 117, *214*
Korn, L., 7, *58*
Korpela, T., 397, *439*
Korshunova, G. A., 426, *445*
Koshland, D. E., Jr., 297, *339*
Koshland, M. E., 38, *62*
Kossoy, A., 400, *435*
Kostyuchenko, N. P., 420, *447*
Kotai, A., 151, *200*
Kotake, H., 114, *206*, 370, *442*
Kourilsky, P., 26, 55, 56, *60, 61, 62*
Kovács, J., 113, 150, 186, 191, *200, 206*, 218, 221, 237, 267, 272, *281*
Kovacs, K., 133, 151, *200, 209*, 410, *430*
Koyama, K., 89, 92, 105, *109*, 125, 160, *213, 215*
Koyama, M., 382, *437*

Koyama, Y., 81, *108*
Kozuki, S., 288, *338*
Kranenburg, P., 195, *199*
Krassó, A. F., 380, *436*
Kraszewski, A., 3, 13, 22, 25, 27, 29, 37, 38, 39, 43, 47, 50, 54, 56, *59, 60, 62, 64*
Krause, H., 398, 402, *446*
Krchnak, V., 391, *449*
Kreil, G., 37, *61*
Kristensen, E. P., 386, *439*
Kroeff, E. P., 39, 48, *59*
Krogsgaard-Larsen, P., 427, *436*
Krumdieck, C. L., 152, *206*
Krupa, T. S., 416, *434*
Krupicka, J., 169, *211*
Kruse, L., 363, 368, *430*
Krust, A., 55, *62*
Kubiak, T., 189, *205*
Kubo, K., *109*
Künzi, H., 138, *207*, 368, *439*
Kuff, E. L., 21, *62*
Kuhn, R., 156, *206*
Kuike, K., 427, *446*
Kulesha, I. D., 145, 179, *214*, 228, 253, 257, 258, *283*
Kulikov, S. V., 167, *207*
Kum, K., 429, *439*
Kumagai, H., 403, *443*
Kumar, A., 5, *58*
Kumarev, V. P., 53, *61*
Kunce, D., 189, 190, *205*
Kuneko, S., 369, *436*
Kung, H., 37, 39, 44, *63, 64*
Kung, Y. T., 67, *107*
Kunitz, M., 98, 101, *107*
Kupper, H., 25, 53, 54, *60, 61*
Kupryszewski, G., 278, *282*
Kurita, H., 309, *335*
Kurita, M., 397, *438*
Kurita, S., 391, *437*
Kurn, N., 399, 407, 421, *431*
Kurobe, M., 80, *109*
Kuroda, K., 183, *200*, 219, 224, 225, 230, 232, 233, 234, 235, 237, 238, 242, 243, 258, 265, 266, 268, 269, 271, 272, 273, 274, 275, 276, 277, *280*
Kuromizu, K., 157, *207, 208*
Kurz, C., 25, 54, *61*
Kushner, S. R., 23, 25, 53, *61, 64*
Kuss, E., 386, 390, *439*
Kusumi, T., 386, *439*
Kusumoto, S., 222, 226, *282*, 392, *447*
Kutawa, S., 163, *214*
Kutny, R., 179, *214*
Kutscher, W, 416, *436*
Kutschera, I., 362, 377, 390, *436*
Kuttab, S. H., 395, *436*
Kuwabara, T., *283*
Kuwada, M., 87, *107*
Kuwata, S., 272, 277, *282*, 350, 366, 404, 415, 428, 429, *438, 445, 448, 449*
Kuyper, L. F., 289, 313, 315, *336*
Kuziel, A., 189, *214*, 229, *282*
Kwai, H., 176, *213*
Kwei, J. Z., 89, *106*, 144, 146, *199*
Kwoh, D. Y., 33, *59*
Kwoh, T. J., 33, *59*
Kynel, J., 405, *448*

L

Lachman, C., 425, *447*
Lacroute, F., 55, *58, 62*
Laguzza, B. C., 384, *439*
Lahde, E., 189, *211*
Lai, C.–Y., 4, 39, 44, *60, 63*
Laird, W. M., 382, *432*
Laitem, L., 421, *439*
Lambros, T. J., 172, *208*, 243, *281*
Lan, N. C. Y., 27, 53, *63*
Landano, A. P., 44, *64*
Lande, S., 67, 68, *107*, 117, *199*
Landor, S. R., 363, 369, 371, *431*
Langemann, A., 403, *439*
Larscheid, M. E., 418, *436*
Larsen, L. M., 386, *439*
Larsen, P. K., 427, *432*
Larsen, P. O., 397, 398, 400, 402, 403, *430, 439*
Lashkov, V. N., 167, *207*
Lau, H. D., 364, *430*
Lauer, G., 29, 53, *60*
Lauinger, C., 370, 380, *446*
Lautsch, W., 348, 407, *444*
Law, H. D., 400, *441*
Lawesson, S.–O., 364, *432*
Lawler, H. C., 67, *106*
Lawn, R M., 56, *61*
Lazar, J., 354, 373, *439*
Lázár, T., 147, 178, *197*
Lea, P. J., 342, *435, 439*

Leach, S. J., 154, *207*
Lebek, M., 189, *205*
Leclercq, J., 375, *440*
Ledermann, S., 222, 226, *282*
Ledger, R., 174, *207*
Ledis, S. L., 367, *443, 445*
Lee, C. J., 375, *440*
Lee, F., 7, *58*
Lee, F. G. H., 402, *440*
Lee, P. Q., 325, *335*
Lee, S., 288, 289, 301, 308, 317, 318, 319, 320, 330, 331, 332, *335, 338,* 405, *445*
Lee, S. G., 56, *62*
Lee, S. L., 413, *448*
Lee, T. C., 353, 367, 394, *437, 438*
Lee, W. W., 425, *440*
Lee, Y. K., 386, 409, *438, 440*
Leeman, S. E., 74, *106*
Leese, R. A., 347, 368, *439*
Legler, G., 117, *203*
Leimgruber, W., 383, *438*
Leist, T., 44, *58*
Leister, N. A., 184, 185, 186, *207*
Lemaire, S., 127, *207,* 402, *440*
Lenard, J., 142, 175, *207*
Le Nguyen, D., 219, 233, 269, 272, 273, *280, 282*
Lennarz, W., 400, *446*
Leonard, F., 403, *440*
Leplawy, M. T., 120, *207,* 256, *282*
Lequesne, W. J., 151, *207*
Lerner, R. A., 44, *61*
Lesiak, T., 421, *445*
Letham, D. S., 369, 424, *440*
Letsinger, R. L., 13, 14, *62*
Lettré, H., 372, 373, 380, *440*
Leukart, O., 348, 363, 371, 408, *434, 440, 444*
Leung, C. Y., 140, *216*
Leung, D. W., 18, 21, 24, 37, 48, 49, 50, 54, 55, 56, *60, 61, 63, 64*
Levenberg, B., 368, *440*
Levin, Y., 127, 162, *209*
Levine, H. L., 37, 39, 44, 55, 56, *61, 64*
Levine, L., 237, 238, 246, 264, *281*
Levine, S. D., 144, 175, *199*
Levinson, A. D., 21, 55, 56, *61, 62*
Lewin, B., 24, *62*
Lewis, H. M., 18, 24, 55, *59, 61*
Lewis, J. W., 396, *446*
Lewis, R. B., 289, 313, 315, *336*
Leyden, D. E., 386, *438*
Li, C. H., 71, 79, *108,* 122, 125, 126, 127, 133, 136, 138, 158, 159, 160, 161, 178, *199, 201, 204, 207, 209, 210, 215, 216,* 402, *440*
Li, R. I., 290, *338*
Liardon, R., 222, 226, *282*
Liberatori, A., 308, *334*
Liberek, B., 396, *440*
Liberek, B., Jr., 155, 156, 191, *207*
Libert, W., 375, *440*
Lichtenberg, L. A., 222, *282*
Lidaks, M., 424, 425, *440*
Lie, T. S., 153, 169, *198*
Liebman, A. A., 356, 381, 413, *434, 440*
Liefländer, M., 151, *207*
Liesch, J. M., 290, *335*
Lin, C.-C., 55, *61*
Lin, N., 39, 44, 48, *63, 64*
Lindeberg, G., 165, *205,* 388, *431*
Lindenmann, A., 179, *204*
Lindley, H., 154, *207*
Lingens, F., 419, *447*
Lipkin, V. M., 87, *106,* 128, *197*
Lipnik, M., 399, *442*
Lipowski, A. W., 428, *440*
Lipsett, M., 327, *335*
Lipton, S. H., 426, *448*
Liu, F. T., 44, *61*
Liu, T. Y., 67, 68, 72, *107, 108*
Liu, Y. Y., 381, *440*
Livingston, D. M., 56, *62*
Liwshitz, Y., 386, 387, *440, 445*
Lo, T. B., 158, *207*
Löw, M., 87, *109,* 127, 128, 129, 158, 191, *207, 208, 215*
Low, M., 129, 154, 190, *201, 205, 206*
Loffet, A., 127, 129, 136, *207*
Logan, C. J., 172, *197*
Logan, M. A., 409, *442*
Loison, G., 53, *62*
Lokshin, G. B., 288, *335*
Lombardino, J. G., 187, *207*
Lomedico, P., 28, 56, *64*
Loncrini, D. F., 372, *440*
Loring, H. S., 157, 163, *201, 207*
Losse, G., 119, 164, 186, *207,* 352, 410, *442*
Lott, R. S., 176, *207*
Louise, A., 54, *59*
Low, T. L. K., 4, 6, 7, 8, 11, 12, 13, 22, 26, 34, 40, 42, 43, 44, 47, 53, *60, 62, 64*

Loy, R. S., 371, *440*
Lozier, R., 226, *282*
Lucas, T J., 193, *207*
Lucente, G., 121, 168, *201, 207*
Luchi, P., 377, *433*
Ludescher, V., 354, *444*
Lukin, M., 293, *334*
Lundell, J., 397, *439*
Lundin, B. N., 386, *430*
Lundt, B. F., 78, *107,* 125, 128, 133, 158, 160, 165, *203, 207,* 398, *440*
Lunkenheimer, W., 156, *207*
Lunsford, W. B., 14, *62*
Ly, M. G., 397, *434*
Lysenko, Z., 426, 428, 429, *433, 445*
Lyster, M. A., 174, *205*

M

Mabuni, C., 313, *337*
McAdoo, M., 4, *60*
McCandliss, R., 17, 18, 21, 24, 28, 30, 44, 55, *60*
McCapara, F., 309, *335*
McCloskey, J. A., 425, *442*
McClure, J. E., 4, 6, 7, 8, 11, 12, 13, 22, 26, 34, 40, 42, 43, 44, 47, 53, *60, 64*
McCord, T. J., 387, 388, 389, 407, *433, 440*
McCormick, W. M., 359, 400, *439*
McDermott, J. R., 225, 227, 232, 236, 262, 263, 271, 272, *282*
McDevitt, H. O., 22, *59*
McGandy, E. L., 418, *445*
McGee, J. O'D., 409, 410, 413, *440*
McGrath, J. P., 56, *63*
McGregor, A. C., 164, *197*
McGregor, W. H., 173, *207*
Mach, B., 26, *61*
Machova, A., 391, *449*
MacIntyre, I., 364, *446*
McKay, F. C., 67, 69, *107,* 138, 159, 164, 167, 178, *197, 207*
MacKay, P., 54, *58*
McKennis, H., Jr., 347, 428, *434*
McKercher, P. D., 24, 26, 53, *61*
McKerrow, J. H., 154, *208*
Maclaren, J. A., 117, *208,* 262, 263, *282*
McLean, E. W., 417, *439*
McLeod, J. K., 130, *197,* 424, *440*
McLeod, R. S., 121, 195, *202,* 355, 409, *435*
McMorris, T. C., 289, *334*
McMurry, J., 78, *107*
McNeil, M. W., 372, *435*
McRae, G., 348, 399, 401, 402, 406, 407, 408, 422, 423, *442*
Maeda, K., 290, *337,* 392, *437*
Maeda, M., 425, *442*
Maeda, S., 17, 18, 21, 24, 28, 30, 44, 55, *60,* 378, 379, *437, 443*
Maeno, Y., 387, *437, 445*
Magee, M. Z., 179, *204*
Maierhofer, A., 371, *448*
Makarova, H. N., 383, *440*
Maki, Y., 393, 399, *440*
Makisumi, S., 127, 180, *209, 214,* 392, *441*
Makofske, R. C., 172, 179, *208,* 214
Maksakov, V. A., 410, 422, *431*
Maksimov, E. E., 269, *282*
Malek, G., 187, *198*
Malicky, J. L., 402, *432*
Maloň, P., 410, *447*
Maloy, W. L., 347, 368, *439*
Mamont, P., 395, *431*
Mangold, J. B., 395, *436*
Mania, D., 290, *337*
Manian, A. A., 402, *440*
Manley, J. L., 31, *63*
Manneburg, M., 138, *207*
Manning, J. M., 152, 157, *208,* 221, 222, 223, 224, 225, 227, 233, *282,* 378, *447*
Mano, M., 384, *435*
Marbach, P., 358, *443*
Marburg, S., 371, 405, *439*
Marchand, J., 289, *335*
Marchelli, R., 288, 289, 292, 293, *334, 335*
Marchiori, F., 130, *202,* 368, 399, *431*
Marcinal, P., 349, 408, *432*
Marconi, G. G., 293, 294, *334, 335*
Marcus, A., 385, *440*
Marglin, A., 67, *107,* 122, 157, 160, 163, 177, *208*
Mariman, E. C. M., 348, 419, *443*
Markeley, L. D., 166, *201*
Markes, J. H. H., 174, *201*
Märki, W., 387, 401, *440*
Marks, D., 38, 55, *59*
Marks, N., 364, *440*
Markum, A. F., 5, 50, *59*
Markussen, J., 78, *107,* 125, 128, 158, 160, 165, *207,* 398, *440*
Marlborough, D. J., 352, 409, *435*
Marlier, M., 412, *440*

Marmur, J., 53, *59*
Marquardt, O., 25, 54, *61*
Marquet, A., 381, *431*
Marshall, G. R., 127, 140, 153, 176, *204, 208, 210,* 364, 372, 400, *437, 440, 447*
Martial, J. A., 54, *62, 63*
Martin, M., 352, 411, *437*
Martinez, A. P., 425, *440*
Martinez, J., 89, *107,* 113, 126, 134, 146, 147, 160, 170, 172, 182, *199, 208*
Martynov, V. S., 383, *440*
Marx, A. F., 184, *209*
Marzotto, A., 391, *445*
Masaki, M., 288, 303, 309, *335, 338*
Masamune, T., 426, *441*
Massey, D. E., 40, *63*
Massey, T. H., 400, *441*
Massiah, T., 168, *198*
Massy-Westropp, R. A., 288, *334*
Mastalerz, P., 397, *436*
Masugi, T., 395, *440*
Masui, Y., 87, *107,* 129, 160, *200, 208*
Mathiaparanam, P., 289, 312, 313, 315, *337*
Matoni, Y., 231, *282*
Matsuda, S., 86, *108*
Matsuda, Y., 132, *209*
Matsueda, G. R., 127, *213*
Matsui, M., 387, *445*
Matsukura, M., 222, 226, *282*
Matsumoto, K., 288, 308, *333, 336, 338,* 369, 373, 374, 379, 380, 385, 386, *438, 441, 442, 443, 447*
Matsumoto, T., 289, 316, *336*
Matsumura, K., 421, 429, *441, 448*
Matsuo, K., 403, *441*
Matsushita, K., 290, *338, 339*
Matsuura, S., 67, *107,* 299, 327, *335*
Matsuura, T., 403, *441*
Matteucci, M. D., 14, *62*
Matthews, C. N., 396, *448*
Matthews, H. W., 382, *443*
Matthies, D., 376, 377, *441*
Mauger, A. B., 409, *441*
Maurer, B., 396, *439, 441*
Maurer, R. A., 56, *60*
Maurukas, J., 140, *197*
Maxam, A. M., 22, *60*
May, L., 17, 18, 21, 24, 28, 30, 39, 44, 48, 55, *60, 63*
Mauri, F., 409, *432*
Mayama, M., 294, *338*
Mayer, D., 235, 267, *283*
Mayer, F., 381, *448*
Mayer, J., 116, *214*
Mayers, G. L., 186, *206*
Mazanek, J., 117, 121, *210*
Mazur, R. H., 71, *107,* 135, 194, *208,* 308, 324, *335*
Meacock, P. A., 5, 50, *59*
Meagher, R. B., 37, *62*
Means, G. E., 40, *62*
Mechanic, G., 381, *441*
Mecklenberg, R. S., 327, *335*
Medina, A., 54, *63*
Medzihradszky, K., 122, 150, 158, *197, 206, 208*
Medzihradszky-Schweiger, H., 158, *208*
Meese, C. O., 239, *282*
Meienhofer, J., 4, *60,* 67, 105, *107,* 121, 122, 151, 157, 158, 172, 176, 178, 179, 184, 185, 194, *200, 201, 202, 207, 208, 216,* 226, 243, 253, *281, 282,* 352, 356, 387, 409, 413, *430, 434, 441*
Meister, A., 342, 395, *435, 441*
Melchiorre, C., 422, *435*
Melendez, E., 404, *432*
Melenteva, T. M., 290, *338*
Mellander, O., 141, *213*
Melville, J., 151, *208*
Menegatti, E., 176, *210*
Mercereau-Puijalon, O., 55, *62*
Merenyi, R., 428, *441*
Meresar, U., 174, *208*
Meriwether, L., 194, *208*
Merkulov, V. M., 53, *61*
Merregaert, J., 7, *60*
Merrien, M.-A., 289, *337*
Merrifield, R. B., 67, 71, 72, 73, 75, 83, 85, 89, 96, *106, 107, 109,* 113, 120, 121, 122, 125, 126, 134, 136, 145, 146, 149, 152, 156, 158, 160, 163, 165, 171, 177, 186, 189, 192, *198, 201, 202, 203, 208, 213, 214, 216,* 223, 224, 228, 231, 242, 253, 257, 258, 259, 260, 270, *279, 281, 282,* 326, 328, *336,* 402, *434*
Mertes, M. P., 376, *441*
Messenguy, F., 55, *59*
Metcalf, B. W., 397, *432*
Mevarech, M., 21, *62*
Meyer, R., 367, 404, *444*
Meyer, W. L., 289, 313, 315, *336, 338*
Meyers, C., 154, *208*

Meyers, G. L., 221, *281*
Miekeley, A., 141, *198*
Mikhaleva, I. I., 134, *204*
Mikozami, N., 186, *215*
Milewski, S., 384, *431*
Militello, G., 413, *448*
Milkowski, J. D., 158, *214*, 406, 423, *441*
Miller, C. A., 417, *439*
Miller, F. M., 406, 423, *441*
Miller, J. B., 55, *61*
Miller, J. H., 20, 30, *60*, *62*
Miller, M. J., 298, 301, *336*
Miller, S. M., 188, *204*
Milne, G. W. A., 128, *197*
Minagawa, T., 288, *336*
Minami, H., 68, *109*
Minard, F., 405, *448*
Minard, R. D., 396, *448*
Minematsu, Y., 311, *338*
Min Jou, W., 7, *60*
Miozarri, G. F., 4, 17, 18, 21, 24, 28, 30, 44, 54, 55, *60*, *62*
Mirachi, U., 407, *447*
Misaki, S., 405, *447*
Mitani, K., 81, 83, 85, *109*, 138, *215*
Mitchell, A. R., 75, *108*, 136, 156, 186, *208*, 224, 231, *281*, *282*, 328, *336*
Mitin, Y. V., 269, *282*
Mitoma, C., 400, 402, *433*
Mitra, T. K., 393, 394, *432*
Mitsuyasu, N., 143, 179, 180, *208*, *214*
Miura, C., 348, 399, 406, 407, 414, 420, 421, *449*
Miyachi, Y., 327, *335*
Miyake, T., 21, 51, *64*, 289, *335*
Miyamoto, S., 80, *109*
Miyazaki, T., 231, *281*, 288, *336*
Miyazawa, T., 272, 277, *282*, 290, *338*, *339*, 366, 404, *449*
Miyoshi, K., 13, *62*
Miyoshi, M., 165, 175, *211*, *213*, 240, 241, 242, 244, 245, 252, *282* 308, *336*, 353, 369, 373, 374, 379, 380, 385, 386, 394, 424, 425, *437*, *438*, *442*, *443*, *447*
Mizogucchi, T., 156, *204*
Mizokami, N., 68, *109*
Mizuguchi, A., 376, *442*
Mizuno, K., 390, 392, *445*, *448*
Mizuno, Y., 78, *107*
Mizusaki, K., 392, *441*
Mizutani, J., 376, *442*
Mocz, A., 349, 408, *432*
Möschler, H. J., 356, 362, *441*
Mohr, H., 115, *215*, 236, *282*
Mokotoff, M., 377, *432*
Molemans, F., 7, *60*
Molko, D., 51, *64*
Monastyrskaya, G. S., 55, *63*
Money, T., 289, *334*
Monseur, X., 289, *335*
Monsigny, M. L. P., 376, *441*
Montagnoli, G., 417, *441*
Montecucci, P., 79, *106*
Montgomery, D. L., 21, *62*
Montiero, H. J., 395, *441*
Moodie, R. B., 162, *204*
Moore, D. M., 24, 26, 53, *61*
Moore, G. A., 130, *205*
Moore, G. J., 352, *441*
Moore, J. A., 396, 409, *441*, *443*
Moore, R. R., 391, *441*
Moore, S., 96, *108*, 157, *208*, 222, 223, 224, 225, 227, 233, *282*, *283*, 352, 364, 400, 409, *430*, *441*
Mooz, E. D., 343, *441*
Morawiec, J., 237, *283*
Morell, J. L., 290, 291, 295, 296, 320, 325, 326, *334*, *335*, 374, *441*
Morgan, D. O., 24, 26, 53, *61*
Morgenstern, A. P., 403, *441*
Mori, H., 290, 294, 295, *336*
Mori, K., 391, 397, *437*, *438*
Moriga, M., 92, *109*
Morimoto, H., 184, *215*
Morimoto, K., 290, *336*
Morin, R. B., 288, *333*
Morinaga, S., 142, *202*
Morita, A., 406, 407, *449*
Morita, K., 409, *437*
Moritoki, H., 77, *107*, 160, *206*
Moriya, T., 308, *336*, 382, 419, *438*, *441*
Morley, J. S., 343, 347, 350, 418, *434*, *436*, *441*
Moroder, L., 129, 130, *202*, *205*, 277, *283*, 368, 399, *431*
Morris, C. J., 398, 400, *437*, *447*
Morris, J., 386, *433*
Morris, J. A., 54, *63*
Morrison, B. H., Jr., 353, *444*
Morrison, D. C., 408, *441*
Moser, P., 193, *212*, 401, *432*
Moshberg, R., 369, 383, *430*

Mosjov, S., 156, *208*
Moussebois, C., 428, *441*
Mowles, C. T., 356, 413, *434*
Mukunoki, Y., 367, 419, *445*
Mühlhausen, D., 195, *210*
Mühlhauser, R. O., 403, *438*
Müller, G., 119, *207*
Müller, H., 269, *282*
Müller, P., 398, 412, *441*
Murakami, M., 153, *204*
Murakami, N., 92, *109*
Murakoshi, I., 418, *441*
Murakoshi, S., 293, *336*
Muramatsu, I., 117, 192, *209*, 289, 293, 294, *334*
Muraoka, M., 225, 231, *281, 282*
Murphy, R. F., 21, 51, *64*
Murray, K., 54, *58*
Murray, W., 403, *438*
Murti, V. V. S., 195, *216*
Mushika, Y., 353, 394, 424, 425, *437, 442*
Mutt, V., 89, *108*, 160, 172, *199*
Muttini, A., 417, *441*
Myagkova, M. A., 134, *204*

N

Naber, S. P., 28, 56, *64*
Nadkarni, M. V., 353, *444*
Nadolski, D., 164, *207*
Naegeli, P., 173, *215*, 289, *339*
Nagai, W., 417, *441*
Nagai, Y., 121, *211*
Nagamachi, T., 403, *441*
Naganawa, H., 290, *336*
Nagaraj, R., 270, 271, *282*
Nagarajan, G. R., 370, *441*
Nagarajan, R., 289, *335*
Nagasawa, H., 288, 292, 293, *336*
Nagasawa, H. T., 353, 389, 394, 409, 411, *434, 441, 442, 445*
Nagashima, K., 288, *338*
Nagata, A., 290, *336, 338*
Nagata, S., 44, 48, 55, *62, 63*
Nagel, D. W., 288, *336*
Nagy, H., 150, *200*
Nahmias, C., 356, 361, 403, *435*
Naider, F., 159, *209*
Nair, R. M. G., 78, *108*
Nair, V., 409, *430*
Naithani, V. K., 179, *209*
Naito, T., 289, *335*
Najarian, R., 21, 55, *60*
Najarian, R. C., 56, *61*
Najjar, V. A., 80, *108*
Nakagawa, M., 414, *442*
Nakagawa, T., 290, 294, 301, *336*
Nakahara, M., 379, *435*
Nakai, T., 419, *442*
Nakajima, K., 301, *336*, 410, *442*
Nakajima, N., 384, *435*
Nakajima, R., 290, 294, 295, *336*
Nakajima, T., 81, 87, *107, 108, 109*, 427, *446*
Nakamura, I., 410, *436*
Nakamura, M., 160, *215*
Nakamura, S., 77, 85, *107*, 125, 160, *206*, 289, 290, *336, 337*
Nakane, M., 364, *442*
Nakanishi, H., 78, *107*
Nakano, K., 153, *204*, 414, *442*
Nakano, M., 74, 80, *107, 109*
Nakashima, R., 293, *336*
Nakashima, T., 289, 290, 294, 295, 316, *336, 339*
Nakata, Y., 79, *109*
Nakatsu, K., 290, *339*
Nakatsuka, S., 288, *336*
Nakatsuyama, S., 369, 381, *435*
Nakazawa, H., 419, *442*
Nakazawa, T., 290, 294, *336*
Nakita, T., 290, *336*
Nannicini, L., 417, *441*
Naoe, K., 350, 415, *448*
Nara, K., 289, *334*
Narang, S. A., 5, 13, *61*
Narita, K., 141, 142, 179, *197, 202, 209*
Natarajan, S., 89, *106*, 134, 139, 148, *199, 209*, 352, 364, 377, *431, 442*
Nauta, W. T., 403, *441*
Nayak, D. P., 54, *59*
Nebelin, E., 122, *212*, 290, 295, 326, *335*
Neder, A., 371, *447*
Needleman, R. B., 53, *59*
Nefkens, G. H. L., 169, *209*, 381, *446*
Neidhardt, F. C., 37, *62*
Neklyudov, A. D., 156, *212*
Nelson, D. A., 153, *201*
Nestor, J. J., Jr., 348, 364, 399, 401, 402, 406, 407, 408, 422, 423, *438, 442*
Neuberger, M. R., 72, *108*
Neubert, K., 232, 237, 278, *281*, 352, 410, *442*
Neumann, H., 127, 162, *209*

Neumann, R. E., 121, *209*
Newton, C. R., 5, 50, *59*
Newton, G. C. F., 289, *333*
Ney, K. H., 149, 160, 161, *210*
Neya, M., 410, *442*
Neys, R. D., 403, *430*
Niall, H. D., 153, 176, *210, 214*
Nichinaga, A., 403, *441*
Nicholson, G. J., 225, 226, *281*
Nicolaides, E. D., 125, 138, 140, *199, 209,* 347, 399, *442*
Nicolaides, E. P., 396, *441*
Nicolaidou, P., *199*
Nicolella, V., 289, *333*
Nicot-Cutton, C., 132, *200*
Nida, T., 397, *442*
Niemann, C., 173, *204*
Nienburg, H., 121, *197*
Niimura, V., 369, *436*
Nijenhuis, B., 404, *448*
Nilsson, A., 89, *108*
Nimura, Y., 371, 381, *436, 442*
Nisanjan, P., 377, *430*
Nisato, D., 391, *445*
Nishida, Y., 350, 415, *448*
Nishikawa, J., 405
Nishimura, H., 376, *442*
Nishimura, N., 232, 277, *283*
Nishimura, O., 81, *108,* 125, 138, *209, 215*
Nishimura, S., 425, *442*
Nishinaga, A., 403, *441*
Nishioka, K., 80, *108*
Nishioka, R. S., 93, *108*
Nishitani, T., 353, 394, 424, 425, *437, 442*
Nisula, B., 327, *335*
Nitecki, D. E., 136, 166, *203,* 262, 263, 273, *282*
Nitta, K., 145, *213*
Nitz, T. J., 307, 310, 312, *336, 338*
Niu, C. H., 67, *107*
Nivard, R. J. F., 169, *209,* 348, 391, 419, *443, 447*
Nixon, L. N., 388, *445*
Noack, K., 380, *436*
Noble, R. L., 79, *108,* 159, *209*
Noda, K., 127, *209,* 223, 231, 233, *282,* 289, 299, 318, 327, 328, *335, 336*
Noda, T., 290, *336, 339*
Node, M., 77, *108*
Noguchi, J., 138, 157, *198, 203*
Noguchi, M., 416, *442*
Nojima, H., 227, 273, *281*
Noll, C. I., 353, *444*
Nollet, A. J. H., 374, 424, 425, *442*
Nolting, H., 193, *212*
Nomoto, S., 289, 290, 299, *336, 338,* 383, *446*
Norris, C. P., 187, *207*
Norris, K., 160, *209*
Norton, S. J., 350, 415, *442, 446*
Notani, J., 227, 273, *281*
Notation, A. D., 416, *446*
Novikova, M. A., 426, *445*
Nowak, K., 190, *212,* 237, 238, *283*
Noyes, B. E., 18, 21, *58, 62*
Nozoe, S., 369, 381, *435*
Nulu, J. R., 412, *430*
Nunami, K., 370, *442*
Nunberg, J. H., 28, 53, 57, *59*
Nutt, R. F., 343, *447*

O

Obayashi, M., 227, 228, 273, *281*
Obermeier, R., 118, *214*
O'Brien, B. C., 401, *444*
O'Donnell, J. P., 396, *432*
Odstrchel, G., 176, *202*
Öhler, E., 287, 298, 299, 302, 303, 304, 305, 308, 309, 311, *336, 337*
Oettmeier, W., 371, 372, *448*
Offe, H. A., 298, *337*
Offord, R. E., 51, *62,* 127, *210*
Ogawa, H., 67, 72, 76, 80, 87, *107, 108, 109,* 125, 129, 159, 162, *204, 209, 215*
Ogawa, Y., 290, 294, 295, *336,* 397, *442*
Ogilvie, K. K., 13, *62*
Ogiso, T., 395, *440*
Ogle, T. D., 409, *442*
Ogura, H., 298, 301, *336*
Ohashi, Z., 425, *442*
Ohhashi, J., 379, *442*
Ohmiya, S., 418, *441*
Ohmori, M., 391, 397, *437, 438*
Ohnishi, M., 164, *206*
Ohnishi, T., 165, *211*
Ohno, K., 179, *197*
Ohno, M., 127, *209,* 367, 419, *442*
Ohta, M., 288, 303, 309, *335, 338*
Ohta, T., 419, *442*
Ohta, Y., 386, *437*
Ohtsuka, A., 297, 311, *338*
Ohtsuka, E., 5, *58*
Okurkura, K., *447*

Oishi, M., 83, 85, *109*, 125, 138, *215*
Oka, O., 427, *438*
Oka, Y., 289, *335*
Okabe, H., 290, *339*
Okabe, K., 290, *338*
Okada, M., 67, 68, 71, 85, *108*, 125, *211*
Okada, Y., 68, *109*, 182, 186, *209*, *215*
Okai, H., 223, 233, *282*
Okamoto, K., 331, *333*
Okamoto, M., 158, *215*
Okamoto, T., 378, *437*
Okawa, K., 126, 140, *209*, 301, *336*, 410, *442*
Okawara, T., 373, *442*
Oki, K., 367, *442*
Okuda, T., 67, *108*
Okumura, K., 165, *211*, 373, *442*
Okumura, S., 419, *442*
Okuno, T., 289, 316, *336*
Olah, G. A., 174, *204*
Olsen, O., 386, *439*
Olsen, R., 373, *446*
Olsen, R. K., 297, 311, 312, *338*
Olsen, S., 180, *210*
Olson, K., 39, 48, *63*
Olson, R. E., 387, *449*
Olsuf'eva, E. N., 424, 425, *445*
Omenn, G. S., 160, *210*
Omori, Y., 86, *108*, 132, *209*
Ondetti, M. A., 117, 121, 123, 140, 143, 145, 157, 165, 175, 184, *199*, *209*, 240, 251, 252, 257, *280*, 352, 364, *442*
Ong, H. H., 403, *442*
Ono, M., 426, *441*
Oppermann, H., 55, *61*
Oppliger, M., 387, 401, *440*, *442*
Oppolzer, W., 173, *215*, 289, *339*
Orezzi, P., 289, *333*
Orlandoni, A., 422, *435*
Osano, T., 289, *335*
Osato, R. L., 184, 186, *214*
Osgerby, J., 408, *443*
Oshima, T., 158, *215*
Otani, T. T., 138, *216*, 376, *443*
Otsuka, H., 142, *204*, 290, *338*, *339*
Ott, U., 222, 226, *282*
Ottenheijm, H. C. J., 299, *335*
Otterburn, M. S., 387, *430*
Otvos, J. D., 52, *58*
Overberger, C. G., 409, *443*
Owen, T., 364, *446*
Ozaki, Y., 369, 373, 379, 380, 385, 386, *438*, *441*, *443*
Ozasa, T., 387, *439*

P

Pachler, K. G. R., 288, *336*
Padmanabhan, P., 10, 11, *61*
Padyukova, N. Sh., 426, *445*
Paegle, R., 424, 425, *440*
Paganov, A., 89, *109*
Paik, W. K., 222, *282*
Pais, M., 289, *335*
Pajetta, P., 130, *202*
Palacz, Z., 418, *436*
Palaveda, W. J., Jr., 117, 151, 188, *201*, *204*
Pallai, P., 321, *336*
Pandit, U. K., 374, 386, 410, 424, 425, *436*, *438*, *442*
Pang, P. C., 402, *446*
Panneman, H. J., 184, *209*
Panthier, J. J., 53, *62*
Papp, G., 410, *430*
Paradisi, M. P., 353, 412, *449*
Park, W., 352, *432*
Park, W. K., 353, 393, 400, *443*
Parker, C. W., 424, *440*
Parrish, P. R., 409, *445*
Pasanen, P., 397, *439*
Pascard, C., 290, *337*
Pasini, A., 410, *432*
Patchornik, A., 122, 155, 157, *209*, *210*, *213*, *215*, 286, 311, 325, *336*, 396, *448*
Patel, R. P., 194, *208*
Patel, T. P., 18, 24, 55, *59*, *61*
Paterson, B. M., 21, *62*
Patthy, A., 138, *214*
Patzer, E. J., 55, *61*
Paul, R., 119, 126, 137, 155, 192, *197*, *201*, *209*, *210*
Paulay, Z., 147, 179, *197*
Pauson, P., 408, *443*
Pearson, D., 93, *108*
Pearson, R. G., 76, *108*
Peckham, W. D., 137, *204*
Peggion, E., 347, *443*
Peled, N., 348, 398, 418, *431*
Pelka, J., 189, *205*
Penke, B., 133, *209*
Pennica, D., 21, 55, *60*, *62*
Pence, S., 289, *333*

Perkins, L. M., 371, 405, *439*
Perkone, I., 167, *214*
Perlman, D., 382, *443*
Perlman, K. L., 382, *443*
Perlow, D., 354, 364, *435*
Perri, G., 419, *430*
Perry, L. J., 37, 39, 44, 55, 56, *61, 64*
Pestka, S., 17, 18, 21, 24, 28, 30, 39, 44, 55, *60, 63*
Petermann, C., 366, *434*
Petitcler, C., 223, *283*
Petrini, F., 410, *435*
Petrovskii, P. V., 410, 422, *431*
Petrzilka, T., 376, *443*
Pettee, J. M., 157, 163, *213*
Pettee, R. M., 39, 40, 48, *60*
Pettit, G. R., 343, 416, *434, 443*
Pezzuto, J. M., 52, *62*
Pfaender, P., 252, *280*
Pfister, R. W., 160, *200*
Phelps, D. N., 313, 315, *336*
Philip, R. P., 409, *443*
Phillipps, M., 419, *430*
Phillips, S., 51, *60, 61*
Phocas, I., 156, *209, 210, 216*
Photaki, I., 137, 142, 156, *209, 216*, 286, 297, 298, 316, 321, 325, 330, *336, 337*
Piantadosi, C., 426, *437*
Piché, L., 138, 157, 168, *198*
Pickering, A., 364, *446*
Pieroni, O., 417, *441*
Pietta, P. J., 153, 176, *210*
Pigott, E., 418, *436*
Pinder, R. M., 395, *443*
Pinder, U., 414, *443*
Pinker, T. G., 393, *443*
Piozzi, L., 293, *334*
Pirelli, A., 289, *333*
Pirrung, M. C., 352, 411, *443*
Pitha, J., 424, 425, *433*
Pitner, T. P., 294, *334*
Planet, G., *429*
Plata, M., 424, 425, *440*
Platt, T., 7, *58*
Pleiss, M. A., 395, *436*
Pless, J., 67, *108*, 125, 127, 129, 138, 160, *198, 210*
Pliška, V., 358, *443*
Plöchl, J., 296, *337*
Plotnikoff, N., 405, *448*
Plume, G., 71, *107*
Pluscec, J., 121, 123, 145, *209, 210*
Pochini, A., 288, 289, 292, *333, 334, 335*
Podgorski, M., 399, *443*
Podkoscielny, W., 399, *443*
Podraza, K. F., 410, *446*
Poduška, K., 388, 416, *443*
Poisel, H., 287, 298, 302, 305, 308, 309, 311, *337*
Polisky, B., 26, *62*
Poll, E. H. A., 348, 401, *447*
Polonsky, J., 289, *337*
Polzhofer, K. P., 149, 160, 161, *210*
Pope, B. M., 164, *213*
Popenoe, E. A., 67, *106*
Poráth, J., 118, 165, *201, 205*
Poritere, S., 424, *440*
Porter, A. G., 18, 54, *59, 61*
Porter, T. H., 370, 397, 406, *443*
Poskiene, R., 401, *443*
Pospíšek, J., 120, *210*, 346, 349, 366, 408, *443*
Potts, J. T., 153, *210*
Poulsen, K., 144, *202*
Powers, D., 52, *60*
Powers, J. C., 343, *443*
Pozerauskas, A., 401, *443*
Pracejus, H., 366, *443*
Prange, T., 290, *337*
Prasad, K. U., 364, *444*
Prasmickiene, G., 357, 400, *438*
Pravda, Z., 152, 162, *211, 214*
Preau, J. N., 289, *335*
Prietner, G., 136, *199*
Prelog, V., 180, *210*
Prendęr, G., 39, 48, *63*
Preston, J., 130, *197*, 393, *439*
Previero, A., 127, 131, 132, *209, 210*
Prevot, D., 219, 233, 269, 272, 273, *282*
Pritchard, A. E., 229, *283*
Probst, G. W., 289, *337*
Prokof'ev, M. A., 426, *445*
Prota, A., 132, *210*
Prox, A., 228, 231, 232, 234, 236, 239, 272, *283*
Prudchenko, A. T., 401, *443*
Prystowsky, M. B., 193, *207*
Przybylski, J., 278, *282*
Psaro, R., 410, *432*
Ptashne, M., 29, 53, 55, 56, *60, 62, 63*
Pucher , G. W., 152, *214*
Pungs, E., 191, *200*

Purdie, J. E., 174, *210*
Purick, R. M., 371, *435*
Pushkarera, Z. V., 390, *430*

Q

Quilico, A., 293, *334*

R

Rabinsohn, Y., 386, *440*
Radics, L., 414, *431*
Raeymaekers, A., 7, *60*
Raftery, M. A., 122, *198*
Ragnarsson, U., 165, *205*
Rahn, W., 226, *282*
Rajbhandary, U. L., 5, *58*
Rajh, H. M., 348, 419, 420, 421, *443*
Rakhshinda, M. A., 375, 388, 389, *443*
Ramachandran, G. N., 193, *210*
Ramachandran, J., 122, 126, 158, 163, *207*, *210*
Ramage, R., 130, 173, *205*, *215*
Ramage, W. I., 133, 190, *198*, *201*, 222, 261, *281*, 289, *339*
Rambach, A., 53, *62*
Ramel, A. H., 4, *60*
Ramirez, F., 159, *210*
Ramsey, A. A., 376, *441*
Ranganathan, S., 173, *215*. 289, *339*
Rao, G. S., 404, *445*
Rao, Y. S., 305, 312, *337*, 404, *434*
Rapaka, R. S., 262, 263, 273, *282*
Rapaka, S. R., 367, *438*
Rapoport, H., 361, 368, 399, 400, *429*, *437*
Rapp, P., 403, *443*
Rasmussen, R., 405, *448*
Ratcliffe, M., 429, *444*
Ratcliffe, R. W., 288, *333*
Ratcliffe, S. J., 125, *200*
Ratledge, C., 289, *337*
Ratner, S., 413, *443*
Ratzkin, B., 3, 53, 54, 56, *62*
Ratzkin, H., 155, *210*
Ravdel, G. A., 159, *216*
Ravel, J. M., 369, *434*
Razin, A., 51, *62*
Rebek, J., 236, 242, *281*, *282*
Redding, T. W., 401, 418, *432*
Redfield, B., 37, *64*
Reedy, A., 400, *446*
Rees, A. R., 127, *210*
Regoli, D., 353, 393, 400, *443*
Reid, J., 352, 364, *442*
Reimann, E., 406, 422, *444*
Reinartz, M. L., 252, *280*
Reinhold, D. F., 371, *435*
Reinhoudt, D. N., 169, *204*
Reinstein, M., 184, *214*
Remaut, E., 25, 55, *59*
Reissmann, S., 380, 404, *430*
Reist, E., 419, *435*
Remli, M., 373, *430*
Renick, R. J., 115, 186, *206*
Rennerts, W., 428, *441*
Renyei, M., 155, *206*
Ressler, C., 66, 67, *106*, 122, 155, 157, 177, *201*, *205*, *210*, 347, 370, 377, 380, *430*, *441*, *444*, *446*
Rexona, L., 123, 128, *205*
Reynolds, H., 177, *214*
Reynolds, J. J., 151, *198*
Reznikova, M. B., 426, *445*
Rheiner, A., 137, *204*
Rhodes, J. B., 365, *436*
Rhodes, R. E., 288, *333*
Rich, D. H., 189, *210*, 242, 248, 250, 260, 278, *282*, 289, 299, 302, 312, 313, 315, 316, 321, *337*, 393, *444*
Richards, F. M., 96, *108*
Richards, J. D., 133, *200*
Richards, K. D., 311, 312, *338*
Richards, R. W., 384, *444*
Rickards, R. W., 288, *334*
Rickert, R. C., 403, *434*
Ried, W., 364, *444*
Riemen, M. W., 146, *213*
Riggs, A. D., 3, 13, 22, 25, 26, 27, 29, 31, 32, 37, 38, 39, 43, 47, 50, 51, 54, 56, *60*, *61*, *62*, *64*
Riley, G., 142, *210*
Rinaldi, A., 362, 378, 413, *433*, *444*
Rinehart, K. L., 288, 290, *335*
Riniker, B., 67, 70, *108*, 134, 147, 148, 154, 158, 174, 176, 179, 182, 192, *210*, *212*, 222, 269, 272, 273, *282*, *283*
Rink, H., 134, 174, 192, *210*, *212*
Rinke, H., 138, *198*
Rinno, H., 142, *214*
Rioux, F., 353, 393, 400, *443*
Rittel, W., 67, 70, *108*, 137, 147, 154, 158, 176, 179, *210*, *212*, 222, 269, *282*, *283*

Ritter, A., 397, *431*
Rivers, R. V. P., 402, *436*
Rivett, D. E., 382, *444*
Rivkin, M. I., 53, *61*
Roach, D., 225, *282*
Roark, E., 379, *430*
Roberts, B. E., 21, *62*
Roberts, C. W., 66, 67, *106*, 157, 177, *201*
Roberts, D. C., 361, 362, 371, 400, *439*, *444*, *446*
Roberts, J. E., 186, *206*
Roberts, J. L., 27, 53, *63*
Roberts, T. M., 29, 53, 55, 56, *60*, *62*, *63*
Robertson, A. V., 352, 409, 410, *430*, *437*, *443*, *444*
Robertson, B. H., 24, 26, 53, *61*
Robinson, A. B., 87, *108*, 127, 154, 160, *208*, *210*, *212*, 226, *282*
Robinson, J. C., 144, 150, *198*
Rocchi, R., 130, 156, 176, *202*, *203*, *210*, *212*
Rodbell, M., 362, *448*
Rodriguez, L. A. M., 375, *440*
Rodriguez, R. L., 23, *58*
Rodwell, J. L., 384, *444*
Roeske, R. W., 154, 158, 174, *210*, 364, *444*
Roffman, C., 418, *431*
Rogers, F. F., 237, 248, *280*
Rogers, L. A., 320, *337*
Roget, A., 51, *64*
Rohr, G., 368, 374, 409, *448*
Romeo, A., 121, *201*, 410, *435*
Rosamond, J. D., 327, *337*, 352, *444*
Rosazza, J. P., 396, *432*
Rose, J. K., 54, *62*
Rosenstein, R. D., 418, *445*
Rosenthal, A., 429, *444*
Rosenthal, G. A., 392, *444*
Rosner, A., 54, *61*
Ross, M. J., 3, 18, 24, 39, 44, 48, 54, 56, *59*, *60*, *63*, *64*
Ross, R. B., 353, *444*
Ross, W. C. J., 353, *444*
Rossi, D., 121, *207*
Rossio, J., 4, *60*
Ross-Petersen, K. J., 157, *197*
Roth, M., 309, *335*
Roth, R. A., 38, *62*
Roth, R. W., 169, *212*
Rothe, M., 117, 121, 188, 195, *210*, *211*
Rothgeb, T., 79, *108*
Rotman, A., 400, *444*
Rougeon, F., 26, *61*
Rowlands, D. A., 151, *211*
Roy, J., 299, *339*
Roy, S. C., 149, *201*
Royal, A., 55, *62*
Roychoudhury, R., 56, *62*
Rubin, B., 307, 310, 312, *336*, 352, *442*
Rubin, E. M., 56, *63*
Rudinger, J., 96, *107*, 115, 122, 150, 152, 155, 157, 158, 162, 168, 169, 177, 180, 186, *204*, *208*, *211*, *216*, 342, 344, 346, 347, 350, 351, 358, 360, 367, 368, 373, 378, 388, 390, 399, 416, *434*, *437*, *438*, *443*, *444*, *449*
Rudzats, R., 367, *435*
Ruff, F., 189, *214*
Rupp, W. D., 37, *63*
Rupprecht, K. M., 417, *436*
Ruswinkle, L. J., 288, *333*
Rutter, W. J., 54, *59*, *63*
Ryabtsev, M. N., 328, *336*
Ryan, C. A., 297, *333*
Ryan, J. W., 311, 324, *334*, 352, 409, *435*
Rybakov, V. N., 53, *61*
Ryder, M A., 397, *434*
Rydon, H. N., 142, 147, 162, 174, 194, *198*, *201*, *203*, *204*, *211*, 416, *436*
Ryle, A. P., 156, *211*
Rzeszotarska, B., 165, 189, *211*, *214*, 229, *282*

S

Saakyan, L. A., 385, *445*
Sabo, E. F., 121, *209*
Sachs, H., 151, *211*
Sadeh, T., 390, 429, *435*, *444*
Said, S. I., 89, 91, *106*, *108*
St. John, A. C., 31, 33, *60*
Saito, T., 114, 125, 141, 164, *206*, *211*, *215*, 289, *335*, 370, *442*
Sakakibara, S., 67, 68, 71, 80, 85, 86, 87, *107*, *108*, 121, 125, 129, 133, 136, 140, 142, 149, 160, 165, 175, *200*, *202*, *208*, *211*, *212*, 223, 224, 278, *283*, 290, *339*, 385, 387, 389, *436*, *448*
Sakamura, S., 382, 393, *437*, *445*
Sakan, T., 387, *437*, *445*
Sakarellos, C., 400, *444*
Sakata, T., 429, *448*
Sakazaki, R., 288, *338*

Sakiyama, F., 133, *211*
Sakuma, H., 416, *442*
Sakurai, H., 87, *108, 109*
Salcher, O., 419, *447*
Salemnick, G., 420, *446*
Salomon, D., 54, *58*
Salvatori, S., 176, *210*
Saman, E., 25, 55, *59*
Samanen, J., 361, 400, *444*
Sammes, P., 364, *436*
Samouilidis, I., 321, *336, 337*
Sancar, A., 37, *63*
Sanders, E., 415, *442*
Sandrin, E., 127, *199*
Sands, T. H., 289, *335*
Sandusky, W. R., 401, *444*
Saneii, H., 364, *446*
Sanger, F., 156, *211*
Sano, A., 299, 323, *336, 337*
Sano, S., 72, *108,* 149, *211*
Sano, Y., 194, *208*
Santoni, C., 368, 399, *431*
Santoso, S., 370, *444*
Saperstein, R., 343, 354, 364, 386, *435, 447*
Sarges, R., 186, *211*
Sarid, S., 122, *215*
Sarin, P. S., 289, *334*
Sarkar, F. H., 44, *63*
Sarkozi, M., 154, *206*
Sasaki, A. W., 389, *444*
Sasaki, T., 75, 79, 87, *106, 108, 109,* 127, 129, 136, 145, 149, *202, 209, 213,* 289, 308, *335, 337*
Satati, I., 398, 406, 407, 426, *431*
Sato, H., 382, *437*
Sato, M., 391, 395, 397, 405, *437, 438*
Sato, N., 378, *430*
Sato, O., 298, 301, *336*
Sato, S., 127, *209*
Sato, S., 293, *336*
Sato, Y., 369, 381, *435*
Satoh, P. S., 80, *108*
Satomi, M., 83, *107,* 231, *281*
Saul, M. W., 23, 25, 56, *60*
Saver, R., 153, *210*
Savrda, J., 120, *211*
Savige, W. E., 157, *208*
Savignac, P., 397, *447*
Sawai, K., 289, 316, *336*
Sawano, S., 406, 407, 414, *449*
Sawlewicz, P., 384, *431*
Sawyer, W. H., 347, 370, *430, 444*
Scaife, J., 24, *58*
Scallenberg, E. E., 68, *108*
Scanlon, D., 177, *214*
Scanlon, D. B., 5, 50, *59*
Scatturin, A., 176, *210*
Schafer, D. J., 139, *202*
Schallenberg, E. E., 135, *211*
Schaller, H., 25, 54, *61*
Schafer, D. J., 124, 175, *211*
Schally, A. V., 78, *108,* 175, *207,* 400, 401, 418, *432*
Scharf, R., 70, *109,* 128, *215*
Schattenkerk, G., 415, *447*
Schatz, V. B., 401, *444*
Schechter, I., 54, *58*
Scheele, G., 38, *63*
Scheer, M., 403, *439*
Scheidl, F., 418, *436*
Scheidtmann, K. H., 44, *64*
Schell, M. A., 54, *63*
Schellenberg, P., 115, *211*
Schenk, W., 411, *444*
Scheraga, H. A., 101, *106*
Schermer, D., 374, 409, *448*
Schiller, P. W., 347, 348, 353, 354, 364, 400, *433, 434*
Schimke, R. T., 28, 52, 57, *59*
Schimmack, G., 359, 402, *434*
Schindler, W., 195, *210*
Schirmer, E. W., 39, *59*
Schlatter, J. M., 135, 194, *208*
Schletter, I., 427, *439*
Schlingoff, G., 262, *282*
Schlossman, S. F., 136, *216*
Schmalzl, K. J., 384, *444*
Schmidhammer, L., 228, 234, 239, *279, 283*
Schmidt, E., 189, 190, *211,* 364, *444*
Schmidt, I., 129, *205*
Schmidt, K., 396, *430*
Schmidt, U., 287, 298, 299, 302, 303, 304, 305, 308, 309, 311, *336, 337,* 370, 409, *436, 444*
Schmidtberg, G., 188, *211*
Schnabel, E., 67, *108,* 125, 133, 136, 140, 142, 152, 153, 158, 165, 174, 178, 185, *202, 207, 211, 216,* 237, 238 253, *282,* 298, *337*
Schneider, F., 179, 180, *211*
Schneider, G., 403, *444*
Schneider, W., 142, 147, 175, *211, 212*
Schöberl, A., 376, *444*
Schögl, K., 117, *211, 214*

Schöllkopf, U., 367, 393, 404, *444*
Schön, I., 91, *108*, 143, 145, 154, 155, 161, *206*, *211*
Schoenewaldt, E. F., 117, 151, 188, *201*, *204*, 371, *433*
Schold, M., 51, *64*
Scholton, H. P. H., 299, *335*
Scholz, D., 370, *444*
Schou, O., 122, *212*
Schreiber, W., 348, 407, *444*
Schrenk, W. J., 56, *62*
Schröder, E., 162, *212*
Schroeder, H. W., 292, *338*
Schuch, W., 5, 50, *59*
Schüssler, H., 174, 183, *211*, *212*, 242, *282*
Schütte, H. R., 398, 411, 412, *441*, *444*
Schütze, G., 371, *436*
Schultz, J., 48, *58*
Schvijt, C., 403, *441*
Schvo, Y., 118, *212*
Schwahn, H., 368, 404, 405, 406, *437*
Schwam, H., 117, 151, 188, *201*, *204*
Schwartz, E. I., 182, *204*
Schwartz, I. L., 154, *208*, 388, *436*
Schwartz, J. L., 358, *448*
Schwarz, H., 89, *108*
Schwimmer, J., 362, 377, 390, *436*
Schwyzer, R., 40, *63*, 67, 69, 70, 71, *108*, 138, 144, 147, 148, 154, 165, 179, 182, 193, *203*, *204*, *205*, *210*, *212*, 346, 347, 348, 354, 356, 359, 361, 362, 363, 368, 371, 387, 400, 401, 408, *432*, *433*, *434*, *440*, *441*, *442*, *444*
Sciarini, L. J., 387, *432*
Scoffone, E., 130, 150, 156, *200*, *202*, *212*, 391, *445*
Scopes, P. M., 138, *212*
Scotchler, J., 226, *282*
Scott, A. I., 379, *445*
Scott, J. W., 409, 418, *436*, *445*
Scott, P. M., 289, *337*
Seebeck, E., 376, *446*
Seeburg, P. H., 17, 18, 21, 24, 28, 30, 44, 54, 55, 56, *60*, *61*, *62*, *63*
Seela, F., 424, *445*
Seely, J. H., 146, 173, *205*, 262, *281*
Seeman, N. C., 418, *445*
Segawa, T., 74, 79, 80, *107*, *109*
Sehring, R., 183, 184, 187, *215*
Sela, M., 126, 147, 188, *198*, *205*
Self, R., 382, *432*
Selva, A., 288, 292, *333*
Semararo, R. J., 154, *213*
Semple, J. E., 426, *445*
Senda, S., *283*
Senoh, S., 387, *437*, *445*
Sergheraert, C., 349, 408, *432*
Serif, G. S., 375, *440*
Sethi, M. L., 404, *445*
Seto, S., 145, *197*
Seto, T., 405, *447*
Seto, Y., 404, 428, *438*, *445*
Sgaramella, V., 5, *58*, *63*
Shaffer, J., 21, 51, *64*
Shakhnazaryan, G. M., 385, *445*
Shalavina, I. F., 385, *434*
Shalitin, Y., 146, *198*, *212*
Shalygina, O. D., 420, *447*
Shankman, S., 118, 119, *212*
Shanks, L., 373, *435*
Shannon, L. M., 385, *440*
Shapiro, J., 6, 7, 8, 11, 12, 13, 22, 26, 34, 40, 42, 43, 44, 47, 53, *64*
Sharp, D. E., 423, *437*
Sharp, J. J., 87, *108*, 127, 160, *212*
Sharpe, R., 364, *446*
Shaw, G., 425, *433*
Shaw, G. J., 388, *445*
Shchukina, L. A., 156, 159, *212*, *216*
Sheehan, J. C., 133, 169, 183, 184, 189, 190, 191, *212*, 237, *282*, 290, *337*, 367, 374, 409, 413, *445*
Sheehan, J. T., 117, 118, 123, 137, 139, 140, 145, *199*, *209*, *212*
Shemyakin, M. F., 55, *63*
Shenhar, A., 361, 400, 402, *435*
Shepard, H. M., 18, 21, 24, 29, 37, 48, 49, 50, 54, 55, *60*, *63*, *64*
Sheppard, R. C., 120, 126, 130, 132, 150, 172, *197*, *200*, *207*, 219, 224, 228, 233, 253, 256, 257, 258, 259, 260, *279*, *280*, 393, 409, *433*, *439*
Sheppard, W. A., 354, 373, *439*
Sheradsky, T., 397, *435*
Sherwood, P. J., 21, 55, *60*
Shiba, T., 142, 151, *212*, *214*, 222, 226, *282*, 289, 290, 299, 323, *336*, *337*, *338*, *339*, 367, 381, 383, 387, 389, 390, 392, 415, 419, *445*, *447*, *448*
Shiina, A., 76, *107*
Shimida, N., 290, *336*
Shimohigashi, Y., 287, 289, 297, 306, 308, 309, 310, 311, 312, 317, 319, 320, 324, 325, 331, 332, *334*, *337*, *338*, 405, *445*

Shimonishi, S., 67, 68, 71, 80, 85, *108*
Shimonishi, Y., 86, *108,* 125, 132, 149, 165, 175, *203, 209, 211*
Shin, C., 287, 288, 297, 303, 304, 305, 307, 308, 309, 311, *338*
Shin, K. H., 142, 175, *211, 212*
Shin, M., 165, 180, 182, *204, 211, 212*
Shinagawa, S., 76, 86, *106,* 125, 141, 159, *202, 204,* 227, 228, 273, *281*
Shine, J., 27, 28, 53, *63*
Shinko, K., 323, *337*
Shinnick, T. M., 44, *61*
Shinozaki, K., 299, *339*
Shioiri, T., 179, *212*
Shirafuji, H., 289, *334*
Shiraishi, K., 393, *437, 445*
Shire, J., 54, *63*
Shire, W., 389, *433*
Shirota, F. N., 353, 389, 394, 409, *442, 445*
Shive, W., 369, 370, 379, 397, 406, 415, *429, 434, 442, 443*
Shively, J. E., 39, 44, *64,* 93, *108*
Shizuo, H., 387, *445*
Shoji, J., 288, 290, 294, *336, 338*
Shrift, A., 377, *445*
Shvachkin, Y. P., 424, 425, 426, *445*
Shvachkin, Yu. P., 126, 139, 142, *202*
Sieber, P., 67, 69, 70, *108,* 128, 146, 158, 160, 167, 174, 176, 193, *212,* 222, 269, 272, 273, *282, 283*
Siedel, W., 68, 105, *107,* 153, *202*
Siemion, I. Z., 190, *212,* 237, 238, *283*
Sievertsson, H., 428, *431, 445*
Sifferd, R. H., 66, 67, *108,* 163, *212*
Sigel, C. W., 313, 315, *336, 338*
Sigler, G. F., 91, *106,* 143, 193, *199, 200*
Signor, A., 391, *445*
Sila, B., 421, *445*
Silaev, A. B., 290, *338,* 419, *430*
Silva de Sol, B., 221, *283*
Silverman, R. B., 427, *445*
Silverstein, R., 237, 248, *280*
Simmonds, S., 180, *212,* 347, 428, *434*
Simonsen, C. C., 21, 55, *60*
Simpson, R., 348, 399, 401, 402, 406, 407, 408, *442*
Simpson, R. J., 72, *108*
Simpson, W. R. J., 352, 409, 410, *430, 437*
Singerman, A., 386, 387, *440, 445*
Singh, J., 189, *210,* 242, 248, 250, 260, 278, *282*
Sivanandaiah, K. M., 163, *197*
Skala, G., 428, *446*
Skelton, F. S., 422, *437*
Skinner, C. G., 369, 386, 415, *434, 436, 442*
Skinner, W. A., 388, 400, 402, *433*
Skophova, J., 391, *449*
Slater, G. R., 293, *336*
Sletzinger, M., 371, *433*
Slinker, B., 39, 44, *64*
Sloane, N. H., 400, *446*
Sloma, A., 17, 18, 21, 24, 28, 30, 44, 55, *60*
Slouka, J., 401, *445*
Sluke, J., 424, *440*
Small, B., 24, 26, 52, *61*
Smart, N. A., 228, *283*
Smeby, R R., 121, *206,* 347, 352, 368, *432, 439*
Smeets, P. J. H., 348, 401, *447*
Smirnova, M., 401, *438*
Smith, A. J., 388, *435*
Smith, A. J. H., 22, *63*
Smith, C. W., 352, 409, 428, *441, 446*
Smith, E. E., 48, *58*
Smith, E. L., 121, 137, *209, 212, 214*
Smith, G. C., 221, *283*
Smith, G. M., 365, *436*
Smith, G. R., 151, 187, *206*
Smith, H. O., 399, 401, *434*
Smith, J. C., 18, *61*
Smith, J. L., 289, *333*
Smith, L. R., 188, *213*
Smith, M. W., 21, 37, 51, *60, 61, 62, 64*
Smith, P. W. G., 194, *211*
Smith, S. C., 400, *446*
Smith, T. A., 287, 290, 311, *334*
Smithers, M. J., 160, *204*
Smolarsky, M., 399, 407, 421, *431*
Smolikova, J., 410, *447*
Smulkowska, E., 399, *443*
Smulkowski, M., 271, 272, *280,* 370, 384, *431, 434*
Smyth, D. G., 40, *63,* 96, *108*
Smyth, R. D., 384, *430*
Snider, B. B., 369, *446*
Snider, C., 39, 48, *63*
Snow, G. A., 289, *337*
Snow, M. L., 370, 380, *446*
Snyder, H., 400, *446*
Snyder, H. R., 422, *437*
Snyder, J. P., 323, *335*
Sørensen, H., 386, *439*
Sørup, P., 125, *213*
Sohar, P., 371, *433*

Sohár, P., 129, *207*
Soine, P., 395, 408, *436*
Soine, W. H., 408, *436*
Sokoloff, S., 386, *440*
Sokolovska, T., 150, *213*
Sokolovsky, M., 157, *212, 213,* 286, 299, 311, 325, *336*
Sokolowska, T., 189, *197,* 228, 229, 235, 269, 271, 273, 274, 275, *279,* 363, 370, 382, 383, *438*
Solenov, E. I., 53, *61*
Soltvedt, B. C., 33, *59*
Soma. G.-L., 369, *436*
Sondheimer, E., 153, 154, 178, *213*
Sonenburg, M., 145, *214,* 228, 253, 257, 258, *283*
Songstad, J., 76, *108*
Sood, S., 403, *435*
Soriano, D. S., 410, *446*
Šorm, F., 123, 128, *205,* 346, 364, 367, 368, *434, 449*
Soroka, M., 397, *436*
Souchleris, I., 147, *213*
Southard, G. L., 157, 163, *212, 213*
Spach, G., 125, *214*
Spackman, D. H., 223, 227, *283*
Spande, T. F., 419, *442*
Spanninger, P. A., 126, *213*
Sparrow, J. T., 328, *338*
Spatola, A. F., 364, *446*
Spears, C., 37, *64*
Speciale, A. J., 188, *213*
Spencer, I. D., 416, *446*
Spencer, R., 419, *435*
Spencer, R. P., 402, *431*
Springer, R. H., 425, *436, 446*
Squires, C., 7, *58*
Squires, C. L., 7, *58*
Srinivasan, A., 297, 311, 312, *338,* 373, *446*
Sroka, W., 67, *108,* 151, *216*
Staab, H. A., 192, *213*
Stachulski, A. V., 133, *201,* 261, *281,* 352, 410, *430*
Staehelin, T., 39, 44, *63*
Stahl, S., 53, 54, *60*
Stalla, K., 362, 373, 390, *436*
Stammer, C. H., 176, *207,* 306, 307, 308, 309, 310, 311, 312, 324, 325, *334, 335, 336, 337, 338,* 386, 389, 395, 405, *437, 438, 446*
Stammer, J., 155, *213,* 287, *337*
Stanssens, P., 25, 55, *59*
Starcher, B., 369, *438*
Stebbing, N., 17, 18, 21, 28, 30, 37, 39, 44, 47, 48, 49, 50, 55, *60, 63, 64*
Stedman, R. J., 150, 155, 158, 168, *202, 210, 213*
Steglich, W., 124, 128, 160, 162, 190, *214,* 235, 258, 259, 264, 265, 267, *283,* 366, 371, 372, *446, 448*
Stein, R., 21, *62*
Stein, S. J., 427, *439*
Stein, W. H., 96, *108,* 223, 227, *283*
Steinauer, R., 234, *283*
Steiner, D. F., 18, 38, *58, 59*
Stekol, J. A., 160, *213*
Stelakatos, G. C., 89, *109,* 170, *213*
Stephensen, R. W., 297, *338,* 373, *446*
Stern, F., 296, 305, *333*
Steuben, K. C., 117, 121, 124, *203*
Stewart, A. G., 18, *61*
Stewart, F. H. C., 134, 158, 174, 191, *207, 210, 213,* 382, *444*
Stewart, J. M., 127, 140, *213,* 216, 347, 428, *433*
Stewart, W. E., 44, 48, 55, *63*
Steyn, P. S., 288, *336*
Stickings, C. E., 288, *334*
Stipanovic, R. D., 292, *338*
Stock, A., 424, *448*
Stock, J. A., 290, *337,* 357, 400, *431*
Stoessl, A., 289, *334*
Stoev, S. B., 377, *430, 446*
Stöhrer, G., 420, *446*
Stoll, A., 376, *446*
Stoltefuss, J., 298, *337*
Stonard, R. J., 289, *338*
Strachan, R. G., 151, 188, *201, 204,* 385, *447*
Stracher, A., 295, *338*
Strasorier, L., 347, *443*
Straukas, I., 380, *446*
Streuli, M., 48, 55, *63*
Striewsky, W., 190, *211*
Strohmaier, K., 25, 54, *61*
Strong, F. M., 426, *448*
Stuart, O., 409, *441*
Stubbs, L., 143, *214*
Studer, R. O., 138, *207,* 368, *439*
Struble, M. E., 14, *59*
Struhl, K., 3, *63*
Sturm, K., 153, *202*
Sturm, M., 419, *448*

Su, H. C. F., 407, *447*
Subramanian, V. H., 152, *198*
Suda, K., 361, 400, *444*
Suefuji, M., 405, *447*
Sugano, H., 176, *213*
Sugawara, Y., 289, *338*
Suggs, S. V., 21, *63*
Sugihara, H., 67, 68, 71, 85, *108*, 125, *211*
Sugiura, M., 87, *108*
Sugiyama, H., 145, *197*
Sullivan, C. B., 415, *446*
Sullivan, P. T., 350, 415, *442*, *446*
Summons, R. E., 424, *440*
Sun, M., 132, *213*
Sun, R. C., 418, *436*
Sunada, Y., 427, *438*
Sutcliffe, J. G., 7, 44, *61*, *63*
Suvorov, N. N., 156, *212*, 420, *447*
Suzuki, A., 288, 292, 293, *336*
Suzuki, K., 67, 89, *107*, *109*, 127, 145, 149, 189, *213*, 370, *442*
Suzuki, M., 289, *338*, 370, *442*
Suzuki, S., 386, *439*
Suzuki, T., 297, 311, *338*
Suzuki, V., 173, *201*
Sverdlov, E. D., 55, *63*
Swamy, K. H. S., 31, 32, *63*
Swan, J. M., 66, 67, *106*, 157, 177, *201*, *208*, *213*
Swodenk, W., 174, *214*
Sykes, B. D., 52, *63*
Symons, R. H., 2, 15, *61*
Synge, L. M., 382, *432*
Synodis, J., 362, 371, *446*
Syrier, J. L. M., 160, *213*
Szilagyi, L., 414, *431*, *446*
Szirtes, T., 154, *206*
Syrtsova, L. A., 426, *445*
Szelke, M., 364, *446*
Szilagyi, L., *446*
Szwarc, M., 188, *213*

T

Tabor, J. M., 17, 18, 21, 24, 28, 30, 44, 55, *60*
Taborsky, R. G., 354, *433*
Tachibana, S., 419, *439*
Tacon, W. C. A., 54, *59*
Tada, M., 163, *214*
Taguchi, Y., 176, *213*
Tahilraman, R., 348, 422, 423, *442*
Taira, H., 44, 55, *62*, *63*
Tait, R. C., 37, *62*
Takada, K., 165, *211*
Takahashi, M., 308, 309, *338*
Takahashi, Y., 288, 289, *338*
Takai, K., 227, 273, *281*, 410, *442*
Takamatsu, N., 190, *204*
Takashima, H., 152, 195, *213*
Takashima, K., 366, 404, *449*
Takashima, T., 391, *437*
Takaya, T., 223, 224, 278, *283*
Take, T., 290, *336*, *339*
Takeda, K., 298, 301, *336*
Takemoto, T., 427, *446*
Takeyama, M., 81, 89, 92, 105, *108*, *109*, 125, 138, *213*, *215*
Takita, T., 380, *438*
Takomasa, K., 421, *441*
Taleisnik, S., 78, *106*
Talmadge, K., 29, 37, 38, 56, *63*
Tam, J. P., 146, *213*, 253, 258, 259, 260, 270, *283*, 299, 302, 313, 321, *337*, 393, *444*
Tamaki, E., 416, *442*
Tamura, M., 368, *446*
Tamura, S., 288, 292, 293, *336*
Tanaka, A., 160, *215*
Tanaka, K., 288, *338*, 384, *435*
Tanaka, S., 51, *64*
Tanaka, T., 410, *442*
Tanenbaum, S. W., 143, *213*
Tanida, H., 405, *447*
Taniguchi, M., 414, *446*
Taniguchi, T., 29, 51, 55, *63*
Taniyama, H., 387, *439*
Tanner, H., 235, 267, *283*
Tanzer, M. L., 381, *441*
Tarbell, D. S., 164, 182, 184, 185, 186, *207*, *213*
Tardif, C., 395, *431*
Tartar, A., 192, *213*, 349, 408, *432*
Tarumi, Y., 142, *214*
Taschner, E., 150, 189, *213*, *214*, 229, 271, 272, *280*, *282*
Tashiro, H., 421, *441*
Tatarinova, G. P., 390, *430*
Tatemoto, K., 134, 139, *199*
Tautz, W., 417, *446*
Taylor, J., 156, *216*, 364, *436*

Taylor, J. B., 396, *446*
Taylor, N., 424, 425, *433*
Taylor, P. J., 394, *432*
Taylor, S. P., Jr., 158, *201*
Tedro, S., 154, *210*
Teitei, T., 383, 416, *436, 446*
Teitel, S. 417, *446*
Templeton, G. E., 289, 313, 315, *336, 338*
Teng, T. A., 402, *446*
Teoule, R., 51, *64*
Terui, Y., 290, *339*
Teshima, T,. 289, 290, *336, 337, 338,* 381, 383, 387, 389, 390, 392, 415, *446, 448*
Tesser, G. I., 136, 169, 171, *209, 213,* 348, 381, 391, 400, 401, 419, 420, 421, *432, 443, 446, 447*
Teuber, H. J., 398, 402, *446*
Thamm, P., 129, *205, 207*
Thanassi, J. W., 416, *447*
Thanei, P., 368, 387, 401, *433, 440*
Theisen, M. C., 400, 402, *433*
Theodoropoulos, D. M., 86, *109,* 127, 133, 141, 147, 170, 187, *213, 216*
Thern, E., 381, *440*
Theyson, R., 195, *210*
Thierauch, K. H., 358, 359, 398, *434*
Thomas, R. J., 229, 234, 277, *280*
Thomas, R. M., 44, *58*
Thomas, W. A., 229, *280*
Thompson, J. F., 398, 400, *437*
Thompson, R. M., 364, *444*
Thompson, R. Q., 293, *338*
Thompson, T. A., 182, *204*
Thorsen, M., 364, *432*
Thummel, C. S., 56, *63*
Thurman, G. B., 4, 6, 7, 8, 11, 12, 13, 22, 26, 34, 40, 42, 43, 44, 47, 53, *60, 64*
Tietzmann, J. E., 305, *334*
Tijhuis, M. W., 299, *335*
Tilak, M., 67, *107,* 122, 186, *205, 214*
Timmis, K. N., 4, *63*
Ting, Y. F., 237, *281*
Tiollais, P., 54, *59*
Titherley, A W., 143, *214*
Titlestad, K., 193, 195, *214*
Tizard, R., 28, 56, *64*
Tjian, R., 56, *63*
Tjoeng, F. S., 146, *213,* 425, *447*
Tobe, T., 89, 105, *109*
Todd, L., 289, *334*
Toennis, G., 159, *214*
Tokura, K., 290, *338*
Tokuyama, T., 387, *437, 445*
Tolle, J. C., 85, 89, *106,* 119, 126, 139, 145, 147, 160, 172, 186, *199, 208*
Tolman, V., 385, 389, 392, *447*
Toma, S., 349, 408, *443*
Tomatis, R., 156, 176, *203, 210*
Tometsko, A., 39, *61,* 67, *107,* 122, 140, *205*
Tomida, I., 232, 269, 272, 273 276, 277, *283*
Tomida, T., 267, *283*
Tomlinson, G., 389, *447*
Tong, J. H., 223, *283*
Toniolo, C., 132, 150, *200, 202*
Torchiana, M. L., 385, *447*
Tori, K., 290, *338, 339,* 405, *447*
Torii, K., 428, *445*
Tortora, J. A., 383, *438, 439*
Townsend, J. M., 418, *436*
Trakatellis, A. C., 39, *61,* 122, *205*
Traynham, J. G., 384, *447*
Tregear, G. W., 153, 177, *210, 214*
Treuth, G., 167, *202*
Trifonova, Zh. P., 290, *338*
Trippett, S., 376, *447*
Trischmann, H., 368, *448*
Tritsch, G. L., 136, 138, *203, 214*
Trivedi, D., 360, *431, 437*
Trka, A., 410, *447*
Trollope, M. L., 409, *432*
Trout, G. E., 417, *447*
Trowitzsch, W., 370, *444*
Trudelle, Y., 125, *214*
Trzeciak, A., 368, *439*
Tschannen, W., 403, *440*
Tsou, K. C., 407, *447*
Tsuchihashi, G., 419, *437*
Tsuda, K., 87, *108*
Tsuda, Y., 182, *209*
Tsuji, N., 288, *338*
Tsuji, S., 392, *447*
Tsuji, T., 405, *447*
Tsukamoto, S., 127, *209*
Tsukerman, B. V., 167, *207*
Tsukiara, H., 289, *335*
Tsuno, T., 301, *336*
Tsuruoka, T., 397, *442*
Tsushima, T., 405, *447*
Tsutsumi, M., 347, 370, *444*
Tuchida, S., 370, *442*
Tun-Kyi, A., 130, 193, *212, 214,* 363, 371, 408, *440, 444*

Turán, A., 128, 138, 154, 175, *197, 206, 214,* 378, *447*
Turnbull, J. H., 142, *210*
Turner, R. B., 407, *447*

U

Uchiyama, A., 138, *198*
Uchiyama, M., 424, *447*
Udenfriend, S., 409, 410, 413, *440*
Ueda, H., 382, *439*
Ueki, M., 299, *339*
Ueno, T., 289, 290, 294, 295, 316, 318, *335, 336, 338, 339,* 403, *443*
Ueyanagi, J., 427, *438*
Ugi, I., 265, *283*
Uitzetter, J. H., 419, 420, 421, *443*
Ujike, T., 386, *437*
Ukawa, K., 77, 83, 85, *107,* 125, *206*
Ukita, T., 390, 392, *445, 448*
Ulichny, C., 360, *437*
Ullrich, A., 17, 18, 21, 24, 28, 30, 44, 54, 55, *60, 63,* 115, *211*
Umezawa, H., 289, 290, *336,* 380, 392, *437, 438*
Umezawa, S., 394, *439*
Unoki, K., 304, 307, 308, *338*
Upham, R. A., 157, *204*
Uphaus, R. A., 86, *109,* 131, *214*
Urabe, Y., 369, 373, 374, 380, *438, 447*
Uritskaya, M. Y., 420, *430*
Urry, D. W., 294, *337, 339*
Usher, J. J., 379, *447*
Uskert, A., 371, *447*

V

Vaculik, M., 376, *441*
Vajda, T., 189, *214*
Vale, W. W., 364, *446*
Valentine, D., Jr., 409, 418, *436, 445*
Valenzuela, P., 54, *59, 63*
Van den Berghe, A., 7, *60*
Van den Drics, C. L., 419, 420, 421, *443*
van der Hoeven, M. G., 404, *448*
Van de Sande, J. H., 5, *58, 63*
van Dorsselaer, V., 395, *431*
Van Etten, C. H., 412, *433*
Van Nispen, J. W., 348, 391, 400, 401, *432, 446, 447*
Van Opdenbosch, N., 364, *440*
Van Orden, H. O., 137, *214*
Van Pee, K. H., 419, *447*
Van Thach, T., 350, 418, *447*
Van Veldhuizen, C. J., 153,, *198*
van Zon, A., 186, *214*
Vapnek, D., 23, 53, *64*
Varga, S. L., 158, *214*
Varlet, J. M., 397, *447*
Vasella, A., 413, *447*
Vasser, M. P., 14, 25, *59*
Vaughan, J. R., Jr., 184, 186, *214*
Vdovina, R. G., 424, *447*
Veber, D. F., 77, 96, *106,* 117, 138, 151, 158, 188, *201, 202, 204, 214,* 261, 343, 354, 364, 385, *435, 447*
Vecchio, G. L., 428, *447*
Veda, M., 54, *59*
Vegners, R., 167, *214*
Vehar, G. A., 55, *62*
Verbiscar, A. J., 409, *447*
Vereš, K., 385, *447*
Vergona, R., 352, 362, 409, 410, *434*
Verlander, M., 193, *200*
Veselova, L. N., 350, 415, *447*
Vičar, J., 410, *447*
Vichez-Martinez, J. A., 400, *432*
Vickery, B., 348, 399, 401, 402, 406, 407, 408, 422, 423, *442*
Vickery, H. B., 152, *214,* 342, *447*
Vickrey, P. E., 389, *433*
Vida, J. A., 403, *448*
Viehe, H. G., 184, *214*
Villa-Komaroff, L., 3, 28, 56, *60, 64*
Villemoes, P., 125, *213*
Vincze, A., 425, *447*
Vine, W. H., 372, *447*
Vining, L. C., 379, *433*
Vinograd, L. K., 420, *447*
Virtanen, A. J., 413, *433*
Visser, G. W. M., 403, *447*
Visser, J., 79, *106*
Visser, J. P., 349, *437*
Viswamitra, M. A., 290, *333*
Viswanatha, V., 355, 389, 402, *431, 447*
Vita, A., 40, *61*
Vlasov, G. P., 167, *207*
Vleggaar, R., 288, 312, *336, 339*
Voeffray, R., 413, *447*
Vogler, K., 184, *215*
Volckaert, G., 7, *60*
Volk, A., 138, 153, *202, 206*
Volpina, O. M., 134, *204*
Volund, A., 78, *107,* 128, 158, 160, 165, *207*

von Bogelen, R. J., 37, *62*
von Rosenberg, J. L., 126, *213*
Vorbrüggen, H., 173, *215*, 289, *339*
Voskamp, D., 195, *199*
Voskuyl-Holtkamp, I., 415, *447*
Voss, D., 406, 422, *444*
Vulkova, A. T., 377, *446*

W

Wade, R., 124, 142, 143, 151, 175, *200, 206, 211*, 364, 393, 400, 403, 419, *430, 441, 443*
Wade, T. N., 372, 405, *448*
Wälti, M., 194, *214*
Waisuisz, J. M., 404, *448*
Wajngurt, A., 403, *440*
Wakamitsu, M., 141, *202*
Wakamiya, T., 142, *214*, 289, 290, 311, 321, 323, *336, 337, 338, 339*, 383, 387, 389, 390, 392, 415, *445, 448*
Wakasaka, Y., 294, *338*
Waki, M., 143, 172, 179, 180, *208, 214*, 289, 311, 318, 330, 332, *333, 335, 338*, 387, *448*
Wakimasu, M., 86, *106*, 384, *435*
Walborsky, H. M., 372, *440*
Walker, M. D., 160, 172, *199*
Walker, R. T., 424, 425, *433*
Wallace, D. M., 21, 55, *60*
Wallace, R. B., 21, 51, *63, 64*
Waller, P. J., 154, *199*
Walshaw, K. B., 138, *212*
Walter, G., 44, *64*
Walter, R., 78, *106*, 154, *208*, 299, 323, *339*, 350, 352, 358, 377, 388, 409, 428, *436, 441, 446, 448*
Walter, W., 239, *282*
Walton, E., 288, *333*
Wang, B. S. H., 253, 258, 259, 260, 270, *283*
Wang, C. T., 356, 413, *434*
Wang, D. C., 426, *445*
Wang, K. T., 127, 179, *199, 200*
Wang, P.-C., 428, 429, *433*
Wang, S.-S., 4, 47, *60, 64*
Wang, S. S., 145, 179, *214*, 228, 253, 257, 258, 259, 260, 270, *283*
Wang, S. W., 228, 231, 234, *281*
Wang, T. S. T., 403, *448*
Wanner, M. J., 386, *436*
Ward, C. A., 55, *62*
Warm, R., 428, *438*
Warren, C. B., 396, *448*
Wasielewski, C., 150, *213*
Wasylyk, B., 51, *64*
Watanabe, H., 80, *109*, 125, 163, *214, 215*, 350, 366, 404, 415, 428, 429, *438, 445, 448, 449*
Watanabe, K., 182, *204*, 272, 277, *282*
Watanabe, S., 289, *335*
Watson, R. N., 407, *440*
Weaver, E. R., 121, *209, 210*
Webb, R. G., 389, *446*
Webb, R. J., 398, *436*
Weber, H., 5, *58*
Weber, K., 30, *60*
Weck, P. K., 39, 40, 48, 49, 55, *61, 64*
Weiber, O., 129, *215*
Weigele, M., 383, *439*
Wein, J., 150, *200*
Weiner, H., 297, *339*
Weiner, J. H., 52, *63*
Weinges, K., 398, *448*
Weinkam, R. J., 355, 417, *448*
Weinman, F., 141, *198*
Weinstein, B., 229, 271, *283*
Weinstein, D. A., 398, 406, *432*
Weisel, Y., 386, *440*
Weisleder, D., 412, *433*
Weiss, B., 380, *448*
Weiss, E., 156, *216*
Weiss, J., 38, 56, *59*
Weiss, K., 183, 184, *215*
Weissbach, H., 37, *64*, 384, *430*
Weissmann, C., 44, 48, 51, 55, *62, 63*
Weitl, F. L., 364, *444*
Welcher, A. D., 230, *279*
Welford, M., 138, *212*
Wellner, D., 222, *282*
Wemple, J., 405, *432*
Wendelberger, G., 277, *283*
Wessels, P. L., 288, 312, *336, 339*
Wessely, F., 116, 117, *214*
Westall, R. G., 152, *200, 214*
Westerik, J. O., 381, *448*
Westheimer, F. H., 194, *208*
Westerhuis, L. W., 419, 420, 421, *443*
Westland, R. D., 396, *441*
Wetzel, R., 3, 6, 7, 9, 11, 12, 13, 22, 26, 27, 34, 38, 39, 40, 42, 43, 44, 47, 50, 53, 56, *59, 64*
Weustink, R. J. M., 389, *438*

Weygand, F., 118, 124, 128, 136, 142, 160, 162, 167, 170, 174, 183, 184, 190, *214, 215,* 228, 231, 232, 234, 235, 236, 239, 264, 265, 267, 272, *283,* 366, 371, 372, 381, *446, 448*
Whelan, W., 48, *58*
White, F. H., Jr., 100, *109*
White, W. H., 297, *339*
Whitlock, B. J., 426, *448*
Whitney, J. G., 409, *445*
Wiberley, S. E., 288, *334*
Wick, M., 117, *203*
Wickner, R. B., 287, *311, 339*
Wieczorkowska, E., 398, 400, 402, *439*
Wieland, A., 25, *59*
Wieland, P., 180, *210*
Wieland, T., 114, 115, 121, 129, 180, 183, 184, 185, 187, *202, 215,* 359, 368, 374, 381, 409, 410, 419, *435, 438, 448*
Wierenga, W., 427, *439*
Wightman, R. H., 5, 13, *61*
Wilchek, M., 98, *109,* 122, 155, 157, *213, 215,* 396, *448*
Wiley, R. A., 403, *438*
Wilkinson, A. J., 51, *64*
Wilkinson, T. J., 379, *445*
Willhardt, I., 362, 377, 390, 418, *436*
Williams, B. J., 172, 176, *197, 215,* 219, 228, 233, 253, 257, 258, 259, 260, *279, 280*
Williams, D. H., 289, *334*
Williams, M. K., 229, 234, *280*
Williams, M. W., 228, 234, *283*
Williams, N. J., 121, 144, 175, *199, 209*
Williams, U. R., 384, *447*
Wilson, D. B., 54, *63*
Wilson, G. A., 54, 56, *63*
Wilson, R. M., 384, *430*
Wilson, W., 142, *210*
Windridge, G. C., 123, 175, *215,* 225, 260, 261, 275, 276, *284,* 367, *438*
Winitz, M., 138, 156, *216,* 222, *281,* 286, 305, *334,* 342, 343, 366, 367, 368, 369, 374, 375, 377, 381, 384, 385, 386, 388, 389, 390, 391, 392, 398, 399, 401, 402, 403, 405, 406, 411, 417, 419, 421, 427, *436*
Winn, M., 405, *448*
Winter, D. P., 179, *214*
Winter, G., 51, *64*
Winter, S., 366, *443*
Wion, K. L., 56, *61*
Wirth, R., 37, *62*
Wissman, H., 195, *205*
Witkop, B., 141, 186, *201, 211,* 352, 389, 409, 411, 419, *435, 437, 441, 442, 444, 447*
Witte, C., 296, 305, *333*
Wittier, E. O., 320, *337*
Wittig, G., 409, *448*
Wittle, E. C., 396, *441*
Witty, M. J., 190, *198,* 219, 240, 242, 246, 247, 249, 252, 257, 261, *279, 281, 284*
Woenckhaus, C., 424, *448*
Wojtanis, J., 421, *445*
Wölcke, U., 372, 373, 380, *440*
Wold, F., 38, 40, *64*
Wolfe, S., 413, *448*
Wolfenden, R., 381, *448*
Wolfgang, S., 372, *448*
Wong, C. H., 179, *200*
Wong, F. F., 413, *432*
Wong, T. W., 146, *213*
Woodford, T. A., 40, *64*
Woodhead, S. H., 289, 313, 315, *336*
Woods, B. L., 289, *337*
Woodward, R. B., 173, *215,* 289, *339*
Wooldridge, K. R. H., 407, *429*
Woolley, D. W., 134, 138, 179, 189, *208, 214*
Work, T. S., 118, *203*
Wright, D. E., 362, *448*
Wright, J., 403, *438*
Wright, S., 348, 400, *438*
Wu, R., 10, 11, *61*
Wünsch, E., 70, 87, 105, *109,* 124, 127, 128, 129, 130, 147, 169, 191, *203, 205, 207, 215,* 277, *283*
Wyler, H., 412, *449*

Y

Yabe, Y., 348, 399, 406, 407, 414, 420, 421, *449*
Yaffe, A., 55, *61*
Yagyu, M., 182, *209, 210*
Yajima, H., 67, 68, 72, 74, 75, 76, 78, 79, 80, 81, 83, 85, 86, 87, 89, 92, 93, 94, 95, 104, 105, *106, 107, 108, 109,* 122, 125, 127, 129, 133, 136, 138, 141, 157, 158, 159, 160, 163, 182, 186, 187, *202, 204, 206, 209, 213, 215*
Yakhontov, L. N., 420, *430*
Yamada, H., 403, 419, *442, 443*

Yamada, S., 179, *212*, 398, *449*
Yamada, T., 5, *58*, 272, 277, *282*, 366, 404, *438*, *449*
Yamamoto, M., 86, *108*, 132, *209*, 404, *438*
Yamamoto, Y., 164, *213*, 417, *438*
Yamasaki, M., 288, 292, *335*
Yamashiro, D., 79, 88, *108*, *109*, 125, 127, 136, 138, 159, 161, 195, *204*, *207*, *209*, *215*, *216*, 231, 232, 278, *284*, 402, *440*
Yamashita, I., *109*
Yamashita, K., 387, *445*
Yanagida, S., 188, *216*
Yanagisawa, H., 394, *439*
Yanaihara, Y., 67, 68, *107*
Yang, C. C., 89, *109*, 145, *212*, *216*, 228, 253, 257, 258, *283*
Yang, D. D. H., 374, 413, *445*
Yang, R., 383, *438*, *439*
Yankeelov, J. A., 364, 377, *446*, *449*
Yano, K., 422, *437*
Yanofsky, C., 7, 24, *58*, *64*
Yansura, D. G., 3, 18, 22, 24, 25, 26, 27, 29, 37, 38, 39, 43, 47, 50, 53, 54, 56, *59*, *60*, *61*, *62*
Yariv, J., *209*
Yaron, A., 136, *216*
Yasuhara, T., 81, 87, *107*, *108*
Yeh, Y. L., 133, 140, *212*
Yelverton, E., 17, 18, 21, 24, 28, 29, 30, 44, 54, 55, *60*, *62*, *63*, *64*
Yeung, K. W., 387, *430*
Yiotakis, A. E., 89, *106*, 133, 137, 139, *199*, *209*
Yocum, R. R., 56, *62*
Yoneda, M., 289, 308, *334*, *335*, *336*, 382, *438*
Yoneda, N., 419, *441*
Yonehara, H., 289, *336*
Yonemitsu, O., 174, *216*
Yonezawa, Y., 304, 307, 308, 309, *338*
Yoshida, H., 87, *107*, 419, *442*
Yoshida, N., 231, *282*
Yoshimura, J., 297, 304, 307, 308, 309, 311, *338*
Yoshimura, Y., 290, *338*
Yoshioka, H., 290, *339*
Yoshioka, R., 398, *449*
Young, F. E., 56, *63*
Young, G. T., 124, 125, 138, 139, 151, 175, 176, 190, *200*, *201*, *202*, *207*, *211*, *212*, *215*, 228, 234, 252, 271, *281*, *283*, 347, 368, 393, *435*, *443*
Young, H., 369, *440*
Young, J. D., 140, *216*
Young, R. W., 230, 234, *279*
Yovanidis, C., 156, *209*, *216*
Ysebaert, M., 7, *60*
Yu, S. D., 38, 56, *59*

Z

Zabel, R., 67, *108*, 139, *216*
Zaborowsky, B. R., 157, 163, *213*
Zabrocki, J., 364, *440*
Zahn, H., 67, *108*, 125, 132, 136, 139, 142, 151, 153, 156, 183, 188, 189, *206*, *207*, *211*, *216*, 242, *282*
Zakarian, S., 40, *63*
Zalut, C., 39, *61*, 122, 140, *205*
Zamir, A., 54, *58*
Zanetti, G., 160, *204*
Zanotti, G., 121, *201*, 419, *448*
Zaoral, M., 115, 155, 163, 168, 169, 185, 186, 187, *201*, *211*, *216*, 362, 364, 390, 391, *432*, *436*, *449*
Zarucki-Schulz, T., 37, *64*
Zaslavsky, V. G., 54, *61*
Zdansky, G., 350, 375, 377, 378, *449*
Zecchini, G. P., 353, 412, *449*
Zee-Cheng, R. K. Y., 387, *449*
Zeelon, E. P., 54, *58*
Zeller, P., 380, *436*
Zemel, O., 54, *58*
Zenker, M., 406, 423, *441*
Zerner, B., 142, *198*
Zervas, L., 66, 67, 89, *106*, *109*, 138, 151, 156, 157, 161, 163, 170, *198*, *209*, *216*, 321, *336*, *337*, *339*
Zhukova, G. F., 159, *216*
Zhuze, A. L., 399, *449*
Ziegler, P., 223, *281*
Zigman, S., 132, *213*
Zikan, J., 123, 128, *205*
Zilkha, A., 361, 400, 402, *435*, *444*, *449*
Zimmerman, J. E., 228, *279*
Zimmerman, R. E., 39, 40, 48, *60*
Zipser, D., 33, *59*
Zobeley, S., 368, 399, 401, *434*, *448*
Zoller, M., 51, *64*
Zora, J. G., 397, *433*
Zuber, H., 67, *108*, 149, 154, 179, *212*, 359, *434*
Zwei, J. Z., *106*
Zwick, A., 147, *215*

Subject Index

A

A-128-OP, 290
A-128-P, 290
A-3302-A, 294
A-3302-B, 294
N^{δ}-Acetimidoylornithine, 393
N^{α}-Acetyltryptophan, cyclization, 131
ACTH, *see* Corticotropin
Actinomycin D, synthesis, side reactions, 194
Acylamino acids, symmetrical anhydrides, 253–256, 259
3-(1-Adamantyl)alanine, 368
3-(9-Adeninyl)alanine, 424
4-Adeninylproline, 410
Albonoursin, 288
2-Alkoxy-4-alkyl-5(4*H*)oxazolones, in peptide synthesis, 239–253
6-Alkoxy-3-amino-1,2,3,4-tetrahydrocarbazole-3-carboxylic acid, 395
N-Alkoxycarbonylamino acids
  coupling without racemization, 251
  racemization, during esterification to resin supports, 257–259
    during peptide bond formation, 260, 261
  reaction with carbodiimides, 242–244
N-Alkoxycarbonylhistidine, racemization, 261, 263
2-Alkoxy-5(4*H*)-oxazolones
  aminolysis and racemization, 246
  formation from symmetrical anhydrides and tertiary amines, 248, 249
  implication in carbodiimide-mediated coupling reactions, 251
    in carbodiimide-mediated reactions in absence of nitrogen nucleophiles, 249
  preparation from chloride-forming reagents, 241, 242
    and reactions, 245, 246
    from soluble carbodiimides, 242–244
  reactions and chiral properties, 244–247
Alkylation, *see also* Indolealkylation
  in methionine-containing peptides, 158–161
2-(5-Alkyl-2-furyl)glycines, 426
tert-Alkylglycines, 367
2-Alkyl-5(4*H*)-oxazolones, reactions, 246
4-Alkyl-5(2*H*)-oxazolones, in peptide synthesis, 238, 239
β-Alkylphenylalanines, ring-substituted, 404
2-(5-Alkyl-2-tetrahydrofuryl)glycines, 426
3-Alkylthiotryptophan, 420
(β-Allenyl)alanine, *see* 2-Amino-4,5-hexadienoic acid
Alliine, *see* 3-(2-Propenylsulfinyl)alanine
Allylglycine, *see* 2-Amino-4-pentenoic acid
Alternaria mali, AM-toxins, 316
Alternaria tenuis, tentoxin, 313
Alternariolide, *see* AM-Toxin 1
Amides, reaction with α-keto acids, 304, 305
N-Amidinocitrulline, 392
L-Amino acid oxidase, 222
Amino acids, *see also* Mutant DNA natural amino acids (For unusual amino acids available for peptide synthesis, with structures and references, see the Appendix, pages 341–449.)
  amidino, 391–393
  aromatic series, replacements, 347, 348
  bicyclic, in peptide synthesis, 353
  carbohydrate-containing, 429
  chalcogen-containing, 374
  chalcogen-containing aliphatic, 374–378
  conformation, effect on peptide synthesis, 351
  fatty, 346, 347
  fluorinated, 354, 355
  guanido, 391–393
  halogenated aliphatic, 371–374
  β-hydroxy, 379
  isofunctional and homofunctional replacements, 346
  isosteric and homosteric replacements, 349
  β-keto, 382

optically pure, preparation, 332
optical purity assessment, amino acid oxidase, 222
conversion to diastereomeric dipeptide, 222–225
gas–liquid chromatography, 225–227
organometallic, 348
5(4*H*)-oxazolone formation, 236–256
oxygenated aliphatic, 378–384
in peptide synthesis, unusual acids, 341–449
polyaminomonocarboxylic, 387–390
polyaminopolycarboxylic, 390, 391
polycarboxylic, 384–387
side-chain functionality, alkylating agents, 357, 358
photoaffinity labeling, 358, 359
silicon-containing, in proton nuclear magnetic resonance spectroscopy, 355
sulfur-containing, functional variants, 350, 351
tetrazole-containing, 350
unsaturated, 368–371
unusual, in peptide synthesis, benefits, 344–346
scope, 343
2-Aminoadamantane-2-carboxylic acid, in peptide synthesis, 353, 394
β-Aminoalanine, 387
2-Aminoalkanedioic acids, 385
2-Aminoalkanoic acids, 366–368
2-Amino-4-alkoxy-3-butenoic acids, 383
2-Amino-4-(2-aminoethoxy)butanoic acid, 381
2-Amino-4-aminooxylbutanoic acid, 390, 397
2-Aminobenzocyclo[2.2.2]octane-2-carboxylic acid, 395
2-Amino-3-bromobutanoic acid, 374
2-Amino-4-bromobutanoic acid, 374
2-Aminobutanedioic acid 4-thionamide, 377
2-Amino-3-butenoic acid, 368
2-Amino-3-butynoic acid, 371
α-Aminobutyric acid, *see* Butyrine
2-Amino-2-carboxyethylcyclobutadiene iron tricarbonyl, 408
2-Amino-2-carboxyethylcyclopentadienyl manganese tricarbonyl, 408
N-(3-Amino-3-carboxypropyl)pyridinium salts, 416
2-Amino-4-(4-carboxy-2-thiazolyl)butanoic acid, 428
2-Amino-3-chlorobutanoic acid, 373
2-Amino-6-chlorohexanoic acid, 374
2-Amino-4-chloro-4-pentenoic acid, 369
2-Amino-3-chloropropanoic acid, 373
1-Aminocycloalkane-1-carboxylic acids, and bicyclic congeners, in peptide synthesis, 353
1-Aminocycloheptanecarboxylic acid, 394
1-Aminocyclohexanecarboxylic acid, 393
1-Amino-1,3-cyclohexanedicarboxylic acid, 395
2-Amino-4-cyclohexylbutanoic acid, 368
α-(1-Aminocyclohexyl)glycine, 388
1-Aminocyclononanecarboxylic acid, 394
1-Aminocyclopentanecarboxylic acid, 393
1-Aminocyclopropanecarboxylic acid, and analogs, 393
2-Aminodecalin-2-carboxylic acid, 394
2-Amino-4,4-dichlorobutanoic acid, 373
2-Amino-4,4-dichloro-3-butenoic acid, 369
2-Amino-3,3-difluorobutanoic acid, 372
2-Amino-5,5-difluorohexanoic acid, 373
2-Amino-3,3-difluoro-3-phenylpropanoic acid, 372
2-Amino-3,4-dihydroxybutanoic acid, 381
2-Amino-5,6-dihydroxyhexanoic acid, 381
2-Amino-4,5-dihydroxy-4-hydroxymethylpentanoic acid, 381
2-Amino-4,5-dihydroxy-3-methylpentanoic acid, 381
2-Amino-4-(3,4-dihydroxyphenyl)butanoic acid, 405
1-Amino-2-(3,4-dihydroxyphenyl)cyclopropanecarboxylic acid, 395
2-Amino-3,3-dimethylbutanoic acid, 366
2-Amino-3,5-dimethylhexanoic acid, 367
2-Amino-4,4-dimethylpentanoic acid, 366
2-Amino-3,3-dimethyl-5-phenylpentanoic acid, 405
α-Amino-1,3-dithiolane-2-alkanoic acids, 376
2-Aminododecanedioic acid, 385
1-Amino-2-ethylcyclopropanecarboxylic acid, 393
O-(2-Aminoethyl)serine, 381
2-Amino-3-fluorobutanoic acid, 371
2-Amino-3-fluorohexanoic acid, 372
2-Amino-3-fluoromethyl-4-fluorobutanoic acid, 372
2-Amino-4-(fluoromethyl)-5-fluoropentanoic acid, 373
2-Amino-3-fluoropentanoic acid, 372
2-Amino-3-guanidobutanoic acid, 391
2-Amino-4-guanidobutanoic acid, 391

2-Amino-4-guanidooxybutanoic acid, 392
2-Amino-4,4,5,5,6,6,6-heptafluorohexanoic acid, 372
2-Amino-3,3,4,4,5,5,5-heptafluoropentanoic acid, 372
2-Aminoheptanedioic acid 7-monoamidine, 392
2-Amino-5-heptenoic acid, 369
2-Amino-6-heptenoic acid, 369
2-Amino-4-hepten-6-ynoic acid, 371
2-Amino-4,5-hexadienoic acid, 371
2-Amino-4-hexenoic acid, 369
2-Amino-4-hexynoic acid, 371
2-Amino-3-hydroxyalkanoic acids, 378
2-Amino-3-hydroxy-5-benzyloxypentanoic acid, 381
2-Amino-3-hydroxybutanoic acid, 379
2-Amino-4-hydroxybutanoic acid, 378
2-Amino-4-hydroxyhexanedioic acid, 386
2-Amino-4-hydroxyhexanoic acid, 379
2-Amino-6-hydroxyhexanoic acid, 379
2-Amino-3-hydroxy-4-hexynoic acid, 381
2-Amino-3-hydroxy-4-methylpentanoic acid, 379
2-Amino-3-hydroxy-5-(methylthio)pentanoic acid, 376
2-Amino-3-hydroxypentanoic acid, 379
2-Amino-3-hydroxy-3-phenylpropanoic acid, *see* 3-Hydroxy-3-phenylalanine
3′-Amino-4′-hydroxytetrahydrothiophene-3-carboxylic acid, 394
2-Aminoindan-2-carboxylic acid, 394
  5-substituted, 395
β-Amino-β-3-indolylalanine, 389
Aminolysis, of oxazolones, racemization and asymmetric induction, 263–265
Aminomalonic acid, 384
Aminomalonic acid mononitrile, 396
2-Aminomalonic acid semialdehyde diethyl acetal, 383
2-Amino-3-mercaptobutanoic acid, 374
2-Amino-5-mercapto-5-methylhexanoic acid, 375
2-Amino-4-methanephosphonylbutanoic acid, 397
2-Amino-5-(4-methoxyphenyl)pentanoic acid, 405
α-Amino-(ω-1)-methylalkanoic acids, 367
2-Amino-3-methylalkanoic acids, 366
2-Amino-3-methylaminobutanoic acid, 388
2-Amino-3-methyl-3-butenoic acid, 368
2-Amino-3-(2-methylenecyclopropyl)propanoic acid, 369
2-Amino-3-methyl-4-fluoropentanoic acid, 373
2-Amino-3-methyl-5-fluoropentanoic acid, 373
2-Amino-4-methylhexanoic acid, 367
2-Amino-4-methyl-4-hexenoic acid, 369
2-Amino-5-methyl-4-hexenoic acid, 369
2-Amino-4-methyl-5-hexenoic acid, 369
2-Amino-3-methyl-4-hydroselenopentanoic acid, 378
2-Amino-3-methyl-4-hydroxybutanoic acid, 379
2-Amino-3-methyl-4-mercaptopentanoic acid, 375
2-Amino-3-methyl-4-(methylseleno)butanoic acid, 378
2-Amino-4-(methylthio)-3-butenoic acid, 376
2-Amino-6-(methylthio)-hexanoic acid, 375
2-Amino-3-methyl-4,4,4-trifluorobutanoic acid, 372
2-Amino-3-(1-naphthyl)pentanoic acid, 406
2-Amino-ω-nitroalkanoic acid, 396
2-Amino-4-(7-nitro-2,1,3-benzoxadiazol-4-ylamino)butanoic acid, 391
2-Amino-3-(*N*-nitrosohydroxylamino)propanoic acid, 397
2-Aminonorbornane-2-carboxylic acid
  and 3-aryl derivatives, 394
  in peptide synthesis, 353
2-Aminooctanedioic acid, 385
β-Aminoornithine, 390
2-Amino-4-oxo-4-(2-amino-4-chlorophenyl)-butanoic acid, 382
2-Amino-5-oxo-6-diazohexanoic acid, 397
2-Amino-8-oxo-9,10-epoxydecanoic acid, 384
2-Amino-4-oxo-4-(2-furyl)butanoic acid, 382
2-Amino-4-oxohexanoic acid, 379
2-Amino-4-oxo-4-(4-hydroxylphenyl)butanoic acid, 382
2-Amino-4-oxo-4-(2-nitrophenyl)butanoic acid, 382
2-Amino-3,3,4,4,4-pentafluorobutanoic acid, 372
2-Amino-4,4,5,5,5-pentafluoropentanoic acid, 372
2-Amino-4-pentenoic acid, 369
2-Amino-4-pentynoic acid, 371
2-Amino-ω-phenoxyalkanoic acids, 406
2-Amino-4-phenoxybutanoic acid, 406
2-Amino-5-phenoxypentanoic acid, 406
β-Aminophenylalanine, 388
  analogs, 389

2-Amino-4-phenylbutanoic acid, 405
2-Amino-4-phenyl-3-butenoic acid, 405
2-Amino-5-phenylpentanoic acid, 405
L-, preparation, 332
4-Aminopipecolic acid, 411
3-(3-Aminopropylseleno)alanine, 378
3-(2-Amino-4-pyrimidinyl)alanine, 426
2-Amino-ω-(1-pyrimidinyl)alkanoic acids, 425
3-Aminopyrrolidine-3-carboxylic acid, 395
2-Amino-ω-(1-pyrryl)alkanoic acids, 416
2-Amino-4-(1-pyrryl)butanoic acid, 416
2-Amino-5-(1-pyrryl)pentanoic acid, 416
2-(6-Amino-9-purinyl)glycine, 424
3-(2-Amino-4-selenazolyl)alanine, 429
2-Amino-3,4,4,4-tetrachlorobutanoic acid, 374
2-Amino-3,4,5,6-tetrahydroxyhexanoic acid, 381
1-Amino-2,2,5,5-tetramethylcyclohexanecarboxylic acid, 393
2-Amino-4-(5-tetrazolyl)butanoic acid, 418
2-Amino-4-thiosulfobutanoic acid, 377
3-(3-Amino-1,2,4-triazol-1-yl)alanine, 418
2-Amino-4,4,4-trichlorobutanoic acid, 373
2-Amino-3-trifluoromethyl-4,4,4-trifluorobutanoic acid, 372
2-Amino-4-trifluoromethyl-5,5,5-trifluoropentanoic acid, 373
2-Amino-5,5,5-trifluoropentanoic acid, 372
2-Amino-4-(3,4,5-trihydroxyphenyl)butanoic acid, 405
2-Amino-3,3,4-trimethyl-4-pentenoic acid, 369
3-Amino-4-trimethylsilyl-3-butynoic acid, 397
AM-toxin I, 289
structure, 316
AM-toxin II, 289
structure, 316
AM-toxin III, 289
structure, 316
AM toxins
hydrogenation, 331
necrotic activity, 319
structure–activity relationships, 319, 320
synthesis, 316–319
Anderson test, for racemization, 231
Angiotensin II, 324
dehydro derivative, 352
Angiotensin-converting enzyme
dehydro derivative, 352
inhibitor, 364
Anhydrides, *see also* *N*-Carboxyanhydrides
mixes (unsymmetrical), side reactions, 184–187
symmetrical, of acylamino acids and *N*-protected peptides, 253–256, 259
side reactions, 183, 184
Anthelvencin A, 289
Anthelvencin B, 289
β-(9-Anthryl)alanine, 407
α-(2-Anthryl)glycine, 407
Antibiotic activity, plasmid, 19
Antrimycin, 290
Arabinose cysteine thioaminal, 414
tert-Aralkylglycines, 404
Arginine
in peptide synthesis, 72
side reactions, 137–139
Arginine-containing peptides, synthesis, 80–84
Asparagine
in peptide amide synthesis, 327, 328
reaction with phosgene, 155
side reactions, in peptide synthesis, 152–156
β-substituted, 387
Asparenomycin A, 288
Asparenomycin B, 288
Asparenomycin C, 288
Aspartic acid, side reactions, in peptide synthesis, 143–148
Aspartic acid-containing peptides, synthesis, 88–92
Aspartic acid 4-nitrile, 396
Aspartic acids, 3-substituted, 386
Aspartic acid γ-semialdehyde, 381
dimethyl acetal, 383
Aspartimide derivatives, 91, 92
β-Aspartylglycine, occurrence in urine, 144
Asymmetric induction
and racemization during aminolysis of oxazolones, 263–265
variables, external, 265, 266, 275–278
internal, 268–275
Attenuation, transcription, 24
Austamide, 288
Autoracemization, oxazolones, 238
5-Azabicyclo[2.1.1]hexane-1-carboxylic acid, 411
5-Azabicyclo[3.1.0]hexane-4-carboxylic acid, 411
Azacycloalkane-2-carboxylic acids, 411

γ-Azalysine, 390
4′-Azatryptophan, 420
7′-Azatryptophan, 420
2-Azetidinecarboxylic acid, 410
  peptides, 352
Azides, preparation of, of amino acids and peptides, 178–180
4-Azidophenylalanine, 359
2-Aziridinecarboxylic acid, 410
Azlactones [5(4*H*)-oxazolones]
  synthesis, 296
    from glycine, 305
    from β-phenylserine, and other amino acids, 306–308

B

Bacterial genetics, 3
α-Benzenesulfonylglycine, 377
Benzhydrylalanine, 406
3-(Benzimidazol-2-yl)alanines, 422
2-(Benzimidazol-5-yl)glycine, 423
2-(Benzisoxazol-3-yl)glycines, 422
3-(Benzoselenol-3-yl)alanine, 421
Benzothiazol-2-ylalanines, 423
3-(Benzothiophen-3-yl)alanine, 421
Benzoxazol-2-ylalanines, 423
S-Benzylcysteine, cleavage, 92
2-Benzyloxy-4-benzyl-5(4*H*)-oxazolone, preparation, 242
Benzyloxycarbonylamino acids, reaction with carbodiimides, 243
Benzyloxycarbonylasparagine pentafluorophenyl ester, cyclization, 154
Benzyloxycarbonyl-β-benzyl-L-aspartyl-L-serine, 147
1-Benzyloxycarbonyl-3-benzyl-2-aziridinone, 241, 242
N-Benzyloxycarbonyl-*N*-(benzyloxycarbonylglycyl)glycine, 114, 115
N^{α}-Benzyloxycarbonyldehydroamino acid, synthesis, 304
Benzyloxycarbonylglutamine hydrazide, 154
Benzyloxycarbonylglycine, side reactions with phosphorus oxychloride, 114, 115
Benzyloxycarbonyl group (Z), 66–69, 71–74
  cleavage, 77, 78
  introduction and removal, side reactions, 161–164
N^{ϵ}-Benzyloxycarbonyloxylysine
  deprotection scavengers, 75
  in peptide synthesis, deprotection procedure, 71–74
Benzyloxycarbonylphenylalanine, reaction with thionyl chloride, 241, 242
Benzyloxycarbonyl-L-phenylalanine, complex formation, 124
Benzyloxycarbonyl-DL-serine, complex formation, 143
Benzyloxycarbonyl-DL-valine, reaction with thionyl chloride, 242
2-Benzyloxy-4-isopropyl-5(4*H*)-oxazolone
  preparation, 243, 244
  properties, 244
  racemization, 246
  symmetrical anhydride formation, 254
2-Benzyloxy-5(4*H*)-oxazolone, preparation, and reactions, 245
α-(Benzylthio)glycine, 376
3-Benzyltyrosine, formation, 124–126
Berninamycin A, 290
2-(4-Biphenylyl)propyl(2)oxycarbonyl group (Bpoc), as protecting group, 69, 70, 146
Bishomoleucine, 367
Bishomomethionine, *see* 2-Amino-6-(methylthio)hexanoic acid
Bradykinin, 324
Bradykinin analogs, 324
2-Bromobenzyloxycarbonyl group, 136
4-Bromobenzyloxycarbonyl-L-phenylalanine, reaction with thionyl chloride, 242
3-(4-Bromo-3-hydroxy-5-isoxazolyl)alanine, 427
3-(1-Bromo-2-naphthyl)alanine, 407
tert-Butoxycarbonyl-*S*-acetamidomethylcysteine sulfoxide, cleavage, 94
tert-Butoxycarbonylamino acids, reaction with carbodiimides, 243
N^{α}-*tert*-Butoxycarbonyl-*O*-dichlorodehydrotyrosine methyl ester, synthesis, 308
tert-Butoxycarbonylglutamine *N*-hydroxysuccinimide ester, 154
tert-Butoxycarbonyl group, introduction and removal, side reaction, 164–167
N^{ϵ}-tert-Butoxycarbonyl group, 69
tert-Butoxycarbonyllysine, in peptide synthesis, 69
N^{α}-*tert*-Butoxycarbonyl-*S*-phenylthiocysteine, formation, 94

tert-Butoxycarbonyl-L-prolyl-L-proline,
preparation, 120
2-*tert*-Butoxy-4-isopropyl-5(4*H*)-oxazolone
formation, 247
isolation, 251
preparation, 243, 244
properties, 244
racemization, 246
2-*tert*-Butoxy-5(4*H*)-oxazolones
formation, 250, 252, 253
from anhydrides and tertiary amines, 247
tert-Butylglycine, *see* 2-Amino-3,3-dimethylbutanoic acid
tert-Butyloxy-, *see tert*-Butoxy-
Butyrine
precursor for dehydroaminobutyric acid, 302

C

C-2801X, 289
Calcitonin, synthesis, 70
Canaline, *see* 2-Amino-4-aminooxybutanoic acid
Canavanine, *see* 2-Amino-4-guanidooxybutanoic acid
Capreomycin 1A, 289
Capreomycin 1B, 289
Capreomycin IIA, 289
Capreomycin IIB, 289
Carbodiimides
in peptide synthesis, side reactions, 189–192
reaction with *N*-alkoxycarbonylamino acids, 242, 249, 250, 251
β-Carboline-3-carboxylic acids, 414
β-Carbolines, formation from tryptophan, 131, 132
β-*o*-Carboranylalanine, 408
N-(5-Carboxy-5-aminopentyl)pyridinium chloride, 416
N-Carboxyanhydride
β-cyanoalanine, 155
glutamine, 155
glycine, rearrangement reaction, 117, 118
serine, 141
side reactions in peptide synthesis, 187, 188
β-Carboxyaspartic acid, 387
γ-Carboxyglutamic acid, 387
3-(1-Carboxy-4-hydroxy-2-cyclohexenyl) alanine, 386
S-[1-Carboxy-2-(4-imidazolyl)ethyl]cysteine, 377
Carboxyl group, protection, 173, 174
3-Carboxylysine, 390
3-(2-Carboxy-6-oxo-6*H*-pyranyl)alanine, 387
Celenamide A, 289
Celenamide B, 289
Cells, transformed, 4
Cephalosporin C, 289
Cephamycin A, 289
Cephamycin B, 289
Cherylline, synthesis, 76
3-Chloroalanine, *see* 2-Amino-3-chloropropanoic acid
2-Chlorobenzyloxycarbonyl group, 136
4-Chlorobenzyloxycarbonyl-L-phenylalanine, reaction with thionyl chloride, 242
5-Chloro-4-bromo-3-indolyl-β-D-galactoside, plasmid indicator, 20
β-Chloroglutamic acid, 386
2-(3-Chloro-Δ^2-isoxazolin-5-yl)glycine, 427
6-Chloro-4-methyl-7-azatryptophan, 420
3-(1-Chloro-2-napththyl)alanine, 406
2-(6-Chloro-9-purinyl)glycine, 424
2-(5-Chloro-2-pyridyl)glycine, 416
Chlorosis, 313
Chorismic acid, *see* 3-(1-Carboxy-4-hydroxy-2-cyclohexenyl)alanine
Cinnamycin, 291
Cleavage of protecting groups, *see* Deprotection
Clones, detection, 22
Cloning
foreign genes into *E. coli*, 3, 4
gene purification, 18–22
restriction mapping, 20
Complementary deoxyribonucleic acid, synthesis, 14–18
Complementary deoxyribonucleic acid clone, semisynthetic approach, 18
Configuration, dehydropeptides, 311
Conformation, amino acid, effect on peptide synthesis, 351
Corticotropin
synthesis, 67, 70
deprotecting agents, 68
3-(3-Coumarinyl)alanine, 422
Coumermycin A_1, 289
Courmermycin A_2, 289
Coupling methods, effect on racemization, 277, 278
Curtius rearrangement, in peptide azide synthesis, 180–182

α-Cyanoglycine, *see* Aminomalonic acid mononitrile
Cyclization
  of *N*-alkoxycarbonylamino acids, 251-252
  in arginine reactions, 137
  in asparagine reactions, 152–154
  in aspartic acid reactions, 143–148
  in glutamic acid reactions, 150–152
  in glutamine reactions, 152–154
  in peptide synthesis, 89, 256
    oxazolone formation, 235–241
    side reactions, 193, 194
α-(1-Cycloalkenyl)glycines, 370
β-Cycloarginine, *see* (2-Iminohexahydropyrimidin-4-yl)glycine
γ-Cycloarginine, *see* 3-(2-Iminoimidazolidin-4-yl)alanine
2-(7-Cycloheptatrienyl)glycine, 371
3-(1-Cycloheptenyl)alanine, 370
3-(1,4-Cyclohexadienyl)alanine, 370
3-(2,5-Cyclohexadienyl)alanine, 370
3-(1-Cyclohexenyl)alanine, 370
3-(2-Cyclohexenyl)alanine, 370
2-(2-Cyclohexenyl)glycine, 370
3-Cyclohexylalanine, 368
1-Cyclohexyl-2-cyclohexylamino-4,5-dihydroimidazolin-5-one, 117
α-Cyclohexylglycine, 368
Cycloleucine, *see* 1-Aminocyclopentanecarboxylic acid
3-(2-Cyclopentenyl)alanine, 370
3-(3-Cyclopentenyl)alanine, 370
2-(2-Cyclopentenyl)glycine, 370
α-Cyclopentylglycine, 367
Cystathionine, 390
Cysteic acid, 377
Cysteic acid derivatives, 377
Cysteine
  precursor for dehydroalanine, 299, 300
  side reactions, in peptide synthesis, 156–158
Cysteine-containing peptides, synthesis, 92–95
Cysteinesulfinic acid, 377
Cystine, side reactions, in peptide synthesis, 156–158
3-(1-Cytosinyl)alanines, 425
2-(1-Cytosinyl)glycines, 425

D

Deacetoxycephalosporin C, 289
Deacetylcephalospolin C, 289
Dehydroalanine
  occurrence, 287
  in peptide amide synthesis, 326
  synthesis, from cysteine and other amino acids, 299, 300
    from serine, 297–299
    side reactions, 298
Dehydroalanine peptides, synthesis, 297–300
α,β-Dehydroamino acids, 285–339
  coupling reactions, 309, 310
  hydrogenation, in cyclic peptides, 330–332
  as precursors, 287, 291
  synthesis, and peptide synthesis, 296–309
    with β-substituents, 308
  utility in peptide chemistry, 325–332
  in vivo synthesis, 302
α,β-Dehydroamino acid moiety
  configuration determination, 311, 312
  identification in dehydropeptides, 310, 311
α,β-Dehydro-α-aminobutyric acid
  L-, preparation, 332
  synthesis from threonine and other amino acids, 300–302, 304
Dehydroaminoundecanoic acid, synthesis, 308
Dehydroleucine synthesis, 303–305
4,5-Dehydrolysine, *see* 2,6-Diamino-4-hexenoic acid
Δ^3-Dehydromethionine, *see* 2-Amino-4-(methylthio)-3-butenoic acid
Dehydronorleucine, synthesis, 304, 305, 308
Dehydronorvaline, synthesis, 304, 308
α,β-Dehydropeptides, 285–339
  analytical methods, 310–312
  biologically active, synthesis, 312–325
  hydrogenation of cyclic, 330–332
  properties, 287
  structure–bioactivity relatioships, 332, 333
  structure and biological activities, 291–296
  synthesis, 309, 310
Dehydrophenylalanine, synthesis, 296, 305–308
α,β-Dehydrophenylalanine azlactone
  from glycine, 305
  from β-phenylserine and other amino acids, 306
α,β-Dehydrophenylalanine peptides, synthesis, 305–308
α,β-Dehydropiperazinediones, 308, 309
2,3-Dehydroproline, 308
3,4-Dehydroproline, 352
α,β-Dehydrotryptophan esters, *N*-acyl, synthesis, 308

Dehydrovaline, synthesis, 302, 303
Deoxyribonucleic acid
  chemical–enzymatic synthesis, 5–14
  sequencing, 22
Deprotecting agents in peptide synthesis, 67, 68
Deprotection
  acidolytic, in peptide synthesis, 65–109
    side reactions, 196
  of carboxyl groups, 174
  hard–soft concept, 76
  of methionine-containing peptides, 158, 160
  push–pull mechanism, 77
  scavengers, 75, 83–87, 125, 126, 149, 160
  of side-chain functions, 175–177
  side reactions, 161–174
  thioanisole-mediated trifluoroacetic acid, 105
Desacetylthymosin α_1
  amino acid analysis, 43
  analysis and purification, 11
  design of gene coding, 5–10
  detection, 22
  purification, 41–43, 46
  synthesis, 4
    by β-galactosidase fusion approach, 26
  synthetic route, for fragment T_{15}, 9
Desacetylthymosin α_1 gene
  ligation scheme for construction, 12, 13
  synthetic route, 9–11
5,6-Dialkoxy-2-aminoindan-2-carboxylic-acids, 396
2,4-Dialkyl-5(4*H*)-oxazolones
  aminolysis, racemization and asymmetric induction, 263–265
  in peptide synthesis, 236–238
Diamino acids, 387–390
2,3-Diaminobutanoic acid, 387
2,4-Diaminobutanoic acid, 388
1,4-Diaminocyclohexanecarboxylic acid, 395
2,4-Diaminoheptanoic acid, 388
2,6-Diamino-4-hexenoic acid, 389
2,6-Diamino-4-hexynoic acid, 389
2,4-Diamino-3-methylbutanoic acid, 388
2,7-Diaminooctanedioic acid, 390
2,4-Diamino-3-phenylbutanoic acid, 388
α,β-Diaminopropionic acid, dehydroalanine synthesis, 299
O-Diazoacetylserine, 396
N^{α},N^{im}-Dibenzyloxycarbonylhistidine, 133
2,4-Dichlorobenzyloxycarbonyl group, 136
3,4-Dichlorobenzyloxycarbonyl group, 136
Dicyclohexylcarbodiimide, coupling reactions, 309
3,3-Diethoxyalanine, 383
β,β-Diethylalanine, 367
β,β-Difluoroaspartic acid, 386
ω,ω′-Difluoroleucine, *see* 2-Amino-4-(fluoromethyl)-5-fluoropentanoic acid
5,5-Difluorolysine, 389
β,β-Difluorophenylalanine, *see* 2-Amino-3,3-difluoro-3-phenylpropionic acid
ω,ω′-Difluorovaline, *see* 2-Amino-3-fluoromethyl-4-fluorobutanoic acid
N^{α},N'-Diformyltryptophan, 131
3-(2,3-Dihydrobenzofuran-3-yl)alanine, 420
3,4-Dihydrocarboline-3-carboxylic acid, 131
2-(1,3-Dihydro-2,2-dioxo-2,1,3-benzothiadiazol-5-yl)glycine, 423
2-(1,3-Dihydro-2,2-dioxoisobenzothiophen-5-yl)glycine, 423
2′,5′-Dihydro-*O*-methyltyrosine, 383
2′,3′-Dihydrotryptophan, 419
4,5-Dihydroxy-2-aminoindan-2-carboxylic acid, 396
5,6-Dihydroxy-2-aminotetralin-2-carboxylic acid, 396
5,6-Dihydroxy-2,3-dihydroindole-2-carboxylic acid, 412
3,4-Dihydroxyglutamic acid, 386
ω,ω′-Dihydroxyleucine, 381
6,7-Dihydroxy-1-methyl-1,2,3,4-tetrahydroisoquinoline-3-carboxylic acid, 412
3,4-Dihydroxyphenylalanine, ring-substituted derivatives, 403
4,5-Dihydroxypipecolic acid, 412
3-(4,5-Dihydroxypyrimidin-2-yl)alanine, 426
6,7-Dihydroxy-1,2,3,4-tetrahydroisoquinoline-3-carboxylic acid, 412
1-(4-Dimethylaminophenyl)-1,2,3,4,4a,9a-hexahydro-β-carboline-3-carboxylic acid, 414
4-Dimethylaminopyridine, effect on racemization of *N*-alkoxycarbonylamino acids, 260
β,β-Dimethylaspartic acid, 384
3-(2,5-Dimethyl-3,6-dioxo-1,4-cyclohexadienyl)alanine, 383
5,5-Dimethyllysine, 389
2,2-Dimethylthiazolidine-4-carboxylic acid, 413
β-Dimethyl(trimethylsilylmethyl)silylalanine, 397

3-(3,5-Dioxo-1,2,4-oxadiazolin-2-yl)alanine, 427
(1,3-Dioxy-4,4,5,5-tetramethylimidazolin-2-yl)alanine, 417
Dipeptide isosteres, 364
Dipeptides
  conformationally constrained, 353, 354
  synthesis, 309
β,β-Diphenylalanine, 404
Distamycin A, 289
Disulfide bonds, polypeptide, 38, 39
DNA, *see* Deoxyribonucleic acid
cDNA, *see* Complementary deoxyribonucleic acid
Dopa, ring-substituted derivatives, 403
Duramycin, 291

E

Echinulin, isolation and structure, 293
Endonucleases, *see* Restricted endonucleases
Endoracididine *see* 3-(2-Iminoimidazolidin-4-yl)alanine
Enkephalin, 324
Enkephalin analogs, 324, 325, 364
Epimerization, definition, 220
3-(2,3-Epoxycyclohexyl)alanine, 384
α-(2,3-Epoxycyclohexyl)glycine, 384
3-(2,3-Epoxy-4-oxocyclohexyl)alanine, 384
Escherichia coli
  electron micrographs of transformed, 35
  phase-contrast microscopy of transformed, 34
  polypeptide synthesis, 3
  recombinant DNA research, 1
Esterification, of *N*-alkoxycarbonylamino acids, racemization, 257–259
Esters, racemization during saponification, 262, 263
N-Ethoxycarbonyl-2-ethoxy-1,2-dihydroquinoline, coupling reagent, 219
2-Ethoxy-4-isopropyl-5(4*H*)-oxazolone, preparation, 244
α-(1-Ethylcyclohexyl)glycine, 368
3-Ethylthreonine, *see* 3-Hydroxyisoleucine
Ethynylglycine, *see* 2-Amino-3-butynoic acid

F

β-Ferrocenylalanine, 408
3-(2-Fluorenyl)alanine, 408
3-(4-Fluorenyl)alanine, 408
N-9-Fluorenylmethyloxycarbonylamino acid anhydrides, preparation, 243
9-Fluorenylmethyloxycarbonyl group, 136, 146
  introduction and removal, side reactions, 170–172
2-(9-Fluorenylmethyloxy)-4-isopropyl-5(4*H*)-oxazolone, preparation, 244
Fluorine-19 nuclear magnetic resonance spectroscopy, peptide, 354, 355
3-Fluoroalanine, 371
γ-Fluoroarginine, 392
β-Fluoroaspartic acid, 385
γ-Fluoroglutamic acid, 385
γ-Fluoroisoleucine, *see* 2-Amino-3-methyl-4-fluoropentanoic acid
ω-Fluoroisoleucine, *see* 2-Amino-3-methyl-5-fluoropentanoic acid
5-Fluorolysine, 389
4-Fluoroornithine, 389
β-Fluorophenylalanine, 405
Fluoroproline, 355
4-Fluorothreonine, 380
β-Fluorovaline, 372
β-Formylalanine, *see* Aspartic acid γ-semialdehyde
N^{ϵ}-Formyllysine, in peptide synthesis, 68
N^{α}-Formyltryptophan, 131
β-(2-Furyl)alanine, 427
2-(2-Furyl)glycine, 428

G

Gas–liquid chromatography, in optical purity assessment, 225–227
Genes
  chemical synthesis, 22
  cloned, 3
  cloning foreign, into *E. coli*, 3, 4
  coding design, 5–10, 17
  expression of foreign, in microorganisms, 52–57
  purification by cloning, 18–22
  semisynthetic, 18
Glucagon, synthesis, 70
S-(β-Glucopyranosyl)cysteine, 376
Glutamic acid
  side reactions, in peptide synthesis, 148–152
  3-substituted, 390
  3- and 4-substituted, 385
L-Glutamic acid *N*-carboxyanhydride, in enantiomer assessment, 223, 224

Glutamic acid 5-nitrile, 396
Glutamine
 in peptide amide synthesis, 327, 328
 reaction with phosgene, 155
 side reactions, in peptide synthesis, 152–156
Glycine
 α,β-dehydrophenylalanine azlactone synthesis, 305
 side reactions in peptide synthesis, 114–118
Gramicidin S, analog, hydrogenation, 331
Granuliberin R, synthesis, 81, 82
Griseoviridin, 290
Growth hormone, *see* Somatotropin
Guanidino group, Guanido group, 137
β-Guanidoalanine, 391
4-Guaninylproline, 410

H

Heptamycin A, 290, 294, 295
Heptamycin B, 290, 294, 295
ω-Hexafluoroleucine, *see* 2-Amino-4-trifluoromethyl-5,5,5-trifluoropentanoic acid
ω-Hexafluorovaline, *see* 2-Amino-3-trifluoromethyl-4,4,4-trifluorobutanoic acid
1,2,3,4,4a,9a-Hexahydro-β-carboline-3-carboxylic acid, 414
Histidine
 N-protected, racemization, 260–263
 side reactions, in peptide synthesis, 132–135
L-Histidine ammonia lyase, 290
Histidine analogs, 417
Histidine isosteres, in peptide synthesis, 349
Homoarginine, 391
Homocitrulline, 391
Homocysteine, 374
Homo-dopa, *see* 2-Amino-4-(3,4-dihydroxyphenyl)butanoic acid
Homohistidine, 417
Homoisoleucine, *see* 2-Amino-4-methylhexanoic acid
Homolysine, 388
Homomethionine, 375
Homothreonine, *see* 2-Amino-3-methyl-4-hydroxybutanoic acid
Hormones, *see* Peptide hormone analogs
 growth, *see* Somatotropin
Hybridization, plasmid, 21
Hydantoic acids, glycine side reaction, 117
Hydantoins, in glycine side reactions, 116, 117
Hydrazine acetate, as deprotecting agent, 68
Hydrazinolysis, in peptide synthesis, 178, 179
Hydrochloric acid, as deprotecting agent in peptide synthesis, 68, 69
Hydrogenation, of α,β-dehydroamino acids in cyclic peptides, 330–332
Hydrogen fluoride
 deprotecting procedure, 71, 72
 as deprotection agent, 100, 102
3-Hydroxyalanine, and analogs, 379
γ-Hydroxyarginine, 392
β-Hydroxyasparagine, 387
β-Hydroxyaspartic acid, 379, 386
3-(4-Hydroxybenzothiazol-6-yl)alanine, 423
3-(5-Hydroxybenzothiophen-3-yl)alanine, 421
β-(*p*-Hydroxybenzoyl)alanine, 382
3-Hydroxy-3-[3-bis(2-chloroethyl)amino]-phenylalanine, 380
3-Hydroxy-3-[4-bis(2-chloroethyl)amino]-phenylalanine, 380
3-(1-Hydroxycyclohexyl)alanine, 380
α-(1-Hydroxycyclopropyl)glycine, 380
3-Hydroxy-3-(3,4-dihydroxyphenyl)alanine, 380
β-Hydroxydopa, *see* 3,3′,4′-Trihydroxyphenylalanine
γ-Hydroxyglutamic acid, 386
3-Hydroxyisoleucine, 379
3-(3-Hydroxy-5-isoxazolyl)alanines, 427
Hydroxylamine hydrochloride, as deprotecting agent, 68
3-Hydroxyleucine, 379
β-Hydroxylysine, 389
γ-Hydroxylysine, 389
3-Hydroxy-3-(3,4-methylenedioxyphenyl)alanine, 380
3-(3-Hydroxy-4-methyl-5-isoxazolyl)alanine, 427
2-(3-Hydroxy-4-methyl-5-isoxazolyl)glycine, 427
2-(3-Hydroxy-5-methyl-4-isoxazolyl)glycine, 427
6-Hydroxy-1-methyl-1,2,3,4-tetrahydroisoquinoline-3-carboxylic acid, 412
3-(Hydroxymethyl)valine, 379
Hydroxyminaline, 288
3-(4-Hydroxy-1-naphthyl)alanine, 407

3-Hydroxy-3-(*p*-nitrophenyl)alanine, 379
γ-Hydroxynorleucine, 378
δ-Hydroxynorleucine, 378
ε-Hydroxynorleucine, 378
β-Hydroxyornithine, 389
γ-Hydroxyornithine, 389
N^{δ}-Hydroxyornithine, 391
3-(3-Hydroxy-4-oxo-1,4-dihydro-1-pyridyl)-alanine, analogs, 416
3-Hydroxy-3-phenylalanine, 379, 380
α,β-dehydrophenylalanine synthesis, 306
S-4-Hydroxyphenylcysteine, formation, 93
3-(3-(4-Hydroxyphenyl)-1,2,4-oxadiazol-5-yl)alanine, 428
5-Hydroxypipecolic acid, 411
3-(3-Hydroxypropyl)aspartic acid, 386
3-Hydroxy-3-(3-pyridyl)alanine, 379
3-(8-Hydroxy-5-quinolyl)alanine, 421
3-Hydroxyvaline, 379
4-Hypoxanthinylproline, 410

I

3-(1-Imidazolyl)alanine, 417
3-(2-Imidazolyl)alanine, 417
3-(2-Iminohexahydropyrimidin-4-yl)alanine, 392
α-(2-Iminohexahydropyrimidin-4-yl)glycine, 392
3-(2-Iminoimidazolidin-4-yl)alanine, 392
2-Imino-3-methylbutyric acid ethyl ester, synthesis, 303
6-Imino-2,5,7-triazabicyclo[3.2.1]octane-3-carboxylic acid, 415
α-(2-Indanyl)glycine, 406
Indole alkylation
scavengers, 87
in tryptophan-containing peptides, 86–88
in tryptophan reactions, 128, 129
2-Indolecarboxylic acid derivatives, 412, 414
Insulin, synthesis, 57, 58
Interferon A
leukocyte, purification, 44
synthesis, 4, 5
Interferon αA, synthesis, 57
Interferon αD, synthesis, 57
Interferon β, synthesis, 57
Interferons
assay, 46
hybrid leukocyte, 48, 49
Isoechinulin A, 288
effect on silkworm growth, 293
isolation and structure, 292
Isoechinulin B, 288
isolation and structure, 292
Isoechinulin C, 288
isolation and structure, 292
Isoleucine, side reactions in peptide synthesis, 118–120
α-Isopropenylglycine, *see* 2-Amino-3-methyl-3-butenoic acid
Isoquinoline alkaloids, synthesis, 76
Isoquinoline-3-carboxylic acid derivatives, 412
Isoracemization, 221
Izumiya test, for racemization, 231

K

Kassinin, synthesis, 80
α-Keto acids, reactions with amides, 304, 305
Kikumycin A, 289
Kikumycin B, 289

L

β-Lactamase, 25
Lanthionine, 291, 295
Lasiodine A, 289
Leuchs' anhydrides, *see* Carboxyanhydrides
tert-Leucine, *see* 2-Amino-3,3-dimethyl-butanoic acid
Leukocite interferon A, *see* Interferon A
Lysine, side reactions, in peptide synthesis, 135, 136
Lysine-containing peptides, synthesis, 74, 75
Lysinoalanine, 291

M

Mastoparan X, synthesis, 87, 88
α-Melanotropin (α-MSH), synthesis, 67
β-Melanotropin (β-MSH), synthesis, 67
(1-Mercaptocycloalkyl)glycines, 375
3-Mercaptoisoleucine, *see* 3-Mercaptonorvaline
3-Mercaptoleucine, 375
3-Mercaptonorvaline, 374
3-Mercaptovaline, *see* Penicillamine
Mesitylenesulfonyl group (Mts), cleavage, 81, 83, 84

Messenger-ribonucleic acid
  structure, 30
  translation, 28
Methanesulfonic acid (MSA)
  as deprotection agent, 97–100, 102
  deprotection procedure, 72–74
Methionine
  in peptide synthesis, 72
  side reactions, in peptide synthesis, 158–161
Methionine-containing peptides
  deprotection, 158, 160
  synthesis, cleavage of ether based on hard–soft concept, 76
    cleavage of methyloxycarbonyl group, 78
    deprotection and push–pull mechanism, 77
    without *S*-protection, 78, 79
    with *S*-protection, 79, 80
7-Methoxycephalosporin C, 289
β-Methylaspartic acid, 384
4-Methyl-2-azetidinecarboxylic acid, 410
1-Methylcarboline-3-carboxylic acid, 131
Methylcyclohexylglycine, 368
β-Methylcysteine, *see* 2-Amino-3-mercaptobutanoic acid
3-(3-Methyl-5,7-dialkylbenzofuran-2-yl)-alanines, 421
2-(5-Methyl-2,5-dihydro-2-furyl)glycine, 426
β-Methyleneaspartic acid, 385
2,3-Methylene-dopa, *see* 1-Amino-2-(3,4-dihydroxyphenyl)cyclopropanecarboxylic acid
γ-Methyleneglutamic acid, 385
β-Methylenephenylalanine, 405
2,4-Methyleneproline, 411
3,4-Methyleneproline, 411
3,4-Methylenethreonine, *see* α-(1-Hydroxycyclopropyl)glycine
N-Methylenkephalinol, synthesis, 76, 77
γ-Methylglutamic acid, 384
S-(2-Methyl-4-hydroxy-2-butyl)cysteine, 376
β-Methyllanthionine, 291, 295
β-Methylleucine, 367
3-(Methylmercapto)phenylalanine, 405
β-Methylornithine, 388
Methyloxybenzenesulfonyl group (Mbs), cleavage, 80–84
S-4-Methyloxybenzylcysteine, sulfoxide, formation, and cleavage, 93–95
Methyloxycarbonyl group, cleavage, 78
β-Methylphenylalanine, 404
Methylsulfonylethyloxycarbonyl group, 136
3-Methylthreonine, *see* 3-Hydroxyvaline
3-(6-Methyl-3-tropolonyl)alanine, 383
β-Methyltryptophan, 419
Micrococcin P_1, 290
Micrococcin P_2, 290
Minaline, 288
Monohomoleucine, 367
Mutant-DNA natural amino acids
  alterations using restriction sites, 51
  chemical synthesis, 50
  random mutagenesis, 50
  semisynthesis, 50
  specific mutagenesis, 51
Mycerianamide, 288

N

3-(1-Naphthyl)alanine, 406
  derivatives, 407
3-(2-Naphthyl)alanine, 407
α-(β-Naphthyl)glycine, 406
Neoechinulin, 288
  isolation and structure, 292
Neoechinulin A, 288
  isolation and structure, 292
Neoechinulin B, 288
  isolation and structure, 292
Neoechinulin C, 288
  isolation and structure, 292
Neoechinulin D, 289
  structure, 292
Neoechinulin E, 289
  structure, 292
Netropsin, 289
Neurotensin, synthesis, 74, 80, 83, 84
Nisin, 290, 291, 295, 296
  structure, 320
  synthesis, 320–323
Nitroarginine-containing peptides, 137, 138, 178
2-Nitrophenylsulfenyl chloride, reactions with tryptophan residues, 130
2-Nitrophenylsulfenylglutamine *N*-hydroxysuccinimide ester, 154
2-Nitrophenylsulfenyl group, introduction and removal, side reactions, 167
2-(2-Nitrophenylsulfenyl)tryptophan, formation, 130
N^{δ}-(5-Nitro-2-pyrimidinyl)ornithine, 391

Nocobactin NA, 289
Norcitrulline, 397
Nosiheptide, 290
Nuclear magnetic resonance spectroscopy, fluorinated peptides, 354, 355

O

Oganomycins, 289
Oligonucleotides, synthesis, 10, 13, 14
Ostreogrycin A, 289
5-Oxahomolysine, *see* 2-Amino-4-(2-aminoethoxy)butanoic acid
Oxaline, 288
4-Oxalysine, *see* *O*-(2-Aminoethyl)serine
δ-Oxaornithine, *see* 2-Amino-4-aminooxybutanoic acid
1,2-Oxazolidine-3-carboxylic acid, 413
1,3-Oxazolidine-4-carboxylic acid, 413
5(4*H*)-Oxazolones
  2-alkoxy-4-alkyl, in peptide synthesis, 239–253
  2-alkoxy, preparation, 241–244
  4-alkyl-, in peptide synthesis, 238, 239
  amination and racemization, 246
  autoracemization, 238
  2,4-dialkyl-, in peptide synthesis, 236–238
  2,4-disubstituted, preparation, 256
  purification, 237, 238
  synthesis, 219
2-(2-Oxobenzimidazol-5-yl)glycine, 423
3-(4-Oxo-1-cyclohexenyl)alanine, 382
3-(4-Oxocyclohexyl)alanine, 382
2-Oxo-2′,3′-dihydrotryptophan, 419
4-Oxoisoleucine, 382
2-(3-Oxo-5-isoxazolidinyl)glycine, 427
4-Oxolysine, 390
Oxytocein, 193
Oxytocin
  dehydro derivative, 352
  inactivation by acetone, 195
  solid-phase synthesis, 328, 329
  synthesis, 66
    side reactions, 193, 194
Oxytocin analogs, synthesis, 155, 157

P

Pencolide, 288
Penicillamine, 374
Pentafluorophenylalanine, 354
Peptide amides, synthesis, 326–329
Peptide bond formation, *see* Peptide synthesis
  azide method, 177–182
  Curtius rearrangement, 180–182
  side reactions, 177–192
Peptide esters, racemization during saponification, 262, 263
Peptide hormone analogs, α,β-dehydroamino acid-containing, 323–325
Peptide isosteres, 363–365
Peptides, *see also* Polypeptides
  natural, containing α,β-dehydroamino acids, 287–291
  N-protected, symmetrical anhydrides, 253–256, 259
  side-chain functionality, receptor interactions, 356–359
    synthetic transformations, 359–363
  stability (instability) in solution, 194–196
  structural variants, 343
Peptide synthesis, *see also* Solid-phase peptide synthesis
  acidolytic deprotecting procedures, 65–109
  amino acids in (unusual acids), 341–449
  with anhydrides, 182–187
  asymmetric induction, 263–278
  carbodiimides in, side reactions, 189–192
  comparative evaluation, 104, 105
  cyclization or anhydride formation, 256
    side reactions, 89, 193, 194
  from α,β-dehydroamino acids, 296–309
  α,β-dehydroamino acids utility, 325–332
  oxazolone formation, 235–241
  prognosis, 105
  racemization, during peptide bond formation, 259
    quantitation and sequence dependence, 217–284
  side reactions, 111–216
Peptidomimetics, nonpeptidic, synthesis, 365
Perfluoroalkylalanines, 372
α-Perfluoroethylglycine, *see* 2-Amino-3,3,4,4,4-pentafluorobutanoic acid
Perhydro-1,3-thiazine-2-carboxylic acid, 413
Perhydro-1,4-thiazine-3-carboxylic acid, 413
3-(2-Phenothiazinyl)alanine, 422
Phenylalanine
  D-, preparation, 332
  side reactions, in peptide synthesis, 123, 124
  β-substituted derivatives, 404

L-Phenylalanine ammonia lyase, 290
Phenylalanine congeners, 404
Phenylalanine derivatives, aromatic-substituted, 399–402
(*S*)-2-Phenyl-4-butyl-5(4*H*)-oxazolone, reaction with aniline, 264
Phenylglycine derivatives, aromatic-substituted, 398
2-Phenyl-4-isopropyl-5(4*H*)-oxazolone, anyhydride formation, 255, 256
3-(3-Phenyl-5-isoxazolyl)alanine, 428
β-Phenylmethionine, 375
γ-Phenylmethionine, 405
β-Phenylserine, *see* 3-Hydroxy-3-phenylalanine
2-Phenylthiazolidine-4-carboxylic acid, 414
β-Phosphoalanine, 397
Phthalyl group, Phthaloyl group, introduction and removal, side reactions, 169
Pipecolic acid, 410
  peptides, 352
Pipecolic acid derivatives, 411, 412
Piperazinediones, amino acid-containing, coupling reactions, 308
α-(2-Piperidyl)glycine, 388
Plasmids, 3, 4, 12
  antibiotic resistance, 19
  construction, 12, 13
  hybridization methods, 21
  indicator plates, 20
  replication, 23
  screening, 20
Polyaminomonocarboxylic acids, 387–389
Polyaminopolycarboxylic acids, 390
Polypeptides
  analogs, synthesis by cloning, 48
  biochemical synthesis, 52
  characterization, 47
  posttranslational processing, amino-terminal acetylation, 40
    amino-terminal methionine, 39
    disulfide bonds, 38, 39
    glycosylation, 40
    proteolytic processing, 40
  purification, 45
  semisynthesis, chemical, 51
  synthesis by recombinant DNA methods, 1–64
  in vivo stability, of fusion proteins, 31
    product secretion, 33–37
Primocarcin, 288
  structure, 291
Proinsulin, assay, 46
Proinsulin analog, synthesis, 50
Proline, side reactions, in peptide synthesis, 120–123
Proline derivatives, 408–410
  racemization, 270
Proline isologs, in peptide synthesis, 352, 353
Propargylglycine, 371
3-(1-Propenylsulfinyl)alanine, 376
3-(2-Propenylsulfinyl)alanine, 376
Protecting groups, *see also* Deprotection
  for arginine, 137, 138
  for aspartic acid, 146
  benzyl esters, 144, 145
  benzyloxycarbonyl, 66, 67, 68
  2-(4-biphenylyl)propyl(2)oxycarbonyl group, 69, 70
  tert-butyloxycarbonyl group, 68
  cleavage by methanesulfonic acid and trifluoromethanesulfonic acid, 73
  cyclohexyl and cyclopentyl esters, 146
  for cysteine, 156
  for imidazole ring, 133, 134
  for lysine, 136
  phenacyl esters, 145, 146
  side reactions in introduction and removal, 161–174
  for tryptophan, 130
Proteins
  detection in clones, 22
  synthesis, 3, 4
Proton nuclear magnetic resonance spectroscopy
  peptide, 354, 355
  in racemization assessment, 229, 230
Pseudodipeptides, 364
3-(3-Purinyl)alanine, 6-substituted, 424
3-(6-Purinyl)alanine, 424
2-(9-Purinyl)glycines, 6-substituted, 424
3-(1-Pyrazolyl)alanine, 418
3-(3-Pyrazolyl)alanine, 418
α-(4-Pyrazolyl)glycine derivatives, 418
3-(2-Pyridyl)alanine, and analogs, 415
3-(3-Pyridyl)alanine, 415
3-(4-Pyridyl)alanine, 415
Pyridylalanines, in peptide synthesis, 350
3-(2-Pyrimidinyl)alanine, 426
3-(5-Pyrimidinyl)alanine, 425

Pyrrolo[2,3-*b*]indole-2-carboxylic acid, tetrahydro derivative, 414
Pyrroloindoles, formation from tryptophan, 132
3-(1-Pyrryl)alanine, 416
3-(2-Pyrryl)alanine, 416

Q

Quinoline-2-carboxylic acid derivatives, 412
3-(4-Quinolyl)alanine, 421
3-(6-Quinolyl)alanine, 421

R

Racemization
  of *N*-alkoxycarbonylamino acids, 257–260
  Anderson test, 231
  assessment methods, 221
  and asymmetric induction during aminolysis of oxazolones, 263–265
  and coupling of *N*-alkoxycarbonylamino acids, 251–256
  during coupling of configurational isomers, 274
  and coupling method, 277, 278
  and cyclization, 252
  definition, 220
  determination, of amino acids, 226
    proton nuclear magnetic resonance spectroscopy, 229, 230
  Izumiya test, 231
  model systems for study, acylamino acids, 228–230
    comparison, 234, 235
    isoleucine as test residue, 227
    protected dipeptides, 230–234
  during peptide bond formation, 259, 260
  in peptide synthesis, mechanisms, 235, 236
    sequence dependence, 217–284
  of *N*-protected histidine, 260–263
  during saponification of peptide esters, 262, 263
  Young test, 228
Recombinant DNA methods
  contributions, 48
  polypeptide synthesis, 1–64
Replication, plasmid, 23
Restriction endonucleases, 7
Restriction mapping, cloning, 20
3-(β-Ribofuranosyl)alanine, 429
Ribonuclease A
  crystals of synthetic, 103
  deprotection of synthetic bovine, 95–104
    with liquid hydrogen fluoride, 100, 102
    with methanesulfonic acid, 97–100, 102
    with trifluoromethanesulfonic acid, 101, 102
  synthesis, 93
mRNA, *see* Messenger-ribonucleic acid
Roquefortine, 289

S

Salmonella typhimurium, recombinant DNA research, 1
Saralasine, 324
Scavengers
  in deprotection procedures, 75, 83, 84, 85, 125, 126, 149, 160
  for indolealkylation suppression, 87
γ-Selenahomoglutamic acid, 378
γ-Selenahomolysine, *see* 3-(3-Aminopropylseleno)alanine, 378
γ-Selenalysine, 378, 390
Selenazolidine-4-carboxylic acid, 413
Selenocysteine, 377
3-(2-Selenolyl)alanine, 429
Selenomethionine, and *Se*-alkyl congeners, 378
Serine
  precursor for dehydroalanine, 297–299
  side reactions, in peptide synthesis, 139–143
Serine-containing peptides, synthesis, 86
Side-chain functionality
  in peptide synthesis, alkylating agents, 357, 358
    aromatic side chains, 361
    photoaffinity labeling, 358, 359
    receptor interactions, 356
    sulfur-containing side chains, 361, 362
    synthetic transformations, 359–363
    unsaturated side chains, 362, 363
Side-chain functions, protection and deprotection, 175–177
Side reactions
  in arginine-containing peptide synthesis, 81, 82
  in aspartic acid-containing peptide synthesis, 89, 91

of carbodiimides in peptide synthesis, 189–192
N-carboxyanhydrides, in peptide synthesis, 187, 188
in cyclization in peptide synthesis, 193, 194
in dehydroalanine synthesis from serine, 298
in deprotection with HF, 72
mixed (unsymmetrical) anhydrides, in peptide synthesis, 184–187
in peptide bond formation, 177–192
in peptide synthesis, 111–216
arginine, 137–139
asparagine, 152–156
aspartic acid, 143–148
cysteine, 156–158
cystine, 156–158
glutamic acid, 148–152
glutamine, 152–156
glycine, 114–118
histidine, 132–135
isoleucine, 118–120
lysine, 135, 136
methionine, 158–161
phenylalanine, 123, 124
proline, 120–123
serine, 139–143
threonine, 139–143
tryptophan, 127–132
tyrosine, 124–126
valine, 118–120
in protecting group introduction and removal, 161–174
in solid-phase peptide synthesis, 192, 193
symmetrical anhydrides in peptide synthesis, 183
Siomycin A, 290
Siomycin B, 290
Siomycin C, 290
Siomycin D_1, 290
Solid-phase peptide synthesis
peptide amides, 326
principle of excess, 196
side reactions, 192, 193
with tyrosine, 125
Solvent
effect on asymmetric induction, 265, 266, 276, 277
effect on peptides, 195, 196
Somatostatin, gene for human, 3
Somatotropin, synthesis, 57
L-Stendomycidine, 294
Stendomycin, 290, 293, 294
Stereomutation, definition, 221
Streptococcus lactis, nisin, 320
Structural reporter groups
for peptide nuclear magnetic resonance spectroscopy, fluorinated amino acids, 354, 355
radioactive labels, 356
spin labels, 355
Styrylglycine, *see* 2-Amino-4-phenyl-3-butenoic acid
Subtilin, 290, 291
isolation and structure, 295, 296
β-Sulfinylalanine, *see* Cysteinesulfinic acid

T

Telluromethionine, 378
Telomycin, 290
Temperature, effect on asymmetric induction, 265, 266, 275, 276
Tentoxin, 289
analogs, 314–316
structure, 313
synthesis, 313, 314
Tetradepsipeptide, cyclization of linear esters, 317
Tetrafluorotyrosine, 354
4,5,6,7-Tetrahydrobenzimidazol-2-ylalanine, 423
1,2,3,6-Tetrahydropicolinic acid, 411
2,3,3a,8a-Tetrahydropyrrolo[2,3-b]indole-2-carboxylic acid, 414
1,2,3,4-Tetrahydroquinoline-2-carboxylic acid, 412
peptides, 353
2-(5,6,7,8-Tetrahydroquinol-5-yl)glycine, 422
α-(1-Tetralyl)glycine, 406
Tetrazole-containing amino acids, in peptide synthesis, 350
β-(Tetrazol-5-yl)alanine, 418
3-(8-Theobrominyl)alanine, 424
Thia amino acids, 376
γ-Thiahomoglutamic acid *S,S*-dioxide, 377
γ-Thialysine, 390
γ-Thialysine *S,S*-dioxide, 377
1,3-Thiazine-2-carboxylic acid, perhydro, 413
1,4-Thiazine-3-carboxylic acid, perhydro, 413

Thiazolidine-4-carboxylic acid, 413
  peptides, 352
3-(2-Thiazolyl)alanine, 428
3-(4-Thiazolyl)alanine, 429
2-(2-Thiazolyl)glycine, 428
Thienamycin, 288
3-(Thieno[3,2-*b*]pyrrol-3-yl)alanine, 422
3-(2-Thienyl)alanine, 347, 428
2-(2-Thienyl)glycine, 428
Thioanisole, as scavenger, 83, 84, 85, 129, 160
γ-Thioasparagine, 377
Thiocillin I, 290
Thiocillin II, 290
Thiocillin III, 290
Thiopeptin A_1, 290
Thiopeptin B, 290
Thiophosphoalanine, 397
Thiostrepton, 290
Thiostrepton B, 290
3-(2-Thiouracil-6-yl)alanines, 426
Threonine
  dehydroanimobutyric acid synthesis, 300, 301
  side reactions, in peptide synthesis, 139–143
Threonine-containing peptides, synthesis, 86
Thyronine, ring-substituted derivatives, 403
4-Toluenesulfonyl group, Tosyl group, introduction and removal, side reactions, 167–169
2-(*p*-Tolyl)thiazolidine-4-carboxylic acid, 414
N-Tosylglycyltosylglycine anilide, 115
Tosyl group, *see* *p*-Toluenesulfonyl group
Transcription
  alternate cleavage systems, 27
  direct expression, 27
  fusion systems, 26
  recombinant DNA techniques, 23–25
Translation
  messenger-ribonucleic acid structure, 30
  protein product structure, 31
  ribosome binding sites, 28, 29
  signal sequences, 29, 30
Transpeptidation, 150, 151, 154
2,5,7-Tri-*tert*-butyltryptophan, preparation, 129
4,4,4-Trichlorothreonine, 380
Tricholomic acid, *see* 2-(3-Oxo-5-isoxazolidinyl)glycine
Trifluoroacetic acid (TFA)
  as deprotecting agent, 69–71
  deprotecting procedure, 70
  thioanisole-mediated deprotection, 105
Trifluoroacetyl group, 136
3,3,3-Trifluoroalanine, 371
Trifluoromethanesulfonic acid
  as deprotection agent, 101, 102
  deprotection procedure, 72–74
Trifluoromethionine, 354
ω,ω,ω-Trifluorovaline, *see* 2-Amino-3-methyl-4,4,4-trifluorobutanoic acid
3,3′,4′-Trihydroxyphenylalanine, 380
1,2,5-Trimethyl-4-(2-amino-2-carboxy-1-hydroxyethyl)pyridinium salt, 416
β-Trimethylsilylalanine, 397
Triphenylmethyl group, Trityl group, introduction and removal, side reactions, 170
Trishomoleucine, 367
S-Tritylcysteine, oxidation, 94
Trityl group, *see* Triphenylmethyl group
3-(4-Tropolonyl)alanine, 383
3-(5-Tropolonyl)alanine, 383
Tryptophan
  in peptide synthesis, 72
  side reactions, in peptide synthesis, 127–132
Tryptophan-containing peptides, synthesis, 86–88
Tryptophan derivatives, 418, 419
Tuberactinomycin A, 290
Tuberactinomycin B, 290
Tuberactinomycin N, 290
Tuberactinomycin O, 290
Tyrosine
  in peptide synthesis, 72
  ring-substituted derivatives, 402, 403
  side reactions, in peptide synthesis, 124–126
Tyrosine-containing peptides, synthesis, 85

U

3-(1-Uracilyl)alanines, 425
3-(6-Uracilyl)alanines, 425
2-(1-Uracilyl)glycines, 425
Ureides, formation in peptide synthesis, 119, 120
β-Ureidoalanine, 397

4-Ureidobutanoic acid, *see* Norcitrulline
Urotensin II, synthesis, and purification, 92, 93

V

Valine, side reactions in peptide synthesis, 118–120
Vasoactive intestinal polypeptide (VIP), synthesis, 89–92
Vasopressin analogs, synthesis, 155, 157
Versimide, 288
α-Vinylglycine, *see* 2-Amino-3-butenoic acid

W

WS-3442B, 289

X

3′-(8-Xanthinyl)-3′*H*-tryptophan, 420

Y

Young test for racemization, 228